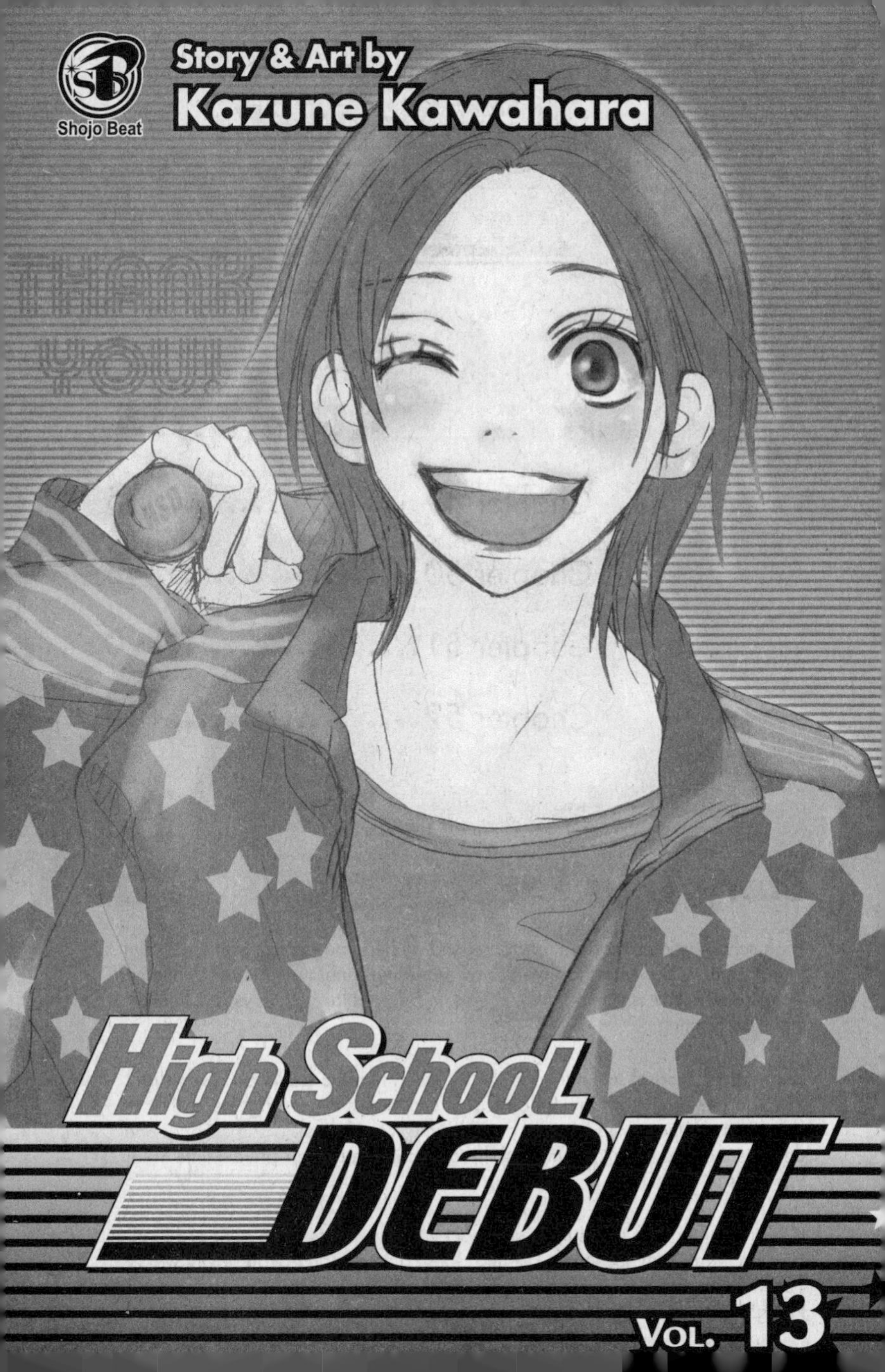
Shojo Beat
Story & Art by
Kazune Kawahara
THANK YOU!
High School
DEBUT
VOL. 13

High School DEBUT

Contents

Story Thus Far...

High school student Haruna used to spend all her time playing softball in junior high, but now she wants to give her all to finding true love instead! While her "love coach" Yoh is training her on how to be popular with guys, the two of them start dating.

During their second summer vacation together, Haruna books an away trip to celebrate Yoh's birthday. It's only after she makes the arrangements that she realizes what could happen between the two of them. Is she ready?! She decides that she is, but Asami and the others interrupt their private time. Their trip ends in chaos!

It's winter now and Yoh is thinking about what he wants to do after graduation. Haruna wants to help! While Haruna does some research, Yoh slowly works out what he wants to do and decides on a college. However, it's in Tokyo! The thought of a long-distance relationship is weighing heavily on Haruna's mind...

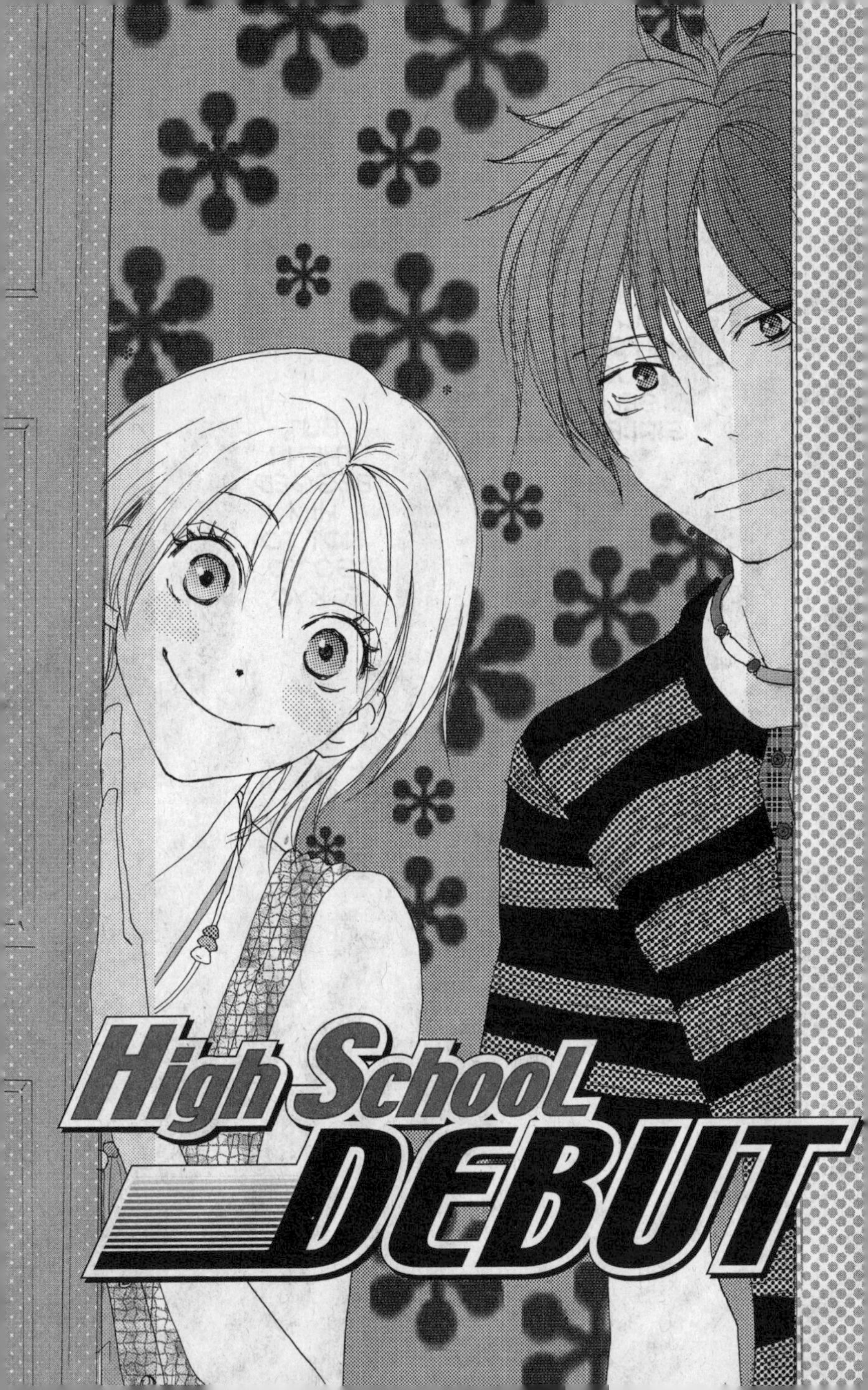
High School
DEBUT

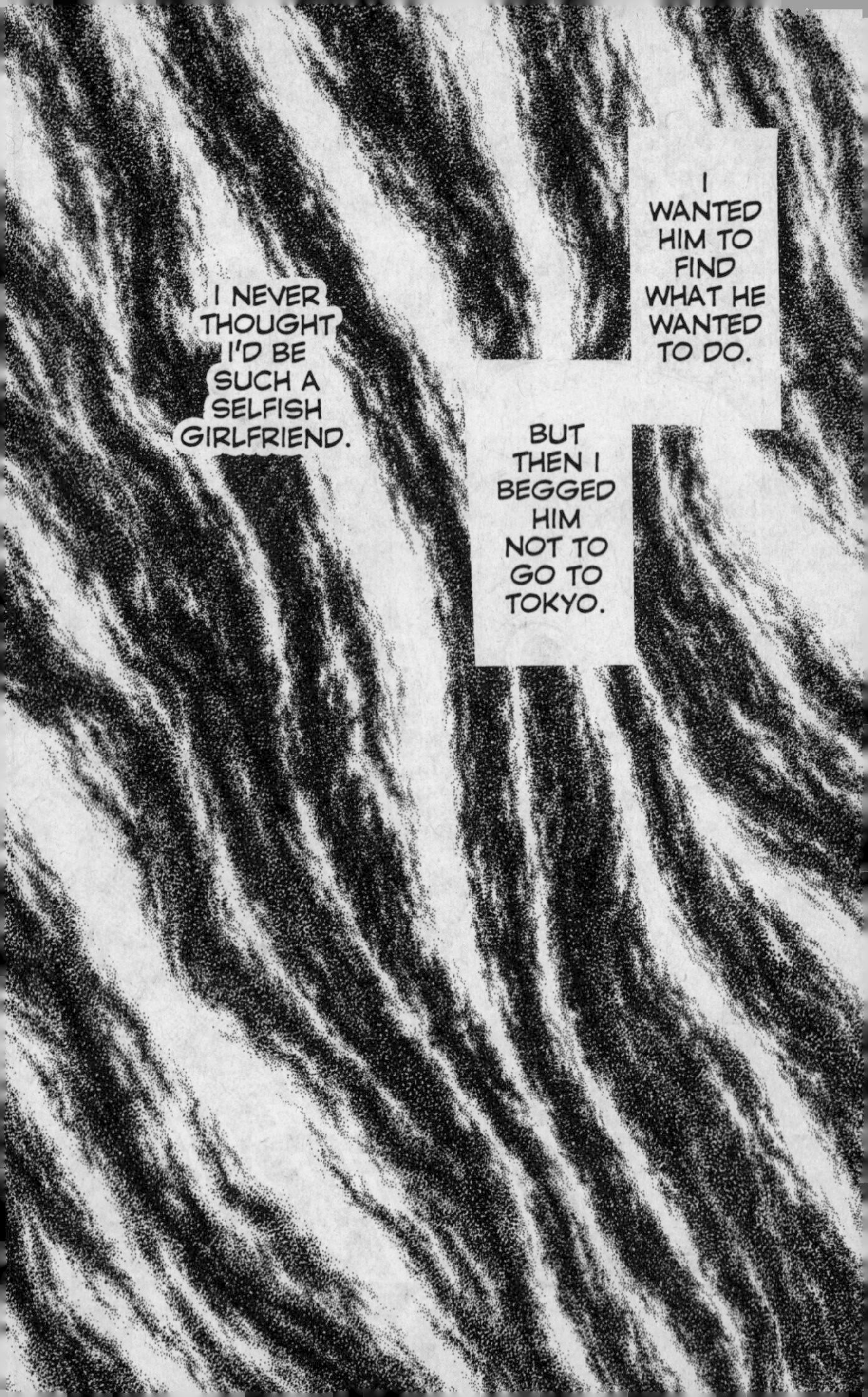
I WANTED HIM TO FIND WHAT HE WANTED TO DO.
BUT THEN I BEGGED HIM NOT TO GO TO TOKYO.
I NEVER THOUGHT I'D BE SUCH A SELFISH GIRLFRIEND.

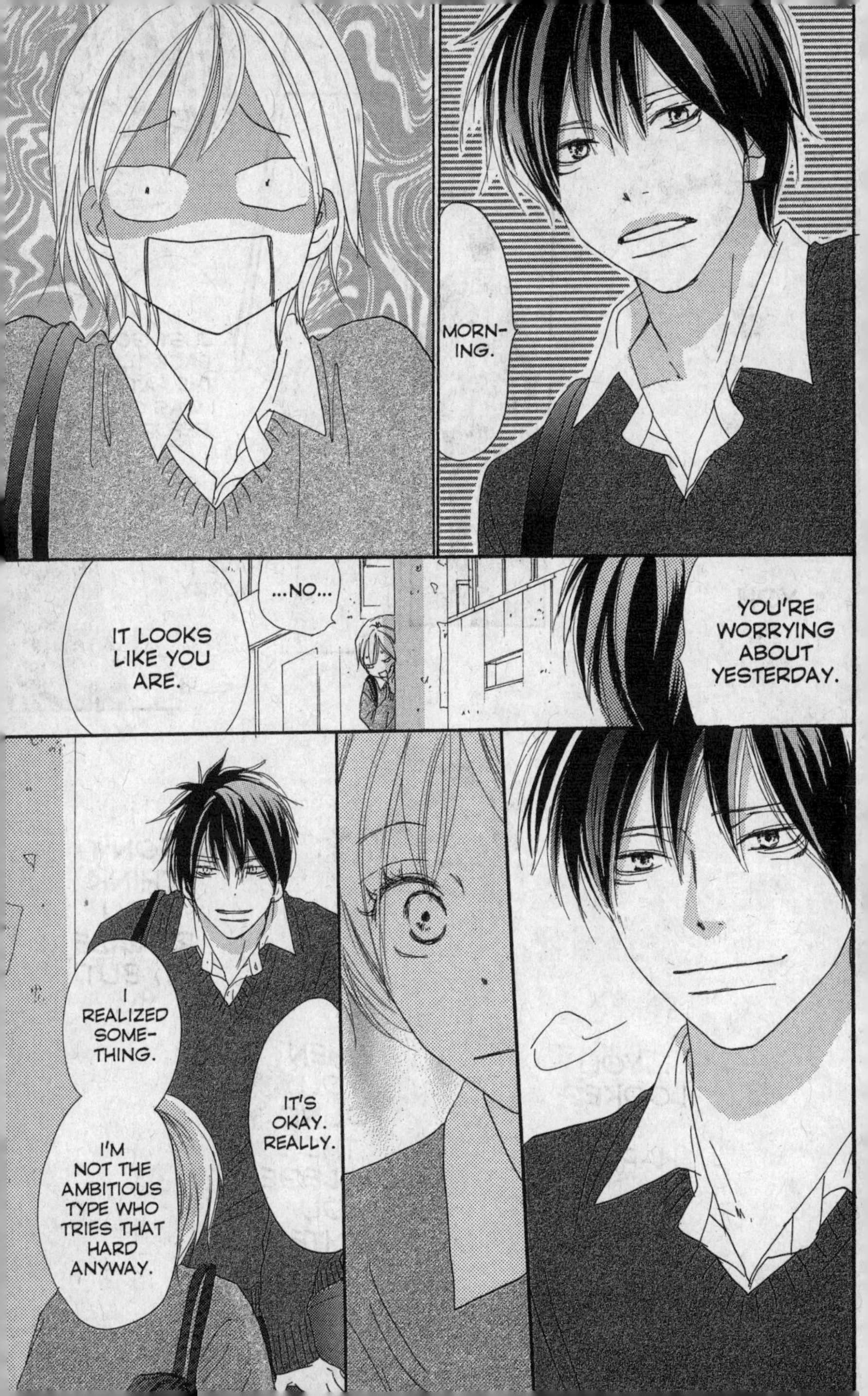
MORN-ING.
YOU'RE WORRYING ABOUT YESTERDAY.
...NO...
IT LOOKS LIKE YOU ARE.
IT'S OKAY. REALLY.
I REALIZED SOME-THING.
I'M NOT THE AMBITIOUS TYPE WHO TRIES THAT HARD ANYWAY.

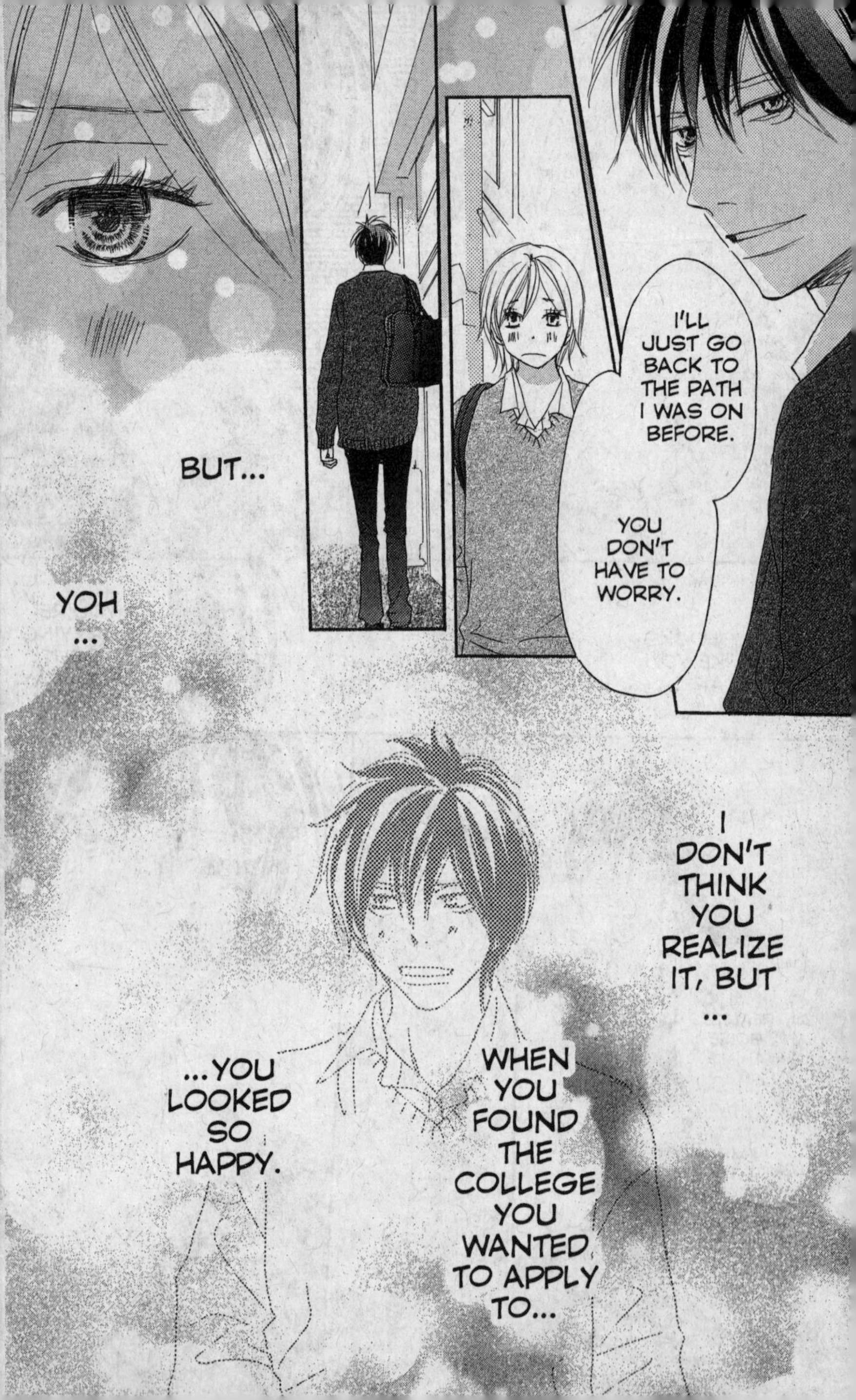
I'LL JUST GO BACK TO THE PATH I WAS ON BEFORE.
YOU DON'T HAVE TO WORRY.
BUT...
YOH ...
I DON'T THINK YOU REALIZE IT, BUT ...
WHEN YOU FOUND THE COLLEGE YOU WANTED TO APPLY TO...
...YOU LOOKED SO HAPPY.

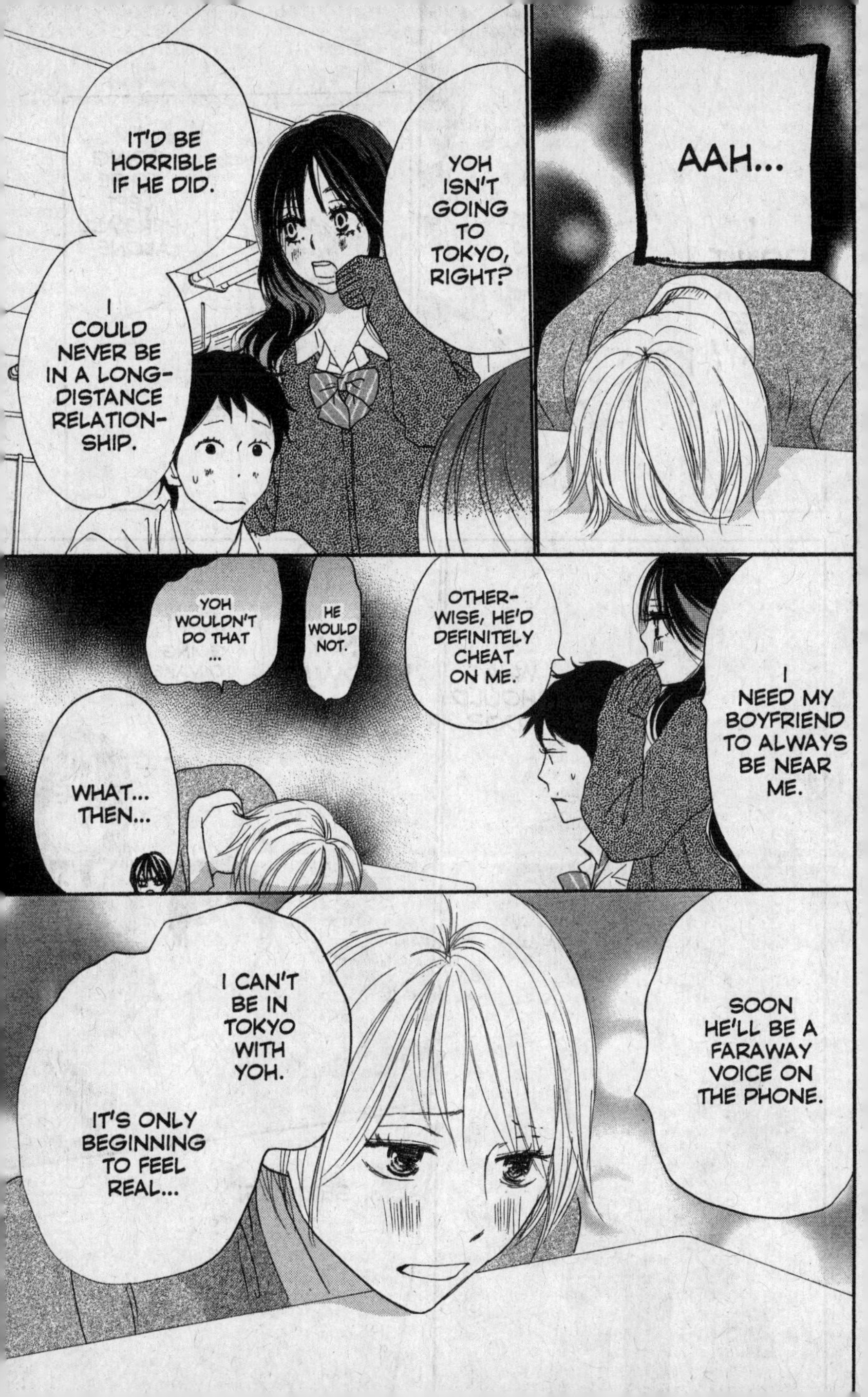
AAH...
YOH ISN'T GOING TO TOKYO, RIGHT?
IT'D BE HORRIBLE IF HE DID.
I COULD NEVER BE IN A LONG-DISTANCE RELATIONSHIP.
I NEED MY BOYFRIEND TO ALWAYS BE NEAR ME.
OTHERWISE, HE'D DEFINITELY CHEAT ON ME.
HE WOULD NOT.
YOH WOULDN'T DO THAT ...
WHAT... THEN...
SOON HE'LL BE A FARAWAY VOICE ON THE PHONE.
I CAN'T BE IN TOKYO WITH YOH.
IT'S ONLY BEGINNING TO FEEL REAL...

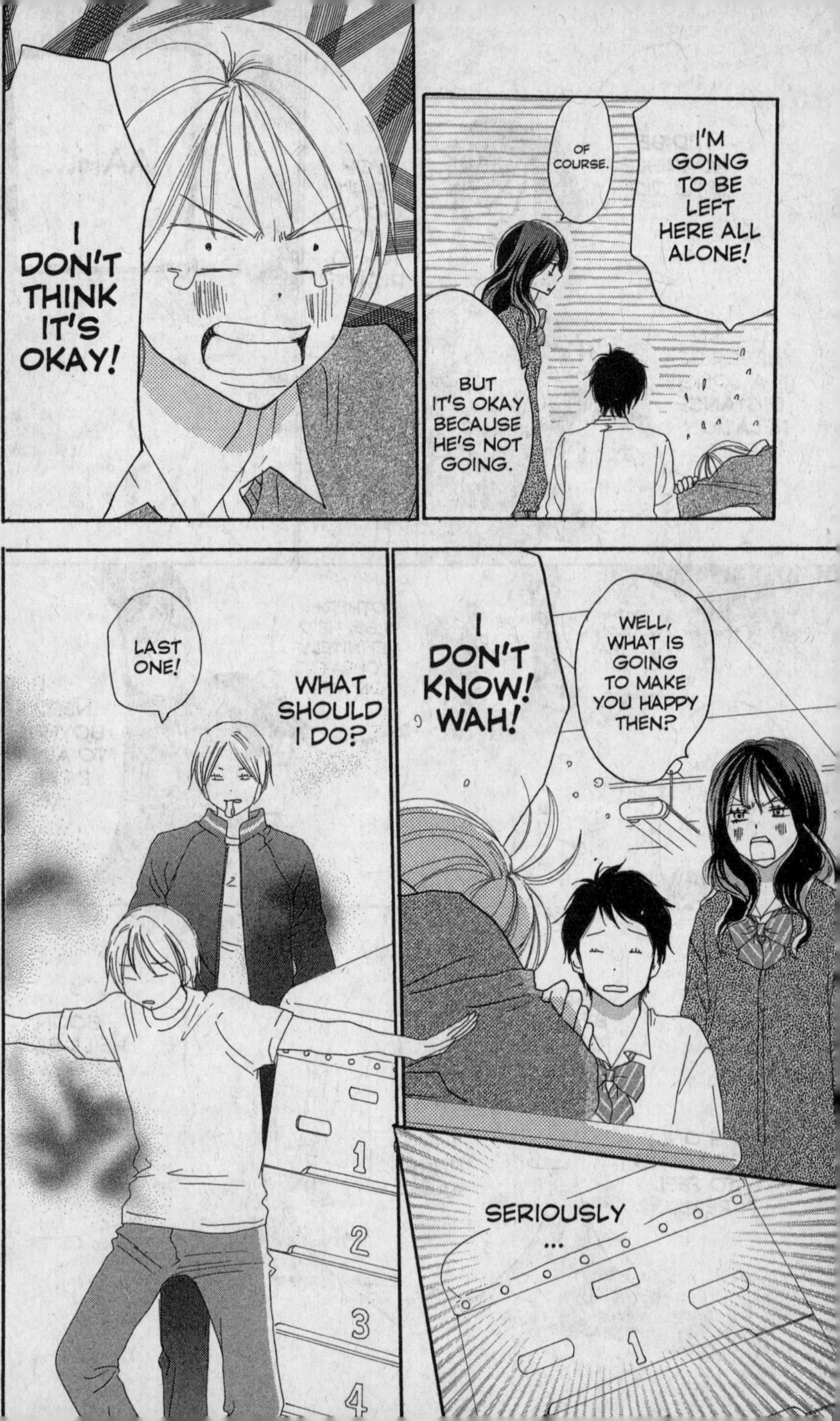
I'M GOING TO BE LEFT HERE ALL ALONE!
OF COURSE.
BUT IT'S OKAY BECAUSE HE'S NOT GOING.
I DON'T THINK IT'S OKAY!
WELL, WHAT IS GOING TO MAKE YOU HAPPY THEN?
I DON'T KNOW! WAH!
SERIOUSLY ...
WHAT SHOULD I DO?
LAST ONE!

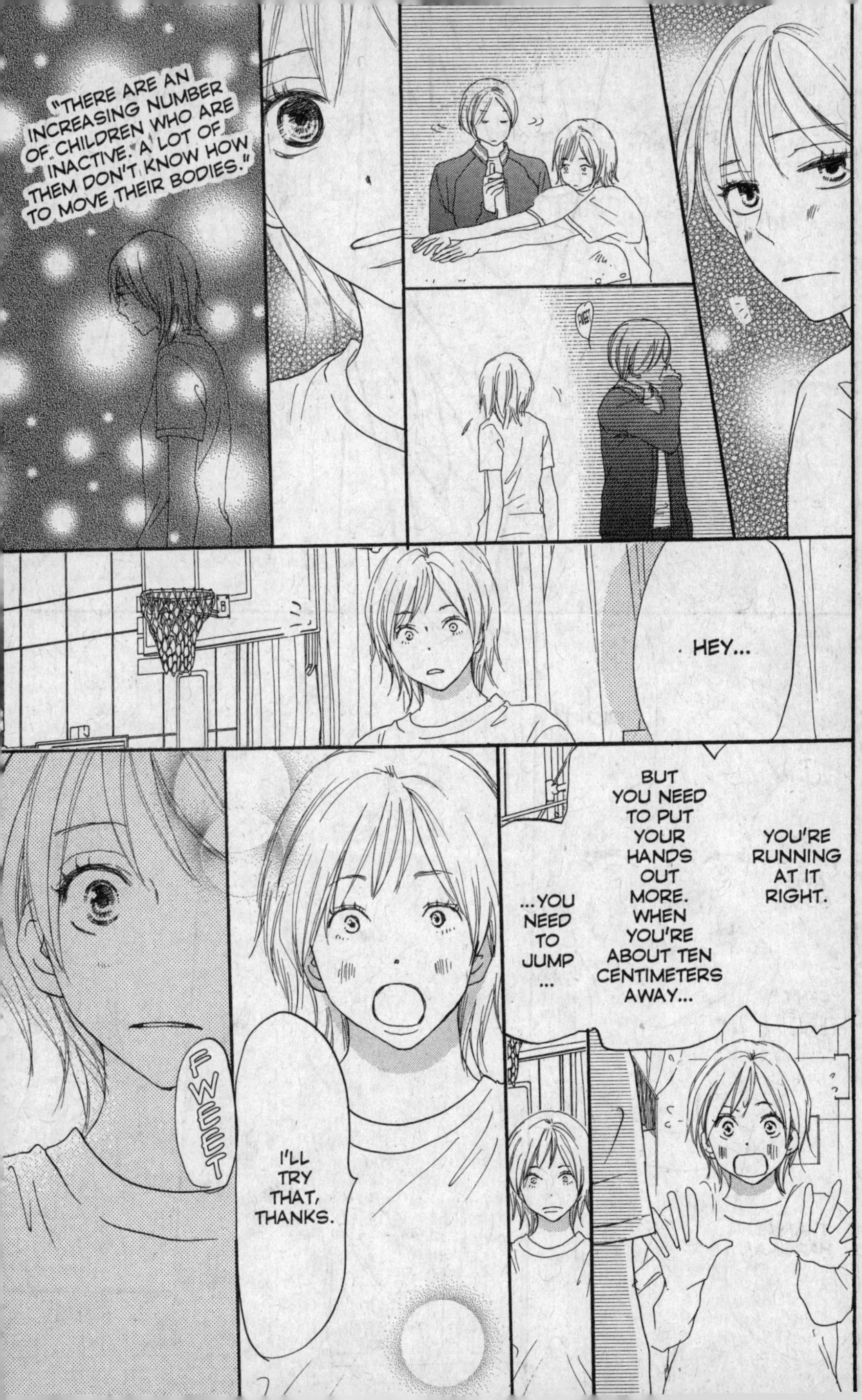
FWEET
"THERE ARE AN INCREASING NUMBER OF CHILDREN WHO ARE INACTIVE. A LOT OF THEM DON'T KNOW HOW TO MOVE THEIR BODIES."
HEY...
YOU'RE RUNNING AT IT RIGHT.
BUT YOU NEED TO PUT YOUR HANDS OUT MORE. WHEN YOU'RE ABOUT TEN CENTIMETERS AWAY...
...YOU NEED TO JUMP...
I'LL TRY THAT, THANKS.
FWEET

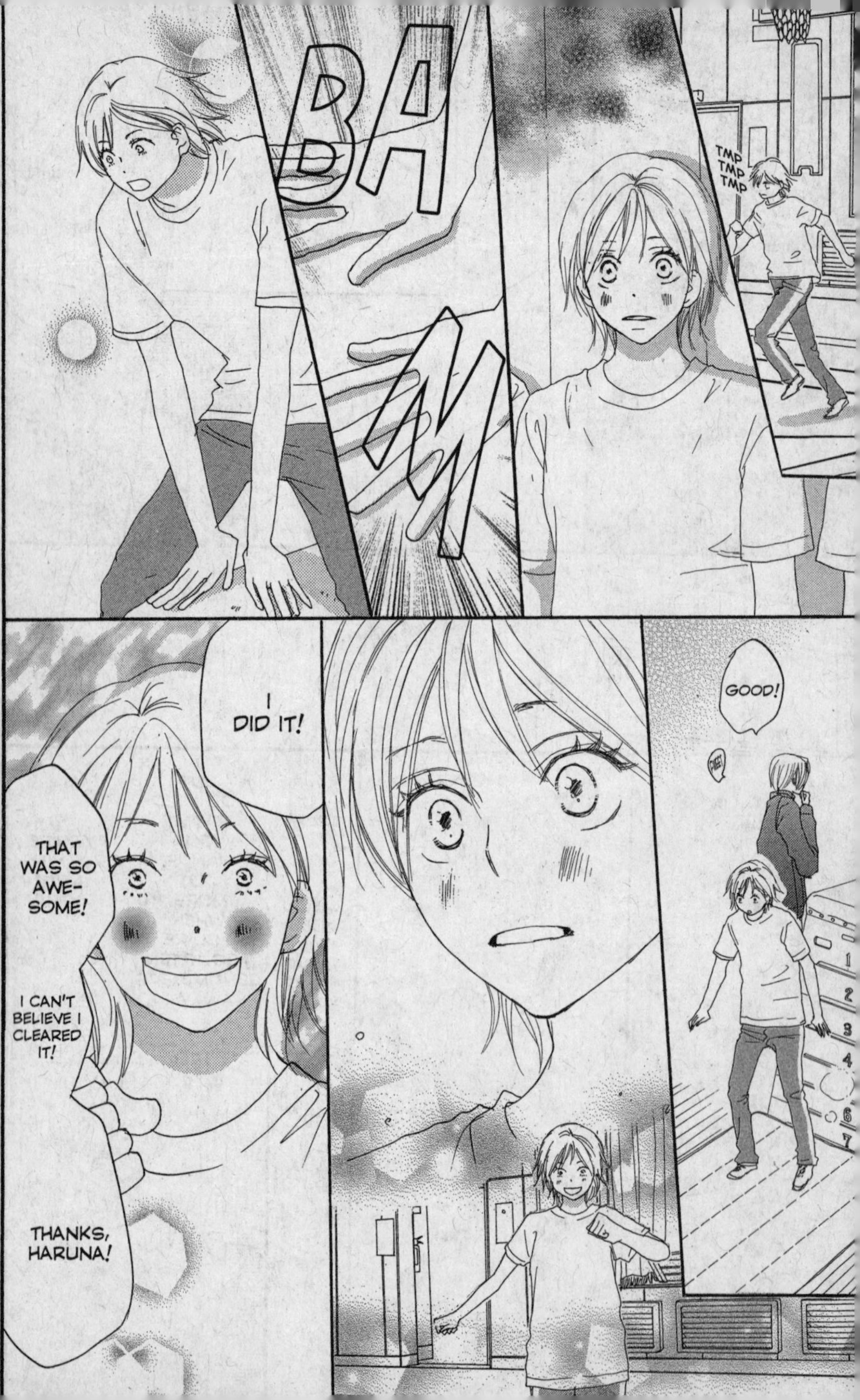

TMP
TMP
TMP
BAM
GOOD!
I DID IT!
THAT WAS SO AWE-SOME!
I CAN'T BELIEVE I CLEARED IT!
THANKS, HARUNA!

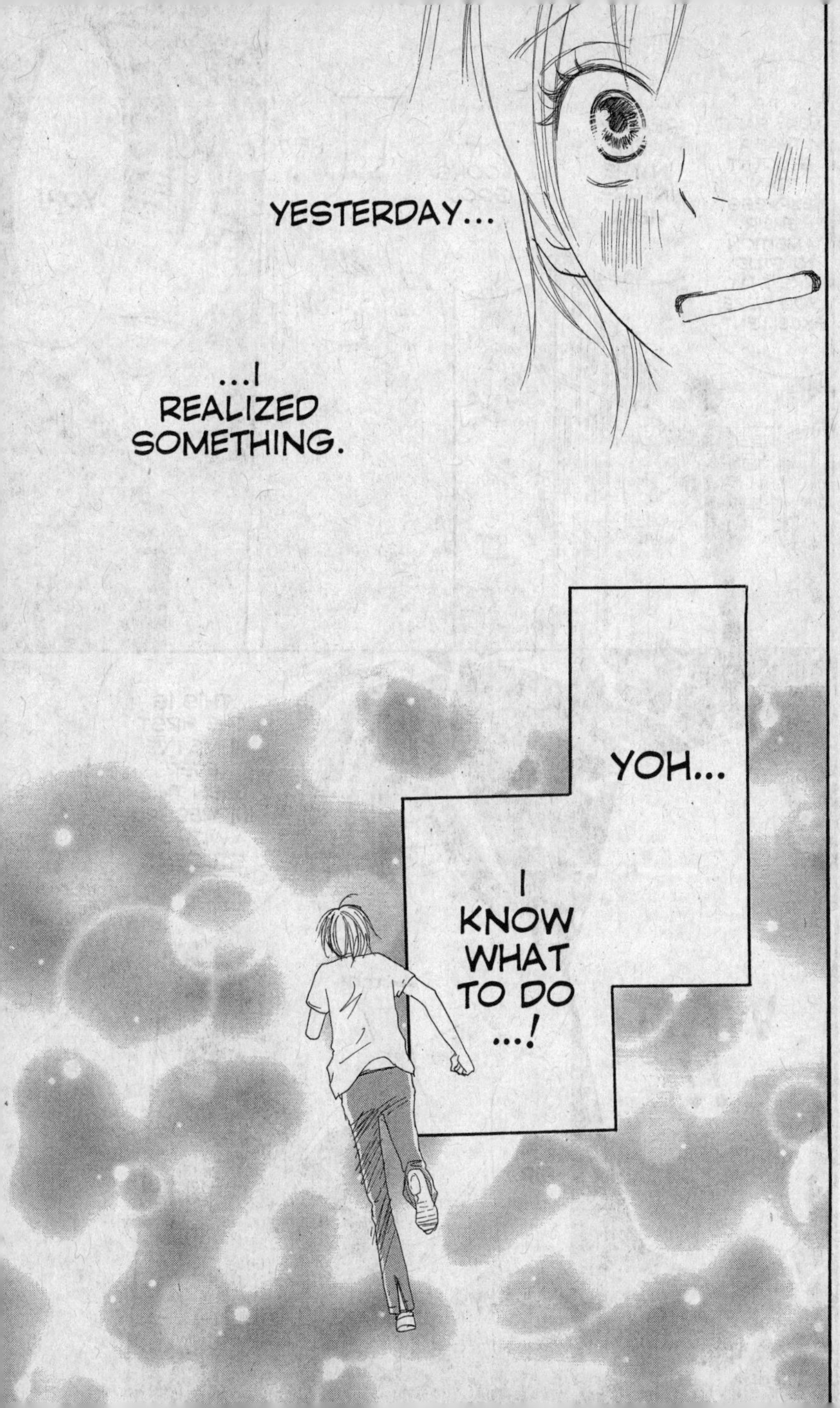
YESTERDAY...
...I REALIZED SOMETHING.
YOH...
I KNOW WHAT TO DO ...!

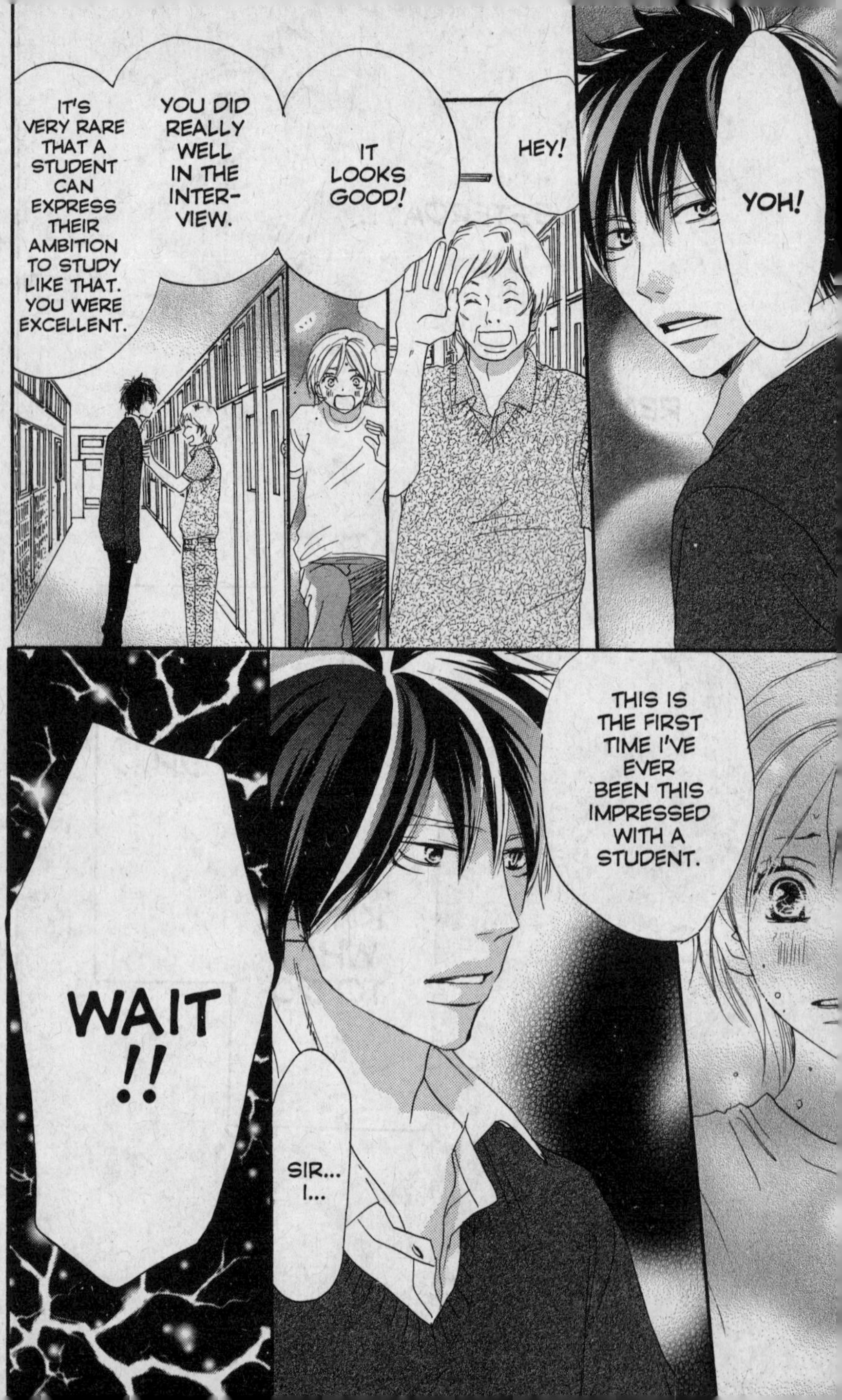
YOH!
HEY!
IT LOOKS GOOD!
YOU DID REALLY WELL IN THE INTERVIEW.
IT'S VERY RARE THAT A STUDENT CAN EXPRESS THEIR AMBITION TO STUDY LIKE THAT. YOU WERE EXCELLENT.
THIS IS THE FIRST TIME I'VE EVER BEEN THIS IMPRESSED WITH A STUDENT.
SIR... I...
WAIT!!

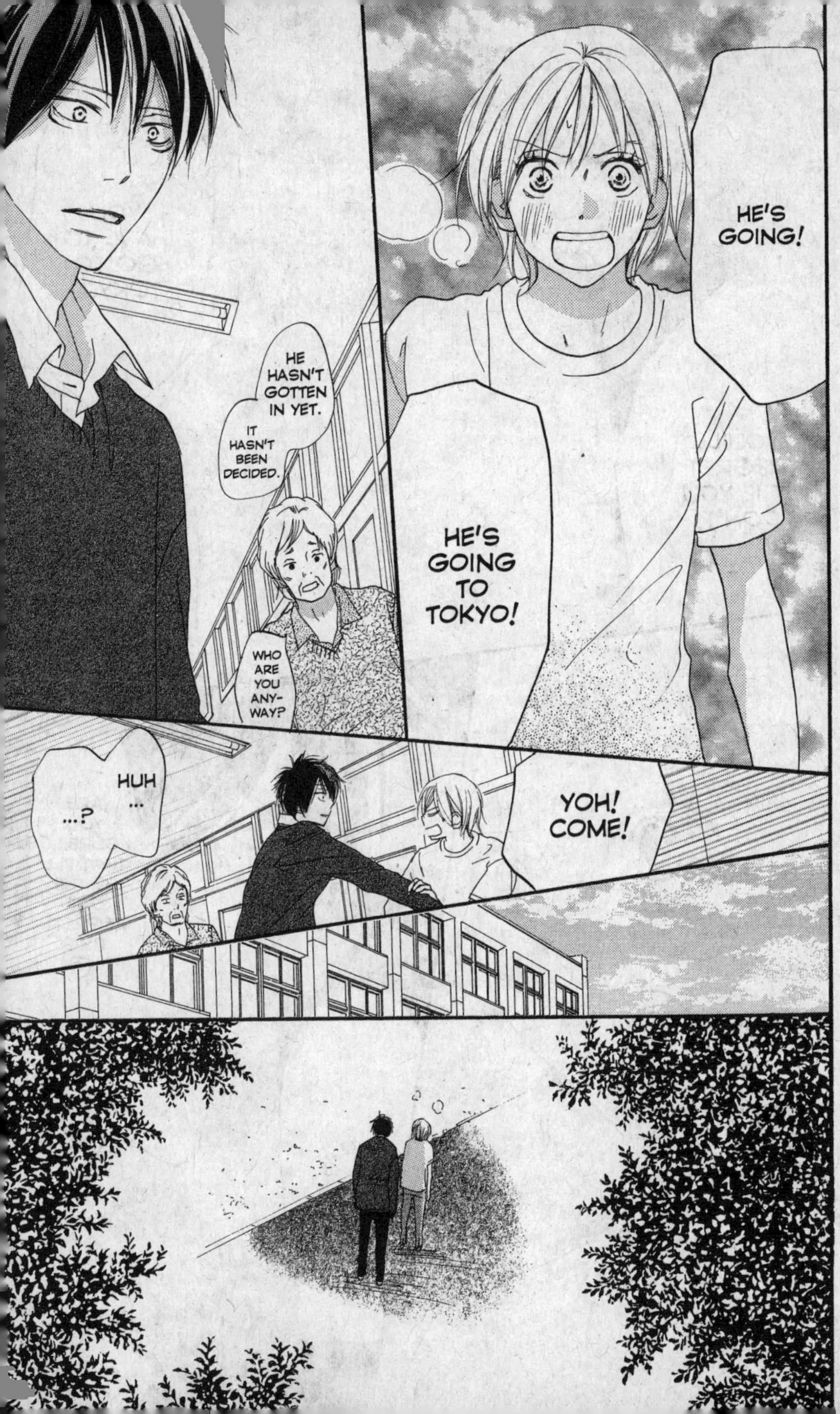
HE'S GOING!
HE'S GOING TO TOKYO!
HE HASN'T GOTTEN IN YET.
IT HASN'T BEEN DECIDED.
WHO ARE YOU ANYWAY?
YOH! COME!
HUH ... ...?

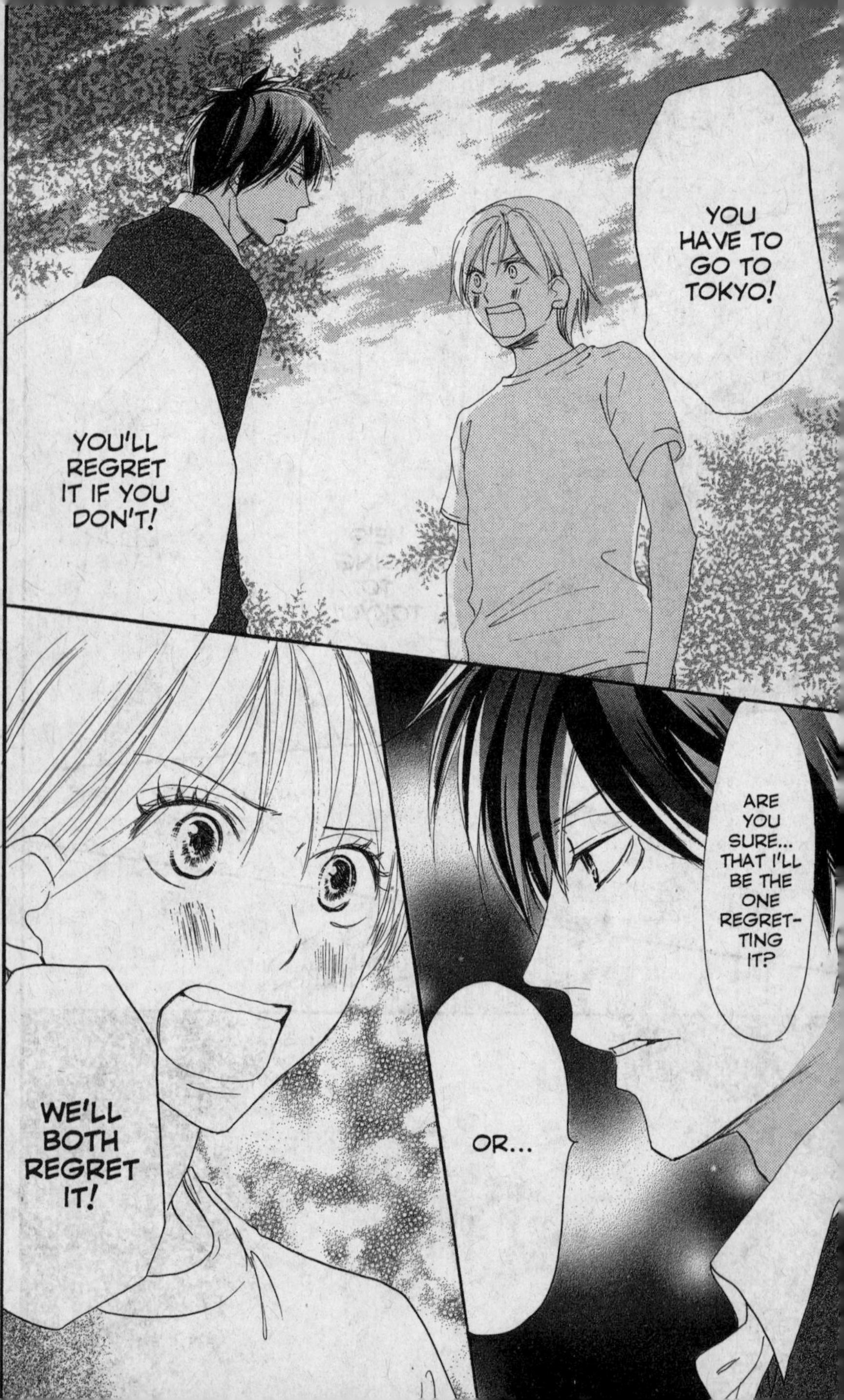
YOU HAVE TO GO TO TOKYO!
YOU'LL REGRET IT IF YOU DON'T!
ARE YOU SURE... THAT I'LL BE THE ONE REGRET-TING IT?
OR...
WE'LL BOTH REGRET IT!

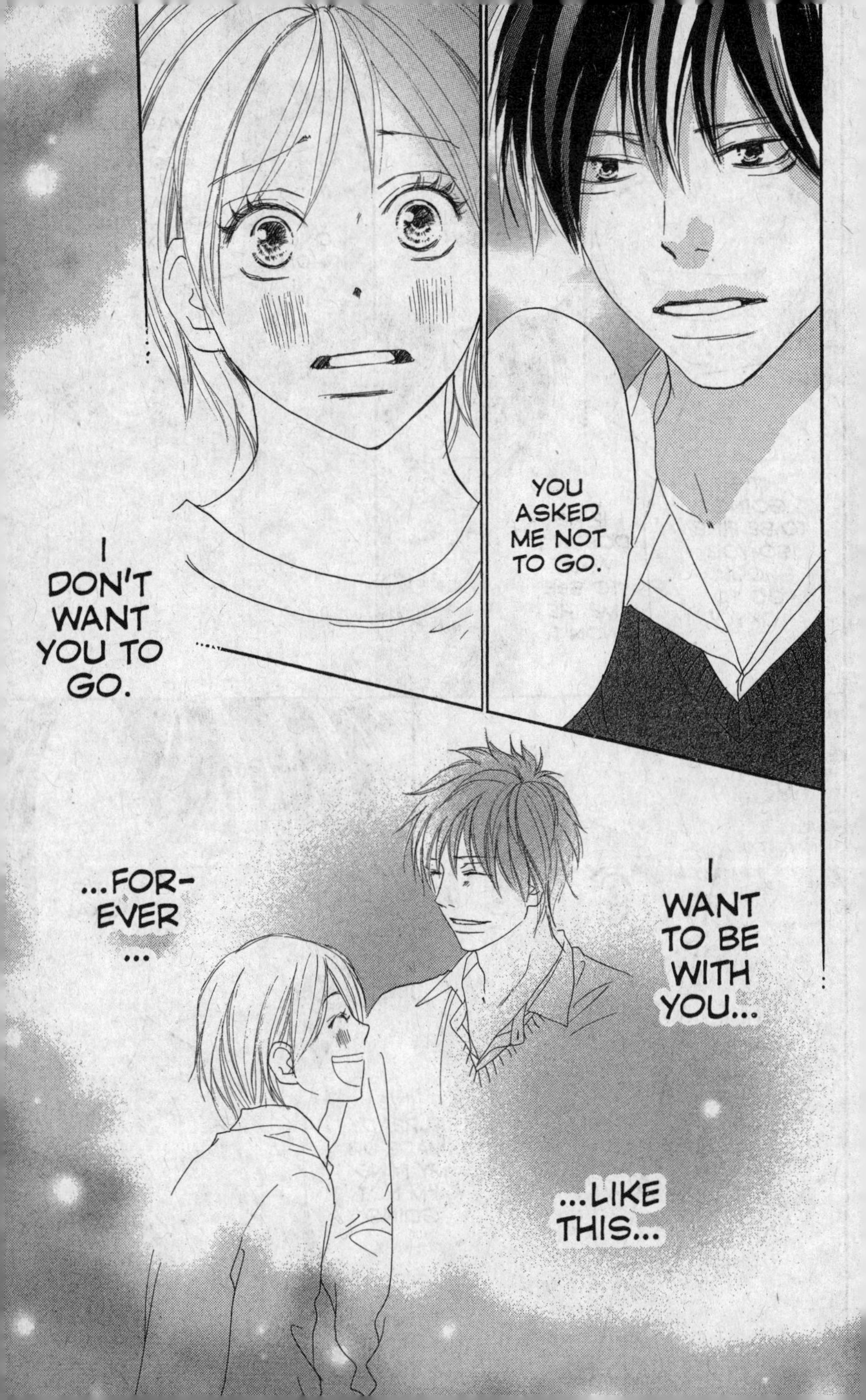
YOU ASKED ME NOT TO GO.
I DON'T WANT YOU TO GO.
I WANT TO BE WITH YOU...
...FOR-EVER...
...LIKE THIS...

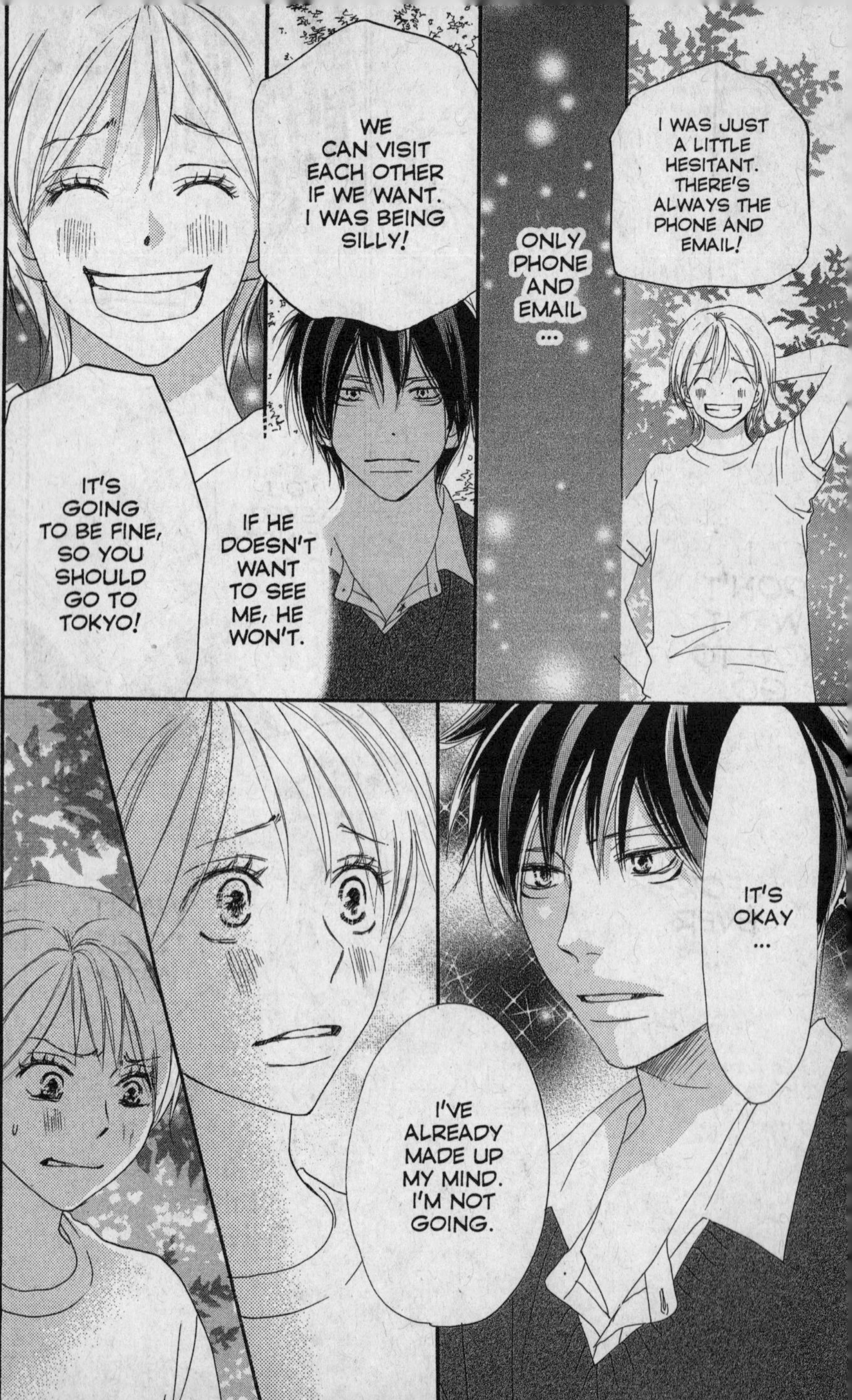
I WAS JUST A LITTLE HESITANT. THERE'S ALWAYS THE PHONE AND EMAIL!
ONLY PHONE AND EMAIL...
WE CAN VISIT EACH OTHER IF WE WANT. I WAS BEING SILLY!
IF HE DOESN'T WANT TO SEE ME, HE WON'T.
IT'S GOING TO BE FINE, SO YOU SHOULD GO TO TOKYO!
IT'S OKAY...
I'VE ALREADY MADE UP MY MIND. I'M NOT GOING.

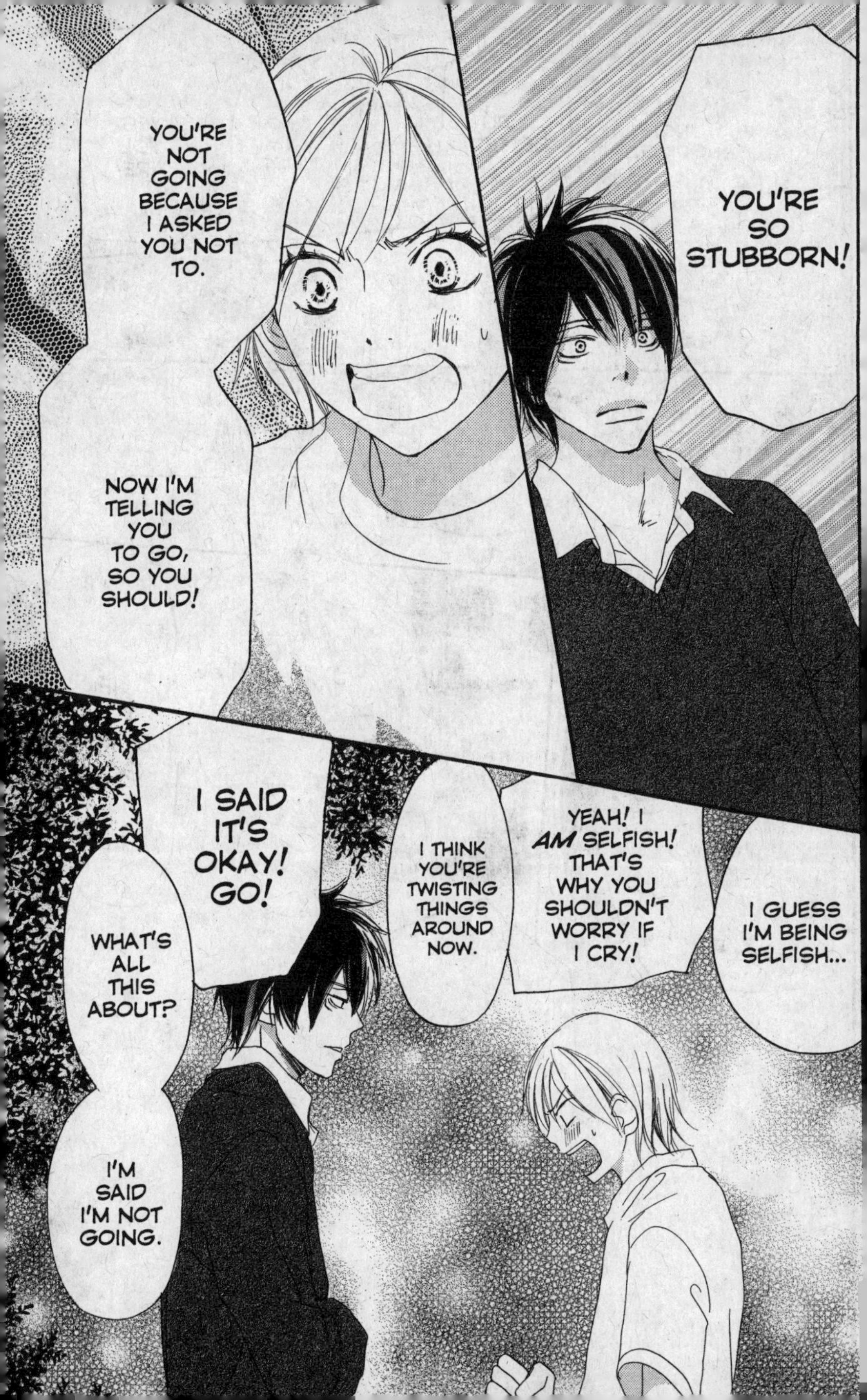
YOU'RE SO STUBBORN!
YOU'RE NOT GOING BECAUSE I ASKED YOU NOT TO.
NOW I'M TELLING YOU TO GO, SO YOU SHOULD!
I GUESS I'M BEING SELFISH...
YEAH! I *AM* SELFISH! THAT'S WHY YOU SHOULDN'T WORRY IF I CRY!
I THINK YOU'RE TWISTING THINGS AROUND NOW.
I SAID IT'S OKAY! GO!
WHAT'S ALL THIS ABOUT?
I'M SAID I'M NOT GOING.

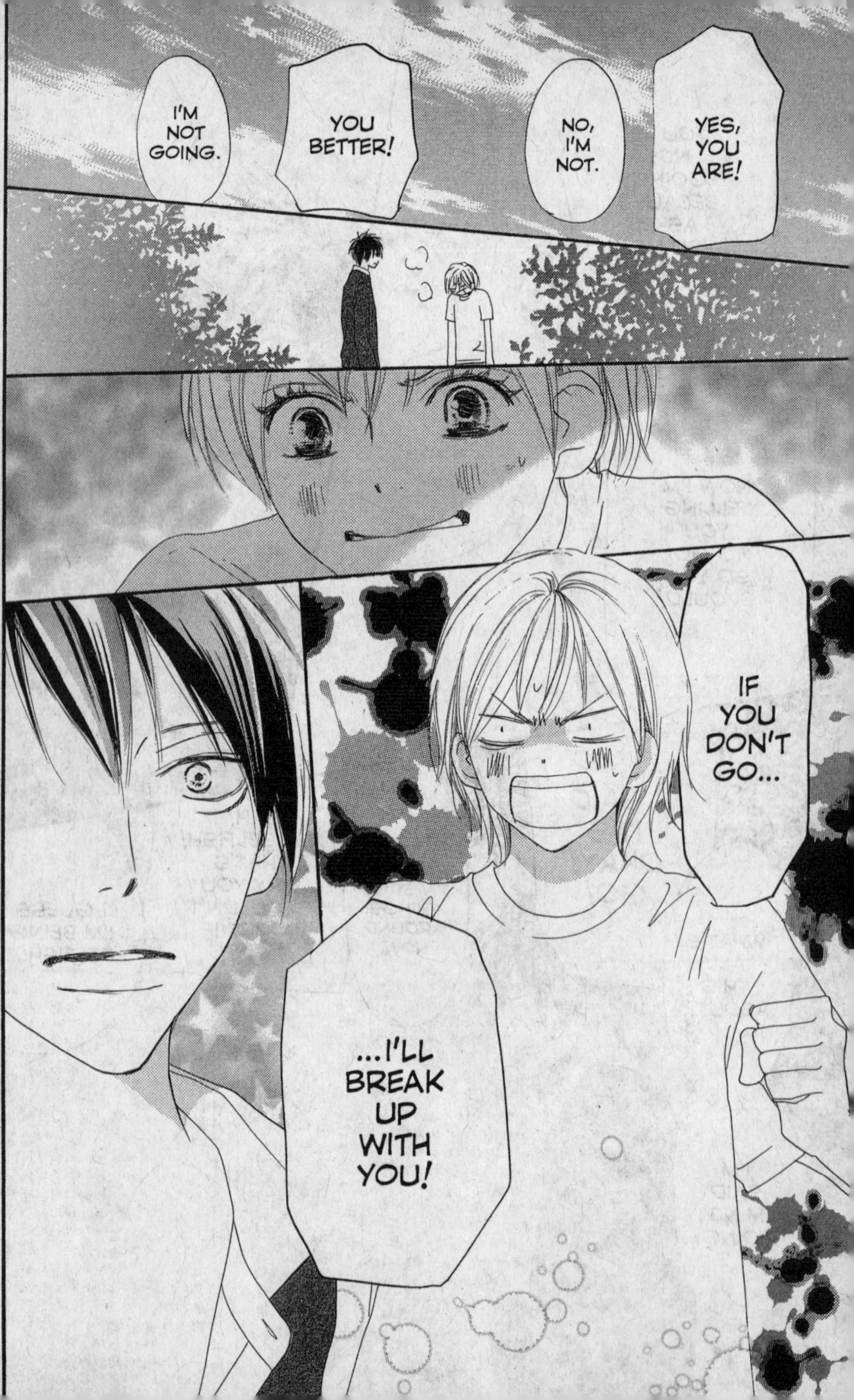
YES, YOU ARE!
NO, I'M NOT.
YOU BETTER!
I'M NOT GOING.
IF YOU DON'T GO...
...I'LL BREAK UP WITH YOU!

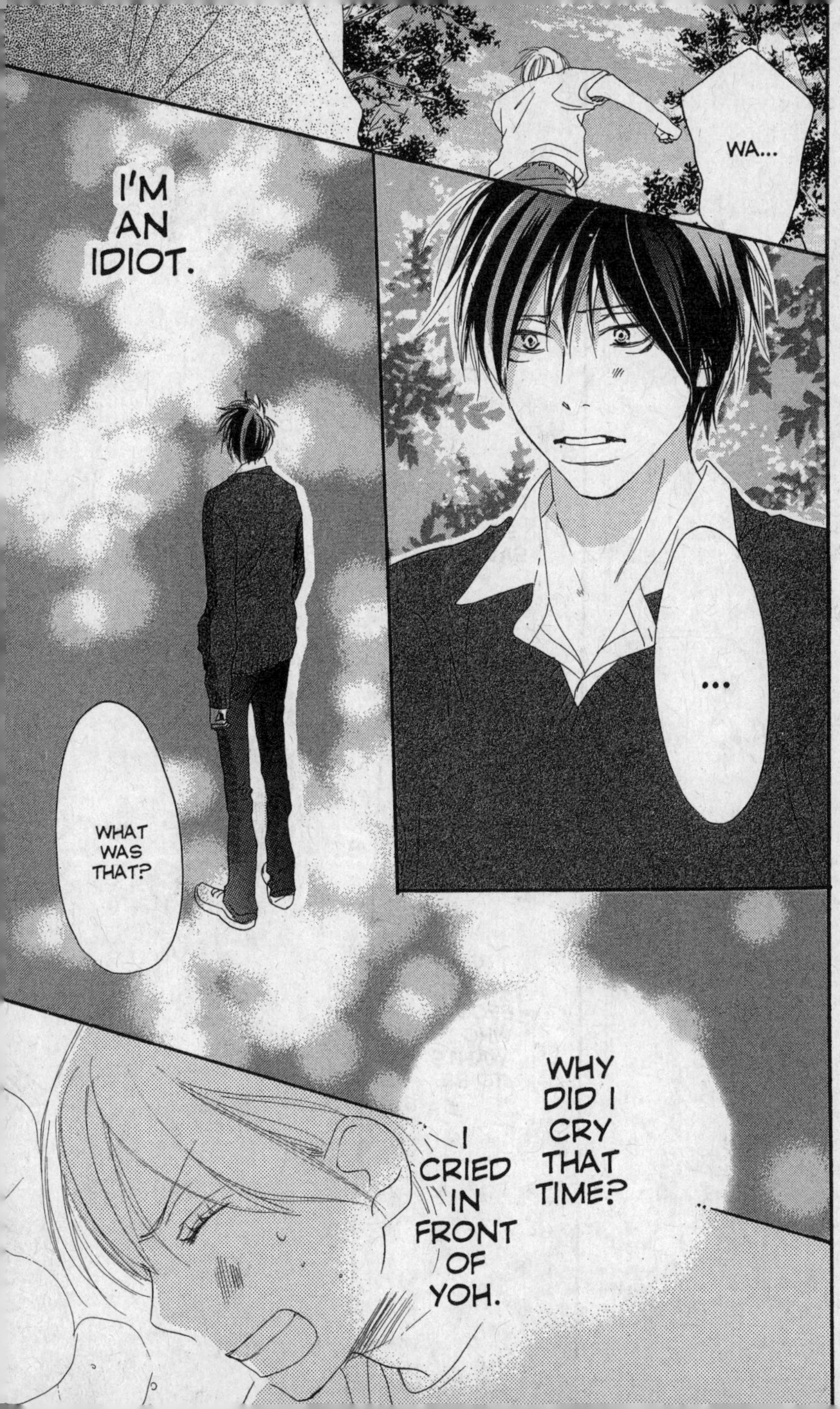
WA...
...
I'M AN IDIOT.
WHAT WAS THAT?
WHY DID I CRY THAT TIME?
I CRIED IN FRONT OF YOH.

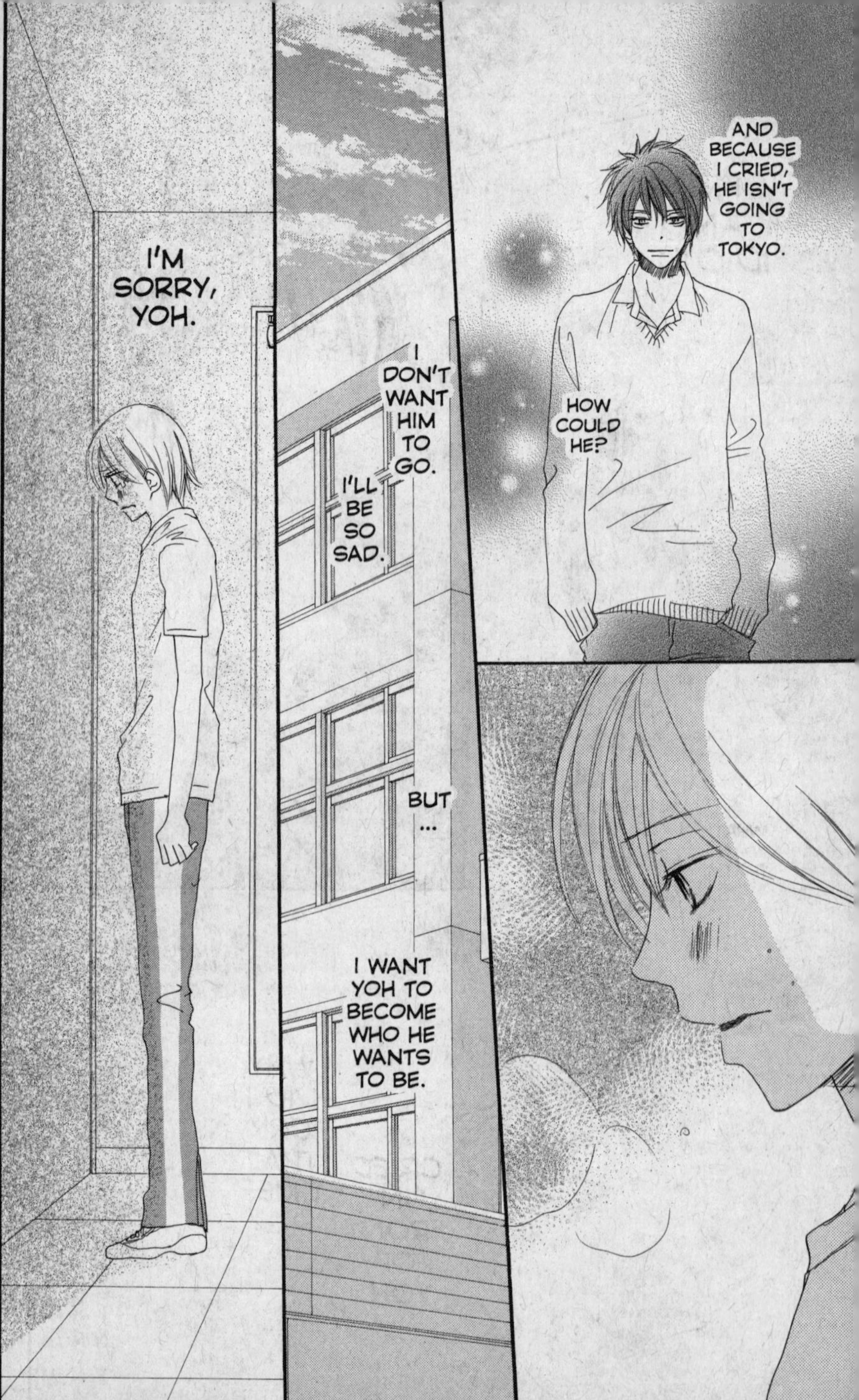
AND BECAUSE I CRIED, HE ISN'T GOING TO TOKYO.
HOW COULD HE?
I DON'T WANT HIM TO GO.
I'LL BE SO SAD.
BUT...
I WANT YOH TO BECOME WHO HE WANTS TO BE.
I'M SORRY, YOH.

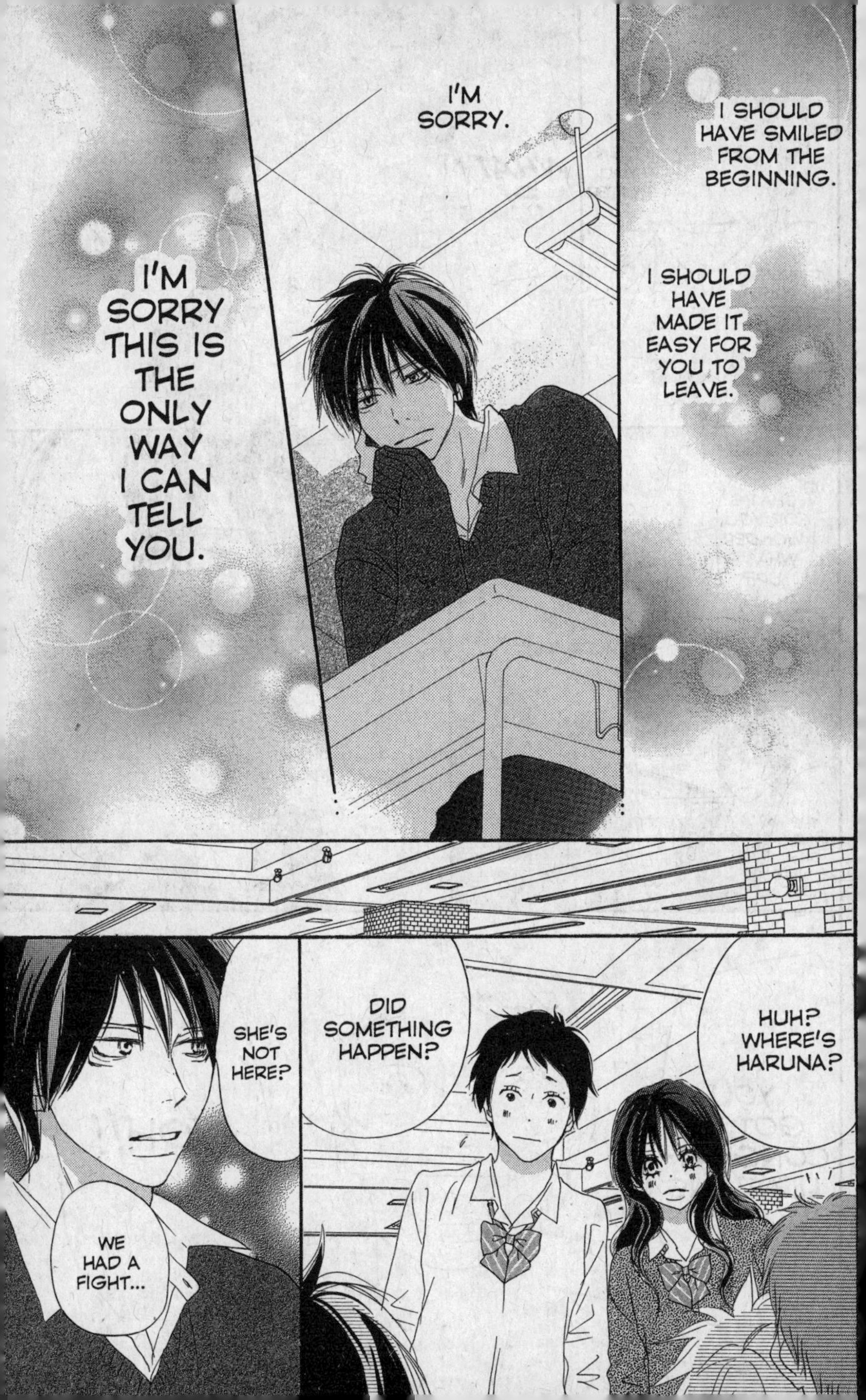
I SHOULD HAVE SMILED FROM THE BEGINNING.
I SHOULD HAVE MADE IT EASY FOR YOU TO LEAVE.
I'M SORRY.
I'M SORRY THIS IS THE ONLY WAY I CAN TELL YOU.
HUH? WHERE'S HARUNA?
DID SOMETHING HAPPEN?
SHE'S NOT HERE?
WE HAD A FIGHT...

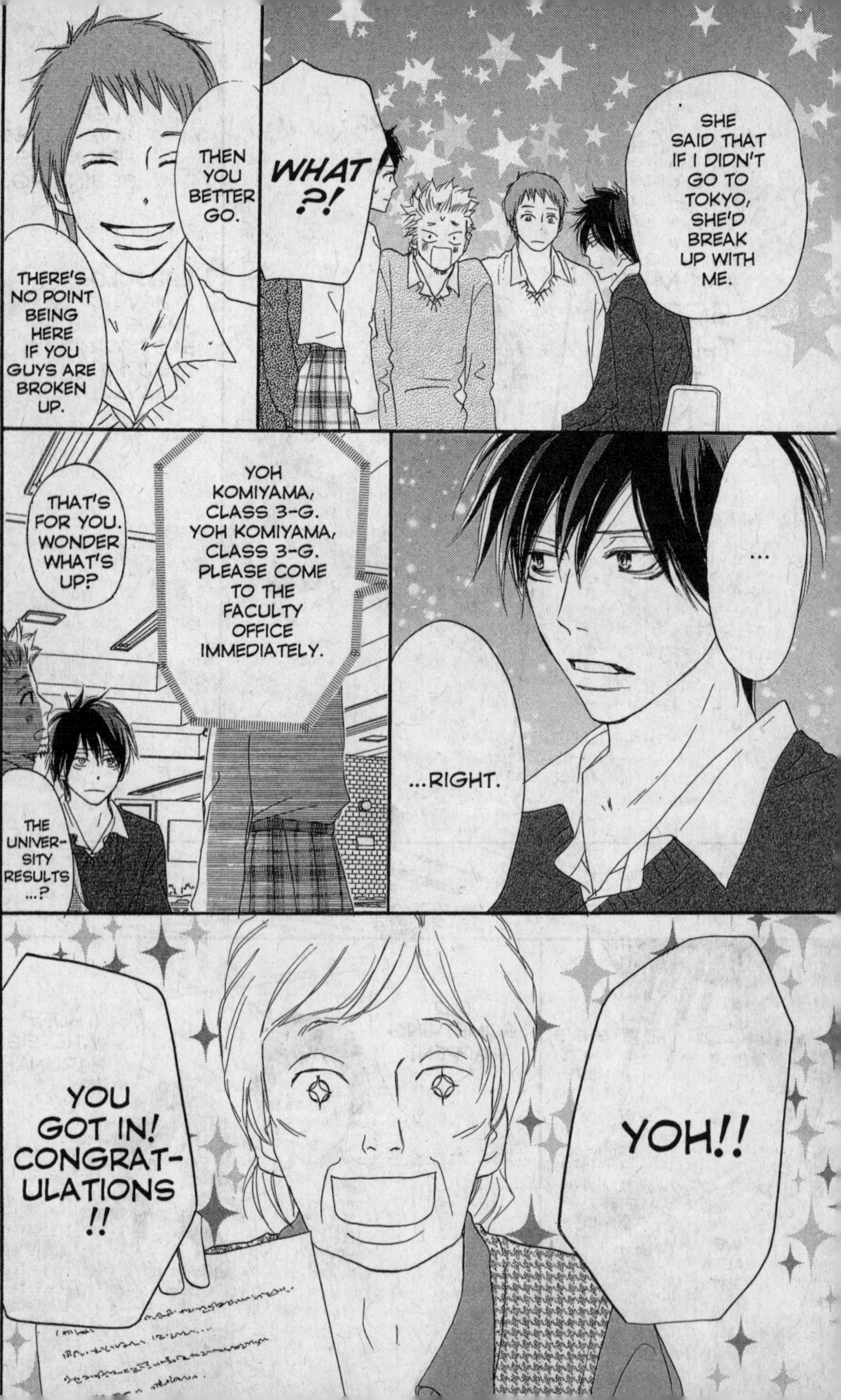
SHE SAID THAT IF I DIDN'T GO TO TOKYO, SHE'D BREAK UP WITH ME.
WHAT?!
THEN YOU BETTER GO.
THERE'S NO POINT BEING HERE IF YOU GUYS ARE BROKEN UP.
...
...RIGHT.
YOH KOMIYAMA, CLASS 3-G. YOH KOMIYAMA, CLASS 3-G. PLEASE COME TO THE FACULTY OFFICE IMMEDIATELY.
THAT'S FOR YOU. WONDER WHAT'S UP?
THE UNIVERSITY RESULTS ...?
YOH!!
YOU GOT IN! CONGRATULATIONS!!

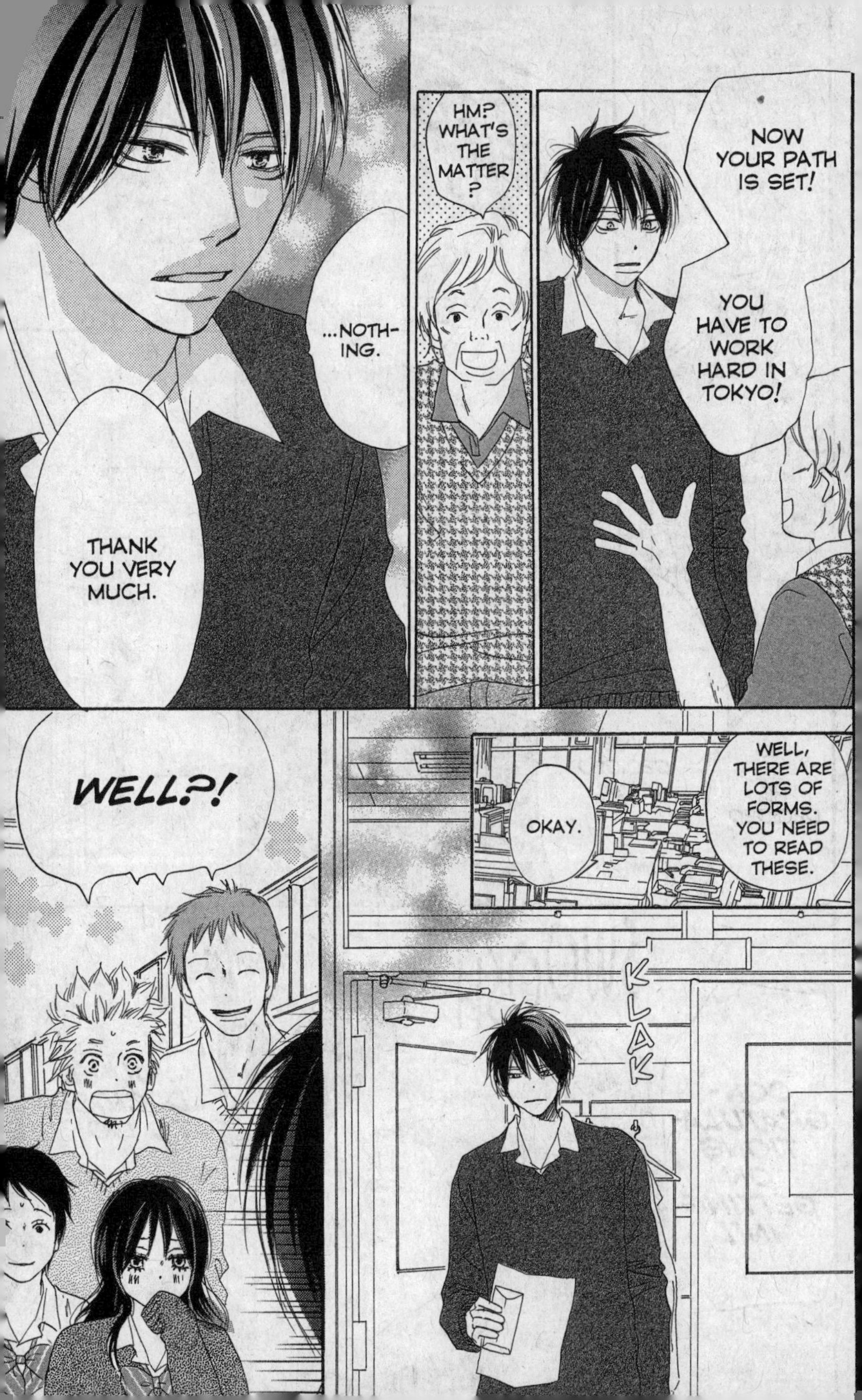
NOW YOUR PATH IS SET!
YOU HAVE TO WORK HARD IN TOKYO!
HM? WHAT'S THE MATTER?
...NOTHING.
THANK YOU VERY MUCH.
WELL, THERE ARE LOTS OF FORMS. YOU NEED TO READ THESE.
OKAY.
KLAK
WELL?!

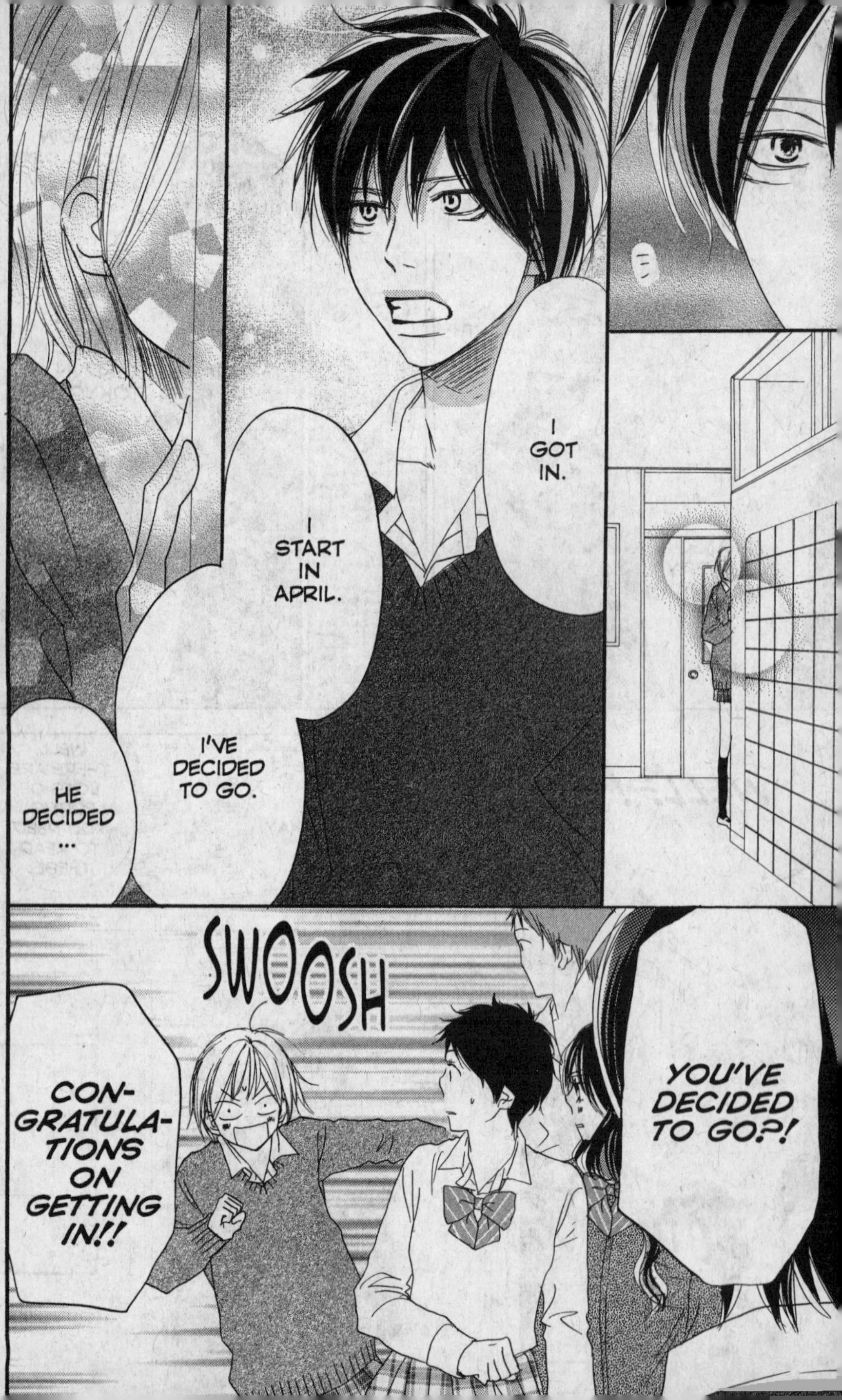
I GOT IN.
I START IN APRIL.
I'VE DECIDED TO GO.
HE DECIDED ...
YOU'VE DECIDED TO GO?!
SWOOSH
CON-GRATULA-TIONS ON GETTING IN!!

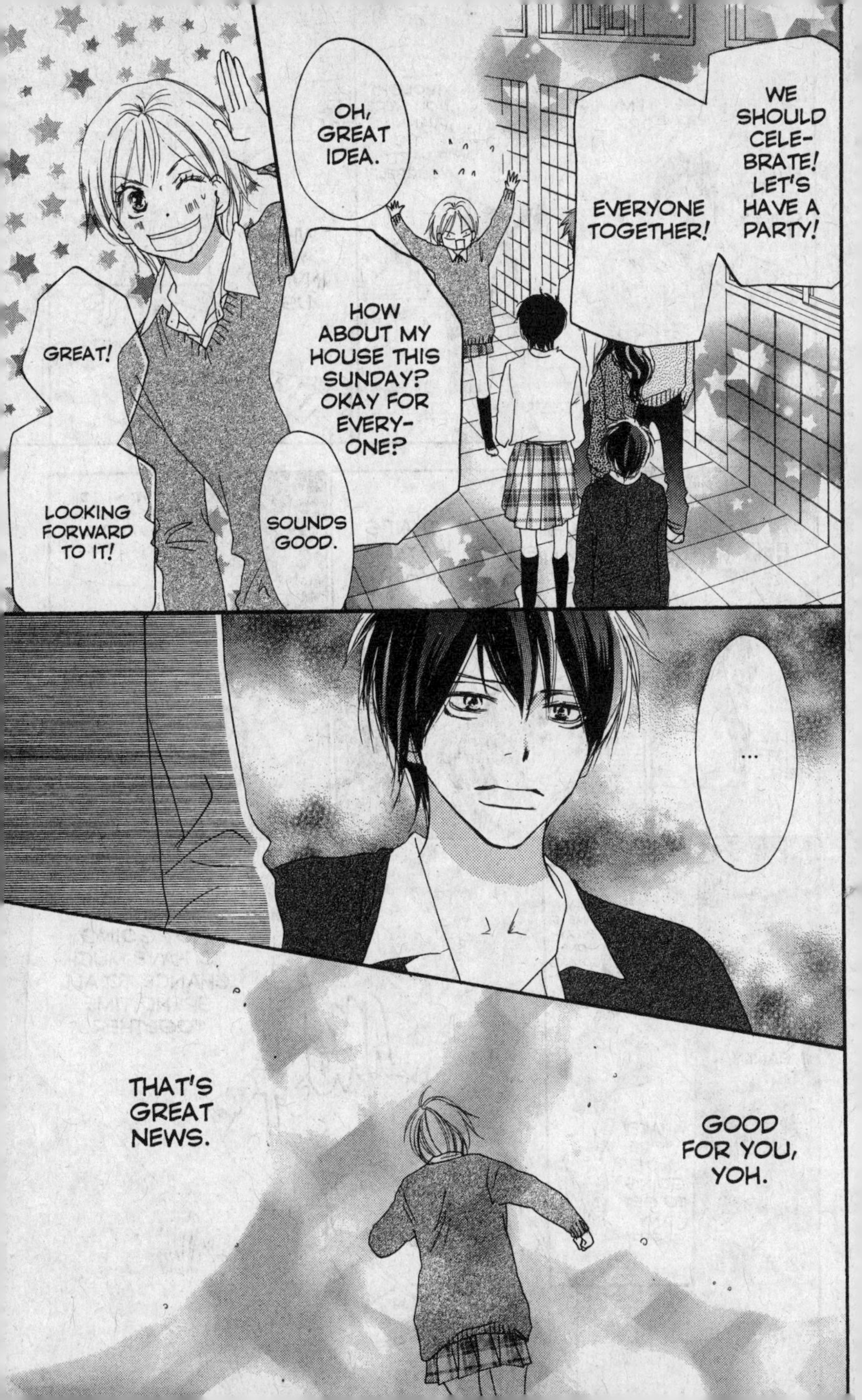
WE SHOULD CELEBRATE! LET'S HAVE A PARTY!
EVERYONE TOGETHER!
OH, GREAT IDEA.
HOW ABOUT MY HOUSE THIS SUNDAY? OKAY FOR EVERYONE?
SOUNDS GOOD.
GREAT!
LOOKING FORWARD TO IT!
...
GOOD FOR YOU, YOH.
THAT'S GREAT NEWS.

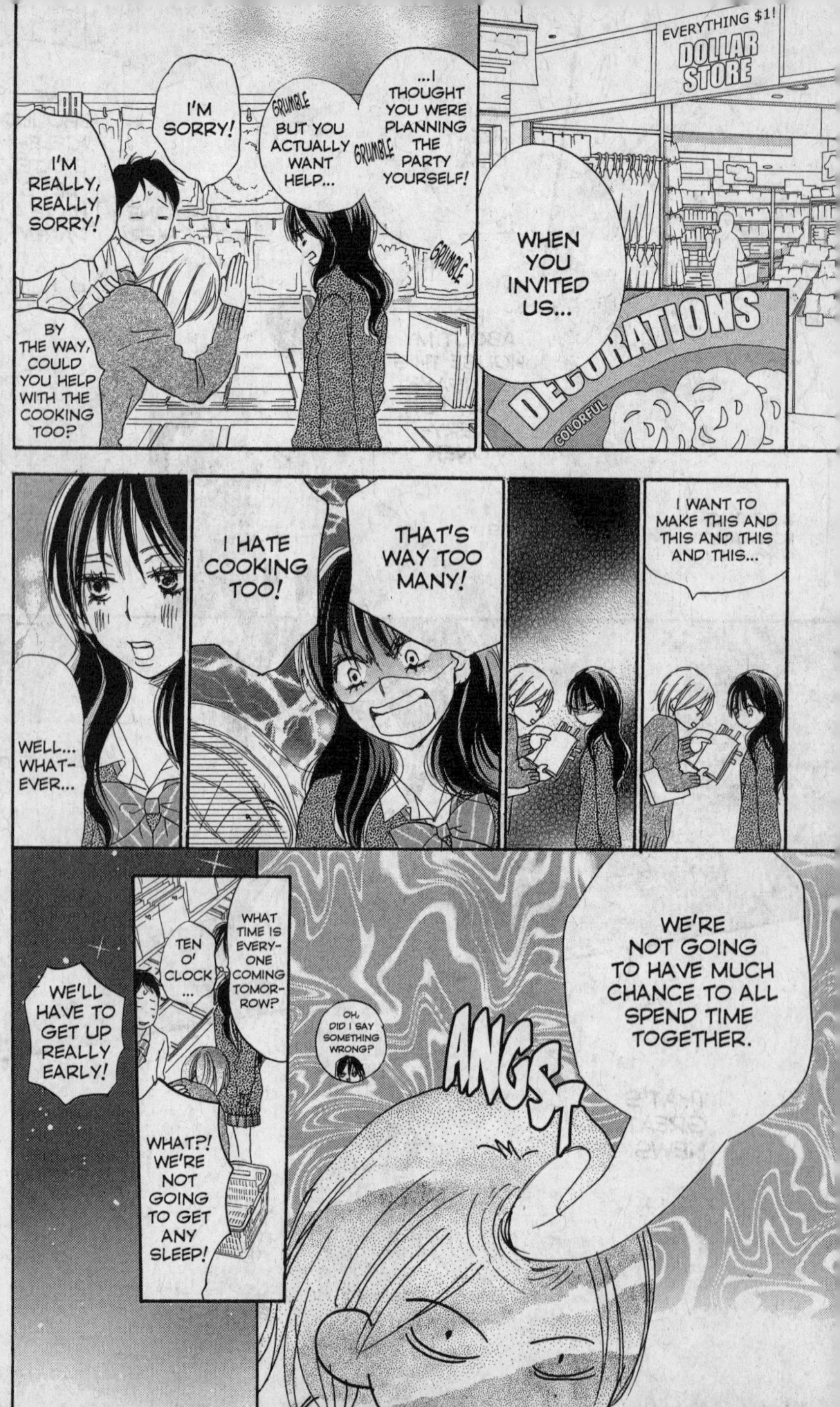
EVERYTHING $1!
DOLLAR STORE
WHEN YOU INVITED US...
DECORATIONS
COLORFUL
...I THOUGHT YOU WERE PLANNING THE PARTY YOURSELF!
GRUMBLE
GRUMBLE
BUT YOU ACTUALLY WANT HELP...
GRUMBLE
I'M SORRY!
I'M REALLY, REALLY SORRY!
BY THE WAY, COULD YOU HELP WITH THE COOKING TOO?
I WANT TO MAKE THIS AND THIS AND THIS AND THIS...
THAT'S WAY TOO MANY!
I HATE COOKING TOO!
WELL... WHATEVER...
WE'RE NOT GOING TO HAVE MUCH CHANCE TO ALL SPEND TIME TOGETHER.
ANGST
OH, DID I SAY SOMETHING WRONG?
WHAT TIME IS EVERYONE COMING TOMORROW?
TEN O' CLOCK...
WHAT?! WE'RE NOT GOING TO GET ANY SLEEP!
WE'LL HAVE TO GET UP REALLY EARLY!

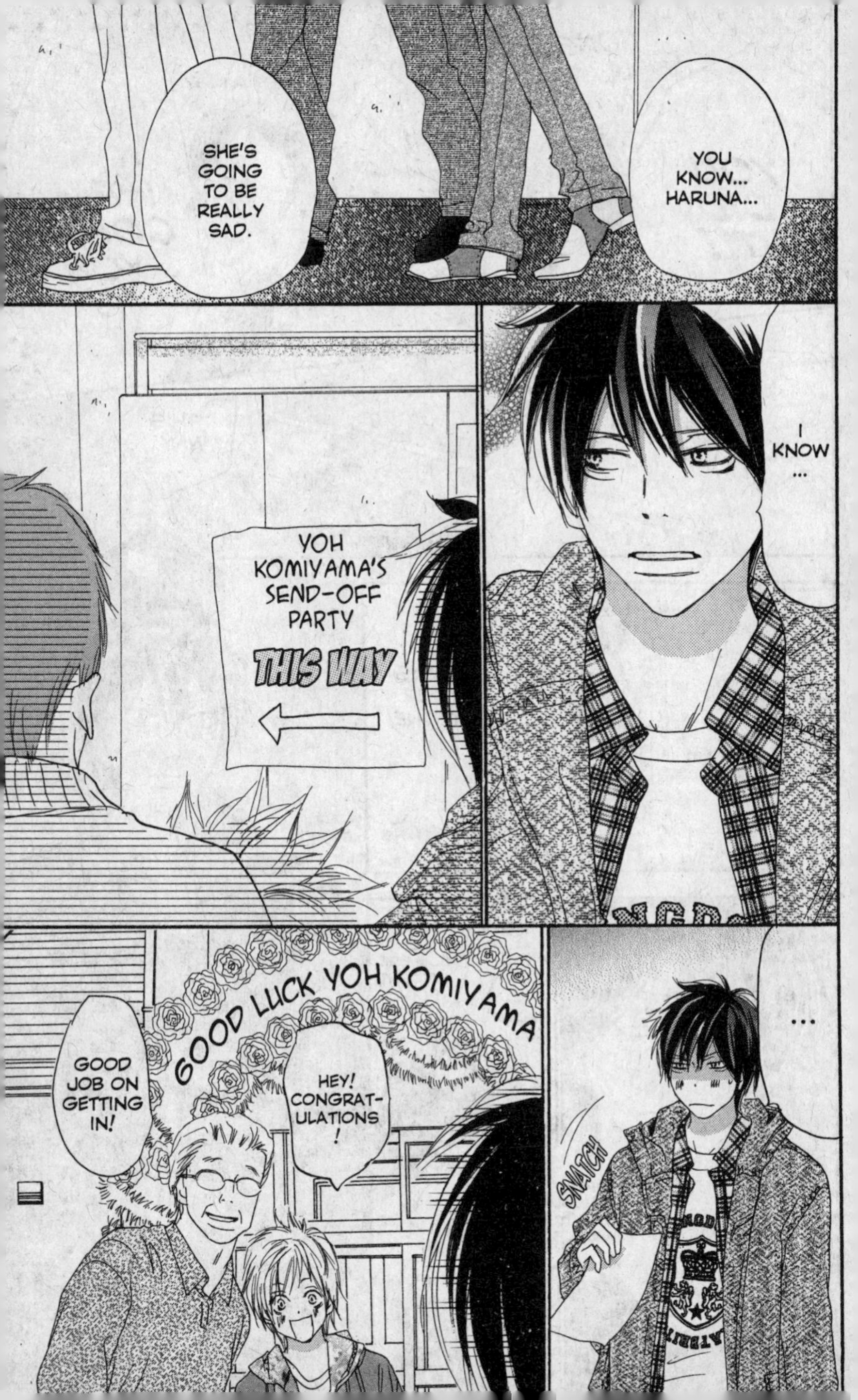
YOU KNOW... HARUNA...
SHE'S GOING TO BE REALLY SAD.
I KNOW ...
YOH KOMIYAMA'S SEND-OFF PARTY
THIS WAY
...
SNATCH
GOOD LUCK YOH KOMIYAMA
HEY! CONGRAT-ULATIONS!
GOOD JOB ON GETTING IN!

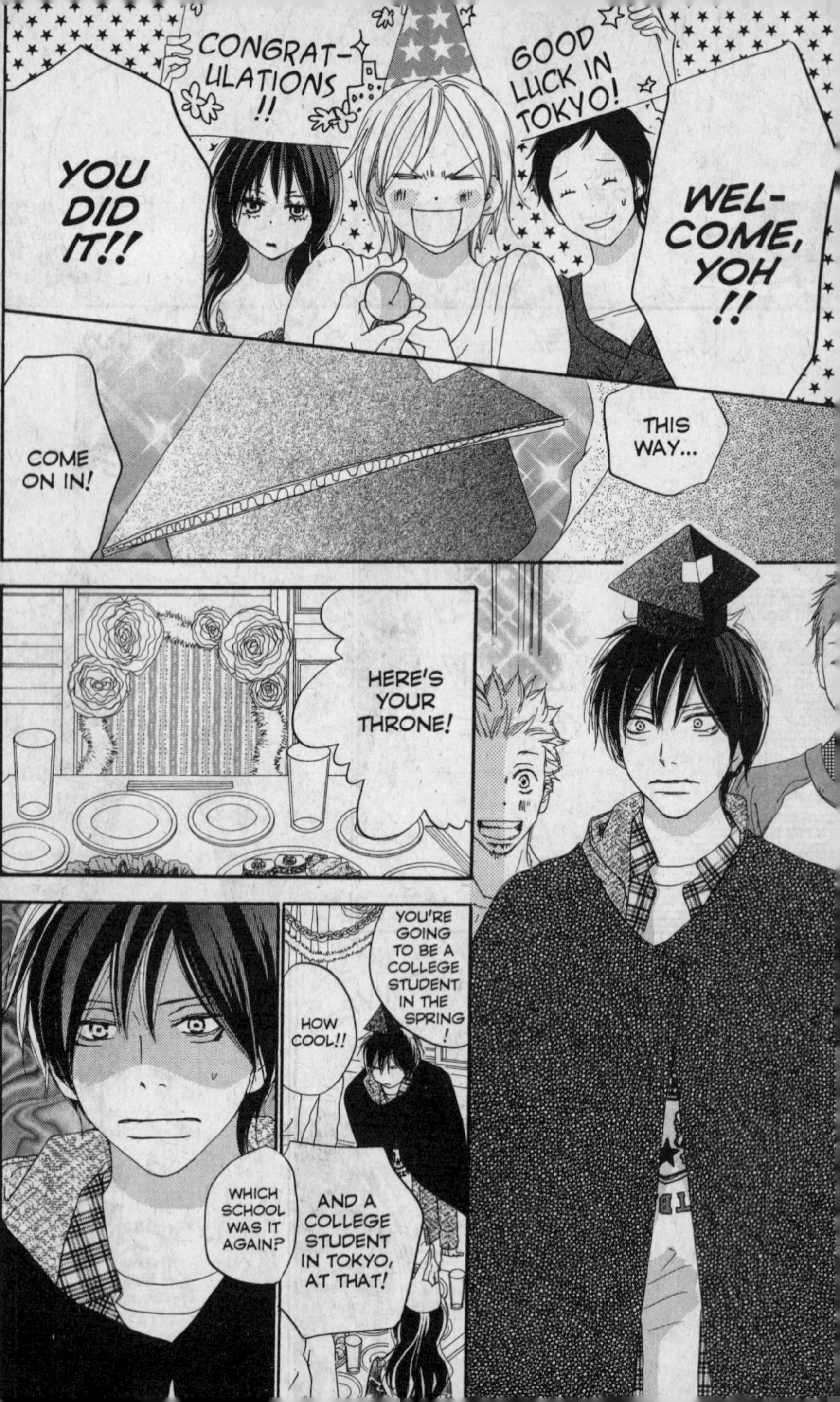
WEL-COME, YOH!!
GOOD LUCK IN TOKYO!
CONGRAT-ULATIONS!!
YOU DID IT!!
THIS WAY...
COME ON IN!
HERE'S YOUR THRONE!
YOU'RE GOING TO BE A COLLEGE STUDENT IN THE SPRING!
HOW COOL!!
AND A COLLEGE STUDENT IN TOKYO, AT THAT!
WHICH SCHOOL WAS IT AGAIN?

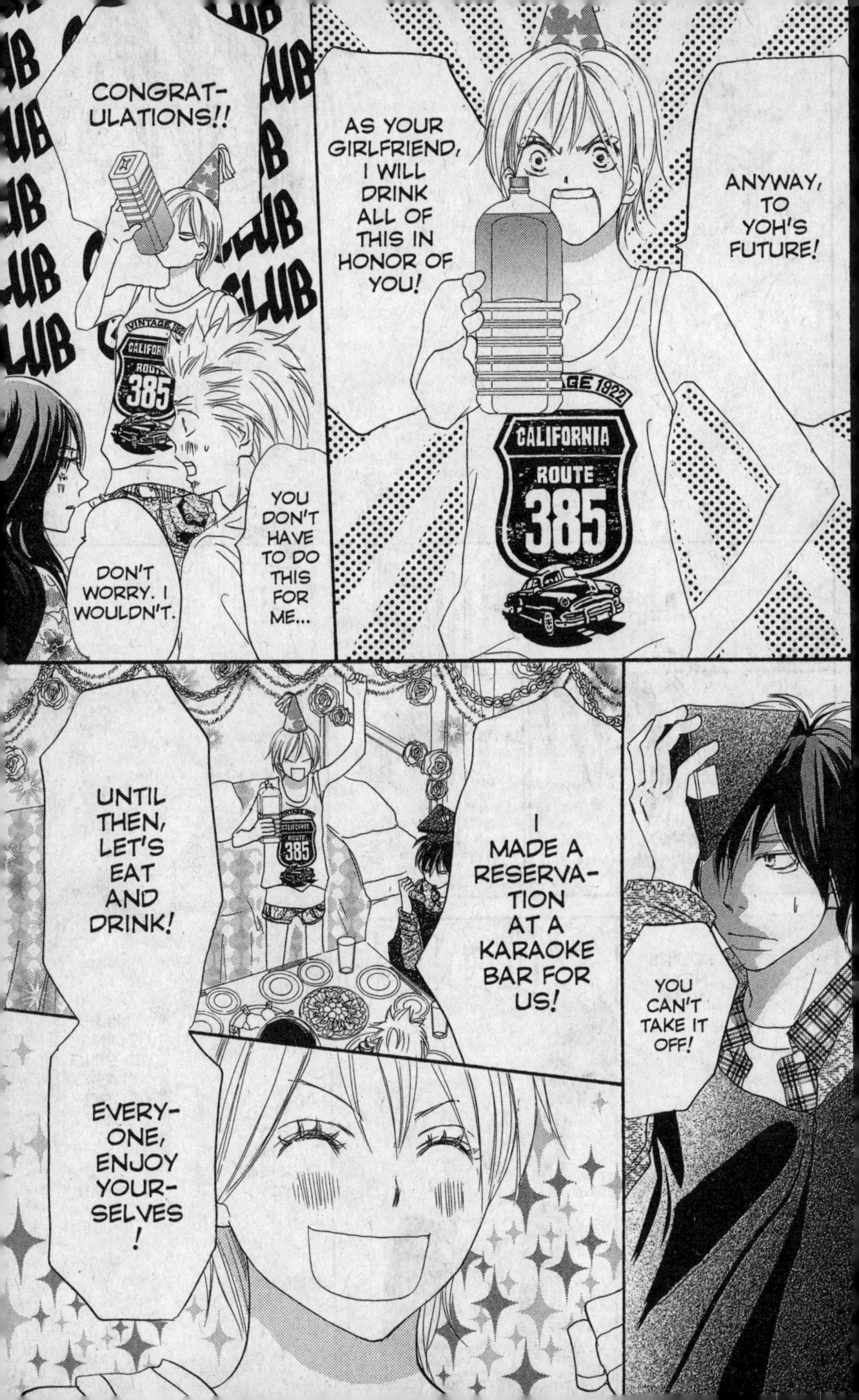
ANYWAY, TO YOH'S FUTURE!
AS YOUR GIRLFRIEND, I WILL DRINK ALL OF THIS IN HONOR OF YOU!
CONGRATULATIONS!!
YOU DON'T HAVE TO DO THIS FOR ME...
DON'T WORRY. I WOULDN'T.
YOU CAN'T TAKE IT OFF!
I MADE A RESERVATION AT A KARAOKE BAR FOR US!
UNTIL THEN, LET'S EAT AND DRINK!
EVERYONE, ENJOY YOURSELVES!

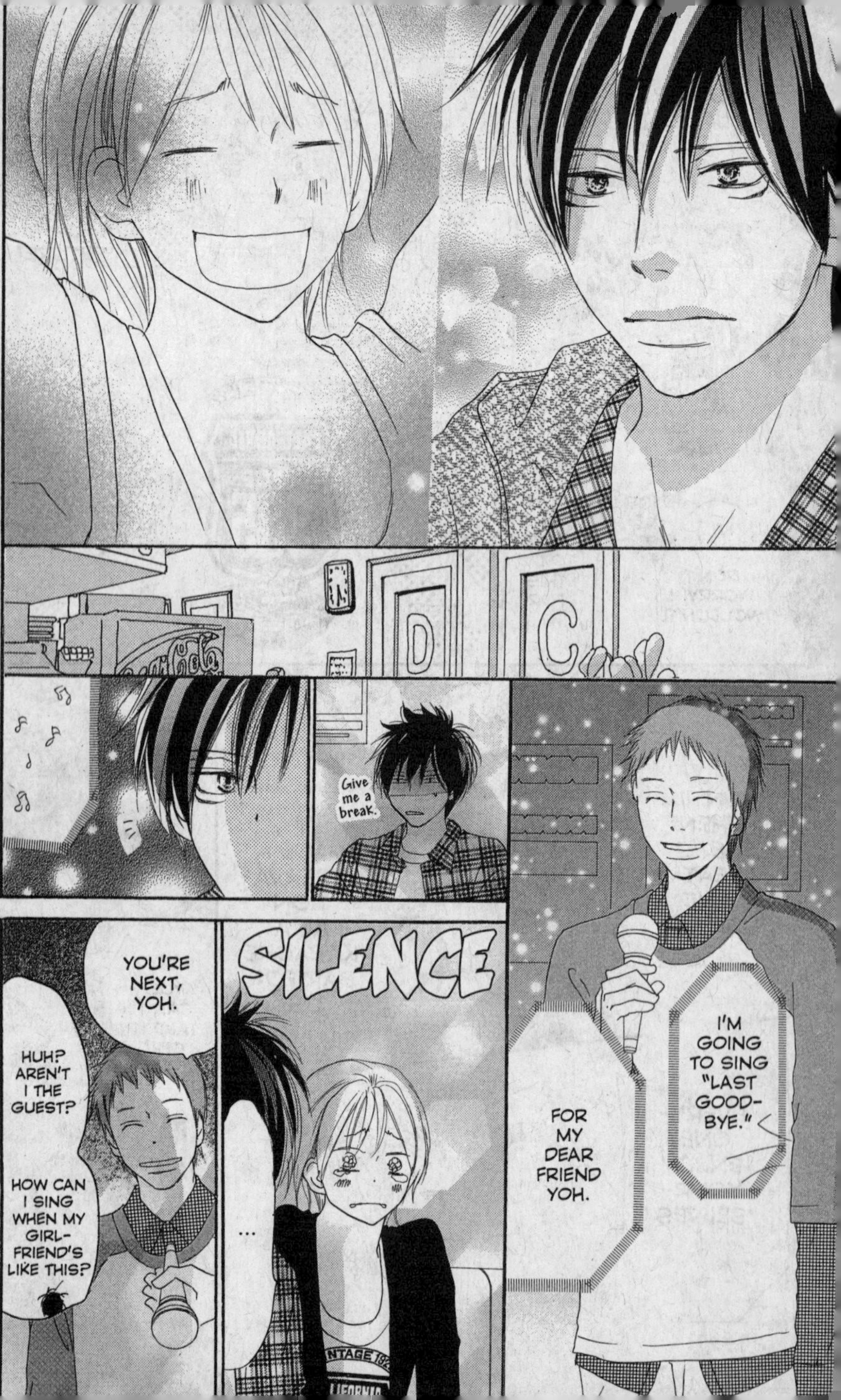

C
D
I'M GOING TO SING "LAST GOOD-BYE."
FOR MY DEAR FRIEND YOH.
Give me a break.
SILENCE
...
YOU'RE NEXT, YOH.
HUH? AREN'T I THE GUEST?
HOW CAN I SING WHEN MY GIRL-FRIEND'S LIKE THIS?

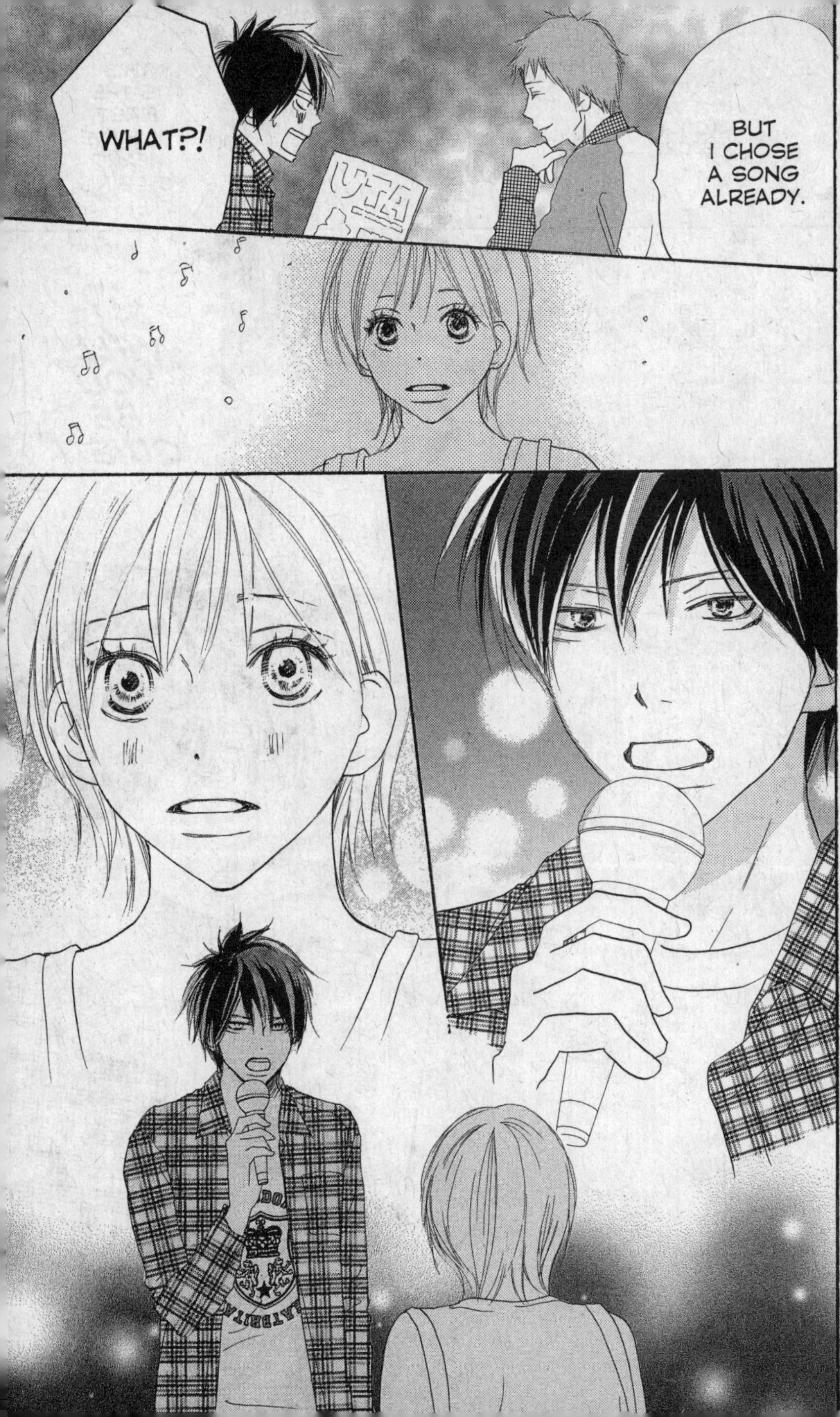
BUT I CHOSE A SONG ALREADY.
WHAT?!

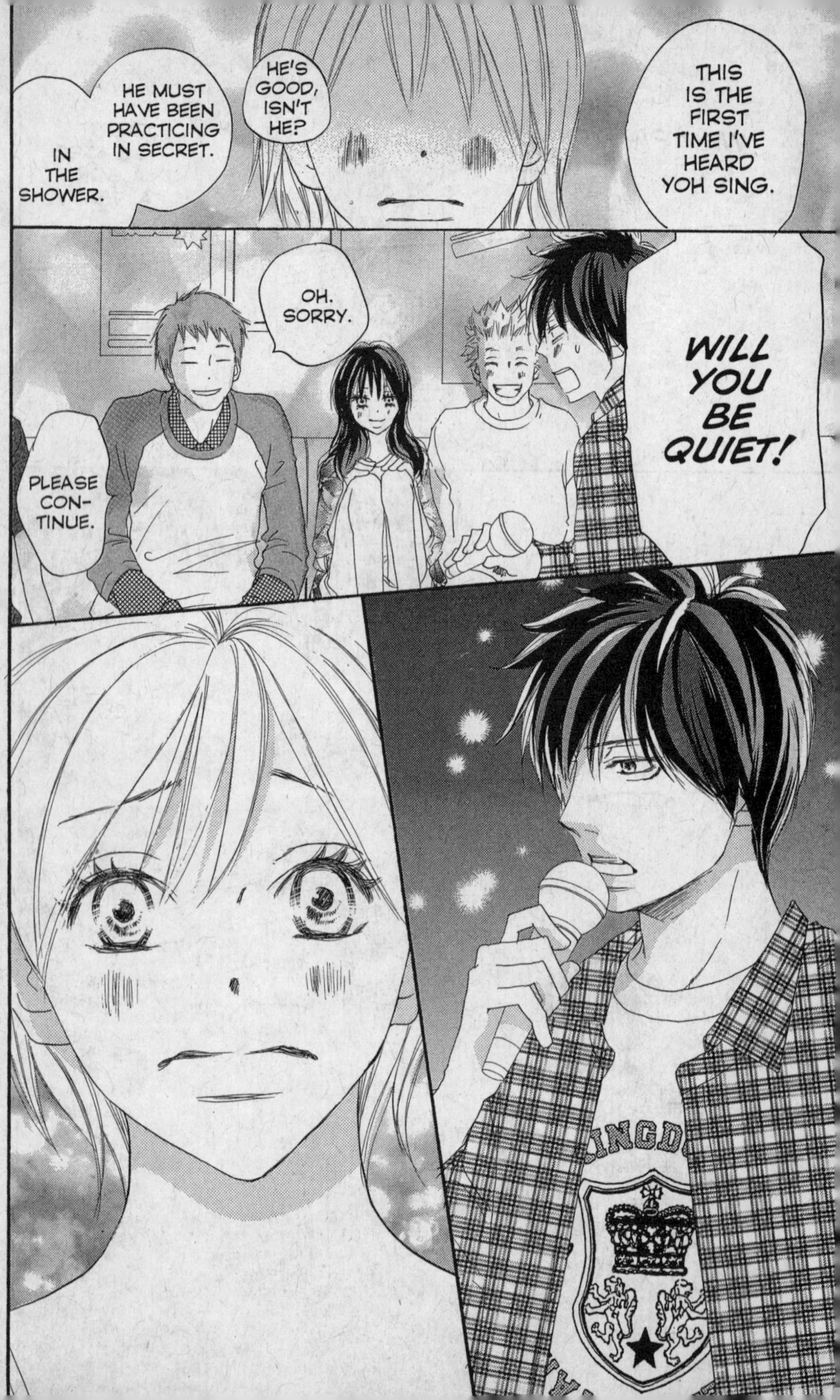
THIS IS THE FIRST TIME I'VE HEARD YOH SING.
HE'S GOOD, ISN'T HE?
HE MUST HAVE BEEN PRACTICING IN SECRET.
IN THE SHOWER.
WILL YOU BE QUIET!
OH. SORRY.
PLEASE CONTINUE.

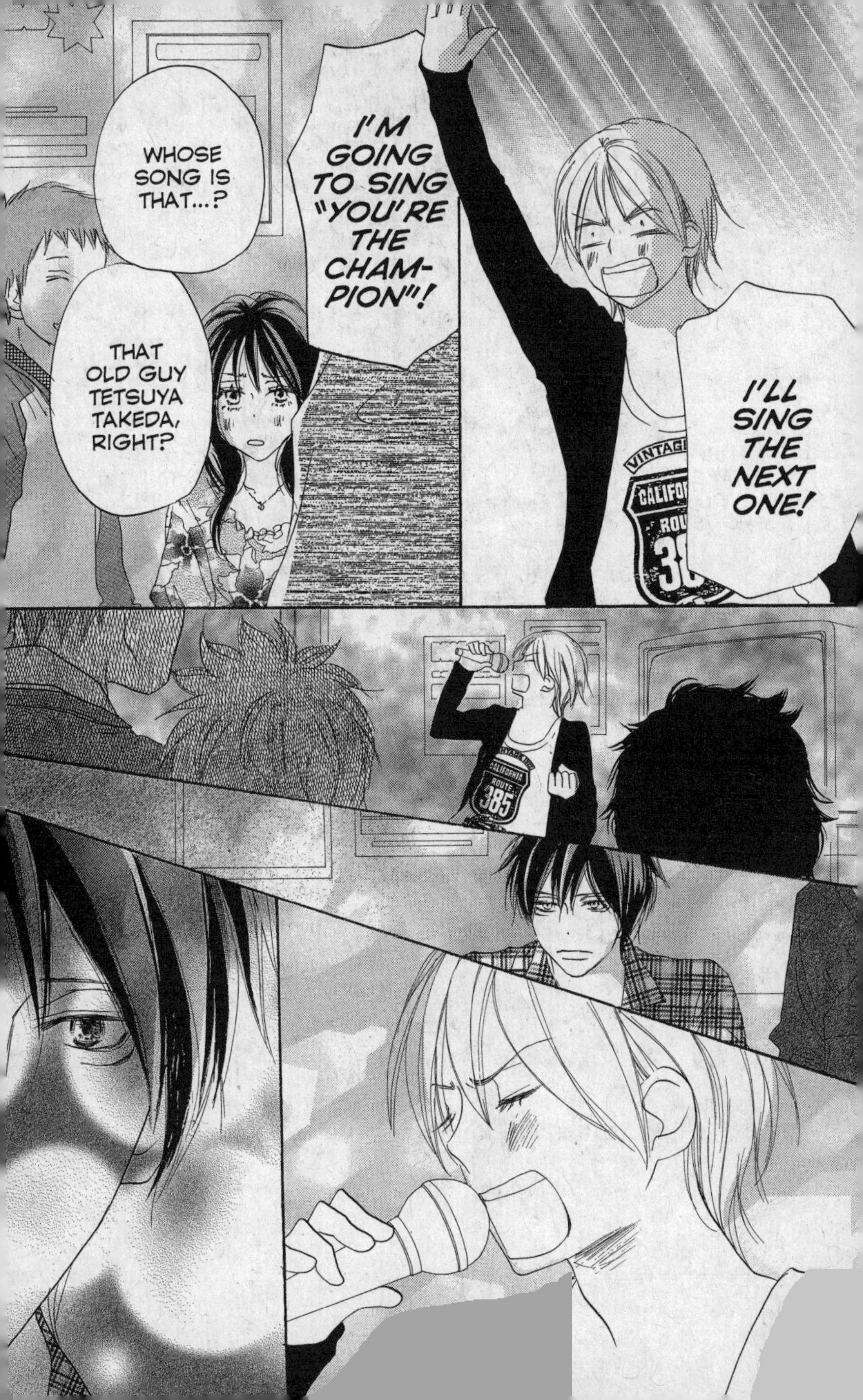
I'LL SING THE NEXT ONE!
I'M GOING TO SING "YOU'RE THE CHAMPION"!
WHOSE SONG IS THAT...?
THAT OLD GUY TETSUYA TAKEDA, RIGHT?

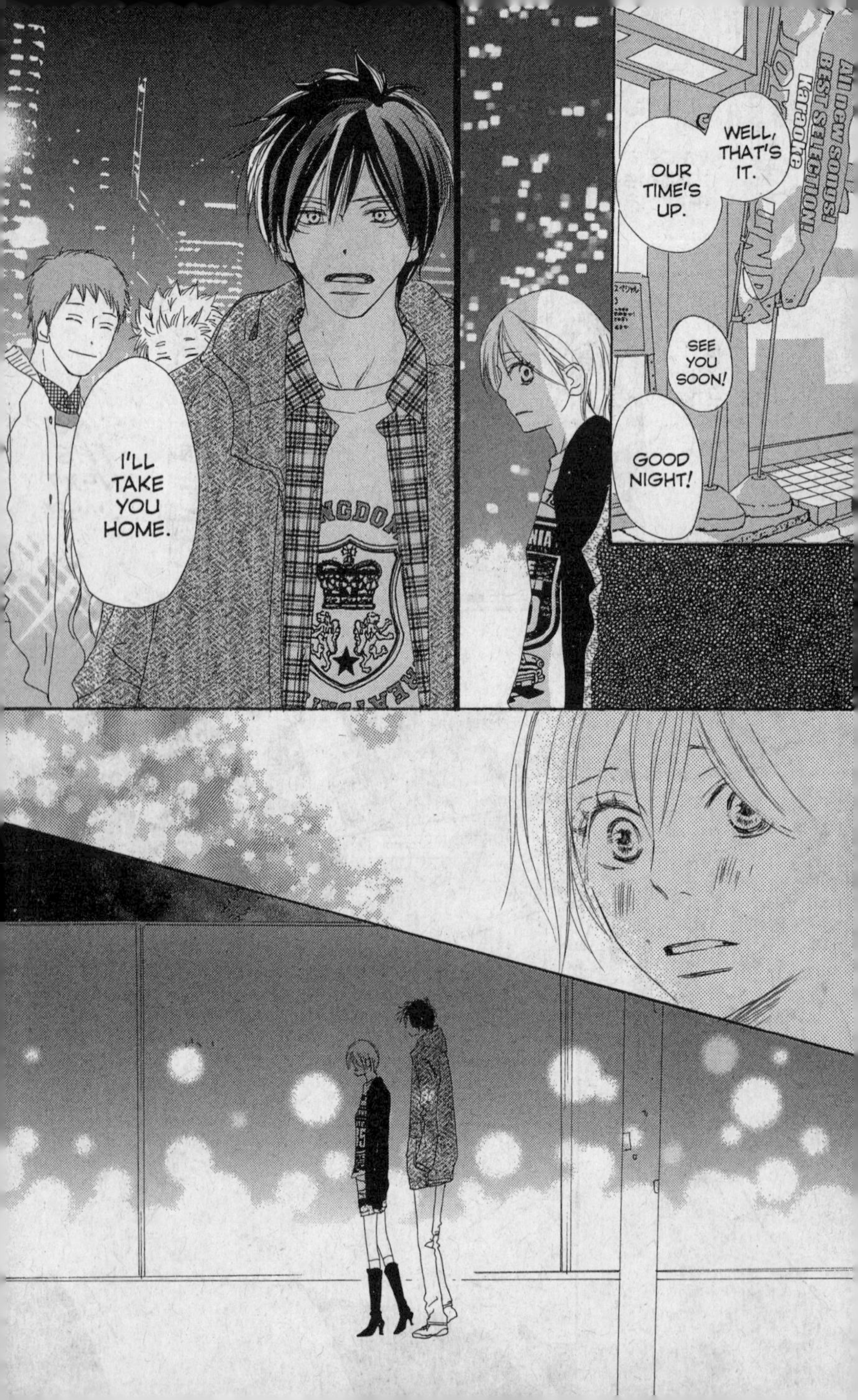
All new songs!
BEST SELECTION!
Karaoke
WELL, THAT'S IT.
OUR TIME'S UP.
SEE YOU SOON!
GOOD NIGHT!
I'LL TAKE YOU HOME.

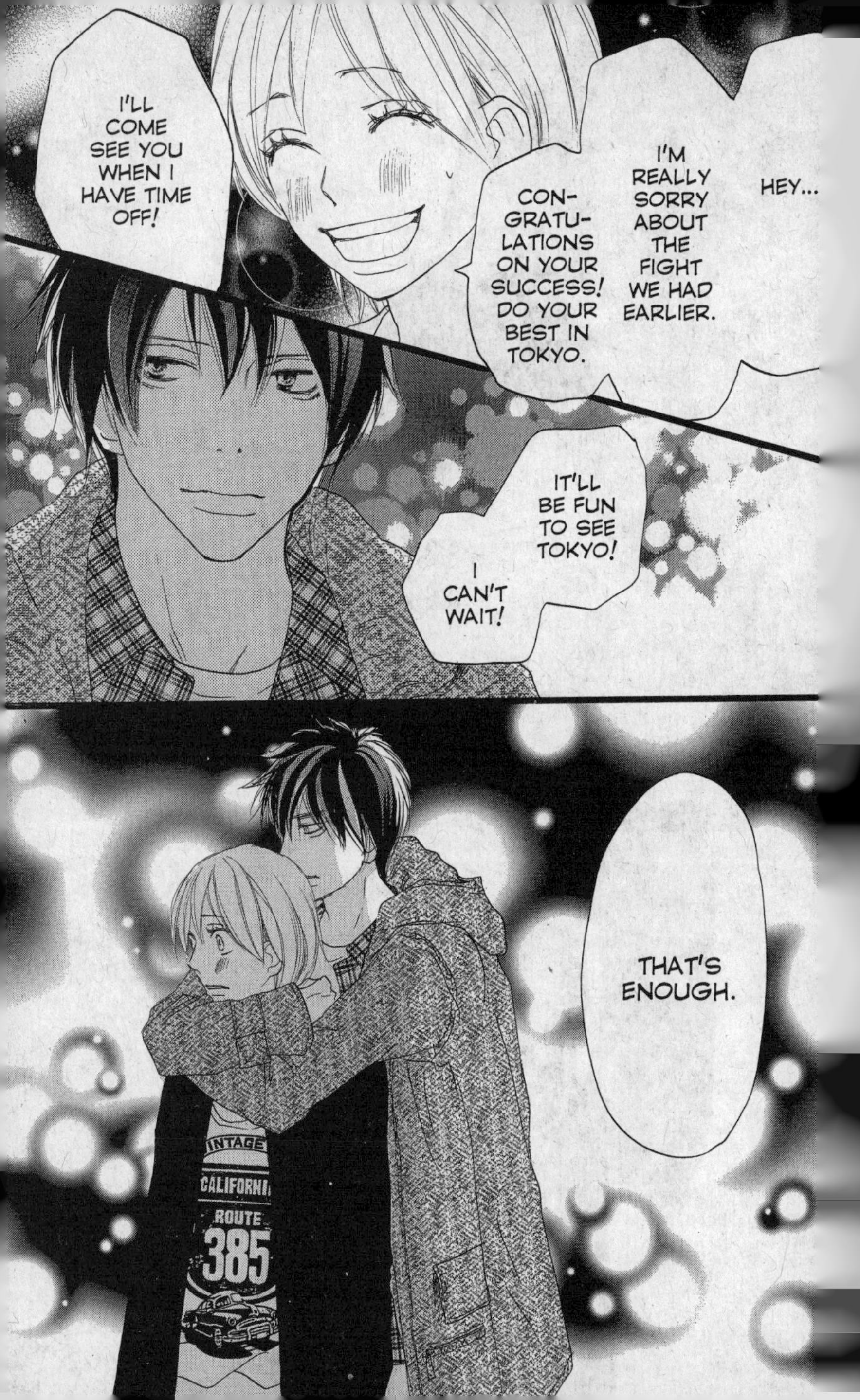
HEY...
I'M REALLY SORRY ABOUT THE FIGHT WE HAD EARLIER.
CONGRATULATIONS ON YOUR SUCCESS! DO YOUR BEST IN TOKYO.
I'LL COME SEE YOU WHEN I HAVE TIME OFF!
IT'LL BE FUN TO SEE TOKYO!
I CAN'T WAIT!
THAT'S ENOUGH.
INTAGE
CALIFORNI
ROUTE
385

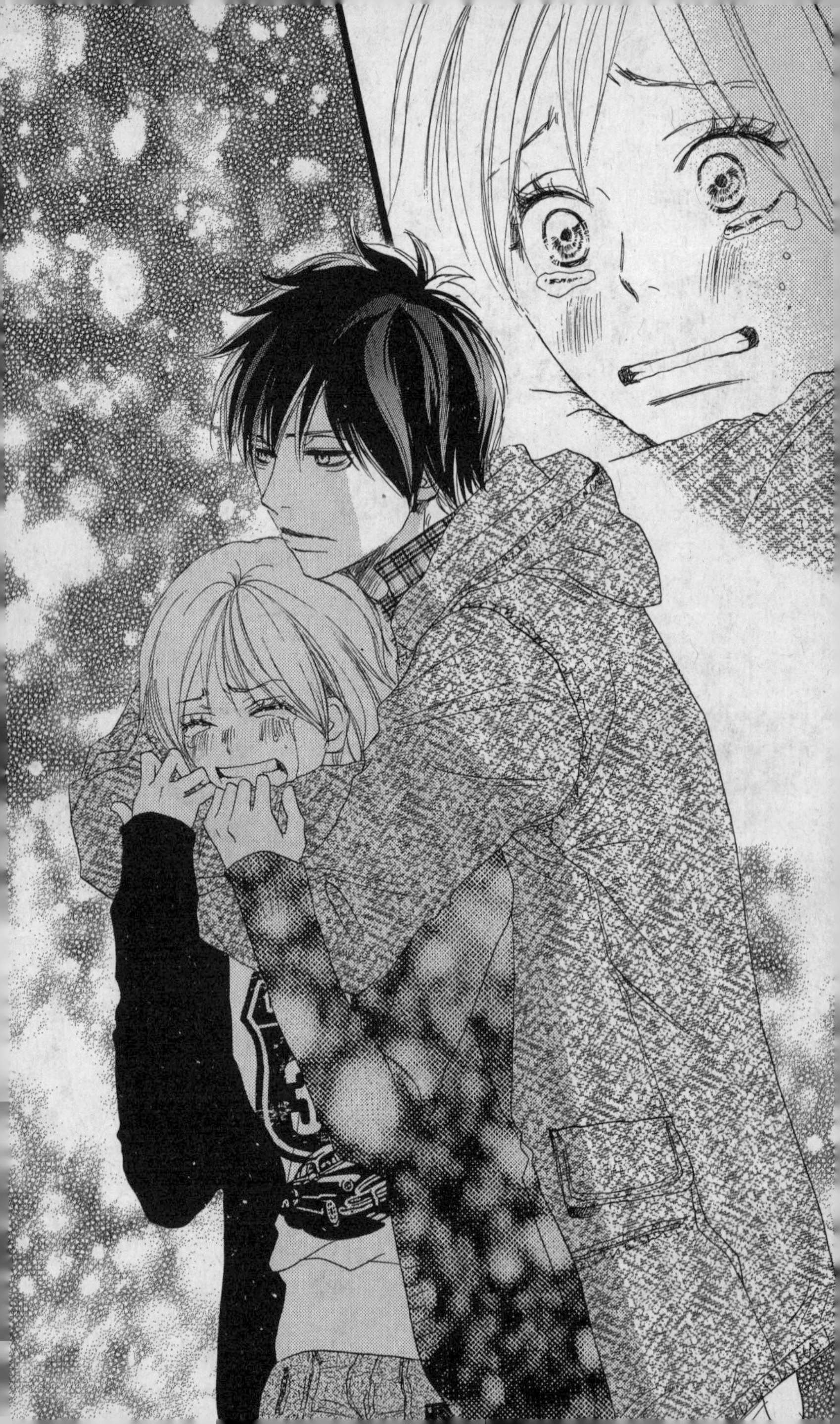

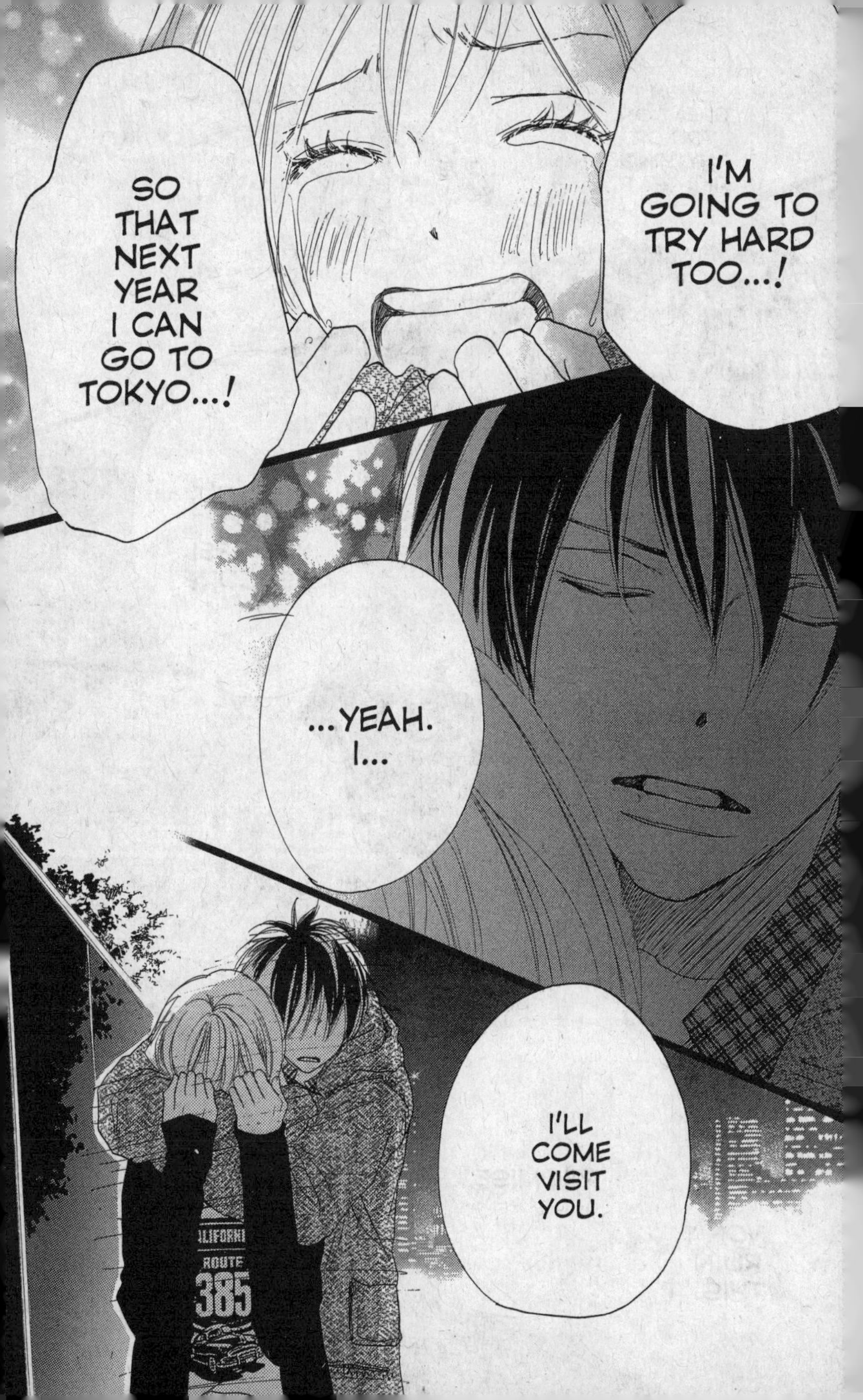
I'M GOING TO TRY HARD TOO...!
SO THAT NEXT YEAR I CAN GO TO TOKYO...!
...YEAH. I...
I'LL COME VISIT YOU.
ROUTE
385

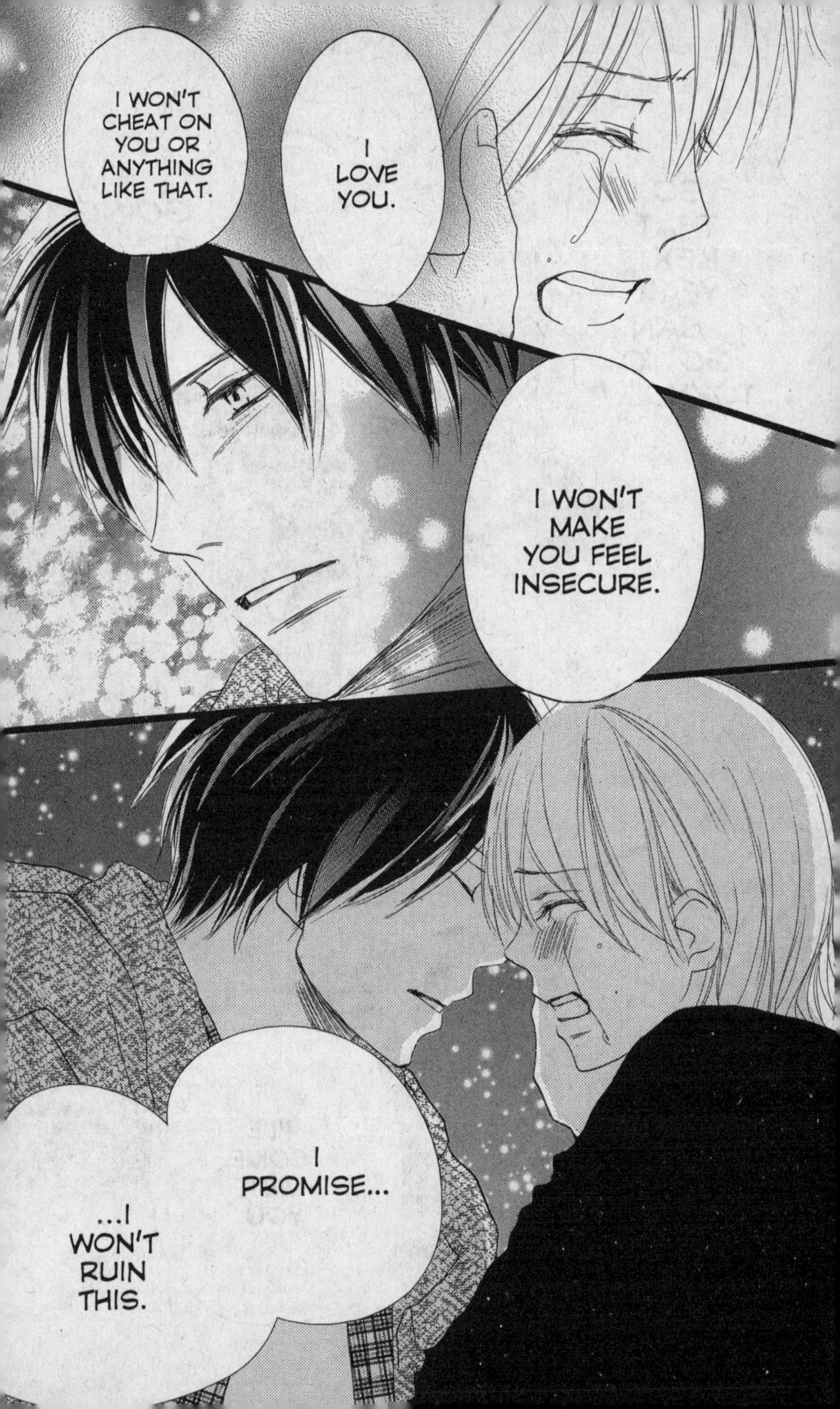
I LOVE YOU.
I WON'T CHEAT ON YOU OR ANYTHING LIKE THAT.
I WON'T MAKE YOU FEEL INSECURE.
I PROMISE...
...I WON'T RUIN THIS.

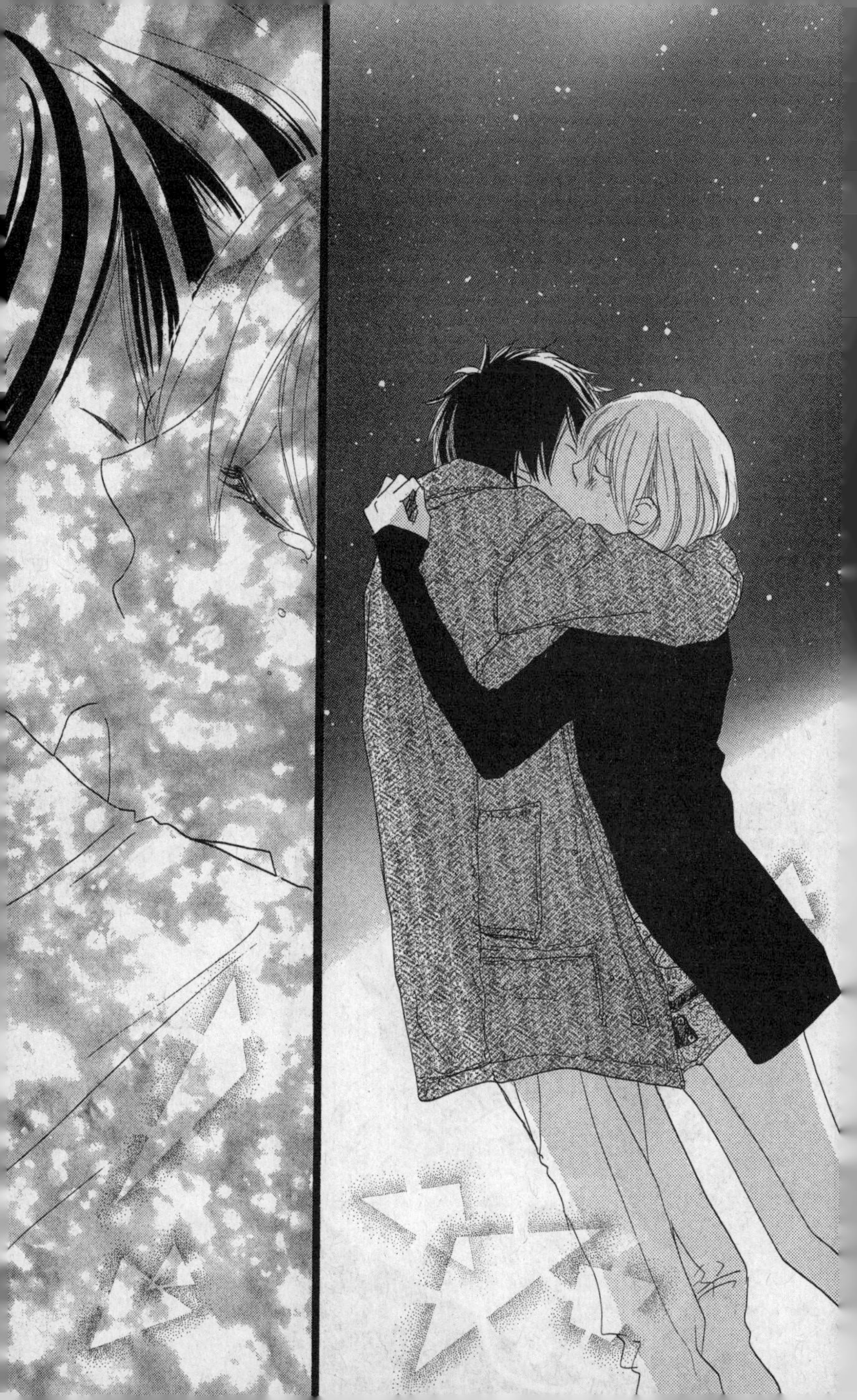

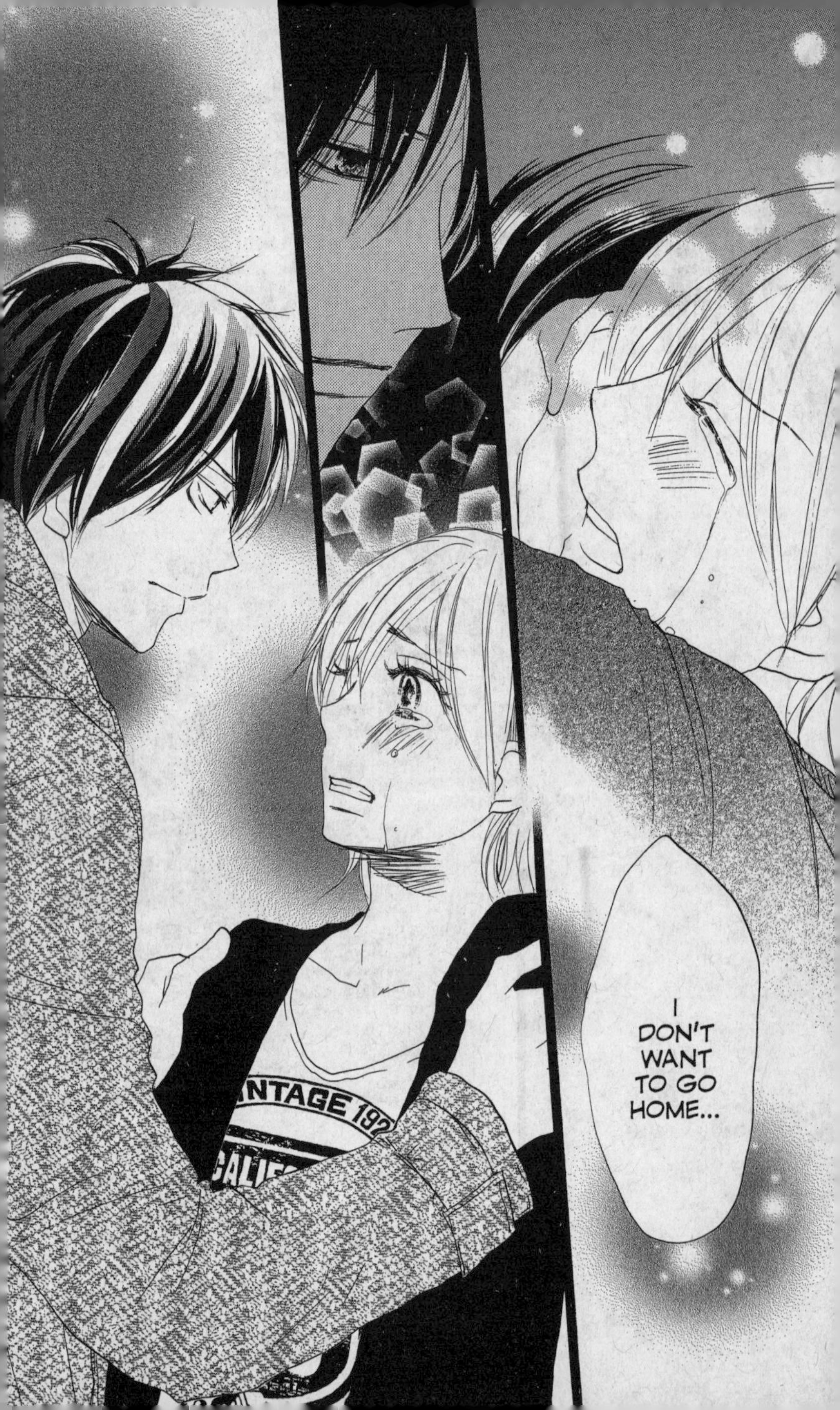
I DON'T WANT TO GO HOME...

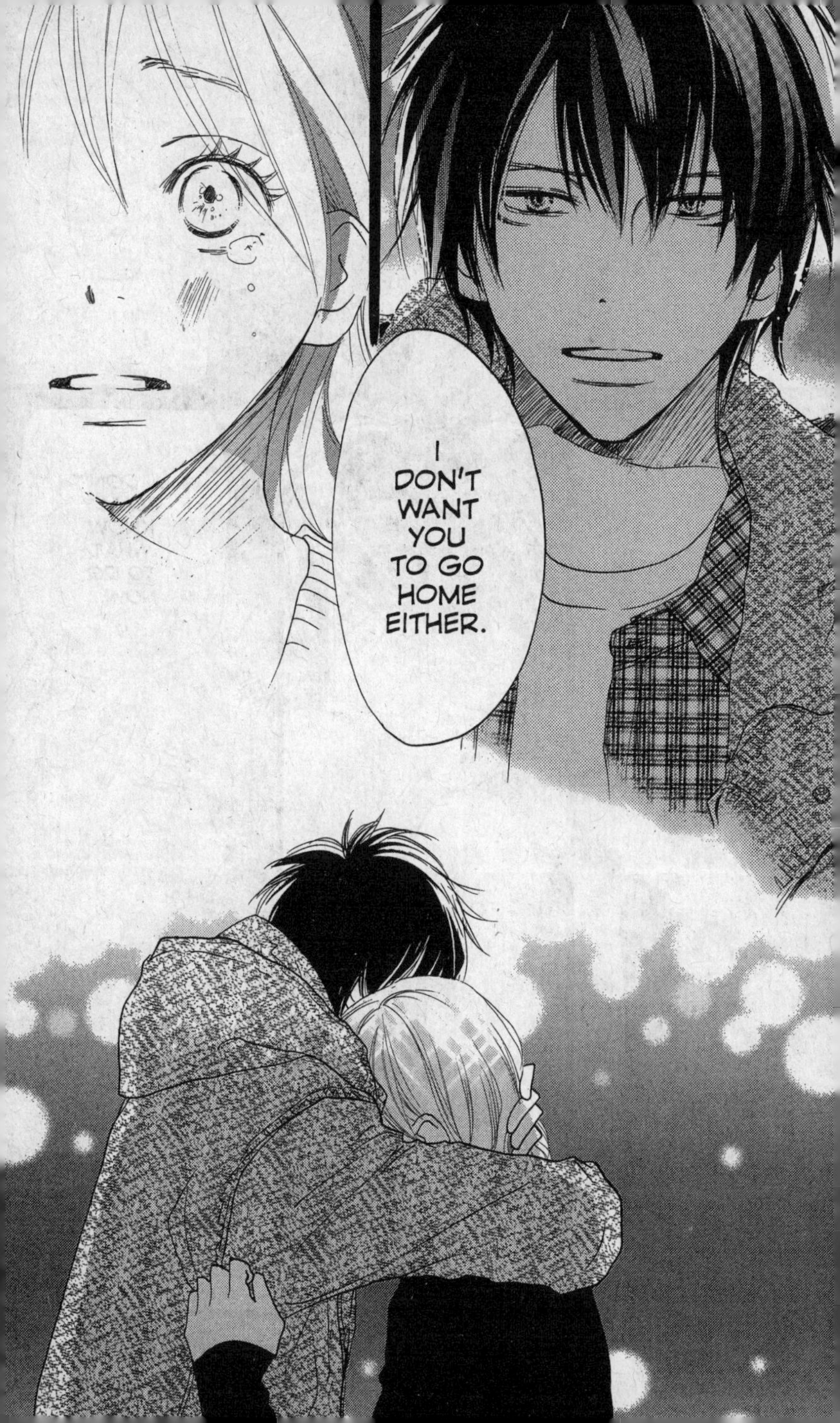
I DON'T WANT YOU TO GO HOME EITHER.

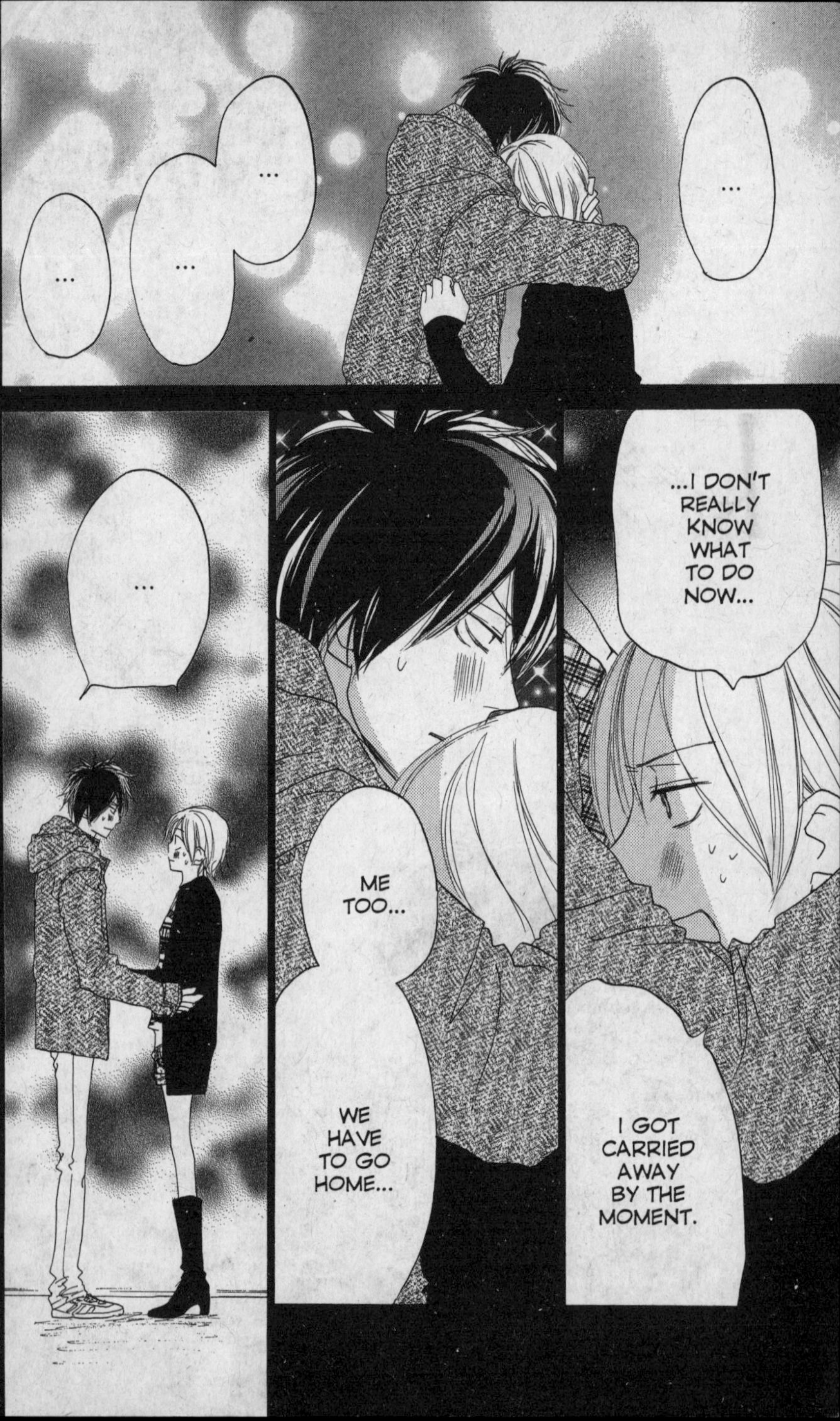
...
...
...
...
...I DON'T REALLY KNOW WHAT TO DO NOW...
I GOT CARRIED AWAY BY THE MOMENT.
ME TOO...
WE HAVE TO GO HOME...
...

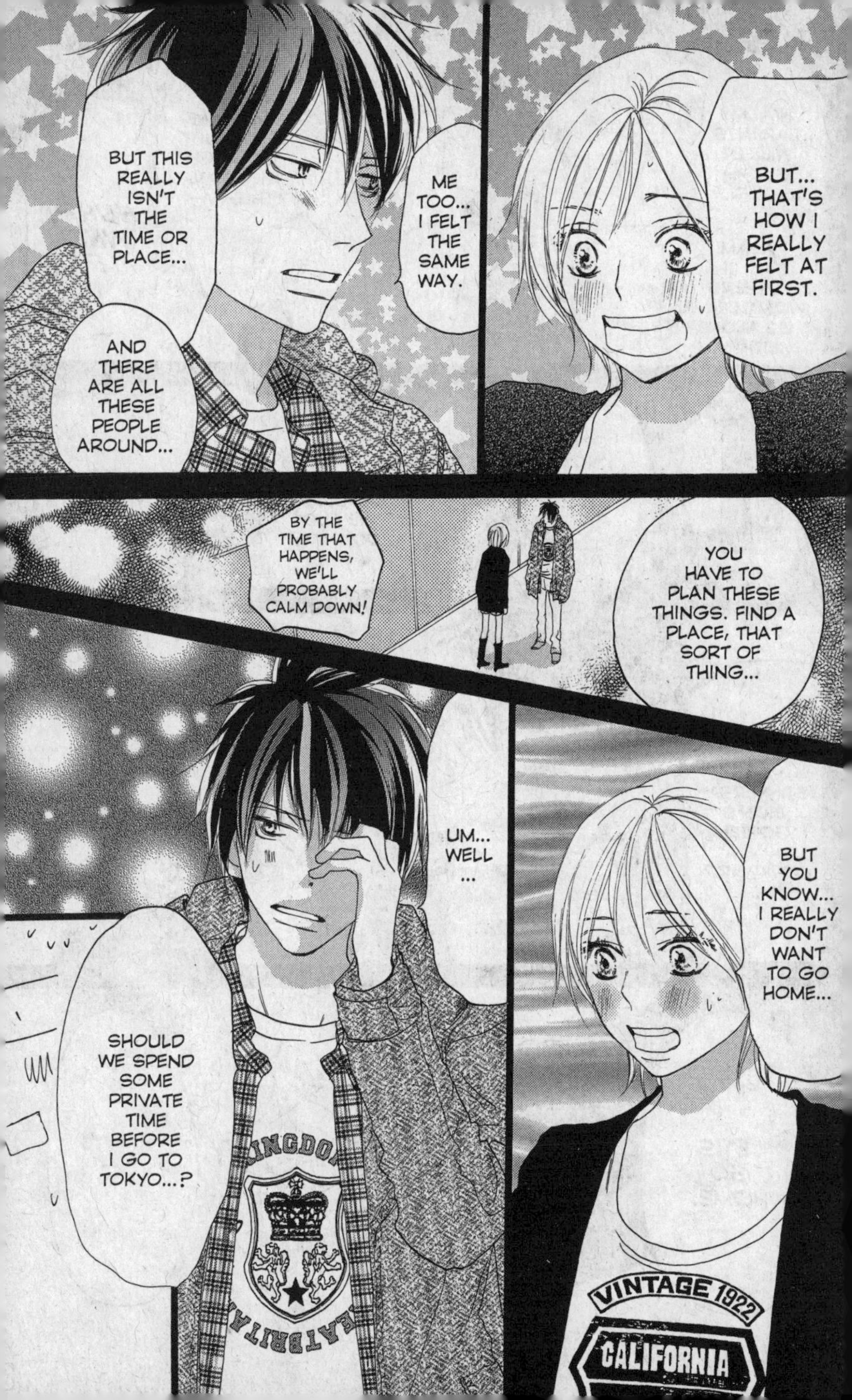
BUT... THAT'S HOW I REALLY FELT AT FIRST.
ME TOO... I FELT THE SAME WAY.
BUT THIS REALLY ISN'T THE TIME OR PLACE...
AND THERE ARE ALL THESE PEOPLE AROUND...
YOU HAVE TO PLAN THESE THINGS. FIND A PLACE, THAT SORT OF THING...
BY THE TIME THAT HAPPENS, WE'LL PROBABLY CALM DOWN!
BUT YOU KNOW... I REALLY DON'T WANT TO GO HOME...
VINTAGE 1922
CALIFORNIA
UM... WELL ...
SHOULD WE SPEND SOME PRIVATE TIME BEFORE I GO TO TOKYO...?

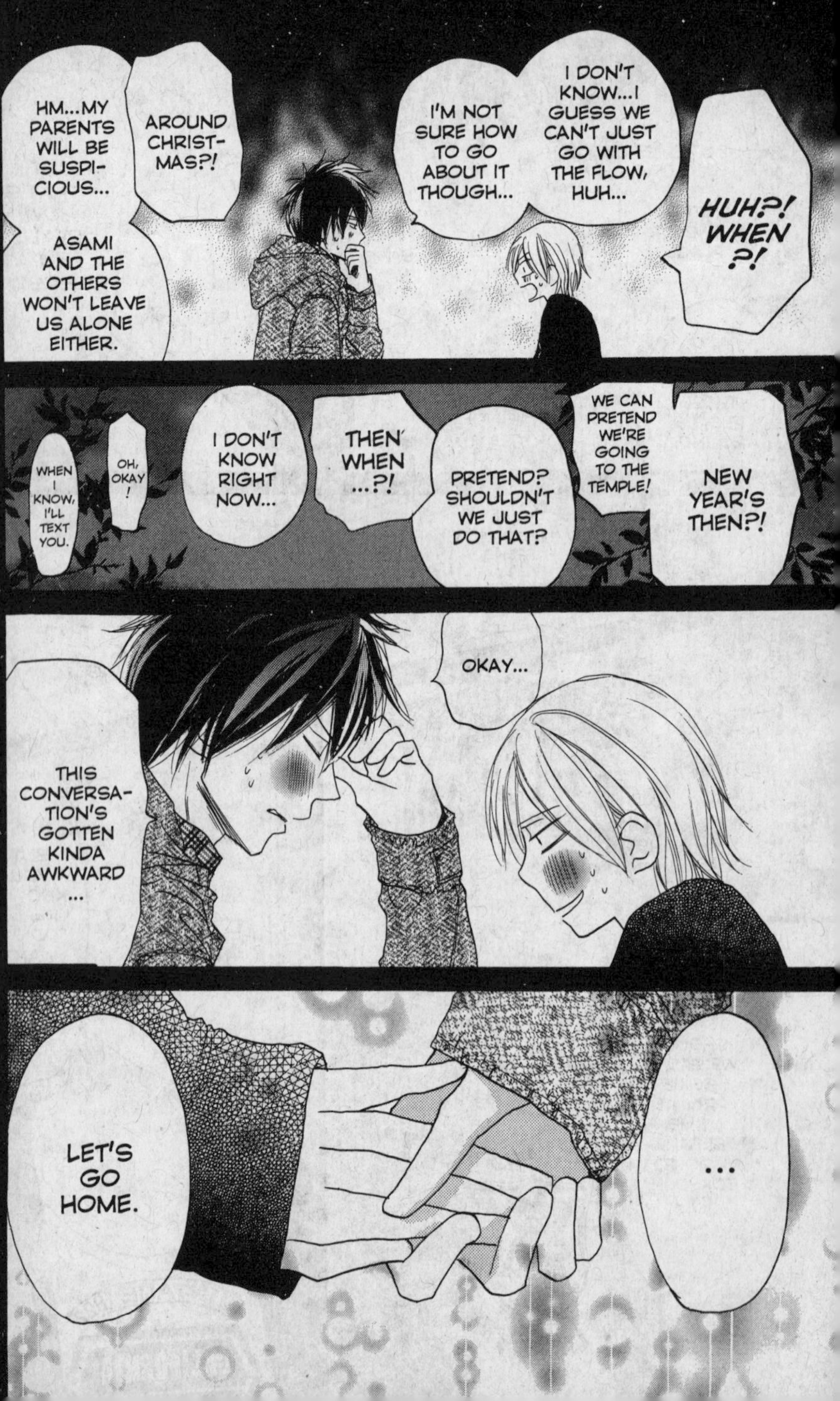
HUH?! WHEN ?!
I DON'T KNOW...I GUESS WE CAN'T JUST GO WITH THE FLOW, HUH...
I'M NOT SURE HOW TO GO ABOUT IT THOUGH...
AROUND CHRIST-MAS?!
HM...MY PARENTS WILL BE SUSPI-CIOUS...
ASAMI AND THE OTHERS WON'T LEAVE US ALONE EITHER.
NEW YEAR'S THEN?!
WE CAN PRETEND WE'RE GOING TO THE TEMPLE!
PRETEND? SHOULDN'T WE JUST DO THAT?
THEN WHEN ...?!
I DON'T KNOW RIGHT NOW...
OH, OKAY!
WHEN I KNOW, I'LL TEXT YOU.
OKAY...
THIS CONVERSA-TION'S GOTTEN KINDA AWKWARD ...
...
LET'S GO HOME.

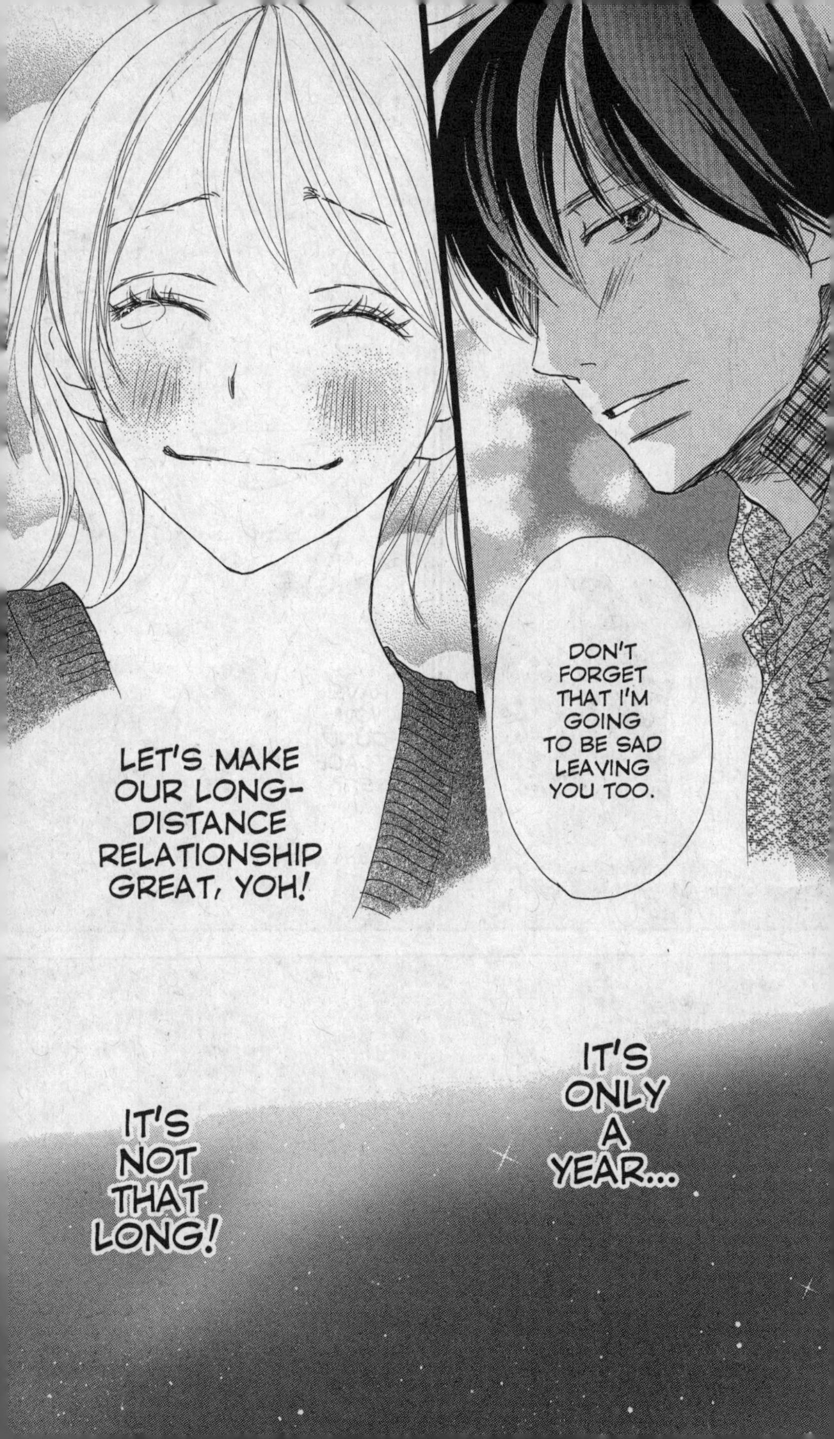
DON'T FORGET THAT I'M GOING TO BE SAD LEAVING YOU TOO.
LET'S MAKE OUR LONG-DISTANCE RELATIONSHIP GREAT, YOH!
IT'S ONLY A YEAR...
IT'S NOT THAT LONG!

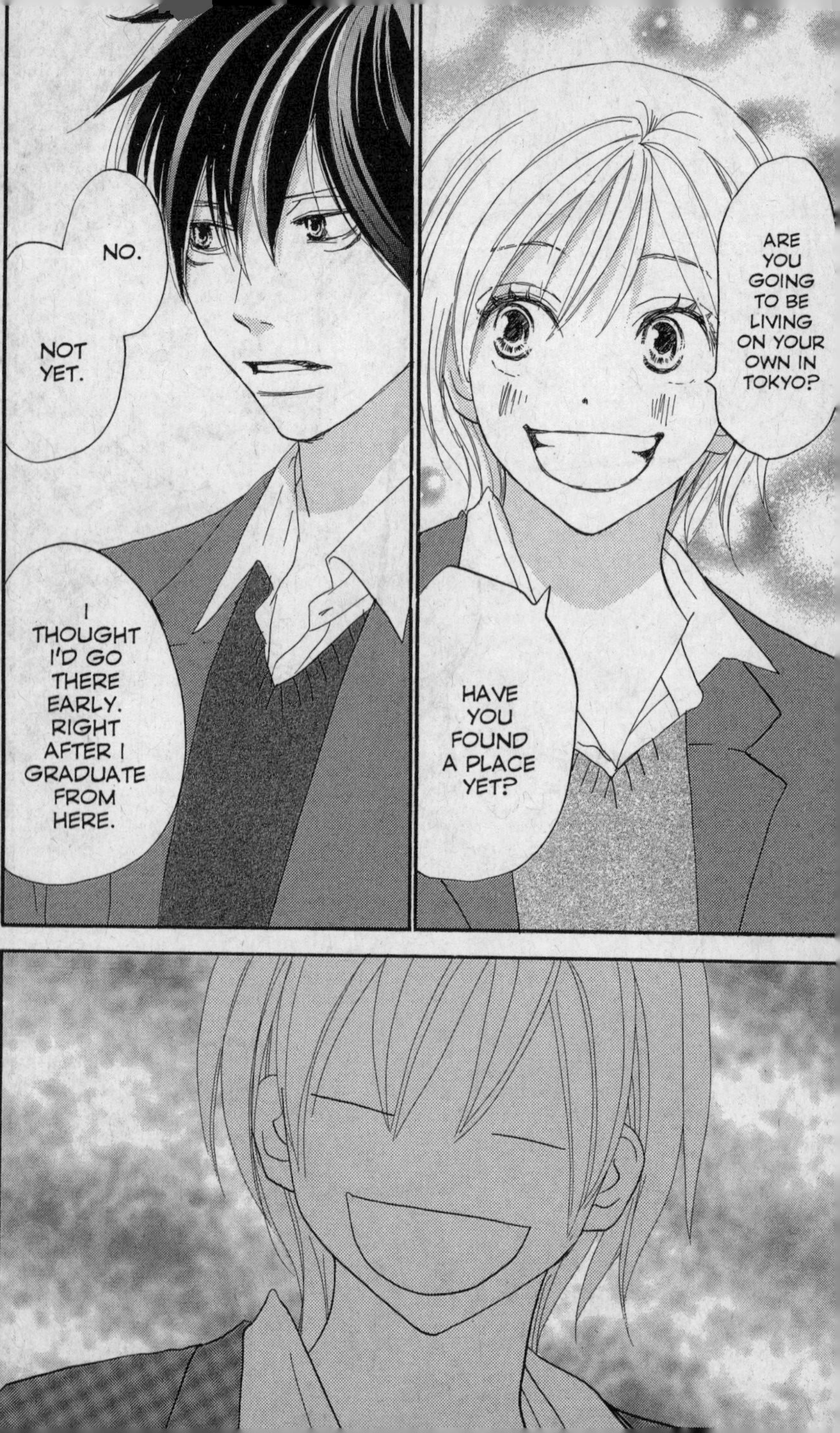
ARE YOU GOING TO BE LIVING ON YOUR OWN IN TOKYO?
HAVE YOU FOUND A PLACE YET?
NO.
NOT YET.
I THOUGHT I'D GO THERE EARLY. RIGHT AFTER I GRADUATE FROM HERE.

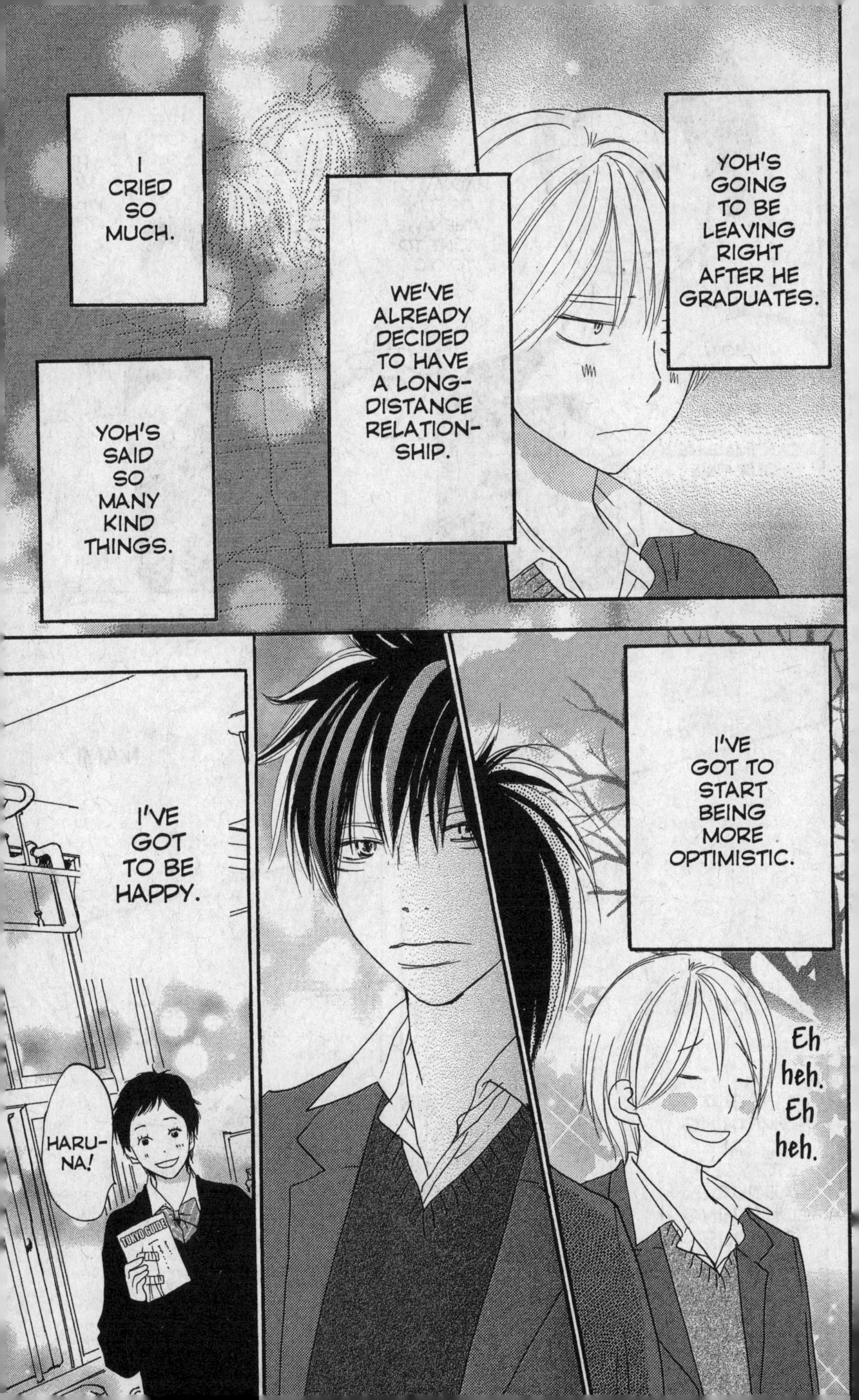
YOH'S GOING TO BE LEAVING RIGHT AFTER HE GRADUATES.
WE'VE ALREADY DECIDED TO HAVE A LONG-DISTANCE RELATION-SHIP.
I CRIED SO MUCH.
YOH'S SAID SO MANY KIND THINGS.
I'VE GOT TO START BEING MORE OPTIMISTIC.
Eh heh. Eh heh.
I'VE GOT TO BE HAPPY.
HARU-NA!
TOKYO GUIDE

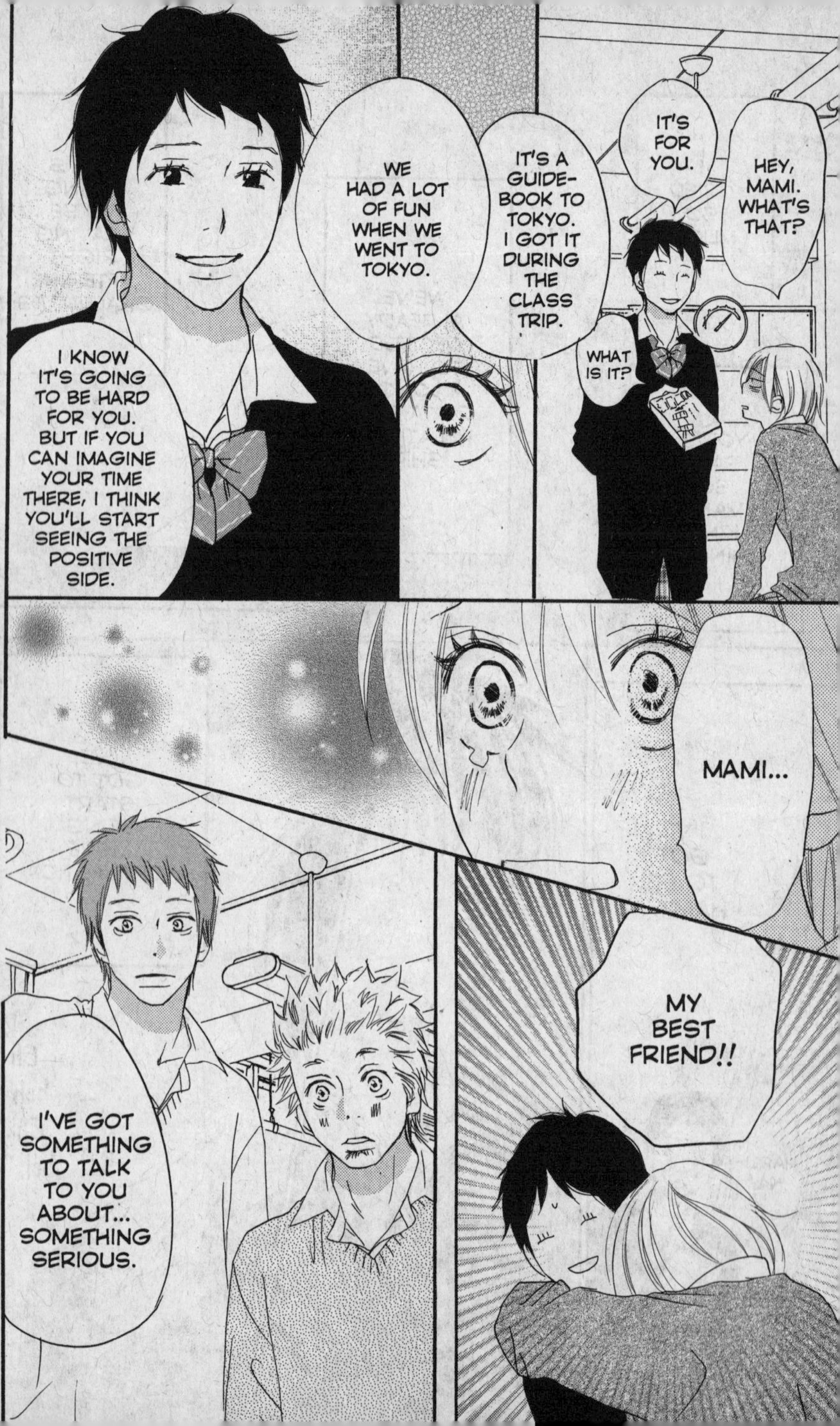
HEY, MAMI. WHAT'S THAT?
IT'S FOR YOU.
WHAT IS IT?
IT'S A GUIDE-BOOK TO TOKYO. I GOT IT DURING THE CLASS TRIP.
WE HAD A LOT OF FUN WHEN WE WENT TO TOKYO.
I KNOW IT'S GOING TO BE HARD FOR YOU. BUT IF YOU CAN IMAGINE YOUR TIME THERE, I THINK YOU'LL START SEEING THE POSITIVE SIDE.
MAMI...
MY BEST FRIEND!!
I'VE GOT SOMETHING TO TALK TO YOU ABOUT... SOMETHING SERIOUS.

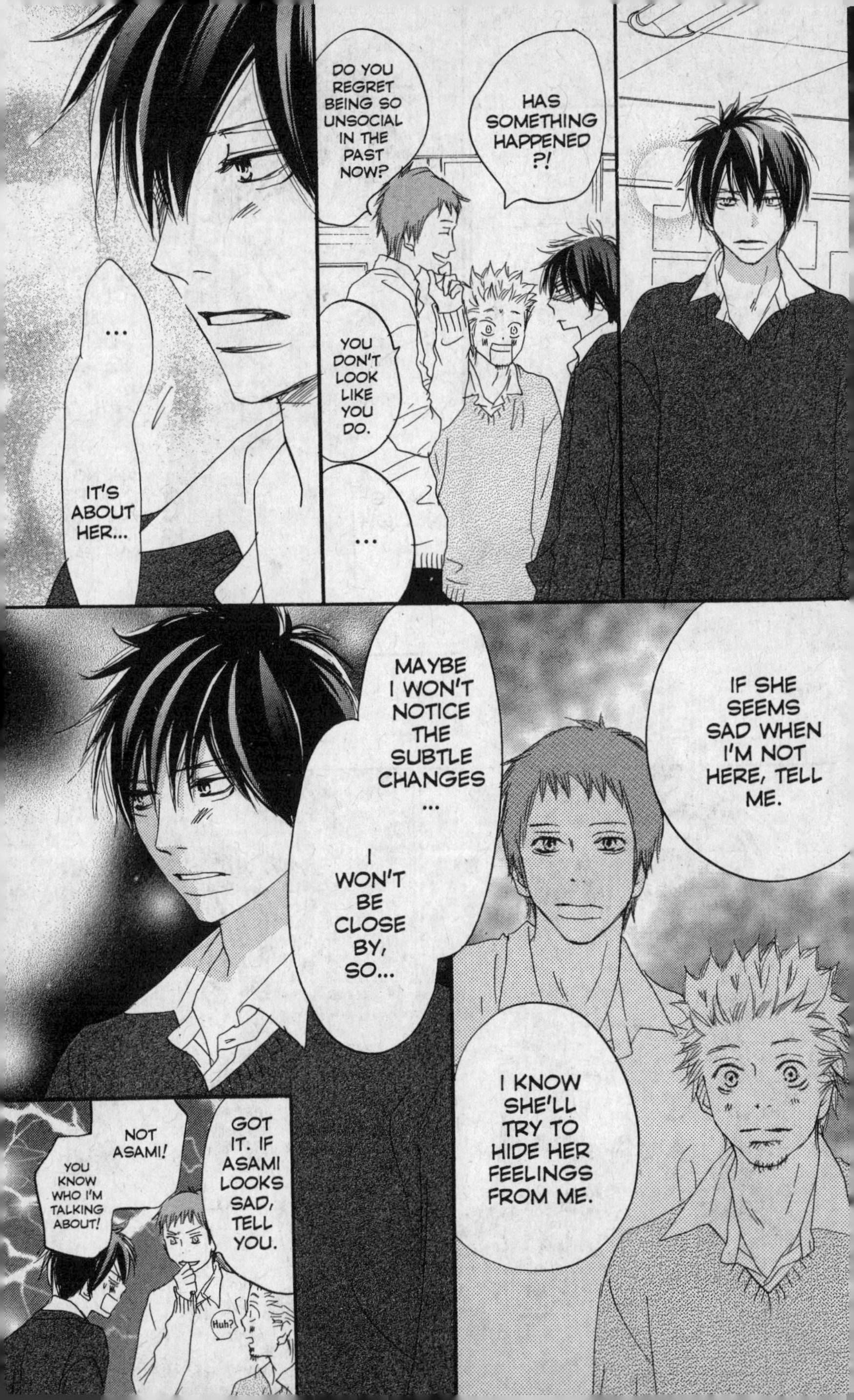
HAS SOMETHING HAPPENED ?!
DO YOU REGRET BEING SO UNSOCIAL IN THE PAST NOW?
YOU DON'T LOOK LIKE YOU DO.
...
...
IT'S ABOUT HER...
IF SHE SEEMS SAD WHEN I'M NOT HERE, TELL ME.
MAYBE I WON'T NOTICE THE SUBTLE CHANGES ...
I WON'T BE CLOSE BY, SO...
I KNOW SHE'LL TRY TO HIDE HER FEELINGS FROM ME.
GOT IT. IF ASAMI LOOKS SAD, TELL YOU.
NOT ASAMI!
YOU KNOW WHO I'M TALKING ABOUT!
Huh?

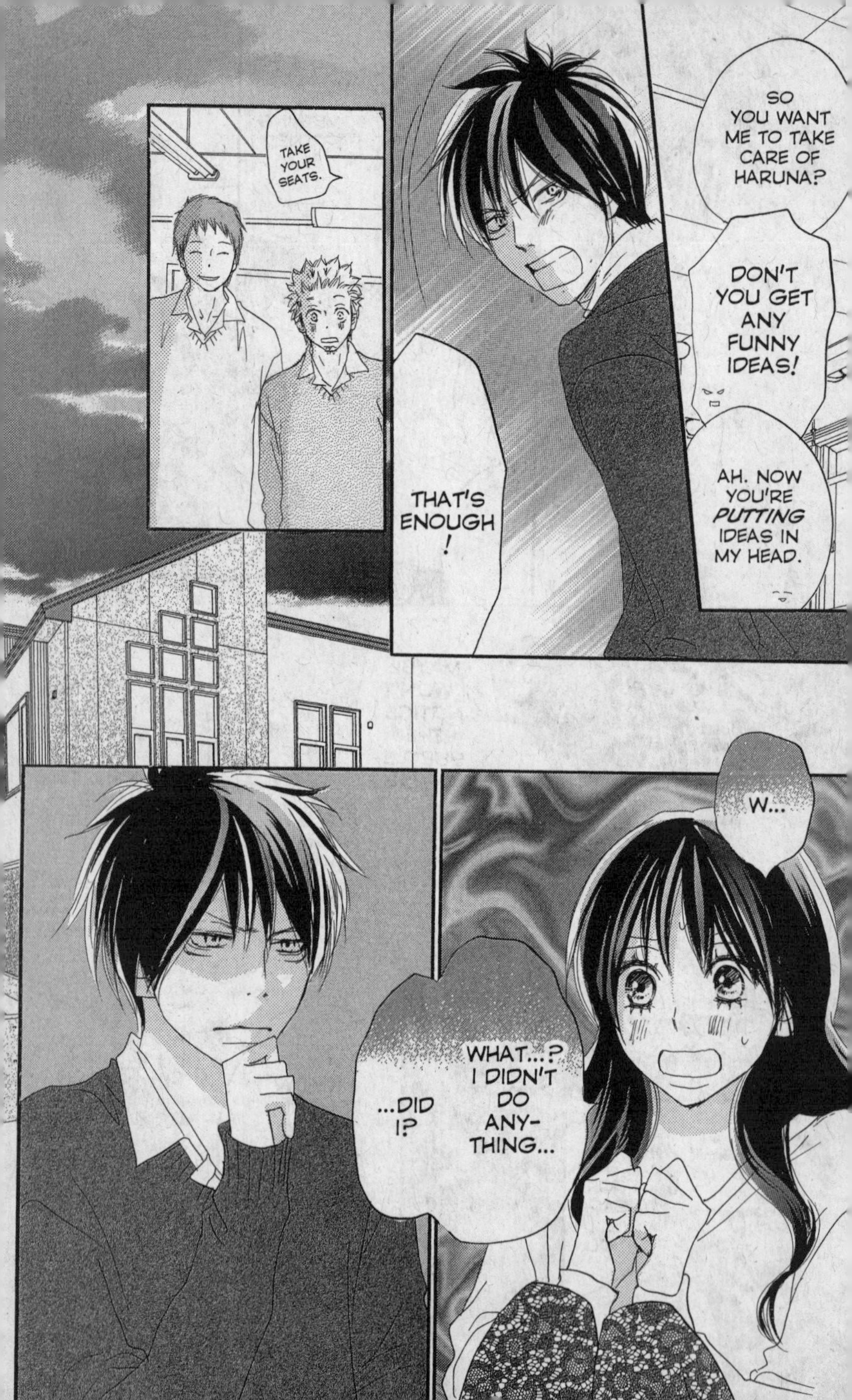
SO YOU WANT ME TO TAKE CARE OF HARUNA?
DON'T YOU GET ANY FUNNY IDEAS!
AH. NOW YOU'RE *PUTTING* IDEAS IN MY HEAD.
THAT'S ENOUGH!
TAKE YOUR SEATS.
W...
WHAT...? I DIDN'T DO ANYTHING...
...DID I?

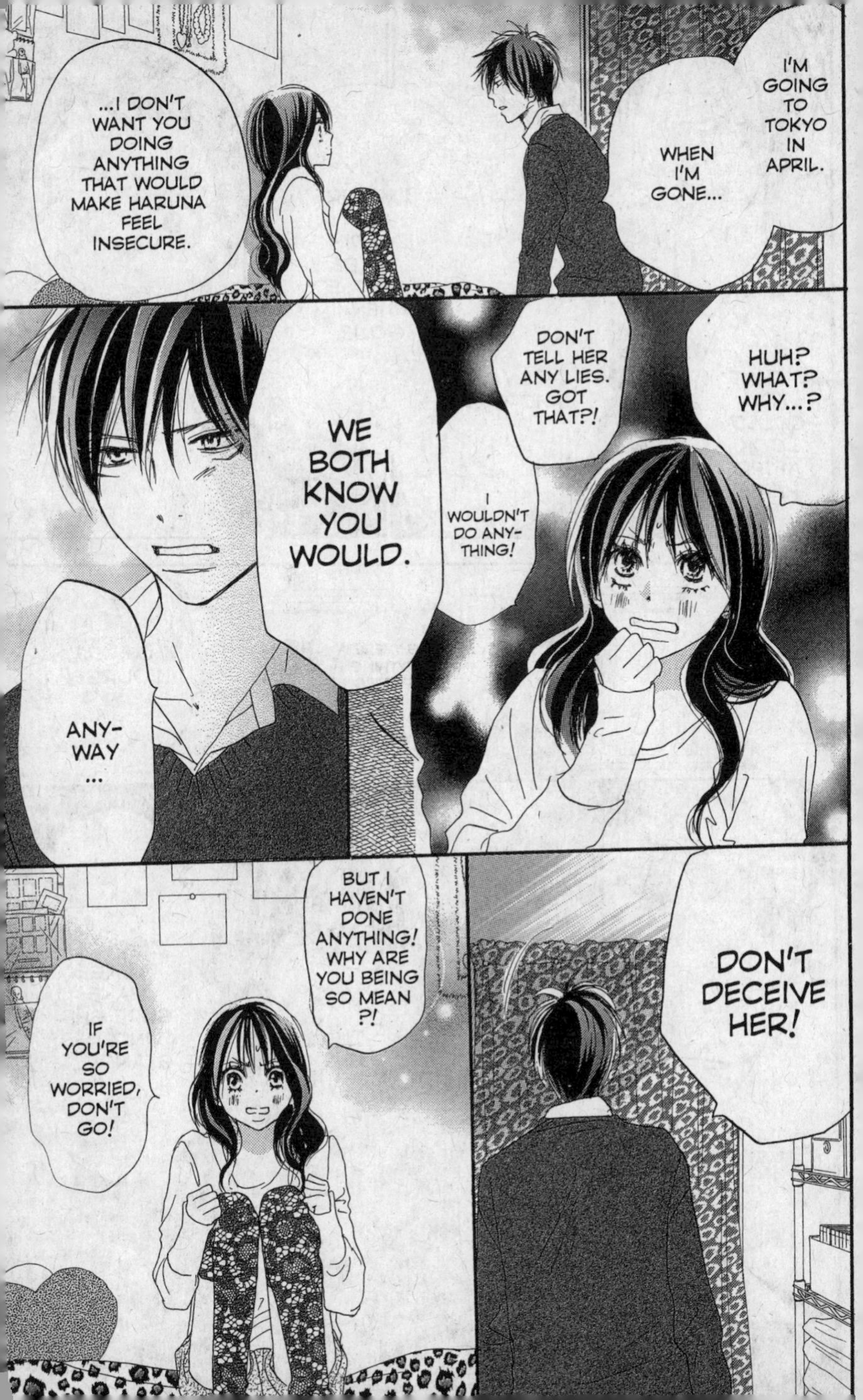
I'M GOING TO TOKYO IN APRIL.
WHEN I'M GONE...
...I DON'T WANT YOU DOING ANYTHING THAT WOULD MAKE HARUNA FEEL INSECURE.
HUH? WHAT? WHY...?
DON'T TELL HER ANY LIES. GOT THAT?!
I WOULDN'T DO ANYTHING!
WE BOTH KNOW YOU WOULD.
ANYWAY...
DON'T DECEIVE HER!
BUT I HAVEN'T DONE ANYTHING! WHY ARE YOU BEING SO MEAN?!
IF YOU'RE SO WORRIED, DON'T GO!

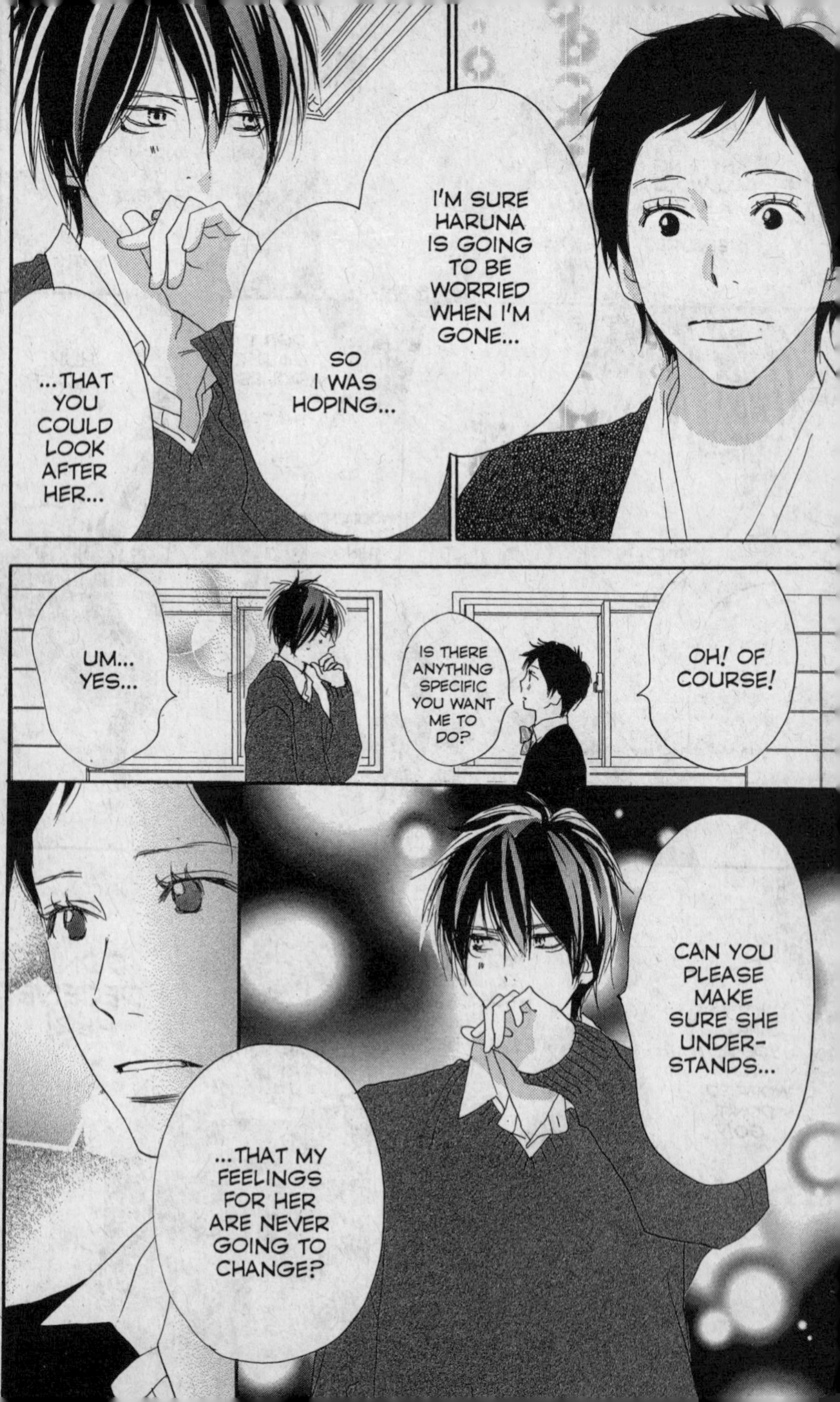
I'M SURE HARUNA IS GOING TO BE WORRIED WHEN I'M GONE...
SO I WAS HOPING...
...THAT YOU COULD LOOK AFTER HER...
OH! OF COURSE!
IS THERE ANYTHING SPECIFIC YOU WANT ME TO DO?
UM... YES...
CAN YOU PLEASE MAKE SURE SHE UNDER-STANDS...
...THAT MY FEELINGS FOR HER ARE NEVER GOING TO CHANGE?

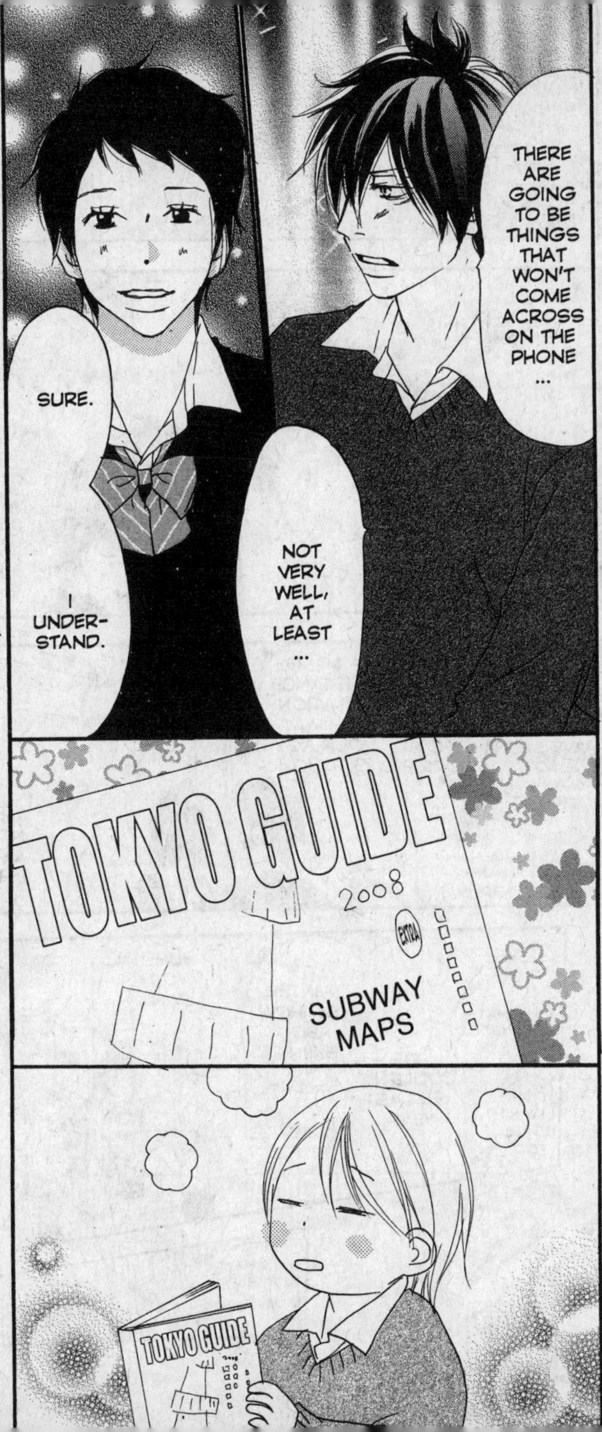
THERE ARE GOING TO BE THINGS THAT WON'T COME ACROSS ON THE PHONE ...
NOT VERY WELL, AT LEAST ...
SURE.
I UNDERSTAND.
TOKYO GUIDE
2008
EXTRA
SUBWAY MAPS
TOKYO GUIDE

There are only two notes in this volume. 1

Hello! This is the last volume! Thank you for sticking with me over such a long time. It's all because of you readers that this series reached 13 volumes. A really, really, really big

THANK YOU!

I'm not sure if I should write this here, but I'd like to thank my assistants who helped me out with this series!

Just about all of the nice backgrounds... (Not just about... All the pretty ones... Sorry, let me start again!) All of the pretty backgrounds were drawn by them. All the bad ones were by me.

I really don't know how manga works. Really! A lot of my friends who can draw well helped me out too. That's why I can still sleep ten hours a day even on a deadline... I'm sorry! What should I do with myself...?

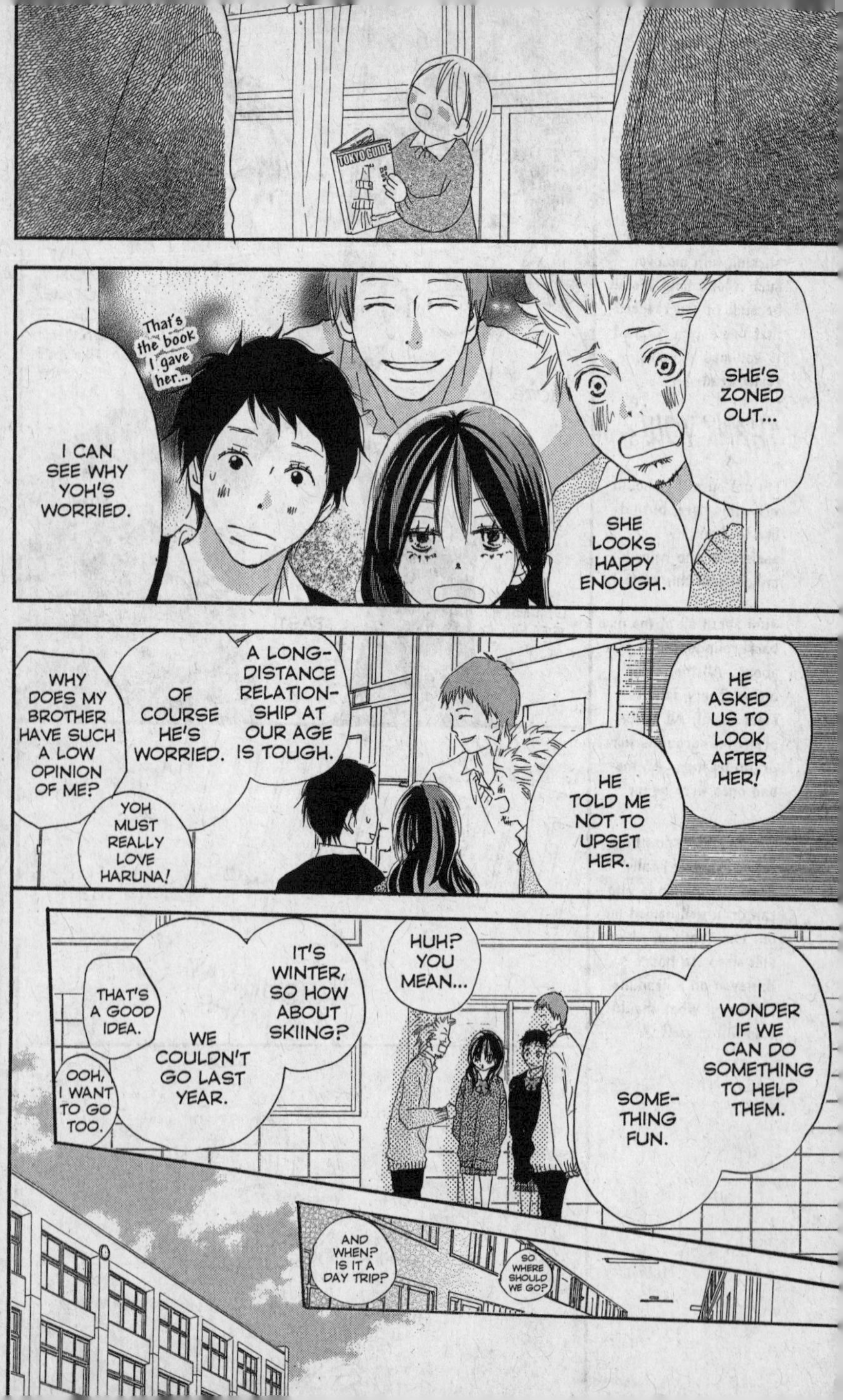
TOKYO GUIDE
SHE'S ZONED OUT...
SHE LOOKS HAPPY ENOUGH.
That's the book I gave her...
I CAN SEE WHY YOH'S WORRIED.
HE ASKED US TO LOOK AFTER HER!
HE TOLD ME NOT TO UPSET HER.
A LONG-DISTANCE RELATIONSHIP AT OUR AGE IS TOUGH.
OF COURSE HE'S WORRIED.
WHY DOES MY BROTHER HAVE SUCH A LOW OPINION OF ME?
YOH MUST REALLY LOVE HARUNA!
I WONDER IF WE CAN DO SOMETHING TO HELP THEM.
SOMETHING FUN.
HUH? YOU MEAN...
IT'S WINTER, SO HOW ABOUT SKIING?
WE COULDN'T GO LAST YEAR.
THAT'S A GOOD IDEA.
OOH, I WANT TO GO TOO.
SO WHERE SHOULD WE GO?
AND WHEN? IS IT A DAY TRIP?

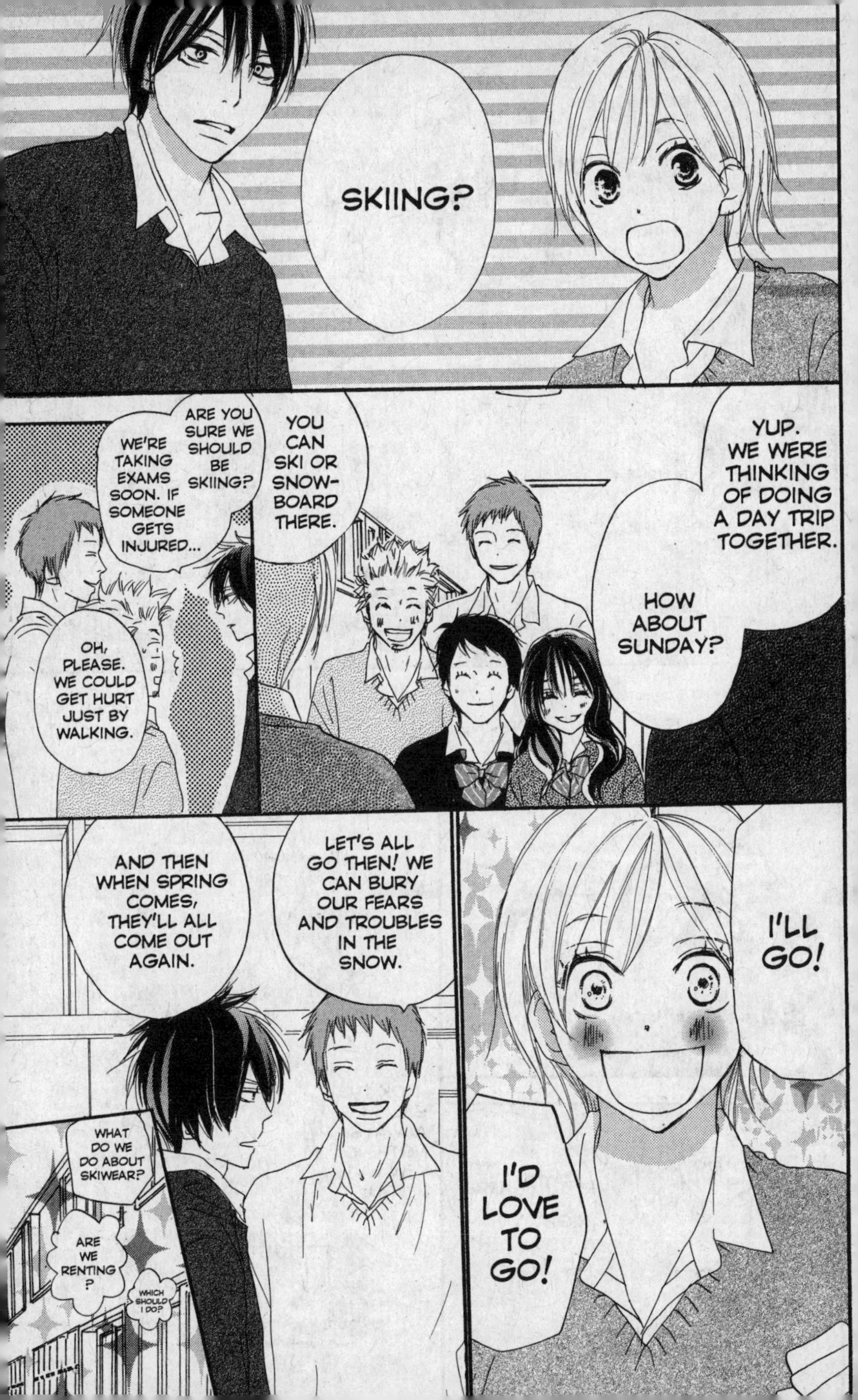
SKIING?
YUP. WE WERE THINKING OF DOING A DAY TRIP TOGETHER.
HOW ABOUT SUNDAY?
YOU CAN SKI OR SNOW-BOARD THERE.
ARE YOU SURE WE SHOULD BE SKIING?
WE'RE TAKING EXAMS SOON. IF SOMEONE GETS INJURED...
OH, PLEASE. WE COULD GET HURT JUST BY WALKING.
I'LL GO!
I'D LOVE TO GO!
LET'S ALL GO THEN! WE CAN BURY OUR FEARS AND TROUBLES IN THE SNOW.
AND THEN WHEN SPRING COMES, THEY'LL ALL COME OUT AGAIN.
WHAT DO WE DO ABOUT SKIWEAR?
ARE WE RENTING?
WHICH SHOULD I DO?

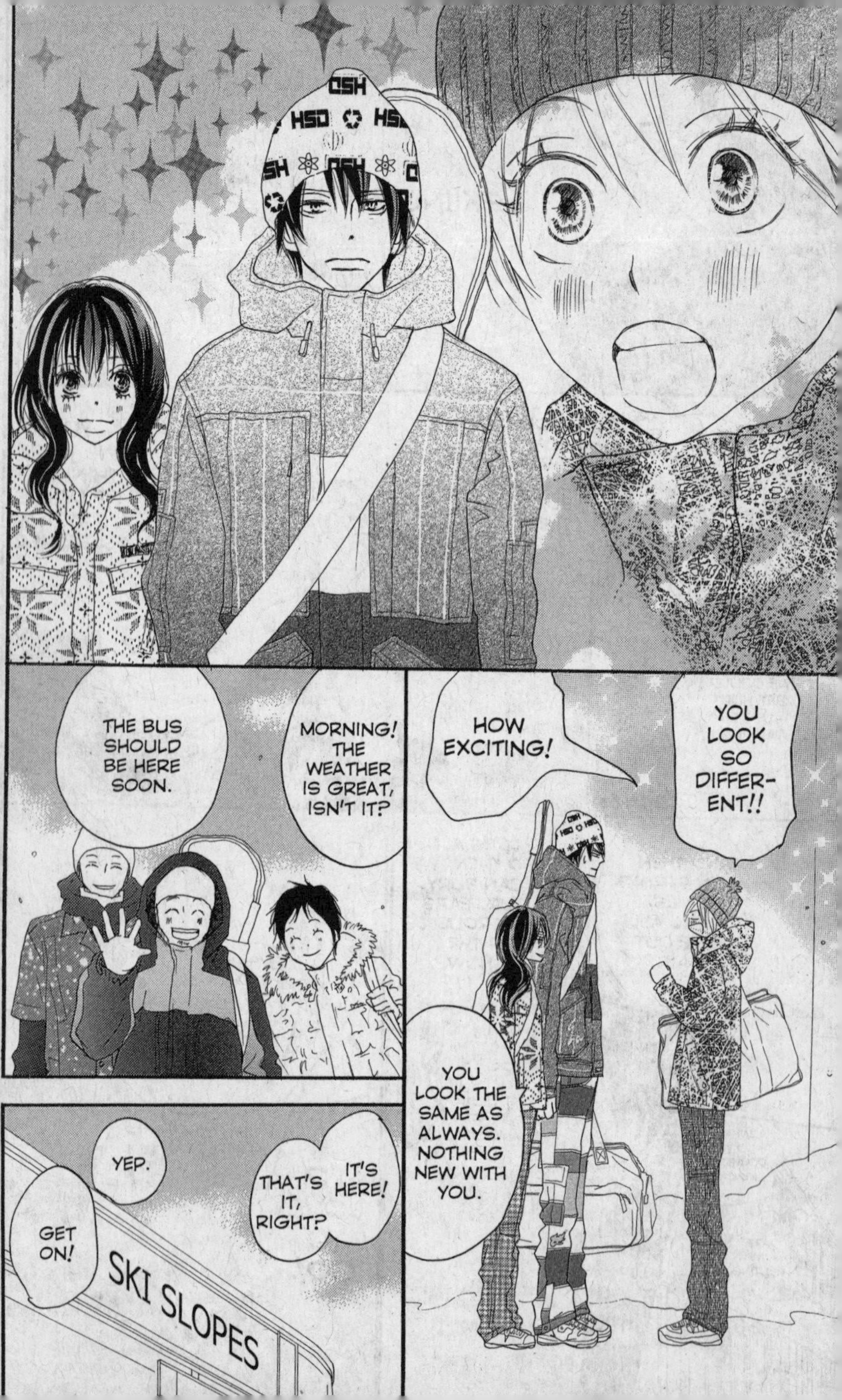
YOU LOOK SO DIFFERENT!!
HOW EXCITING!
YOU LOOK THE SAME AS ALWAYS. NOTHING NEW WITH YOU.
MORNING! THE WEATHER IS GREAT, ISN'T IT?
THE BUS SHOULD BE HERE SOON.
IT'S HERE!
THAT'S IT, RIGHT?
YEP.
GET ON!
SKI SLOPES

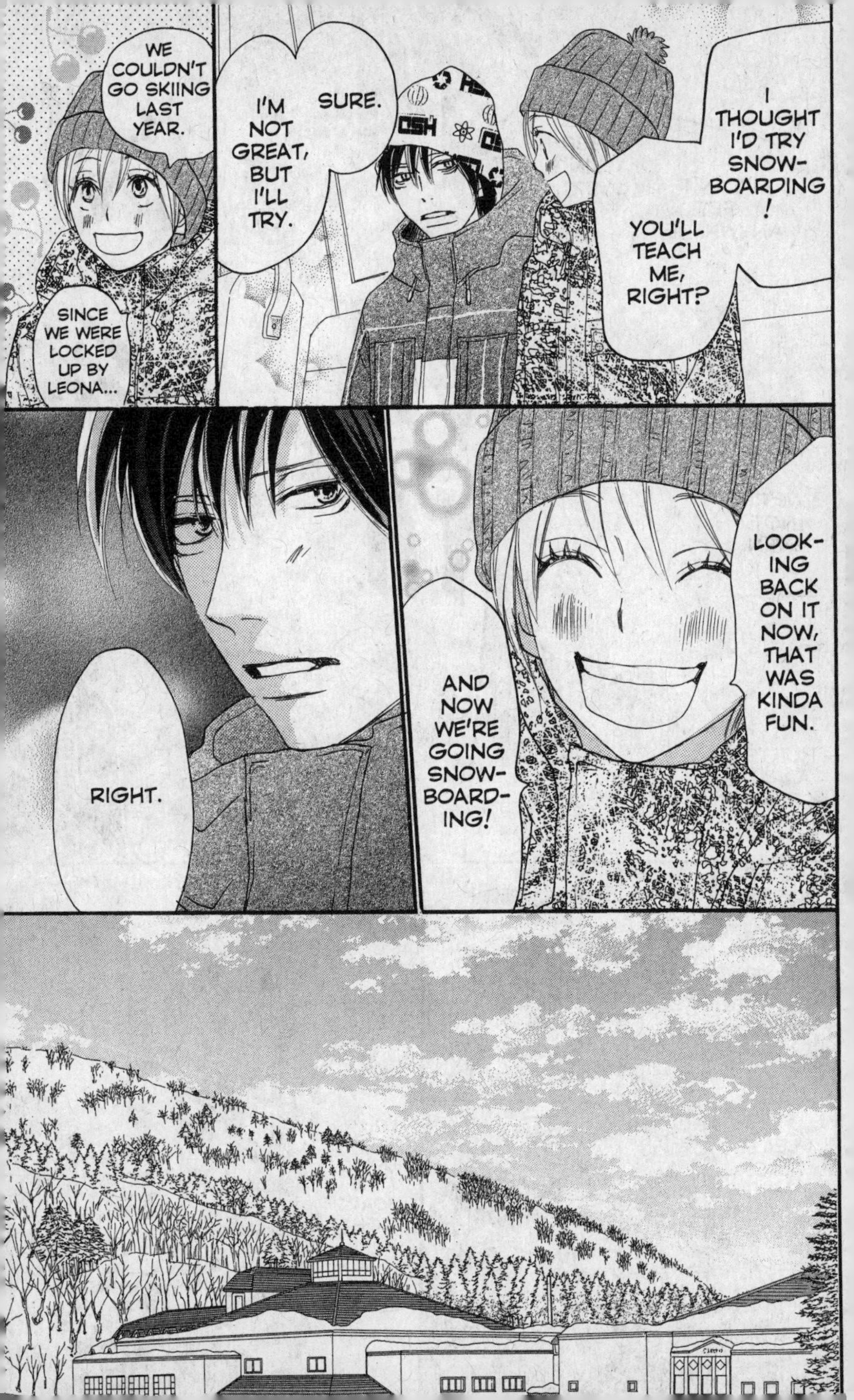
I THOUGHT I'D TRY SNOW-BOARDING!
YOU'LL TEACH ME, RIGHT?
SURE.
I'M NOT GREAT, BUT I'LL TRY.
WE COULDN'T GO SKIING LAST YEAR.
SINCE WE WERE LOCKED UP BY LEONA...
LOOK-ING BACK ON IT NOW, THAT WAS KINDA FUN.
AND NOW WE'RE GOING SNOW-BOARD-ING!
RIGHT.

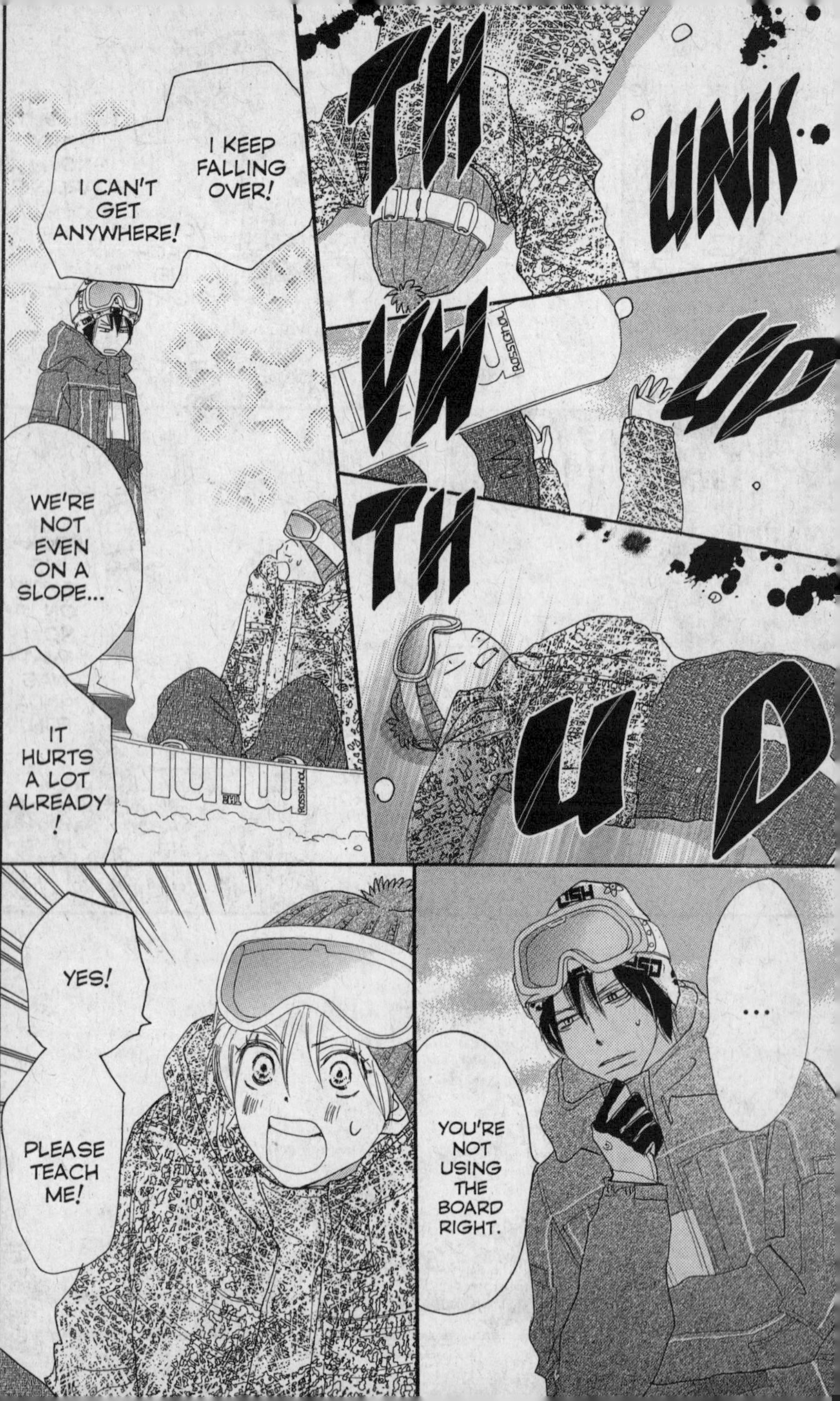
TH
UNK
VW
UP
TH
UD
I KEEP FALLING OVER!
I CAN'T GET ANYWHERE!
WE'RE NOT EVEN ON A SLOPE...
IT HURTS A LOT ALREADY!
...
YOU'RE NOT USING THE BOARD RIGHT.
YES!
PLEASE TEACH ME!

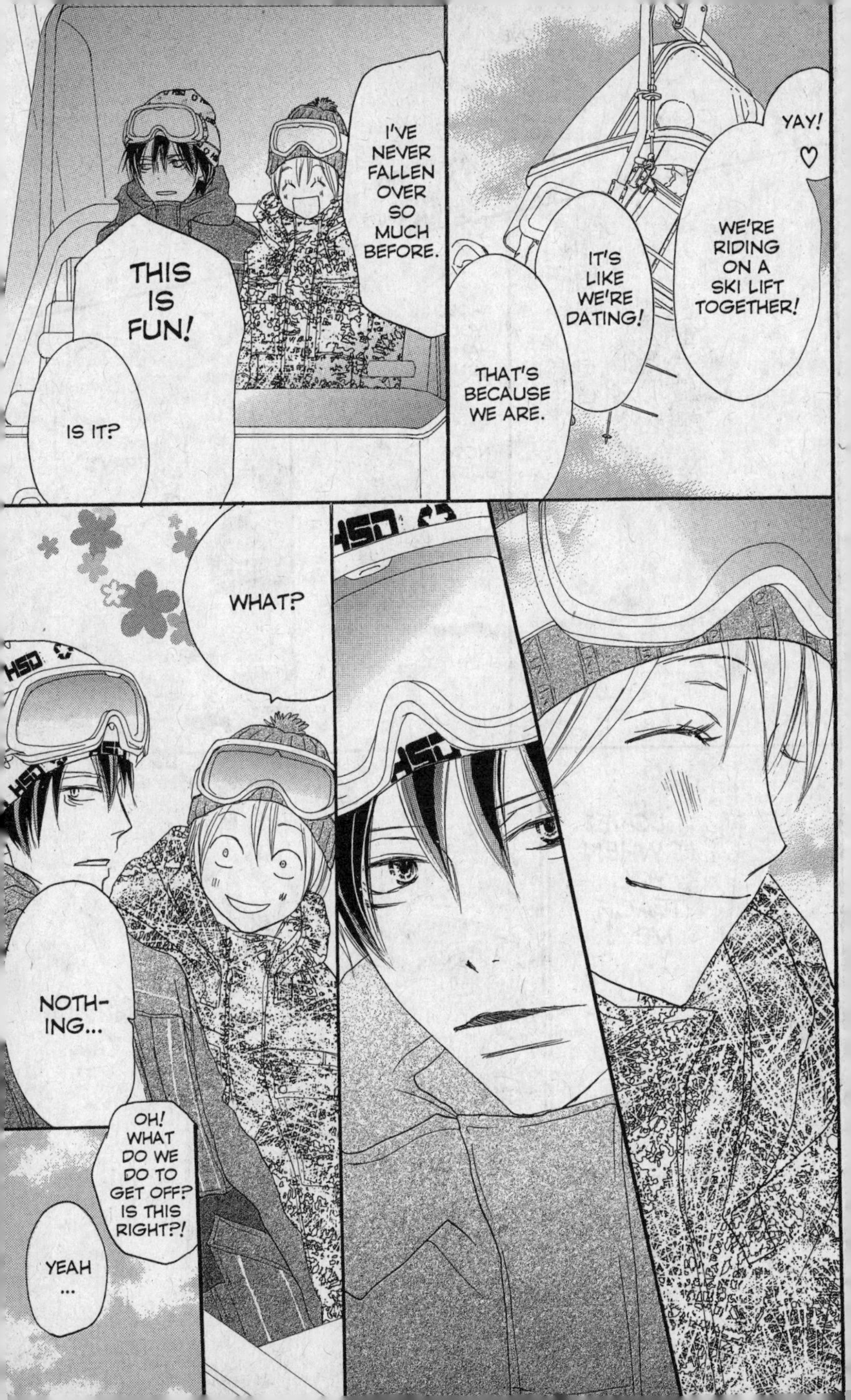
YAY! ♡
WE'RE RIDING ON A SKI LIFT TOGETHER!
IT'S LIKE WE'RE DATING!
THAT'S BECAUSE WE ARE.
I'VE NEVER FALLEN OVER SO MUCH BEFORE.
THIS IS FUN!
IS IT?
WHAT?
NOTH-ING...
OH! WHAT DO WE DO TO GET OFF? IS THIS RIGHT?!
YEAH...

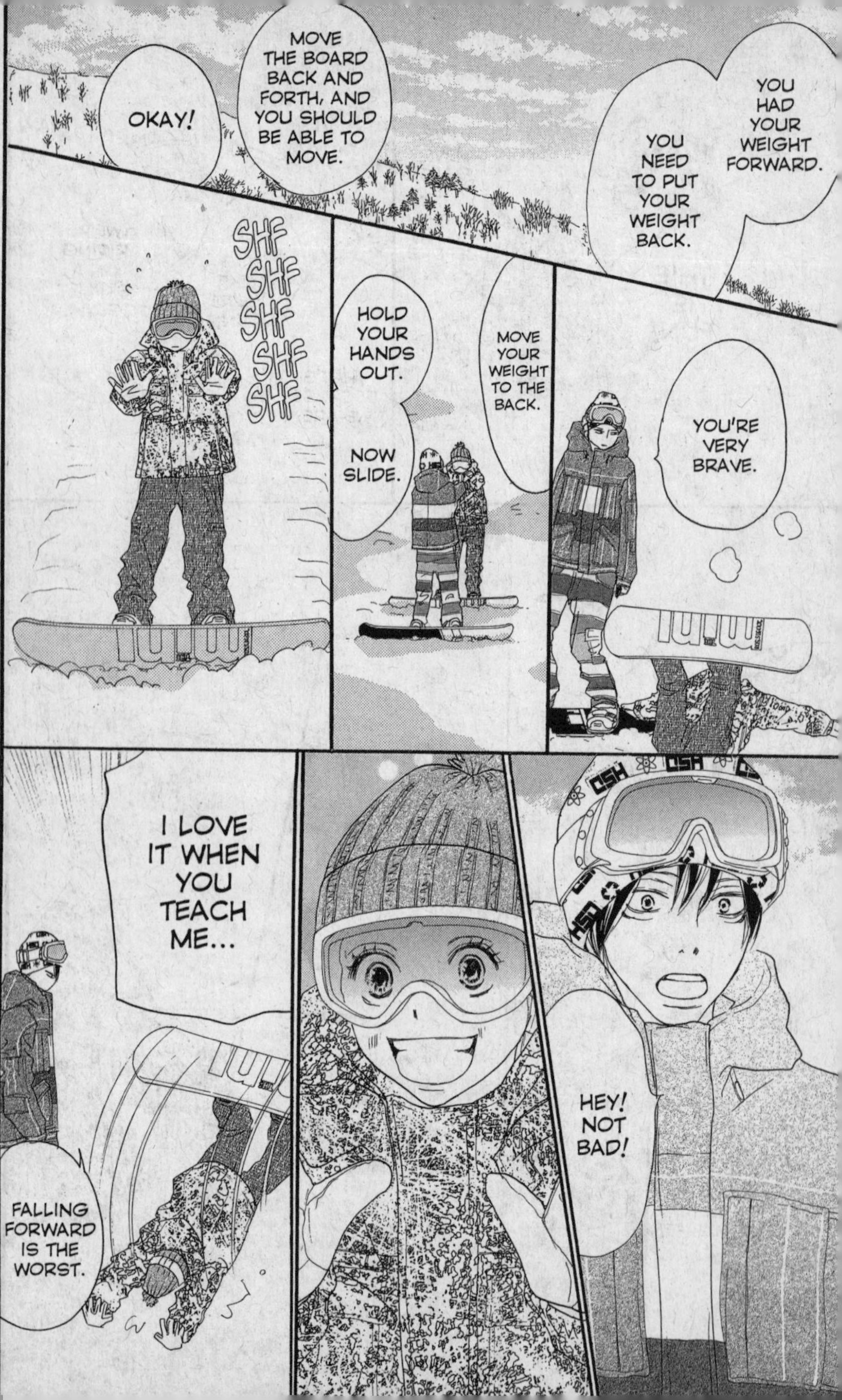
YOU HAD YOUR WEIGHT FORWARD.
YOU NEED TO PUT YOUR WEIGHT BACK.
MOVE THE BOARD BACK AND FORTH, AND YOU SHOULD BE ABLE TO MOVE.
OKAY!
YOU'RE VERY BRAVE.
MOVE YOUR WEIGHT TO THE BACK.
HOLD YOUR HANDS OUT.
NOW SLIDE.
SHF SHF SHF SHF SHF
HEY! NOT BAD!
I LOVE IT WHEN YOU TEACH ME...
FALLING FORWARD IS THE WORST.

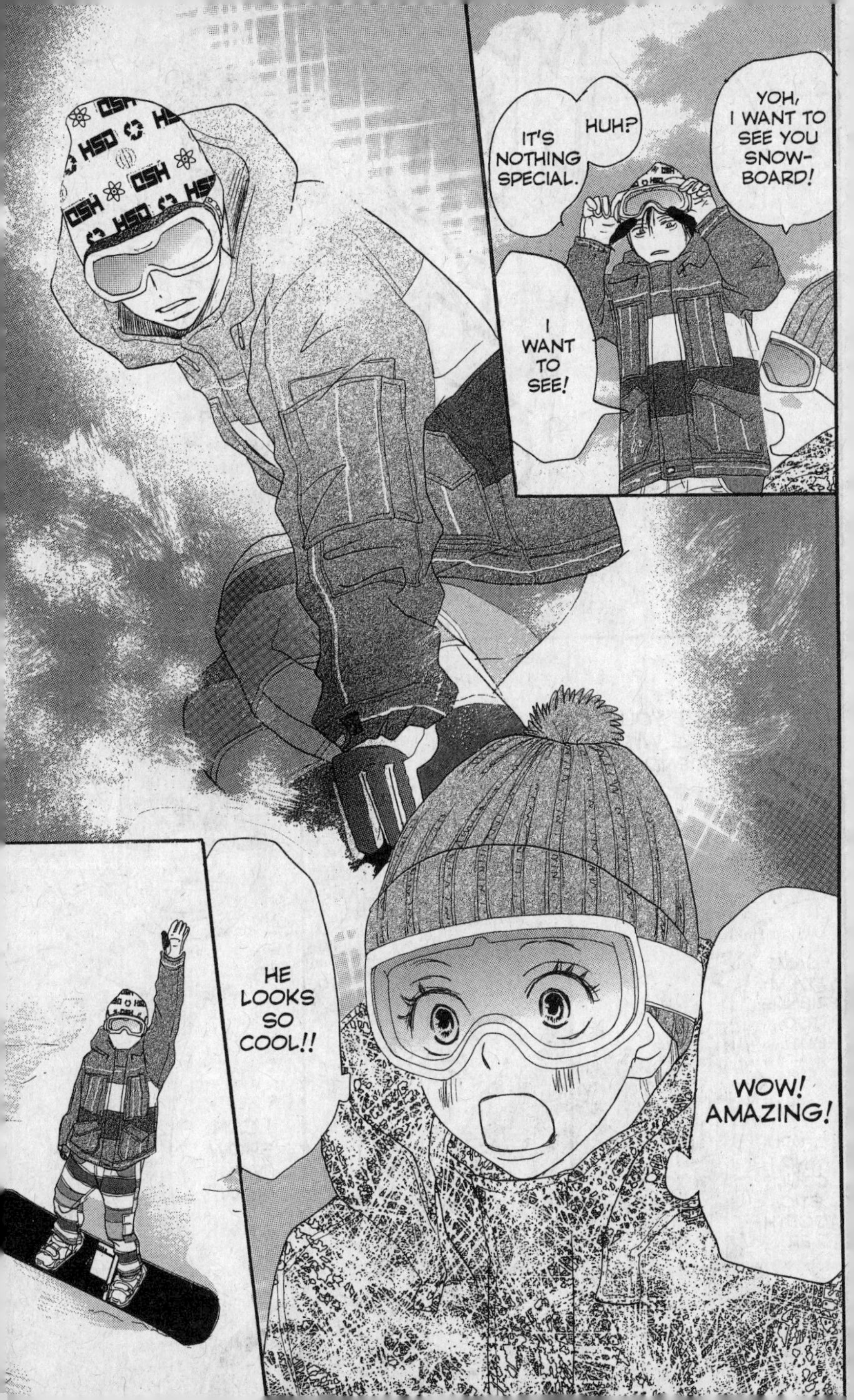
YOH, I WANT TO SEE YOU SNOWBOARD!
HUH?
IT'S NOTHING SPECIAL.
I WANT TO SEE!
WOW! AMAZING!
HE LOOKS SO COOL!!

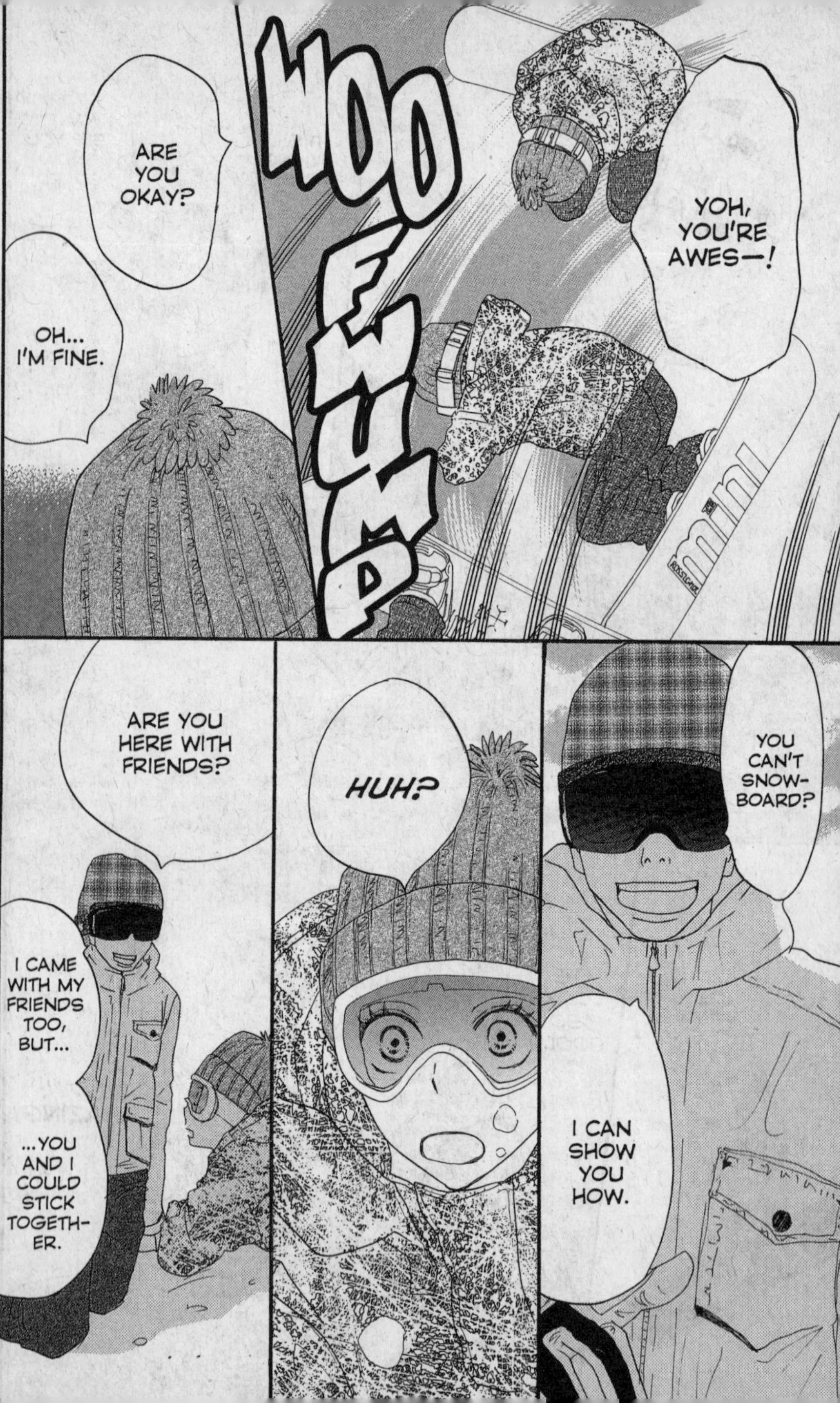
YOH, YOU'RE AWES—!
WOOFWUMP
ARE YOU OKAY?
OH... I'M FINE.
YOU CAN'T SNOW-BOARD?
I CAN SHOW YOU HOW.
HUH?
ARE YOU HERE WITH FRIENDS?
I CAME WITH MY FRIENDS TOO, BUT...
...YOU AND I COULD STICK TOGETH-ER.

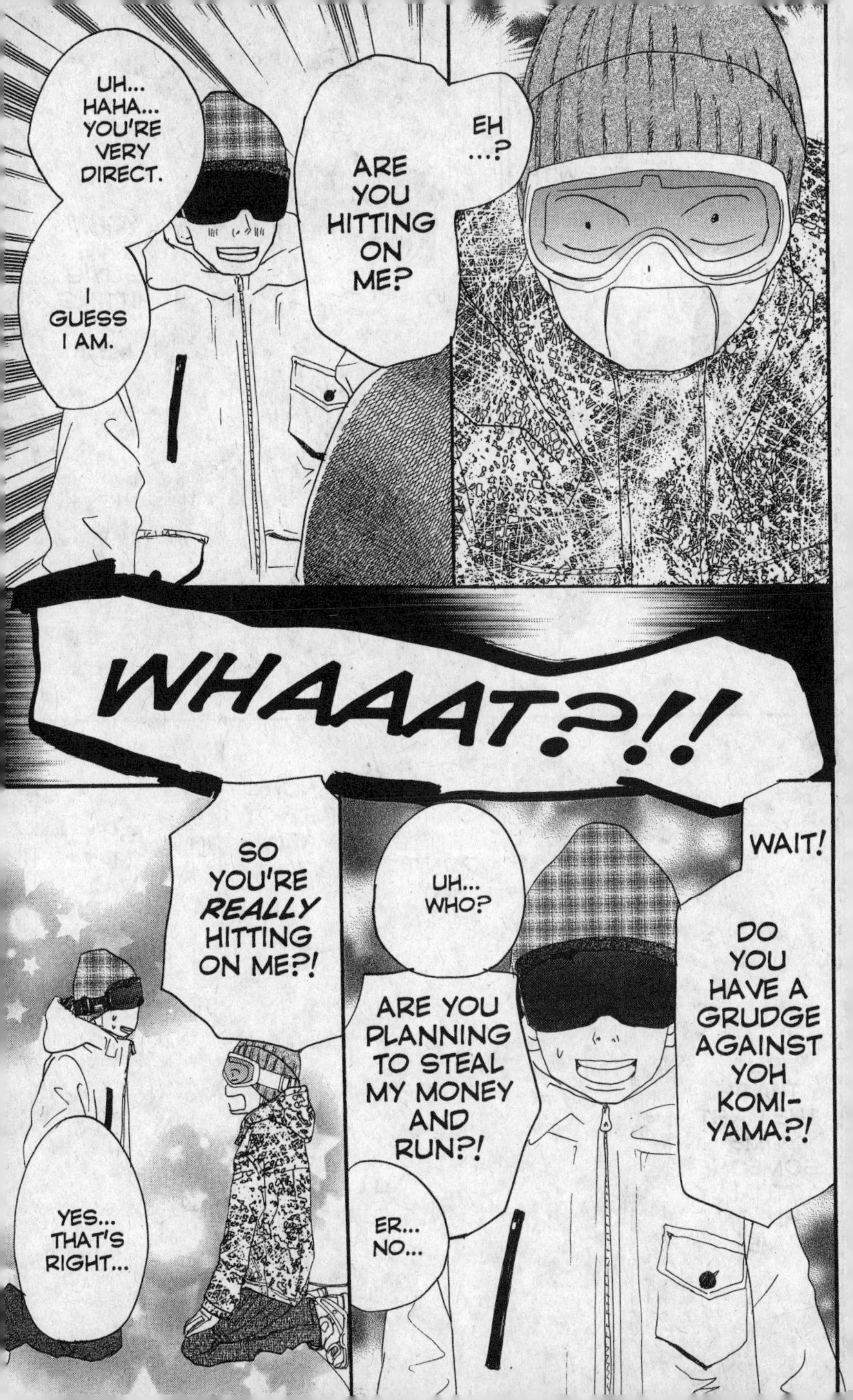
EH ...?
ARE YOU HITTING ON ME?
UH... HAHA... YOU'RE VERY DIRECT.
I GUESS I AM.
WHAAAT?!!
WAIT!
DO YOU HAVE A GRUDGE AGAINST YOH KOMI-YAMA?!
UH... WHO?
ARE YOU PLANNING TO STEAL MY MONEY AND RUN?!
ER... NO...
SO YOU'RE *REALLY* HITTING ON ME?!
YES... THAT'S RIGHT...

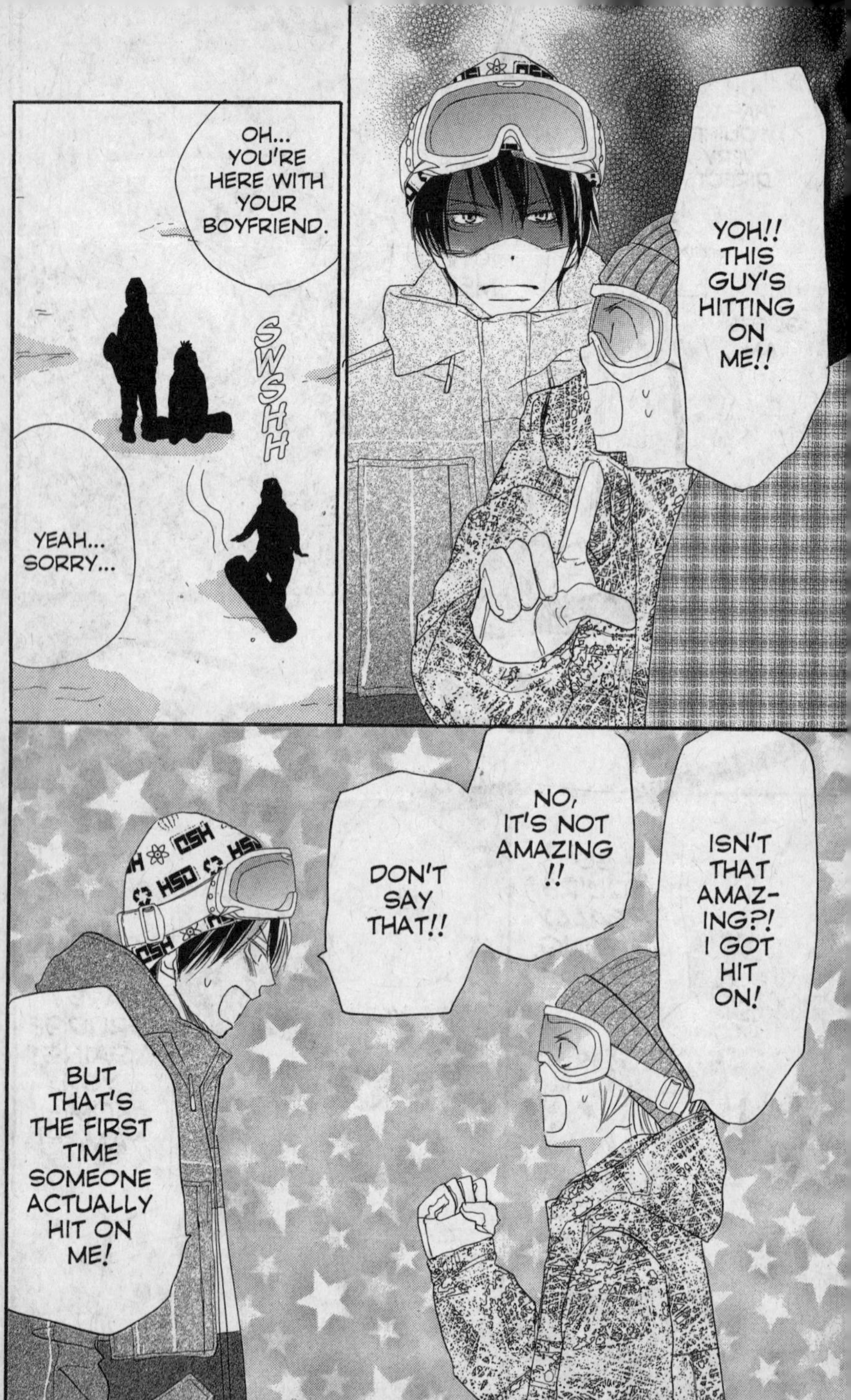
YOH!! THIS GUY'S HITTING ON ME!!
OH... YOU'RE HERE WITH YOUR BOYFRIEND.
SWSHH
YEAH... SORRY...
ISN'T THAT AMAZ-ING?! I GOT HIT ON!
NO, IT'S NOT AMAZING!!
DON'T SAY THAT!!
BUT THAT'S THE FIRST TIME SOMEONE ACTUALLY HIT ON ME!

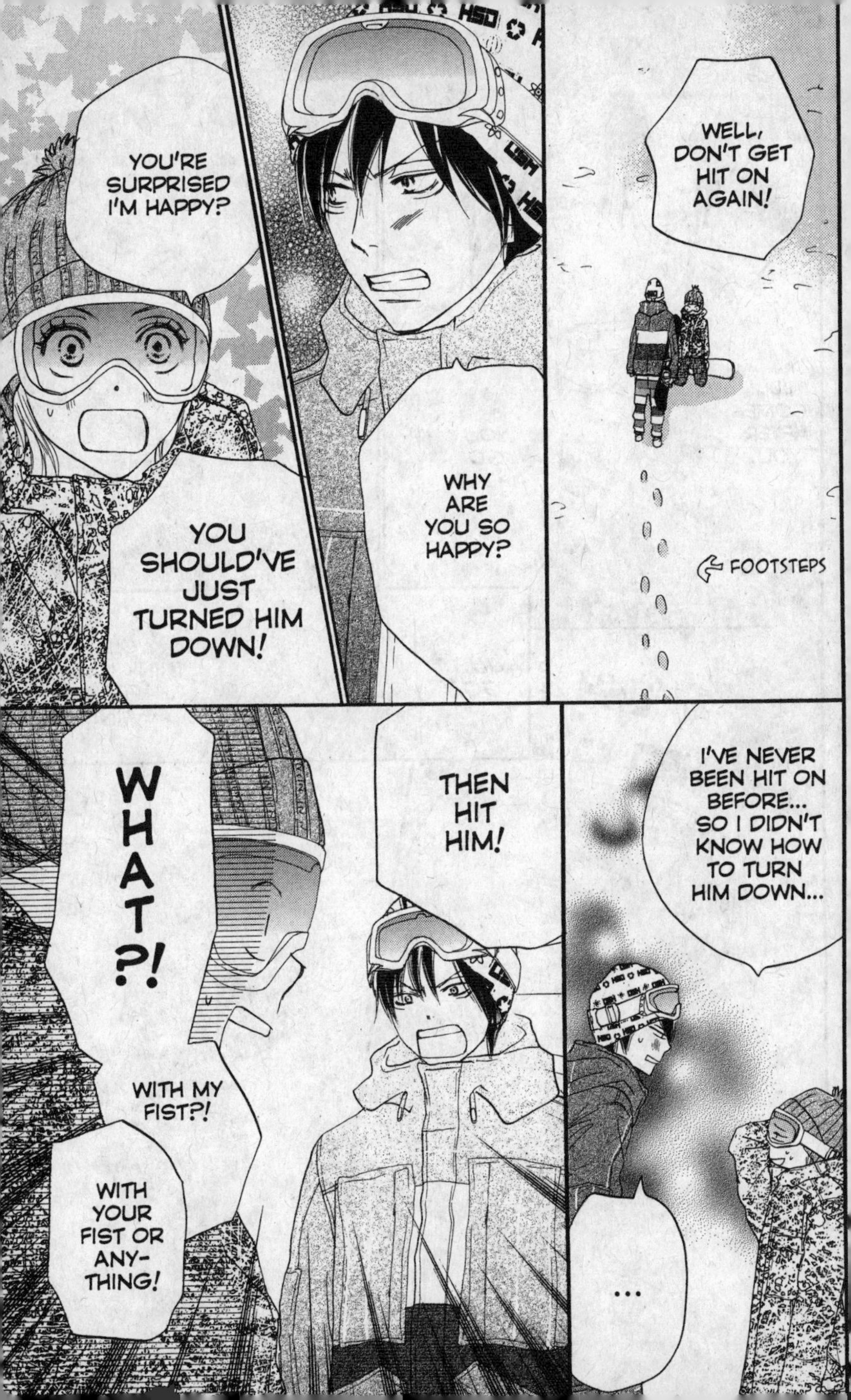
WELL, DON'T GET HIT ON AGAIN!
FOOTSTEPS
WHY ARE YOU SO HAPPY?
YOU'RE SURPRISED I'M HAPPY?
YOU SHOULD'VE JUST TURNED HIM DOWN!
I'VE NEVER BEEN HIT ON BEFORE... SO I DIDN'T KNOW HOW TO TURN HIM DOWN...
...
THEN HIT HIM!
WHAT?!
WITH MY FIST?!
WITH YOUR FIST OR ANY-THING!

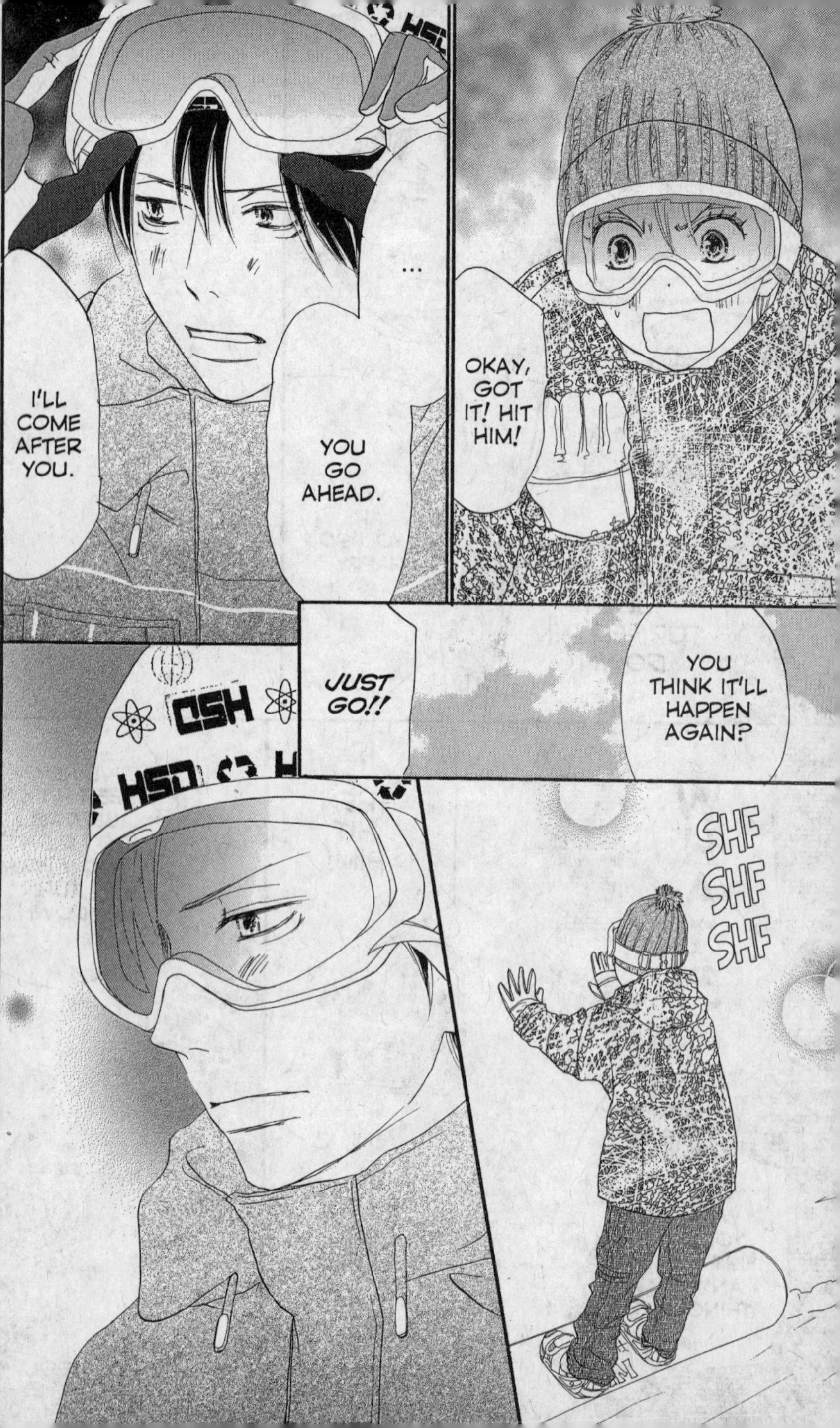
OKAY, GOT IT! HIT HIM!
...
YOU GO AHEAD.
I'LL COME AFTER YOU.
YOU THINK IT'LL HAPPEN AGAIN?
JUST GO!!
SHF SHF SHF

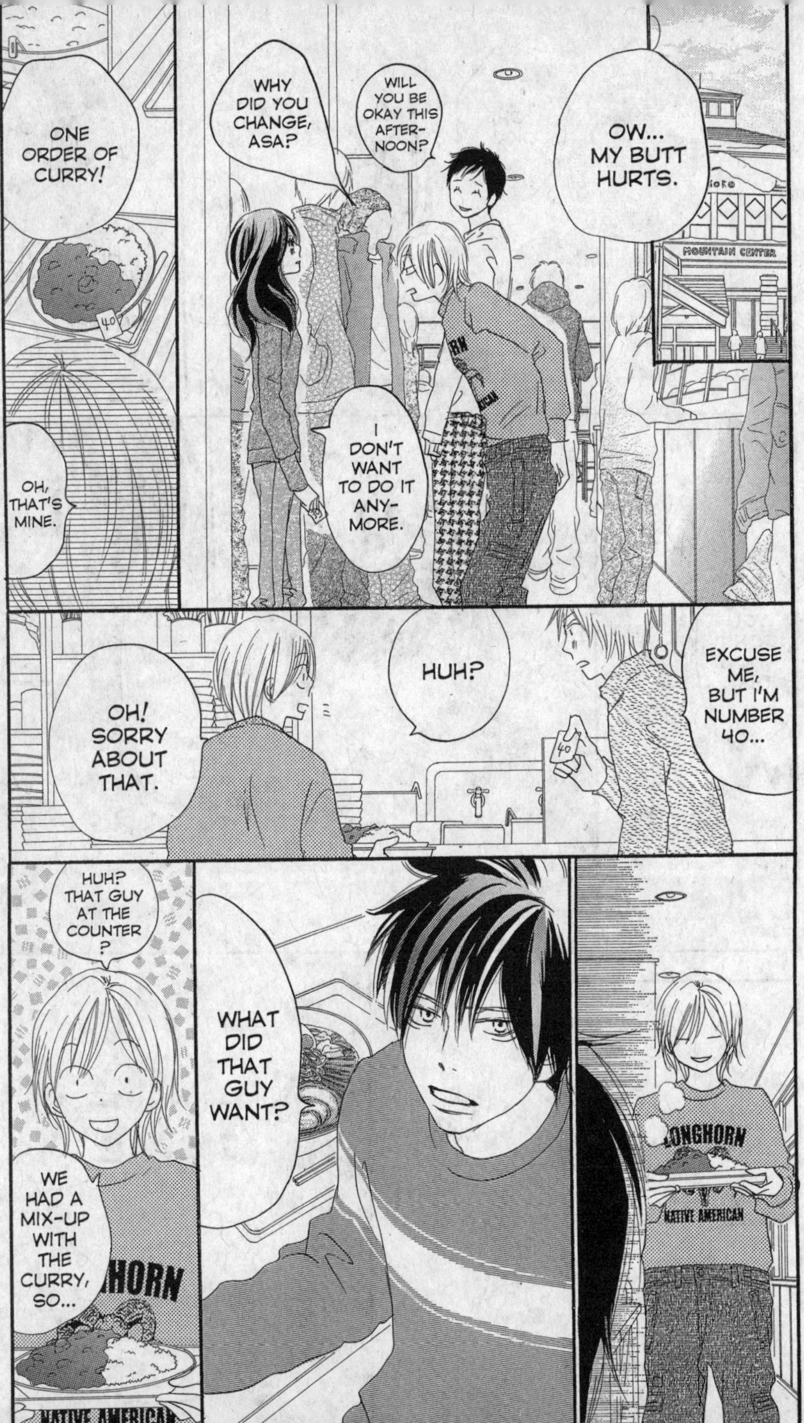

OW... MY BUTT HURTS.
MOUNTAIN CENTER
WILL YOU BE OKAY THIS AFTERNOON?
WHY DID YOU CHANGE, ASA?
I DON'T WANT TO DO IT ANYMORE.
ONE ORDER OF CURRY!
OH, THAT'S MINE.
EXCUSE ME, BUT I'M NUMBER 40...
HUH?
OH! SORRY ABOUT THAT.
NATIVE AMERICAN
WHAT DID THAT GUY WANT?
HUH? THAT GUY AT THE COUNTER?
WE HAD A MIX-UP WITH THE CURRY, SO...
NATIVE AMERICAN

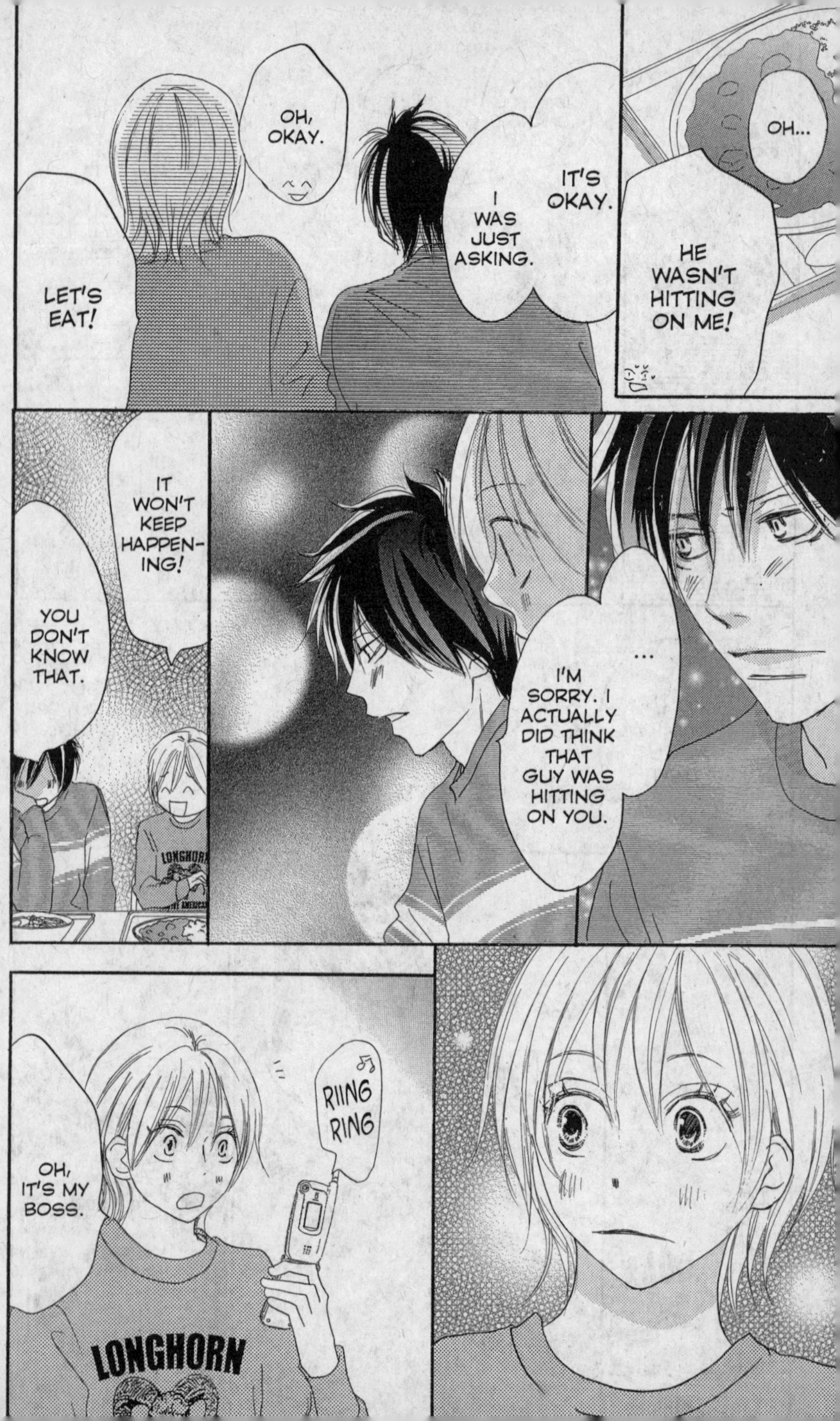
OH...
HE WASN'T HITTING ON ME!
IT'S OKAY.
I WAS JUST ASKING.
OH, OKAY.
LET'S EAT!
...
I'M SORRY. I ACTUALLY DID THINK THAT GUY WAS HITTING ON YOU.
IT WON'T KEEP HAPPENING!
YOU DON'T KNOW THAT.
RIING RING
OH, IT'S MY BOSS.
LONGHORN

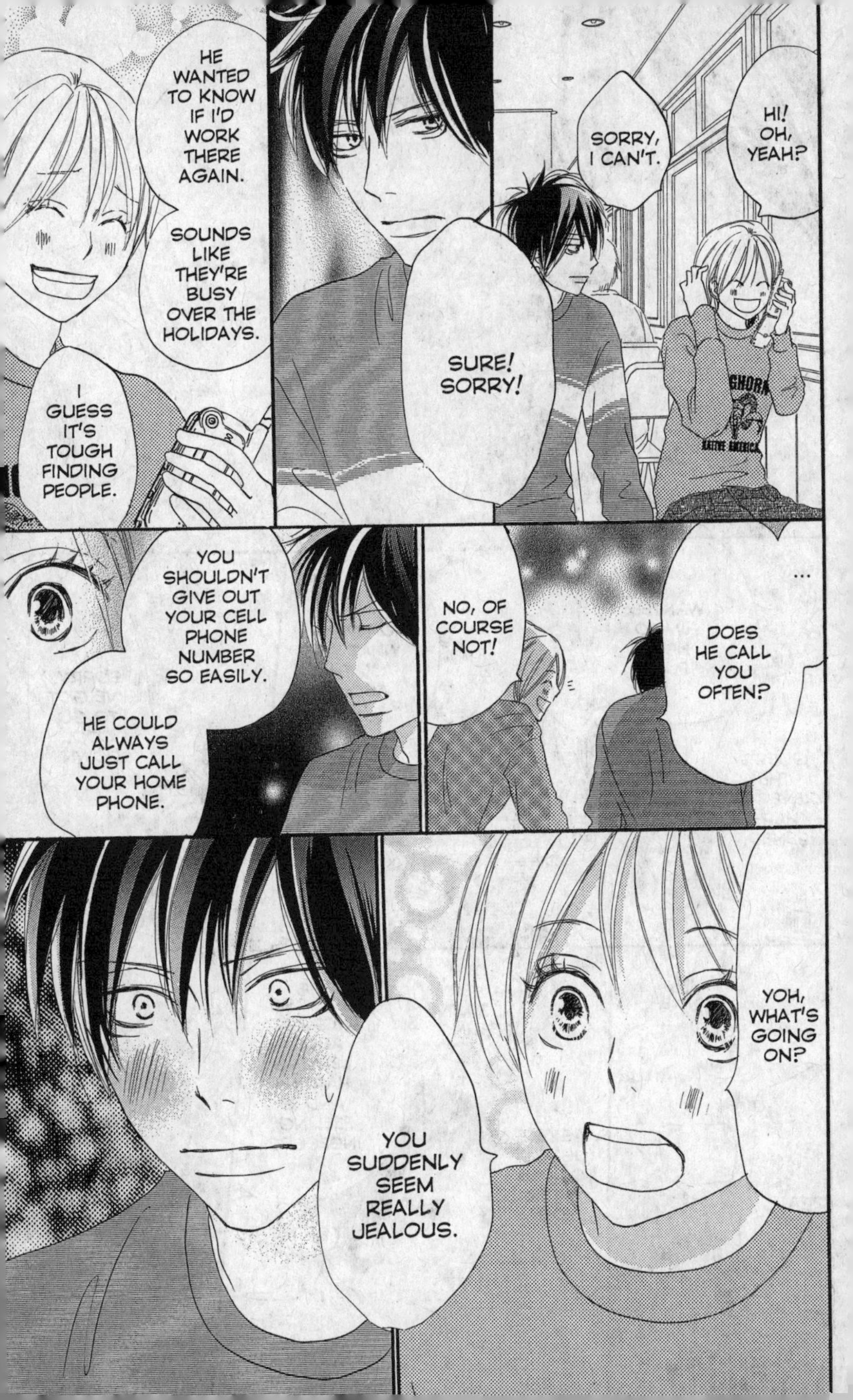
HI! OH, YEAH?
SORRY, I CAN'T.
SURE! SORRY!
HE WANTED TO KNOW IF I'D WORK THERE AGAIN.
SOUNDS LIKE THEY'RE BUSY OVER THE HOLIDAYS.
I GUESS IT'S TOUGH FINDING PEOPLE.
...
DOES HE CALL YOU OFTEN?
NO, OF COURSE NOT!
YOU SHOULDN'T GIVE OUT YOUR CELL PHONE NUMBER SO EASILY.
HE COULD ALWAYS JUST CALL YOUR HOME PHONE.
YOH, WHAT'S GOING ON?
YOU SUDDENLY SEEM REALLY JEALOUS.

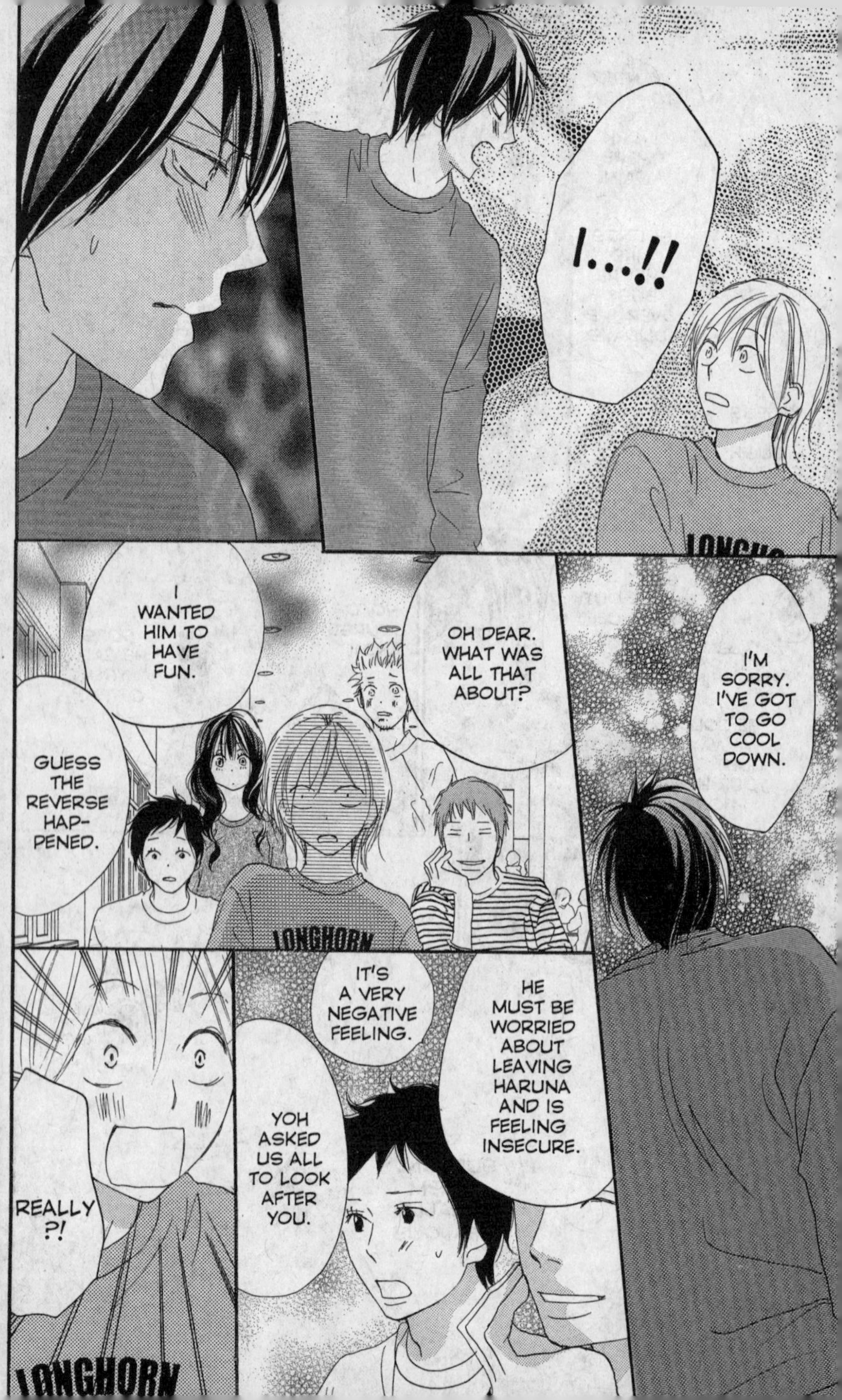
I...!!
I'M SORRY. I'VE GOT TO GO COOL DOWN.
OH DEAR. WHAT WAS ALL THAT ABOUT?
I WANTED HIM TO HAVE FUN.
GUESS THE REVERSE HAP-PENED.
LONGHORN
HE MUST BE WORRIED ABOUT LEAVING HARUNA AND IS FEELING INSECURE.
IT'S A VERY NEGATIVE FEELING.
YOH ASKED US ALL TO LOOK AFTER YOU.
REALLY?!
LONGHORN

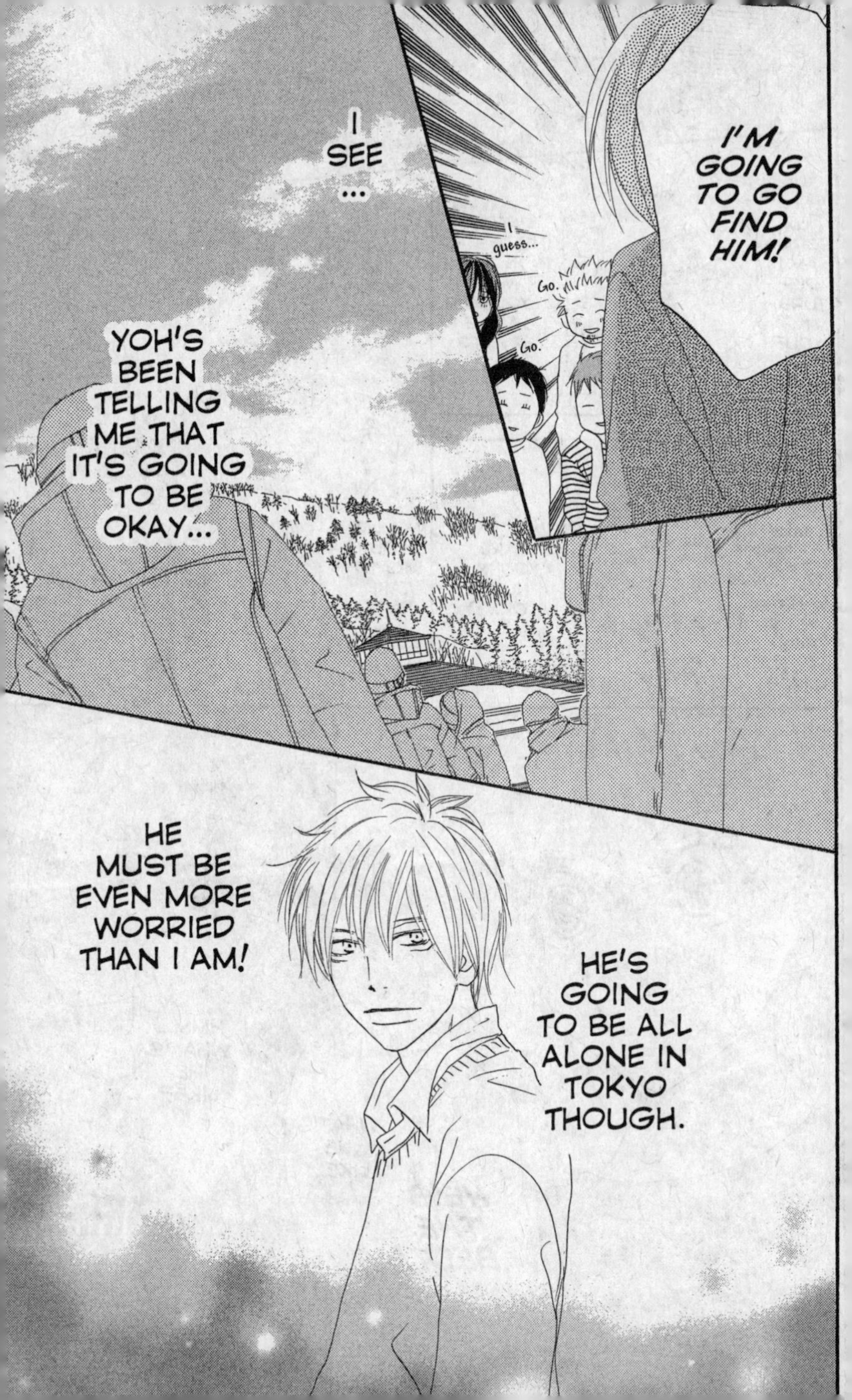
I'M GOING TO GO FIND HIM!
I guess...
Go.
Go.
I SEE...
YOH'S BEEN TELLING ME THAT IT'S GOING TO BE OKAY...
HE'S GOING TO BE ALL ALONE IN TOKYO THOUGH.
HE MUST BE EVEN MORE WORRIED THAN I AM!

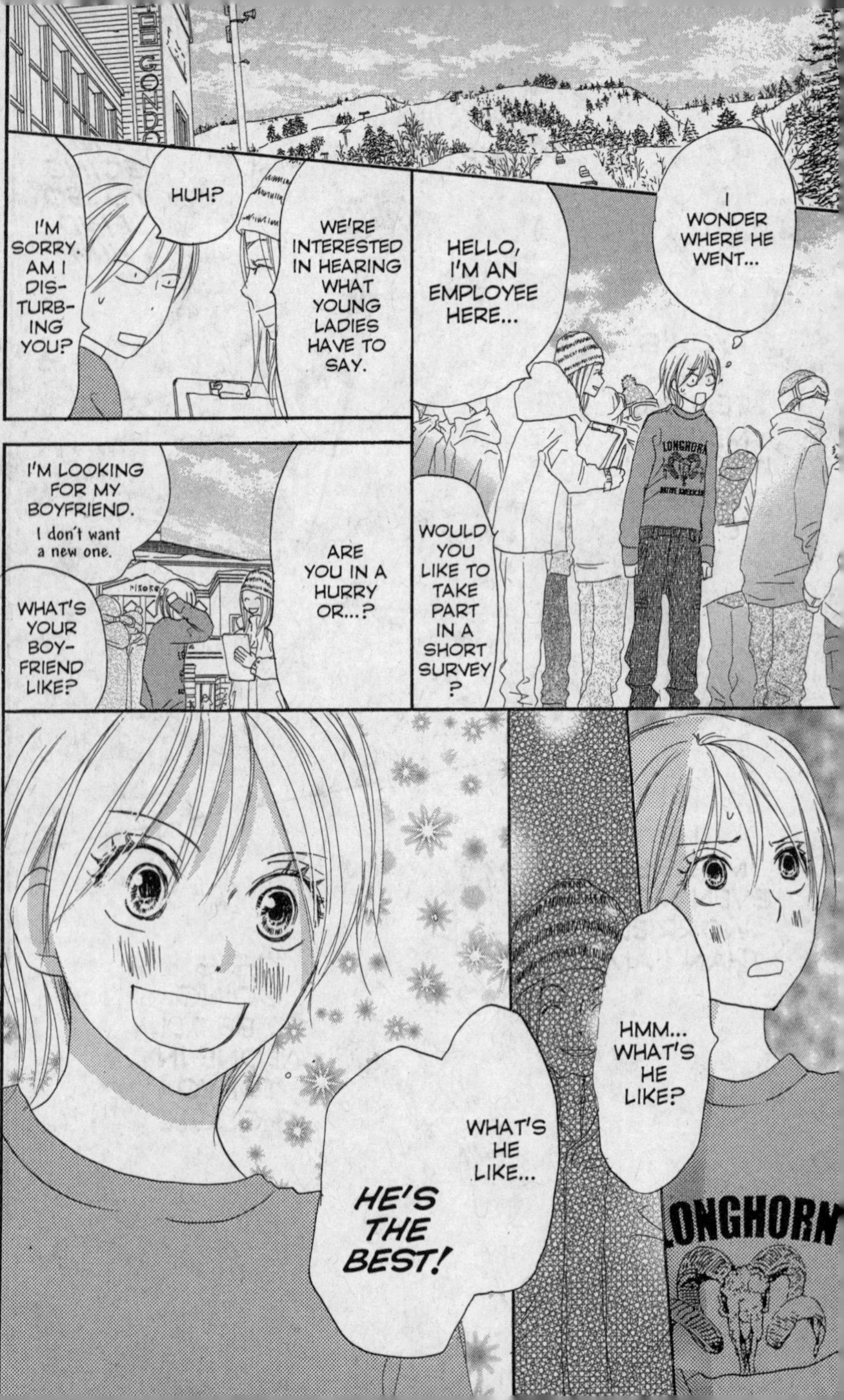

I WONDER WHERE HE WENT...
HELLO, I'M AN EMPLOYEE HERE...
WOULD YOU LIKE TO TAKE PART IN A SHORT SURVEY?
HUH?
WE'RE INTERESTED IN HEARING WHAT YOUNG LADIES HAVE TO SAY.
I'M SORRY. AM I DIS-TURB-ING YOU?
ARE YOU IN A HURRY OR...?
I'M LOOKING FOR MY BOYFRIEND.
I don't want a new one.
WHAT'S YOUR BOY-FRIEND LIKE?
HMM... WHAT'S HE LIKE?
WHAT'S HE LIKE...
HE'S THE BEST!
LONGHORN

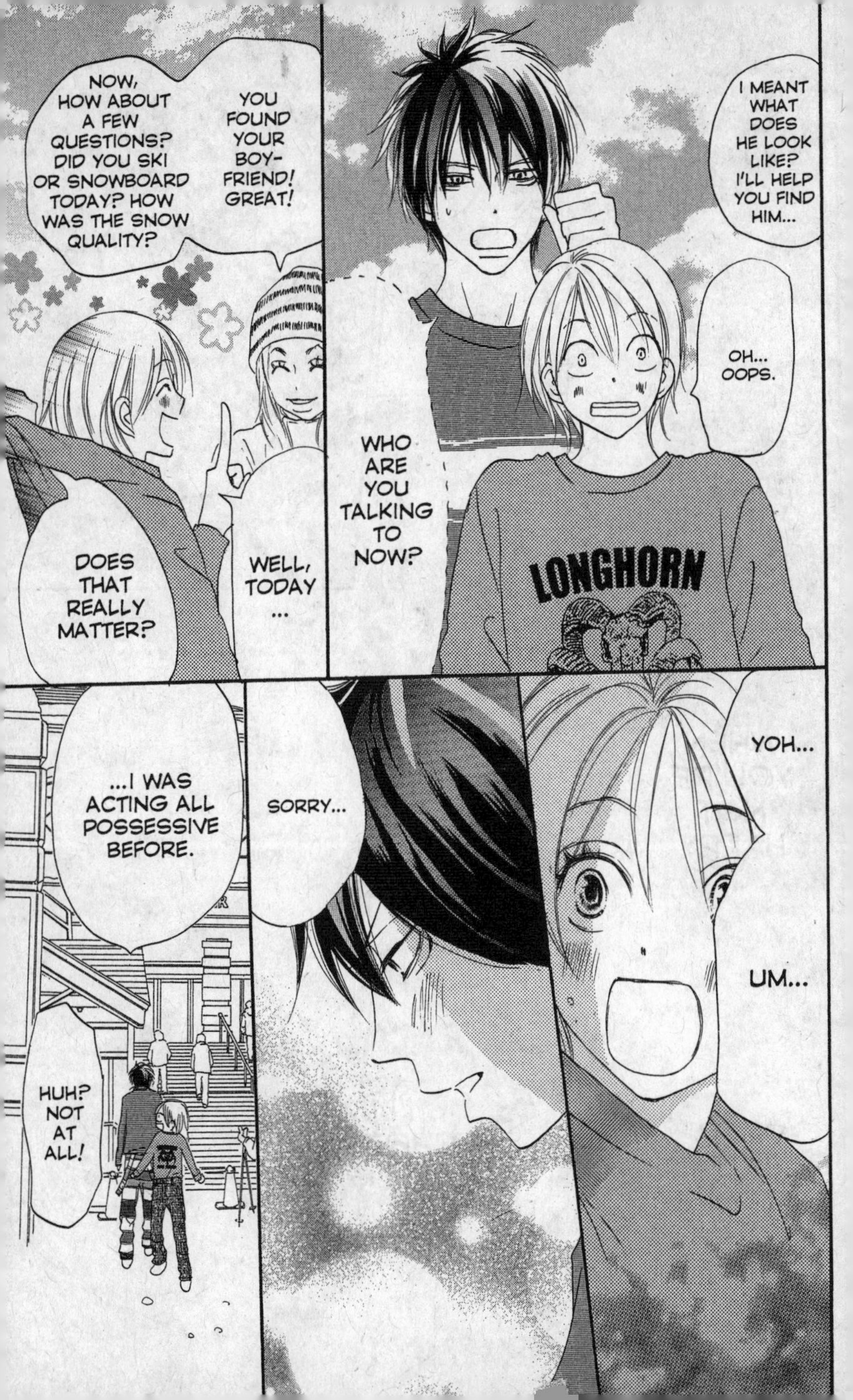

I MEANT WHAT DOES HE LOOK LIKE? I'LL HELP YOU FIND HIM...
WHO ARE YOU TALKING TO NOW?
OH... OOPS.
LONGHORN
YOU FOUND YOUR BOY-FRIEND! GREAT!
NOW, HOW ABOUT A FEW QUESTIONS? DID YOU SKI OR SNOWBOARD TODAY? HOW WAS THE SNOW QUALITY?
WELL, TODAY ...
DOES THAT REALLY MATTER?
YOH...
UM...
SORRY...
...I WAS ACTING ALL POSSESSIVE BEFORE.
HUH? NOT AT ALL!

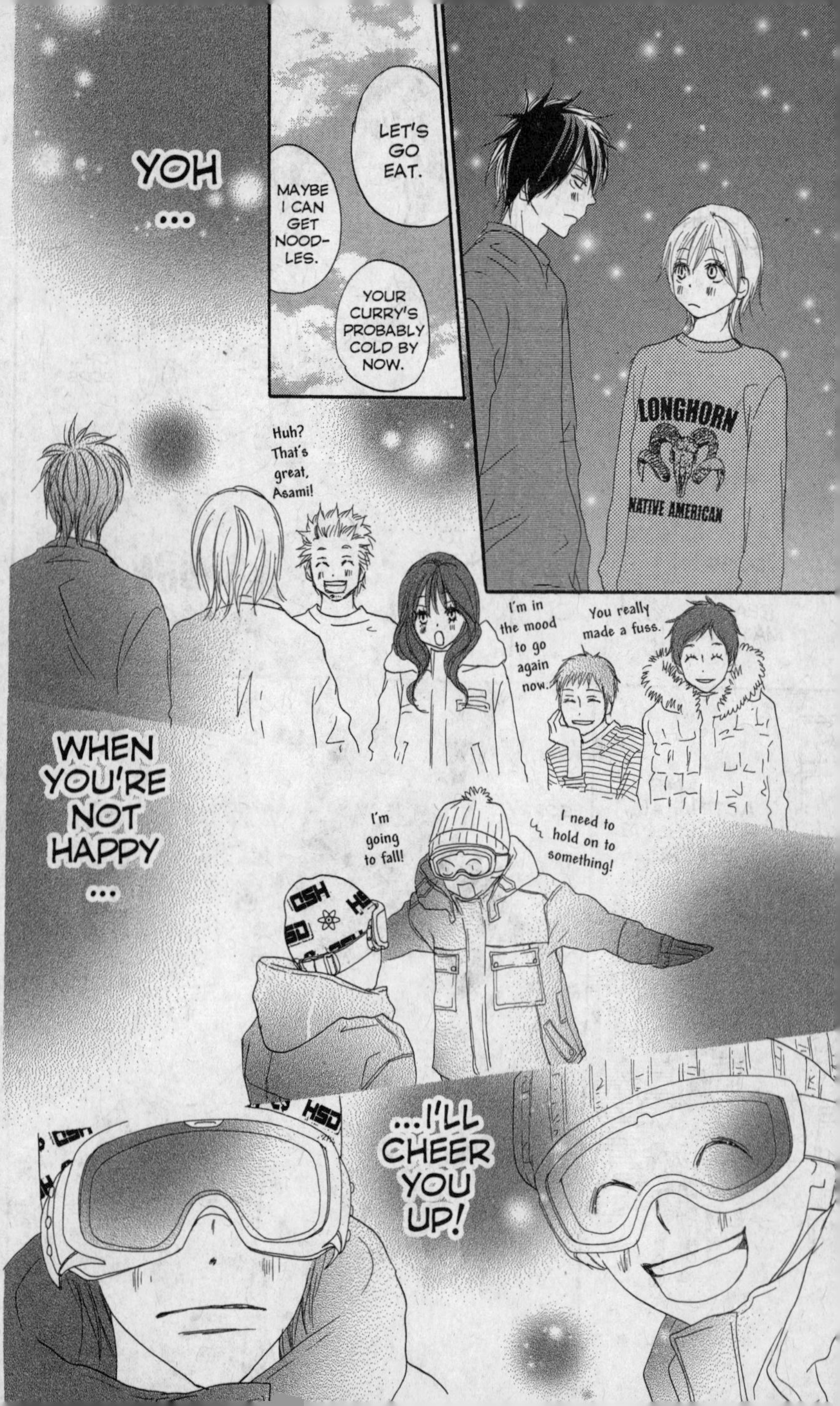
LET'S GO EAT.
MAYBE I CAN GET NOOD-LES.
YOUR CURRY'S PROBABLY COLD BY NOW.
YOH ...
LONGHORN
NATIVE AMERICAN
You really made a fuss.
I'm in the mood to go again now.
Huh? That's great, Asami!
WHEN YOU'RE NOT HAPPY ...
I need to hold on to something!
I'm going to fall!
...I'LL CHEER YOU UP!

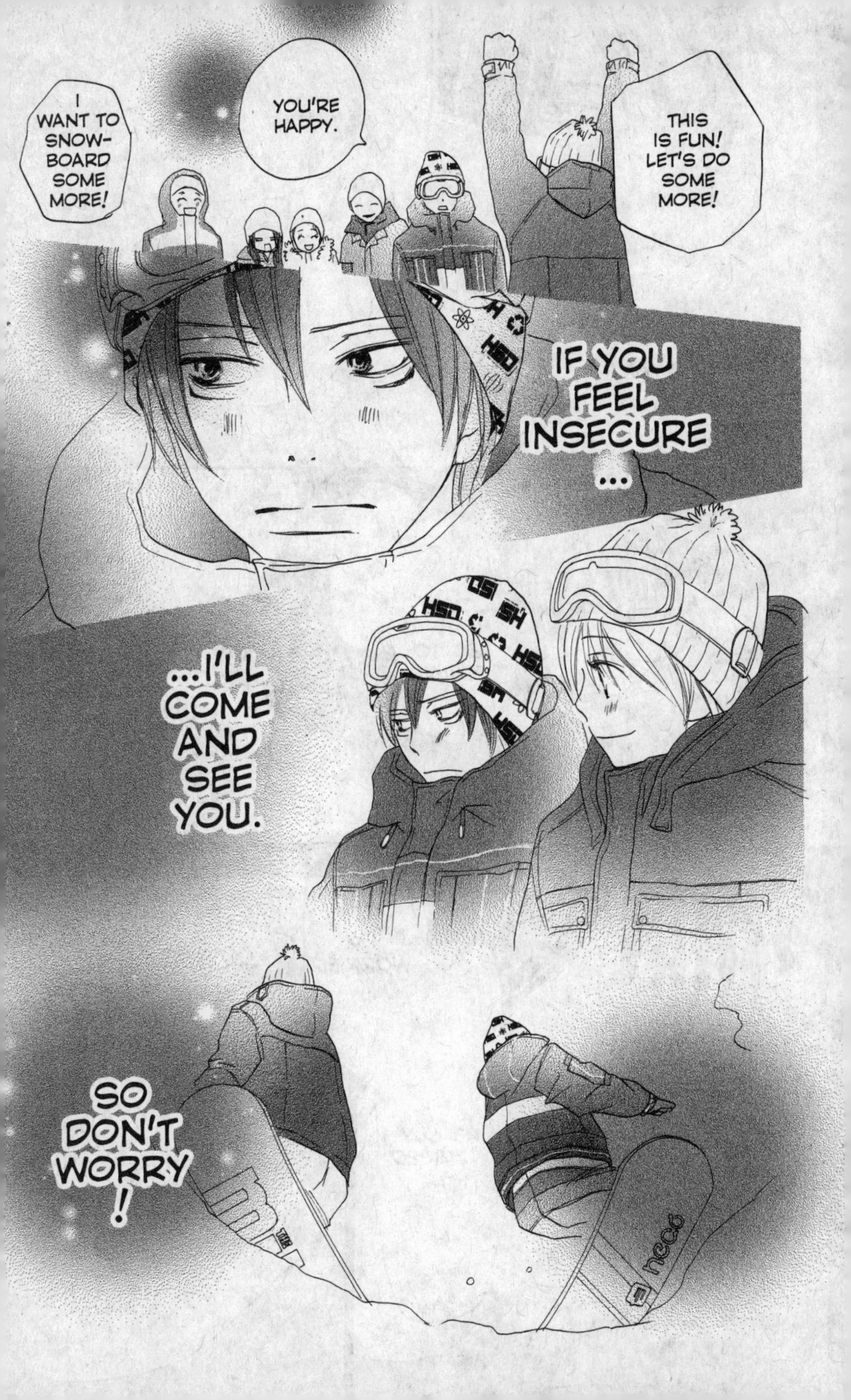
THIS IS FUN! LET'S DO SOME MORE!
YOU'RE HAPPY.
I WANT TO SNOW-BOARD SOME MORE!
IF YOU FEEL INSECURE ...
...I'LL COME AND SEE YOU.
SO DON'T WORRY!

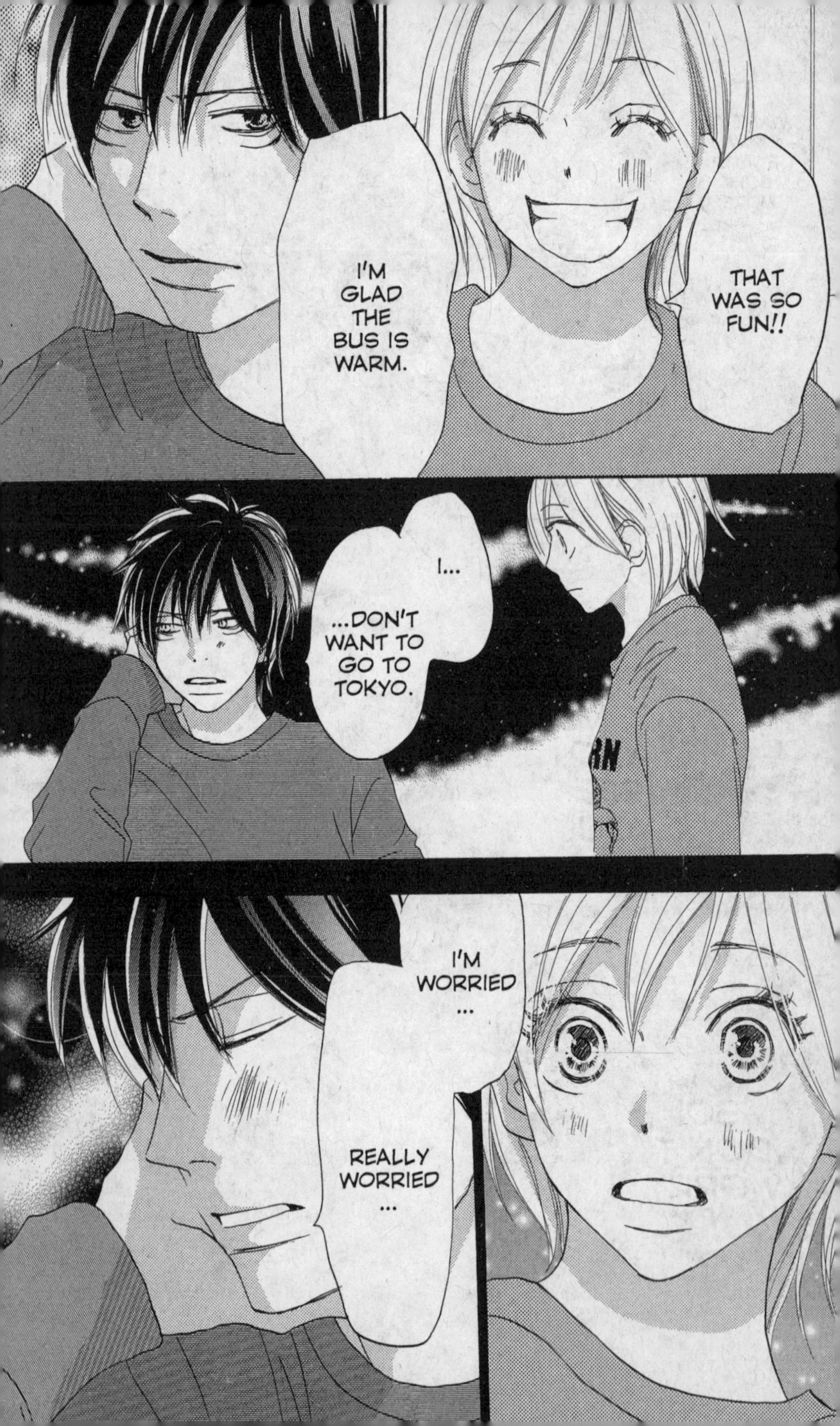
THAT WAS SO FUN!!
I'M GLAD THE BUS IS WARM.
I...
...DON'T WANT TO GO TO TOKYO.
I'M WORRIED ...
REALLY WORRIED ...

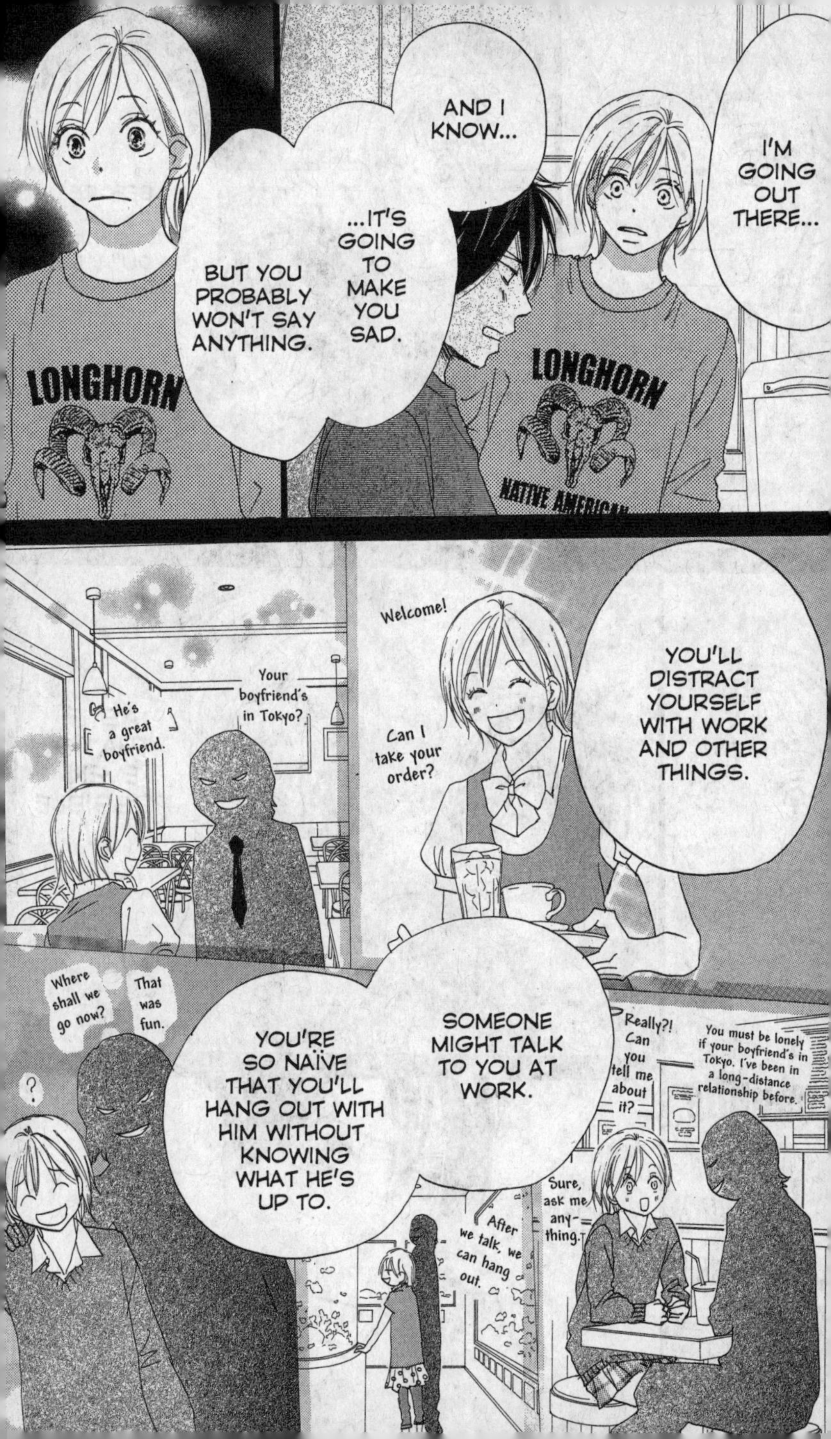
I'M GOING OUT THERE...
AND I KNOW...
...IT'S GOING TO MAKE YOU SAD.
BUT YOU PROBABLY WON'T SAY ANYTHING.
LONGHORN
LONGHORN
NATIVE AMERICAN
YOU'LL DISTRACT YOURSELF WITH WORK AND OTHER THINGS.
Welcome!
Can I take your order?
Your boyfriend's in Tokyo?
He's a great boyfriend.
SOMEONE MIGHT TALK TO YOU AT WORK.
YOU'RE SO NAÏVE THAT YOU'LL HANG OUT WITH HIM WITHOUT KNOWING WHAT HE'S UP TO.
You must be lonely if your boyfriend's in Tokyo. I've been in a long-distance relationship before.
Really?! Can you tell me about it?
Sure, ask me any-thing.
After we talk, we can hang out.
That was fun.
Where shall we go now?
?

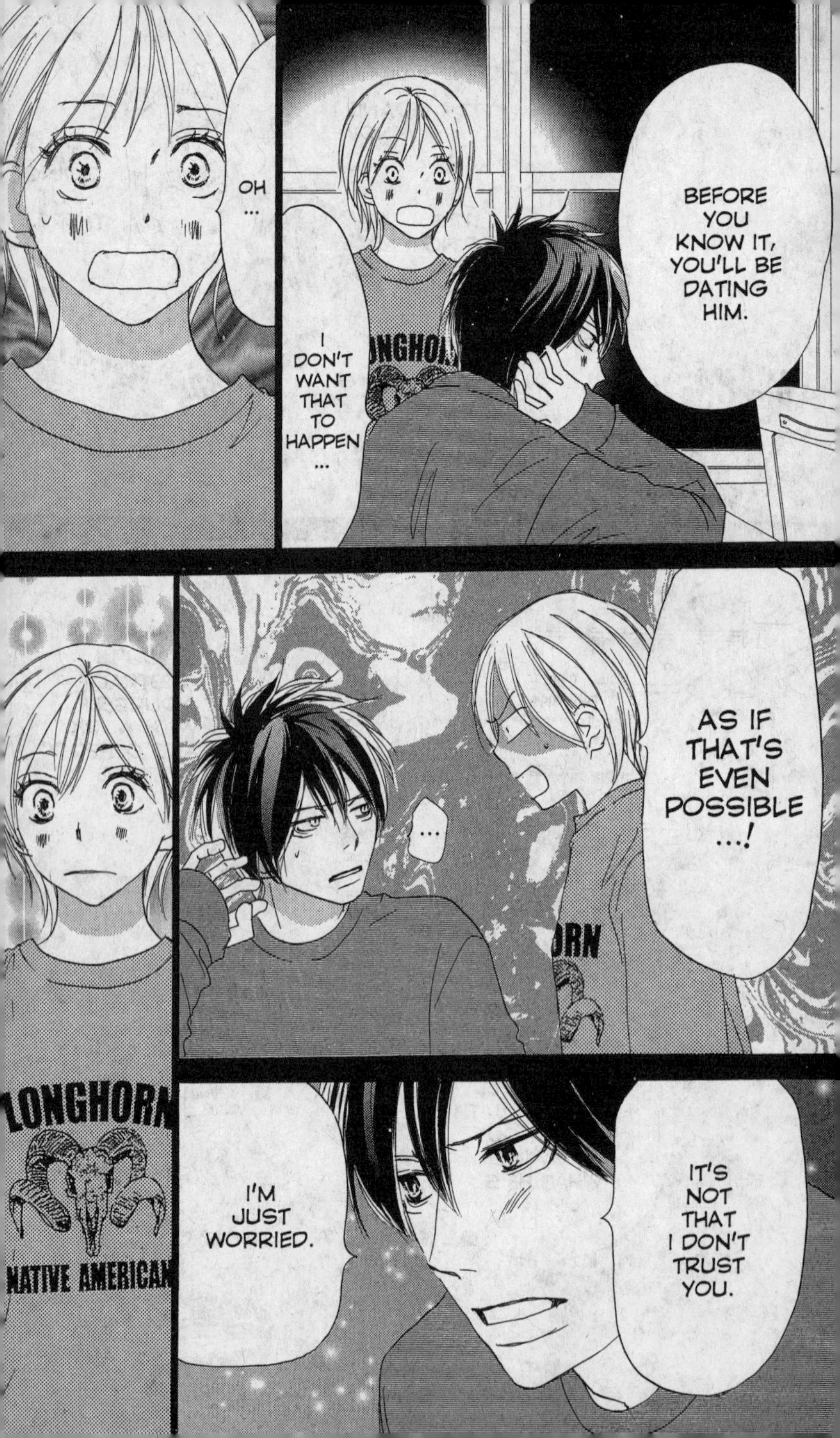
BEFORE YOU KNOW IT, YOU'LL BE DATING HIM.
I DON'T WANT THAT TO HAPPEN ...
OH ...
AS IF THAT'S EVEN POSSIBLE ...!
...
IT'S NOT THAT I DON'T TRUST YOU.
I'M JUST WORRIED.
LONGHORN
NATIVE AMERICAN

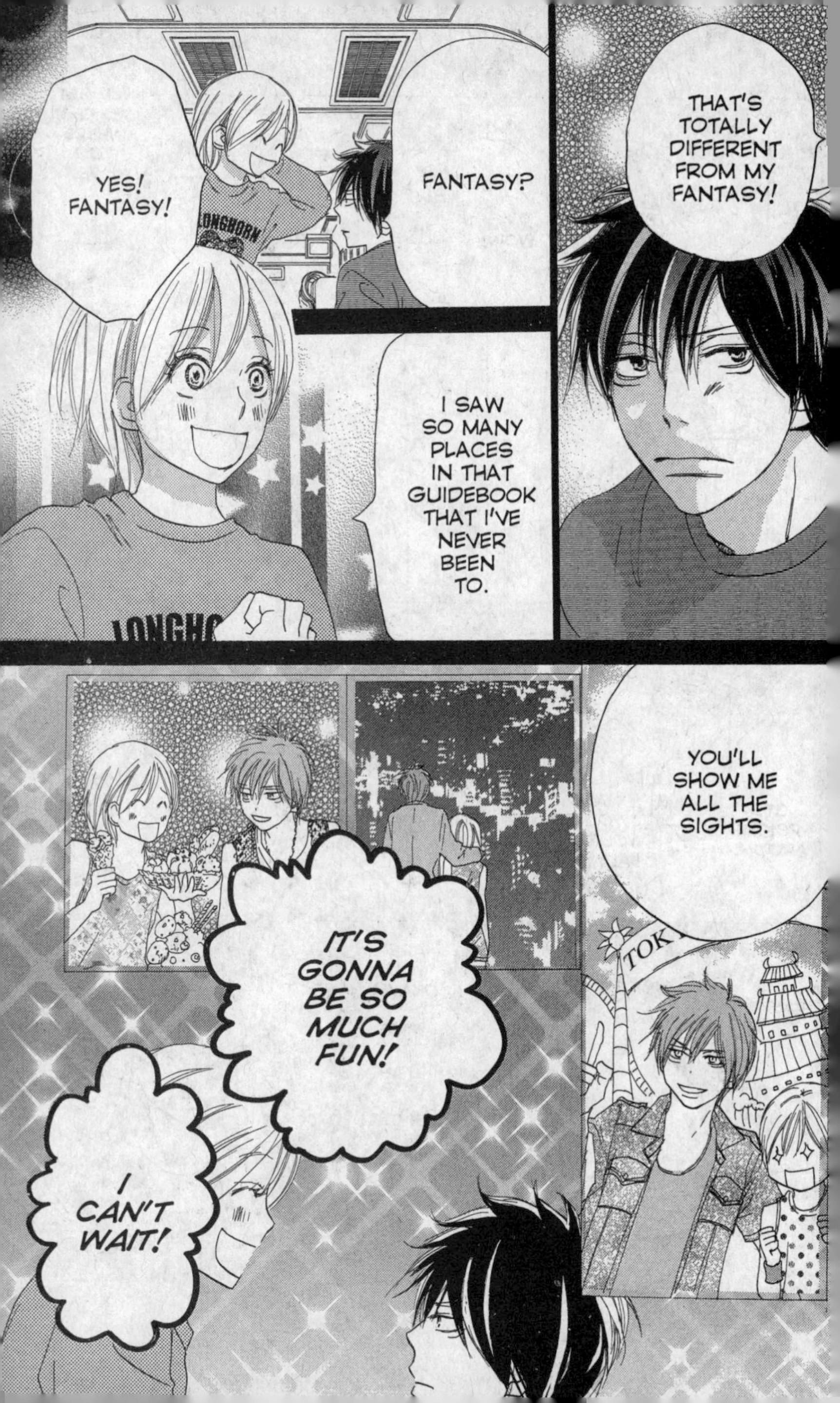
THAT'S TOTALLY DIFFERENT FROM MY FANTASY!
FANTASY?
YES! FANTASY!
I SAW SO MANY PLACES IN THAT GUIDEBOOK THAT I'VE NEVER BEEN TO.
YOU'LL SHOW ME ALL THE SIGHTS.
IT'S GONNA BE SO MUCH FUN!
I CAN'T WAIT!

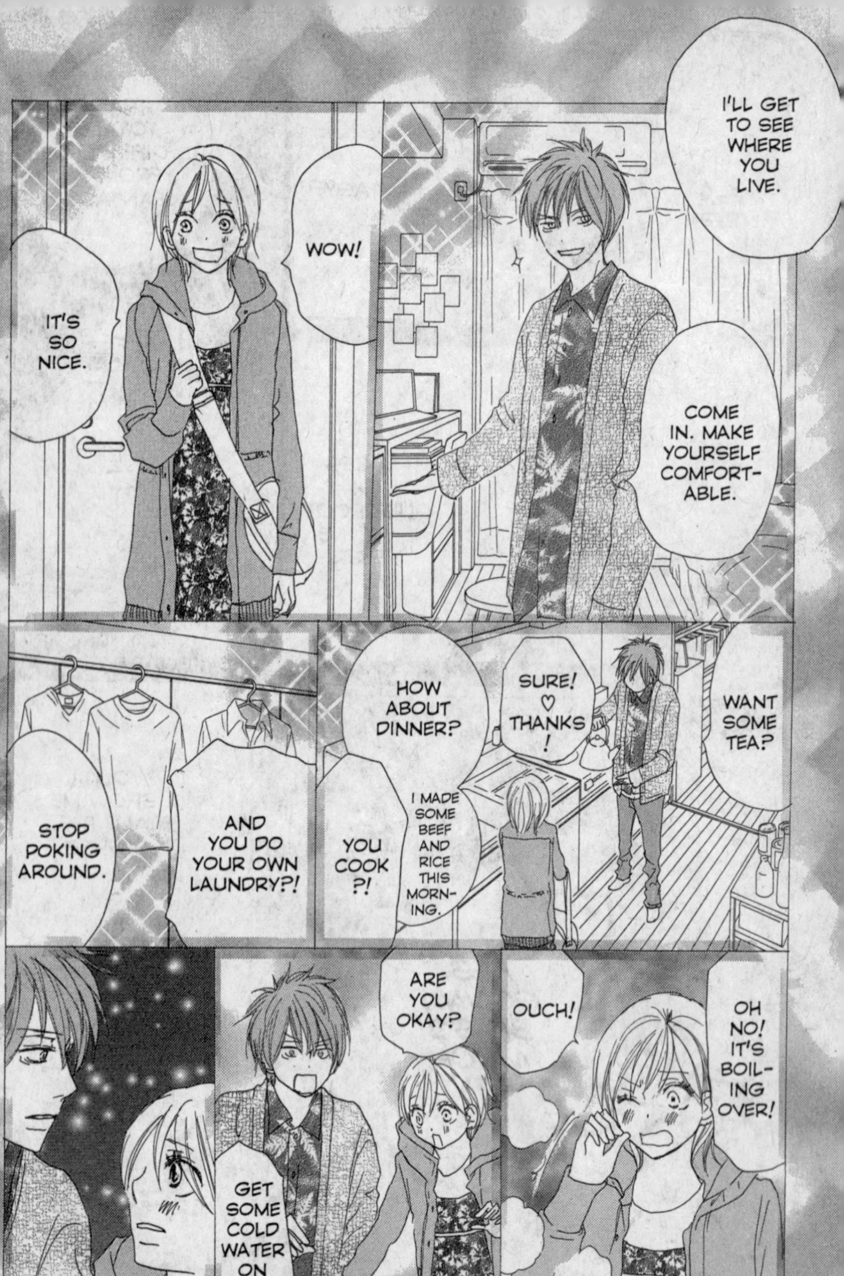
I'LL GET TO SEE WHERE YOU LIVE.
COME IN. MAKE YOURSELF COMFORTABLE.
WOW!
IT'S SO NICE.
WANT SOME TEA?
SURE! ♡ THANKS!
HOW ABOUT DINNER?
I MADE SOME BEEF AND RICE THIS MORNING.
YOU COOK?!
AND YOU DO YOUR OWN LAUNDRY?!
STOP POKING AROUND.
OH NO! IT'S BOILING OVER!
OUCH!
ARE YOU OKAY?
GET SOME COLD WATER ON IT!

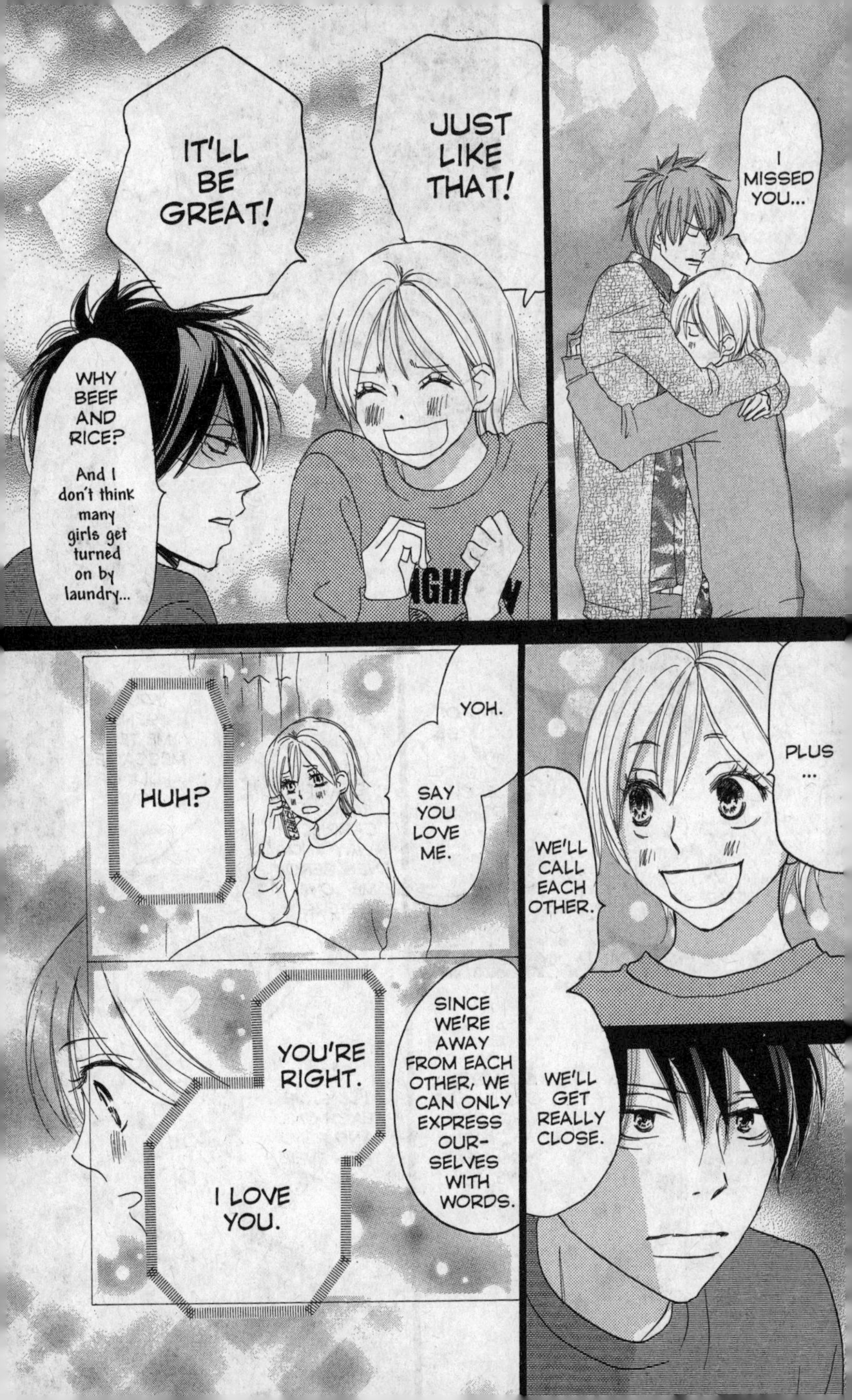
I MISSED YOU...
JUST LIKE THAT!
IT'LL BE GREAT!
WHY BEEF AND RICE?
And I don't think many girls get turned on by laundry...
PLUS ...
WE'LL CALL EACH OTHER.
WE'LL GET REALLY CLOSE.
YOH.
SAY YOU LOVE ME.
HUH?
SINCE WE'RE AWAY FROM EACH OTHER, WE CAN ONLY EXPRESS OURSELVES WITH WORDS.
YOU'RE RIGHT.
I LOVE YOU.

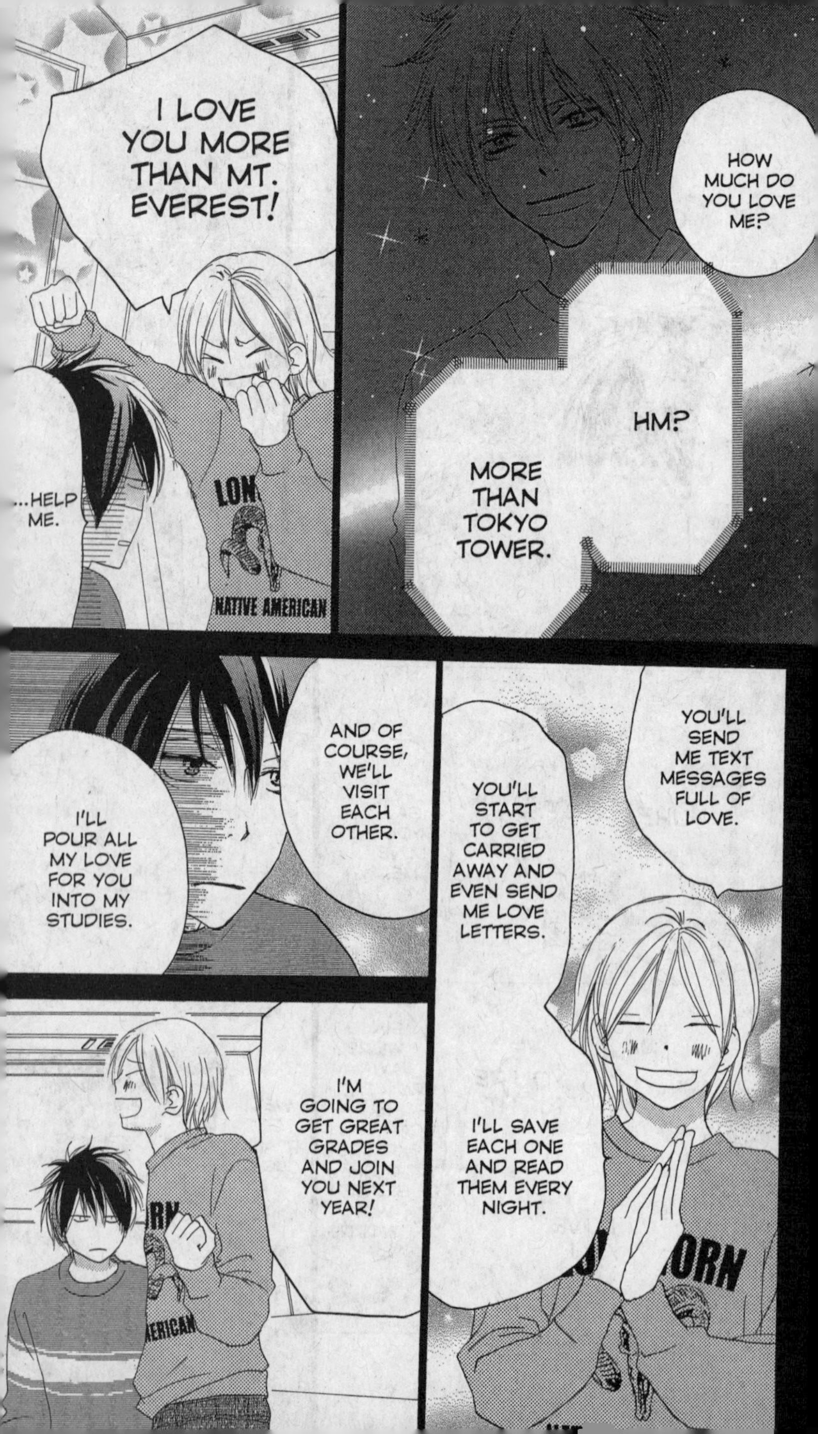
HOW MUCH DO YOU LOVE ME?
HM?
MORE THAN TOKYO TOWER.
I LOVE YOU MORE THAN MT. EVEREST!
...HELP ME.
YOU'LL SEND ME TEXT MESSAGES FULL OF LOVE.
YOU'LL START TO GET CARRIED AWAY AND EVEN SEND ME LOVE LETTERS.
I'LL SAVE EACH ONE AND READ THEM EVERY NIGHT.
AND OF COURSE, WE'LL VISIT EACH OTHER.
I'LL POUR ALL MY LOVE FOR YOU INTO MY STUDIES.
I'M GOING TO GET GREAT GRADES AND JOIN YOU NEXT YEAR!

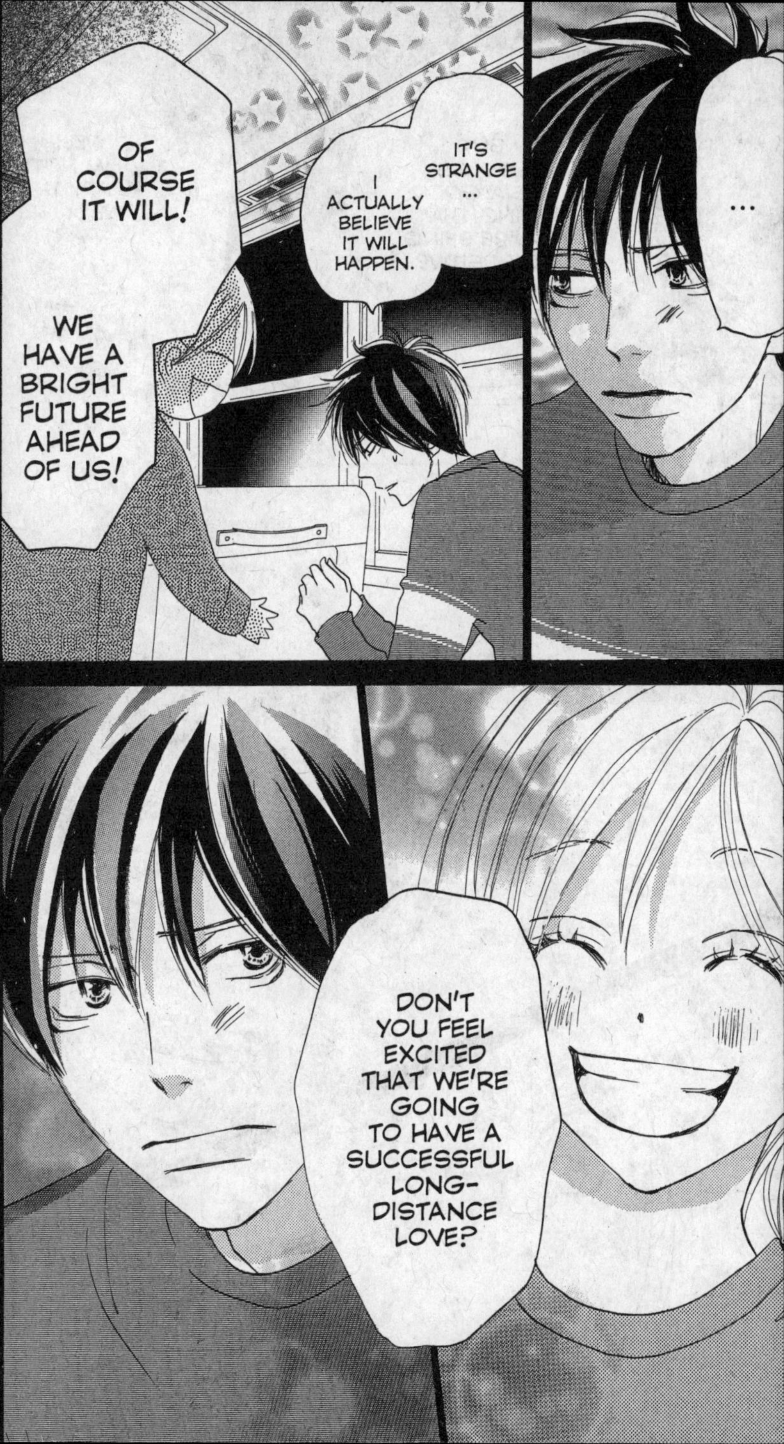
...
IT'S STRANGE...
I ACTUALLY BELIEVE IT WILL HAPPEN.
OF COURSE IT WILL!
WE HAVE A BRIGHT FUTURE AHEAD OF US!
DON'T YOU FEEL EXCITED THAT WE'RE GOING TO HAVE A SUCCESSFUL LONG-DISTANCE LOVE?

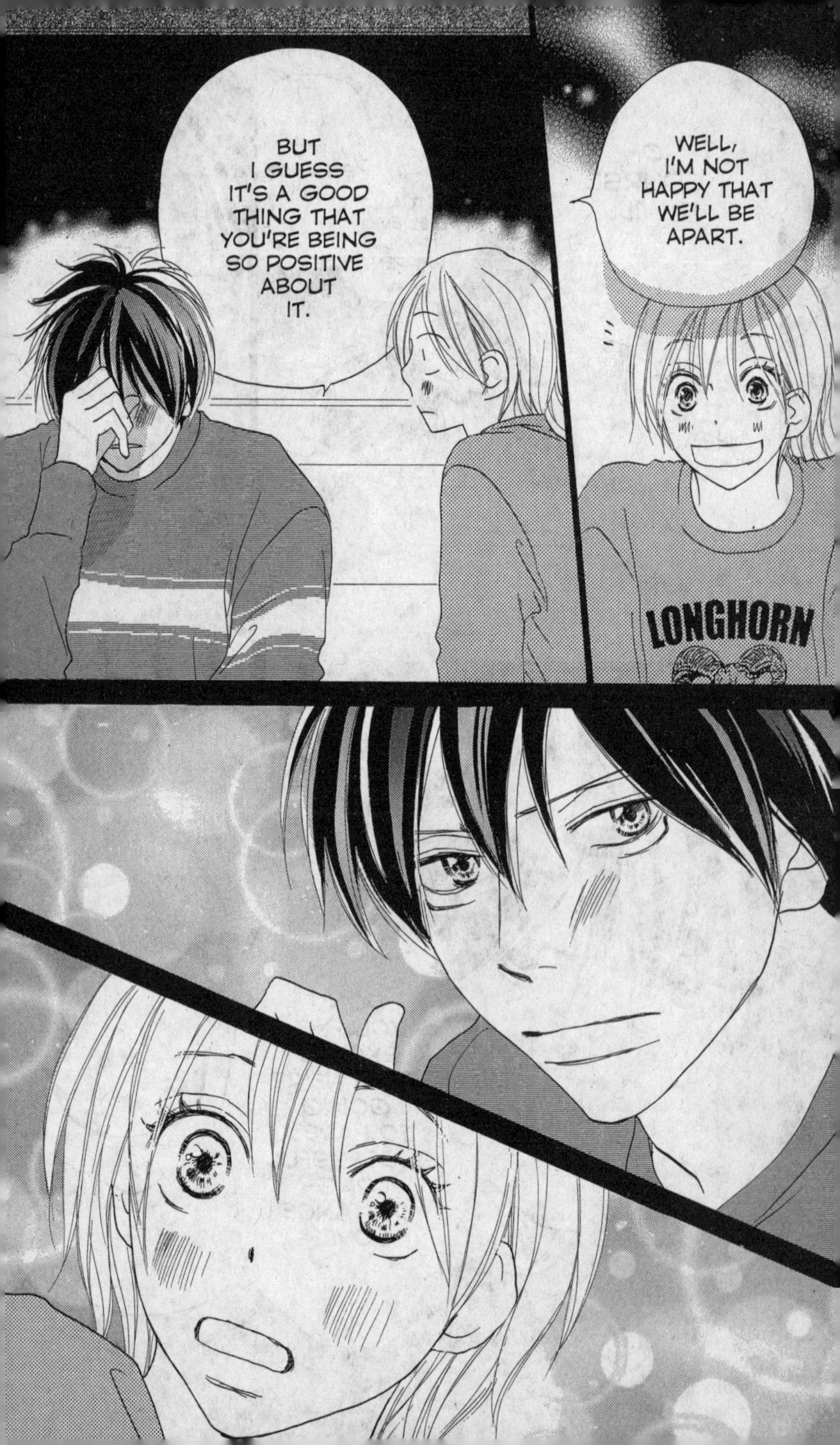
WELL, I'M NOT HAPPY THAT WE'LL BE APART.
LONGHORN
BUT I GUESS IT'S A GOOD THING THAT YOU'RE BEING SO POSITIVE ABOUT IT.

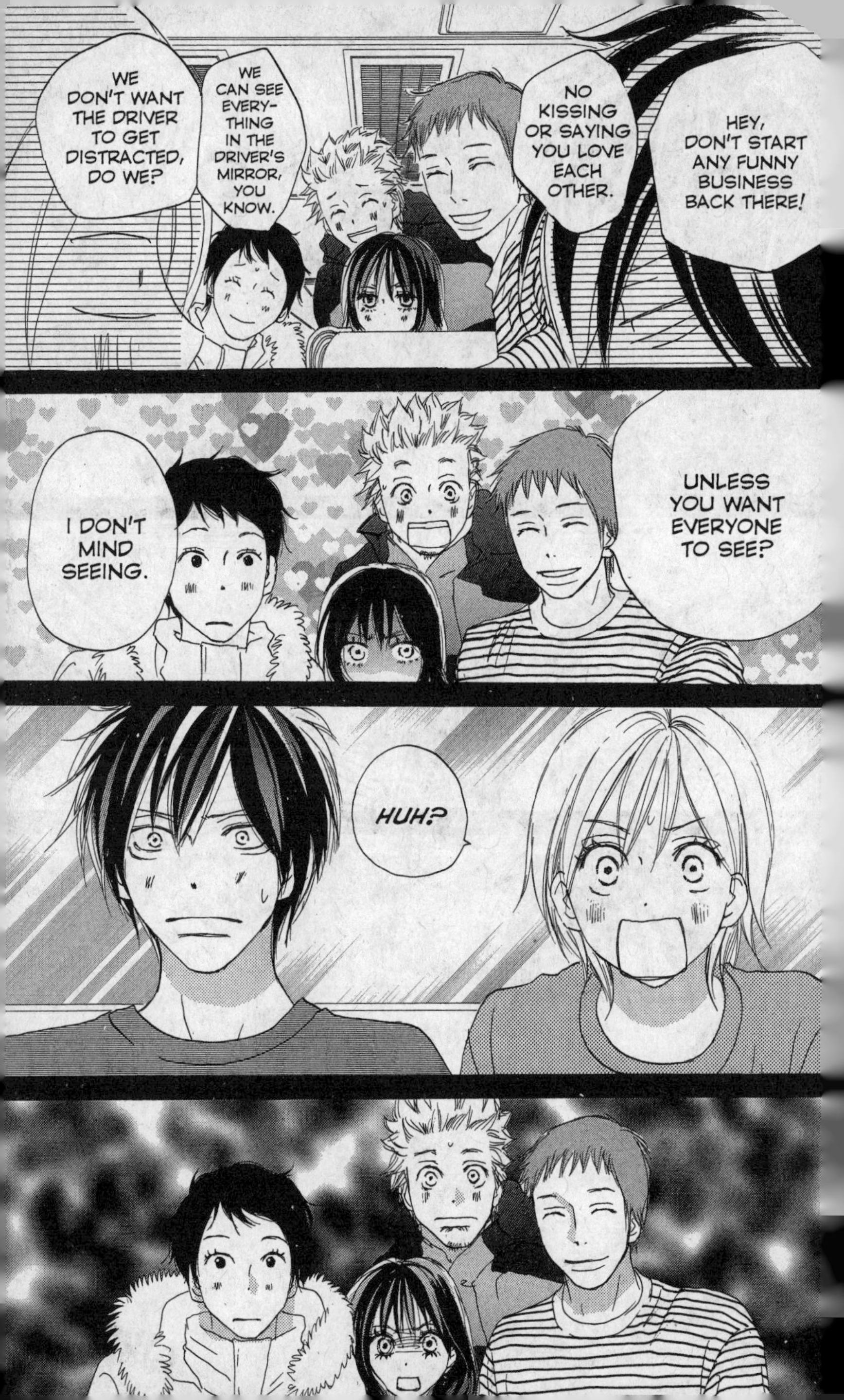
HEY, DON'T START ANY FUNNY BUSINESS BACK THERE!
NO KISSING OR SAYING YOU LOVE EACH OTHER.
WE CAN SEE EVERY-THING IN THE DRIVER'S MIRROR, YOU KNOW.
WE DON'T WANT THE DRIVER TO GET DISTRACTED, DO WE?
UNLESS YOU WANT EVERYONE TO SEE?
I DON'T MIND SEEING.
HUH?

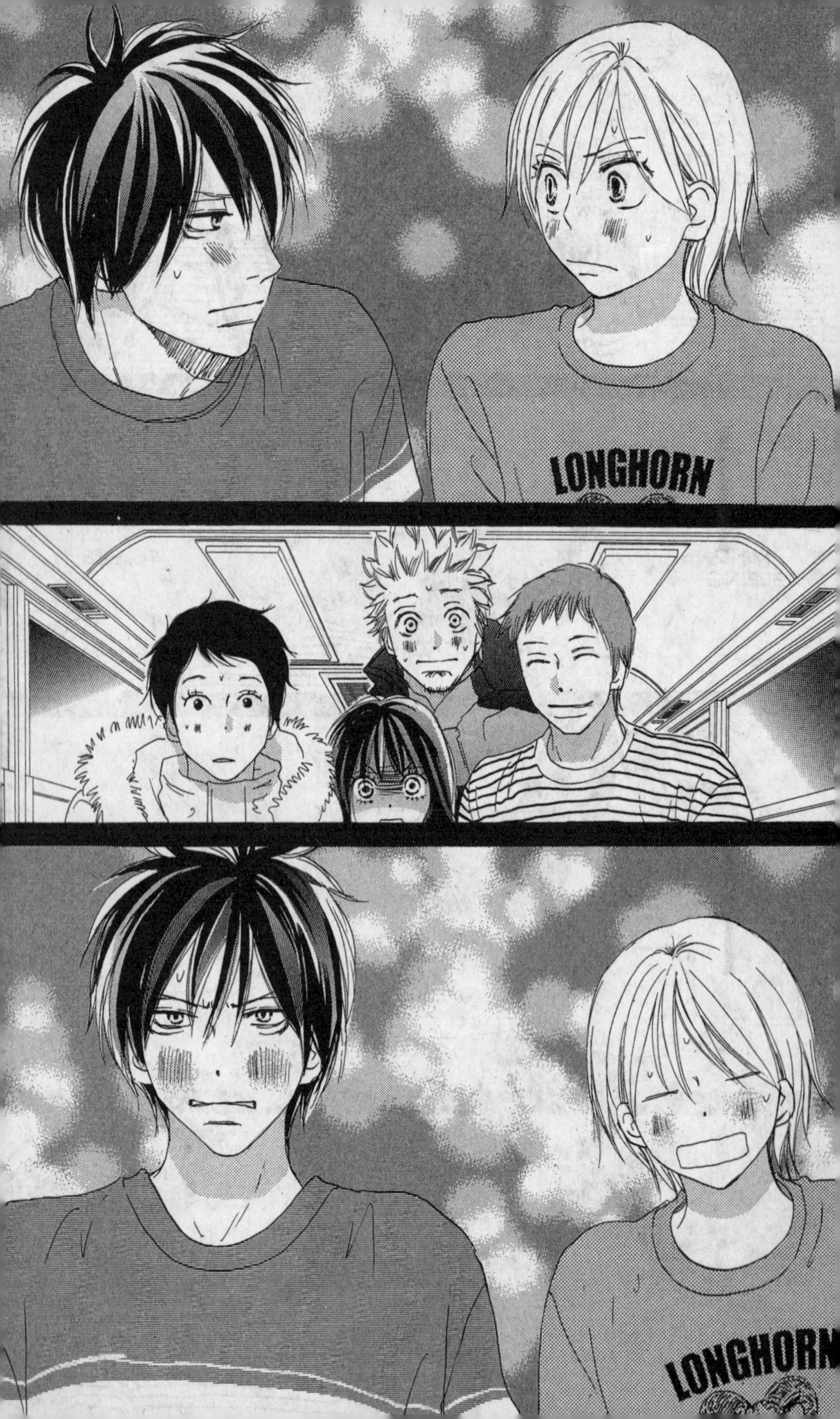
LONGHORN
LONGHORN

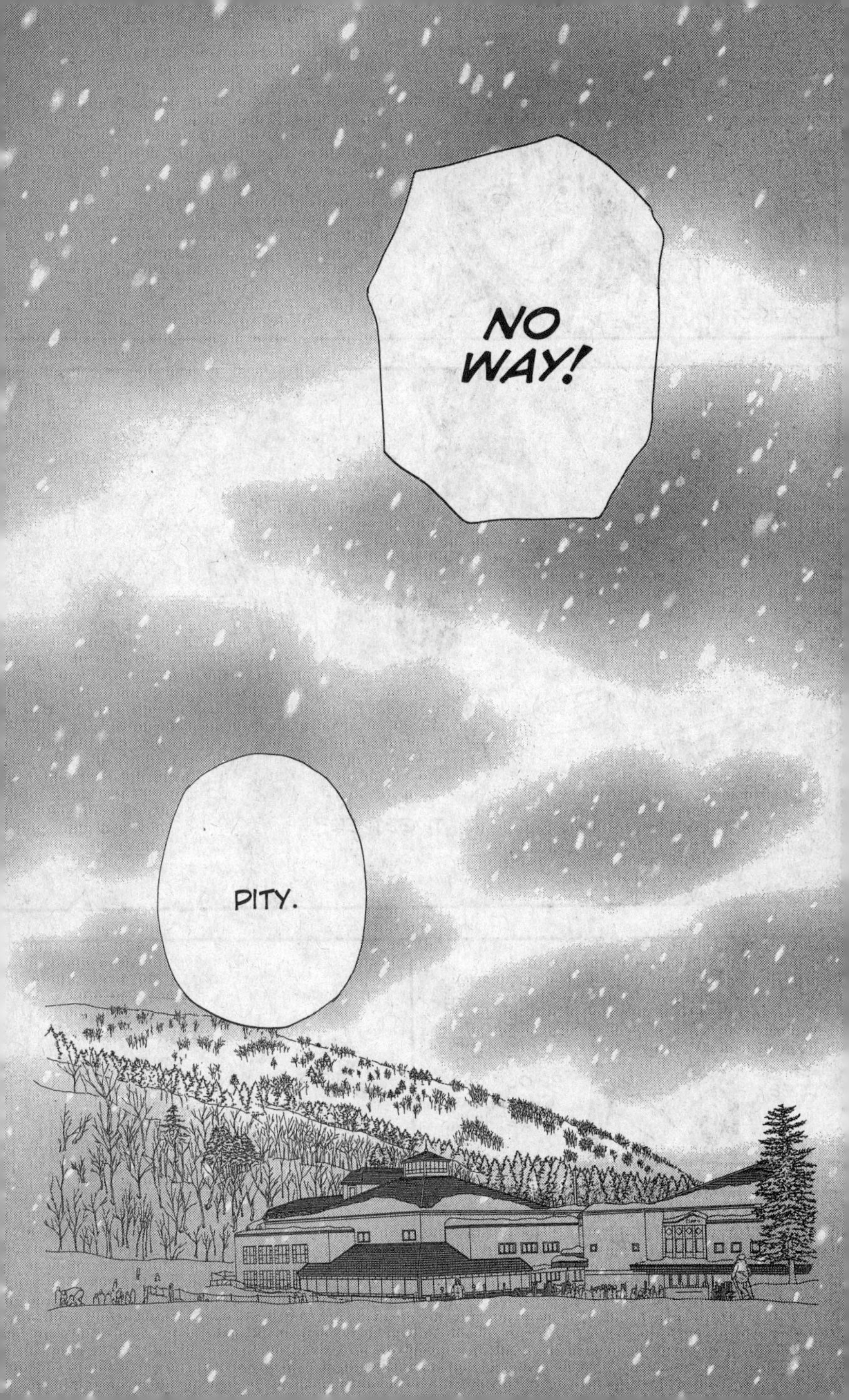
NO WAY!
PITY.

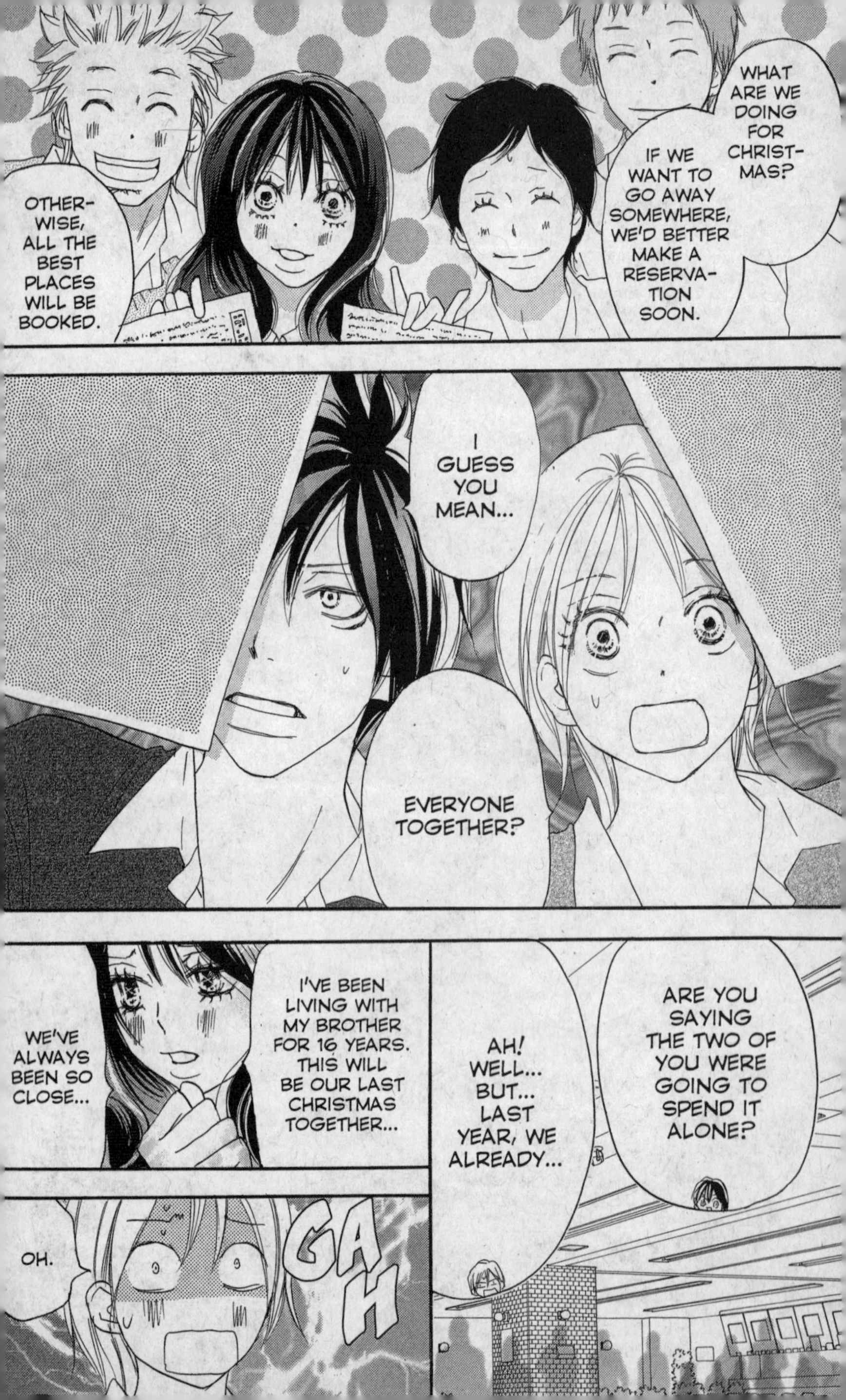
WHAT ARE WE DOING FOR CHRISTMAS?
IF WE WANT TO GO AWAY SOMEWHERE, WE'D BETTER MAKE A RESERVATION SOON.
OTHERWISE, ALL THE BEST PLACES WILL BE BOOKED.
I GUESS YOU MEAN...
EVERYONE TOGETHER?
ARE YOU SAYING THE TWO OF YOU WERE GOING TO SPEND IT ALONE?
AH! WELL... BUT... LAST YEAR, WE ALREADY...
I'VE BEEN LIVING WITH MY BROTHER FOR 16 YEARS. THIS WILL BE OUR LAST CHRISTMAS TOGETHER...
WE'VE ALWAYS BEEN SO CLOSE...
GAH
OH.

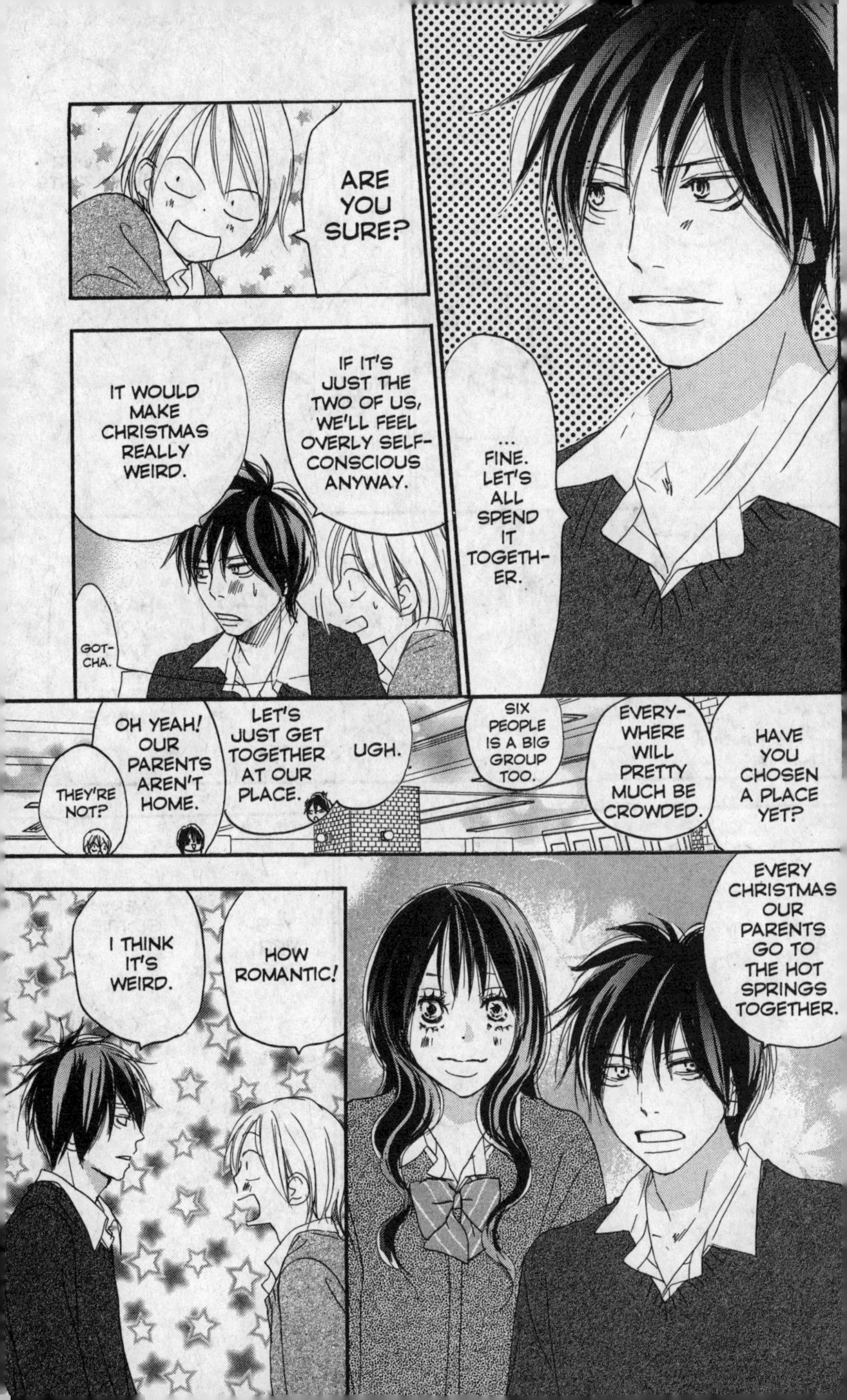

... FINE. LET'S ALL SPEND IT TOGETH-ER.
ARE YOU SURE?
IF IT'S JUST THE TWO OF US, WE'LL FEEL OVERLY SELF-CONSCIOUS ANYWAY.
IT WOULD MAKE CHRISTMAS REALLY WEIRD.
GOT-CHA.
HAVE YOU CHOSEN A PLACE YET?
EVERY-WHERE WILL PRETTY MUCH BE CROWDED.
SIX PEOPLE IS A BIG GROUP TOO.
UGH.
LET'S JUST GET TOGETHER AT OUR PLACE.
OH YEAH! OUR PARENTS AREN'T HOME.
THEY'RE NOT?
EVERY CHRISTMAS OUR PARENTS GO TO THE HOT SPRINGS TOGETHER.
HOW ROMANTIC!
I THINK IT'S WEIRD.

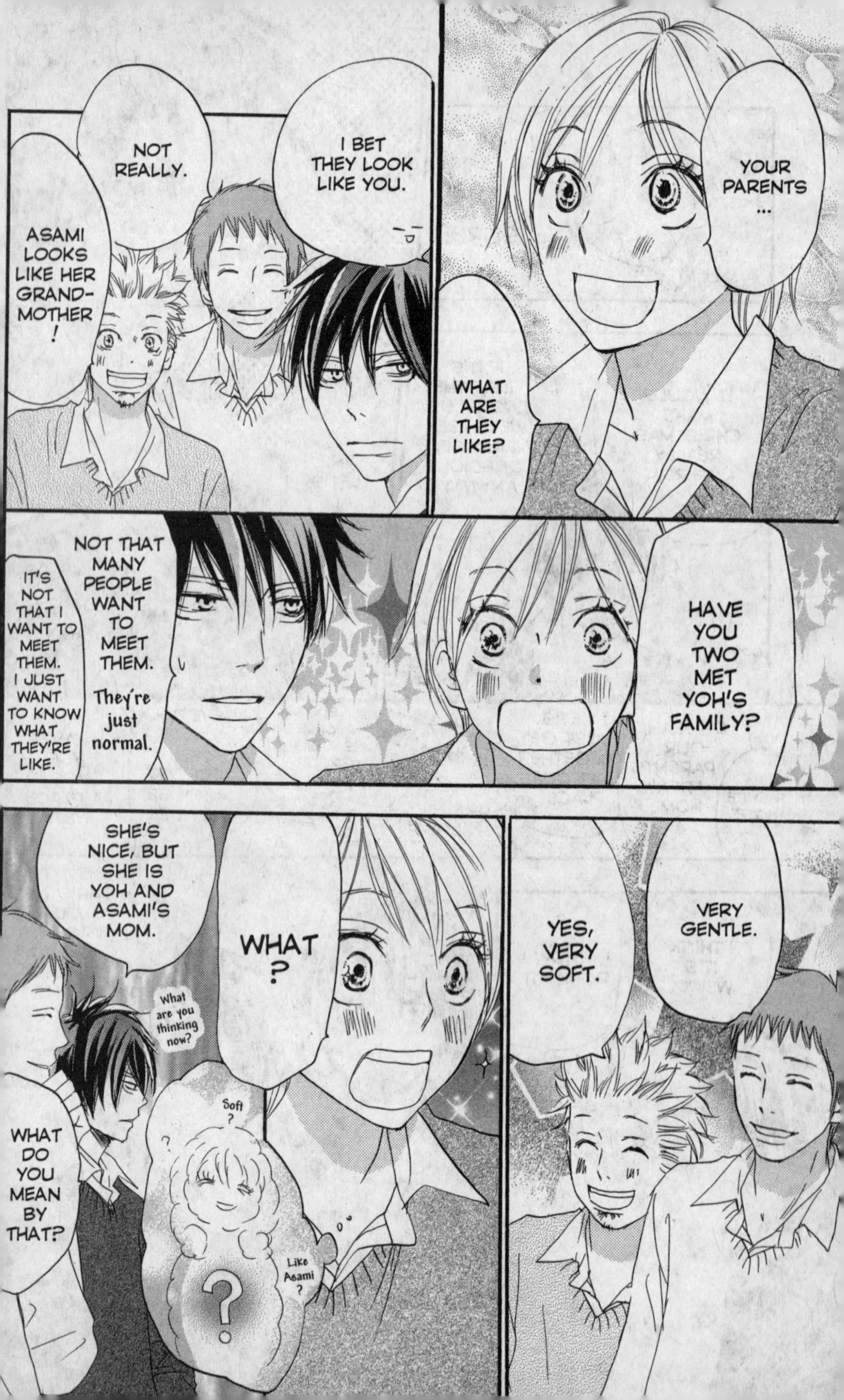
YOUR PARENTS ...
WHAT ARE THEY LIKE?
I BET THEY LOOK LIKE YOU.
NOT REALLY.
ASAMI LOOKS LIKE HER GRAND-MOTHER!
HAVE YOU TWO MET YOH'S FAMILY?
NOT THAT MANY PEOPLE WANT TO MEET THEM.
They're just normal.
IT'S NOT THAT I WANT TO MEET THEM. I JUST WANT TO KNOW WHAT THEY'RE LIKE.
VERY GENTLE.
YES, VERY SOFT.
WHAT?
SHE'S NICE, BUT SHE IS YOH AND ASAMI'S MOM.
What are you thinking now?
Soft?
Like Asami?
WHAT DO YOU MEAN BY THAT?

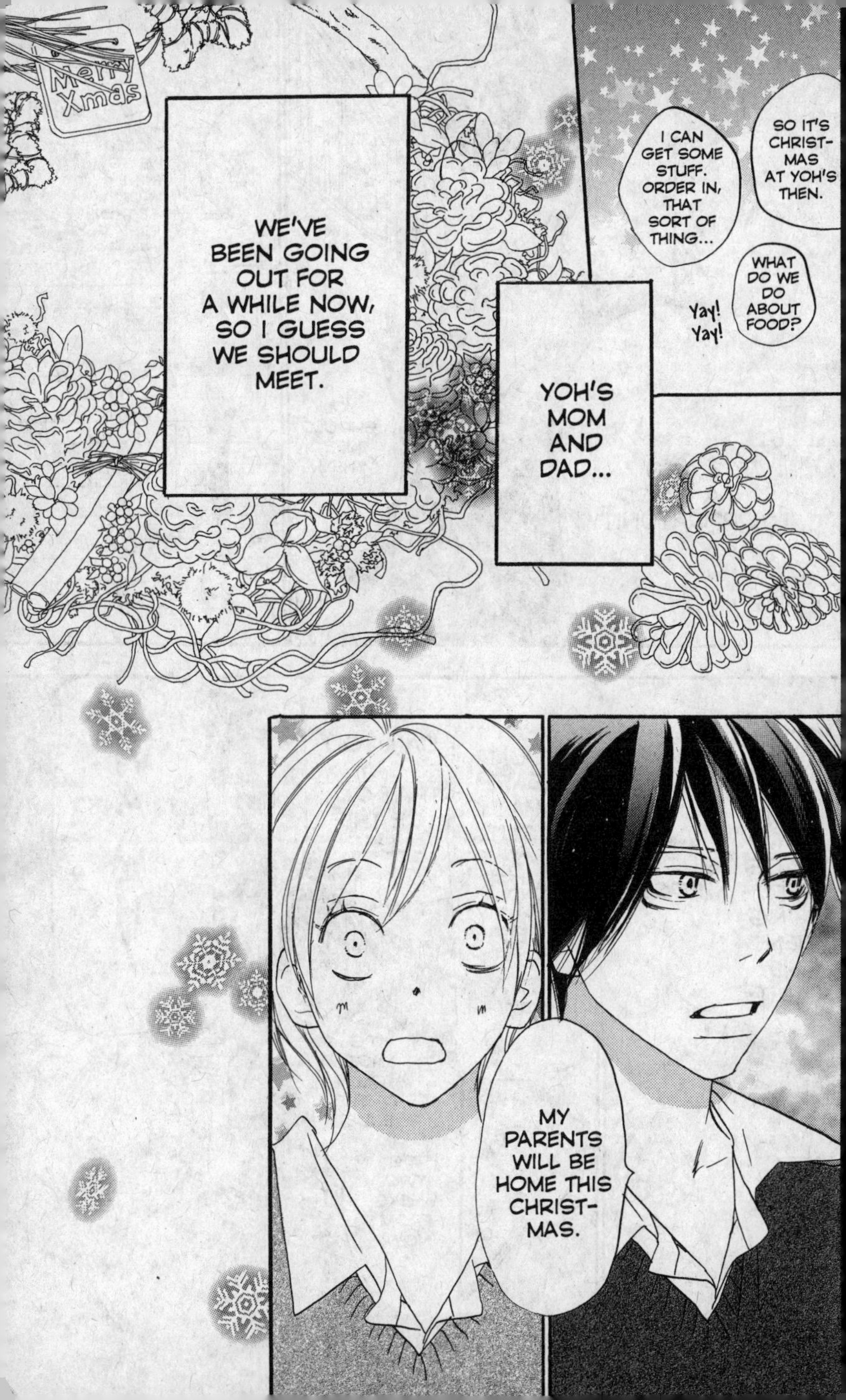
SO IT'S CHRIST-MAS AT YOH'S THEN.
I CAN GET SOME STUFF. ORDER IN, THAT SORT OF THING...
WHAT DO WE DO ABOUT FOOD?
Yay! Yay!
Merry Xmas
YOH'S MOM AND DAD...
WE'VE BEEN GOING OUT FOR A WHILE NOW, SO I GUESS WE SHOULD MEET.
MY PARENTS WILL BE HOME THIS CHRIST-MAS.

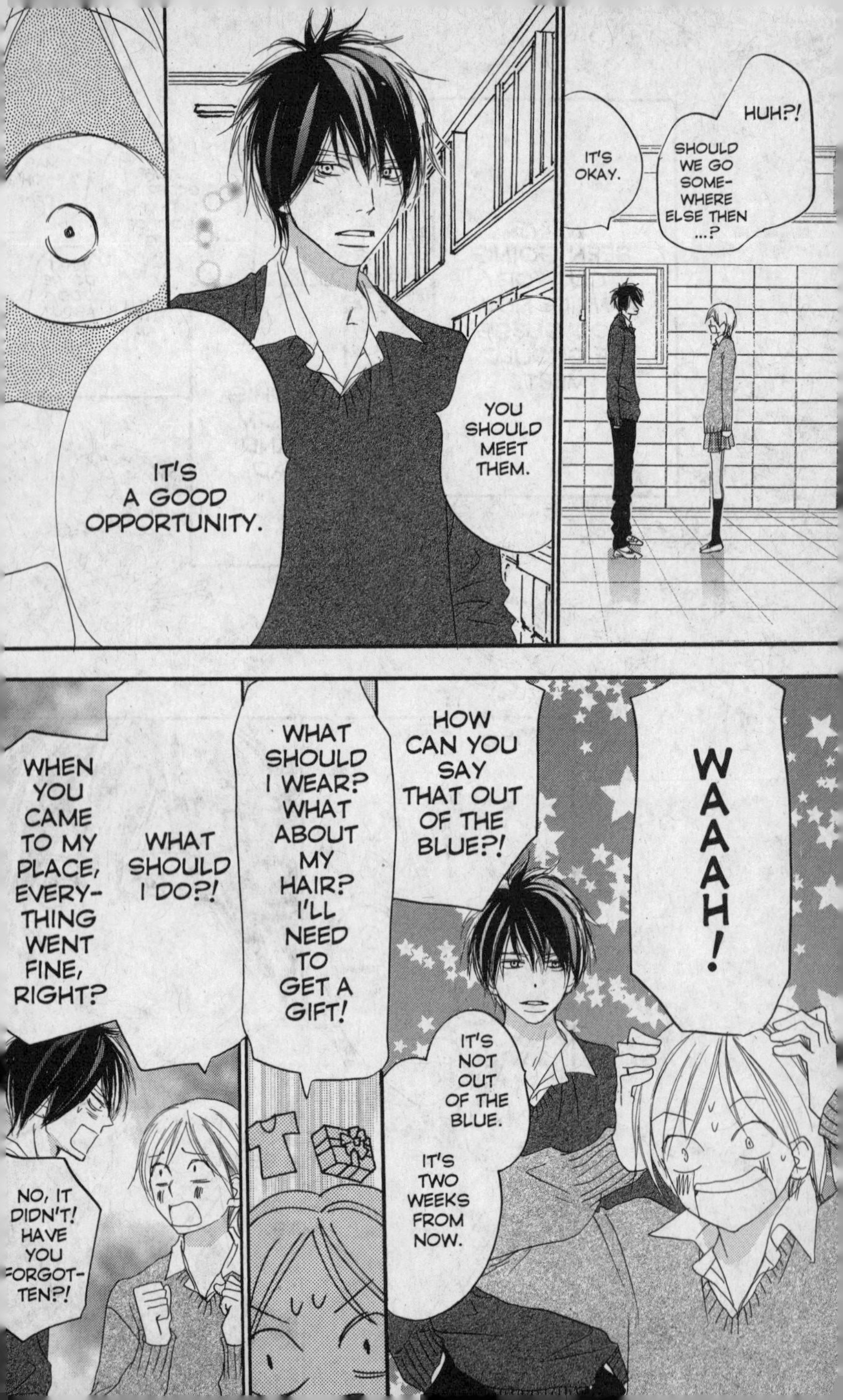
HUH?!
SHOULD WE GO SOMEWHERE ELSE THEN ...?
IT'S OKAY.
YOU SHOULD MEET THEM.
IT'S A GOOD OPPORTUNITY.
WAAAH!
HOW CAN YOU SAY THAT OUT OF THE BLUE?!
IT'S NOT OUT OF THE BLUE.
IT'S TWO WEEKS FROM NOW.
WHAT SHOULD I WEAR? WHAT ABOUT MY HAIR? I'LL NEED TO GET A GIFT!
WHAT SHOULD I DO?!
WHEN YOU CAME TO MY PLACE, EVERYTHING WENT FINE, RIGHT?
NO, IT DIDN'T! HAVE YOU FORGOTTEN?!

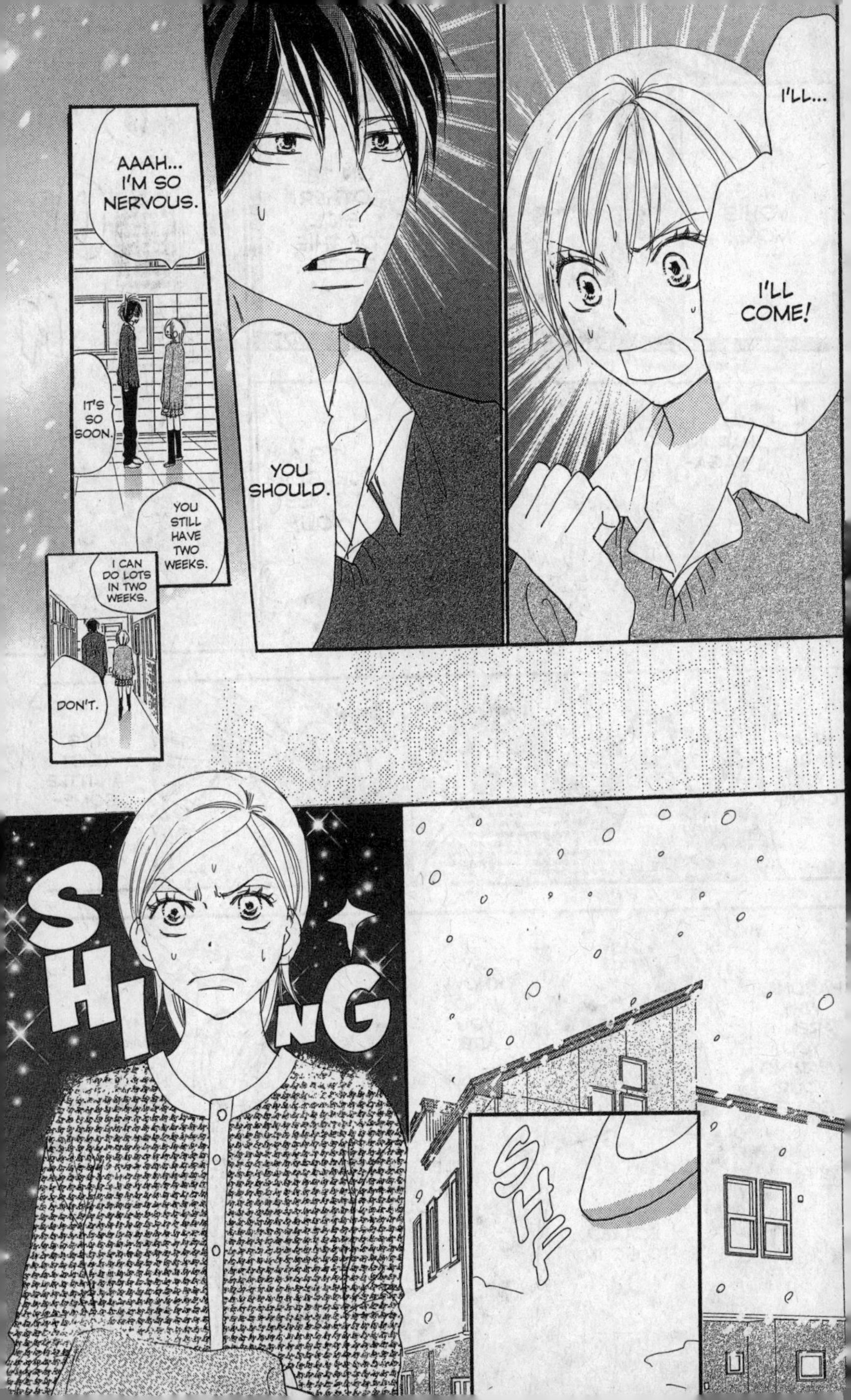
I'LL...
I'LL COME!
YOU SHOULD.
AAAH... I'M SO NERVOUS.
IT'S SO SOON.
YOU STILL HAVE TWO WEEKS.
I CAN DO LOTS IN TWO WEEKS.
DON'T.
SHF
SHING

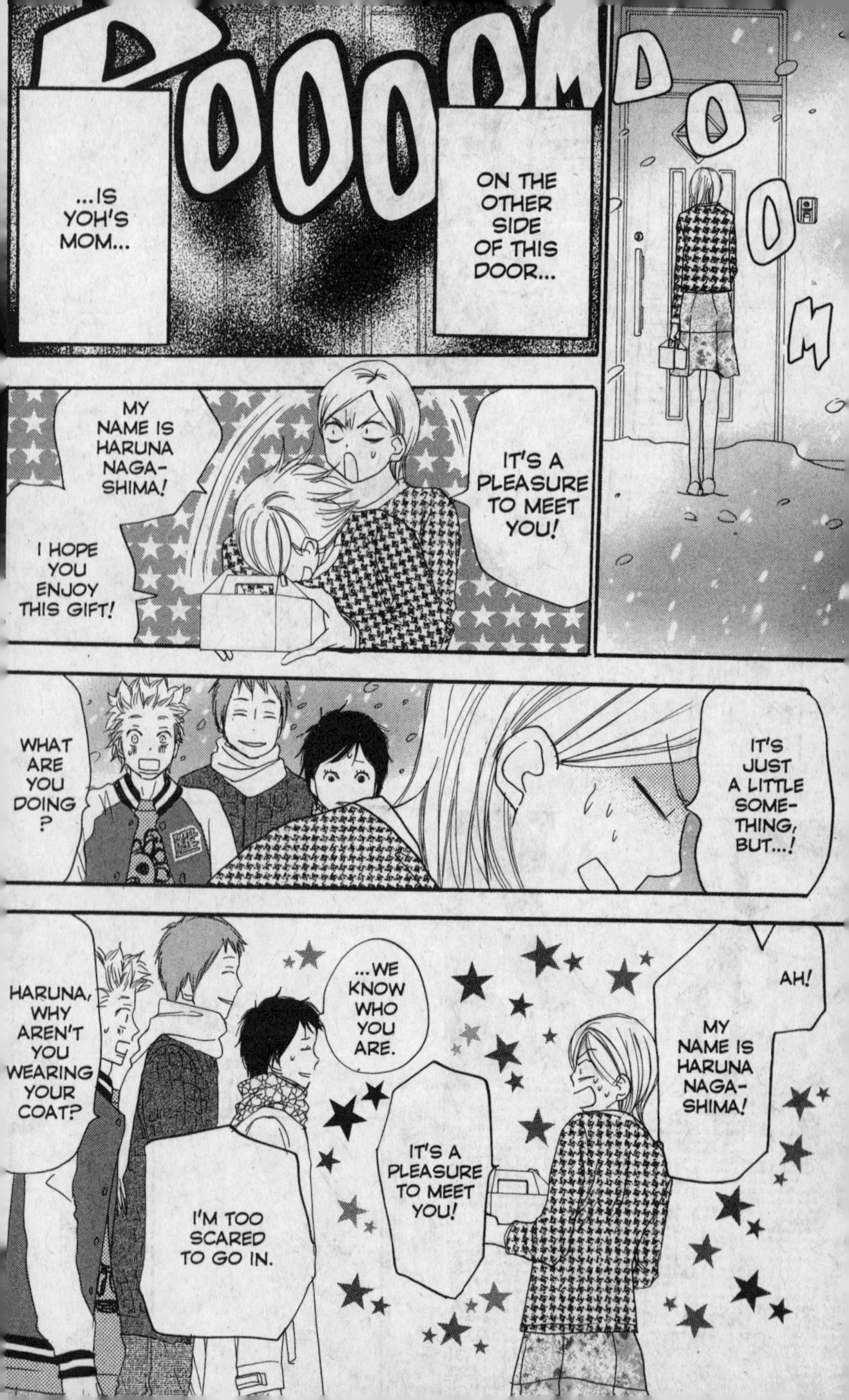
DOOOOM DOOOM
ON THE OTHER SIDE OF THIS DOOR...
...IS YOH'S MOM...
IT'S A PLEASURE TO MEET YOU!
MY NAME IS HARUNA NAGA-SHIMA!
I HOPE YOU ENJOY THIS GIFT!
IT'S JUST A LITTLE SOME-THING, BUT...!
WHAT ARE YOU DOING?
AH!
MY NAME IS HARUNA NAGA-SHIMA!
IT'S A PLEASURE TO MEET YOU!
...WE KNOW WHO YOU ARE.
HARUNA, WHY AREN'T YOU WEARING YOUR COAT?
I'M TOO SCARED TO GO IN.

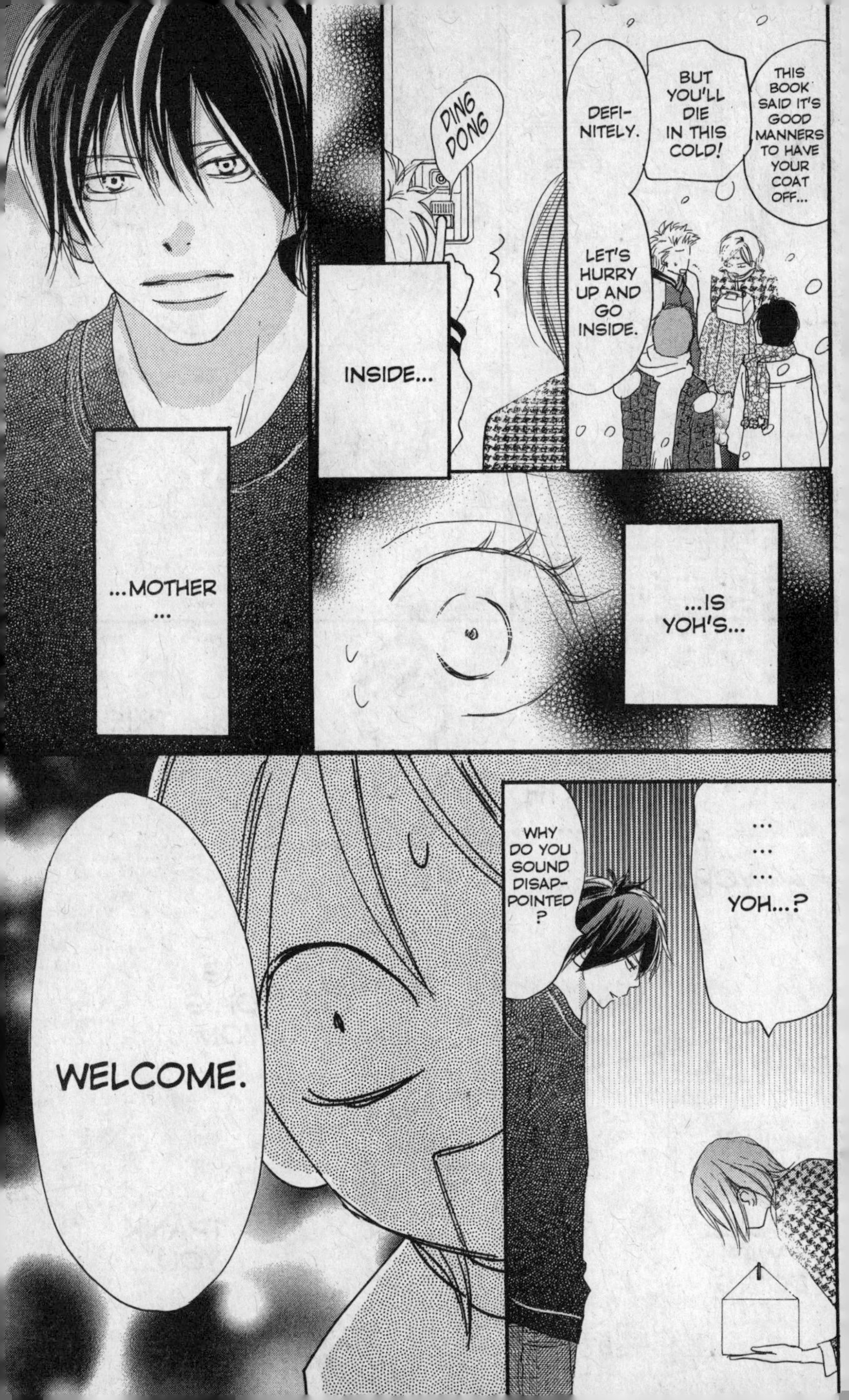
THIS BOOK SAID IT'S GOOD MANNERS TO HAVE YOUR COAT OFF...
BUT YOU'LL DIE IN THIS COLD!
DEFI-NITELY.
LET'S HURRY UP AND GO INSIDE.
DING DONG
INSIDE...
...IS YOH'S...
...MOTHER ...
... ... YOH...?
WHY DO YOU SOUND DISAP-POINTED ?
WELCOME.

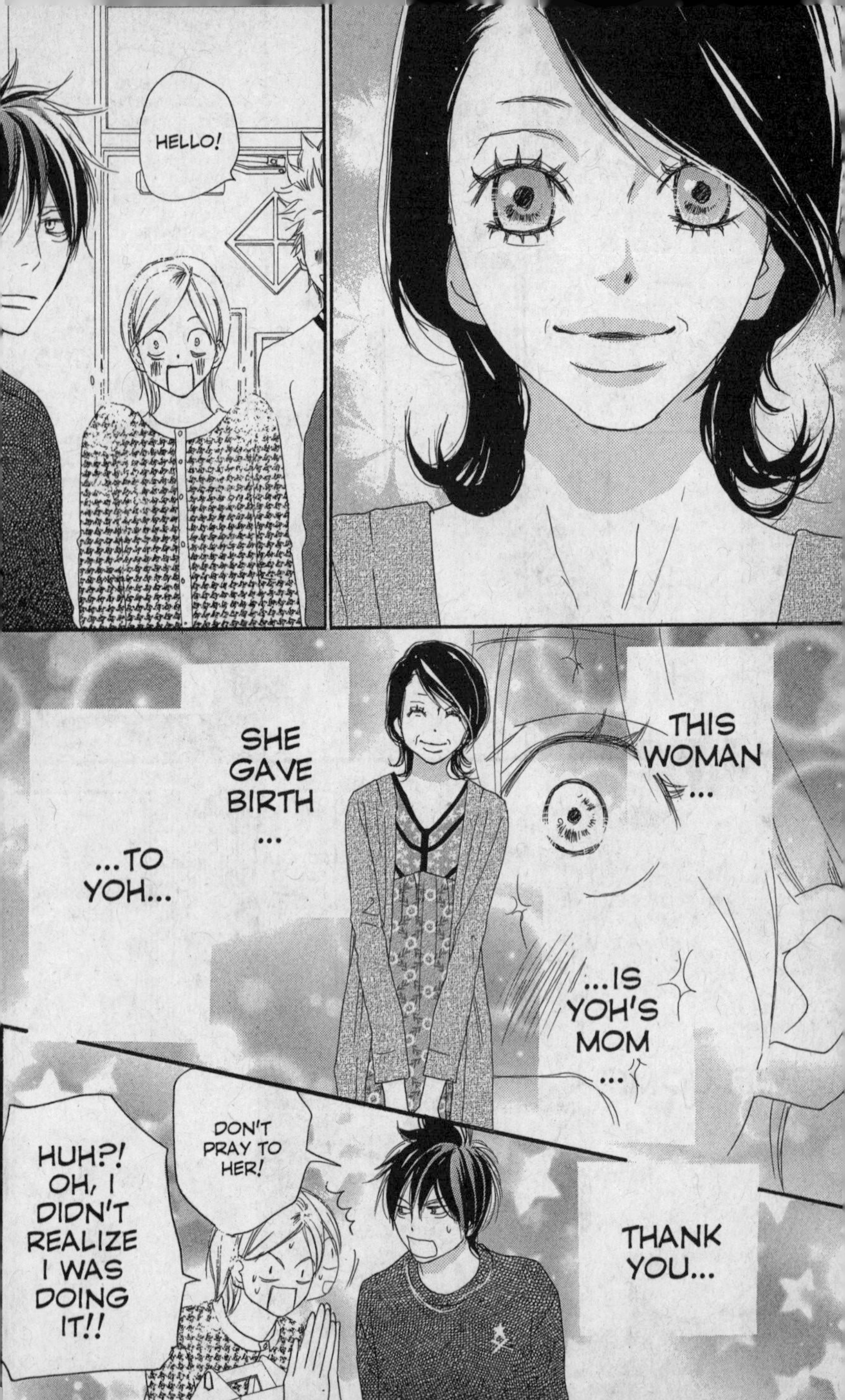

HELLO!
THIS WOMAN...
...IS YOH'S MOM...
SHE GAVE BIRTH...
...TO YOH...
THANK YOU...
DON'T PRAY TO HER!
HUH?! OH, I DIDN'T REALIZE I WAS DOING IT!!

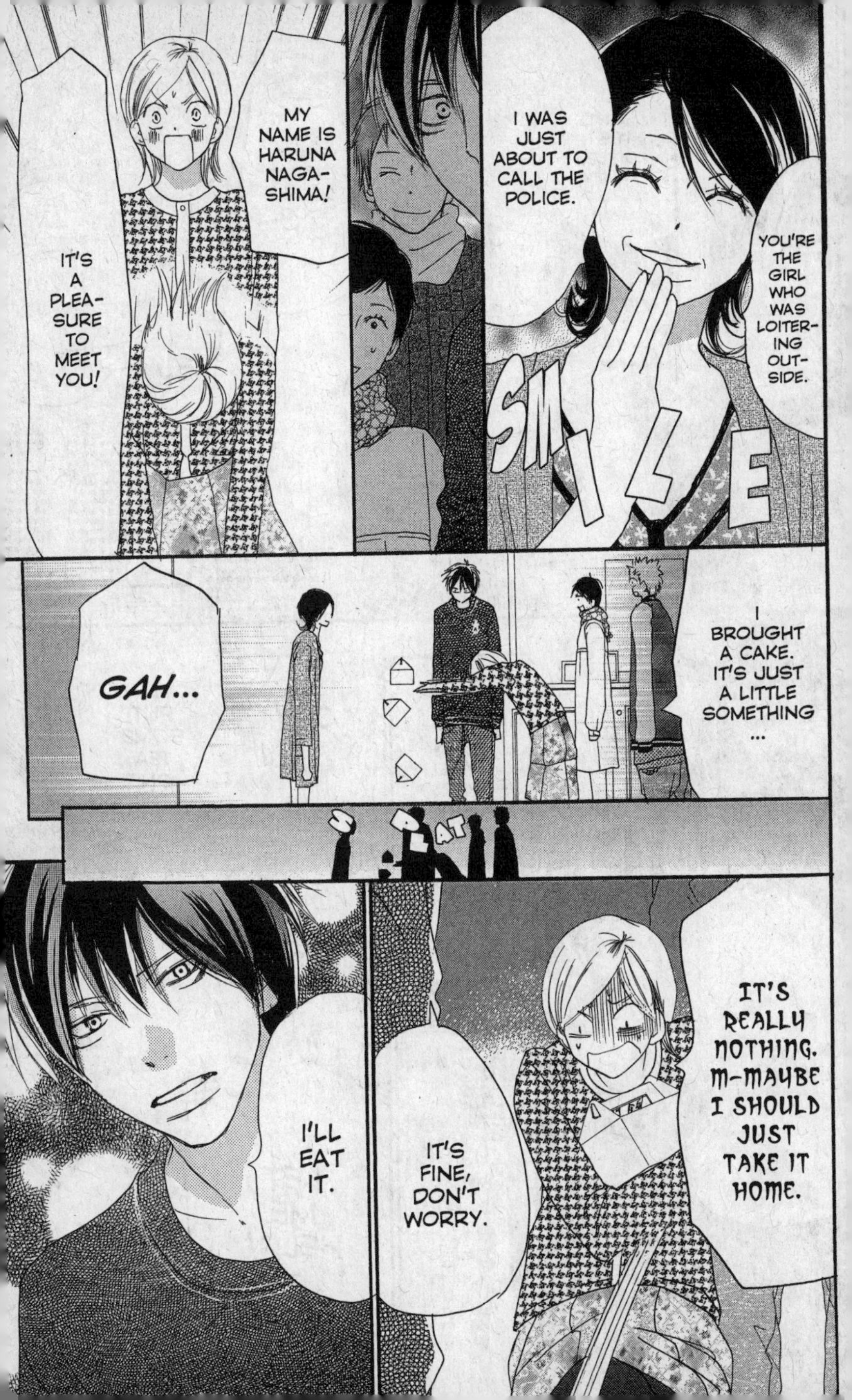
YOU'RE THE GIRL WHO WAS LOITERING OUTSIDE.
I WAS JUST ABOUT TO CALL THE POLICE.
SMILE
MY NAME IS HARUNA NAGASHIMA!
IT'S A PLEASURE TO MEET YOU!
I BROUGHT A CAKE. IT'S JUST A LITTLE SOMETHING...
GAH...
SPLAT
IT'S REALLY NOTHING. M-MAYBE I SHOULD JUST TAKE IT HOME.
IT'S FINE, DON'T WORRY.
I'LL EAT IT.

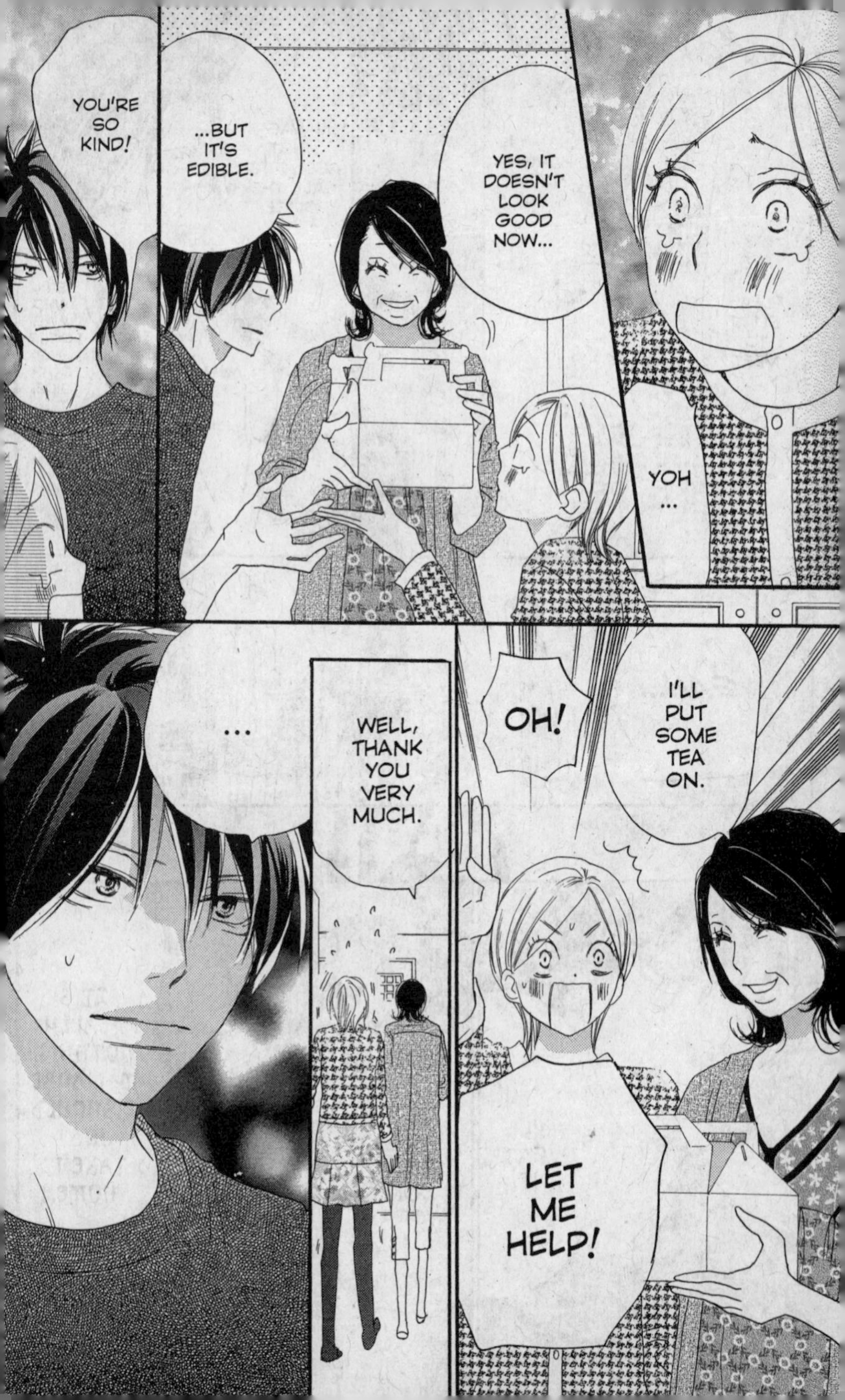
YOH ...
YES, IT DOESN'T LOOK GOOD NOW...
...BUT IT'S EDIBLE.
YOU'RE SO KIND!
I'LL PUT SOME TEA ON.
OH!
LET ME HELP!
WELL, THANK YOU VERY MUCH.
...

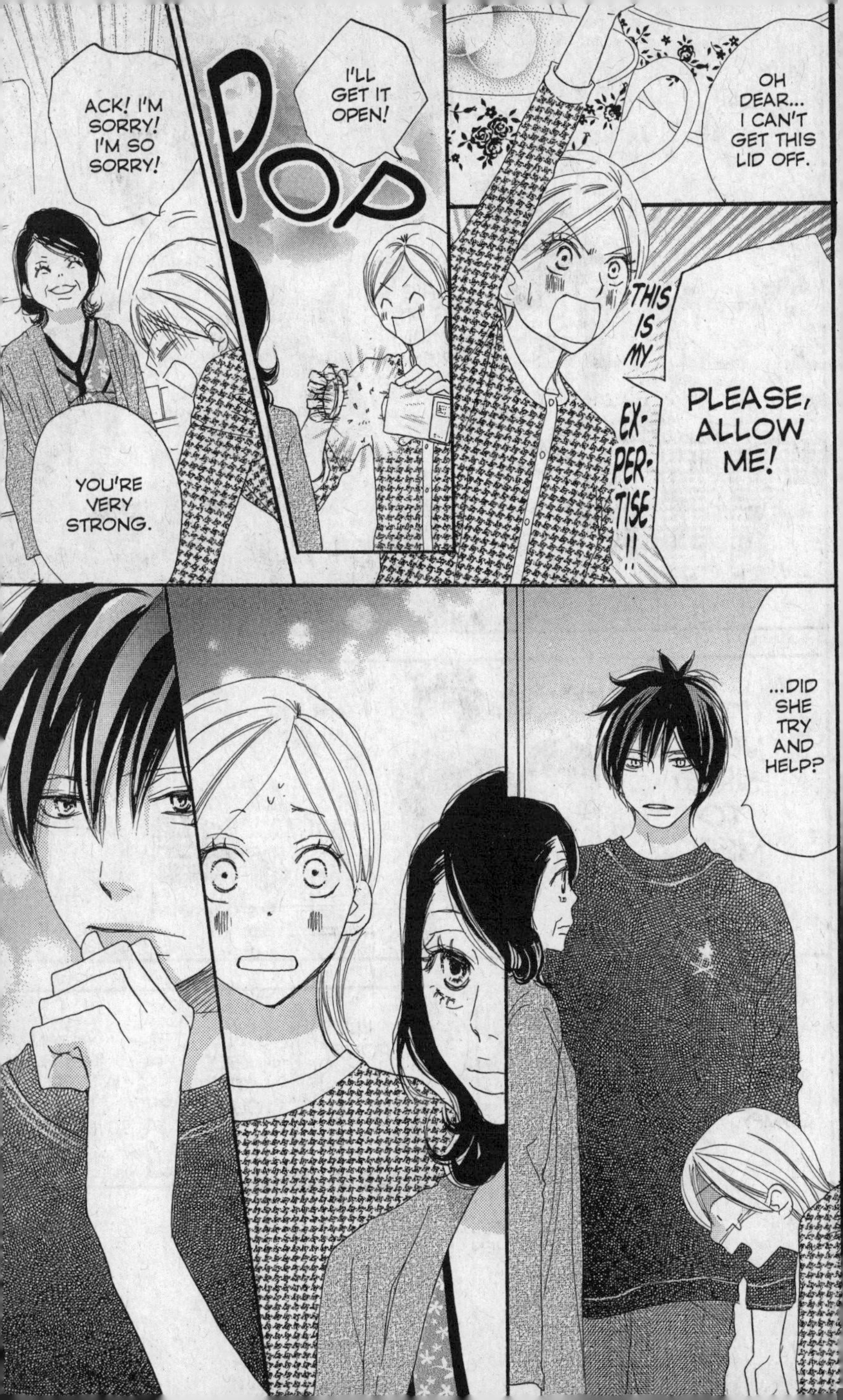
OH DEAR... I CAN'T GET THIS LID OFF.
PLEASE, ALLOW ME!
THIS IS MY EX-PER-TISE!!
I'LL GET IT OPEN!
POP
ACK! I'M SORRY! I'M SO SORRY!
YOU'RE VERY STRONG.
...DID SHE TRY AND HELP?

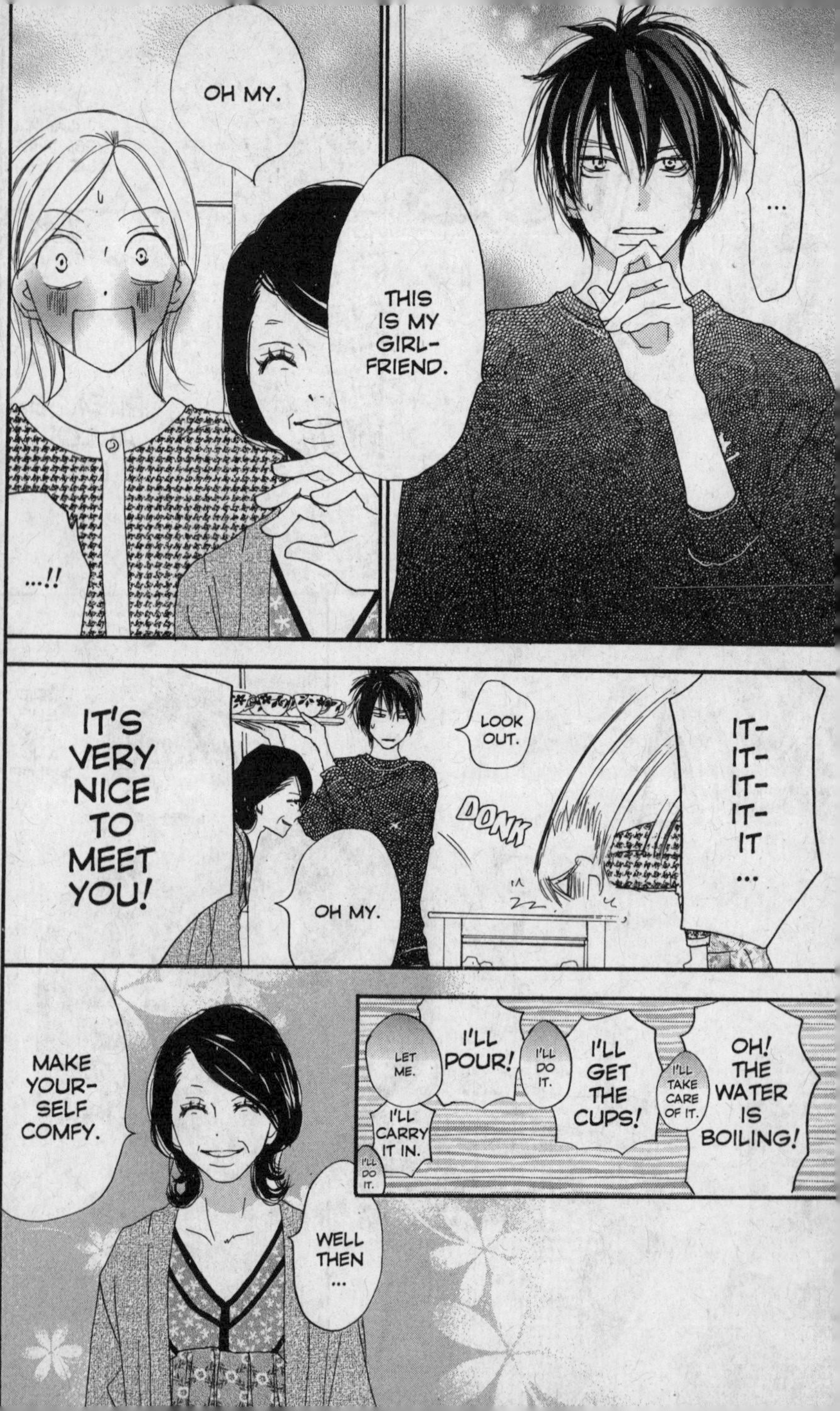
...
THIS IS MY GIRL-FRIEND.
OH MY.
...!!
IT-IT-IT-IT-IT...
DONK
LOOK OUT.
OH MY.
IT'S VERY NICE TO MEET YOU!
OH! THE WATER IS BOILING!
I'LL TAKE CARE OF IT.
I'LL GET THE CUPS!
I'LL DO IT.
I'LL POUR!
LET ME.
I'LL CARRY IT IN.
I'LL DO IT.
WELL THEN...
MAKE YOUR-SELF COMFY.

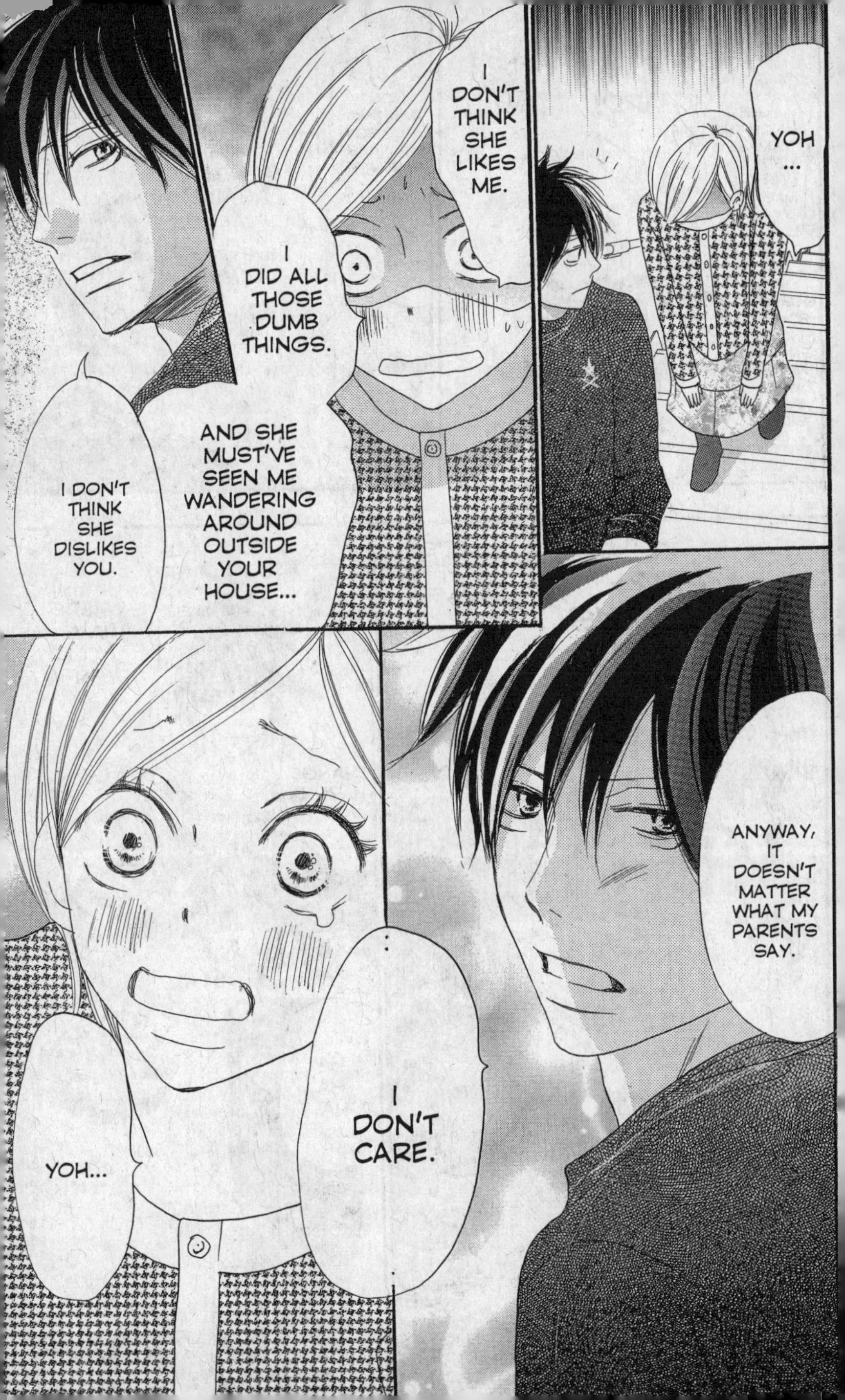
YOH ...
I DON'T THINK SHE LIKES ME.
I DID ALL THOSE DUMB THINGS.
AND SHE MUST'VE SEEN ME WANDERING AROUND OUTSIDE YOUR HOUSE...
I DON'T THINK SHE DISLIKES YOU.
ANYWAY, IT DOESN'T MATTER WHAT MY PARENTS SAY.
I DON'T CARE.
YOH...

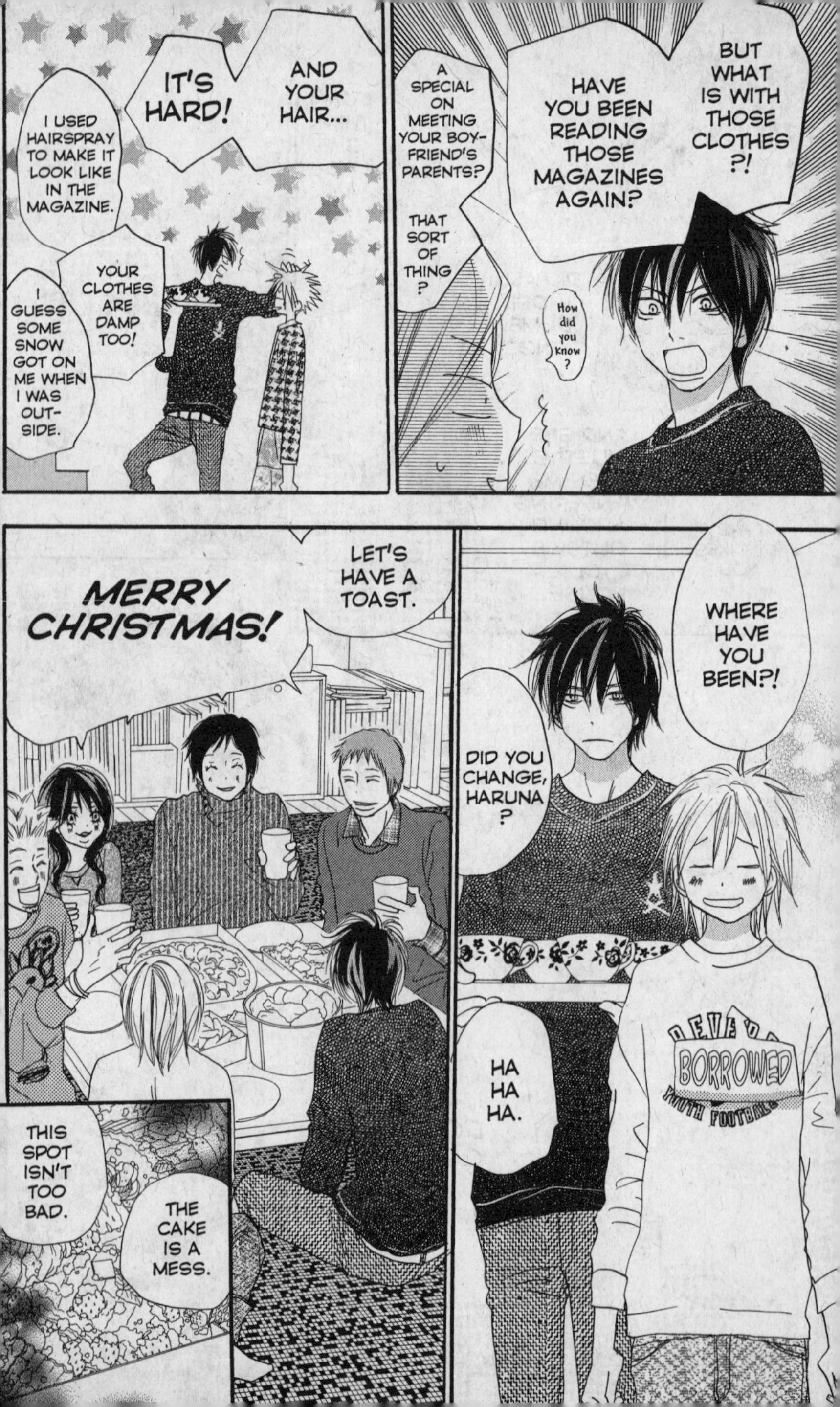
BUT WHAT IS WITH THOSE CLOTHES?!
HAVE YOU BEEN READING THOSE MAGAZINES AGAIN?
A SPECIAL ON MEETING YOUR BOY-FRIEND'S PARENTS?
THAT SORT OF THING?
How did you know?
AND YOUR HAIR...
IT'S HARD!
I USED HAIRSPRAY TO MAKE IT LOOK LIKE IN THE MAGAZINE.
YOUR CLOTHES ARE DAMP TOO!
I GUESS SOME SNOW GOT ON ME WHEN I WAS OUT-SIDE.
WHERE HAVE YOU BEEN?!
DID YOU CHANGE, HARUNA?
HA HA HA.
BORROWED
LET'S HAVE A TOAST.
MERRY CHRISTMAS!
THIS SPOT ISN'T TOO BAD.
THE CAKE IS A MESS.

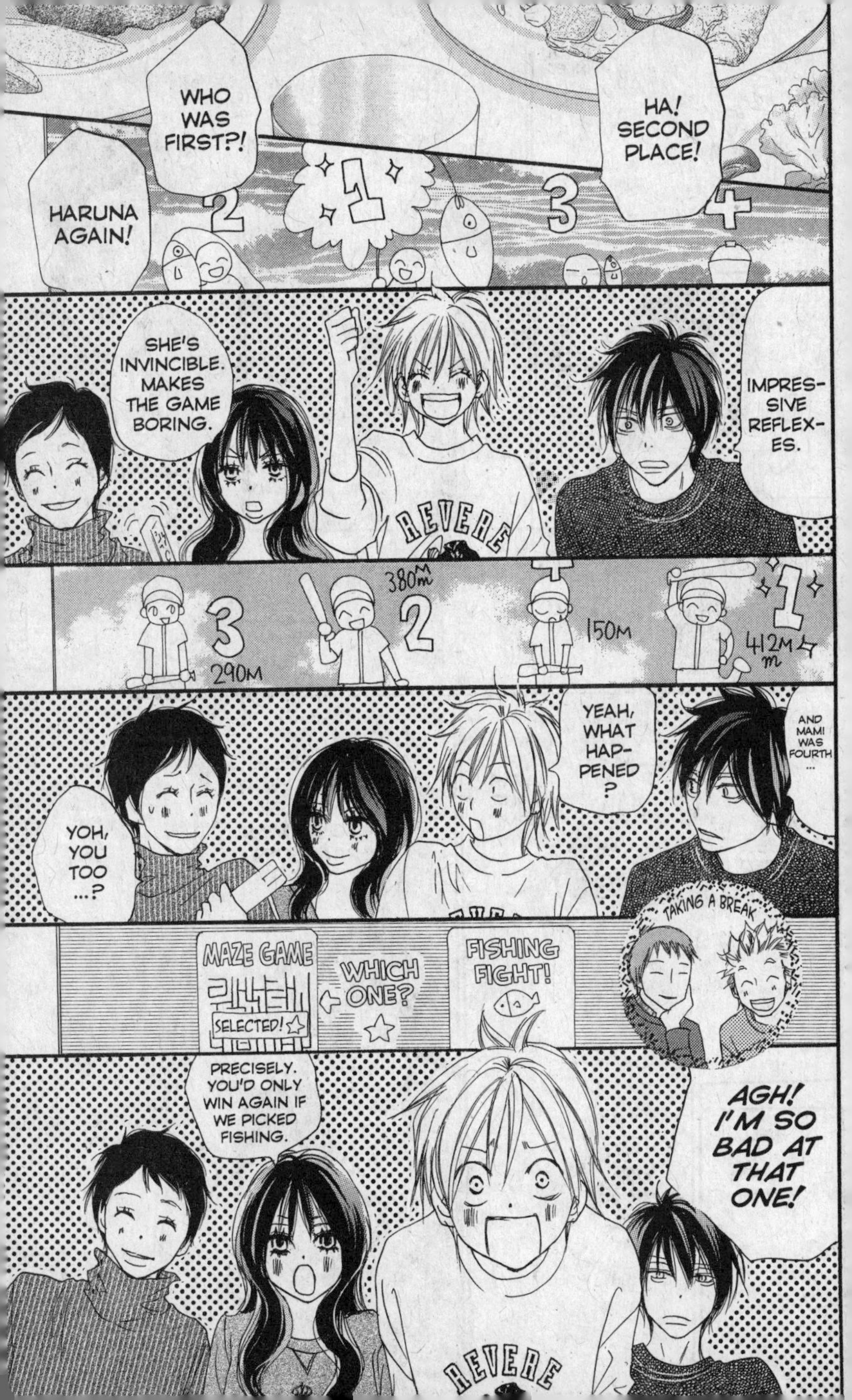
HA! SECOND PLACE!
WHO WAS FIRST?!
HARUNA AGAIN!
IMPRESSIVE REFLEXES.
REVERE
SHE'S INVINCIBLE. MAKES THE GAME BORING.
1 412M
150M
2 380M
3 290M
AND MAMI WAS FOURTH...
YEAH, WHAT HAPPENED?
YOH, YOU TOO...?
TAKING A BREAK
FISHING FIGHT!
WHICH ONE?
MAZE GAME
SELECTED!
AGH! I'M SO BAD AT THAT ONE!
PRECISELY. YOU'D ONLY WIN AGAIN IF WE PICKED FISHING.
REVERE

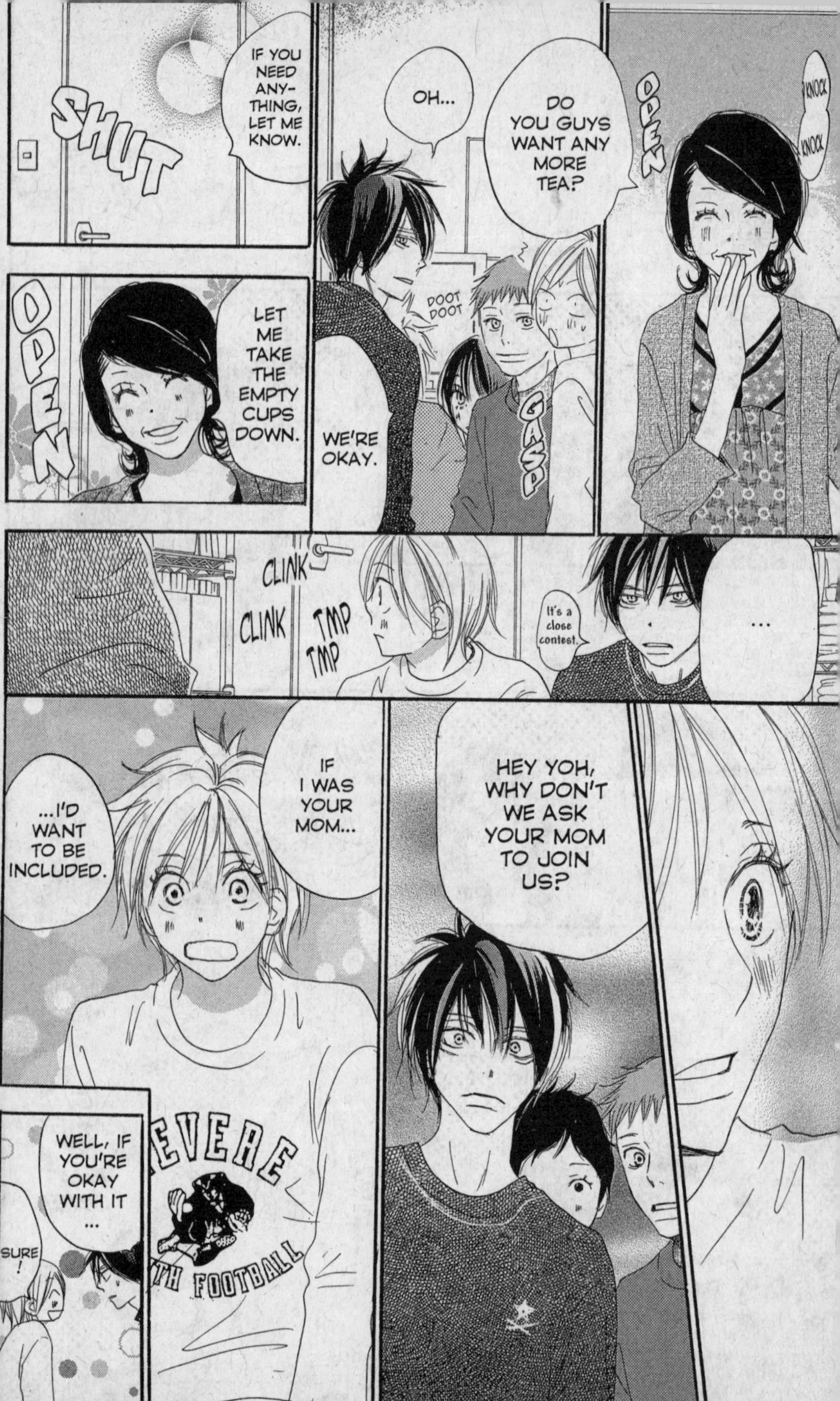
KNOCK
KNOCK
OPEN
DO YOU GUYS WANT ANY MORE TEA?
OH...
DOOT DOOT
GASP
WE'RE OKAY.
IF YOU NEED ANYTHING, LET ME KNOW.
SHUT
LET ME TAKE THE EMPTY CUPS DOWN.
OPEN
...
It's a close contest.
TMP TMP
CLINK
CLINK
HEY YOH, WHY DON'T WE ASK YOUR MOM TO JOIN US?
IF I WAS YOUR MOM...
...I'D WANT TO BE INCLUDED.
WELL, IF YOU'RE OKAY WITH IT...
SURE!

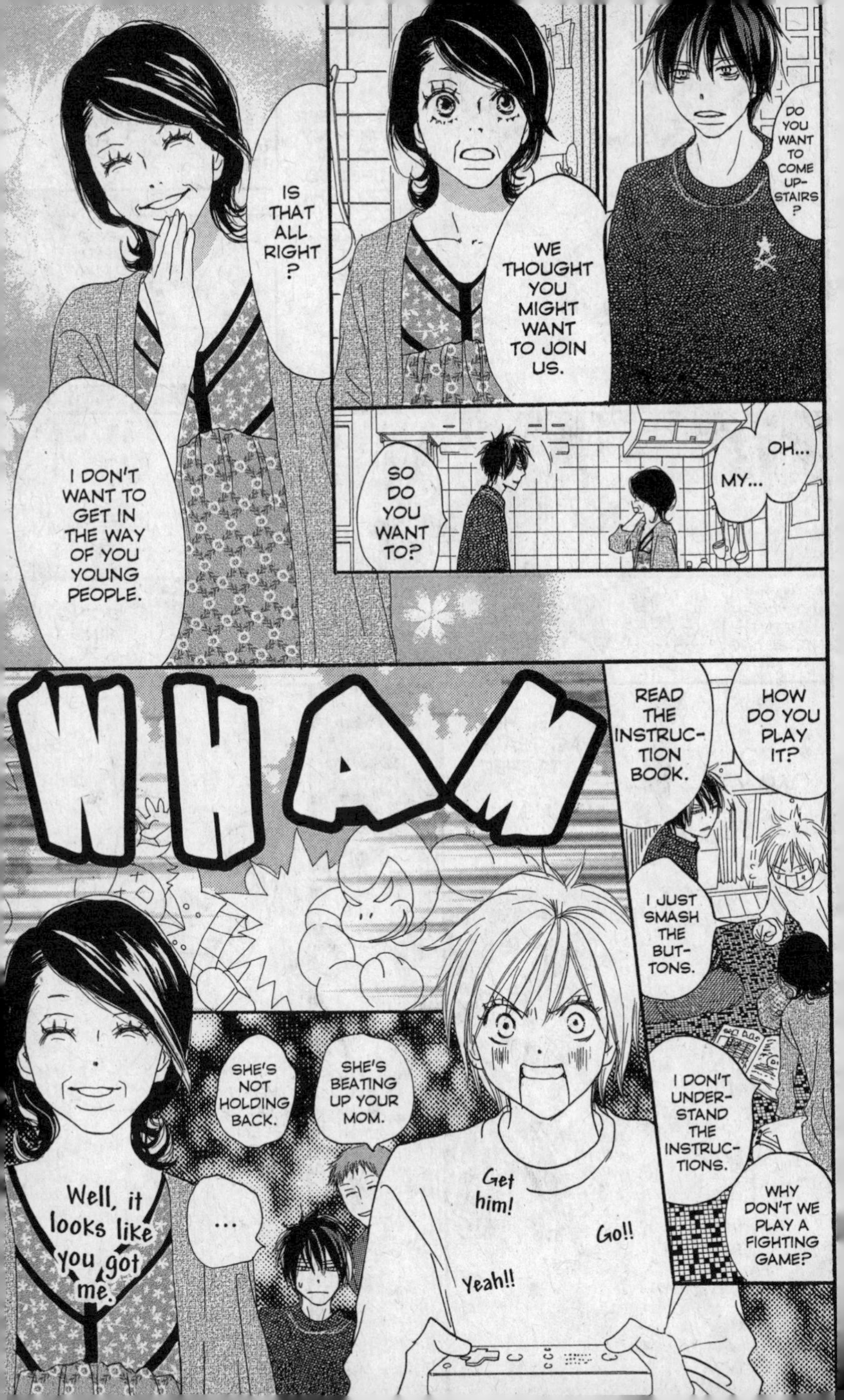
DO YOU WANT TO COME UP-STAIRS?
WE THOUGHT YOU MIGHT WANT TO JOIN US.
OH... MY...
SO DO YOU WANT TO?
IS THAT ALL RIGHT?
I DON'T WANT TO GET IN THE WAY OF YOU YOUNG PEOPLE.
HOW DO YOU PLAY IT?
READ THE INSTRUC-TION BOOK.
I JUST SMASH THE BUT-TONS.
WHY DON'T WE PLAY A FIGHTING GAME?
I DON'T UNDER-STAND THE INSTRUC-TIONS.
WHAM
Go!!
Get him!
Yeah!!
SHE'S BEATING UP YOUR MOM.
SHE'S NOT HOLDING BACK.
...
Well, it looks like you got me.

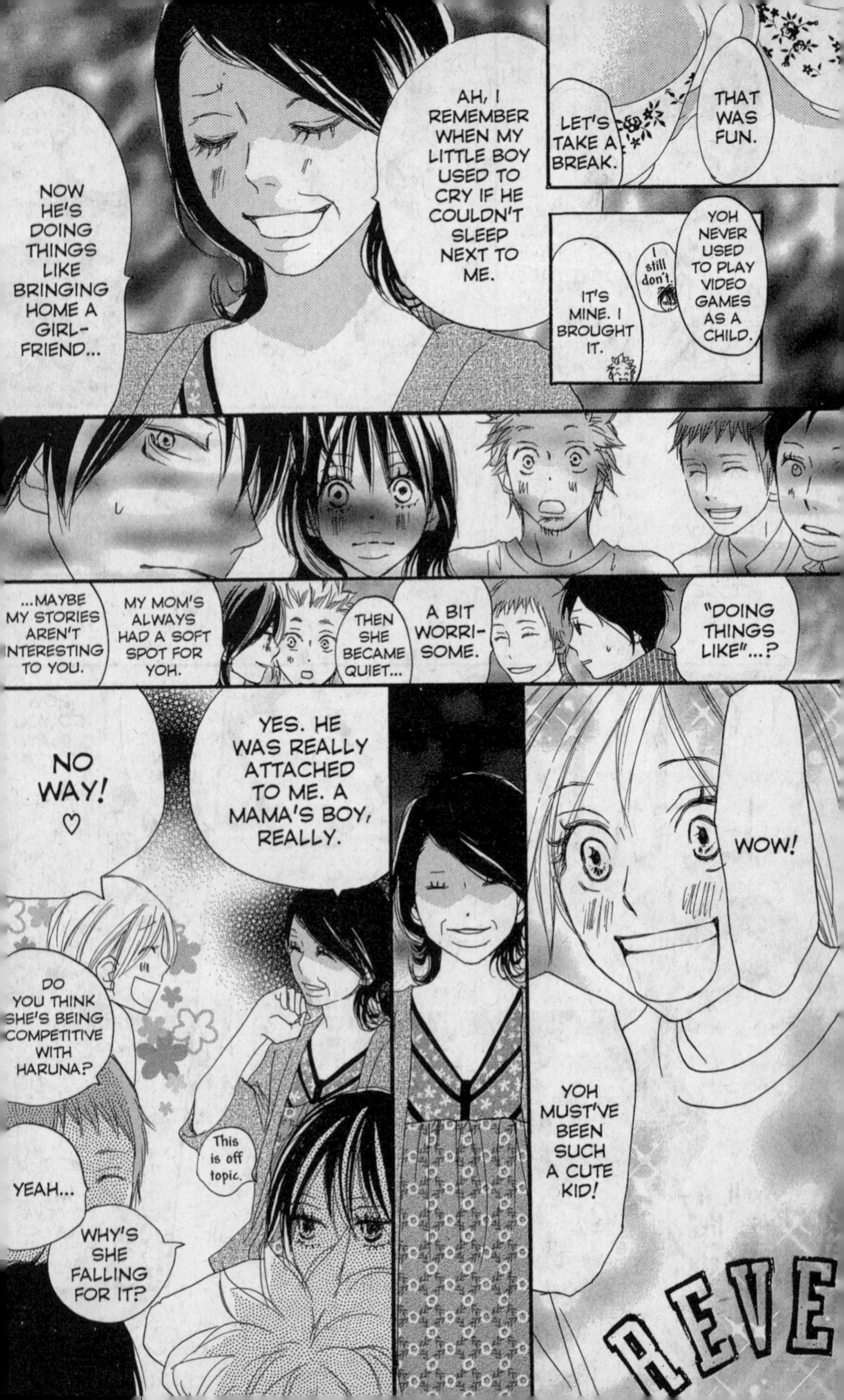
THAT WAS FUN.
LET'S TAKE A BREAK.
YOH NEVER USED TO PLAY VIDEO GAMES AS A CHILD.
I still don't.
IT'S MINE. I BROUGHT IT.
AH, I REMEMBER WHEN MY LITTLE BOY USED TO CRY IF HE COULDN'T SLEEP NEXT TO ME.
NOW HE'S DOING THINGS LIKE BRINGING HOME A GIRL-FRIEND...
"DOING THINGS LIKE"...?
A BIT WORRI-SOME.
THEN SHE BECAME QUIET...
MY MOM'S ALWAYS HAD A SOFT SPOT FOR YOH.
...MAYBE MY STORIES AREN'T INTERESTING TO YOU.
WOW!
YOH MUST'VE BEEN SUCH A CUTE KID!
REVE
YES. HE WAS REALLY ATTACHED TO ME. A MAMA'S BOY, REALLY.
NO WAY! ♡
This is off topic.
DO YOU THINK SHE'S BEING COMPETITIVE WITH HARUNA?
YEAH...
WHY'S SHE FALLING FOR IT?

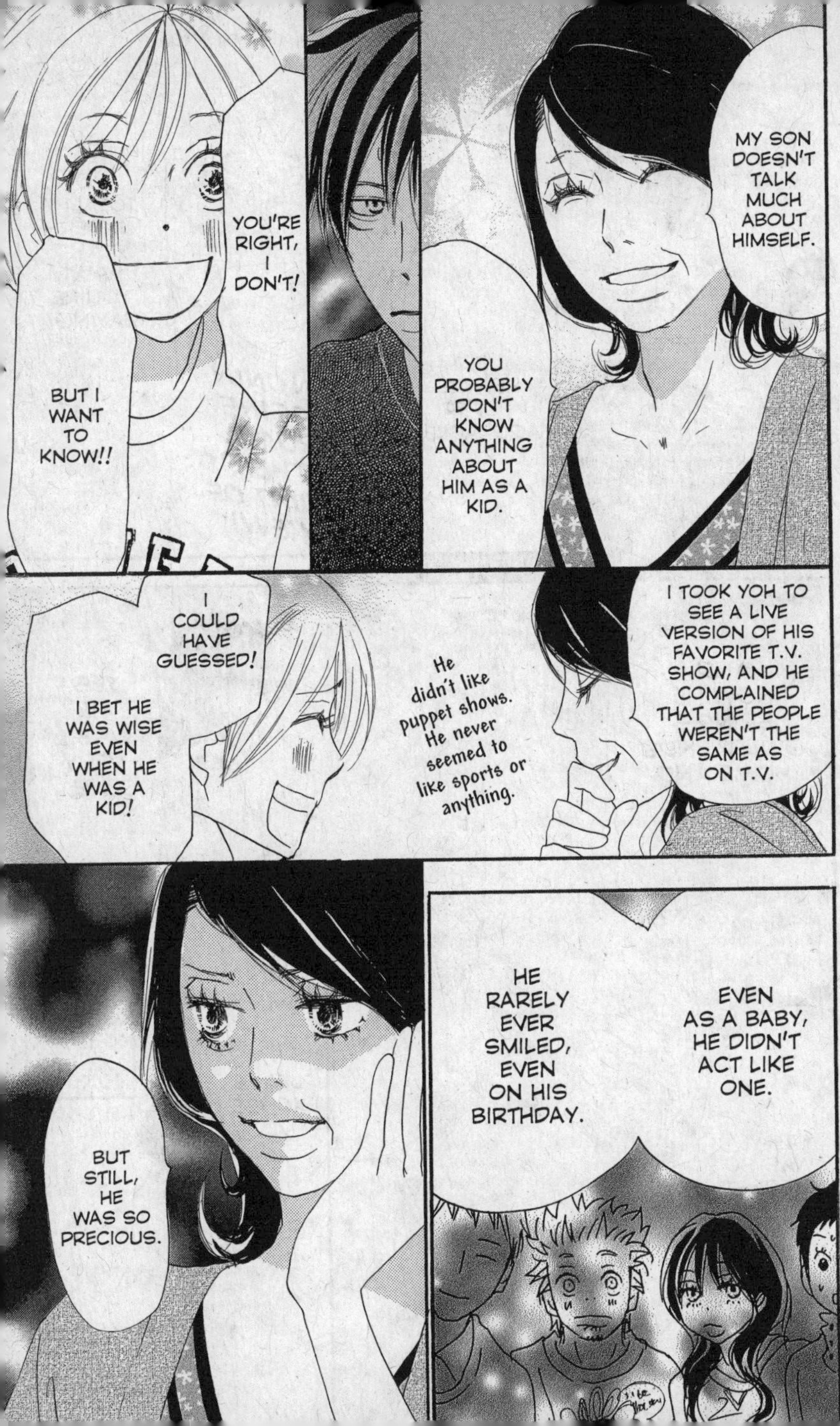
MY SON DOESN'T TALK MUCH ABOUT HIMSELF.
YOU PROBABLY DON'T KNOW ANYTHING ABOUT HIM AS A KID.
YOU'RE RIGHT, I DON'T!
BUT I WANT TO KNOW!!
I TOOK YOH TO SEE A LIVE VERSION OF HIS FAVORITE T.V. SHOW, AND HE COMPLAINED THAT THE PEOPLE WEREN'T THE SAME AS ON T.V.
He didn't like puppet shows. He never seemed to like sports or anything.
I COULD HAVE GUESSED!
I BET HE WAS WISE EVEN WHEN HE WAS A KID!
EVEN AS A BABY, HE DIDN'T ACT LIKE ONE.
HE RARELY EVER SMILED, EVEN ON HIS BIRTHDAY.
BUT STILL, HE WAS SO PRECIOUS.

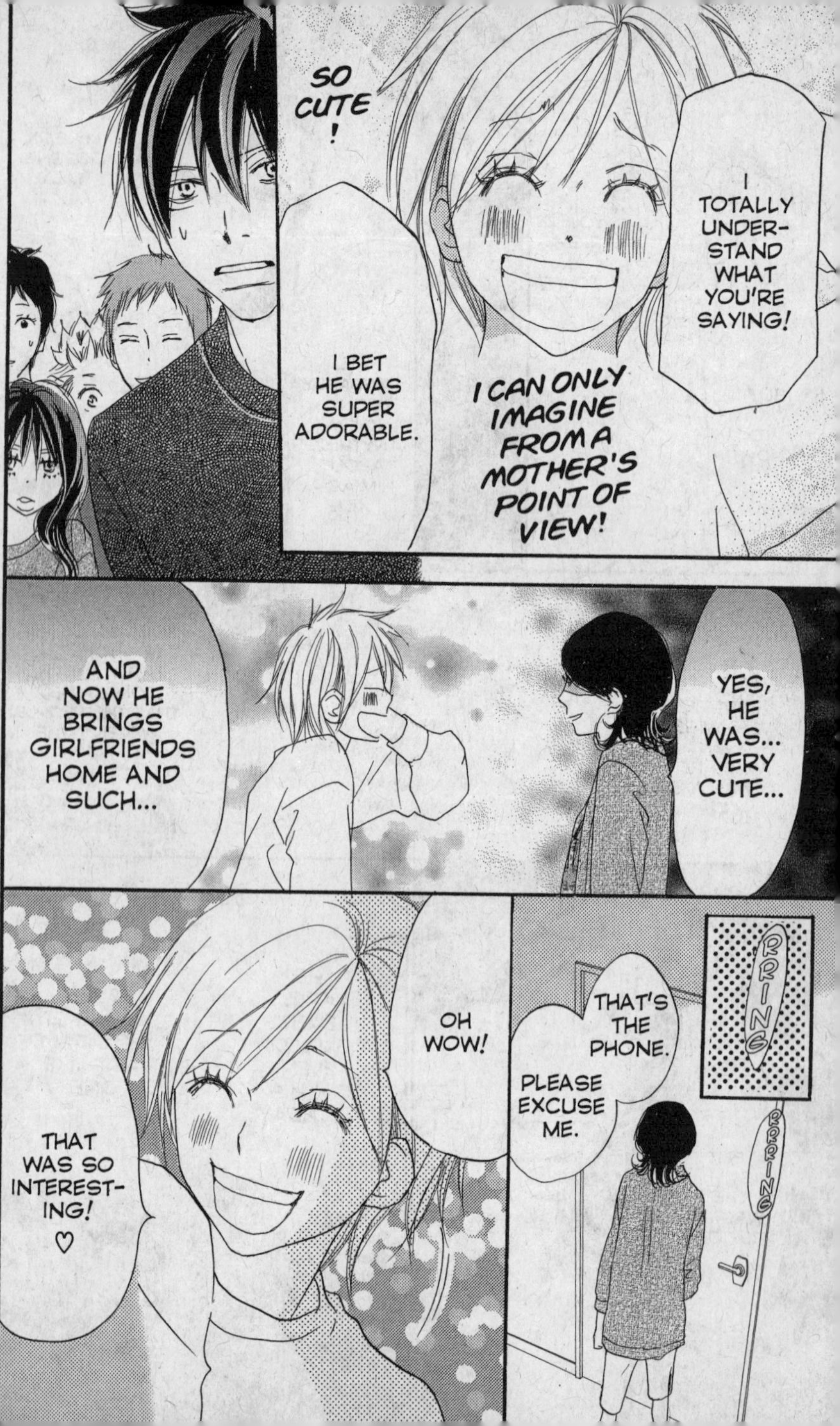
I TOTALLY UNDERSTAND WHAT YOU'RE SAYING!
I CAN ONLY IMAGINE FROM A MOTHER'S POINT OF VIEW!
I BET HE WAS SUPER ADORABLE.
SO CUTE!
YES, HE WAS... VERY CUTE...
AND NOW HE BRINGS GIRLFRIENDS HOME AND SUCH...
RRRING
THAT'S THE PHONE.
PLEASE EXCUSE ME.
RRRING
OH WOW!
THAT WAS SO INTEREST-ING! ♡

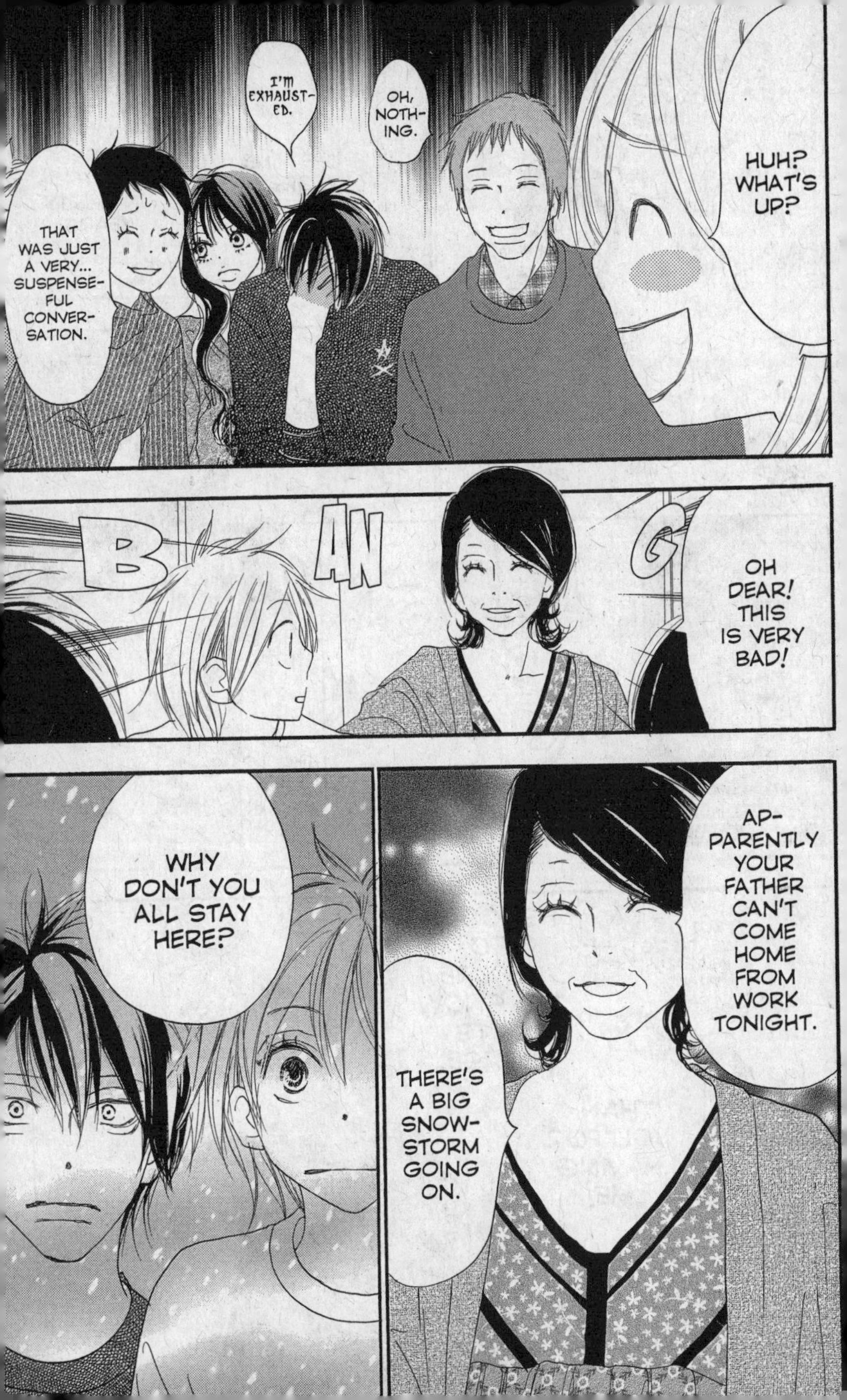
HUH? WHAT'S UP?
OH, NOTHING.
I'M EXHAUSTED.
THAT WAS JUST A VERY... SUSPENSEFUL CONVERSATION.
BANG
OH DEAR! THIS IS VERY BAD!
APPARENTLY YOUR FATHER CAN'T COME HOME FROM WORK TONIGHT.
THERE'S A BIG SNOWSTORM GOING ON.
WHY DON'T YOU ALL STAY HERE?

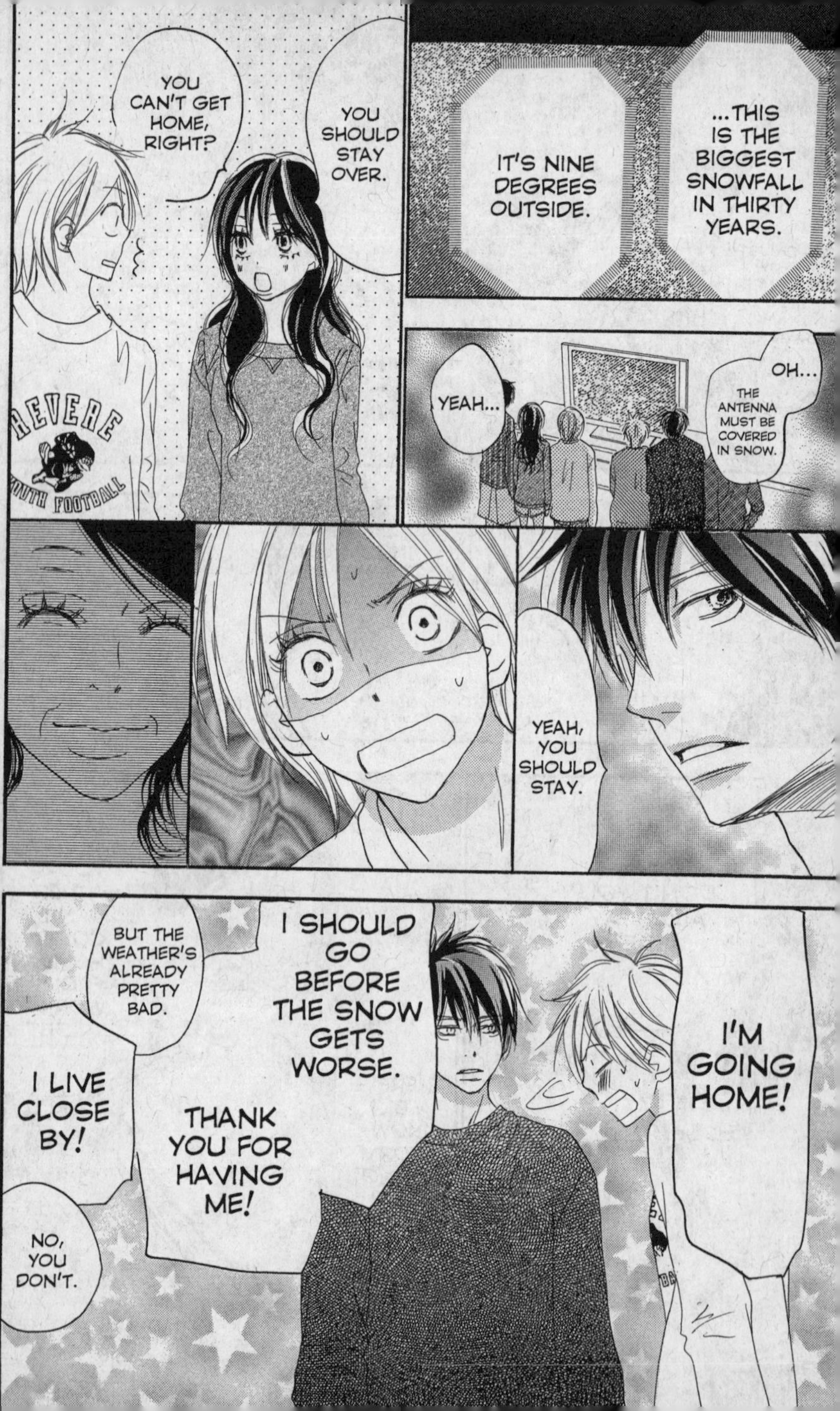
...THIS IS THE BIGGEST SNOWFALL IN THIRTY YEARS.
IT'S NINE DEGREES OUTSIDE.
OH... THE ANTENNA MUST BE COVERED IN SNOW.
YEAH...
YOU SHOULD STAY OVER.
YOU CAN'T GET HOME, RIGHT?
YEAH, YOU SHOULD STAY.
I'M GOING HOME!
I SHOULD GO BEFORE THE SNOW GETS WORSE.
BUT THE WEATHER'S ALREADY PRETTY BAD.
THANK YOU FOR HAVING ME!
I LIVE CLOSE BY!
NO, YOU DON'T.

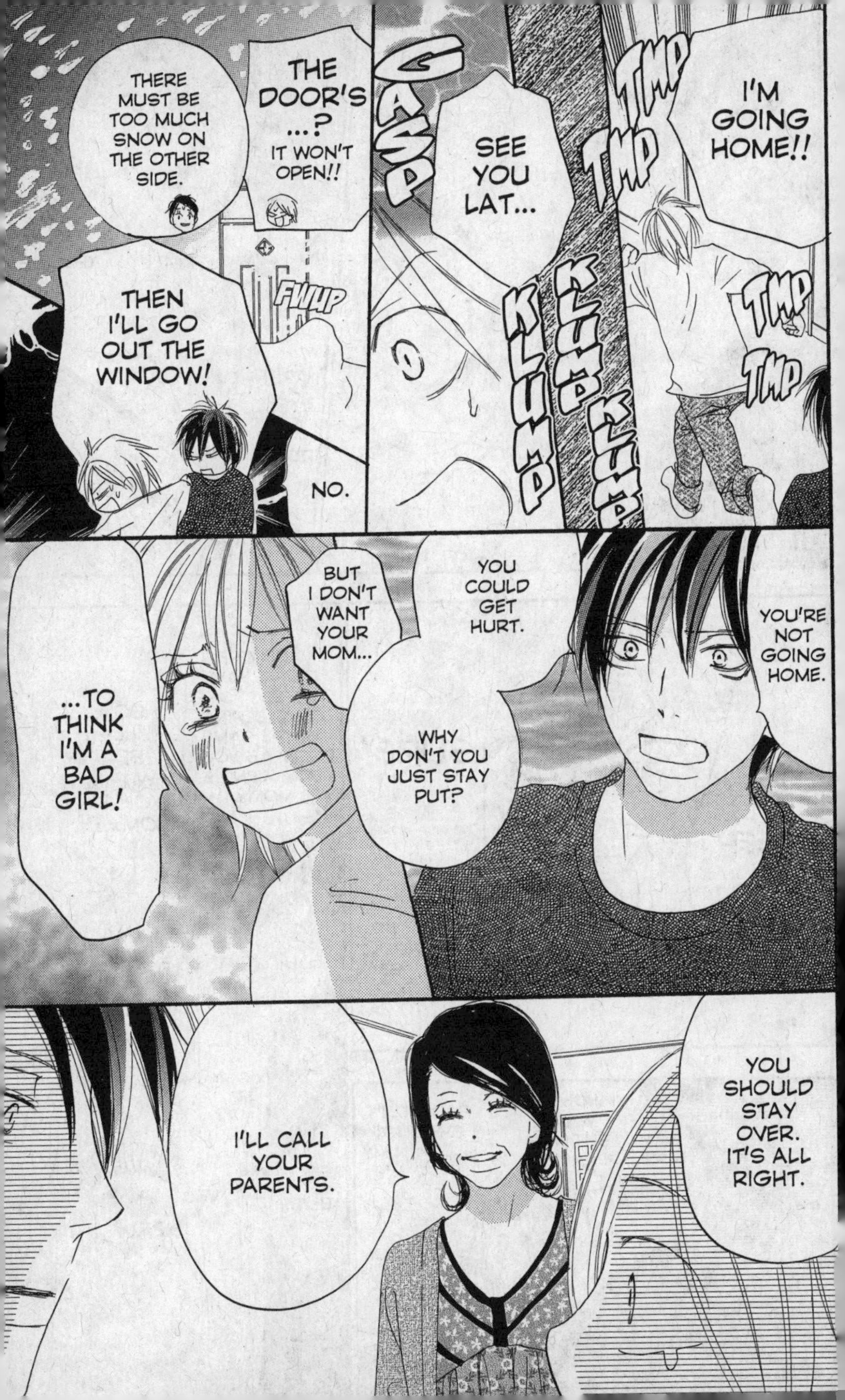
I'M GOING HOME!!
TMP
TMP
TMP
TMP
KLUMP
KLUMP
KLUMP
GASP
SEE YOU LAT...
THE DOOR'S ...? IT WON'T OPEN!!
THERE MUST BE TOO MUCH SNOW ON THE OTHER SIDE.
THEN I'LL GO OUT THE WINDOW!
FWUP
NO.
YOU'RE NOT GOING HOME.
YOU COULD GET HURT.
WHY DON'T YOU JUST STAY PUT?
BUT I DON'T WANT YOUR MOM...
...TO THINK I'M A BAD GIRL!
YOU SHOULD STAY OVER. IT'S ALL RIGHT.
I'LL CALL YOUR PARENTS.

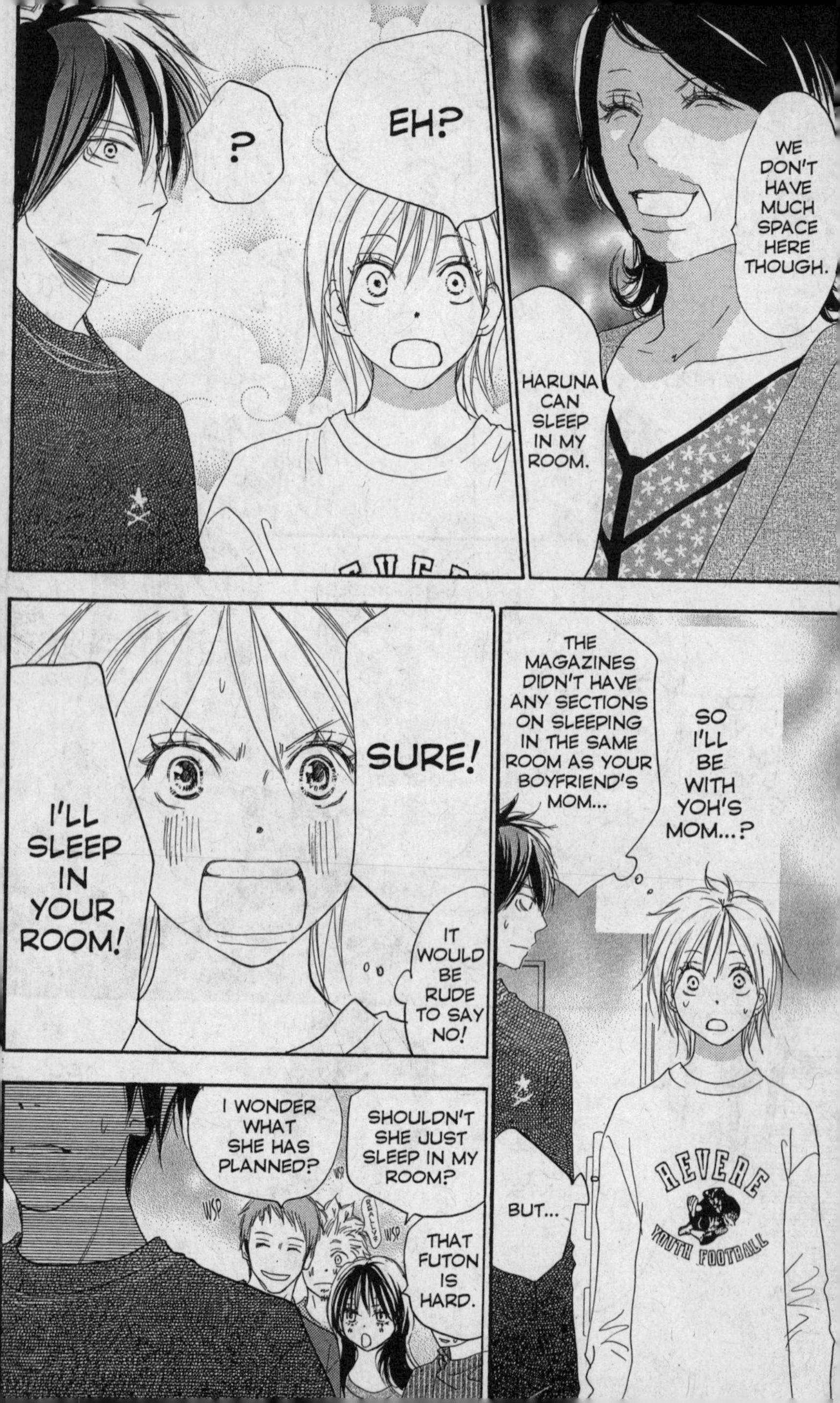
WE DON'T HAVE MUCH SPACE HERE THOUGH.
HARUNA CAN SLEEP IN MY ROOM.
EH?
?
SO I'LL BE WITH YOH'S MOM...?
THE MAGAZINES DIDN'T HAVE ANY SECTIONS ON SLEEPING IN THE SAME ROOM AS YOUR BOYFRIEND'S MOM...
BUT...
SURE!
I'LL SLEEP IN YOUR ROOM!
IT WOULD BE RUDE TO SAY NO!
SHOULDN'T SHE JUST SLEEP IN MY ROOM?
I WONDER WHAT SHE HAS PLANNED?
WSP
REALLY?
WSP
THAT FUTON IS HARD.

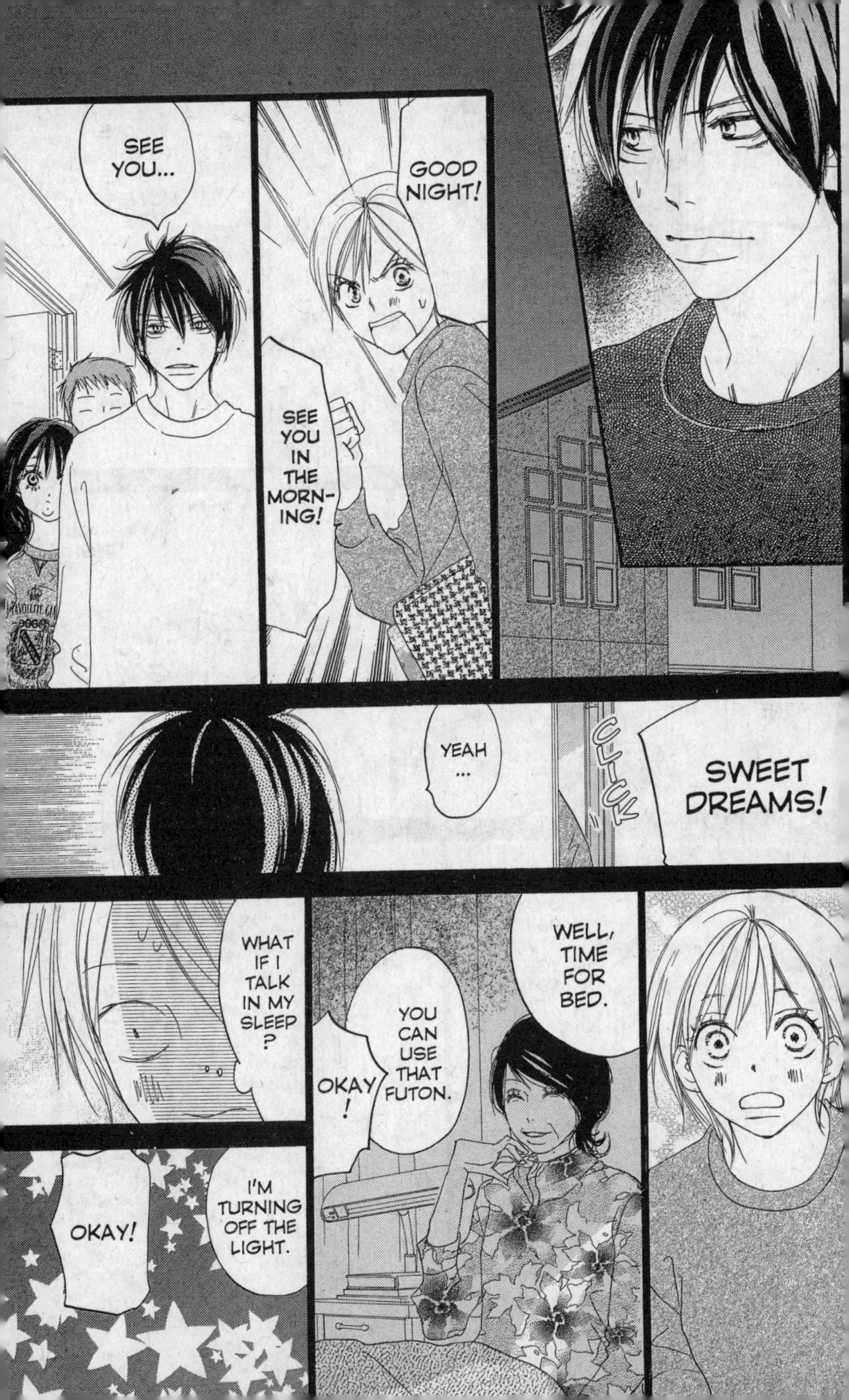
GOOD NIGHT!
SEE YOU IN THE MORNING!
SEE YOU...
CLICK
SWEET DREAMS!
YEAH ...
WELL, TIME FOR BED.
YOU CAN USE THAT FUTON.
OKAY!
WHAT IF I TALK IN MY SLEEP?
I'M TURNING OFF THE LIGHT.
OKAY!

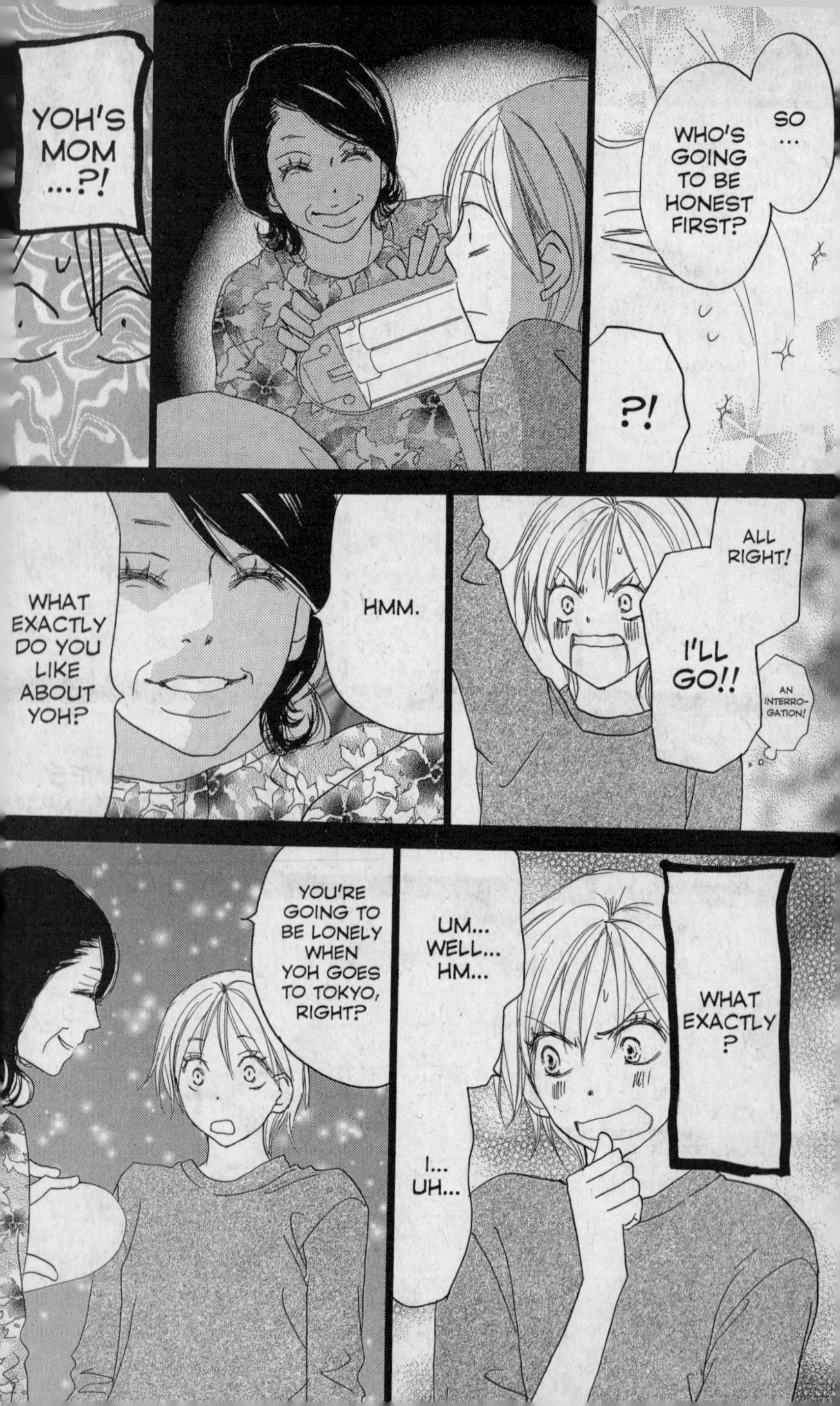

SO ... WHO'S GOING TO BE HONEST FIRST?
?!
YOH'S MOM ...?!
ALL RIGHT! I'LL GO!!
AN INTERROGATION!
HMM.
WHAT EXACTLY DO YOU LIKE ABOUT YOH?
WHAT EXACTLY?
UM... WELL... HM...
I... UH...
YOU'RE GOING TO BE LONELY WHEN YOH GOES TO TOKYO, RIGHT?

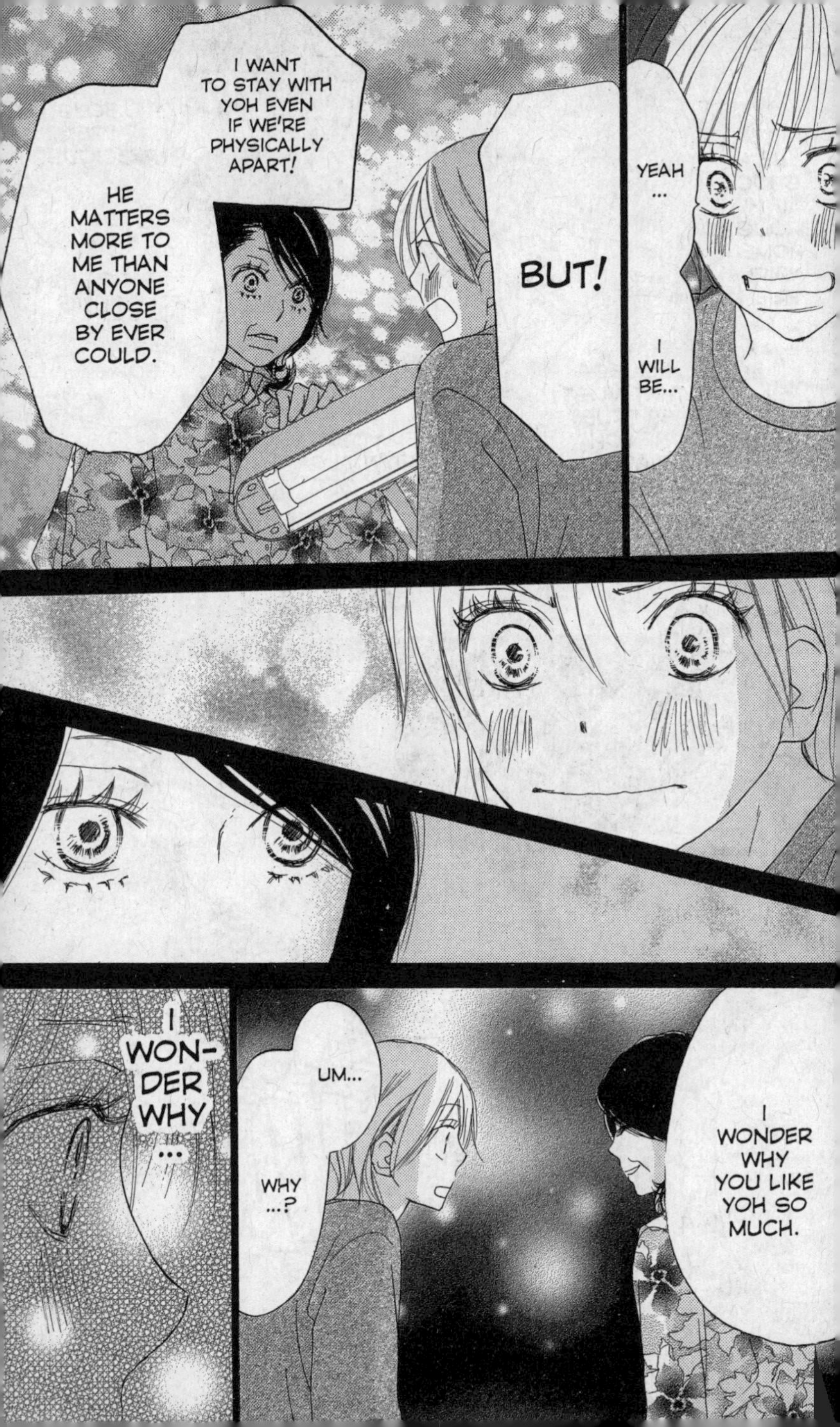
YEAH ...
I WILL BE...
BUT!
I WANT TO STAY WITH YOH EVEN IF WE'RE PHYSICALLY APART!
HE MATTERS MORE TO ME THAN ANYONE CLOSE BY EVER COULD.
I WONDER WHY YOU LIKE YOH SO MUCH.
UM...
WHY ...?
I WONDER WHY ...

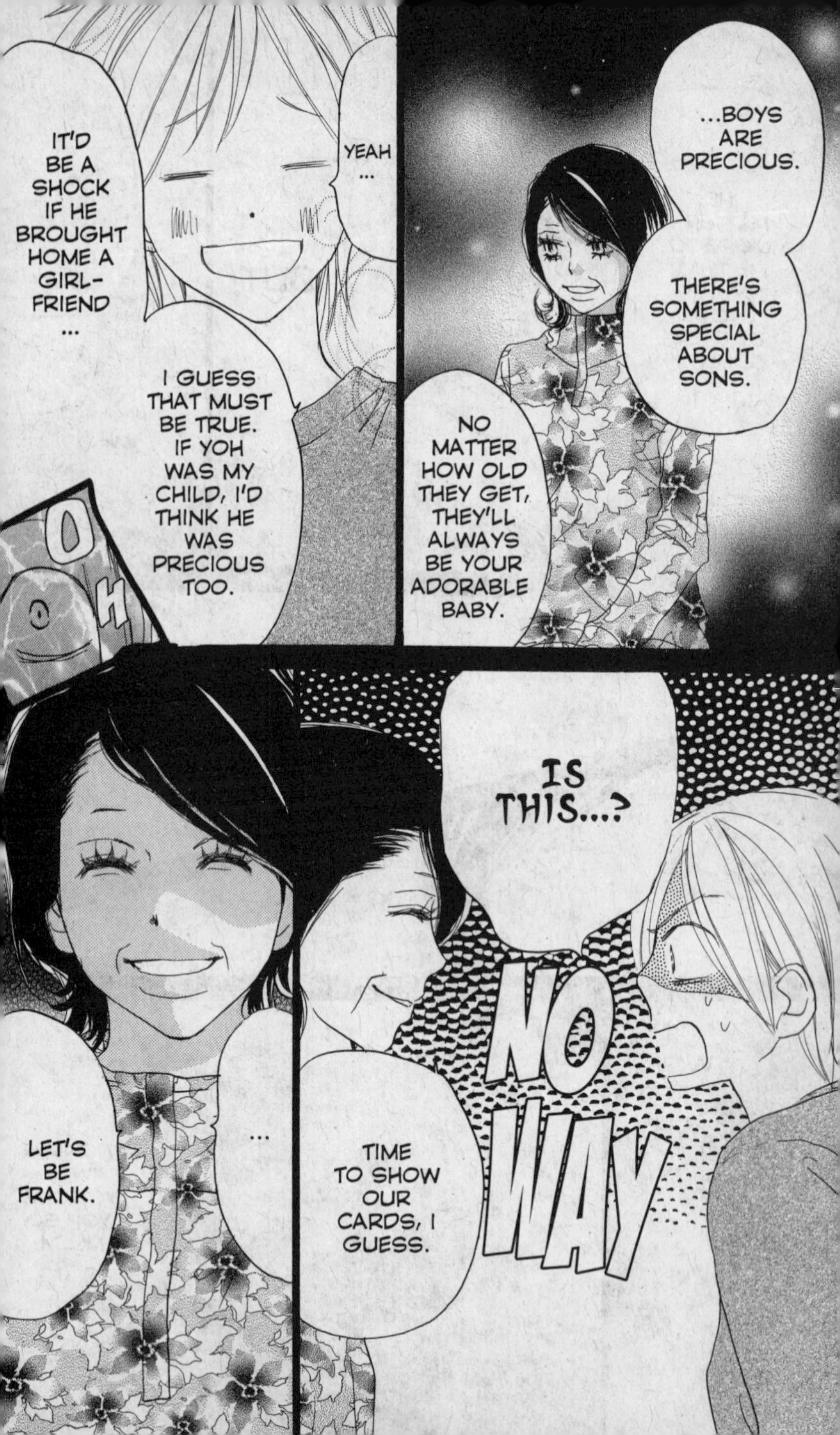
...BOYS ARE PRECIOUS.
THERE'S SOMETHING SPECIAL ABOUT SONS.
NO MATTER HOW OLD THEY GET, THEY'LL ALWAYS BE YOUR ADORABLE BABY.
YEAH ...
IT'D BE A SHOCK IF HE BROUGHT HOME A GIRL-FRIEND ...
I GUESS THAT MUST BE TRUE. IF YOH WAS MY CHILD, I'D THINK HE WAS PRECIOUS TOO.
OH
IS THIS...?
NO WAY
TIME TO SHOW OUR CARDS, I GUESS.
...
LET'S BE FRANK.

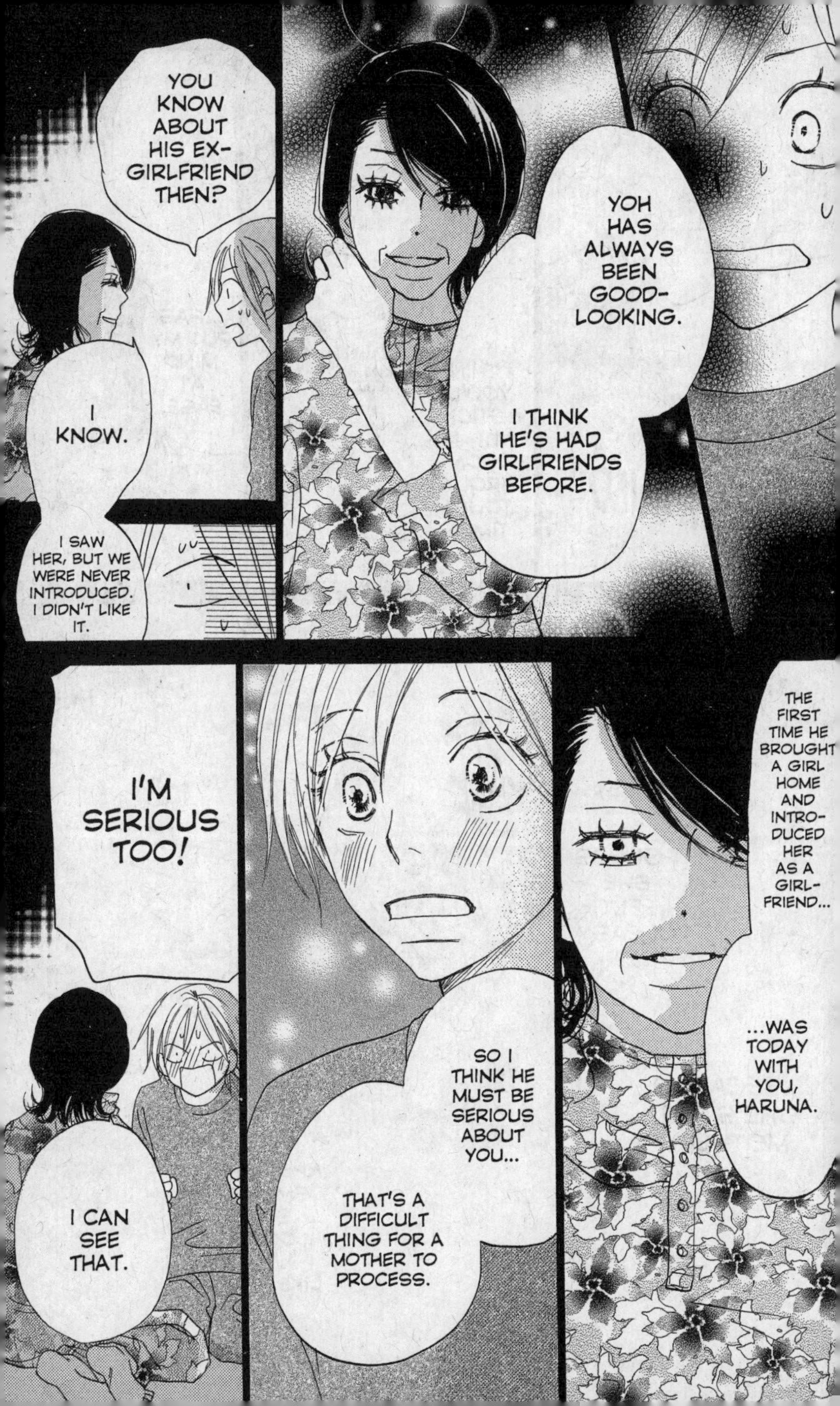
YOH HAS ALWAYS BEEN GOOD-LOOKING.
I THINK HE'S HAD GIRLFRIENDS BEFORE.
YOU KNOW ABOUT HIS EX-GIRLFRIEND THEN?
I KNOW.
I SAW HER, BUT WE WERE NEVER INTRODUCED. I DIDN'T LIKE IT.
THE FIRST TIME HE BROUGHT A GIRL HOME AND INTRODUCED HER AS A GIRLFRIEND...
...WAS TODAY WITH YOU, HARUNA.
SO I THINK HE MUST BE SERIOUS ABOUT YOU...
THAT'S A DIFFICULT THING FOR A MOTHER TO PROCESS.
I'M SERIOUS TOO!
I CAN SEE THAT.

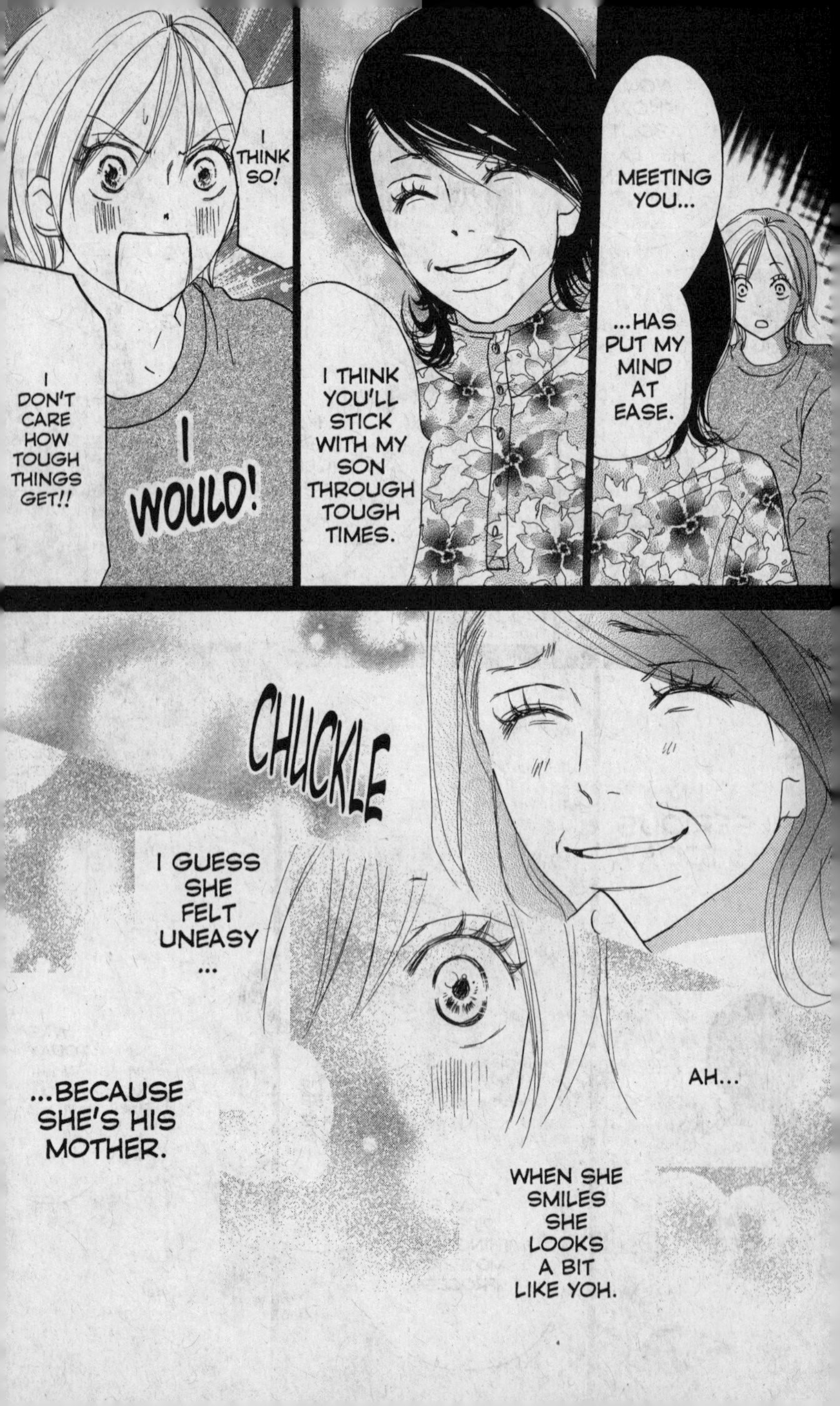
MEETING YOU...
...HAS PUT MY MIND AT EASE.
I THINK YOU'LL STICK WITH MY SON THROUGH TOUGH TIMES.
I THINK SO!
I WOULD!
I DON'T CARE HOW TOUGH THINGS GET!!
CHUCKLE
AH...
I GUESS SHE FELT UNEASY...
...BECAUSE SHE'S HIS MOTHER.
WHEN SHE SMILES SHE LOOKS A BIT LIKE YOH.

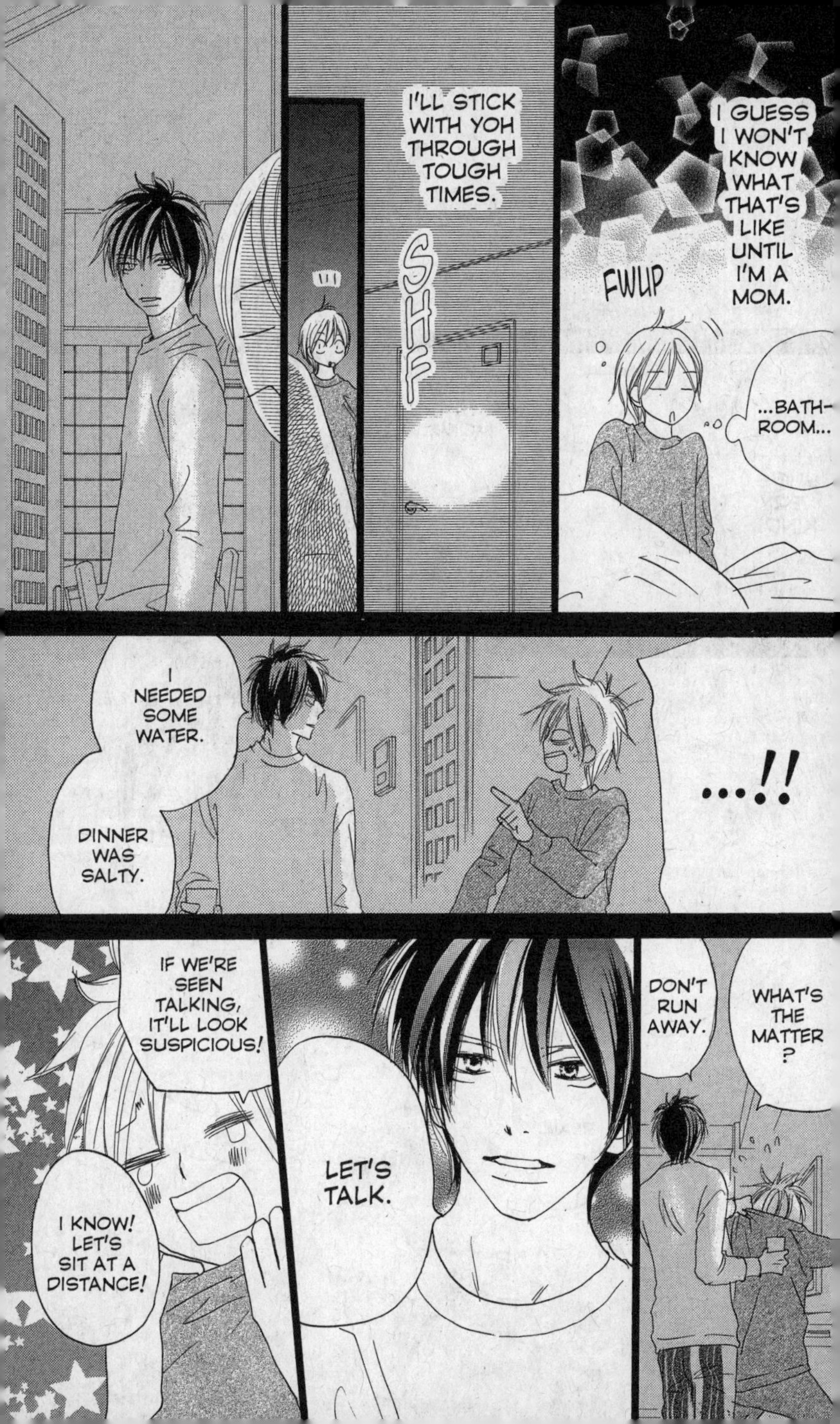
I GUESS I WON'T KNOW WHAT THAT'S LIKE UNTIL I'M A MOM.
FWUP
...BATH-ROOM...
I'LL STICK WITH YOH THROUGH TOUGH TIMES.
SHF
...!!
I NEEDED SOME WATER.
DINNER WAS SALTY.
WHAT'S THE MATTER?
DON'T RUN AWAY.
LET'S TALK.
IF WE'RE SEEN TALKING, IT'LL LOOK SUSPICIOUS!
I KNOW! LET'S SIT AT A DISTANCE!

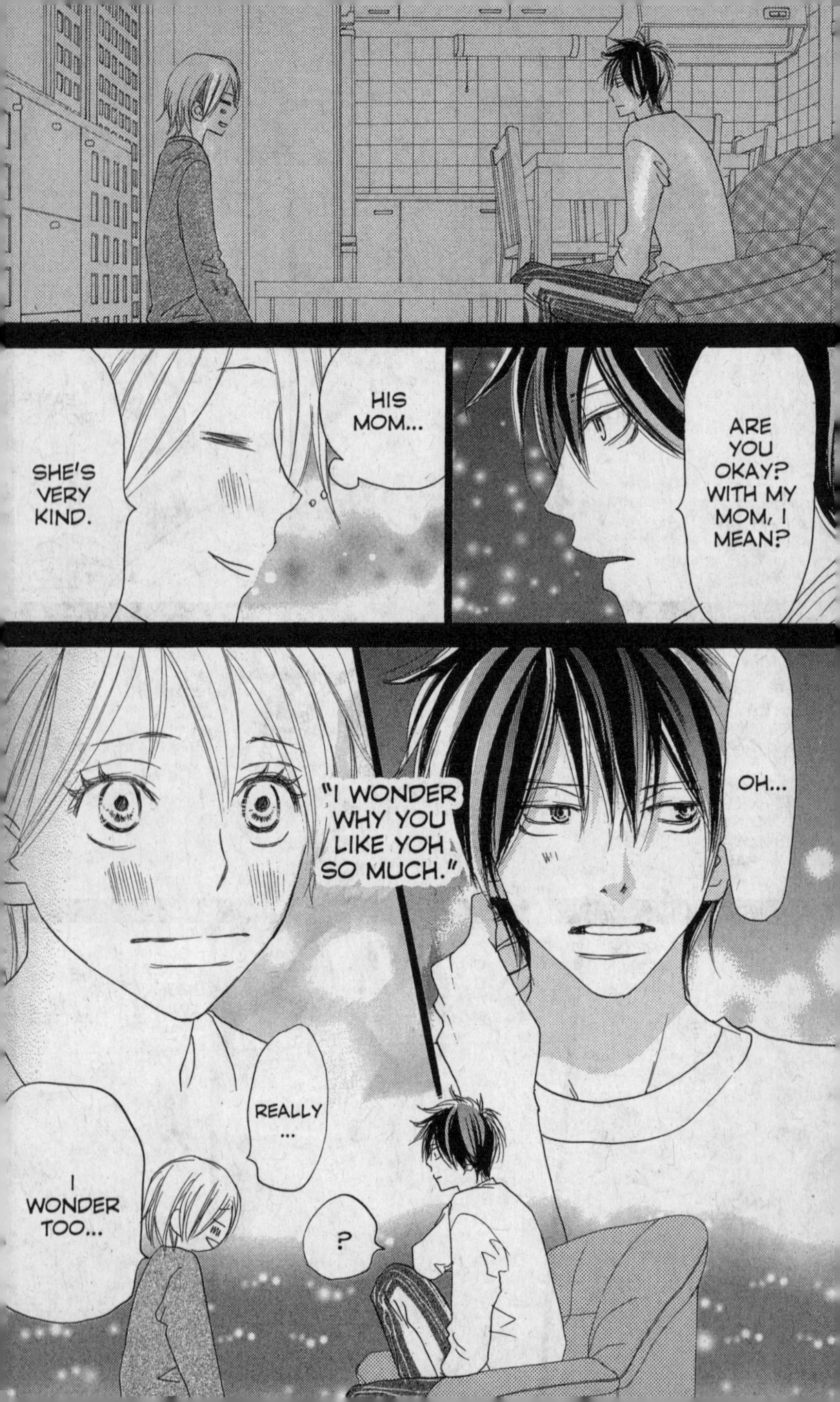
ARE YOU OKAY? WITH MY MOM, I MEAN?
HIS MOM...
SHE'S VERY KIND.
OH...
"I WONDER WHY YOU LIKE YOH SO MUCH."
REALLY ...
?
I WONDER TOO...

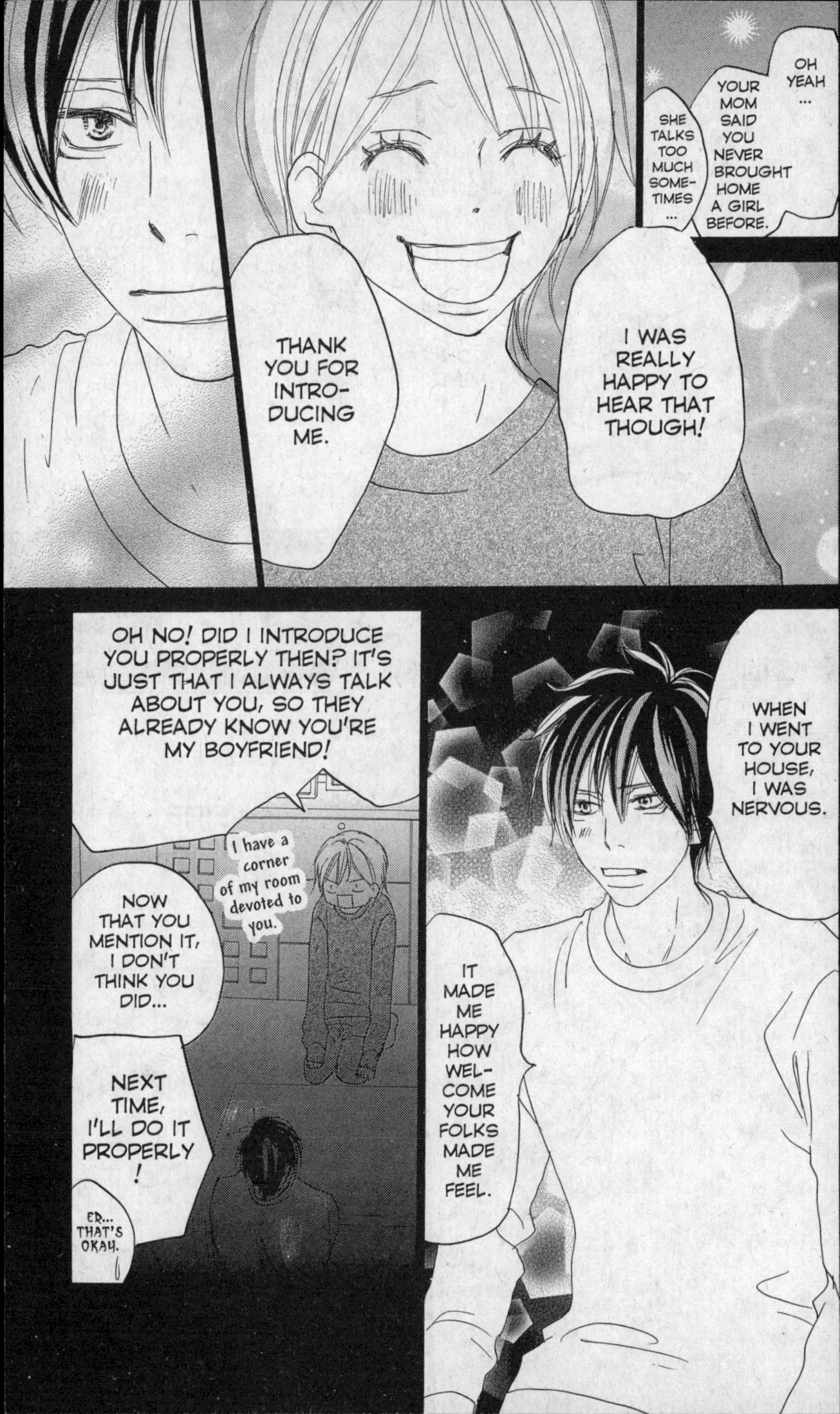
OH YEAH ...
YOUR MOM SAID YOU NEVER BROUGHT HOME A GIRL BEFORE.
SHE TALKS TOO MUCH SOME-TIMES ...
I WAS REALLY HAPPY TO HEAR THAT THOUGH!
THANK YOU FOR INTRO-DUCING ME.
WHEN I WENT TO YOUR HOUSE, I WAS NERVOUS.
IT MADE ME HAPPY HOW WEL-COME YOUR FOLKS MADE ME FEEL.
OH NO! DID I INTRODUCE YOU PROPERLY THEN? IT'S JUST THAT I ALWAYS TALK ABOUT YOU, SO THEY ALREADY KNOW YOU'RE MY BOYFRIEND!
I have a corner of my room devoted to you.
NOW THAT YOU MENTION IT, I DON'T THINK YOU DID...
NEXT TIME, I'LL DO IT PROPERLY!
ER... THAT'S OKAY.

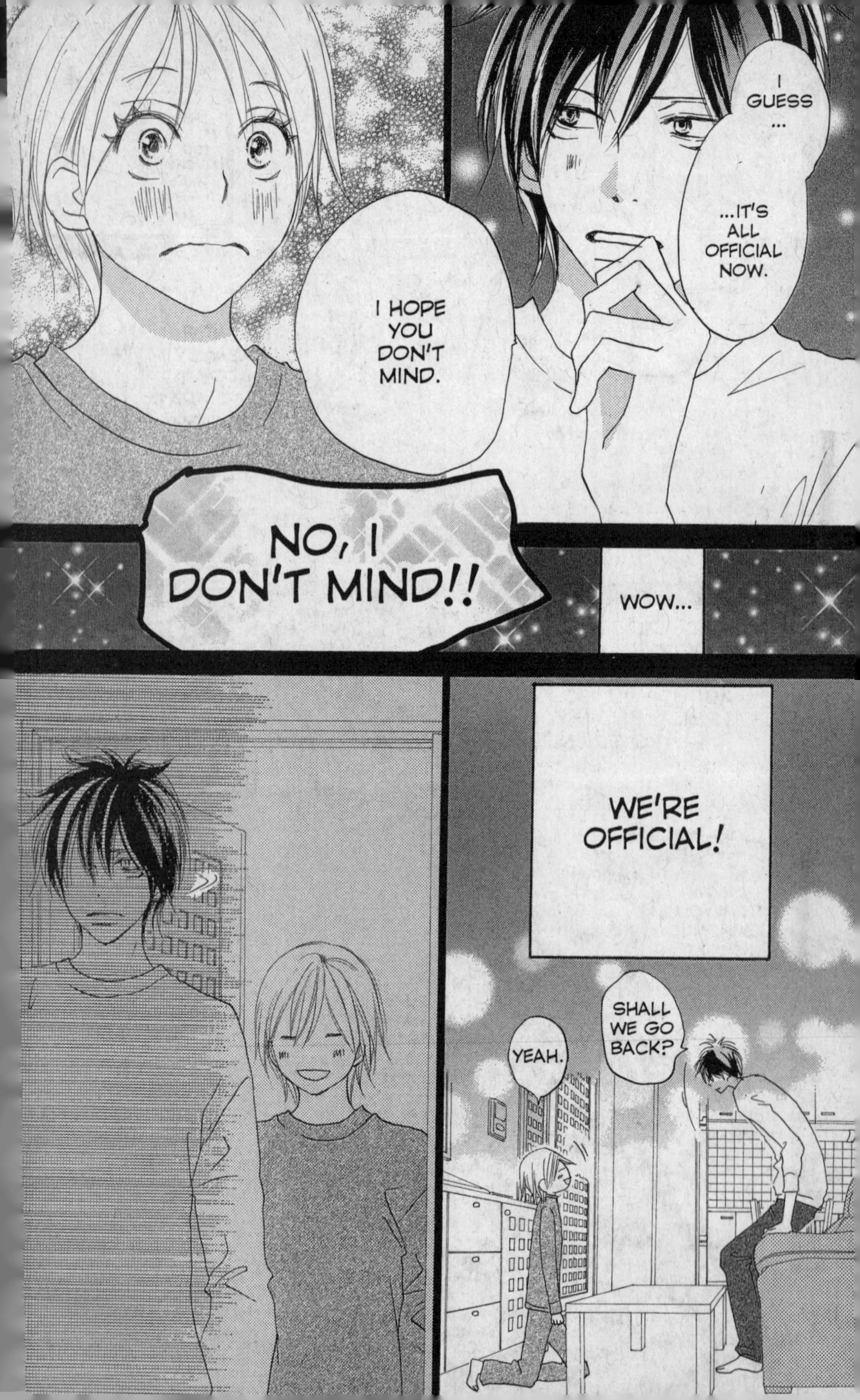

I GUESS...
...IT'S ALL OFFICIAL NOW.
I HOPE YOU DON'T MIND.
NO, I DON'T MIND!!
WOW...
WE'RE OFFICIAL!
SHALL WE GO BACK?
YEAH.

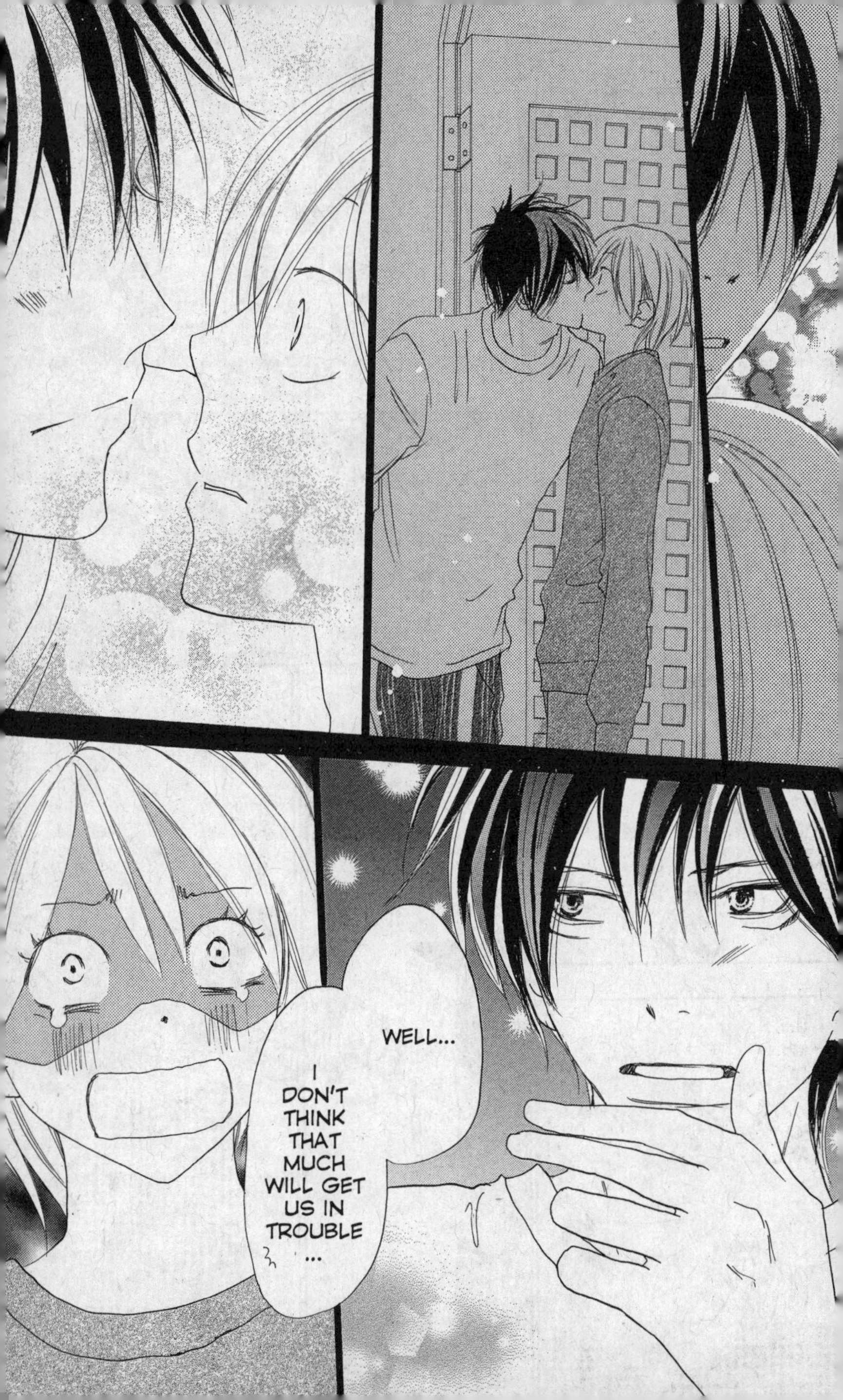
WELL...
I DON'T THINK THAT MUCH WILL GET US IN TROUBLE ...

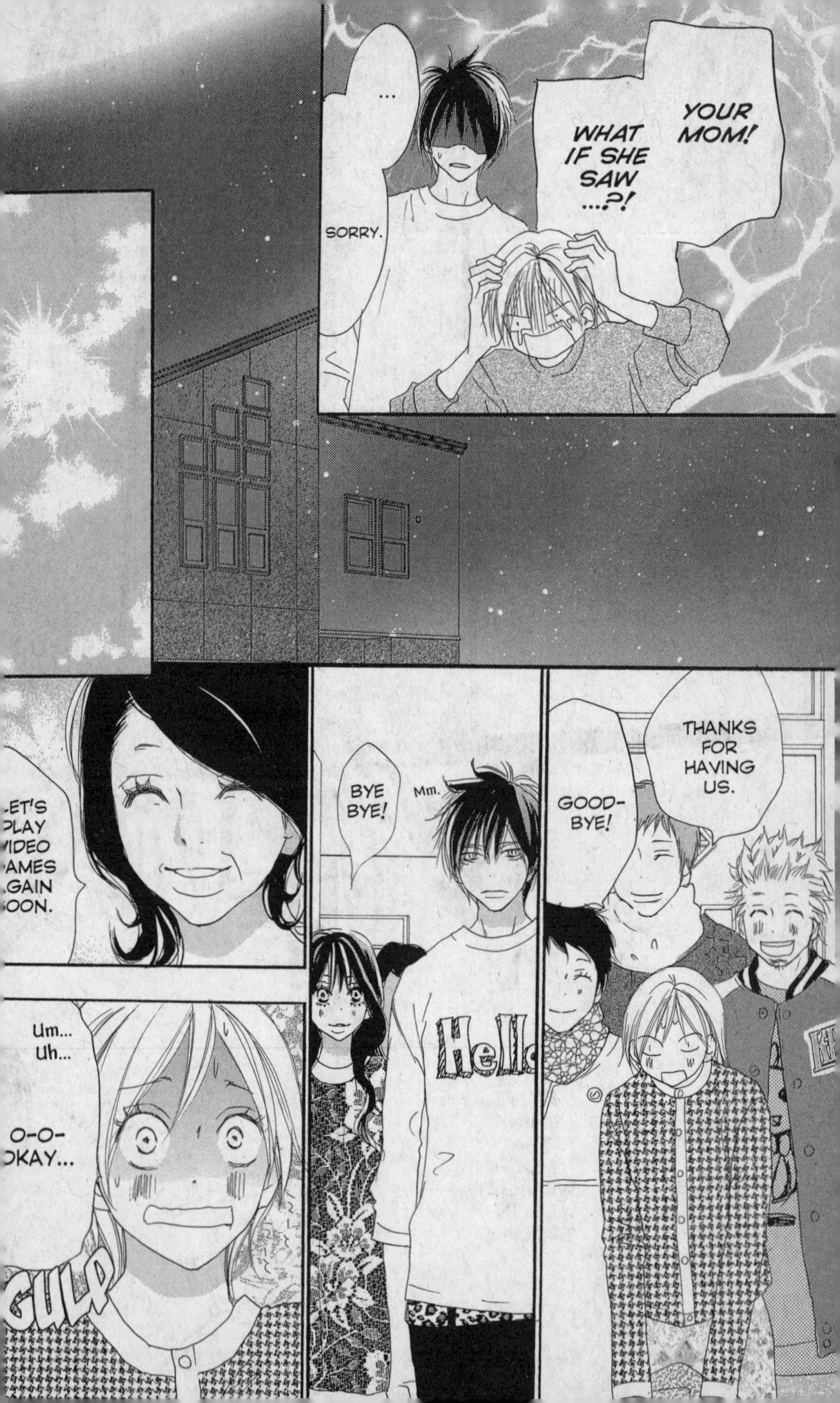
YOUR MOM!
WHAT IF SHE SAW ...?!
...
SORRY.
THANKS FOR HAVING US.
GOOD-BYE!
Mm.
BYE BYE!
LET'S PLAY VIDEO GAMES AGAIN SOON.
Um... Uh...
O-O-OKAY...
GULP

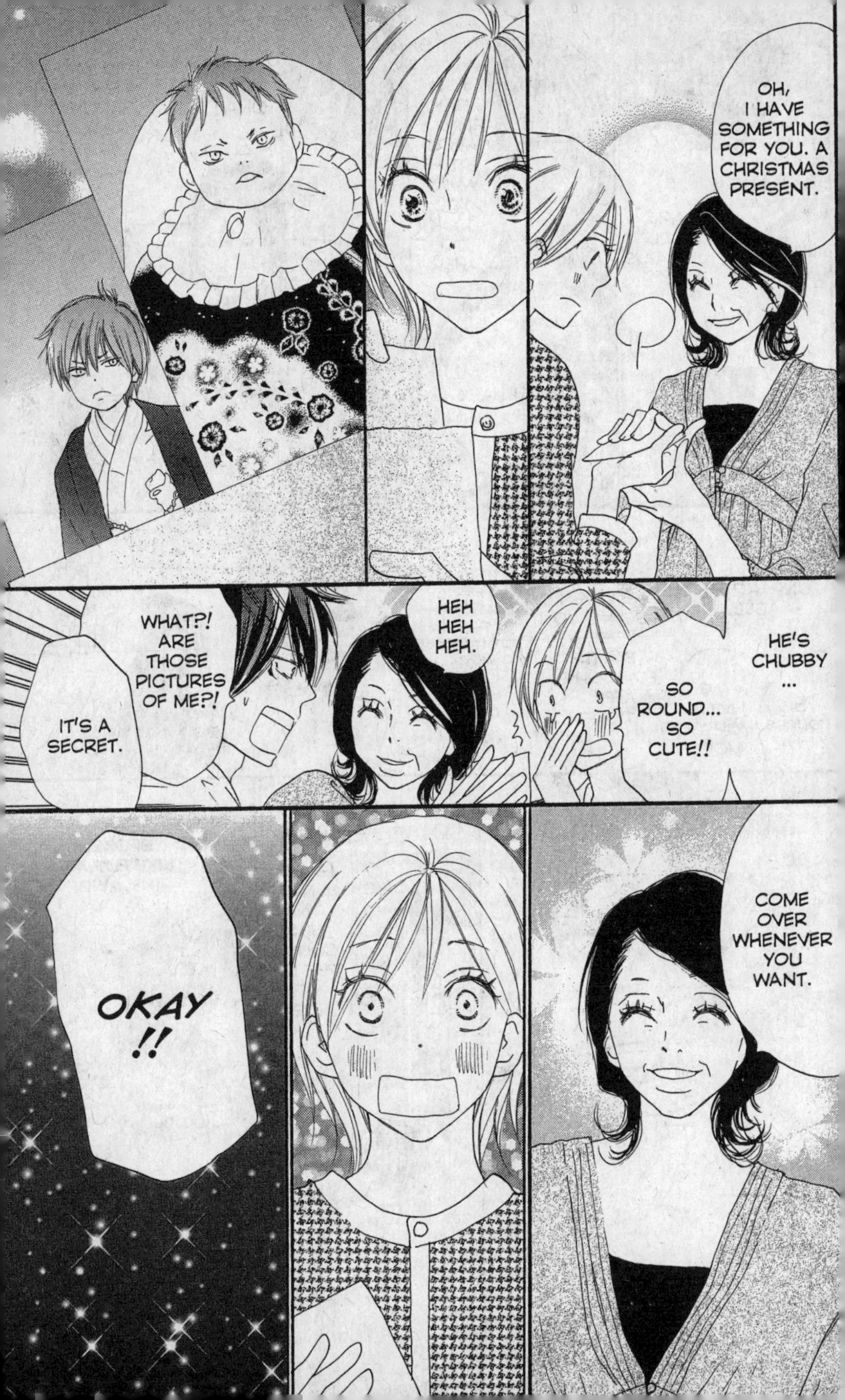
OH, I HAVE SOMETHING FOR YOU. A CHRISTMAS PRESENT.
HE'S CHUBBY ...
SO ROUND... SO CUTE!!
HEH HEH HEH.
WHAT?! ARE THOSE PICTURES OF ME?!
IT'S A SECRET.
COME OVER WHENEVER YOU WANT.
OKAY !!

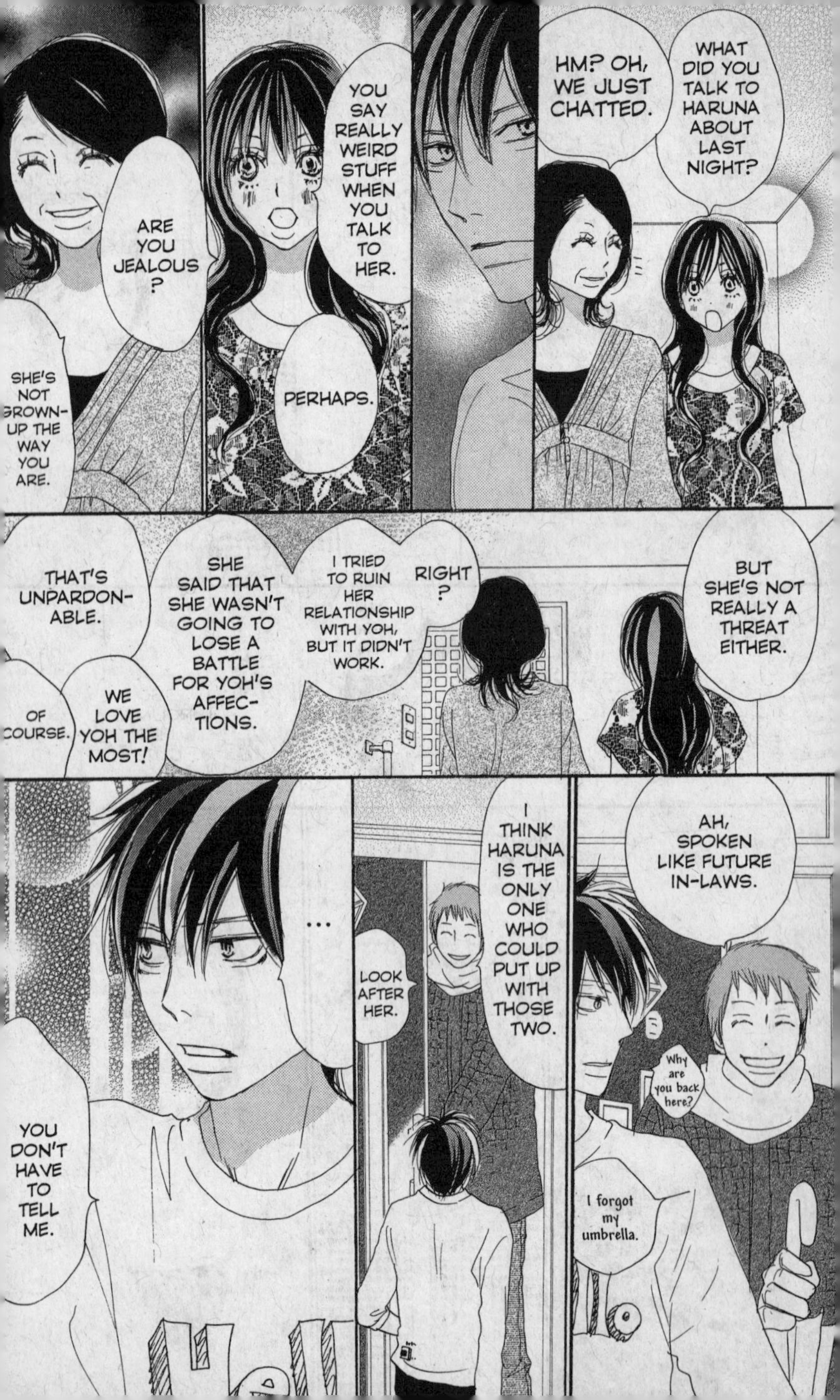
WHAT DID YOU TALK TO HARUNA ABOUT LAST NIGHT?
HM? OH, WE JUST CHATTED.
YOU SAY REALLY WEIRD STUFF WHEN YOU TALK TO HER.
PERHAPS.
ARE YOU JEALOUS?
SHE'S NOT GROWN-UP THE WAY YOU ARE.
BUT SHE'S NOT REALLY A THREAT EITHER.
RIGHT?
I TRIED TO RUIN HER RELATIONSHIP WITH YOH, BUT IT DIDN'T WORK.
SHE SAID THAT SHE WASN'T GOING TO LOSE A BATTLE FOR YOH'S AFFECTIONS.
THAT'S UNPARDONABLE.
WE LOVE YOH THE MOST!
OF COURSE.
AH, SPOKEN LIKE FUTURE IN-LAWS.
Why are you back here?
I forgot my umbrella.
I THINK HARUNA IS THE ONLY ONE WHO COULD PUT UP WITH THOSE TWO.
LOOK AFTER HER.
...
YOU DON'T HAVE TO TELL ME.

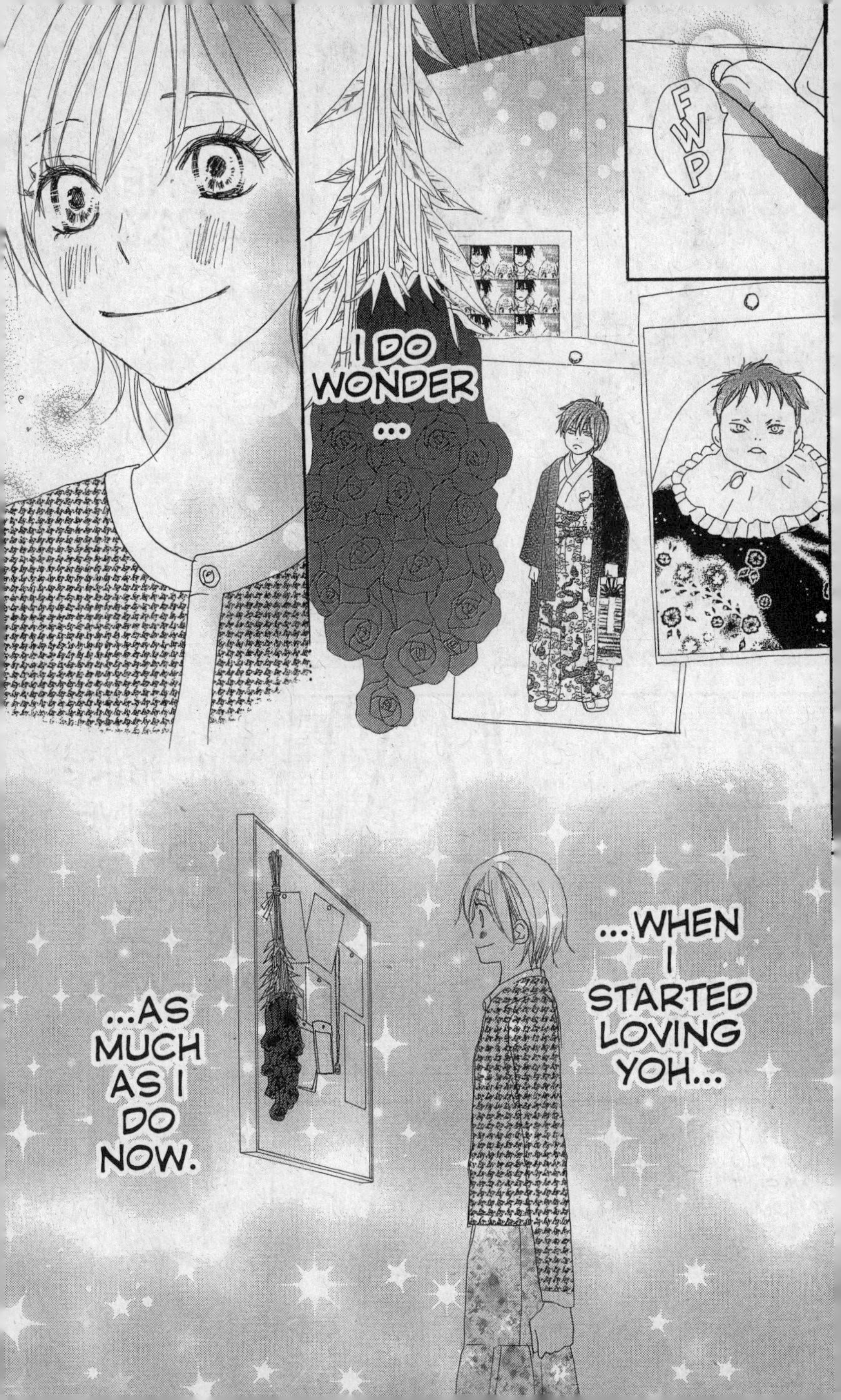
FWP
I DO WONDER...
...WHEN I STARTED LOVING YOH...
...AS MUCH AS I DO NOW.

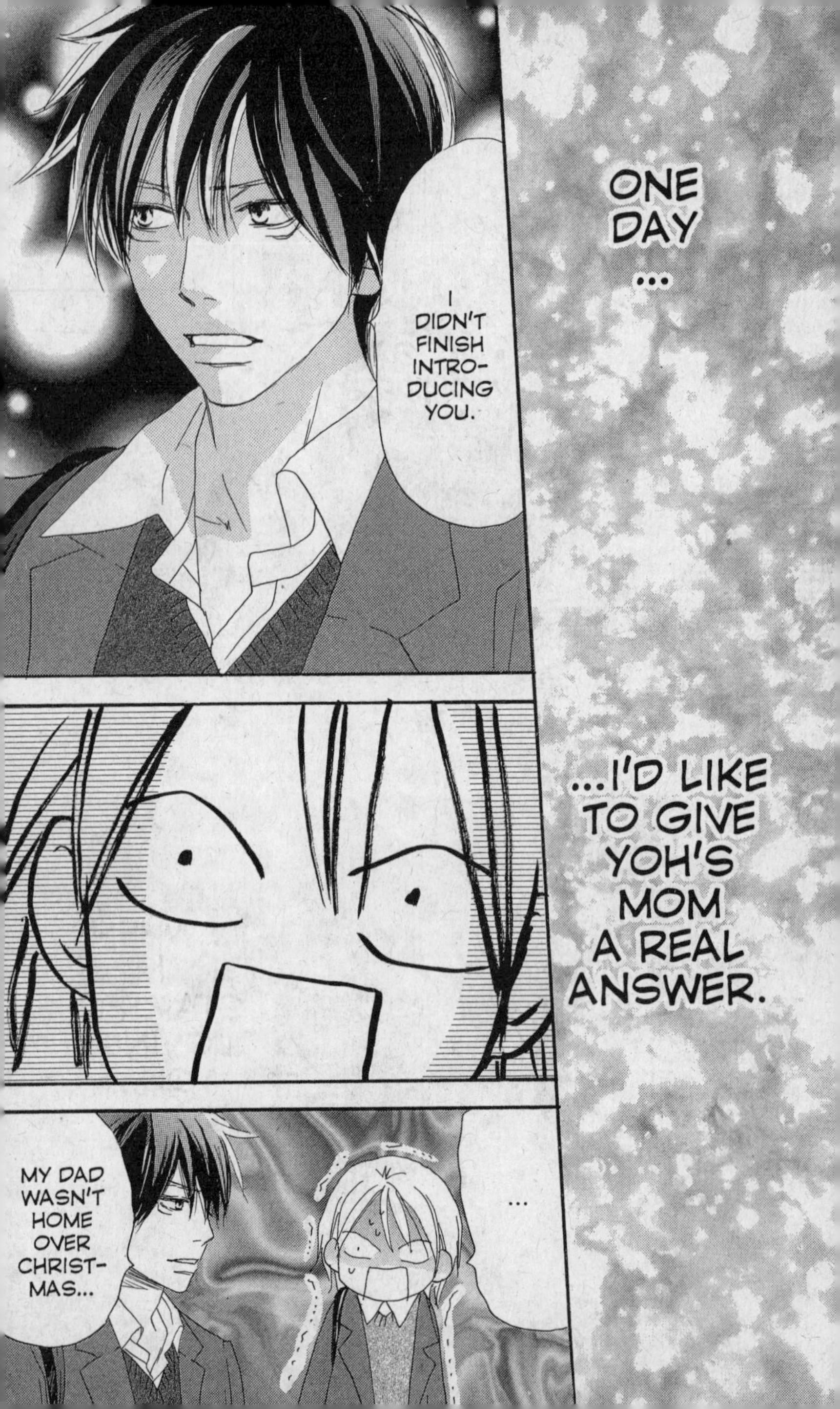
ONE DAY ...
...I'D LIKE TO GIVE YOH'S MOM A REAL ANSWER.
I DIDN'T FINISH INTRO-DUCING YOU.
...
MY DAD WASN'T HOME OVER CHRIST-MAS...

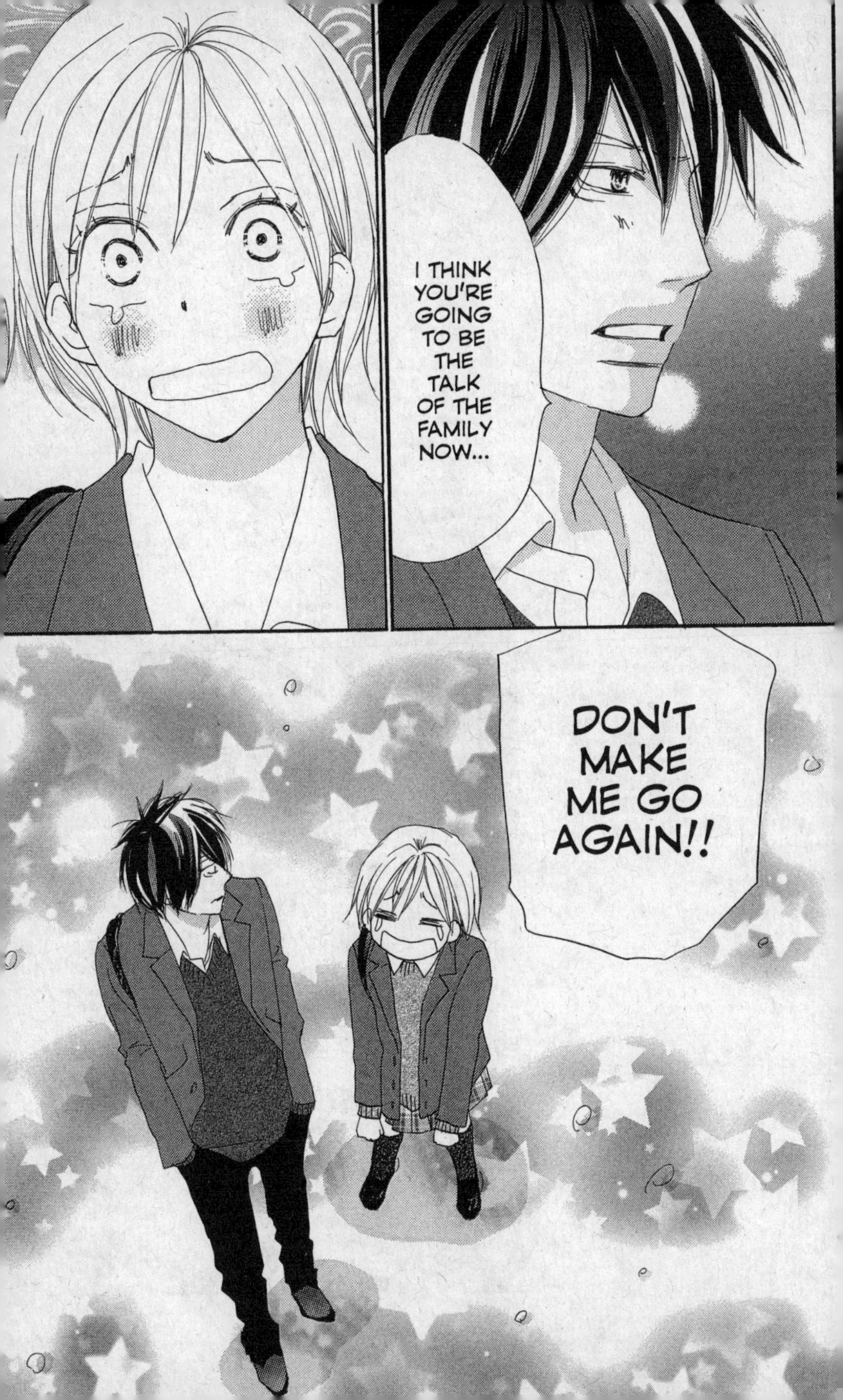
I THINK YOU'RE GOING TO BE THE TALK OF THE FAMILY NOW...
DON'T MAKE ME GO AGAIN!!

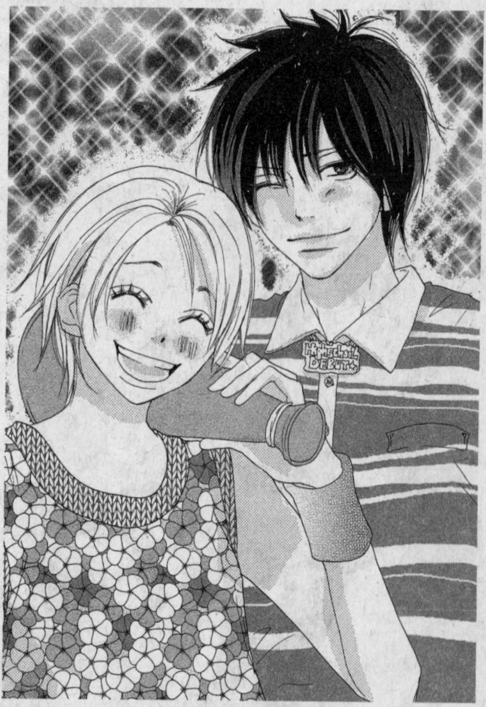
Highschool DEBUT

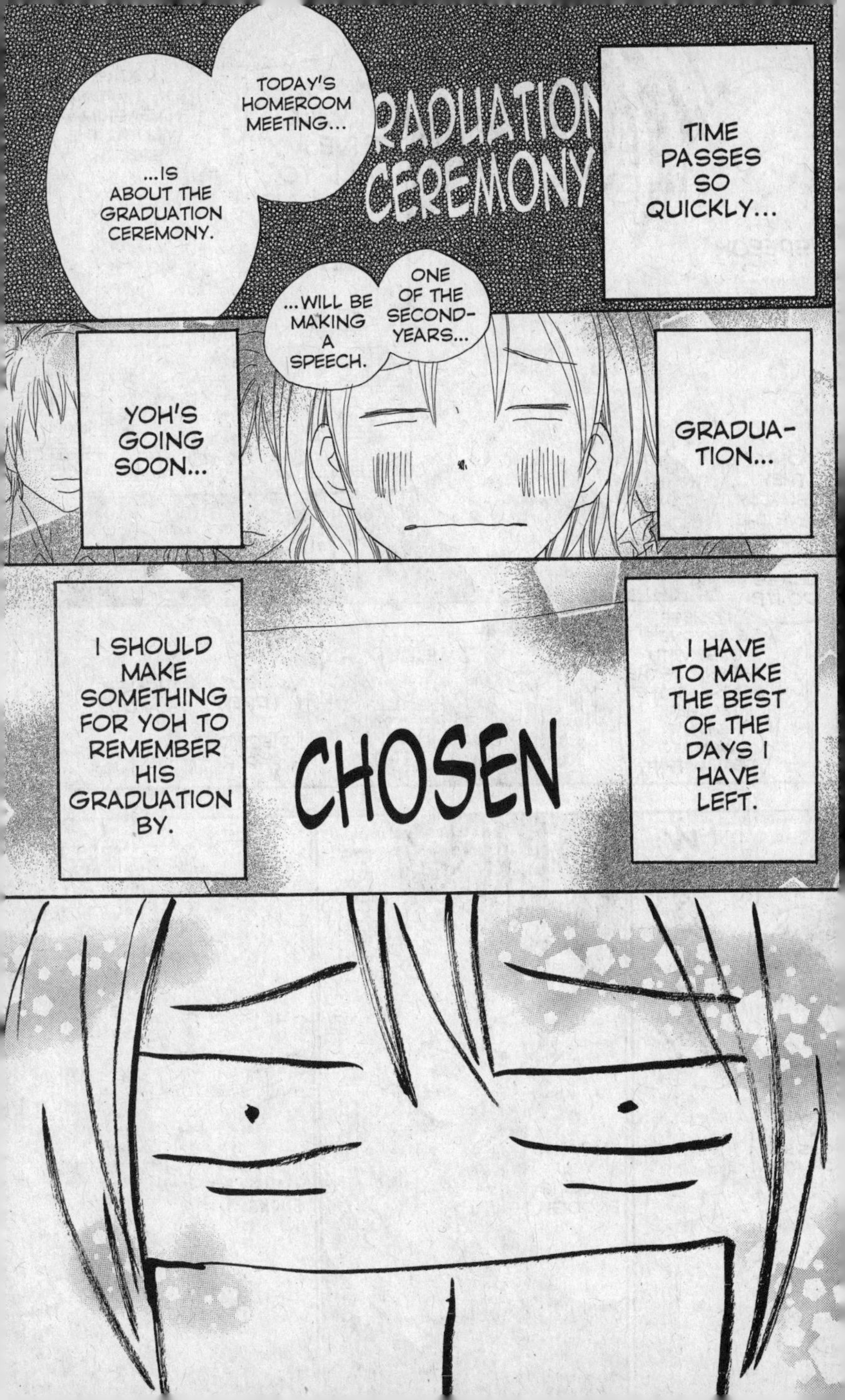
TIME PASSES SO QUICKLY...
GRADUATION CEREMONY
TODAY'S HOMEROOM MEETING...
...IS ABOUT THE GRADUATION CEREMONY.
ONE OF THE SECOND-YEARS...
...WILL BE MAKING A SPEECH.
GRADUA-TION...
YOH'S GOING SOON...
I HAVE TO MAKE THE BEST OF THE DAYS I HAVE LEFT.
CHOSEN
I SHOULD MAKE SOMETHING FOR YOH TO REMEMBER HIS GRADUATION BY.

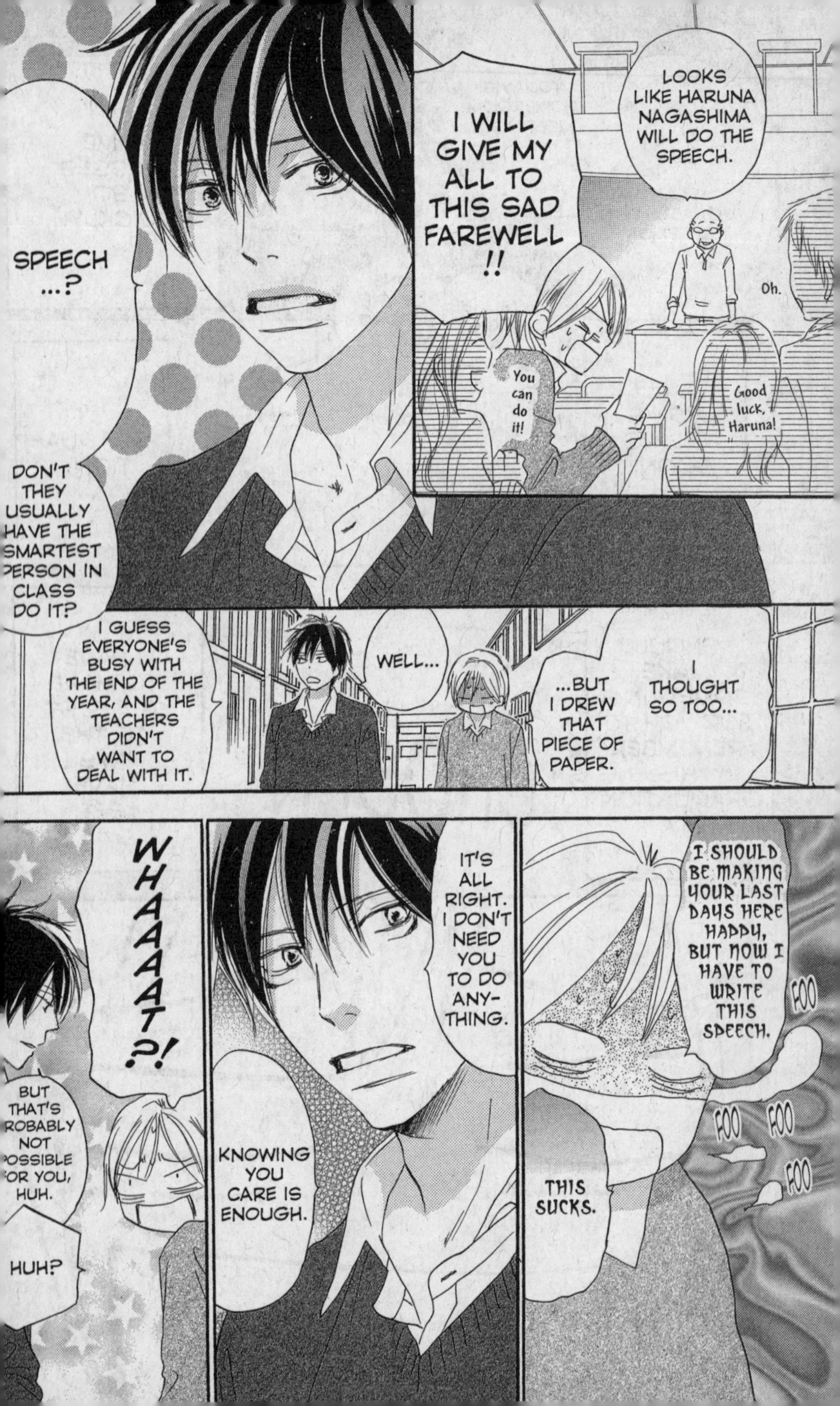
LOOKS LIKE HARUNA NAGASHIMA WILL DO THE SPEECH.
Oh.
Good luck, Haruna!
I WILL GIVE MY ALL TO THIS SAD FAREWELL!!
You can do it!
SPEECH...?
DON'T THEY USUALLY HAVE THE SMARTEST ERSON IN CLASS DO IT?
I THOUGHT SO TOO...
...BUT I DREW THAT PIECE OF PAPER.
WELL...
I GUESS EVERYONE'S BUSY WITH THE END OF THE YEAR, AND THE TEACHERS DIDN'T WANT TO DEAL WITH IT.
I SHOULD BE MAKING YOUR LAST DAYS HERE HAPPY, BUT NOW I HAVE TO WRITE THIS SPEECH.
FOO
FOO FOO
FOO
THIS SUCKS.
IT'S ALL RIGHT. I DON'T NEED YOU TO DO ANYTHING.
KNOWING YOU CARE IS ENOUGH.
WHAAAAT?!
BUT THAT'S ROBABLY NOT OSSIBLE OR YOU, HUH.
HUH?

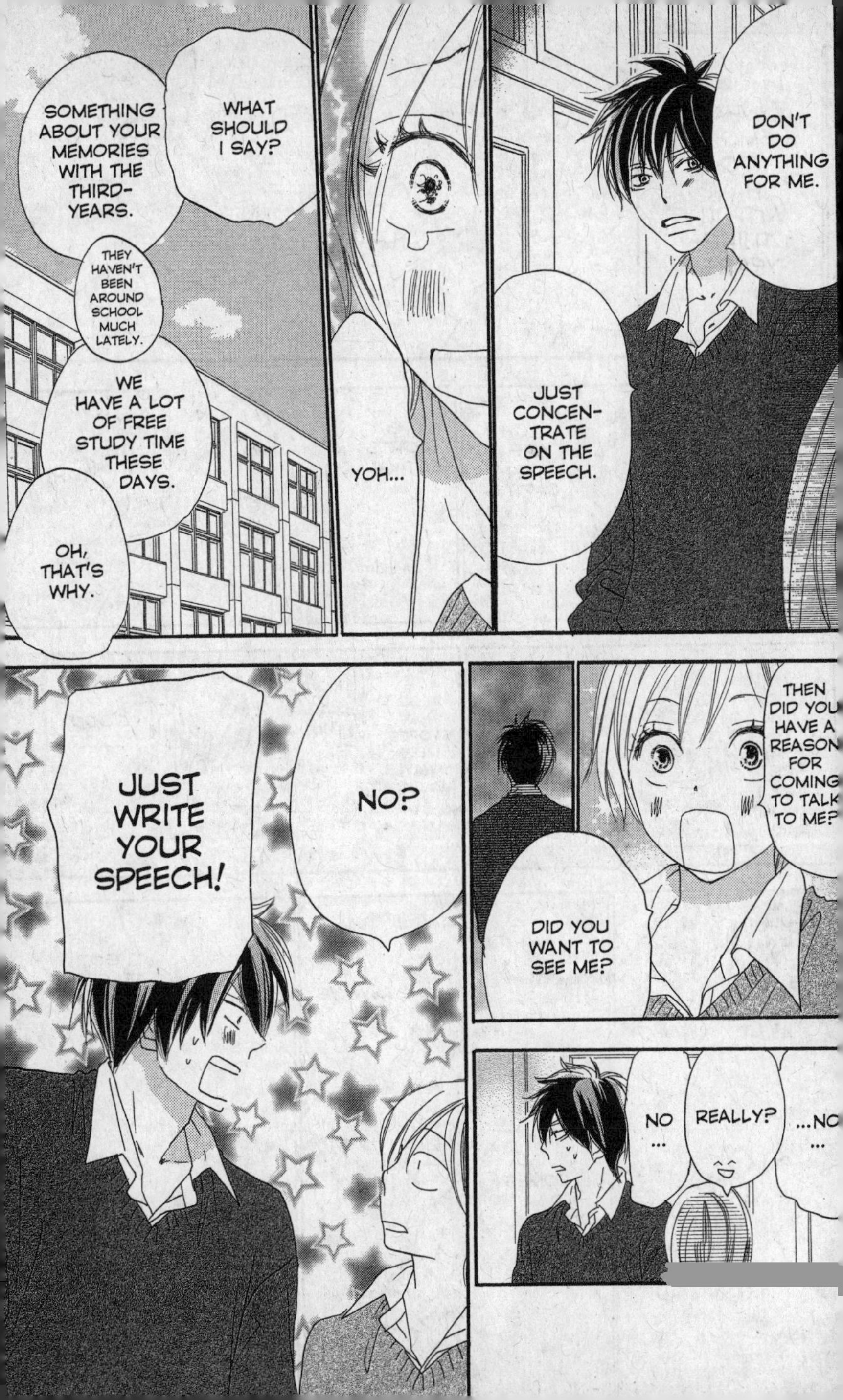
DON'T DO ANYTHING FOR ME.
JUST CONCENTRATE ON THE SPEECH.
YOH...
WHAT SHOULD I SAY?
SOMETHING ABOUT YOUR MEMORIES WITH THE THIRD-YEARS.
THEY HAVEN'T BEEN AROUND SCHOOL MUCH LATELY.
WE HAVE A LOT OF FREE STUDY TIME THESE DAYS.
OH, THAT'S WHY.
THEN DID YOU HAVE A REASON FOR COMING TO TALK TO ME?
DID YOU WANT TO SEE ME?
...NO...
REALLY?
NO...
NO?
JUST WRITE YOUR SPEECH!

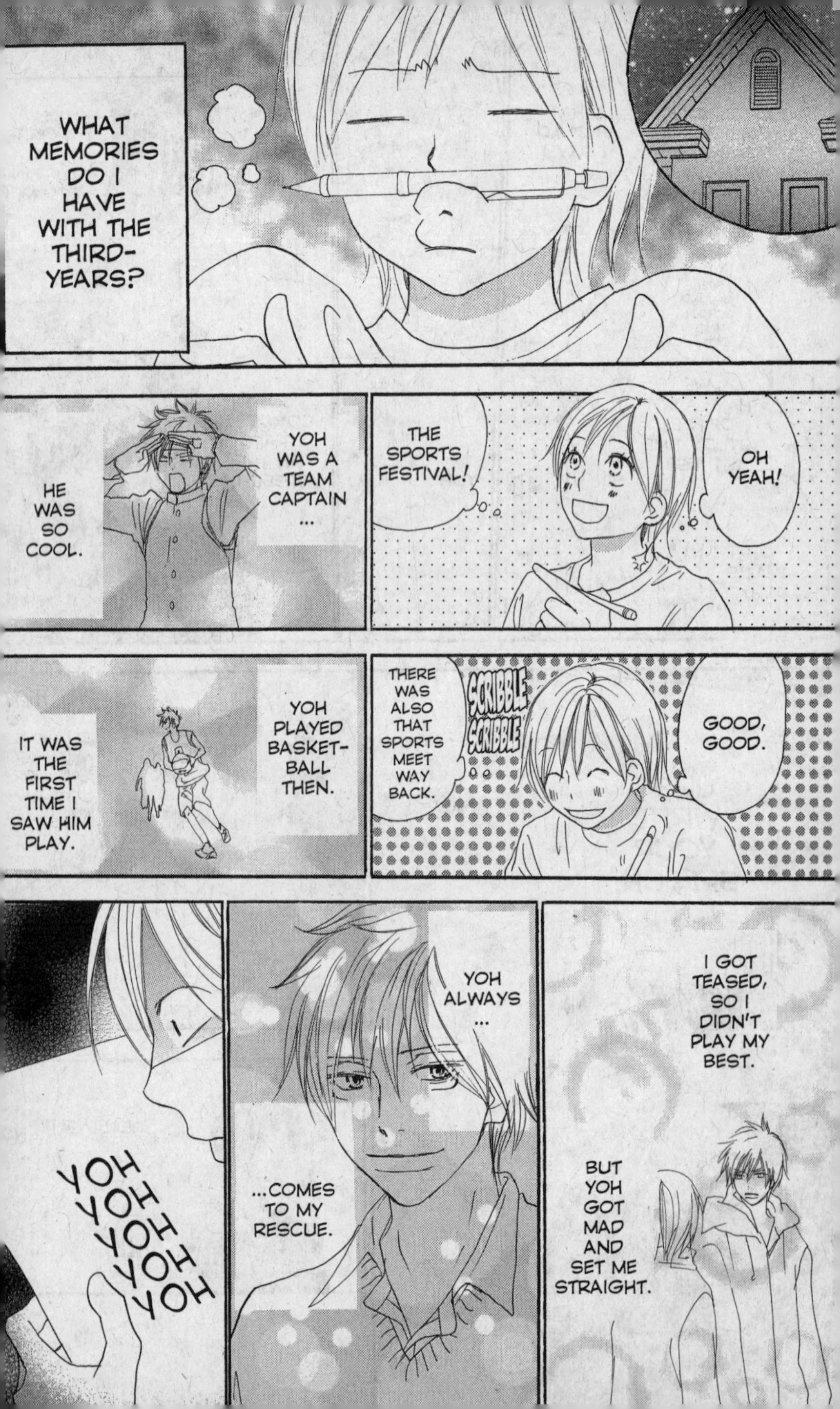
WHAT MEMORIES DO I HAVE WITH THE THIRD-YEARS?
OH YEAH!
THE SPORTS FESTIVAL!
YOH WAS A TEAM CAPTAIN ...
HE WAS SO COOL.
GOOD, GOOD.
SCRIBBLE SCRIBBLE
THERE WAS ALSO THAT SPORTS MEET WAY BACK.
YOH PLAYED BASKET-BALL THEN.
IT WAS THE FIRST TIME I SAW HIM PLAY.
I GOT TEASED, SO I DIDN'T PLAY MY BEST.
BUT YOH GOT MAD AND SET ME STRAIGHT.
YOH ALWAYS ...
...COMES TO MY RESCUE.
YOH YOH YOH YOH YOH

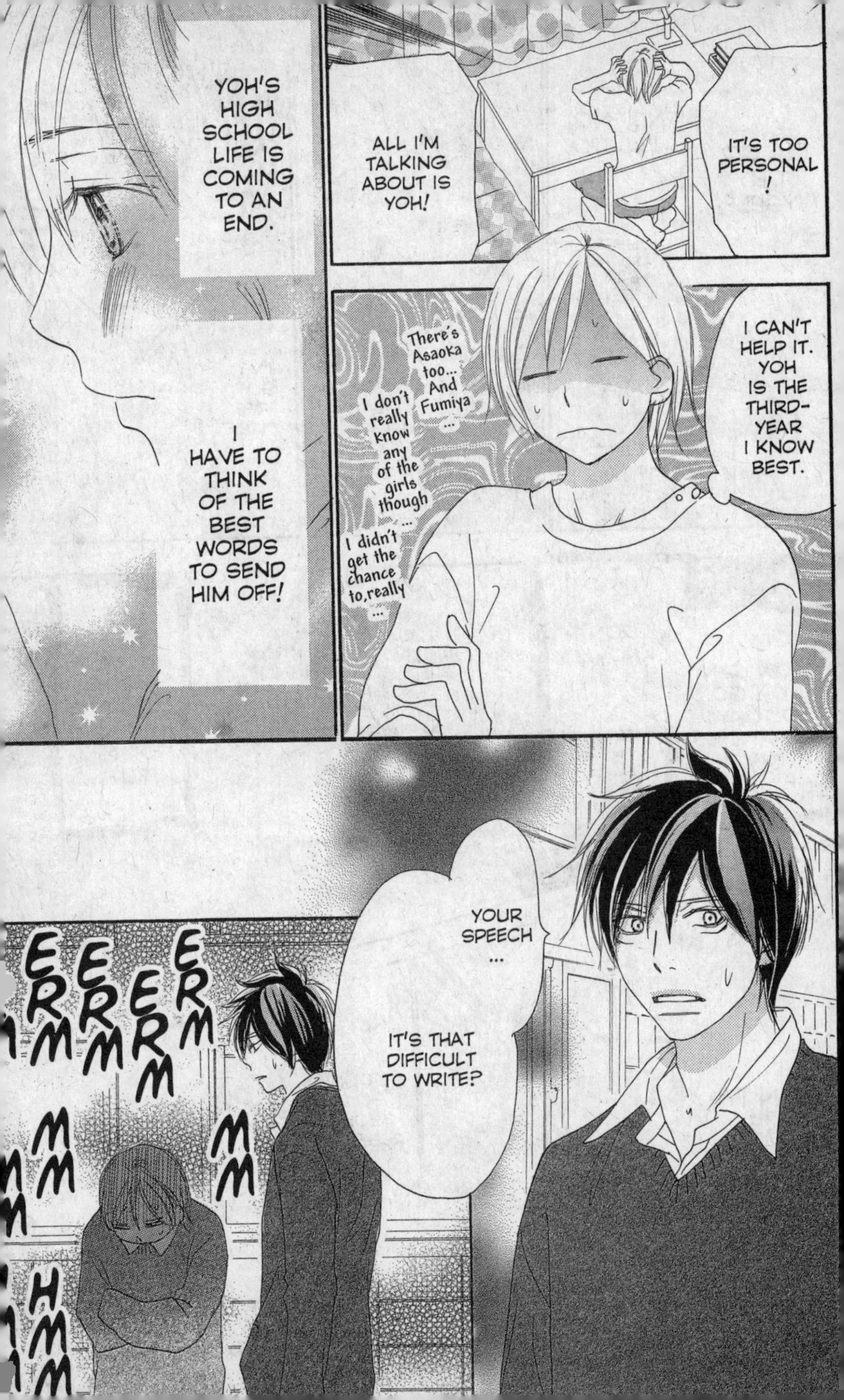
IT'S TOO PERSONAL!
ALL I'M TALKING ABOUT IS YOH!
I CAN'T HELP IT. YOH IS THE THIRD-YEAR I KNOW BEST.
There's Asaoka too... And Fumiya...
I don't really know any of the girls though...
I didn't get the chance to, really...
YOH'S HIGH SCHOOL LIFE IS COMING TO AN END.
I HAVE TO THINK OF THE BEST WORDS TO SEND HIM OFF!
YOUR SPEECH...
IT'S THAT DIFFICULT TO WRITE?
ERMMMM
ERRMMM
ERRMMM
ERMMM
HMMM

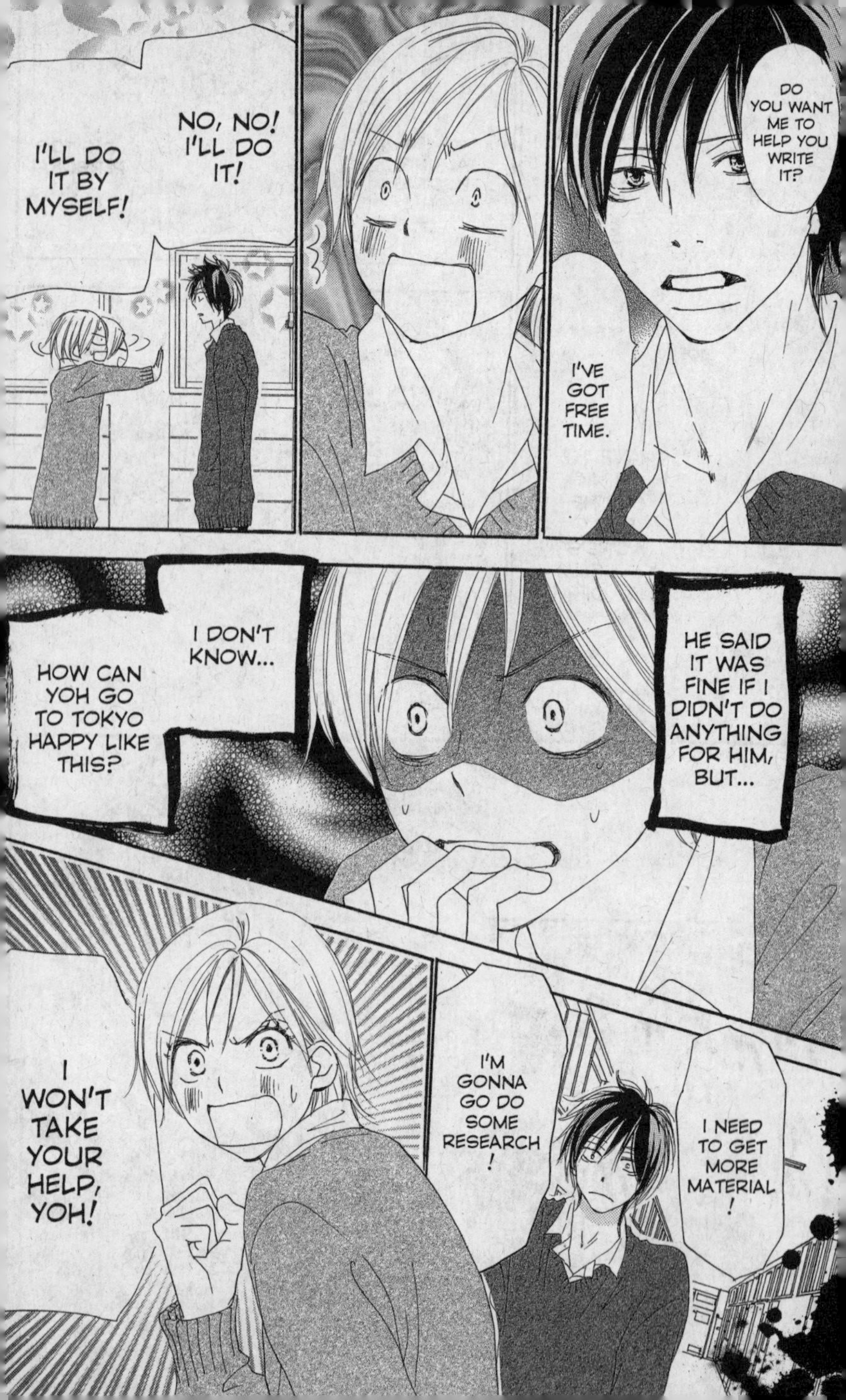
DO YOU WANT ME TO HELP YOU WRITE IT?
I'VE GOT FREE TIME.
NO, NO! I'LL DO IT!
I'LL DO IT BY MYSELF!
HE SAID IT WAS FINE IF I DIDN'T DO ANYTHING FOR HIM, BUT...
I DON'T KNOW...
HOW CAN YOH GO TO TOKYO HAPPY LIKE THIS?
I NEED TO GET MORE MATERIAL!
I'M GONNA GO DO SOME RESEARCH!
I WON'T TAKE YOUR HELP, YOH!

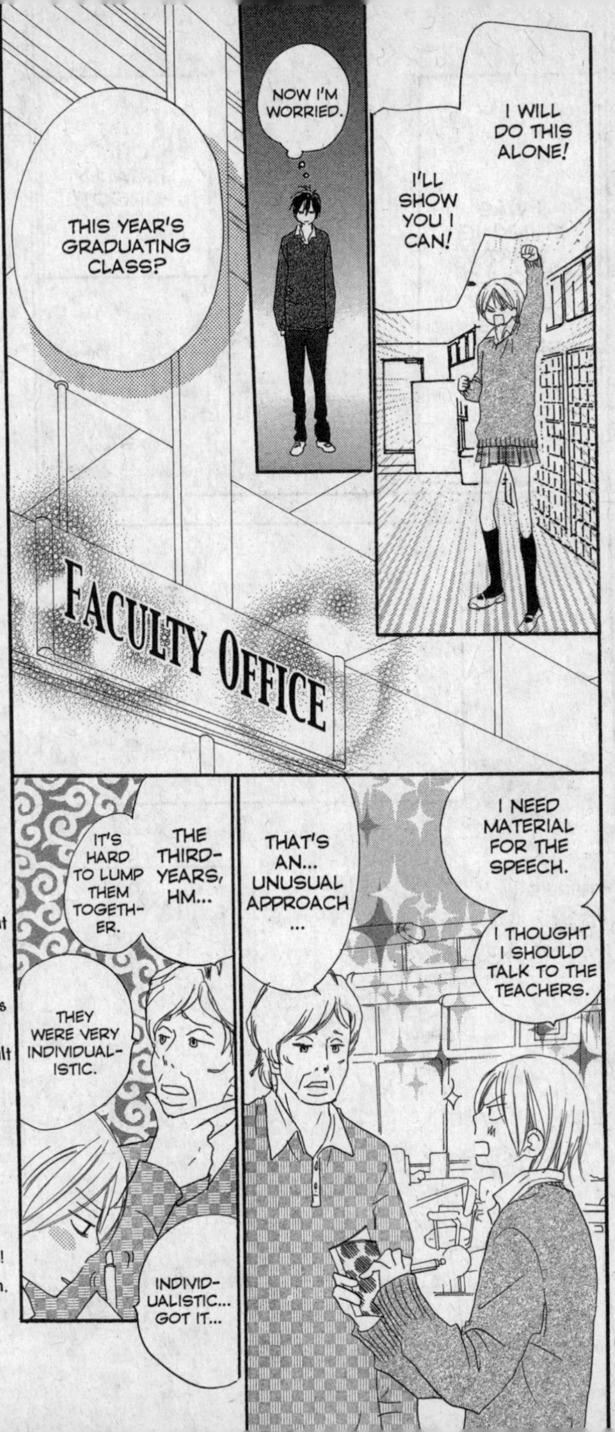
I WILL DO THIS ALONE!
I'LL SHOW YOU I CAN!
NOW I'M WORRIED.
THIS YEAR'S GRADUATING CLASS?
FACULTY OFFICE
I NEED MATERIAL FOR THE SPEECH.
I THOUGHT I SHOULD TALK TO THE TEACHERS.
THAT'S AN... UNUSUAL APPROACH...
THE THIRD-YEARS, HM...
IT'S HARD TO LUMP THEM TOGETHER.
THEY WERE VERY INDIVIDUALISTIC.
INDIVIDUALISTIC... GOT IT...

2 Last!

Thank you to the editors! I'm sorry I forgot my notes so often. I'm sorry I forgot to write notes even. I'm sorry I went to bed early and ignored calls after nine o'clock. I'm sorry for my six o'clock emails.

I also want to thank the designers for the title pages. Thank you for all your hard work on the covers as well. Sorry if I made things hard. (As a result, one of the characters on the original volume 12 cover was squashed. Here she is. ↙)

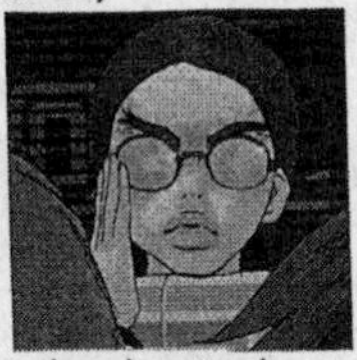

It doesn't matter how many years have passed. I still can't draw well. The bodies are always out of proportion. I'm sorry you had to tell me!

The room I'm sitting in is too cold, so I'm sorry if my handwriting is difficult to read!

Sorry again and thank you! I have so much to say!

Thank you so much!!

One last big thank you!

I'm sure we'll meet again. I hope there will be an announcement for my readers soon!

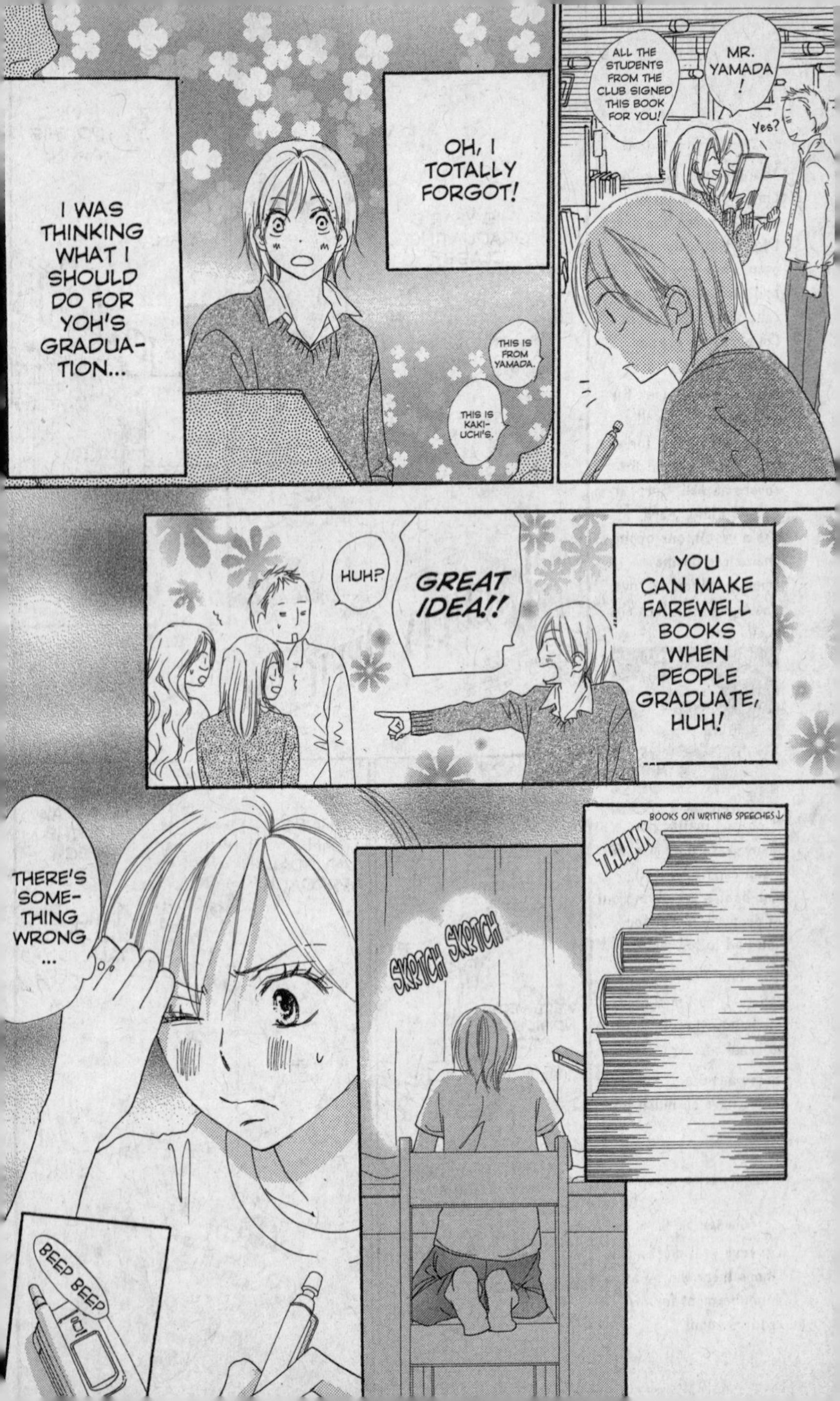

MR. YAMADA!
ALL THE STUDENTS FROM THE CLUB SIGNED THIS BOOK FOR YOU!
Yes?
OH, I TOTALLY FORGOT!
THIS IS FROM YAMADA.
THIS IS KAKI-UCHI'S.
I WAS THINKING WHAT I SHOULD DO FOR YOH'S GRADUA-TION...
YOU CAN MAKE FAREWELL BOOKS WHEN PEOPLE GRADUATE, HUH!
GREAT IDEA!!
HUH?
BOOKS ON WRITING SPEECHES↓
THUNK
SKRTCH SKRTCH
THERE'S SOME-THING WRONG ...
BEEP BEEP

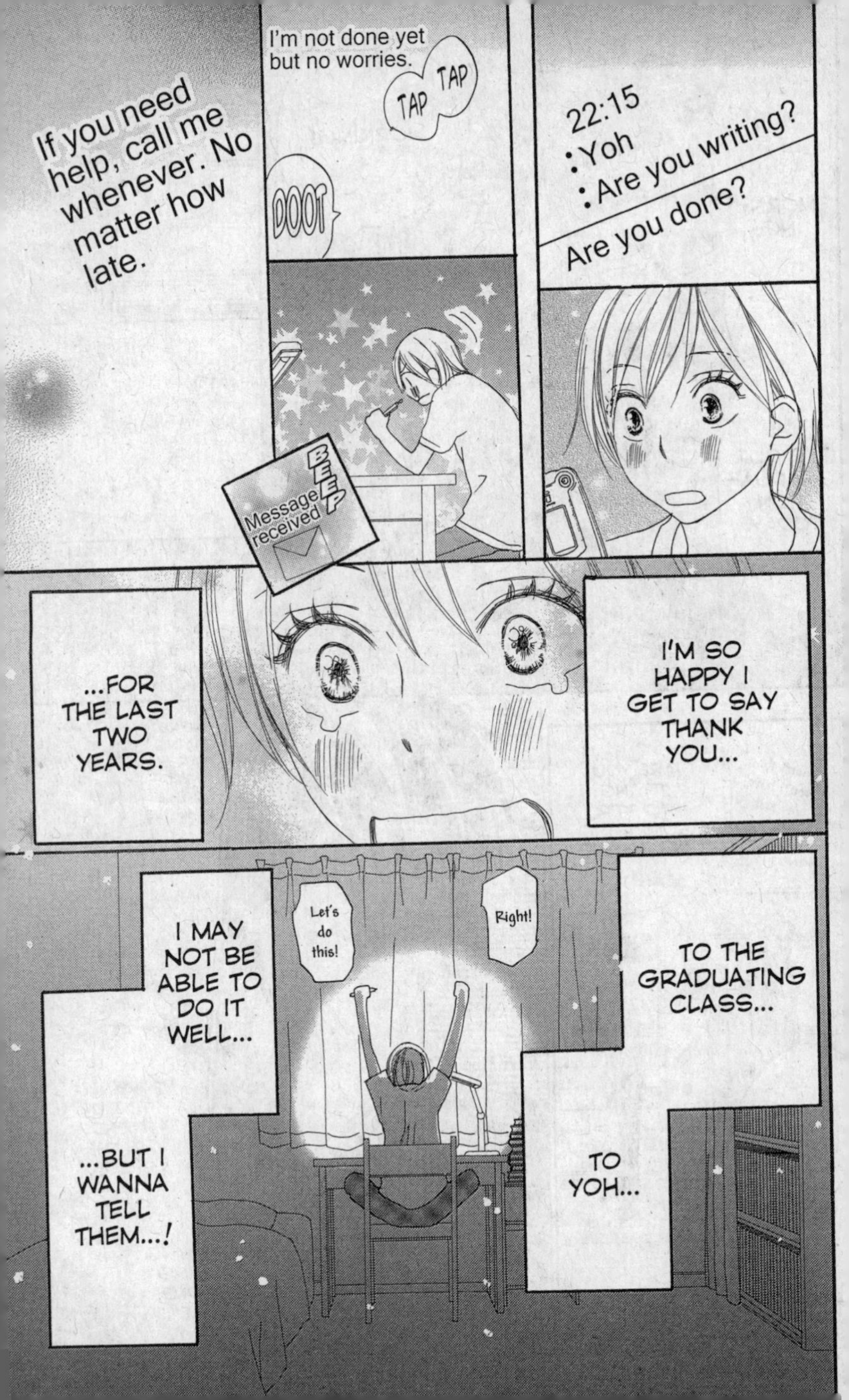
22:15
•Yoh
•Are you writing?
Are you done?
I'm not done yet but no worries.
TAP TAP TAP
DOOT
If you need help, call me whenever. No matter how late.
BEEP
Message received
I'M SO HAPPY I GET TO SAY THANK YOU...
...FOR THE LAST TWO YEARS.
TO THE GRADUATING CLASS...
Right!
Let's do this!
I MAY NOT BE ABLE TO DO IT WELL...
TO YOH...
...BUT I WANNA TELL THEM...!

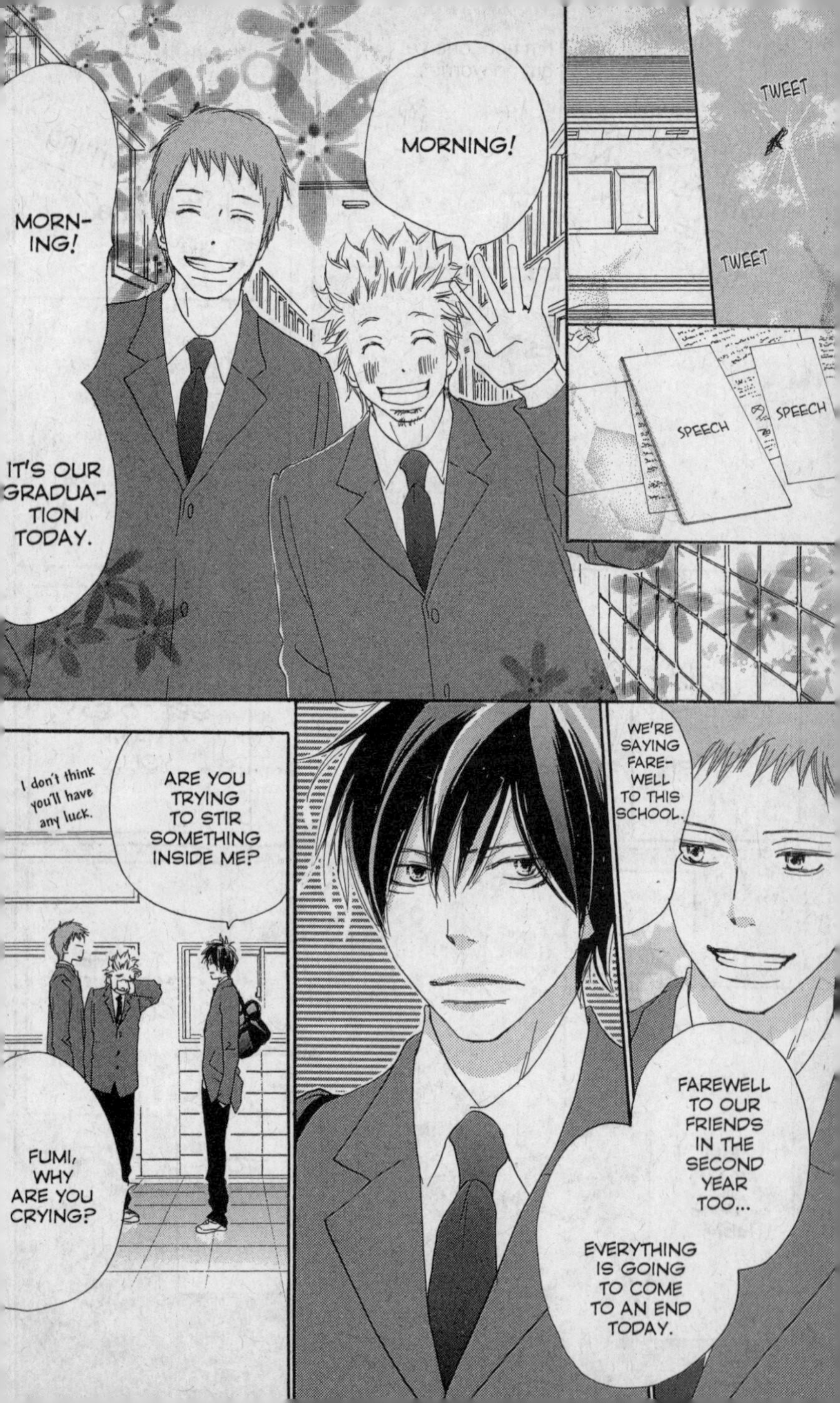
TWEET
TWEET
SPEECH
SPEECH
MORNING!
MORNING!
IT'S OUR GRADUATION TODAY.
WE'RE SAYING FAREWELL TO THIS SCHOOL.
FAREWELL TO OUR FRIENDS IN THE SECOND YEAR TOO...
EVERYTHING IS GOING TO COME TO AN END TODAY.
ARE YOU TRYING TO STIR SOMETHING INSIDE ME?
I don't think you'll have any luck.
FUMI, WHY ARE YOU CRYING?

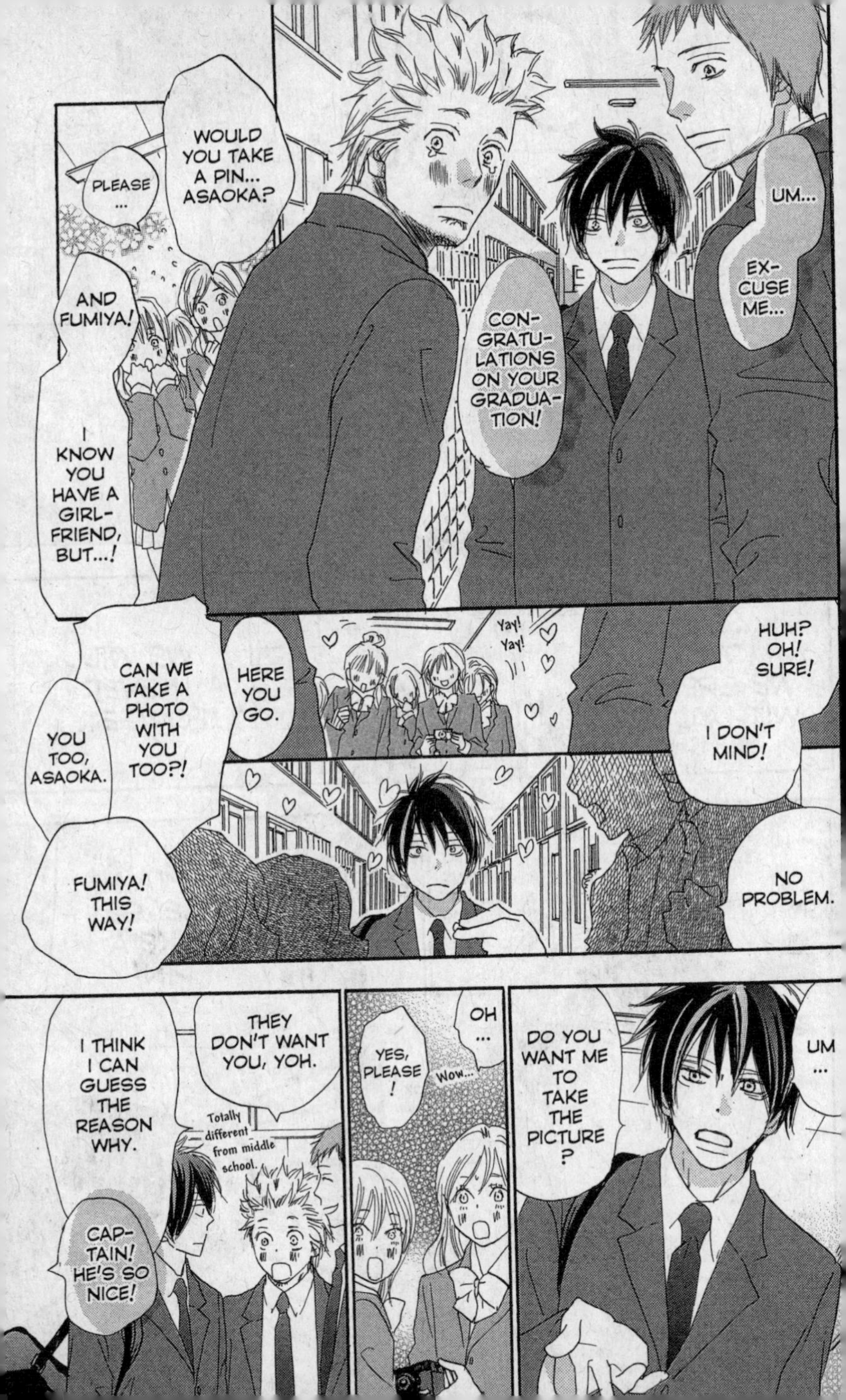
UM...
EXCUSE ME...
CONGRATULATIONS ON YOUR GRADUATION!
WOULD YOU TAKE A PIN... ASAOKA?
PLEASE ...
AND FUMIYA!
I KNOW YOU HAVE A GIRLFRIEND, BUT...!
HUH? OH! SURE!
I DON'T MIND!
Yay! Yay!
HERE YOU GO.
CAN WE TAKE A PHOTO WITH YOU TOO?!
YOU TOO, ASAOKA.
NO PROBLEM.
FUMIYA! THIS WAY!
UM ...
DO YOU WANT ME TO TAKE THE PICTURE?
OH ...
Wow...
YES, PLEASE!
THEY DON'T WANT YOU, YOH.
I THINK I CAN GUESS THE REASON WHY.
Totally different from middle school.
CAPTAIN! HE'S SO NICE!

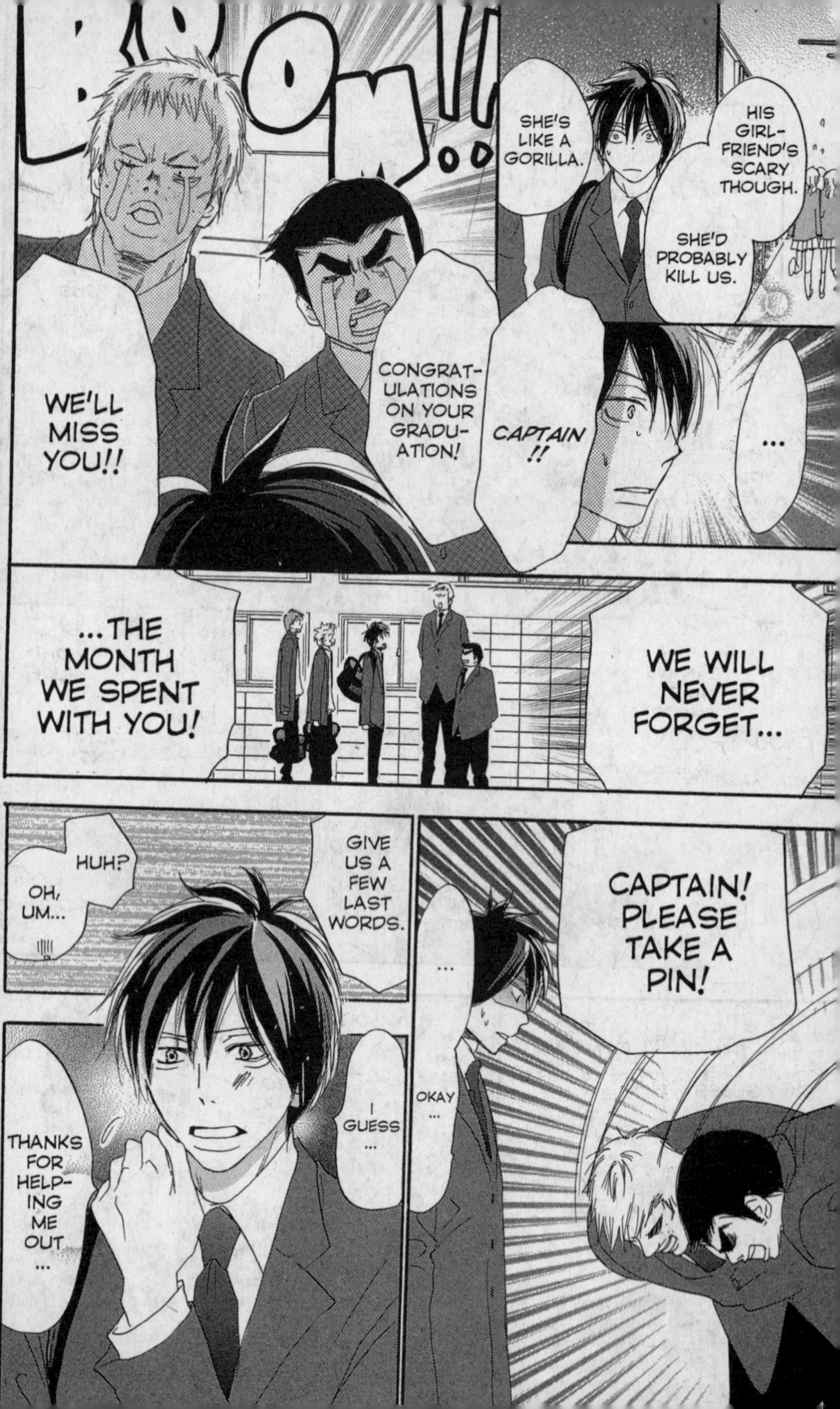
HIS GIRLFRIEND'S SCARY THOUGH.
SHE'D PROBABLY KILL US.
SHE'S LIKE A GORILLA.
...
CAPTAIN!!
BOOM!!
CONGRATULATIONS ON YOUR GRADUATION!
WE'LL MISS YOU!!
WE WILL NEVER FORGET...
...THE MONTH WE SPENT WITH YOU!
CAPTAIN! PLEASE TAKE A PIN!
...
OKAY...
GIVE US A FEW LAST WORDS.
HUH?
OH, UM...
I GUESS...
THANKS FOR HELPING ME OUT...

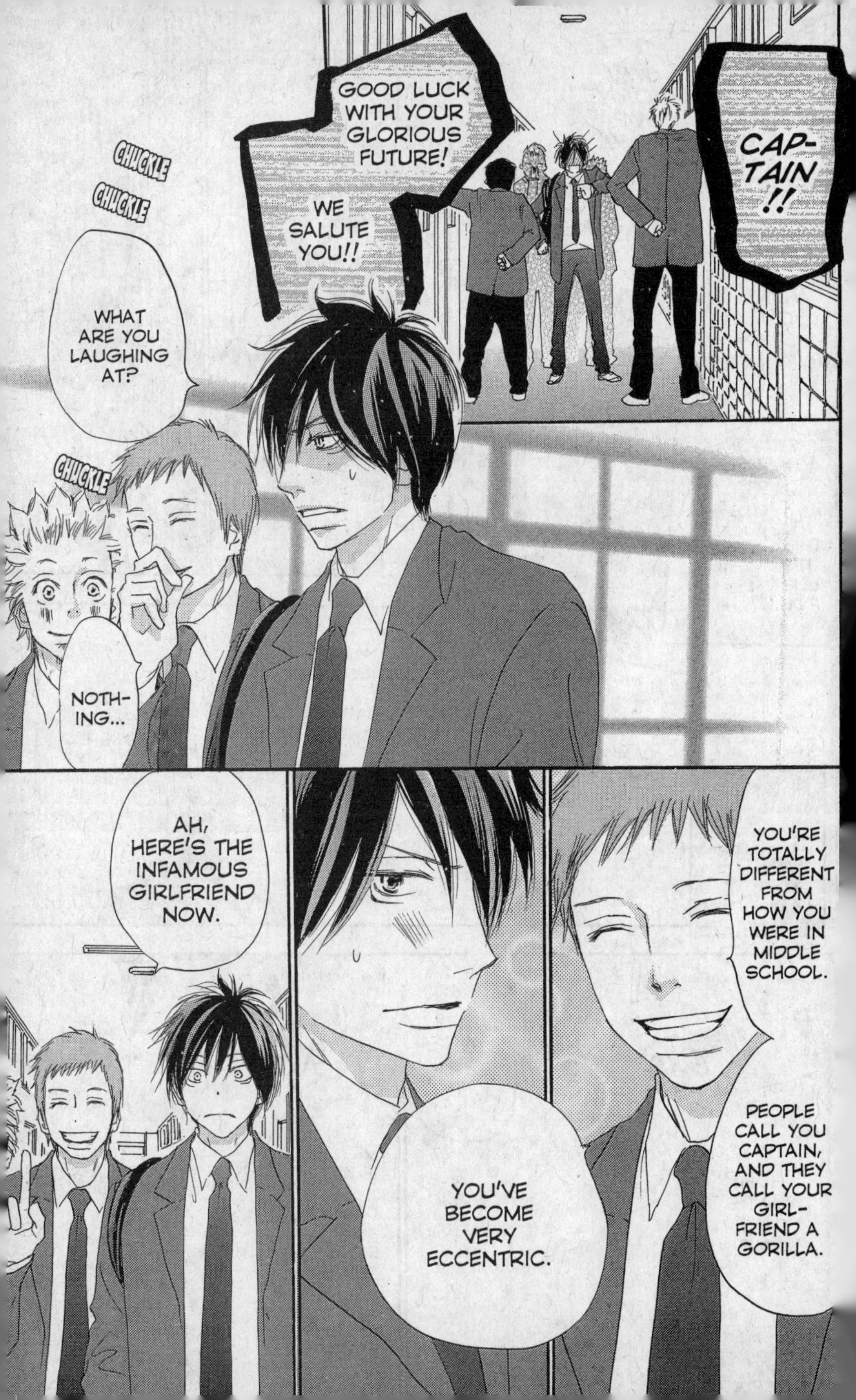
CAP-TAIN!!
GOOD LUCK WITH YOUR GLORIOUS FUTURE!
WE SALUTE YOU!!
CHUCKLE
CHUCKLE
WHAT ARE YOU LAUGHING AT?
CHUCKLE
NOTH-ING...
YOU'RE TOTALLY DIFFERENT FROM HOW YOU WERE IN MIDDLE SCHOOL.
PEOPLE CALL YOU CAPTAIN, AND THEY CALL YOUR GIRL-FRIEND A GORILLA.
YOU'VE BECOME VERY ECCENTRIC.
AH, HERE'S THE INFAMOUS GIRLFRIEND NOW.

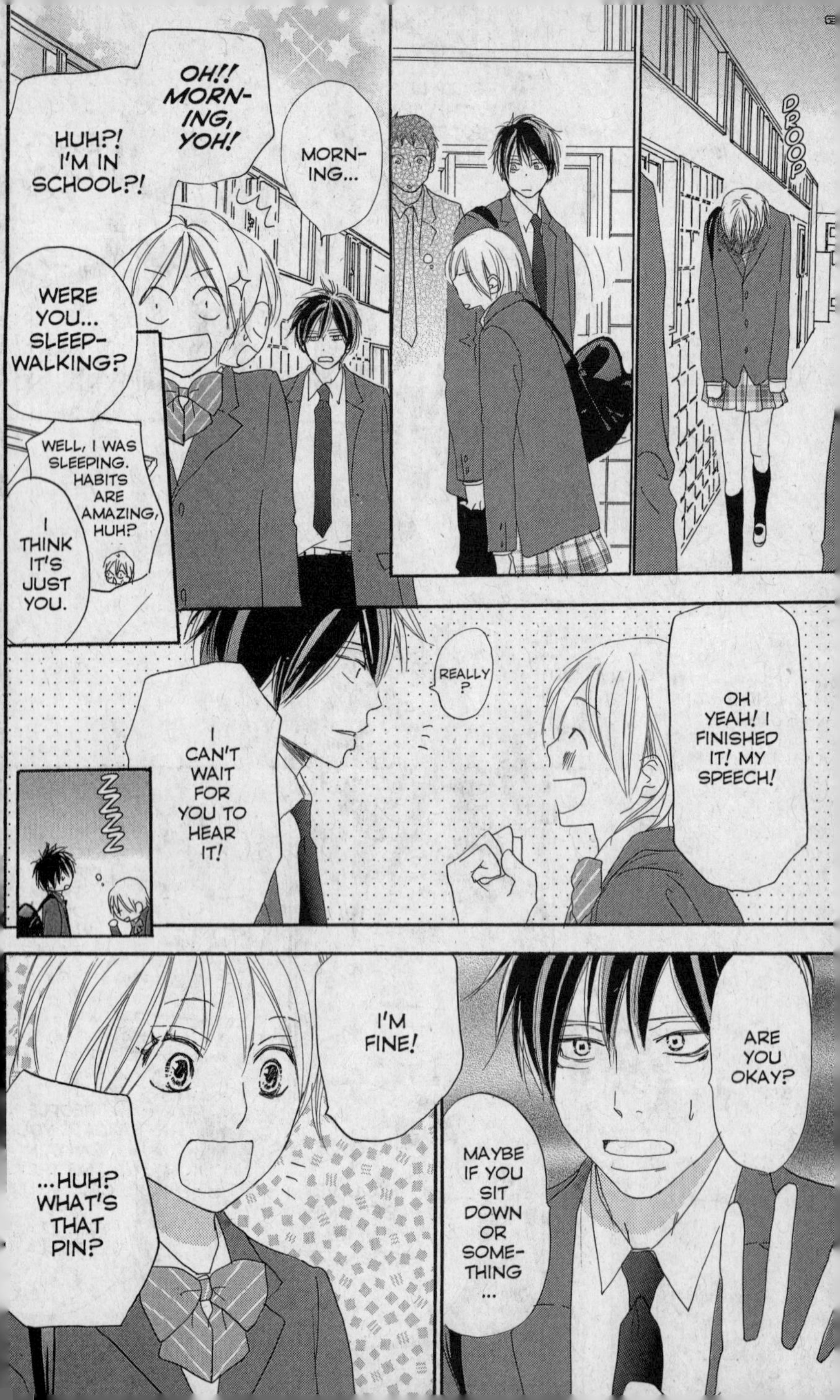
DROOP
OH!! MORN-ING, YOH!
MORN-ING...
HUH?! I'M IN SCHOOL?!
WERE YOU... SLEEP-WALKING?
WELL, I WAS SLEEPING. HABITS ARE AMAZING, HUH?
I THINK IT'S JUST YOU.
OH YEAH! I FINISHED IT! MY SPEECH!
REALLY?
I CAN'T WAIT FOR YOU TO HEAR IT!
ZZZZ
ARE YOU OKAY?
MAYBE IF YOU SIT DOWN OR SOME-THING...
I'M FINE!
...HUH? WHAT'S THAT PIN?

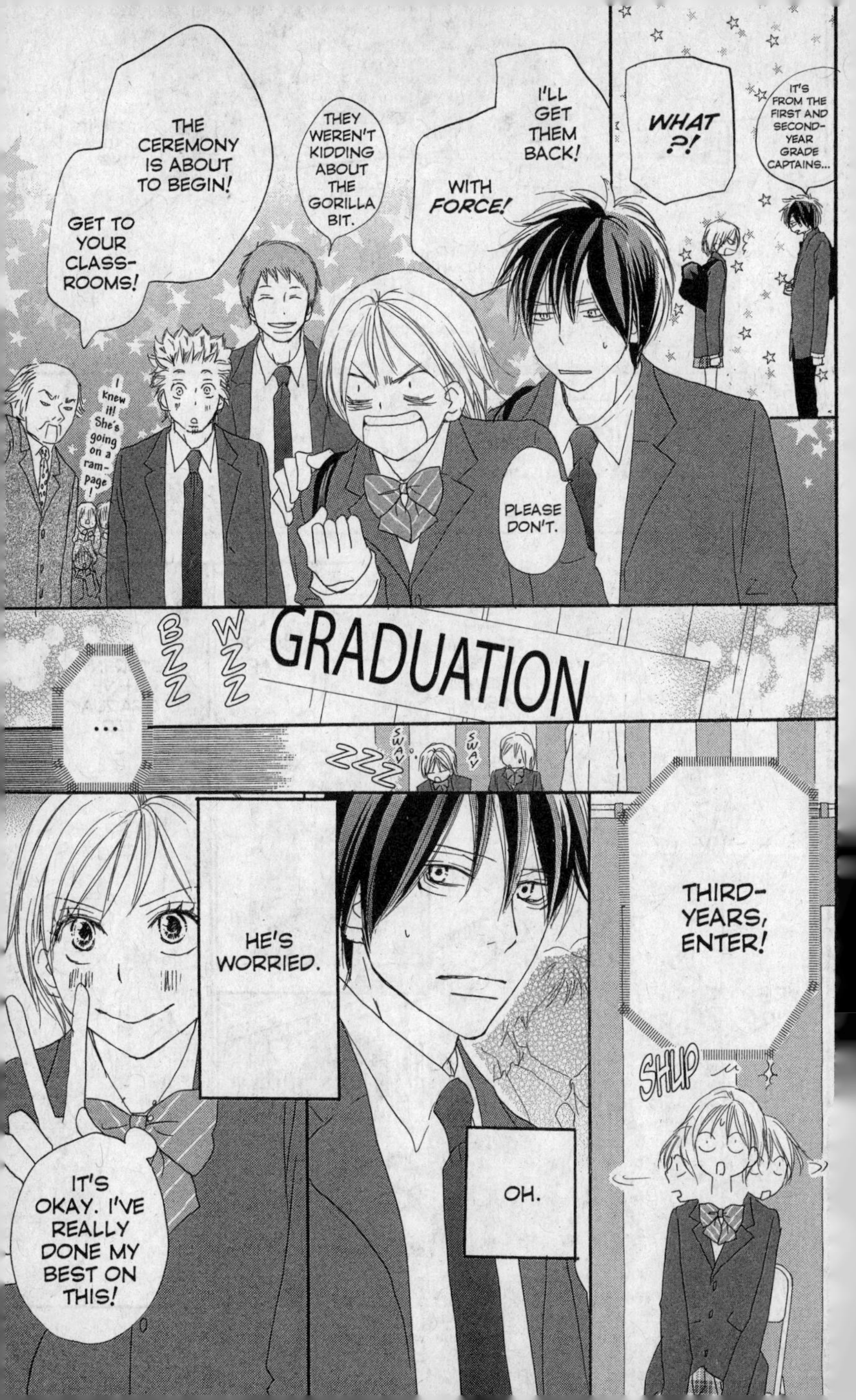
IT'S FROM THE FIRST AND SECOND-YEAR GRADE CAPTAINS...
WHAT ?!
I'LL GET THEM BACK! WITH FORCE!
THEY WEREN'T KIDDING ABOUT THE GORILLA BIT.
THE CEREMONY IS ABOUT TO BEGIN! GET TO YOUR CLASS-ROOMS!
PLEASE DON'T.
I knew it! She's going on a ram-page!
GRADUATION
WZZ
BZZ
...
SWAY
SWAY
ZZZ
THIRD-YEARS, ENTER!
SHUP
OH.
HE'S WORRIED.
IT'S OKAY. I'VE REALLY DONE MY BEST ON THIS!

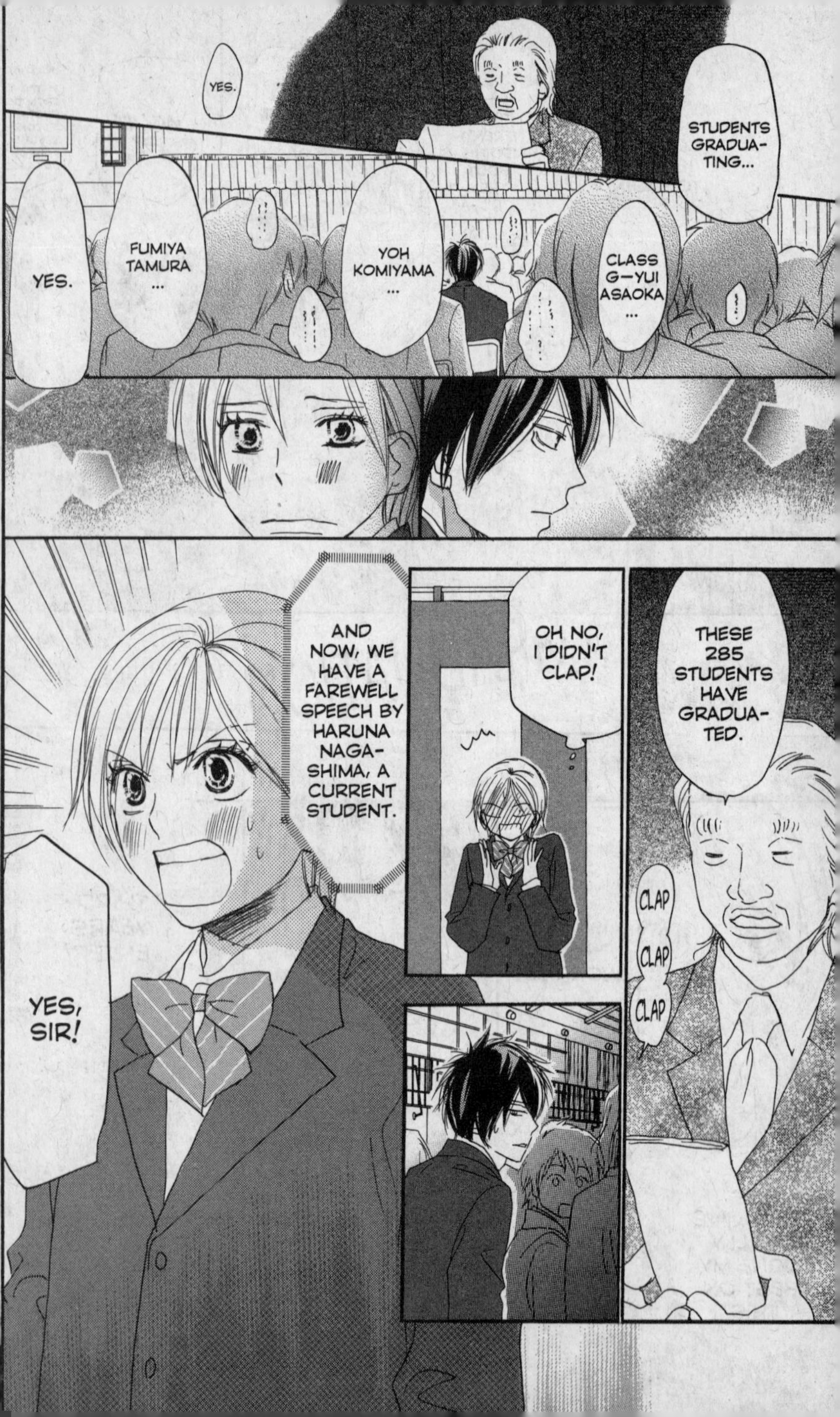
STUDENTS GRADUATING...
YES.
CLASS G—YUI ASAOKA...
YOH KOMIYAMA...
FUMIYA TAMURA...
YES.
THESE 285 STUDENTS HAVE GRADUATED.
CLAP
CLAP
CLAP
OH NO, I DIDN'T CLAP!
AND NOW, WE HAVE A FAREWELL SPEECH BY HARUNA NAGASHIMA, A CURRENT STUDENT.
YES, SIR!

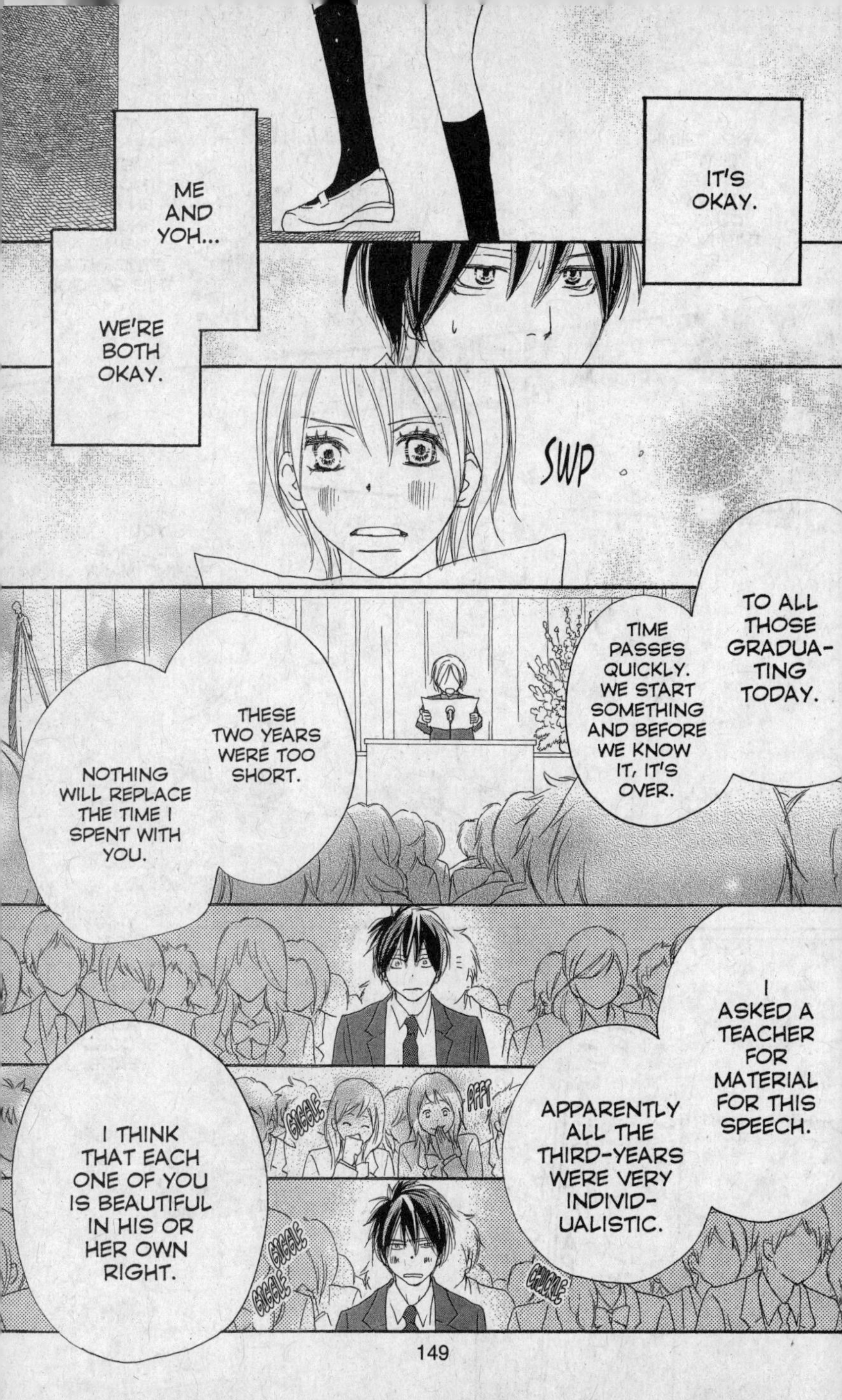

IT'S OKAY.
ME AND YOH...
WE'RE BOTH OKAY.
SWP
TO ALL THOSE GRADUATING TODAY.
TIME PASSES QUICKLY. WE START SOMETHING AND BEFORE WE KNOW IT, IT'S OVER.
THESE TWO YEARS WERE TOO SHORT.
NOTHING WILL REPLACE THE TIME I SPENT WITH YOU.
I ASKED A TEACHER FOR MATERIAL FOR THIS SPEECH.
APPARENTLY ALL THE THIRD-YEARS WERE VERY INDIVIDUALISTIC.
PFFT
GIGGLE
I THINK THAT EACH ONE OF YOU IS BEAUTIFUL IN HIS OR HER OWN RIGHT.
CHUCKLE
GIGGLE
GIGGLE

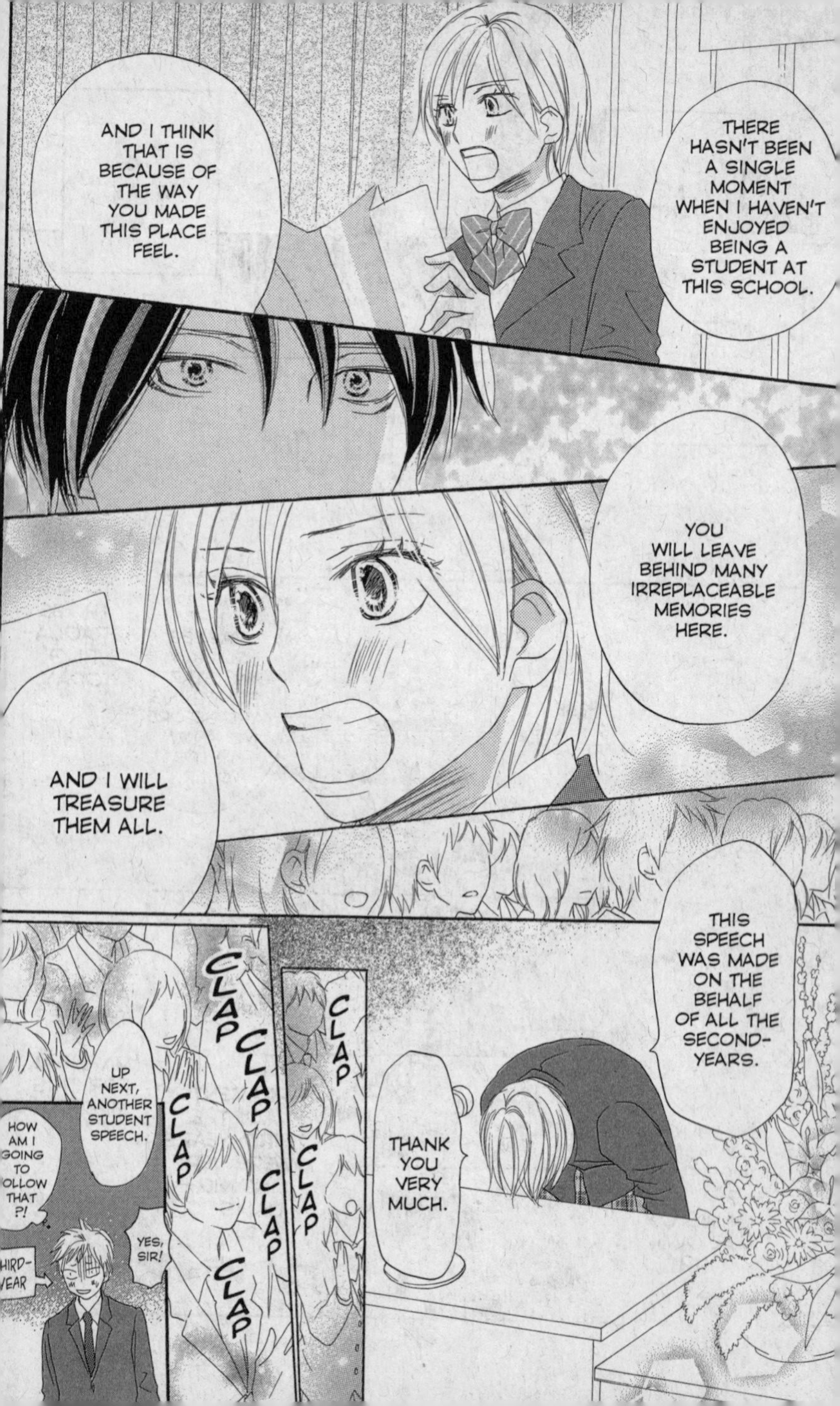
THERE HASN'T BEEN A SINGLE MOMENT WHEN I HAVEN'T ENJOYED BEING A STUDENT AT THIS SCHOOL.
AND I THINK THAT IS BECAUSE OF THE WAY YOU MADE THIS PLACE FEEL.
YOU WILL LEAVE BEHIND MANY IRREPLACEABLE MEMORIES HERE.
AND I WILL TREASURE THEM ALL.
THIS SPEECH WAS MADE ON THE BEHALF OF ALL THE SECOND-YEARS.
THANK YOU VERY MUCH.
CLAP CLAP
CLAP CLAP
CLAP CLAP CLAP CLAP
UP NEXT, ANOTHER STUDENT SPEECH.
YES, SIR!
HOW AM I GOING TO OLLOW THAT?!
HIRD-YEAR

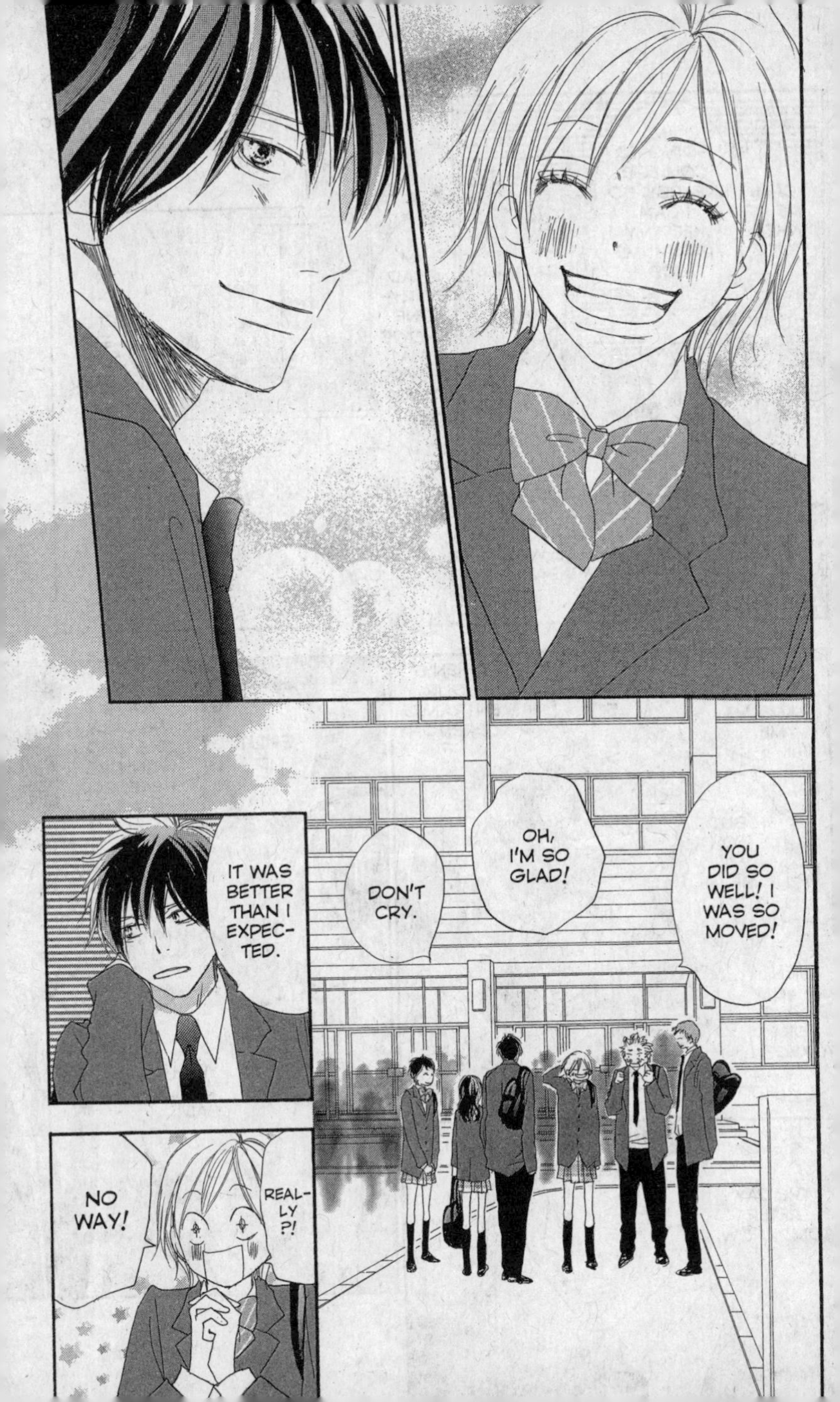
YOU DID SO WELL! I WAS SO MOVED!
OH, I'M SO GLAD!
DON'T CRY.
IT WAS BETTER THAN I EXPECTED.
REALLY?!
NO WAY!

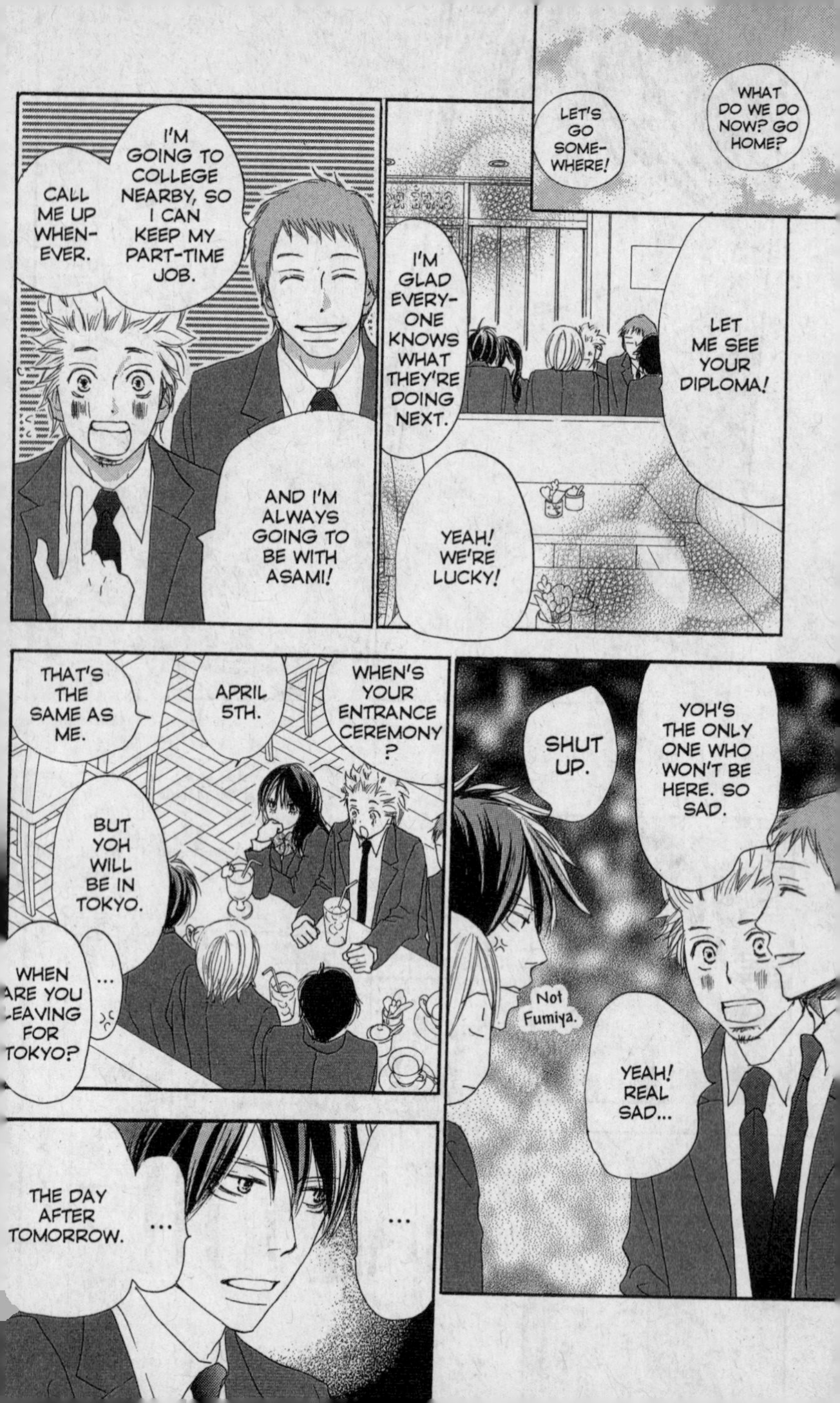

WHAT DO WE DO NOW? GO HOME?
LET'S GO SOME-WHERE!
LET ME SEE YOUR DIPLOMA!
I'M GLAD EVERY-ONE KNOWS WHAT THEY'RE DOING NEXT.
YEAH! WE'RE LUCKY!
I'M GOING TO COLLEGE NEARBY, SO I CAN KEEP MY PART-TIME JOB.
CALL ME UP WHEN-EVER.
AND I'M ALWAYS GOING TO BE WITH ASAMI!
YOH'S THE ONLY ONE WHO WON'T BE HERE. SO SAD.
SHUT UP.
Not Fumiya.
YEAH! REAL SAD...
WHEN'S YOUR ENTRANCE CEREMONY?
APRIL 5TH.
THAT'S THE SAME AS ME.
BUT YOH WILL BE IN TOKYO.
...
WHEN ARE YOU LEAVING FOR TOKYO?
...
...
THE DAY AFTER TOMORROW.

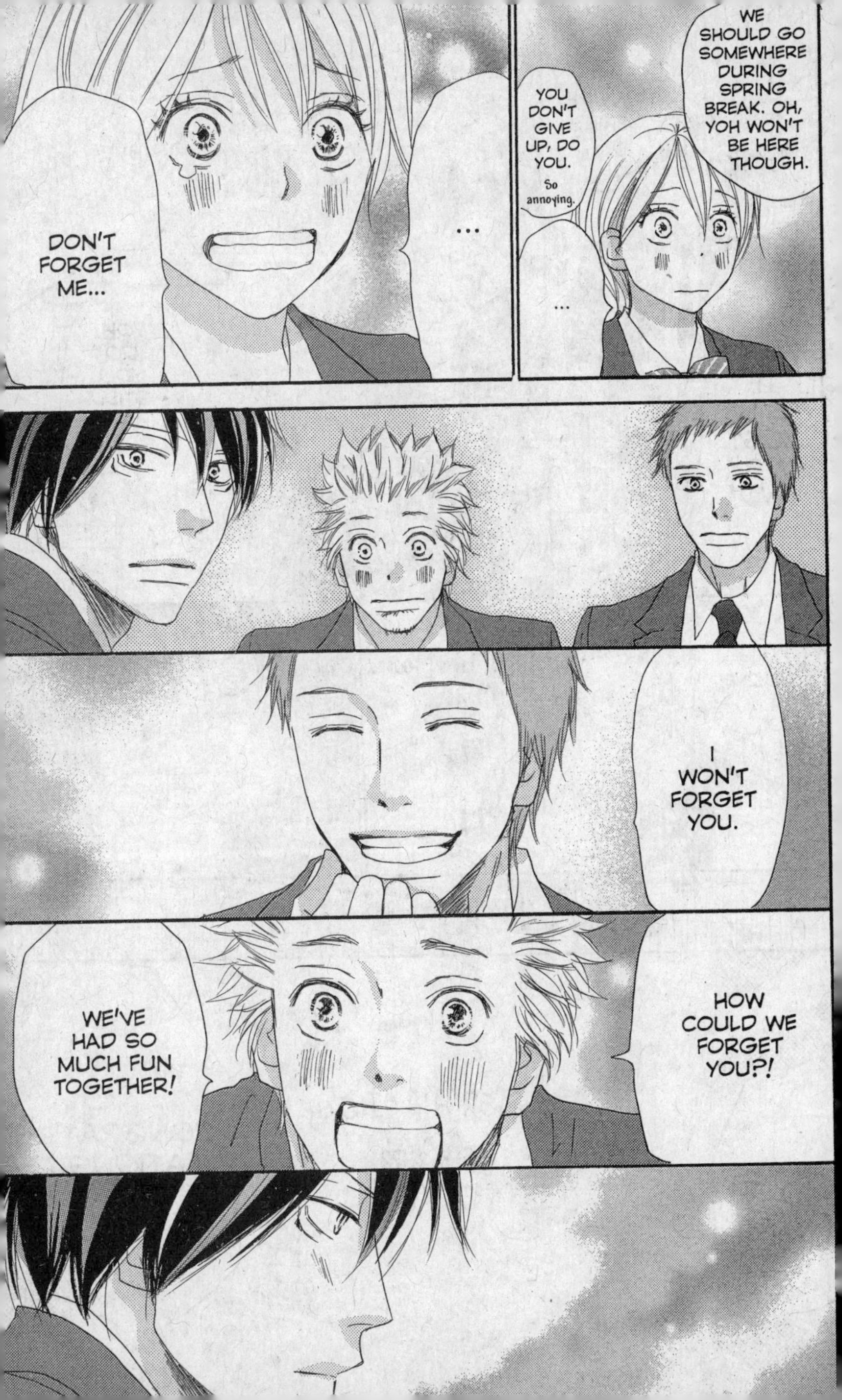
WE SHOULD GO SOMEWHERE DURING SPRING BREAK. OH, YOH WON'T BE HERE THOUGH.
YOU DON'T GIVE UP, DO YOU.
So annoying.
...
...
DON'T FORGET ME...
I WON'T FORGET YOU.
HOW COULD WE FORGET YOU?!
WE'VE HAD SO MUCH FUN TOGETHER!

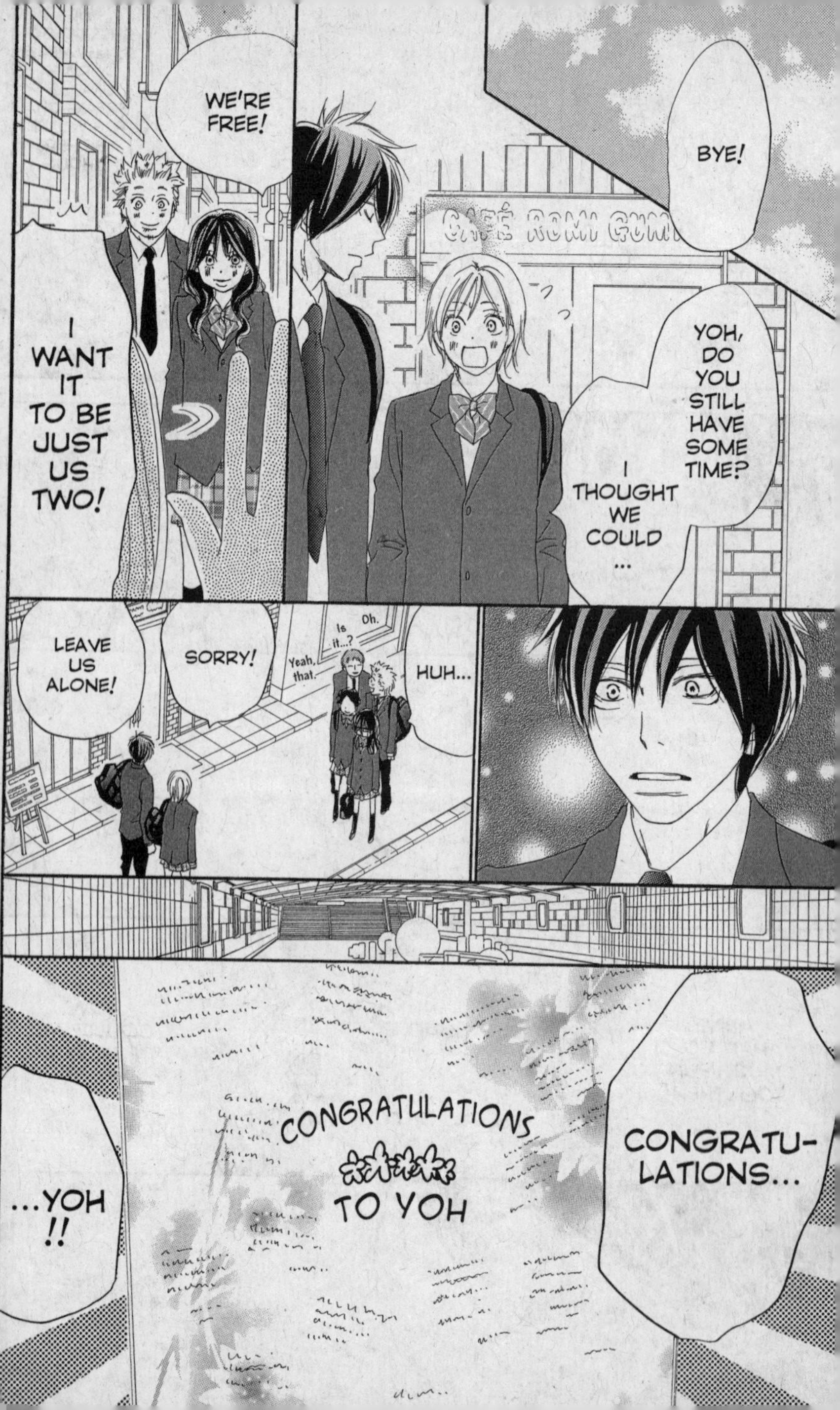
BYE!
YOH, DO YOU STILL HAVE SOME TIME?
I THOUGHT WE COULD...
WE'RE FREE!
I WANT IT TO BE JUST US TWO!
HUH...
Oh.
Is it...?
Yeah, that.
SORRY!
LEAVE US ALONE!
CONGRATU-LATIONS...
CONGRATULATIONS TO YOH
...YOH !!

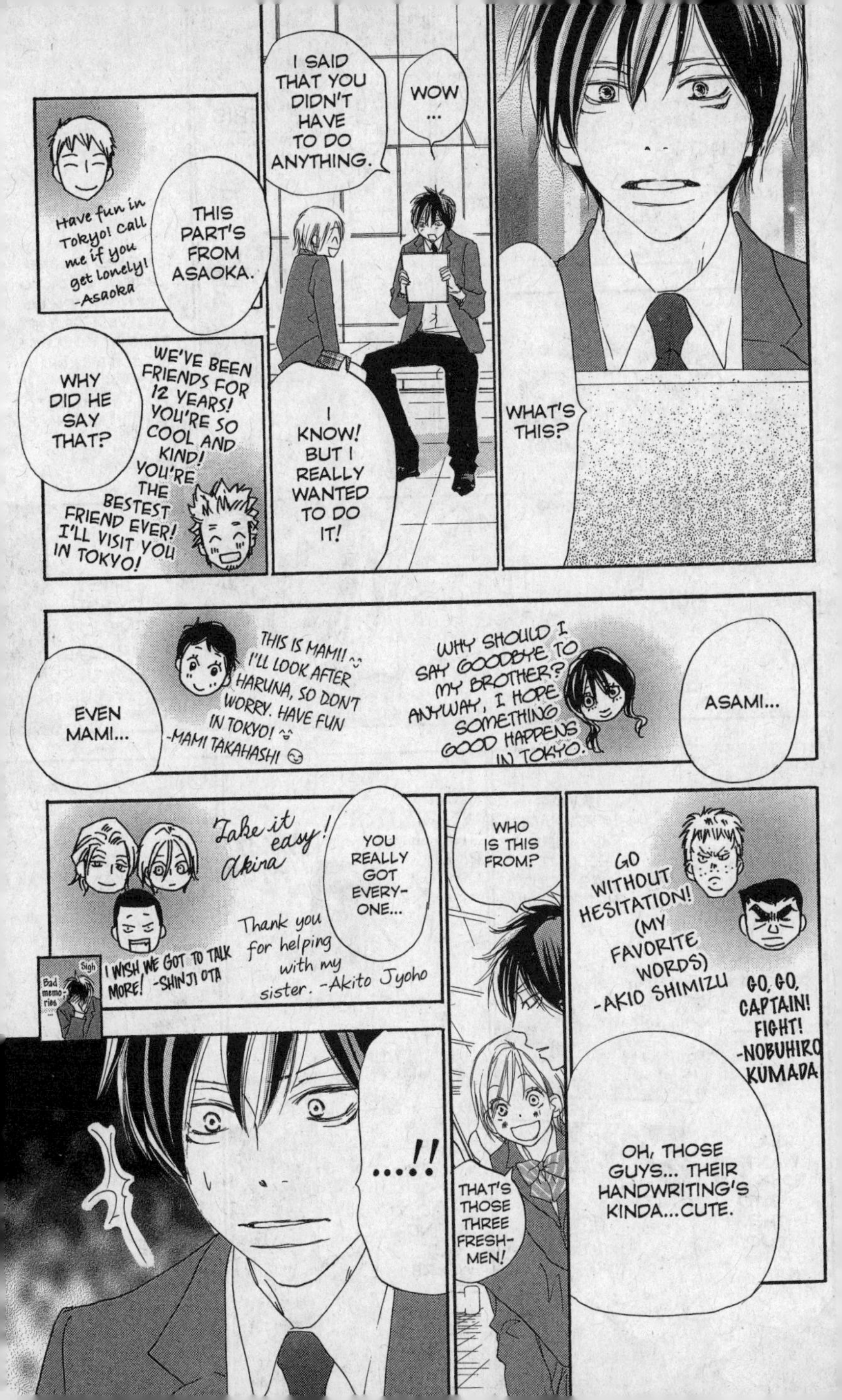
WHAT'S THIS?
WOW...
I SAID THAT YOU DIDN'T HAVE TO DO ANYTHING.
I KNOW! BUT I REALLY WANTED TO DO IT!
THIS PART'S FROM ASAOKA.
Have fun in Tokyo! Call me if you get lonely! -Asaoka
WHY DID HE SAY THAT?
WE'VE BEEN FRIENDS FOR 12 YEARS! YOU'RE SO COOL AND KIND! YOU'RE THE BESTEST FRIEND EVER! I'LL VISIT YOU IN TOKYO!
ASAMI...
WHY SHOULD I SAY GOODBYE TO MY BROTHER? ANYWAY, I HOPE SOMETHING GOOD HAPPENS IN TOKYO.
THIS IS MAMI! I'LL LOOK AFTER HARUNA, SO DON'T WORRY. HAVE FUN IN TOKYO! -MAMI TAKAHASHI
EVEN MAMI...
GO WITHOUT HESITATION! (MY FAVORITE WORDS) -AKIO SHIMIZU
GO, GO, CAPTAIN! FIGHT! -NOBUHIRO KUMADA
WHO IS THIS FROM?
THAT'S THOSE THREE FRESHMEN!
OH, THOSE GUYS... THEIR HANDWRITING'S KINDA...CUTE.
YOU REALLY GOT EVERYONE...
Take it easy! Akira
Thank you for helping with my sister. -Akito Jyoho
I WISH WE GOT TO TALK MORE! -SHINJI OTA
Sigh
Bad memories...
...!!

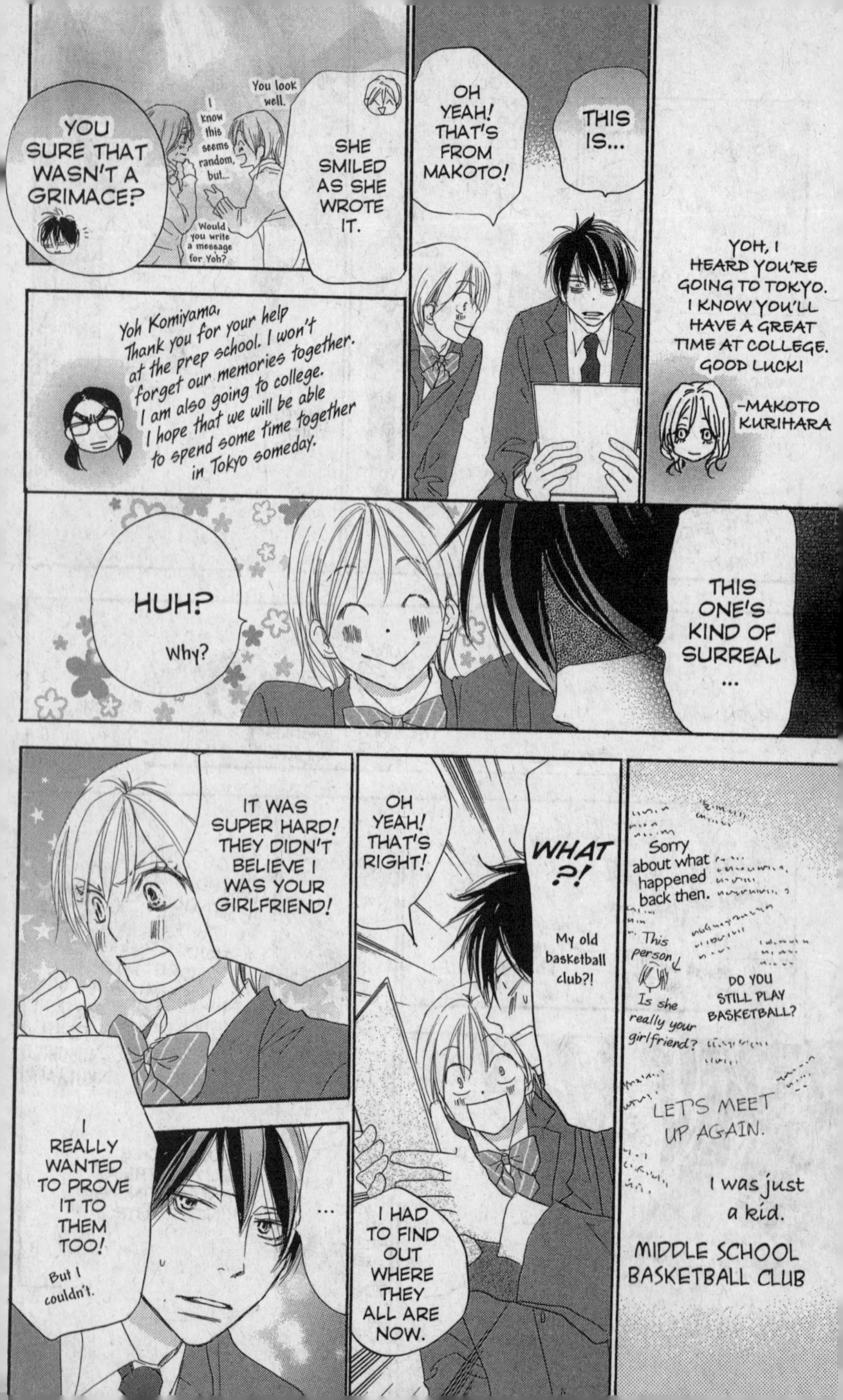
THIS IS...
YOH, I HEARD YOU'RE GOING TO TOKYO. I KNOW YOU'LL HAVE A GREAT TIME AT COLLEGE. GOOD LUCK!
-MAKOTO KURIHARA
OH YEAH! THAT'S FROM MAKOTO!
SHE SMILED AS SHE WROTE IT.
You look well.
I know this seems random, but...
Would you write a message for Yoh?
YOU SURE THAT WASN'T A GRIMACE?
Yoh Komiyama,
Thank you for your help at the prep school. I won't forget our memories together. I am also going to college. I hope that we will be able to spend some time together in Tokyo someday.
THIS ONE'S KIND OF SURREAL ...
HUH?
Why?
Sorry about what happened back then.
This person
Is she really your girlfriend?
DO YOU STILL PLAY BASKETBALL?
LET'S MEET UP AGAIN.
I was just a kid.
MIDDLE SCHOOL BASKETBALL CLUB
WHAT ?!
My old basketball club?!
OH YEAH! THAT'S RIGHT!
I HAD TO FIND OUT WHERE THEY ALL ARE NOW.
IT WAS SUPER HARD! THEY DIDN'T BELIEVE I WAS YOUR GIRLFRIEND!
I REALLY WANTED TO PROVE IT TO THEM TOO!
But I couldn't.
...

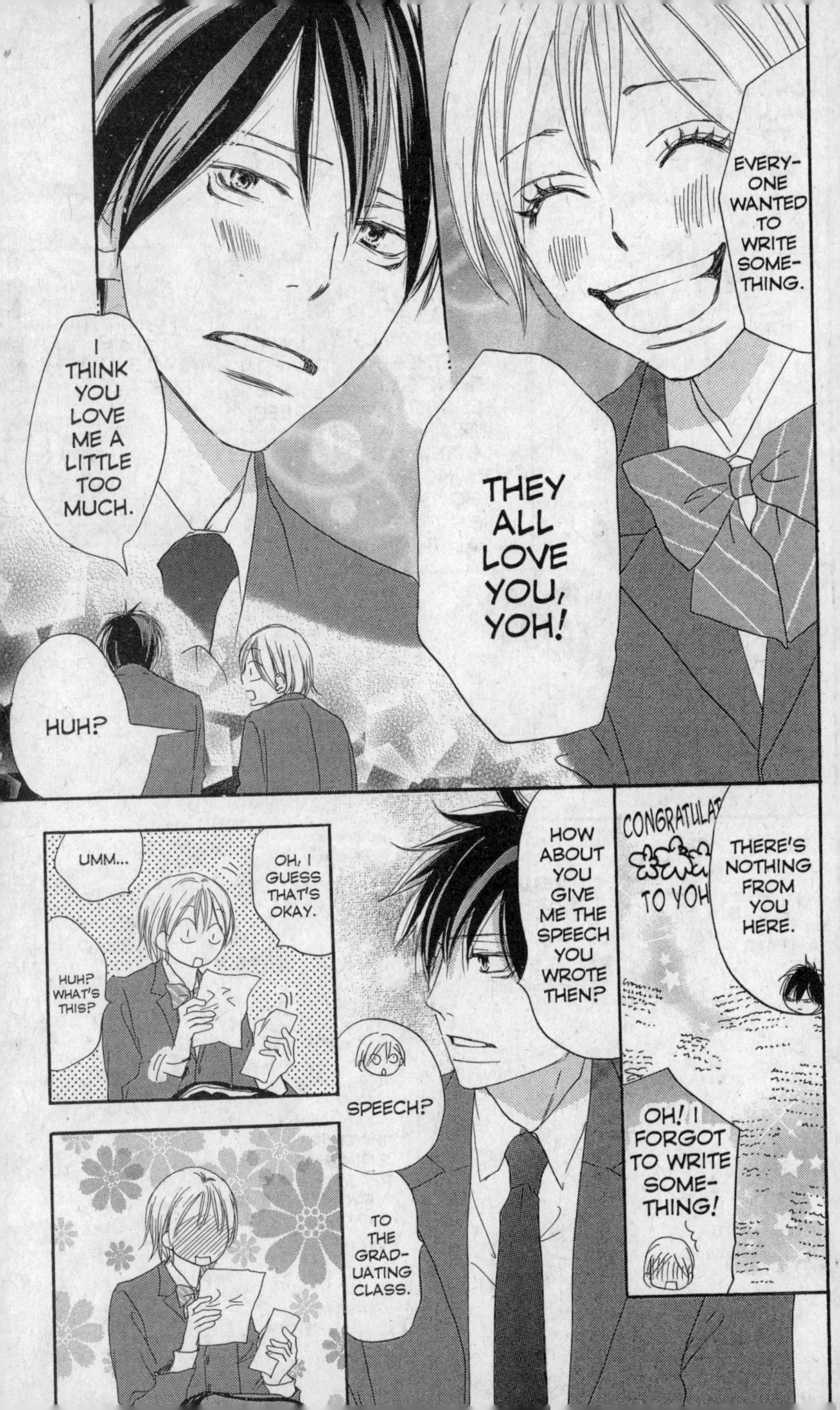
EVERYONE WANTED TO WRITE SOMETHING.
THEY ALL LOVE YOU, YOH!
I THINK YOU LOVE ME A LITTLE TOO MUCH.
HUH?
TO YOH
THERE'S NOTHING FROM YOU HERE.
OH! I FORGOT TO WRITE SOMETHING!
HOW ABOUT YOU GIVE ME THE SPEECH YOU WROTE THEN?
SPEECH?
TO THE GRADUATING CLASS.
OH, I GUESS THAT'S OKAY.
UMM...
HUH? WHAT'S THIS?

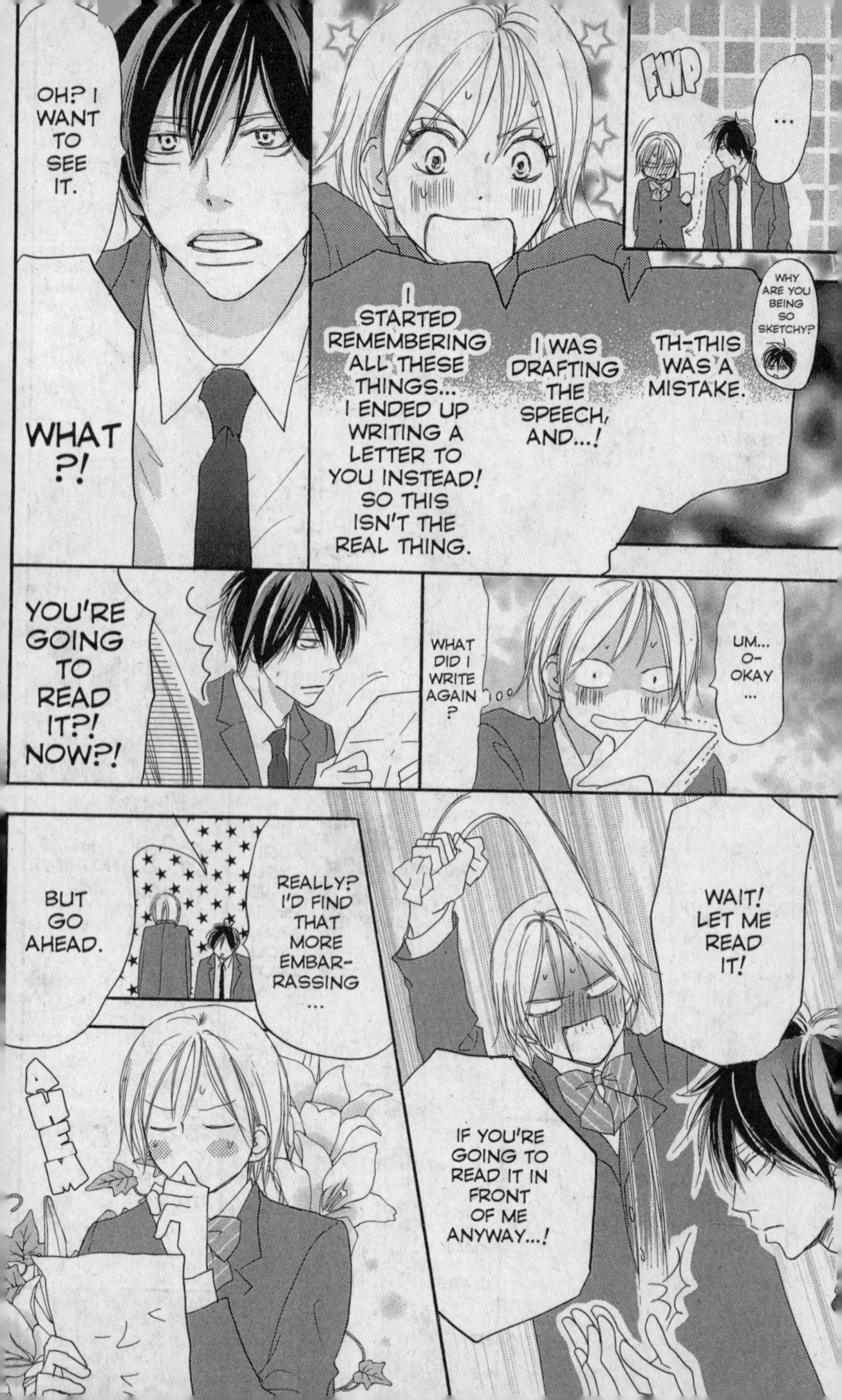
FWP
...
WHY ARE YOU BEING SO SKETCHY?
TH-THIS WAS A MISTAKE.
I WAS DRAFTING THE SPEECH, AND...!
I STARTED REMEMBERING ALL THESE THINGS... I ENDED UP WRITING A LETTER TO YOU INSTEAD! SO THIS ISN'T THE REAL THING.
OH? I WANT TO SEE IT.
WHAT?!
UM... O-OKAY...
WHAT DID I WRITE AGAIN?
YOU'RE GOING TO READ IT?! NOW?!
WAIT! LET ME READ IT!
IF YOU'RE GOING TO READ IT IN FRONT OF ME ANYWAY...!
REALLY? I'D FIND THAT MORE EMBARRASSING...
BUT GO AHEAD.
AHEM

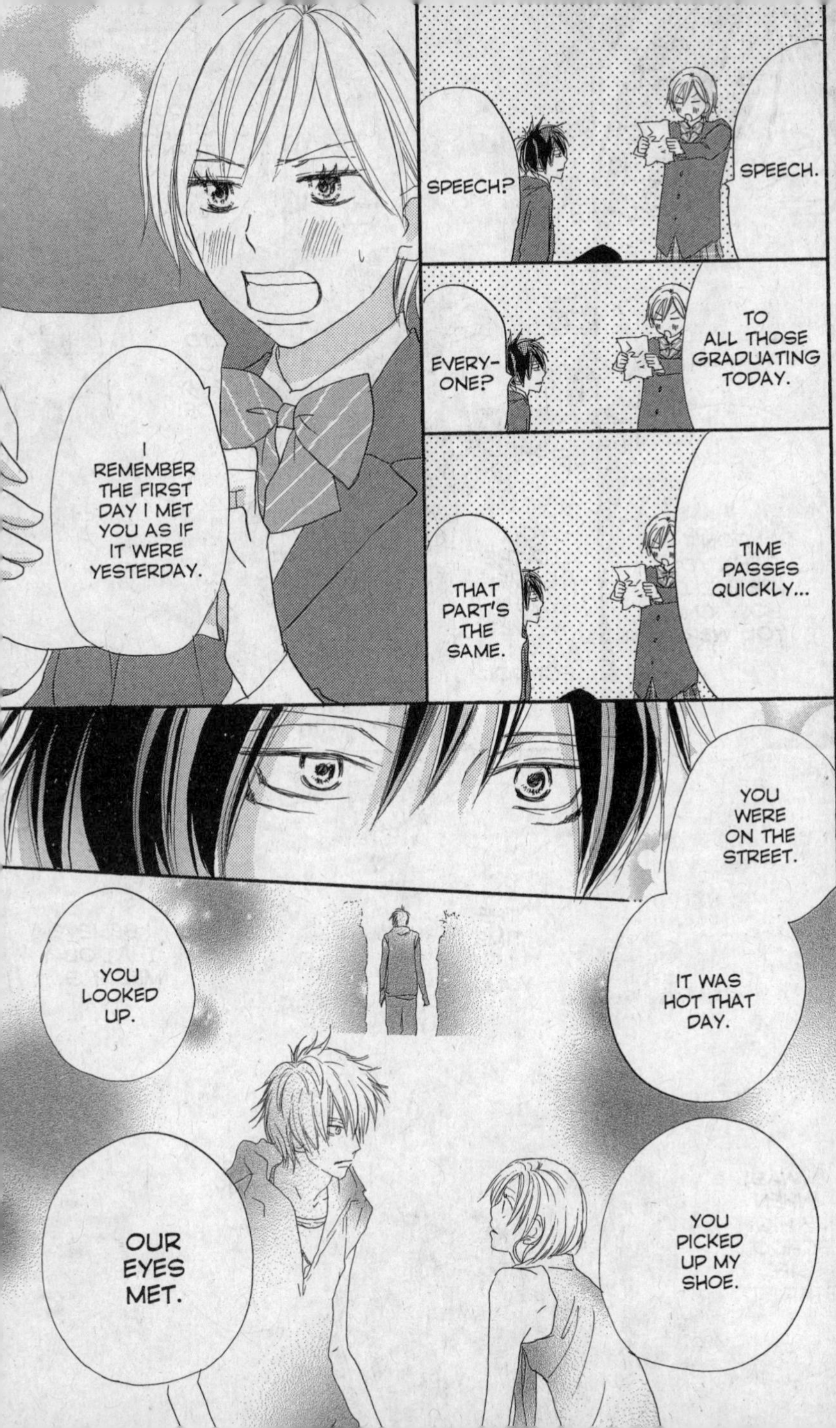
SPEECH.
SPEECH?
TO ALL THOSE GRADUATING TODAY.
EVERY-ONE?
TIME PASSES QUICKLY...
THAT PART'S THE SAME.
I REMEMBER THE FIRST DAY I MET YOU AS IF IT WERE YESTERDAY.
YOU WERE ON THE STREET.
IT WAS HOT THAT DAY.
YOU LOOKED UP.
YOU PICKED UP MY SHOE.
OUR EYES MET.

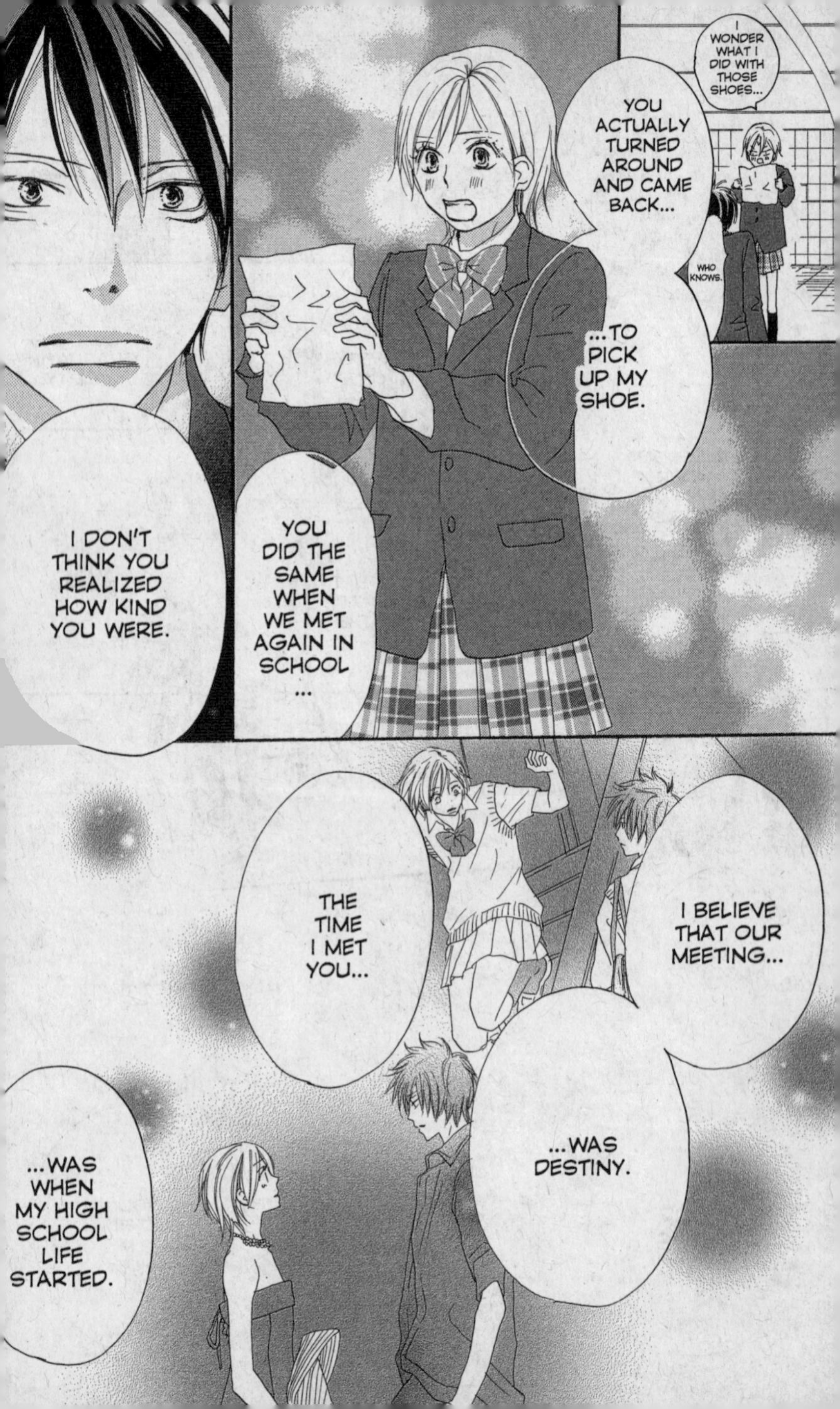
I WONDER WHAT I DID WITH THOSE SHOES...
WHO KNOWS.
YOU ACTUALLY TURNED AROUND AND CAME BACK...
...TO PICK UP MY SHOE.
YOU DID THE SAME WHEN WE MET AGAIN IN SCHOOL ...
I DON'T THINK YOU REALIZED HOW KIND YOU WERE.
I BELIEVE THAT OUR MEETING...
THE TIME I MET YOU...
...WAS DESTINY.
...WAS WHEN MY HIGH SCHOOL LIFE STARTED.

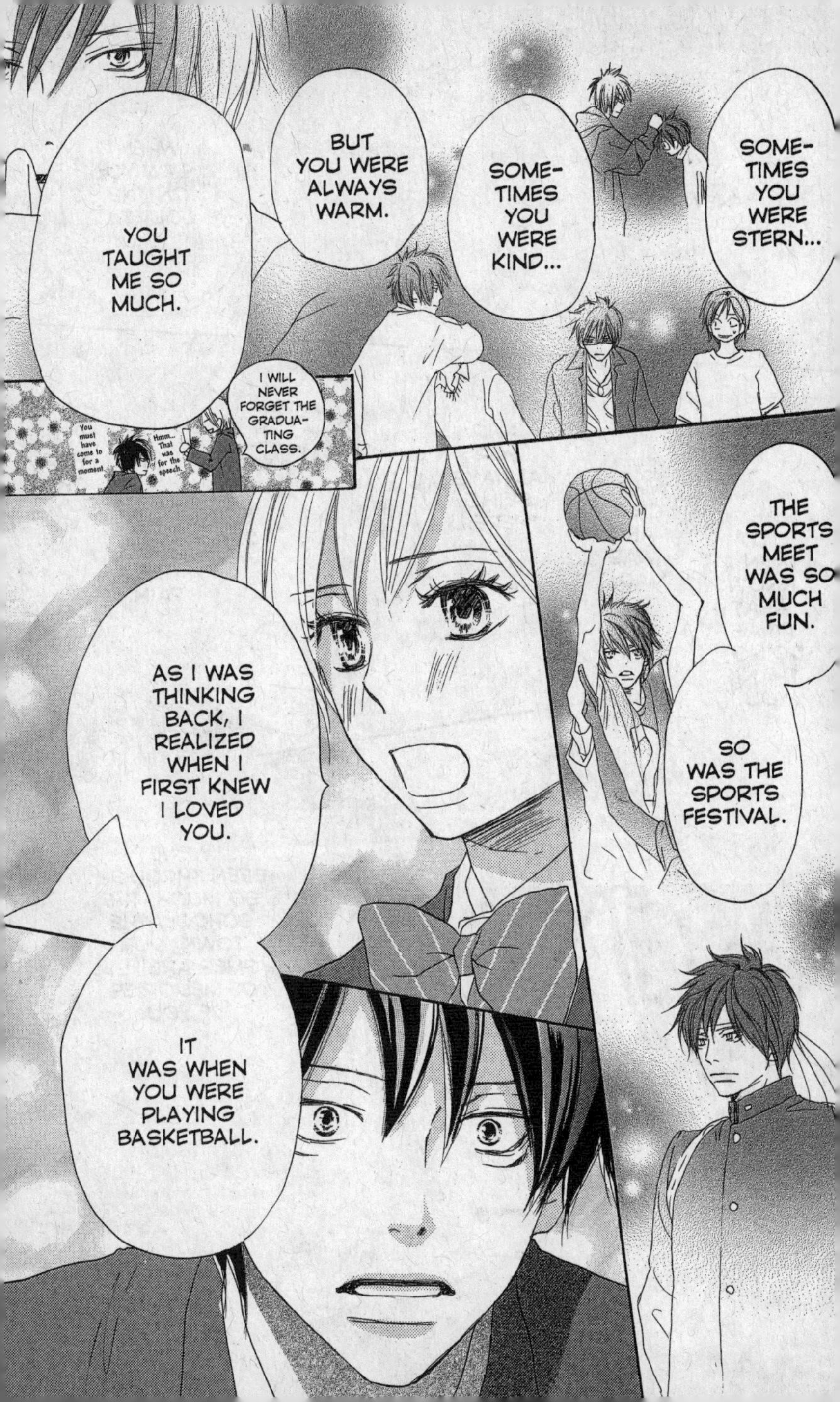
SOME-TIMES YOU WERE STERN...
SOME-TIMES YOU WERE KIND...
BUT YOU WERE ALWAYS WARM.
YOU TAUGHT ME SO MUCH.
I WILL NEVER FORGET THE GRADUA-TING CLASS.
Hmm... That was for the speech.
You must have come to for a moment.
THE SPORTS MEET WAS SO MUCH FUN.
SO WAS THE SPORTS FESTIVAL.
AS I WAS THINKING BACK, I REALIZED WHEN I FIRST KNEW I LOVED YOU.
IT WAS WHEN YOU WERE PLAYING BASKETBALL.

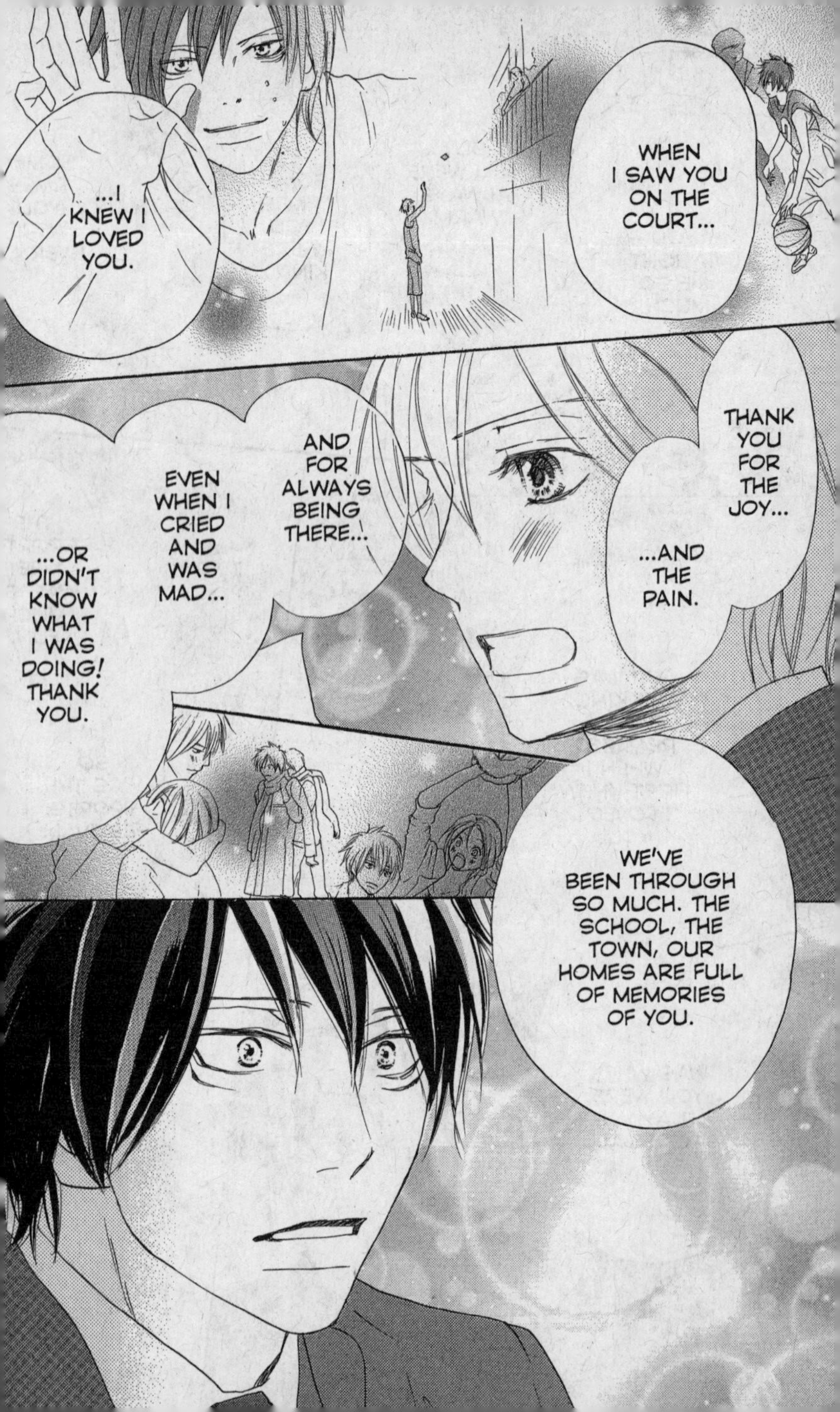
WHEN I SAW YOU ON THE COURT...
...I KNEW I LOVED YOU.
THANK YOU FOR THE JOY...
...AND THE PAIN.
AND FOR ALWAYS BEING THERE...
EVEN WHEN I CRIED AND WAS MAD...
...OR DIDN'T KNOW WHAT I WAS DOING! THANK YOU.
WE'VE BEEN THROUGH SO MUCH. THE SCHOOL, THE TOWN, OUR HOMES ARE FULL OF MEMORIES OF YOU.

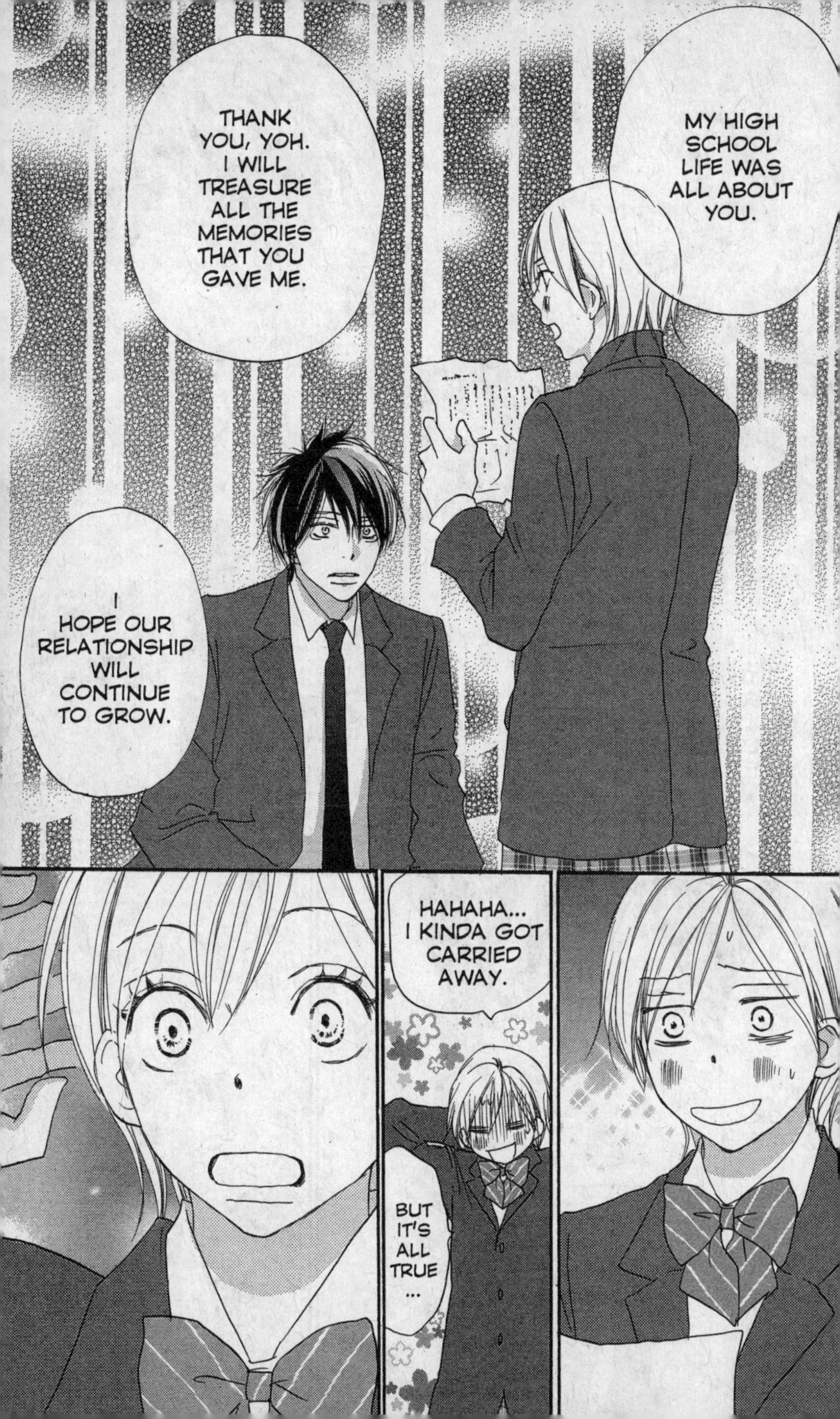
MY HIGH SCHOOL LIFE WAS ALL ABOUT YOU.
THANK YOU, YOH. I WILL TREASURE ALL THE MEMORIES THAT YOU GAVE ME.
I HOPE OUR RELATIONSHIP WILL CONTINUE TO GROW.
HAHAHA... I KINDA GOT CARRIED AWAY.
BUT IT'S ALL TRUE ...

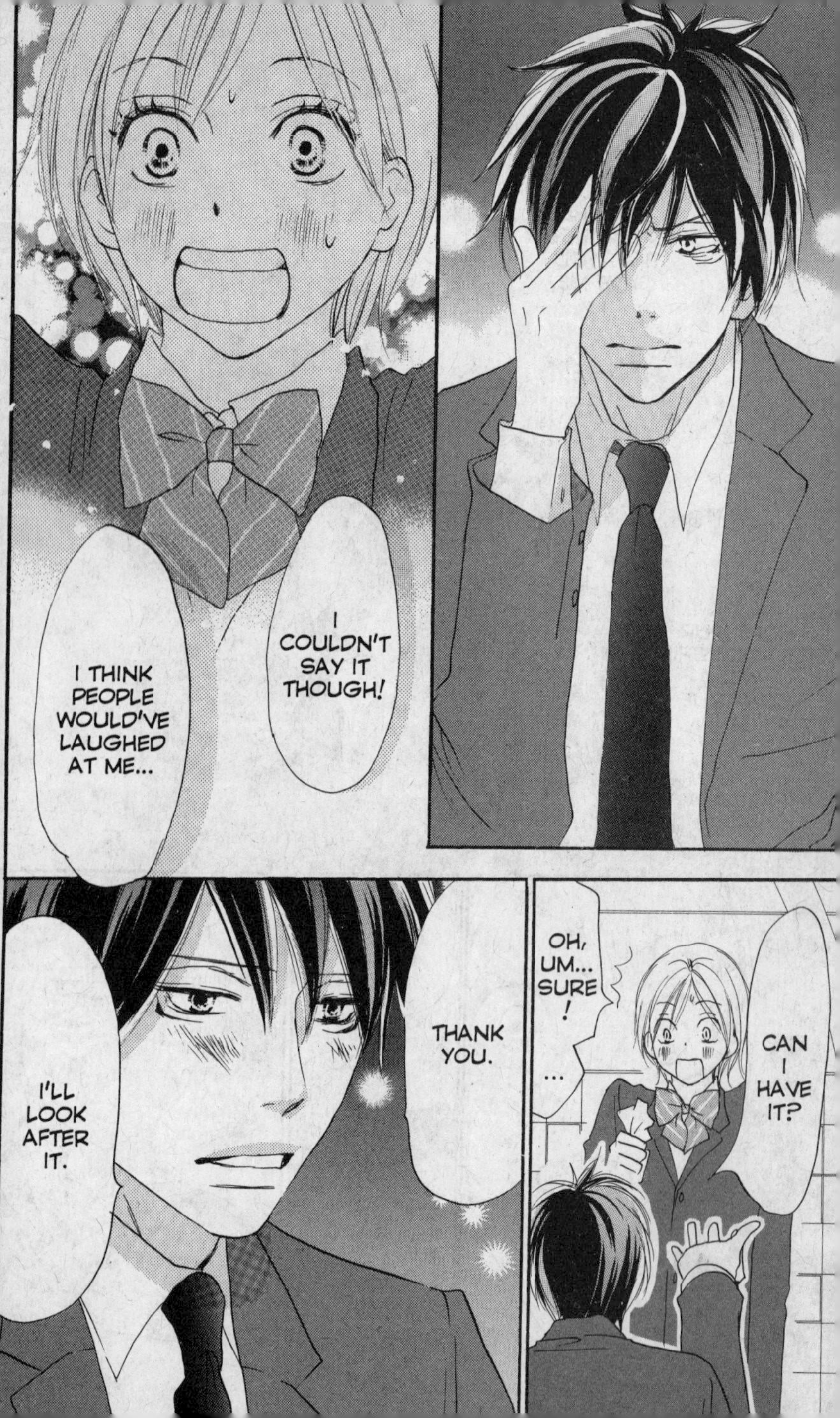
I COULDN'T SAY IT THOUGH!
I THINK PEOPLE WOULD'VE LAUGHED AT ME...
CAN I HAVE IT?
OH, UM... SURE!
...
THANK YOU.
I'LL LOOK AFTER IT.

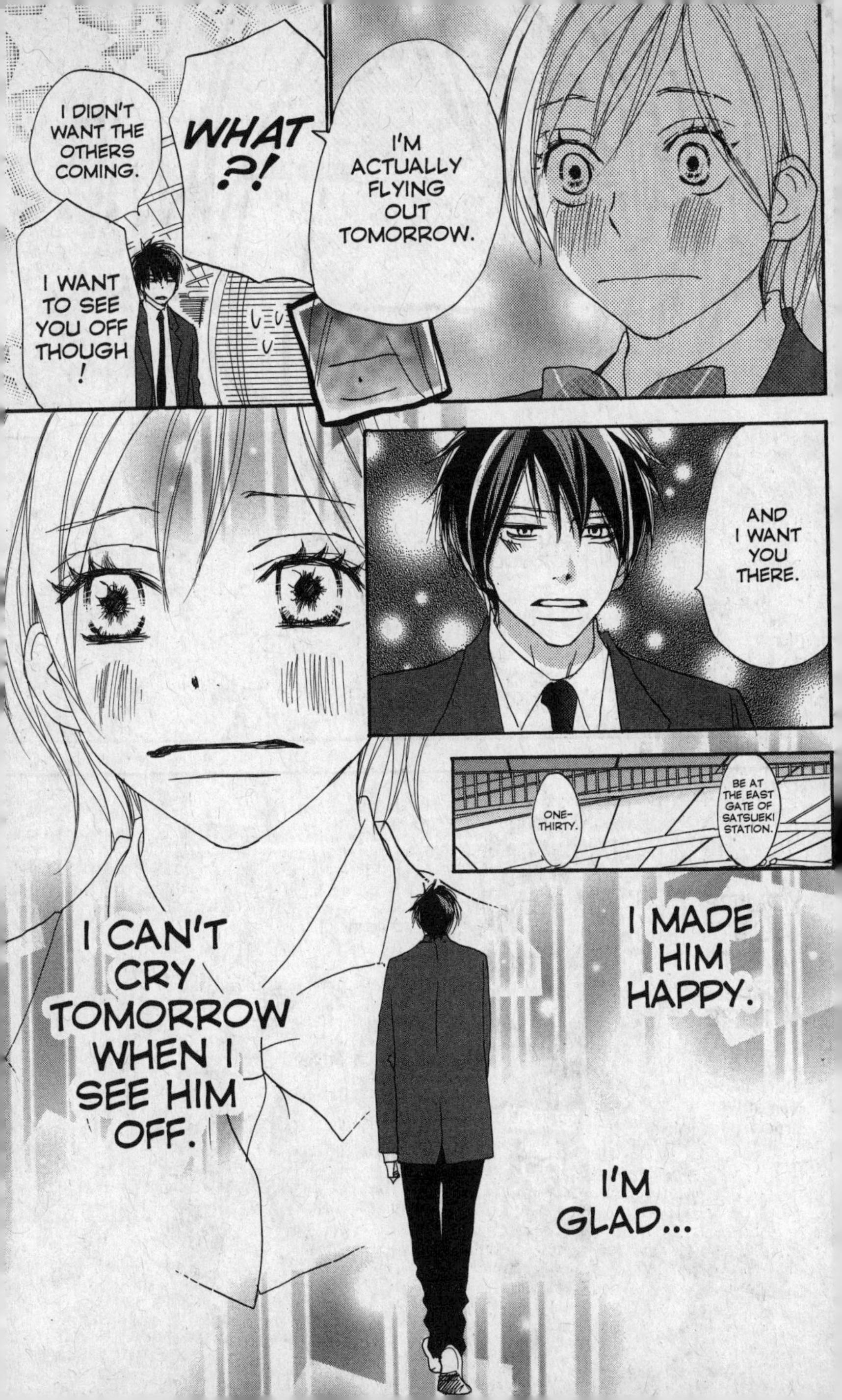
I'M ACTUALLY FLYING OUT TOMORROW.
WHAT?!
I DIDN'T WANT THE OTHERS COMING.
I WANT TO SEE YOU OFF THOUGH!
AND I WANT YOU THERE.
BE AT THE EAST GATE OF SATSUEKI STATION.
ONE-THIRTY.
I MADE HIM HAPPY.
I'M GLAD...
I CAN'T CRY TOMORROW WHEN I SEE HIM OFF.

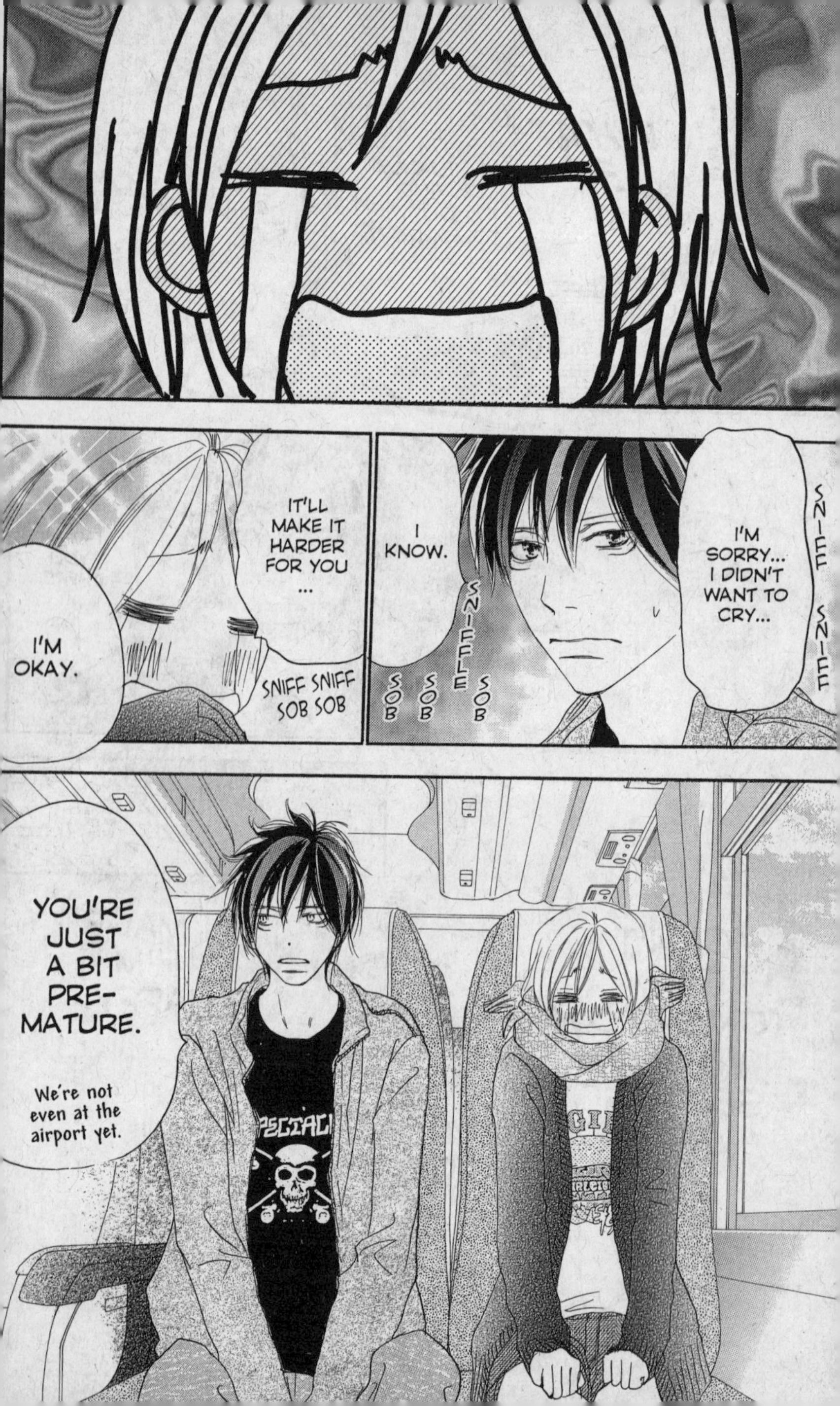
SNIFF SNIFF
I'M SORRY... I DIDN'T WANT TO CRY...
I KNOW.
SNIFFLE
SOB SOB SOB
IT'LL MAKE IT HARDER FOR YOU ...
SNIFF SNIFF SOB SOB
I'M OKAY.
YOU'RE JUST A BIT PRE-MATURE.
We're not even at the airport yet.

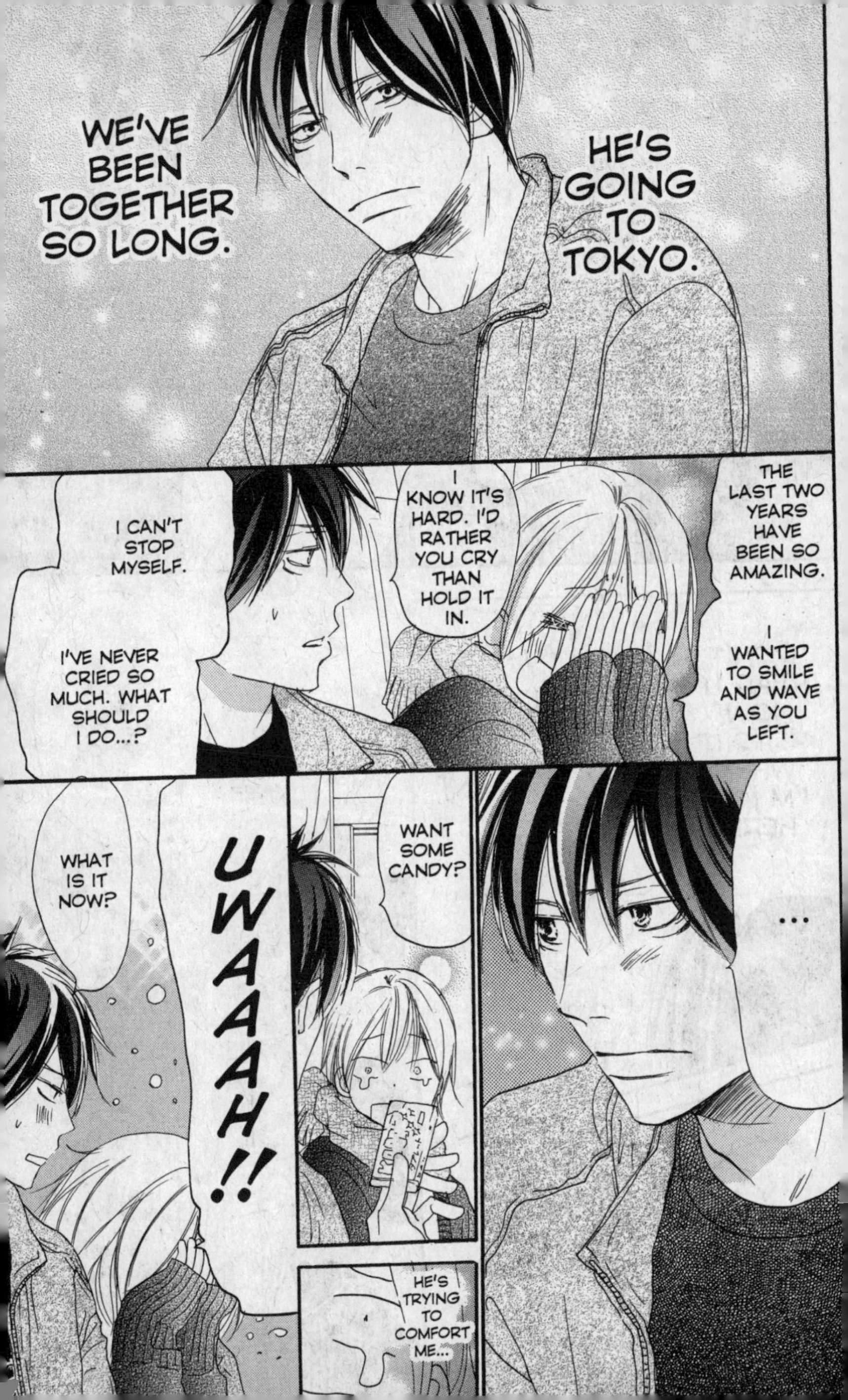
HE'S GOING TO TOKYO.
WE'VE BEEN TOGETHER SO LONG.
THE LAST TWO YEARS HAVE BEEN SO AMAZING.
I WANTED TO SMILE AND WAVE AS YOU LEFT.
I KNOW IT'S HARD. I'D RATHER YOU CRY THAN HOLD IT IN.
I CAN'T STOP MYSELF.
I'VE NEVER CRIED SO MUCH. WHAT SHOULD I DO...?
...
WANT SOME CANDY?
HE'S TRYING TO COMFORT ME...
UWAAAAH!!
WHAT IS IT NOW?

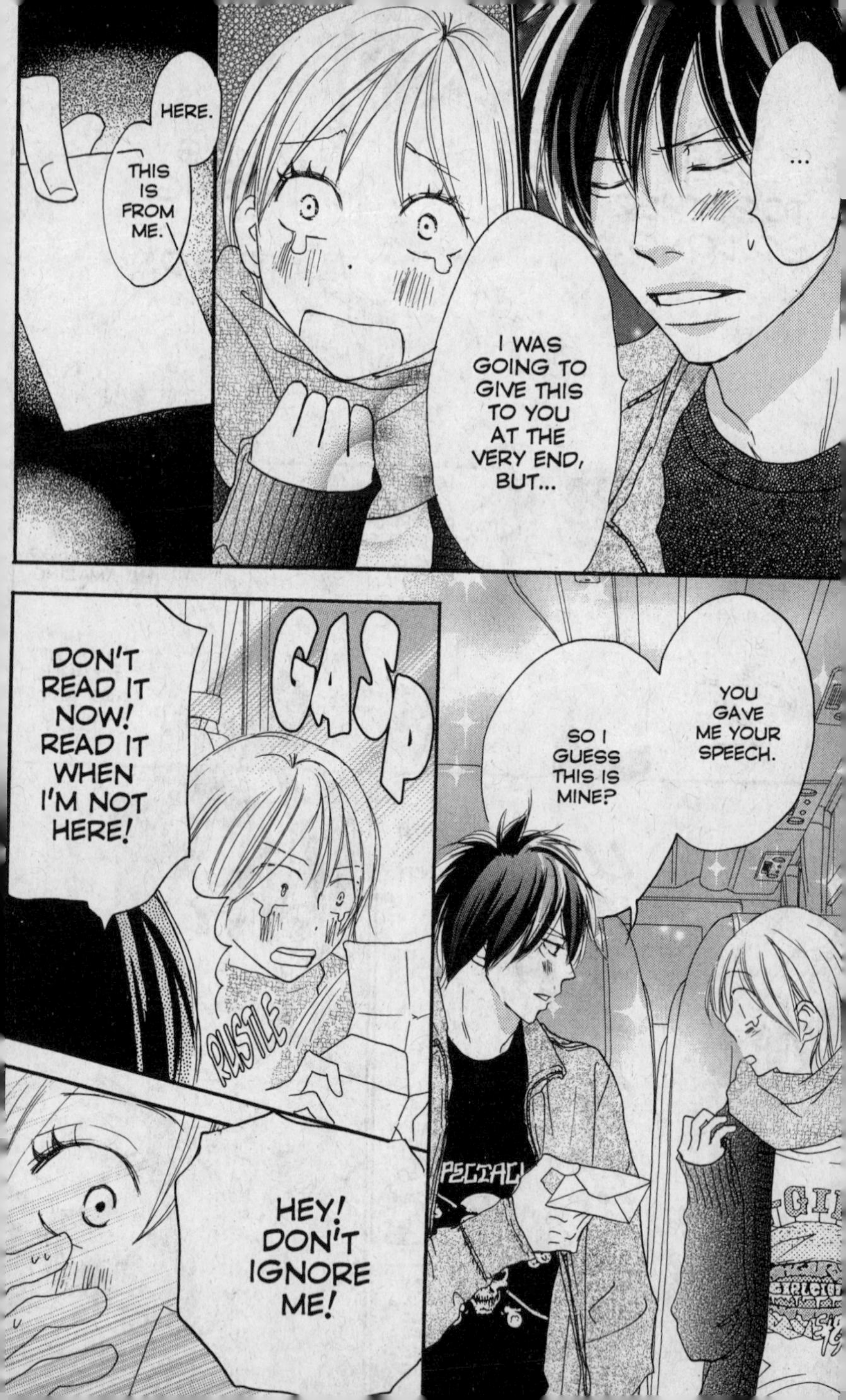
...
I WAS GOING TO GIVE THIS TO YOU AT THE VERY END, BUT...
HERE.
THIS IS FROM ME.
YOU GAVE ME YOUR SPEECH.
SO I GUESS THIS IS MINE?
GASP
DON'T READ IT NOW! READ IT WHEN I'M NOT HERE!
RUSTLE
HEY! DON'T IGNORE ME!

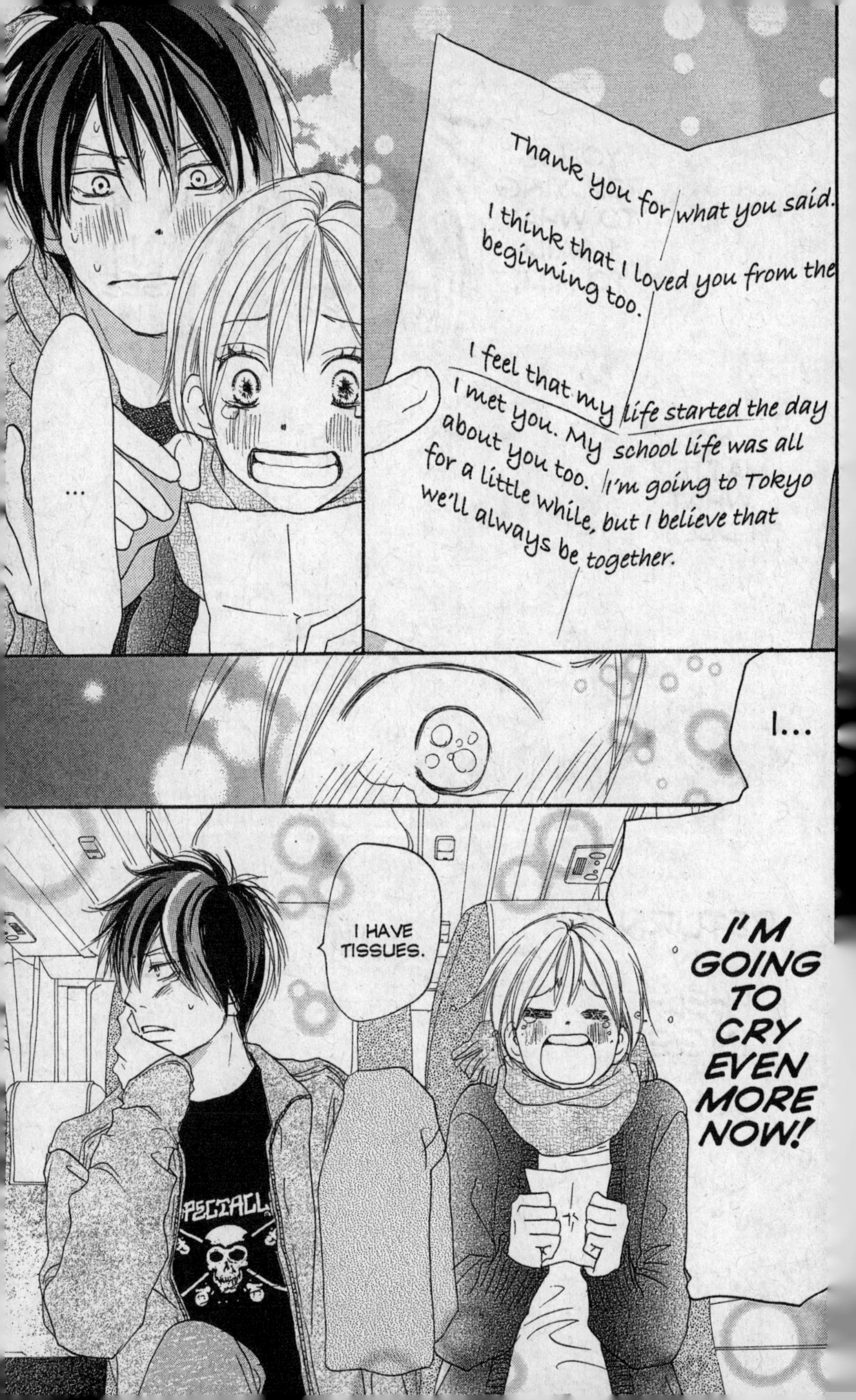
Thank you for what you said. I think that I loved you from the beginning too.
I feel that my life started the day I met you. My school life was all about you too. I'm going to Tokyo for a little while, but I believe that we'll always be together.
...
I...
I'M GOING TO CRY EVEN MORE NOW!
I HAVE TISSUES.

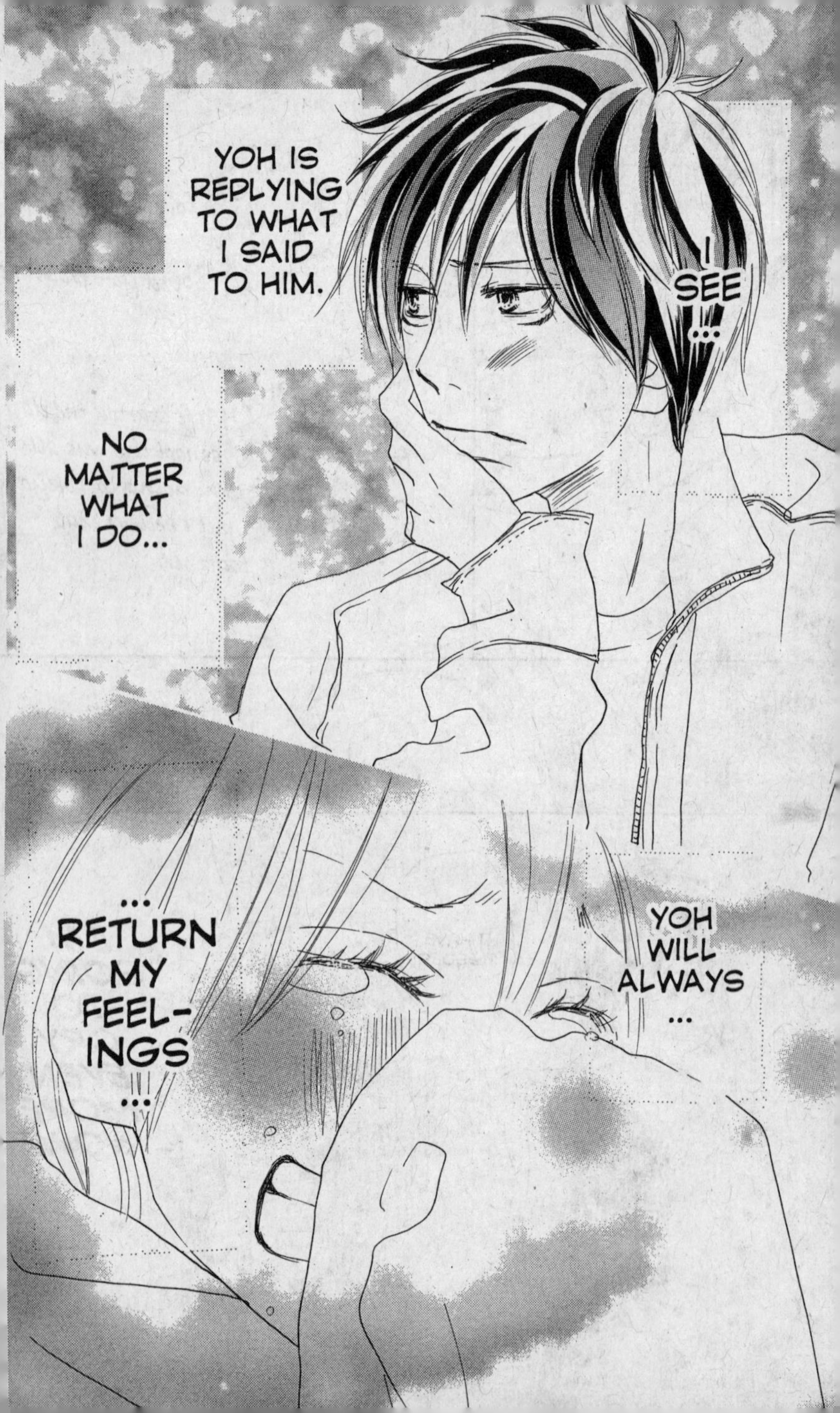
I SEE...
YOH IS REPLYING TO WHAT I SAID TO HIM.
NO MATTER WHAT I DO...
YOH WILL ALWAYS...
...RETURN MY FEEL-INGS...

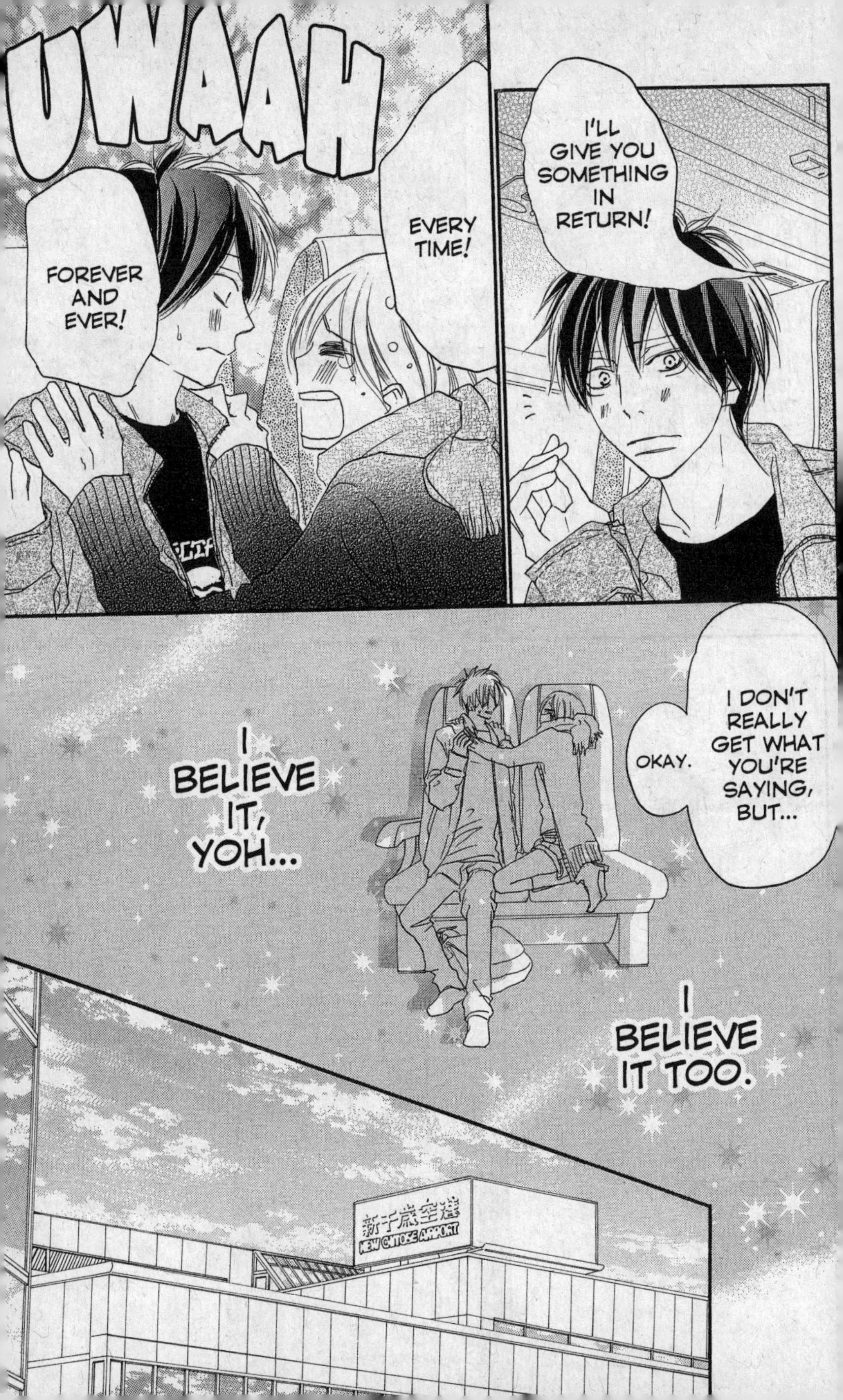
I'LL GIVE YOU SOMETHING IN RETURN!
EVERY TIME!
UWAAH
FOREVER AND EVER!
I DON'T REALLY GET WHAT YOU'RE SAYING, BUT...
OKAY.
I BELIEVE IT, YOH...
I BELIEVE IT TOO.
新千歳空港
NEW CHITOSE AIRPORT

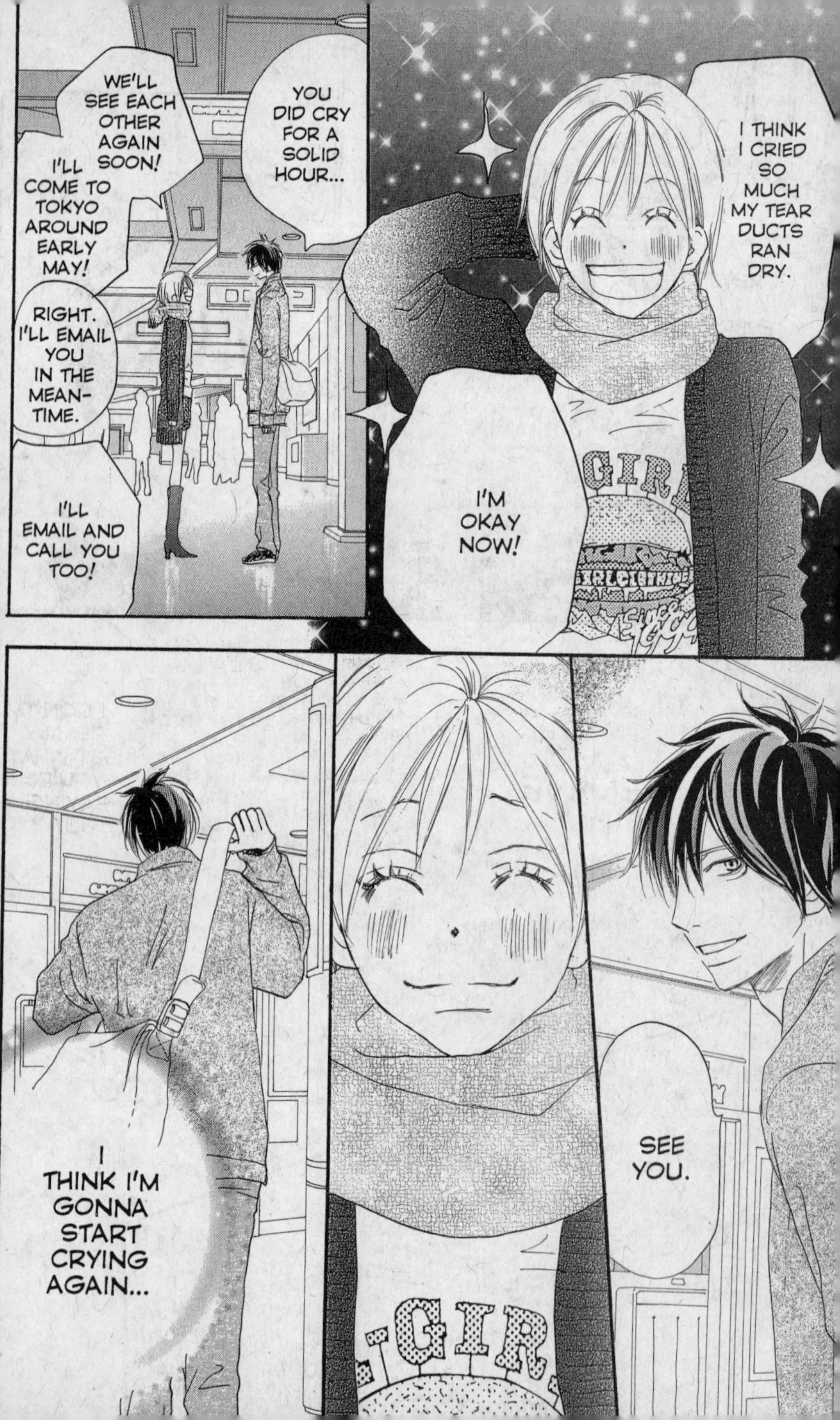
I THINK I CRIED SO MUCH MY TEAR DUCTS RAN DRY.
I'M OKAY NOW!
YOU DID CRY FOR A SOLID HOUR...
WE'LL SEE EACH OTHER AGAIN SOON!
I'LL COME TO TOKYO AROUND EARLY MAY!
RIGHT. I'LL EMAIL YOU IN THE MEAN-TIME.
I'LL EMAIL AND CALL YOU TOO!
SEE YOU.
I THINK I'M GONNA START CRYING AGAIN...

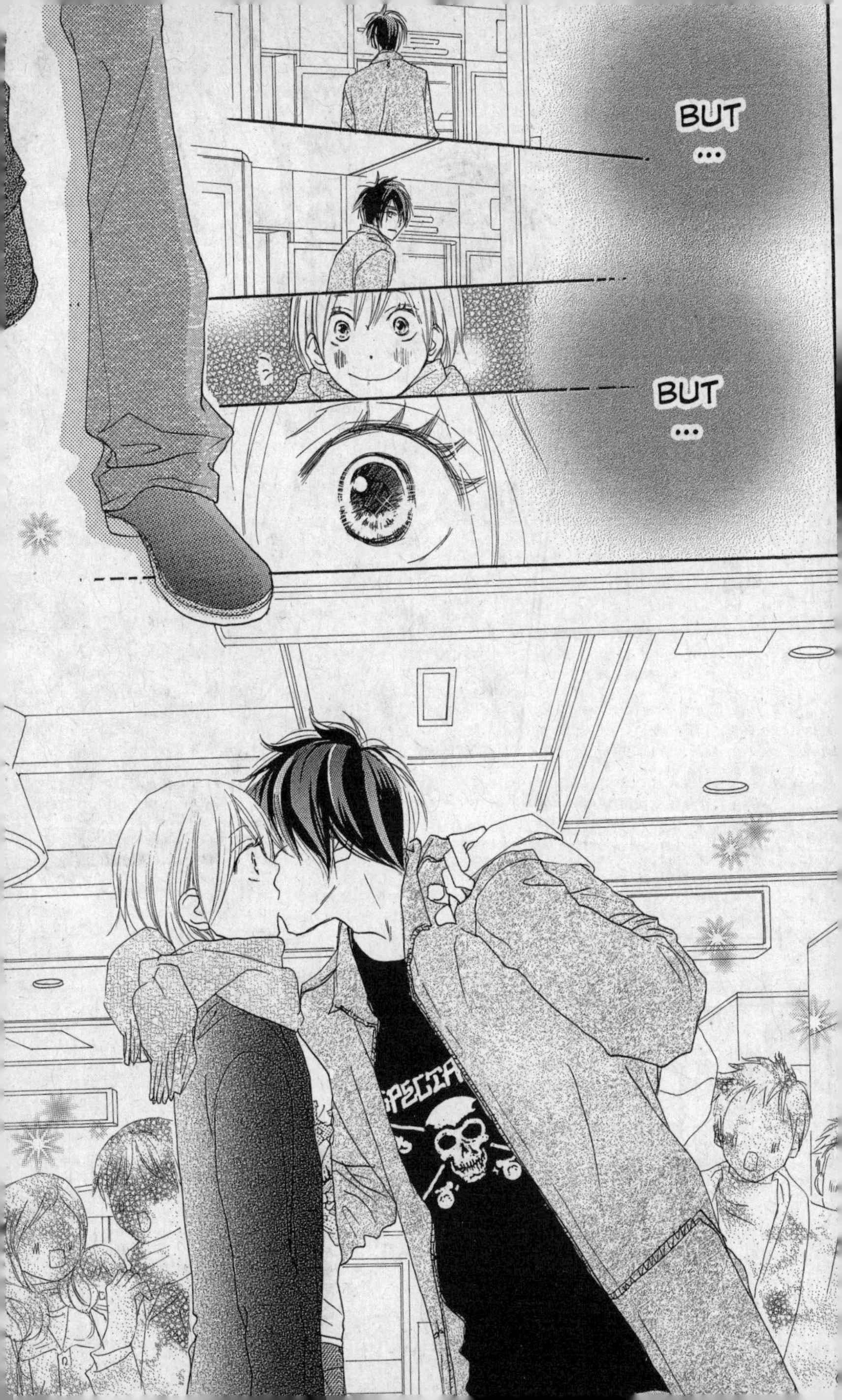
BUT …
BUT …

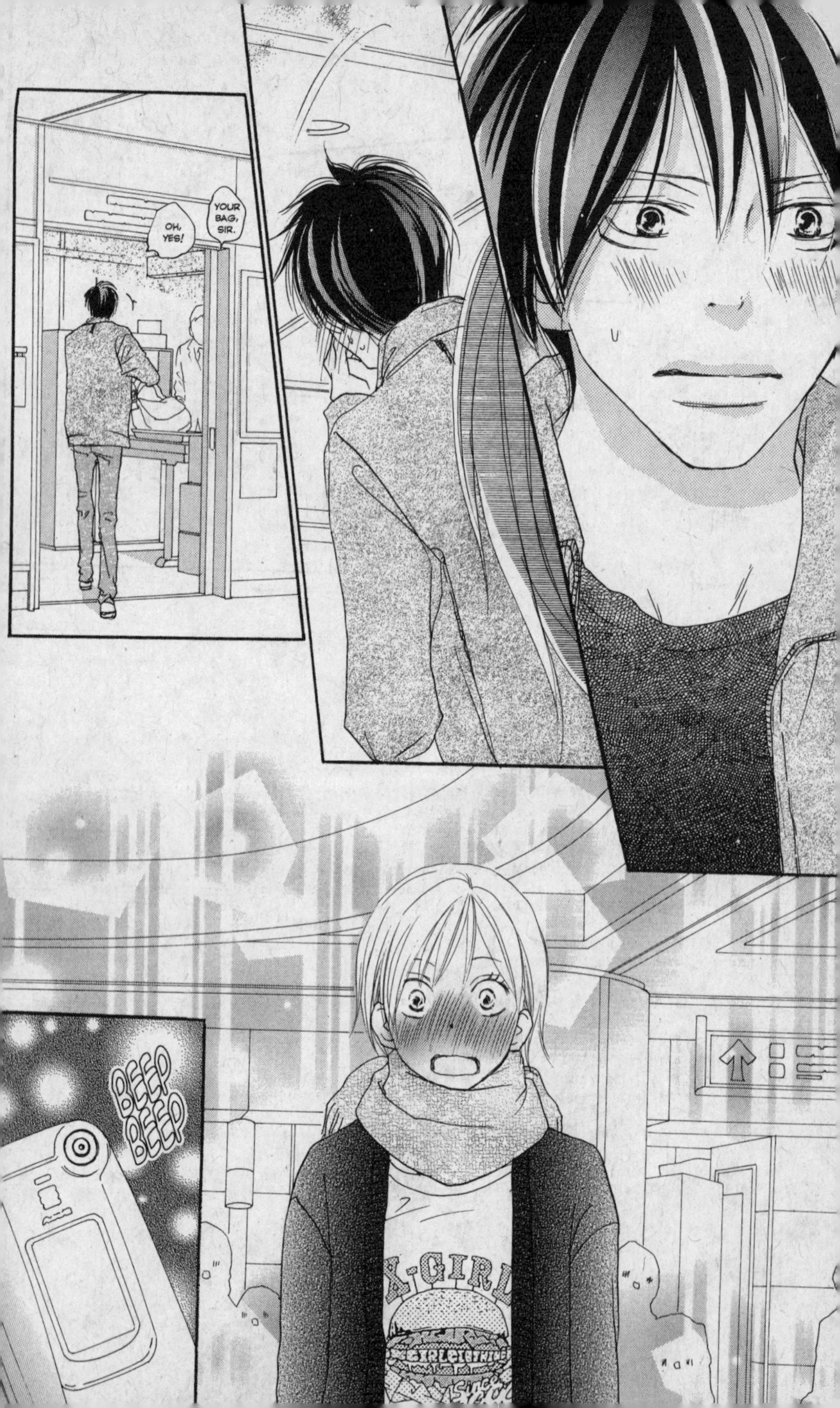
YOUR BAG, SIR.
OH, YES!
BEEP BEEP
X-GIRL

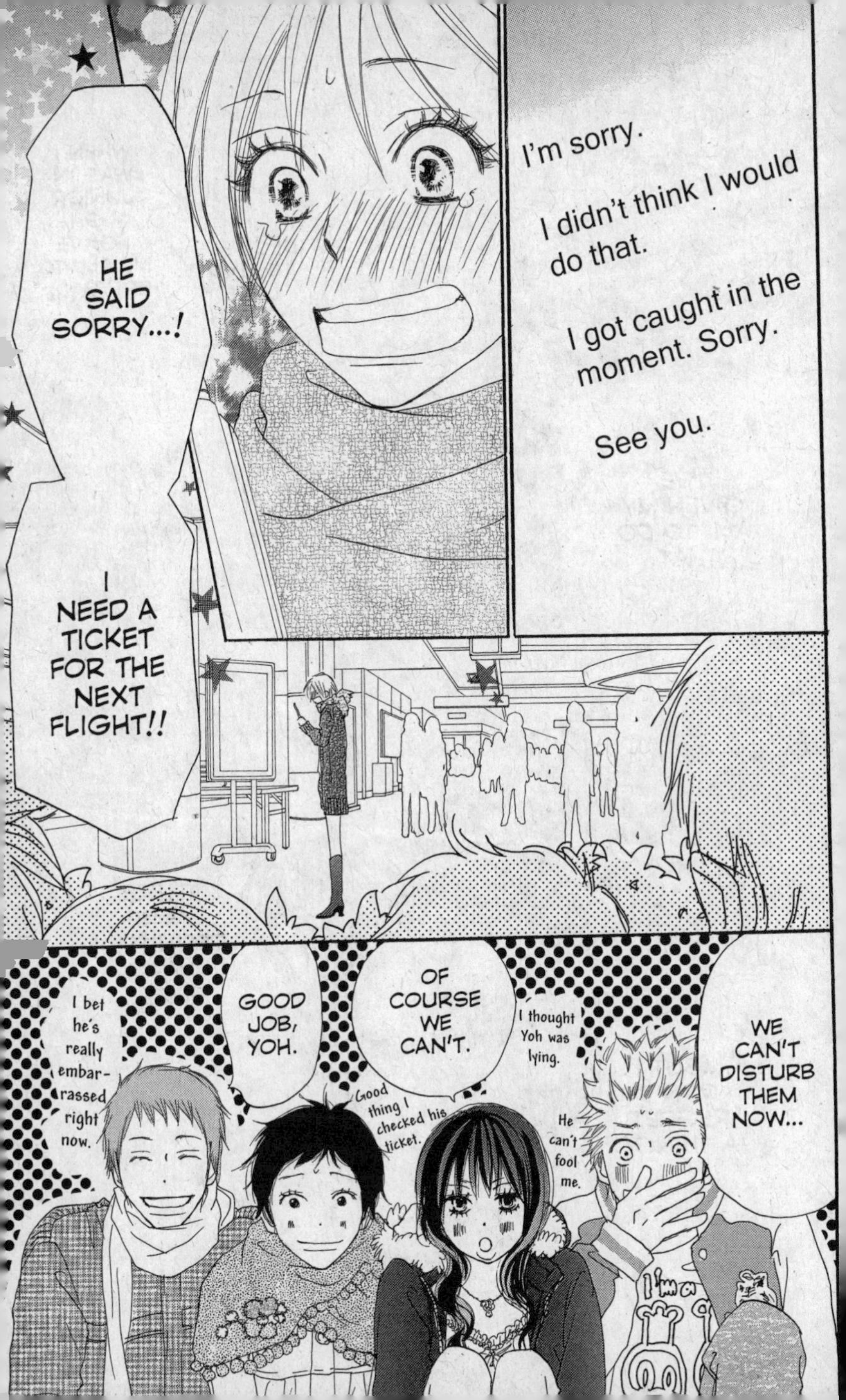
I'm sorry.
I didn't think I would do that.
I got caught in the moment. Sorry.
See you.
HE SAID SORRY...!
I NEED A TICKET FOR THE NEXT FLIGHT!!
WE CAN'T DISTURB THEM NOW...
I thought Yoh was lying.
He can't fool me.
OF COURSE WE CAN'T.
Good thing I checked his ticket.
GOOD JOB, YOH.
I bet he's really embarrassed right now.

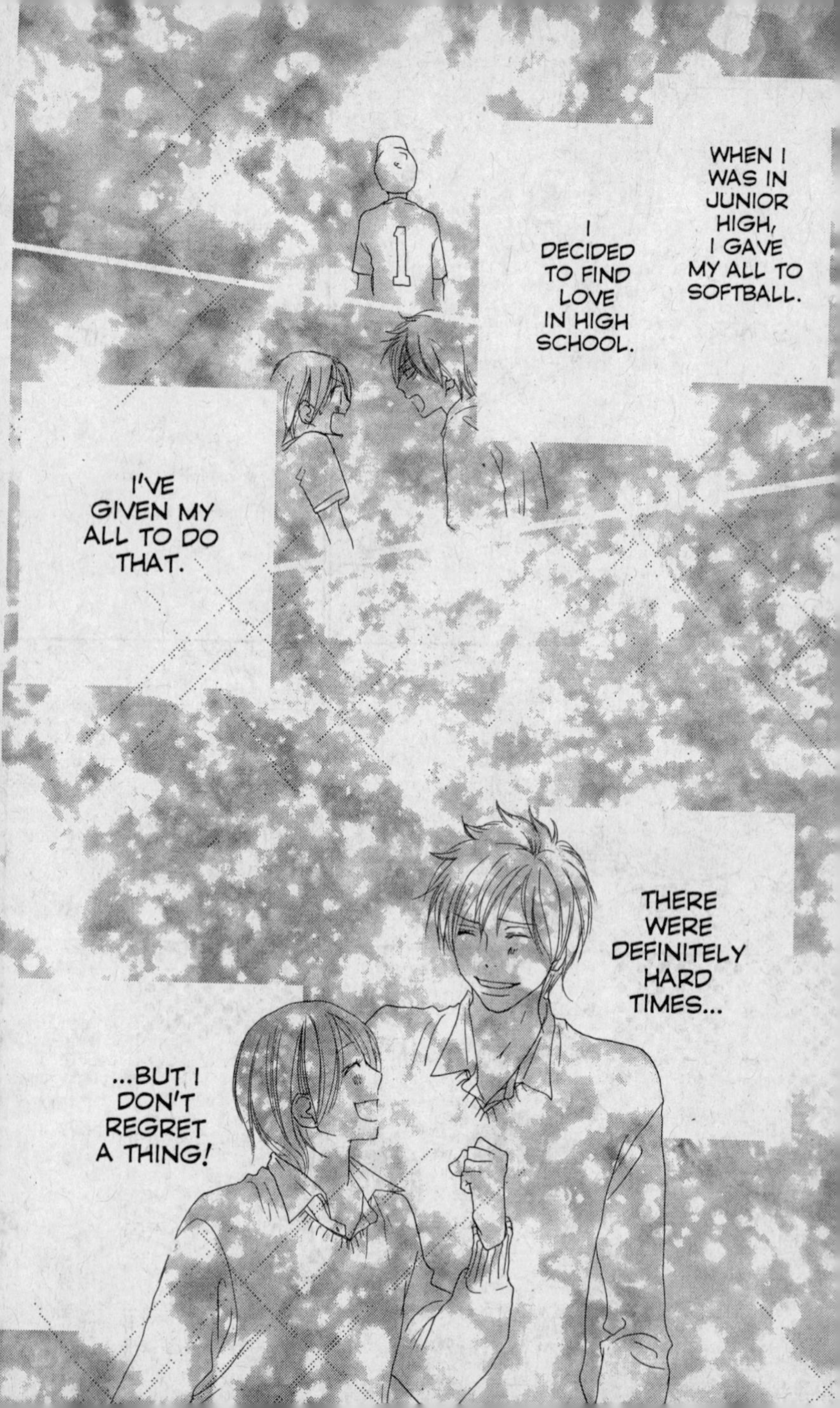
WHEN I WAS IN JUNIOR HIGH, I GAVE MY ALL TO SOFTBALL.
I DECIDED TO FIND LOVE IN HIGH SCHOOL.
I'VE GIVEN MY ALL TO DO THAT.
THERE WERE DEFINITELY HARD TIMES...
...BUT I DON'T REGRET A THING!

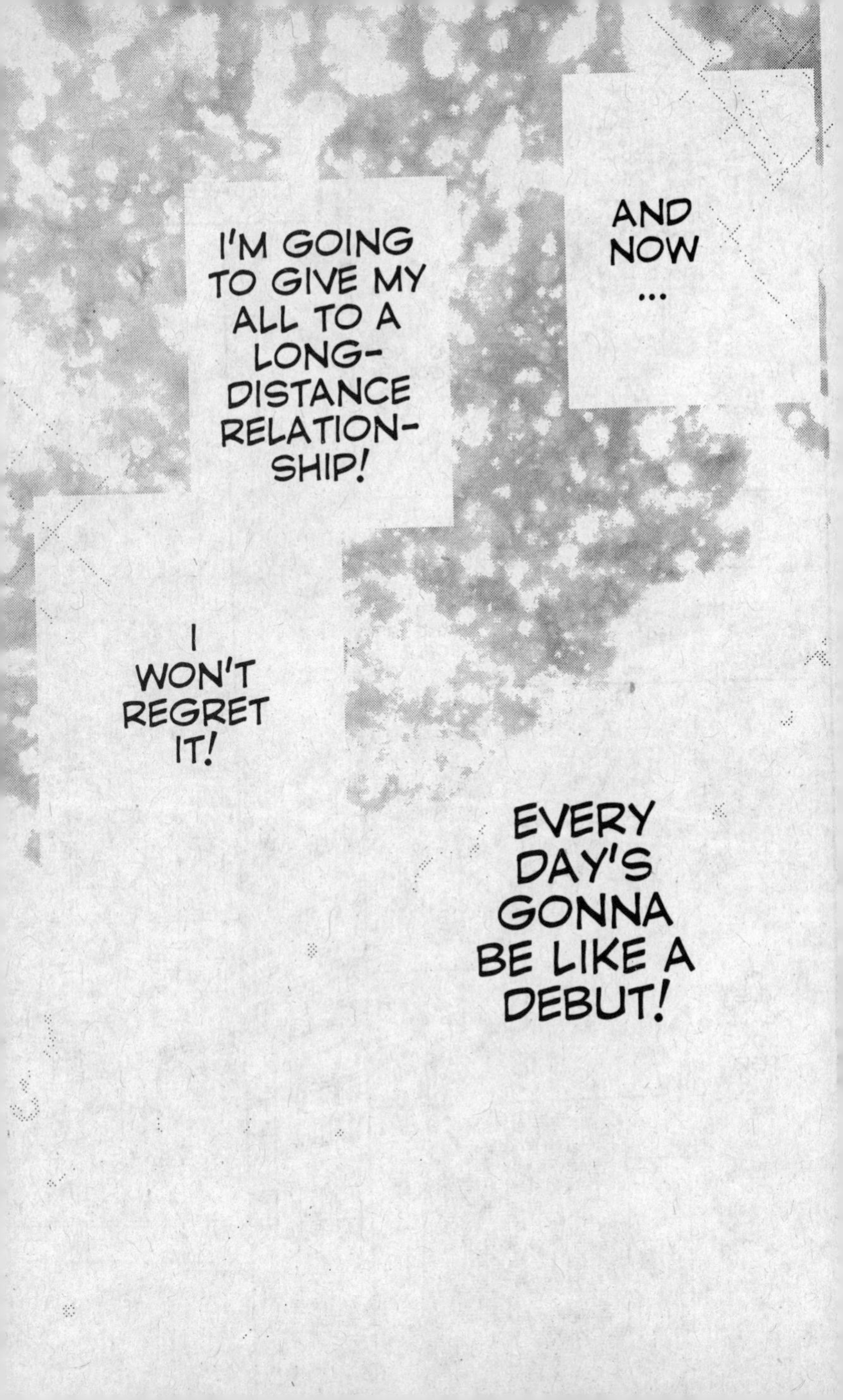
AND NOW ...
I'M GOING TO GIVE MY ALL TO A LONG-DISTANCE RELATION-SHIP!
I WON'T REGRET IT!
EVERY DAY'S GONNA BE LIKE A DEBUT!

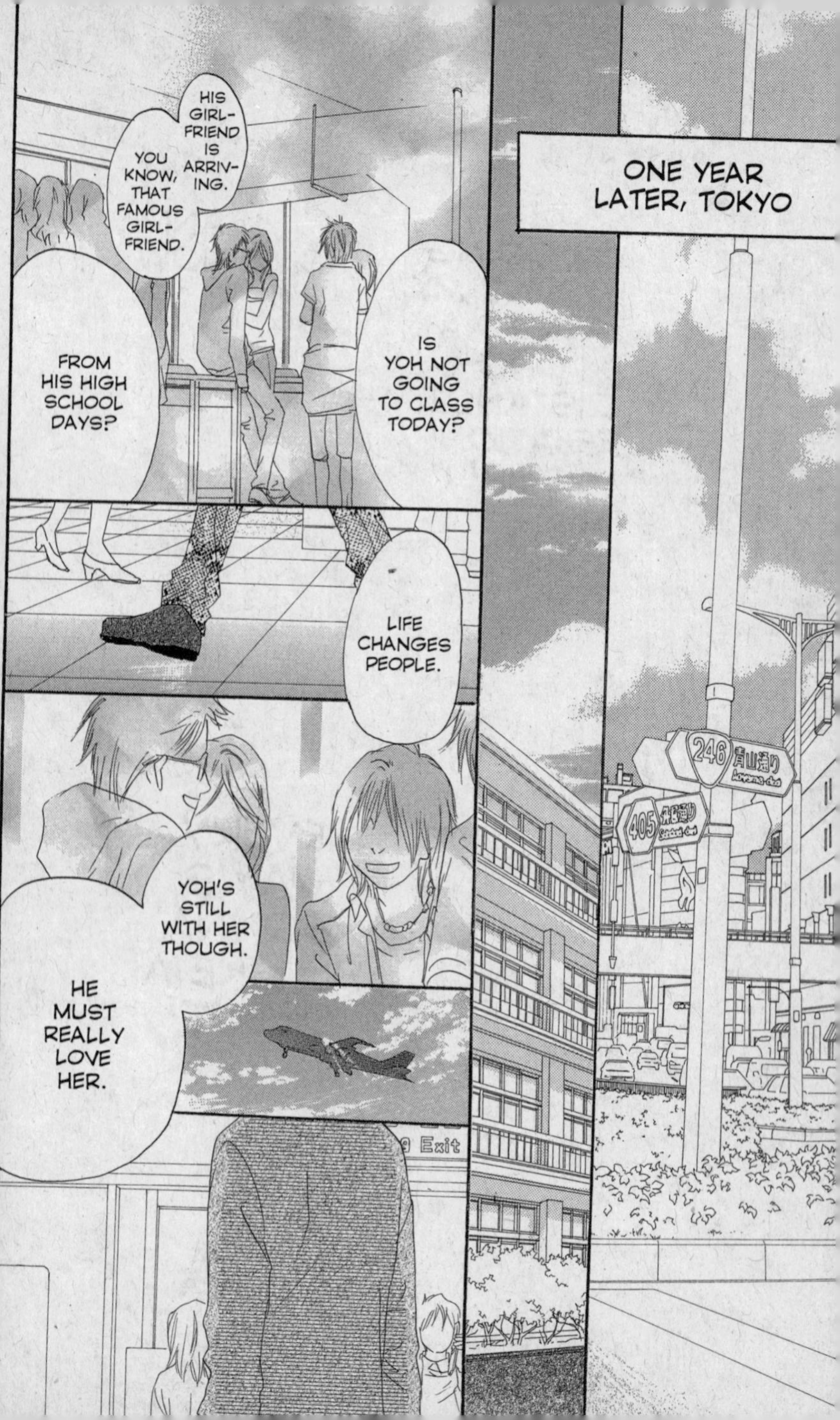
ONE YEAR LATER, TOKYO
246 青山通り
IS YOH NOT GOING TO CLASS TODAY?
HIS GIRL-FRIEND IS ARRIV-ING.
YOU KNOW, THAT FAMOUS GIRL-FRIEND.
FROM HIS HIGH SCHOOL DAYS?
LIFE CHANGES PEOPLE.
YOH'S STILL WITH HER THOUGH.
HE MUST REALLY LOVE HER.
Exit

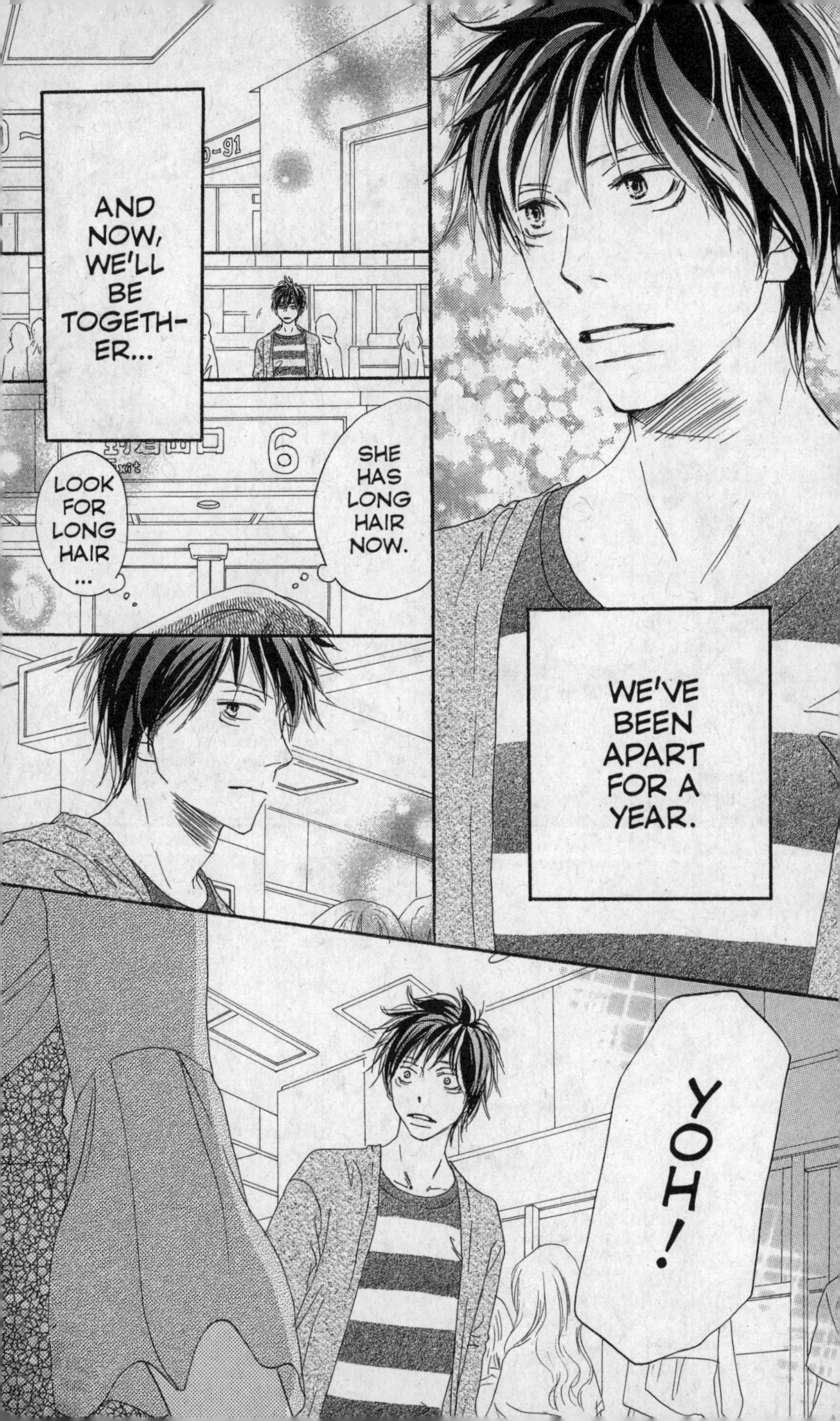
WE'VE BEEN APART FOR A YEAR.
AND NOW, WE'LL BE TOGETH-ER...
SHE HAS LONG HAIR NOW.
LOOK FOR LONG HAIR ...
YOH!

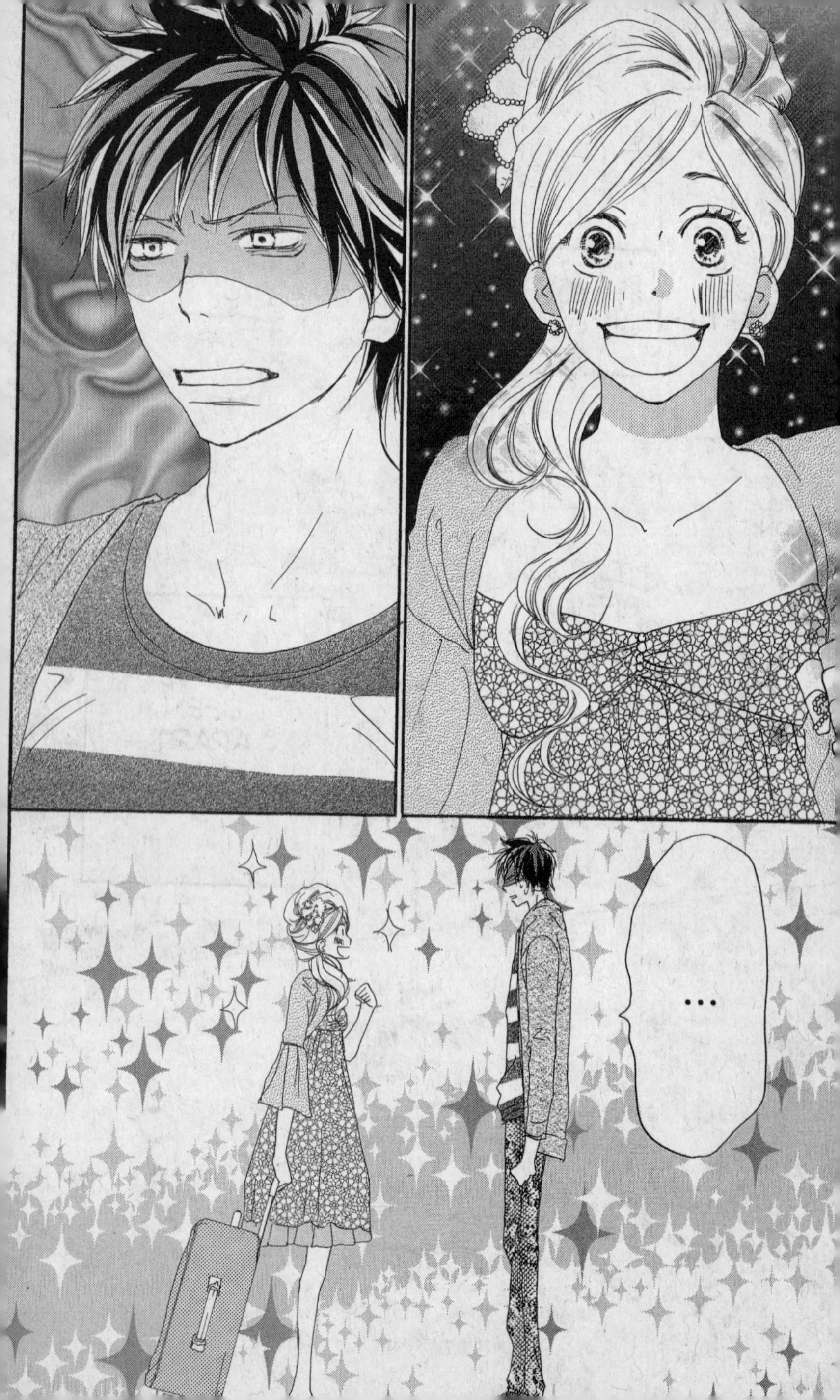
...

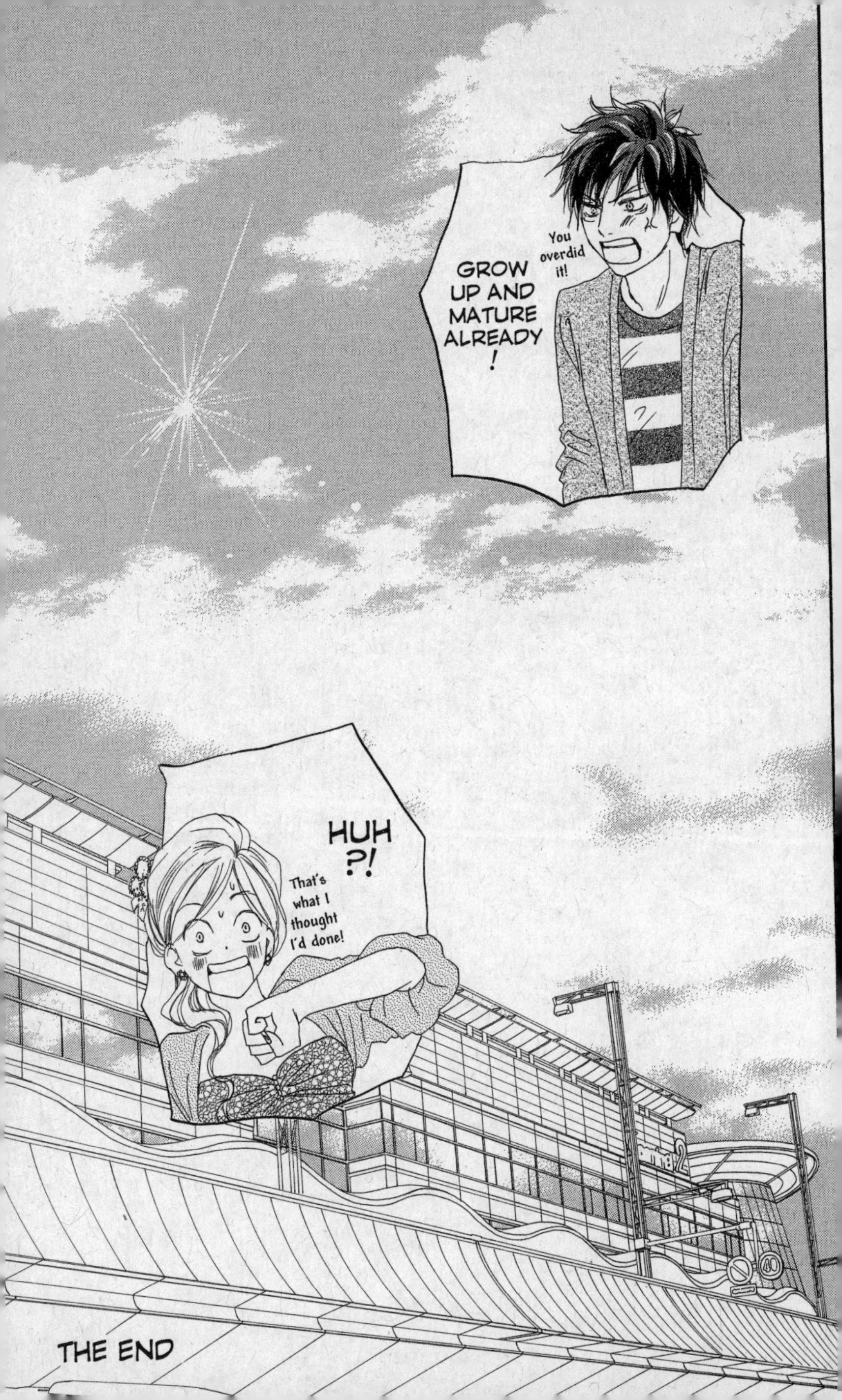
You overdid it!
GROW UP AND MATURE ALREADY!
HUH ?!
That's what I thought I'd done!
THE END

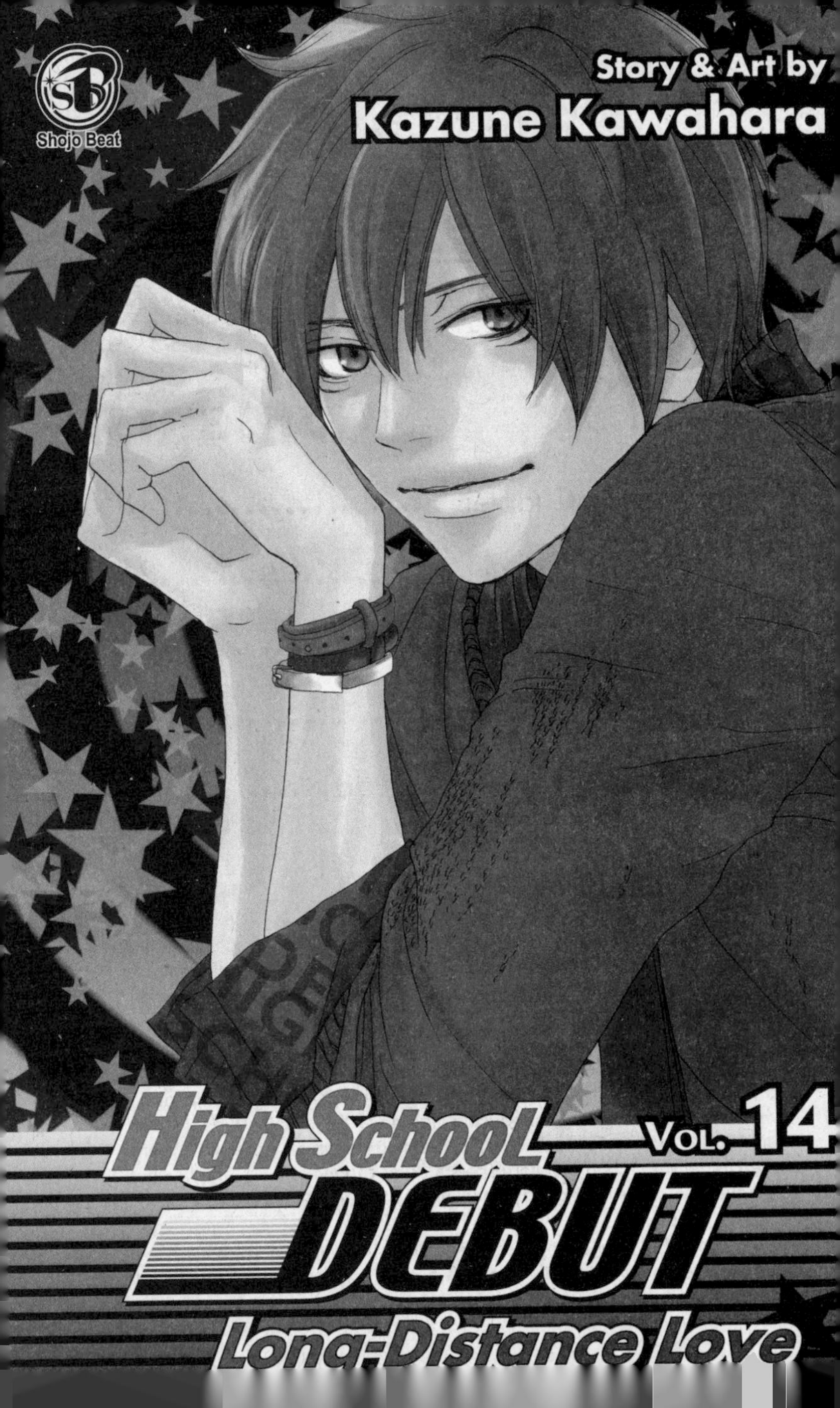
Shojo Beat
Story & Art by
Kazune Kawahara
High School DEBUT
Vol. 14
Long-Distance Love

High School DEBUT
Long-Distance Love

★★ Contents

Story Thus Far...

High school student Haruna used to spend all her time playing softball in junior high, but now she wants to give her all to finding true love instead! While her "love coach" Yoh is training her on how to be popular with guys, the two of them start dating.

With graduation approaching, Yoh decides to go to college in Tokyo. He and Haruna spend their last winter break together skiing with their friends, celebrating Christmas...and introducing Haruna to Yoh's mother! Haruna has no time to be sentimental about Yoh's impending departure since she's been chosen to deliver a congratulatory speech at his graduation. On the day that Yoh leaves, he kisses her goodbye at the airport...

Haruna knows being in a long-distance relationship will be hard, but she's determined to go the extra mile and do whatever it takes to make sure their love survives the separation!

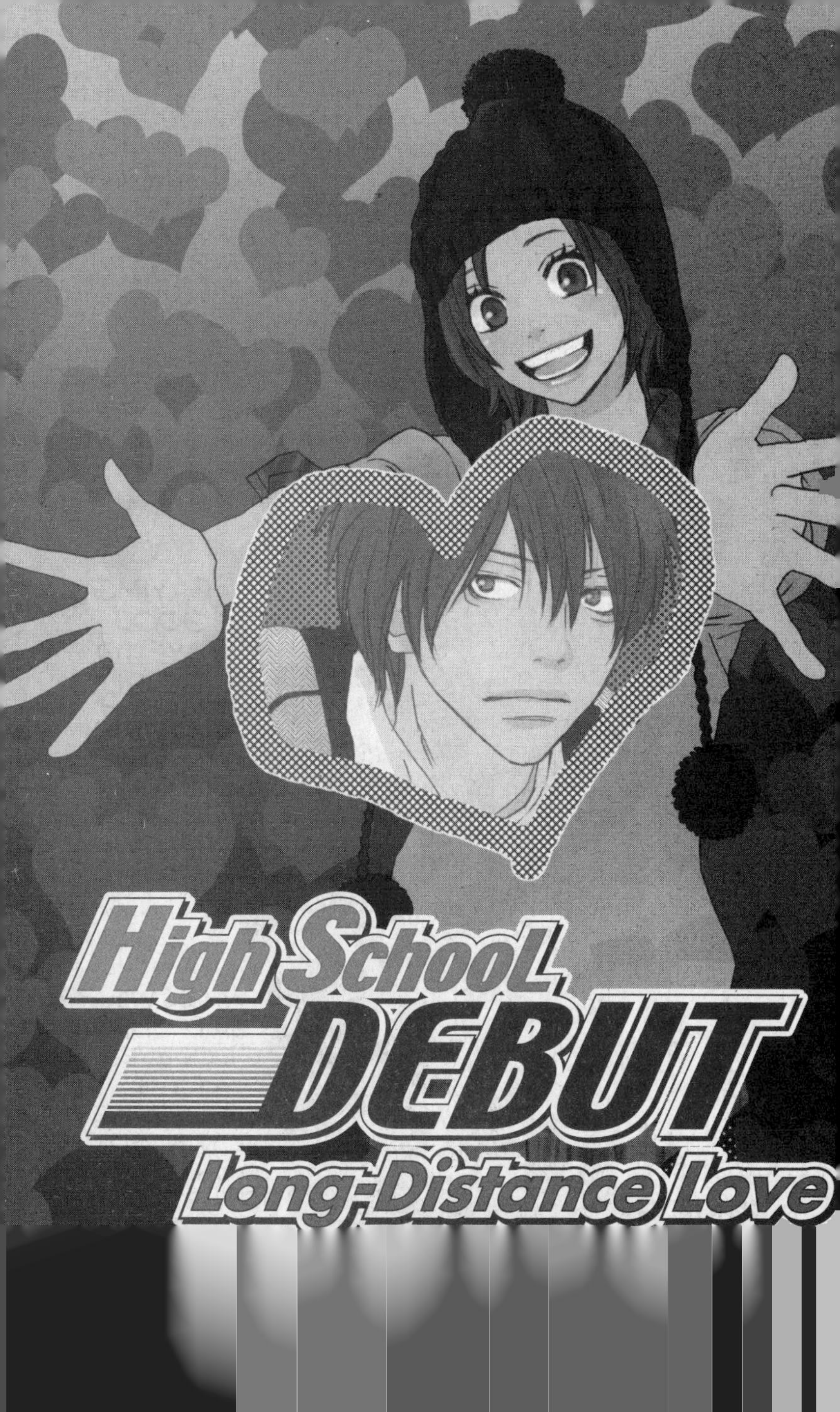
High School
DEBUT
Long-Distance Love

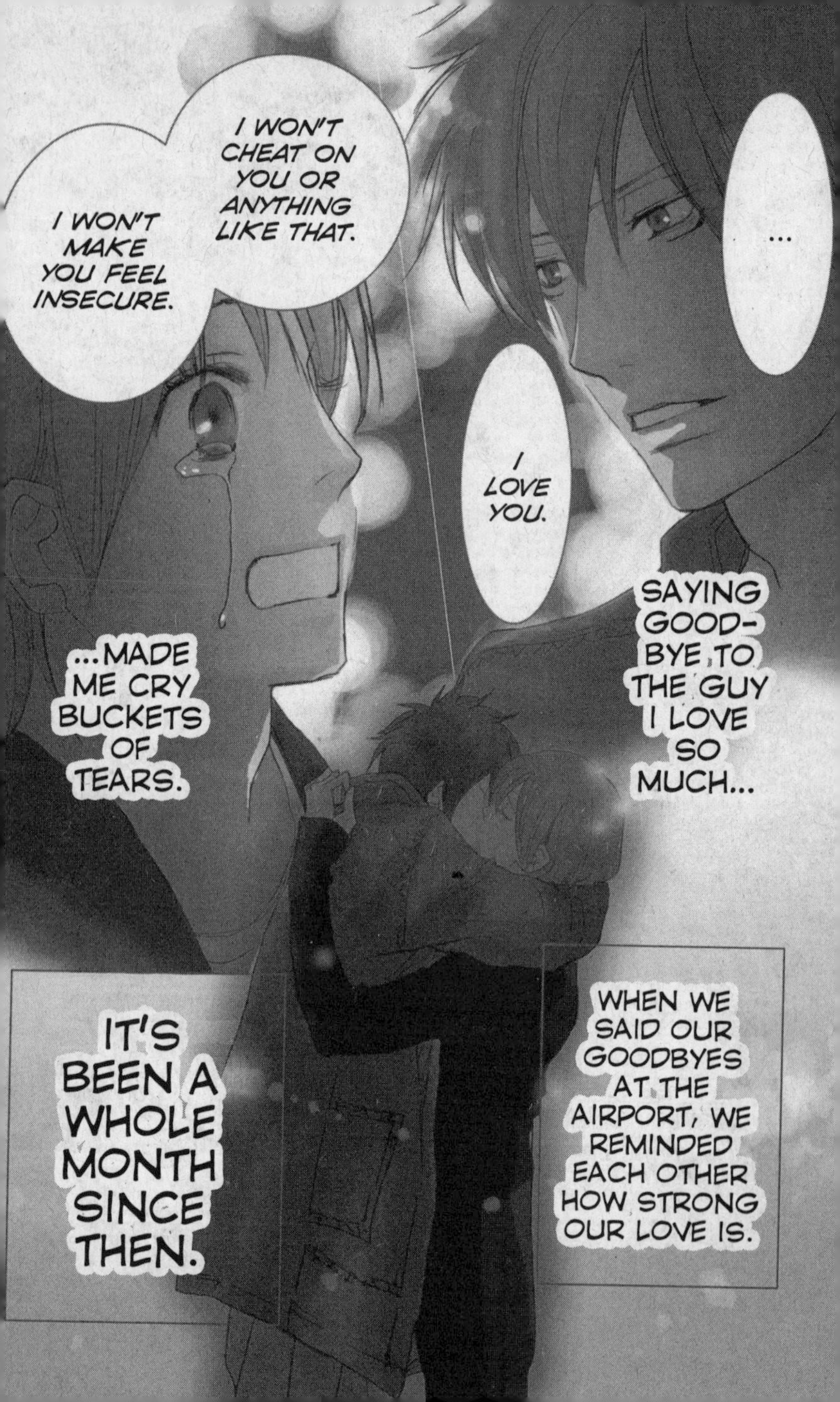
...
I WON'T CHEAT ON YOU OR ANYTHING LIKE THAT.
I WON'T MAKE YOU FEEL INSECURE.
I LOVE YOU.
SAYING GOOD-BYE TO THE GUY I LOVE SO MUCH...
...MADE ME CRY BUCKETS OF TEARS.
WHEN WE SAID OUR GOODBYES AT THE AIRPORT, WE REMINDED EACH OTHER HOW STRONG OUR LOVE IS.
IT'S BEEN A WHOLE MONTH SINCE THEN.

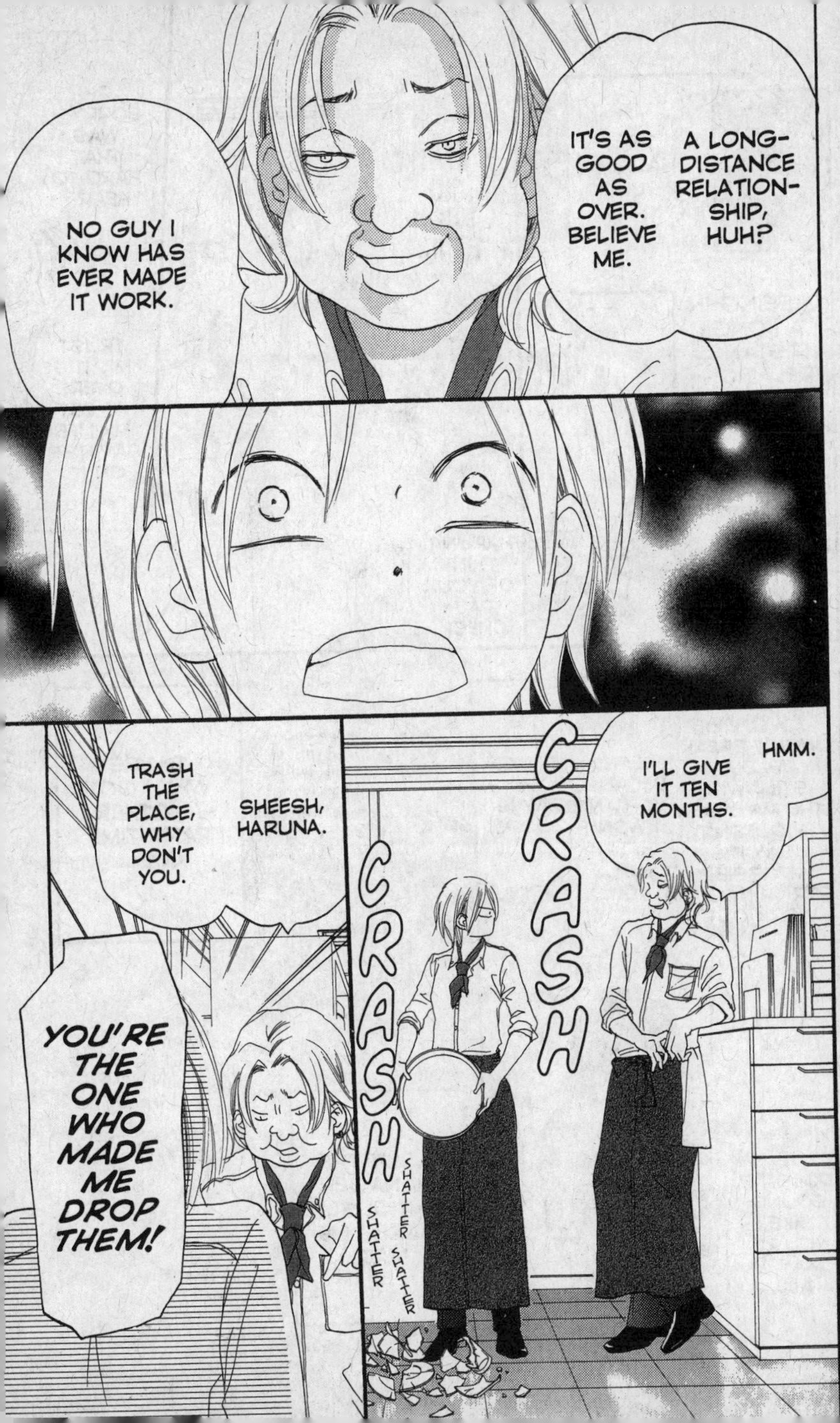
A LONG-DISTANCE RELATIONSHIP, HUH?
IT'S AS GOOD AS OVER. BELIEVE ME.
NO GUY I KNOW HAS EVER MADE IT WORK.
HMM.
I'LL GIVE IT TEN MONTHS.
CRASH
CRASH
SHATTER SHATTER
SHATTER
SHEESH, HARUNA.
TRASH THE PLACE, WHY DON'T YOU.
YOU'RE THE ONE WHO MADE ME DROP THEM!

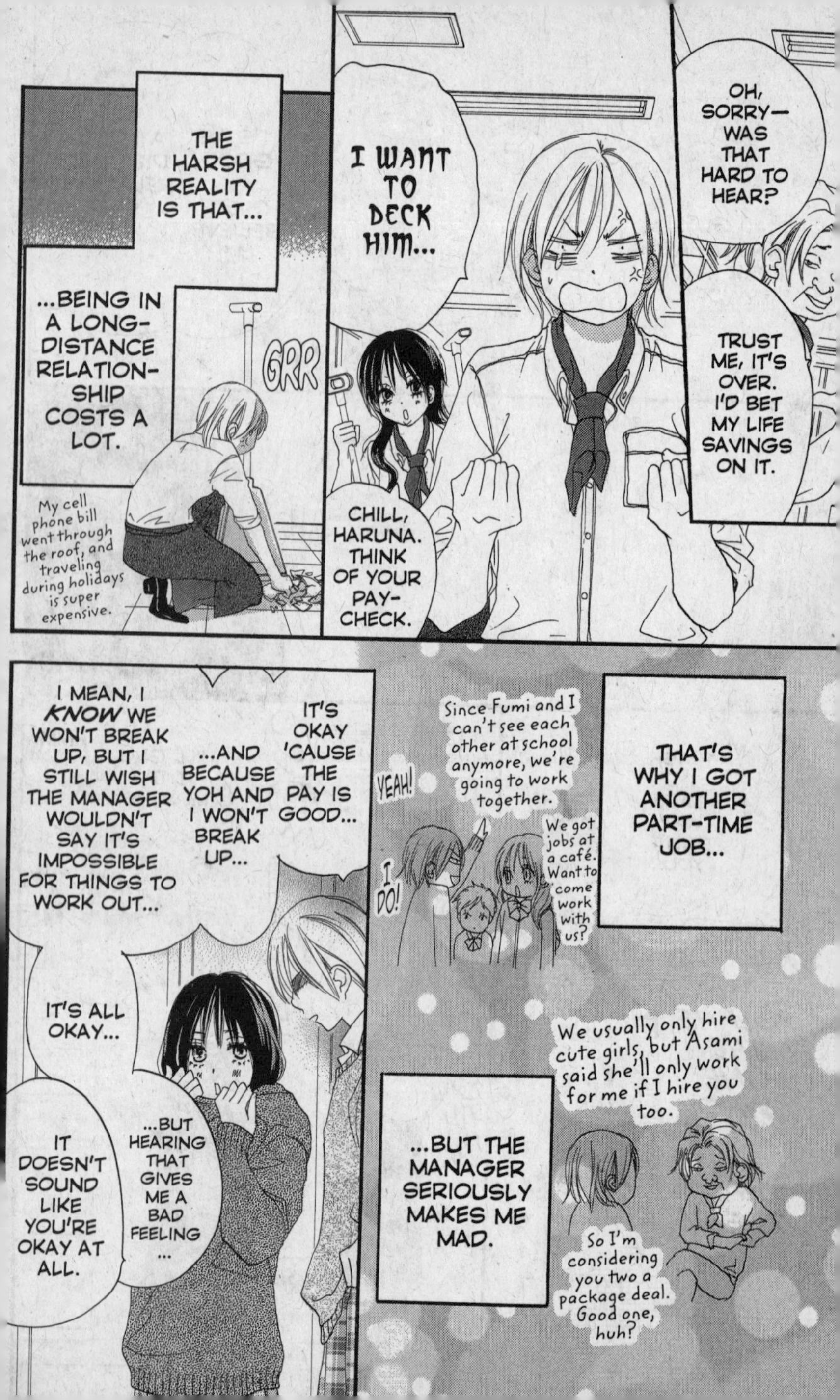

OH, SORRY—WAS THAT HARD TO HEAR?
TRUST ME, IT'S OVER. I'D BET MY LIFE SAVINGS ON IT.
I WANT TO DECK HIM...
CHILL, HARUNA. THINK OF YOUR PAYCHECK.
THE HARSH REALITY IS THAT...
...BEING IN A LONG-DISTANCE RELATIONSHIP COSTS A LOT.
GRR
My cell phone bill went through the roof, and traveling during holidays is super expensive.
THAT'S WHY I GOT ANOTHER PART-TIME JOB...
Since Fumi and I can't see each other at school anymore, we're going to work together.
We got jobs at a café. Want to come work with us?
YEAH!
I DO!
We usually only hire cute girls, but Asami said she'll only work for me if I hire you too.
...BUT THE MANAGER SERIOUSLY MAKES ME MAD.
So I'm considering you two a package deal. Good one, huh?
IT'S OKAY 'CAUSE THE PAY IS GOOD...
...AND BECAUSE YOH AND I WON'T BREAK UP...
I MEAN, I *KNOW* WE WON'T BREAK UP, BUT I STILL WISH THE MANAGER WOULDN'T SAY IT'S IMPOSSIBLE FOR THINGS TO WORK OUT...
IT'S ALL OKAY...
...BUT HEARING THAT GIVES ME A BAD FEELING...
IT DOESN'T SOUND LIKE YOU'RE OKAY AT ALL.

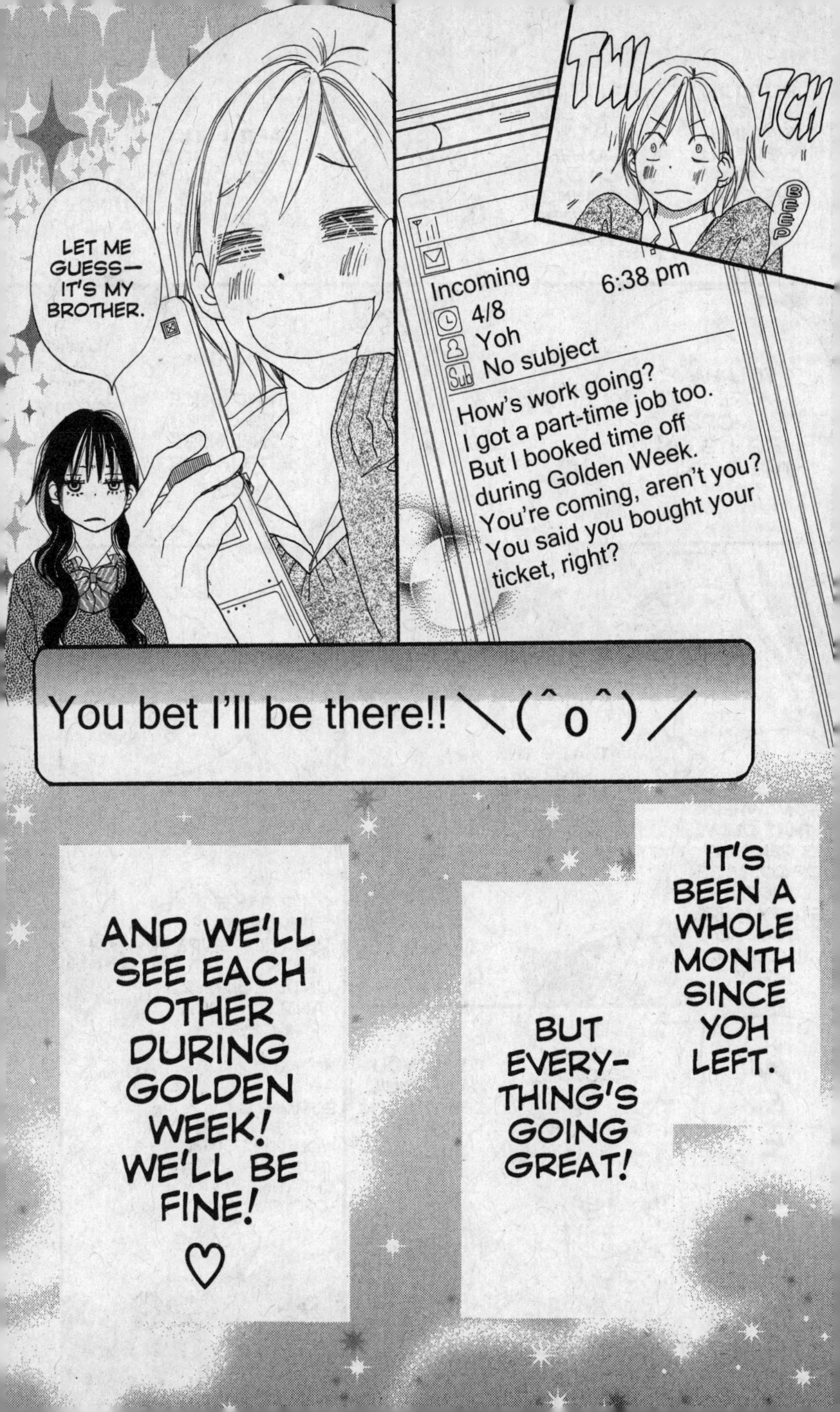
TWITCH
BEEP
Incoming 6:38 pm
4/8
Yoh
No subject
How's work going? I got a part-time job too. But I booked time off during Golden Week. You're coming, aren't you? You said you bought your ticket, right?
LET ME GUESS—IT'S MY BROTHER.
You bet I'll be there!! ＼(^o^)／
IT'S BEEN A WHOLE MONTH SINCE YOH LEFT.
BUT EVERY-THING'S GOING GREAT!
AND WE'LL SEE EACH OTHER DURING GOLDEN WEEK! WE'LL BE FINE! ♡

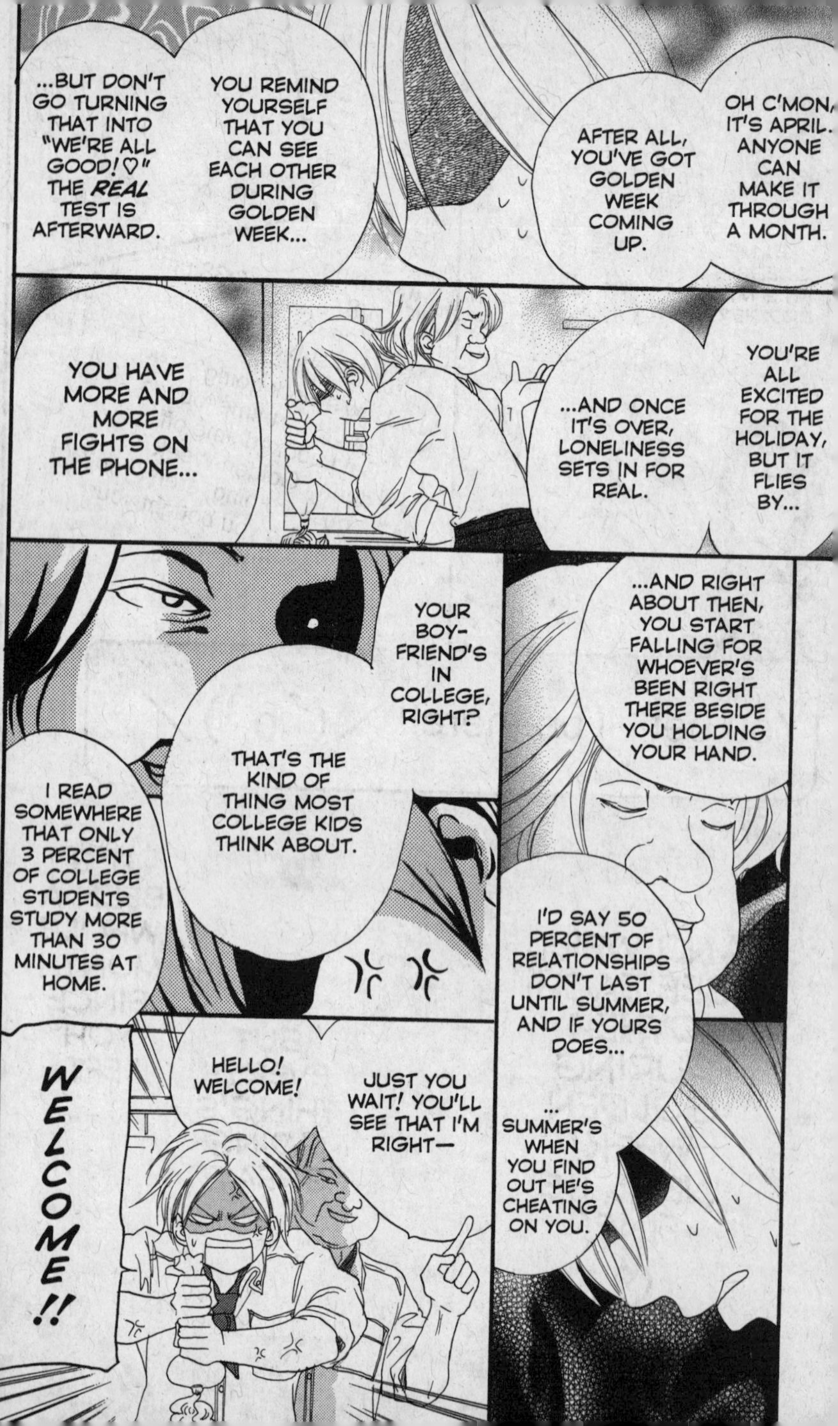
OH C'MON, IT'S APRIL. ANYONE CAN MAKE IT THROUGH A MONTH.
AFTER ALL, YOU'VE GOT GOLDEN WEEK COMING UP.
YOU REMIND YOURSELF THAT YOU CAN SEE EACH OTHER DURING GOLDEN WEEK...
...BUT DON'T GO TURNING THAT INTO "WE'RE ALL GOOD!♡" THE *REAL* TEST IS AFTERWARD.
YOU'RE ALL EXCITED FOR THE HOLIDAY, BUT IT FLIES BY...
...AND ONCE IT'S OVER, LONELINESS SETS IN FOR REAL.
YOU HAVE MORE AND MORE FIGHTS ON THE PHONE...
...AND RIGHT ABOUT THEN, YOU START FALLING FOR WHOEVER'S BEEN RIGHT THERE BESIDE YOU HOLDING YOUR HAND.
I'D SAY 50 PERCENT OF RELATIONSHIPS DON'T LAST UNTIL SUMMER, AND IF YOURS DOES...
...SUMMER'S WHEN YOU FIND OUT HE'S CHEATING ON YOU.
YOUR BOY-FRIEND'S IN COLLEGE, RIGHT?
THAT'S THE KIND OF THING MOST COLLEGE KIDS THINK ABOUT.
I READ SOMEWHERE THAT ONLY 3 PERCENT OF COLLEGE STUDENTS STUDY MORE THAN 30 MINUTES AT HOME.
JUST YOU WAIT! YOU'LL SEE THAT I'M RIGHT—
HELLO! WELCOME!
WELCOME!!

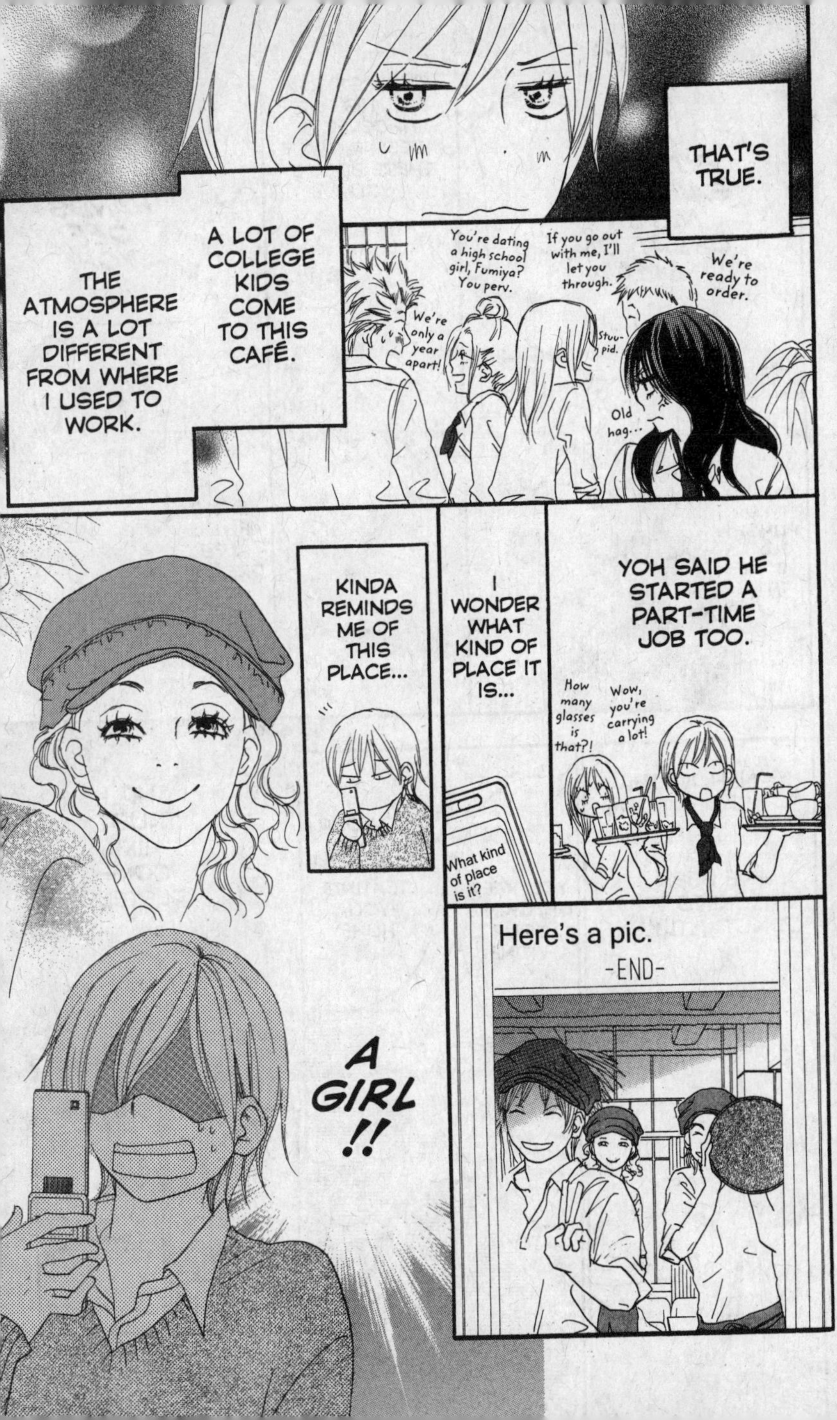
THAT'S TRUE.
A LOT OF COLLEGE KIDS COME TO THIS CAFÉ.
THE ATMOSPHERE IS A LOT DIFFERENT FROM WHERE I USED TO WORK.
We're ready to order.
If you go out with me, I'll let you through.
Stuu-pid.
You're dating a high school girl, Fumiya? You perv.
We're only a year apart!
Old hag...
YOH SAID HE STARTED A PART-TIME JOB TOO.
Wow, you're carrying a lot!
How many glasses is that?!
I WONDER WHAT KIND OF PLACE IT IS...
What kind of place is it?
KINDA REMINDS ME OF THIS PLACE...
Here's a pic.
-END-
A GIRL!!

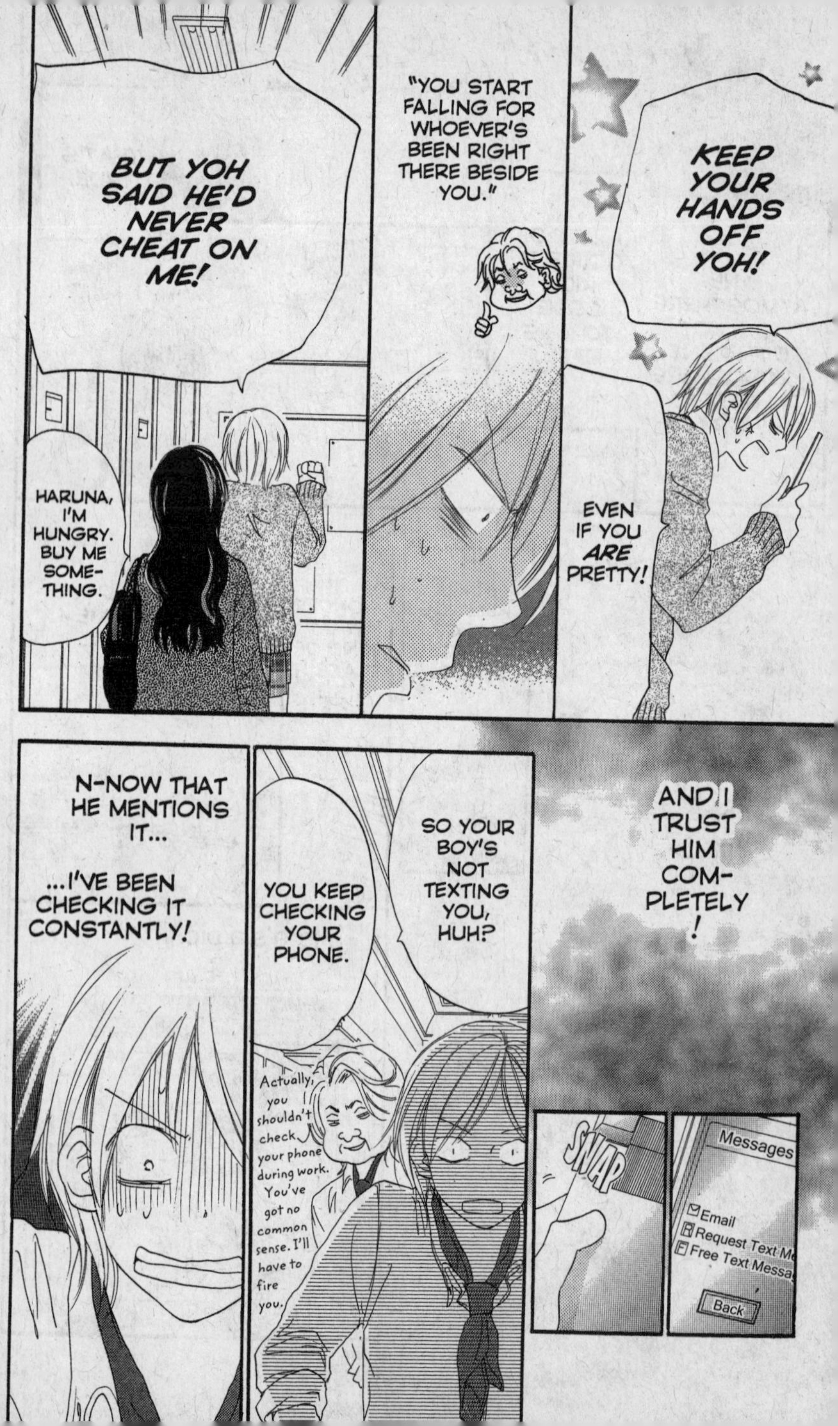
KEEP YOUR HANDS OFF YOH!
EVEN IF YOU *ARE* PRETTY!
"YOU START FALLING FOR WHOEVER'S BEEN RIGHT THERE BESIDE YOU."
BUT YOH SAID HE'D NEVER CHEAT ON ME!
HARUNA, I'M HUNGRY. BUY ME SOME-THING.
AND I TRUST HIM COM-PLETELY!
Messages
Email
Request Text M
Free Text Messa
Back
SNAP
SO YOUR BOY'S NOT TEXTING YOU, HUH?
YOU KEEP CHECKING YOUR PHONE.
Actually, you shouldn't check your phone during work. You've got no common sense. I'll have to fire you.
N-NOW THAT HE MENTIONS IT...
...I'VE BEEN CHECKING IT CONSTANTLY!

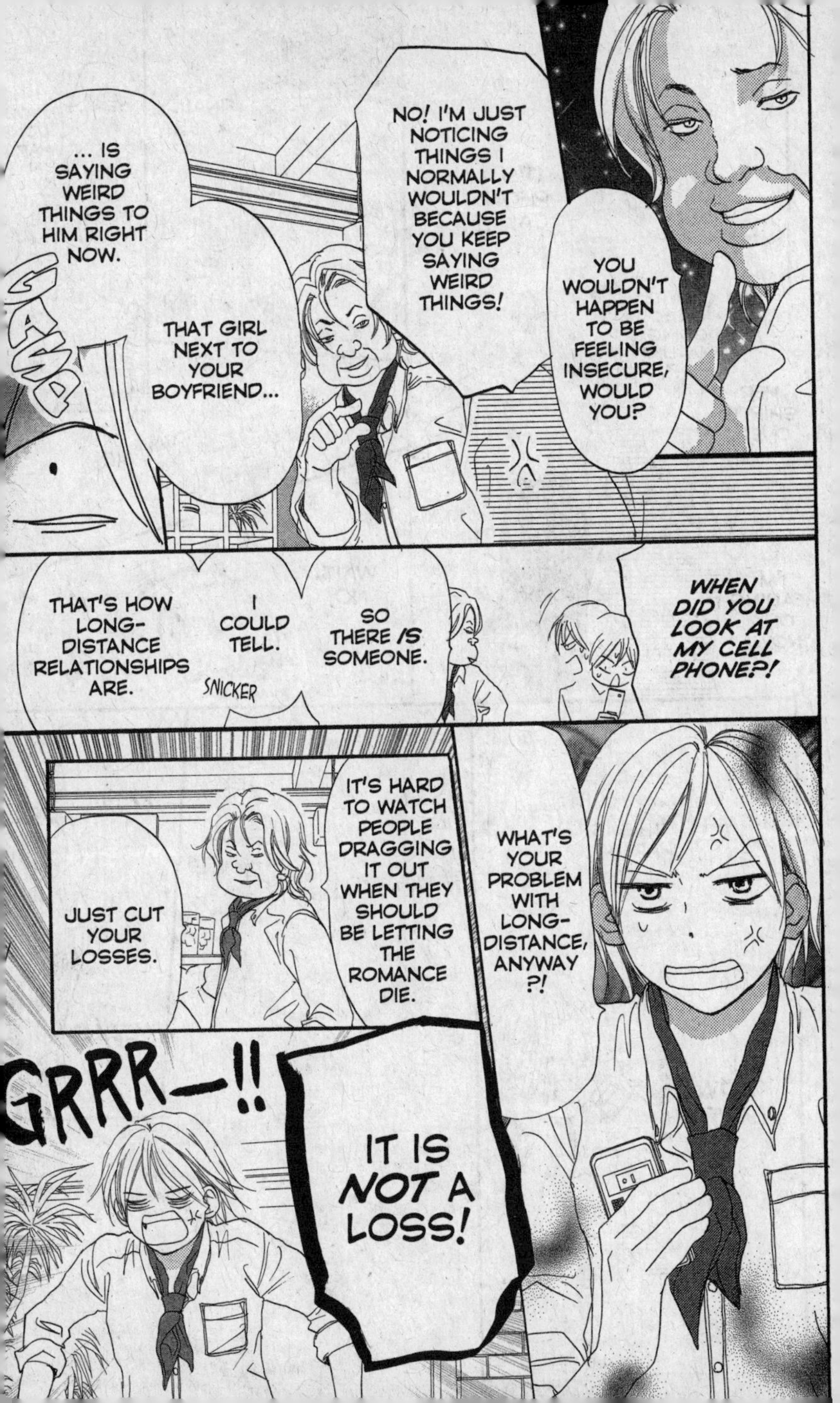
YOU WOULDN'T HAPPEN TO BE FEELING INSECURE, WOULD YOU?
NO! I'M JUST NOTICING THINGS I NORMALLY WOULDN'T BECAUSE YOU KEEP SAYING WEIRD THINGS!
THAT GIRL NEXT TO YOUR BOYFRIEND...
... IS SAYING WEIRD THINGS TO HIM RIGHT NOW.
GASP
WHEN DID YOU LOOK AT MY CELL PHONE?!
SO THERE *IS* SOMEONE.
I COULD TELL.
SNICKER
THAT'S HOW LONG-DISTANCE RELATIONSHIPS ARE.
WHAT'S YOUR PROBLEM WITH LONG-DISTANCE, ANYWAY?!
IT'S HARD TO WATCH PEOPLE DRAGGING IT OUT WHEN THEY SHOULD BE LETTING THE ROMANCE DIE.
JUST CUT YOUR LOSSES.
IT IS *NOT* A LOSS!
GRRR—!!

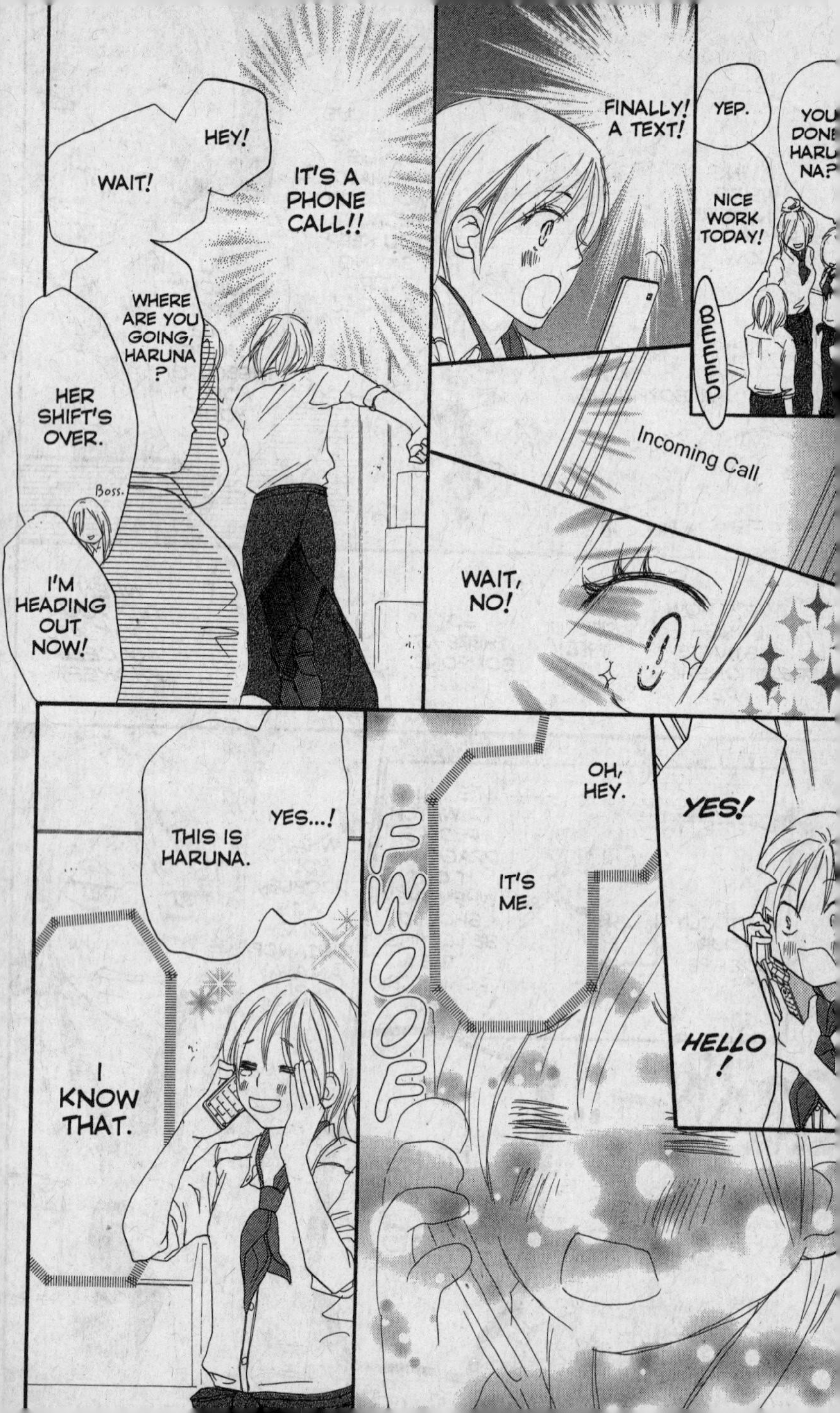
YOU DONE HARU NA?
YEP.
NICE WORK TODAY!
BEEEP
FINALLY! A TEXT!
Incoming Call
WAIT, NO!
IT'S A PHONE CALL!!
HEY!
WAIT!
WHERE ARE YOU GOING, HARUNA?
HER SHIFT'S OVER.
Boss.
I'M HEADING OUT NOW!
YES!
HELLO!
OH, HEY.
IT'S ME.
FWOOF
YES...!
THIS IS HARUNA.
...
I KNOW THAT.

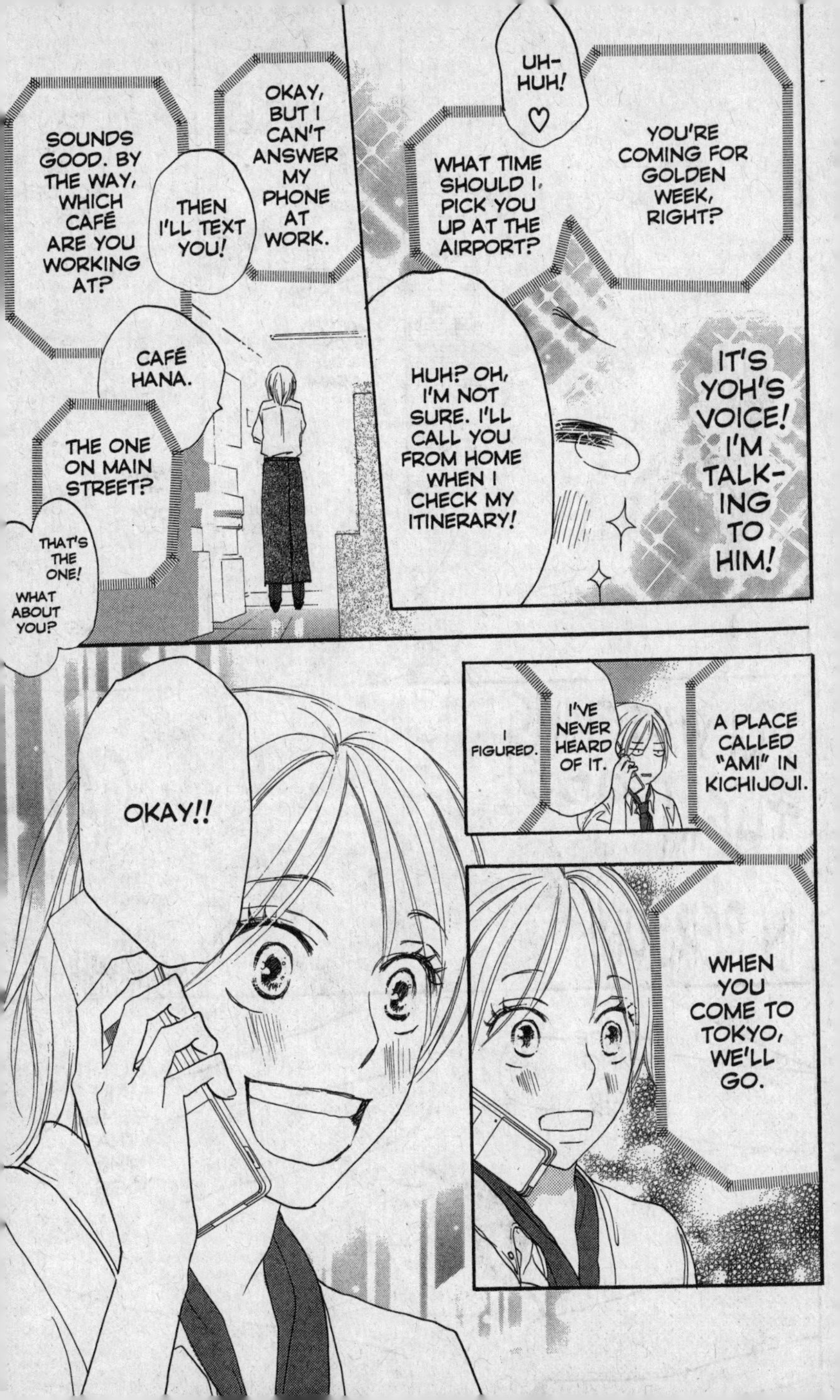
YOU'RE COMING FOR GOLDEN WEEK, RIGHT?
UH-HUH! ♡
WHAT TIME SHOULD I PICK YOU UP AT THE AIRPORT?
IT'S YOH'S VOICE! I'M TALKING TO HIM!
HUH? OH, I'M NOT SURE. I'LL CALL YOU FROM HOME WHEN I CHECK MY ITINERARY!
OKAY, BUT I CAN'T ANSWER MY PHONE AT WORK.
THEN I'LL TEXT YOU!
SOUNDS GOOD. BY THE WAY, WHICH CAFÉ ARE YOU WORKING AT?
CAFÉ HANA.
THE ONE ON MAIN STREET?
THAT'S THE ONE! WHAT ABOUT YOU?
A PLACE CALLED "AMI" IN KICHIJOJI.
I'VE NEVER HEARD OF IT.
I FIGURED.
WHEN YOU COME TO TOKYO, WE'LL GO.
OKAY!!

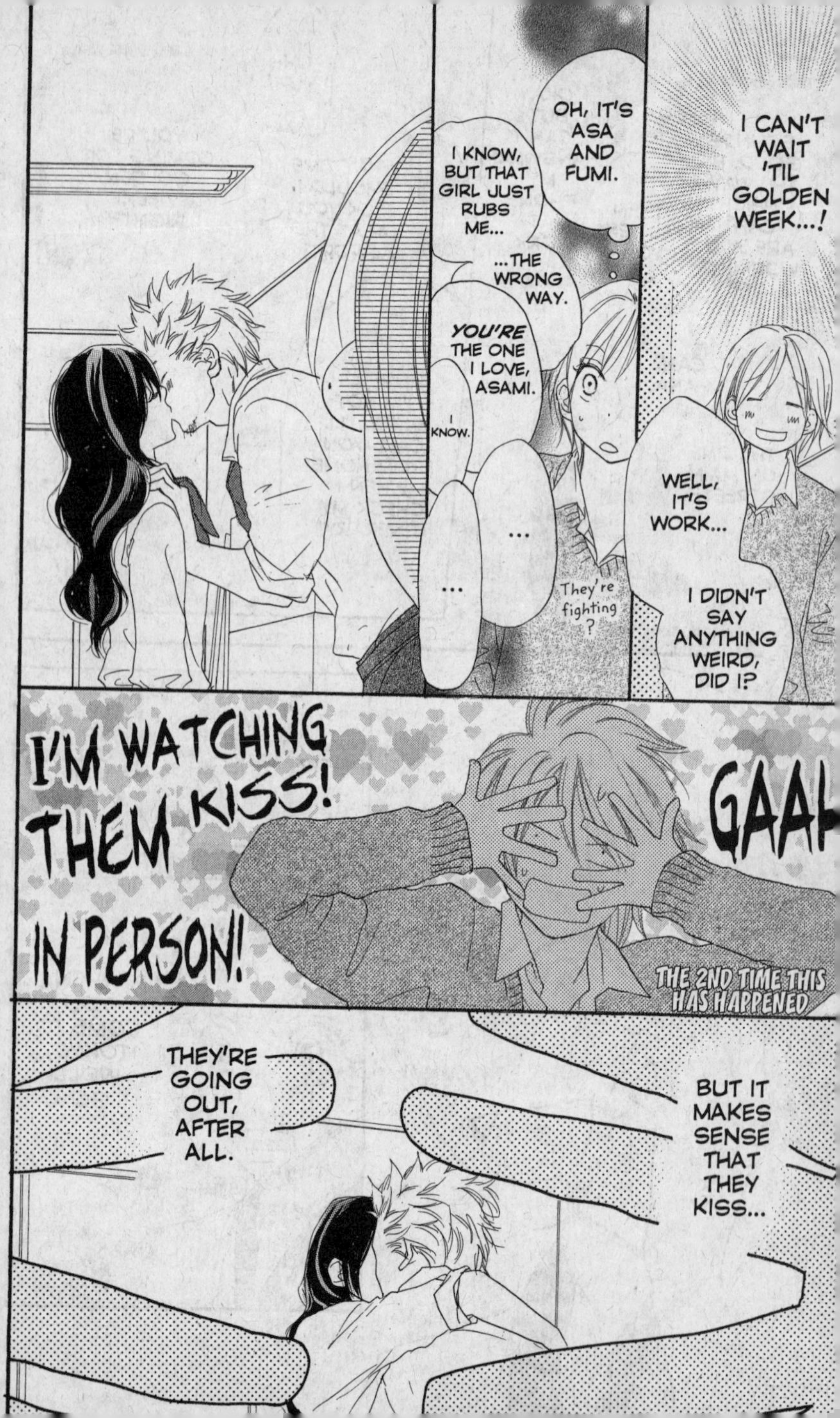
I CAN'T WAIT 'TIL GOLDEN WEEK...!
WELL, IT'S WORK...
I DIDN'T SAY ANYTHING WEIRD, DID I?
OH, IT'S ASA AND FUMI.
They're fighting?
I KNOW, BUT THAT GIRL JUST RUBS ME...
...THE WRONG WAY.
YOU'RE THE ONE I LOVE, ASAMI.
I KNOW.
...
...
GAA
THE 2ND TIME THIS HAS HAPPENED
I'M WATCHING THEM KISS!
IN PERSON!
BUT IT MAKES SENSE THAT THEY KISS...
THEY'RE GOING OUT, AFTER ALL.

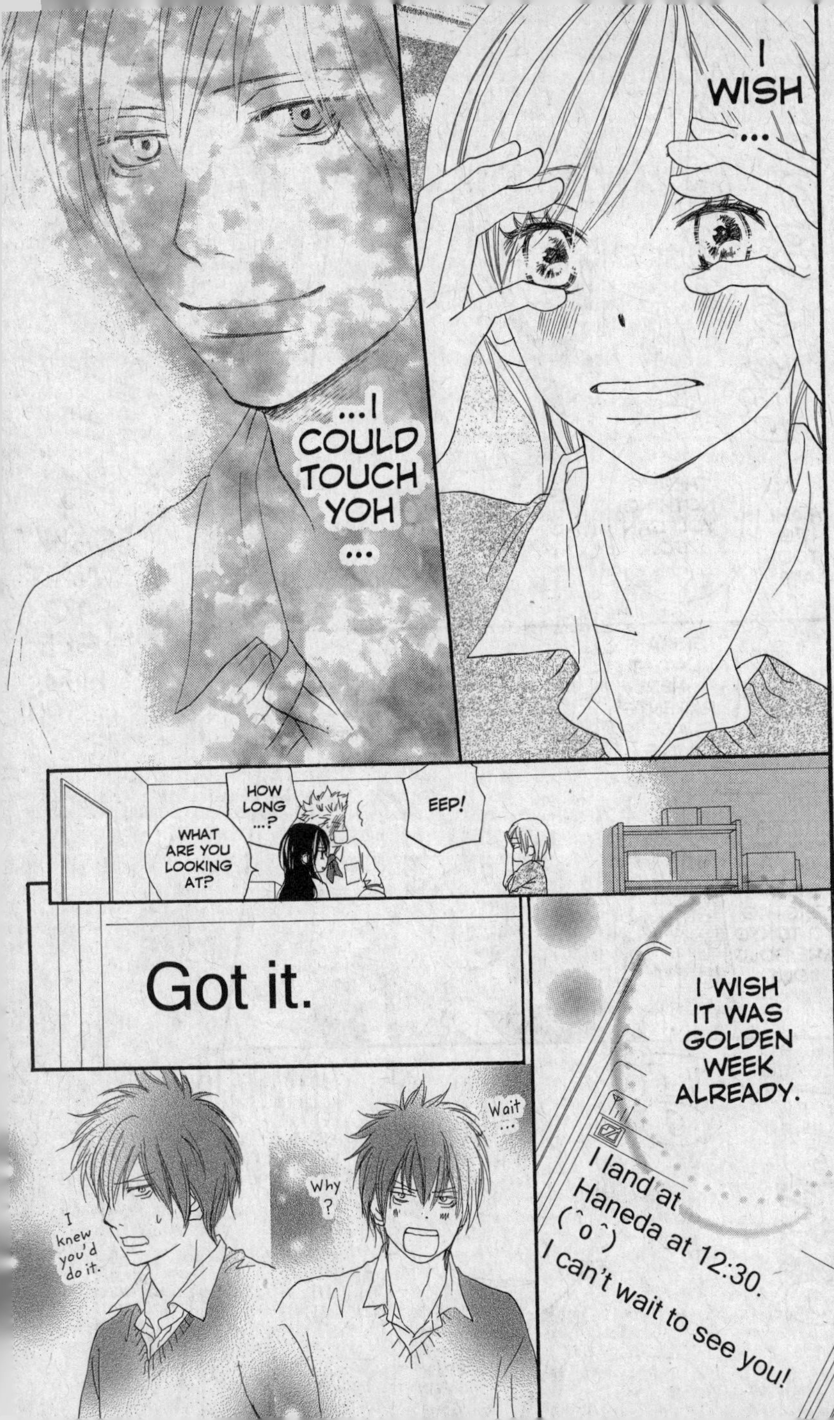

I WISH ...
...I COULD TOUCH YOH ...
EEP!
HOW LONG ...?
WHAT ARE YOU LOOKING AT?
I WISH IT WAS GOLDEN WEEK ALREADY.
I land at Haneda at 12:30. (^o^) I can't wait to see you!
Got it.
Wait ...
Why ?
I knew you'd do it.

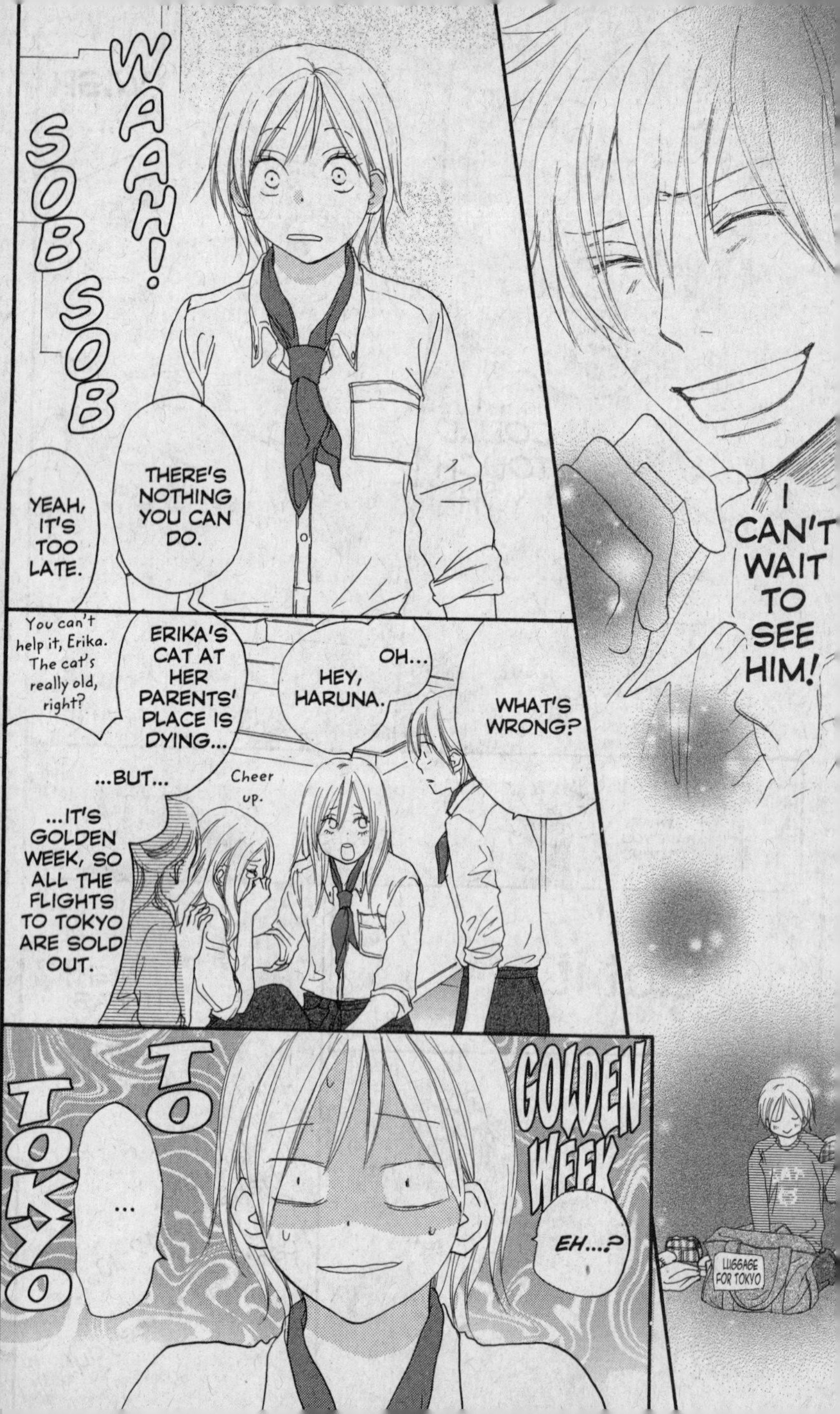

I CAN'T WAIT TO SEE HIM!
LUGGAGE FOR TOKYO
WAAAH!
SOB SOB
THERE'S NOTHING YOU CAN DO.
YEAH, IT'S TOO LATE.
WHAT'S WRONG?
OH... HEY, HARUNA.
ERIKA'S CAT AT HER PARENTS' PLACE IS DYING...
You can't help it, Erika. The cat's really old, right?
Cheer up.
...BUT...
...IT'S GOLDEN WEEK, SO ALL THE FLIGHTS TO TOKYO ARE SOLD OUT.
GOLDEN WEEK
EH...?
TO TOKYO
...

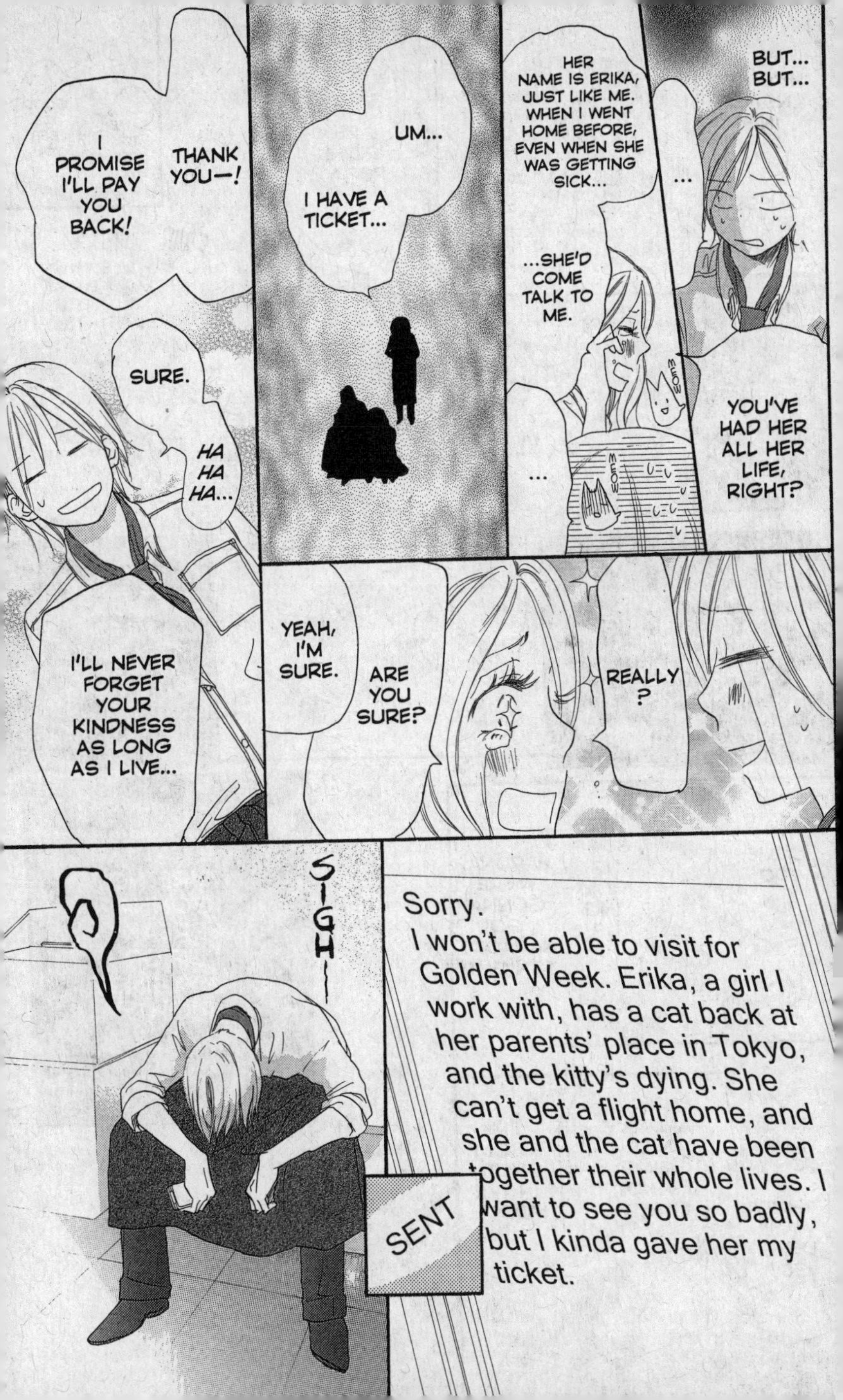
BUT... BUT...
...
YOU'VE HAD HER ALL HER LIFE, RIGHT?
HER NAME IS ERIKA, JUST LIKE ME. WHEN I WENT HOME BEFORE, EVEN WHEN SHE WAS GETTING SICK...
...SHE'D COME TALK TO ME.
MEOW
MEOW
...
UM...
I HAVE A TICKET...
REALLY?
ARE YOU SURE?
YEAH, I'M SURE.
THANK YOU—!
I PROMISE I'LL PAY YOU BACK!
SURE.
HA HA HA...
I'LL NEVER FORGET YOUR KINDNESS AS LONG AS I LIVE...
Sorry.
I won't be able to visit for Golden Week. Erika, a girl I work with, has a cat back at her parents' place in Tokyo, and the kitty's dying. She can't get a flight home, and she and the cat have been together their whole lives. I want to see you so badly, but I kinda gave her my ticket.
SENT
SIGH

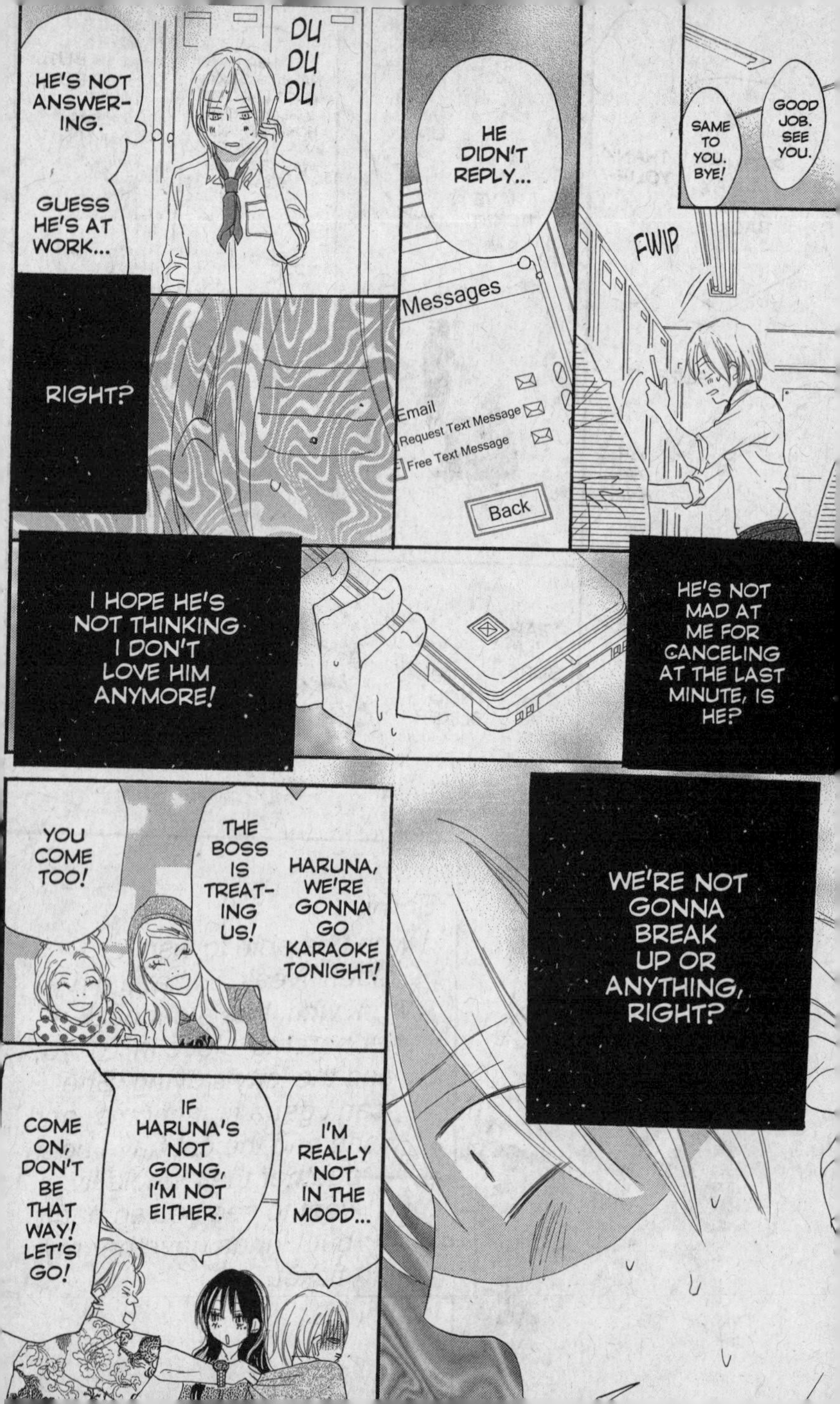
GOOD JOB. SEE YOU.
SAME TO YOU. BYE!
FWIP
HE DIDN'T REPLY...
Messages
Email
Request Text Message
Free Text Message
Back
DU DU DU
HE'S NOT ANSWERING.
GUESS HE'S AT WORK...
RIGHT?
HE'S NOT MAD AT ME FOR CANCELING AT THE LAST MINUTE, IS HE?
I HOPE HE'S NOT THINKING I DON'T LOVE HIM ANYMORE!
WE'RE NOT GONNA BREAK UP OR ANYTHING, RIGHT?
HARUNA, WE'RE GONNA GO KARAOKE TONIGHT!
THE BOSS IS TREATING US!
YOU COME TOO!
I'M REALLY NOT IN THE MOOD...
IF HARUNA'S NOT GOING, I'M NOT EITHER.
COME ON, DON'T BE THAT WAY! LET'S GO!

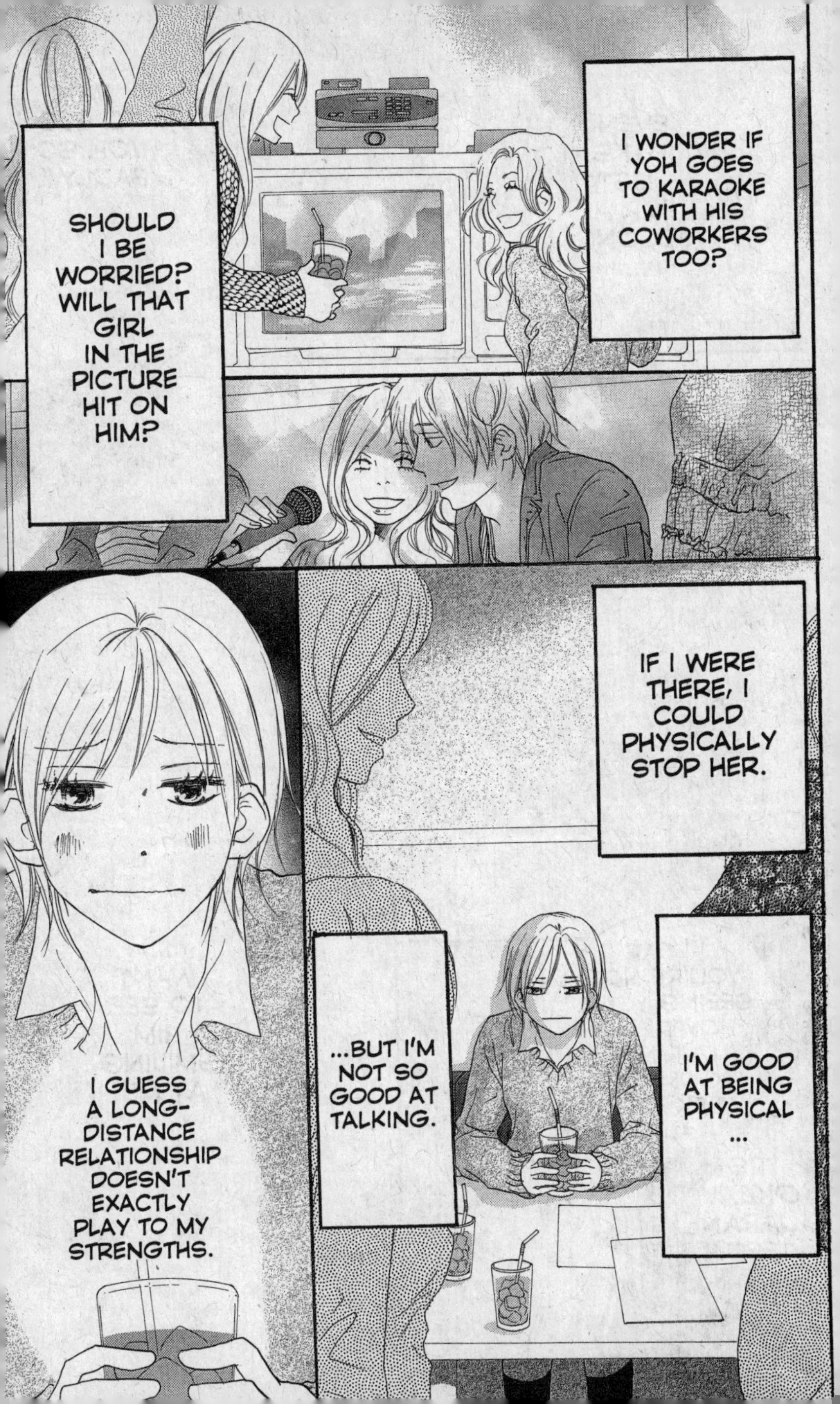
I WONDER IF YOH GOES TO KARAOKE WITH HIS COWORKERS TOO?
SHOULD I BE WORRIED? WILL THAT GIRL IN THE PICTURE HIT ON HIM?
IF I WERE THERE, I COULD PHYSICALLY STOP HER.
I'M GOOD AT BEING PHYSICAL ...
...BUT I'M NOT SO GOOD AT TALKING.
I GUESS A LONG-DISTANCE RELATIONSHIP DOESN'T EXACTLY PLAY TO MY STRENGTHS.

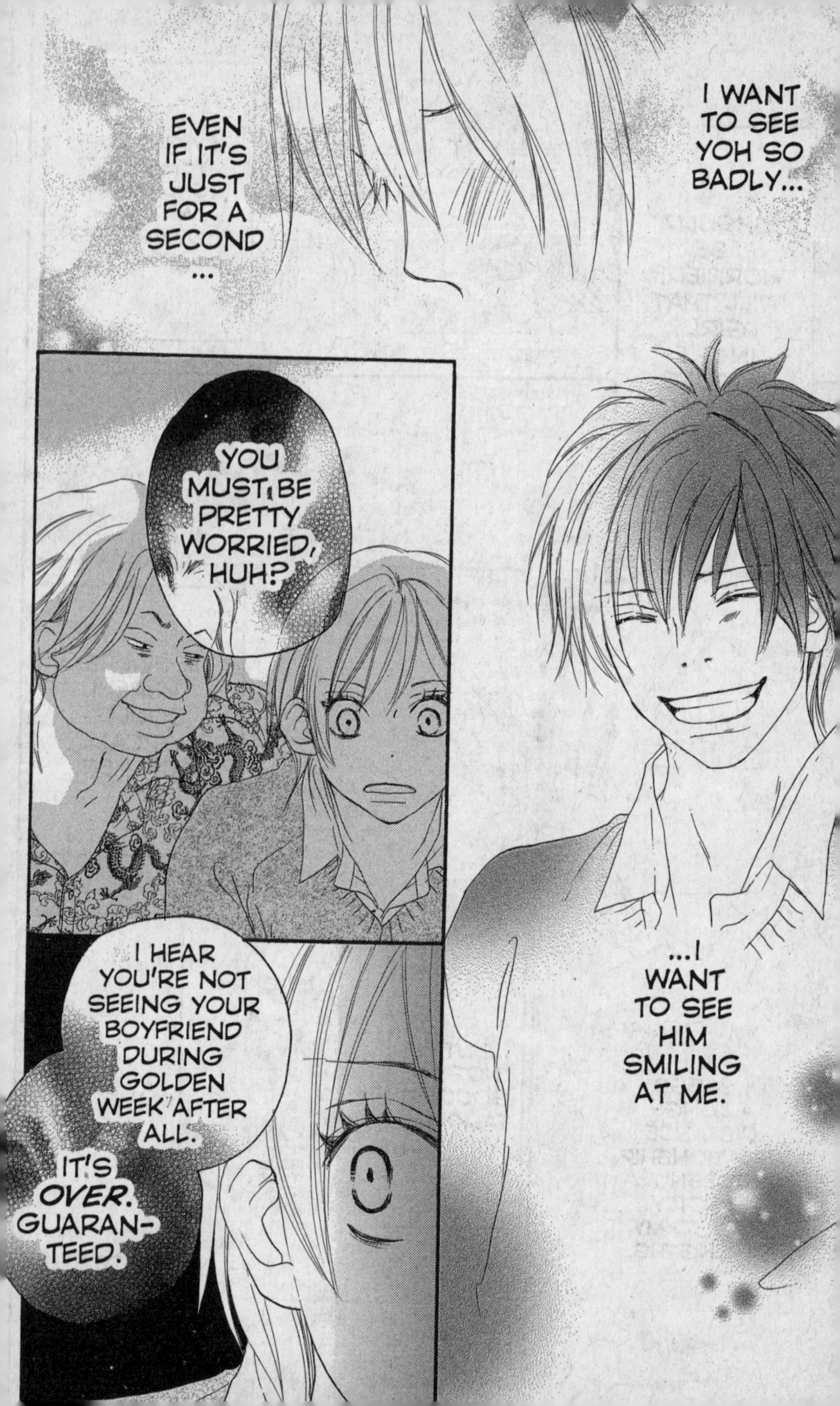
I WANT TO SEE YOH SO BADLY...
EVEN IF IT'S JUST FOR A SECOND...
...I WANT TO SEE HIM SMILING AT ME.
YOU MUST BE PRETTY WORRIED, HUH?
I HEAR YOU'RE NOT SEEING YOUR BOYFRIEND DURING GOLDEN WEEK AFTER ALL.
IT'S *OVER*. GUARAN-TEED.

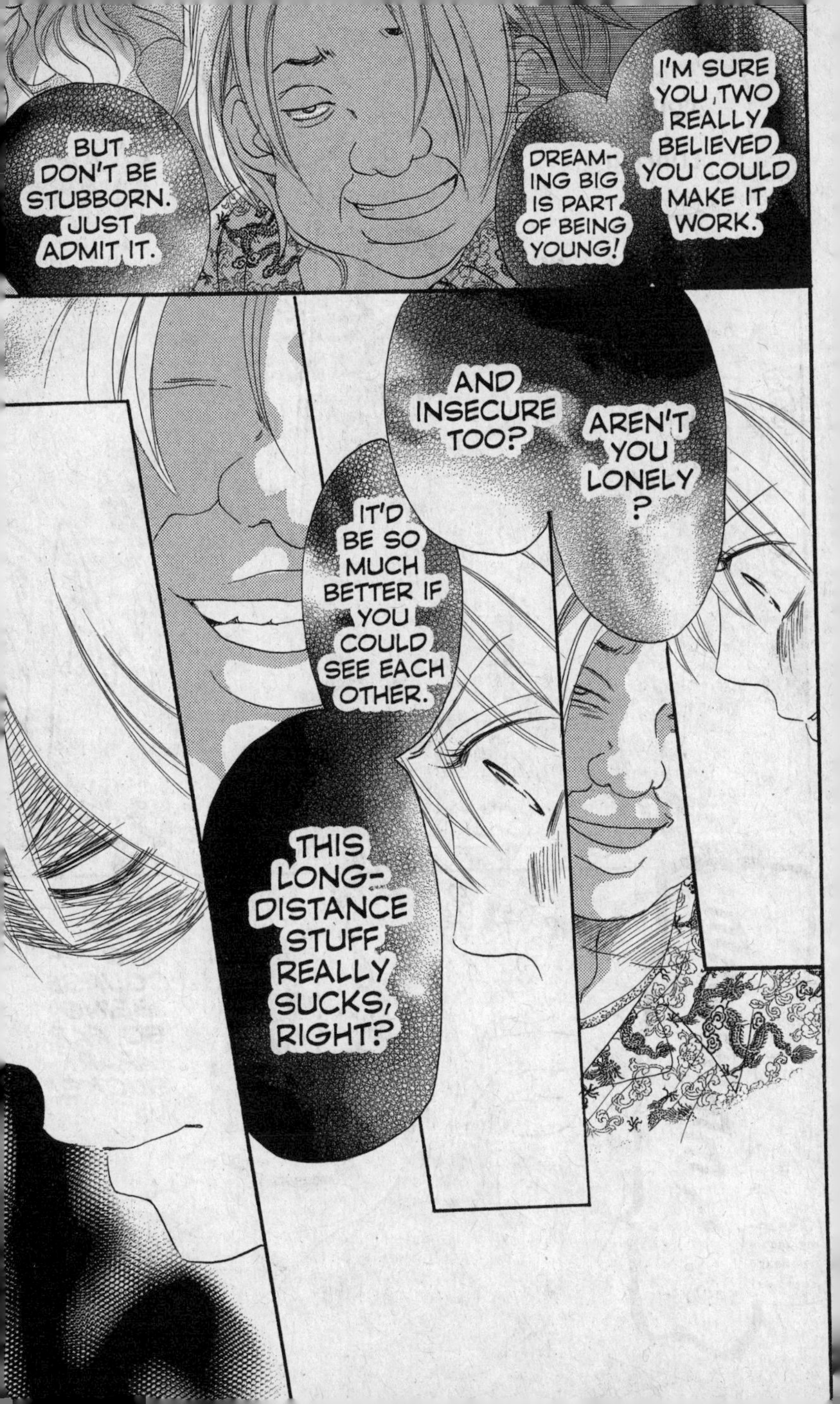
I'M SURE YOU TWO REALLY BELIEVED YOU COULD MAKE IT WORK.
DREAMING BIG IS PART OF BEING YOUNG!
BUT DON'T BE STUBBORN. JUST ADMIT IT.
AREN'T YOU LONELY?
AND INSECURE TOO?
IT'D BE SO MUCH BETTER IF YOU COULD SEE EACH OTHER.
THIS LONG-DISTANCE STUFF REALLY SUCKS, RIGHT?

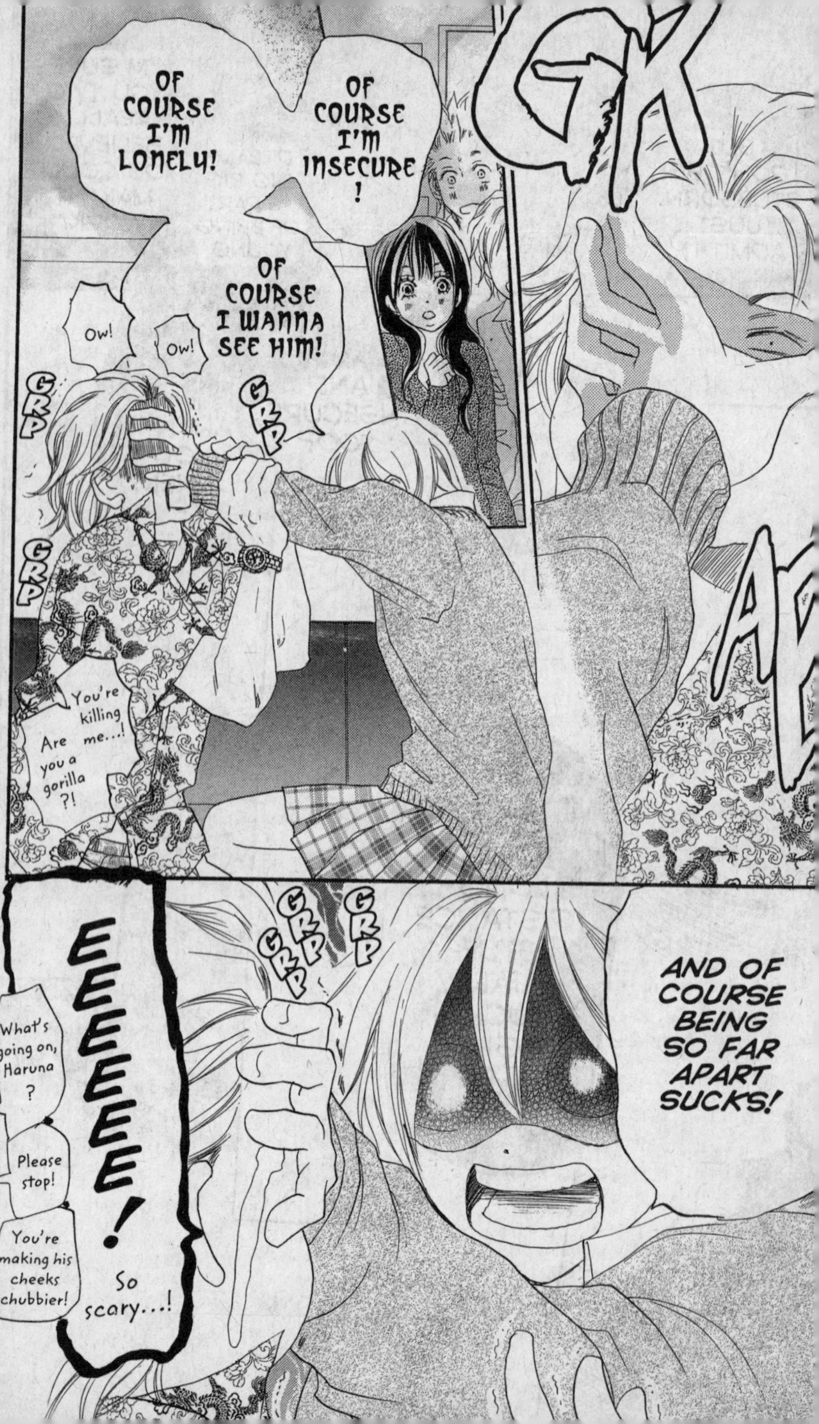
GK
OF COURSE I'M INSECURE!
OF COURSE I'M LONELY!
OF COURSE I WANNA SEE HIM!
GRP GRP
Ow!
Ow!
GRP GRP
You're killing me...!
Are you a gorilla?!
AND OF COURSE BEING SO FAR APART SUCKS!
GRP GRP GRP
EEEEEEE!
So scary...!
What's going on, Haruna?
Please stop!
You're making his cheeks chubbier!

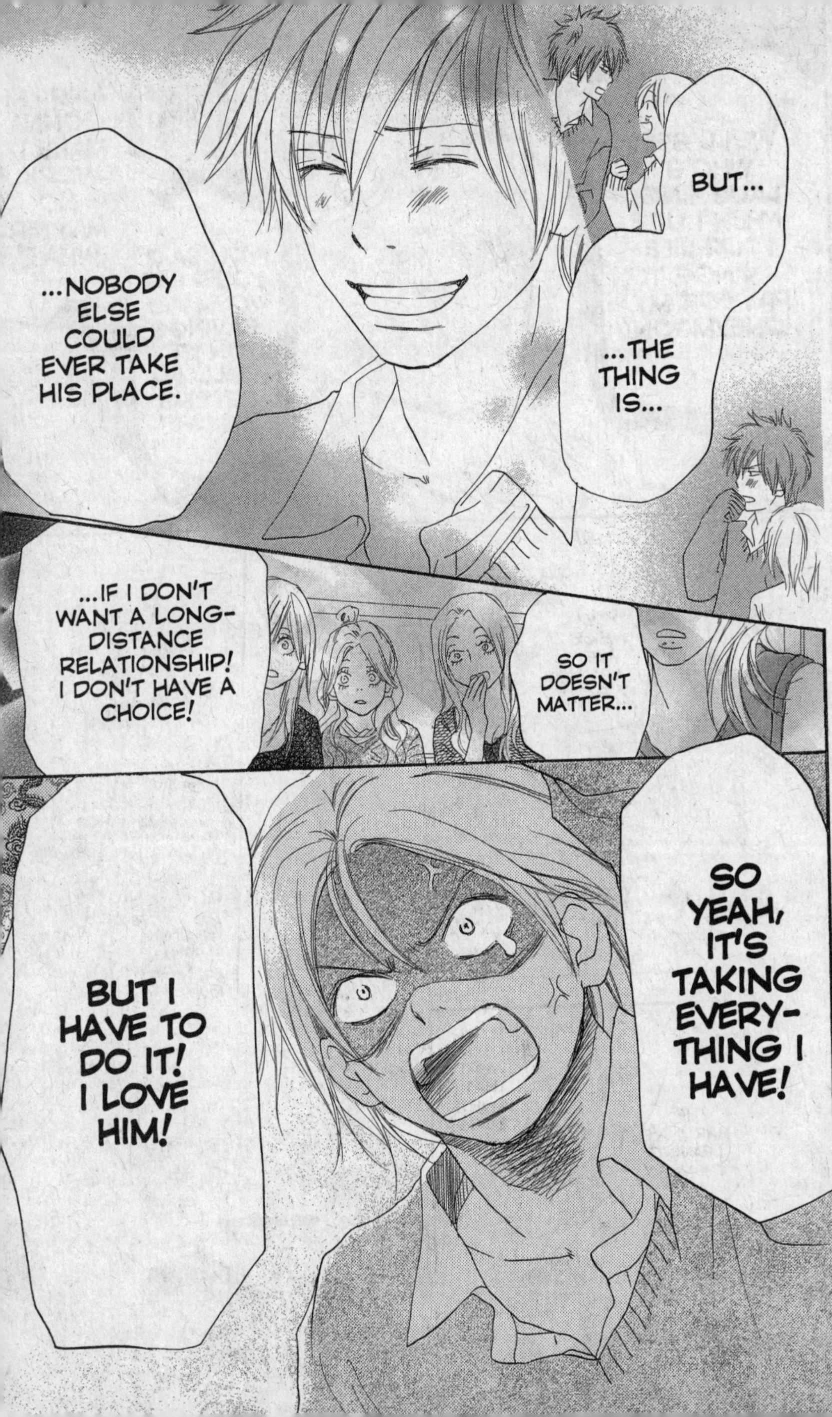
BUT...
...THE THING IS...
...NOBODY ELSE COULD EVER TAKE HIS PLACE.
SO IT DOESN'T MATTER...
...IF I DON'T WANT A LONG-DISTANCE RELATIONSHIP! I DON'T HAVE A CHOICE!
SO YEAH, IT'S TAKING EVERYTHING I HAVE!
BUT I HAVE TO DO IT! I LOVE HIM!

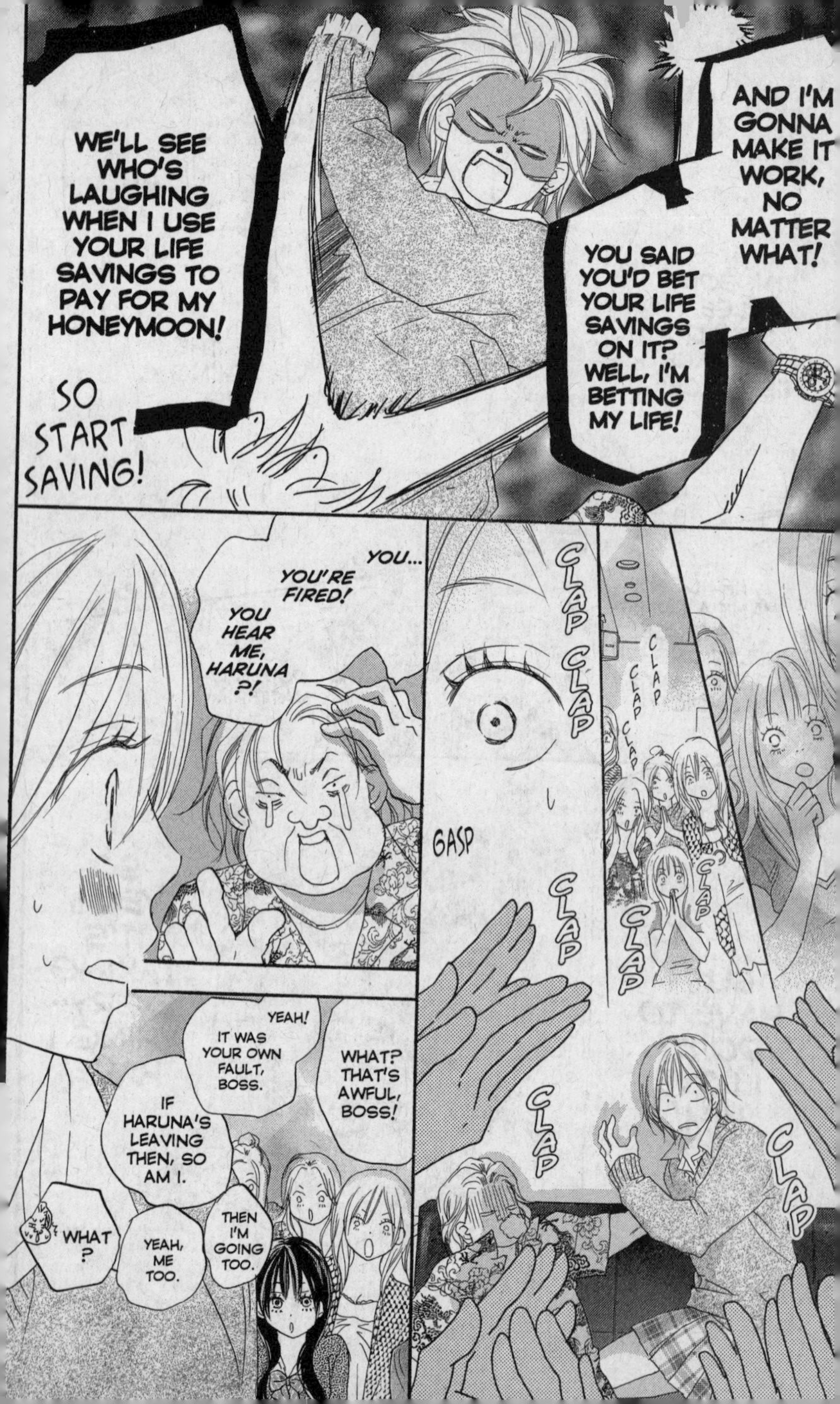
AND I'M GONNA MAKE IT WORK, NO MATTER WHAT!
YOU SAID YOU'D BET YOUR LIFE SAVINGS ON IT? WELL, I'M BETTING MY LIFE!
WE'LL SEE WHO'S LAUGHING WHEN I USE YOUR LIFE SAVINGS TO PAY FOR MY HONEYMOON!
SO START SAVING!
CLAP CLAP CLAP
CLAP
CLAP CLAP
GASP
CLAP CLAP
CLAP CLAP
YOU...
YOU'RE FIRED!
YOU HEAR ME, HARUNA?!
CLAP
CLAP
WHAT? THAT'S AWFUL, BOSS!
YEAH! IT WAS YOUR OWN FAULT, BOSS.
IF HARUNA'S LEAVING THEN, SO AM I.
THEN I'M GOING TOO.
YEAH, ME TOO.
WHAT?

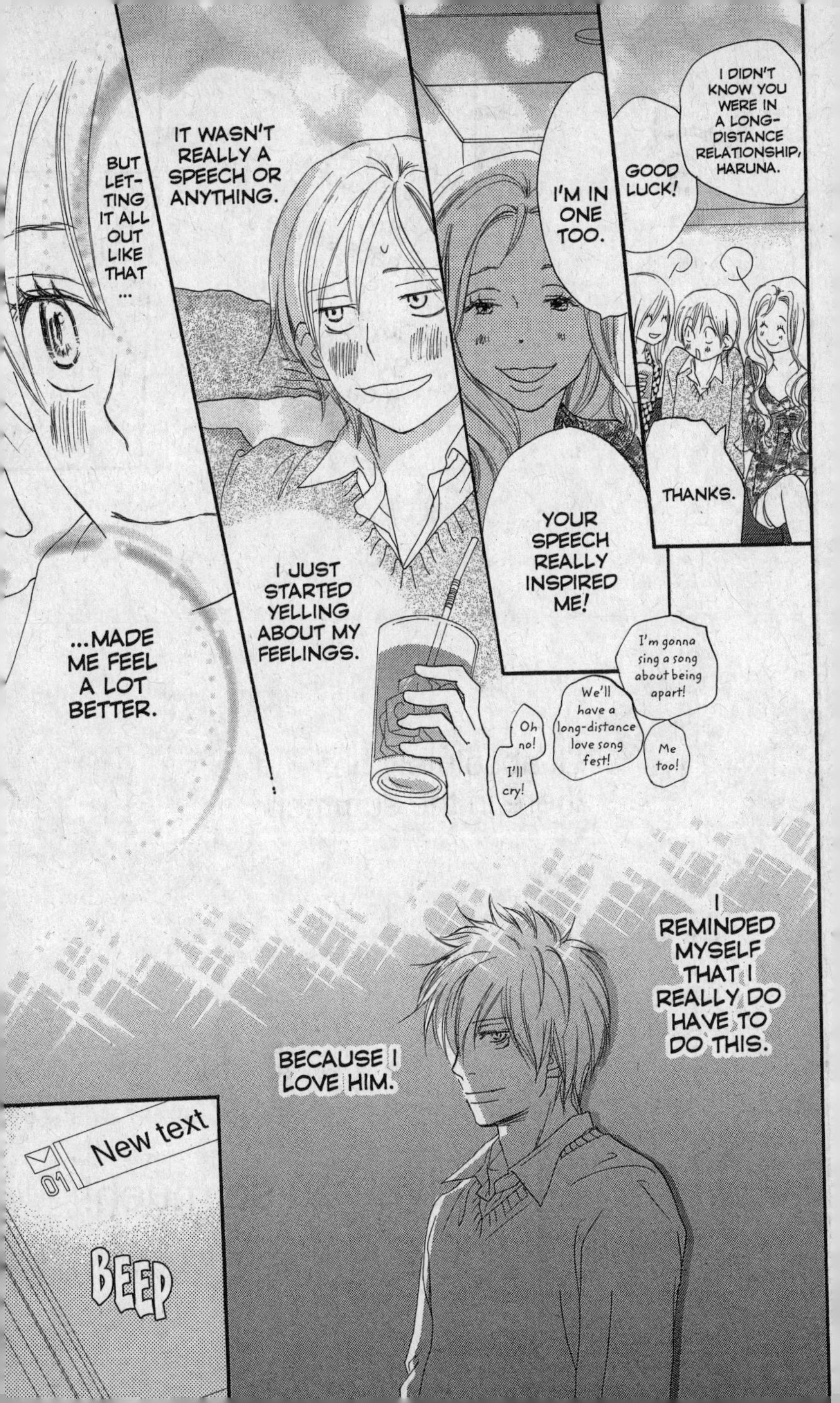
I DIDN'T KNOW YOU WERE IN A LONG-DISTANCE RELATIONSHIP, HARUNA.
GOOD LUCK!
THANKS.
I'M IN ONE TOO.
YOUR SPEECH REALLY INSPIRED ME!
I'm gonna sing a song about being apart!
Me too!
We'll have a long-distance love song fest!
Oh no! I'll cry!
IT WASN'T REALLY A SPEECH OR ANYTHING.
I JUST STARTED YELLING ABOUT MY FEELINGS.
BUT LET-TING IT ALL OUT LIKE THAT...
...MADE ME FEEL A LOT BETTER.
I REMINDED MYSELF THAT I REALLY DO HAVE TO DO THIS.
BECAUSE I LOVE HIM.
New text
01
BEEP

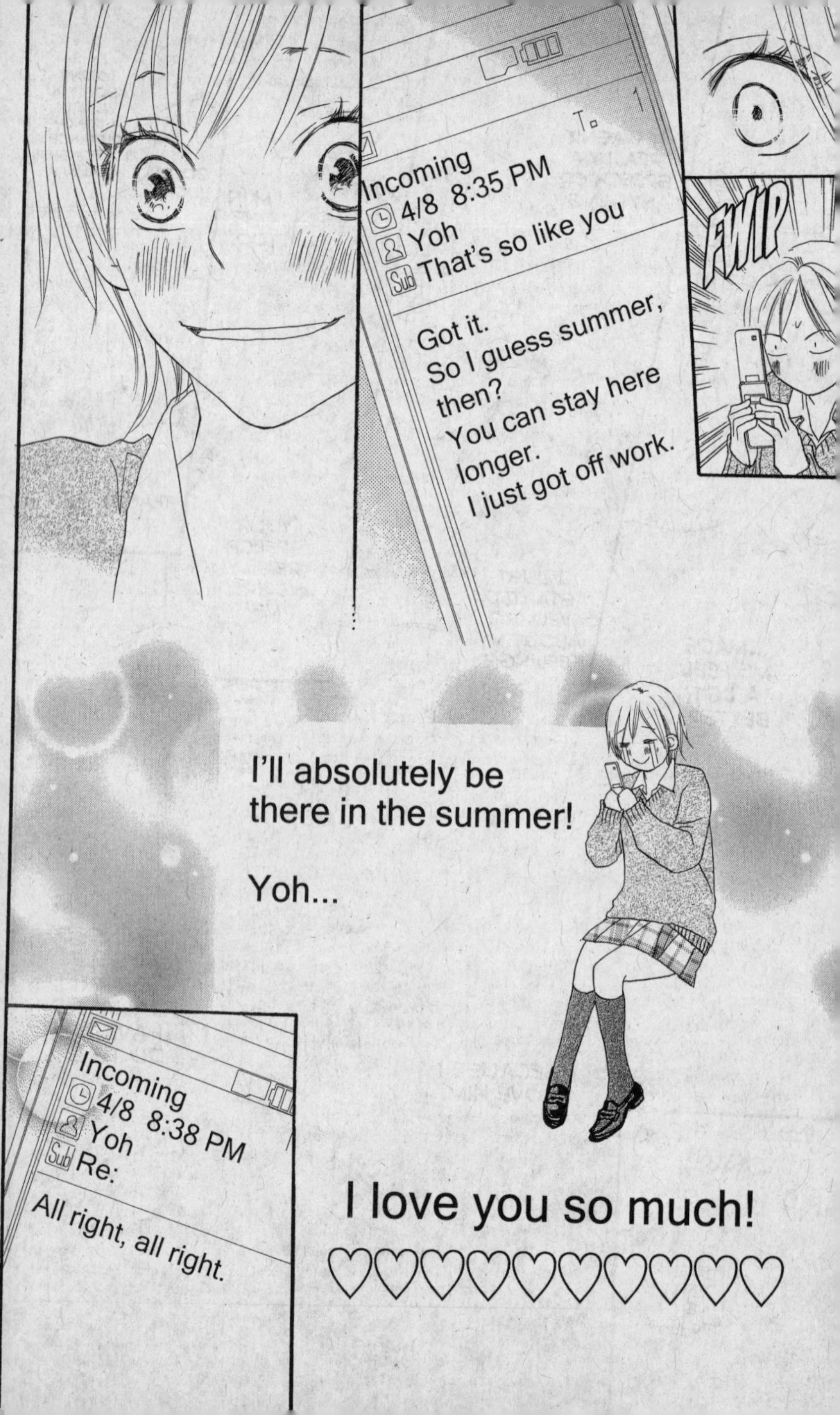
FWIP
Incoming
4/8 8:35 PM
Yoh
Sub That's so like you
Got it.
So I guess summer, then?
You can stay here longer.
I just got off work.
I'll absolutely be there in the summer!
Yoh...
Incoming
4/8 8:38 PM
Yoh
Sub Re:
All right, all right.
I love you so much!
♡♡♡♡♡♡♡♡♡♡

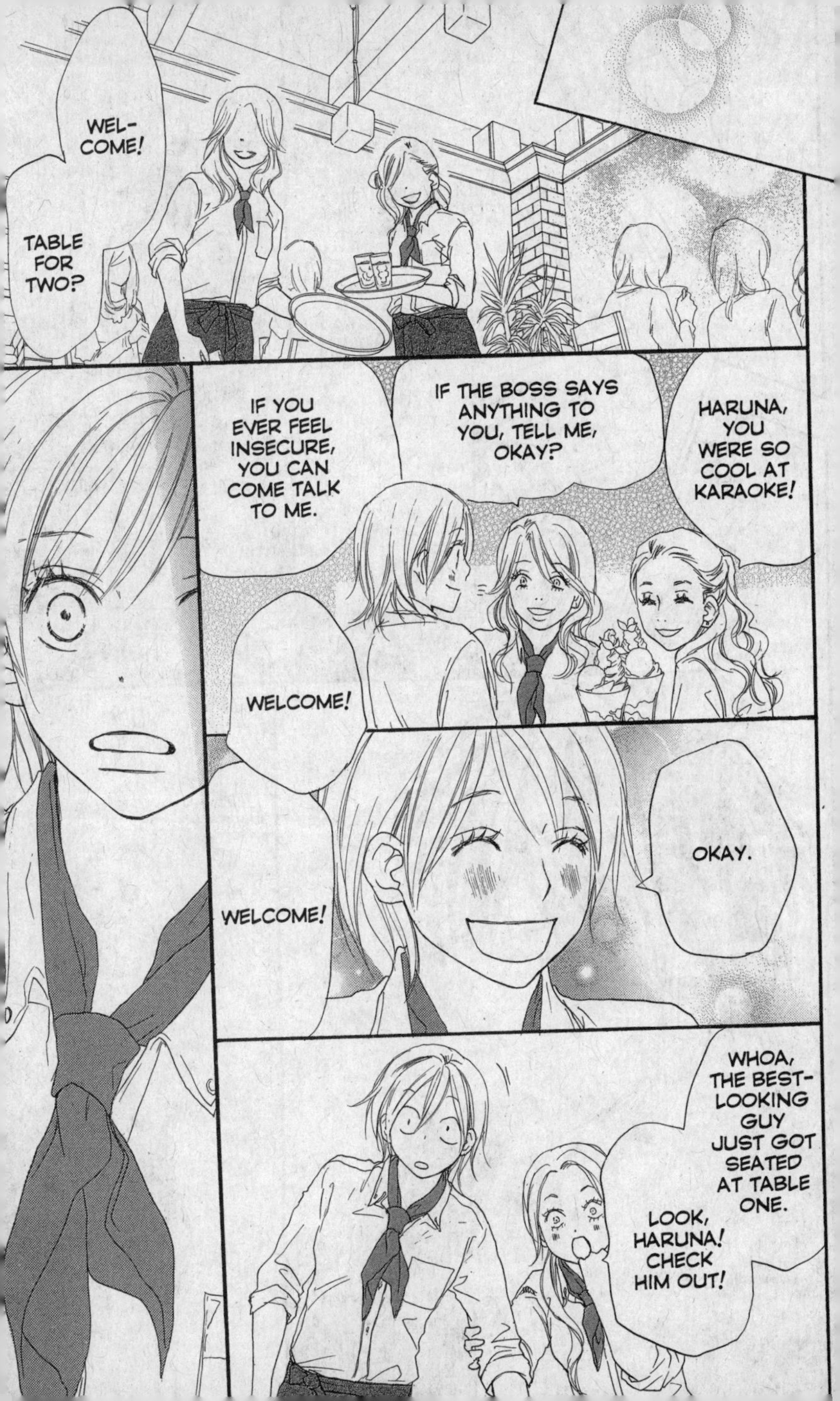
WEL-COME!
TABLE FOR TWO?
HARUNA, YOU WERE SO COOL AT KARAOKE!
IF THE BOSS SAYS ANYTHING TO YOU, TELL ME, OKAY?
IF YOU EVER FEEL INSECURE, YOU CAN COME TALK TO ME.
WELCOME!
OKAY.
WELCOME!
WHOA, THE BEST-LOOKING GUY JUST GOT SEATED AT TABLE ONE.
LOOK, HARUNA! CHECK HIM OUT!

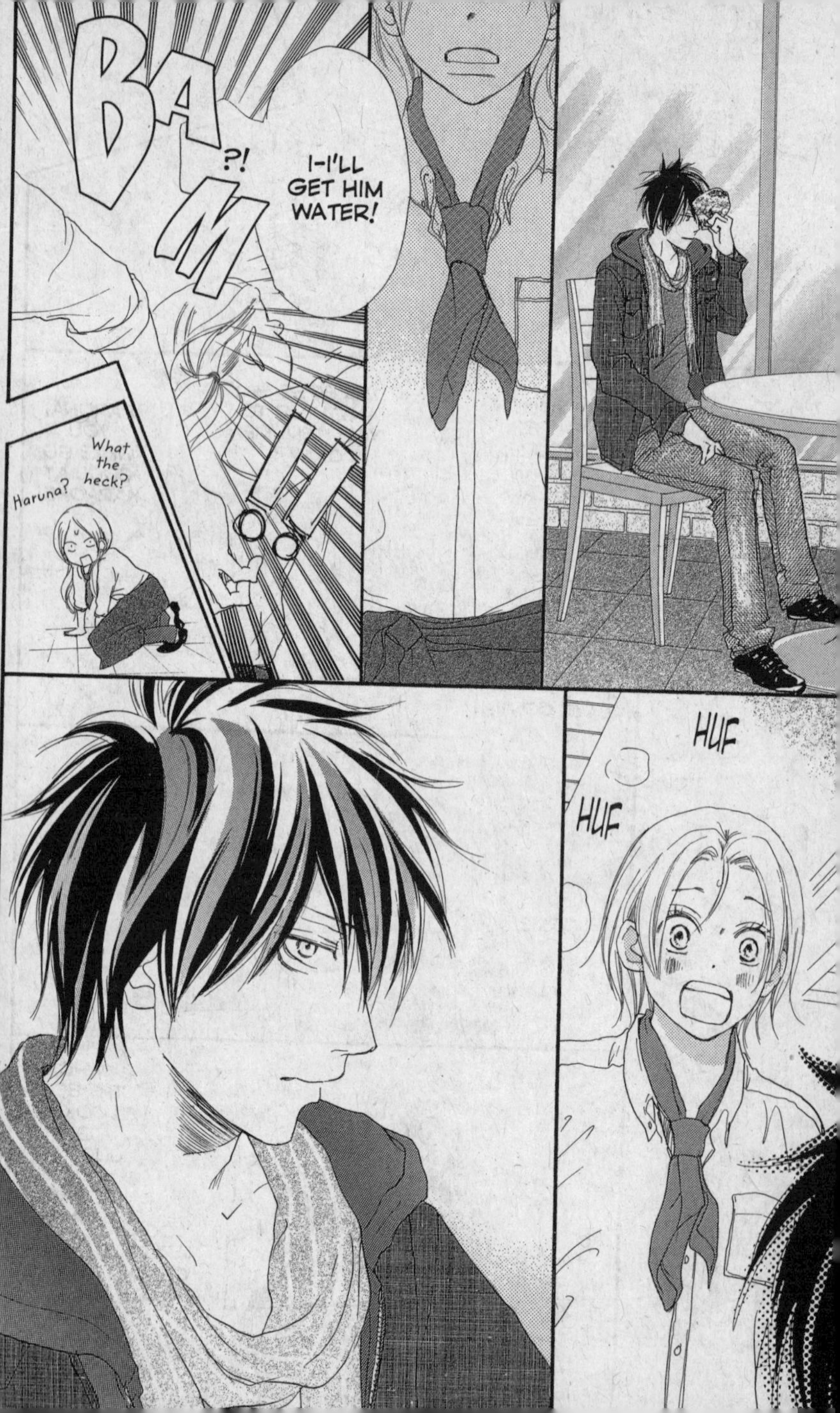
I-I'LL GET HIM WATER!
BAM
?!
What the heck?
Haruna?
HUF
HUF

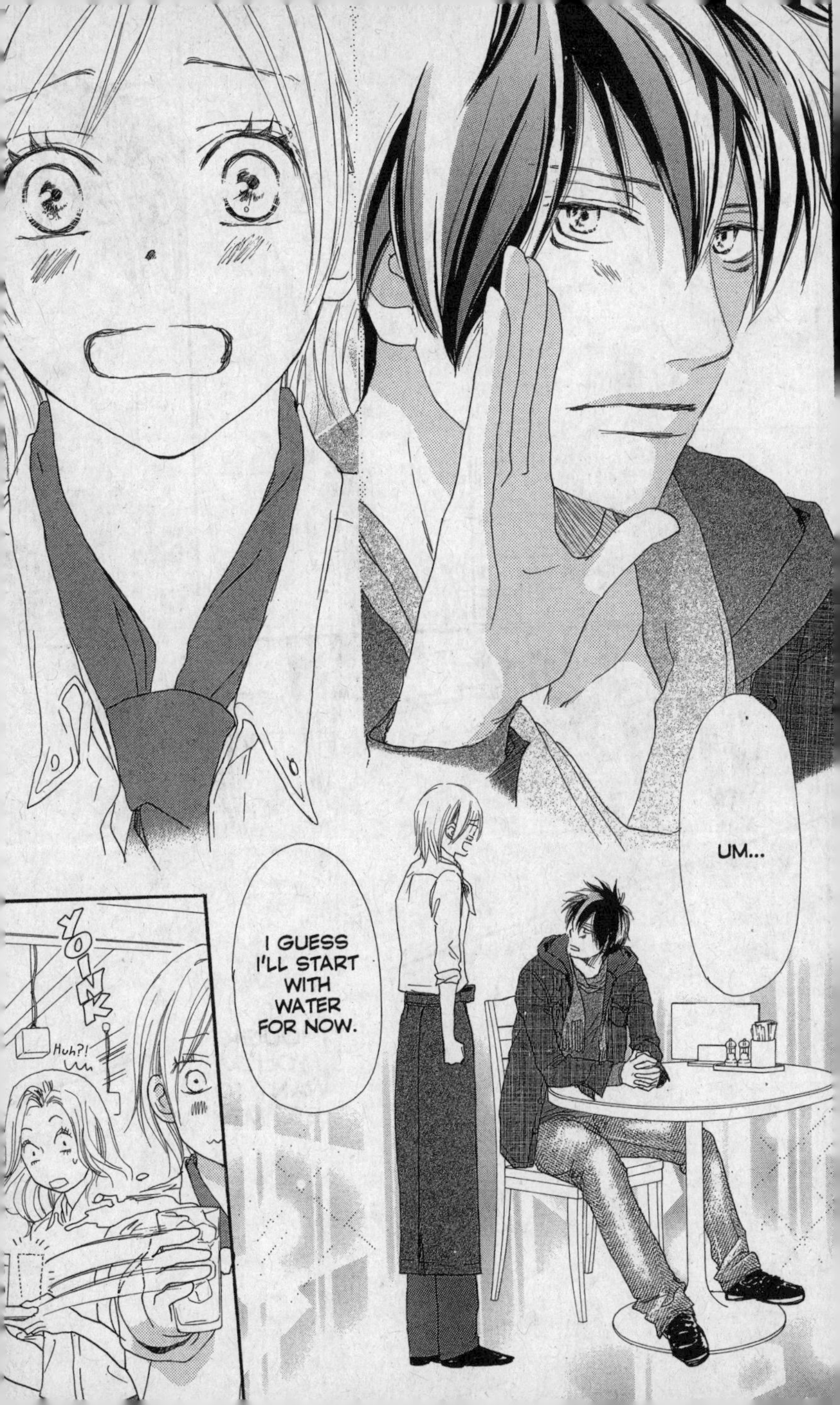
UM...
I GUESS I'LL START WITH WATER FOR NOW.
YOINK
Huh?!

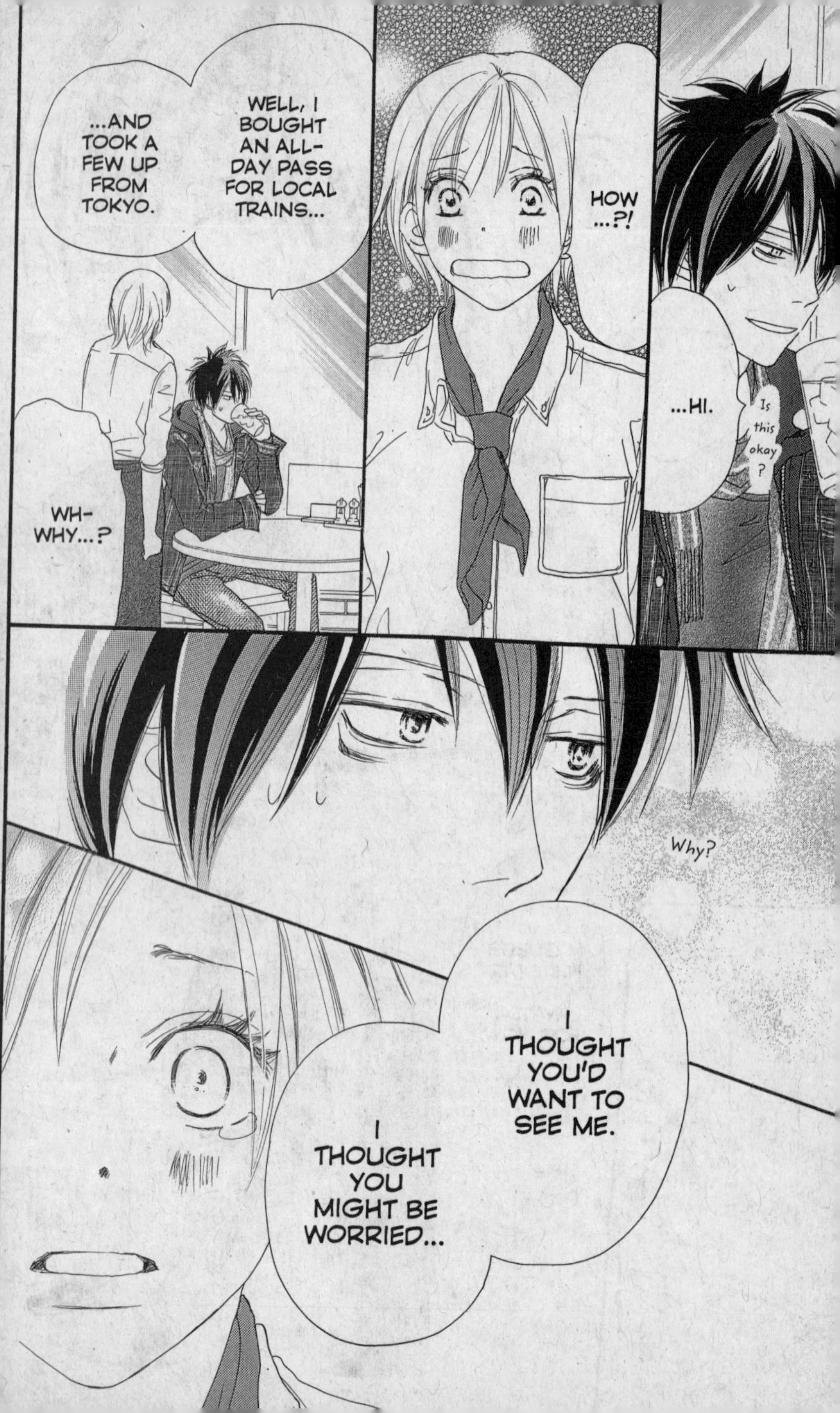
...HI.
Is this okay?
HOW ...?!
WELL, I BOUGHT AN ALL-DAY PASS FOR LOCAL TRAINS...
...AND TOOK A FEW UP FROM TOKYO.
WH- WHY...?
Why?
I THOUGHT YOU'D WANT TO SEE ME.
I THOUGHT YOU MIGHT BE WORRIED...

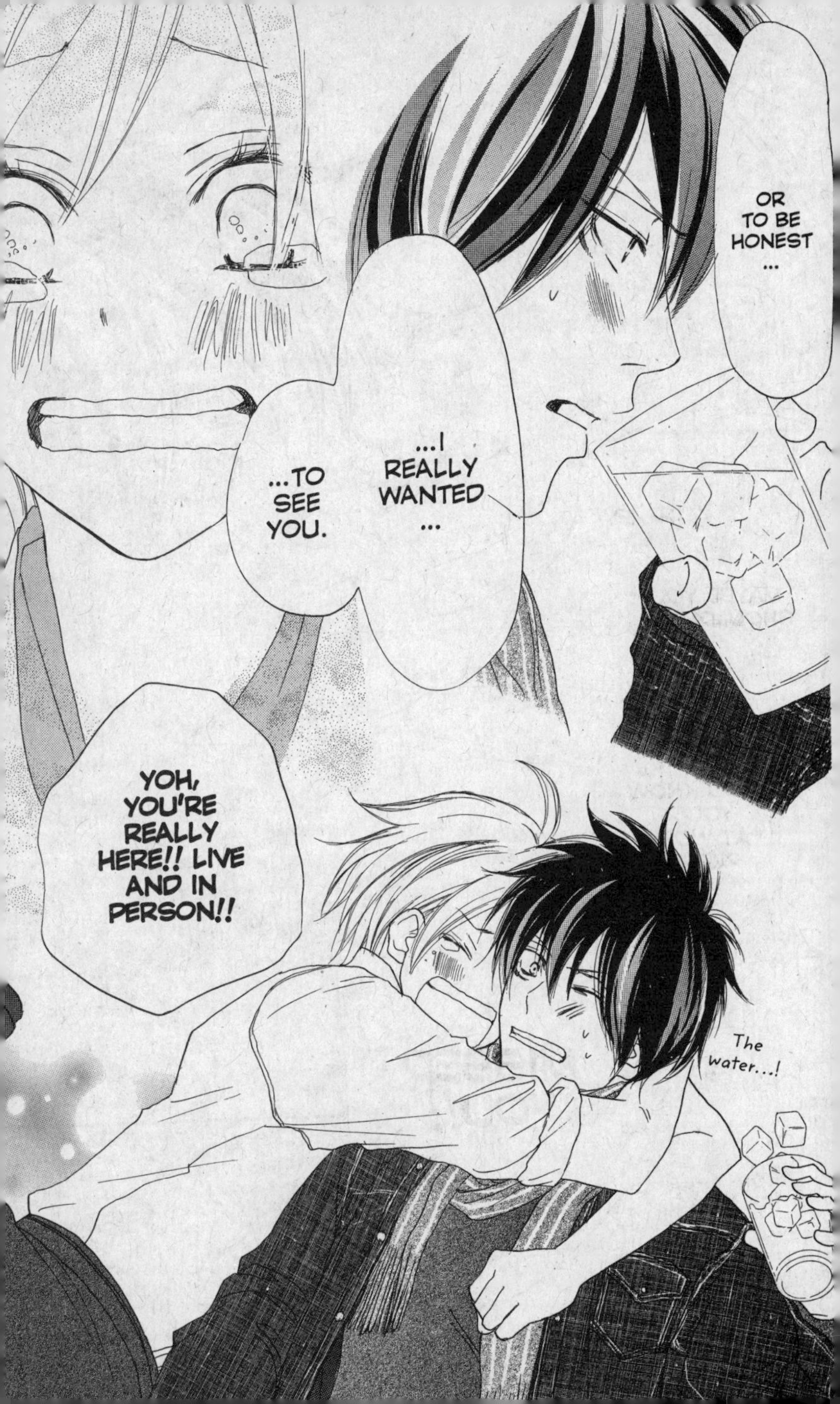
OR TO BE HONEST ...
...I REALLY WANTED ...
...TO SEE YOU.
YOH, YOU'RE REALLY HERE!! LIVE AND IN PERSON!!
The water...!

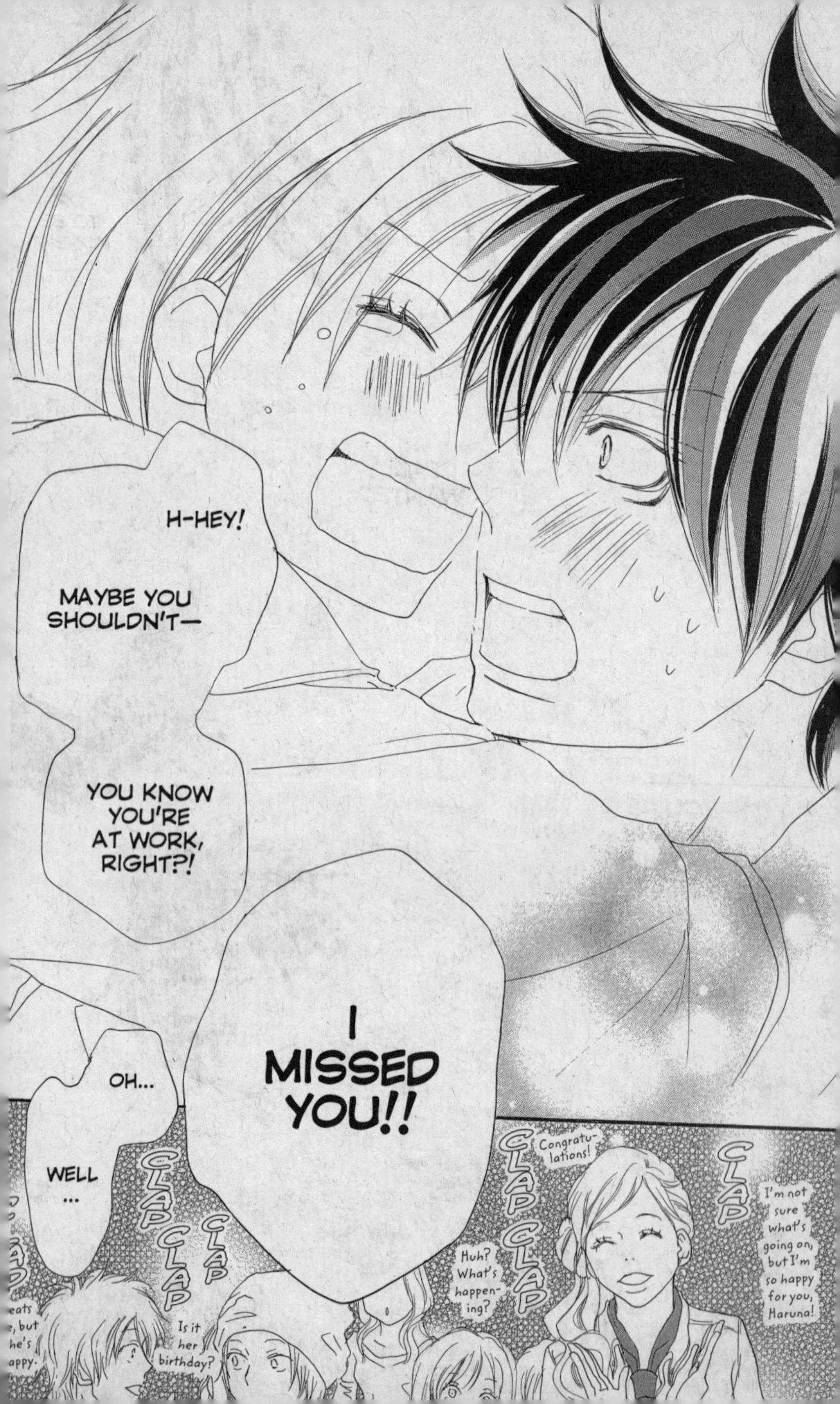
H-HEY!
MAYBE YOU SHOULDN'T—
YOU KNOW YOU'RE AT WORK, RIGHT?!
I MISSED YOU!!
OH...
WELL...
CLAP
I'm not sure what's going on, but I'm so happy for you, Haruna!
CLAP CLAP
Congratu-lations!
Huh? What's happen-ing?
CLAP
CLAP CLAP
Is it her birthday?
eats
e, but
he's
appy.

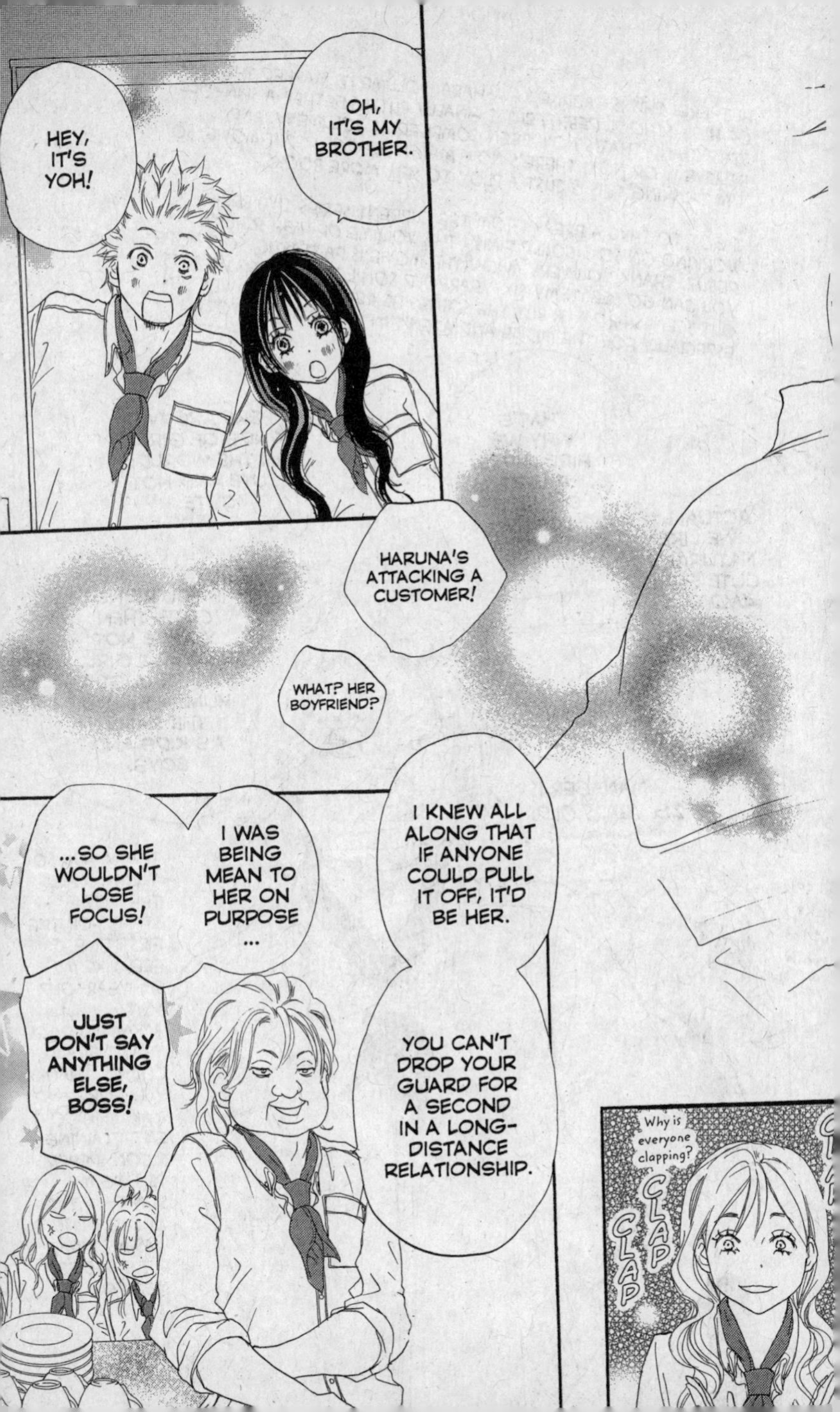
OH, IT'S MY BROTHER.
HEY, IT'S YOH!
HARUNA'S ATTACKING A CUSTOMER!
WHAT? HER BOYFRIEND?
Why is everyone clapping?
CLAP
CLAP
CLAP
I KNEW ALL ALONG THAT IF ANYONE COULD PULL IT OFF, IT'D BE HER.
YOU CAN'T DROP YOUR GUARD FOR A SECOND IN A LONG-DISTANCE RELATIONSHIP.
I WAS BEING MEAN TO HER ON PURPOSE...
...SO SHE WOULDN'T LOSE FOCUS!
JUST DON'T SAY ANYTHING ELSE, BOSS!

HI THERE! THIS IS KAZUNE KAWAHARA. VOLUME 13 MARKED THE END OF *HIGH SCHOOL DEBUT*, BUT I FINALLY PUT TOGETHER A SPIN-OFF STORY, AND THAT'S NOW BEEN COMPILED AS VOLUME 14. AND BELIEVE IT OR NOT, THERE'S NOW A *HIGH SCHOOL DEBUT* MOVIE, SO I'M THINKING THIS IS JUST A PLOY TO SELL MORE BOOKS.

I GOT TO TAKE A BREAK FROM THE CURRENT SERIES I'VE BEEN WORKING ON SO I COULD FINISH THIS VOLUME OF *HIGH SCHOOL DEBUT*. THANK YOU VERY MUCH! THE MOVIE IS FANTASTIC, SO I HOPE YOU CAN GO SEE IT. MY SIX-YEAR-OLD SON LOVES IT, AND HE ACTS OUT SCENES FROM IT. BUT THE SCENES HE REENACTS WERE WRITTEN ESPECIALLY FOR THE MOVIE AND AREN'T IN MY ORIGINAL STORY.

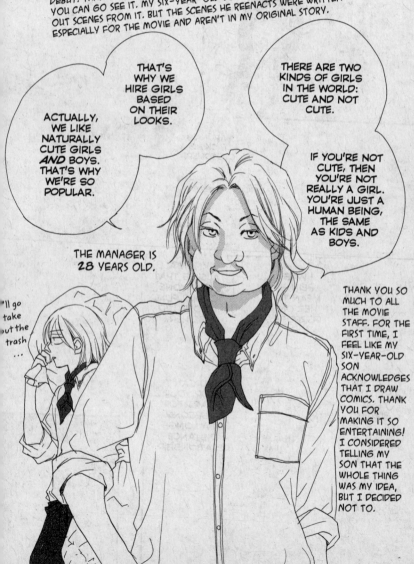

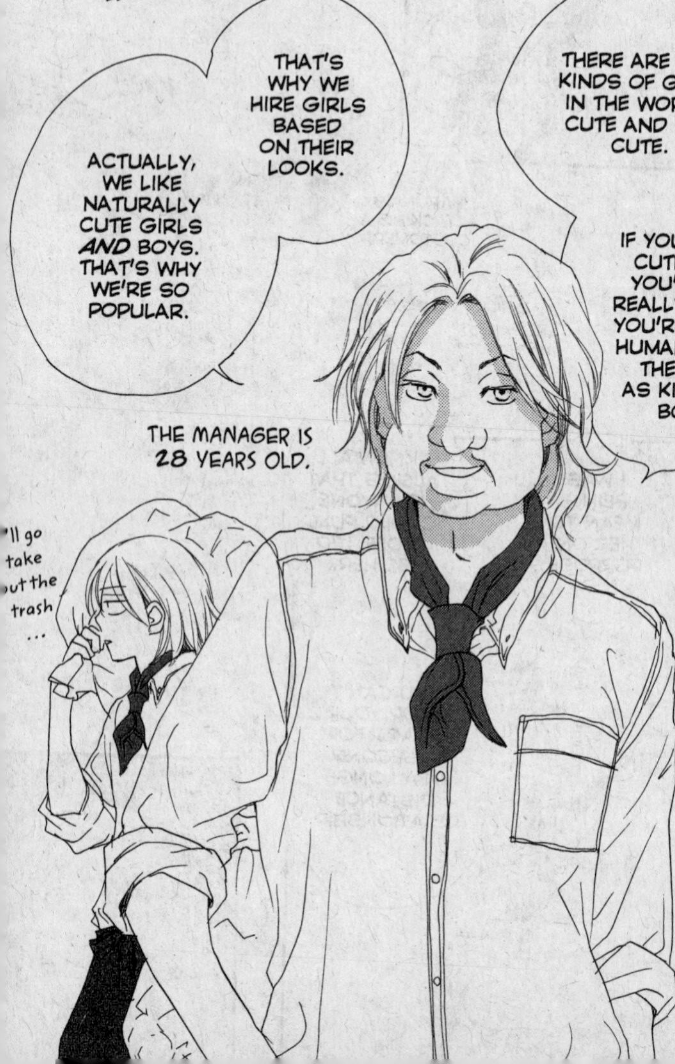
THERE ARE TWO KINDS OF GIRLS IN THE WORLD: CUTE AND NOT CUTE.
IF YOU'RE NOT CUTE, THEN YOU'RE NOT REALLY A GIRL. YOU'RE JUST A HUMAN BEING, THE SAME AS KIDS AND BOYS.
THAT'S WHY WE HIRE GIRLS BASED ON THEIR LOOKS.
ACTUALLY, WE LIKE NATURALLY CUTE GIRLS *AND* BOYS. THAT'S WHY WE'RE SO POPULAR.
THE MANAGER IS 28 YEARS OLD.
'll go take ut the trash ...

THANK YOU SO MUCH TO ALL THE MOVIE STAFF. FOR THE FIRST TIME, I FEEL LIKE MY SIX-YEAR-OLD SON ACKNOWLEDGES THAT I DRAW COMICS. THANK YOU FOR MAKING IT SO ENTERTAINING! I CONSIDERED TELLING MY SON THAT THE WHOLE THING WAS MY IDEA, BUT I DECIDED NOT TO.

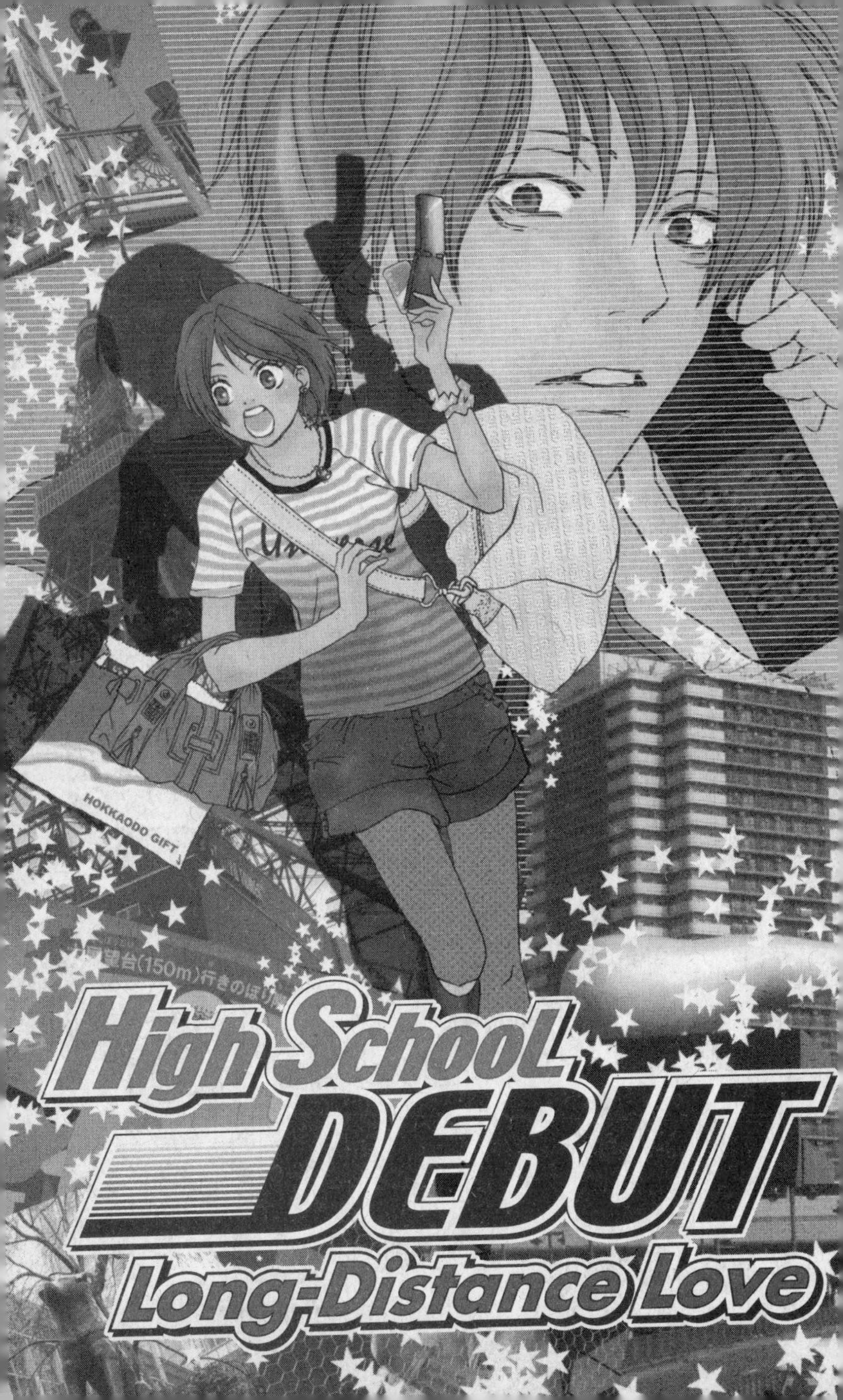
HOKKAODO GIFT
High School
DEBUT
Long-Distance Love

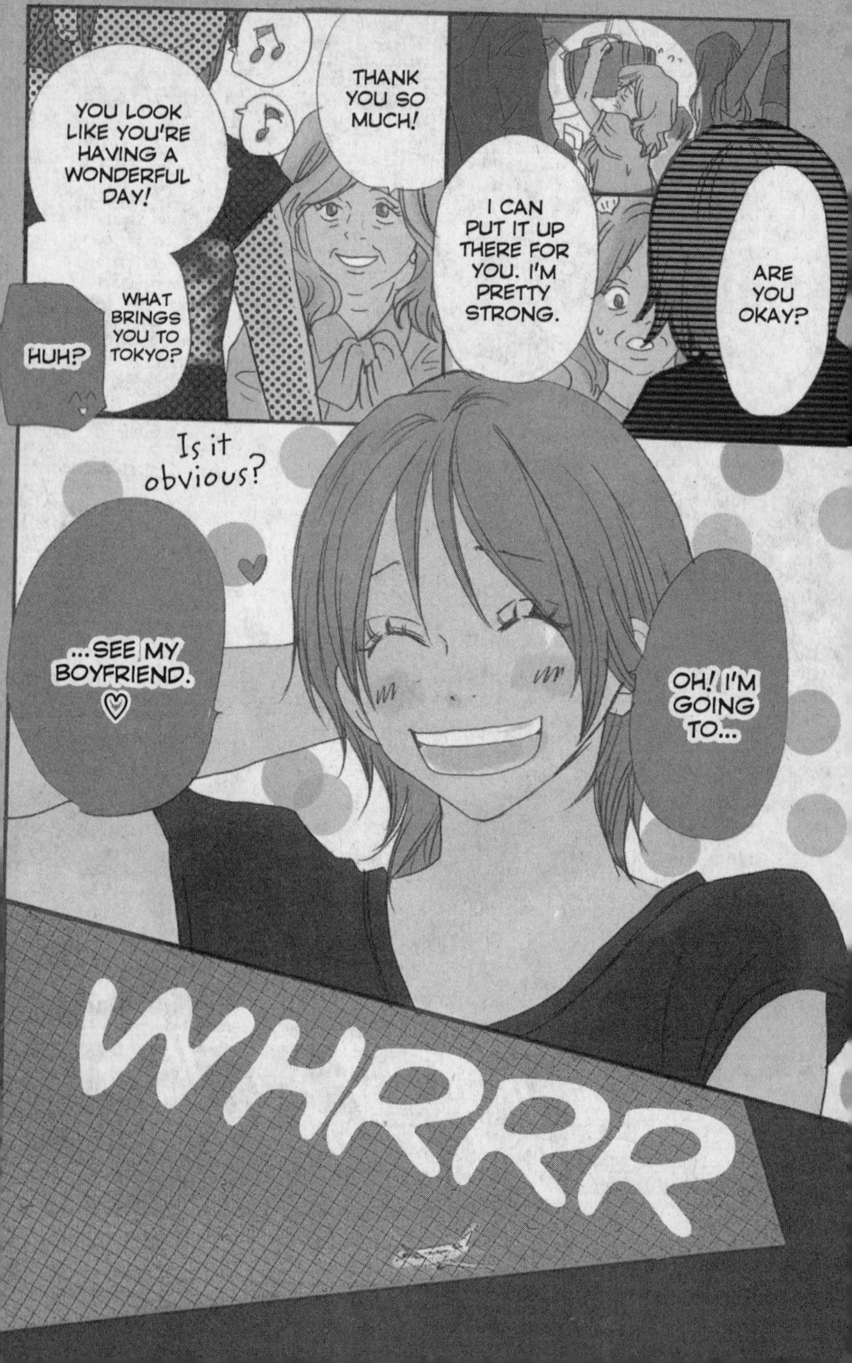
ARE YOU OKAY?
I CAN PUT IT UP THERE FOR YOU. I'M PRETTY STRONG.
THANK YOU SO MUCH!
YOU LOOK LIKE YOU'RE HAVING A WONDERFUL DAY!
WHAT BRINGS YOU TO TOKYO?
HUH?
Is it obvious?
OH! I'M GOING TO...
...SEE MY BOYFRIEND. ♡
WHRRR

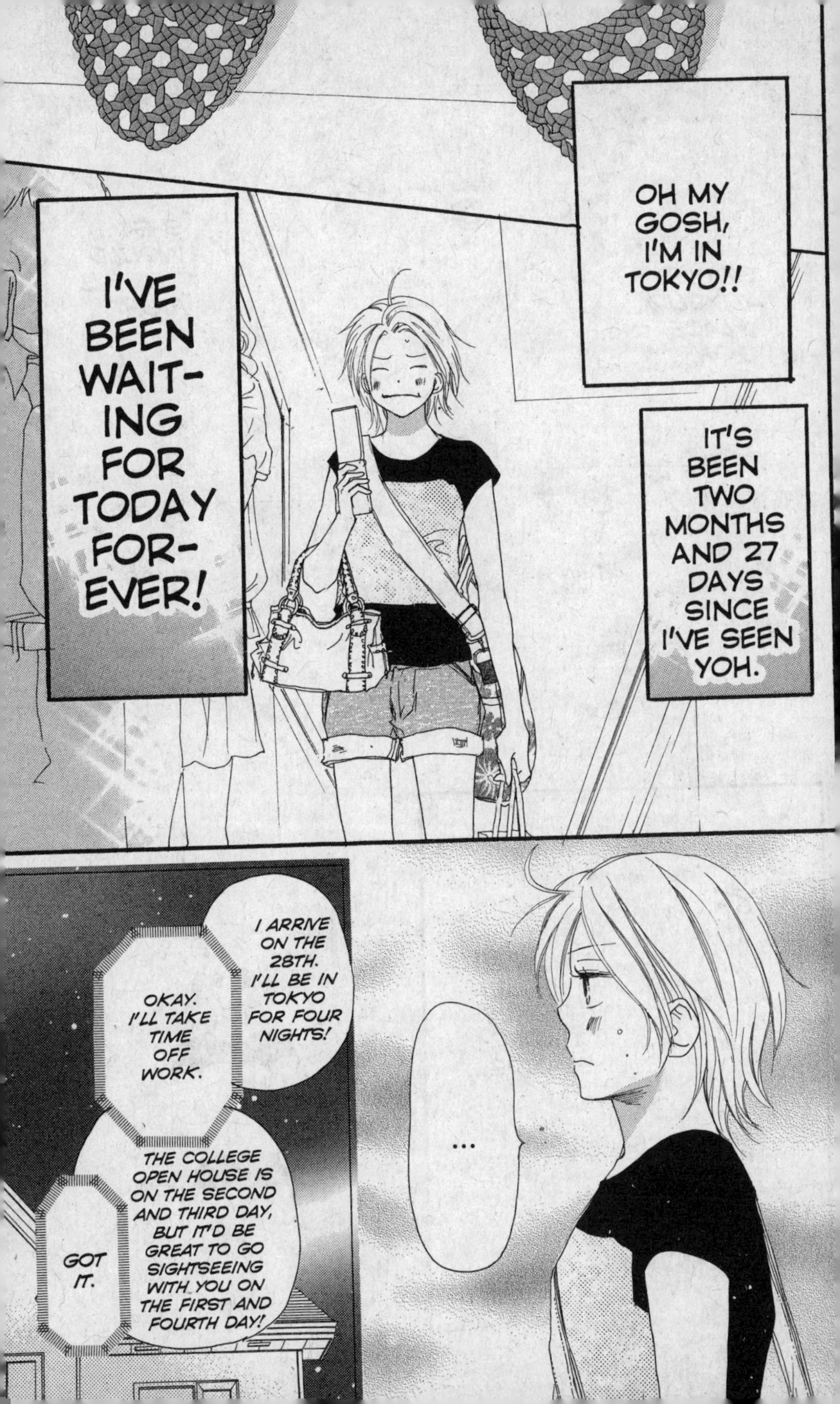
OH MY GOSH, I'M IN TOKYO!!
IT'S BEEN TWO MONTHS AND 27 DAYS SINCE I'VE SEEN YOH.
I'VE BEEN WAIT-ING FOR TODAY FOR-EVER!
...
I ARRIVE ON THE 28TH. I'LL BE IN TOKYO FOR FOUR NIGHTS!
OKAY. I'LL TAKE TIME OFF WORK.
THE COLLEGE OPEN HOUSE IS ON THE SECOND AND THIRD DAY, BUT IT'D BE GREAT TO GO SIGHTSEEING WITH YOU ON THE FIRST AND FOURTH DAY!
GOT IT.

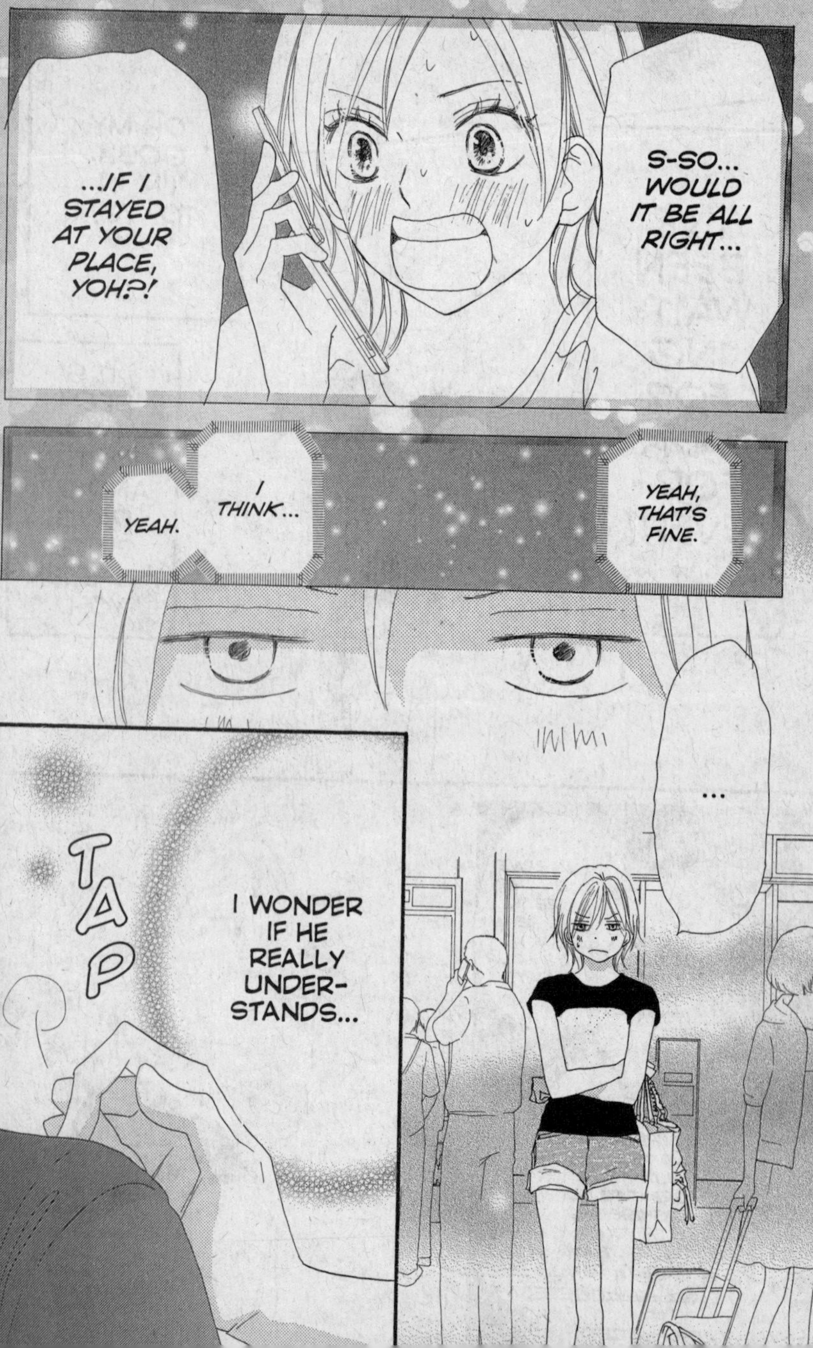
S-SO... WOULD IT BE ALL RIGHT...
...IF I STAYED AT YOUR PLACE, YOH?!
YEAH, THAT'S FINE.
I THINK...
YEAH.
...
I WONDER IF HE REALLY UNDER-STANDS...
TAP

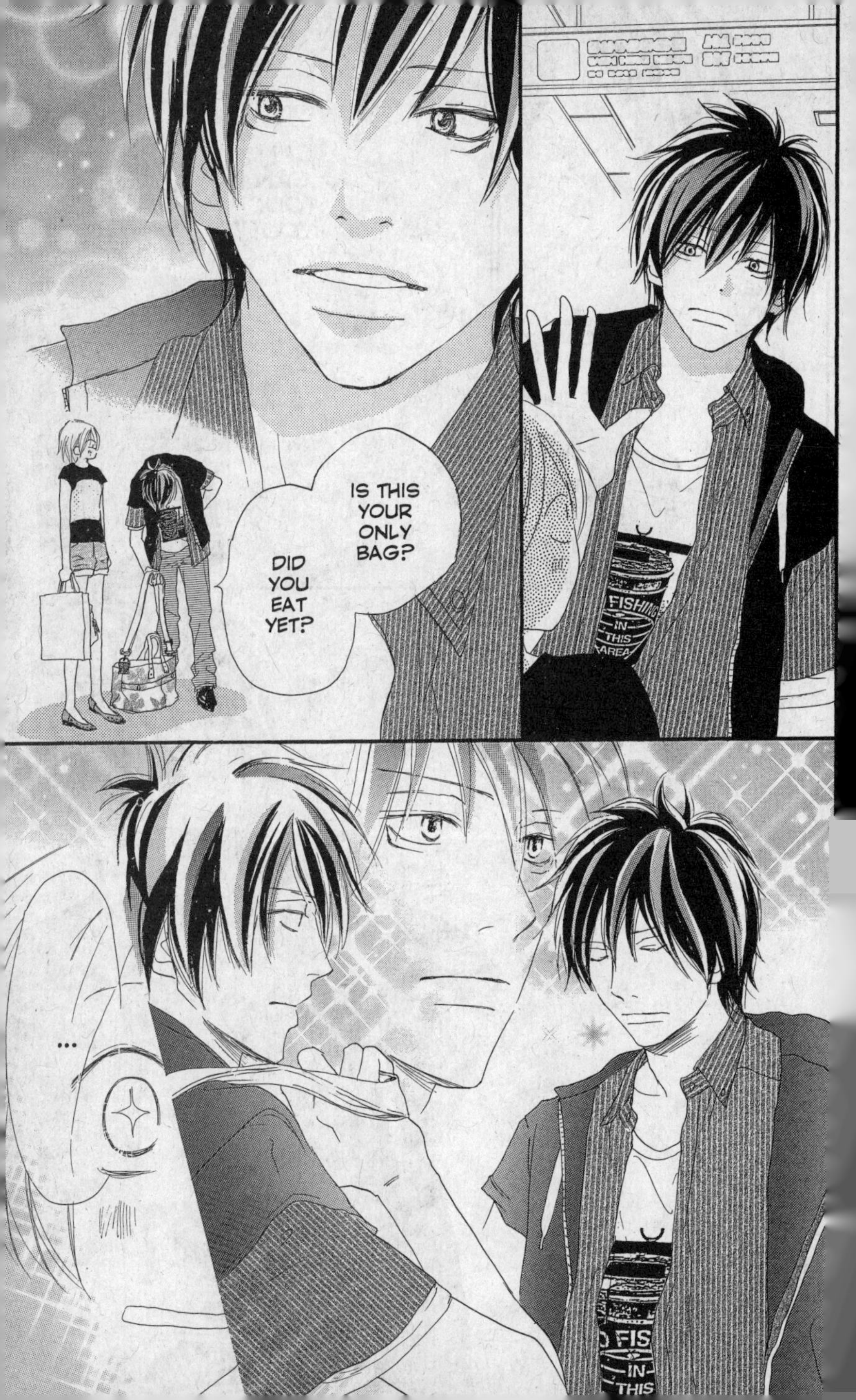
IS THIS YOUR ONLY BAG?
DID YOU EAT YET?
FISHING IN THIS AREA
...
FIS IN THIS

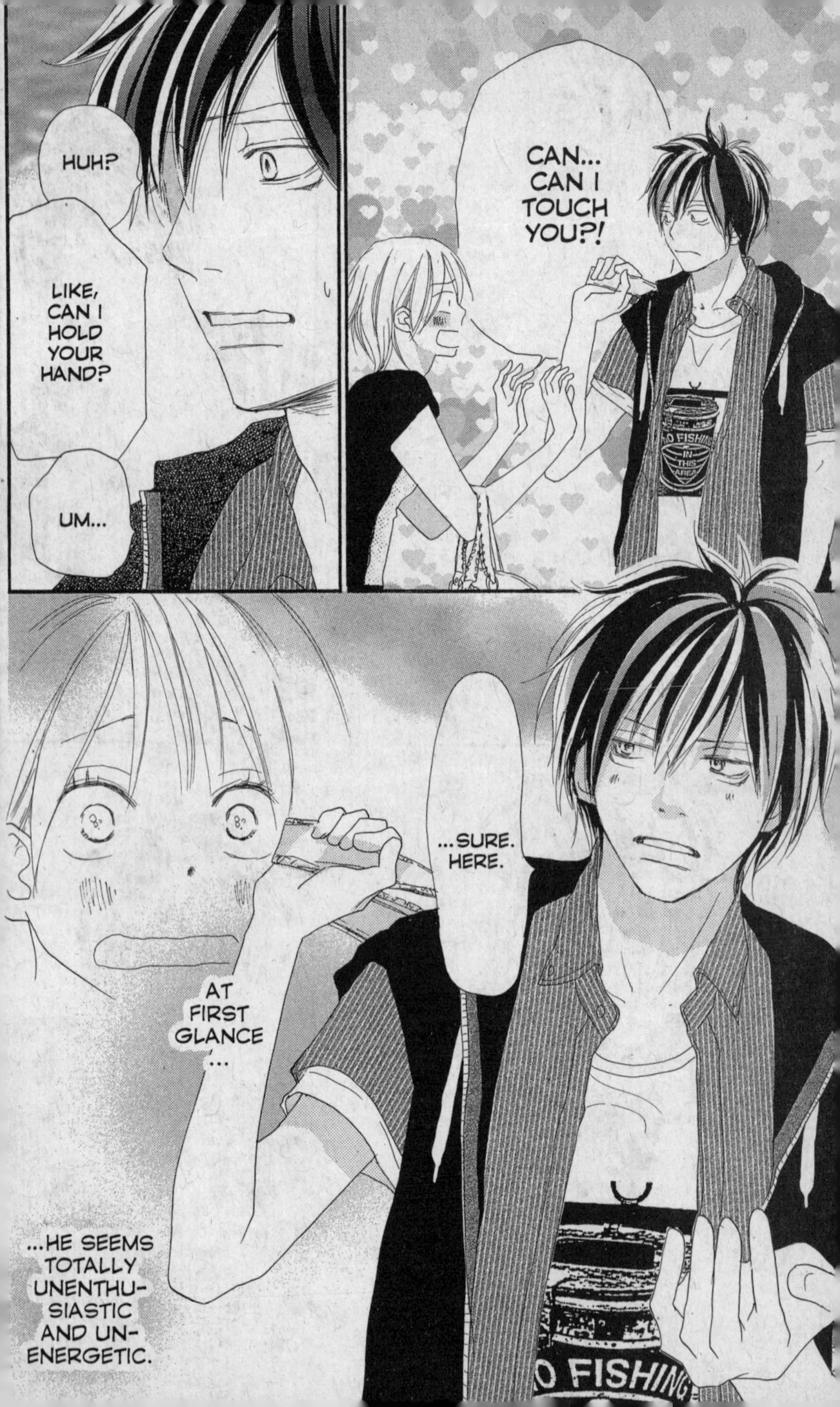
CAN... CAN I TOUCH YOU?!
HUH?
LIKE, CAN I HOLD YOUR HAND?
UM...
...SURE. HERE.
AT FIRST GLANCE...
...HE SEEMS TOTALLY UNENTHUSIASTIC AND UN-ENERGETIC.

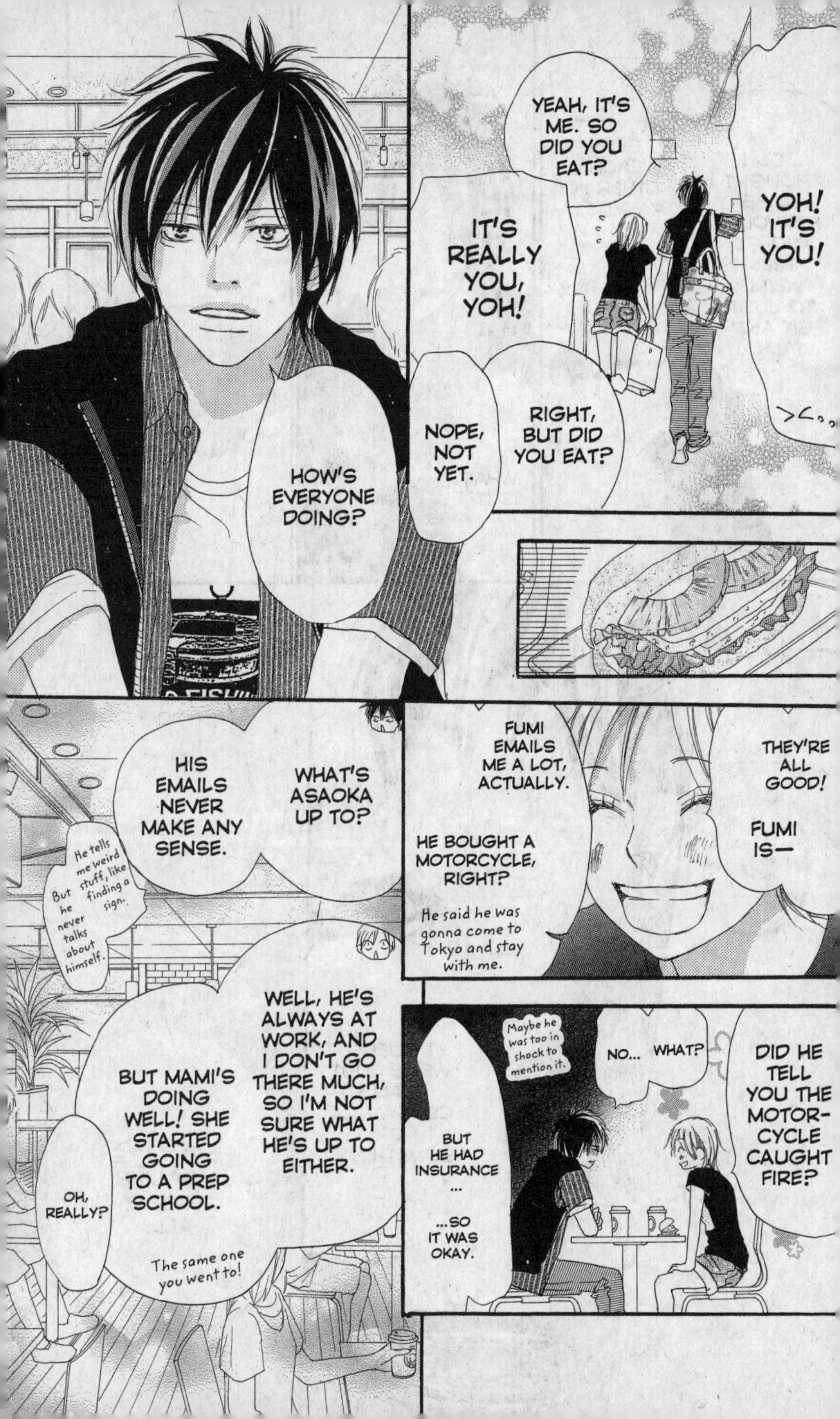
YOH! IT'S YOU!
YEAH, IT'S ME. SO DID YOU EAT?
IT'S REALLY YOU, YOH!
RIGHT, BUT DID YOU EAT?
NOPE, NOT YET.
HOW'S EVERYONE DOING?
THEY'RE ALL GOOD!
FUMI IS—
FUMI EMAILS ME A LOT, ACTUALLY.
HE BOUGHT A MOTORCYCLE, RIGHT?
He said he was gonna come to Tokyo and stay with me.
DID HE TELL YOU THE MOTOR-CYCLE CAUGHT FIRE?
WHAT?
NO...
Maybe he was too in shock to mention it.
BUT HE HAD INSURANCE...
...SO IT WAS OKAY.
WHAT'S ASAOKA UP TO?
HIS EMAILS NEVER MAKE ANY SENSE.
He tells me weird stuff, like finding a sign.
But he never talks about himself.
WELL, HE'S ALWAYS AT WORK, AND I DON'T GO THERE MUCH, SO I'M NOT SURE WHAT HE'S UP TO EITHER.
BUT MAMI'S DOING WELL! SHE STARTED GOING TO A PREP SCHOOL.
The same one you went to!
OH, REALLY?

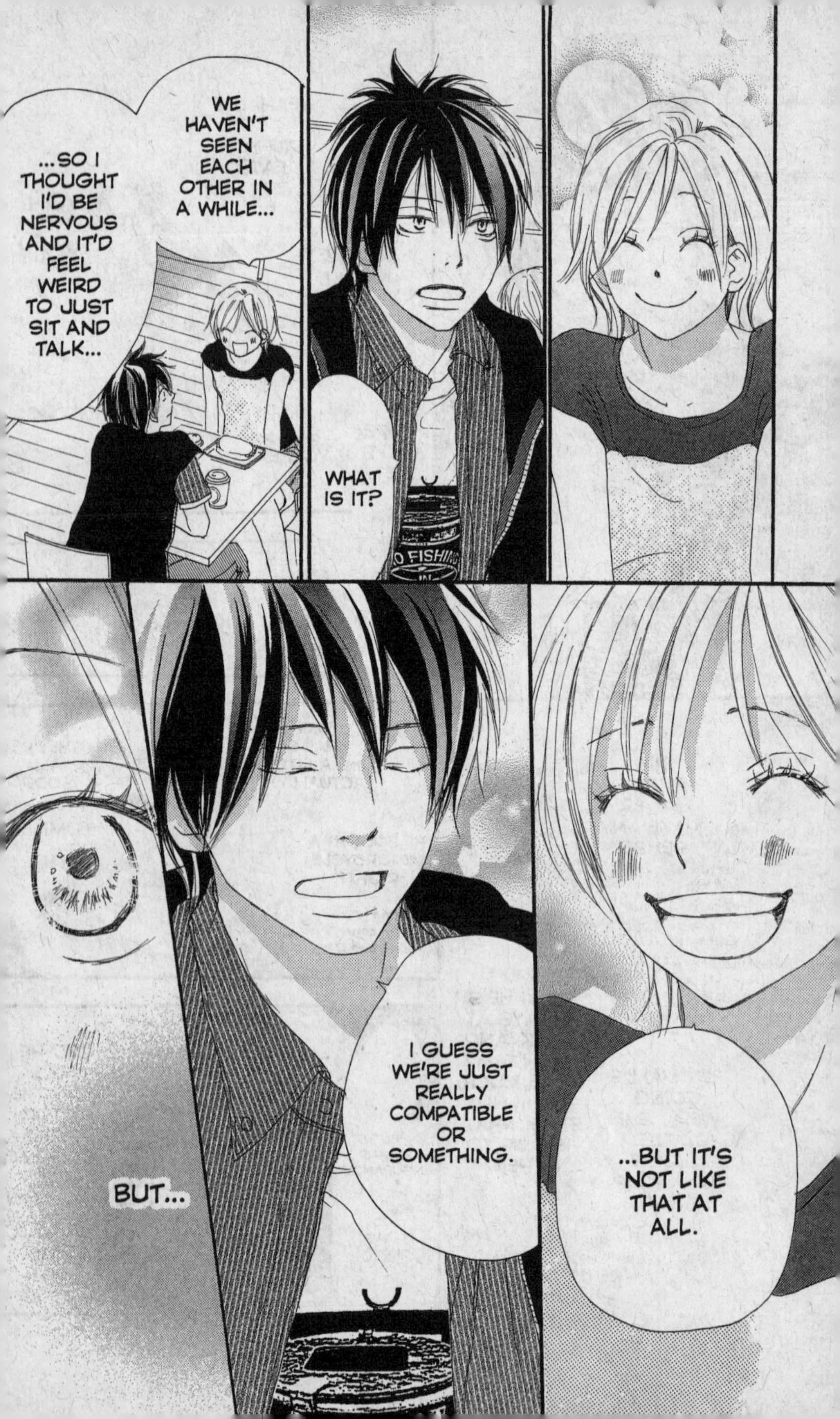
WHAT IS IT?
WE HAVEN'T SEEN EACH OTHER IN A WHILE...
...SO I THOUGHT I'D BE NERVOUS AND IT'D FEEL WEIRD TO JUST SIT AND TALK...
...BUT IT'S NOT LIKE THAT AT ALL.
I GUESS WE'RE JUST REALLY COMPATIBLE OR SOMETHING.
BUT...

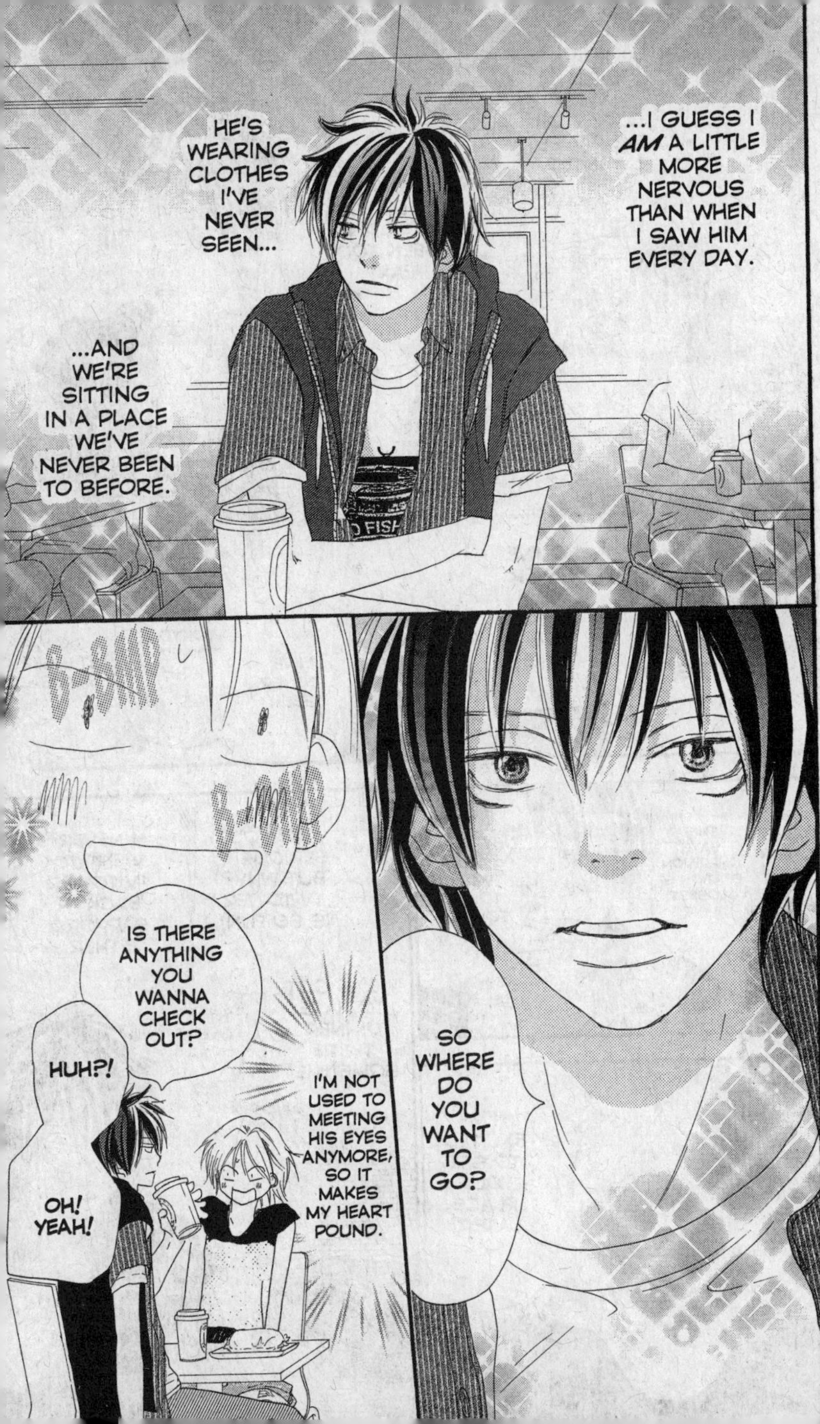
...I GUESS I *AM* A LITTLE MORE NERVOUS THAN WHEN I SAW HIM EVERY DAY.
HE'S WEARING CLOTHES I'VE NEVER SEEN...
...AND WE'RE SITTING IN A PLACE WE'VE NEVER BEEN TO BEFORE.
SO WHERE DO YOU WANT TO GO?
B-BMP
B-BMP
IS THERE ANYTHING YOU WANNA CHECK OUT?
I'M NOT USED TO MEETING HIS EYES ANYMORE, SO IT MAKES MY HEART POUND.
HUH?!
OH! YEAH!

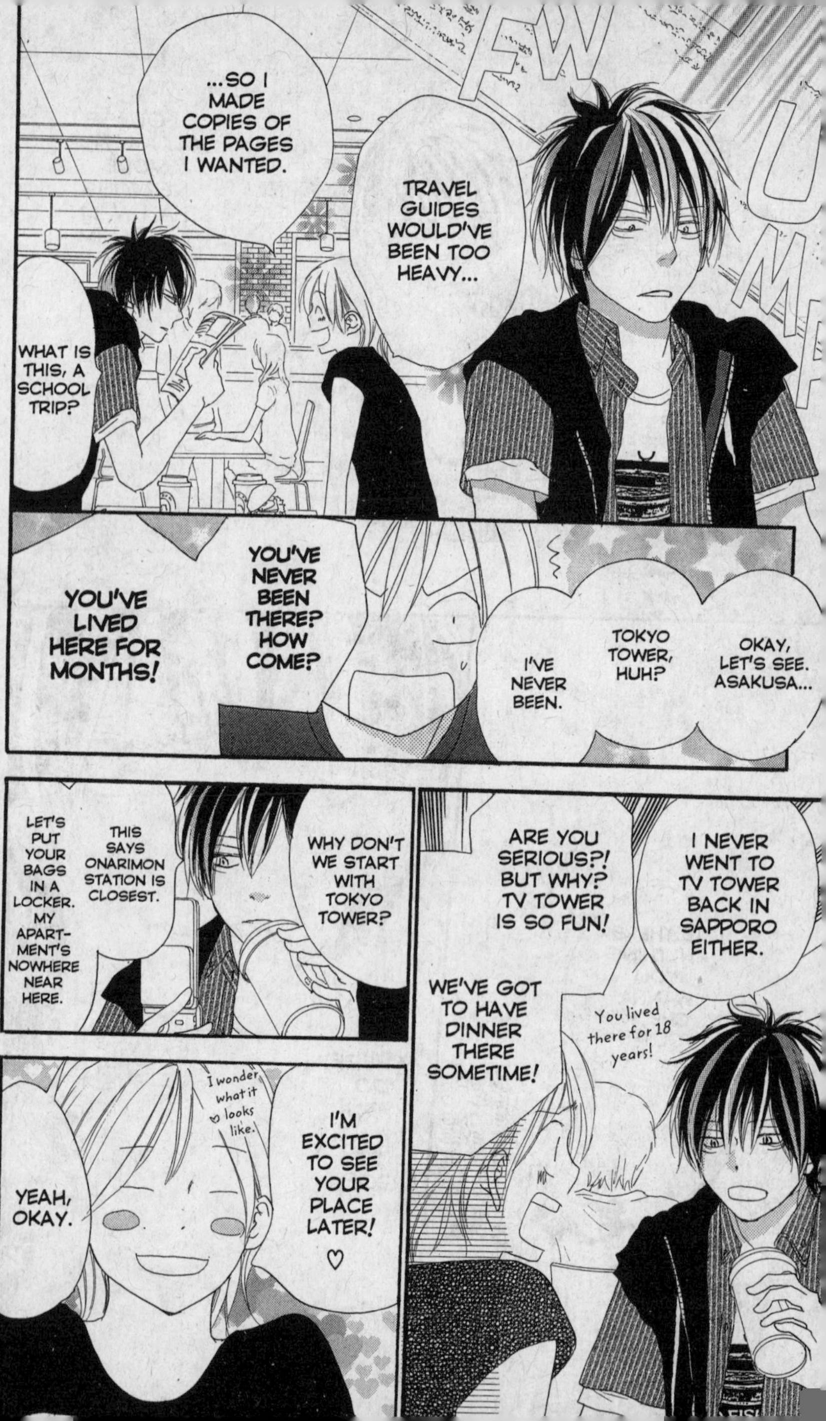
FWUMP
TRAVEL GUIDES WOULD'VE BEEN TOO HEAVY...
...SO I MADE COPIES OF THE PAGES I WANTED.
WHAT IS THIS, A SCHOOL TRIP?
OKAY, LET'S SEE. ASAKUSA...
TOKYO TOWER, HUH?
I'VE NEVER BEEN.
YOU'VE NEVER BEEN THERE? HOW COME?
YOU'VE LIVED HERE FOR MONTHS!
I NEVER WENT TO TV TOWER BACK IN SAPPORO EITHER.
ARE YOU SERIOUS?! BUT WHY? TV TOWER IS SO FUN!
You lived there for 18 years!
WE'VE GOT TO HAVE DINNER THERE SOMETIME!
WHY DON'T WE START WITH TOKYO TOWER?
THIS SAYS ONARIMON STATION IS CLOSEST.
LET'S PUT YOUR BAGS IN A LOCKER. MY APARTMENT'S NOWHERE NEAR HERE.
I'M EXCITED TO SEE YOUR PLACE LATER! ♡
I wonder what it ♡ looks like.
YEAH, OKAY.

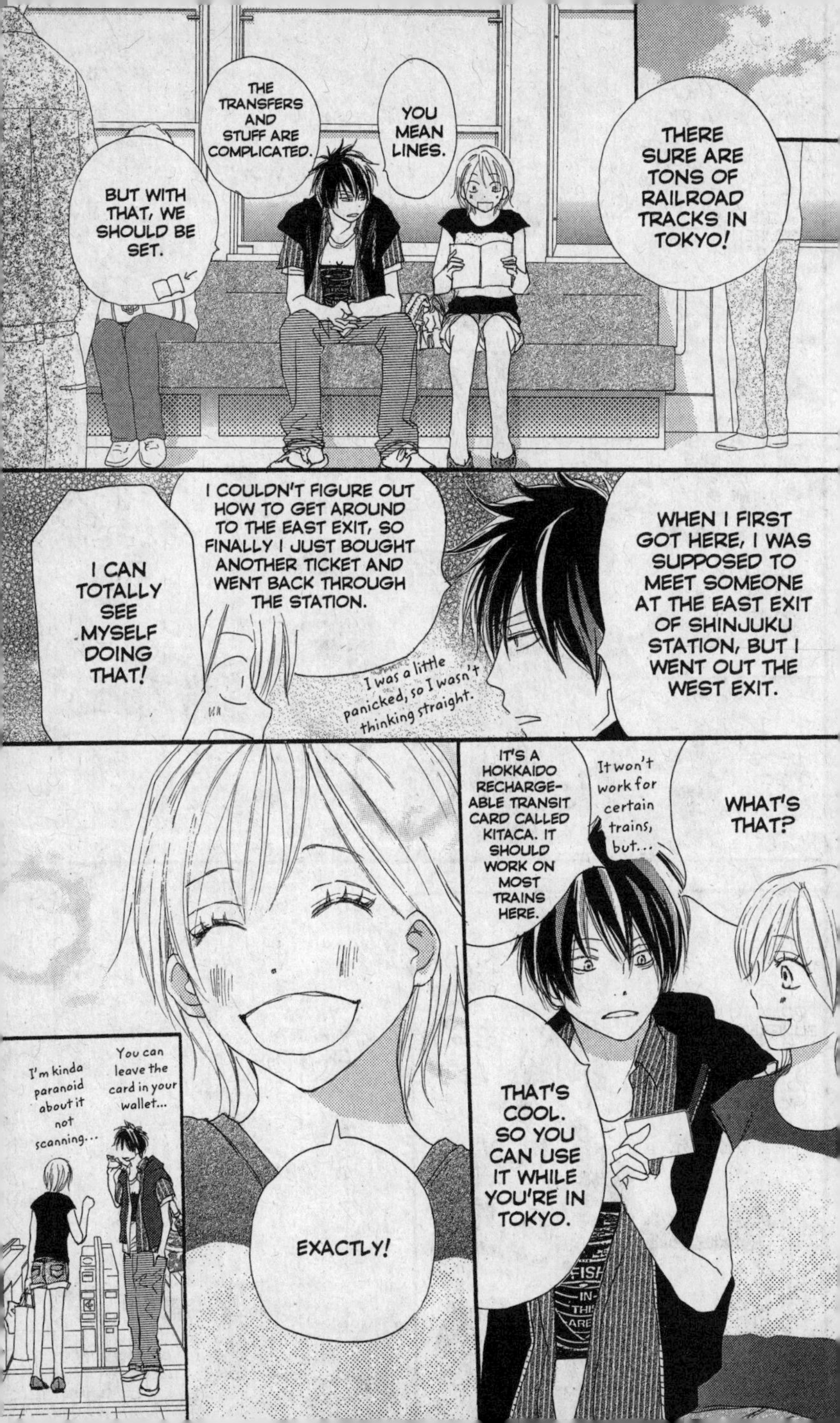
THERE SURE ARE TONS OF RAILROAD TRACKS IN TOKYO!
YOU MEAN LINES.
THE TRANSFERS AND STUFF ARE COMPLICATED.
BUT WITH THAT, WE SHOULD BE SET.
WHEN I FIRST GOT HERE, I WAS SUPPOSED TO MEET SOMEONE AT THE EAST EXIT OF SHINJUKU STATION, BUT I WENT OUT THE WEST EXIT.
I was a little panicked, so I wasn't thinking straight.
I COULDN'T FIGURE OUT HOW TO GET AROUND TO THE EAST EXIT, SO FINALLY I JUST BOUGHT ANOTHER TICKET AND WENT BACK THROUGH THE STATION.
I CAN TOTALLY SEE MYSELF DOING THAT!
WHAT'S THAT?
It won't work for certain trains, but...
IT'S A HOKKAIDO RECHARGE-ABLE TRANSIT CARD CALLED KITACA. IT SHOULD WORK ON MOST TRAINS HERE.
THAT'S COOL. SO YOU CAN USE IT WHILE YOU'RE IN TOKYO.
EXACTLY!
You can leave the card in your wallet...
I'm kinda paranoid about it not scanning...

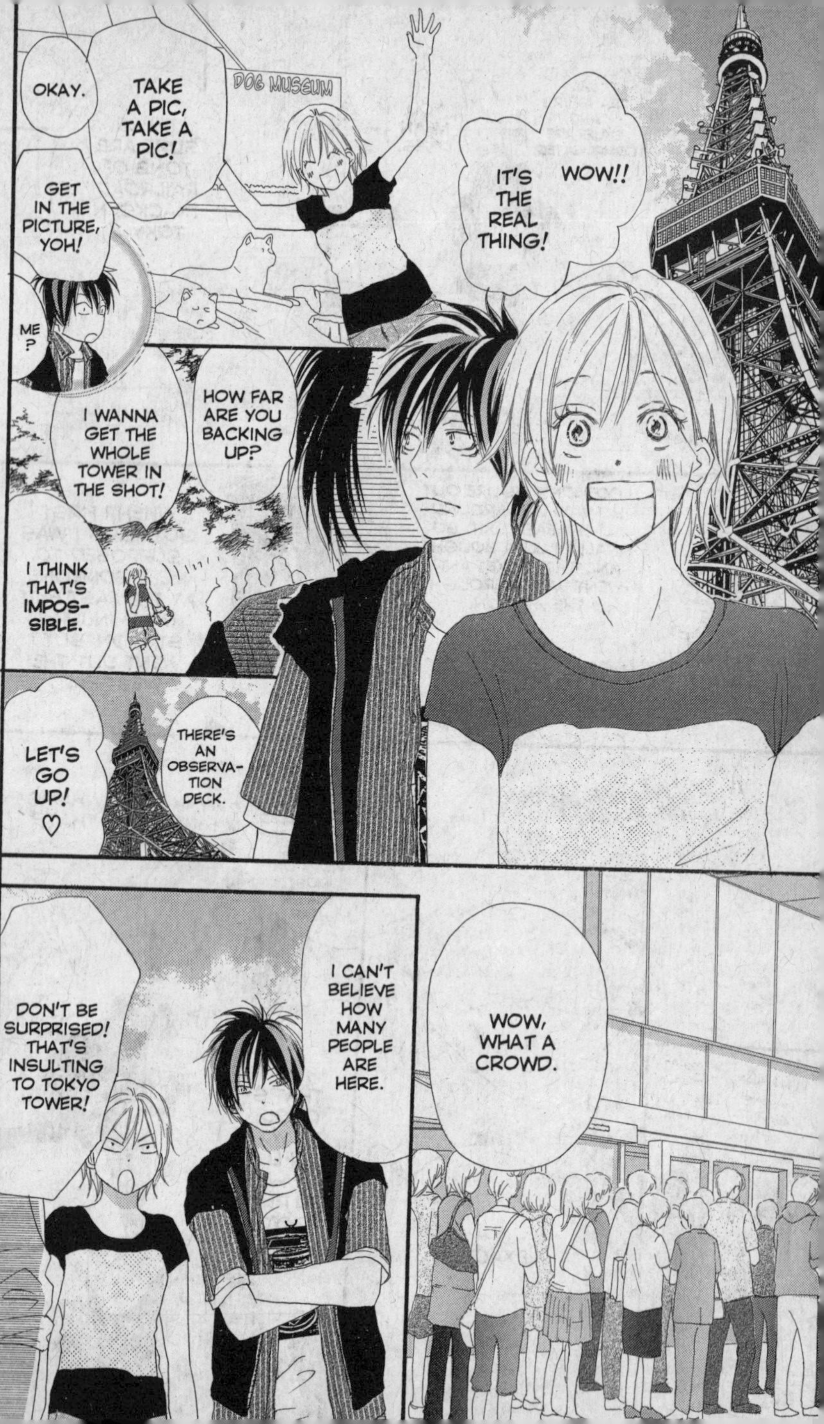
WOW!!
IT'S THE REAL THING!
DOG MUSEUM
TAKE A PIC, TAKE A PIC!
OKAY.
GET IN THE PICTURE, YOH!
ME?
HOW FAR ARE YOU BACKING UP?
I WANNA GET THE WHOLE TOWER IN THE SHOT!
I THINK THAT'S IMPOSSIBLE.
THERE'S AN OBSERVATION DECK.
LET'S GO UP! ♡
WOW, WHAT A CROWD.
I CAN'T BELIEVE HOW MANY PEOPLE ARE HERE.
DON'T BE SURPRISED! THAT'S INSULTING TO TOKYO TOWER!

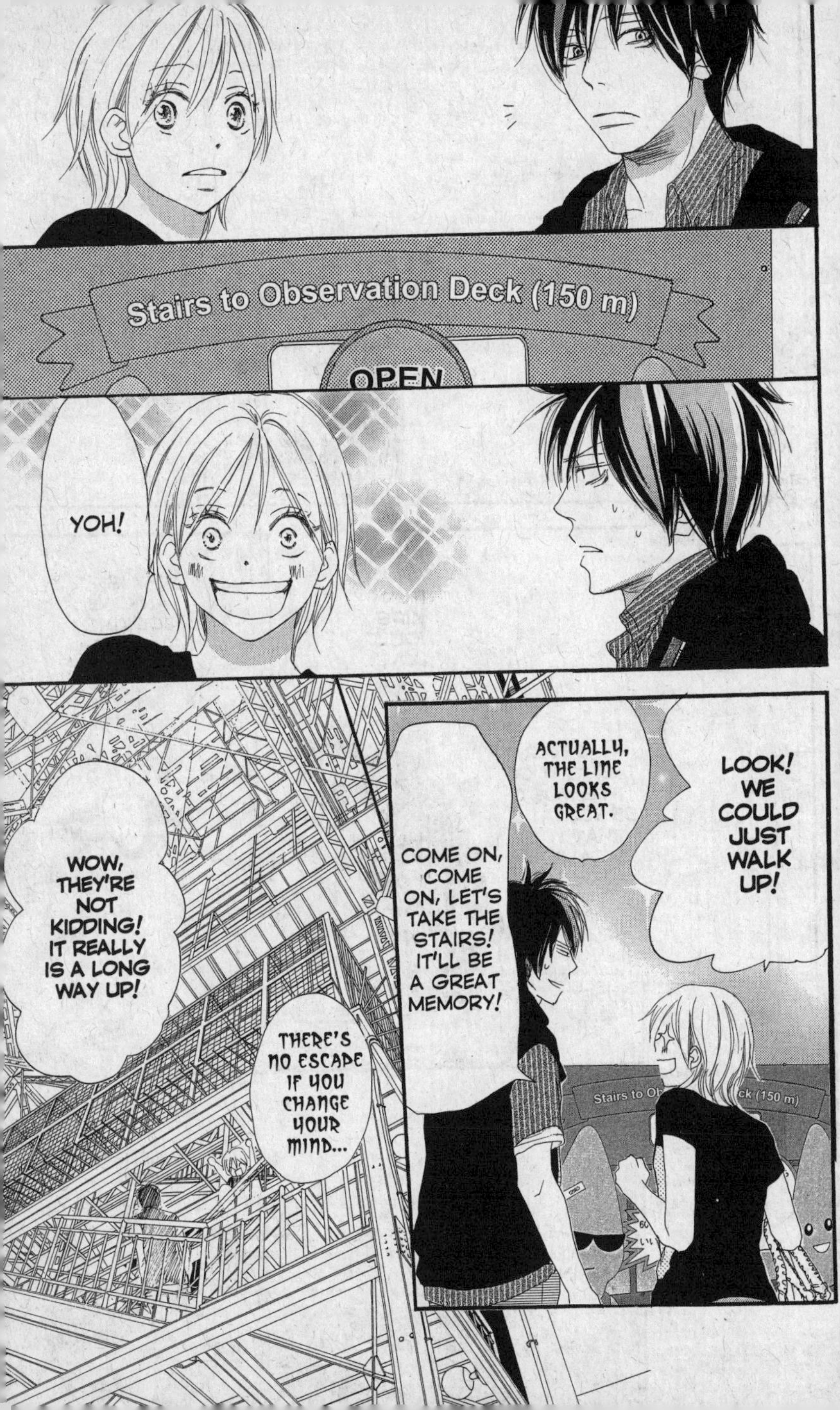
Stairs to Observation Deck (150 m)
OPEN
YOH!
LOOK! WE COULD JUST WALK UP!
ACTUALLY, THE LINE LOOKS GREAT.
COME ON, COME ON, LET'S TAKE THE STAIRS! IT'LL BE A GREAT MEMORY!
WOW, THEY'RE NOT KIDDING! IT REALLY IS A LONG WAY UP!
THERE'S NO ESCAPE IF YOU CHANGE YOUR MIND...

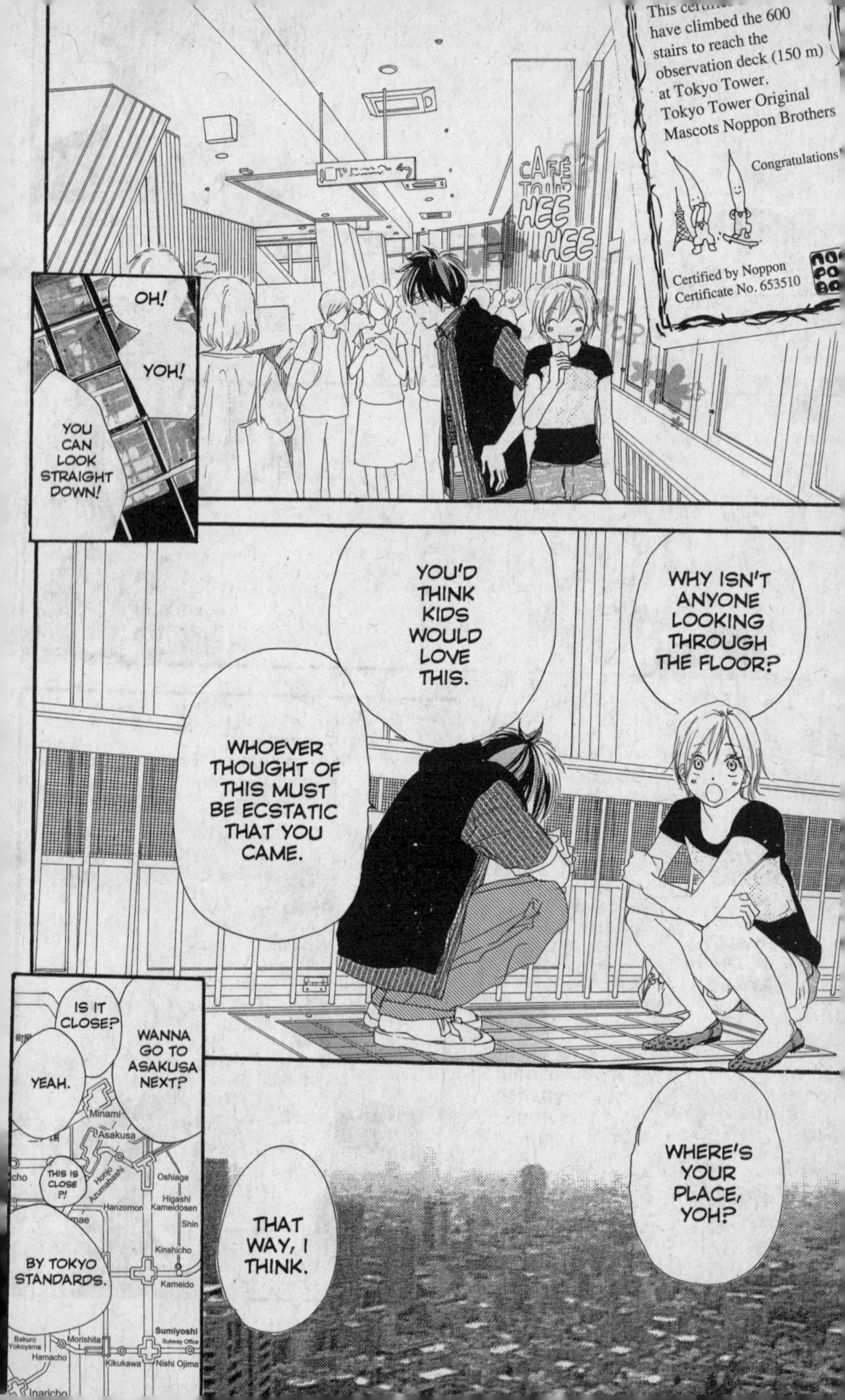

have climbed the 600
stairs to reach the
observation deck (150 m)
at Tokyo Tower.
Tokyo Tower Original
Mascots Noppon Brothers
Congratulations
Certified by Noppon
Certificate No. 653510
HEE HEE
OH!
YOH!
YOU CAN LOOK STRAIGHT DOWN!
WHY ISN'T ANYONE LOOKING THROUGH THE FLOOR?
YOU'D THINK KIDS WOULD LOVE THIS.
WHOEVER THOUGHT OF THIS MUST BE ECSTATIC THAT YOU CAME.
WHERE'S YOUR PLACE, YOH?
THAT WAY, I THINK.
WANNA GO TO ASAKUSA NEXT?
IS IT CLOSE?
YEAH.
THIS IS CLOSE?!
BY TOKYO STANDARDS.
Minami
Asakusa
Honjo Azumabashi
Oshiage
Hanzomon
Higashi Kameidosen
Shin
Kinshicho
Kameido
Sumiyoshi
Subway Office
Bakuro Yokoyama
Morishita
Hamacho
Kikukawa
Nishi Ojima

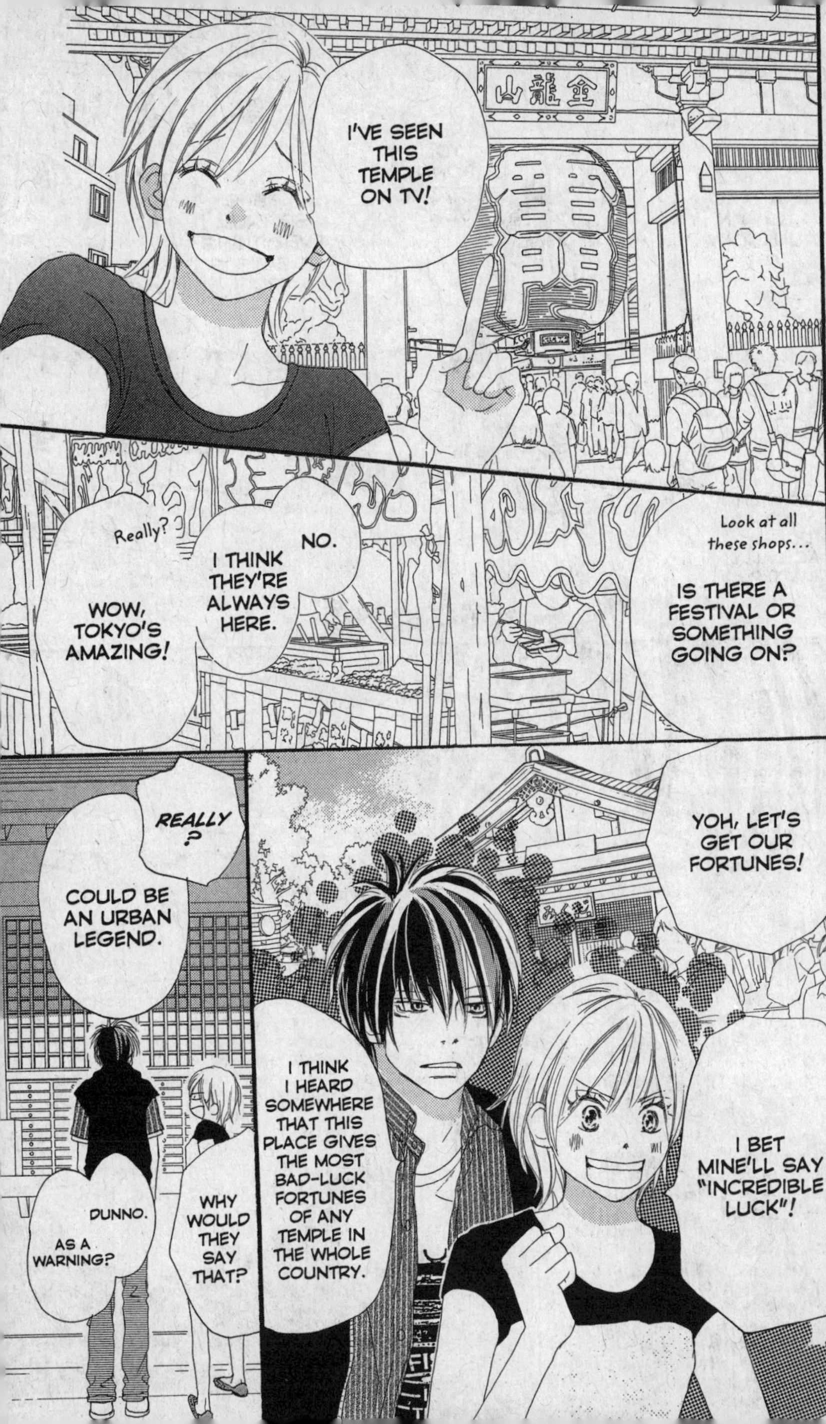
I'VE SEEN THIS TEMPLE ON TV!
Look at all these shops...
IS THERE A FESTIVAL OR SOMETHING GOING ON?
NO.
I THINK THEY'RE ALWAYS HERE.
Really?
WOW, TOKYO'S AMAZING!
YOH, LET'S GET OUR FORTUNES!
I BET MINE'LL SAY "INCREDIBLE LUCK"!
I THINK I HEARD SOMEWHERE THAT THIS PLACE GIVES THE MOST BAD-LUCK FORTUNES OF ANY TEMPLE IN THE WHOLE COUNTRY.
REALLY?
COULD BE AN URBAN LEGEND.
WHY WOULD THEY SAY THAT?
DUNNO.
AS A WARNING?

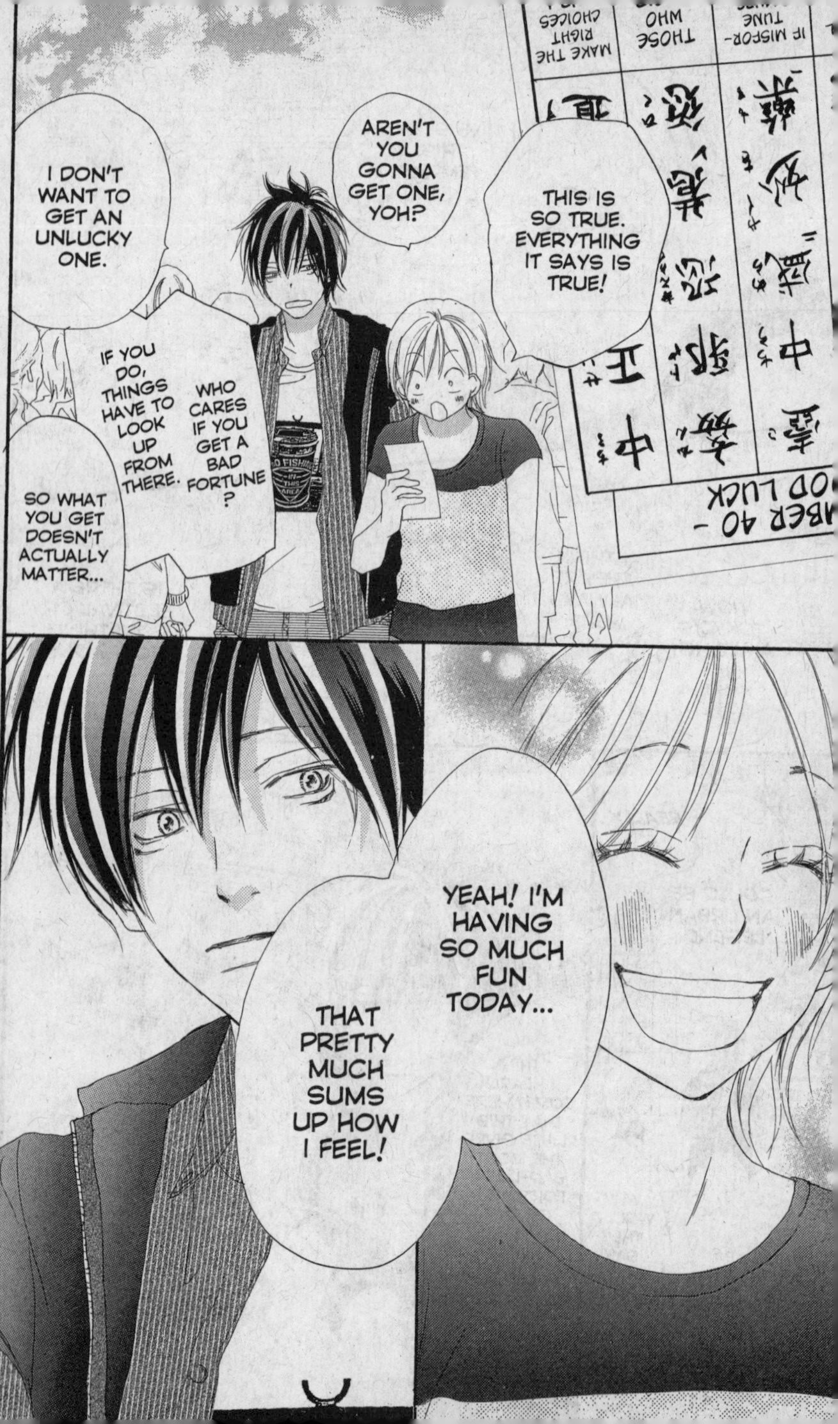
THIS IS SO TRUE. EVERYTHING IT SAYS IS TRUE!
AREN'T YOU GONNA GET ONE, YOH?
I DON'T WANT TO GET AN UNLUCKY ONE.
WHO CARES IF YOU GET A BAD FORTUNE?
IF YOU DO, THINGS HAVE TO LOOK UP FROM THERE.
SO WHAT YOU GET DOESN'T ACTUALLY MATTER...
YEAH! I'M HAVING SO MUCH FUN TODAY...
THAT PRETTY MUCH SUMS UP HOW I FEEL!

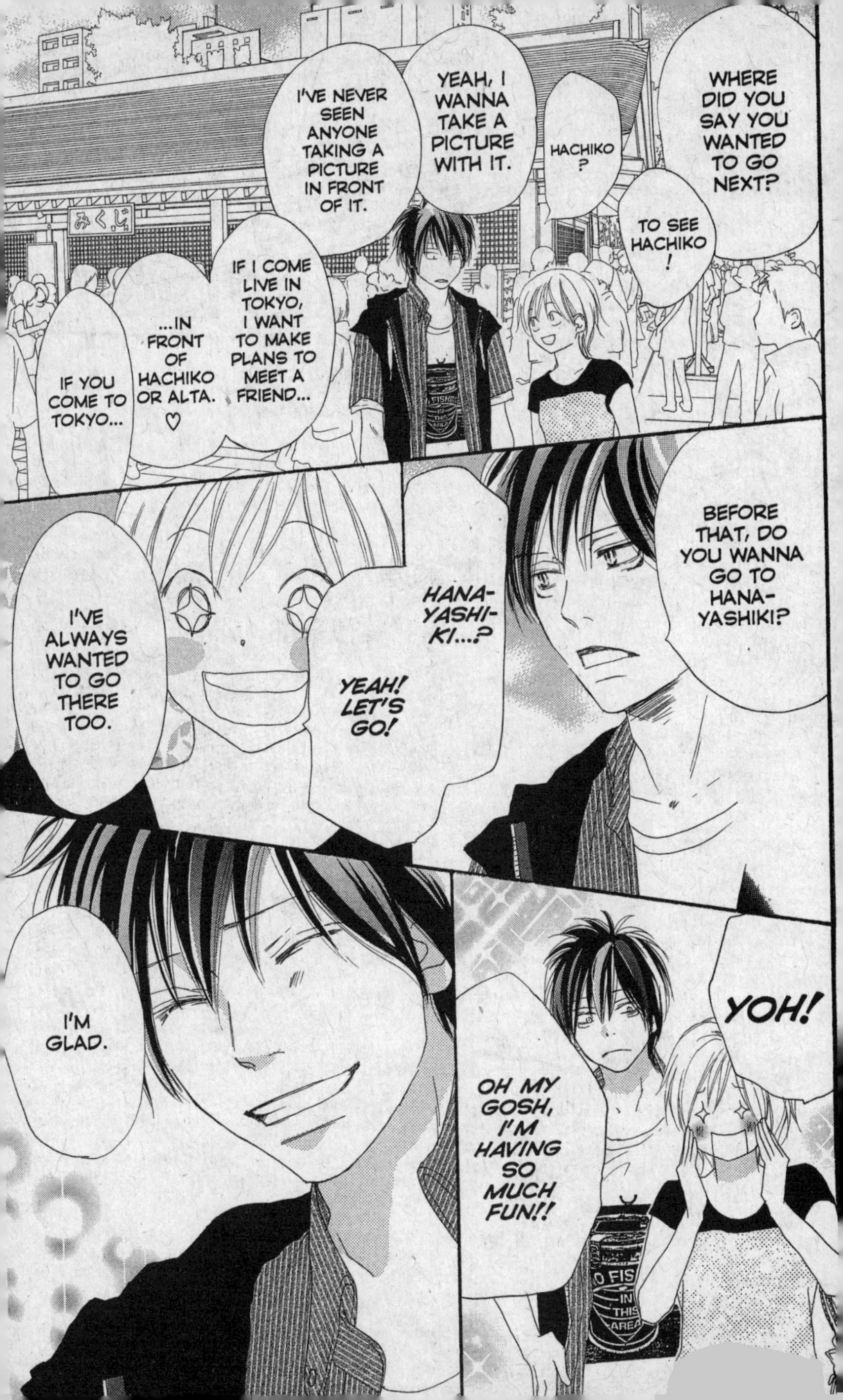
WHERE DID YOU SAY YOU WANTED TO GO NEXT?
TO SEE HACHIKO!
HACHIKO?
YEAH, I WANNA TAKE A PICTURE WITH IT.
I'VE NEVER SEEN ANYONE TAKING A PICTURE IN FRONT OF IT.
みくじ
IF I COME LIVE IN TOKYO, I WANT TO MAKE PLANS TO MEET A FRIEND...
...IN FRONT OF HACHIKO OR ALTA. ♡
IF YOU COME TO TOKYO...
BEFORE THAT, DO YOU WANNA GO TO HANA-YASHIKI?
HANA-YASHIKI...?
YEAH! LET'S GO!
I'VE ALWAYS WANTED TO GO THERE TOO.
YOH!
OH MY GOSH, I'M HAVING SO MUCH FUN!!
I'M GLAD.

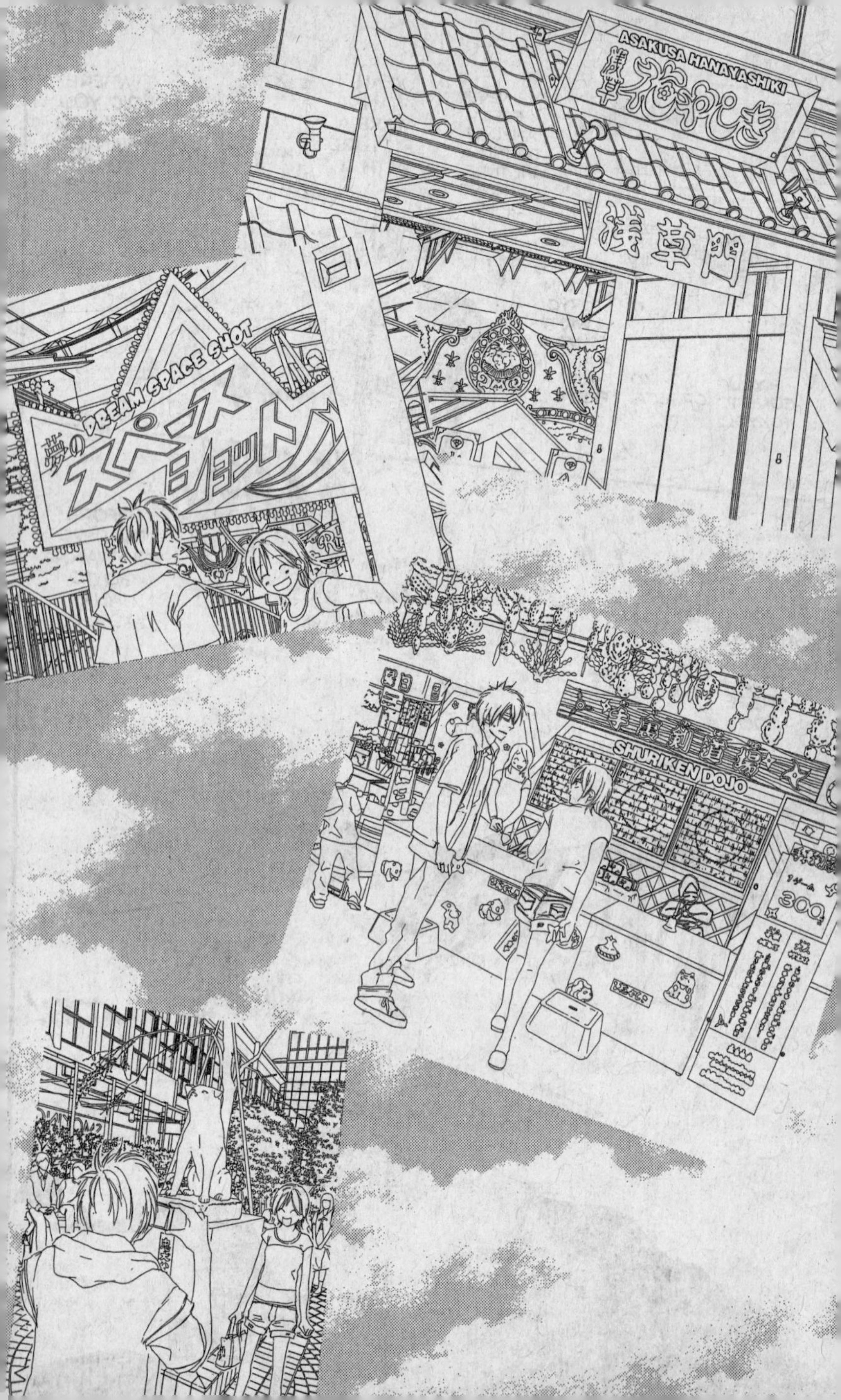
ASAKUSA HANAYASHIKI
浅草花やしき
浅草門
DREAM SPACE SHOT
夢のスペースショット
SHURIKEN DOJO
300

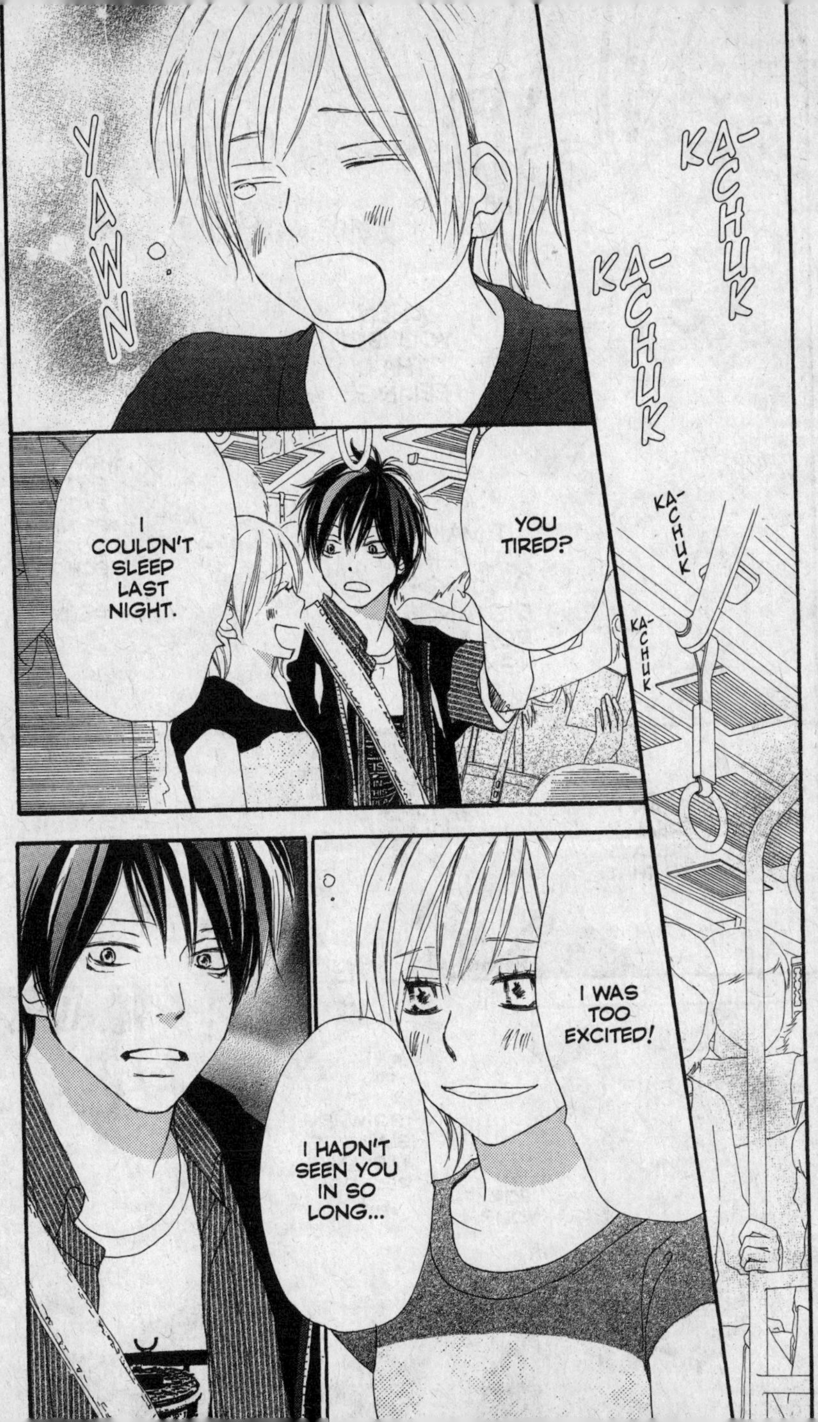
KA-CHUK
KA-CHUK
KA-CHUK
KA-CHUK
YAWN
YOU TIRED?
I COULDN'T SLEEP LAST NIGHT.
I WAS TOO EXCITED!
I HADN'T SEEN YOU IN SO LONG...

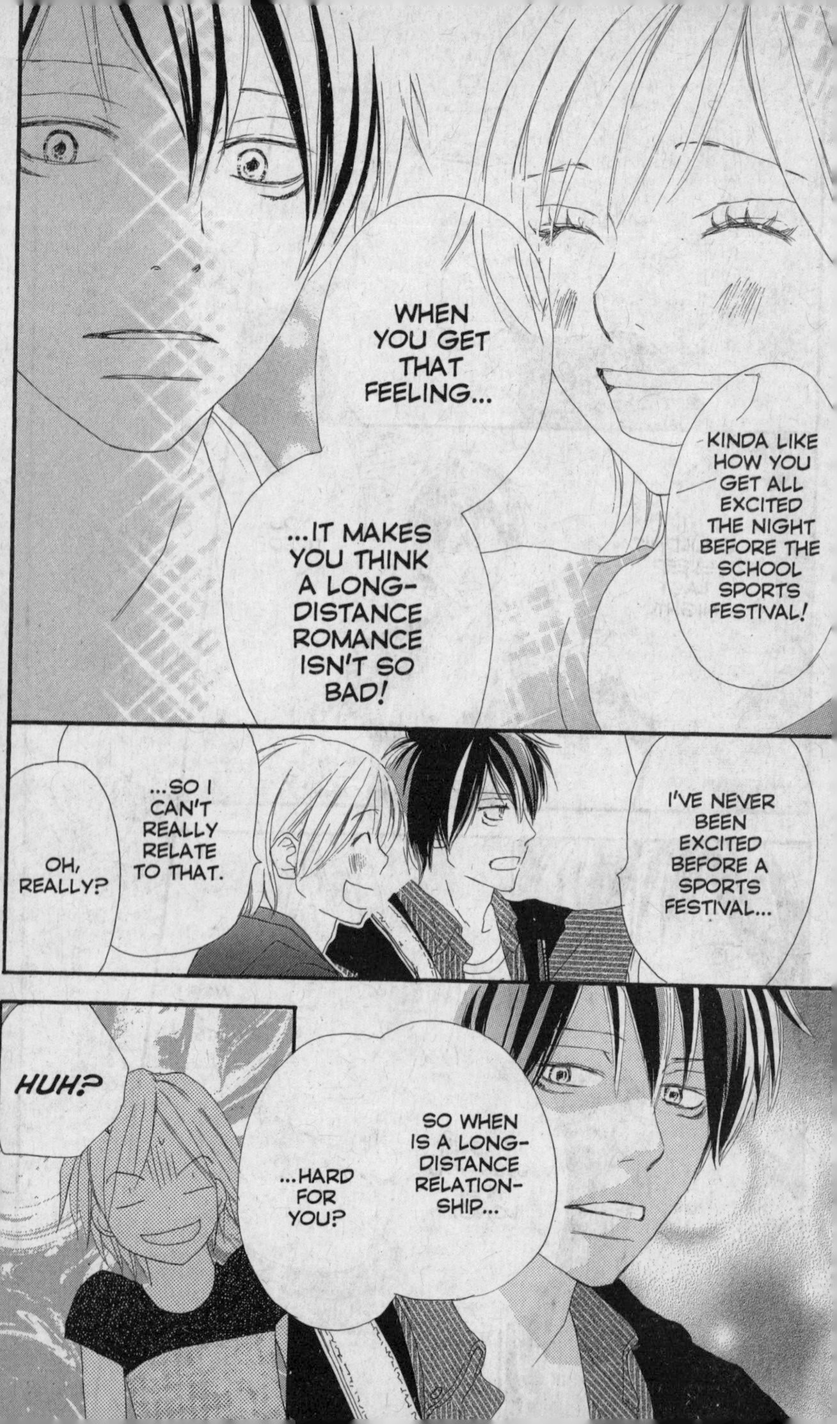
WHEN YOU GET THAT FEELING...
KINDA LIKE HOW YOU GET ALL EXCITED THE NIGHT BEFORE THE SCHOOL SPORTS FESTIVAL!
...IT MAKES YOU THINK A LONG-DISTANCE ROMANCE ISN'T SO BAD!
I'VE NEVER BEEN EXCITED BEFORE A SPORTS FESTIVAL...
...SO I CAN'T REALLY RELATE TO THAT.
OH, REALLY?
SO WHEN IS A LONG-DISTANCE RELATIONSHIP...
...HARD FOR YOU?
HUH?

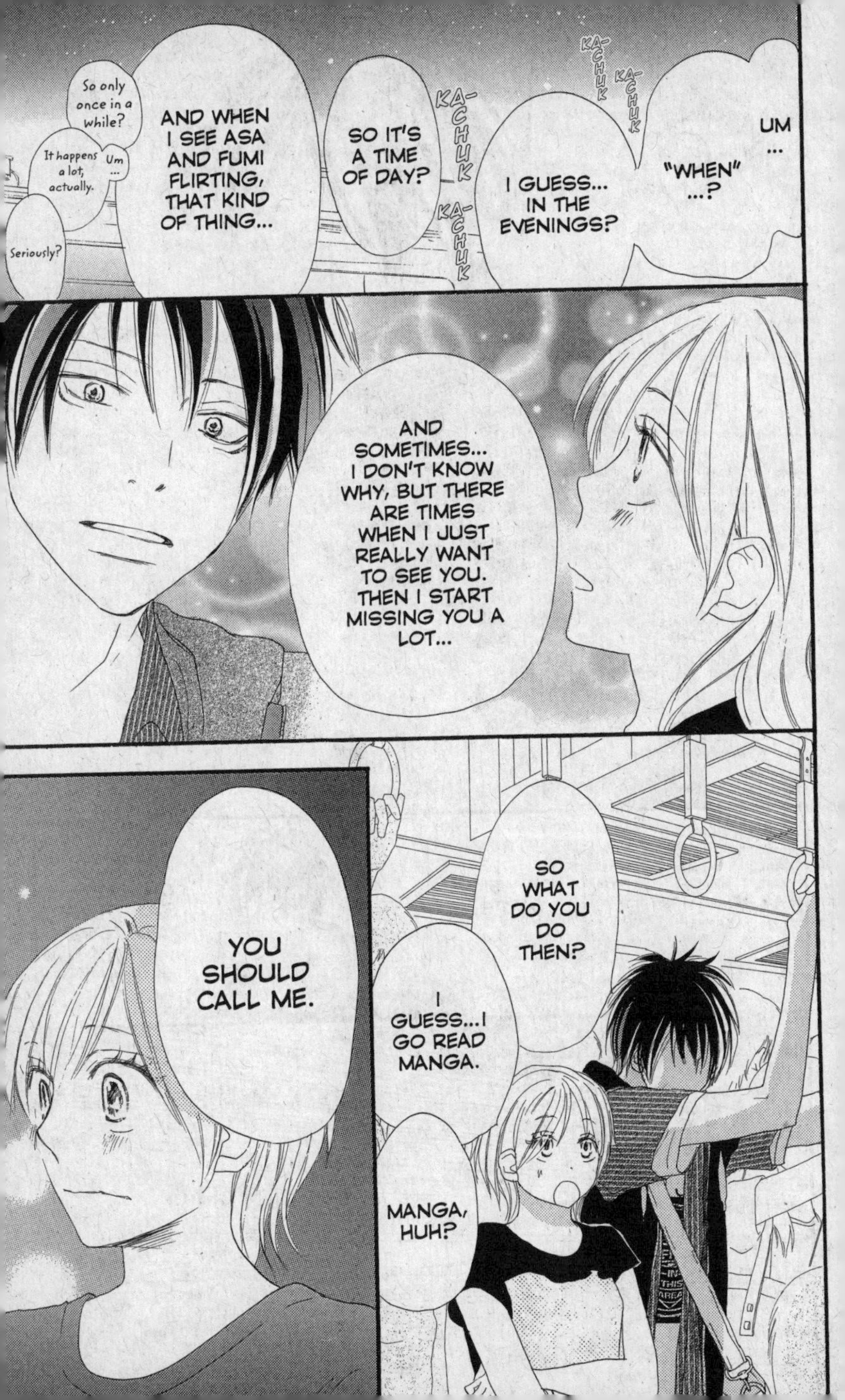
UM ...
"WHEN" ...?
KA-CHUK
KA-CHUK
I GUESS... IN THE EVENINGS?
KA-CHUK
KA-CHUK
SO IT'S A TIME OF DAY?
AND WHEN I SEE ASA AND FUMI FLIRTING, THAT KIND OF THING...
So only once in a while?
Um ...
It happens a lot, actually.
Seriously?
AND SOMETIMES... I DON'T KNOW WHY, BUT THERE ARE TIMES WHEN I JUST REALLY WANT TO SEE YOU. THEN I START MISSING YOU A LOT...
SO WHAT DO YOU DO THEN?
I GUESS...I GO READ MANGA.
MANGA, HUH?
YOU SHOULD CALL ME.

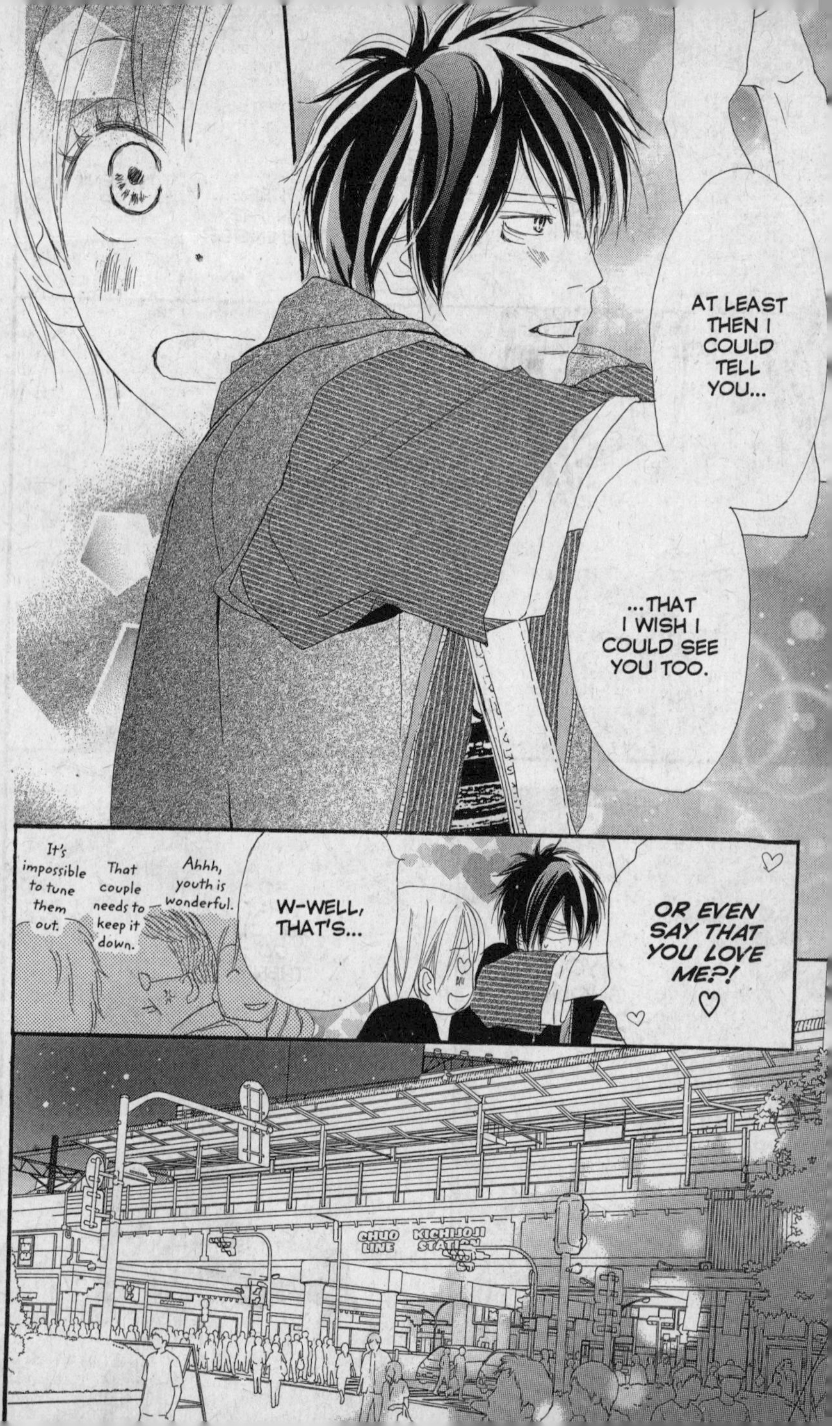
AT LEAST THEN I COULD TELL YOU...
...THAT I WISH I COULD SEE YOU TOO.
OR EVEN SAY THAT YOU LOVE ME?!
W-WELL, THAT'S...
Ahhh, youth is wonderful.
That couple needs to keep it down.
It's impossible to tune them out.
CHUO LINE
KICHIJOJI STATION

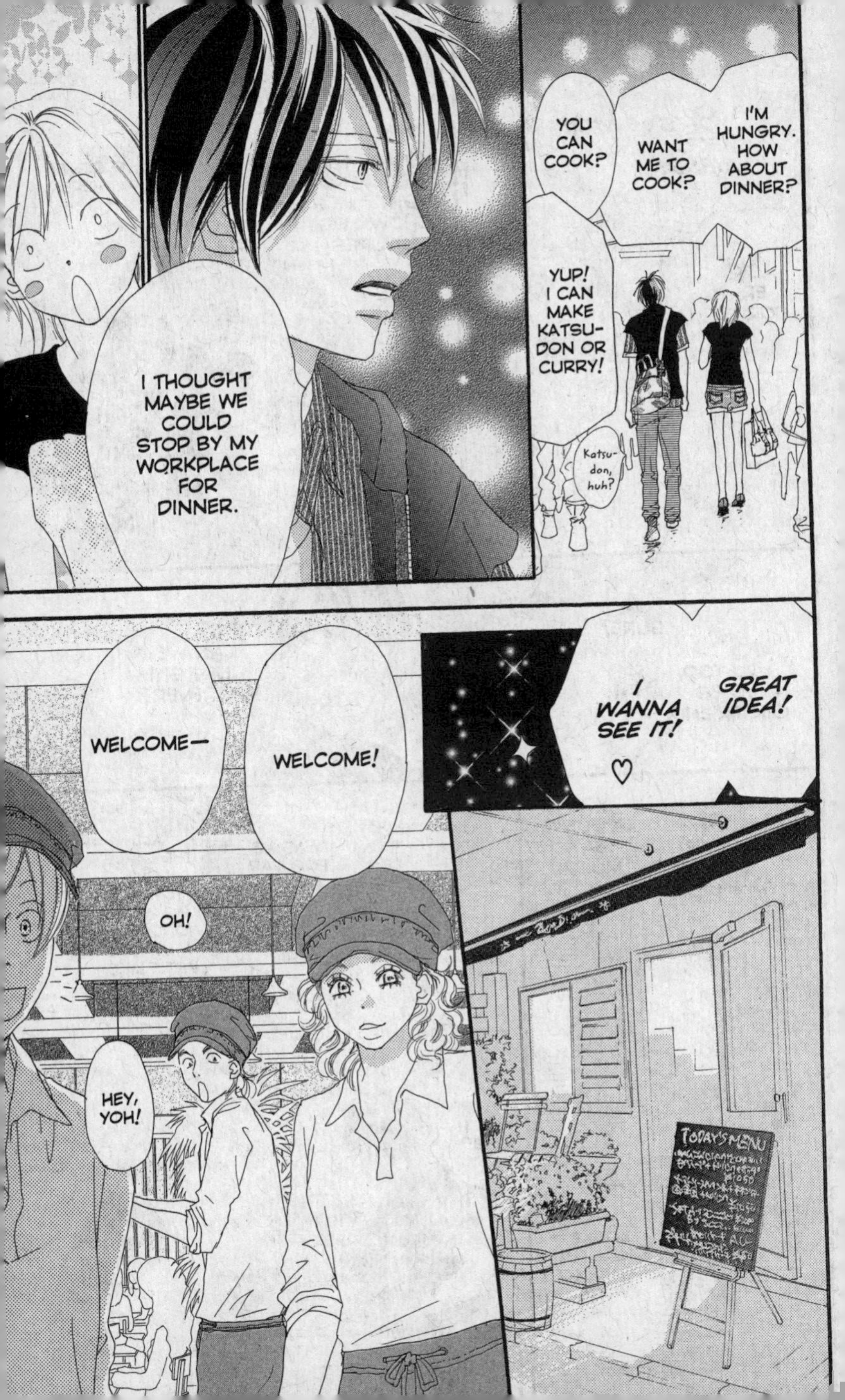
I'M HUNGRY. HOW ABOUT DINNER?
WANT ME TO COOK?
YOU CAN COOK?
YUP! I CAN MAKE KATSU-DON OR CURRY!
Katsu-don, huh?
I THOUGHT MAYBE WE COULD STOP BY MY WORKPLACE FOR DINNER.
GREAT IDEA!
I WANNA SEE IT! ♡
TODAY'S MENU
WELCOME!
WELCOME—
OH!
HEY, YOH!

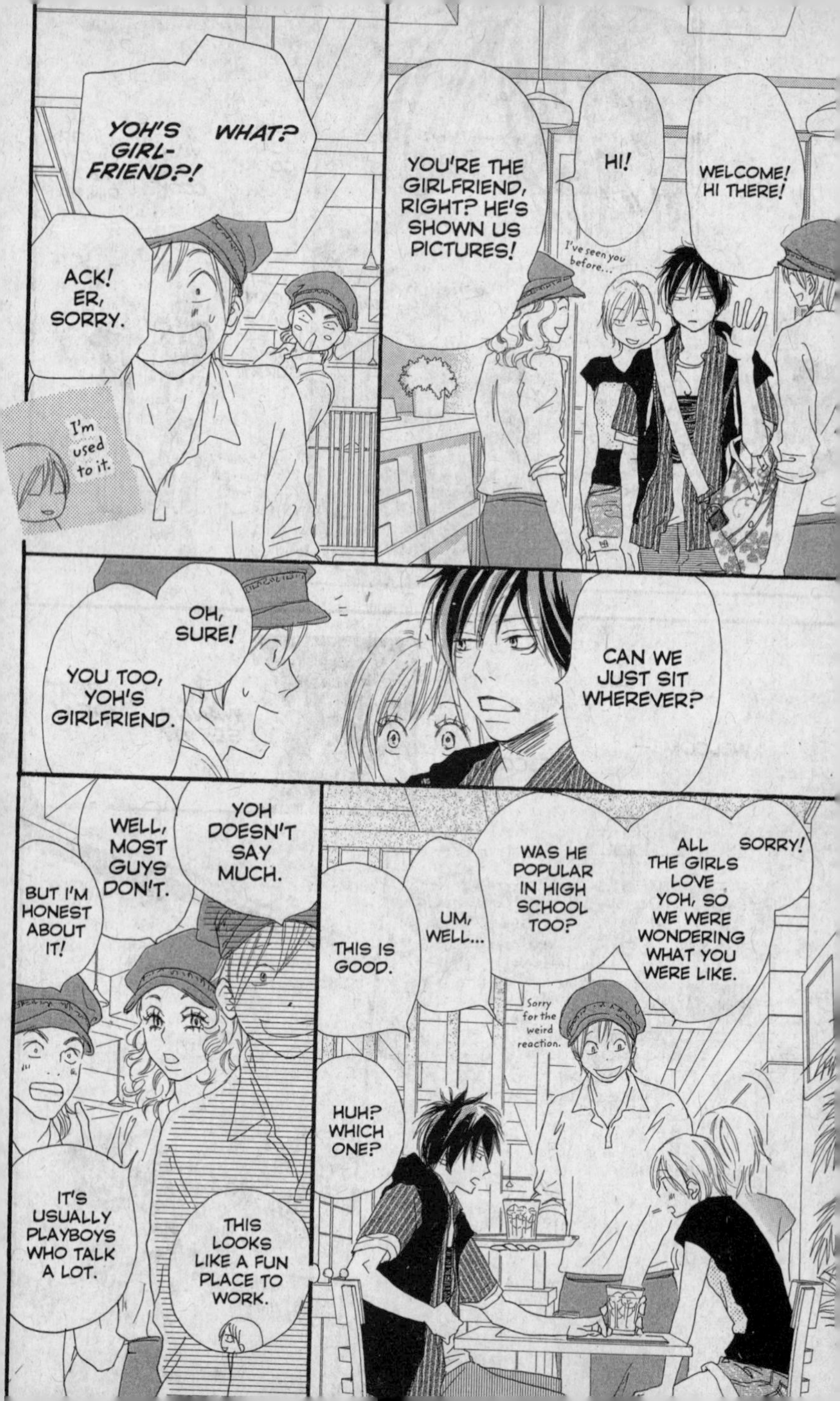
WELCOME! HI THERE!
HI!
I've seen you before...
YOU'RE THE GIRLFRIEND, RIGHT? HE'S SHOWN US PICTURES!
WHAT?
YOH'S GIRL-FRIEND?!
ACK! ER, SORRY.
I'm used to it.
CAN WE JUST SIT WHEREVER?
OH, SURE!
YOU TOO, YOH'S GIRLFRIEND.
SORRY!
ALL THE GIRLS LOVE YOH, SO WE WERE WONDERING WHAT YOU WERE LIKE.
WAS HE POPULAR IN HIGH SCHOOL TOO?
UM, WELL...
THIS IS GOOD.
Sorry for the weird reaction.
HUH? WHICH ONE?
YOH DOESN'T SAY MUCH.
WELL, MOST GUYS DON'T.
BUT I'M HONEST ABOUT IT!
THIS LOOKS LIKE A FUN PLACE TO WORK.
IT'S USUALLY PLAYBOYS WHO TALK A LOT.

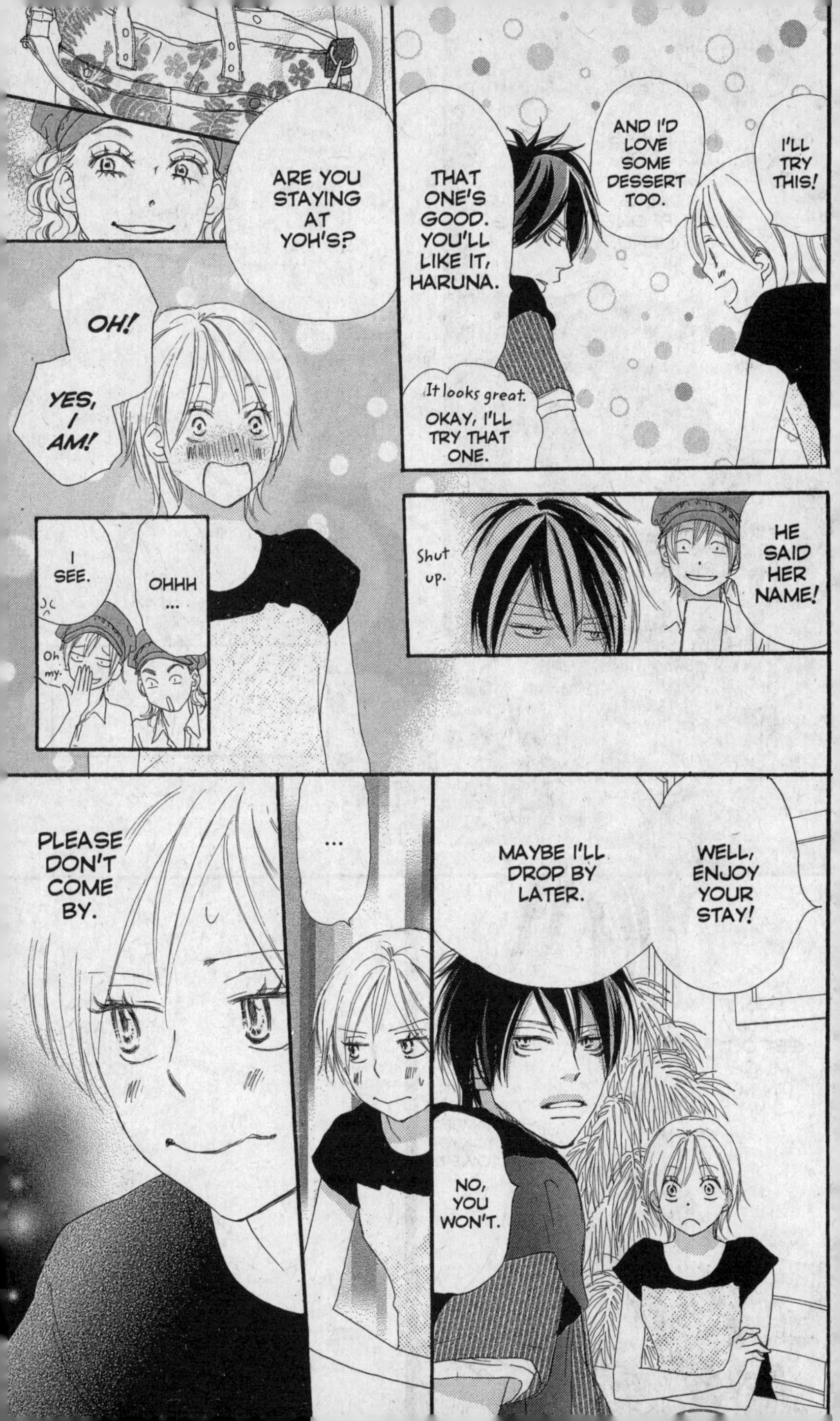
I'LL TRY THIS!
AND I'D LOVE SOME DESSERT TOO.
THAT ONE'S GOOD. YOU'LL LIKE IT, HARUNA.
It looks great.
OKAY, I'LL TRY THAT ONE.
HE SAID HER NAME!
Shut up.
ARE YOU STAYING AT YOH'S?
OH!
YES, I AM!
OHHH...
I SEE.
Oh my.
WELL, ENJOY YOUR STAY!
MAYBE I'LL DROP BY LATER.
NO, YOU WON'T.
...
PLEASE DON'T COME BY.

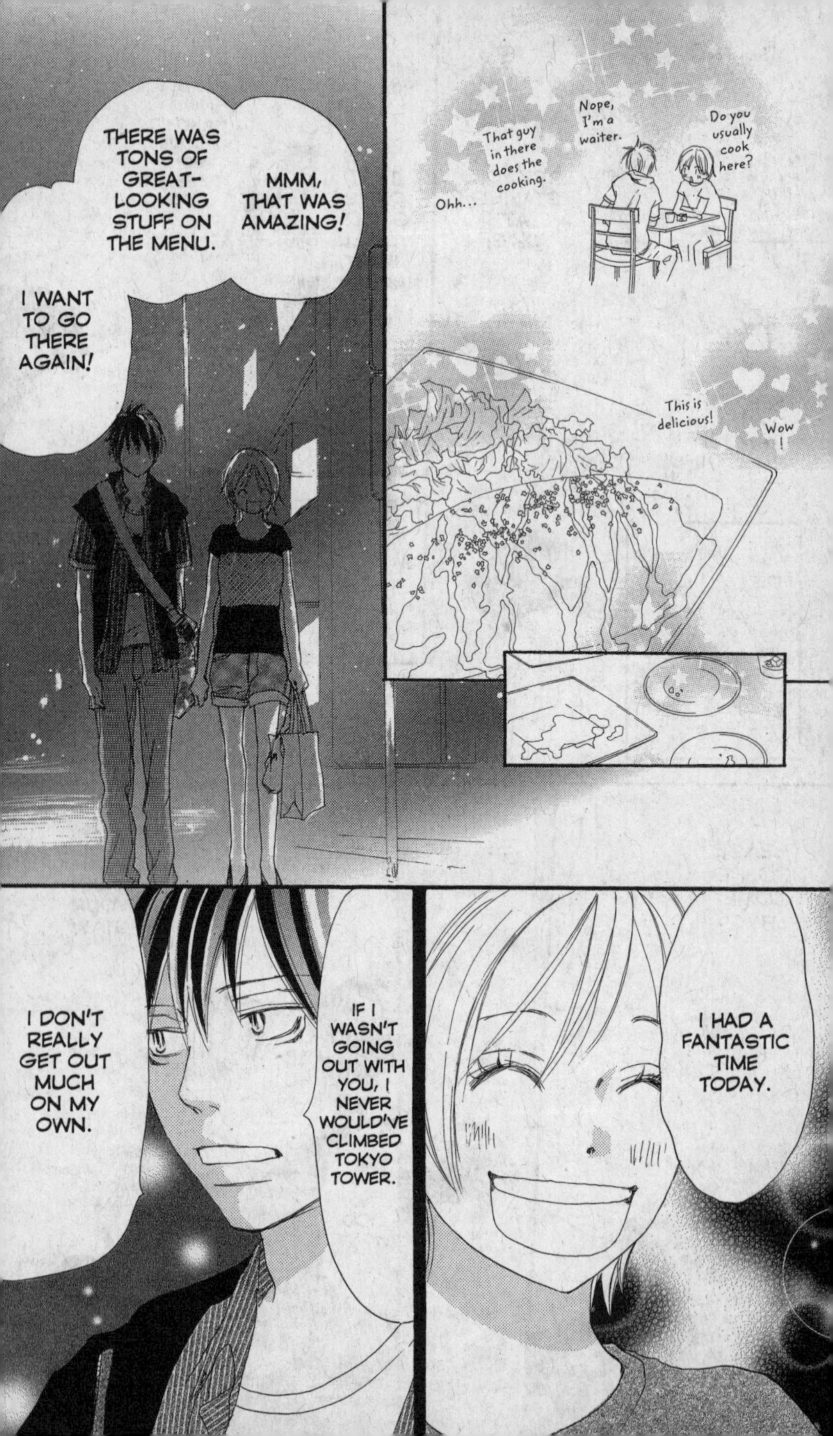
Do you usually cook here?
Nope, I'm a waiter.
That guy in there does the cooking.
Ohh...
Wow!
This is delicious!
MMM, THAT WAS AMAZING!
THERE WAS TONS OF GREAT-LOOKING STUFF ON THE MENU.
I WANT TO GO THERE AGAIN!
I HAD A FANTASTIC TIME TODAY.
IF I WASN'T GOING OUT WITH YOU, I NEVER WOULD'VE CLIMBED TOKYO TOWER.
I DON'T REALLY GET OUT MUCH ON MY OWN.

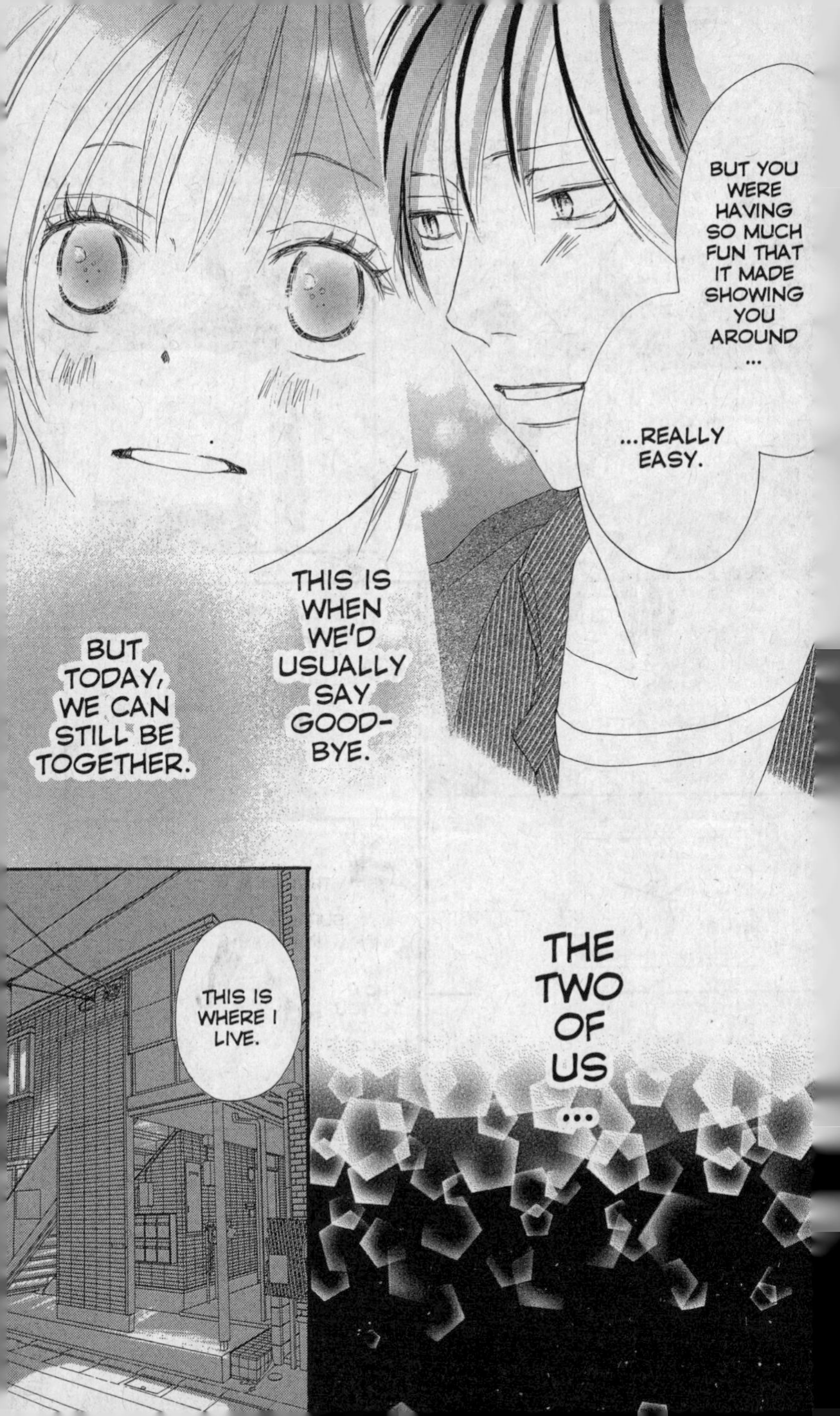
BUT YOU WERE HAVING SO MUCH FUN THAT IT MADE SHOWING YOU AROUND ...
...REALLY EASY.
THIS IS WHEN WE'D USUALLY SAY GOOD-BYE.
BUT TODAY, WE CAN STILL BE TOGETHER.
THE TWO OF US ...
THIS IS WHERE I LIVE.

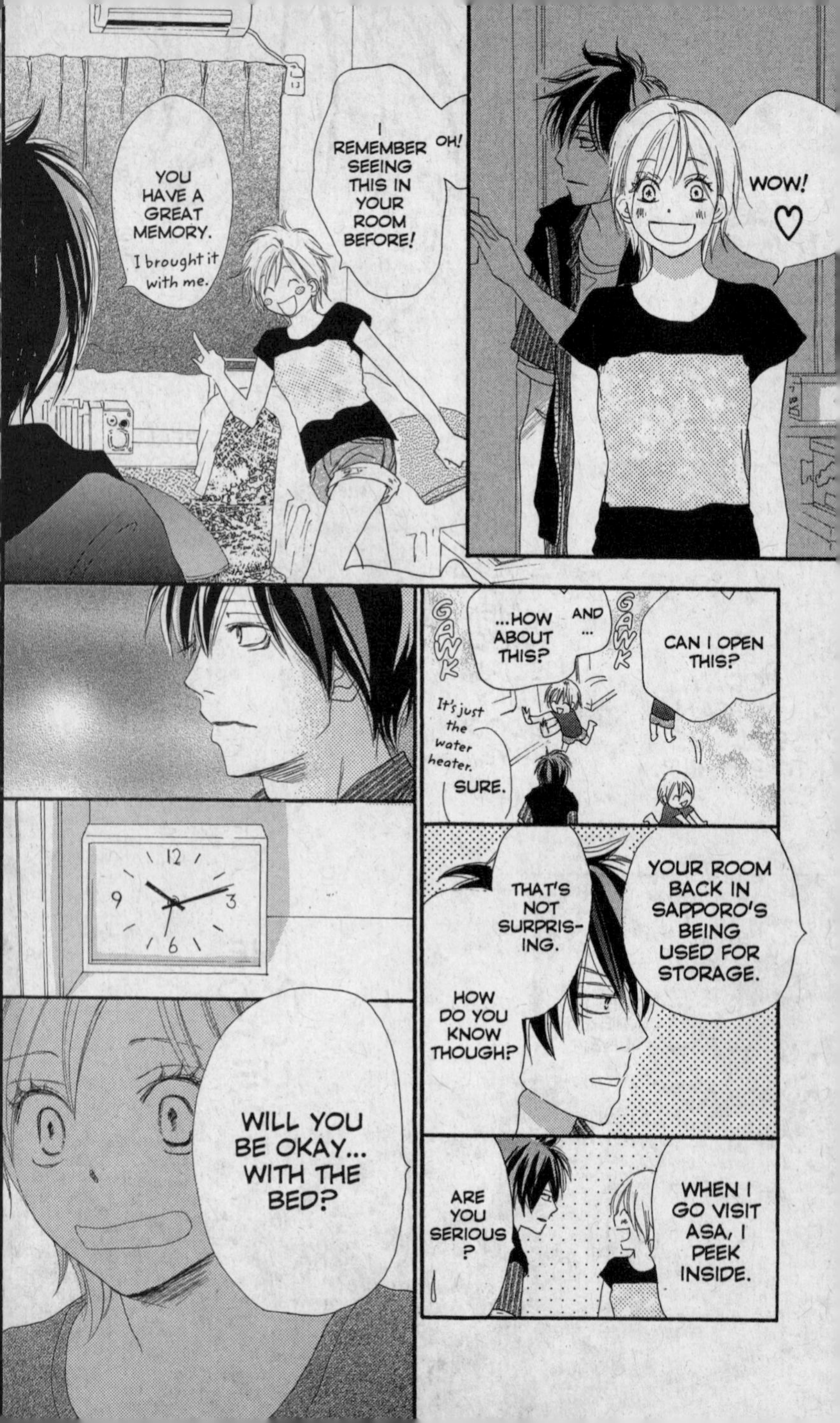
WOW! ♥
OH!
I REMEMBER SEEING THIS IN YOUR ROOM BEFORE!
YOU HAVE A GREAT MEMORY.
I brought it with me.
GAWK
CAN I OPEN THIS?
SURE.
GAWK
AND ...
...HOW ABOUT THIS?
It's just the water heater.
YOUR ROOM BACK IN SAPPORO'S BEING USED FOR STORAGE.
THAT'S NOT SURPRISING.
HOW DO YOU KNOW THOUGH?
WHEN I GO VISIT ASA, I PEEK INSIDE.
ARE YOU SERIOUS?
WILL YOU BE OKAY... WITH THE BED?

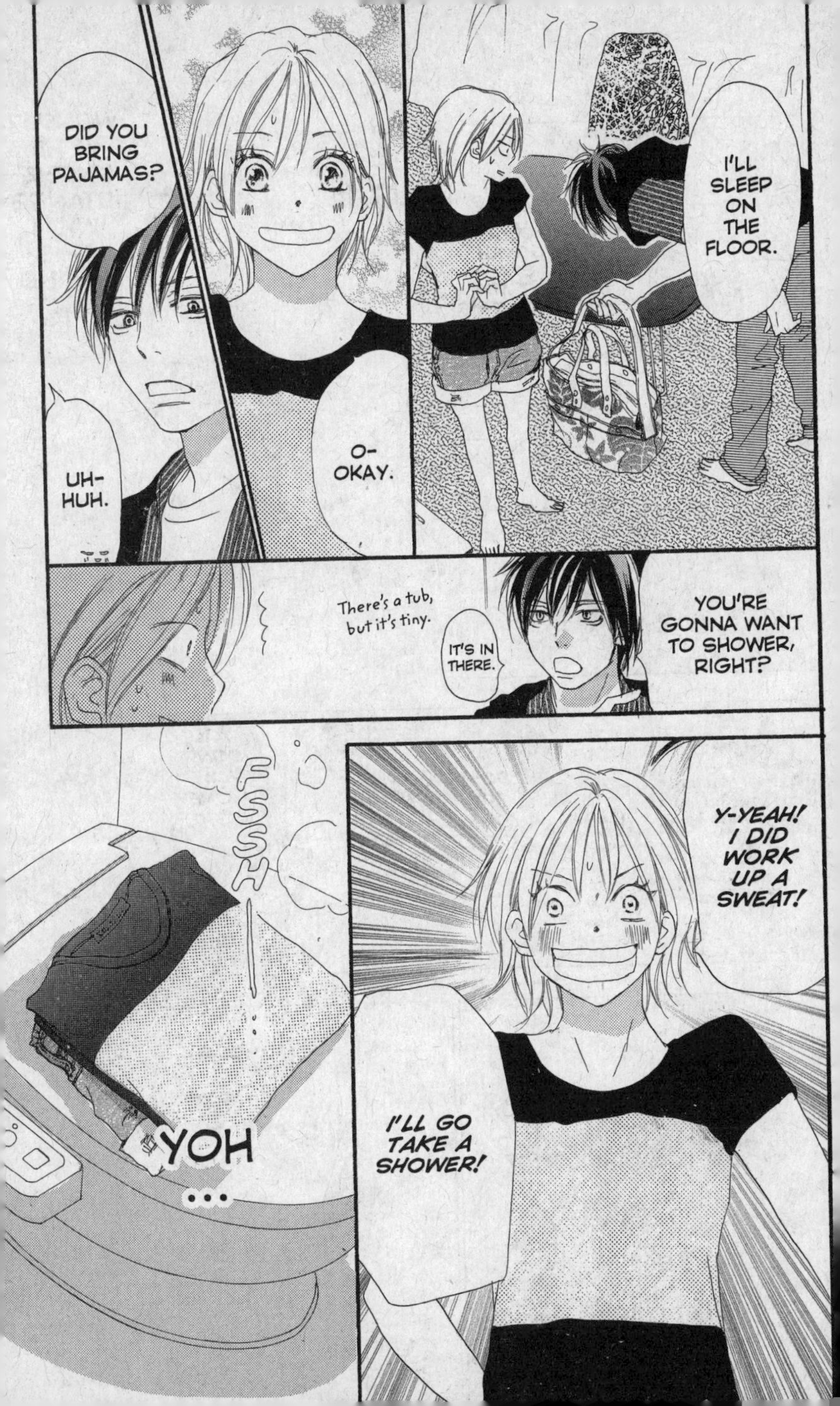
I'LL SLEEP ON THE FLOOR.
O-OKAY.
DID YOU BRING PAJAMAS?
UH-HUH.
YOU'RE GONNA WANT TO SHOWER, RIGHT?
IT'S IN THERE.
There's a tub, but it's tiny.
Y-YEAH! I DID WORK UP A SWEAT!
I'LL GO TAKE A SHOWER!
FSSH
YOH
...

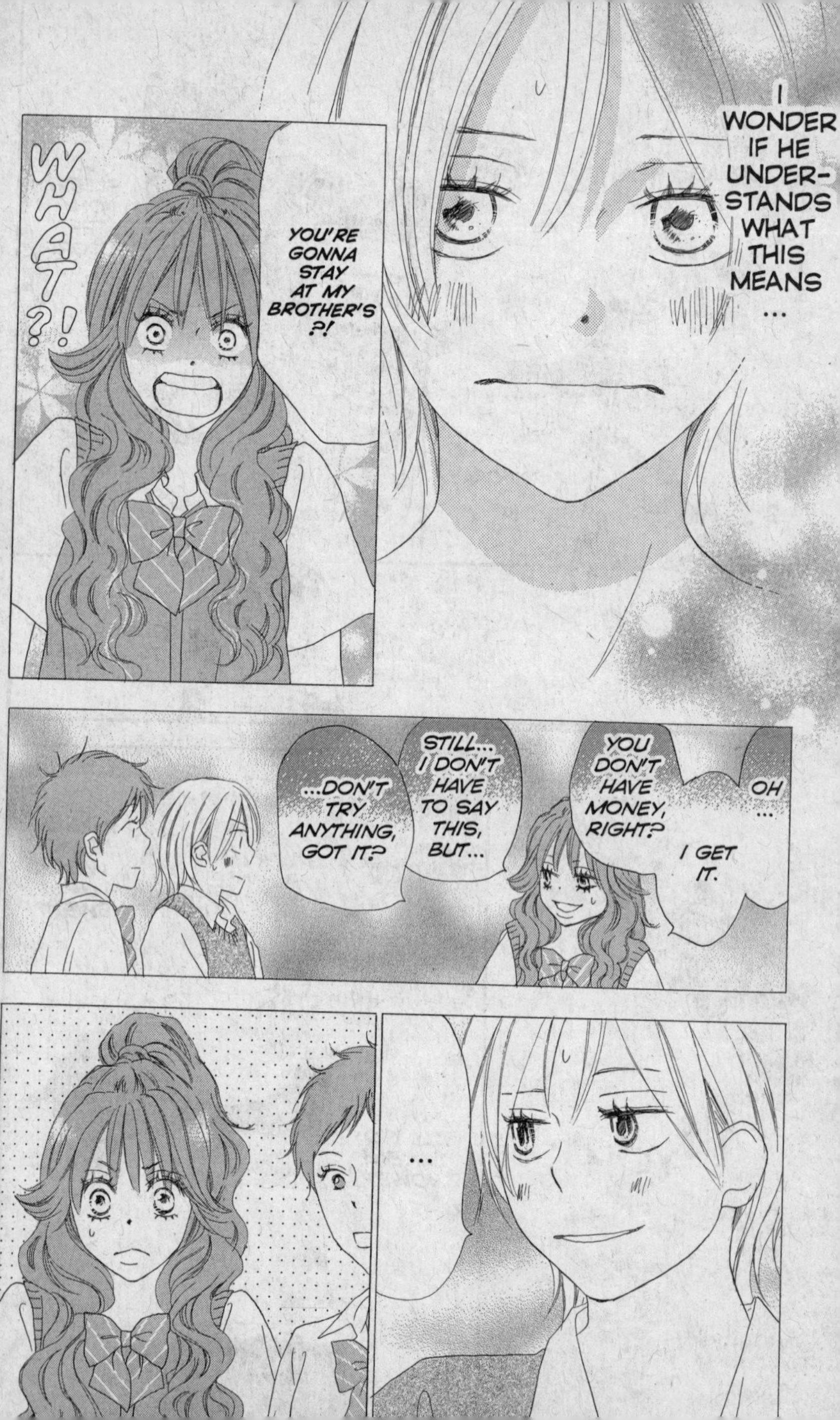
I WONDER IF HE UNDER-STANDS WHAT THIS MEANS ...
YOU'RE GONNA STAY AT MY BROTHER'S ?!
WHAT ?!
OH ...
I GET IT.
YOU DON'T HAVE MONEY, RIGHT?
STILL... I DON'T HAVE TO SAY THIS, BUT...
...DON'T TRY ANYTHING, GOT IT?
...

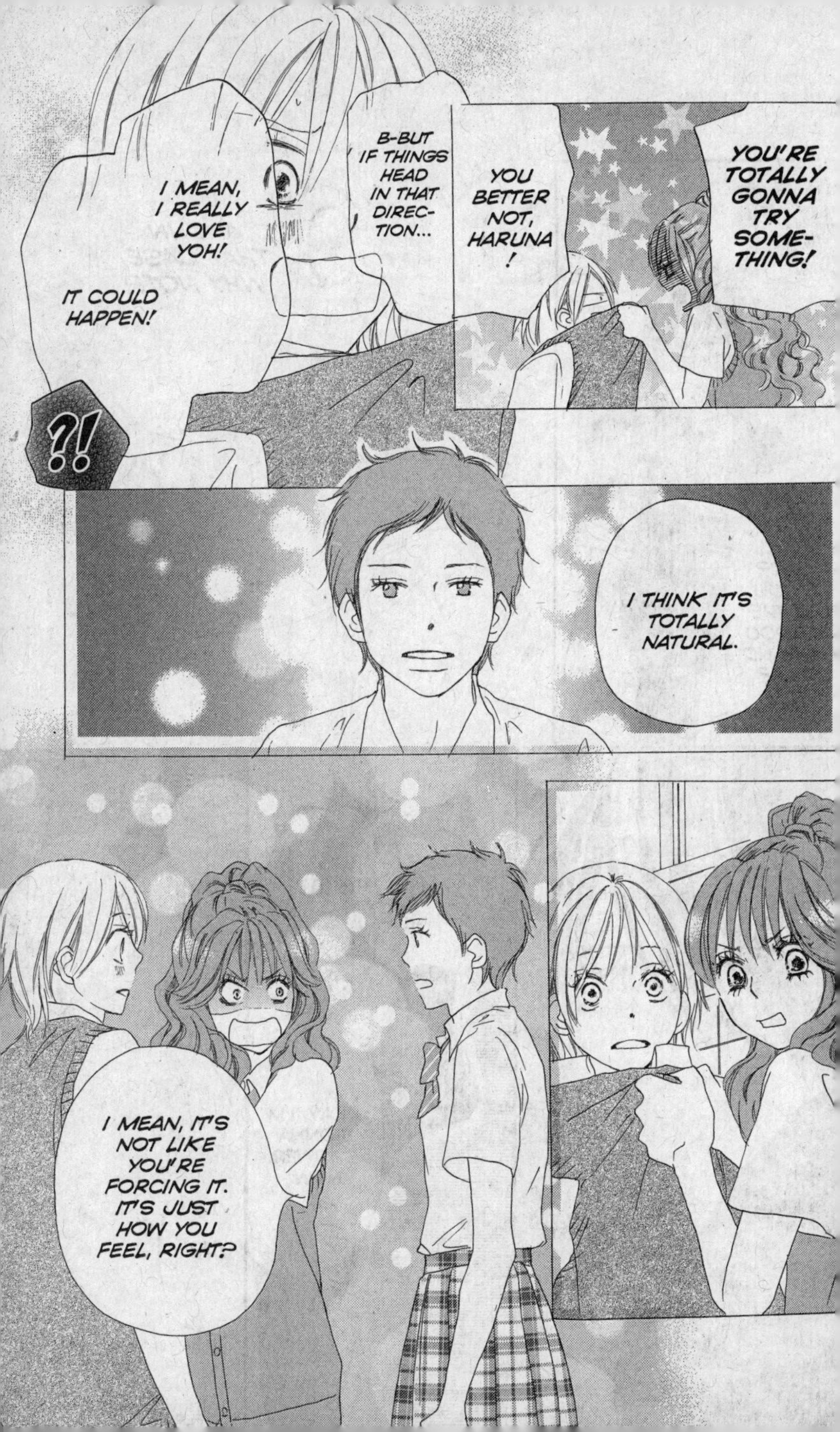
YOU'RE TOTALLY GONNA TRY SOME-THING!
YOU BETTER NOT, HARUNA!
B-BUT IF THINGS HEAD IN THAT DIREC-TION...
I MEAN, I REALLY LOVE YOH!
IT COULD HAPPEN!
?!
I THINK IT'S TOTALLY NATURAL.
I MEAN, IT'S NOT LIKE YOU'RE FORCING IT. IT'S JUST HOW YOU FEEL, RIGHT?

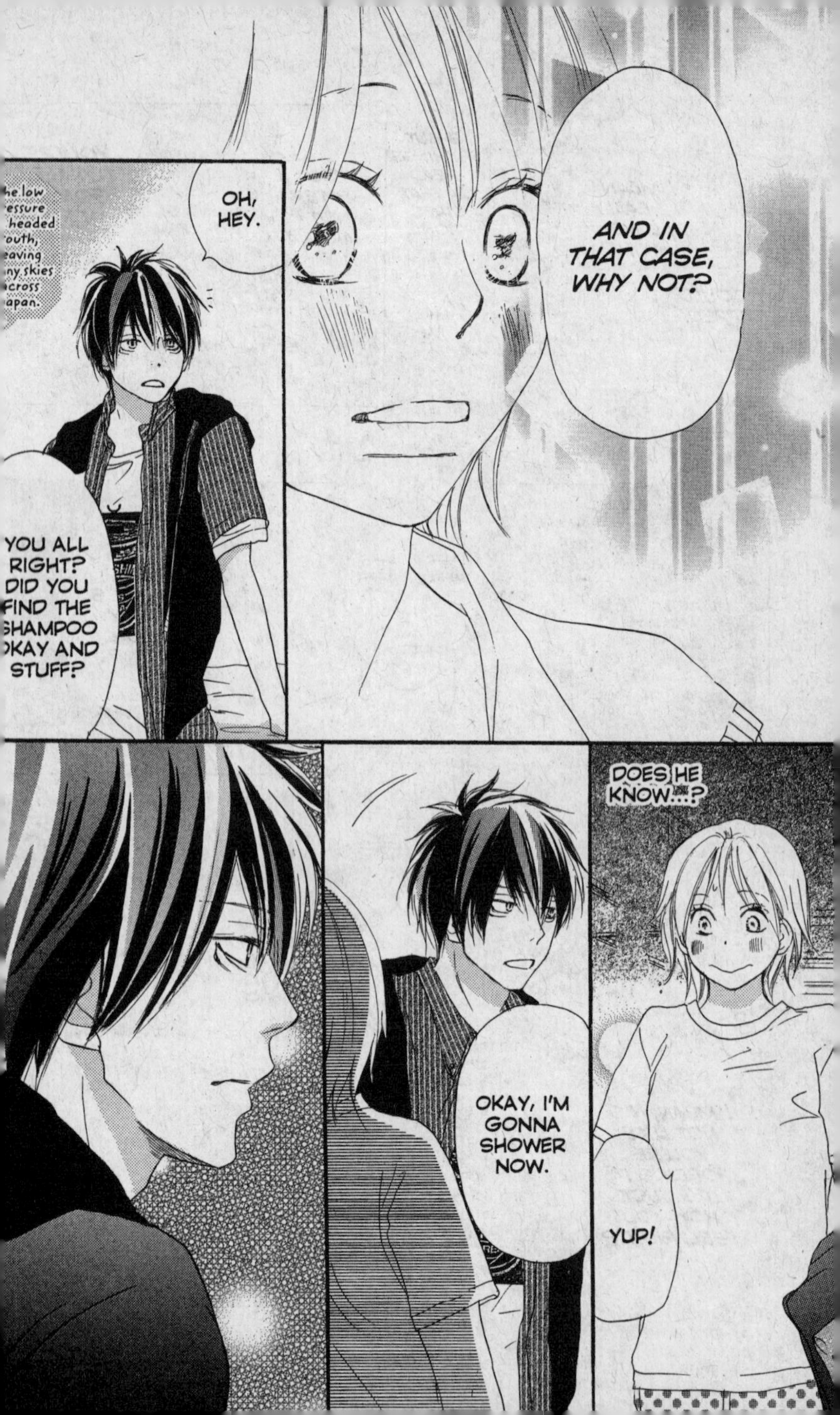
AND IN THAT CASE, WHY NOT?
OH, HEY.
he low essure headed outh, eaving ny skies cross apan.
YOU ALL RIGHT? DID YOU FIND THE SHAMPOO OKAY AND STUFF?
DOES HE KNOW...?
YUP!
OKAY, I'M GONNA SHOWER NOW.

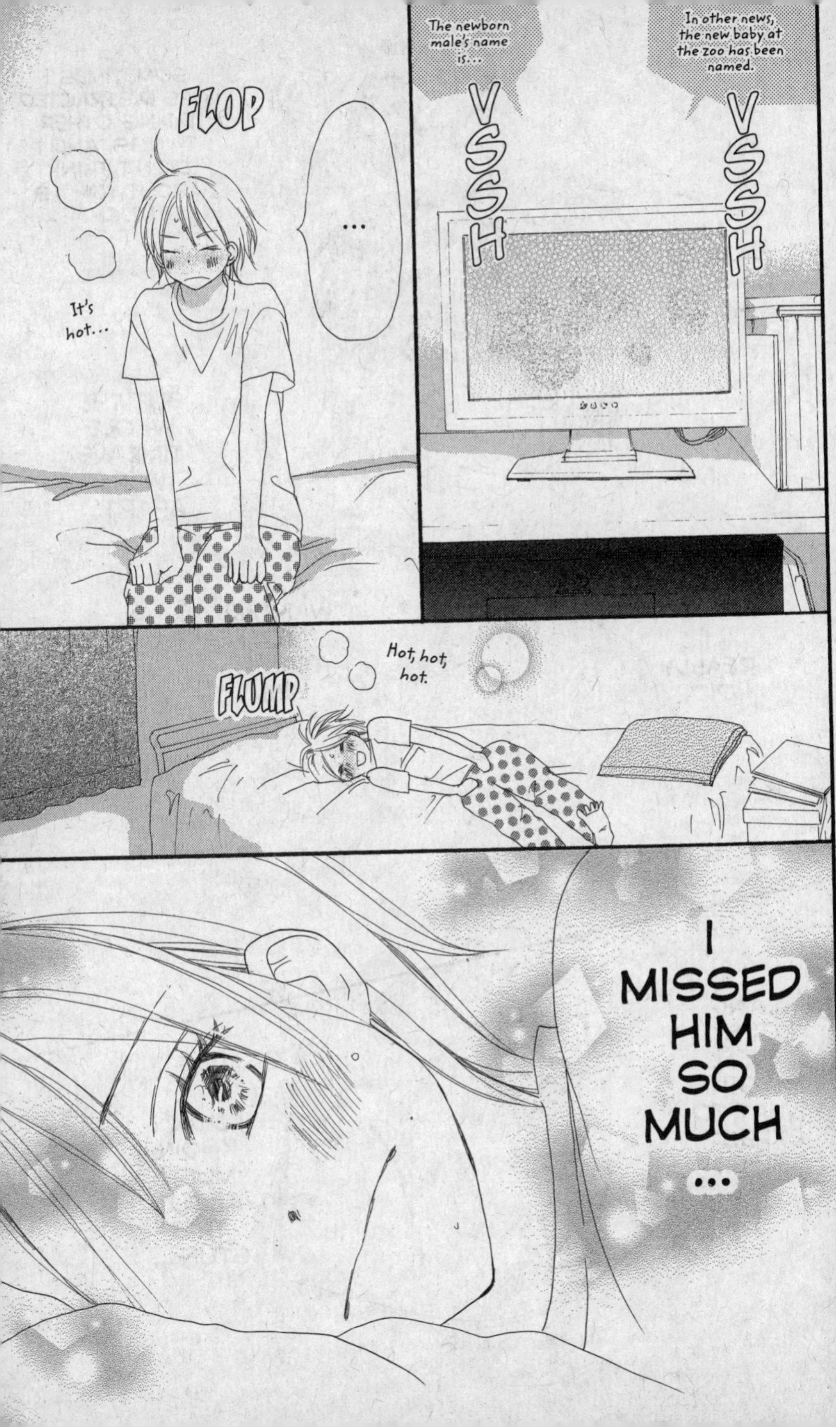
In other news, the new baby at the zoo has been named.
VSSH
The newborn male's name is...
VSSH
...
FLOP
It's hot...
Hot, hot, hot.
FLUMP
I MISSED HIM SO MUCH...

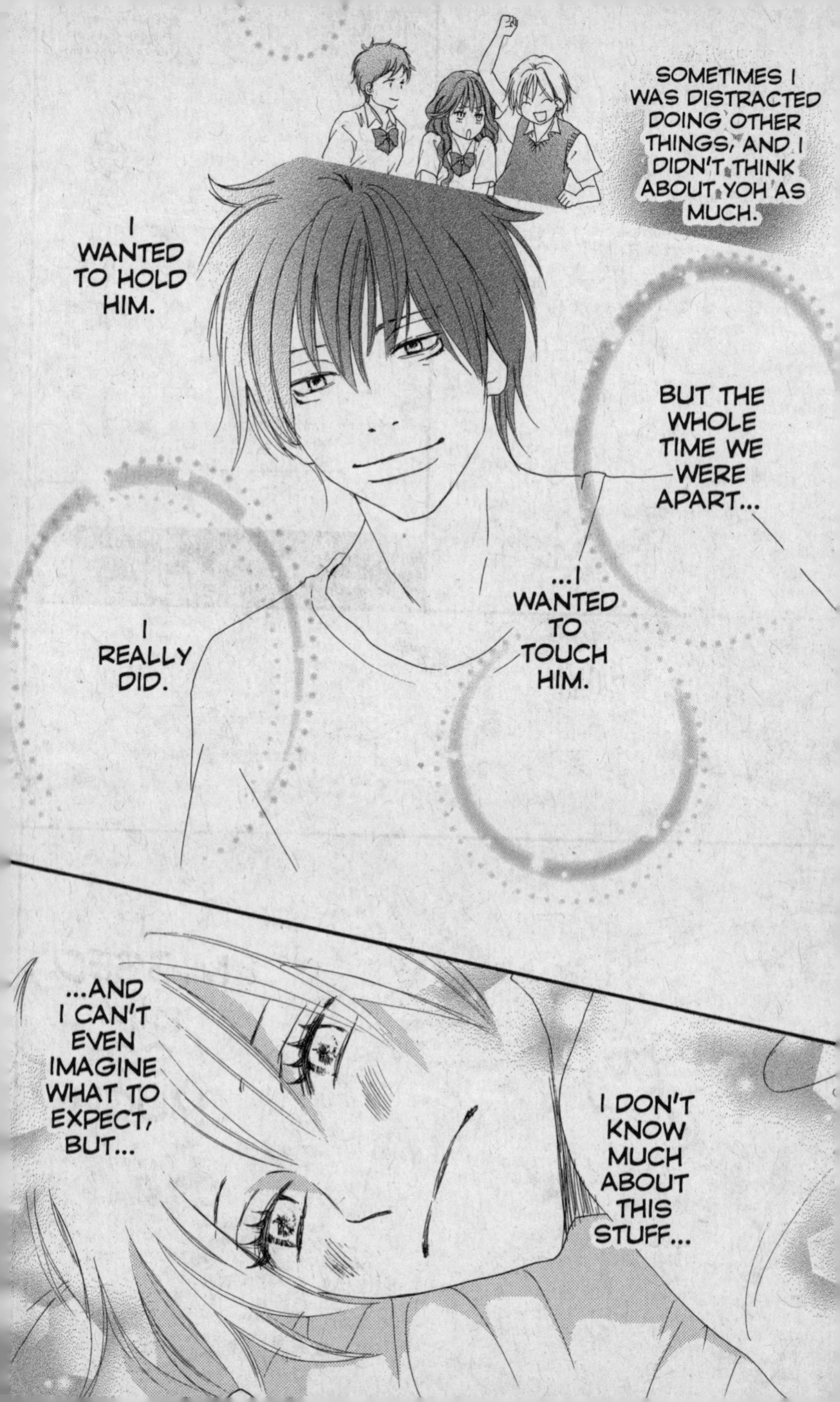
SOMETIMES I WAS DISTRACTED DOING OTHER THINGS, AND I DIDN'T THINK ABOUT YOH AS MUCH.
BUT THE WHOLE TIME WE WERE APART...
...I WANTED TO TOUCH HIM.
I WANTED TO HOLD HIM.
I REALLY DID.
I DON'T KNOW MUCH ABOUT THIS STUFF...
...AND I CAN'T EVEN IMAGINE WHAT TO EXPECT, BUT...

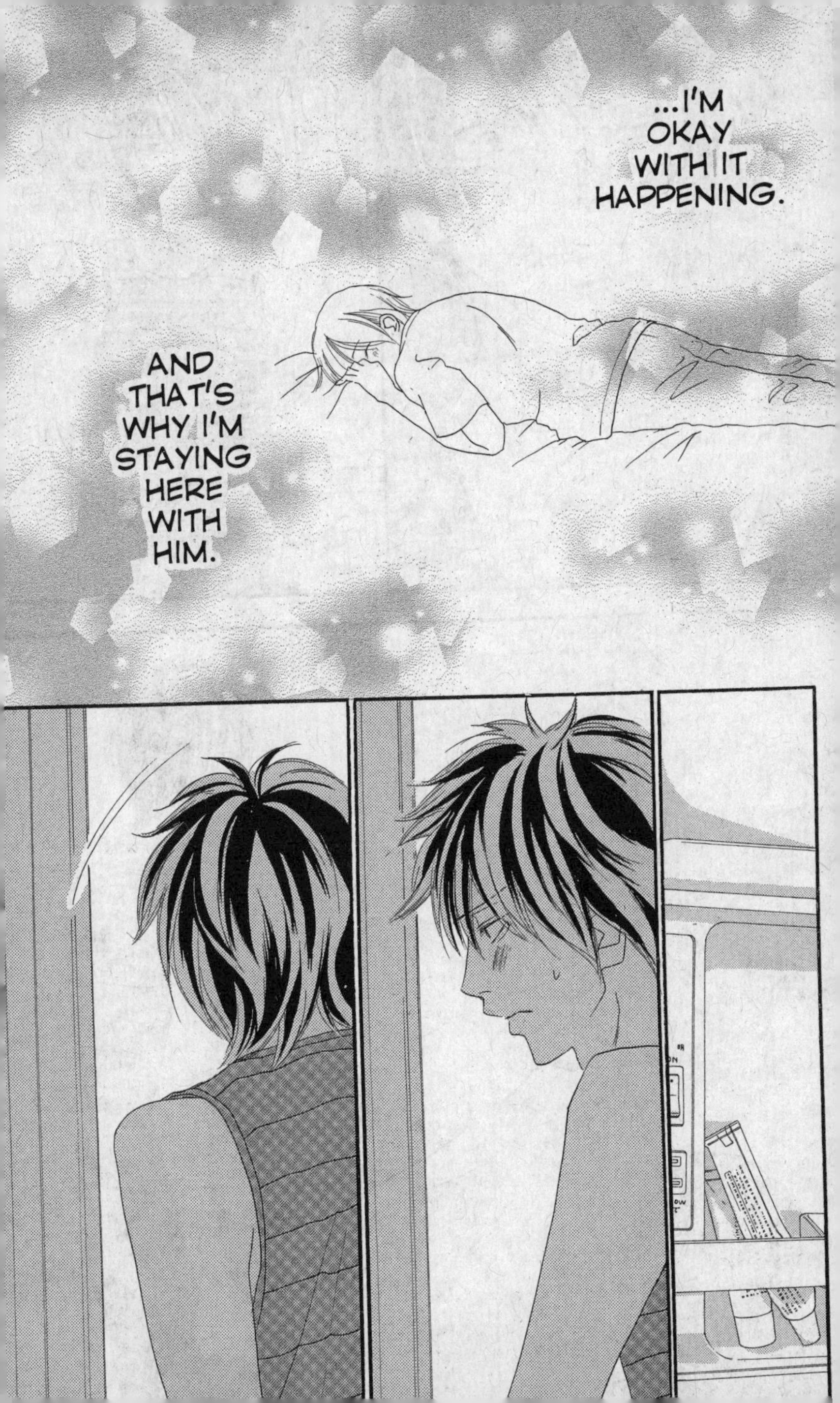
...I'M OKAY WITH IT HAPPENING.
AND THAT'S WHY I'M STAYING HERE WITH HIM.

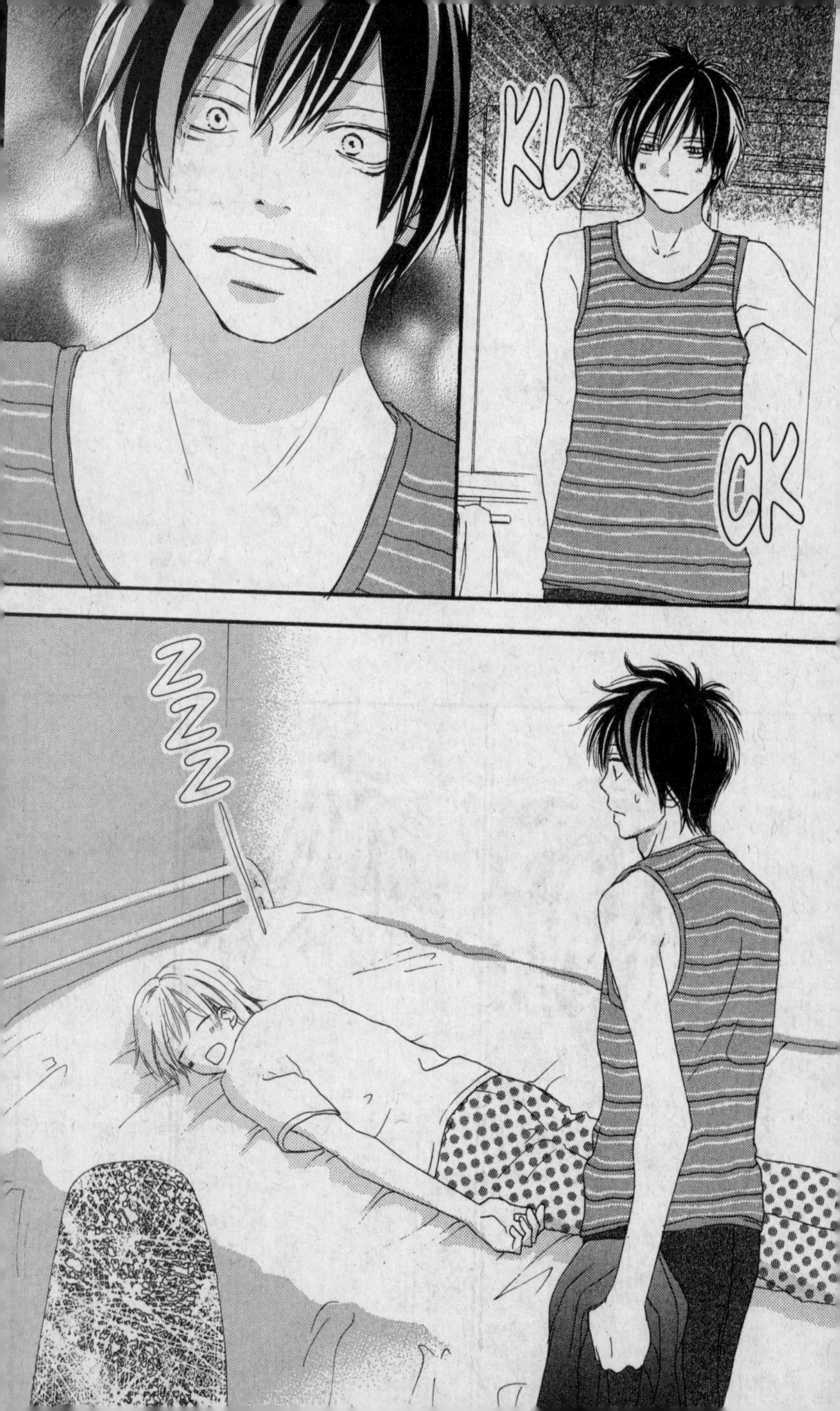
KL
CK
ZZZ

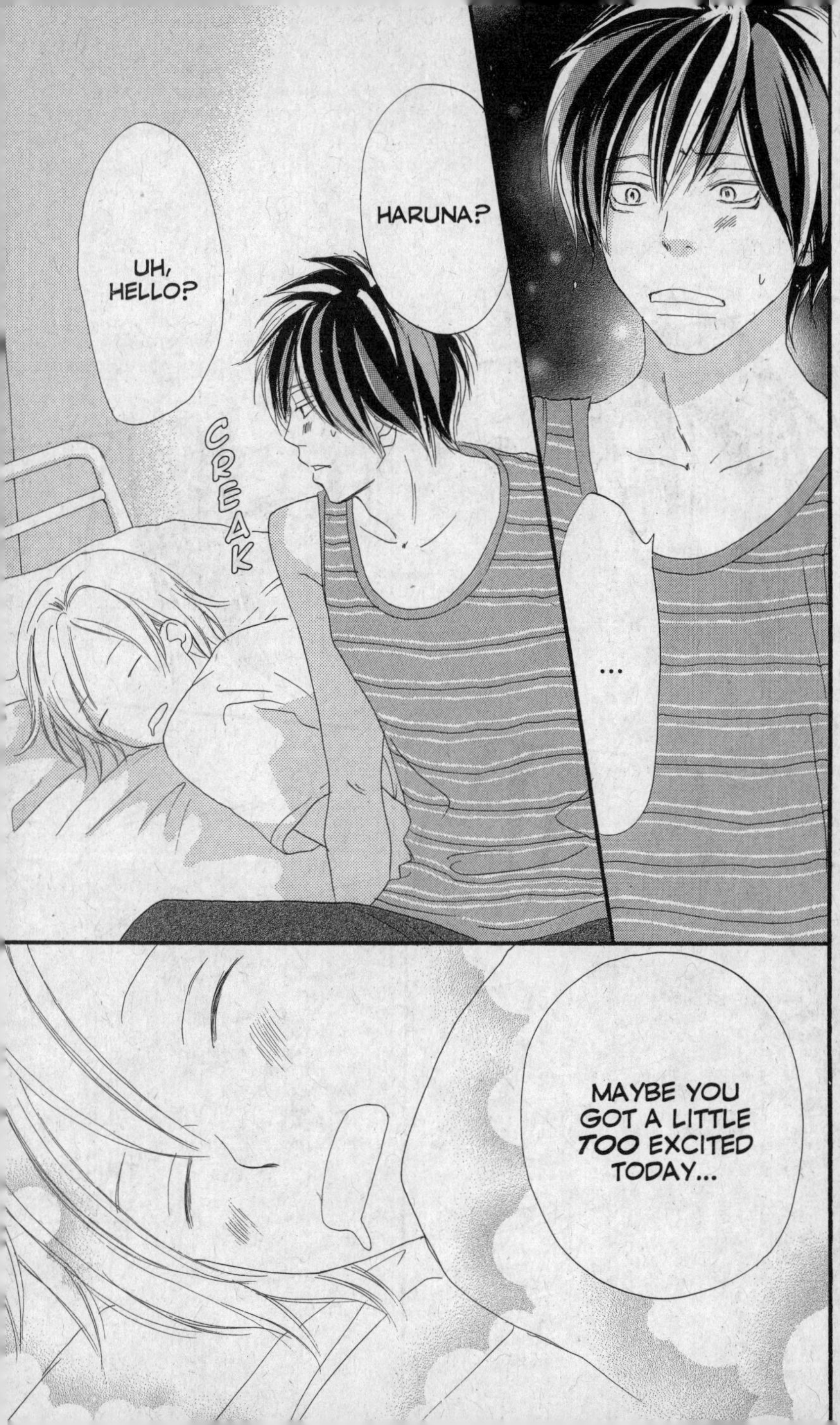
...
HARUNA?
UH, HELLO?
CREAK
MAYBE YOU GOT A LITTLE *TOO* EXCITED TODAY...

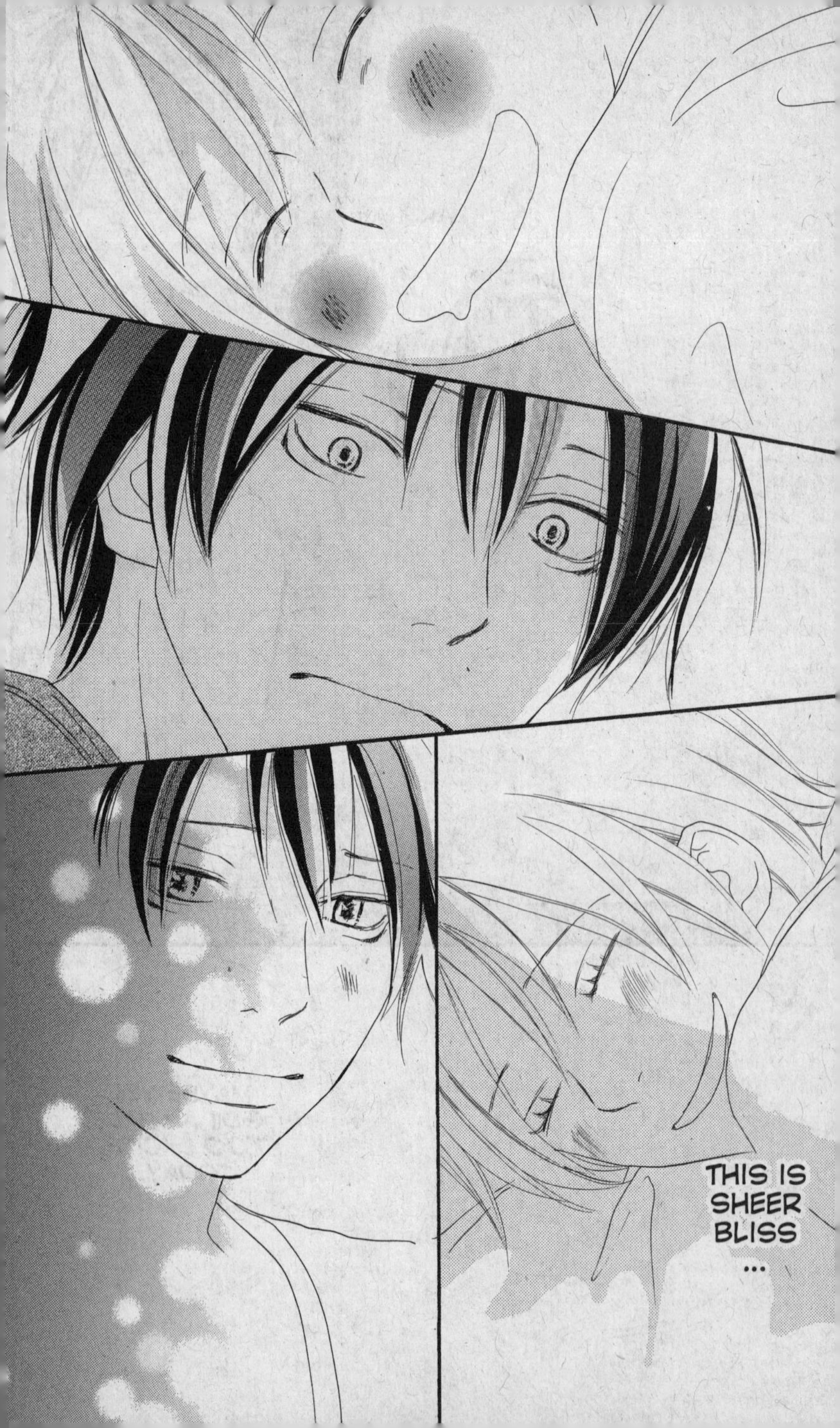
THIS IS SHEER BLISS ...

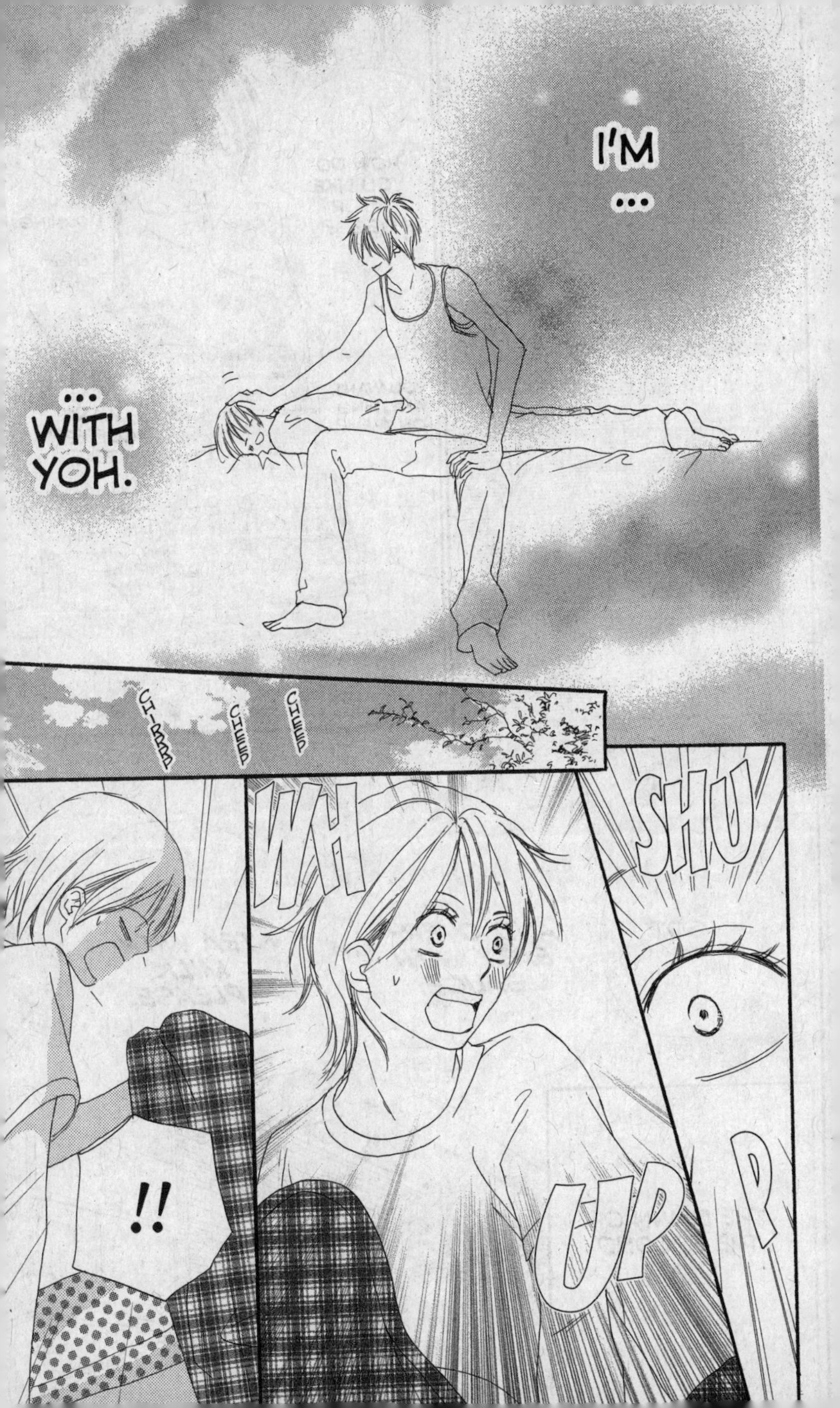
I'M ...
... WITH YOH.
CHEEP
CHEEP
CHIRRR
SHU
P
WH
UP
!!

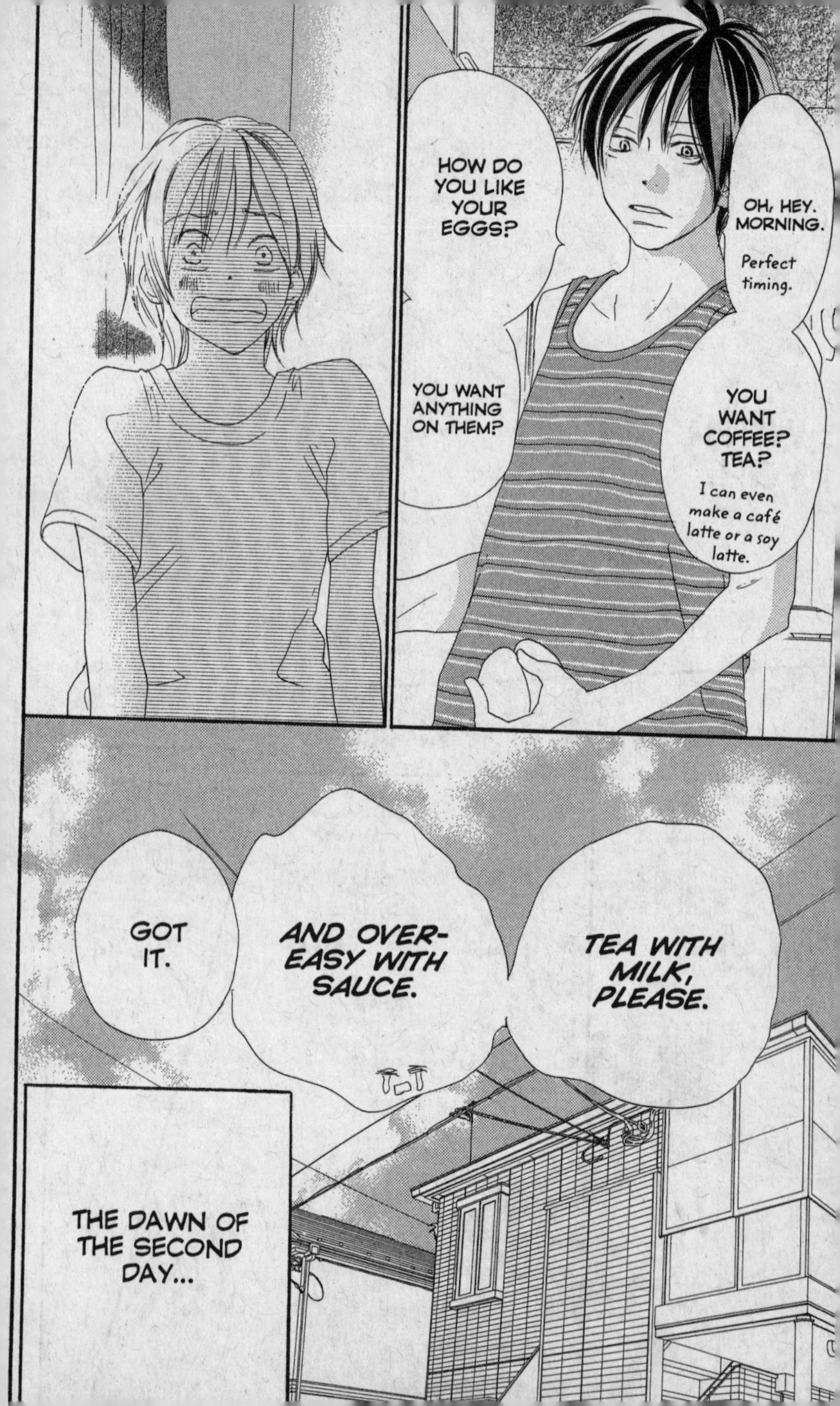
OH, HEY. MORNING.
Perfect timing.
HOW DO YOU LIKE YOUR EGGS?
YOU WANT COFFEE? TEA?
I can even make a café latte or a soy latte.
YOU WANT ANYTHING ON THEM?
TEA WITH MILK, PLEASE.
AND OVER-EASY WITH SAUCE.
GOT IT.
THE DAWN OF THE SECOND DAY...

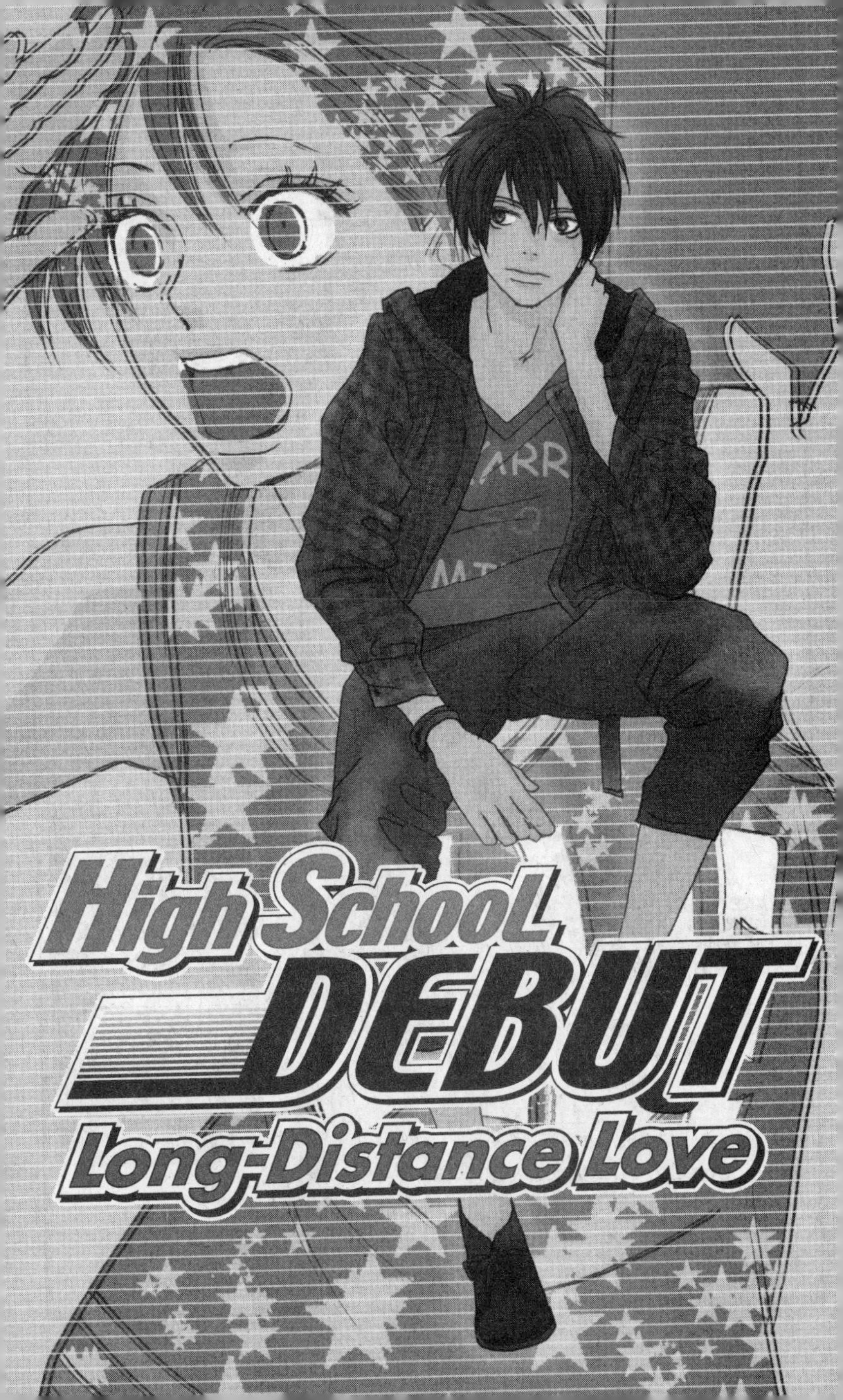
High School
DEBUT
Long-Distance Love

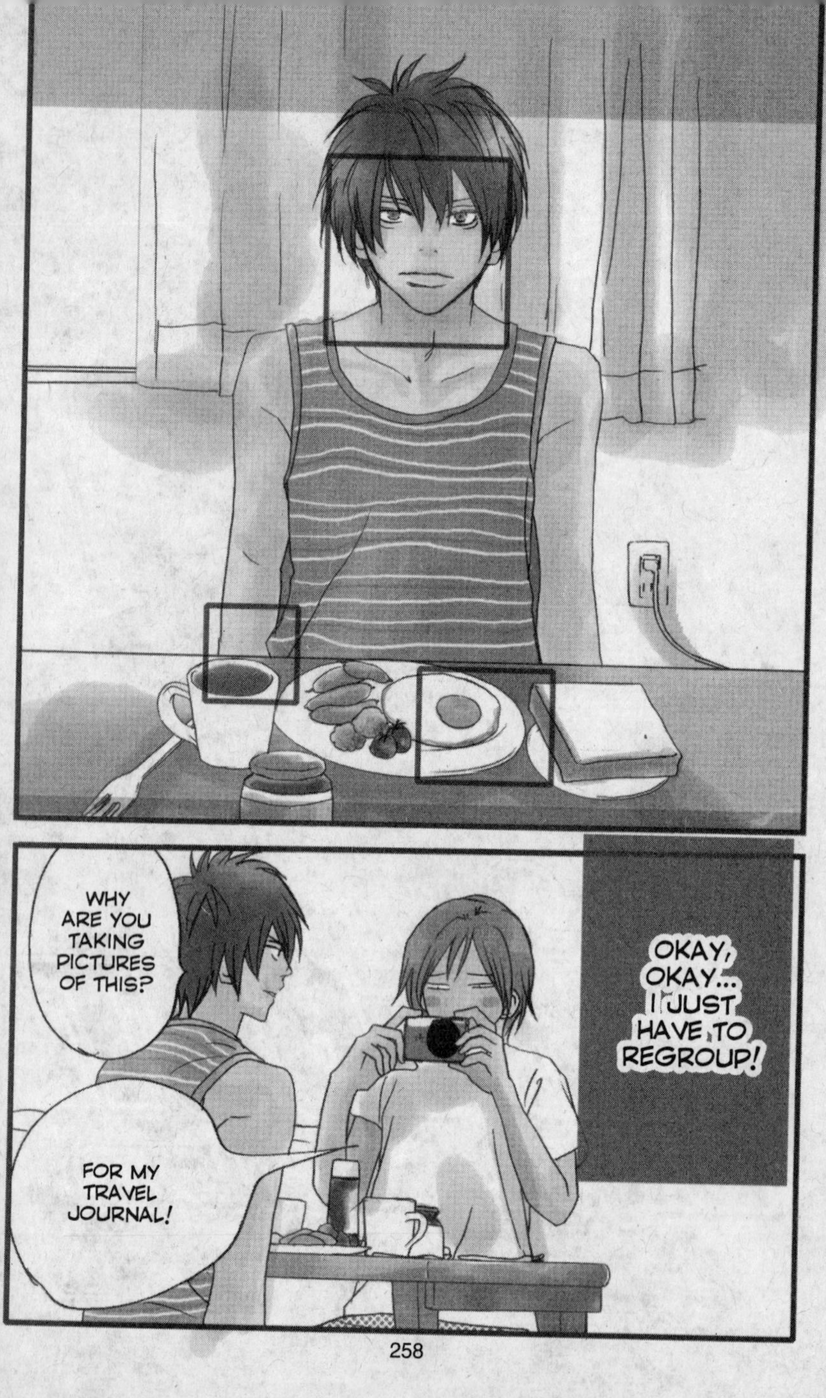
OKAY, OKAY... I JUST HAVE TO REGROUP!
WHY ARE YOU TAKING PICTURES OF THIS?
FOR MY TRAVEL JOURNAL!

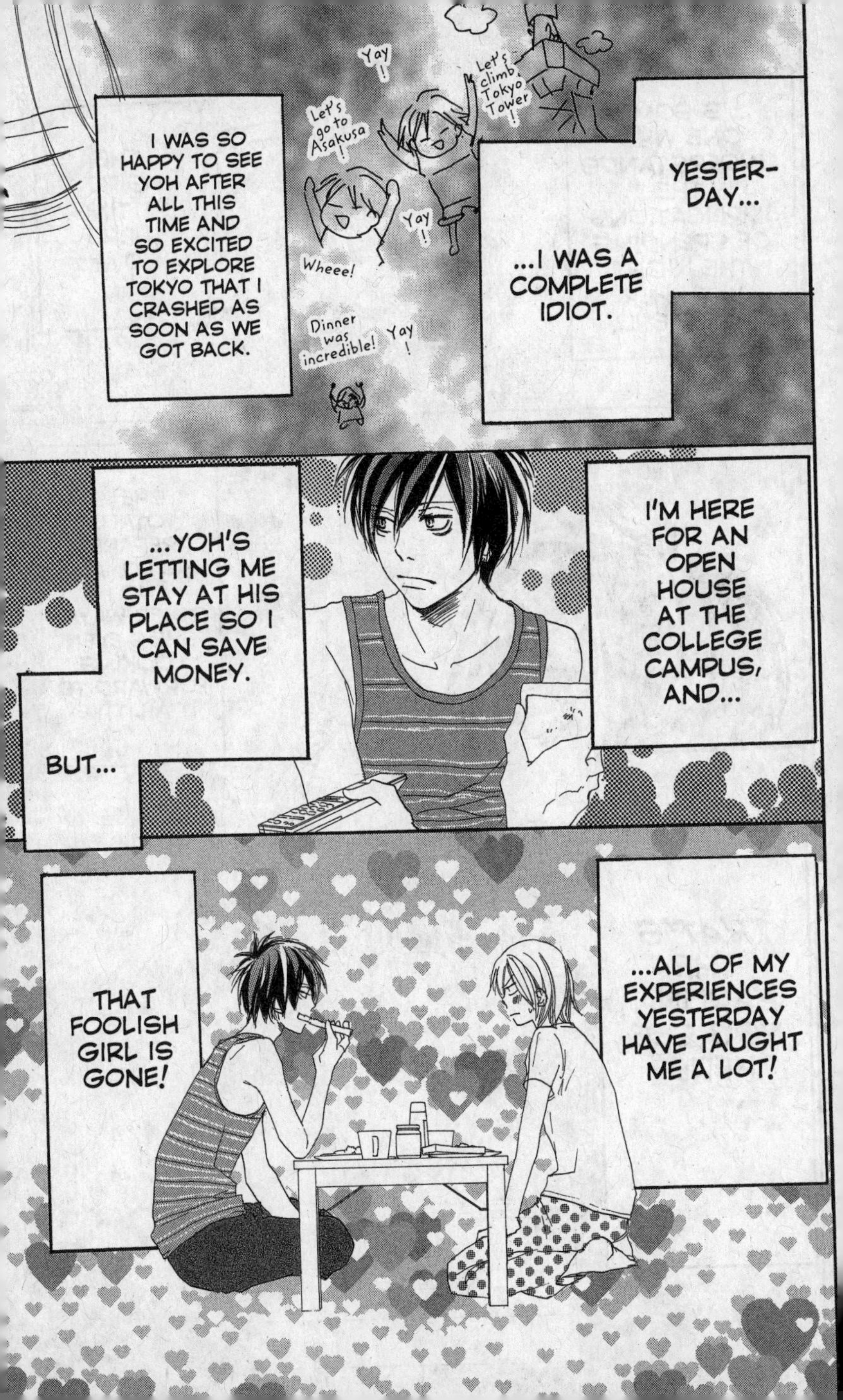
YESTER-DAY...
...I WAS A COMPLETE IDIOT.
Let's climb Tokyo Tower!
Yay!
Let's go to Asakusa!
Yay!
Wheee!
Dinner was incredible!
Yay!
I WAS SO HAPPY TO SEE YOH AFTER ALL THIS TIME AND SO EXCITED TO EXPLORE TOKYO THAT I CRASHED AS SOON AS WE GOT BACK.
I'M HERE FOR AN OPEN HOUSE AT THE COLLEGE CAMPUS, AND...
...YOH'S LETTING ME STAY AT HIS PLACE SO I CAN SAVE MONEY.
BUT...
...ALL OF MY EXPERIENCES YESTERDAY HAVE TAUGHT ME A LOT!
THAT FOOLISH GIRL IS GONE!

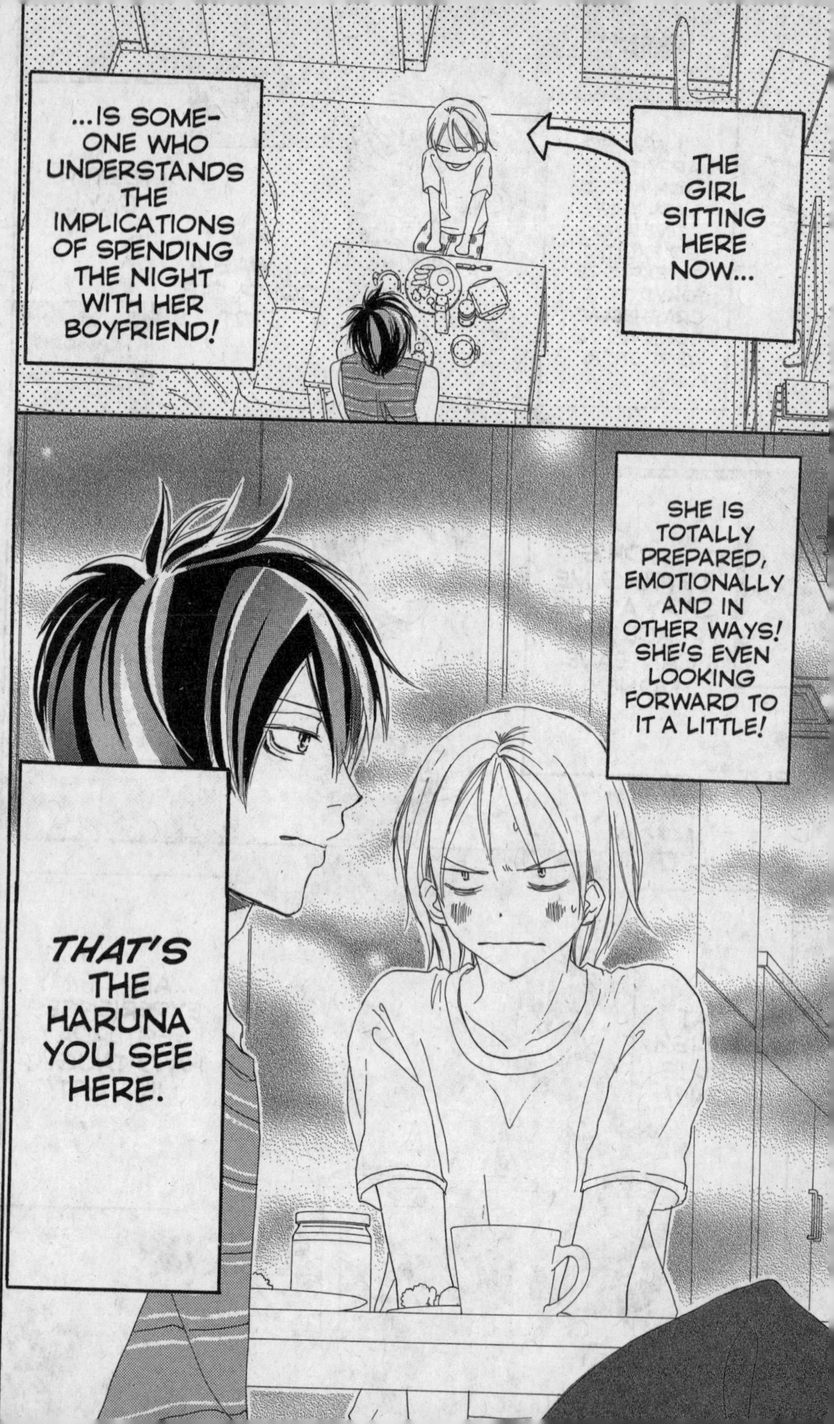
THE GIRL SITTING HERE NOW...
...IS SOME-ONE WHO UNDERSTANDS THE IMPLICATIONS OF SPENDING THE NIGHT WITH HER BOYFRIEND!
SHE IS TOTALLY PREPARED, EMOTIONALLY AND IN OTHER WAYS! SHE'S EVEN LOOKING FORWARD TO IT A LITTLE!
THAT'S THE HARUNA YOU SEE HERE.

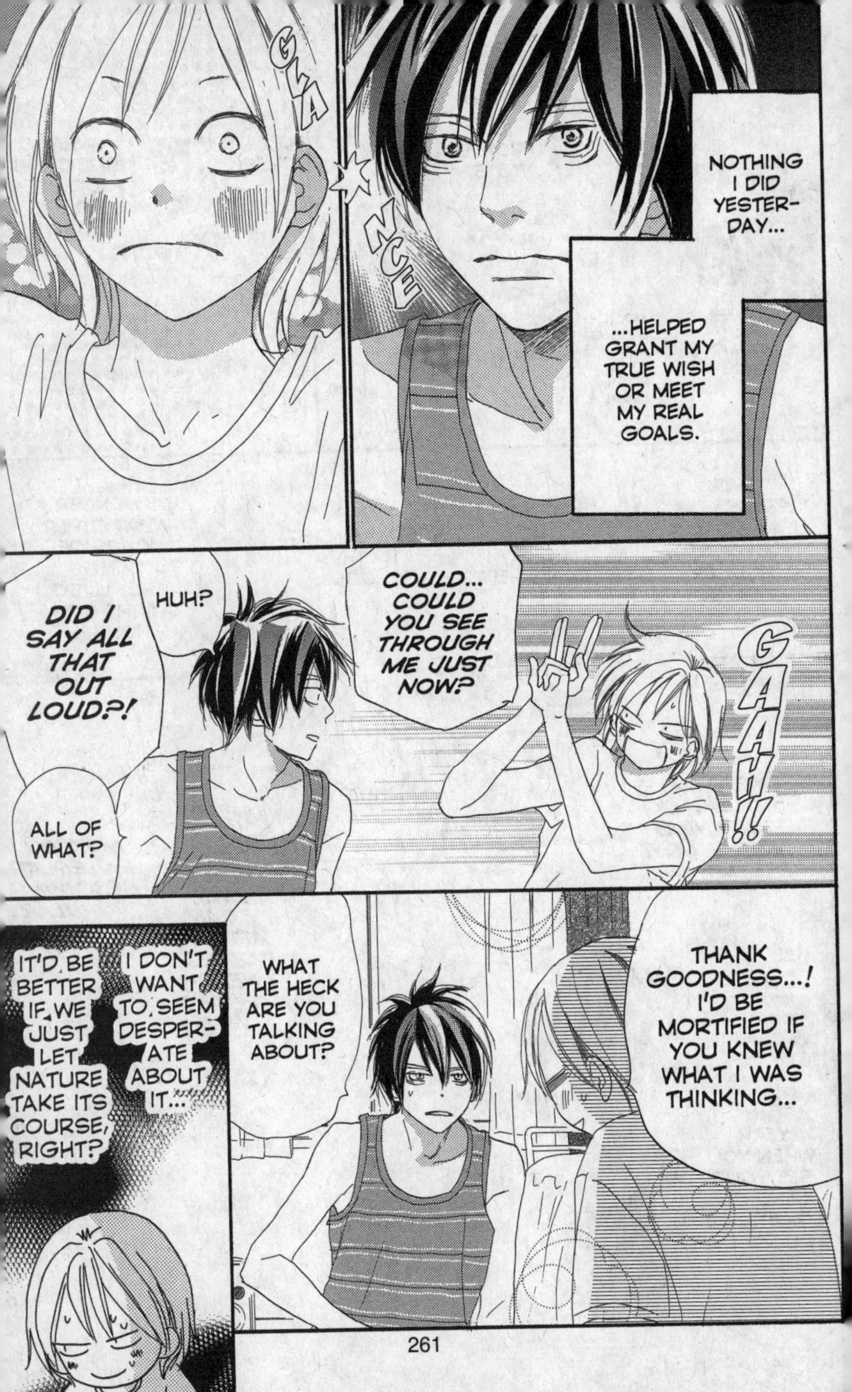
NOTHING I DID YESTERDAY...
...HELPED GRANT MY TRUE WISH OR MEET MY REAL GOALS.
GLANCE
GAAAH!!
COULD... COULD YOU SEE THROUGH ME JUST NOW?
HUH?
DID I SAY ALL THAT OUT LOUD?!
ALL OF WHAT?
THANK GOODNESS...! I'D BE MORTIFIED IF YOU KNEW WHAT I WAS THINKING...
WHAT THE HECK ARE YOU TALKING ABOUT?
I DON'T WANT TO SEEM DESPERATE ABOUT IT...
IT'D BE BETTER IF WE JUST LET NATURE TAKE ITS COURSE, RIGHT?

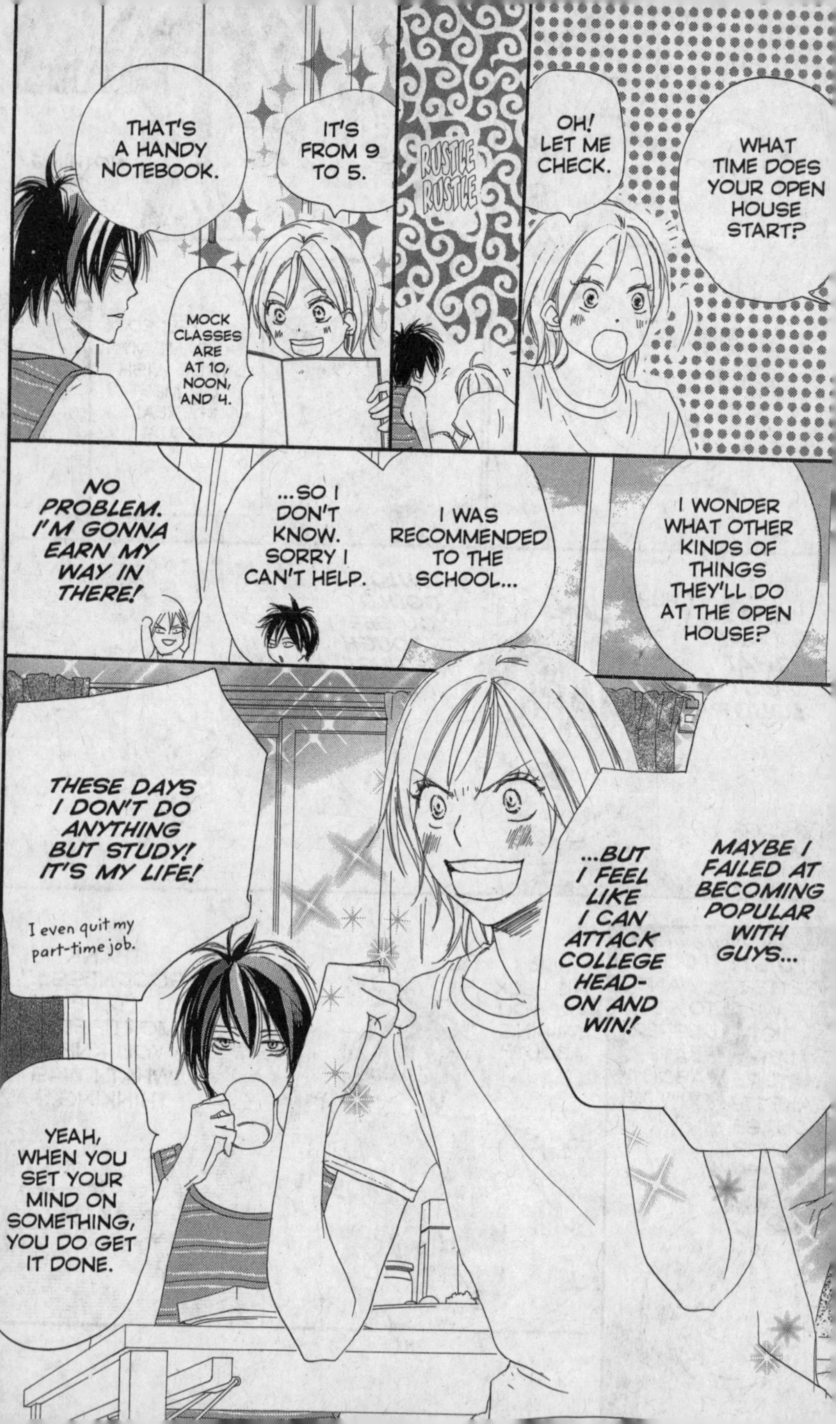
WHAT TIME DOES YOUR OPEN HOUSE START?
OH! LET ME CHECK.
RUSTLE RUSTLE
IT'S FROM 9 TO 5.
MOCK CLASSES ARE AT 10, NOON, AND 4.
THAT'S A HANDY NOTEBOOK.
I WONDER WHAT OTHER KINDS OF THINGS THEY'LL DO AT THE OPEN HOUSE?
I WAS RECOMMENDED TO THE SCHOOL...
...SO I DON'T KNOW. SORRY I CAN'T HELP.
NO PROBLEM. I'M GONNA EARN MY WAY IN THERE!
MAYBE I FAILED AT BECOMING POPULAR WITH GUYS...
...BUT I FEEL LIKE I CAN ATTACK COLLEGE HEAD-ON AND WIN!
THESE DAYS I DON'T DO ANYTHING BUT STUDY! IT'S MY LIFE!
I even quit my part-time job.
YEAH, WHEN YOU SET YOUR MIND ON SOMETHING, YOU DO GET IT DONE.

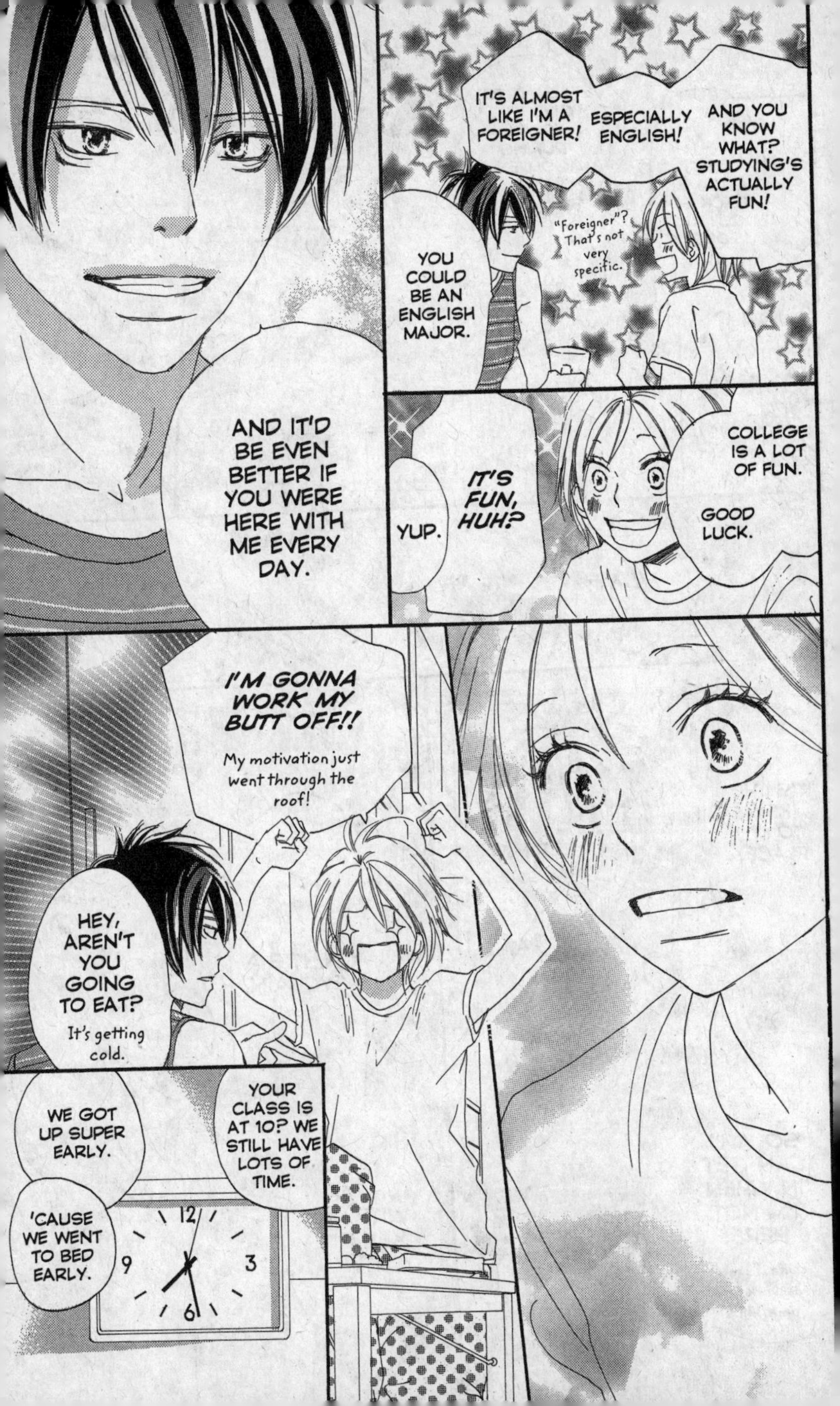
AND YOU KNOW WHAT? STUDYING'S ACTUALLY FUN!
ESPECIALLY ENGLISH!
IT'S ALMOST LIKE I'M A FOREIGNER!
"Foreigner"? That's not very specific.
YOU COULD BE AN ENGLISH MAJOR.
COLLEGE IS A LOT OF FUN.
GOOD LUCK.
IT'S FUN, HUH?
YUP.
AND IT'D BE EVEN BETTER IF YOU WERE HERE WITH ME EVERY DAY.
I'M GONNA WORK MY BUTT OFF!!
My motivation just went through the roof!
HEY, AREN'T YOU GOING TO EAT?
It's getting cold.
YOUR CLASS IS AT 10? WE STILL HAVE LOTS OF TIME.
WE GOT UP SUPER EARLY.
'CAUSE WE WENT TO BED EARLY.

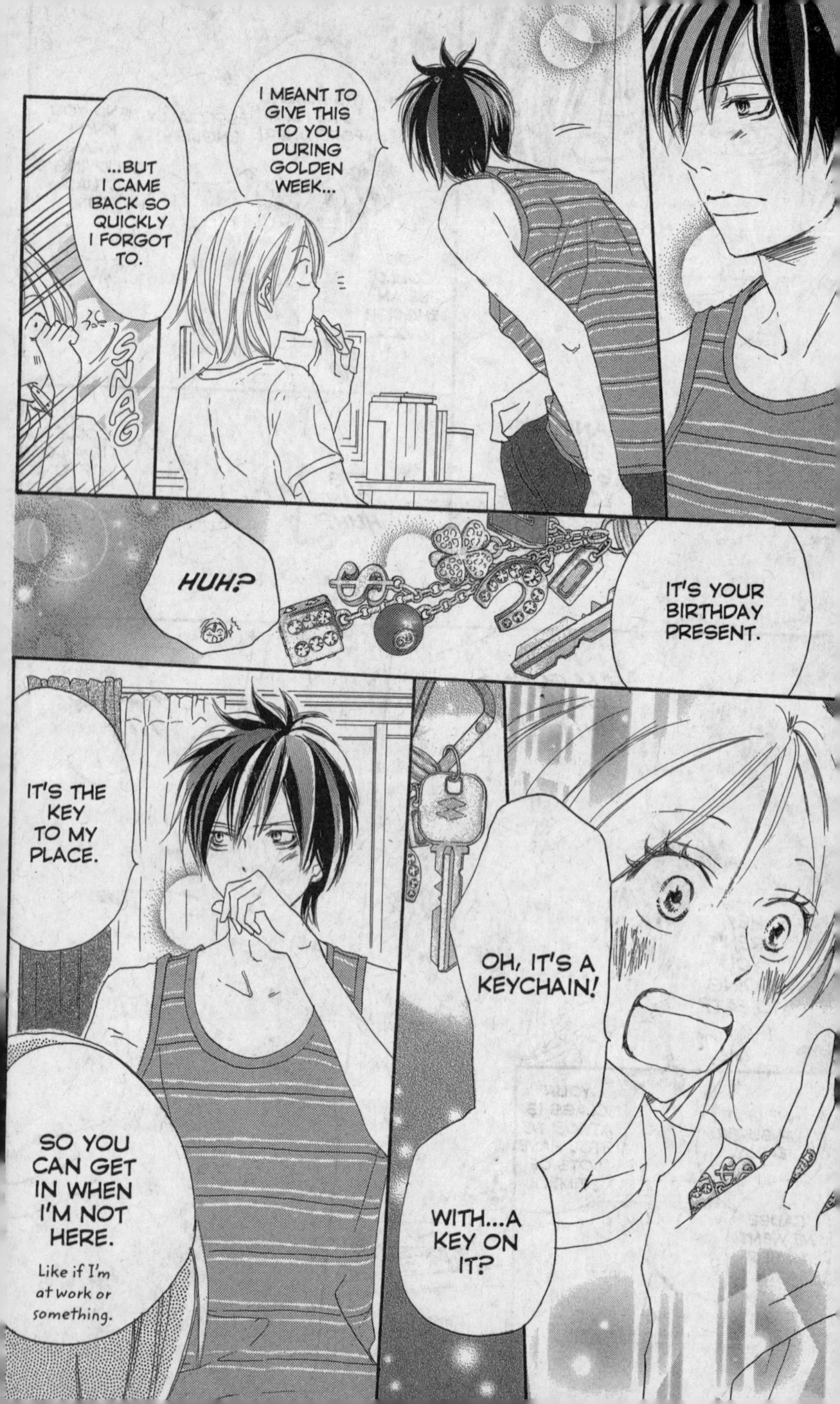
I MEANT TO GIVE THIS TO YOU DURING GOLDEN WEEK...
...BUT I CAME BACK SO QUICKLY I FORGOT TO.
SNAG
IT'S YOUR BIRTHDAY PRESENT.
HUH?
OH, IT'S A KEYCHAIN!
WITH...A KEY ON IT?
IT'S THE KEY TO MY PLACE.
SO YOU CAN GET IN WHEN I'M NOT HERE.
Like if I'm at work or something.

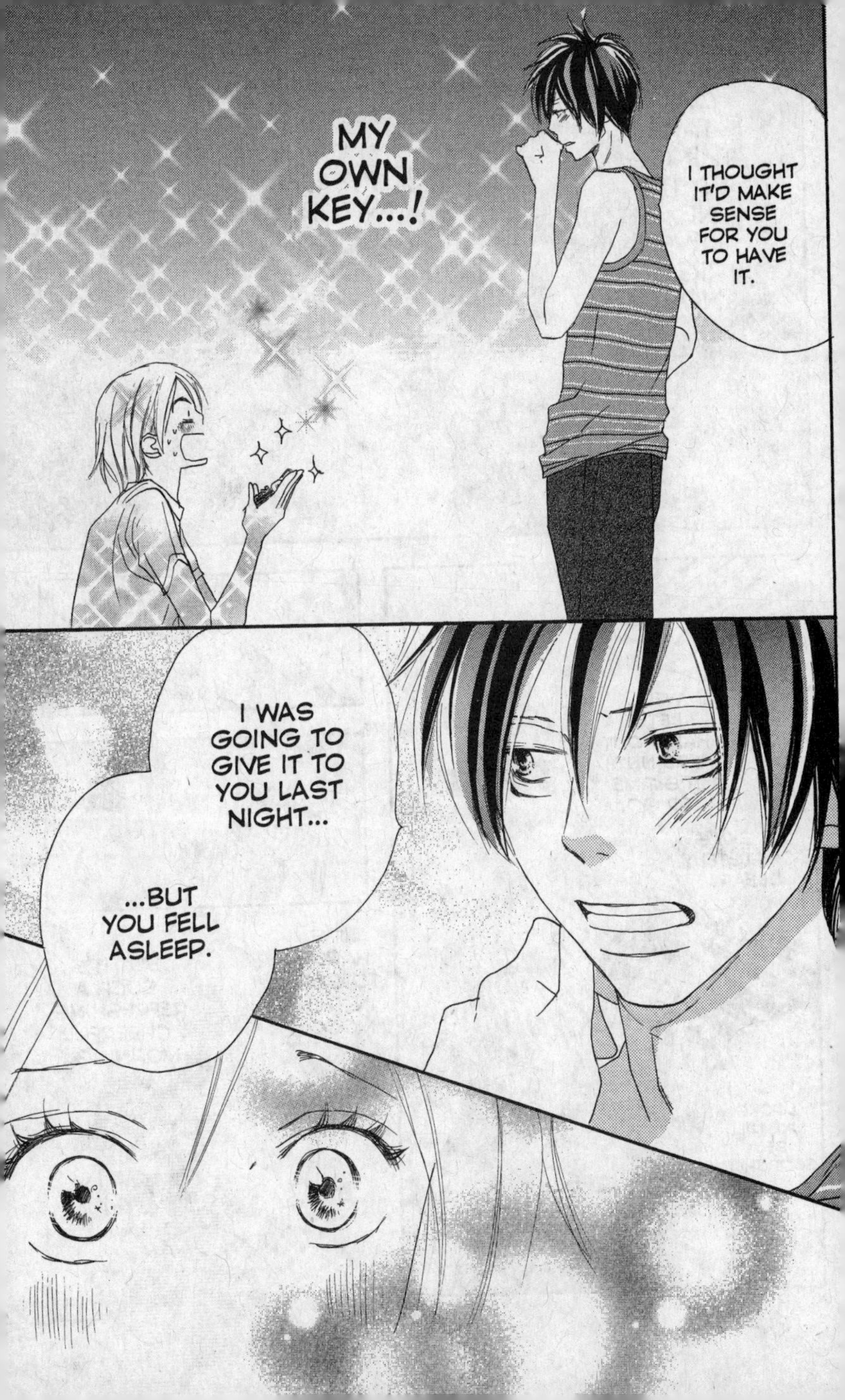
I THOUGHT IT'D MAKE SENSE FOR YOU TO HAVE IT.
MY OWN KEY...!
I WAS GOING TO GIVE IT TO YOU LAST NIGHT...
...BUT YOU FELL ASLEEP.

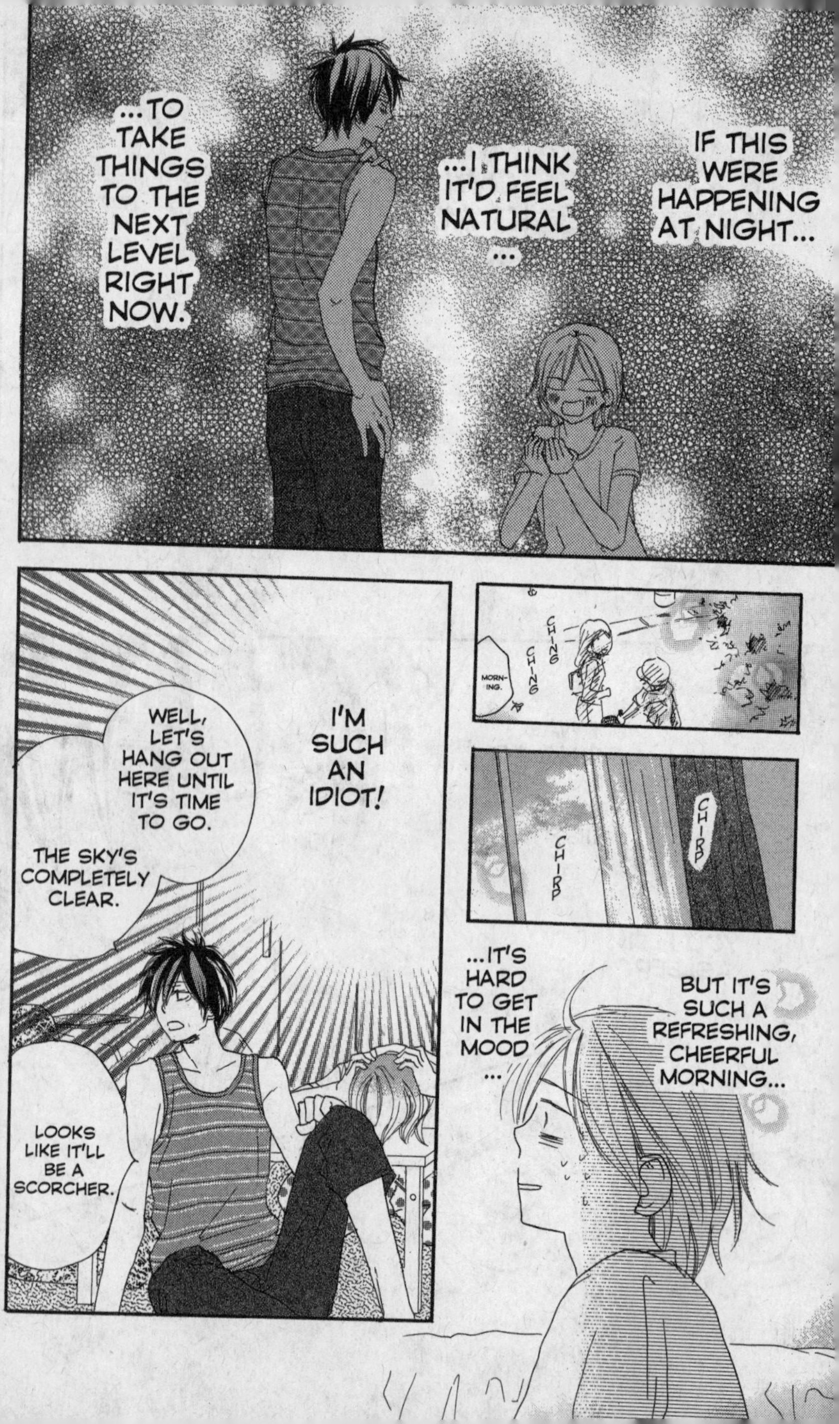
IF THIS WERE HAPPENING AT NIGHT...
...I THINK IT'D FEEL NATURAL...
...TO TAKE THINGS TO THE NEXT LEVEL RIGHT NOW.
CHING CHING
MORN-ING.
CHIRP
CHIRP
BUT IT'S SUCH A REFRESHING, CHEERFUL MORNING...
...IT'S HARD TO GET IN THE MOOD...
I'M SUCH AN IDIOT!
WELL, LET'S HANG OUT HERE UNTIL IT'S TIME TO GO.
THE SKY'S COMPLETELY CLEAR.
LOOKS LIKE IT'LL BE A SCORCHER.

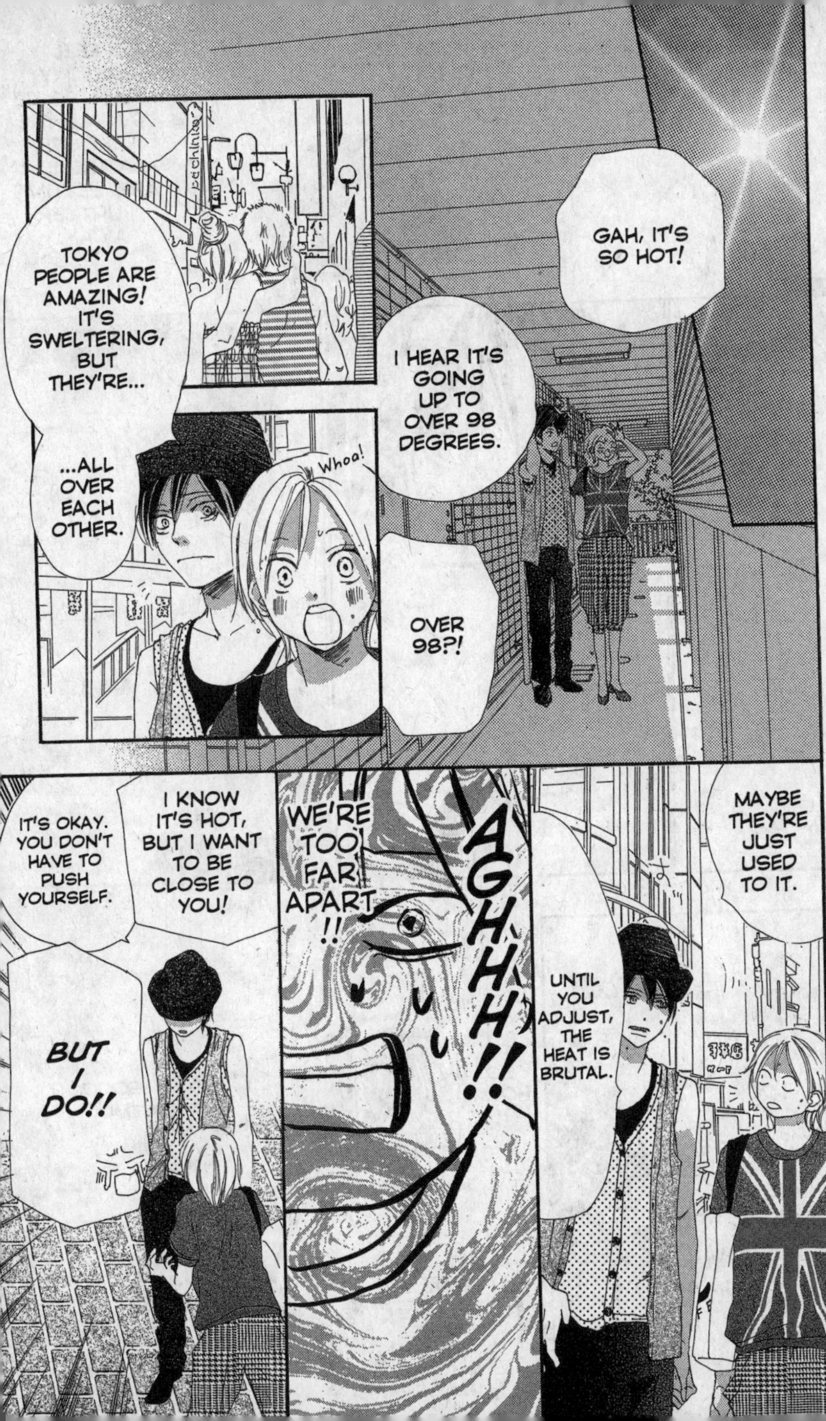
GAH, IT'S SO HOT!
I HEAR IT'S GOING UP TO OVER 98 DEGREES.
OVER 98?!
Whoa!
TOKYO PEOPLE ARE AMAZING! IT'S SWELTERING, BUT THEY'RE...
...ALL OVER EACH OTHER.
MAYBE THEY'RE JUST USED TO IT.
UNTIL YOU ADJUST, THE HEAT IS BRUTAL.
WE'RE TOO FAR APART!!
AGHHH!!
I KNOW IT'S HOT, BUT I WANT TO BE CLOSE TO YOU!
IT'S OKAY. YOU DON'T HAVE TO PUSH YOURSELF.
BUT I DO!!

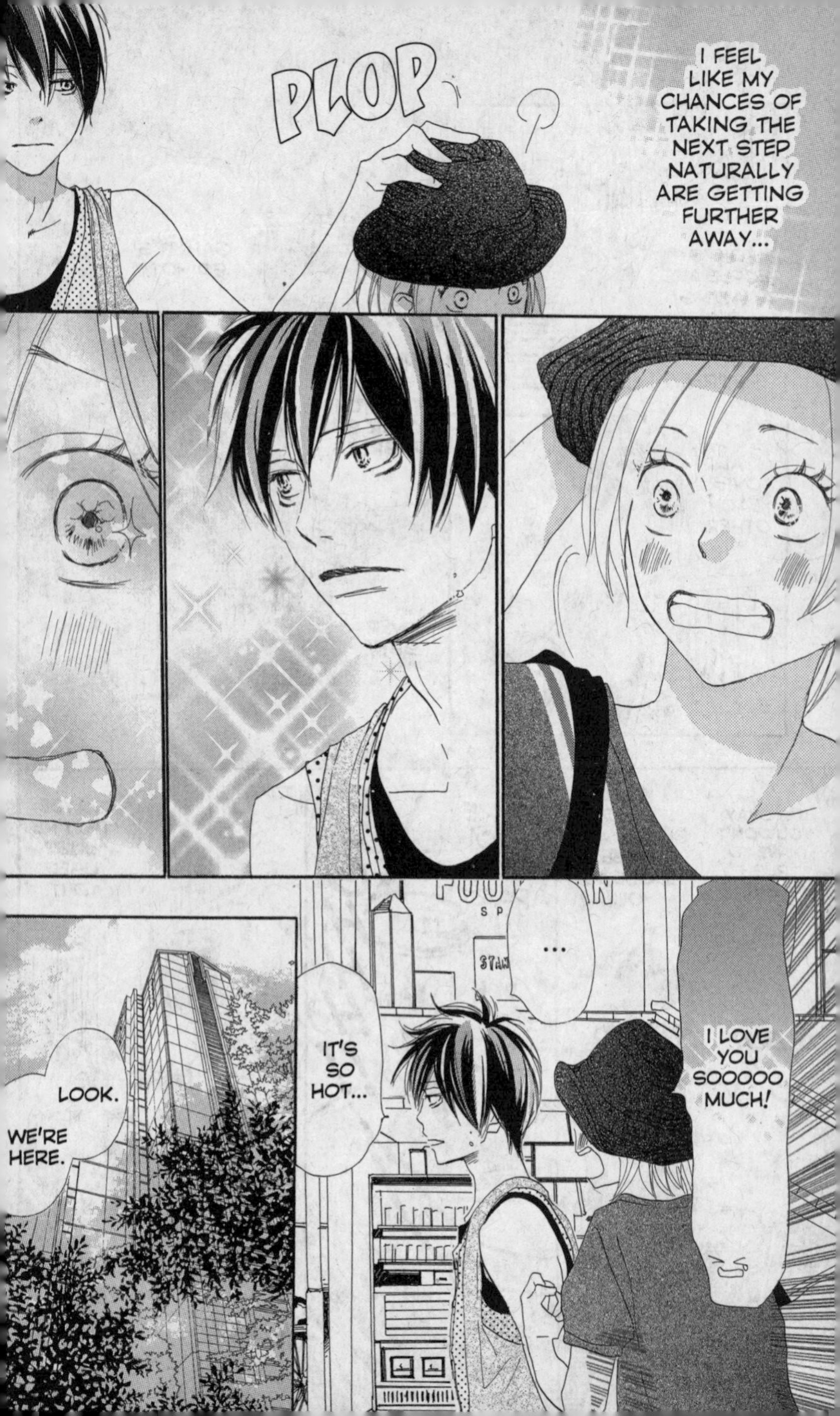
I FEEL LIKE MY CHANCES OF TAKING THE NEXT STEP NATURALLY ARE GETTING FURTHER AWAY...
PLOP
I LOVE YOU SOOOOO MUCH!
...
IT'S SO HOT...
LOOK.
WE'RE HERE.

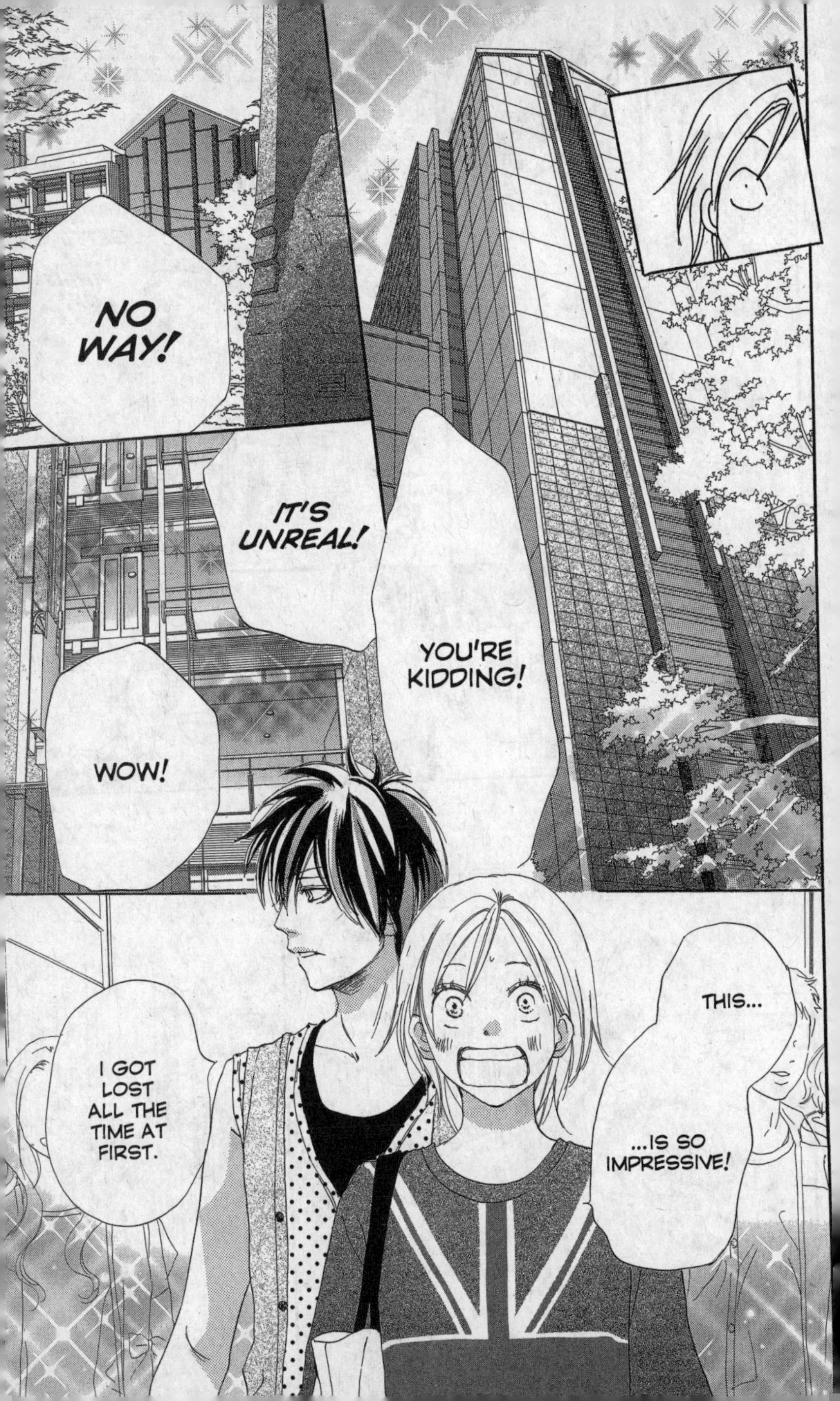
YOU'RE KIDDING!
NO WAY!
IT'S UNREAL!
WOW!
THIS...
...IS SO IMPRESSIVE!
I GOT LOST ALL THE TIME AT FIRST.

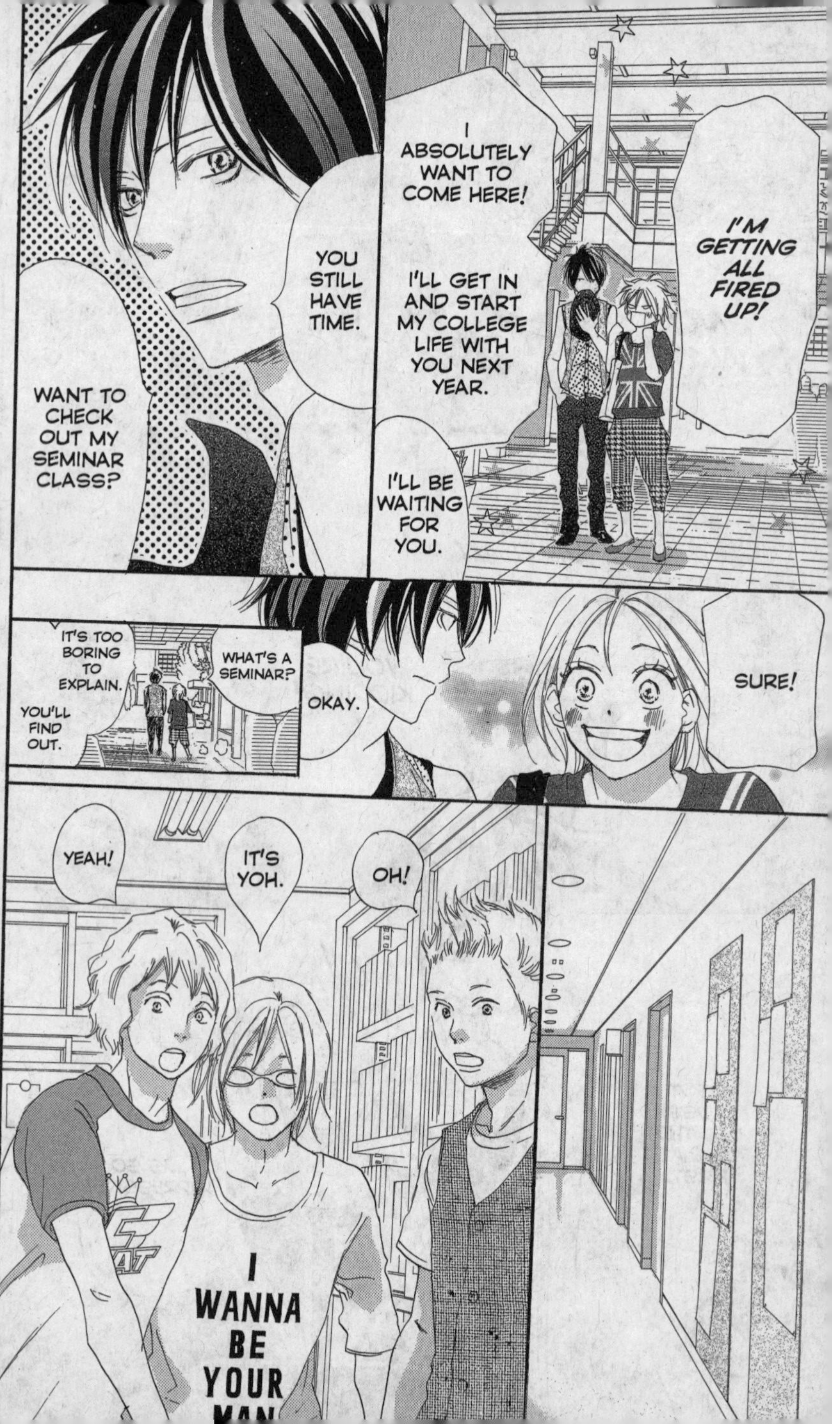

I'M GETTING ALL FIRED UP!
I ABSOLUTELY WANT TO COME HERE!
I'LL GET IN AND START MY COLLEGE LIFE WITH YOU NEXT YEAR.
I'LL BE WAITING FOR YOU.
YOU STILL HAVE TIME.
WANT TO CHECK OUT MY SEMINAR CLASS?
SURE!
OKAY.
WHAT'S A SEMINAR?
IT'S TOO BORING TO EXPLAIN.
YOU'LL FIND OUT.
OH!
IT'S YOH.
YEAH!
I WANNA BE YOUR

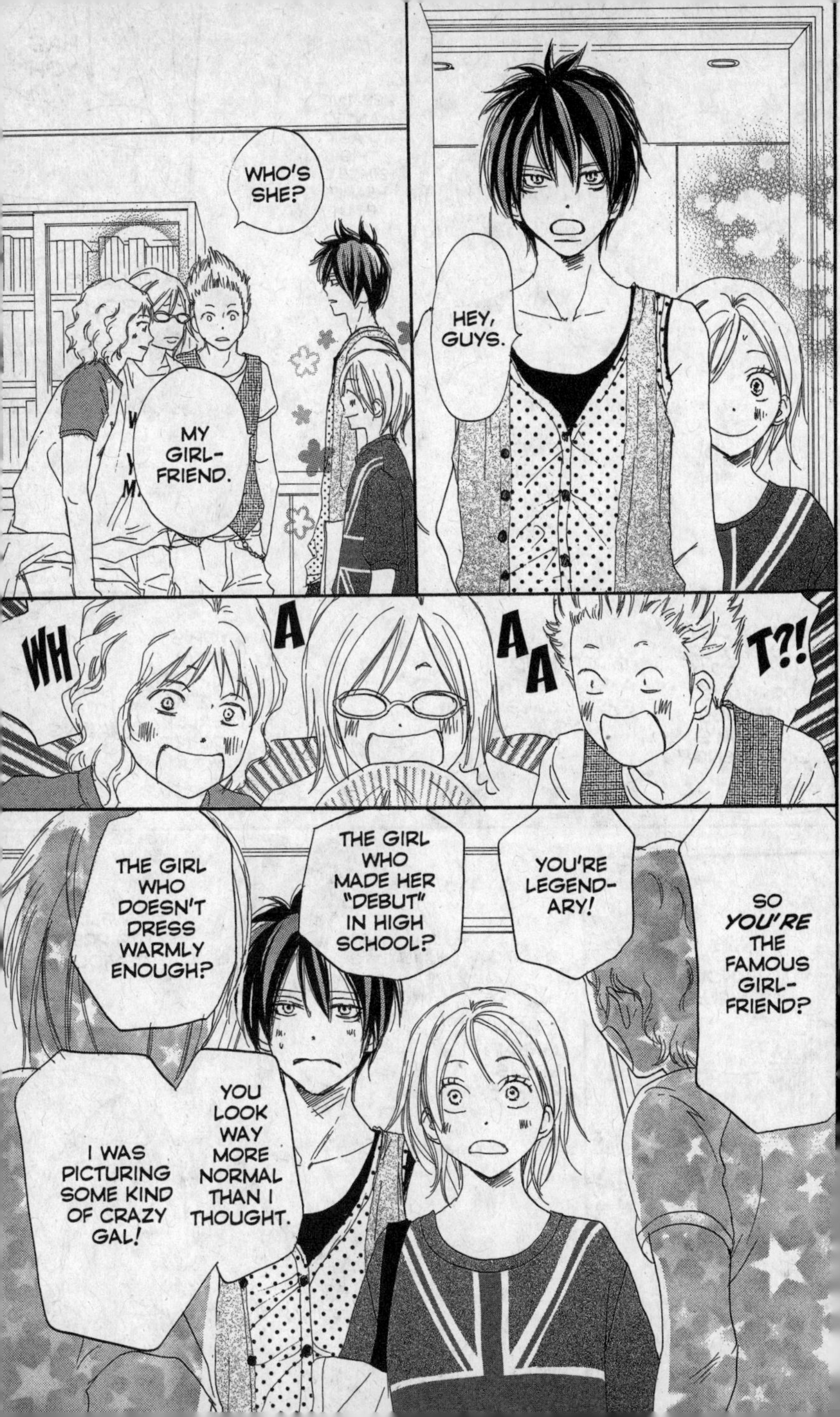
HEY, GUYS.
WHO'S SHE?
MY GIRL-FRIEND.
WHAAAT?!
SO *YOU'RE* THE FAMOUS GIRL-FRIEND?
YOU'RE LEGEND-ARY!
THE GIRL WHO MADE HER "DEBUT" IN HIGH SCHOOL?
THE GIRL WHO DOESN'T DRESS WARMLY ENOUGH?
YOU LOOK WAY MORE NORMAL THAN I THOUGHT.
I WAS PICTURING SOME KIND OF CRAZY GAL!

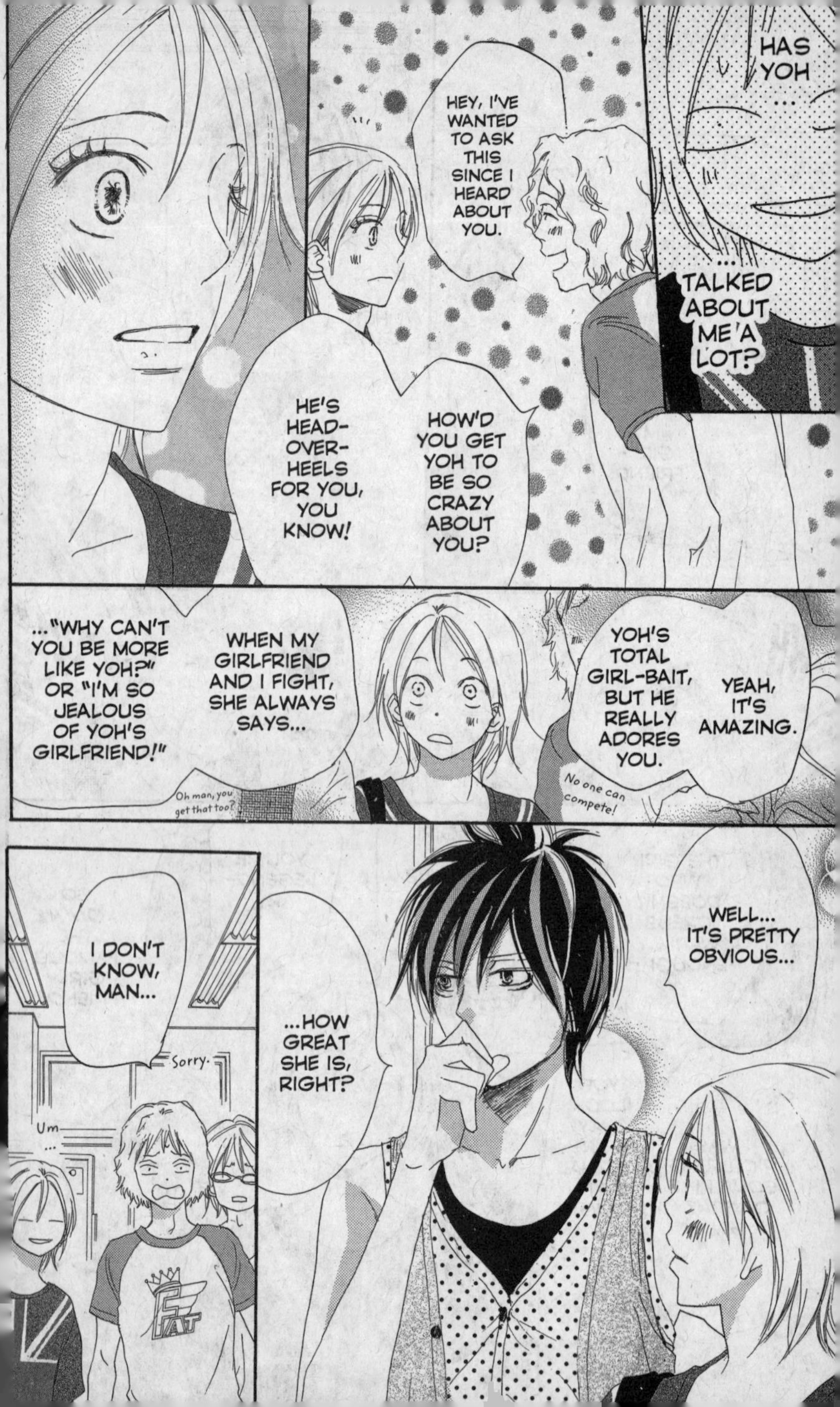
HAS YOH ...
...TALKED ABOUT ME A LOT?
HEY, I'VE WANTED TO ASK THIS SINCE I HEARD ABOUT YOU.
HOW'D YOU GET YOH TO BE SO CRAZY ABOUT YOU?
HE'S HEAD-OVER-HEELS FOR YOU, YOU KNOW!
YEAH, IT'S AMAZING.
YOH'S TOTAL GIRL-BAIT, BUT HE REALLY ADORES YOU.
No one can compete!
WHEN MY GIRLFRIEND AND I FIGHT, SHE ALWAYS SAYS...
..."WHY CAN'T YOU BE MORE LIKE YOH?" OR "I'M SO JEALOUS OF YOH'S GIRLFRIEND!"
Oh man, you get that too?
WELL... IT'S PRETTY OBVIOUS...
...HOW GREAT SHE IS, RIGHT?
I DON'T KNOW, MAN...
Sorry.
Um...

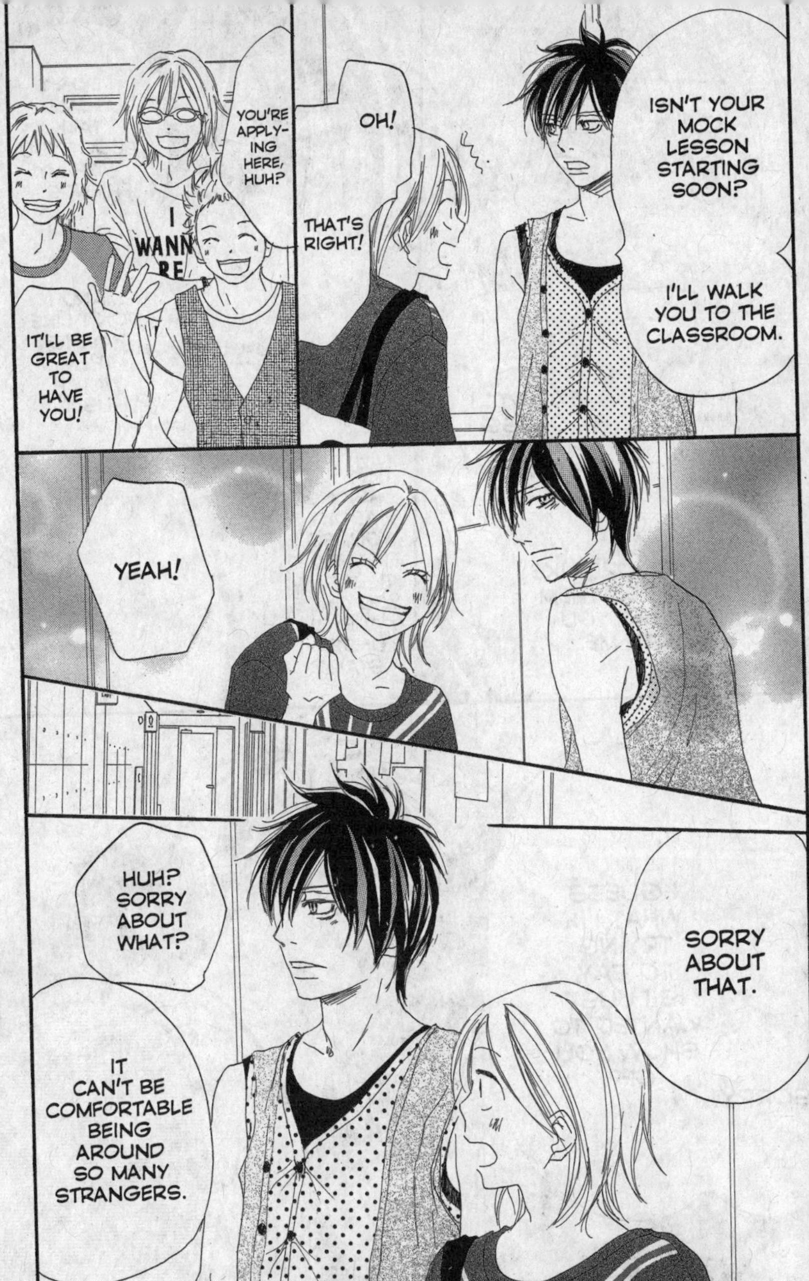
ISN'T YOUR MOCK LESSON STARTING SOON?
I'LL WALK YOU TO THE CLASSROOM.
OH!
THAT'S RIGHT!
YOU'RE APPLY-ING HERE, HUH?
IT'LL BE GREAT TO HAVE YOU!
YEAH!
SORRY ABOUT THAT.
HUH? SORRY ABOUT WHAT?
IT CAN'T BE COMFORTABLE BEING AROUND SO MANY STRANGERS.

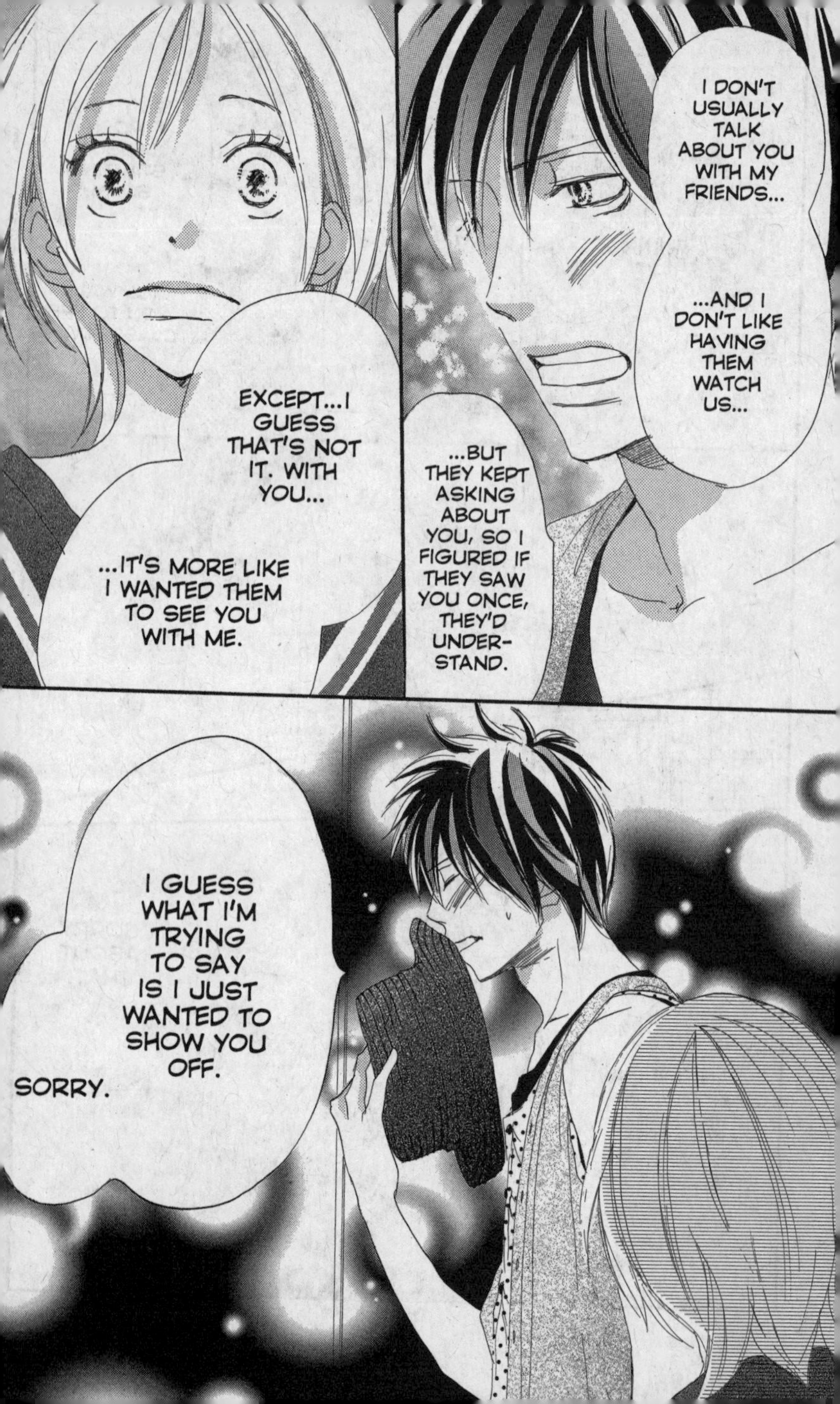
I DON'T USUALLY TALK ABOUT YOU WITH MY FRIENDS...
...AND I DON'T LIKE HAVING THEM WATCH US...
...BUT THEY KEPT ASKING ABOUT YOU, SO I FIGURED IF THEY SAW YOU ONCE, THEY'D UNDER-STAND.
EXCEPT...I GUESS THAT'S NOT IT. WITH YOU...
...IT'S MORE LIKE I WANTED THEM TO SEE YOU WITH ME.
I GUESS WHAT I'M TRYING TO SAY IS I JUST WANTED TO SHOW YOU OFF.
SORRY.

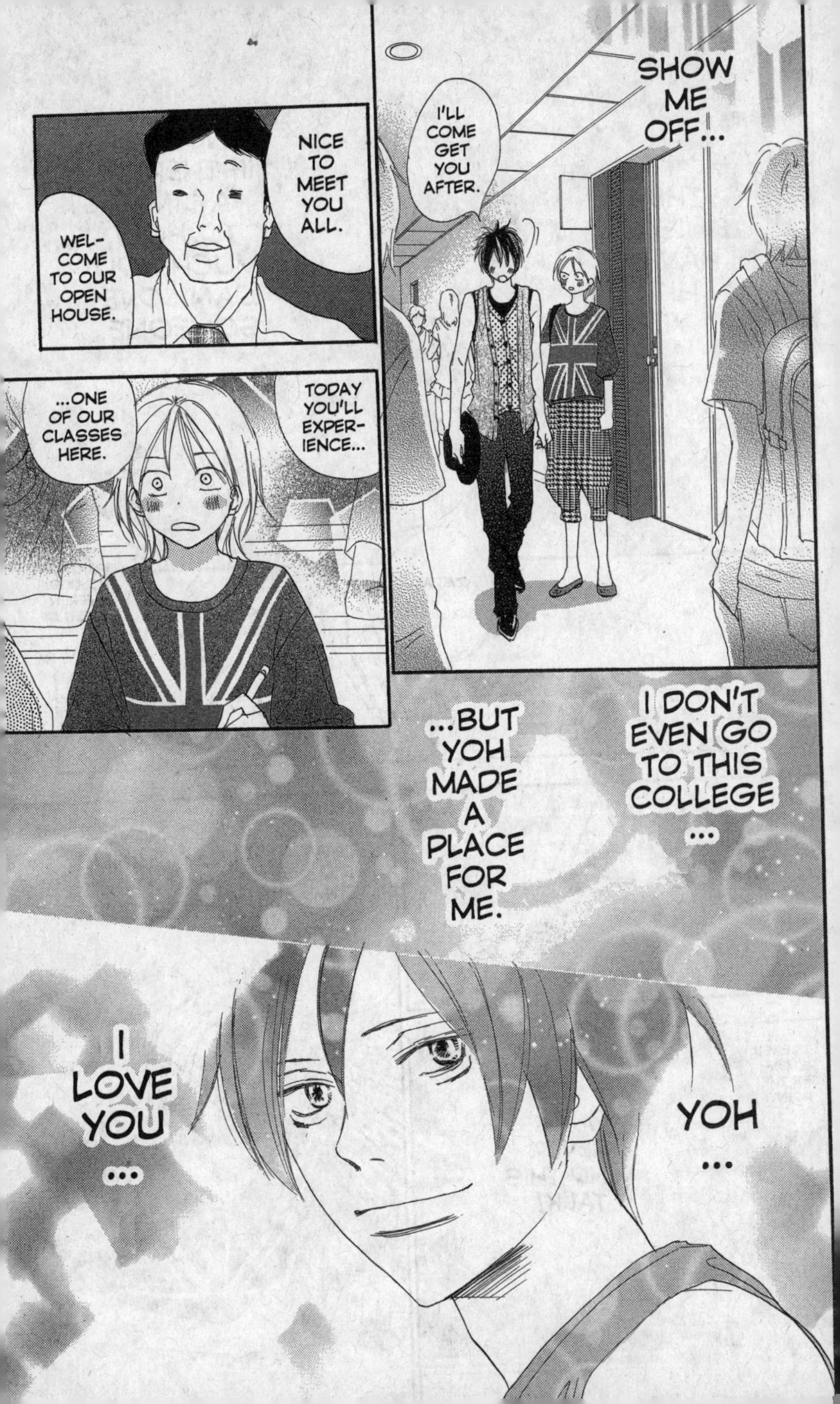
SHOW ME OFF...
I'LL COME GET YOU AFTER.
NICE TO MEET YOU ALL.
WELCOME TO OUR OPEN HOUSE.
TODAY YOU'LL EXPERIENCE...
...ONE OF OUR CLASSES HERE.
I DON'T EVEN GO TO THIS COLLEGE...
...BUT YOH MADE A PLACE FOR ME.
YOH...
I LOVE YOU...

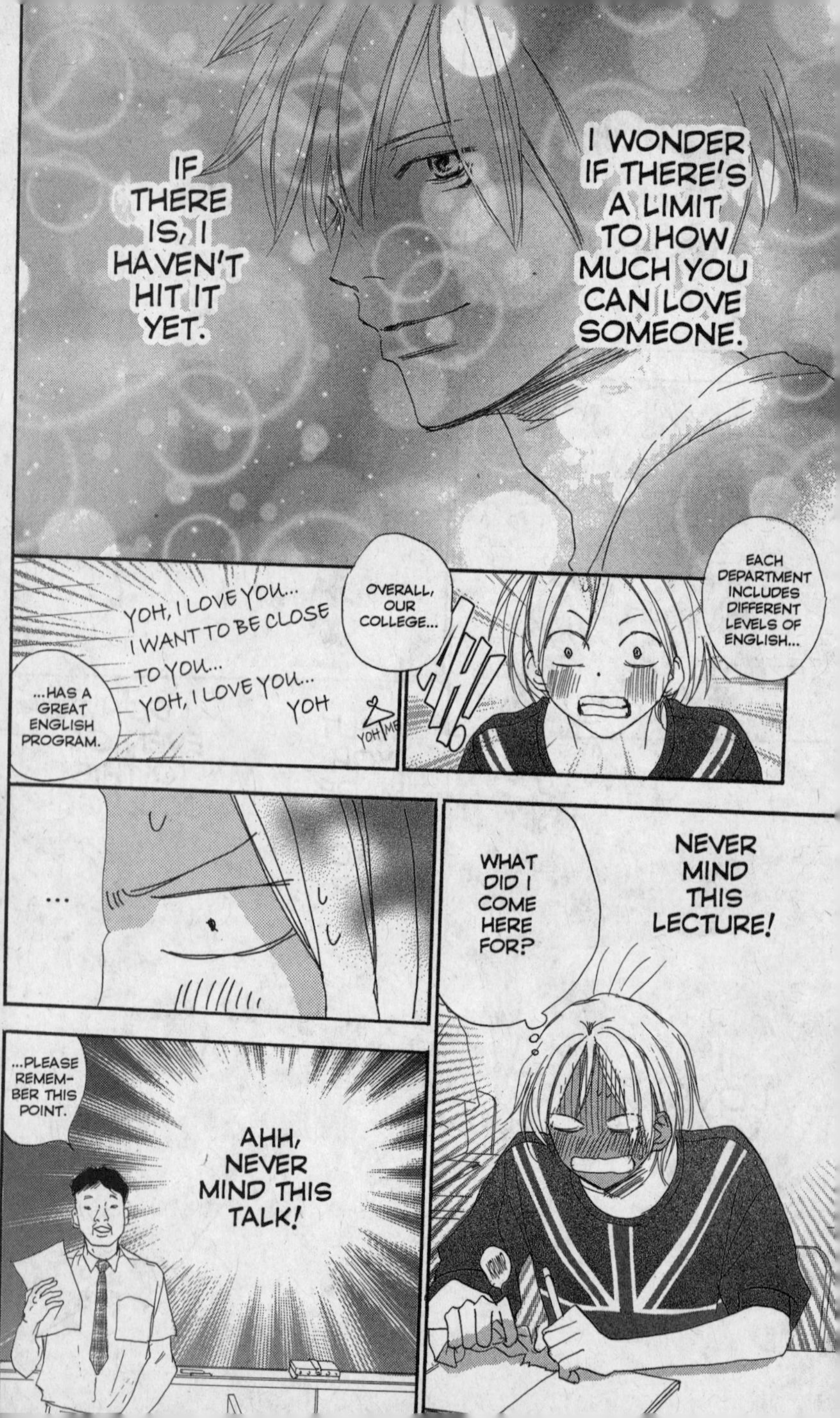
I WONDER IF THERE'S A LIMIT TO HOW MUCH YOU CAN LOVE SOMEONE.
IF THERE IS, I HAVEN'T HIT IT YET.
EACH DEPARTMENT INCLUDES DIFFERENT LEVELS OF ENGLISH...
OVERALL, OUR COLLEGE...
YOH ♥ ME
YOH, I LOVE YOU... I WANT TO BE CLOSE TO YOU... YOH, I LOVE YOU... YOH
...HAS A GREAT ENGLISH PROGRAM.
NEVER MIND THIS LECTURE!
WHAT DID I COME HERE FOR?
...
...PLEASE REMEMBER THIS POINT.
AHH, NEVER MIND THIS TALK!

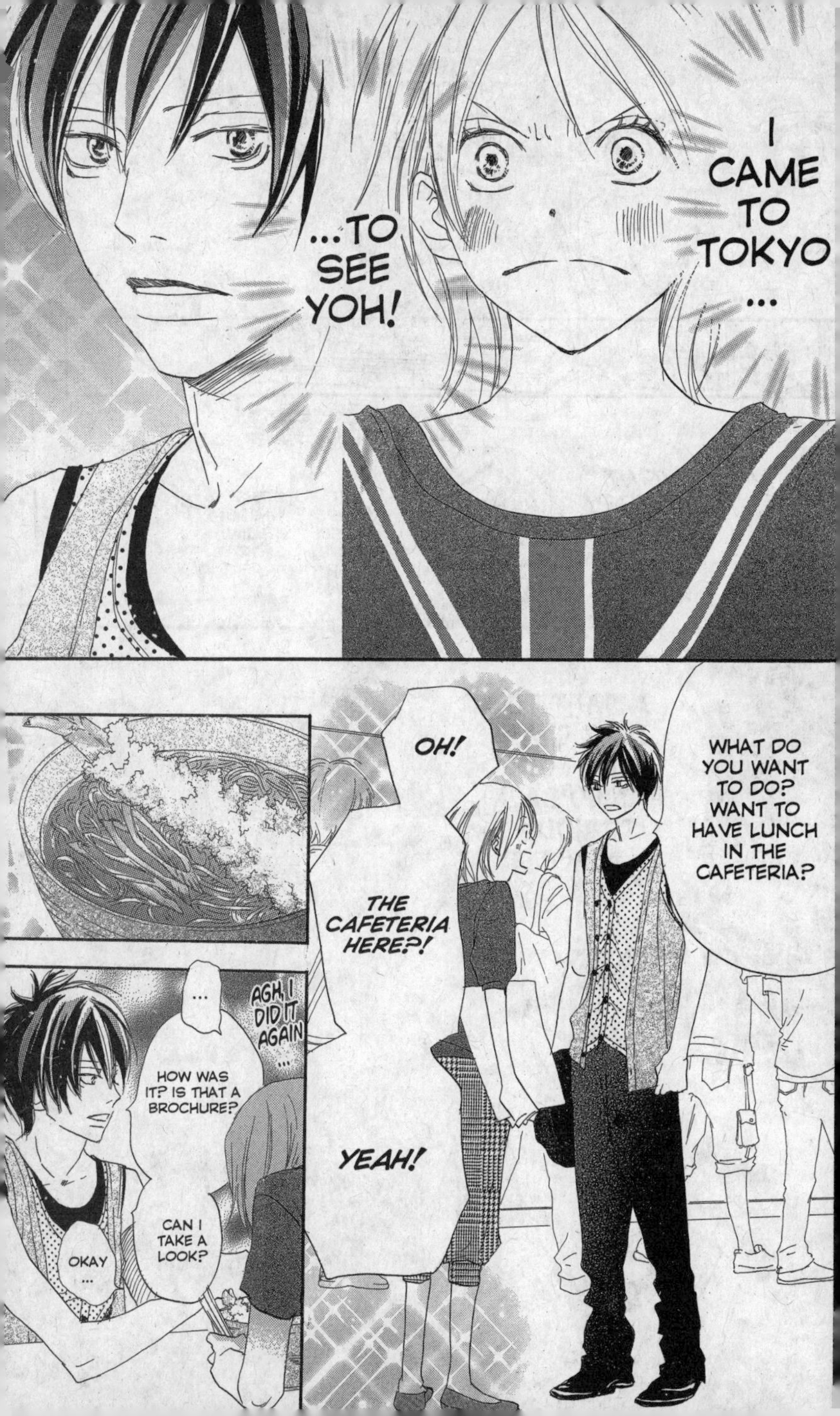
I CAME TO TOKYO ...
...TO SEE YOH!
WHAT DO YOU WANT TO DO? WANT TO HAVE LUNCH IN THE CAFETERIA?
OH!
THE CAFETERIA HERE?!
YEAH!
AGH, I DID IT AGAIN ...
...
HOW WAS IT? IS THAT A BROCHURE?
CAN I TAKE A LOOK?
OKAY ...

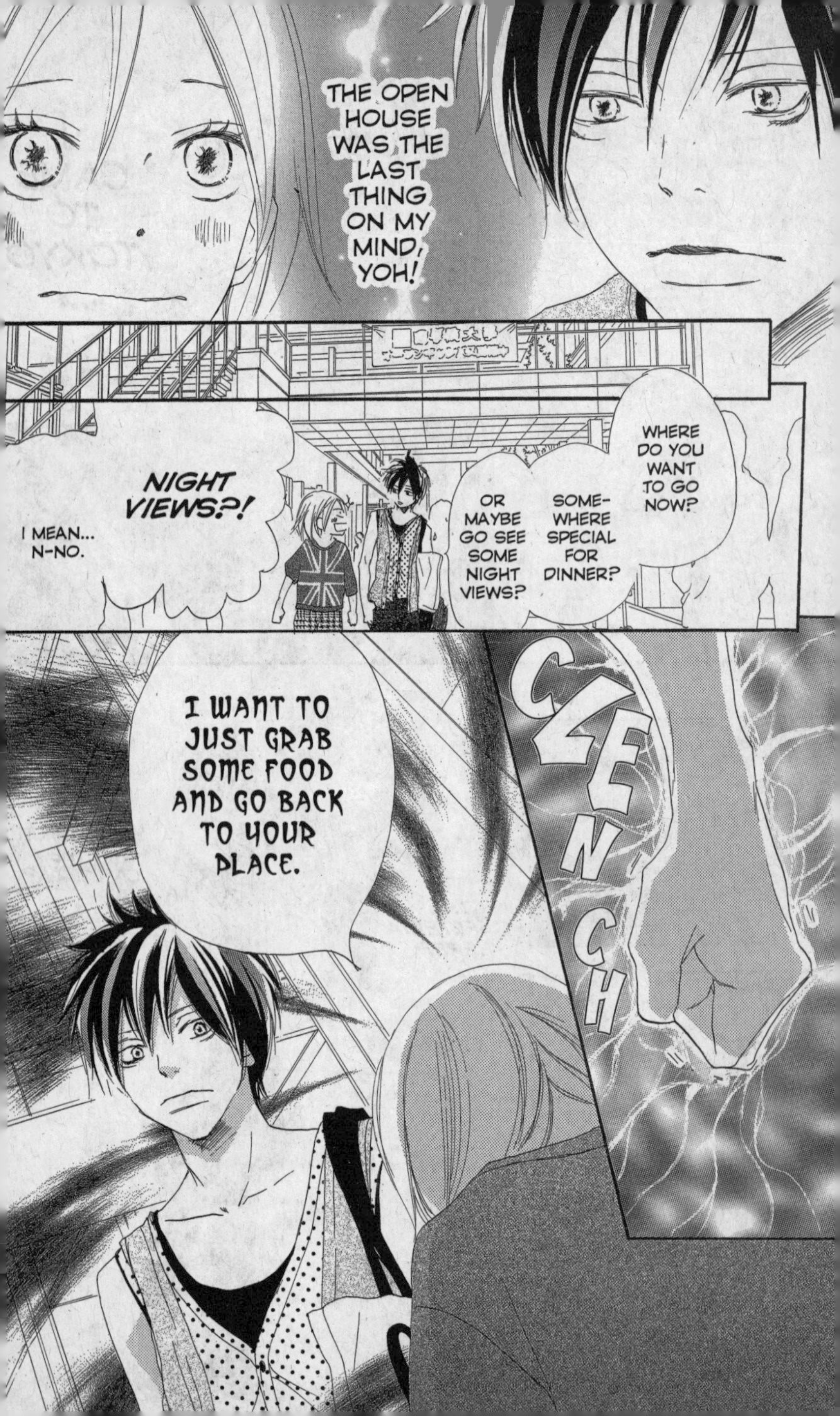
THE OPEN HOUSE WAS THE LAST THING ON MY MIND, YOH!
WHERE DO YOU WANT TO GO NOW?
SOME-WHERE SPECIAL FOR DINNER?
OR MAYBE GO SEE SOME NIGHT VIEWS?
NIGHT VIEWS?!
I MEAN... N-NO.
CLENCH
I WANT TO JUST GRAB SOME FOOD AND GO BACK TO YOUR PLACE.

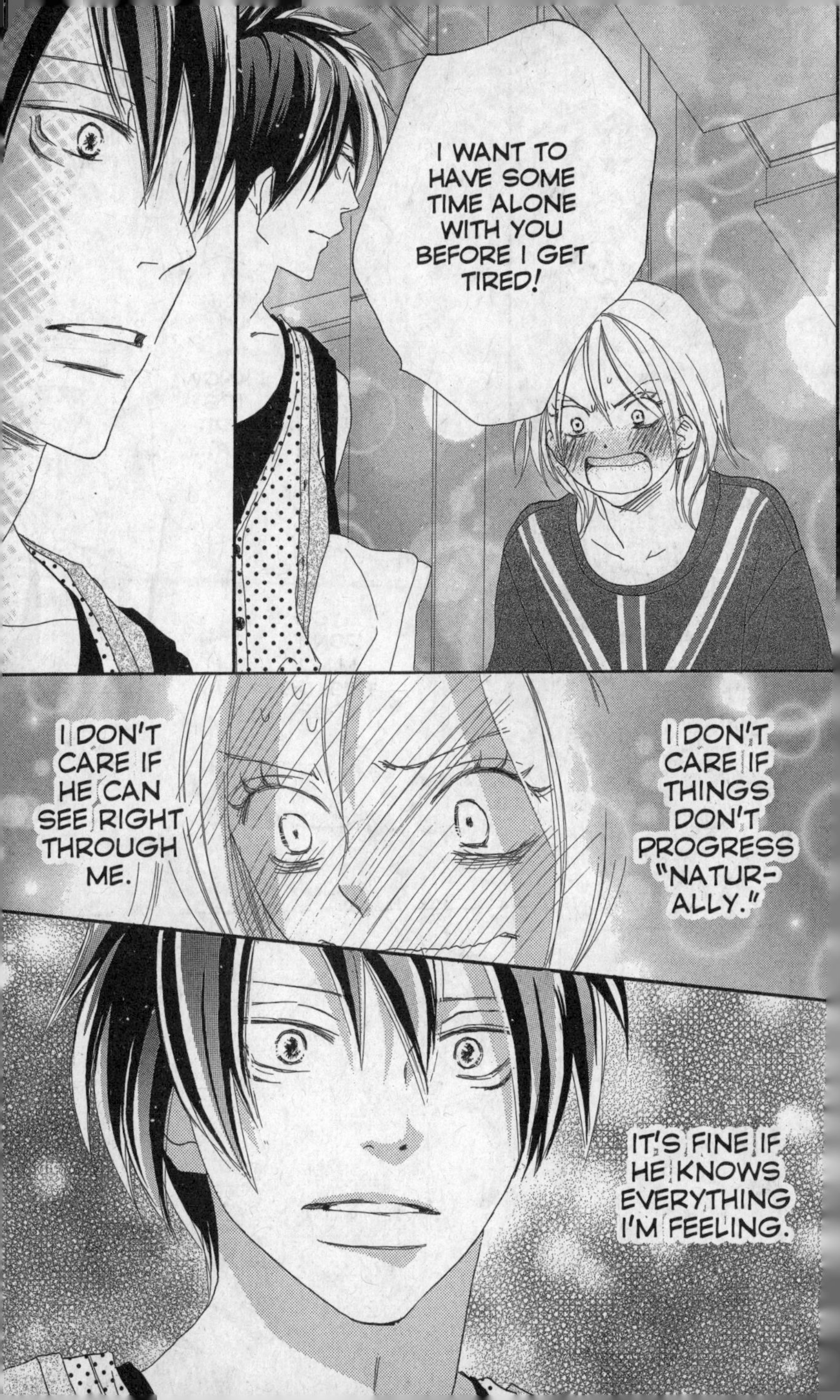
I WANT TO HAVE SOME TIME ALONE WITH YOU BEFORE I GET TIRED!
I DON'T CARE IF THINGS DON'T PROGRESS "NATURALLY."
I DON'T CARE IF HE CAN SEE RIGHT THROUGH ME.
IT'S FINE IF HE KNOWS EVERYTHING I'M FEELING.

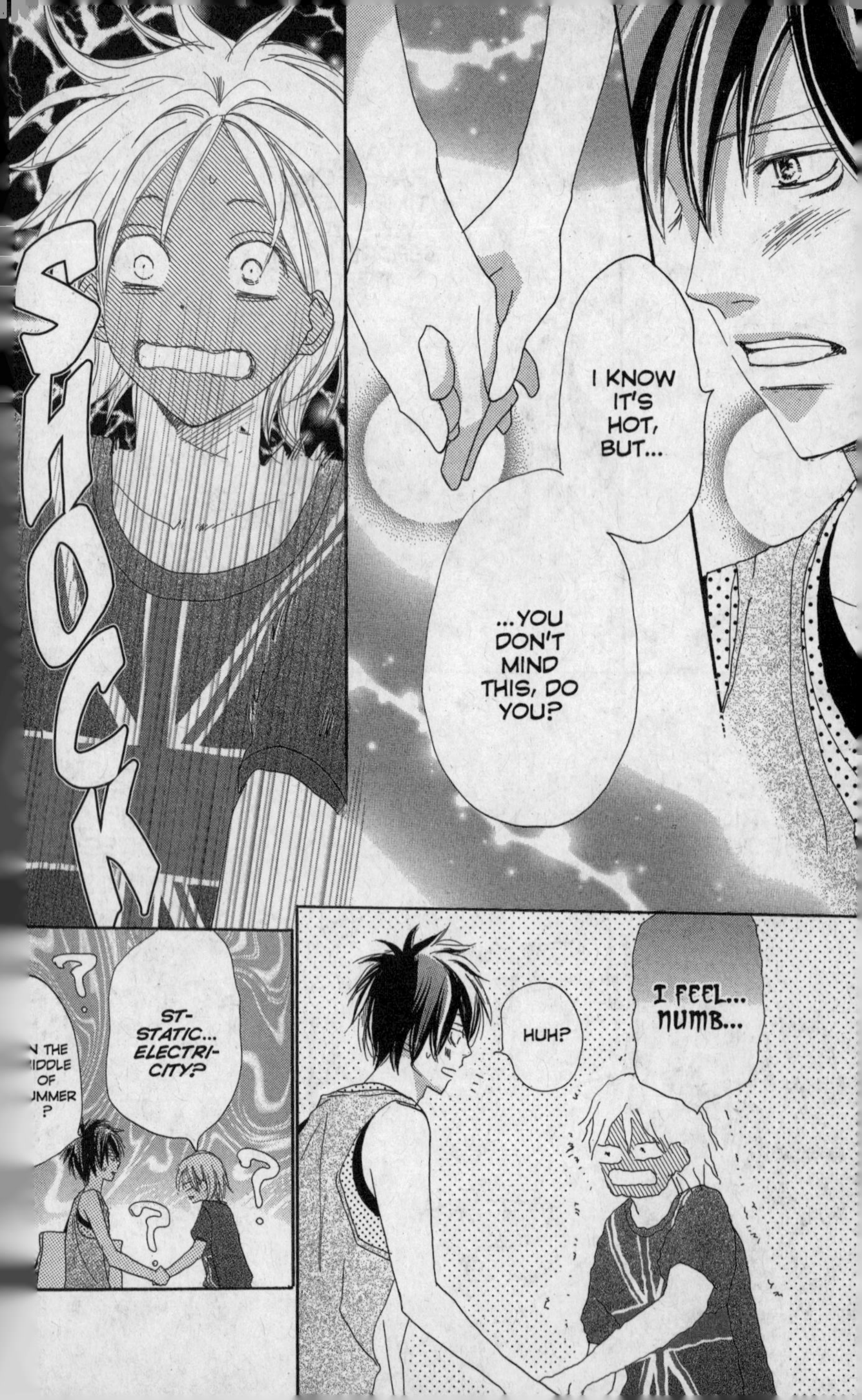
I KNOW IT'S HOT, BUT...
...YOU DON'T MIND THIS, DO YOU?
SHOCK
I FEEL... NUMB...
HUH?
ST-STATIC... ELECTRICITY?
N THE IDDLE OF UMMER ?

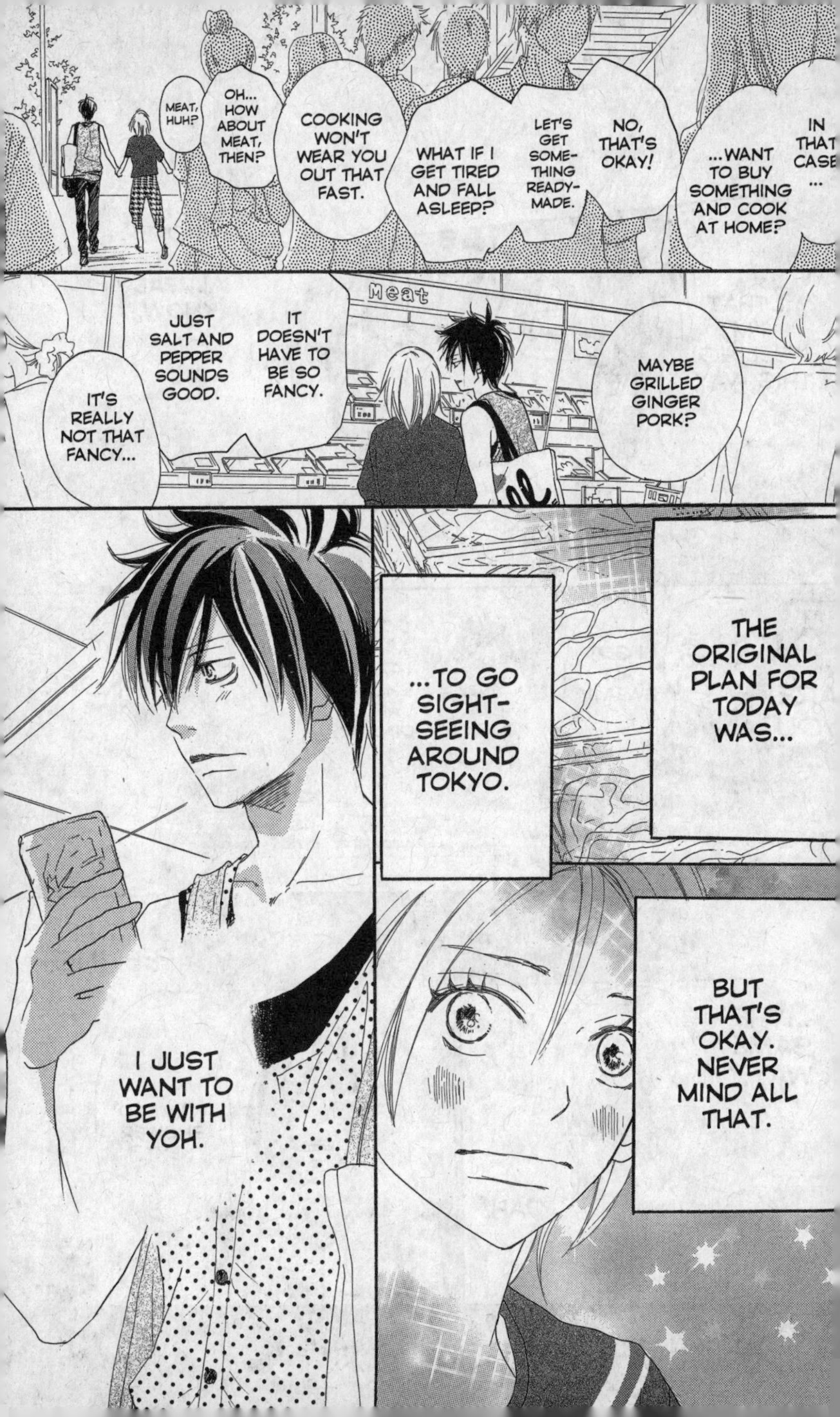
IN THAT CASE...
...WANT TO BUY SOMETHING AND COOK AT HOME?
NO, THAT'S OKAY!
LET'S GET SOME-THING READY-MADE.
WHAT IF I GET TIRED AND FALL ASLEEP?
COOKING WON'T WEAR YOU OUT THAT FAST.
OH... HOW ABOUT MEAT, THEN?
MEAT, HUH?
Meat
MAYBE GRILLED GINGER PORK?
IT DOESN'T HAVE TO BE SO FANCY.
JUST SALT AND PEPPER SOUNDS GOOD.
IT'S REALLY NOT THAT FANCY...
THE ORIGINAL PLAN FOR TODAY WAS...
...TO GO SIGHT-SEEING AROUND TOKYO.
BUT THAT'S OKAY. NEVER MIND ALL THAT.
I JUST WANT TO BE WITH YOH.

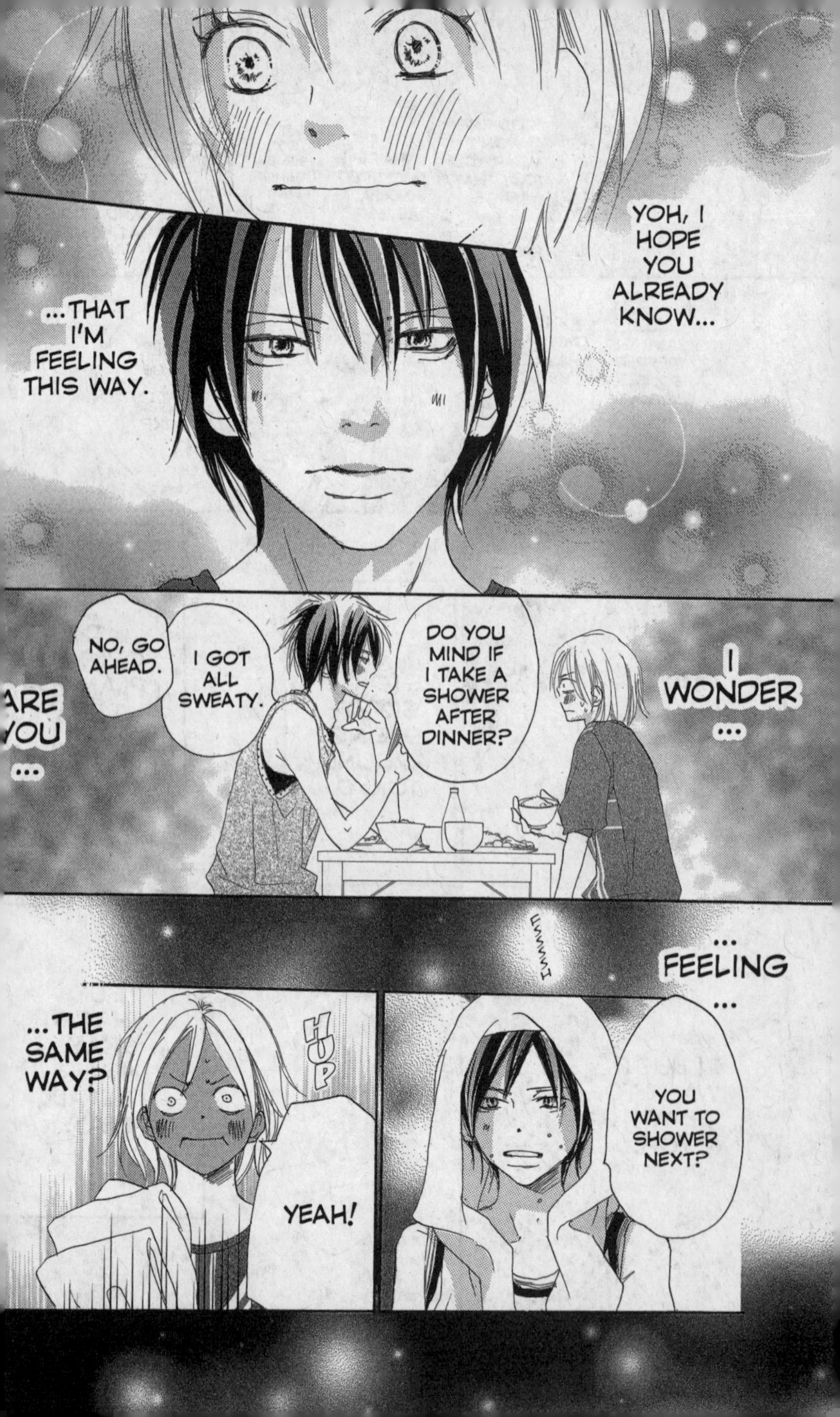
YOH, I HOPE YOU ALREADY KNOW...
...THAT I'M FEELING THIS WAY.
I WONDER ...
DO YOU MIND IF I TAKE A SHOWER AFTER DINNER?
I GOT ALL SWEATY.
NO, GO AHEAD.
ARE YOU ...
... FEELING ...
YOU WANT TO SHOWER NEXT?
HUP
...THE SAME WAY?
YEAH!

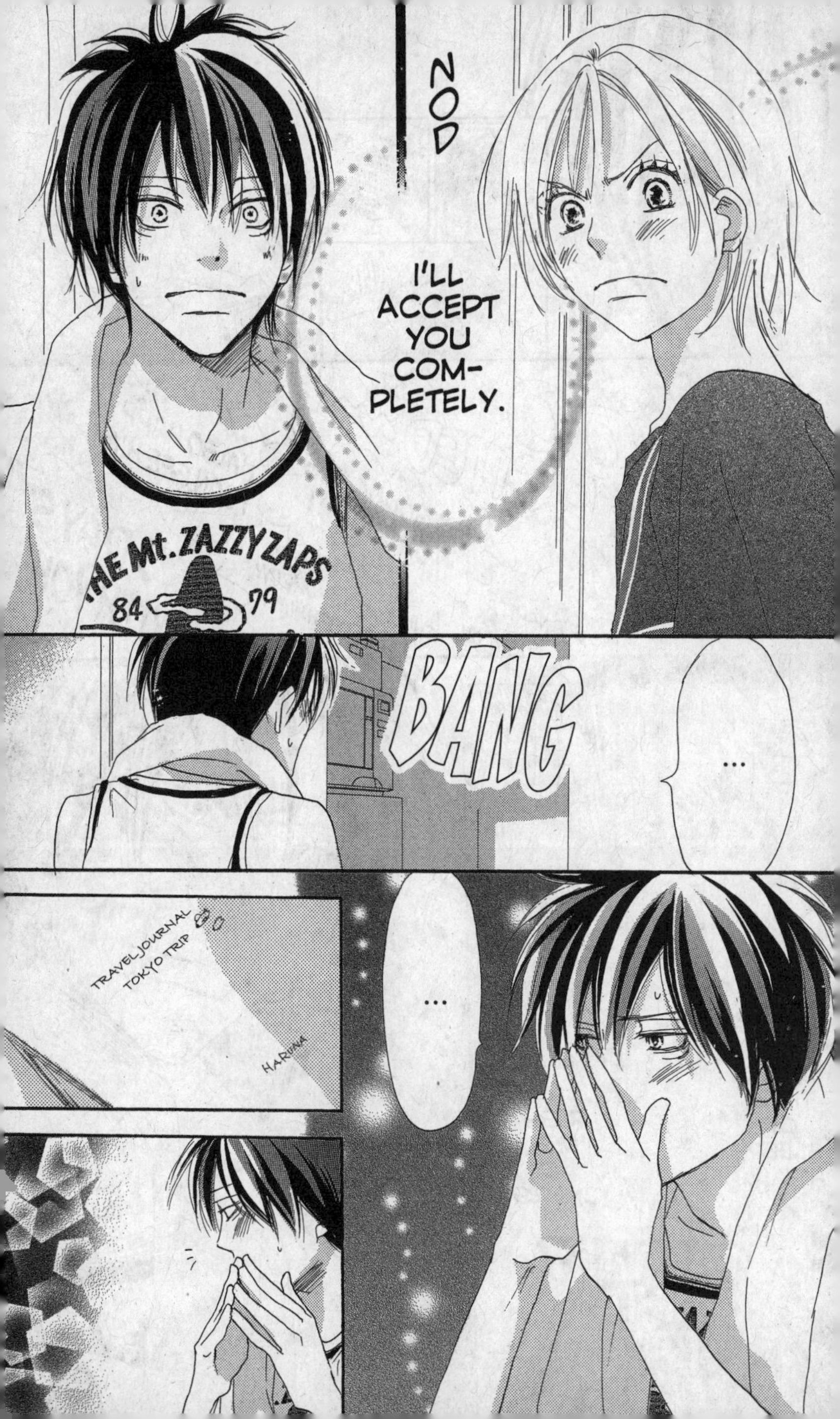
NOD
I'LL ACCEPT YOU COM-PLETELY.
THE Mt. ZAZZY ZAPS 84 79
...
BANG
...
TRAVEL JOURNAL TOKYO TRIP
HARUNA

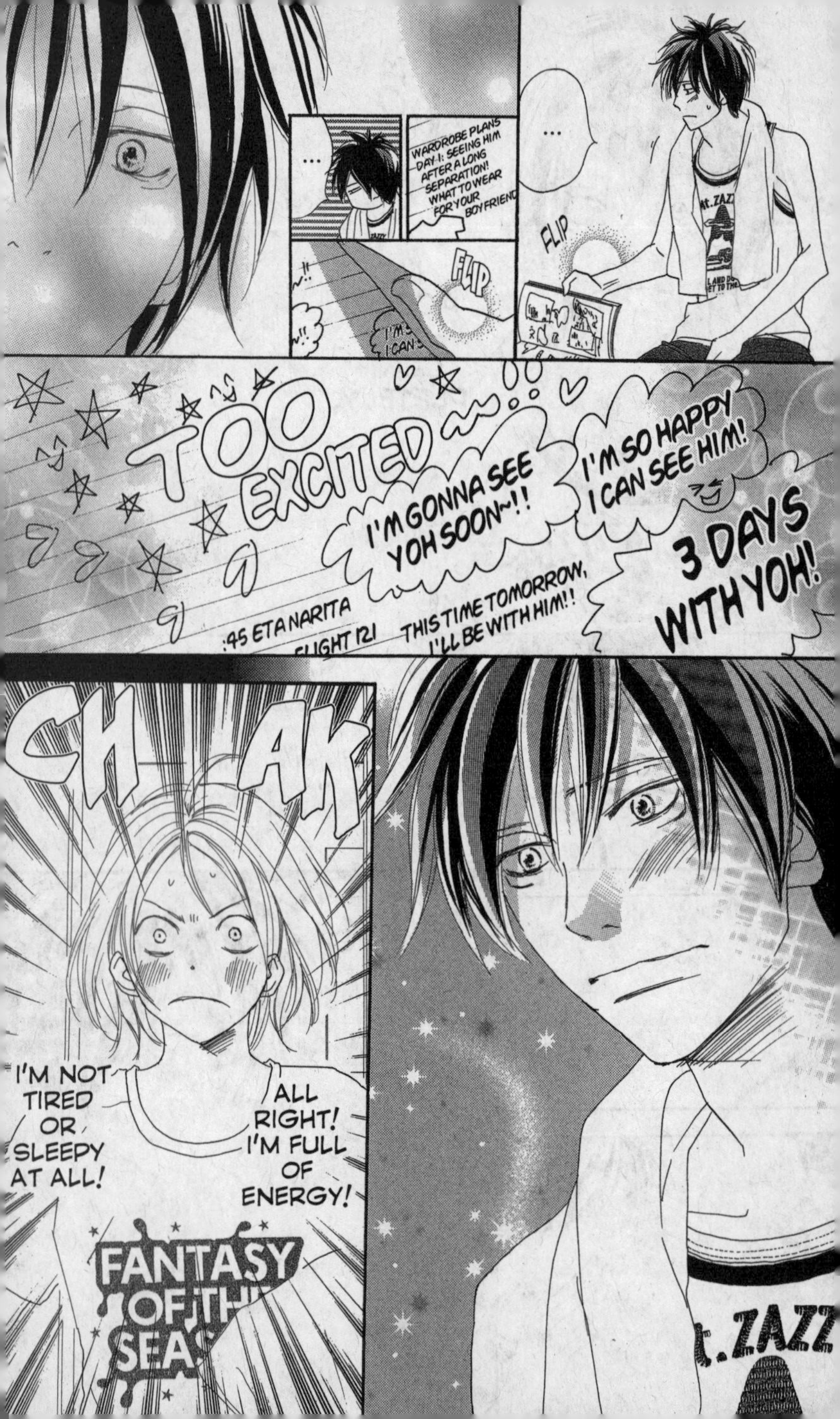
...
FLIP
WARDROBE PLANS DAY 1: SEEING HIM AFTER A LONG SEPARATION! WHAT TO WEAR FOR YOUR BOYFRIEND
...
FLIP
3 DAYS WITH YOH!
I'M SO HAPPY I CAN SEE HIM!
THIS TIME TOMORROW, I'LL BE WITH HIM!!
I'M GONNA SEE YOH SOON~!!
FLIGHT 121
:45 ETA NARITA
TOO EXCITED~
CH AK
ALL RIGHT! I'M FULL OF ENERGY!
I'M NOT TIRED OR SLEEPY AT ALL!
FANTASY

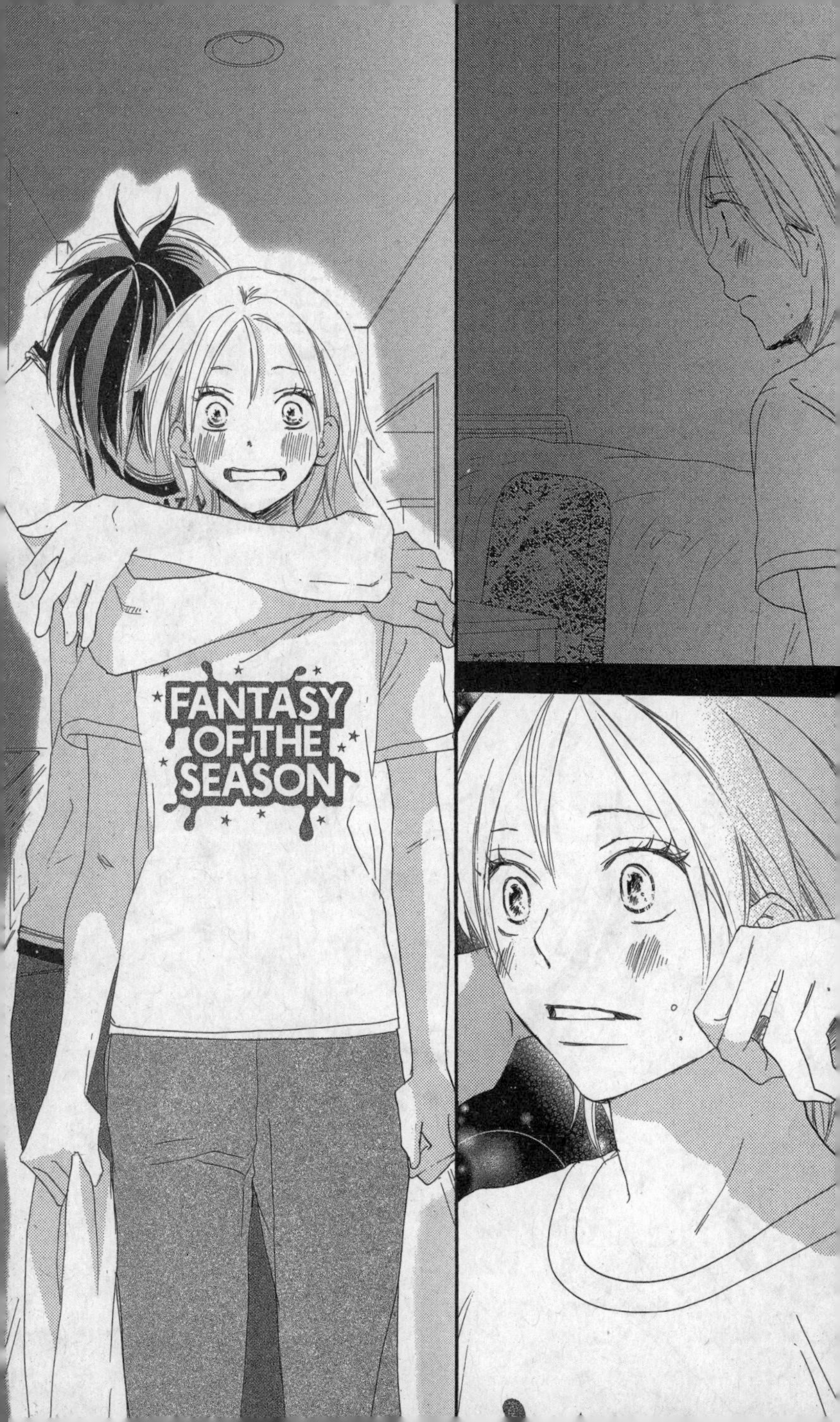
FANTASY OF THE SEASON

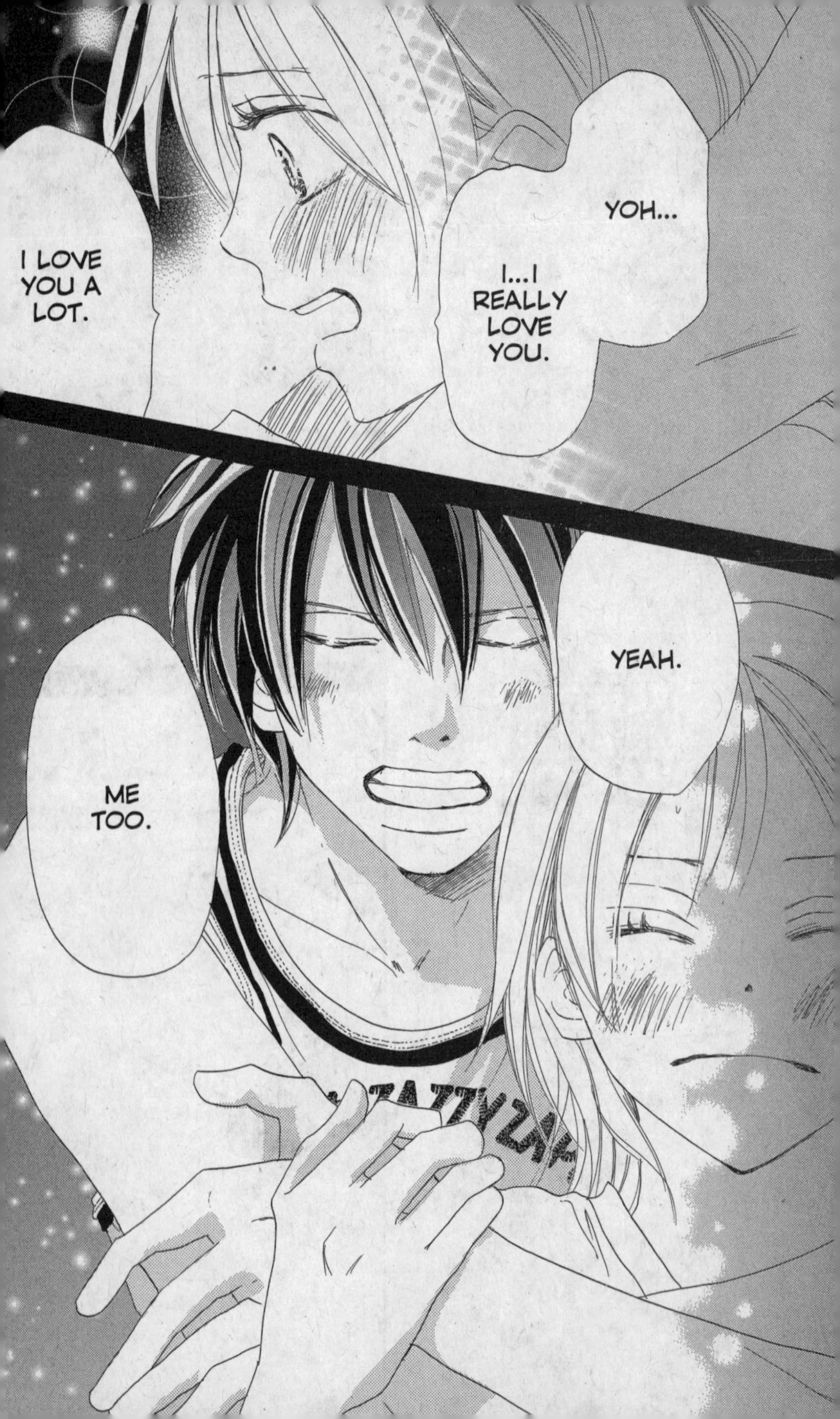
YOH...
I...I REALLY LOVE YOU.
I LOVE YOU A LOT.
YEAH.
ME TOO.

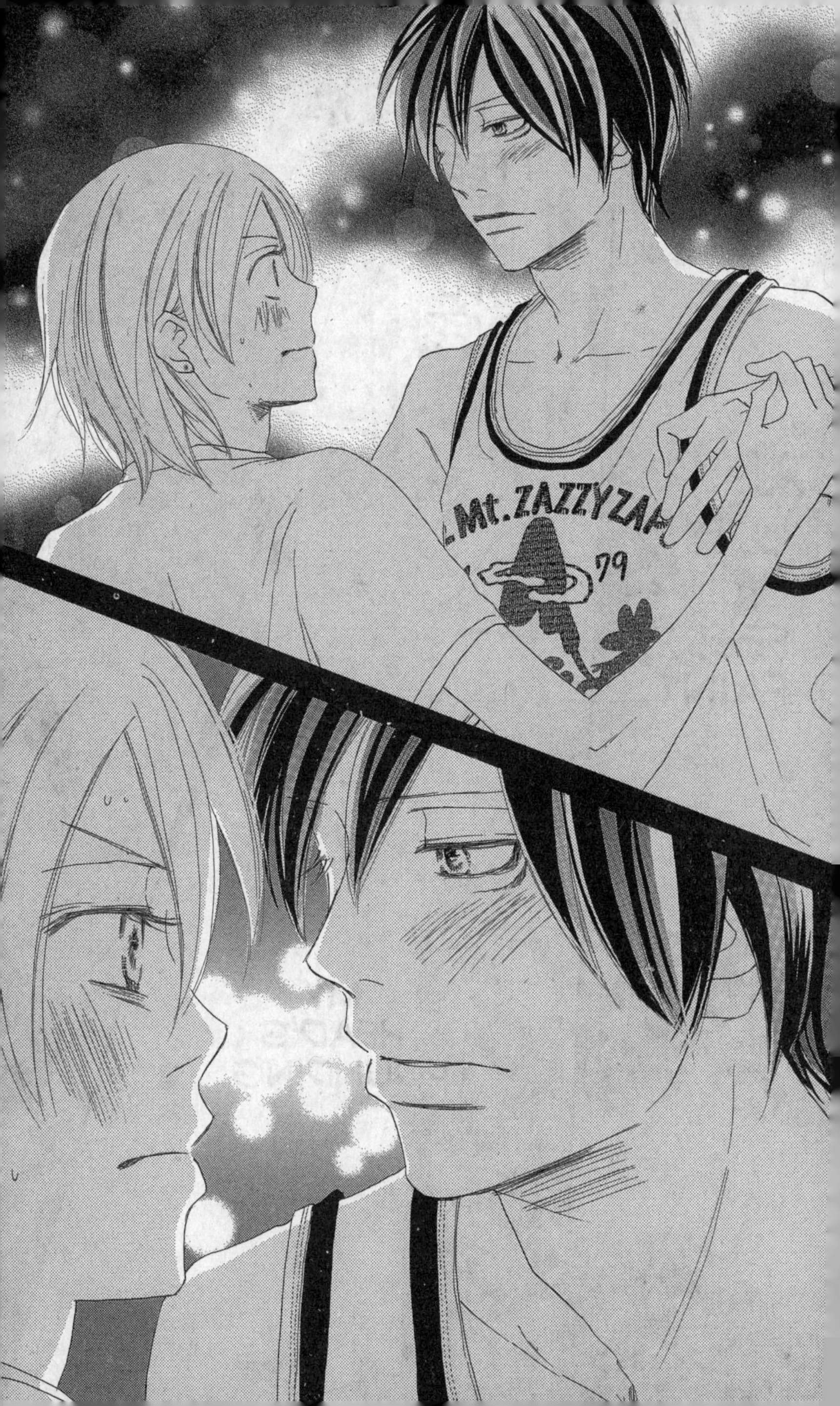
Mt.ZAZZYZA
79

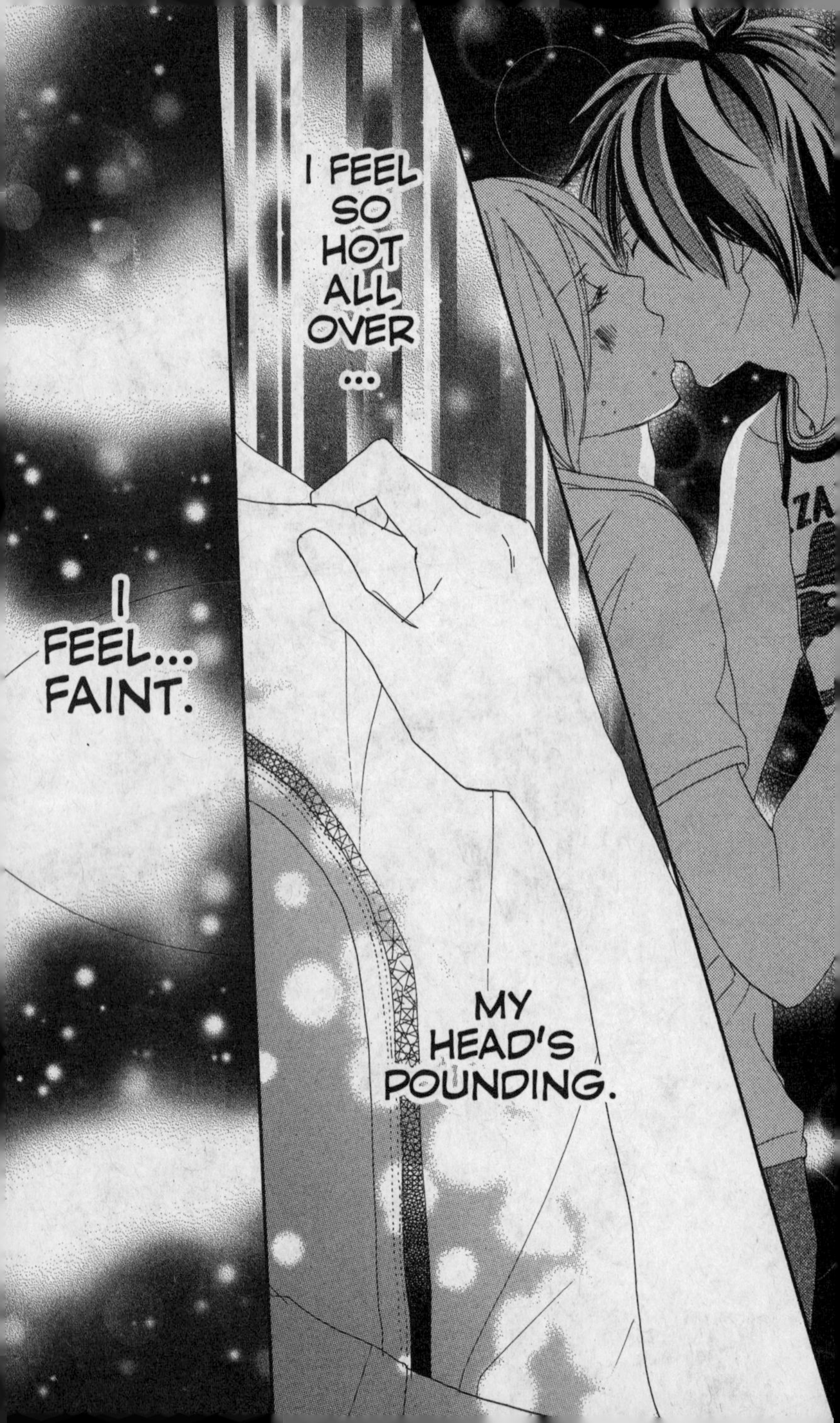
I FEEL SO HOT ALL OVER ...
MY HEAD'S POUNDING.
I FEEL... FAINT.

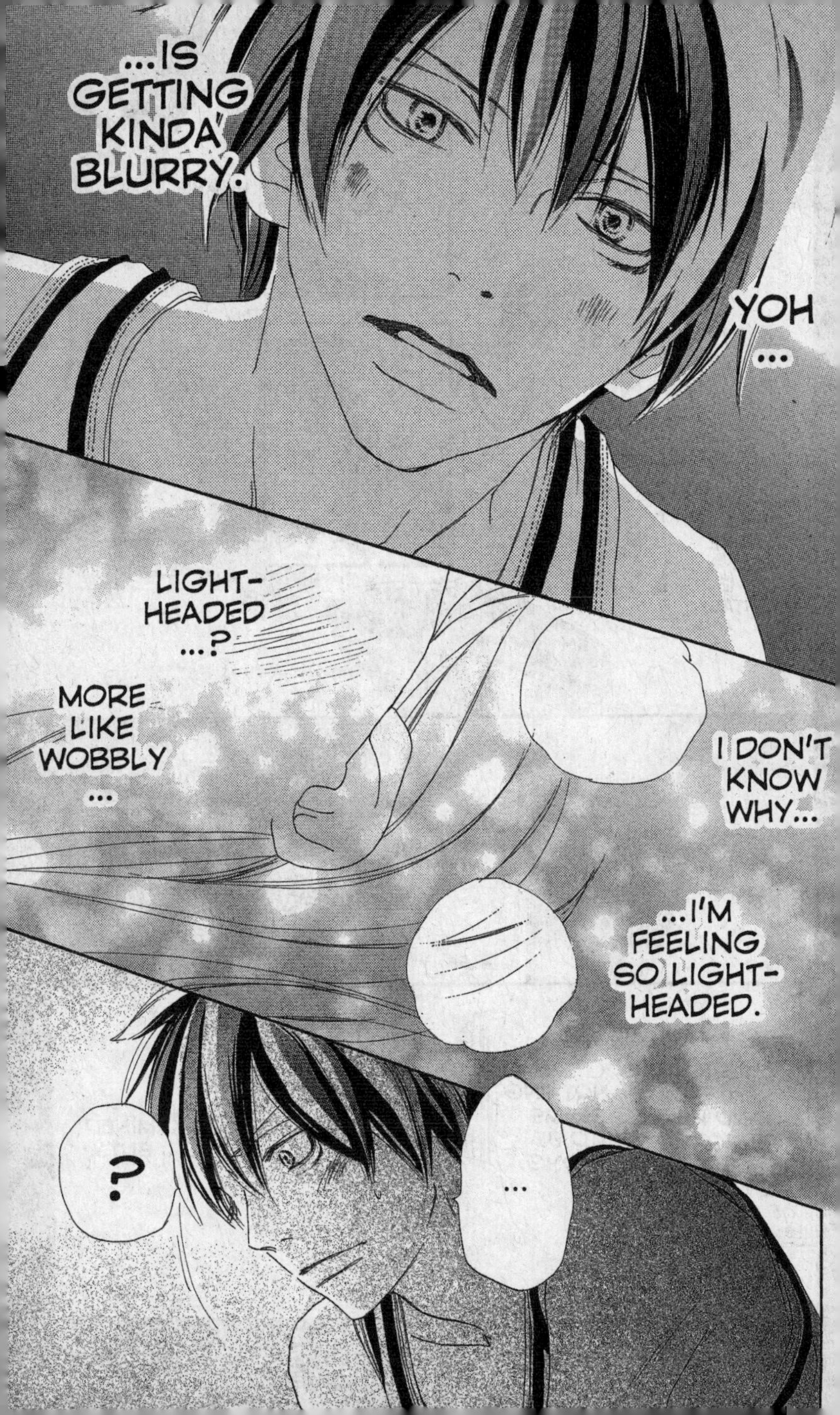
...IS GETTING KINDA BLURRY.
YOH ...
I DON'T KNOW WHY...
...I'M FEELING SO LIGHT-HEADED.
LIGHT-HEADED ...?
MORE LIKE WOBBLY ...
...
?

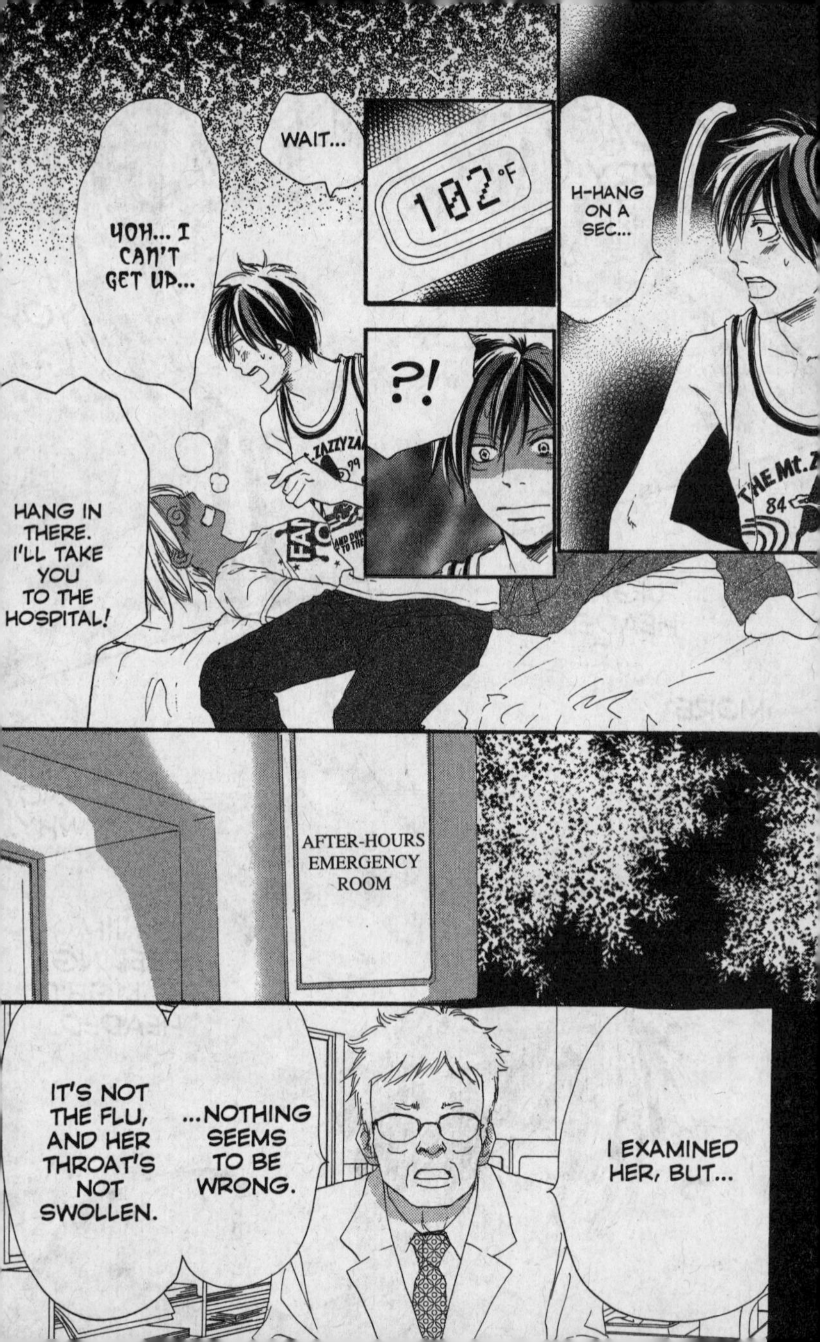
H-HANG ON A SEC...
102°F
WAIT...
?!
YOH... I CAN'T GET UP...
HANG IN THERE. I'LL TAKE YOU TO THE HOSPITAL!
AFTER-HOURS EMERGENCY ROOM
I EXAMINED HER, BUT...
...NOTHING SEEMS TO BE WRONG.
IT'S NOT THE FLU, AND HER THROAT'S NOT SWOLLEN.

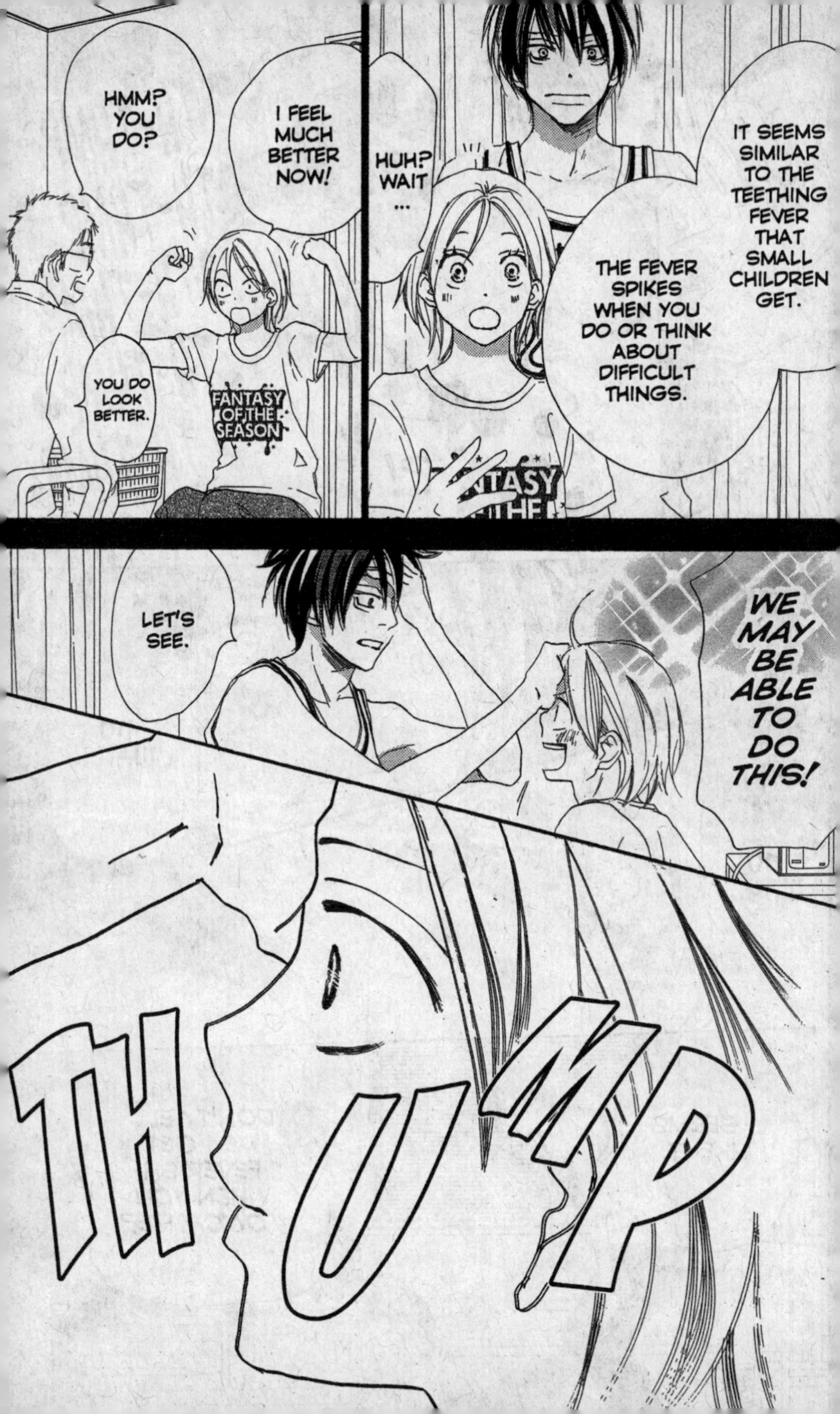
IT SEEMS SIMILAR TO THE TEETHING FEVER THAT SMALL CHILDREN GET.
THE FEVER SPIKES WHEN YOU DO OR THINK ABOUT DIFFICULT THINGS.
HUH? WAIT ...
I FEEL MUCH BETTER NOW!
HMM? YOU DO?
FANTASY OF THE SEASON
YOU DO LOOK BETTER.
WE MAY BE ABLE TO DO THIS!
LET'S SEE.
THUMP

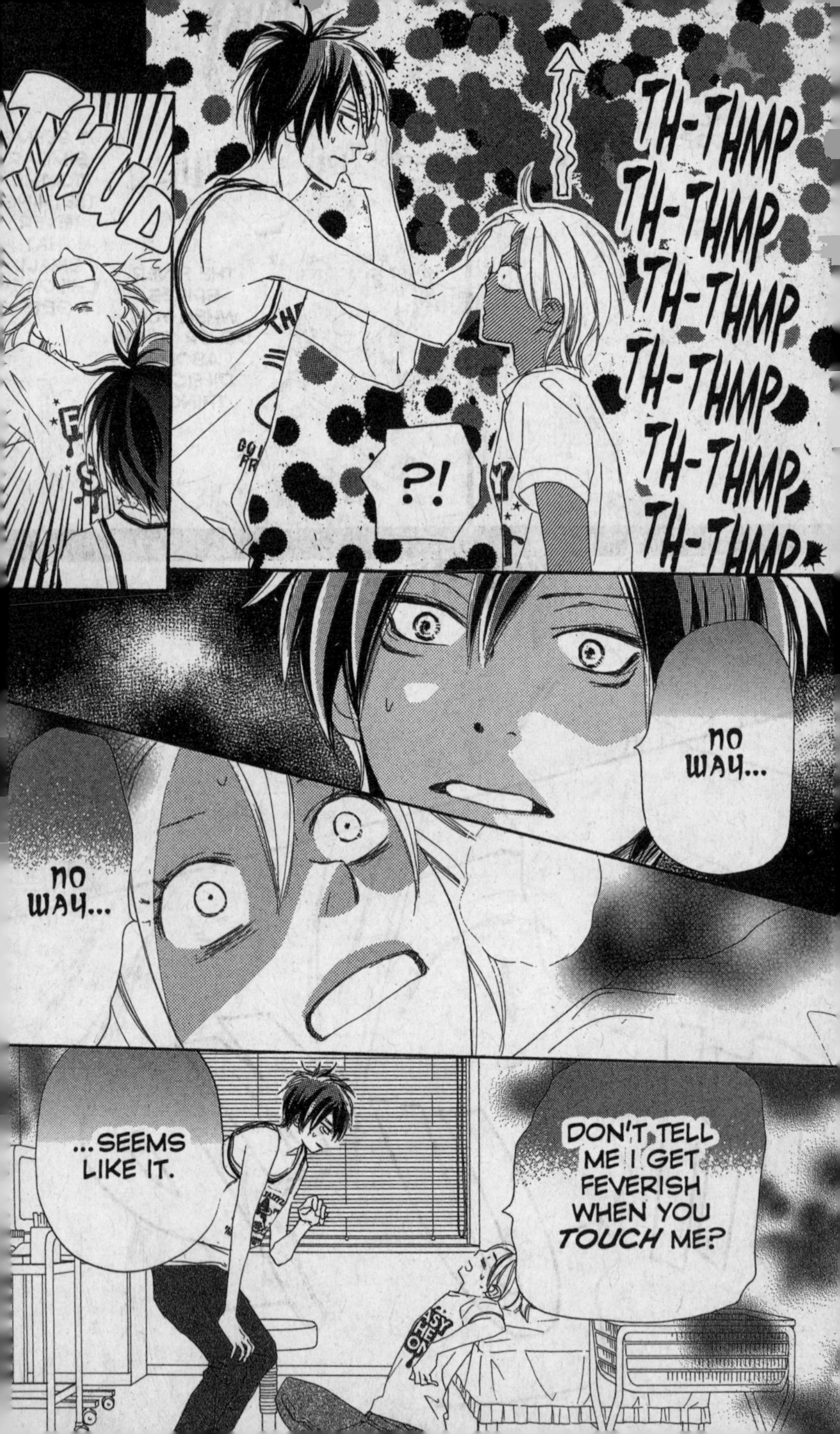
TH-THMP TH-THMP TH-THMP TH-THMP TH-THMP TH-THMP
?!
THUD
no way...
no way...
DON'T TELL ME I GET FEVERISH WHEN YOU *TOUCH* ME?
...SEEMS LIKE IT.

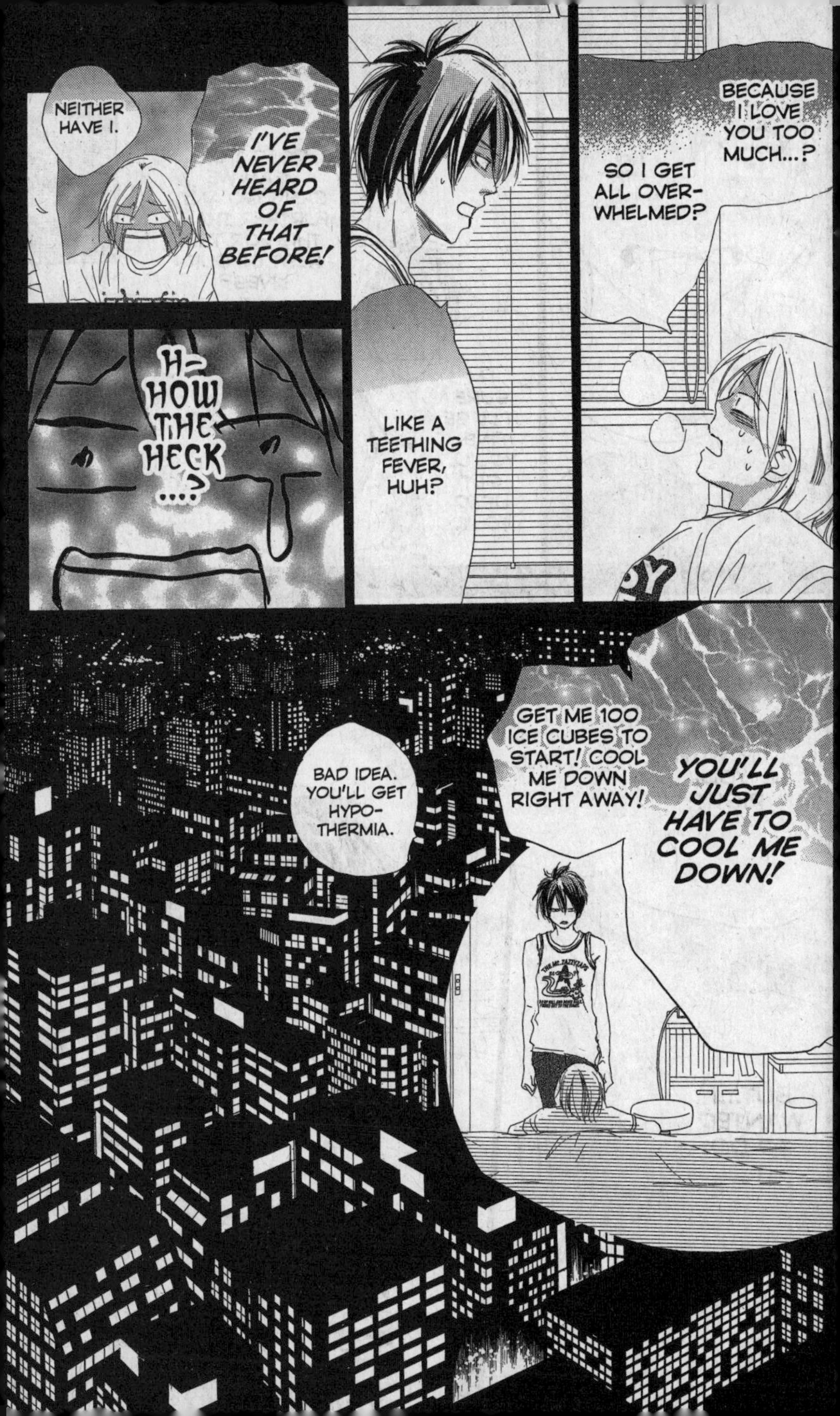
BECAUSE I LOVE YOU TOO MUCH...?
SO I GET ALL OVER-WHELMED?
LIKE A TEETHING FEVER, HUH?
I'VE NEVER HEARD OF THAT BEFORE!
NEITHER HAVE I.
H-HOW THE HECK...?
YOU'LL JUST HAVE TO COOL ME DOWN!
GET ME 100 ICE CUBES TO START! COOL ME DOWN RIGHT AWAY!
BAD IDEA. YOU'LL GET HYPO-THERMIA.

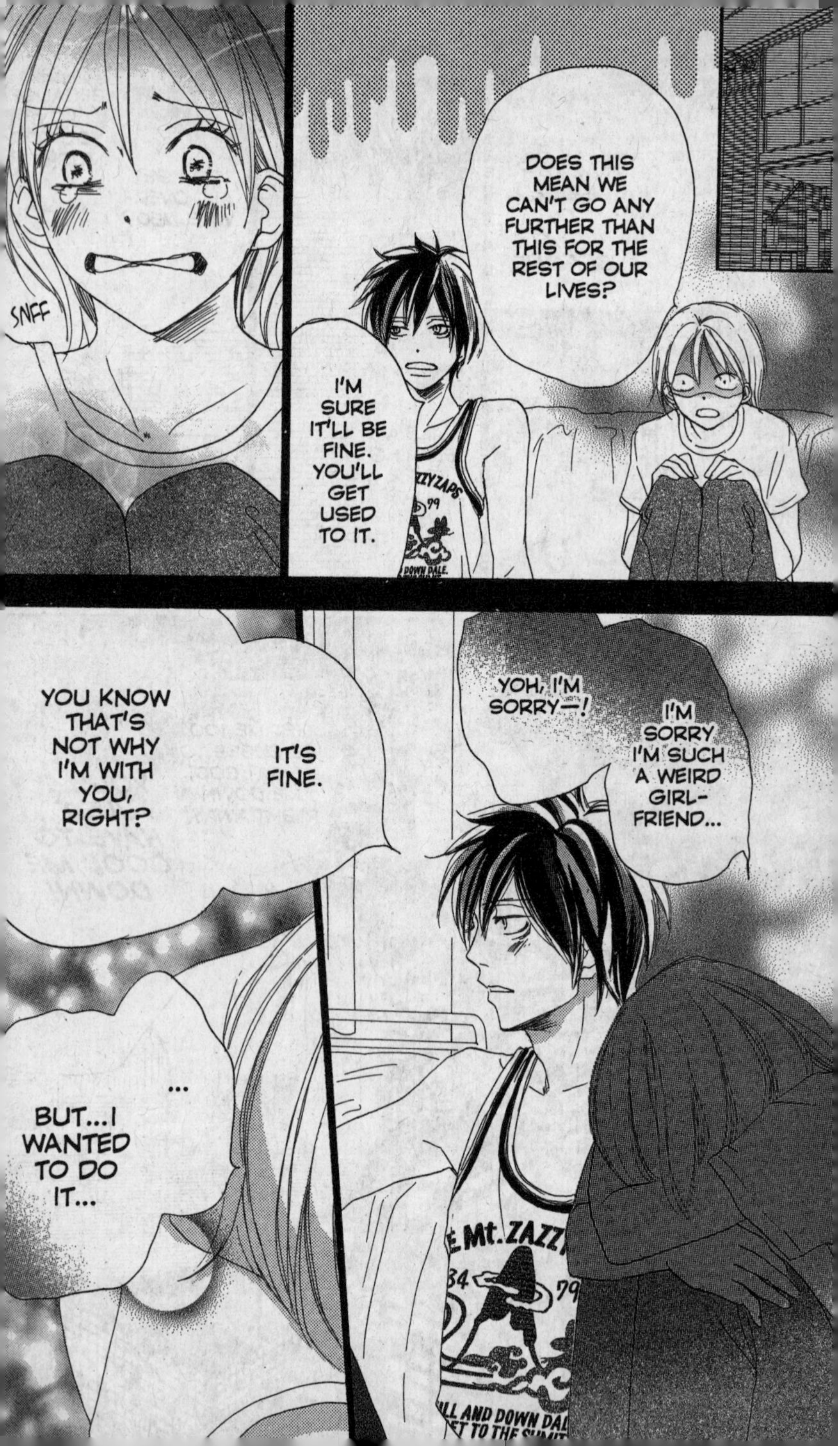
DOES THIS MEAN WE CAN'T GO ANY FURTHER THAN THIS FOR THE REST OF OUR LIVES?
I'M SURE IT'LL BE FINE. YOU'LL GET USED TO IT.
SNFF
YOH, I'M SORRY—!
I'M SORRY I'M SUCH A WEIRD GIRL-FRIEND...
IT'S FINE.
YOU KNOW THAT'S NOT WHY I'M WITH YOU, RIGHT?
...
BUT...I WANTED TO DO IT...

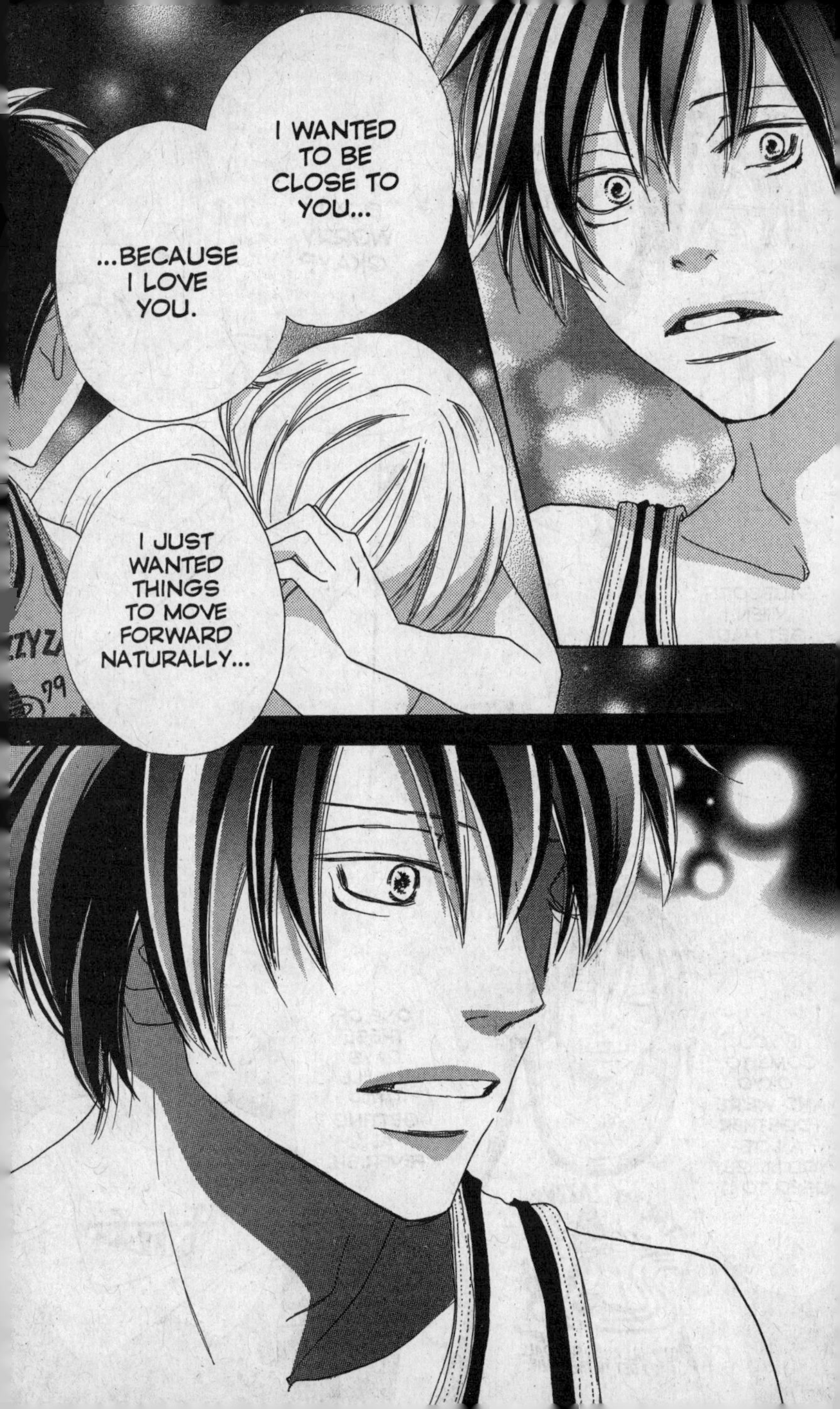
I WANTED TO BE CLOSE TO YOU...
...BECAUSE I LOVE YOU.
I JUST WANTED THINGS TO MOVE FORWARD NATURALLY...

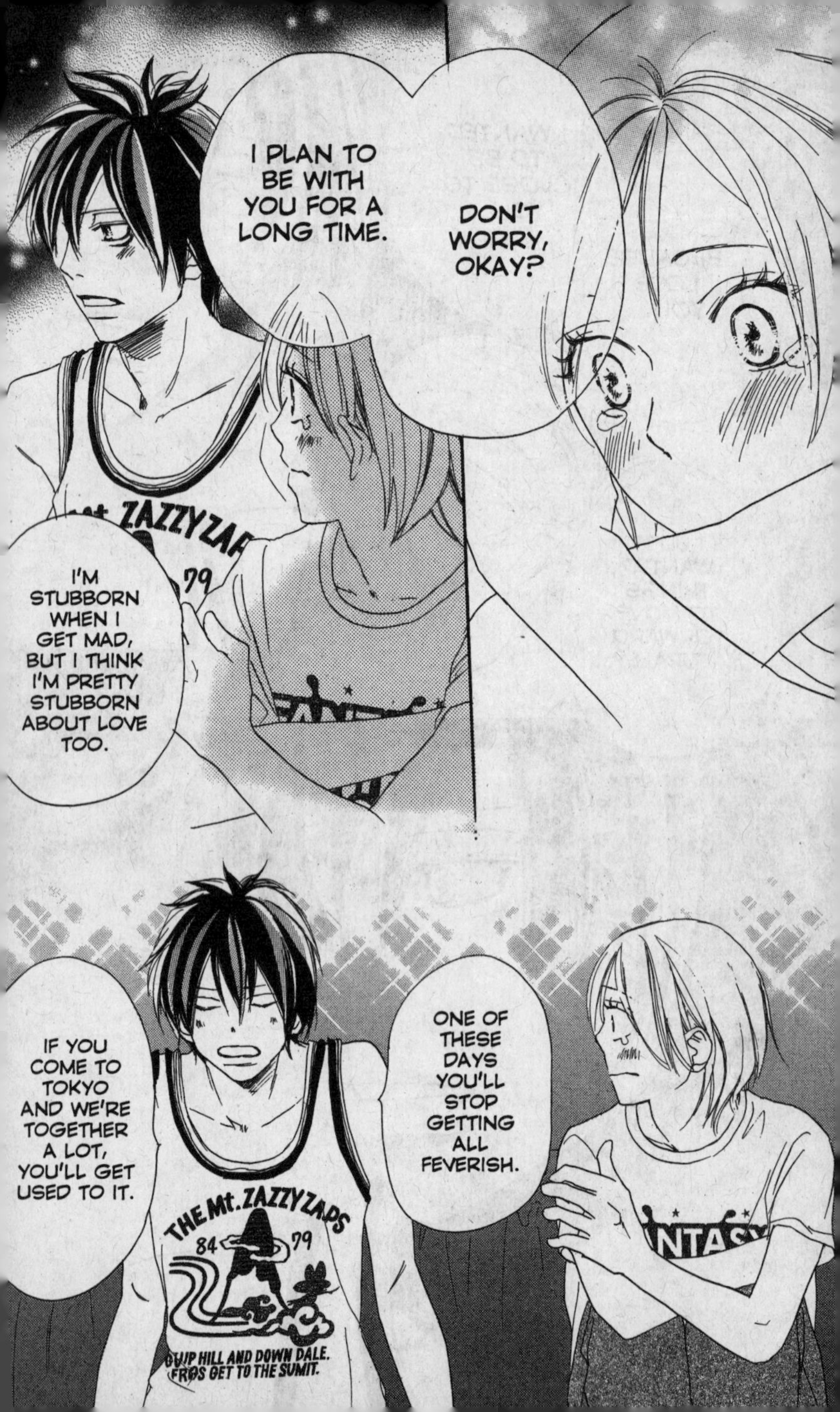
DON'T WORRY, OKAY?
I PLAN TO BE WITH YOU FOR A LONG TIME.
I'M STUBBORN WHEN I GET MAD, BUT I THINK I'M PRETTY STUBBORN ABOUT LOVE TOO.
ONE OF THESE DAYS YOU'LL STOP GETTING ALL FEVERISH.
IF YOU COME TO TOKYO AND WE'RE TOGETHER A LOT, YOU'LL GET USED TO IT.
THE Mt. ZAZZYZAPS
84 79

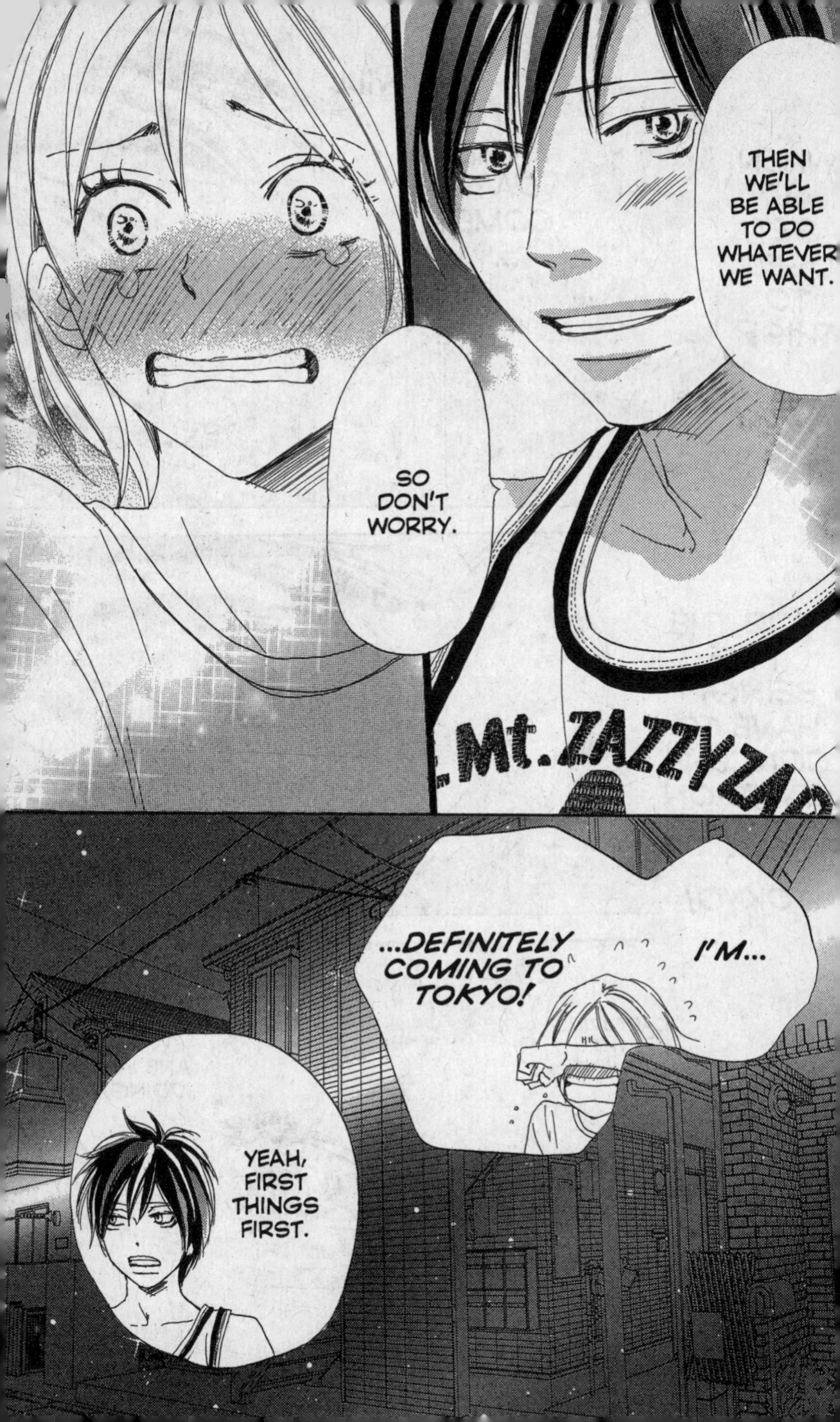
THEN WE'LL BE ABLE TO DO WHATEVER WE WANT.
SO DON'T WORRY.
Mt. ZAZZY
I'M...
...DEFINITELY COMING TO TOKYO!
YEAH, FIRST THINGS FIRST.

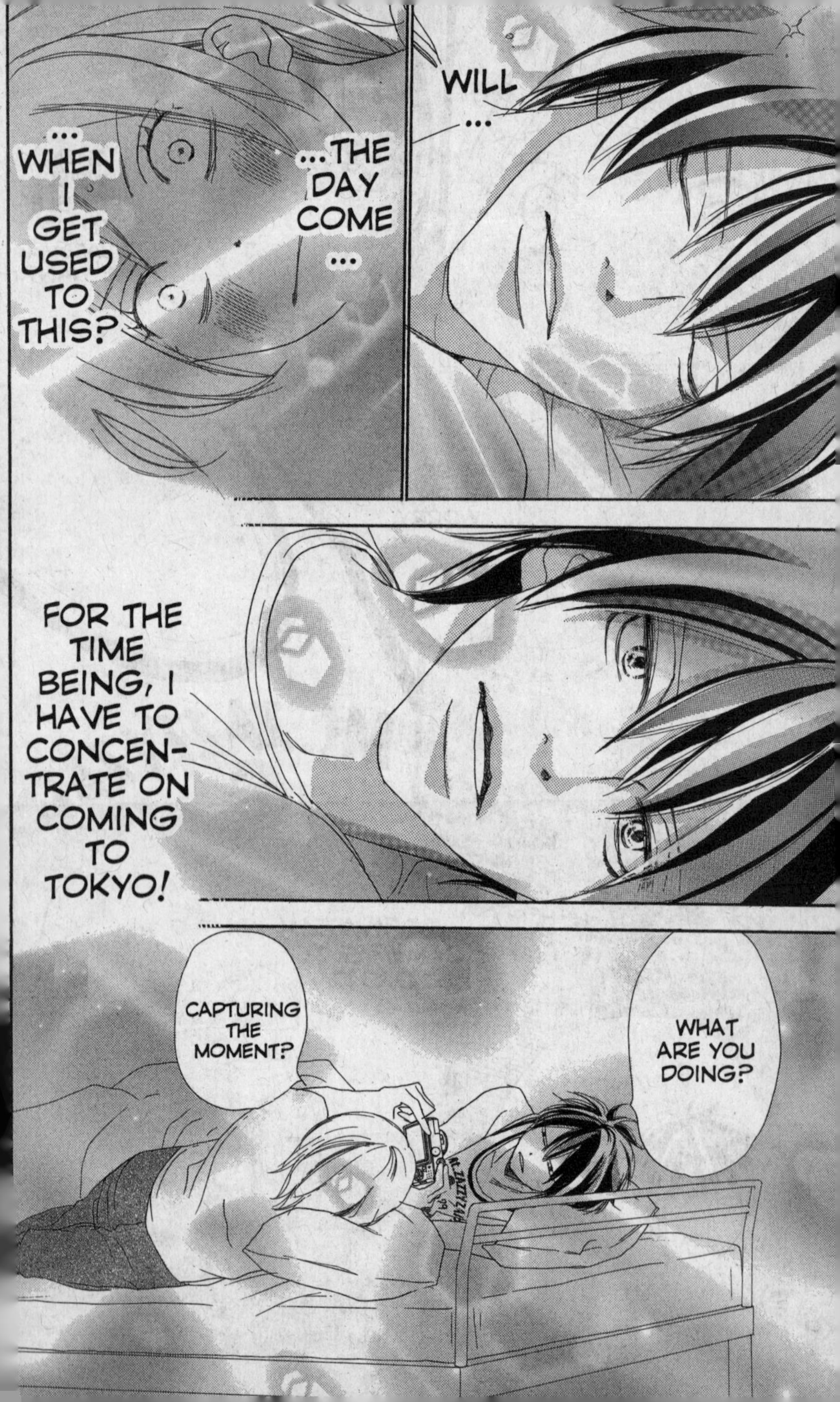
WILL ...
...THE DAY COME ...
... WHEN I GET USED TO THIS?
FOR THE TIME BEING, I HAVE TO CONCENTRATE ON COMING TO TOKYO!
WHAT ARE YOU DOING?
CAPTURING THE MOMENT?

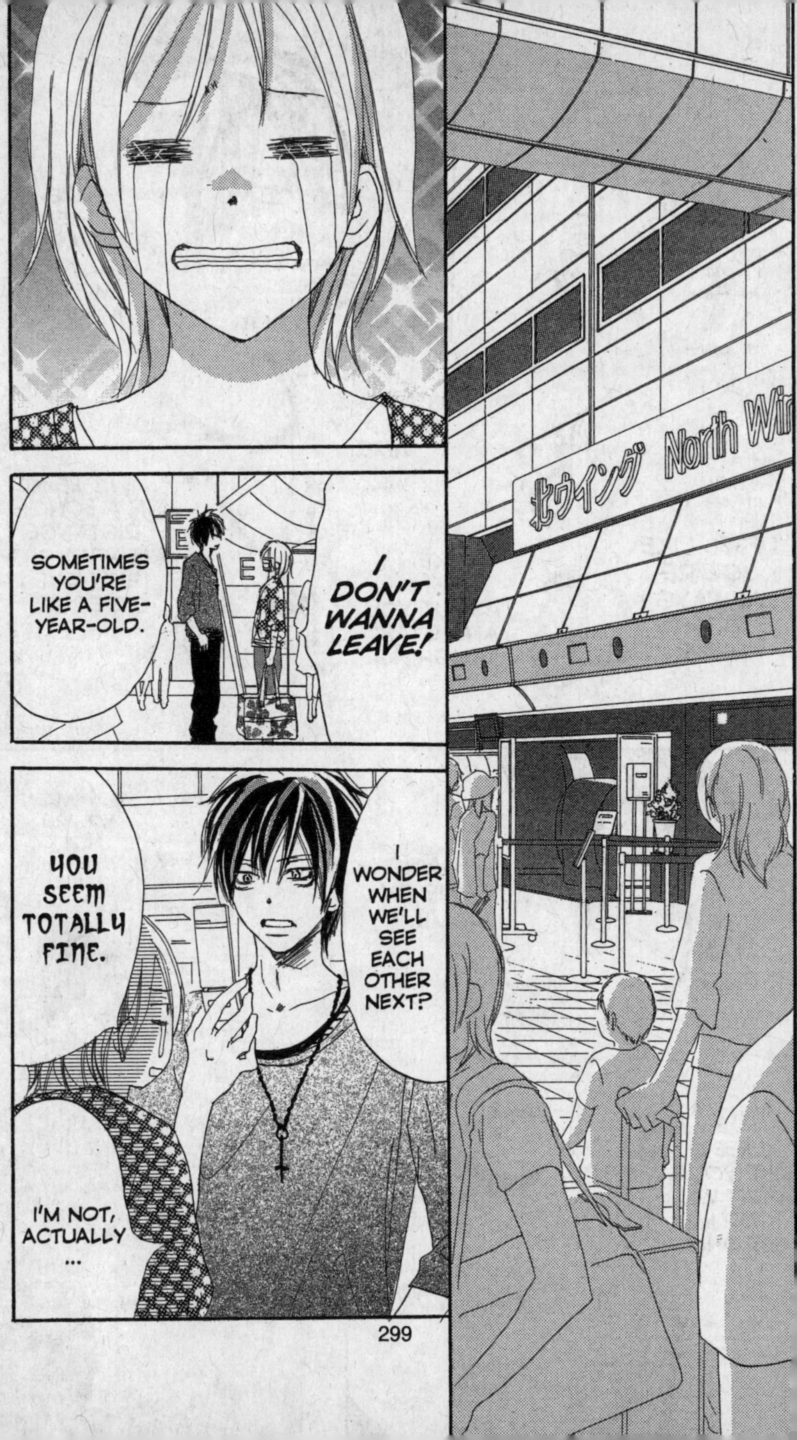
北ウイング North Wi
I DON'T WANNA LEAVE!
SOMETIMES YOU'RE LIKE A FIVE-YEAR-OLD.
I WONDER WHEN WE'LL SEE EACH OTHER NEXT?
YOU SEEM TOTALLY FINE.
I'M NOT, ACTUALLY ...

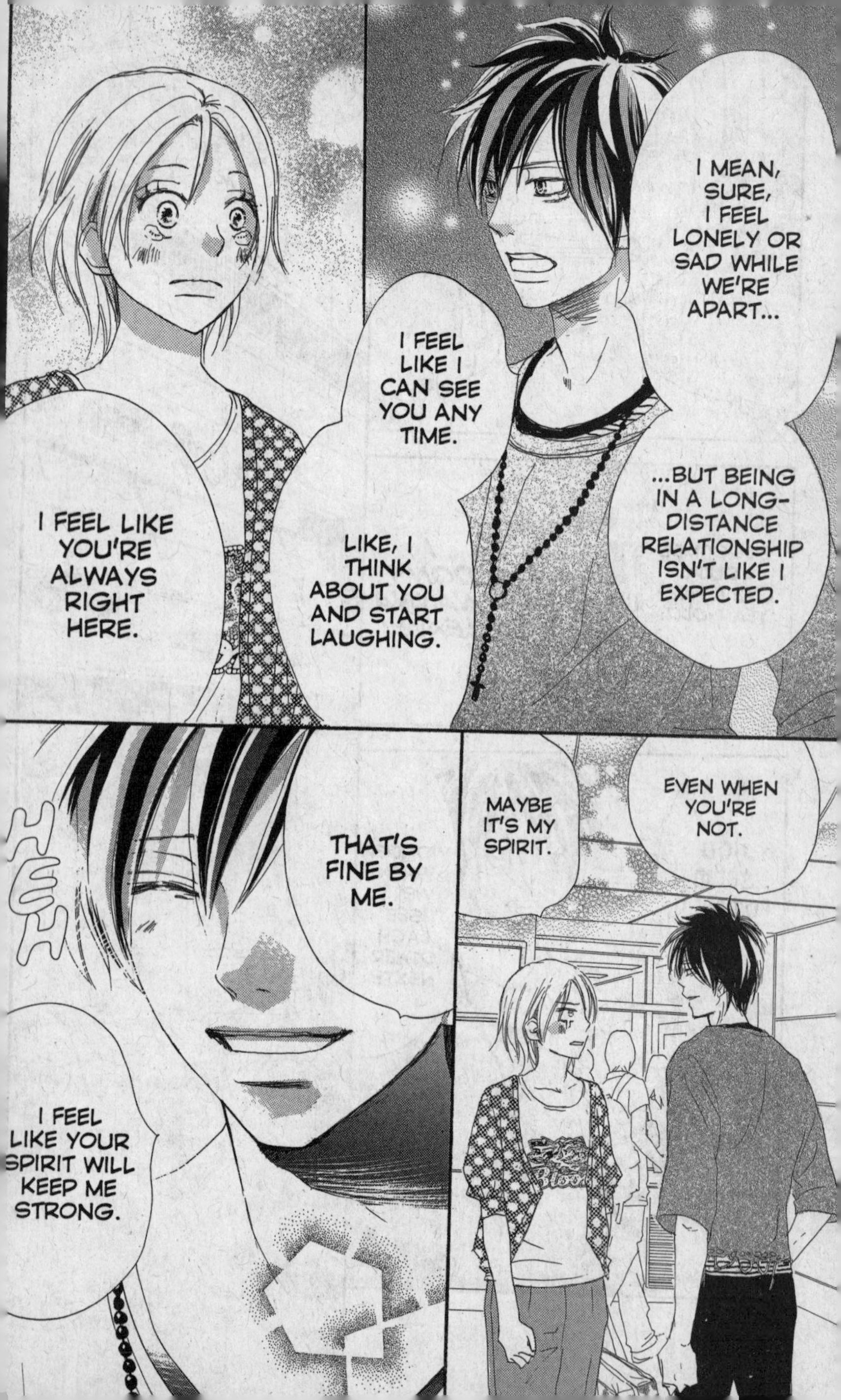
I MEAN, SURE, I FEEL LONELY OR SAD WHILE WE'RE APART...
...BUT BEING IN A LONG-DISTANCE RELATIONSHIP ISN'T LIKE I EXPECTED.
I FEEL LIKE I CAN SEE YOU ANY TIME.
LIKE, I THINK ABOUT YOU AND START LAUGHING.
I FEEL LIKE YOU'RE ALWAYS RIGHT HERE.
EVEN WHEN YOU'RE NOT.
MAYBE IT'S MY SPIRIT.
THAT'S FINE BY ME.
HEH
I FEEL LIKE YOUR SPIRIT WILL KEEP ME STRONG.

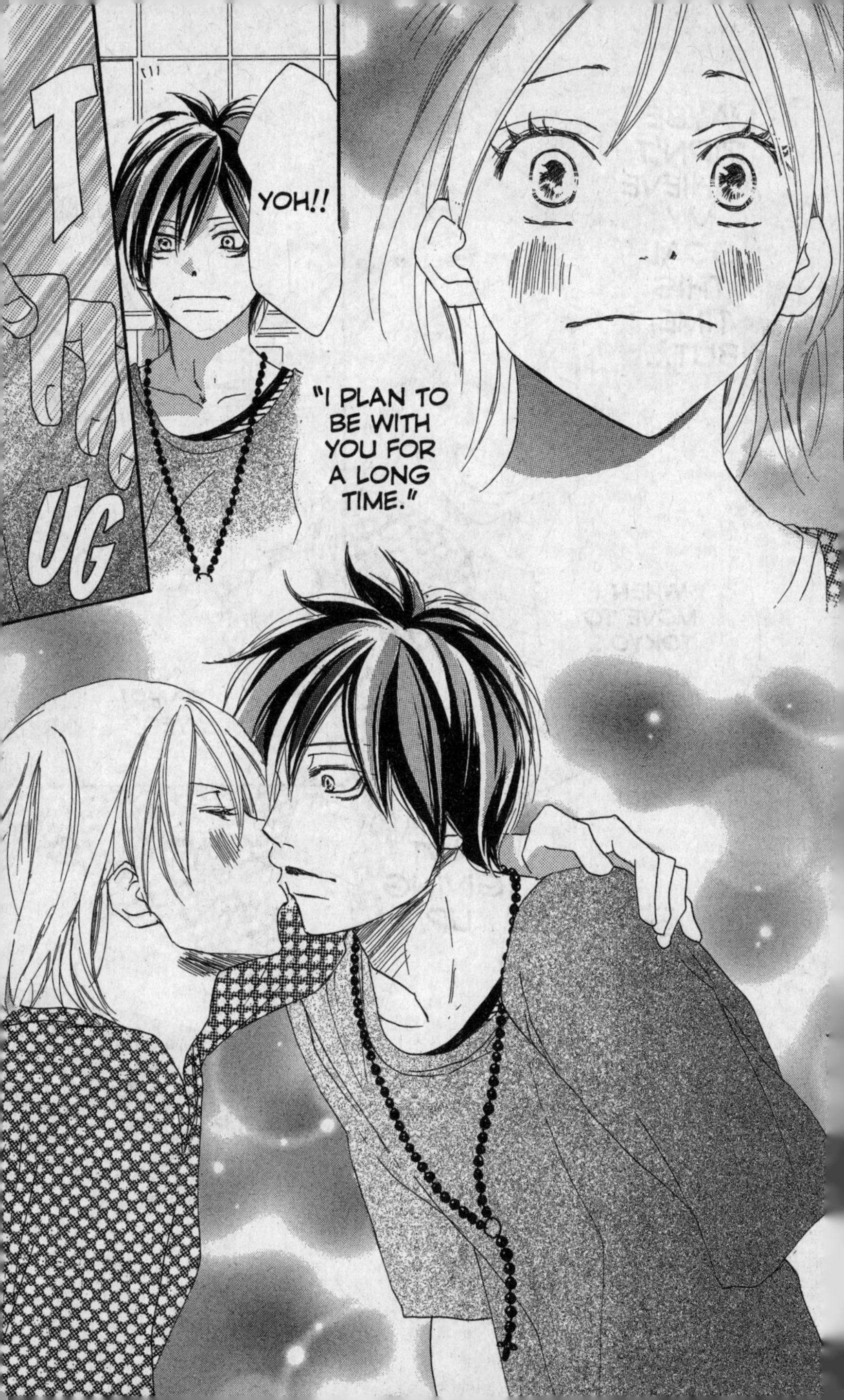
"I PLAN TO BE WITH YOU FOR A LONG TIME."
TUG
YOH!!

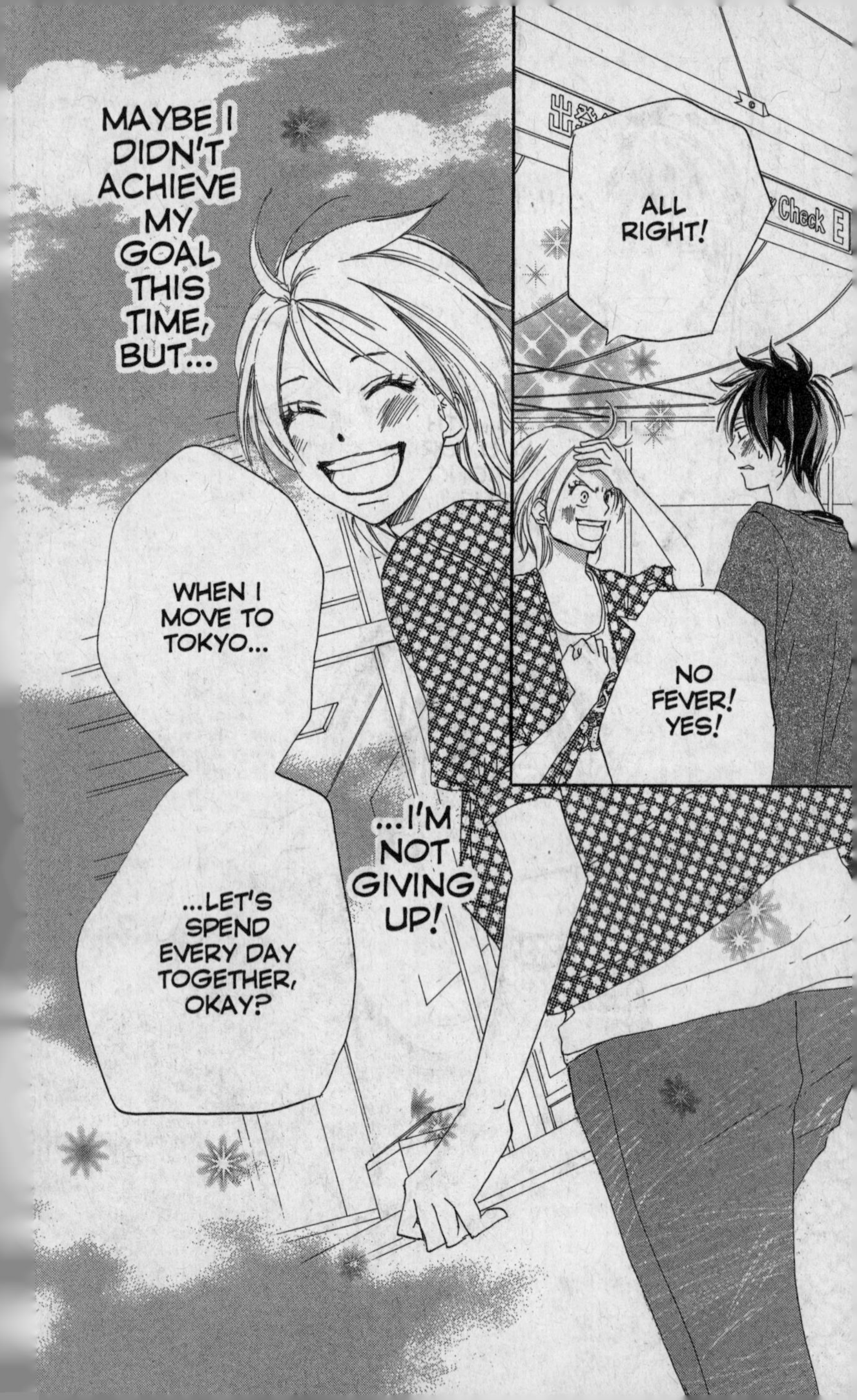
ALL RIGHT!
NO FEVER! YES!
MAYBE I DIDN'T ACHIEVE MY GOAL THIS TIME, BUT...
...I'M NOT GIVING UP!
WHEN I MOVE TO TOKYO...
...LET'S SPEND EVERY DAY TOGETHER, OKAY?

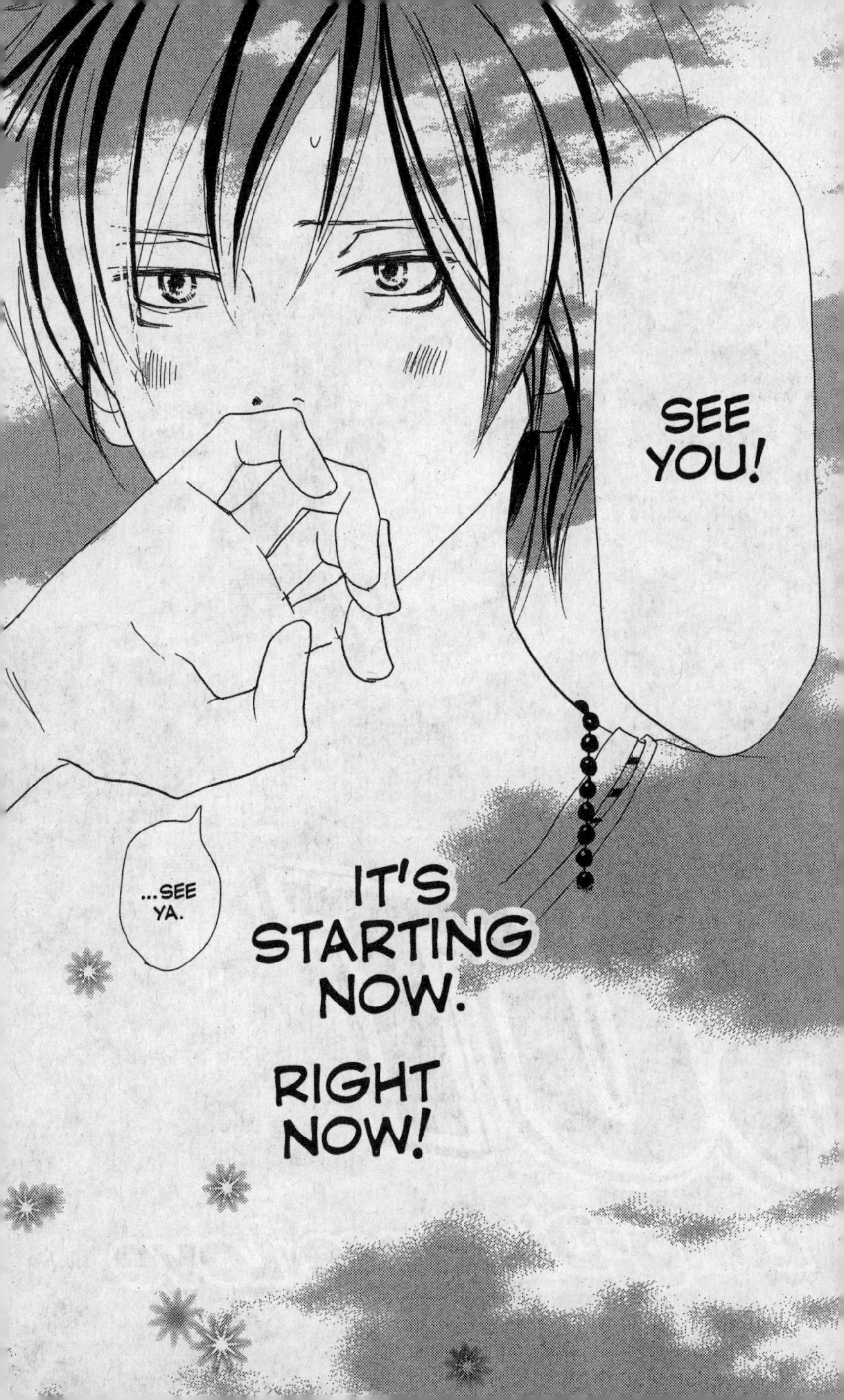
SEE YOU!
...SEE YA.
IT'S STARTING NOW.
RIGHT NOW!

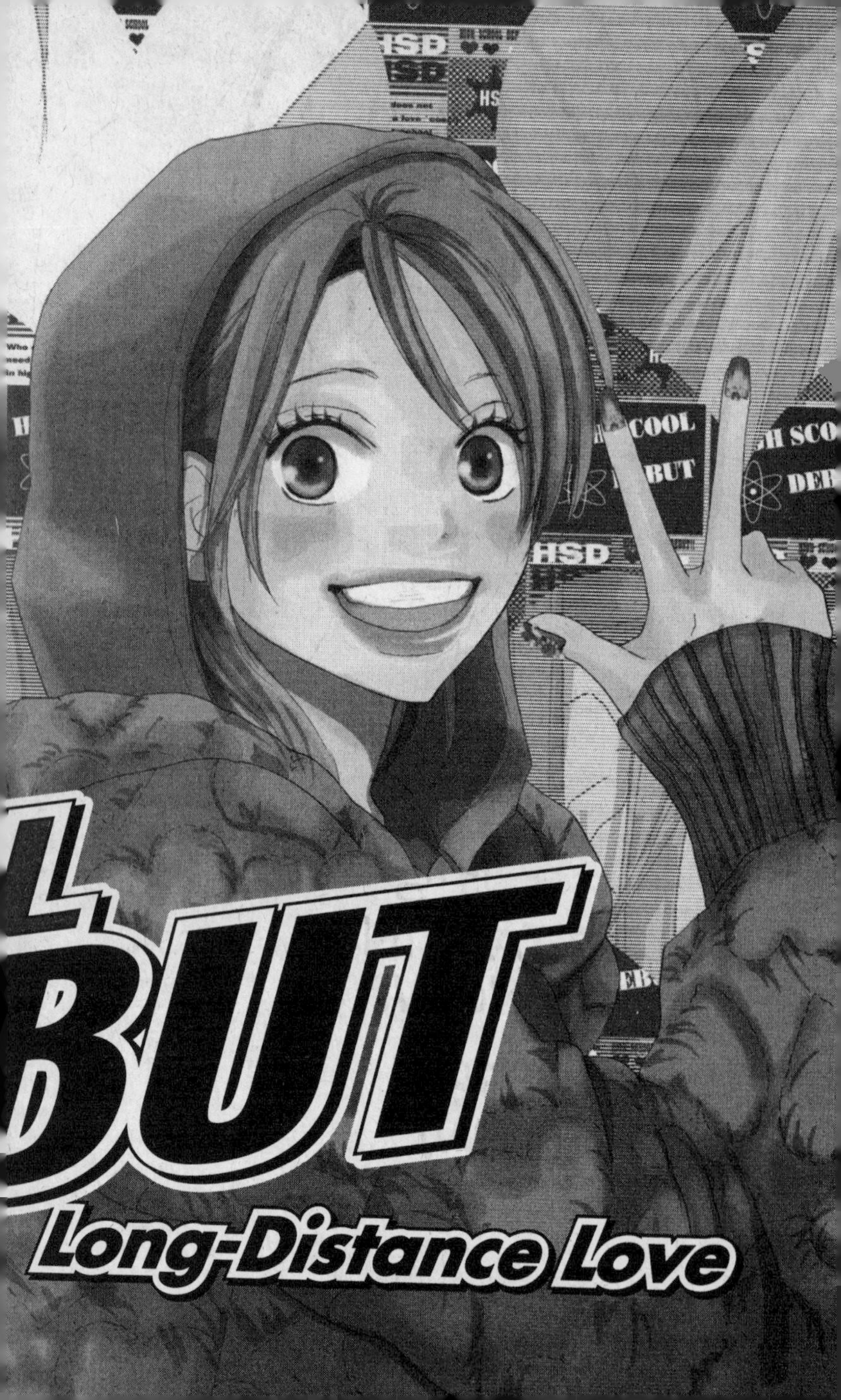
BUT
Long-Distance Love

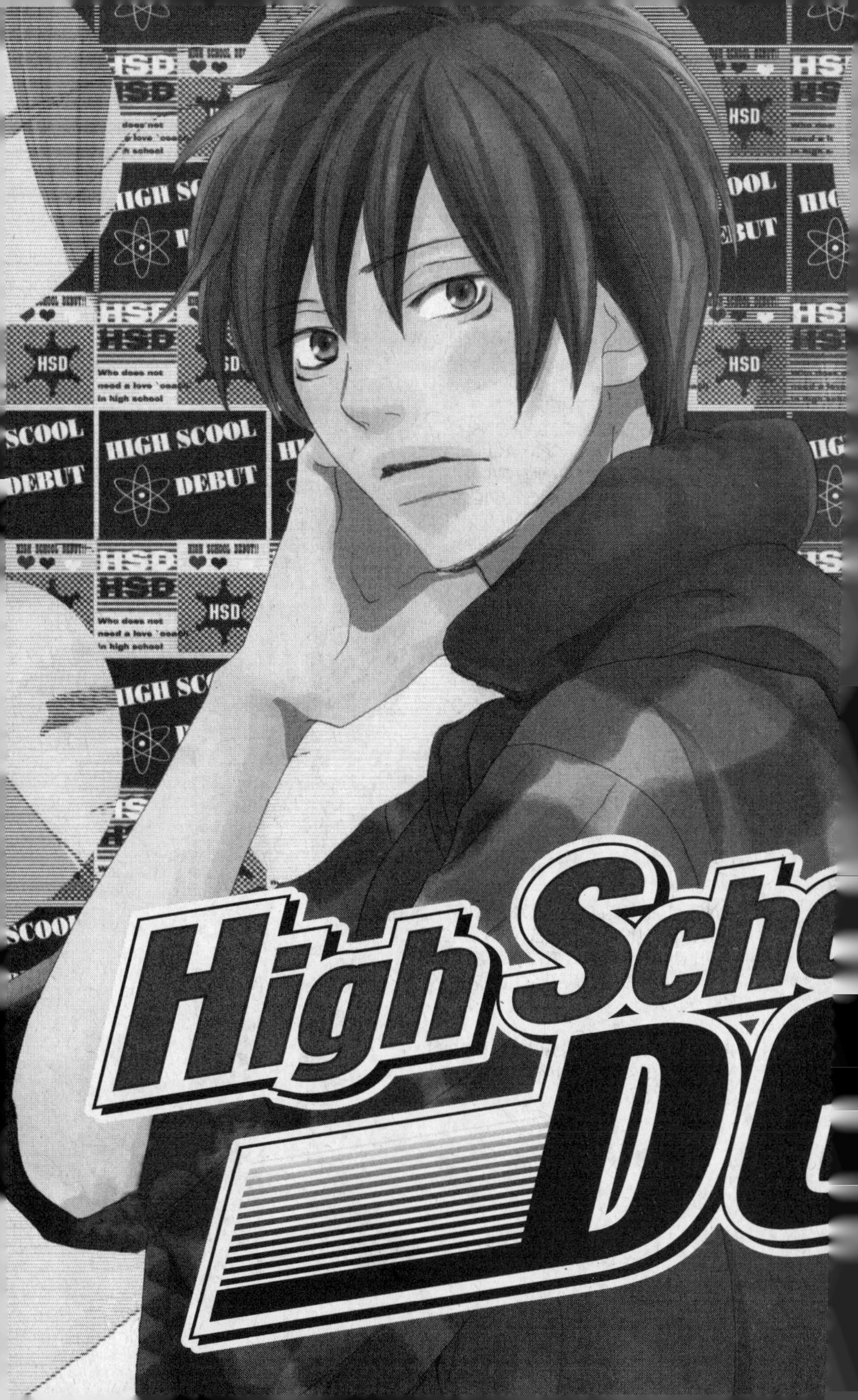
HIGH SCOOL
DEBUT
HSD
Who does not
need a love `coach
in high school
High

I'M SORRY FOR ONLY NOTICING THIS NOW, BUT IF YOU'RE READING THIS STORY AFTER VOLUME 13, IT DOESN'T MAKE SENSE!

SO JUST WEDGE THIS WHOLE STORY IN BETWEEN THE FINAL PAGE OF VOL. 13, WHERE HARUNA GOES TO TOKYO, AND THE PREVIOUS PAGES, WHERE YOH GOES TO TOKYO AFTER HE GRADUATES. AGAIN, I'M SORRY!

THIS STORY OF THEIR LONG-DISTANCE RELATIONSHIP WILL KEEP GOING FOR A WHILE LONGER! BUT I DIDN'T EVEN EXPLAIN THOSE CRITICAL PIECES OF INFO AND JUST KEPT ON WRITING.

A FEW YEARS AGO, I DID SOME JUDGING AT A MANGA SCHOOL, AND I MADE THIS TOTALLY SHAMELESS COMMENT: "MAKE SURE NINE OUT OF TEN READERS UNDERSTAND WHAT YOU'RE WRITING ABOUT!" WAY TO NOT TAKE MY OWN ADVICE, HUH?

BUT WHAT'S DONE IS DONE. I'LL BE MORE CAREFUL FROM NOW ON.

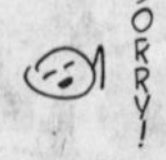
SORRY!

SINCE THE TITLE IS "LONG-DISTANCE LOVE DEBUT," I IMAGINE SOME OF YOU CAUGHT ON, BUT IT'S STILL CONFUSING. IT WAS SO CARELESS OF ME.

BUT DESPITE MY FLAWS, I HOPE YOU'LL KEEP READING MY WORK. THANK YOU.

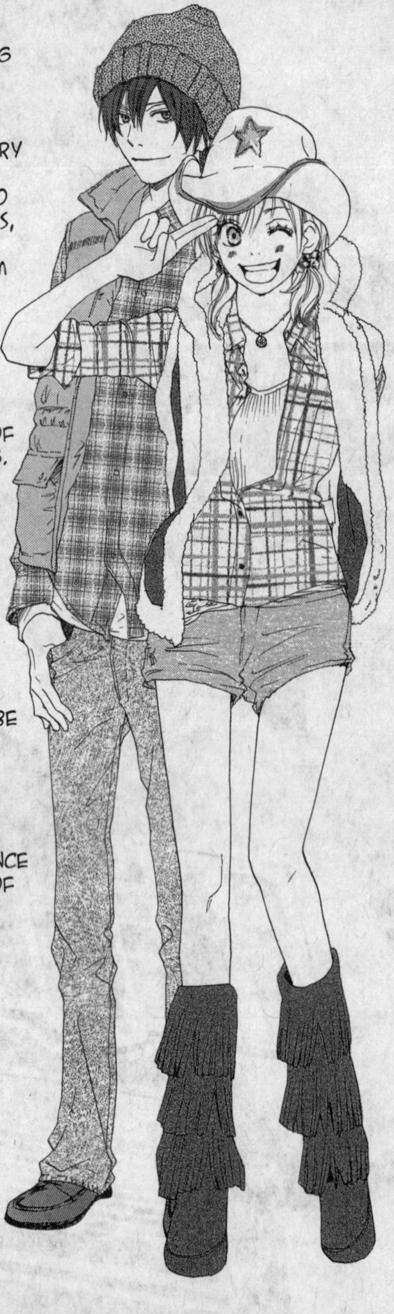

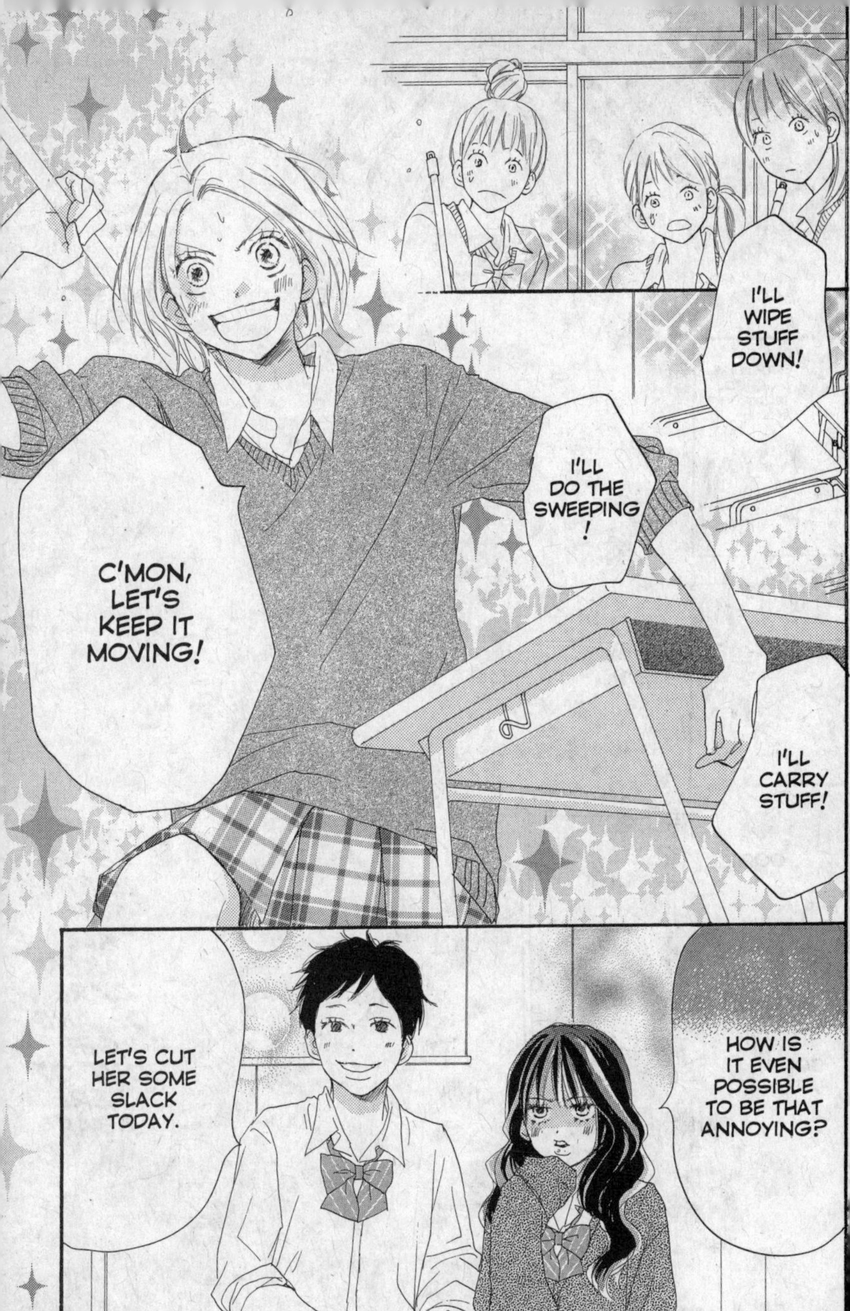
I'LL WIPE STUFF DOWN!
I'LL DO THE SWEEPING!
I'LL CARRY STUFF!
C'MON, LET'S KEEP IT MOVING!
HOW IS IT EVEN POSSIBLE TO BE THAT ANNOYING?
LET'S CUT HER SOME SLACK TODAY.

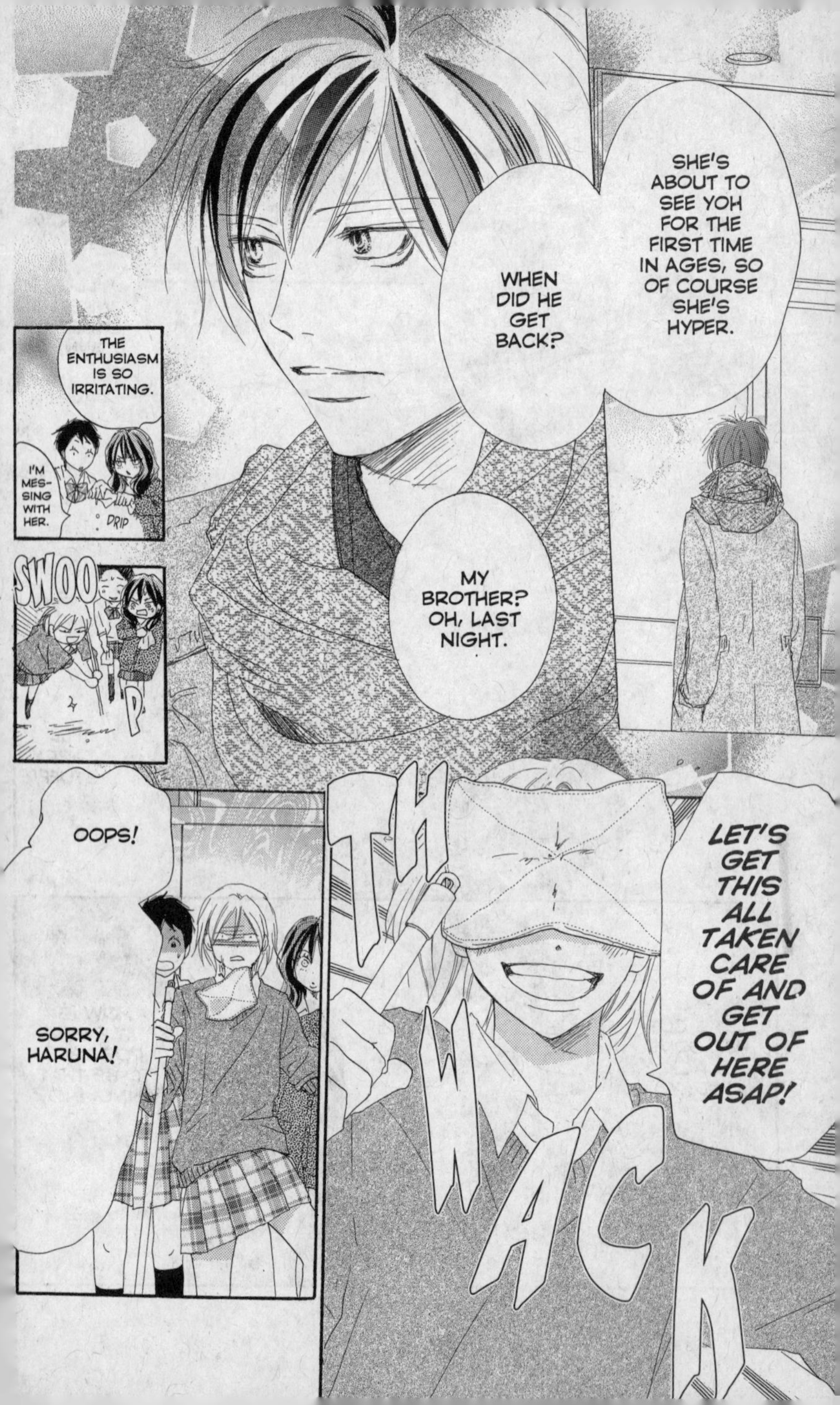
SHE'S ABOUT TO SEE YOH FOR THE FIRST TIME IN AGES, SO OF COURSE SHE'S HYPER.
WHEN DID HE GET BACK?
MY BROTHER? OH, LAST NIGHT.
THE ENTHUSIASM IS SO IRRITATING.
I'M MES-SING WITH HER.
DRIP
SWOOP
LET'S GET THIS ALL TAKEN CARE OF AND GET OUT OF HERE ASAP!
THWACK
OOPS!
SORRY, HARUNA!

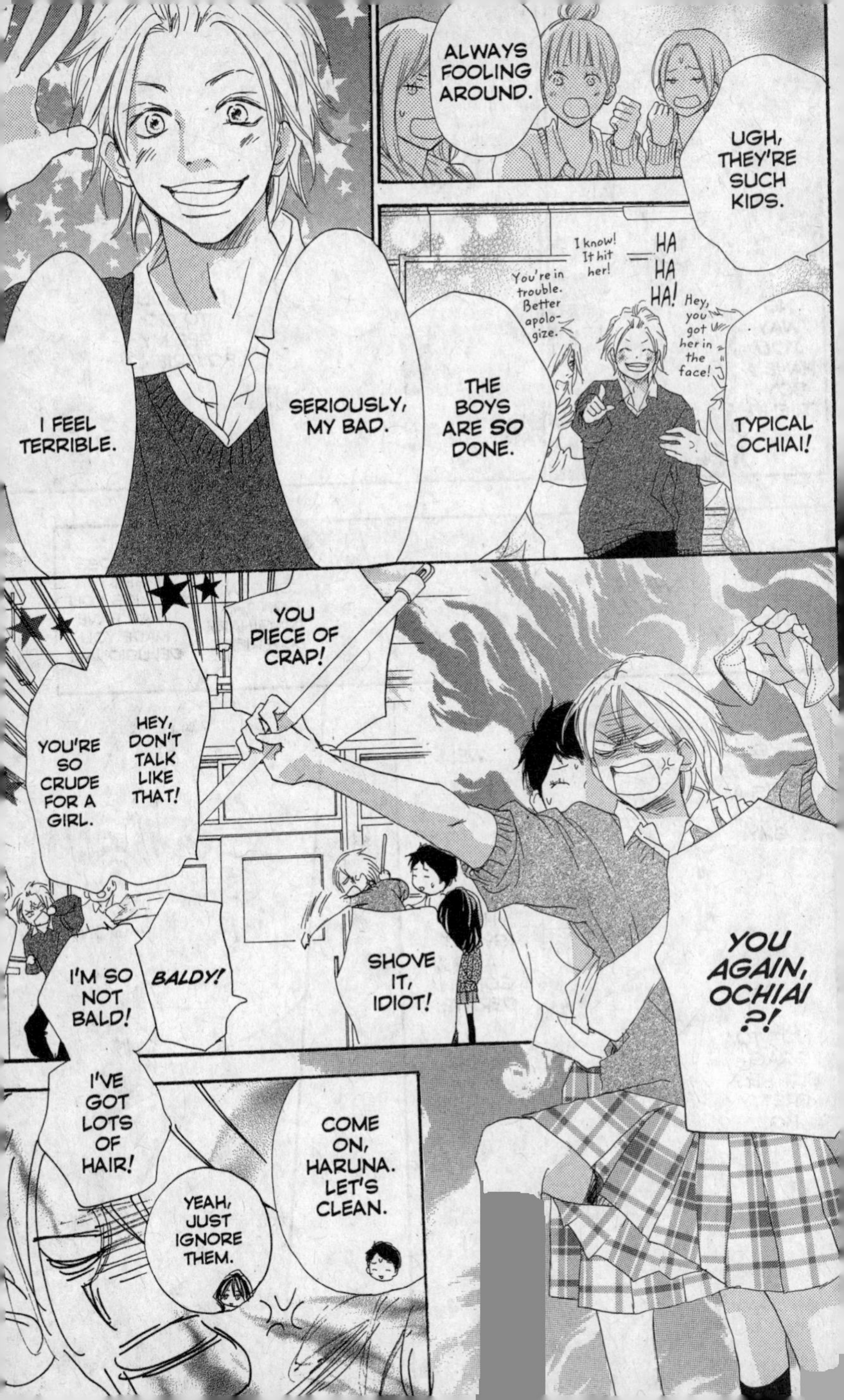
ALWAYS FOOLING AROUND.
UGH, THEY'RE SUCH KIDS.
TYPICAL OCHIAI!
Hey, you got her in the face!
HA HA HA!
I know! It hit her!
You're in trouble. Better apologize.
THE BOYS ARE SO DONE.
SERIOUSLY, MY BAD.
I FEEL TERRIBLE.
YOU AGAIN, OCHIAI?!
SHOVE IT, IDIOT!
YOU PIECE OF CRAP!
HEY, DON'T TALK LIKE THAT!
YOU'RE SO CRUDE FOR A GIRL.
BALDY!
I'M SO NOT BALD!
I'VE GOT LOTS OF HAIR!
COME ON, HARUNA. LET'S CLEAN.
YEAH, JUST IGNORE THEM.

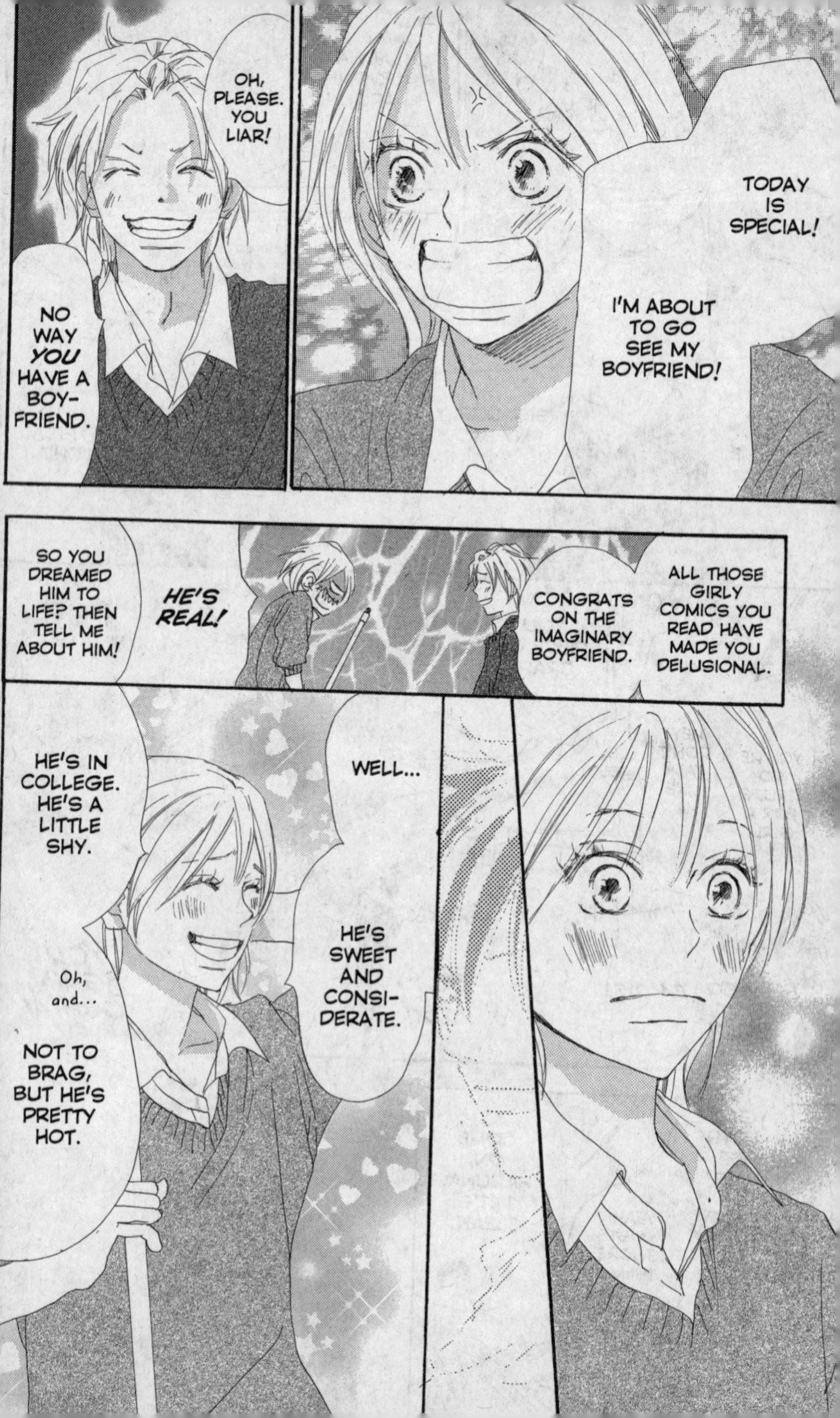
TODAY IS SPECIAL!
I'M ABOUT TO GO SEE MY BOYFRIEND!
OH, PLEASE. YOU LIAR!
NO WAY YOU HAVE A BOY-FRIEND.
ALL THOSE GIRLY COMICS YOU READ HAVE MADE YOU DELUSIONAL.
CONGRATS ON THE IMAGINARY BOYFRIEND.
HE'S REAL!
SO YOU DREAMED HIM TO LIFE? THEN TELL ME ABOUT HIM!
WELL...
HE'S SWEET AND CONSI-DERATE.
HE'S IN COLLEGE. HE'S A LITTLE SHY.
Oh, and...
NOT TO BRAG, BUT HE'S PRETTY HOT.

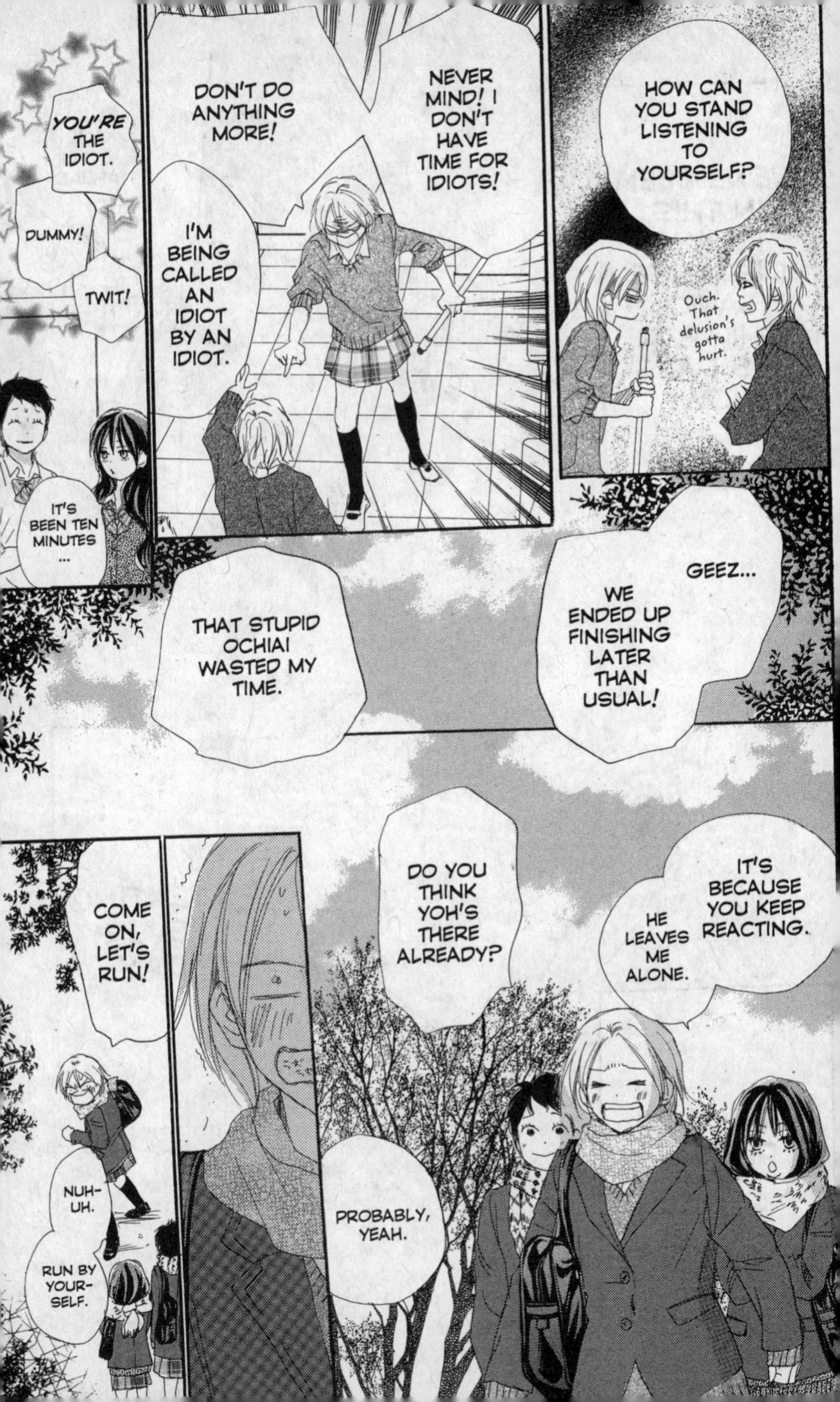
HOW CAN YOU STAND LISTENING TO YOURSELF?
Ouch. That delusion's gotta hurt.
NEVER MIND! I DON'T HAVE TIME FOR IDIOTS!
DON'T DO ANYTHING MORE!
I'M BEING CALLED AN IDIOT BY AN IDIOT.
YOU'RE THE IDIOT.
DUMMY!
TWIT!
IT'S BEEN TEN MINUTES ...
GEEZ...
WE ENDED UP FINISHING LATER THAN USUAL!
THAT STUPID OCHIAI WASTED MY TIME.
IT'S BECAUSE YOU KEEP REACTING.
HE LEAVES ME ALONE.
DO YOU THINK YOH'S THERE ALREADY?
PROBABLY, YEAH.
COME ON, LET'S RUN!
NUH-UH.
RUN BY YOURSELF.

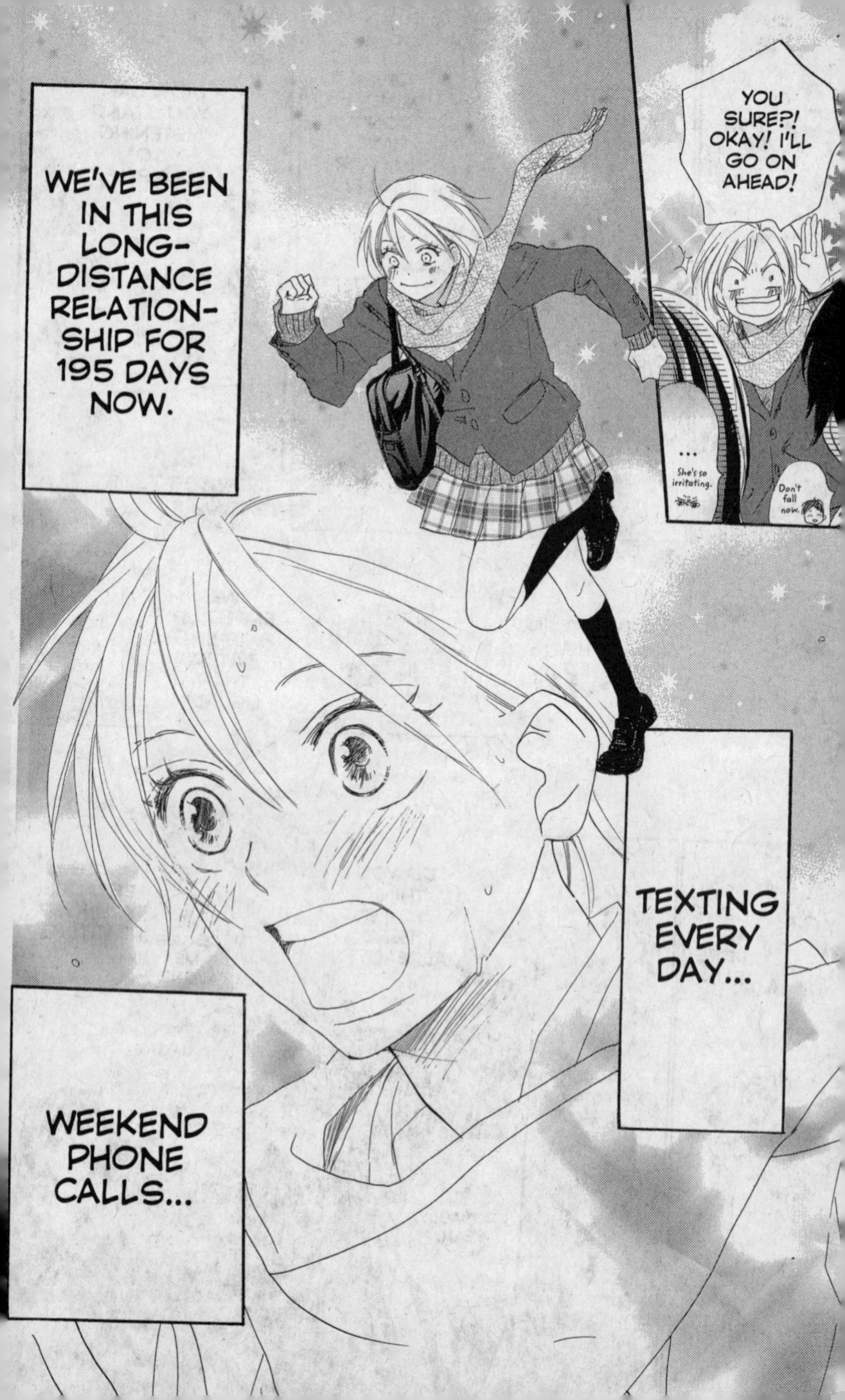
YOU SURE?! OKAY! I'LL GO ON AHEAD!
...
She's so irritating.
Don't fall now.
WE'VE BEEN IN THIS LONG-DISTANCE RELATION-SHIP FOR 195 DAYS NOW.
TEXTING EVERY DAY...
WEEKEND PHONE CALLS...

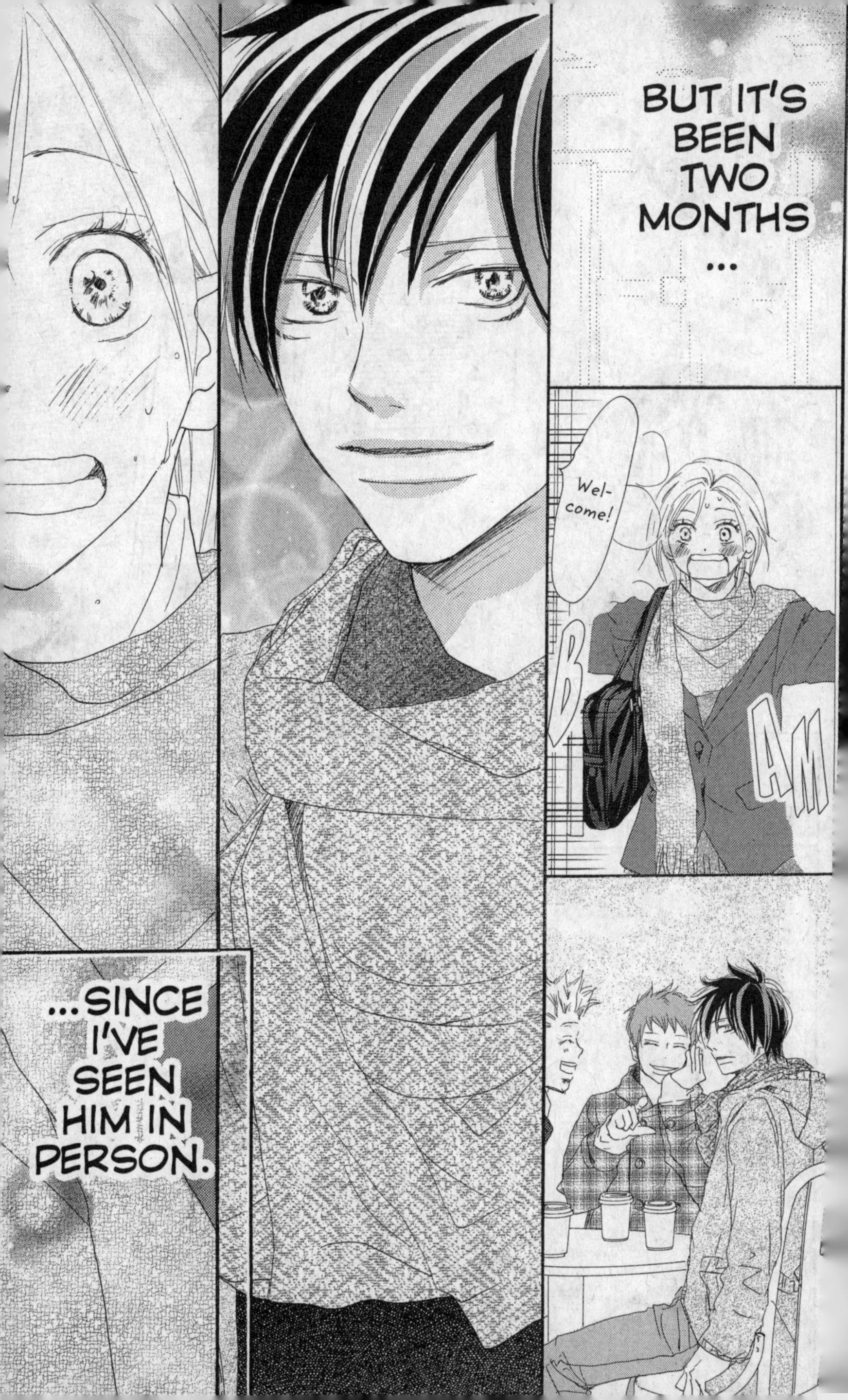
BUT IT'S BEEN TWO MONTHS ...
Wel-come!
BAM
...SINCE I'VE SEEN HIM IN PERSON.

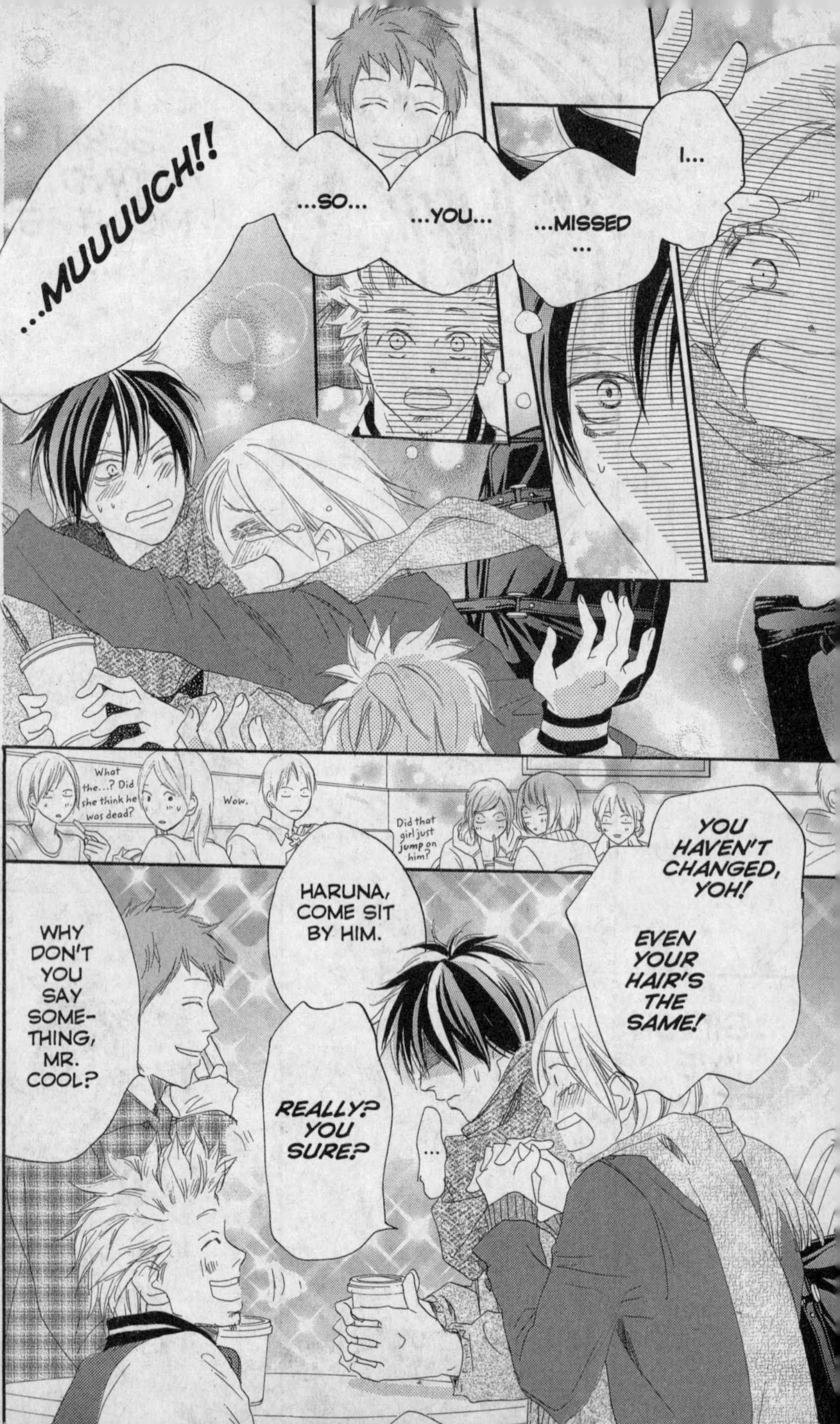
I...
...MISSED ...
...YOU...
...SO...
...MUUUUCH!!
Did that girl just jump on him?
What the...? Did she think he was dead?
Wow.
YOU HAVEN'T CHANGED, YOH!
EVEN YOUR HAIR'S THE SAME!
HARUNA, COME SIT BY HIM.
...
REALLY? YOU SURE?
WHY DON'T YOU SAY SOME-THING, MR. COOL?

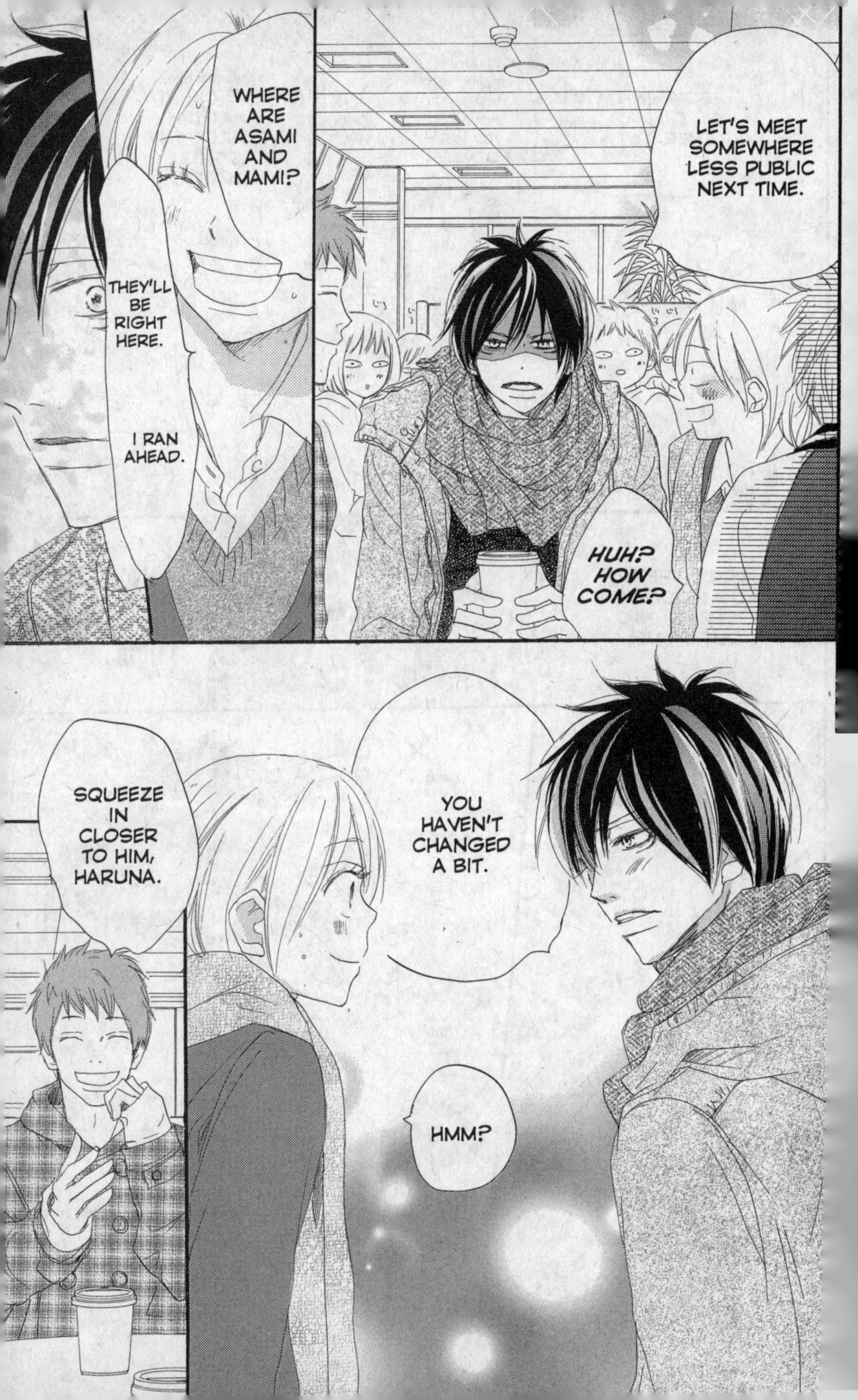
LET'S MEET SOMEWHERE LESS PUBLIC NEXT TIME.
HUH? HOW COME?
WHERE ARE ASAMI AND MAMI?
THEY'LL BE RIGHT HERE.
I RAN AHEAD.
YOU HAVEN'T CHANGED A BIT.
HMM?
SQUEEZE IN CLOSER TO HIM, HARUNA.

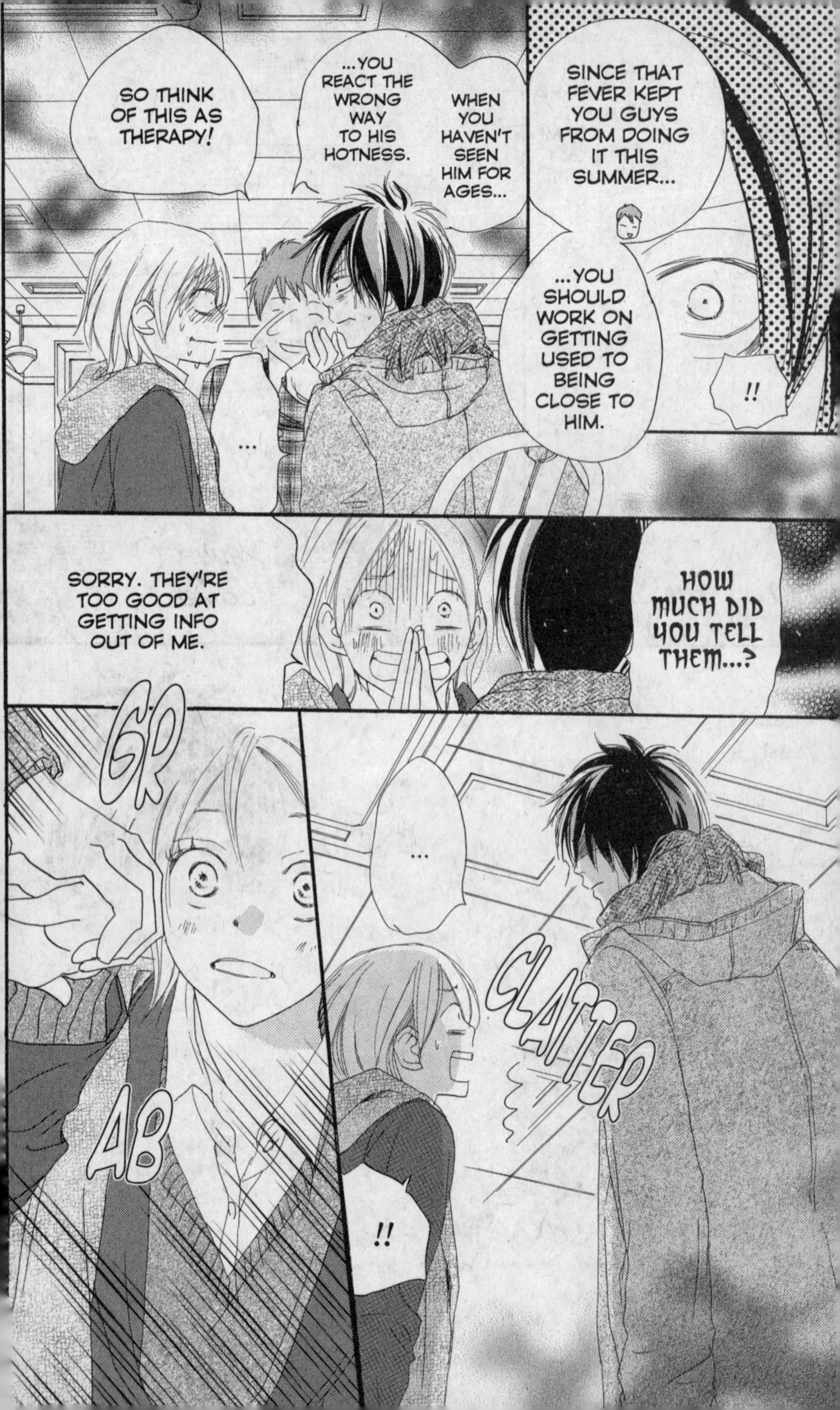
SINCE THAT FEVER KEPT YOU GUYS FROM DOING IT THIS SUMMER...
...YOU SHOULD WORK ON GETTING USED TO BEING CLOSE TO HIM.
!!
WHEN YOU HAVEN'T SEEN HIM FOR AGES...
...YOU REACT THE WRONG WAY TO HIS HOTNESS.
SO THINK OF THIS AS THERAPY!
...
HOW MUCH DID YOU TELL THEM...?
SORRY. THEY'RE TOO GOOD AT GETTING INFO OUT OF ME.
...
CLATTER
!!
GR
AB

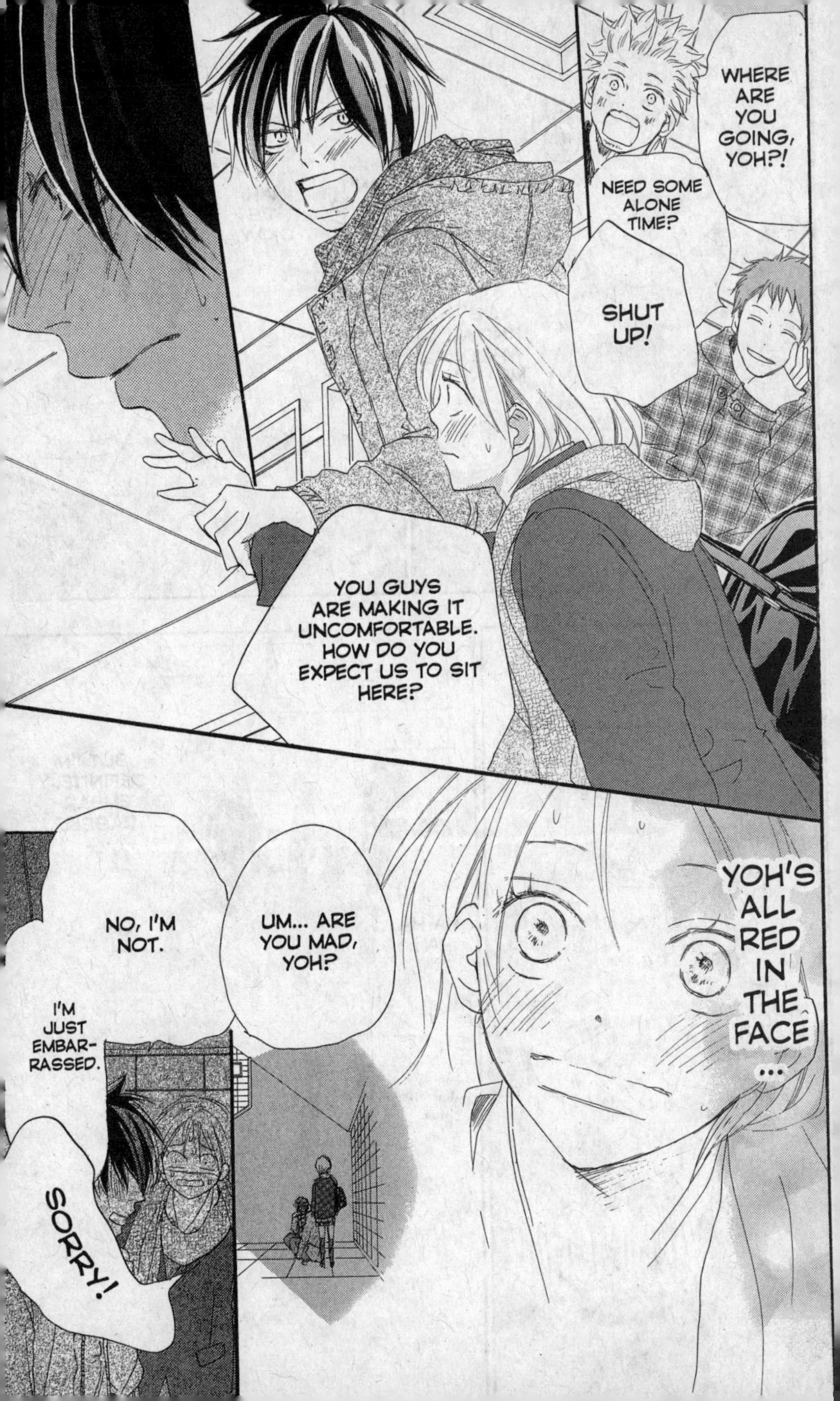
WHERE ARE YOU GOING, YOH?!
NEED SOME ALONE TIME?
SHUT UP!
YOU GUYS ARE MAKING IT UNCOMFORTABLE. HOW DO YOU EXPECT US TO SIT HERE?
YOH'S ALL RED IN THE FACE...
UM... ARE YOU MAD, YOH?
NO, I'M NOT.
I'M JUST EMBARRASSED.
SORRY!

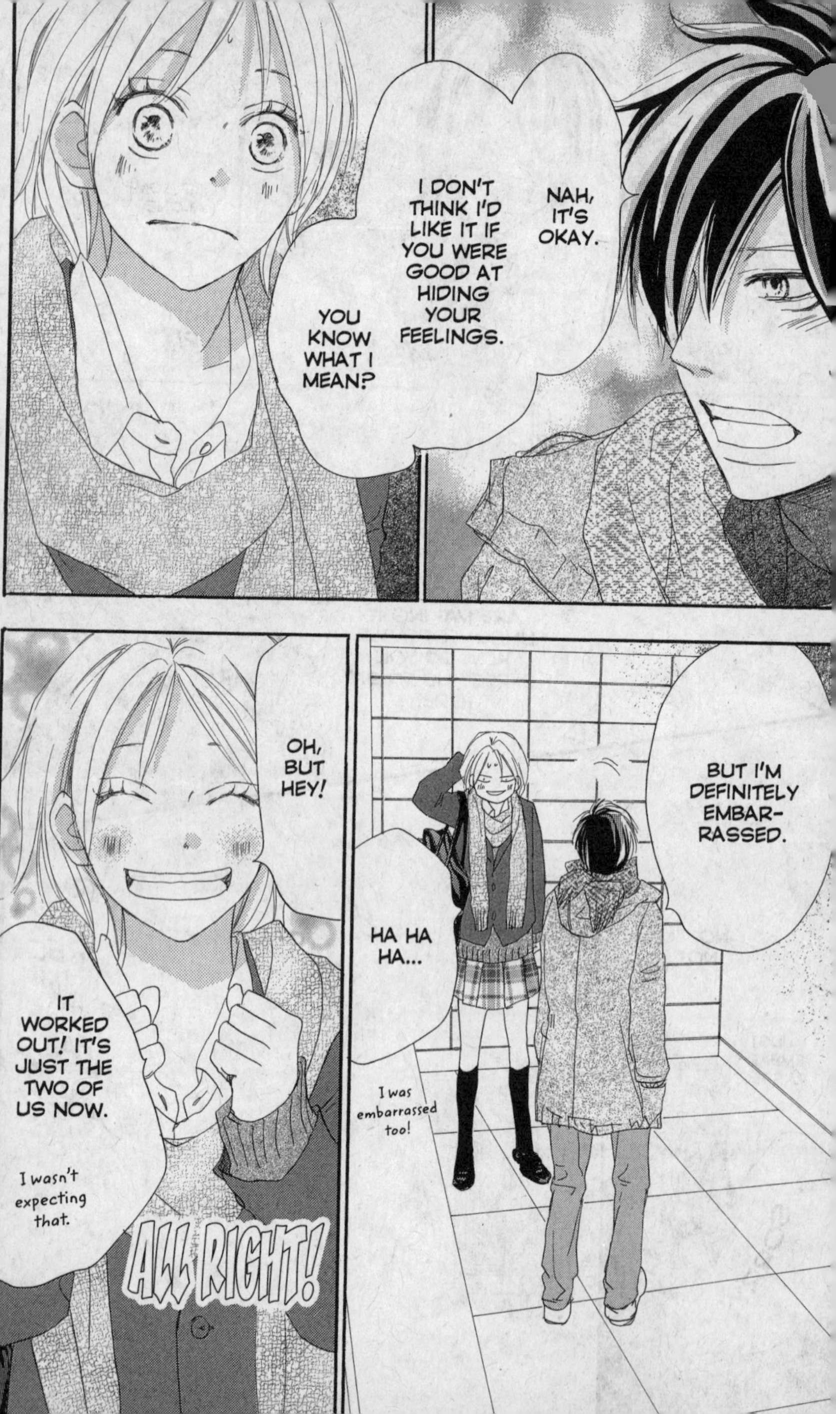
NAH, IT'S OKAY.
I DON'T THINK I'D LIKE IT IF YOU WERE GOOD AT HIDING YOUR FEELINGS.
YOU KNOW WHAT I MEAN?
BUT I'M DEFINITELY EMBARRASSED.
HA HA HA...
I was embarrassed too!
OH, BUT HEY!
IT WORKED OUT! IT'S JUST THE TWO OF US NOW.
I wasn't expecting that.
ALL RIGHT!

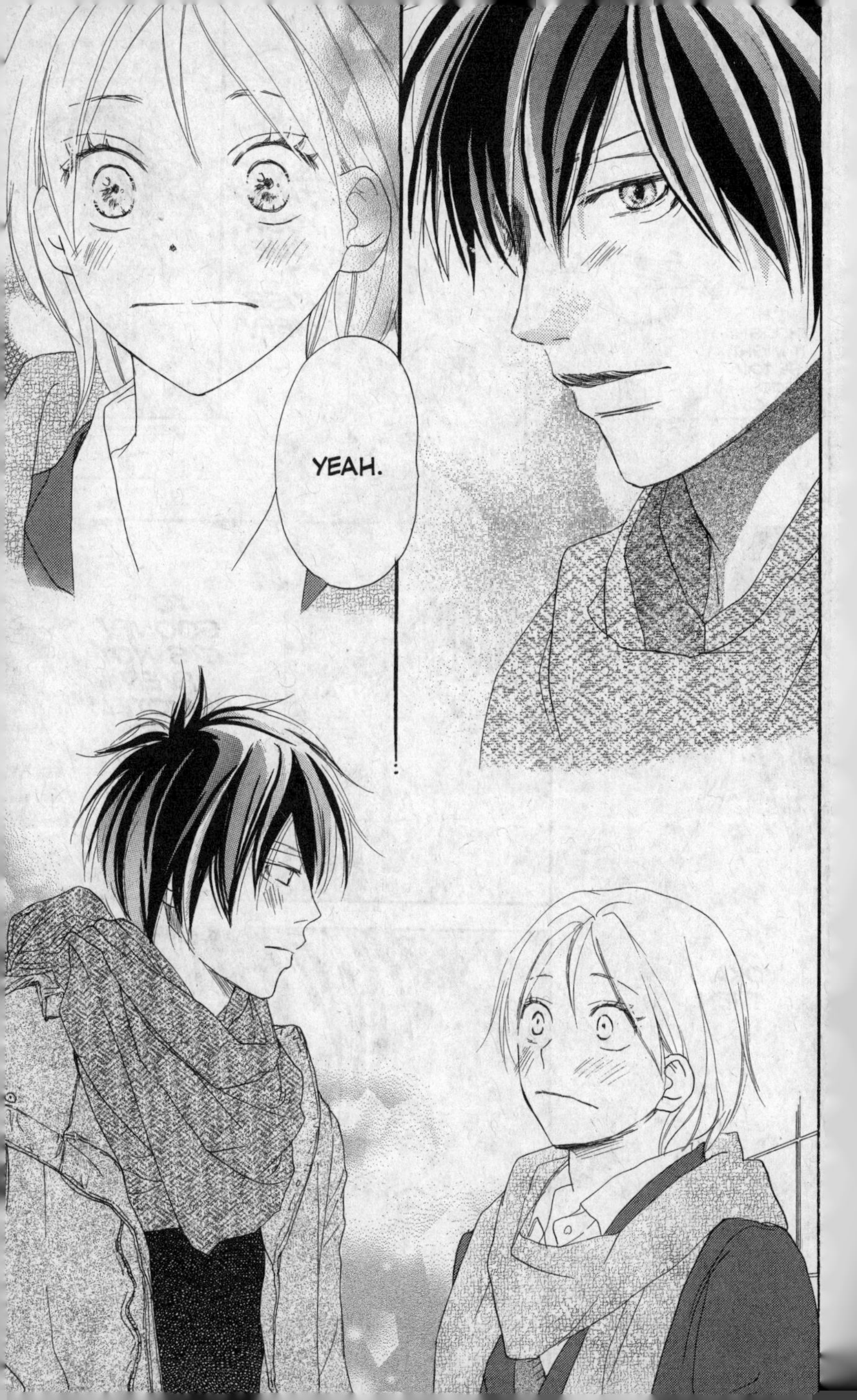
YEAH.

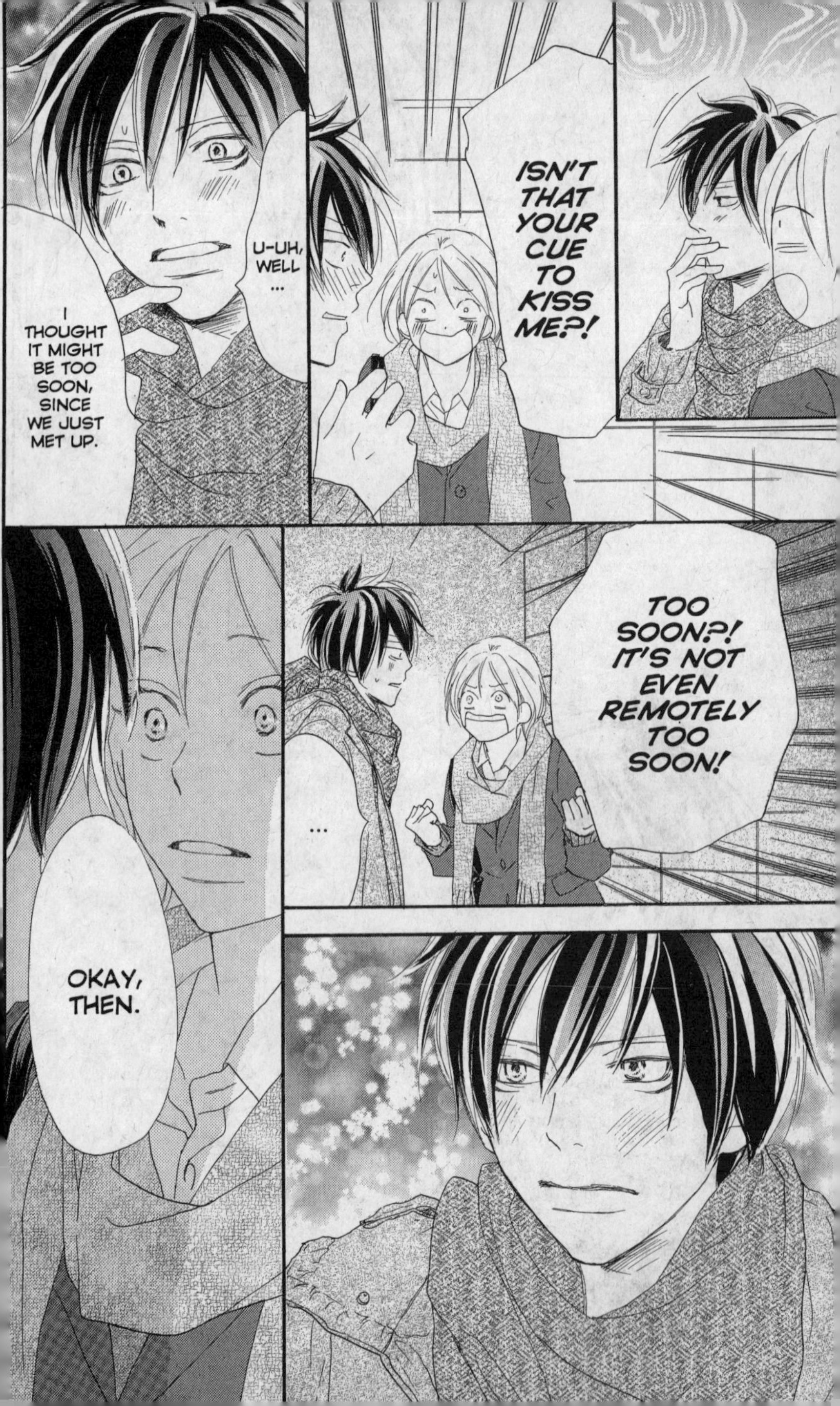
ISN'T THAT YOUR CUE TO KISS ME?!
U-UH, WELL ...
I THOUGHT IT MIGHT BE TOO SOON, SINCE WE JUST MET UP.
TOO SOON?! IT'S NOT EVEN REMOTELY TOO SOON!
...
OKAY, THEN.

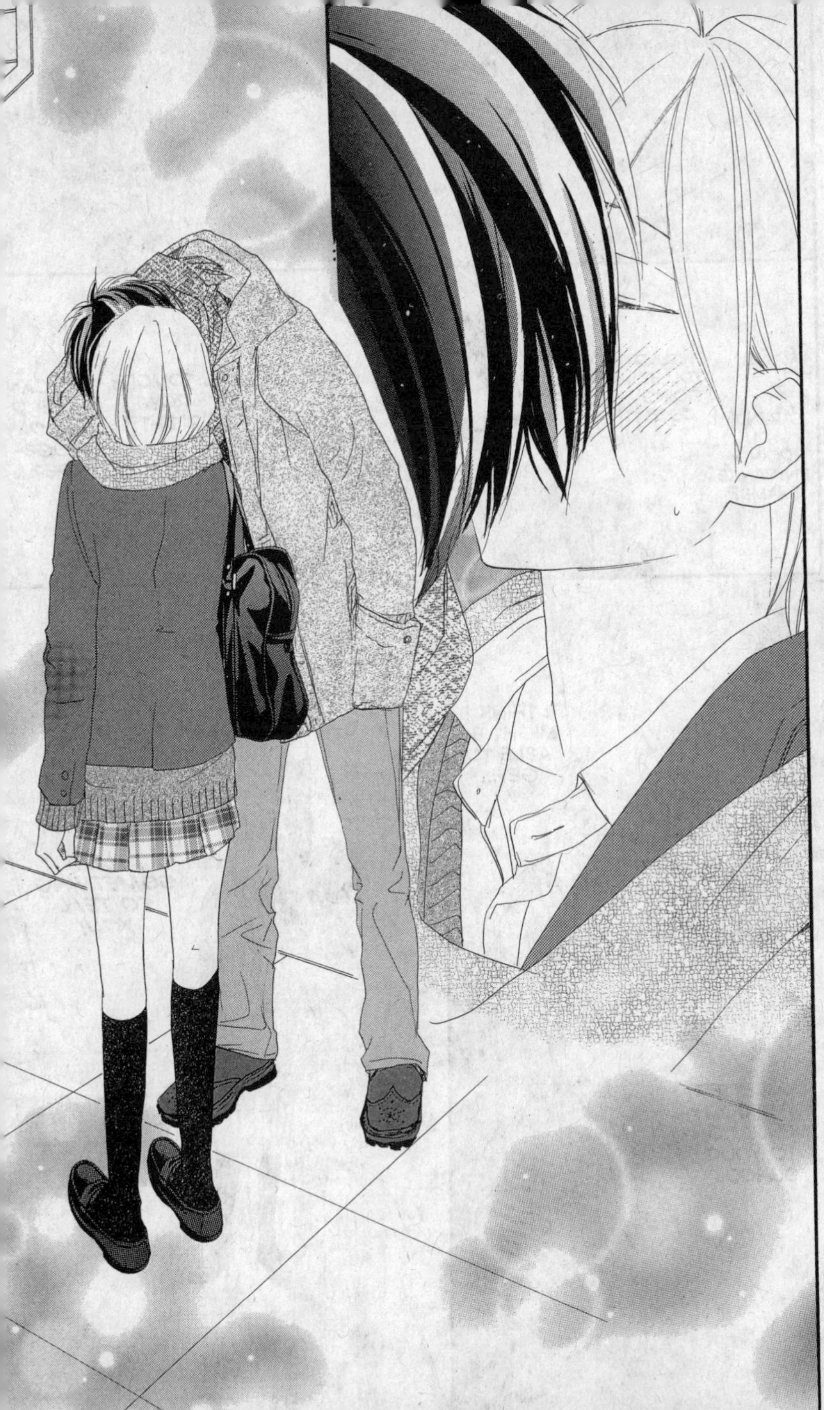

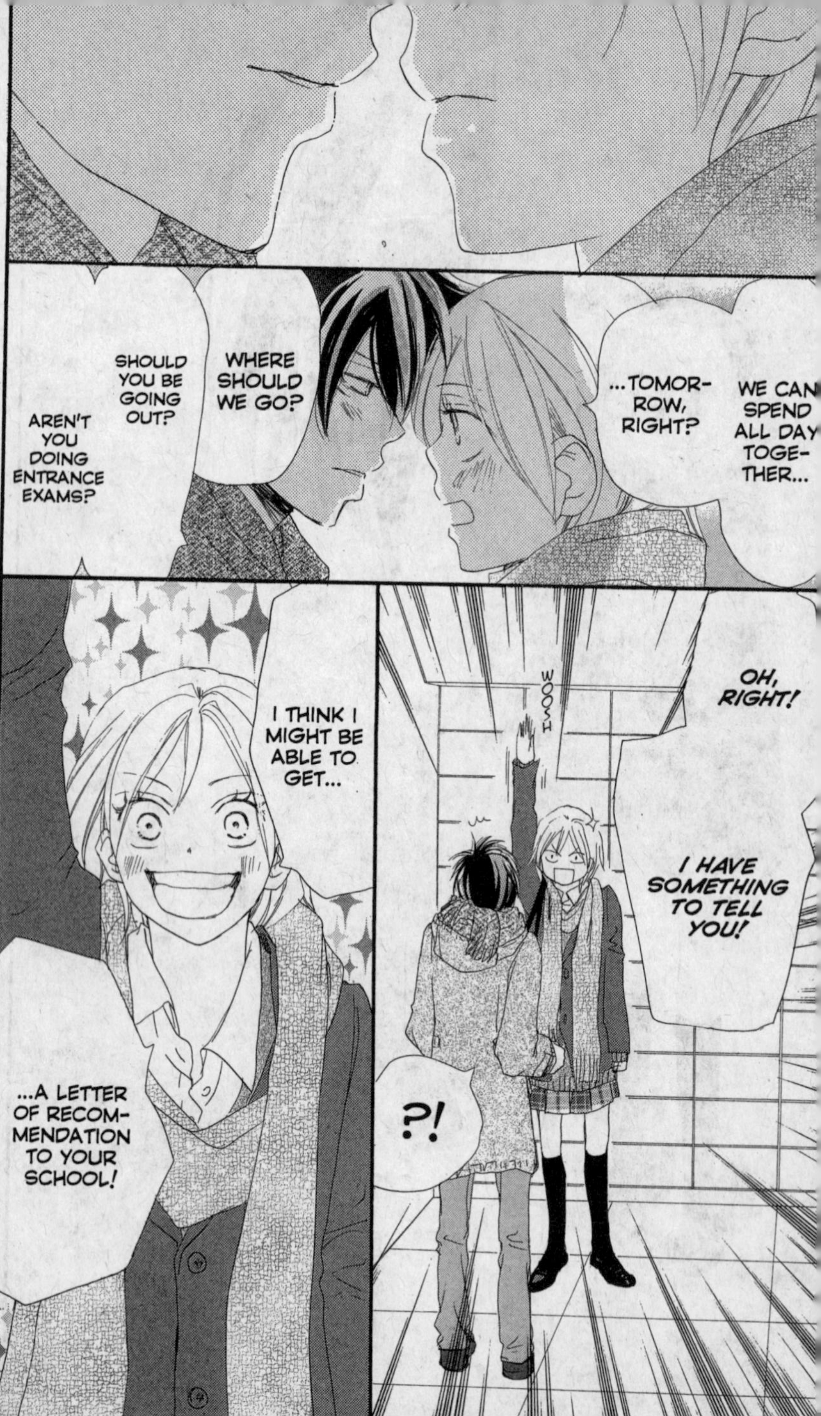
WE CAN SPEND ALL DAY TOGETHER...
...TOMORROW, RIGHT?
WHERE SHOULD WE GO?
SHOULD YOU BE GOING OUT?
AREN'T YOU DOING ENTRANCE EXAMS?
OH, RIGHT!
I HAVE SOMETHING TO TELL YOU!
WOOSH
?!
I THINK I MIGHT BE ABLE TO GET...
...A LETTER OF RECOMMENDATION TO YOUR SCHOOL!

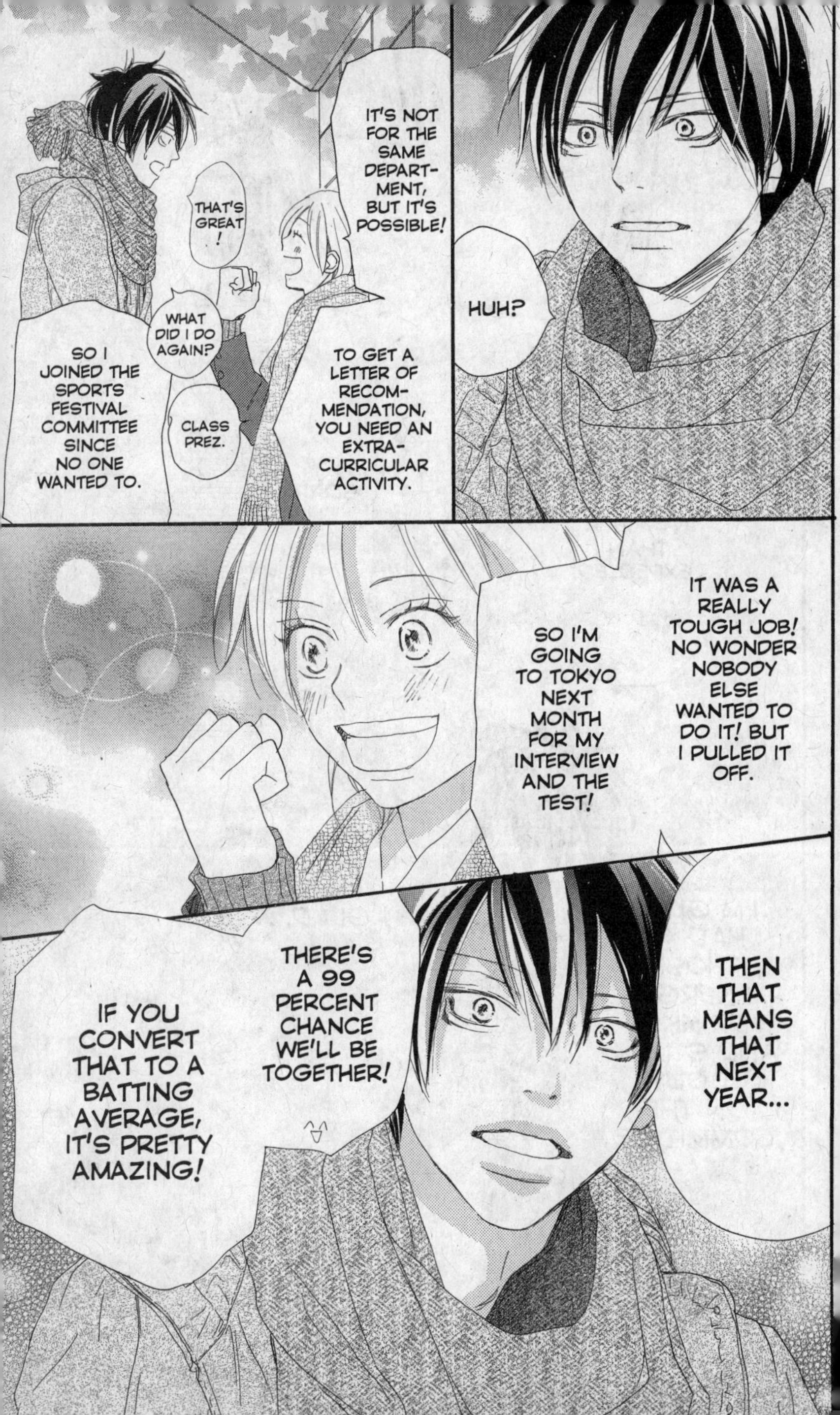
HUH?
IT'S NOT FOR THE SAME DEPARTMENT, BUT IT'S POSSIBLE!
THAT'S GREAT!
TO GET A LETTER OF RECOMMENDATION, YOU NEED AN EXTRACURRICULAR ACTIVITY.
WHAT DID I DO AGAIN?
CLASS PREZ.
SO I JOINED THE SPORTS FESTIVAL COMMITTEE SINCE NO ONE WANTED TO.
IT WAS A REALLY TOUGH JOB! NO WONDER NOBODY ELSE WANTED TO DO IT! BUT I PULLED IT OFF.
SO I'M GOING TO TOKYO NEXT MONTH FOR MY INTERVIEW AND THE TEST!
THEN THAT MEANS THAT NEXT YEAR...
THERE'S A 99 PERCENT CHANCE WE'LL BE TOGETHER!
IF YOU CONVERT THAT TO A BATTING AVERAGE, IT'S PRETTY AMAZING!

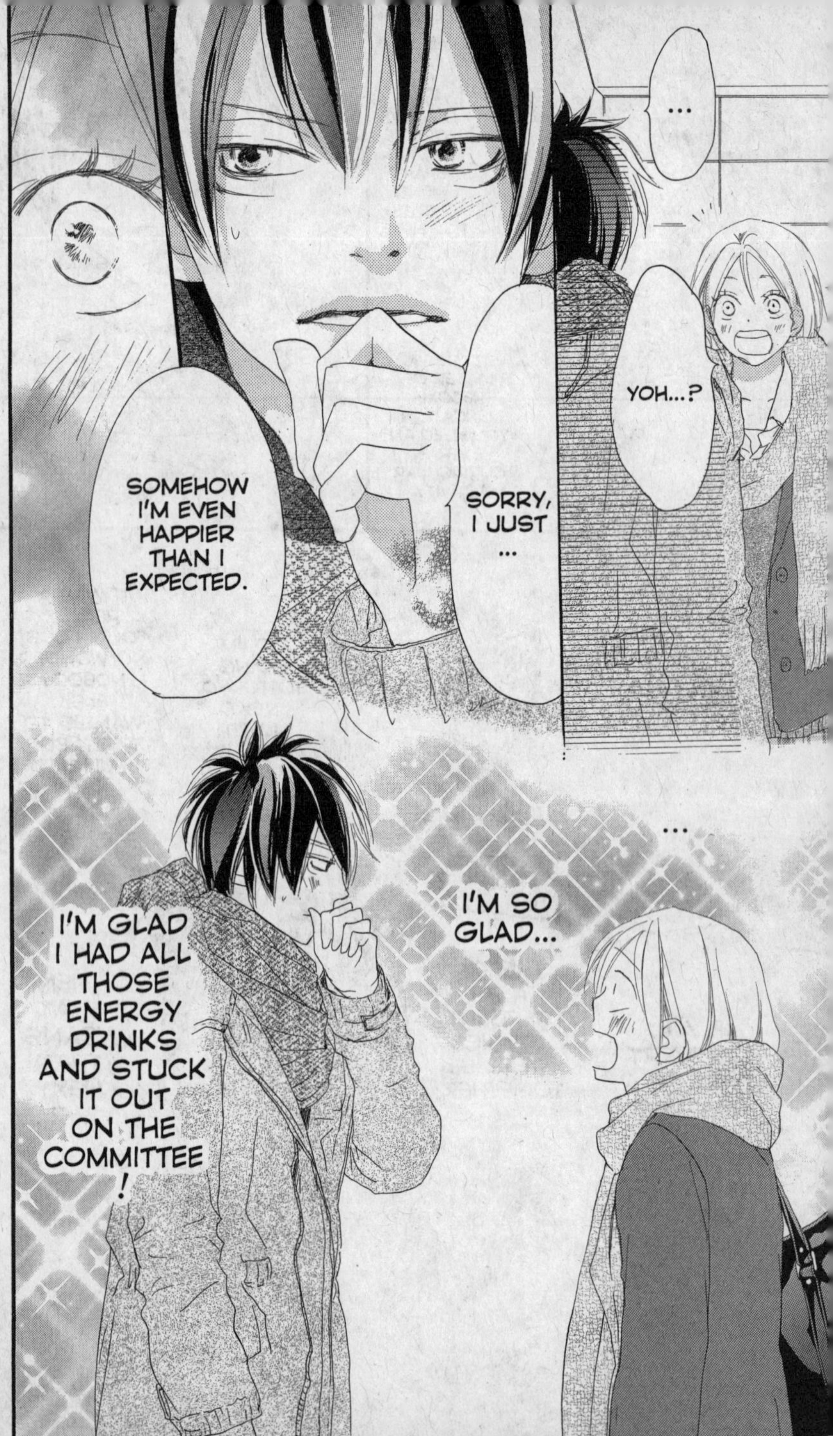
...
YOH...?
SORRY, I JUST ...
SOMEHOW I'M EVEN HAPPIER THAN I EXPECTED.
...
I'M SO GLAD...
I'M GLAD I HAD ALL THOSE ENERGY DRINKS AND STUCK IT OUT ON THE COMMITTEE!

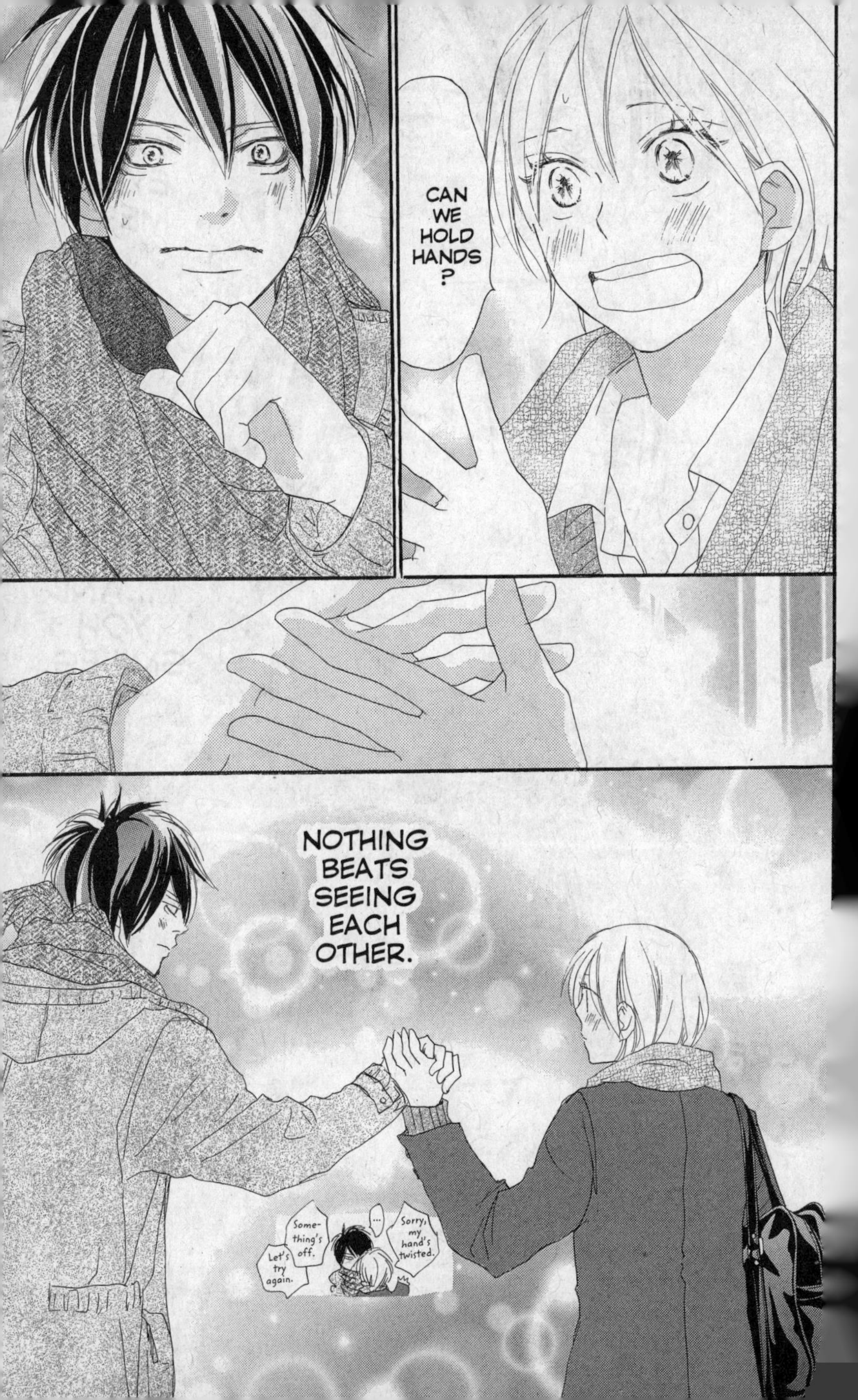
CAN WE HOLD HANDS?
NOTHING BEATS SEEING EACH OTHER.
Sorry, my hand's twisted.
...
Some-thing's off.
Let's try again.

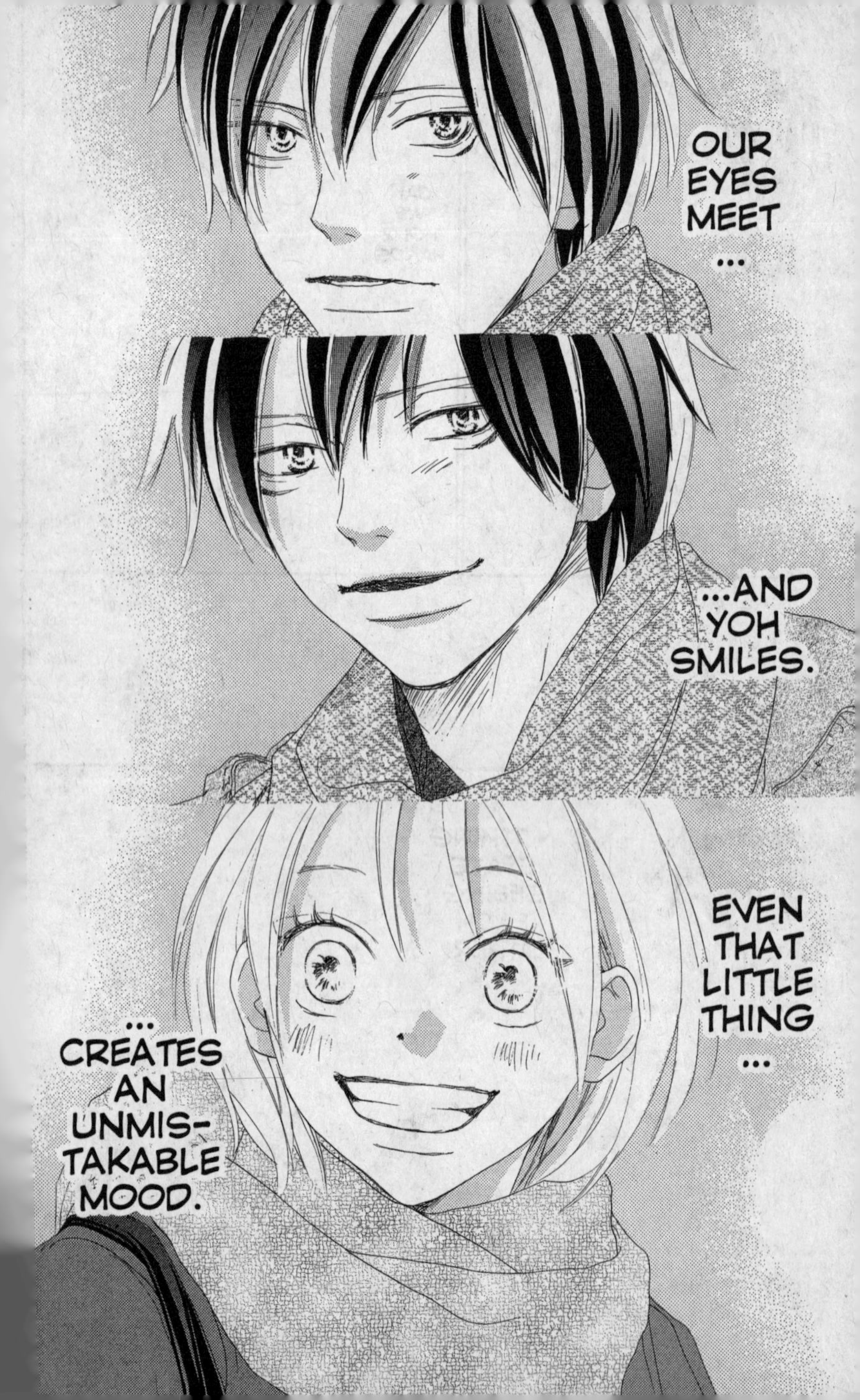
OUR EYES MEET ...
...AND YOH SMILES.
EVEN THAT LITTLE THING ...
... CREATES AN UNMIS-TAKABLE MOOD.

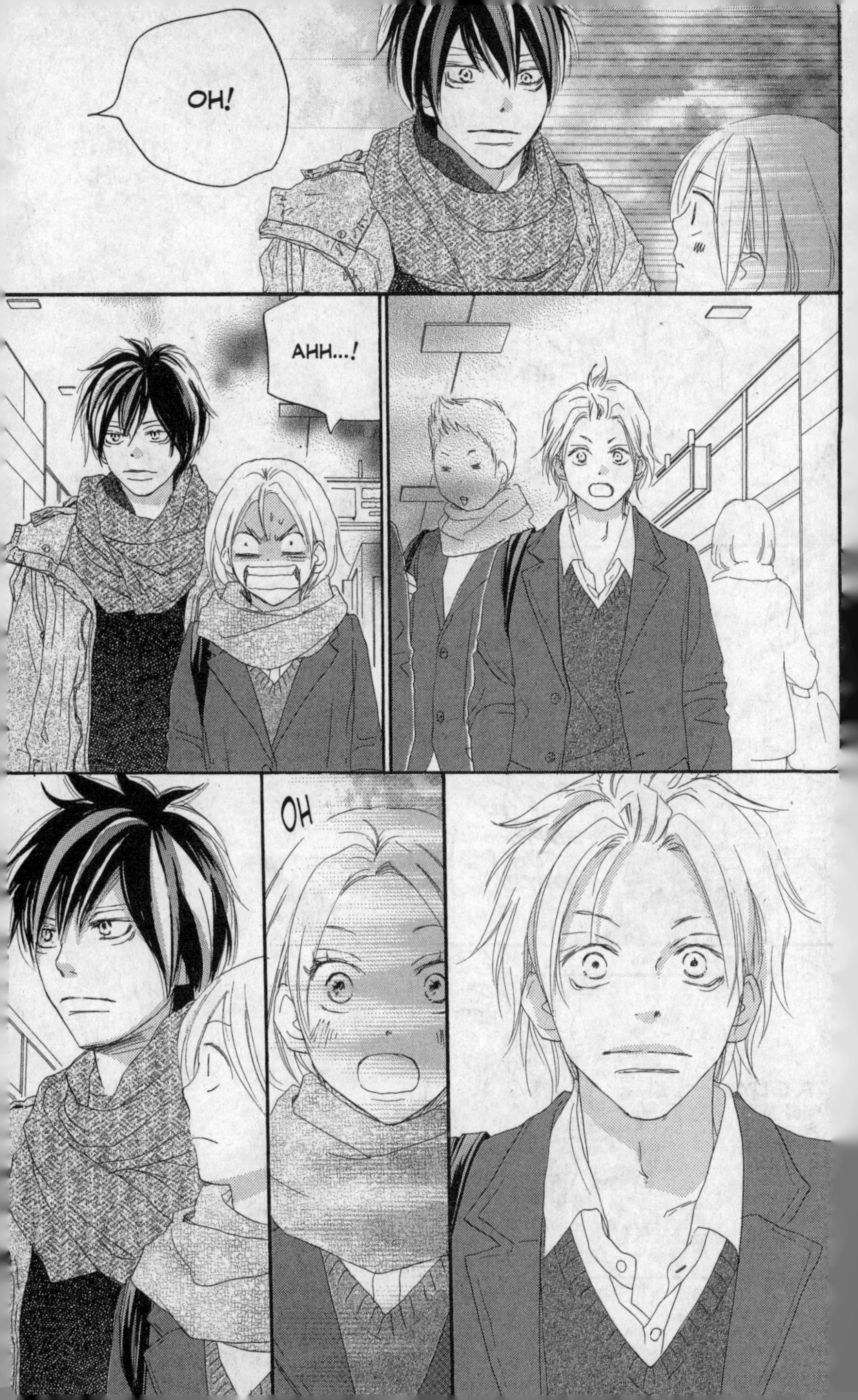
OH!
AHH...!
OH

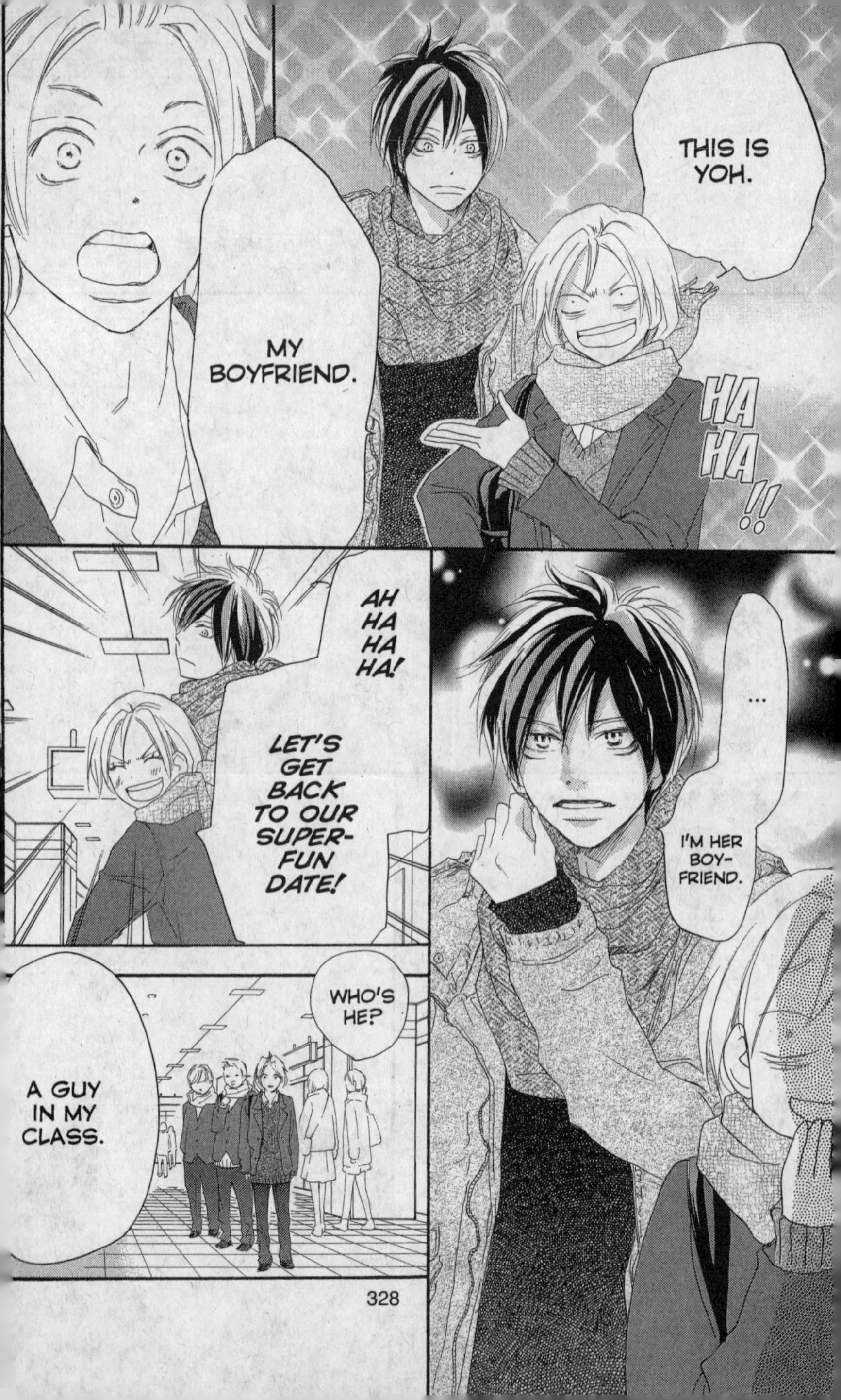
THIS IS YOH.
HA HA!!
MY BOYFRIEND.
...
I'M HER BOY-FRIEND.
AH HA HA HA!
LET'S GET BACK TO OUR SUPER-FUN DATE!
WHO'S HE?
A GUY IN MY CLASS.

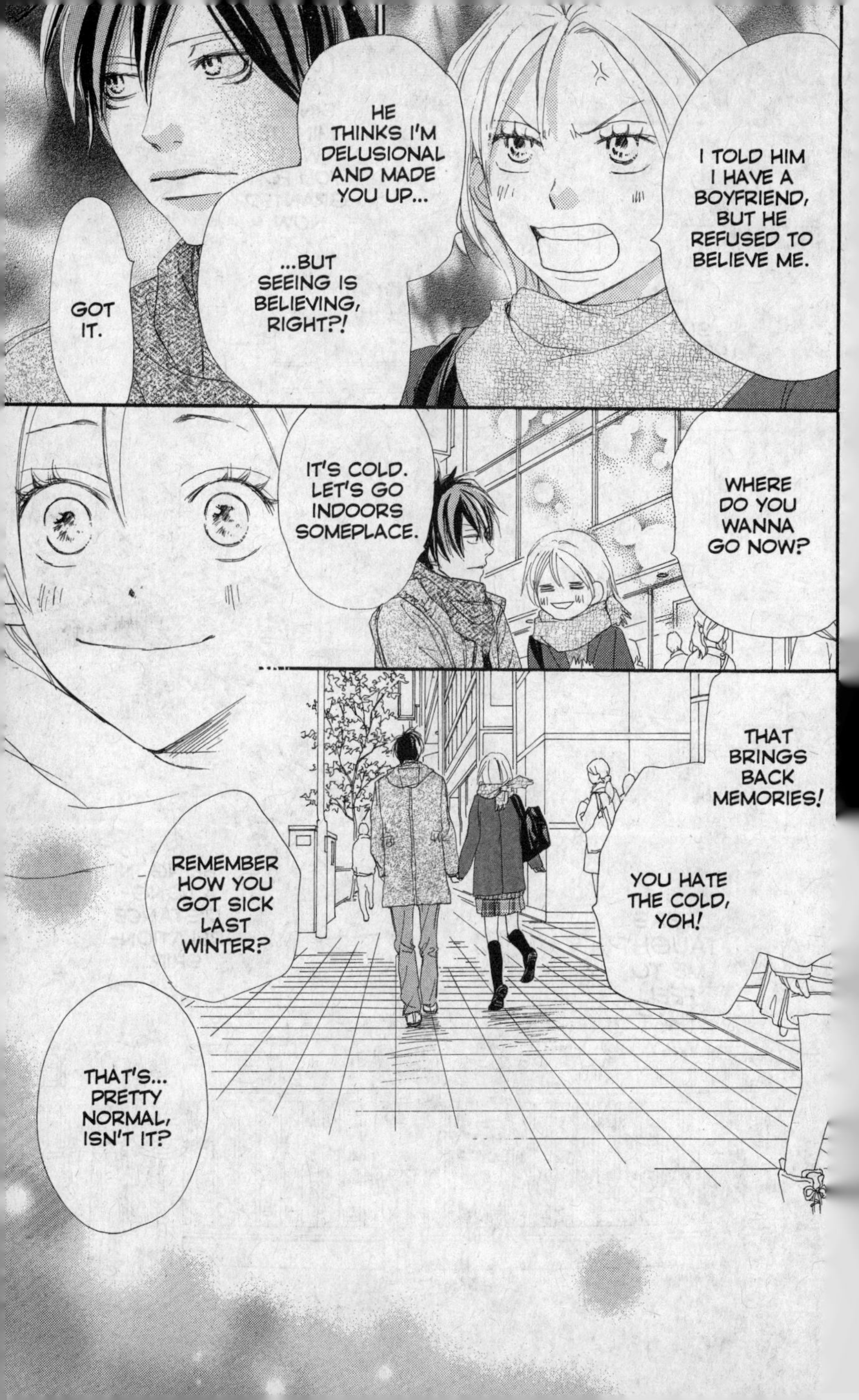
I TOLD HIM I HAVE A BOYFRIEND, BUT HE REFUSED TO BELIEVE ME.
HE THINKS I'M DELUSIONAL AND MADE YOU UP...
...BUT SEEING IS BELIEVING, RIGHT?!
GOT IT.
WHERE DO YOU WANNA GO NOW?
IT'S COLD. LET'S GO INDOORS SOMEPLACE.
THAT BRINGS BACK MEMORIES!
YOU HATE THE COLD, YOH!
REMEMBER HOW YOU GOT SICK LAST WINTER?
THAT'S... PRETTY NORMAL, ISN'T IT?

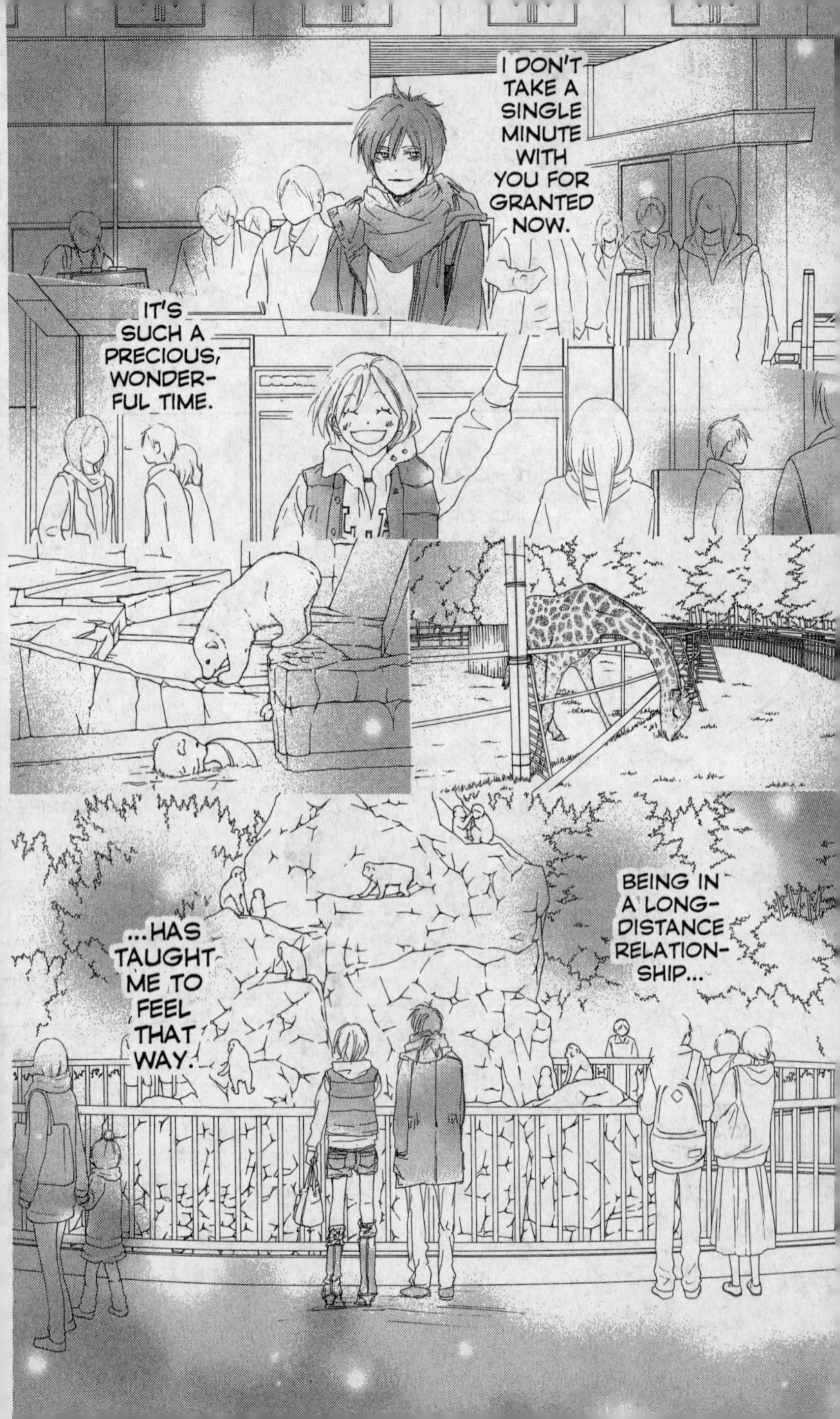
I DON'T TAKE A SINGLE MINUTE WITH YOU FOR GRANTED NOW.
IT'S SUCH A PRECIOUS, WONDERFUL TIME.
BEING IN A LONG-DISTANCE RELATIONSHIP...
...HAS TAUGHT ME TO FEEL THAT WAY.

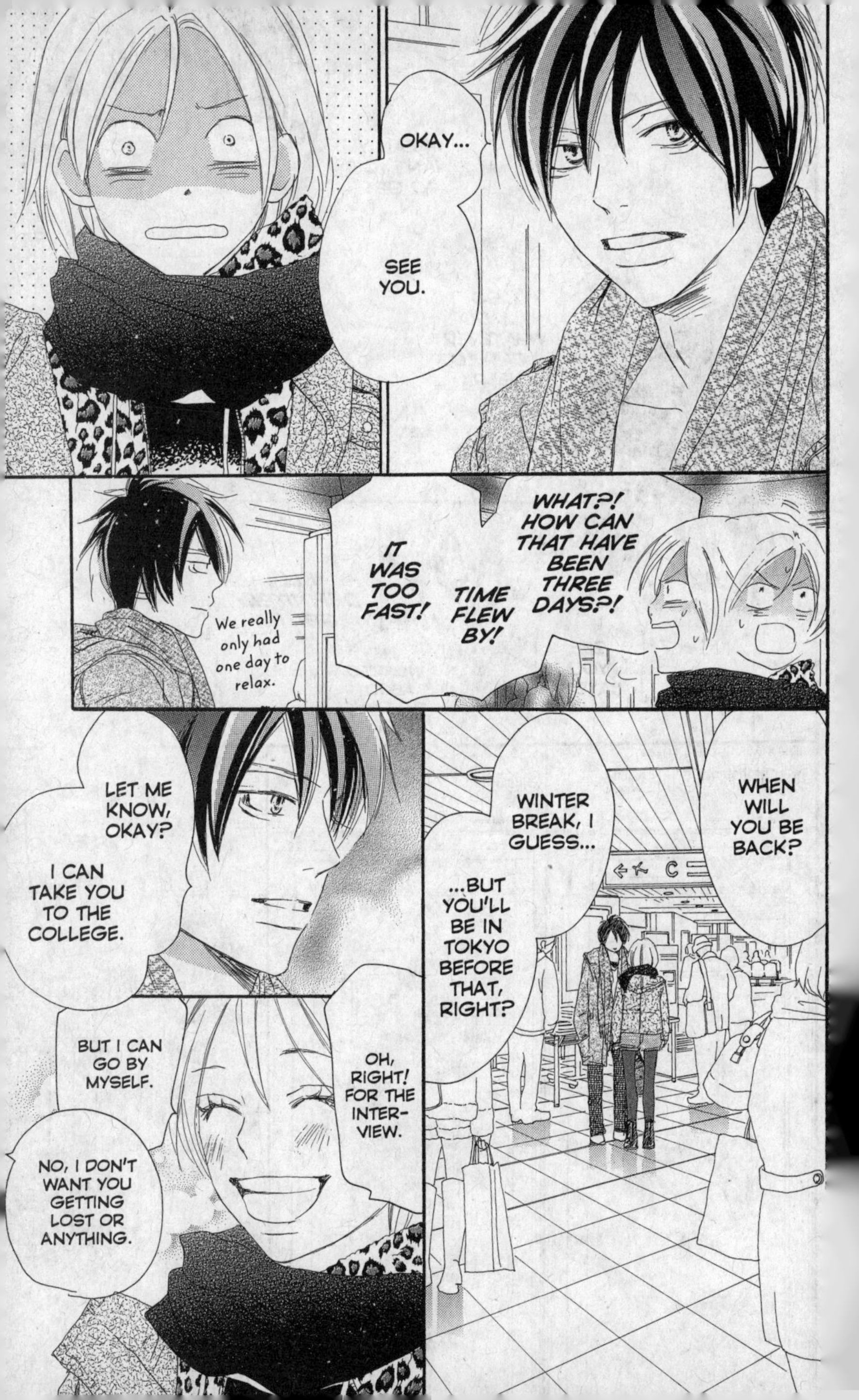
OKAY...
SEE YOU.
WHAT?! HOW CAN THAT HAVE BEEN THREE DAYS?!
TIME FLEW BY!
IT WAS TOO FAST!
We really only had one day to relax.
WHEN WILL YOU BE BACK?
WINTER BREAK, I GUESS...
...BUT YOU'LL BE IN TOKYO BEFORE THAT, RIGHT?
C
LET ME KNOW, OKAY?
I CAN TAKE YOU TO THE COLLEGE.
OH, RIGHT! FOR THE INTER-VIEW.
BUT I CAN GO BY MYSELF.
NO, I DON'T WANT YOU GETTING LOST OR ANYTHING.

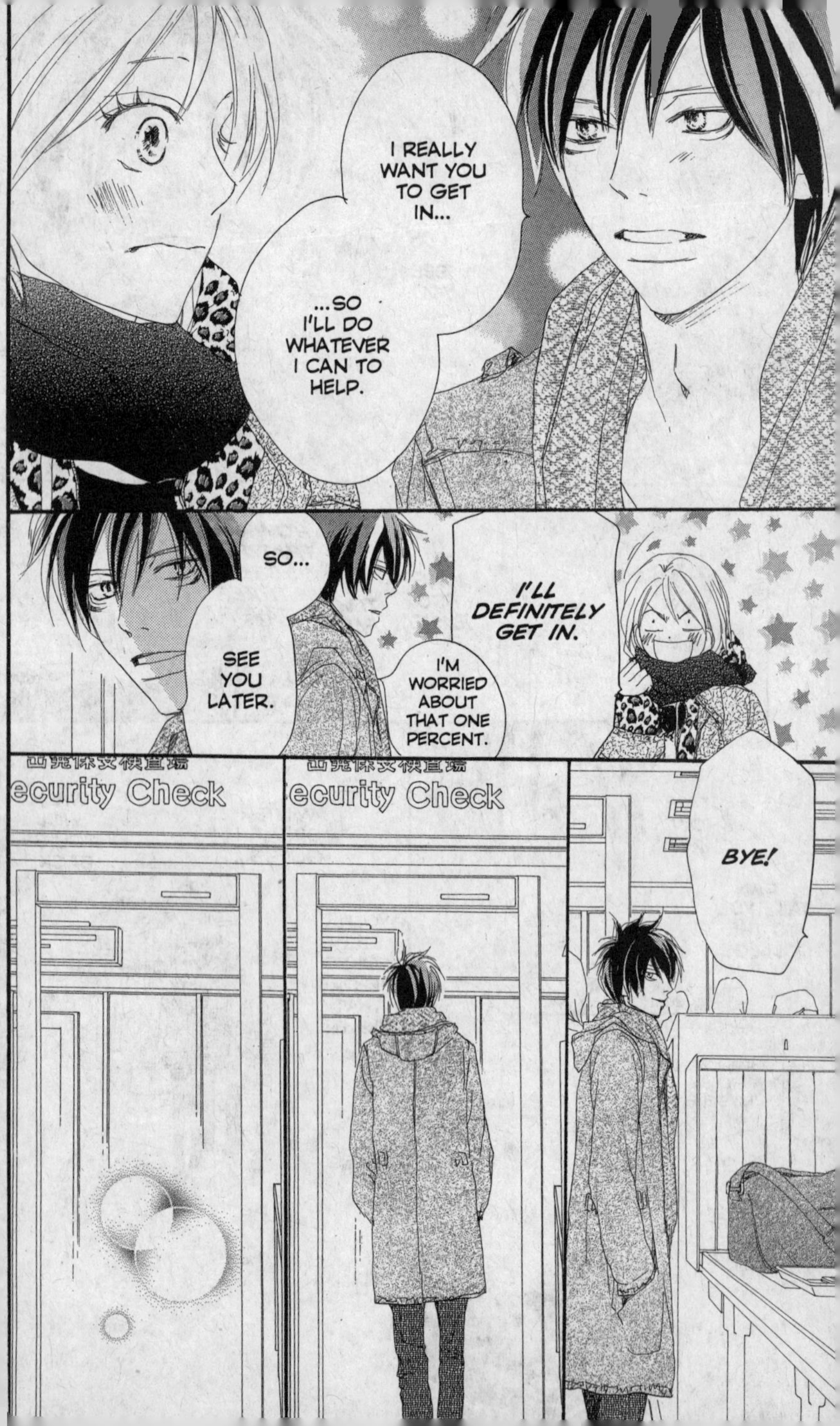
I REALLY WANT YOU TO GET IN...
...SO I'LL DO WHATEVER I CAN TO HELP.
I'LL DEFINITELY GET IN.
I'M WORRIED ABOUT THAT ONE PERCENT.
SO...
SEE YOU LATER.
BYE!
ecurity Check
ecurity Check

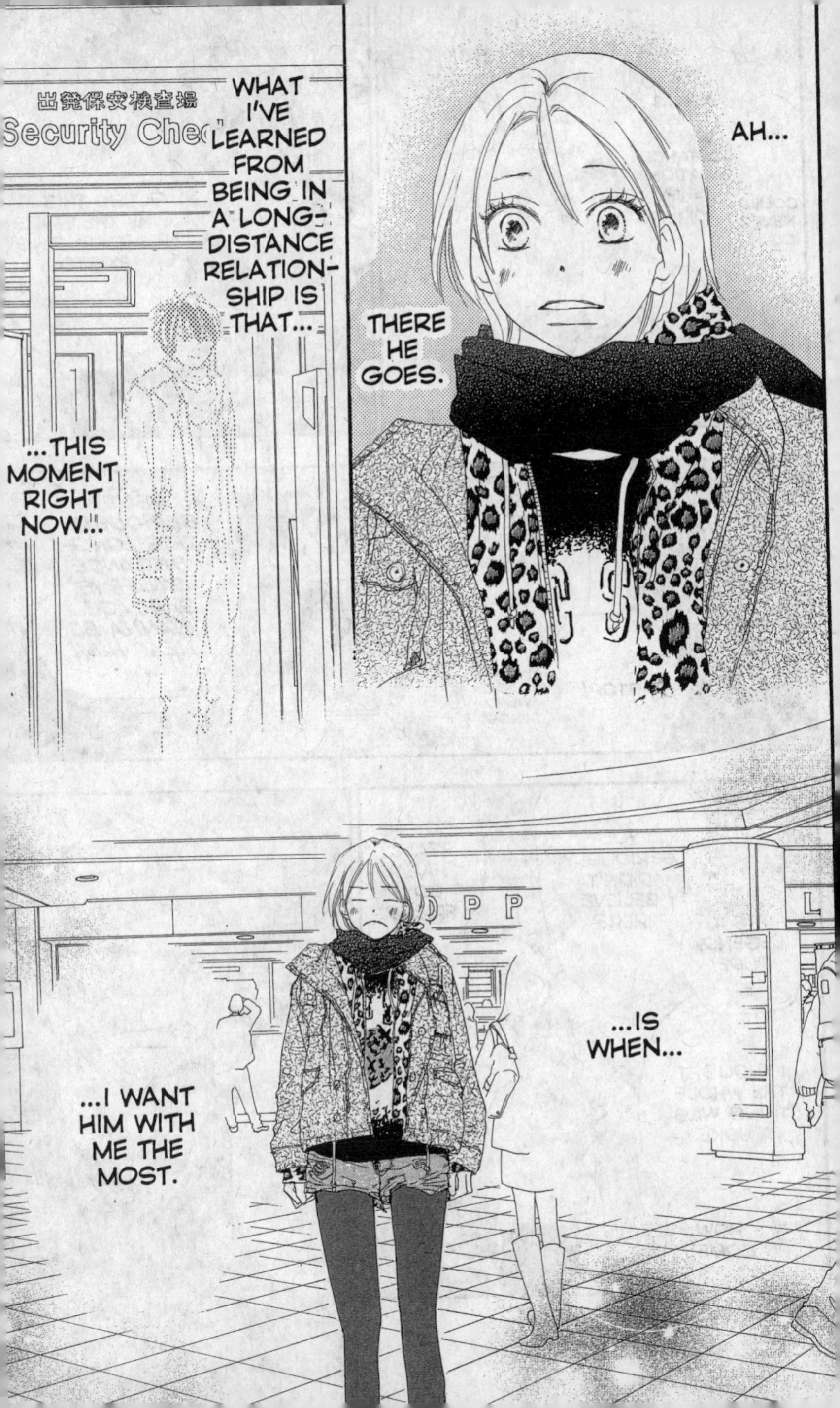
AH...
THERE HE GOES.
出発保安検査場
Security Chec
WHAT I'VE LEARNED FROM BEING IN A LONG-DISTANCE RELATIONSHIP IS THAT...
...THIS MOMENT RIGHT NOW...
...IS WHEN...
...I WANT HIM WITH ME THE MOST.

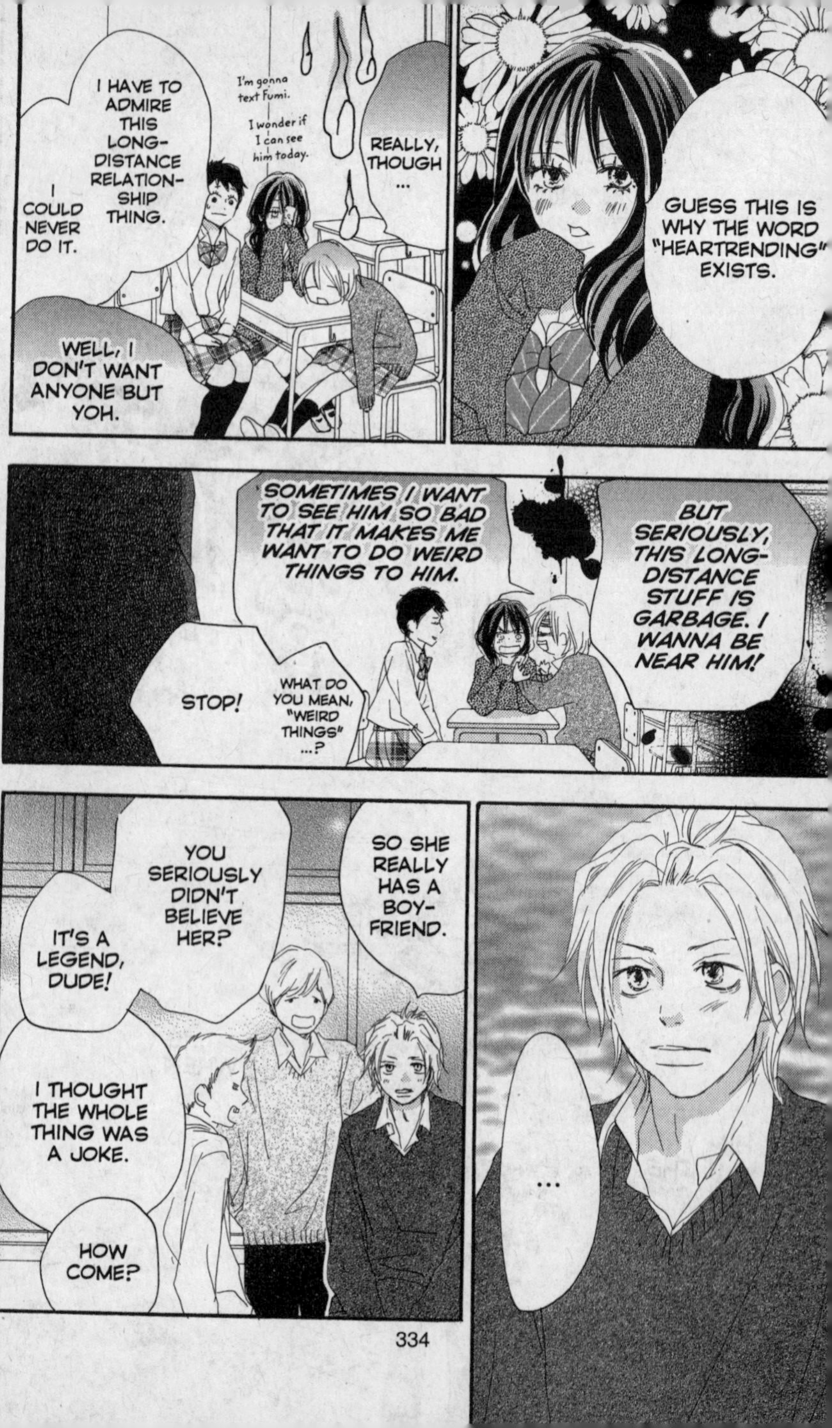
GUESS THIS IS WHY THE WORD "HEARTRENDING" EXISTS.
REALLY, THOUGH ...
I'm gonna text Fumi.
I wonder if I can see him today.
I HAVE TO ADMIRE THIS LONG-DISTANCE RELATIONSHIP THING.
I COULD NEVER DO IT.
WELL, I DON'T WANT ANYONE BUT YOH.
BUT SERIOUSLY, THIS LONG-DISTANCE STUFF IS GARBAGE. I WANNA BE NEAR HIM!
SOMETIMES I WANT TO SEE HIM SO BAD THAT IT MAKES ME WANT TO DO WEIRD THINGS TO HIM.
WHAT DO YOU MEAN, "WEIRD THINGS" ...?
STOP!
...
SO SHE REALLY HAS A BOYFRIEND.
YOU SERIOUSLY DIDN'T BELIEVE HER?
IT'S A LEGEND, DUDE!
I THOUGHT THE WHOLE THING WAS A JOKE.
HOW COME?

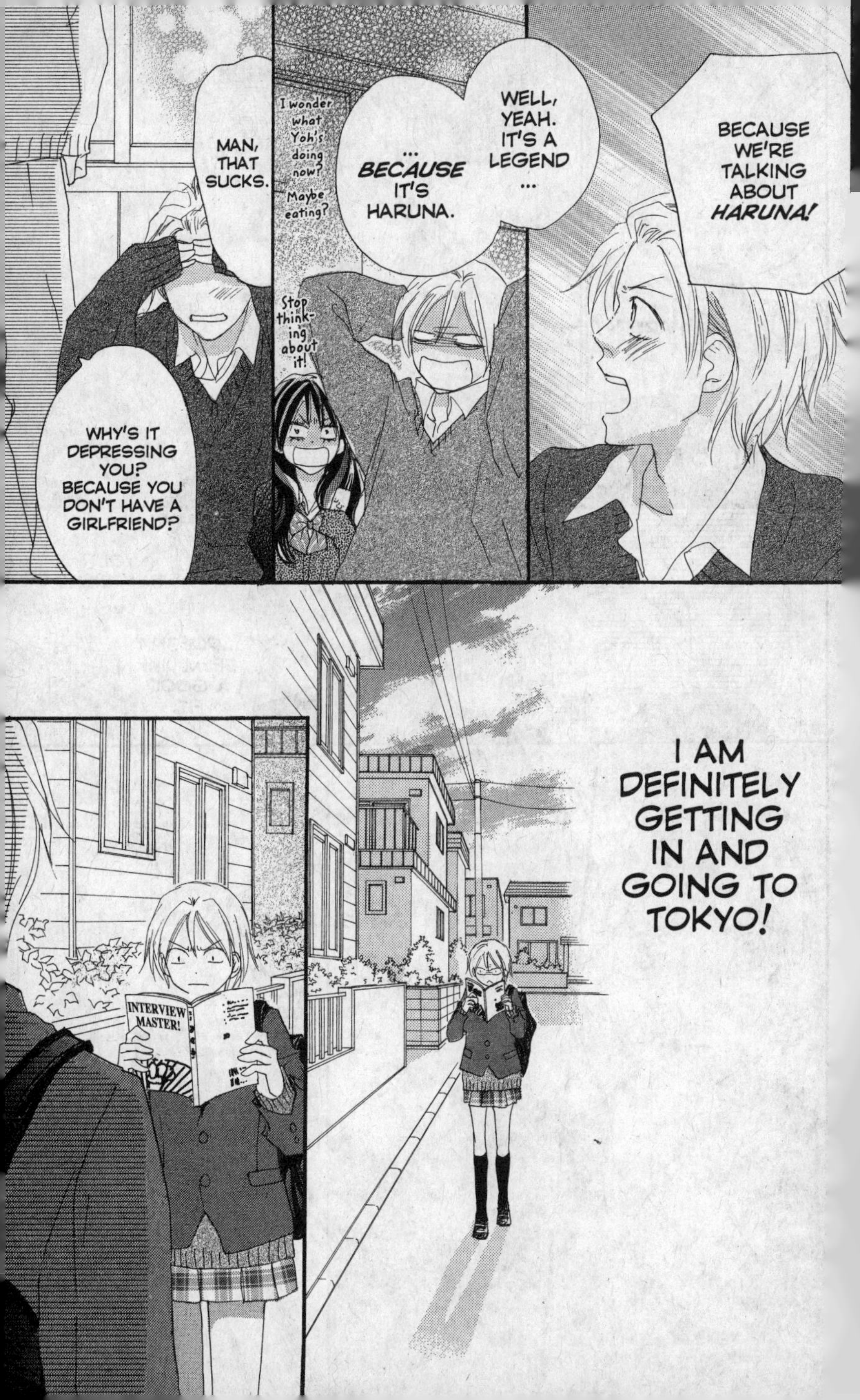
BECAUSE WE'RE TALKING ABOUT *HARUNA!*
WELL, YEAH. IT'S A LEGEND ...
... *BECAUSE* IT'S HARUNA.
I wonder what Yoh's doing now? Maybe eating?
Stop thinking about it!
MAN, THAT SUCKS.
WHY'S IT DEPRESSING YOU? BECAUSE YOU DON'T HAVE A GIRLFRIEND?
I AM DEFINITELY GETTING IN AND GOING TO TOKYO!
INTERVIEW MASTER!

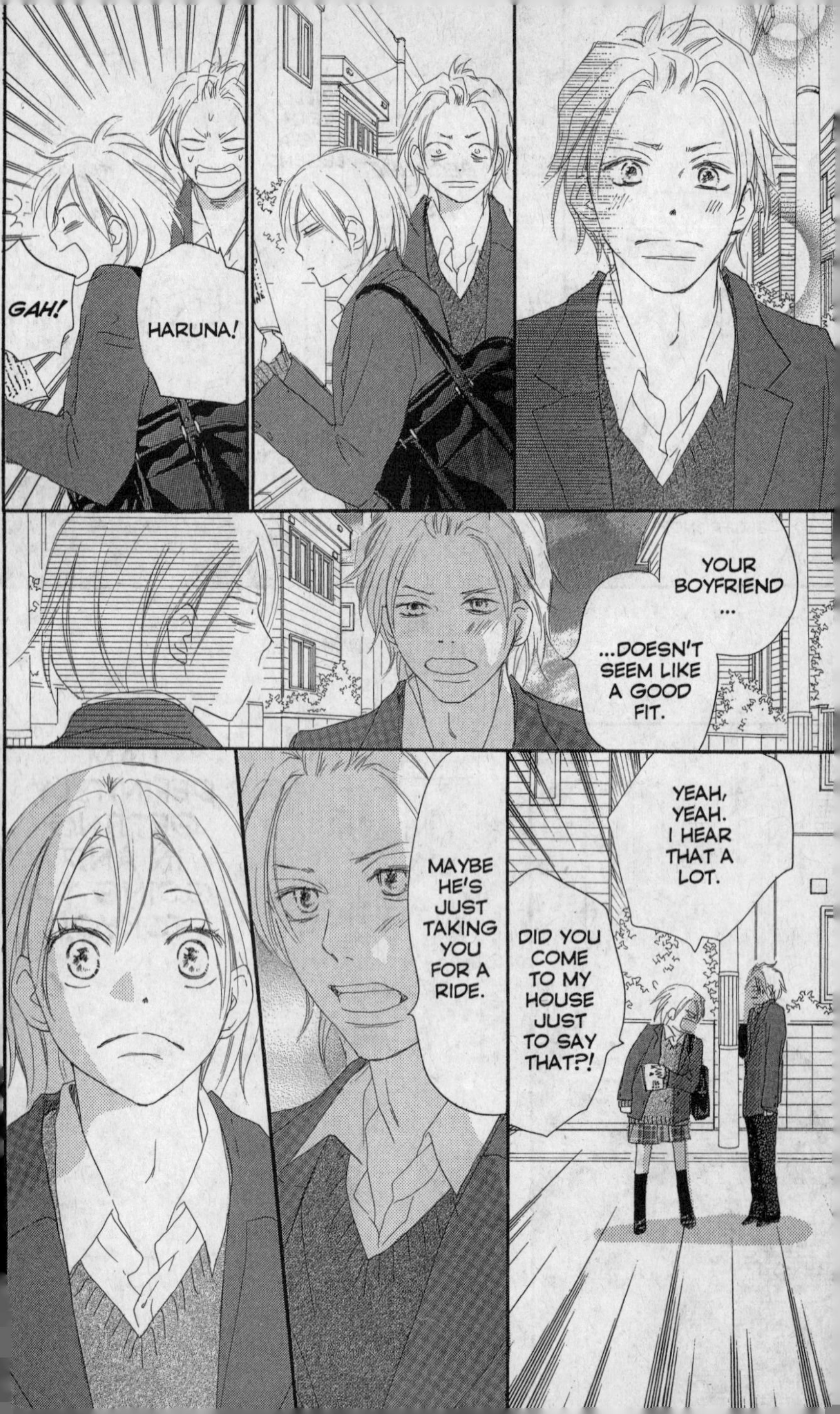
HARUNA!
GAH!
YOUR BOYFRIEND ...
...DOESN'T SEEM LIKE A GOOD FIT.
YEAH, YEAH. I HEAR THAT A LOT.
DID YOU COME TO MY HOUSE JUST TO SAY THAT?!
MAYBE HE'S JUST TAKING YOU FOR A RIDE.

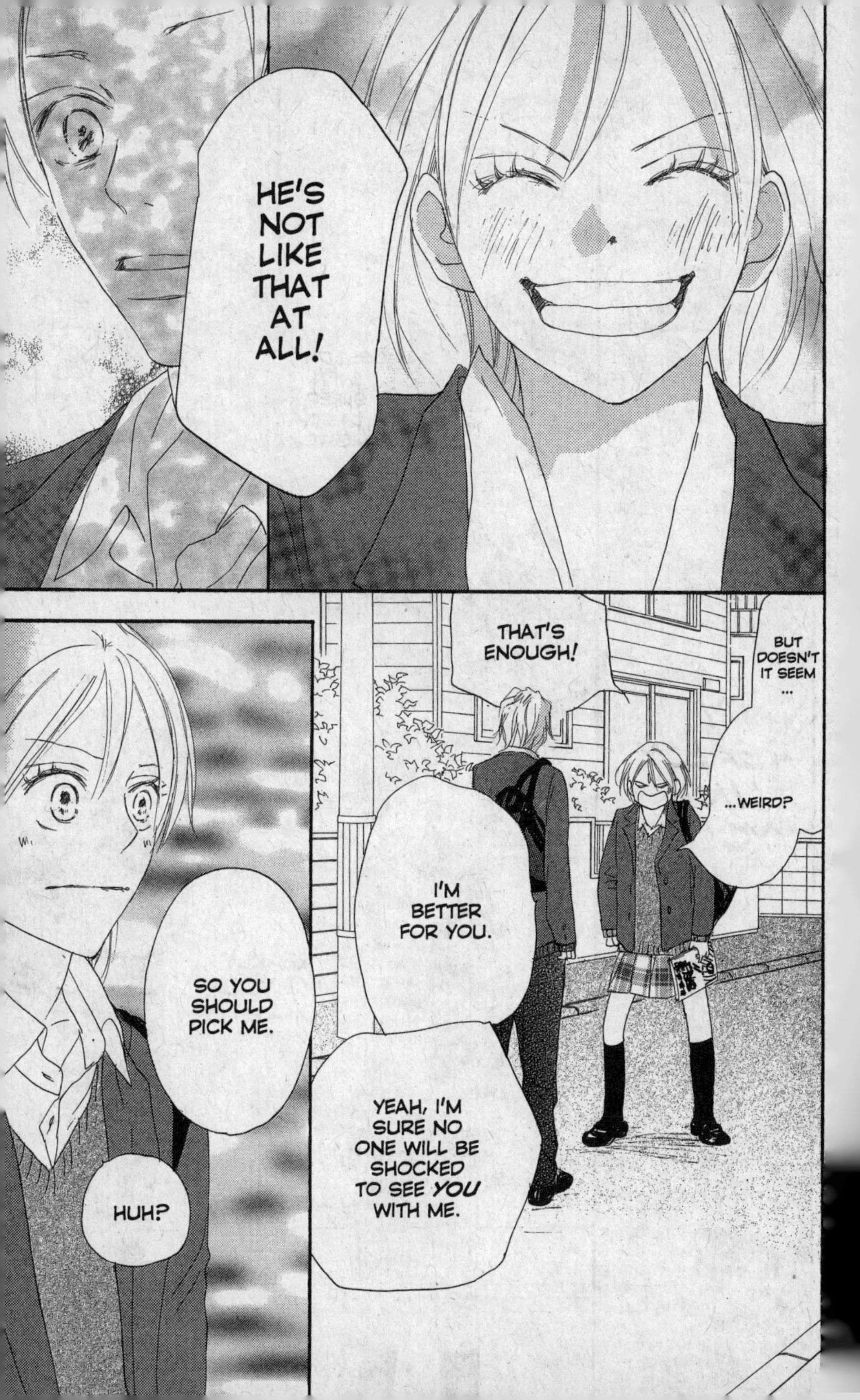
HE'S NOT LIKE THAT AT ALL!
BUT DOESN'T IT SEEM ...
...WEIRD?
THAT'S ENOUGH!
I'M BETTER FOR YOU.
YEAH, I'M SURE NO ONE WILL BE SHOCKED TO SEE *YOU* WITH ME.
SO YOU SHOULD PICK ME.
HUH?

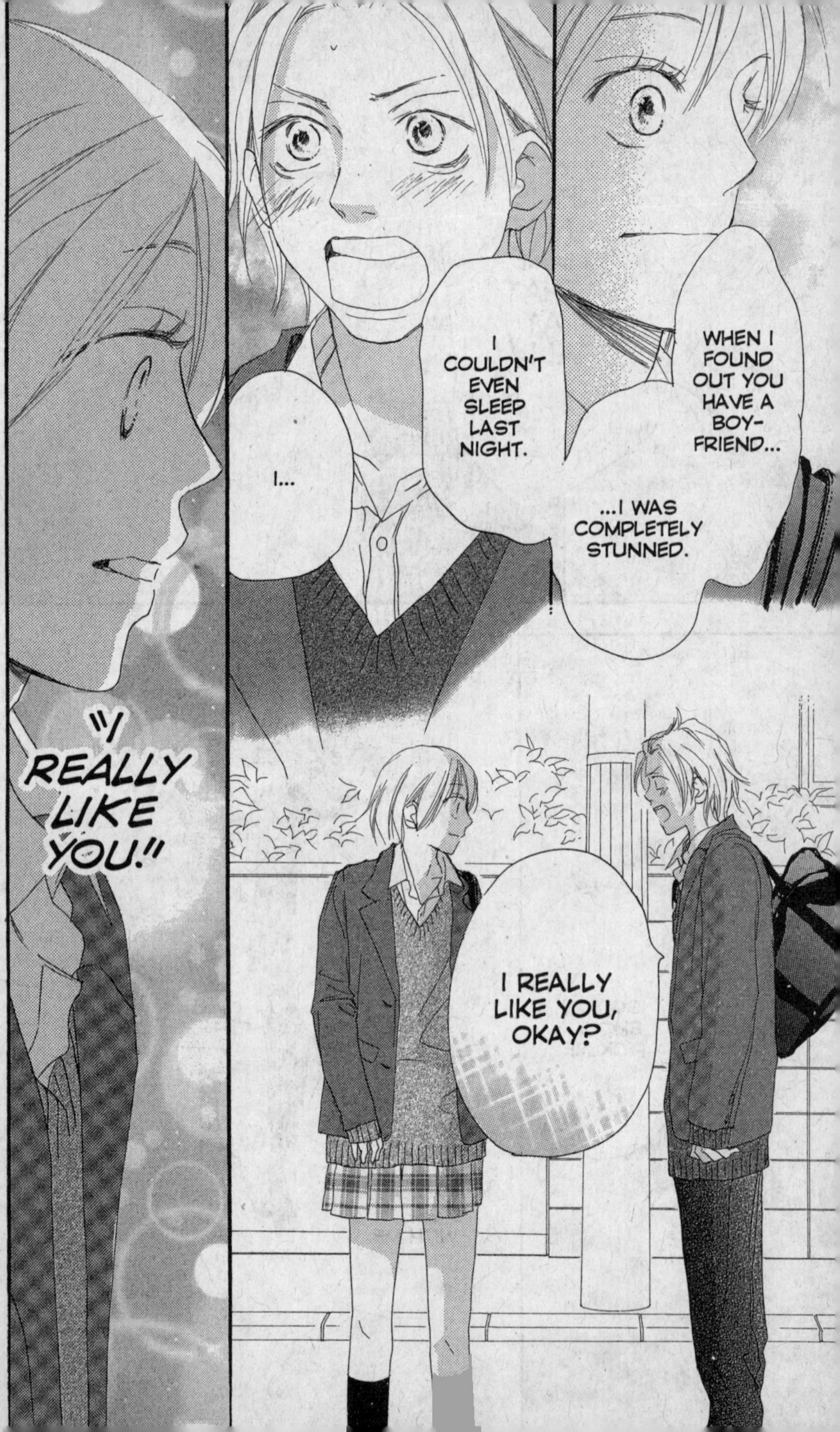
WHEN I FOUND OUT YOU HAVE A BOY-FRIEND...
...I WAS COMPLETELY STUNNED.
I COULDN'T EVEN SLEEP LAST NIGHT.
I...
I REALLY LIKE YOU, OKAY?
"I REALLY LIKE YOU."

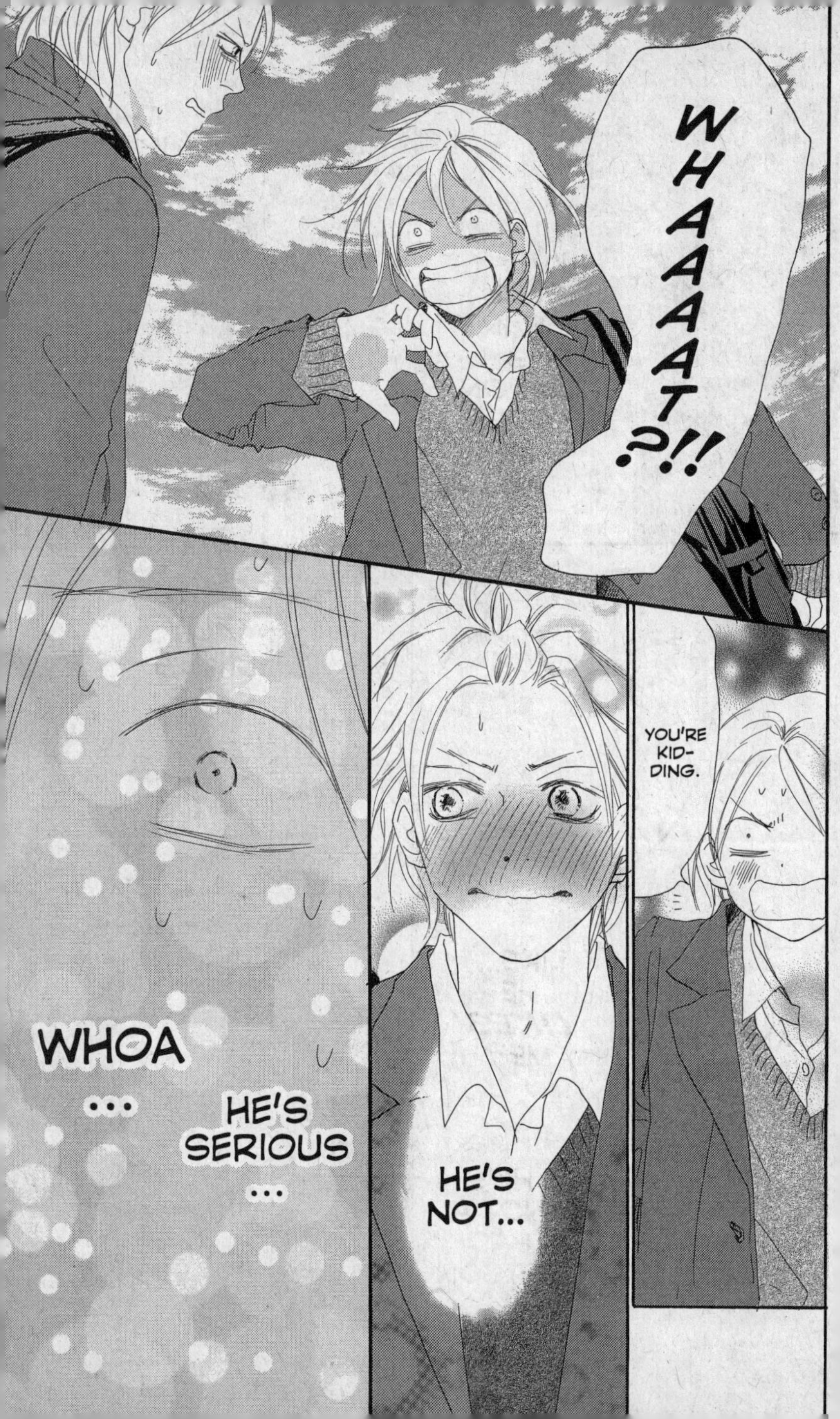
WHAAAAAT?!!
YOU'RE KID-DING.
HE'S NOT...
WHOA ...
HE'S SERIOUS ...

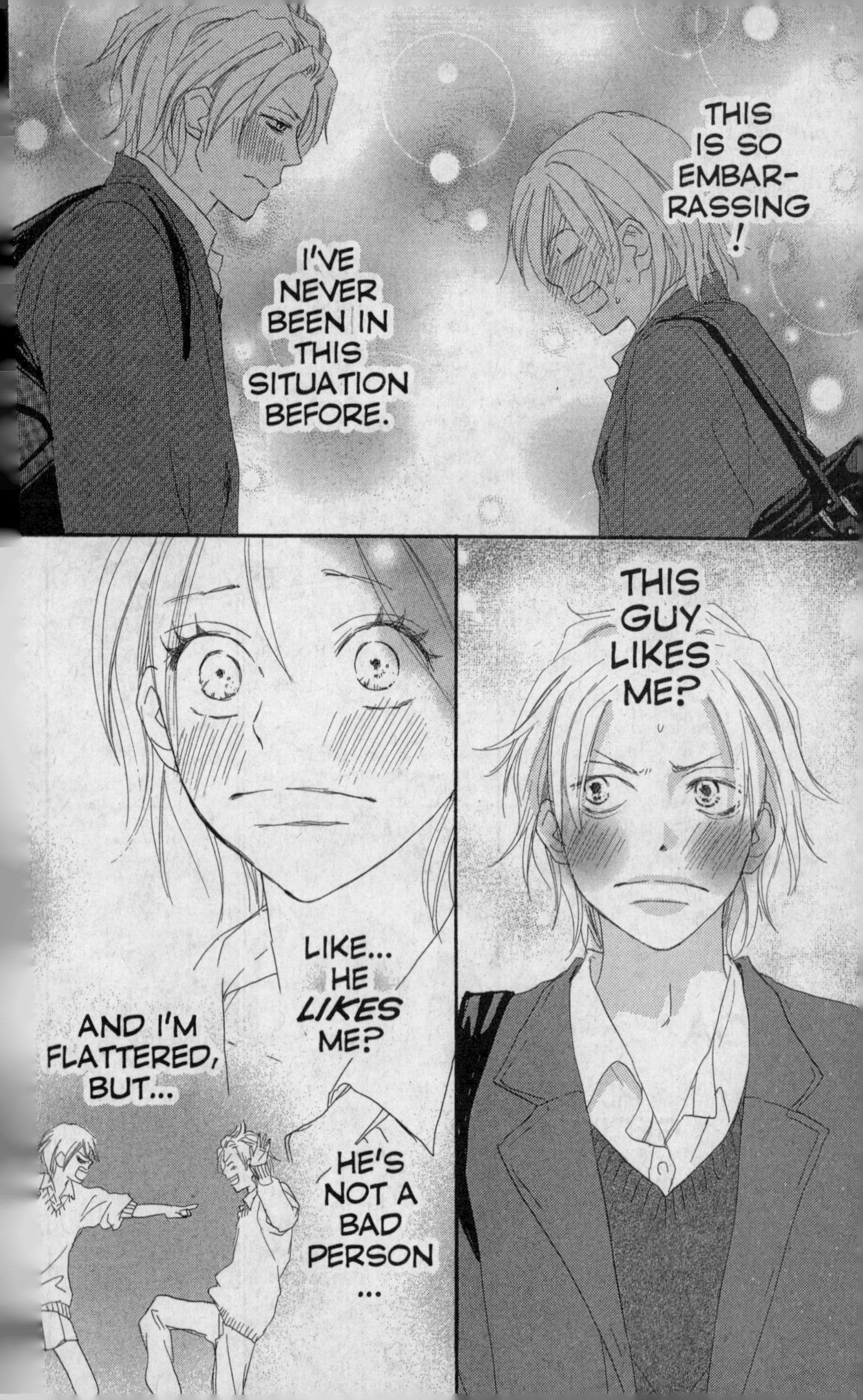
THIS IS SO EMBARRASSING!
I'VE NEVER BEEN IN THIS SITUATION BEFORE.
THIS GUY LIKES ME?
LIKE... HE *LIKES* ME?
AND I'M FLATTERED, BUT...
HE'S NOT A BAD PERSON...

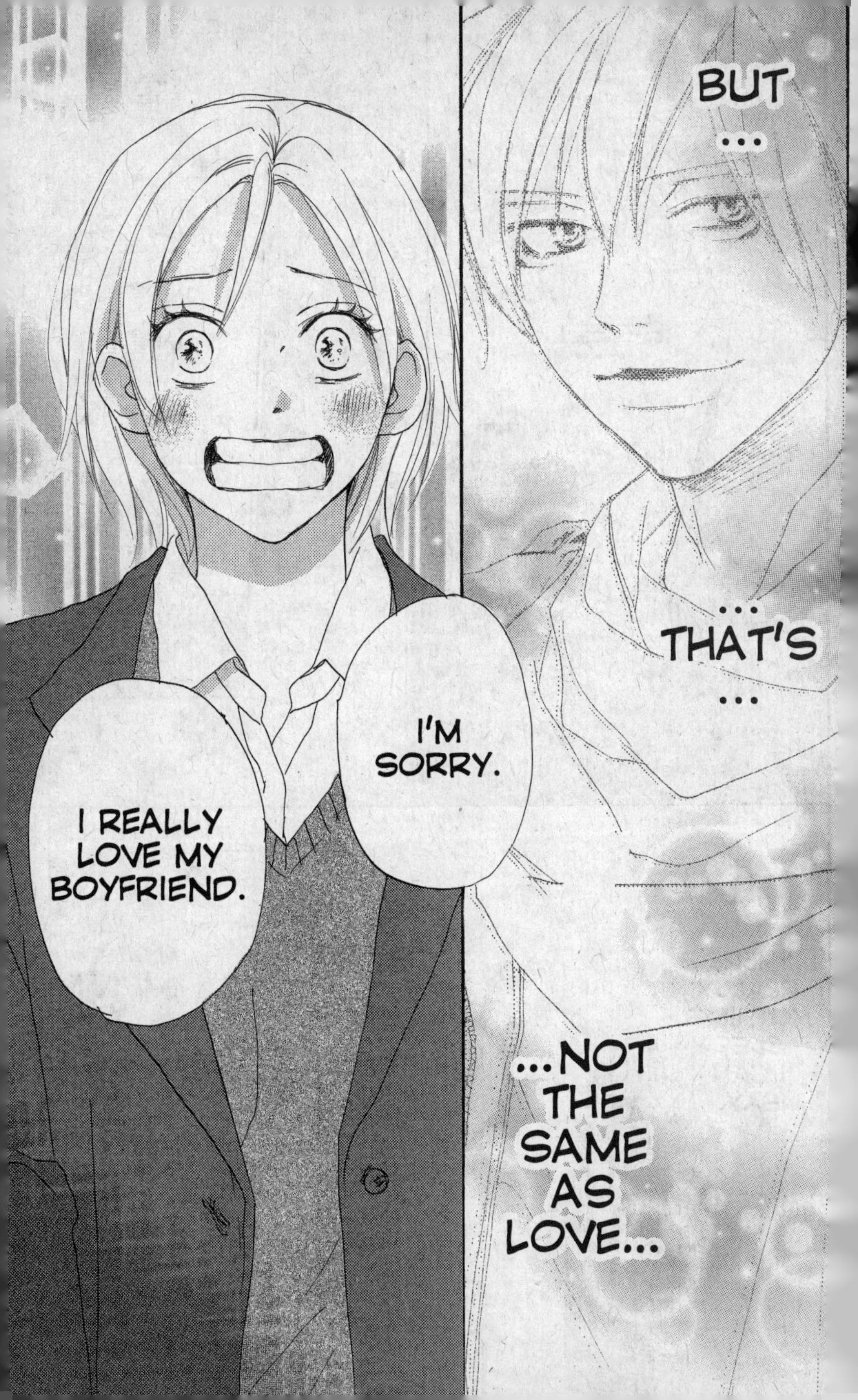
BUT ...
... THAT'S ...
...NOT THE SAME AS LOVE...
I'M SORRY.
I REALLY LOVE MY BOYFRIEND.

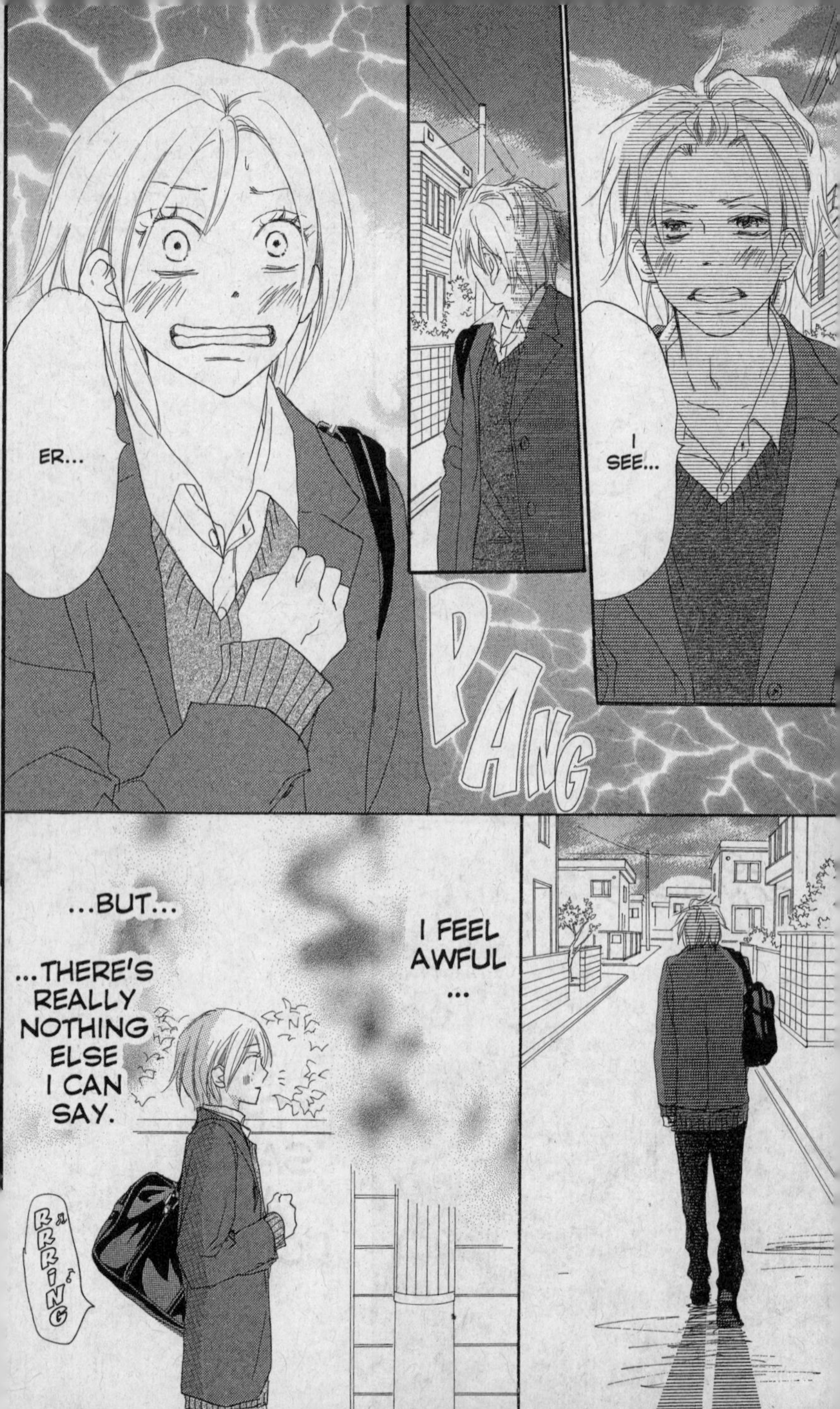
I SEE...
ER...
PANG
I FEEL AWFUL ...
...BUT...
...THERE'S REALLY NOTHING ELSE I CAN SAY.
RRRING

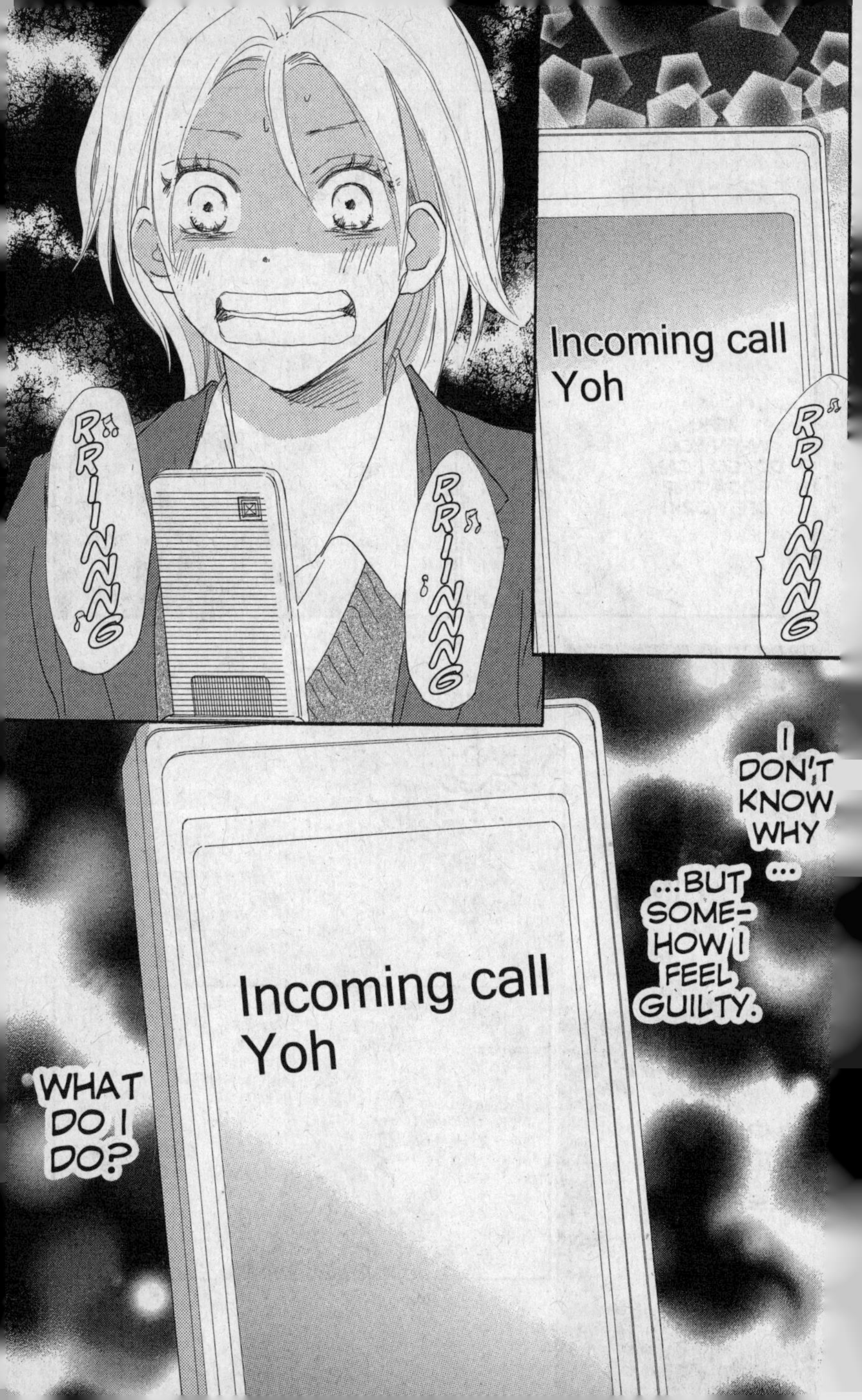
Incoming call Yoh
RRINNNG
RRINNNG
RRINNNG
Incoming call Yoh
I DON'T KNOW WHY...
...BUT SOMEHOW I FEEL GUILTY.
WHAT DO I DO?

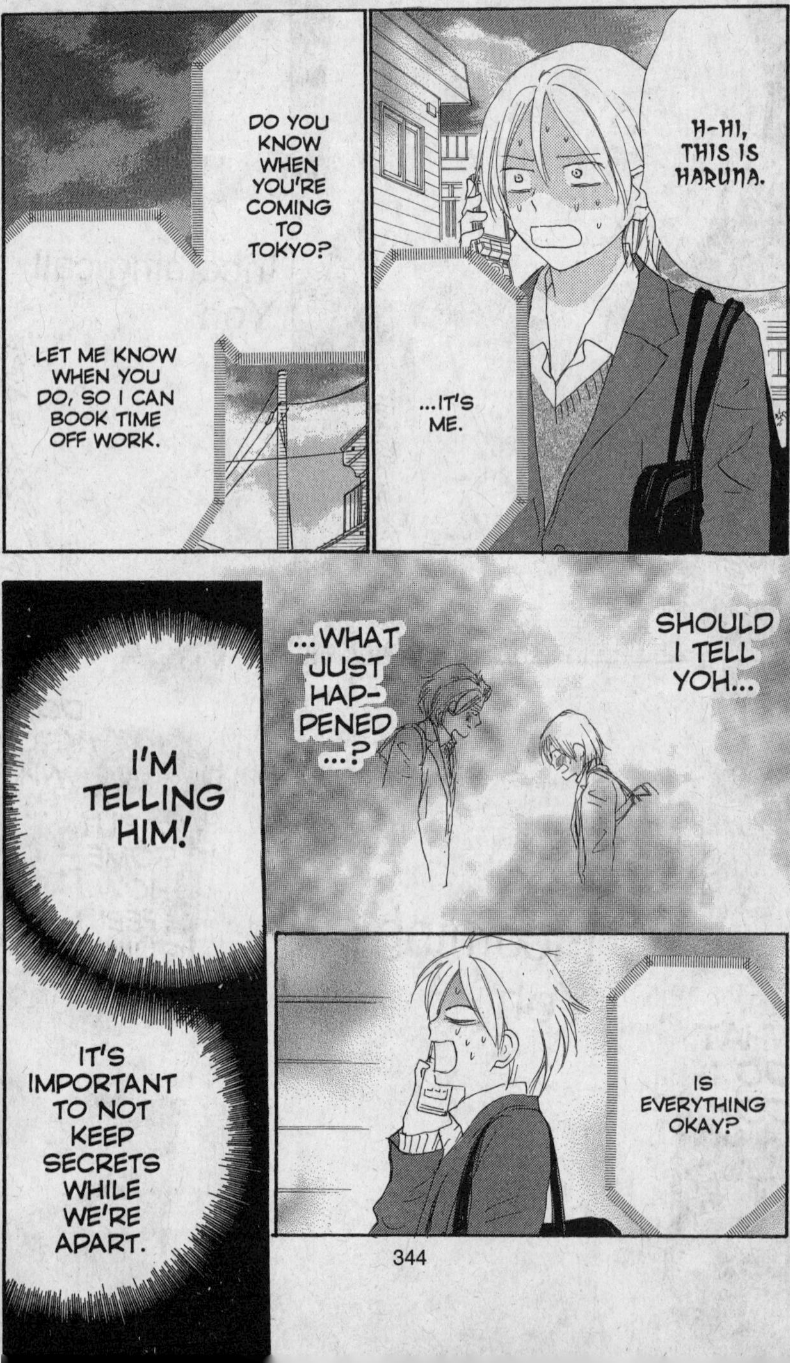
H-HI, THIS IS HARUNA.
...IT'S ME.
DO YOU KNOW WHEN YOU'RE COMING TO TOKYO?
LET ME KNOW WHEN YOU DO, SO I CAN BOOK TIME OFF WORK.
SHOULD I TELL YOH...
...WHAT JUST HAP-PENED...?
IS EVERYTHING OKAY?
I'M TELLING HIM!
IT'S IMPORTANT TO NOT KEEP SECRETS WHILE WE'RE APART.

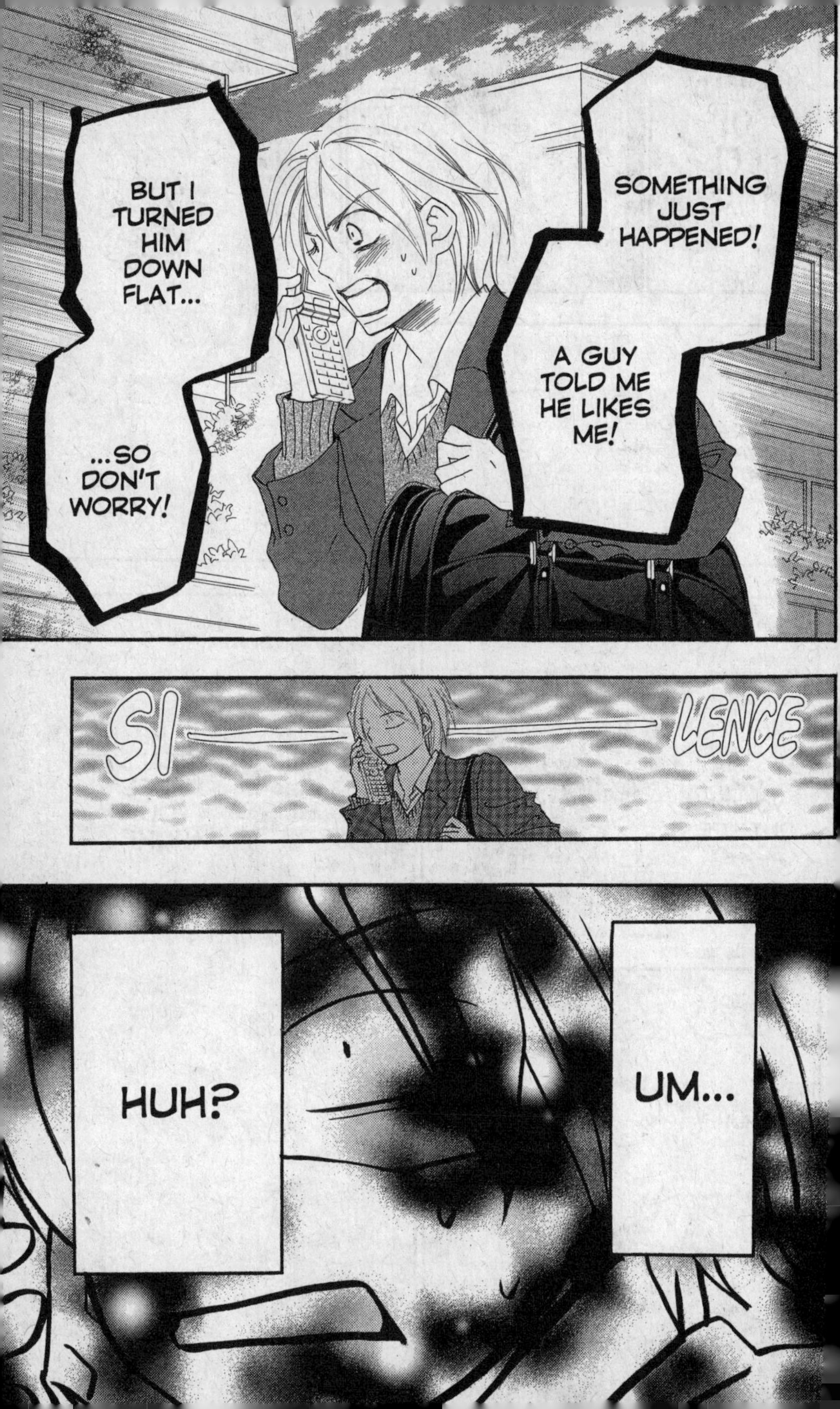
SOMETHING JUST HAPPENED!
A GUY TOLD ME HE LIKES ME!
BUT I TURNED HIM DOWN FLAT...
...SO DON'T WORRY!
SI——LENCE
UM...
HUH?

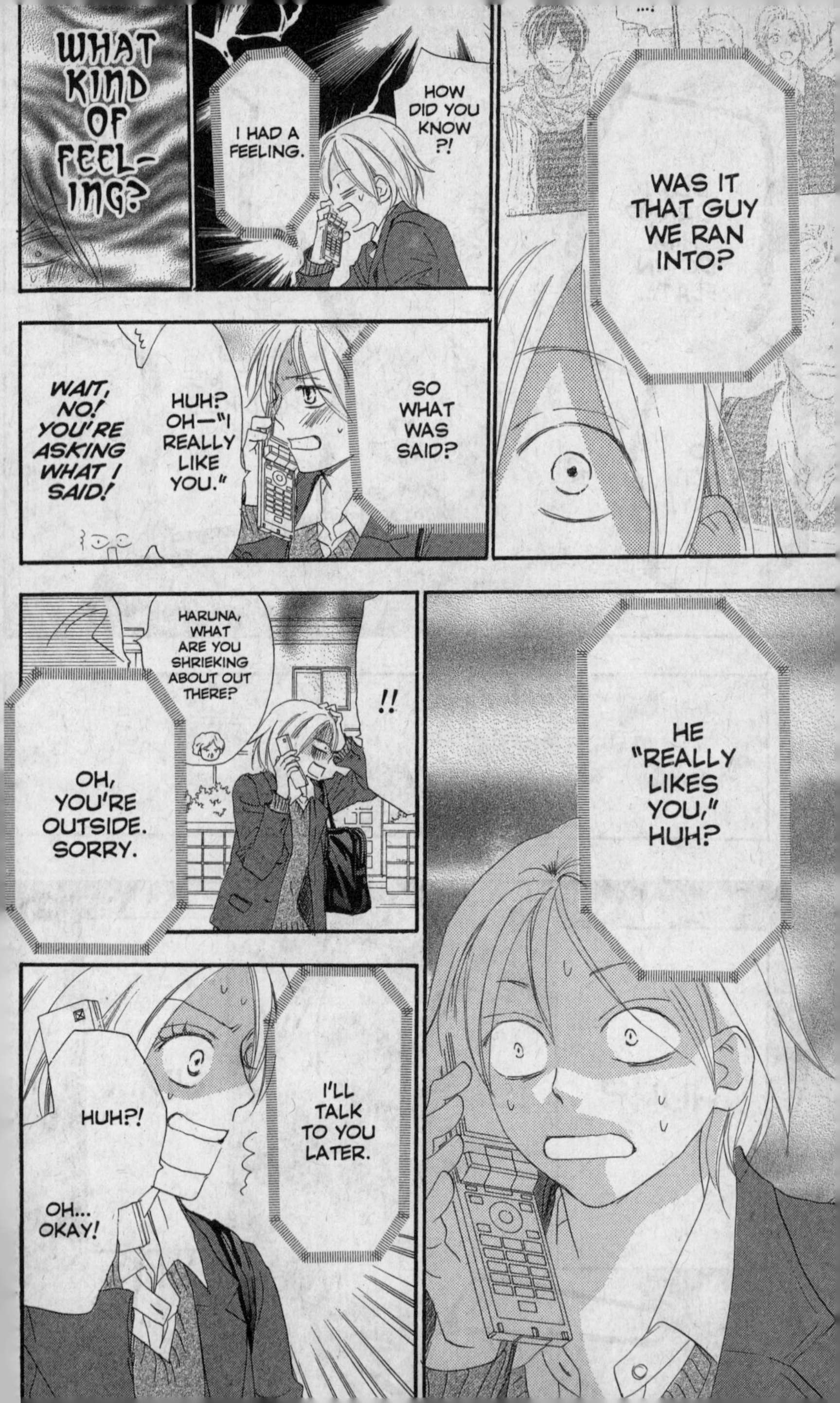
....
WAS IT THAT GUY WE RAN INTO?
HOW DID YOU KNOW ?!
I HAD A FEELING.
WHAT KIND OF FEEL-ING?
SO WHAT WAS SAID?
HUH? OH—"I REALLY LIKE YOU."
WAIT, NO! YOU'RE ASKING WHAT I SAID!
HE "REALLY LIKES YOU," HUH?
HARUNA, WHAT ARE YOU SHRIEKING ABOUT OUT THERE?
!!
OH, YOU'RE OUTSIDE. SORRY.
I'LL TALK TO YOU LATER.
HUH?!
OH... OKAY!

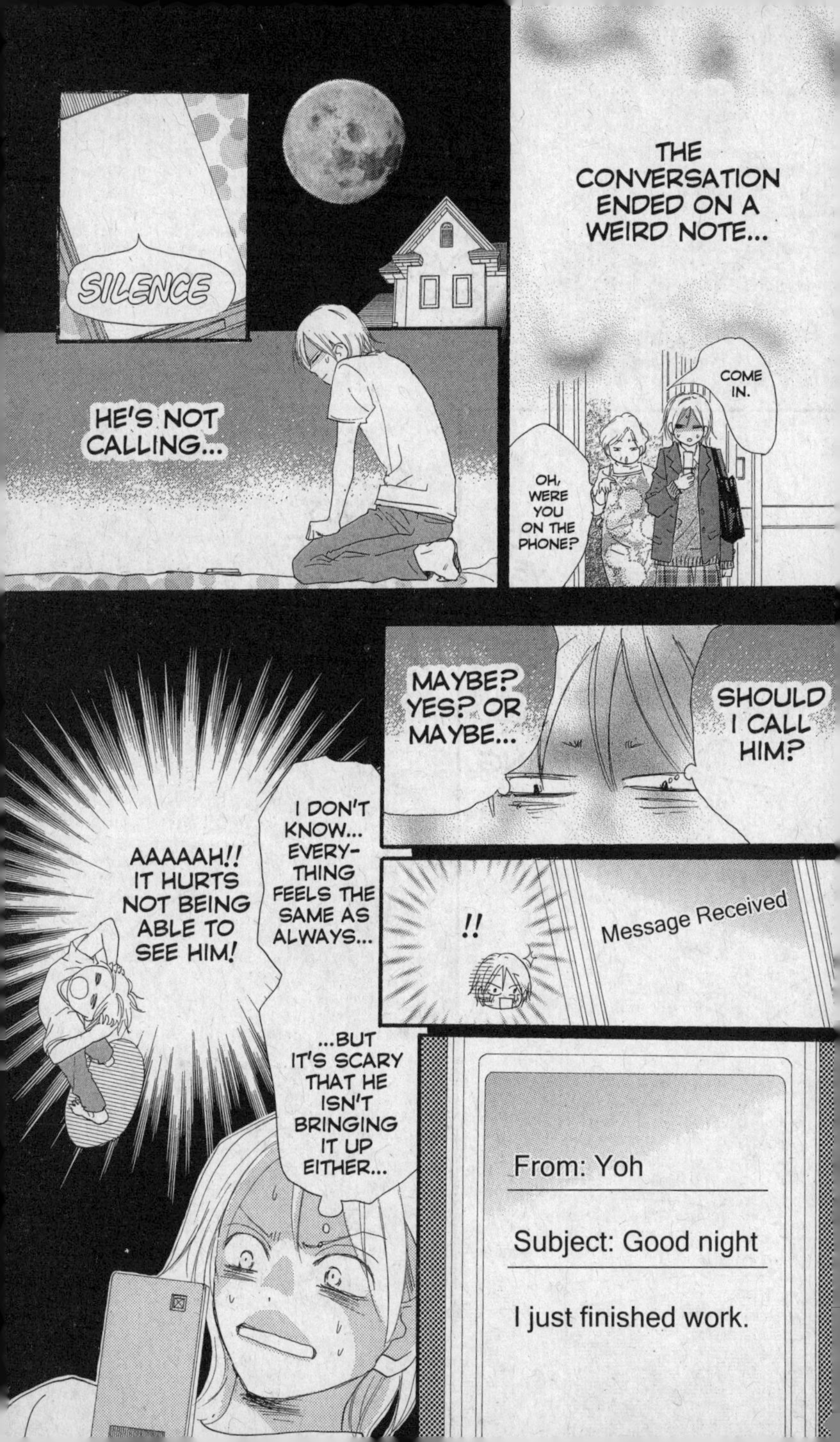
THE CONVERSATION ENDED ON A WEIRD NOTE...
COME IN.
OH, WERE YOU ON THE PHONE?
SILENCE
HE'S NOT CALLING...
SHOULD I CALL HIM?
MAYBE? YES? OR MAYBE...
!!
Message Received
From: Yoh
Subject: Good night
I just finished work.
I DON'T KNOW... EVERYTHING FEELS THE SAME AS ALWAYS...
AAAAAH!! IT HURTS NOT BEING ABLE TO SEE HIM!
...BUT IT'S SCARY THAT HE ISN'T BRINGING IT UP EITHER...

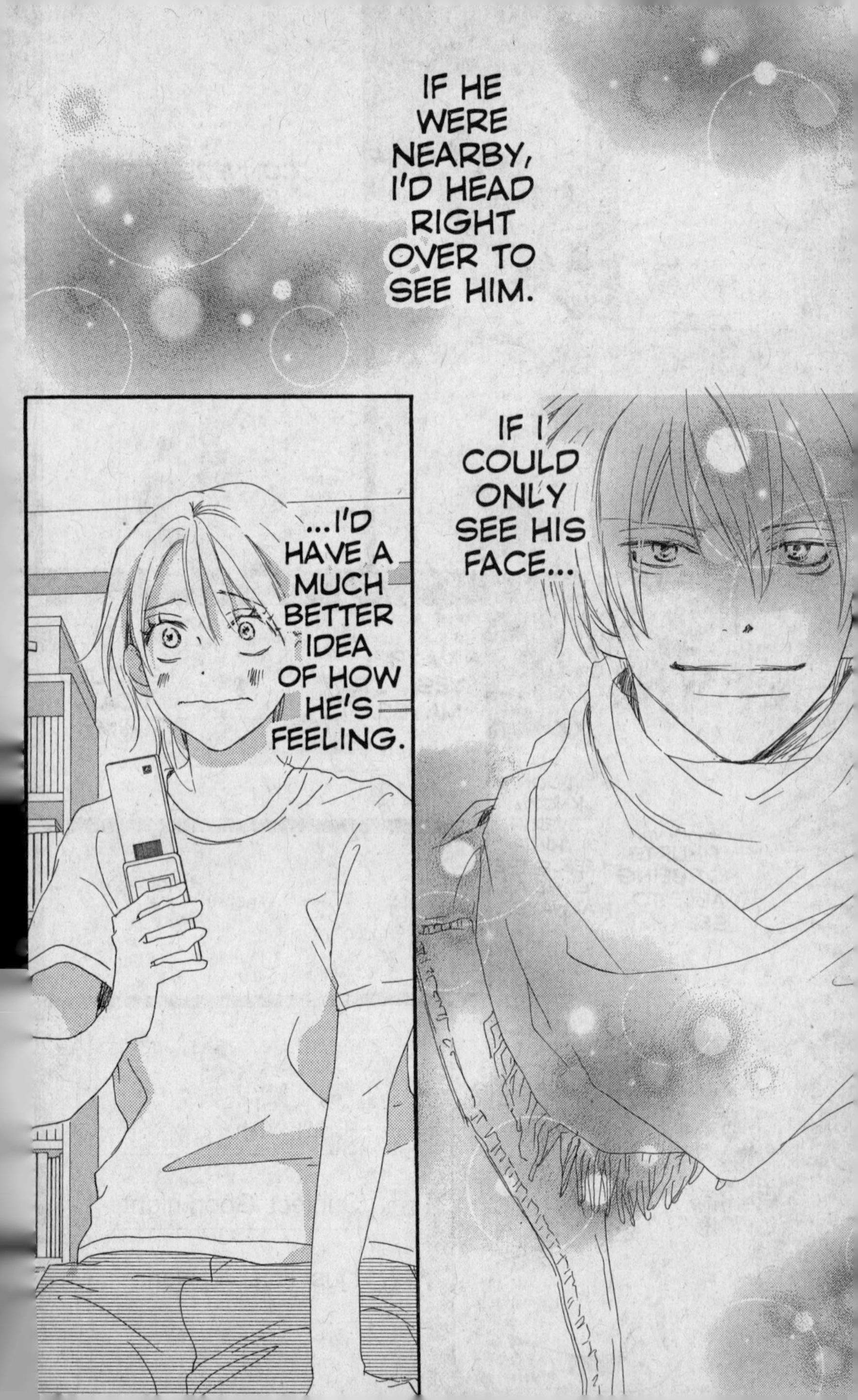
IF HE WERE NEARBY, I'D HEAD RIGHT OVER TO SEE HIM.
IF I COULD ONLY SEE HIS FACE...
...I'D HAVE A MUCH BETTER IDEA OF HOW HE'S FEELING.

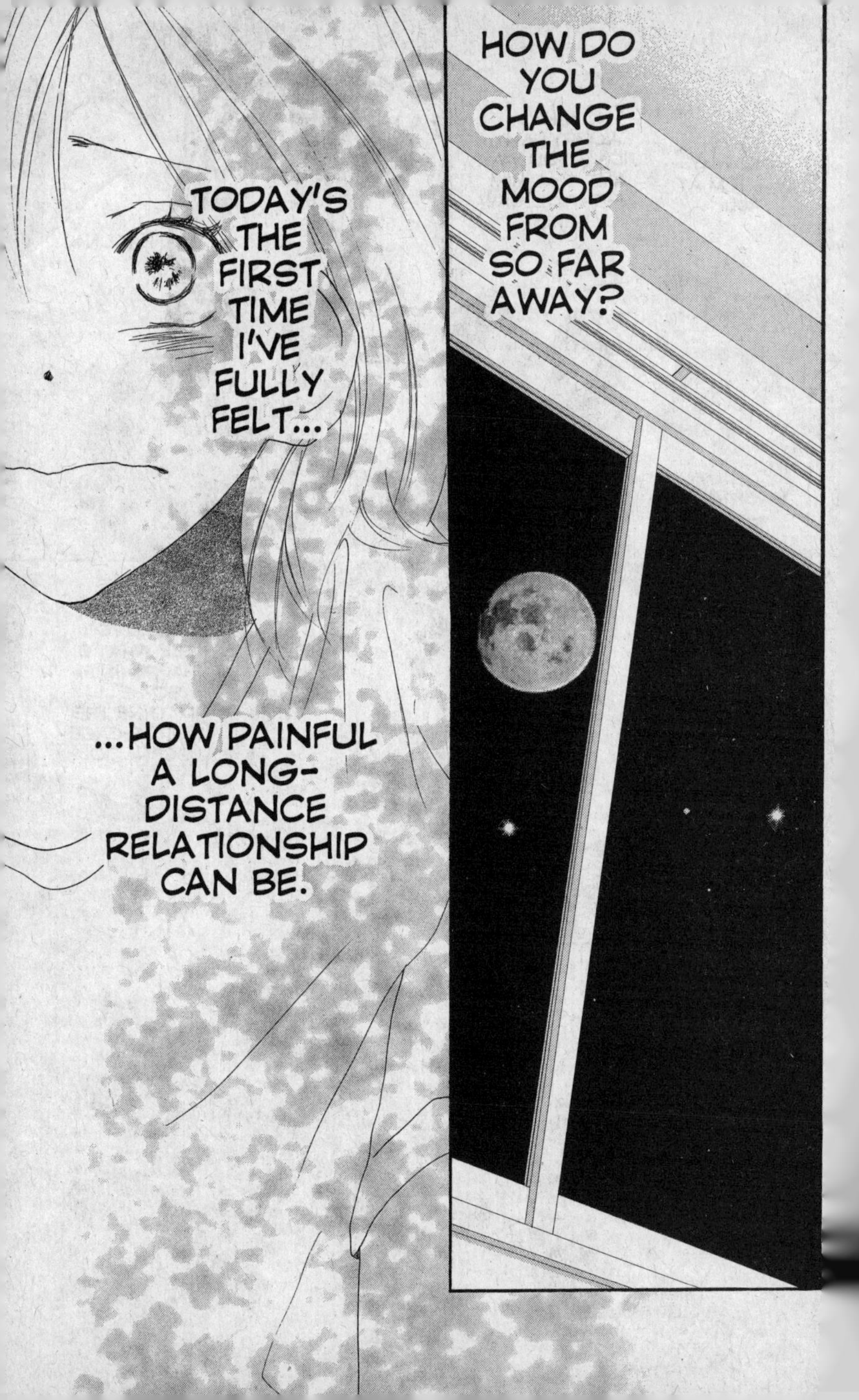
HOW DO YOU CHANGE THE MOOD FROM SO FAR AWAY?
TODAY'S THE FIRST TIME I'VE FULLY FELT...
...HOW PAINFUL A LONG-DISTANCE RELATIONSHIP CAN BE.

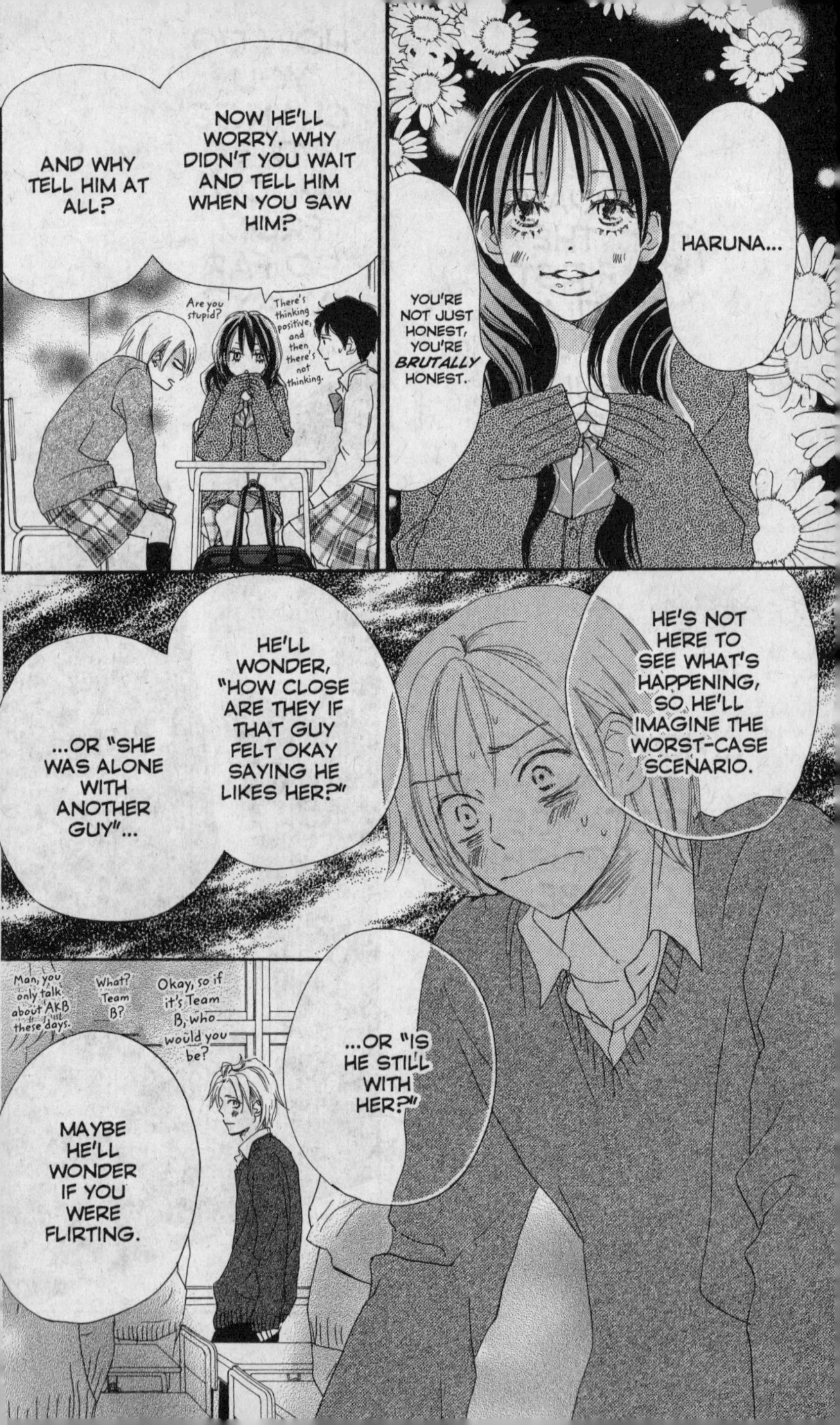
HARUNA...
YOU'RE NOT JUST HONEST, YOU'RE *BRUTALLY* HONEST.
NOW HE'LL WORRY. WHY DIDN'T YOU WAIT AND TELL HIM WHEN YOU SAW HIM?
AND WHY TELL HIM AT ALL?
There's thinking positive, and then there's not thinking.
Are you stupid?
HE'S NOT HERE TO SEE WHAT'S HAPPENING, SO HE'LL IMAGINE THE WORST-CASE SCENARIO.
HE'LL WONDER, "HOW CLOSE ARE THEY IF THAT GUY FELT OKAY SAYING HE LIKES HER?"
...OR "SHE WAS ALONE WITH ANOTHER GUY"...
...OR "IS HE STILL WITH HER?"
Okay, so if it's Team B, who would you be?
What? Team B?
Man, you only talk about AKB these days.
MAYBE HE'LL WONDER IF YOU WERE FLIRTING.

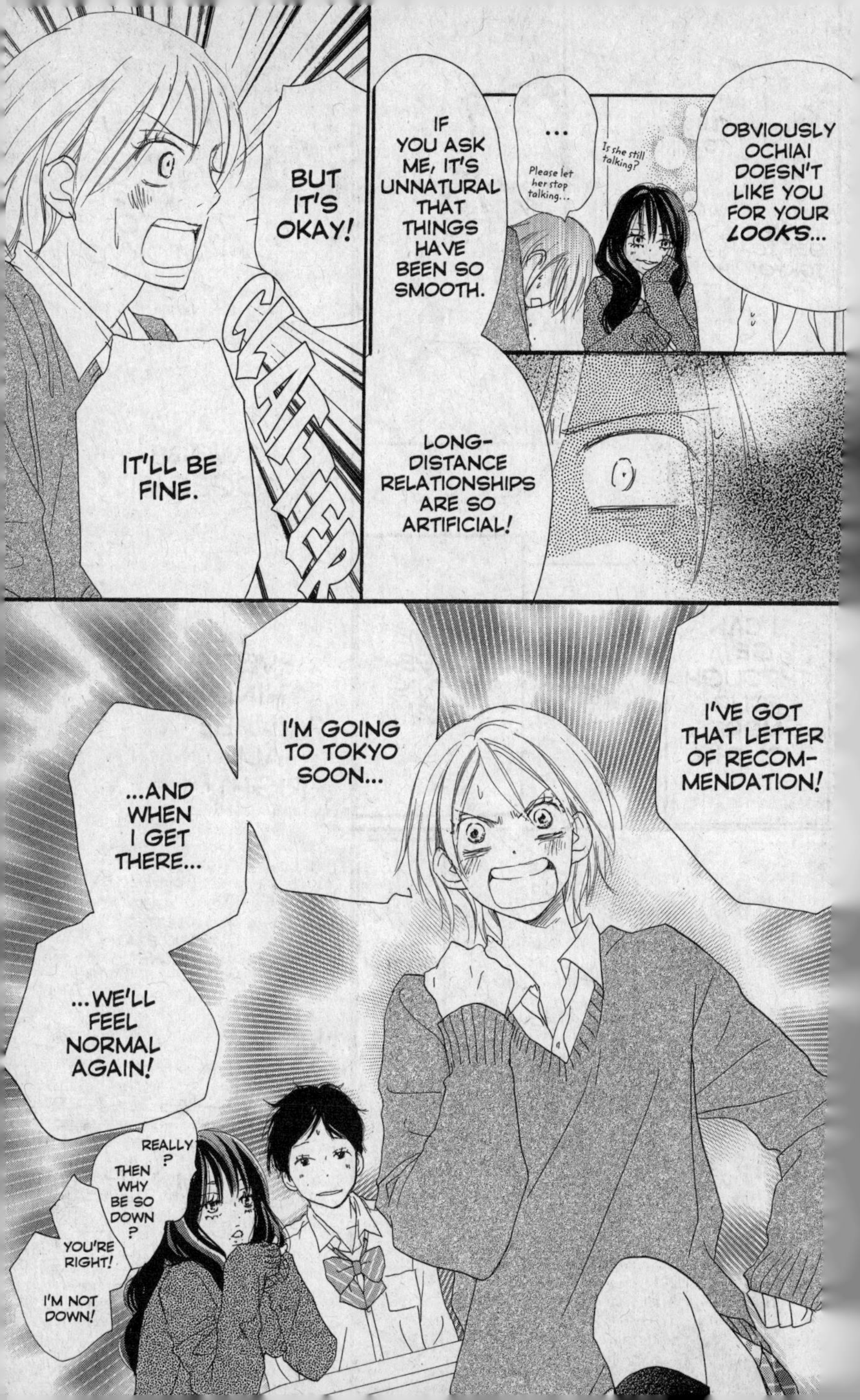
OBVIOUSLY OCHIAI DOESN'T LIKE YOU FOR YOUR *LOOKS*...
Is she still talking?
Please let her stop talking...
...
IF YOU ASK ME, IT'S UNNATURAL THAT THINGS HAVE BEEN SO SMOOTH.
LONG-DISTANCE RELATIONSHIPS ARE SO ARTIFICIAL!
BUT IT'S OKAY!
CLATTER
IT'LL BE FINE.
I'VE GOT THAT LETTER OF RECOM-MENDATION!
I'M GOING TO TOKYO SOON...
...AND WHEN I GET THERE...
...WE'LL FEEL NORMAL AGAIN!
REALLY? THEN WHY BE SO DOWN?
YOU'RE RIGHT!
I'M NOT DOWN!

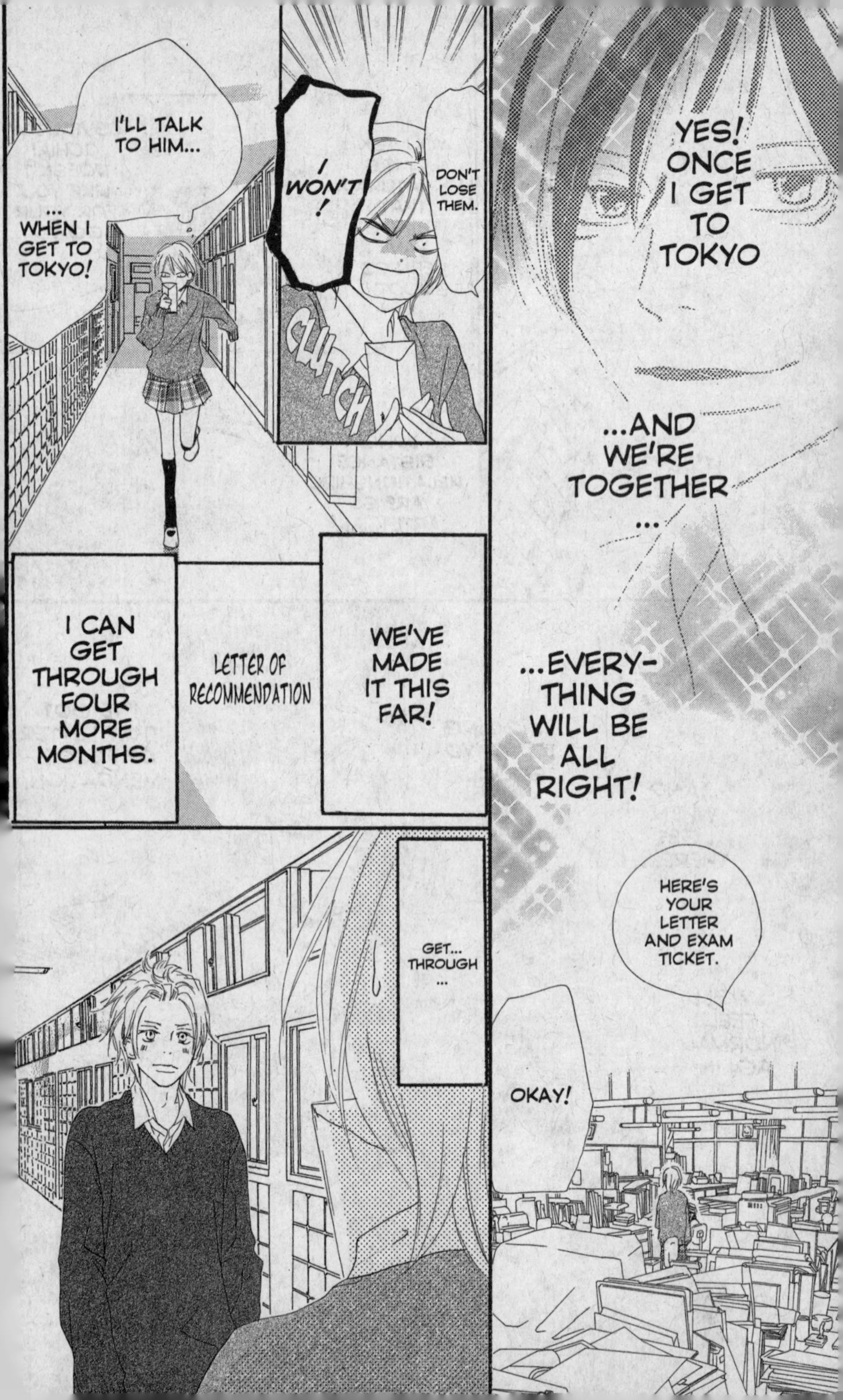
YES! ONCE I GET TO TOKYO
...AND WE'RE TOGETHER...
...EVERYTHING WILL BE ALL RIGHT!
HERE'S YOUR LETTER AND EXAM TICKET.
OKAY!
DON'T LOSE THEM.
I WON'T!
CLUTCH
I'LL TALK TO HIM...
...WHEN I GET TO TOKYO!
WE'VE MADE IT THIS FAR!
LETTER OF RECOMMENDATION
I CAN GET THROUGH FOUR MORE MONTHS.
GET... THROUGH...

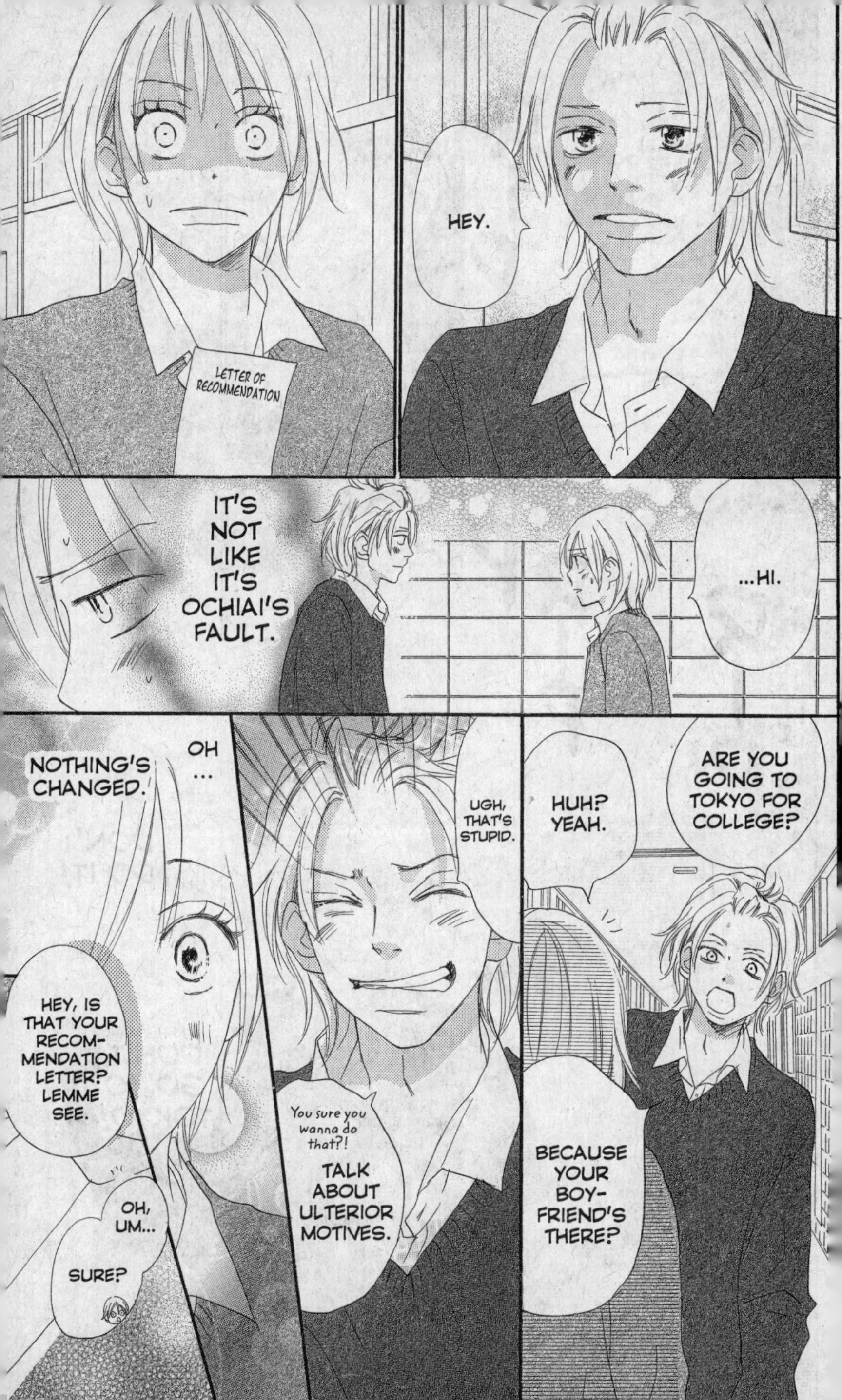
HEY.
LETTER OF RECOMMENDATION
...HI.
IT'S NOT LIKE IT'S OCHIAI'S FAULT.
ARE YOU GOING TO TOKYO FOR COLLEGE?
HUH? YEAH.
BECAUSE YOUR BOY-FRIEND'S THERE?
UGH, THAT'S STUPID.
You sure you wanna do that?!
TALK ABOUT ULTERIOR MOTIVES.
OH ...
NOTHING'S CHANGED.
HEY, IS THAT YOUR RECOM-MENDATION LETTER? LEMME SEE.
OH, UM...
SURE?

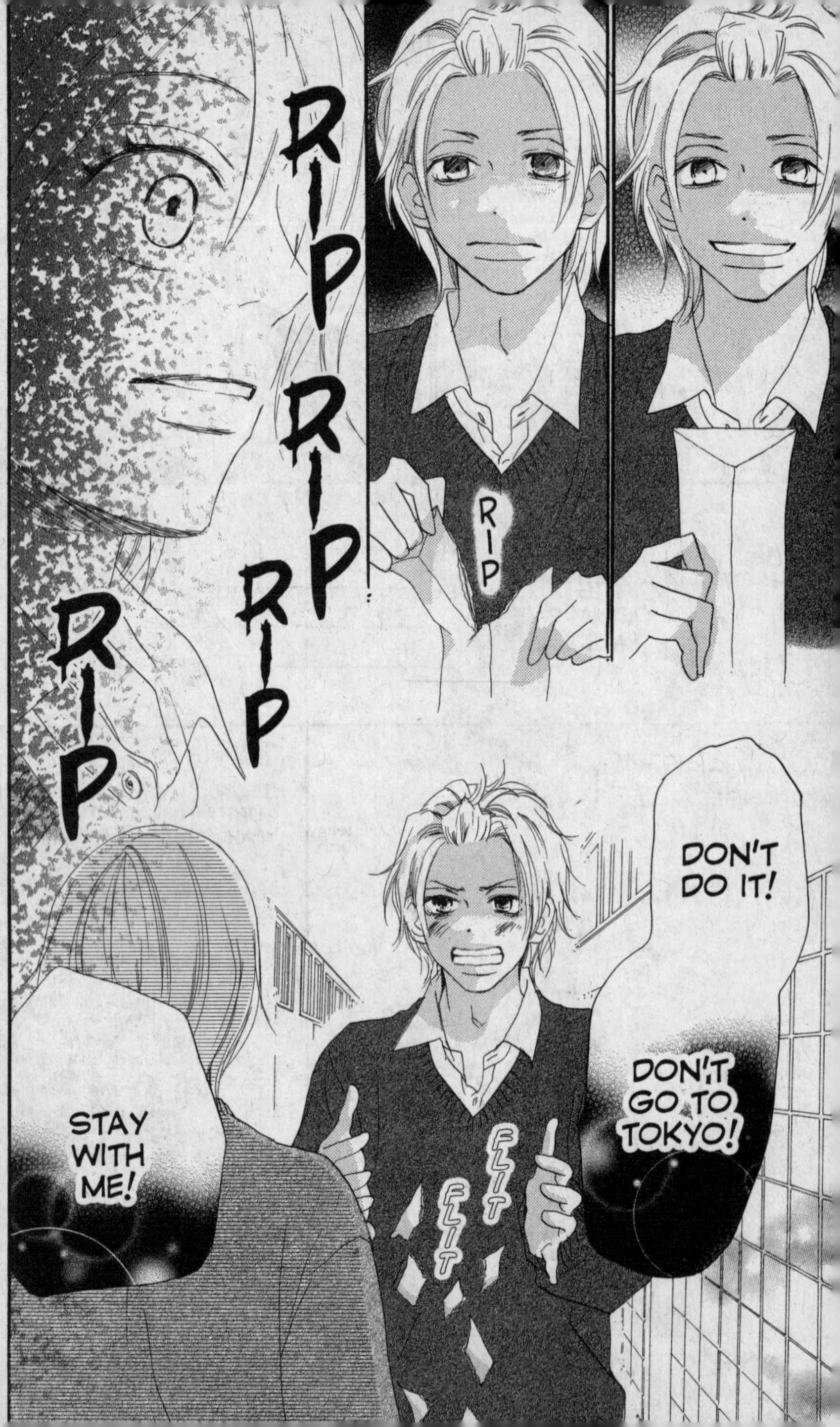
RIP
RIP RIP RIP RIP
DON'T DO IT!
DON'T GO TO TOKYO!
FLIT FLIT
STAY WITH ME!

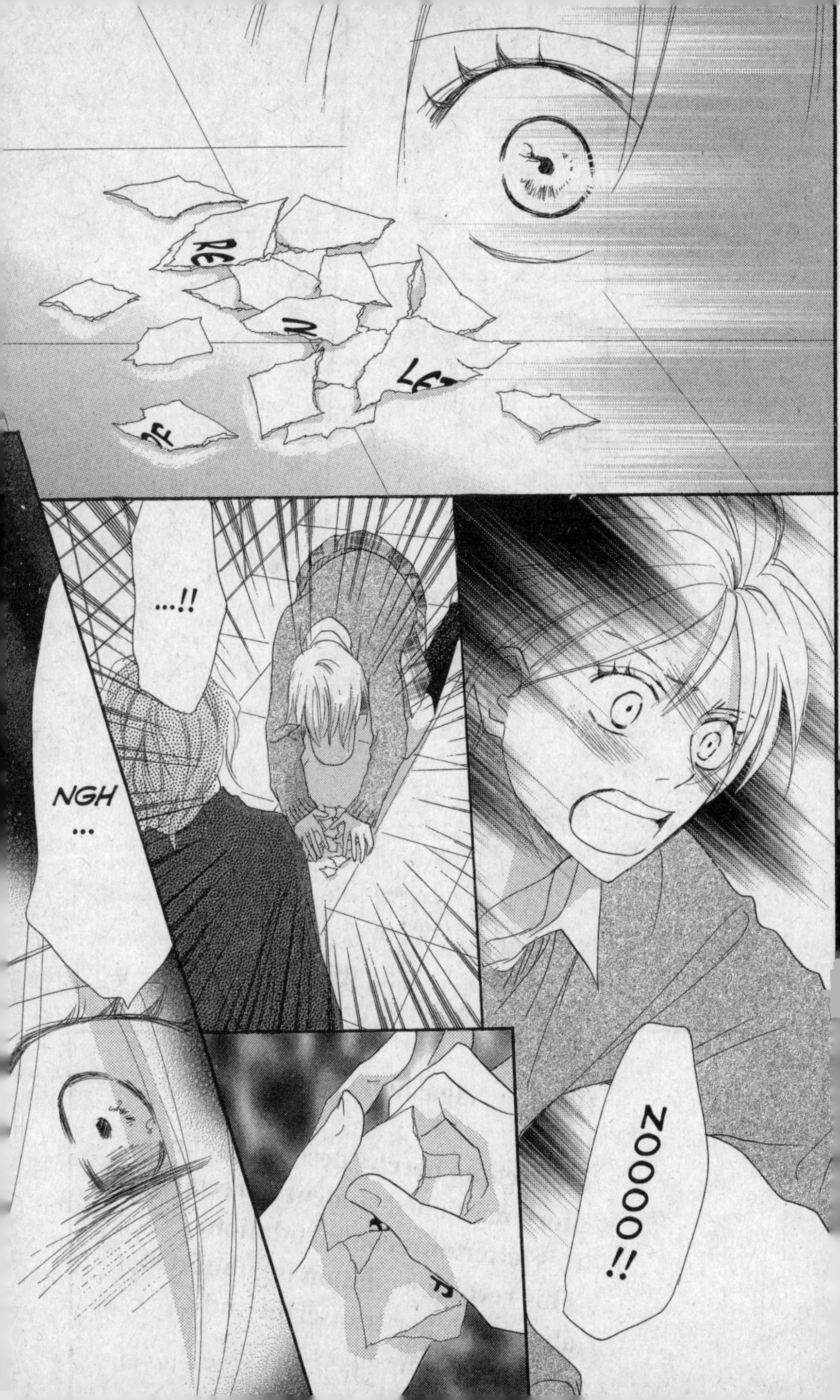
NOOOO!!
...!!
NGH ...

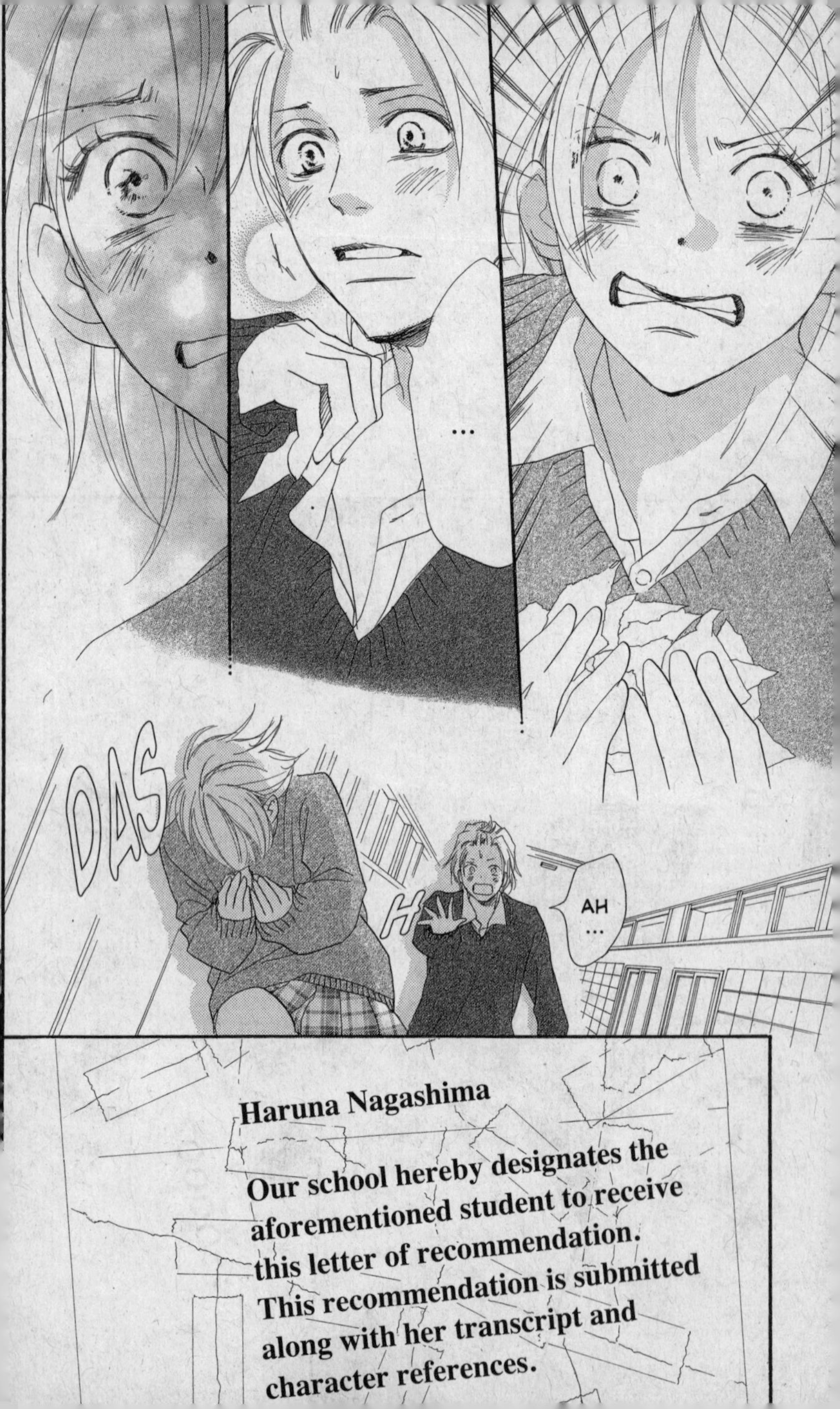
...
DASH
AH ...
Haruna Nagashima
Our school hereby designates the aforementioned student to receive this letter of recommendation. This recommendation is submitted along with her transcript and character references.

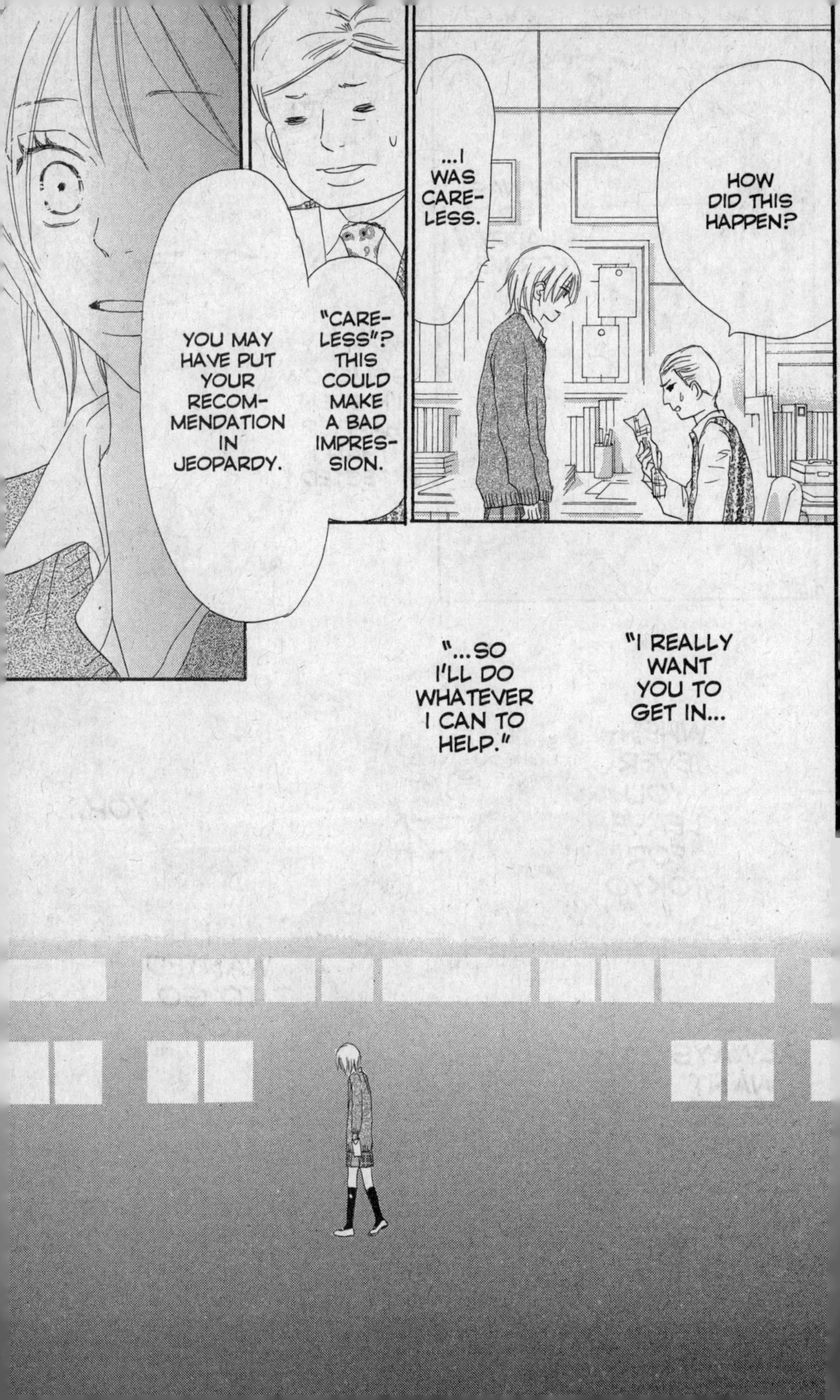
HOW DID THIS HAPPEN?
...I WAS CARELESS.
"CARELESS"? THIS COULD MAKE A BAD IMPRESSION.
YOU MAY HAVE PUT YOUR RECOMMENDATION IN JEOPARDY.
"I REALLY WANT YOU TO GET IN...
"...SO I'LL DO WHATEVER I CAN TO HELP."

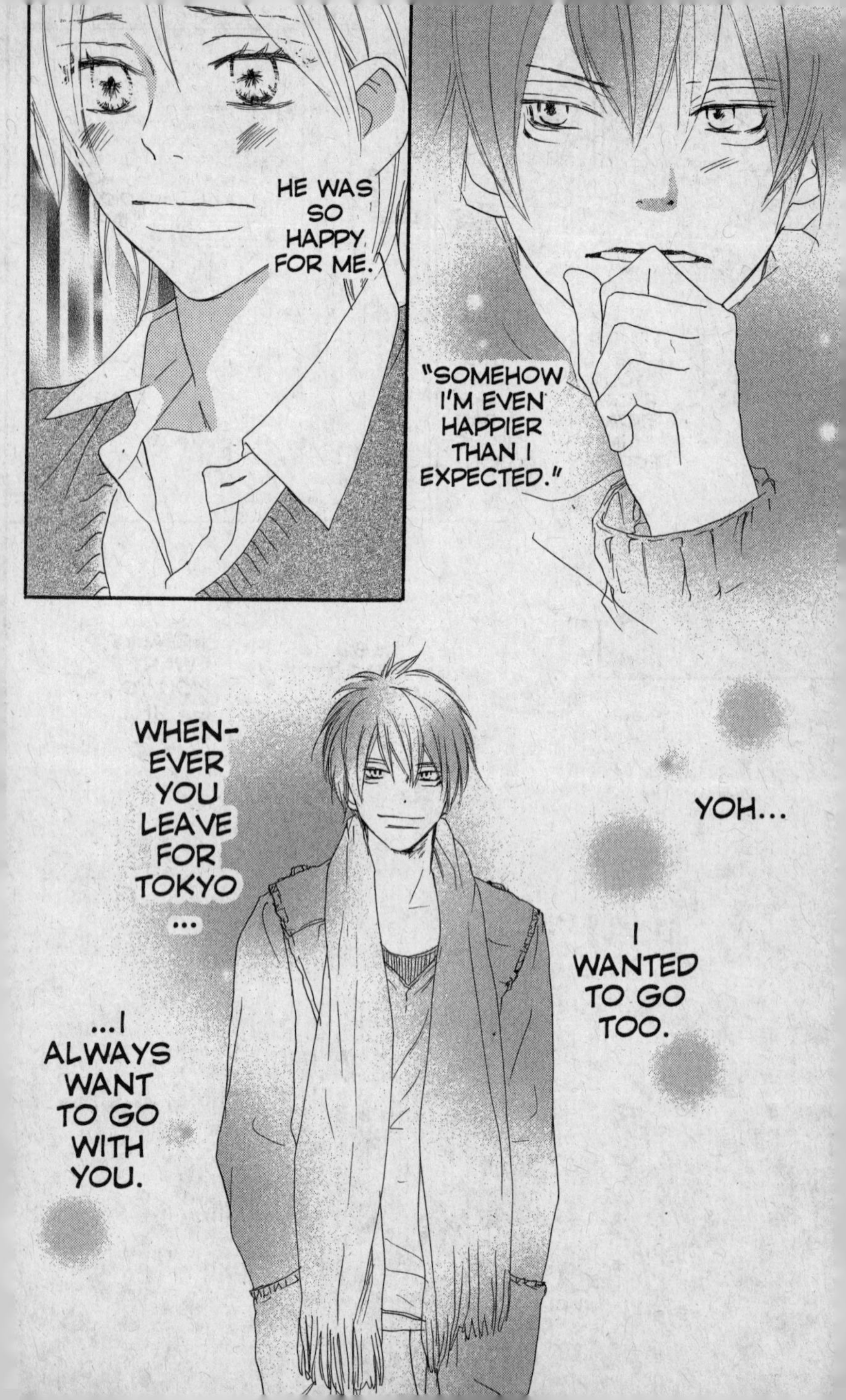
"SOMEHOW I'M EVEN HAPPIER THAN I EXPECTED."
HE WAS SO HAPPY FOR ME.
YOH...
I WANTED TO GO TOO.
WHEN-EVER YOU LEAVE FOR TOKYO...
...I ALWAYS WANT TO GO WITH YOU.

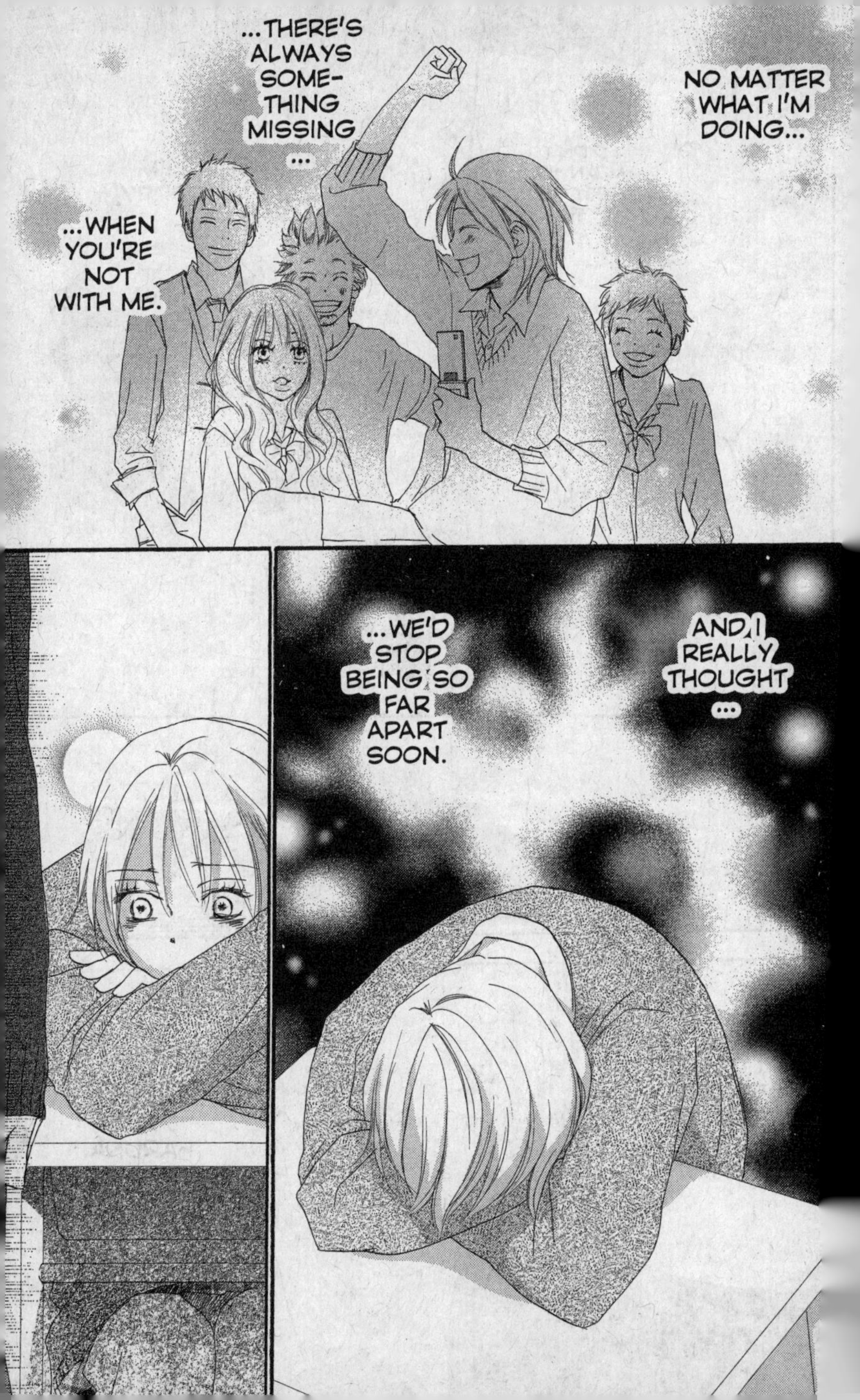
NO MATTER WHAT I'M DOING...
...THERE'S ALWAYS SOME-THING MISSING...
...WHEN YOU'RE NOT WITH ME.
AND I REALLY THOUGHT...
...WE'D STOP BEING SO FAR APART SOON.

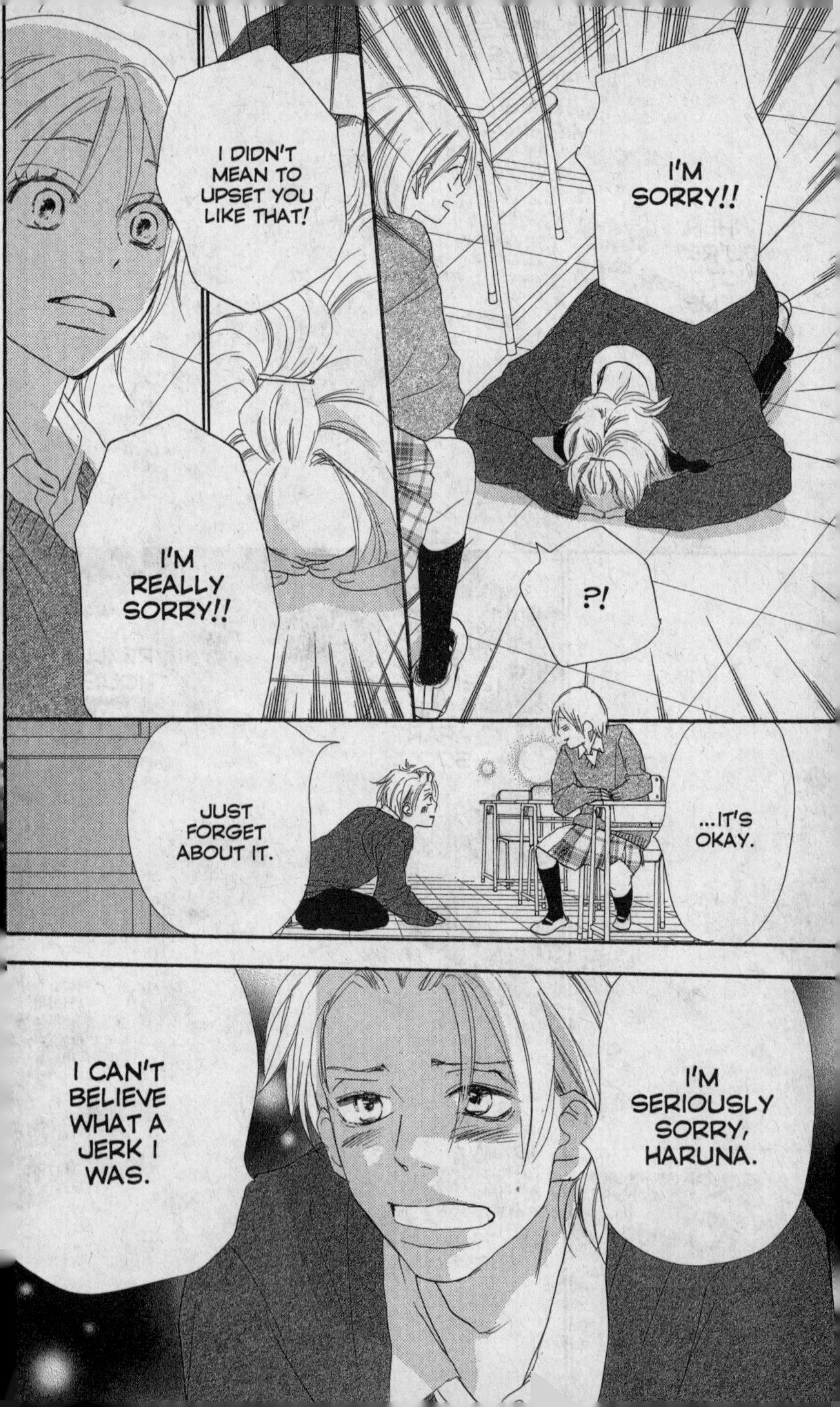
I'M SORRY!!
?!
I DIDN'T MEAN TO UPSET YOU LIKE THAT!
I'M REALLY SORRY!!
...IT'S OKAY.
JUST FORGET ABOUT IT.
I'M SERIOUSLY SORRY, HARUNA.
I CAN'T BELIEVE WHAT A JERK I WAS.

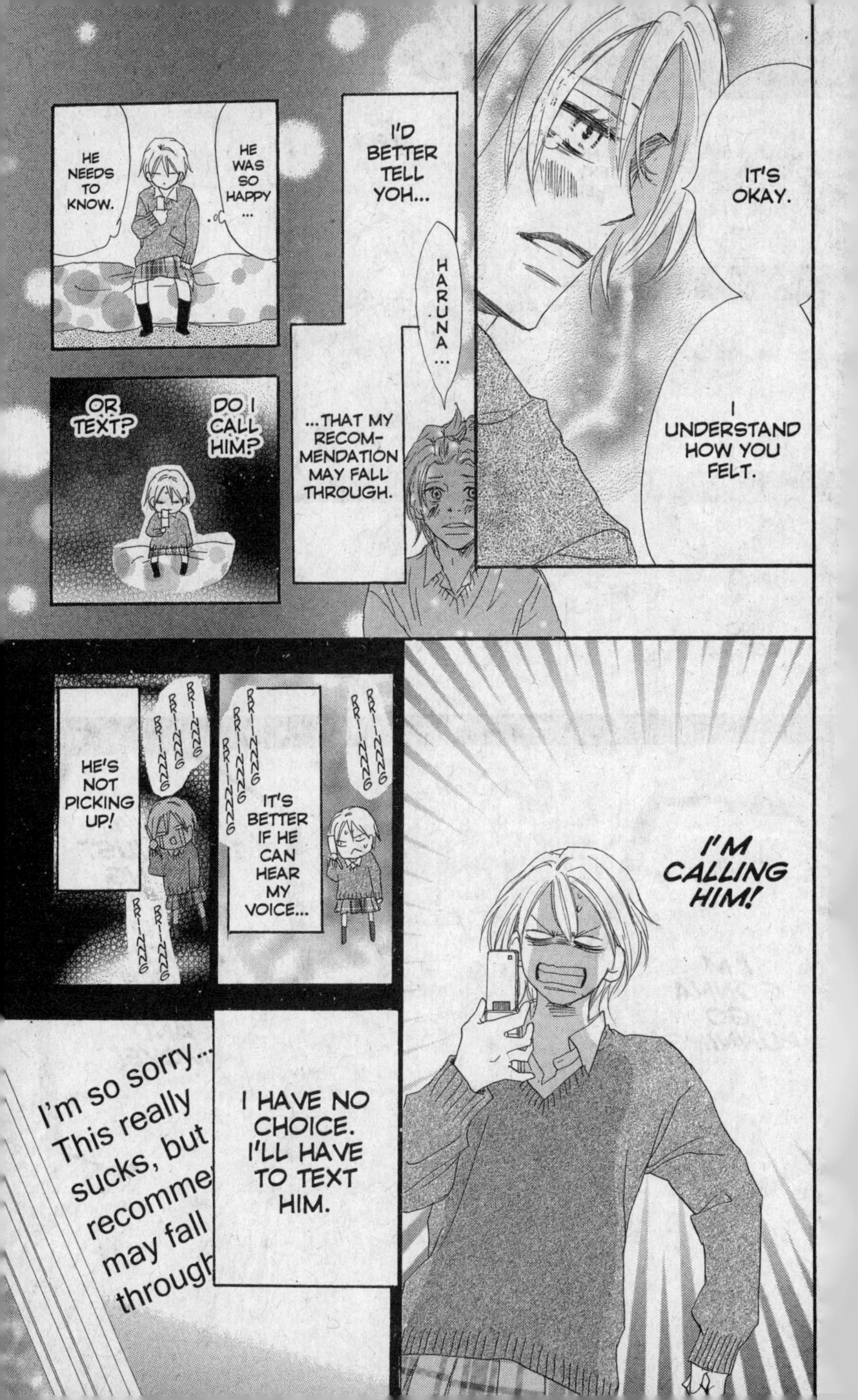
IT'S OKAY.
I UNDERSTAND HOW YOU FELT.
I'D BETTER TELL YOH...
HARUNA...
...THAT MY RECOMMENDATION MAY FALL THROUGH.
HE WAS SO HAPPY...
HE NEEDS TO KNOW.
DO I CALL HIM?
OR TEXT?
I'M CALLING HIM!
RRINNNG RRINNNG
RRINNNG RRINNNG
IT'S BETTER IF HE CAN HEAR MY VOICE...
RRINNNG RRINNNG
HE'S NOT PICKING UP!
RRINNNG RRINNNG
I HAVE NO CHOICE. I'LL HAVE TO TEXT HIM.
I'm so sorry... This really sucks, but recomme may fall through

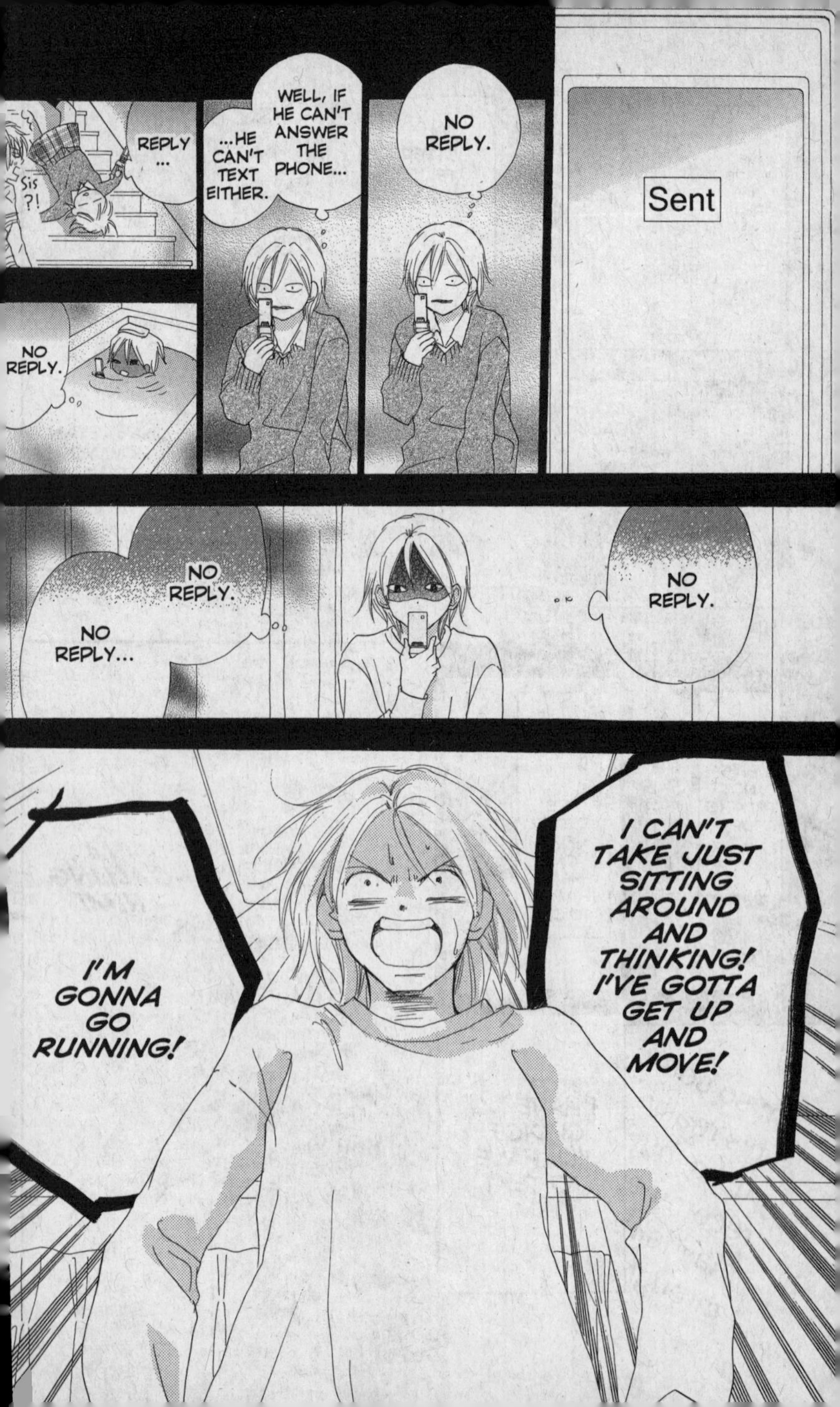
Sent
NO REPLY.
WELL, IF HE CAN'T ANSWER THE PHONE...
...HE CAN'T TEXT EITHER.
REPLY ...
Sis ?!
NO REPLY.
NO REPLY.
NO REPLY.
NO REPLY...
I CAN'T TAKE JUST SITTING AROUND AND THINKING! I'VE GOTTA GET UP AND MOVE!
I'M GONNA GO RUNNING!

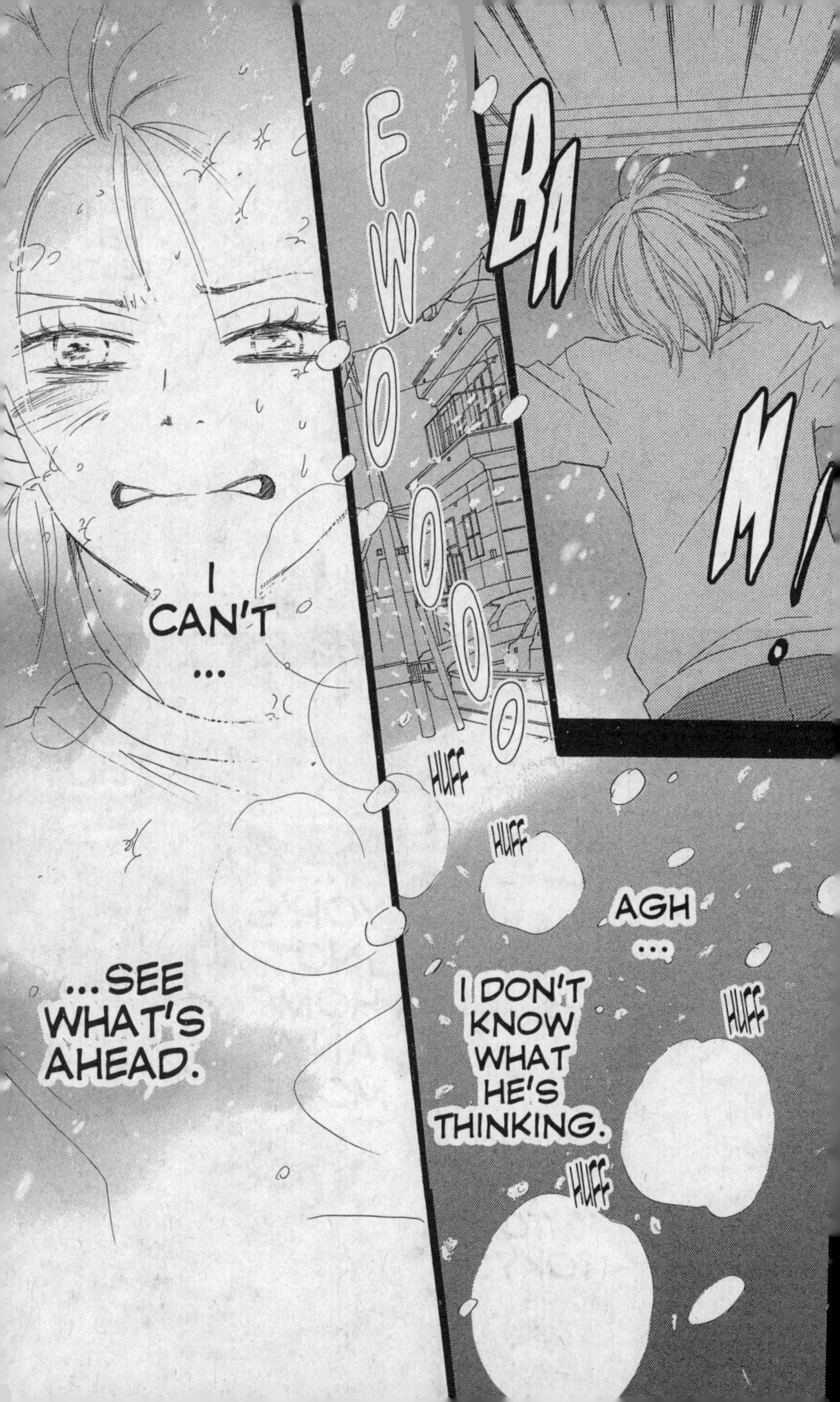
BAM!
HUFF
HUFF
AGH...
I DON'T KNOW WHAT HE'S THINKING.
HUFF
HUFF
FWOOOOOO
I CAN'T...
...SEE WHAT'S AHEAD.

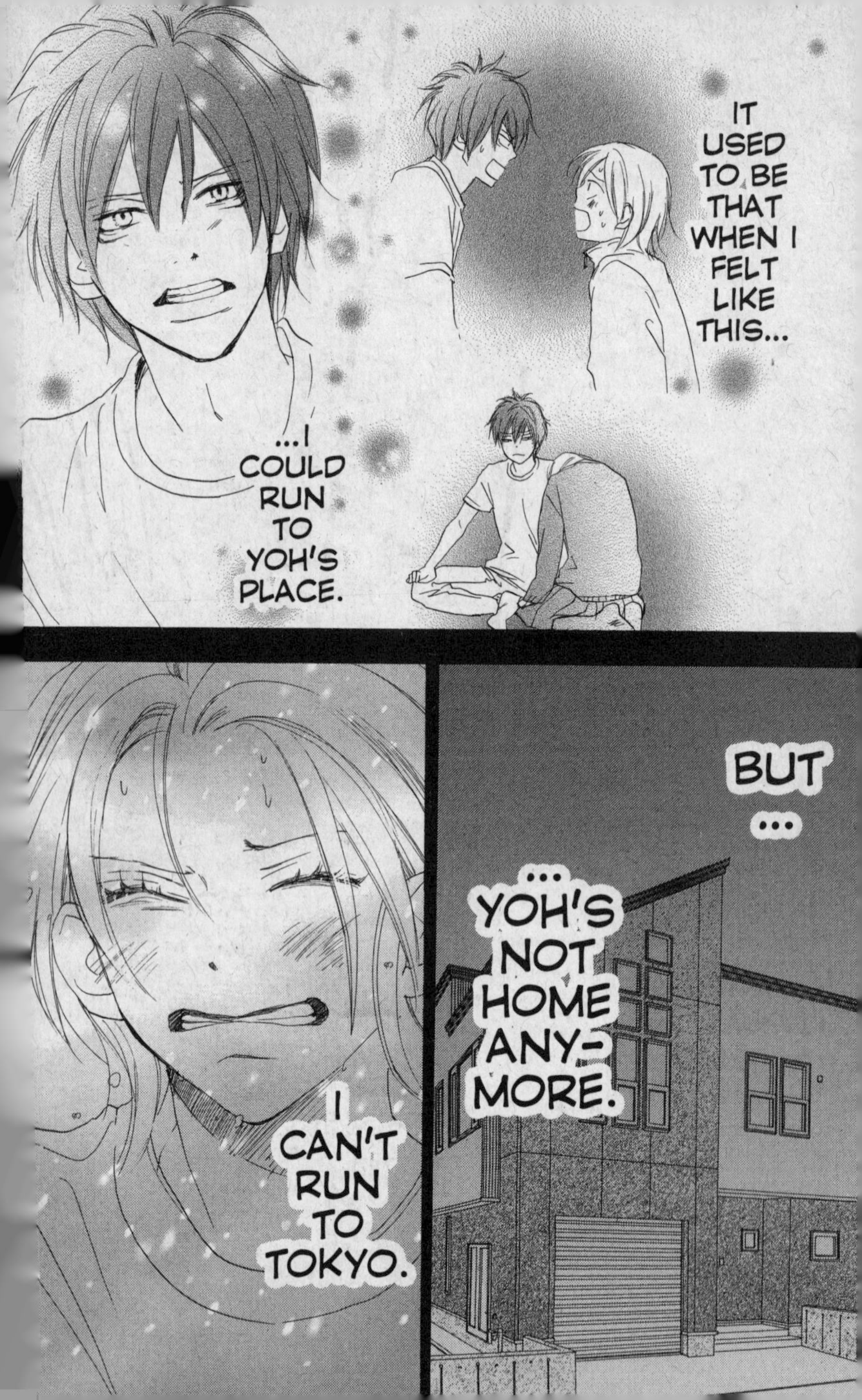
IT USED TO BE THAT WHEN I FELT LIKE THIS...
...I COULD RUN TO YOH'S PLACE.
BUT...
...YOH'S NOT HOME ANY-MORE.
I CAN'T RUN TO TOKYO.

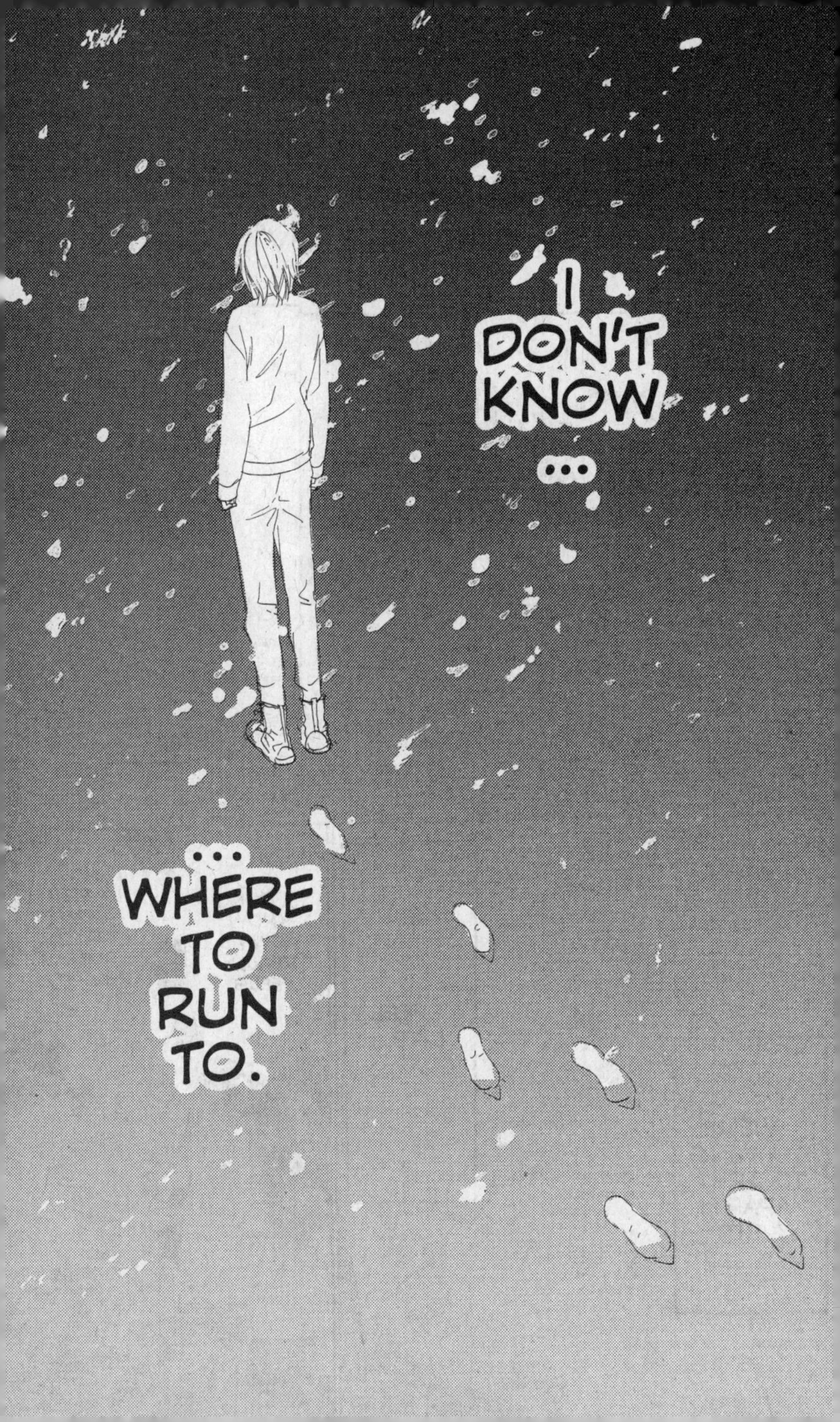
I DON'T KNOW...
...WHERE TO RUN TO.

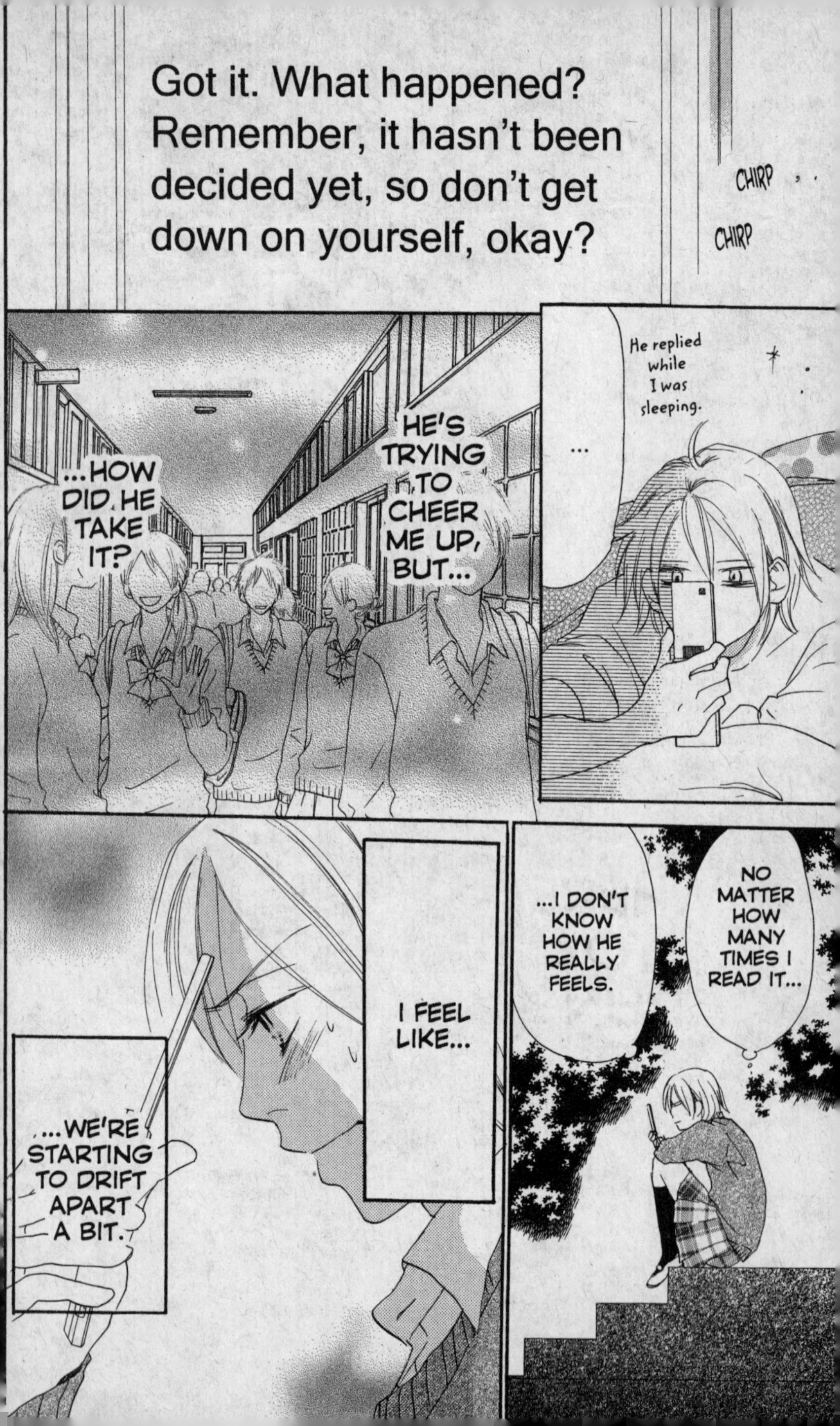
Got it. What happened? Remember, it hasn't been decided yet, so don't get down on yourself, okay?
CHIRP
CHIRP
He replied while I was sleeping.
...
HE'S TRYING TO CHEER ME UP, BUT...
...HOW DID HE TAKE IT?
NO MATTER HOW MANY TIMES I READ IT...
...I DON'T KNOW HOW HE REALLY FEELS.
I FEEL LIKE...
...WE'RE STARTING TO DRIFT APART A BIT.

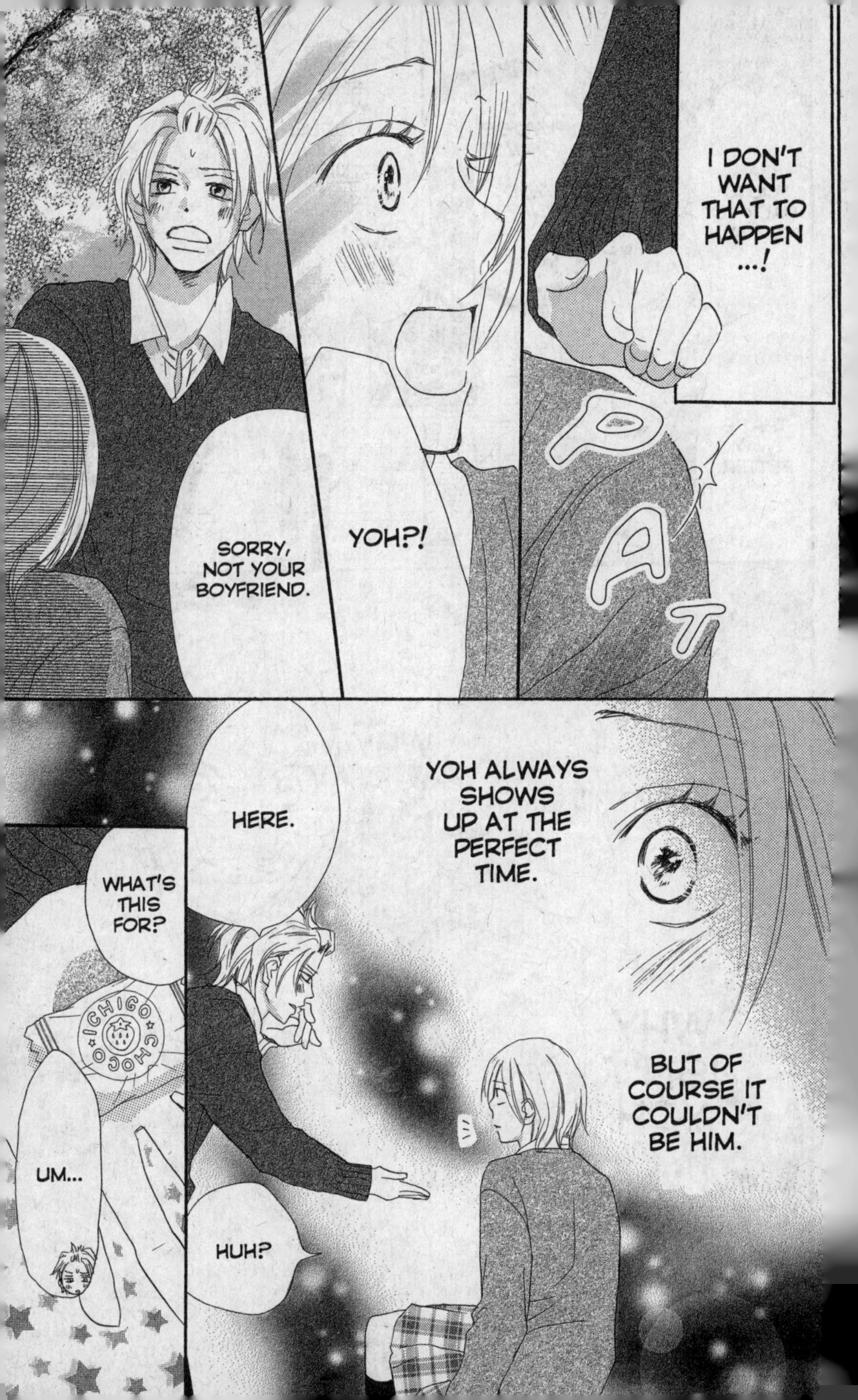
I DON'T WANT THAT TO HAPPEN ...!
PAT
YOH?!
SORRY, NOT YOUR BOYFRIEND.
YOH ALWAYS SHOWS UP AT THE PERFECT TIME.
BUT OF COURSE IT COULDN'T BE HIM.
HERE.
HUH?
WHAT'S THIS FOR?
ICHIGO CHOCO
UM...

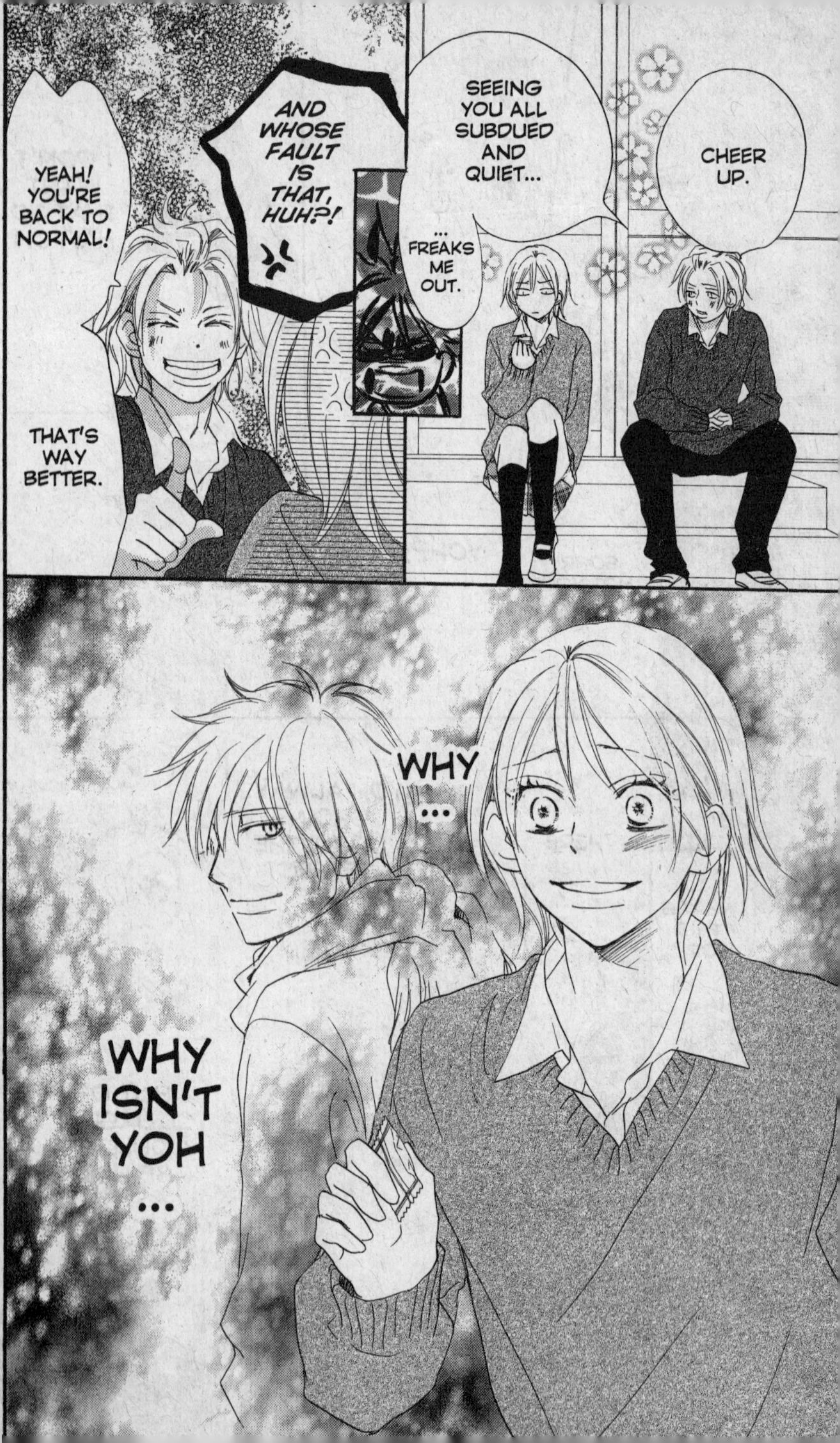
CHEER UP.
SEEING YOU ALL SUBDUED AND QUIET...
... FREAKS ME OUT.
AND WHOSE FAULT IS THAT, HUH?!
YEAH! YOU'RE BACK TO NORMAL!
THAT'S WAY BETTER.
WHY ...
WHY ISN'T YOH ...

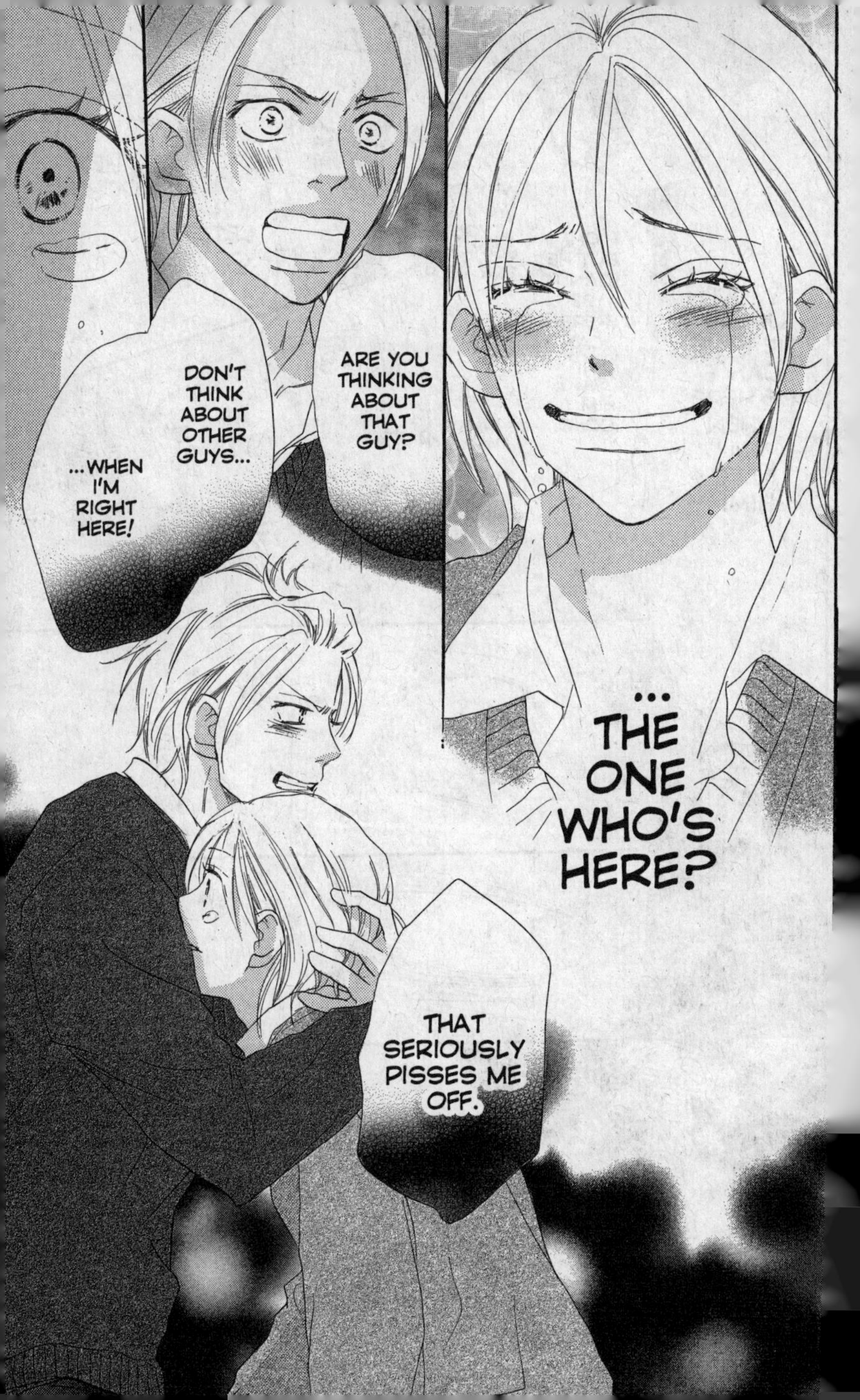
ARE YOU THINKING ABOUT THAT GUY?
DON'T THINK ABOUT OTHER GUYS...
...WHEN I'M RIGHT HERE!
...THE ONE WHO'S HERE?
THAT SERIOUSLY PISSES ME OFF.

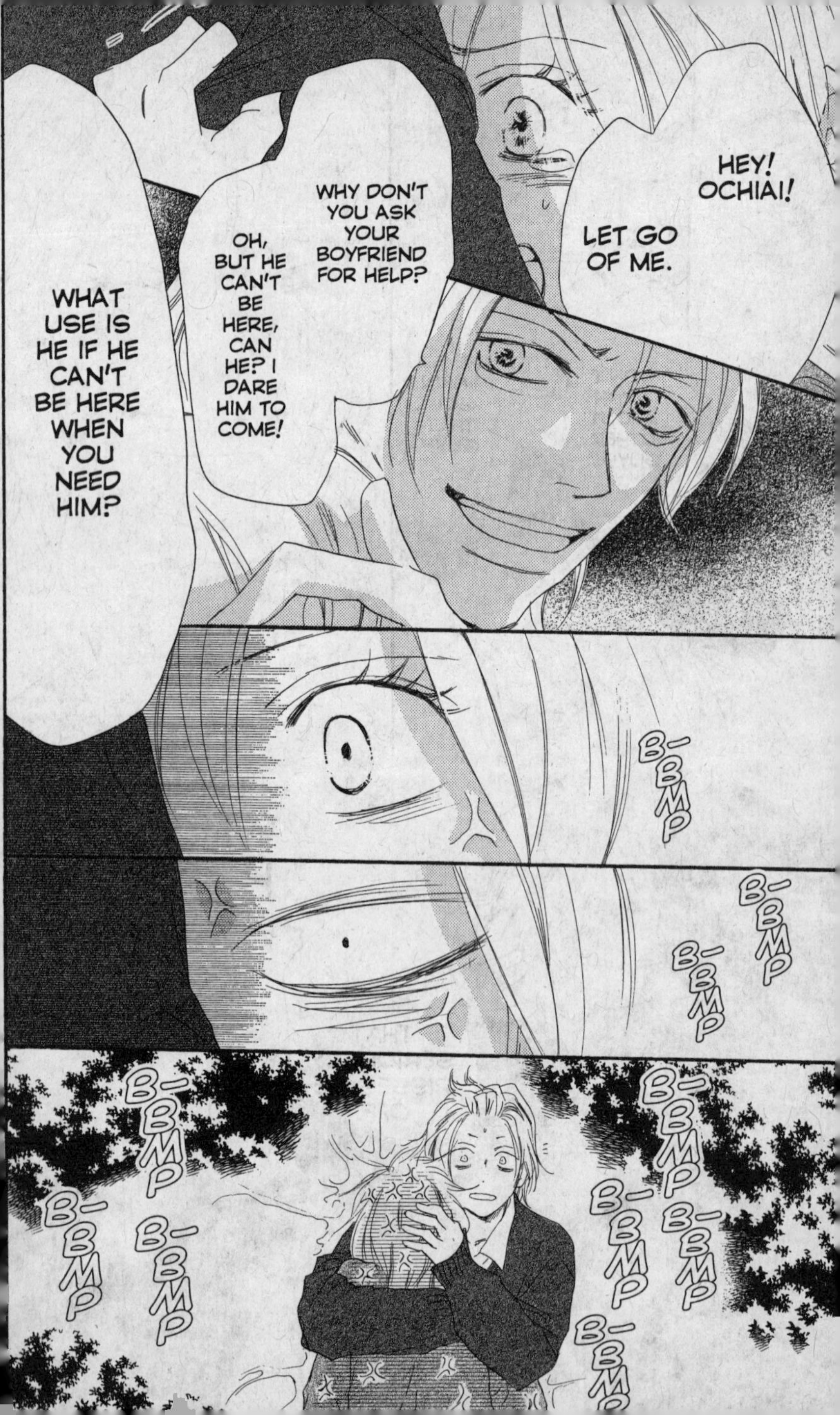

HEY! OCHIAI!
LET GO OF ME.
WHY DON'T YOU ASK YOUR BOYFRIEND FOR HELP?
OH, BUT HE CAN'T BE HERE, CAN HE? I DARE HIM TO COME!
WHAT USE IS HE IF HE CAN'T BE HERE WHEN YOU NEED HIM?
B-BMP
B-BMP
B-BMP
B-BMP
B-BMP
B-BMP
B-BMP
B-BMP
B-BMP

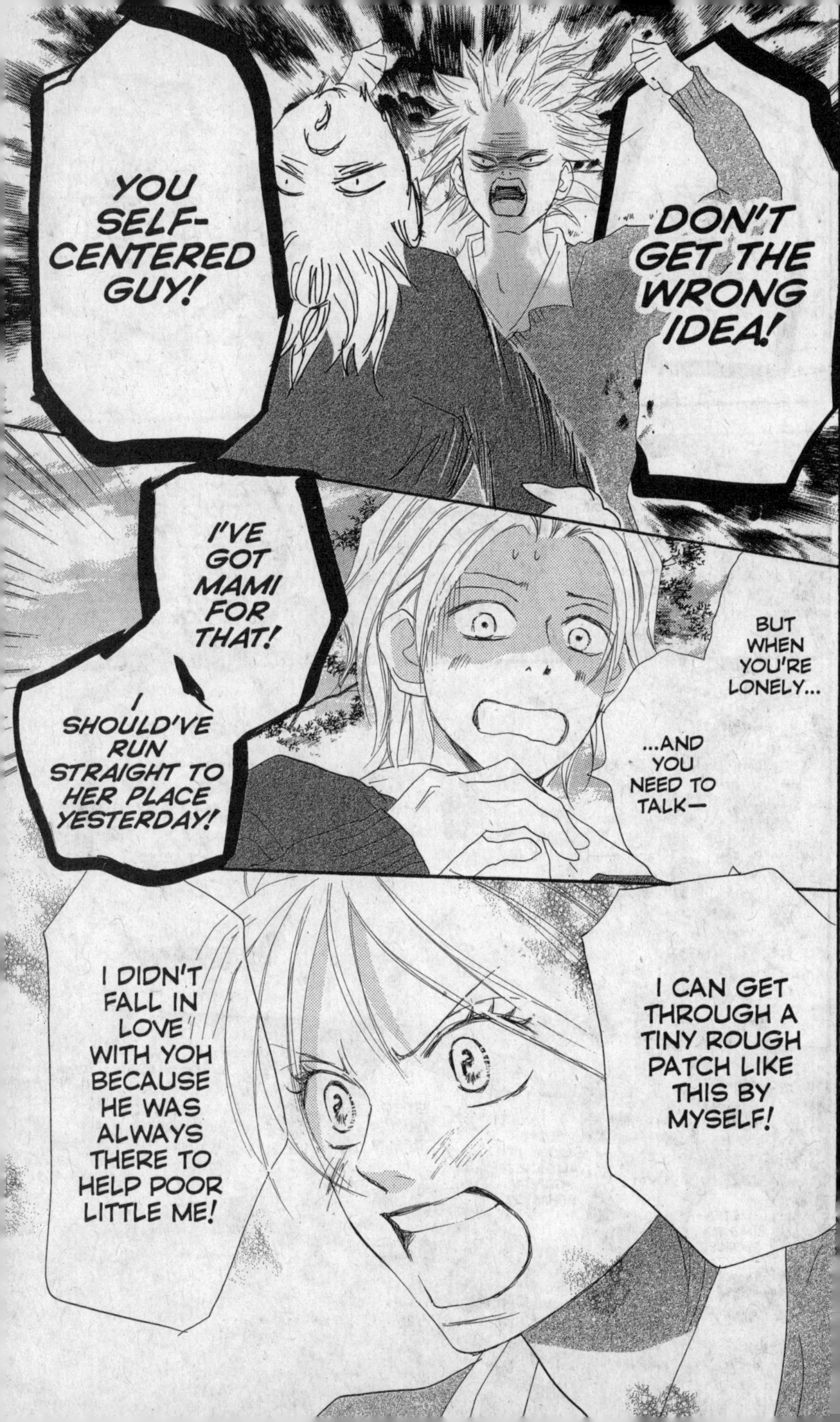
DON'T GET THE WRONG IDEA!
YOU SELF-CENTERED GUY!
BUT WHEN YOU'RE LONELY...
...AND YOU NEED TO TALK—
I'VE GOT MAMI FOR THAT!
I SHOULD'VE RUN STRAIGHT TO HER PLACE YESTERDAY!
I CAN GET THROUGH A TINY ROUGH PATCH LIKE THIS BY MYSELF!
I DIDN'T FALL IN LOVE WITH YOH BECAUSE HE WAS ALWAYS THERE TO HELP POOR LITTLE ME!

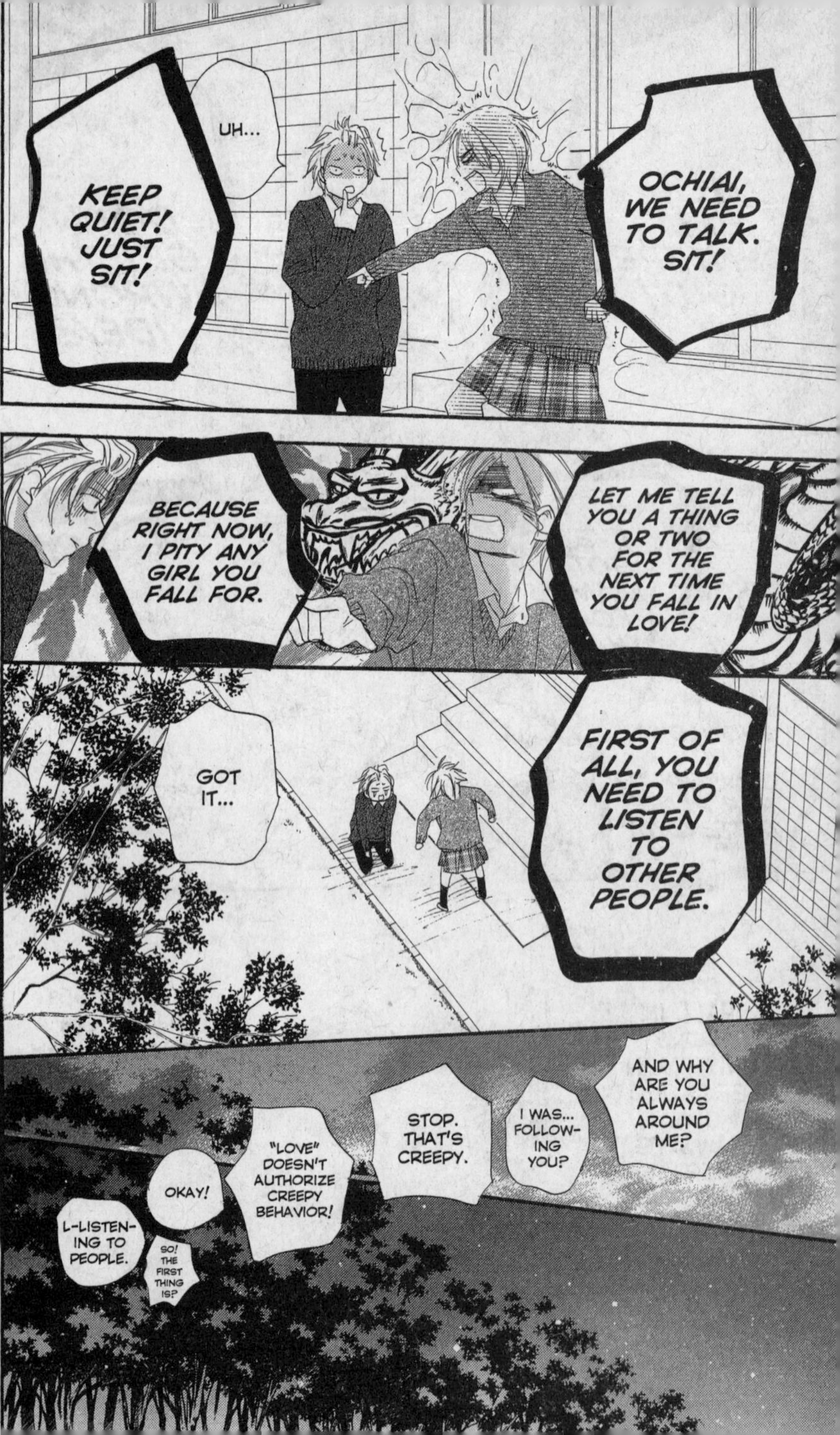
OCHIAI, WE NEED TO TALK. SIT!
UH...
KEEP QUIET! JUST SIT!
LET ME TELL YOU A THING OR TWO FOR THE NEXT TIME YOU FALL IN LOVE!
BECAUSE RIGHT NOW, I PITY ANY GIRL YOU FALL FOR.
FIRST OF ALL, YOU NEED TO LISTEN TO OTHER PEOPLE.
GOT IT...
AND WHY ARE YOU ALWAYS AROUND ME?
I WAS... FOLLOW-ING YOU?
STOP. THAT'S CREEPY.
"LOVE" DOESN'T AUTHORIZE CREEPY BEHAVIOR!
OKAY!
SO! THE FIRST THING IS?
L-LISTEN-ING TO PEOPLE.

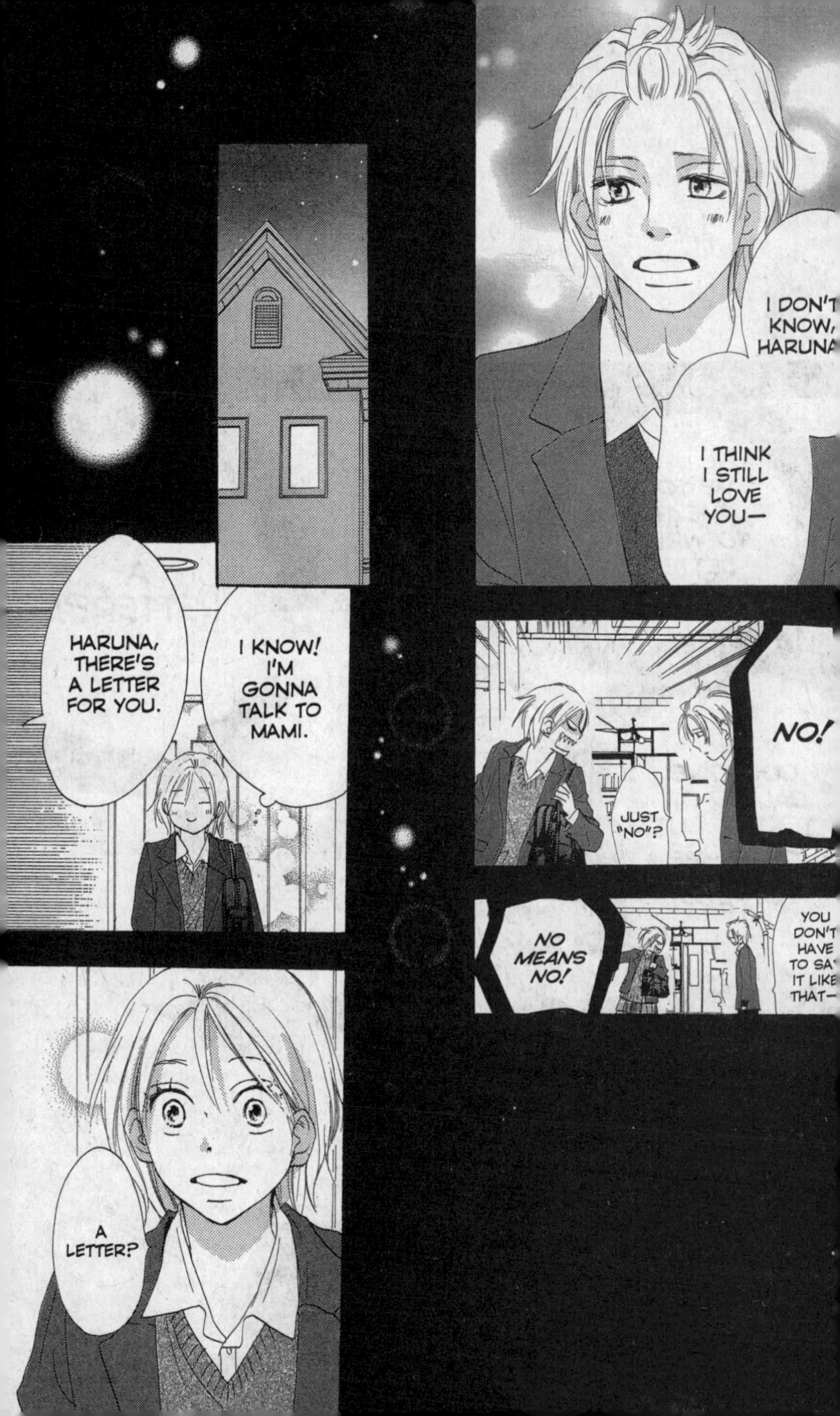
I DON'T KNOW, HARUNA
I THINK I STILL LOVE YOU—
NO!
JUST "NO"?
YOU DON'T HAVE TO SA IT LIKE THAT—
NO MEANS NO!
I KNOW! I'M GONNA TALK TO MAMI.
HARUNA, THERE'S A LETTER FOR YOU.
A LETTER?

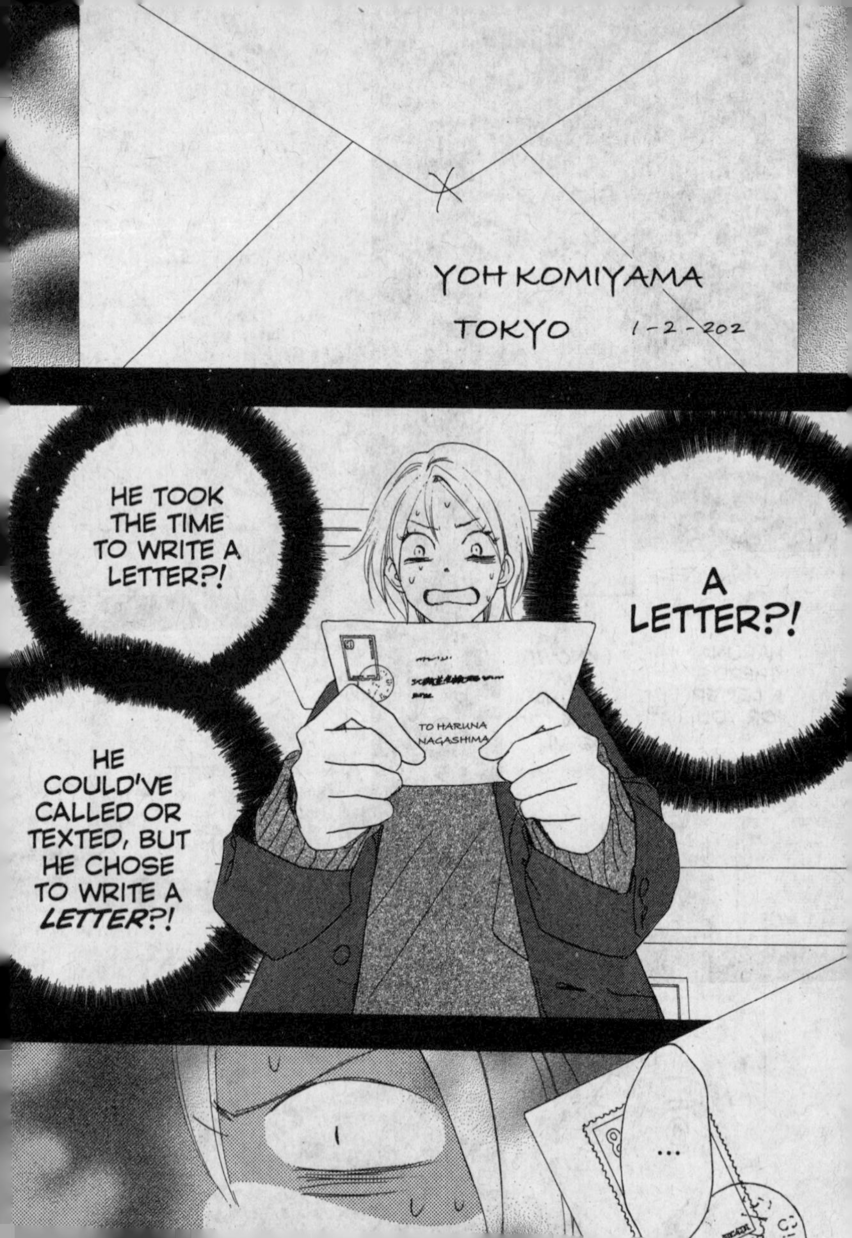
YOH KOMIYAMA
TOKYO 1-2-202
A LETTER?!
HE TOOK THE TIME TO WRITE A LETTER?!
TO HARUNA NAGASHIMA
HE COULD'VE CALLED OR TEXTED, BUT HE CHOSE TO WRITE A *LETTER*?!
...

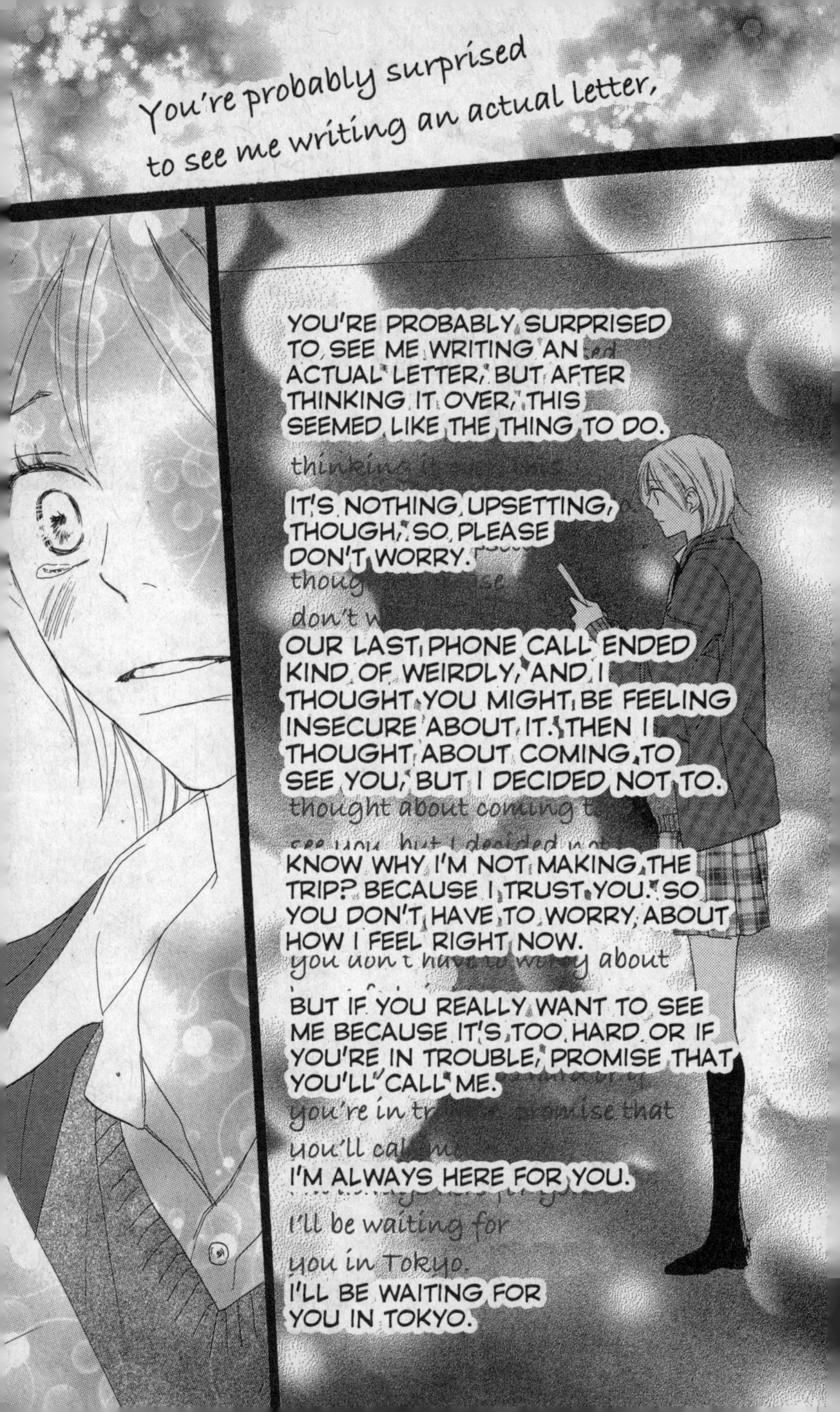
You're probably surprised to see me writing an actual letter,
YOU'RE PROBABLY SURPRISED TO SEE ME WRITING AN ACTUAL LETTER, BUT AFTER THINKING IT OVER, THIS SEEMED LIKE THE THING TO DO.
IT'S NOTHING UPSETTING, THOUGH, SO PLEASE DON'T WORRY.
OUR LAST PHONE CALL ENDED KIND OF WEIRDLY, AND I THOUGHT YOU MIGHT BE FEELING INSECURE ABOUT IT. THEN I THOUGHT ABOUT COMING TO SEE YOU, BUT I DECIDED NOT TO.
KNOW WHY I'M NOT MAKING THE TRIP? BECAUSE I TRUST YOU. SO YOU DON'T HAVE TO WORRY ABOUT HOW I FEEL RIGHT NOW.
BUT IF YOU REALLY WANT TO SEE ME BECAUSE IT'S TOO HARD OR IF YOU'RE IN TROUBLE, PROMISE THAT YOU'LL CALL ME.
I'M ALWAYS HERE FOR YOU.
I'll be waiting for you in Tokyo.
I'LL BE WAITING FOR YOU IN TOKYO.

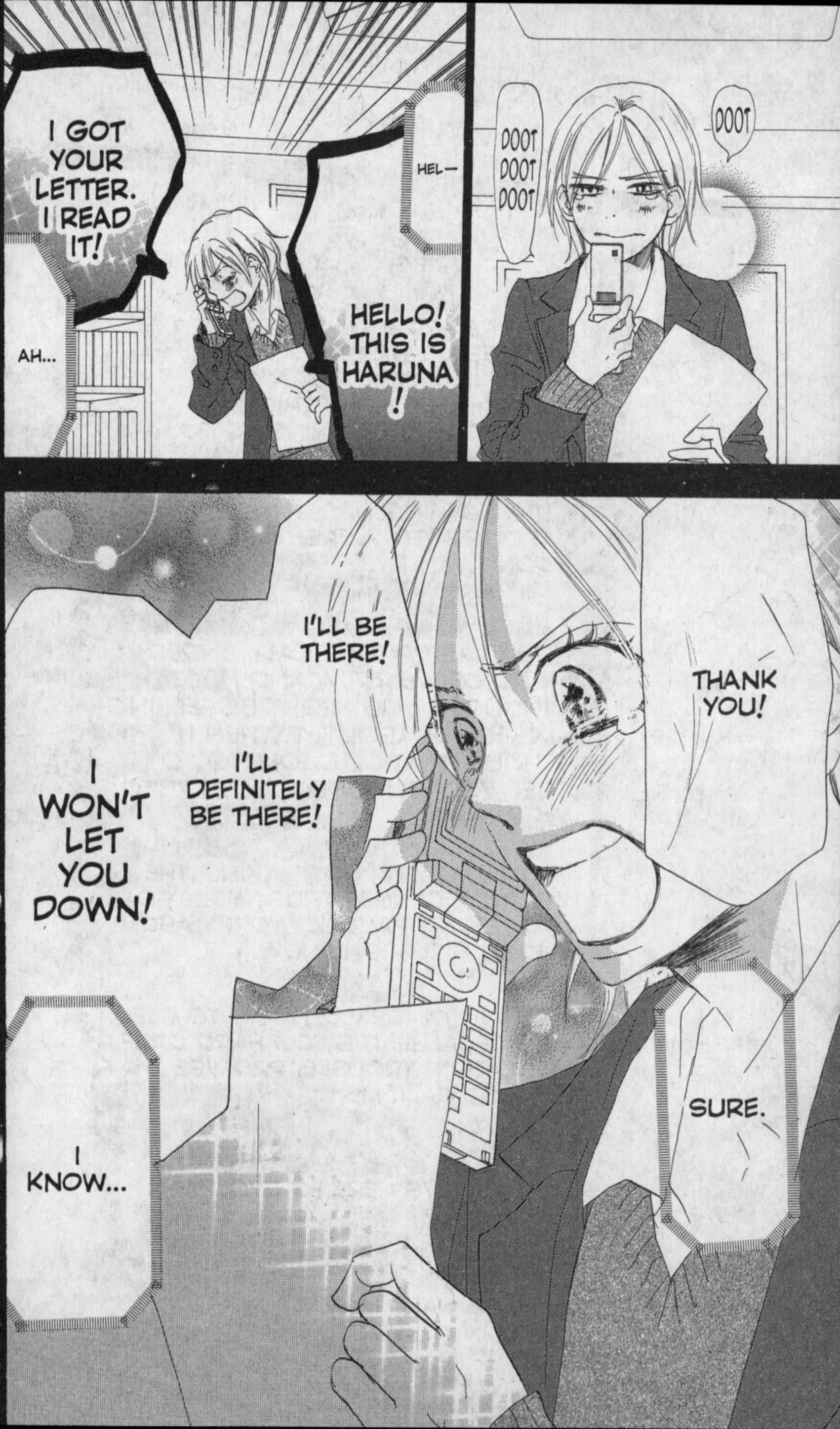
DOOT
DOOT DOOT DOOT
HEL—
HELLO! THIS IS HARUNA!
I GOT YOUR LETTER. I READ IT!
AH...
THANK YOU!
I'LL BE THERE!
I'LL DEFINITELY BE THERE!
I WON'T LET YOU DOWN!
SURE.
I KNOW...

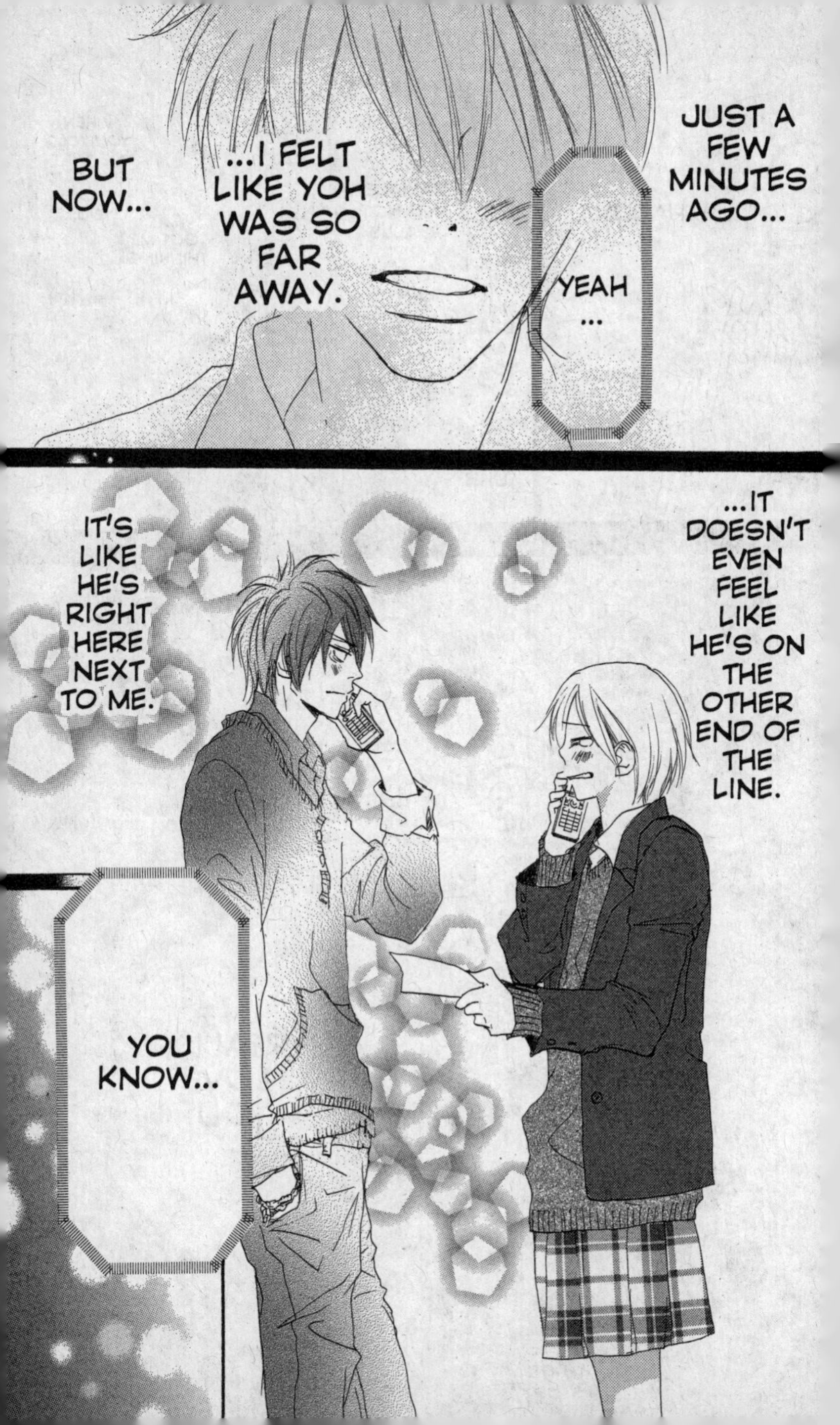
JUST A FEW MINUTES AGO...
YEAH...
...I FELT LIKE YOH WAS SO FAR AWAY.
BUT NOW...
...IT DOESN'T EVEN FEEL LIKE HE'S ON THE OTHER END OF THE LINE.
IT'S LIKE HE'S RIGHT HERE NEXT TO ME.
YOU KNOW...

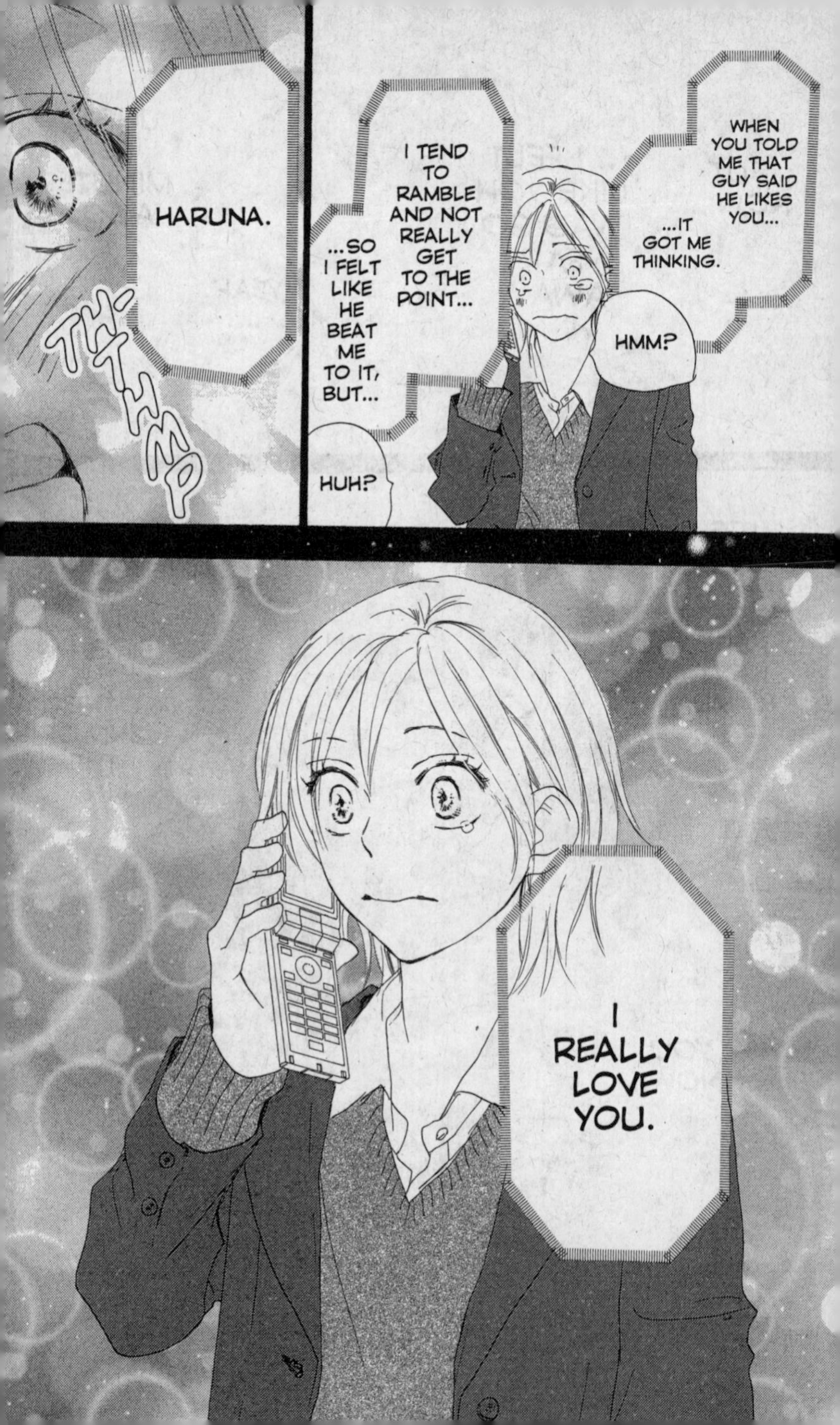
WHEN YOU TOLD ME THAT GUY SAID HE LIKES YOU...
...IT GOT ME THINKING.
HMM?
I TEND TO RAMBLE AND NOT REALLY GET TO THE POINT...
...SO I FELT LIKE HE BEAT ME TO IT, BUT...
HUH?
HARUNA.
TH-THUMP
I REALLY LOVE YOU.

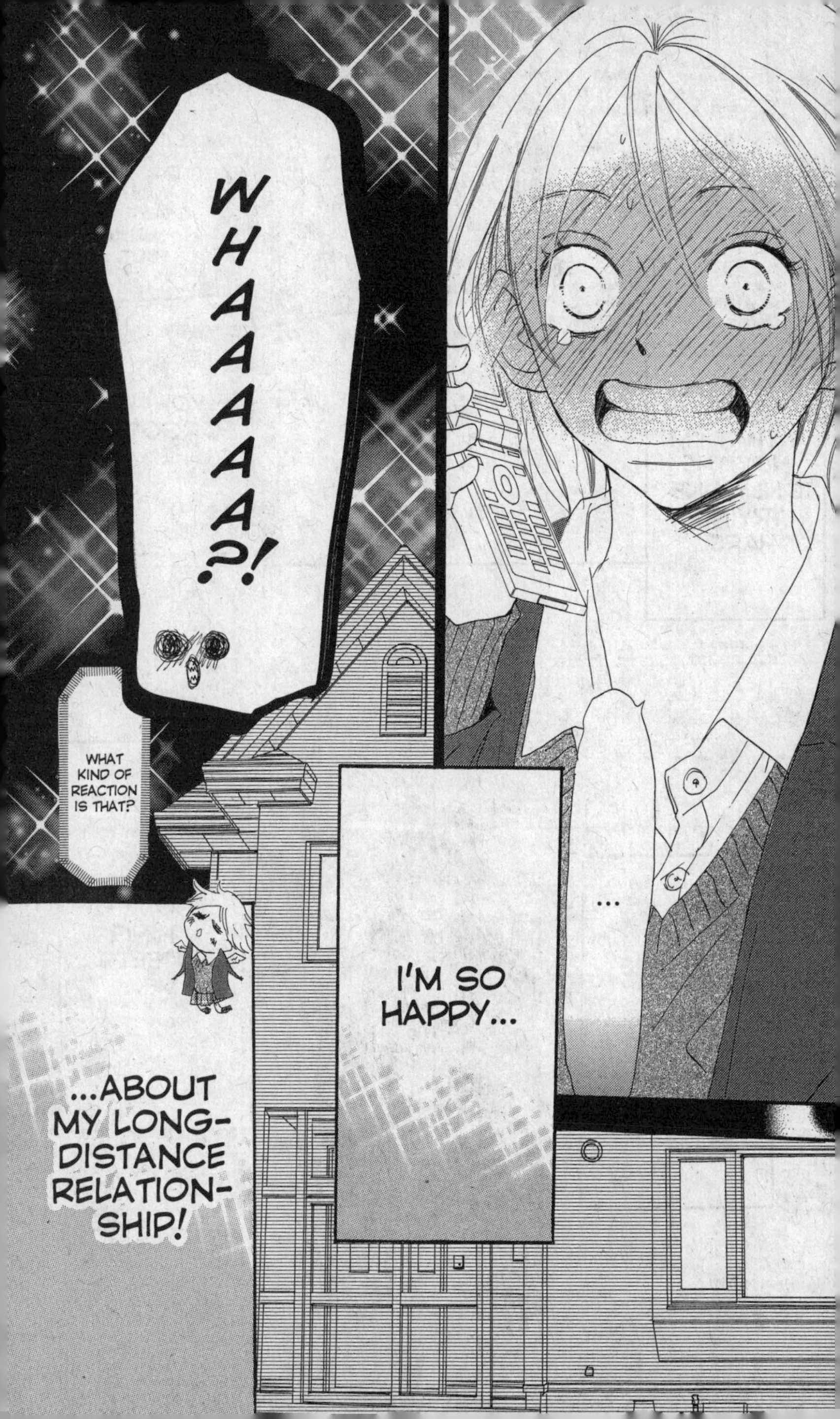
WHAAAAA?!
WHAT KIND OF REACTION IS THAT?
...
I'M SO HAPPY...
...ABOUT MY LONG-DISTANCE RELATIONSHIP!

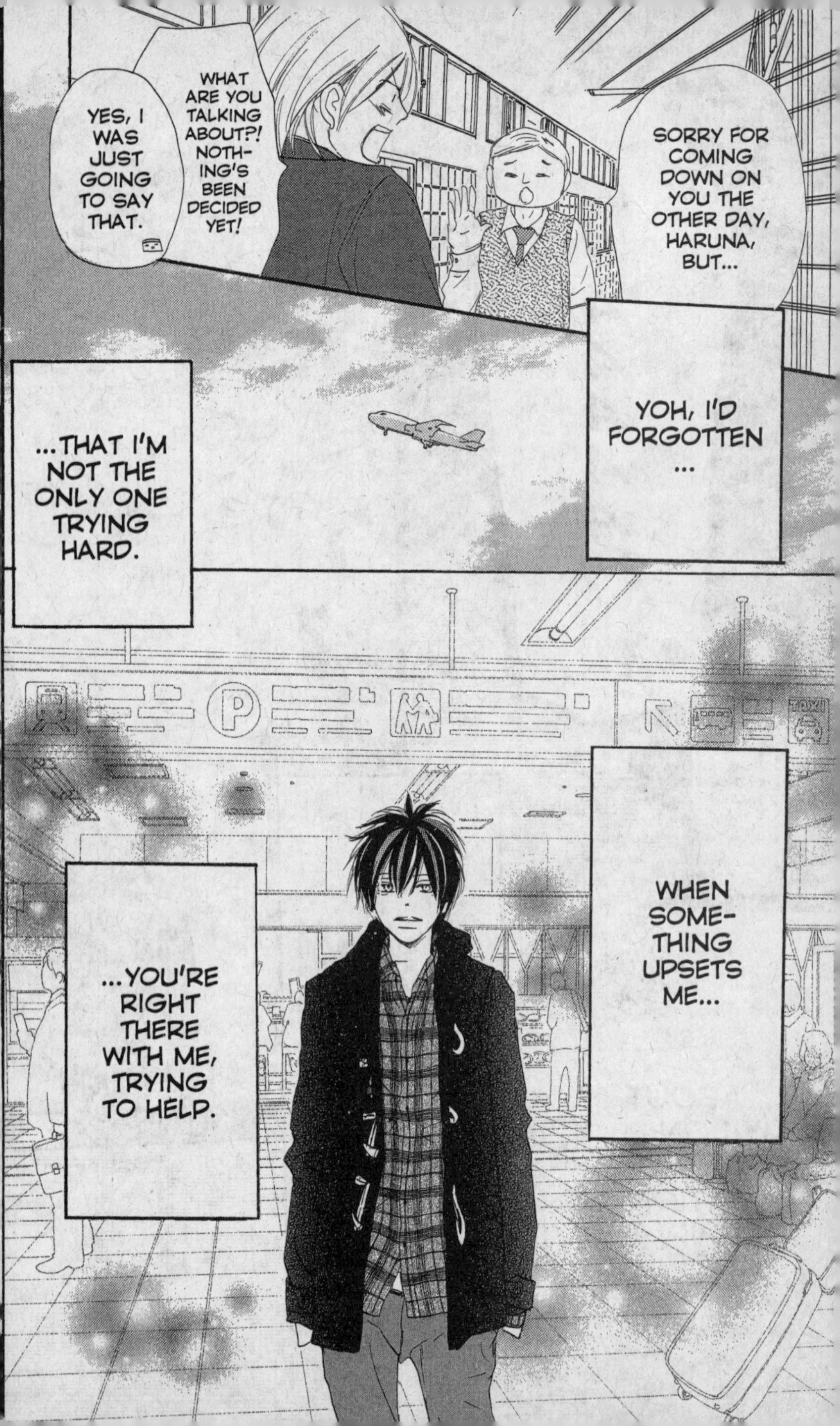
SORRY FOR COMING DOWN ON YOU THE OTHER DAY, HARUNA, BUT...
WHAT ARE YOU TALKING ABOUT?! NOTHING'S BEEN DECIDED YET!
YES, I WAS JUST GOING TO SAY THAT.
YOH, I'D FORGOTTEN...
...THAT I'M NOT THE ONLY ONE TRYING HARD.
WHEN SOMETHING UPSETS ME...
...YOU'RE RIGHT THERE WITH ME, TRYING TO HELP.

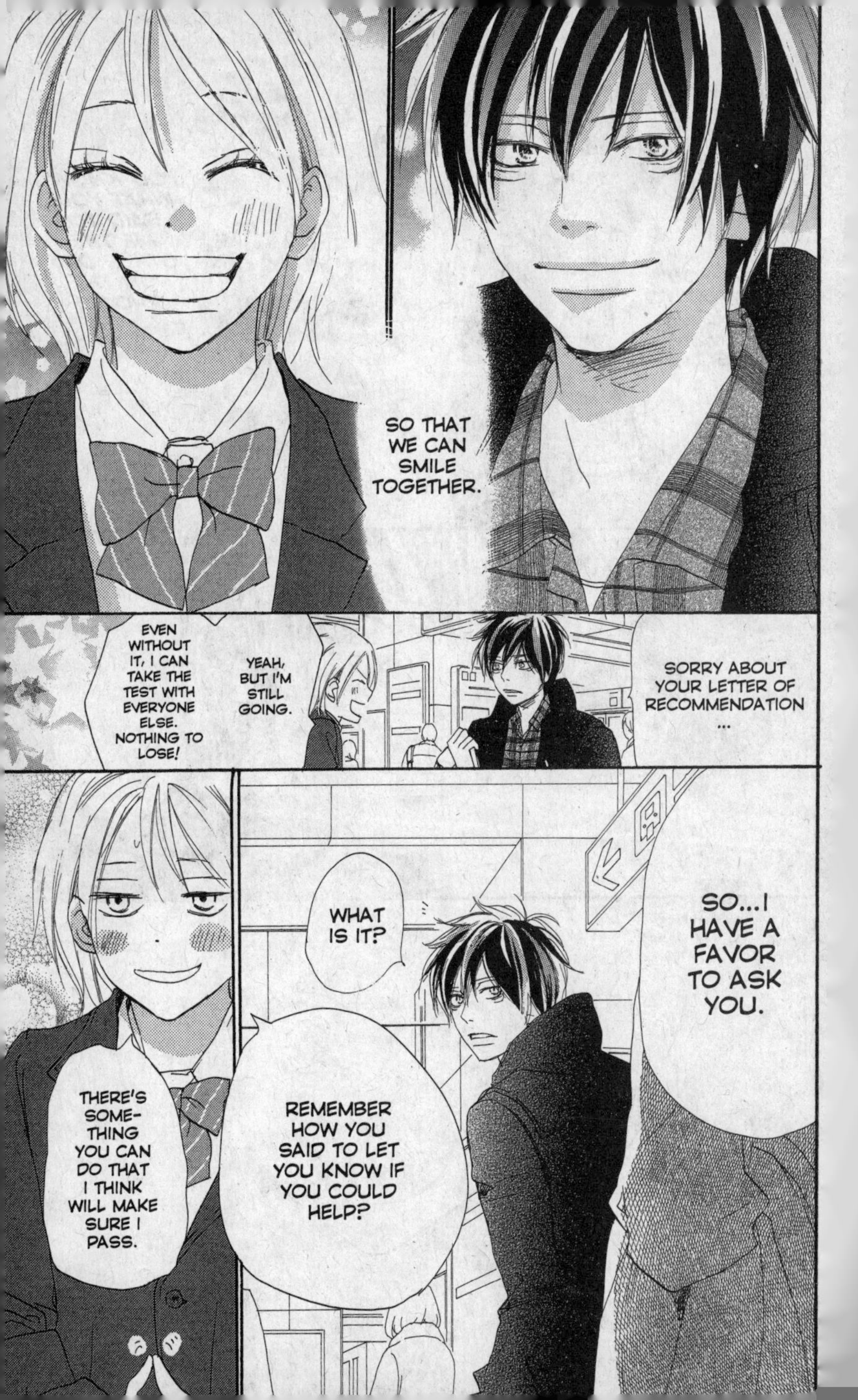
SO THAT WE CAN SMILE TOGETHER.
SORRY ABOUT YOUR LETTER OF RECOMMENDATION ...
YEAH, BUT I'M STILL GOING.
EVEN WITHOUT IT, I CAN TAKE THE TEST WITH EVERYONE ELSE. NOTHING TO LOSE!
SO...I HAVE A FAVOR TO ASK YOU.
WHAT IS IT?
REMEMBER HOW YOU SAID TO LET YOU KNOW IF YOU COULD HELP?
THERE'S SOMETHING YOU CAN DO THAT I THINK WILL MAKE SURE I PASS.

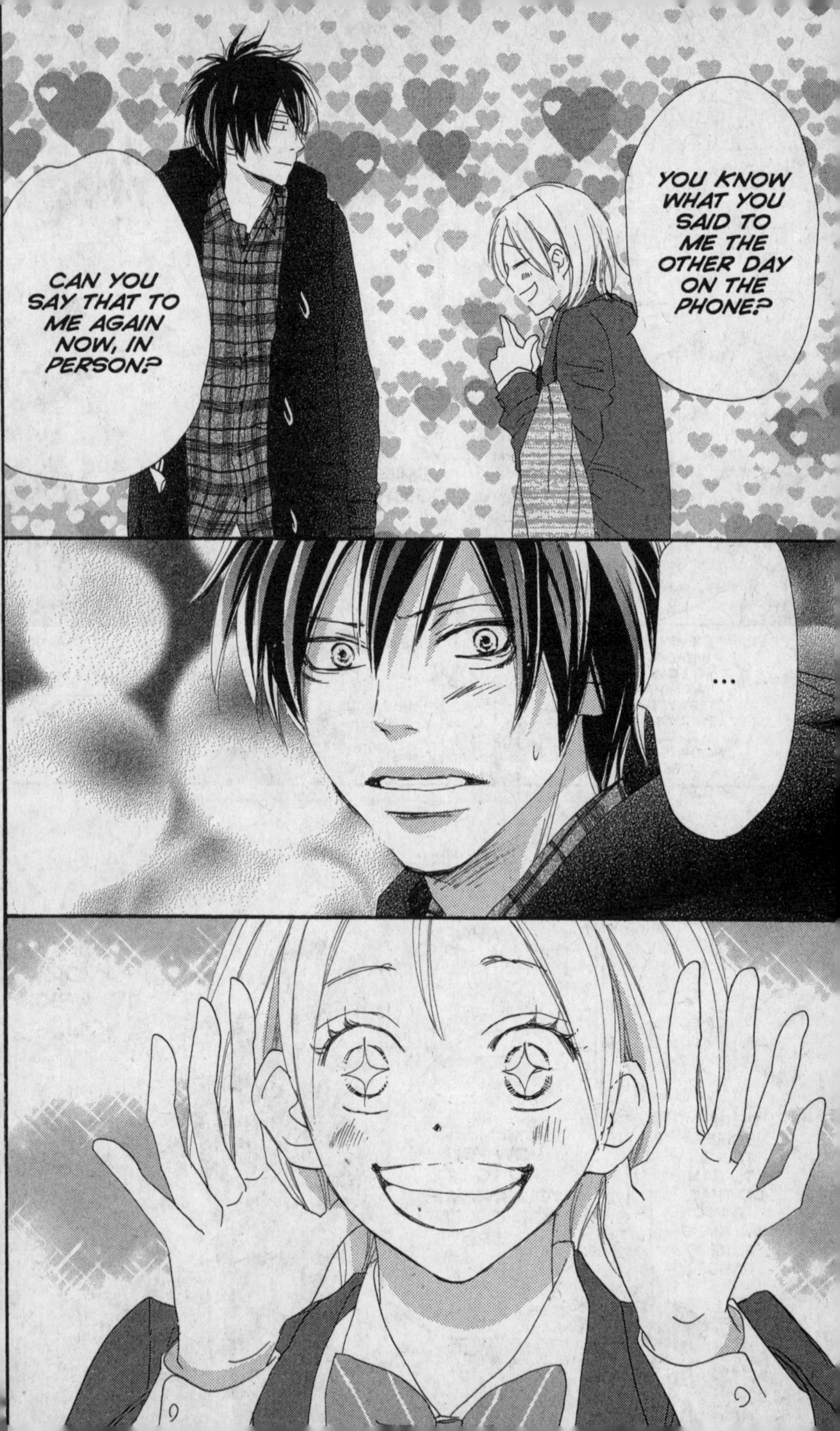
YOU KNOW WHAT YOU SAID TO ME THE OTHER DAY ON THE PHONE?
CAN YOU SAY THAT TO ME AGAIN NOW, IN PERSON?
...

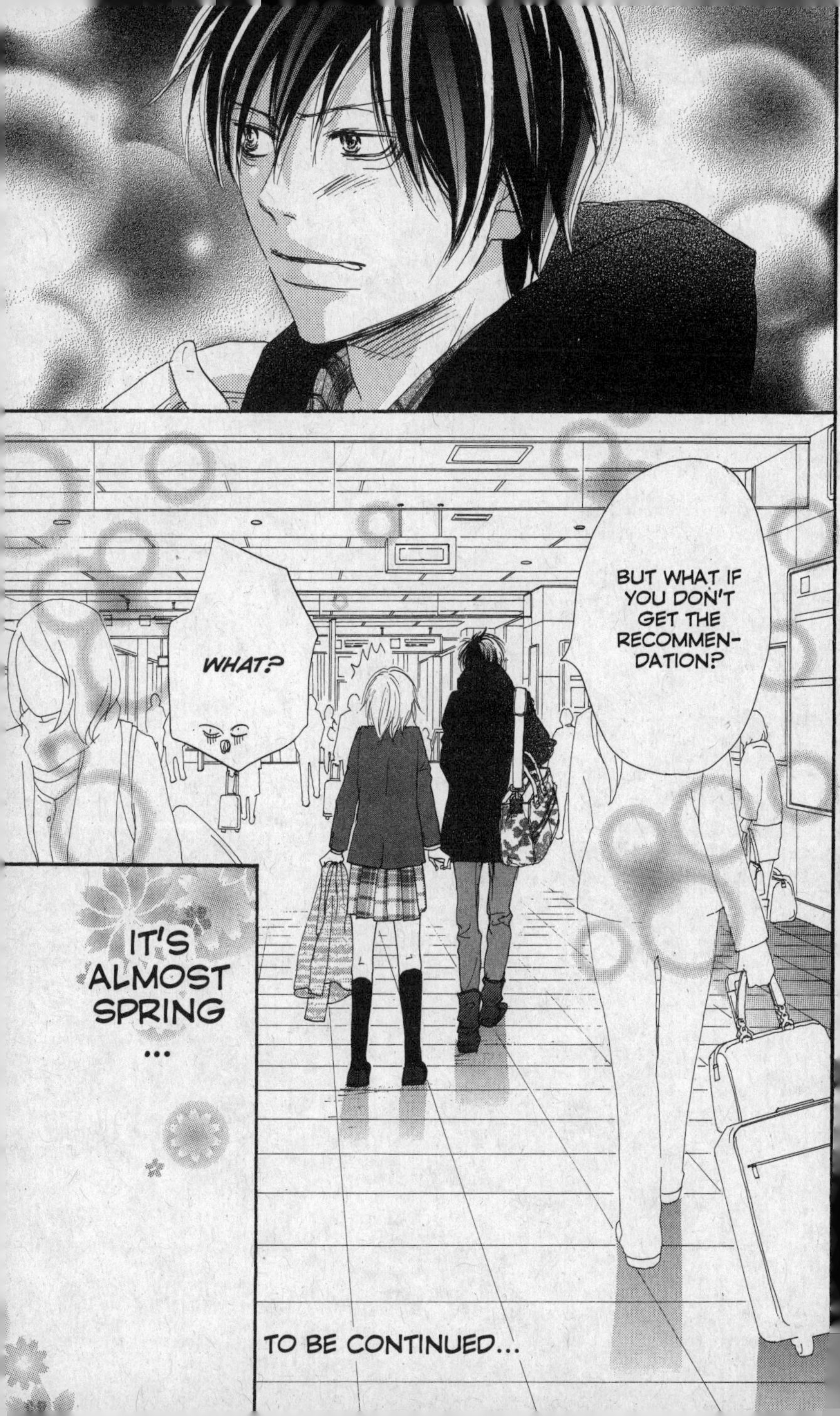
BUT WHAT IF YOU DON'T GET THE RECOMMEN-DATION?
WHAT?
IT'S ALMOST SPRING ...
TO BE CONTINUED...

TO CELEBRATE THE *HIGH SCHOOL DEBUT* MOVIE, MY FELLOW MANGA ARTIST FRIENDS CREATED WONDERFUL TRIBUTE MANGA FOR ME! I'D LIKE TO SHOW THEM OFF. (AT THE END OF THE BOOK)

I'VE DONE MANGA LIKE THIS FOR OTHER PEOPLE, BUT I'D NEVER HAD ANY DONE FOR ME BEFORE, SO I DIDN'T KNOW HOW IT FELT TO GET THEM.

YOU KNOW HOW IT FEELS? WONDERFUL! FROM NOW ON, WHEN SOMEONE ASKS ME TO DO A TRIBUTE MANGA FOR THEM, I'M GOING ALL OUT AND HAVING FUN WITH IT!

I LOVE YOU ALL!

KARUHO SHIINA, I'LL DROP BY WITHOUT WARNING AGAIN SOMETIME, OKAY? I KNOW YOU'RE SUPER BUSY, SO I REALLY APPRECIATE IT!

CHOKO MONSHIRO, I HOPE YOU'LL LET ME COME OVER TO YOUR HOUSE AGAIN. MY SON ADMIRES YOUR LOVELY HOME AND HOW IT'S FULL OF THE THINGS YOU LOVE.

MOMOKO KODA, THANK YOU FOR MAKING YOH LOOK GOOD! LET'S CHAT AGAIN! I'VE BEEN REJECTED BY MY EDITOR BEFORE TOO, SO HANG IN THERE. GOOD LUCK WITH EVERYTHING IN LIFE! THANK YOU SO MUCH.

I'LL NEVER FORGET THIS FAVOR!

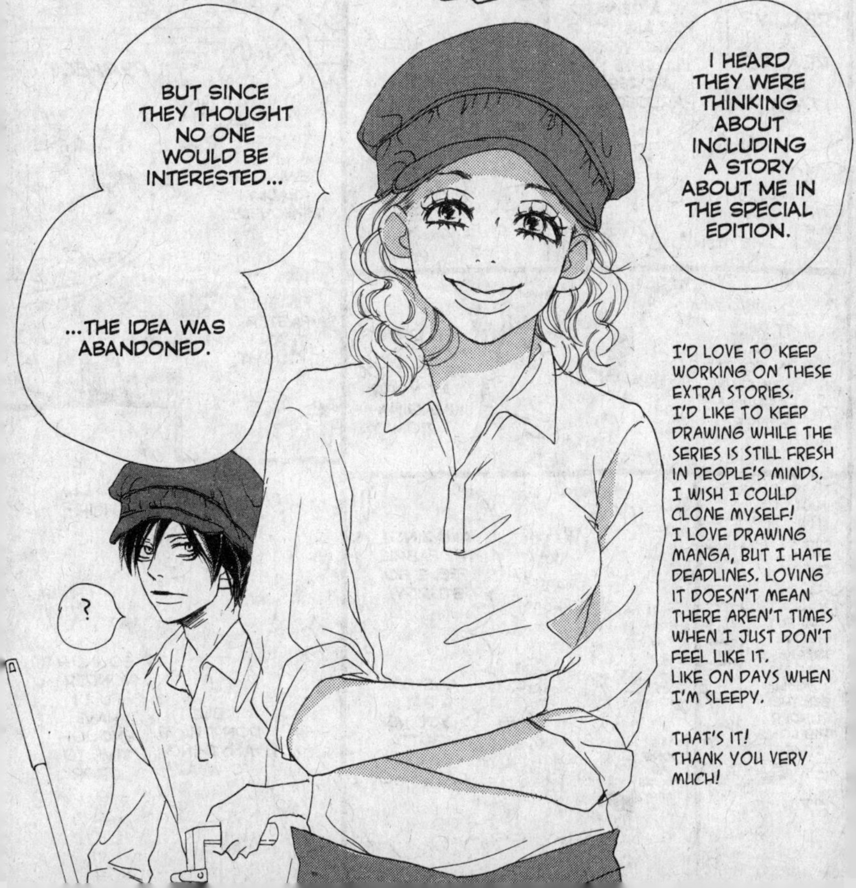
I HEARD THEY WERE THINKING ABOUT INCLUDING A STORY ABOUT ME IN THE SPECIAL EDITION.
BUT SINCE THEY THOUGHT NO ONE WOULD BE INTERESTED...
...THE IDEA WAS ABANDONED.
?

I'D LOVE TO KEEP WORKING ON THESE EXTRA STORIES. I'D LIKE TO KEEP DRAWING WHILE THE SERIES IS STILL FRESH IN PEOPLE'S MINDS. I WISH I COULD CLONE MYSELF! I LOVE DRAWING MANGA, BUT I HATE DEADLINES. LOVING IT DOESN'T MEAN THERE AREN'T TIMES WHEN I JUST DON'T FEEL LIKE IT. LIKE ON DAYS WHEN I'M SLEEPY.

THAT'S IT! THANK YOU VERY MUCH!

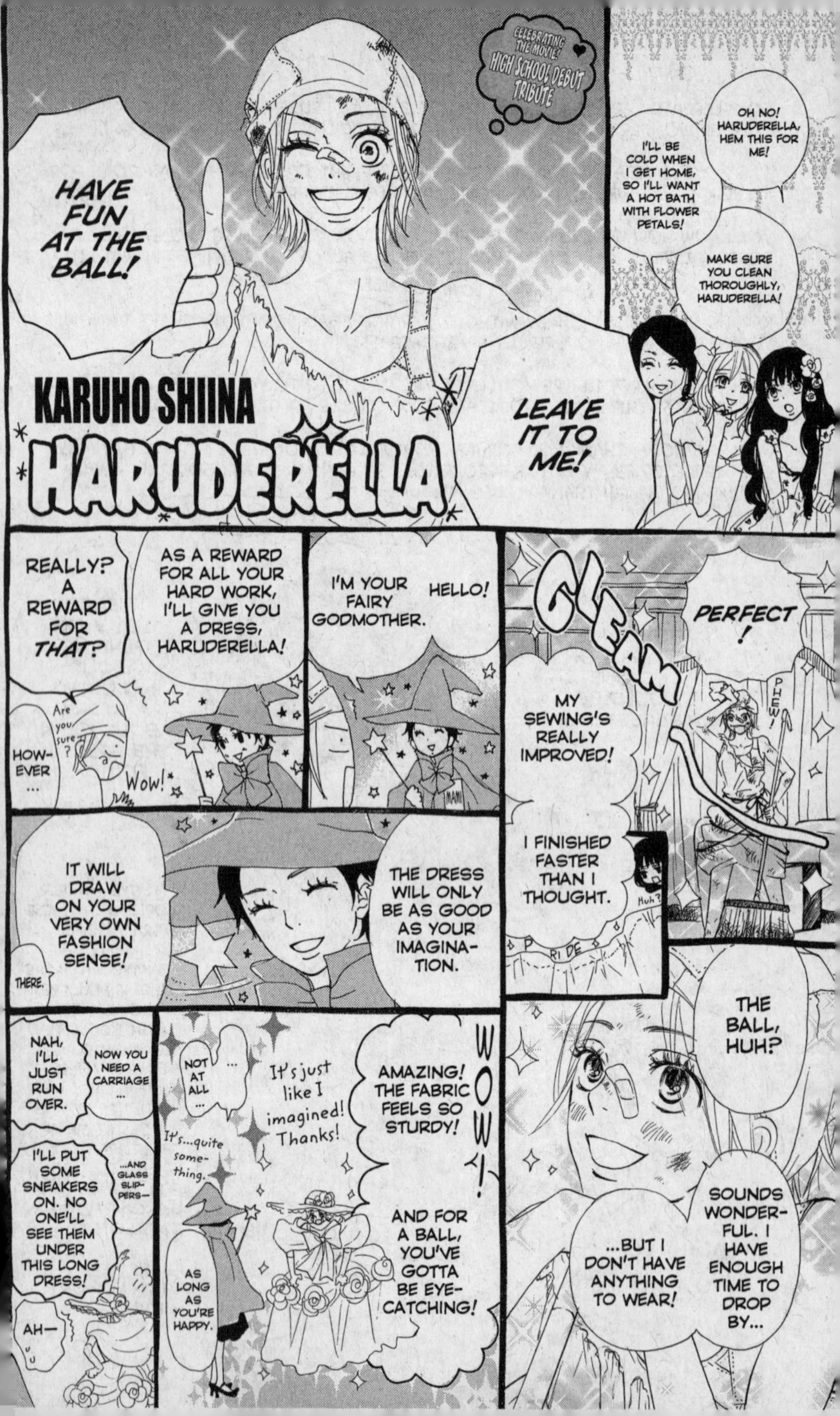

OH NO! HARUDERELLA, HEM THIS FOR ME!
I'LL BE COLD WHEN I GET HOME, SO I'LL WANT A HOT BATH WITH FLOWER PETALS!
MAKE SURE YOU CLEAN THOROUGHLY, HARUDERELLA!
LEAVE IT TO ME!
CELEBRATING THE MOVIE! HIGH SCHOOL DEBUT TRIBUTE
HAVE FUN AT THE BALL!
KARUHO SHIINA
HARUDERELLA
PERFECT!
CLEAM
PHEW!
MY SEWING'S REALLY IMPROVED!
I FINISHED FASTER THAN I THOUGHT.
Huh?
PRIDE
THE BALL, HUH?
SOUNDS WONDERFUL. I HAVE ENOUGH TIME TO DROP BY...
...BUT I DON'T HAVE ANYTHING TO WEAR!
HELLO!
I'M YOUR FAIRY GODMOTHER.
MAMI
AS A REWARD FOR ALL YOUR HARD WORK, I'LL GIVE YOU A DRESS, HARUDERELLA!
Wow!
REALLY? A REWARD FOR THAT?
Are you sure?
HOWEVER...
THE DRESS WILL ONLY BE AS GOOD AS YOUR IMAGINATION.
IT WILL DRAW ON YOUR VERY OWN FASHION SENSE!
THERE.
WOW!
AMAZING! THE FABRIC FEELS SO STURDY!
It's just like I imagined! Thanks!
NOT AT ALL...
It's...quite something.
AND FOR A BALL, YOU'VE GOTTA BE EYE-CATCHING!
AS LONG AS YOU'RE HAPPY.
NOW YOU NEED A CARRIAGE...
NAH, I'LL JUST RUN OVER.
...AND GLASS SLIPPERS—
I'LL PUT SOME SNEAKERS ON. NO ONE'LL SEE THEM UNDER THIS LONG DRESS!
AH—

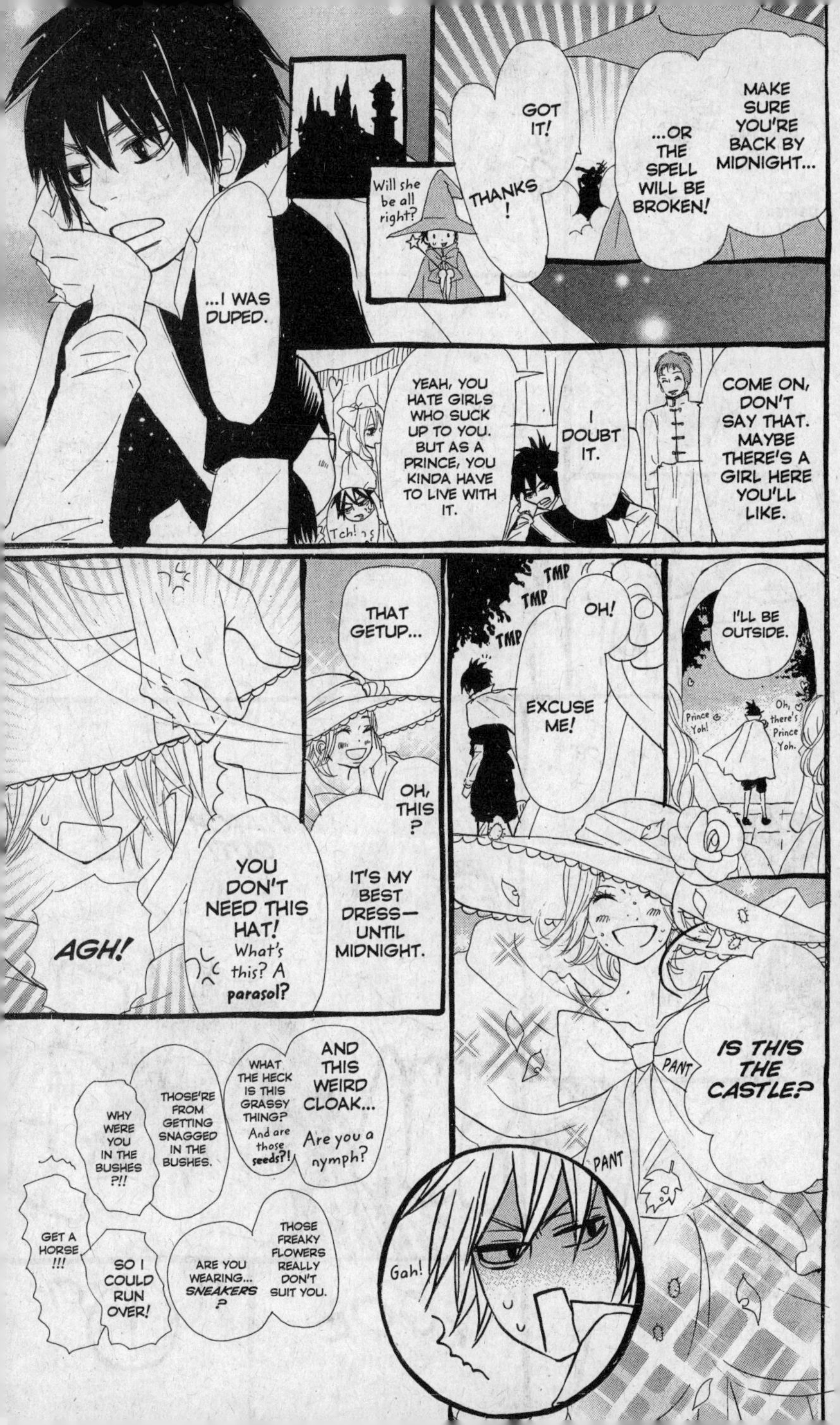

MAKE SURE YOU'RE BACK BY MIDNIGHT...
...OR THE SPELL WILL BE BROKEN!
GOT IT!
THANKS!
Will she be all right?
COME ON, DON'T SAY THAT. MAYBE THERE'S A GIRL HERE YOU'LL LIKE.
I DOUBT IT.
YEAH, YOU HATE GIRLS WHO SUCK UP TO YOU. BUT AS A PRINCE, YOU KINDA HAVE TO LIVE WITH IT.
Tch!
...I WAS DUPED.
I'LL BE OUTSIDE.
Oh, there's Prince Yoh.
Prince Yoh!
TMP
TMP
TMP
OH!
EXCUSE ME!
IS THIS THE CASTLE?
PANT
PANT
THAT GETUP...
OH, THIS?
IT'S MY BEST DRESS—UNTIL MIDNIGHT.
YOU DON'T NEED THIS HAT!
What's this? A parasol?
AGH!
Gah!
AND THIS WEIRD CLOAK...
Are you a nymph?
WHAT THE HECK IS THIS GRASSY THING?
And are those seeds?!
THOSE'RE FROM GETTING SNAGGED IN THE BUSHES.
WHY WERE YOU IN THE BUSHES?!!
THOSE FREAKY FLOWERS REALLY DON'T SUIT YOU.
ARE YOU WEARING... SNEAKERS?
SO I COULD RUN OVER!
GET A HORSE!!!

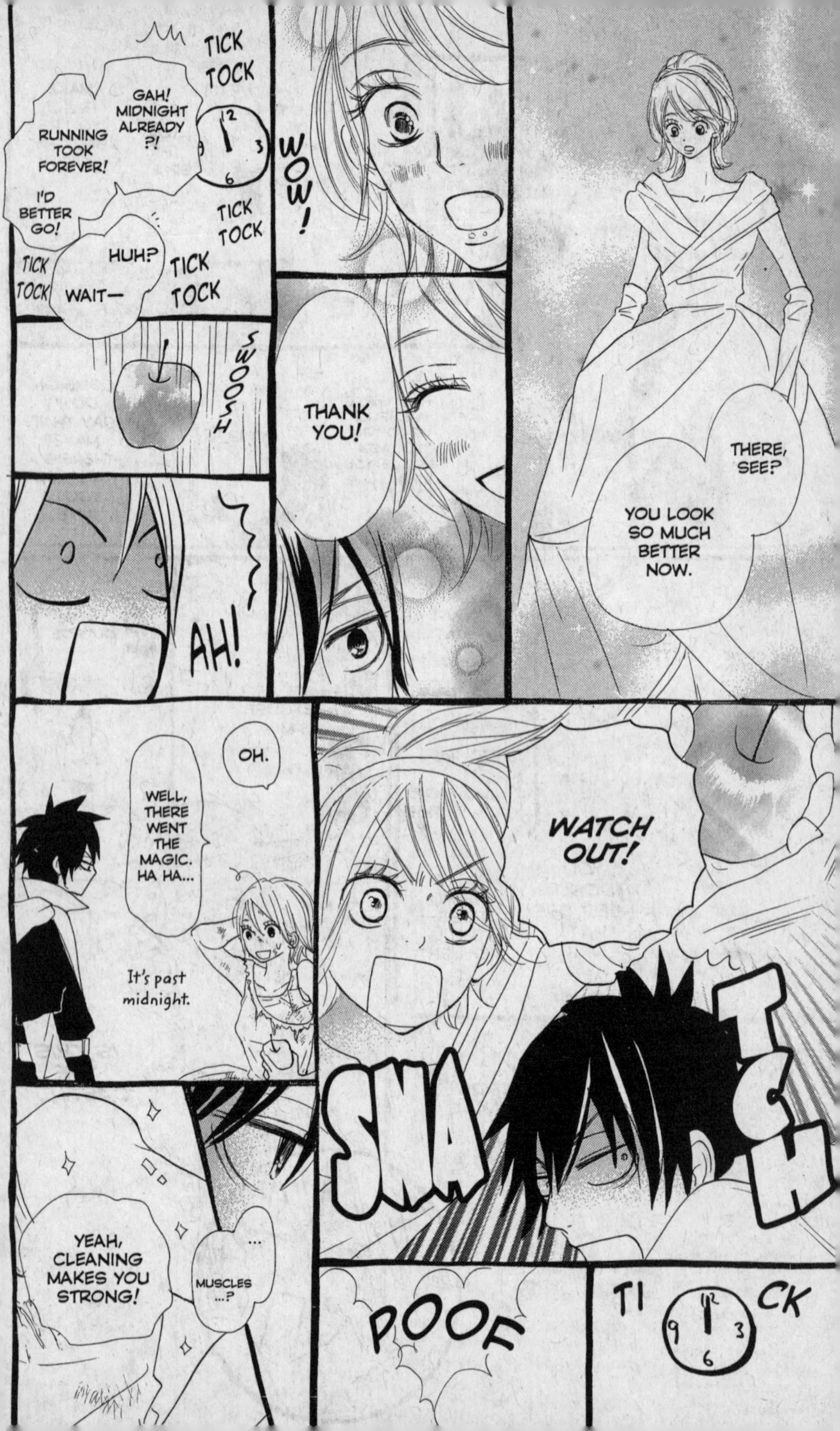
THERE, SEE?
YOU LOOK SO MUCH BETTER NOW.
WOW!
THANK YOU!
TICK TOCK
GAH! MIDNIGHT ALREADY ?!
RUNNING TOOK FOREVER!
TICK TOCK
I'D BETTER GO!
TICK TOCK
HUH?
WAIT—
TICK TOCK
SWOOSH
AH!
WATCH OUT!
SNATCH
TI CK
POOF
OH.
WELL, THERE WENT THE MAGIC. HA HA...
It's past midnight.
...
MUSCLES ...?
YEAH, CLEANING MAKES YOU STRONG!

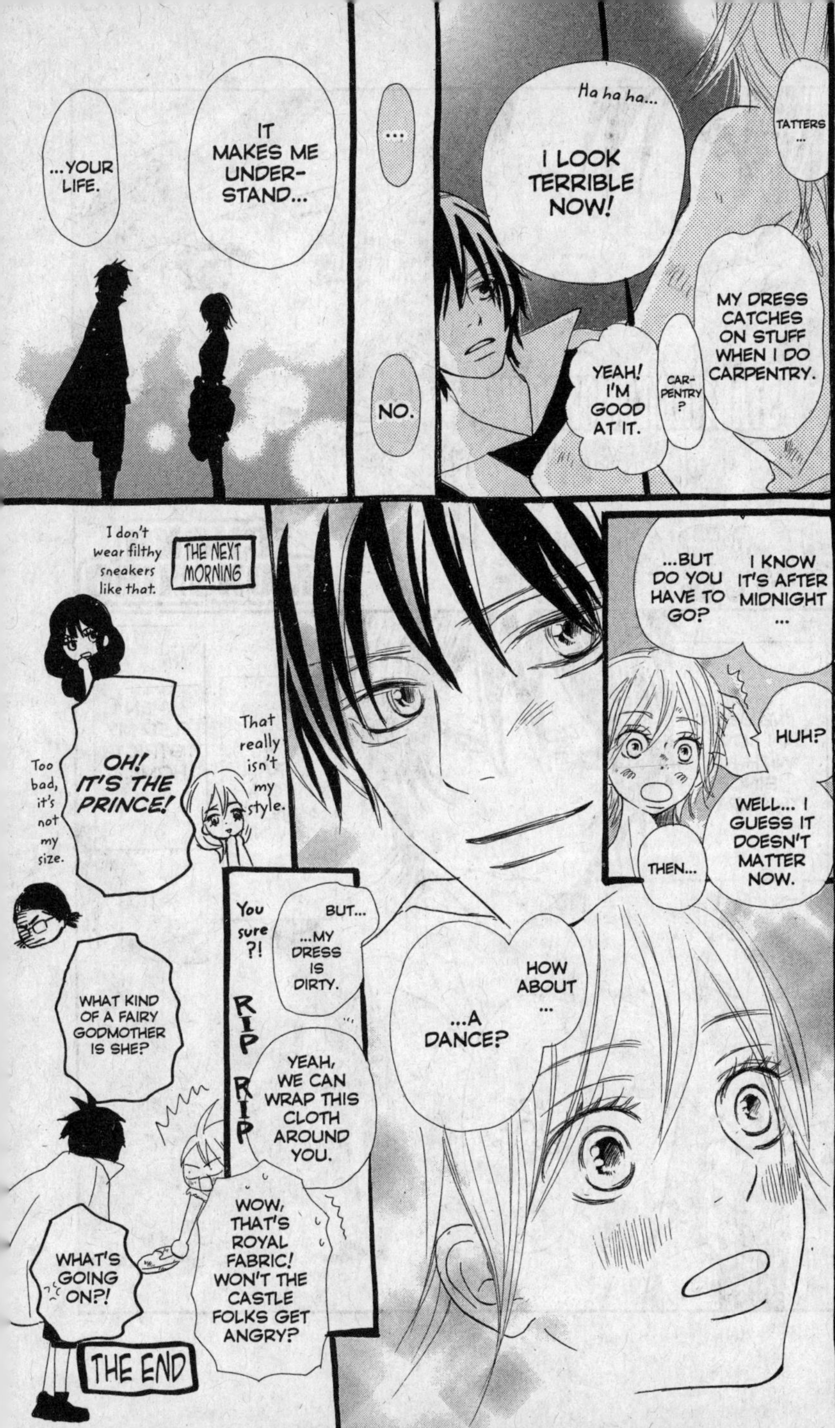
TATTERS...
Ha ha ha...
I LOOK TERRIBLE NOW!
MY DRESS CATCHES ON STUFF WHEN I DO CARPENTRY.
CARPENTRY?
YEAH! I'M GOOD AT IT.
...
NO.
IT MAKES ME UNDERSTAND...
...YOUR LIFE.
I KNOW IT'S AFTER MIDNIGHT...
...BUT DO YOU HAVE TO GO?
HUH?
WELL... I GUESS IT DOESN'T MATTER NOW.
THEN...
HOW ABOUT...
...A DANCE?
BUT...
...MY DRESS IS DIRTY.
You sure?!
RIP RIP
YEAH, WE CAN WRAP THIS CLOTH AROUND YOU.
WOW, THAT'S ROYAL FABRIC! WON'T THE CASTLE FOLKS GET ANGRY?
THE NEXT MORNING
I don't wear filthy sneakers like that.
OH! IT'S THE PRINCE!
That really isn't my style.
Too bad, it's not my size.
WHAT KIND OF A FAIRY GODMOTHER IS SHE?
WHAT'S GOING ON?!
THE END

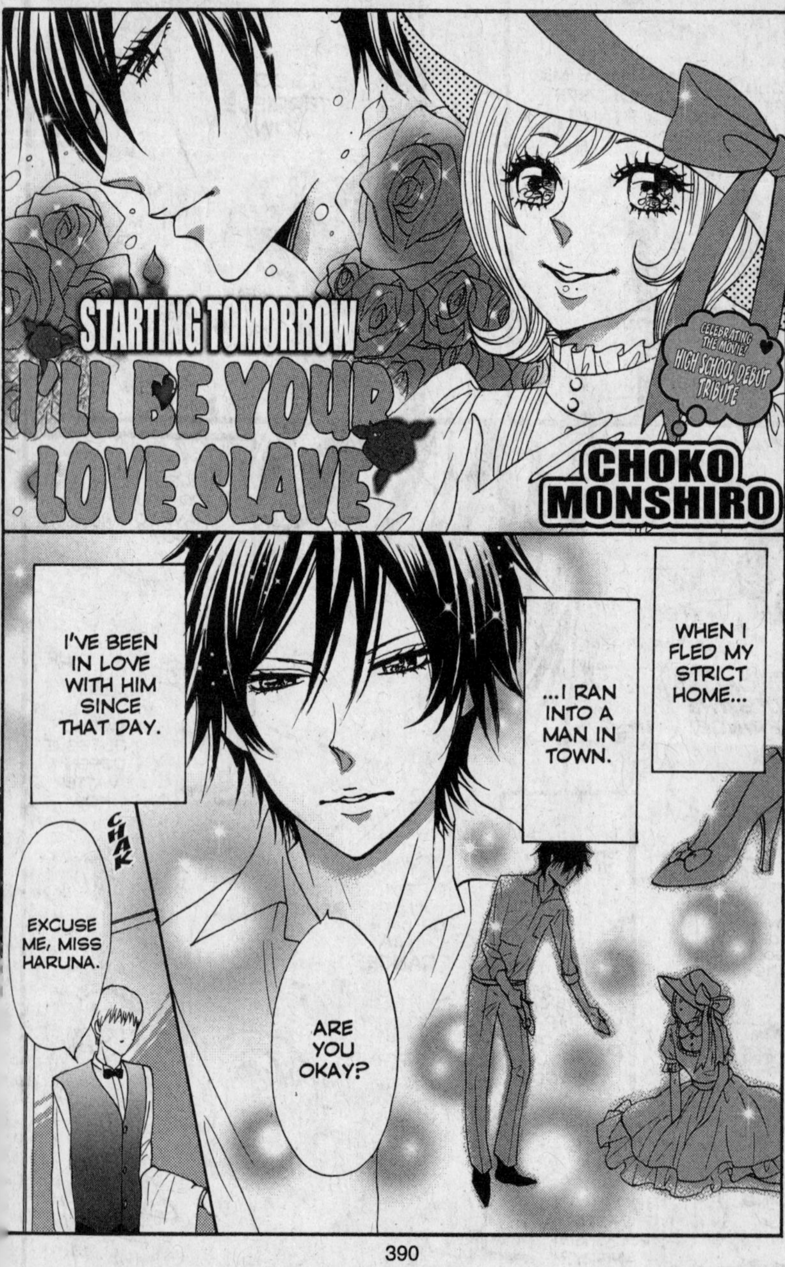
STARTING TOMORROW
I'LL BE YOUR LOVE SLAVE
CELEBRATING THE MOVIE! HIGH SCHOOL DEBUT TRIBUTE
CHOKO MONSHIRO
WHEN I FLED MY STRICT HOME...
...I RAN INTO A MAN IN TOWN.
I'VE BEEN IN LOVE WITH HIM SINCE THAT DAY.
ARE YOU OKAY?
CHAK
EXCUSE ME, MISS HARUNA.

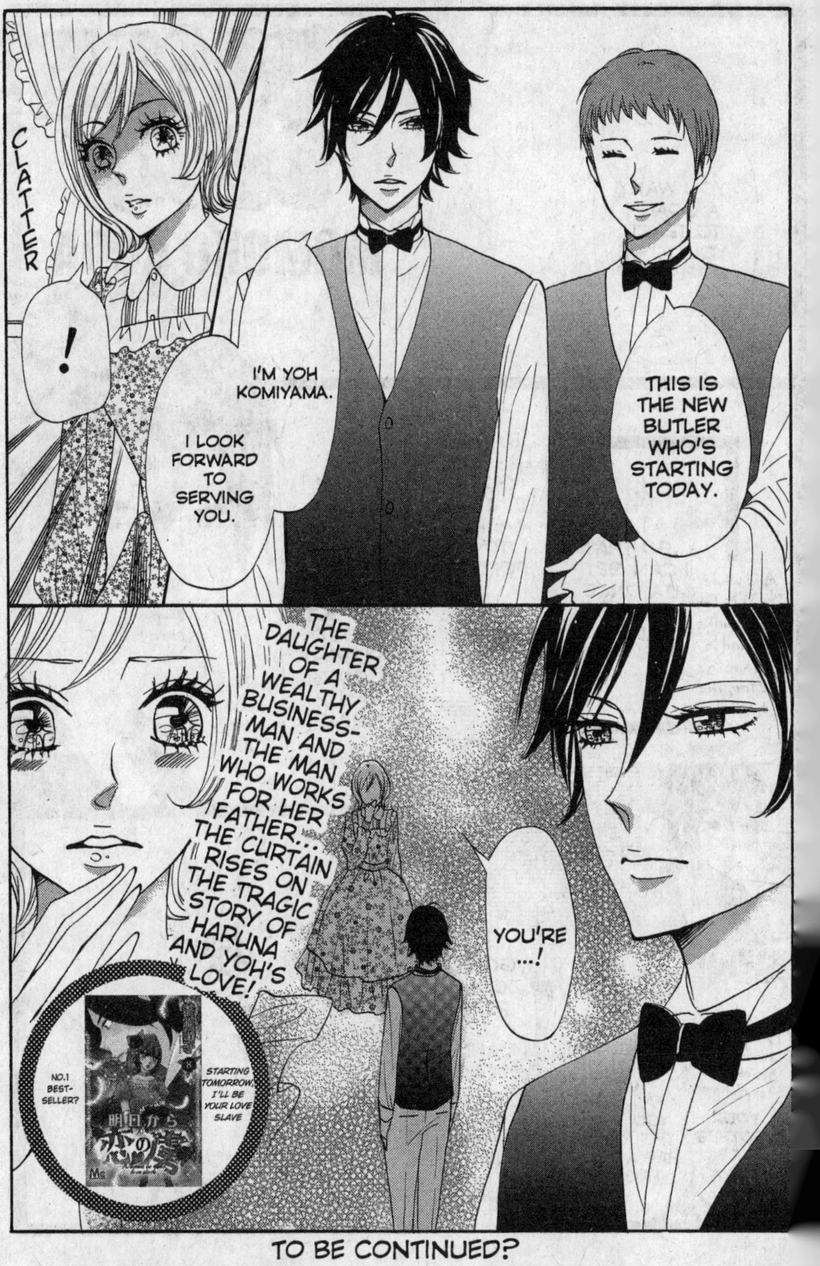
THIS IS THE NEW BUTLER WHO'S STARTING TODAY.
I'M YOH KOMIYAMA.
I LOOK FORWARD TO SERVING YOU.
!
CLATTER
YOU'RE ...!
THE DAUGHTER OF A WEALTHY BUSINESSMAN AND THE MAN WHO WORKS FOR HER FATHER... THE CURTAIN RISES ON THE TRAGIC STORY OF HARUNA AND YOH'S LOVE!
STARTING TOMORROW, I'LL BE YOUR LOVE SLAVE
NO.1 BEST-SELLER?

TO BE CONTINUED?

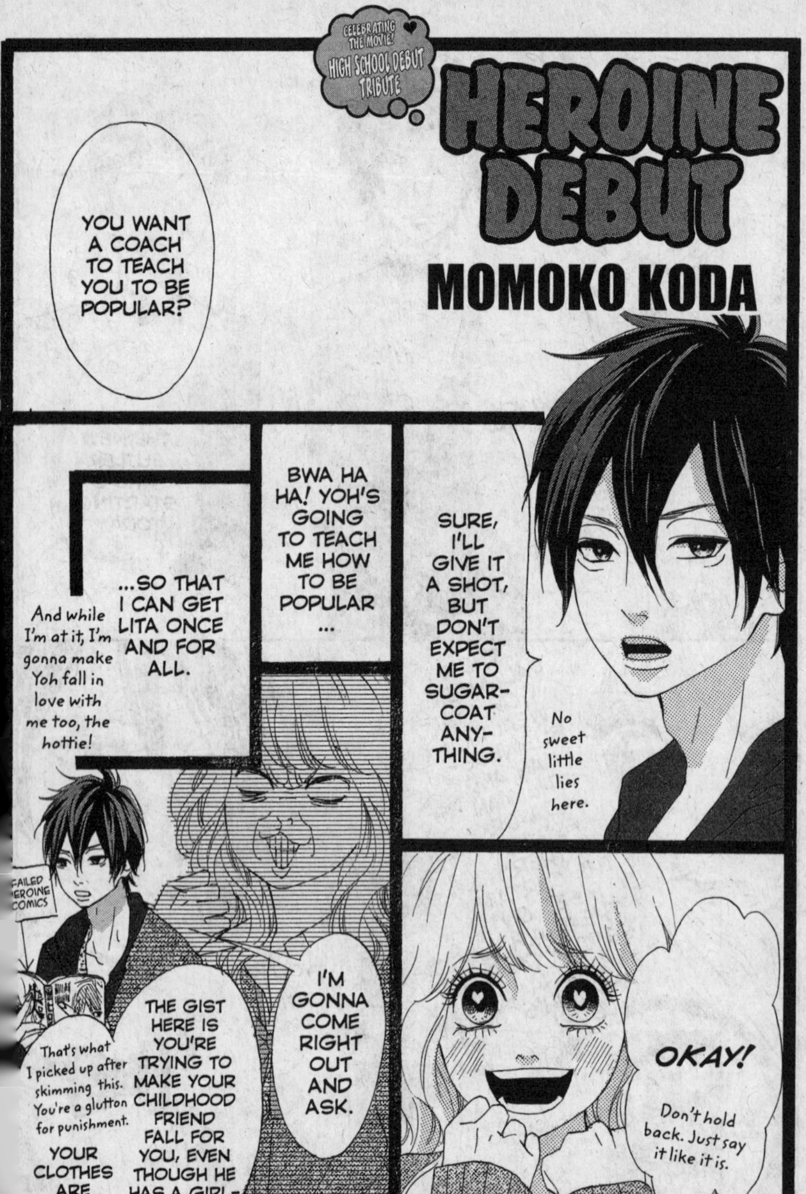
CELEBRATING THE MOVIE! HIGH SCHOOL DEBUT TRIBUTE
HEROINE DEBUT
MOMOKO KODA
YOU WANT A COACH TO TEACH YOU TO BE POPULAR?
SURE, I'LL GIVE IT A SHOT, BUT DON'T EXPECT ME TO SUGAR-COAT ANY-THING.
No sweet little lies here.
BWA HA HA! YOH'S GOING TO TEACH ME HOW TO BE POPULAR ...
...SO THAT I CAN GET LITA ONCE AND FOR ALL.
And while I'm at it, I'm gonna make Yoh fall in love with me too, the hottie!
OKAY!
Don't hold back. Just say it like it is.
I'M GONNA COME RIGHT OUT AND ASK.
THE GIST HERE IS YOU'RE TRYING TO MAKE YOUR CHILDHOOD FRIEND FALL FOR YOU, EVEN THOUGH HE HAS A GIRL-FRIEND?
That's what I picked up after skimming this. You're a glutton for punishment.
YOUR CLOTHES ARE OKAY, BUT...

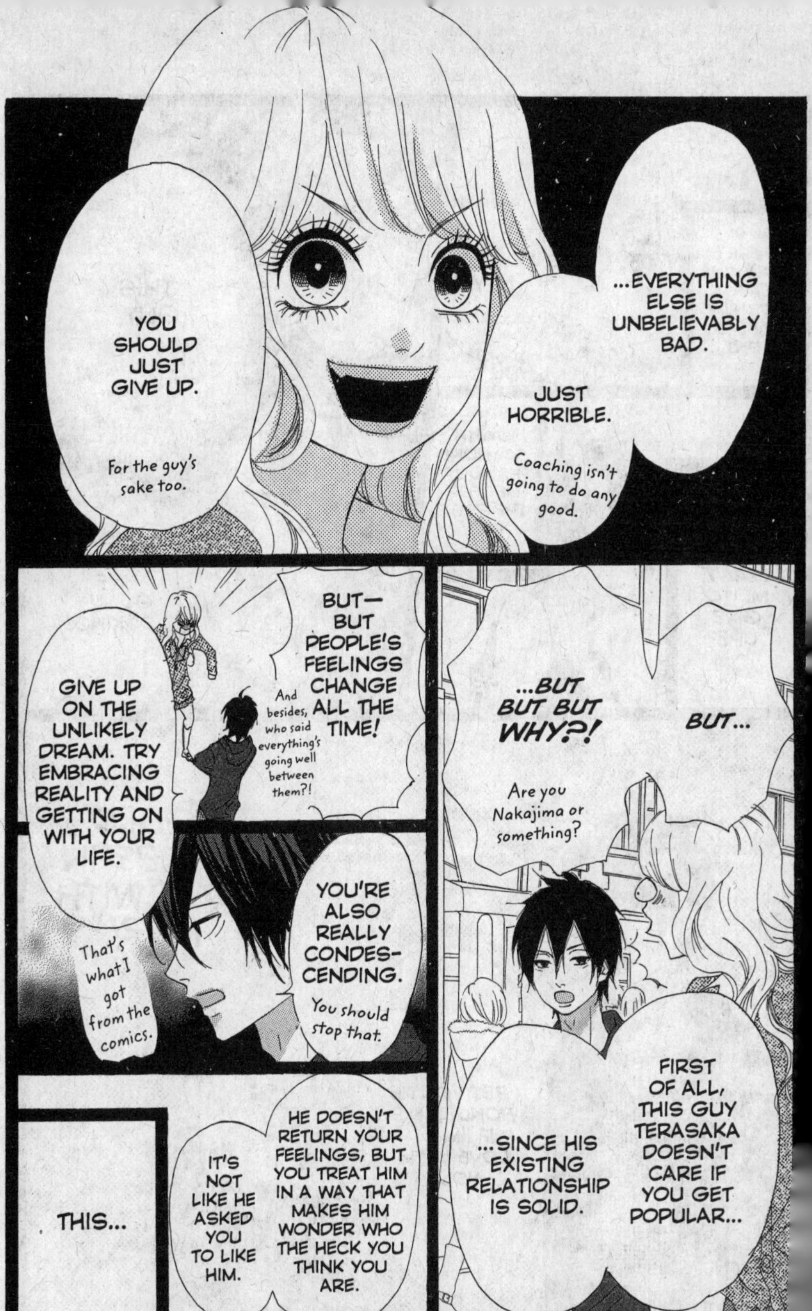
...EVERYTHING ELSE IS UNBELIEVABLY BAD.
JUST HORRIBLE.
Coaching isn't going to do any good.
YOU SHOULD JUST GIVE UP.
For the guy's sake too.
BUT...
...BUT BUT BUT WHY?!
Are you Nakajima or something?
FIRST OF ALL, THIS GUY TERASAKA DOESN'T CARE IF YOU GET POPULAR...
...SINCE HIS EXISTING RELATIONSHIP IS SOLID.
BUT— BUT PEOPLE'S FEELINGS CHANGE ALL THE TIME!
And besides, who said everything's going well between them?!
GIVE UP ON THE UNLIKELY DREAM. TRY EMBRACING REALITY AND GETTING ON WITH YOUR LIFE.
YOU'RE ALSO REALLY CONDESCENDING.
You should stop that.
That's what I got from the comics.
HE DOESN'T RETURN YOUR FEELINGS, BUT YOU TREAT HIM IN A WAY THAT MAKES HIM WONDER WHO THE HECK YOU THINK YOU ARE.
IT'S NOT LIKE HE ASKED YOU TO LIKE HIM.
THIS...

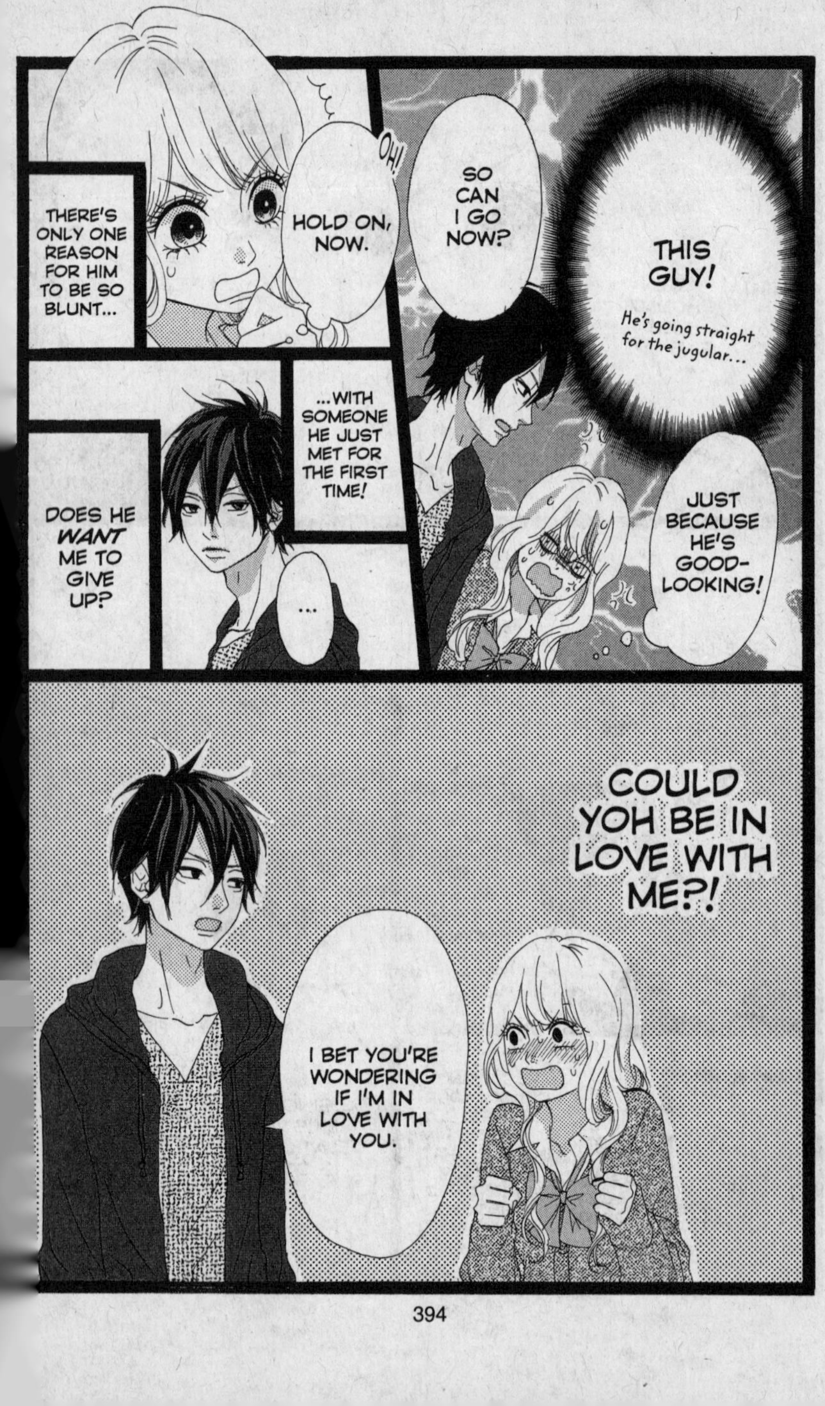
SO CAN I GO NOW?
THIS GUY!
He's going straight for the jugular...
JUST BECAUSE HE'S GOOD-LOOKING!
OH!
HOLD ON, NOW.
THERE'S ONLY ONE REASON FOR HIM TO BE SO BLUNT...
...WITH SOMEONE HE JUST MET FOR THE FIRST TIME!
...
DOES HE *WANT* ME TO GIVE UP?
COULD YOH BE IN LOVE WITH ME?!
I BET YOU'RE WONDERING IF I'M IN LOVE WITH YOU.

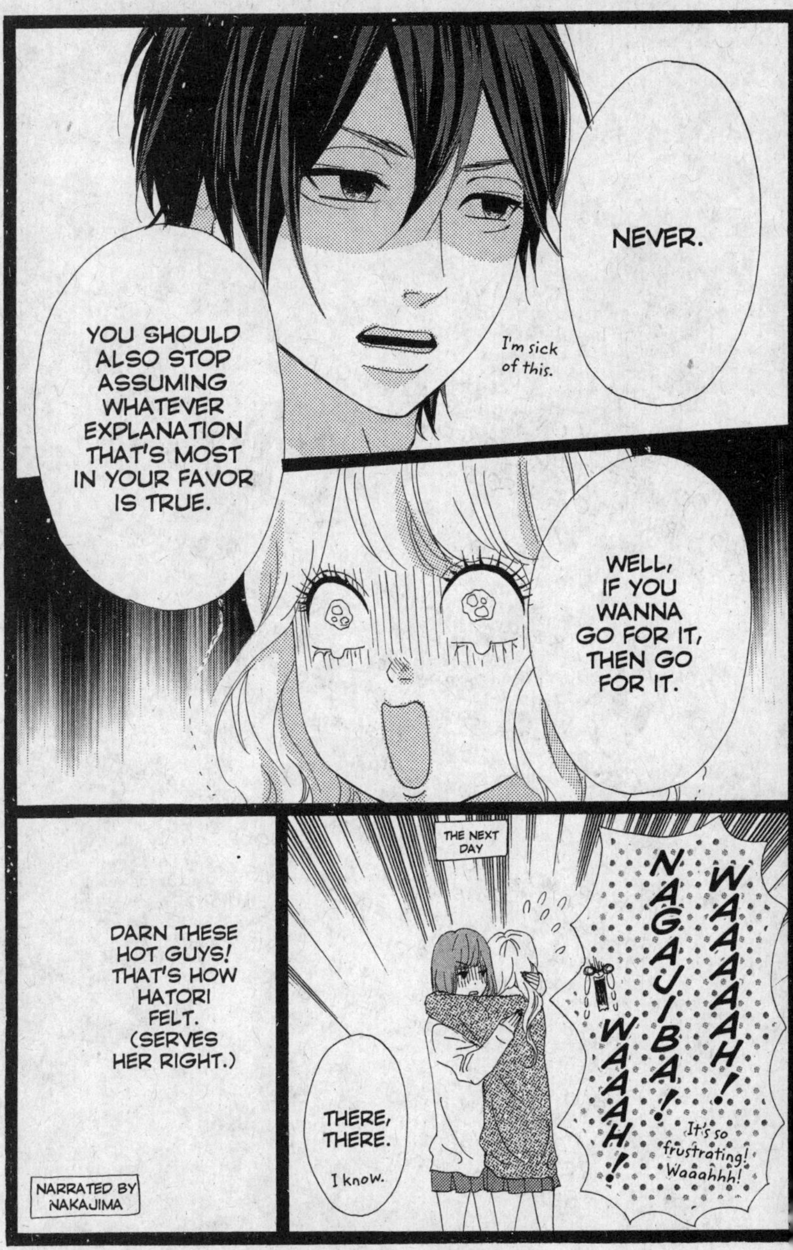
NEVER.
I'm sick of this.
YOU SHOULD ALSO STOP ASSUMING WHATEVER EXPLANATION THAT'S MOST IN YOUR FAVOR IS TRUE.
WELL, IF YOU WANNA GO FOR IT, THEN GO FOR IT.
THE NEXT DAY
WAAAAAH!
NAGAJIBA! WAAAAH!
It's so frustrating! Waaahhh!
THERE, THERE.
I know.
DARN THESE HOT GUYS! THAT'S HOW HATORI FELT. (SERVES HER RIGHT.)
NARRATED BY NAKAJIMA

LET THERE BE HAPPINESS FOR HATORI!

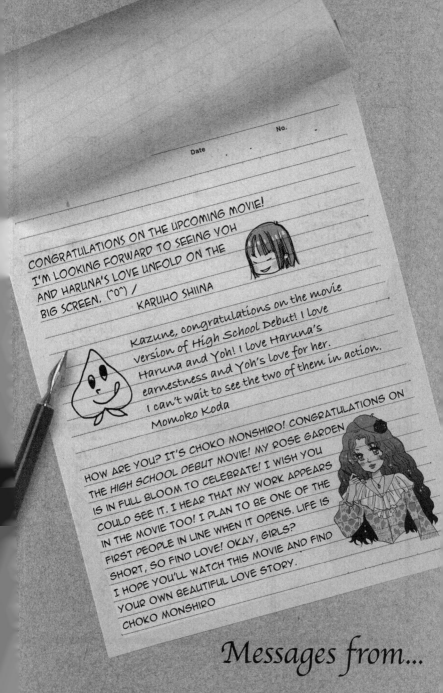

CONGRATULATIONS ON THE UPCOMING MOVIE!
I'M LOOKING FORWARD TO SEEING YOH
AND HARUNA'S LOVE UNFOLD ON THE
BIG SCREEN. (^0^) /

KARUHO SHIINA

Kazune, congratulations on the movie
version of High School Debut! I love
Haruna and Yoh! I love Haruna's
earnestness and Yoh's love for her.
I can't wait to see the two of them in action.

Momoko Koda

HOW ARE YOU? IT'S CHOKO MONSHIRO! CONGRATULATIONS ON
THE HIGH SCHOOL DEBUT MOVIE! MY ROSE GARDEN
IS IN FULL BLOOM TO CELEBRATE! I WISH YOU
COULD SEE IT. I HEAR THAT MY WORK APPEARS
IN THE MOVIE TOO! I PLAN TO BE ONE OF THE
FIRST PEOPLE IN LINE WHEN IT OPENS. LIFE IS
SHORT, SO FIND LOVE! OKAY, GIRLS?
I HOPE YOU'LL WATCH THIS MOVIE AND FIND
YOUR OWN BEAUTIFUL LOVE STORY.

CHOKO MONSHIRO

Messages from...

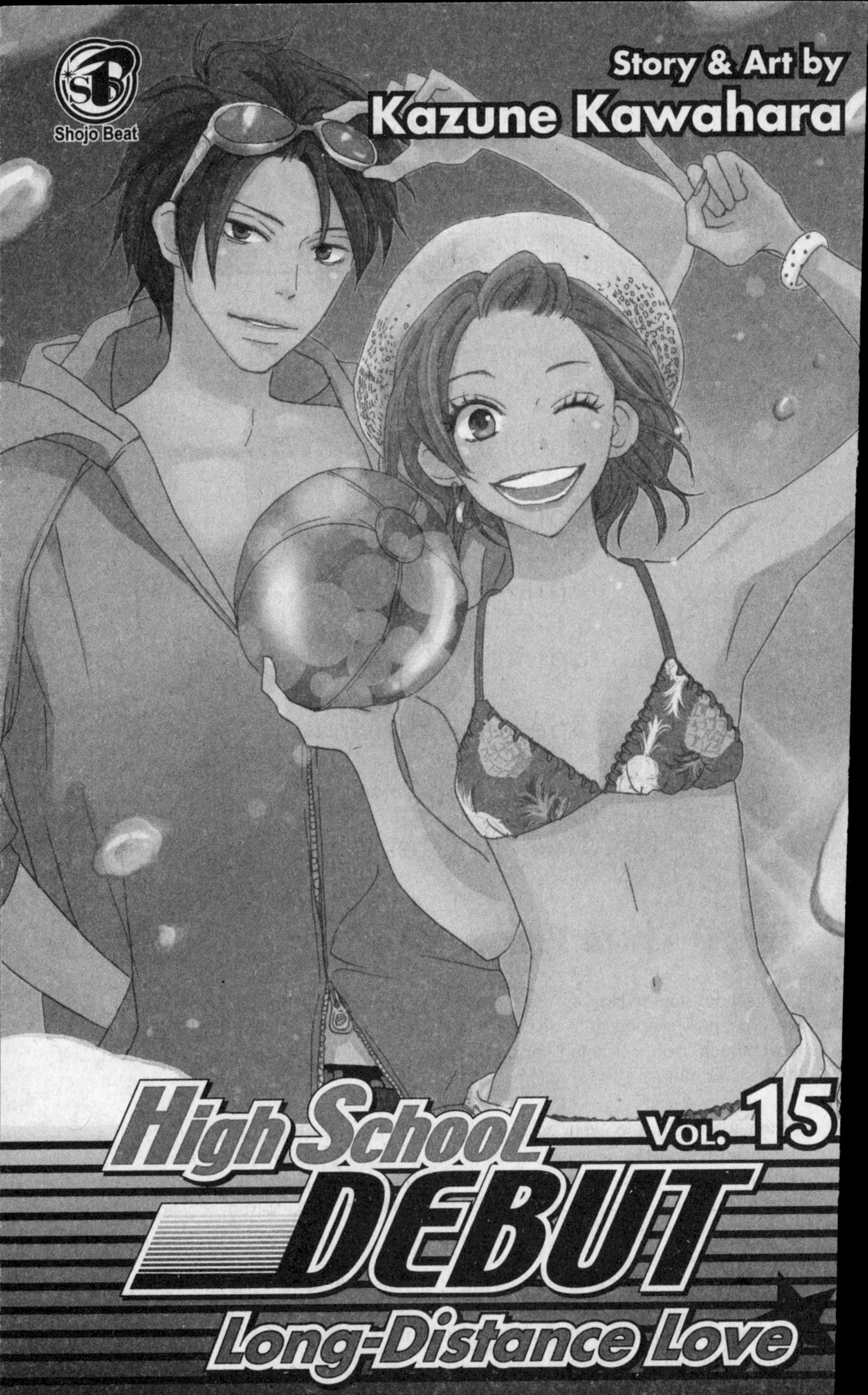
Shojo Beat
Story & Art by
Kazune Kawahara
High School DEBUT
VOL. 15
Long-Distance Love

High School DEBUT
Long-Distance Love

Contents

Story Thus Far...

High school student Haruna used to spend all her time playing softball in junior high, but now she wants to give her all to finding true love instead! While her "love coach" Yoh is training her on how to be popular with guys, the two of them start dating.

When Yoh decides to go to college in Tokyo, Haruna finds herself in a long-distance relationship. Her boss adds to her anxiety by telling her that long-distance relationships never, ever work out. Meanwhile, a boy in her class tells her he loves her—and rips up her letter of recommendation to Yoh's college in an attempt to keep her from leaving!

Life seems to be full of drama everywhere she turns, but when she tells Yoh about her classmate's feelings for her, Yoh tells her he loves her over the phone, and her worries melt away. And now, it's finally time for Haruna's in-person interview at Yoh's college in Tokyo!

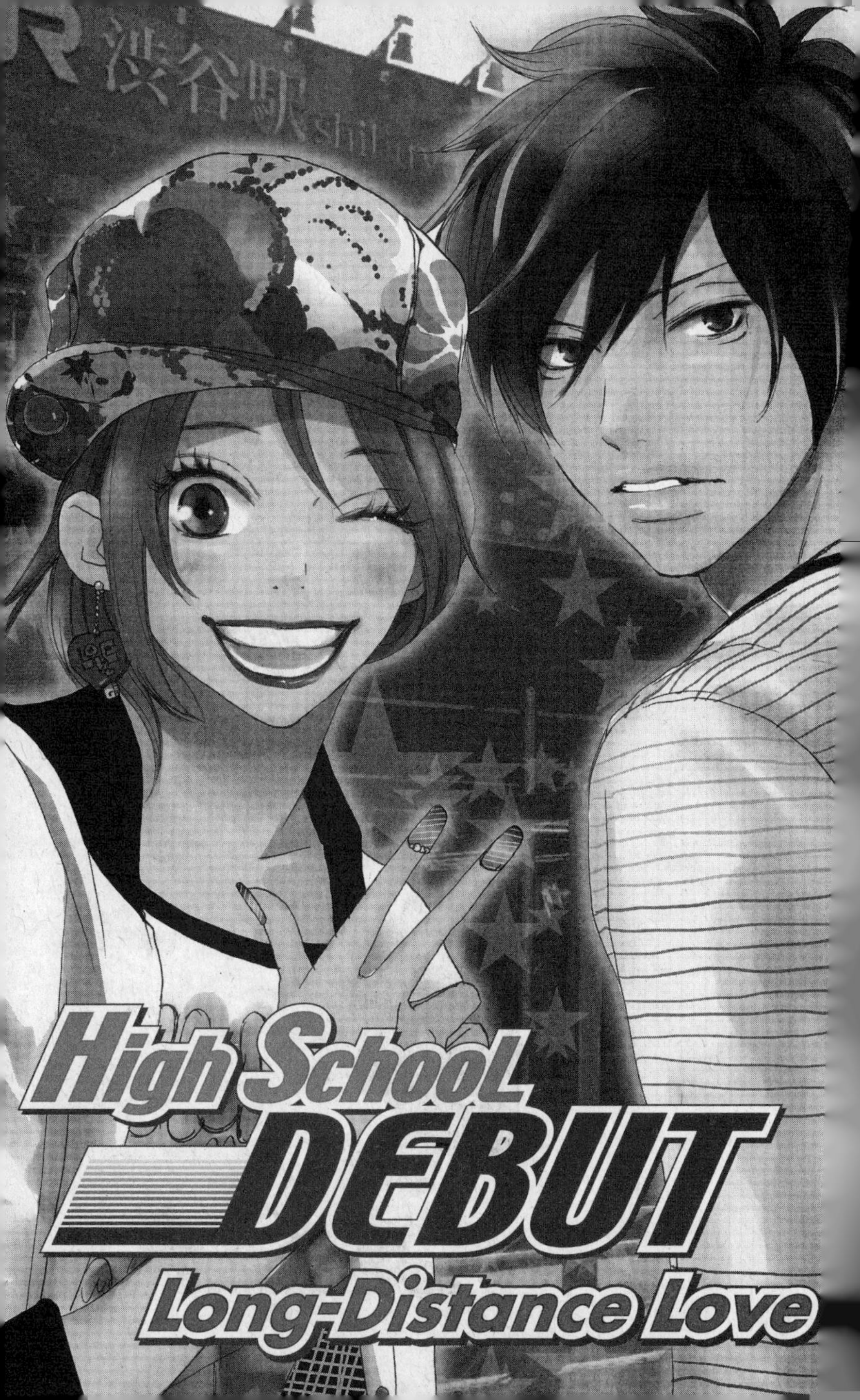
High School
DEBUT
Long-Distance Love

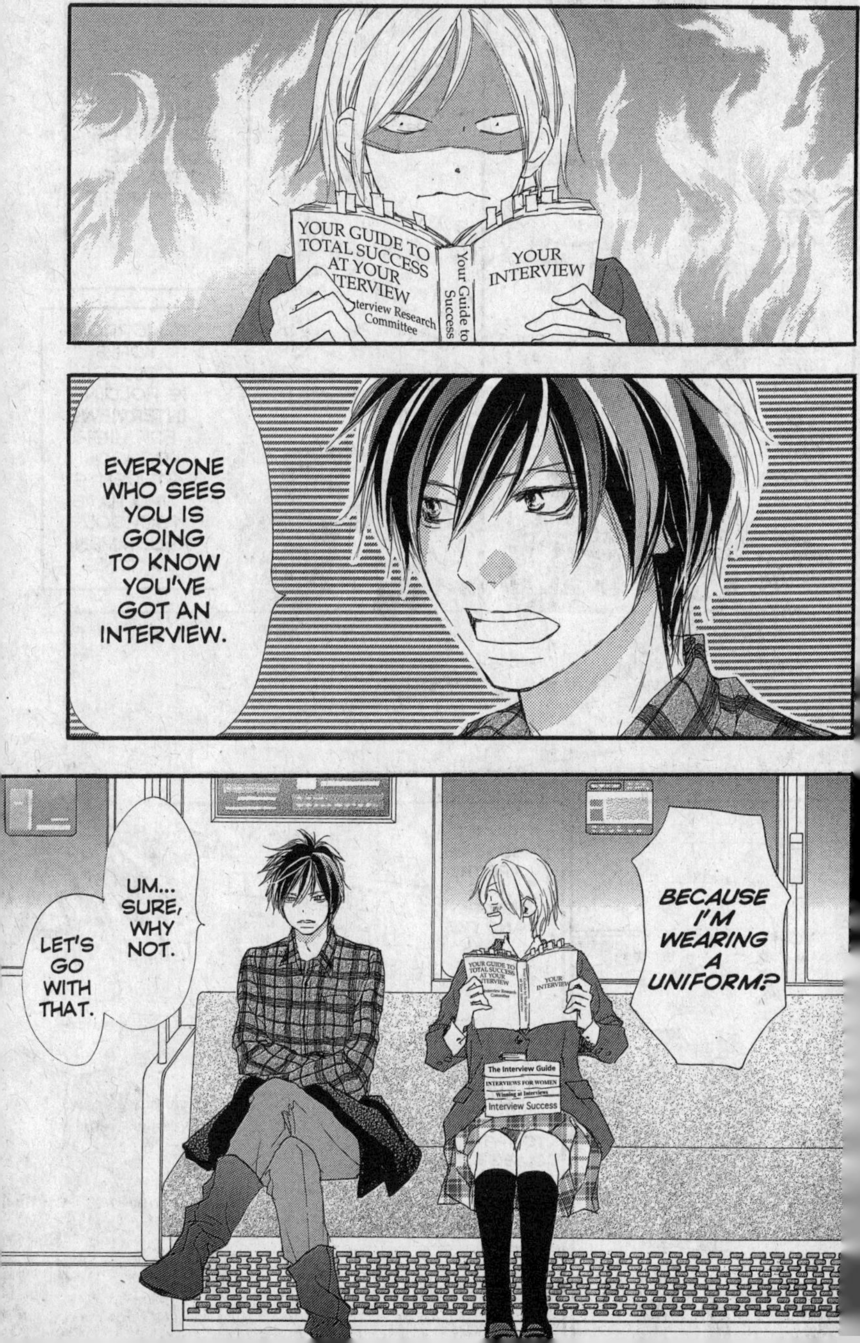
YOUR GUIDE TO TOTAL SUCCESS AT YOUR TERVIEW
terview Research Committee
Your Guide to Success
YOUR INTERVIEW
EVERYONE WHO SEES YOU IS GOING TO KNOW YOU'VE GOT AN INTERVIEW.
BECAUSE I'M WEARING A UNIFORM?
UM... SURE, WHY NOT.
LET'S GO WITH THAT.
The Interview Guide
INTERVIEWS FOR WOMEN
Winning at Interviews
Interview Success

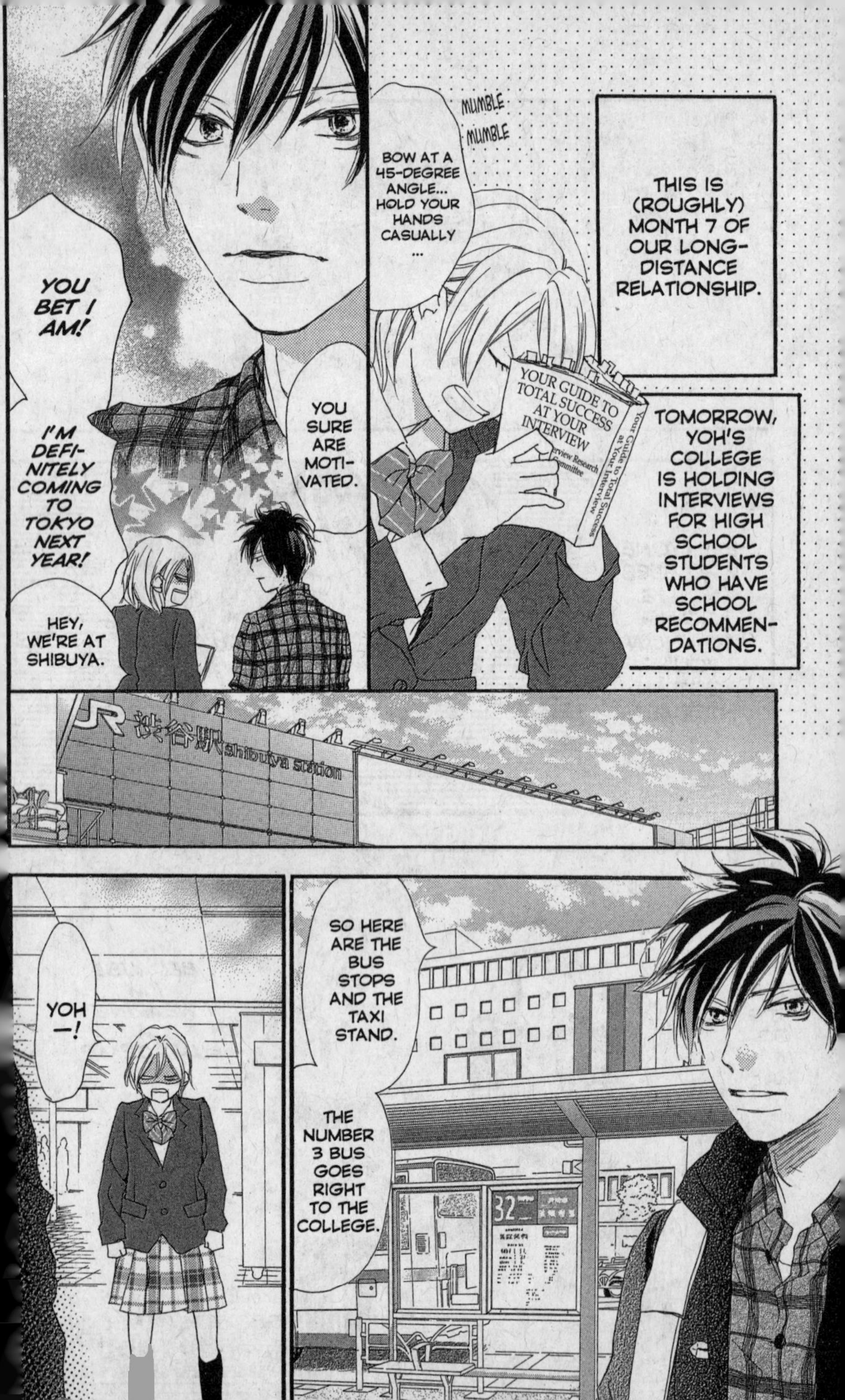

THIS IS (ROUGHLY) MONTH 7 OF OUR LONG-DISTANCE RELATIONSHIP.
TOMORROW, YOH'S COLLEGE IS HOLDING INTERVIEWS FOR HIGH SCHOOL STUDENTS WHO HAVE SCHOOL RECOMMENDATIONS.
MUMBLE
MUMBLE
BOW AT A 45-DEGREE ANGLE... HOLD YOUR HANDS CASUALLY ...
YOUR GUIDE TO TOTAL SUCCESS AT YOUR INTERVIEW
YOU SURE ARE MOTIVATED.
YOU BET I AM!
I'M DEFINITELY COMING TO TOKYO NEXT YEAR!
HEY, WE'RE AT SHIBUYA.
JR 渋谷駅 shibuya station
SO HERE ARE THE BUS STOPS AND THE TAXI STAND.
THE NUMBER 3 BUS GOES RIGHT TO THE COLLEGE.
YOH—!

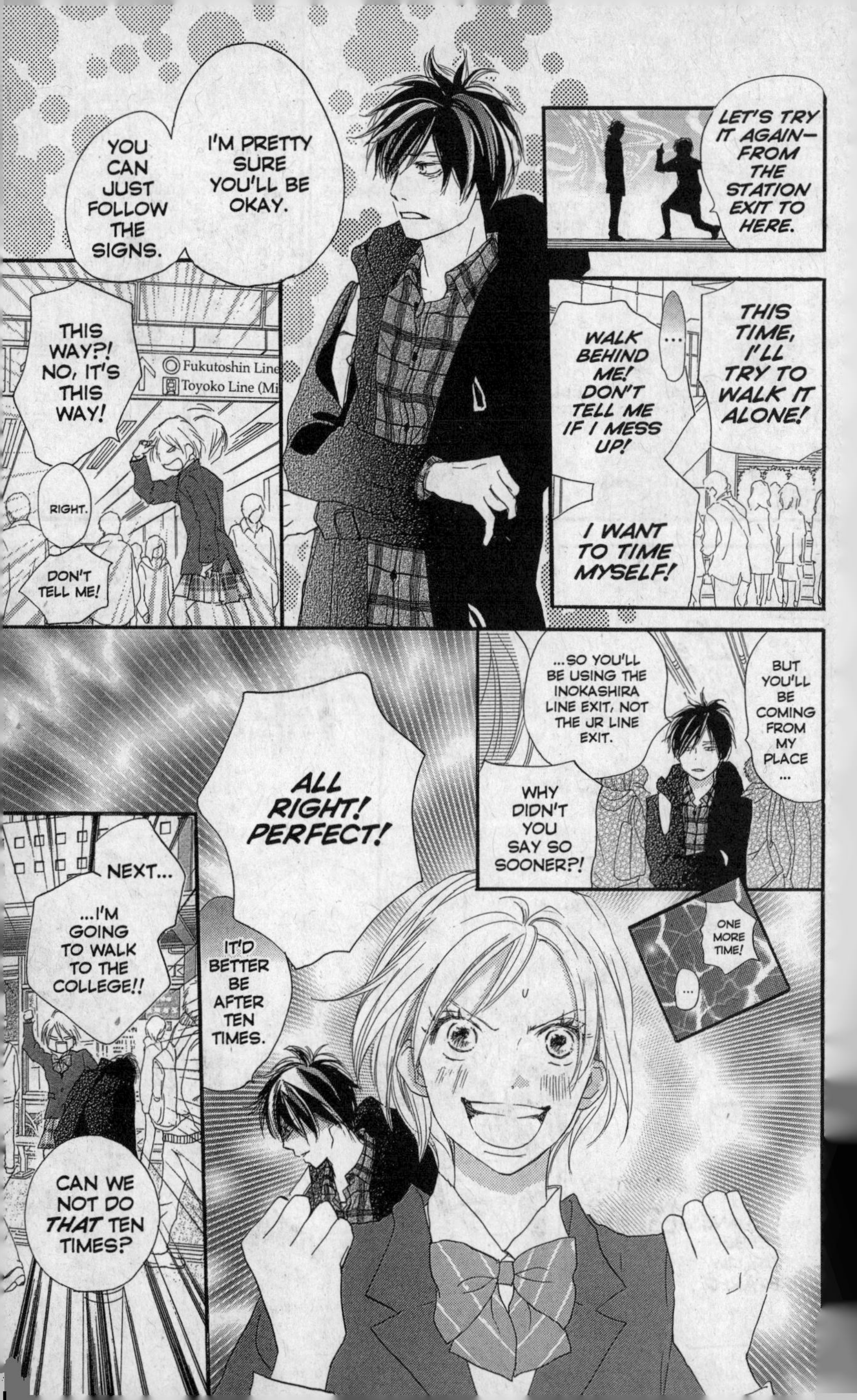
LET'S TRY IT AGAIN—FROM THE STATION EXIT TO HERE.
THIS TIME, I'LL TRY TO WALK IT ALONE!
...
WALK BEHIND ME! DON'T TELL ME IF I MESS UP!
I WANT TO TIME MYSELF!
I'M PRETTY SURE YOU'LL BE OKAY.
YOU CAN JUST FOLLOW THE SIGNS.
Fukutoshin Line
Toyoko Line (Mi
THIS WAY?! NO, IT'S THIS WAY!
RIGHT.
DON'T TELL ME!
BUT YOU'LL BE COMING FROM MY PLACE ...
...SO YOU'LL BE USING THE INOKASHIRA LINE EXIT, NOT THE JR LINE EXIT.
WHY DIDN'T YOU SAY SO SOONER?!
ONE MORE TIME!
...
ALL RIGHT! PERFECT!
IT'D BETTER BE AFTER TEN TIMES.
NEXT...
...I'M GOING TO WALK TO THE COLLEGE!!
CAN WE NOT DO *THAT* TEN TIMES?

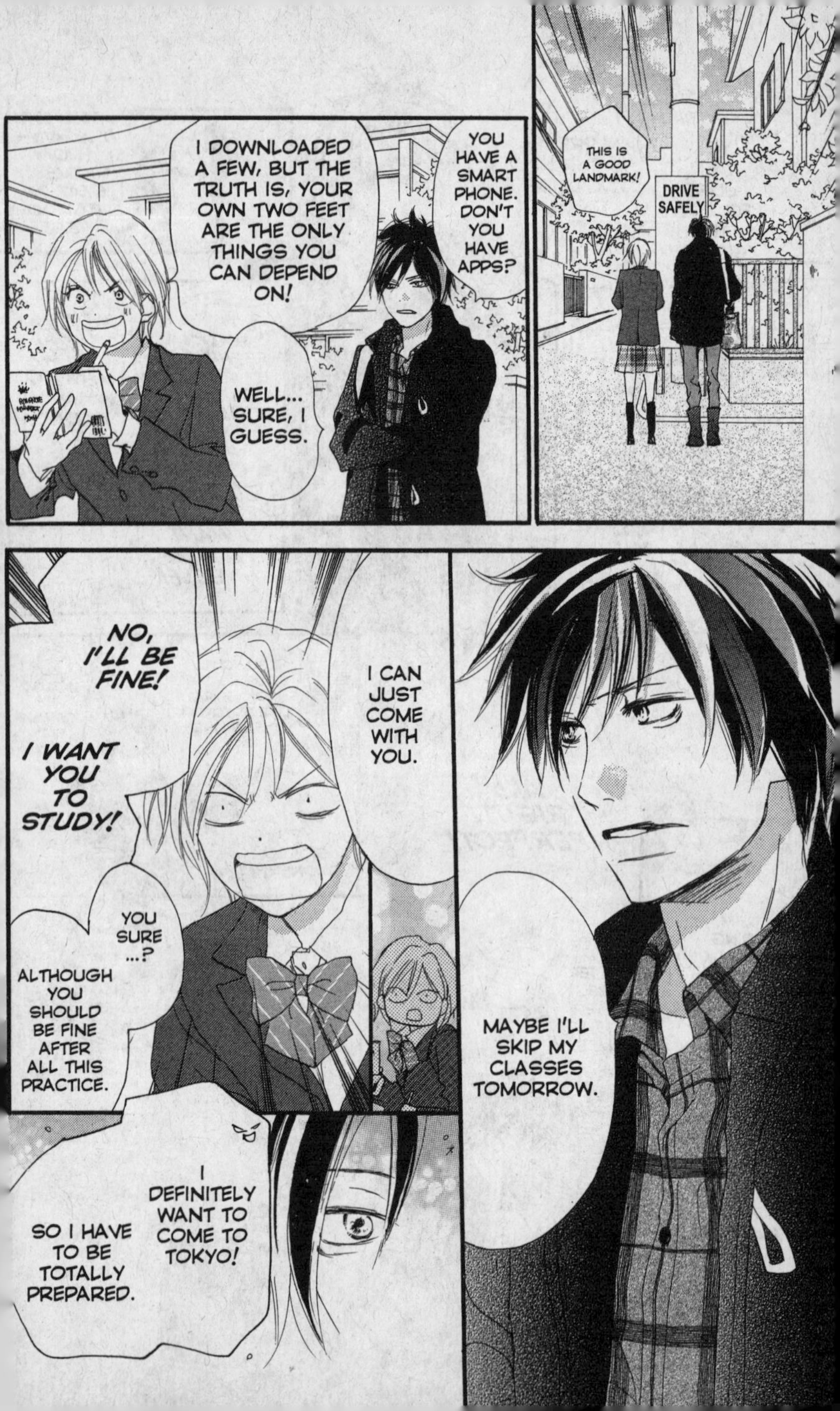
THIS IS A GOOD LANDMARK!
DRIVE SAFELY
YOU HAVE A SMART PHONE. DON'T YOU HAVE APPS?
I DOWNLOADED A FEW, BUT THE TRUTH IS, YOUR OWN TWO FEET ARE THE ONLY THINGS YOU CAN DEPEND ON!
WELL... SURE, I GUESS.
MAYBE I'LL SKIP MY CLASSES TOMORROW.
I CAN JUST COME WITH YOU.
NO, I'LL BE FINE!
I WANT YOU TO STUDY!
YOU SURE ...?
ALTHOUGH YOU SHOULD BE FINE AFTER ALL THIS PRACTICE.
I DEFINITELY WANT TO COME TO TOKYO!
SO I HAVE TO BE TOTALLY PREPARED.

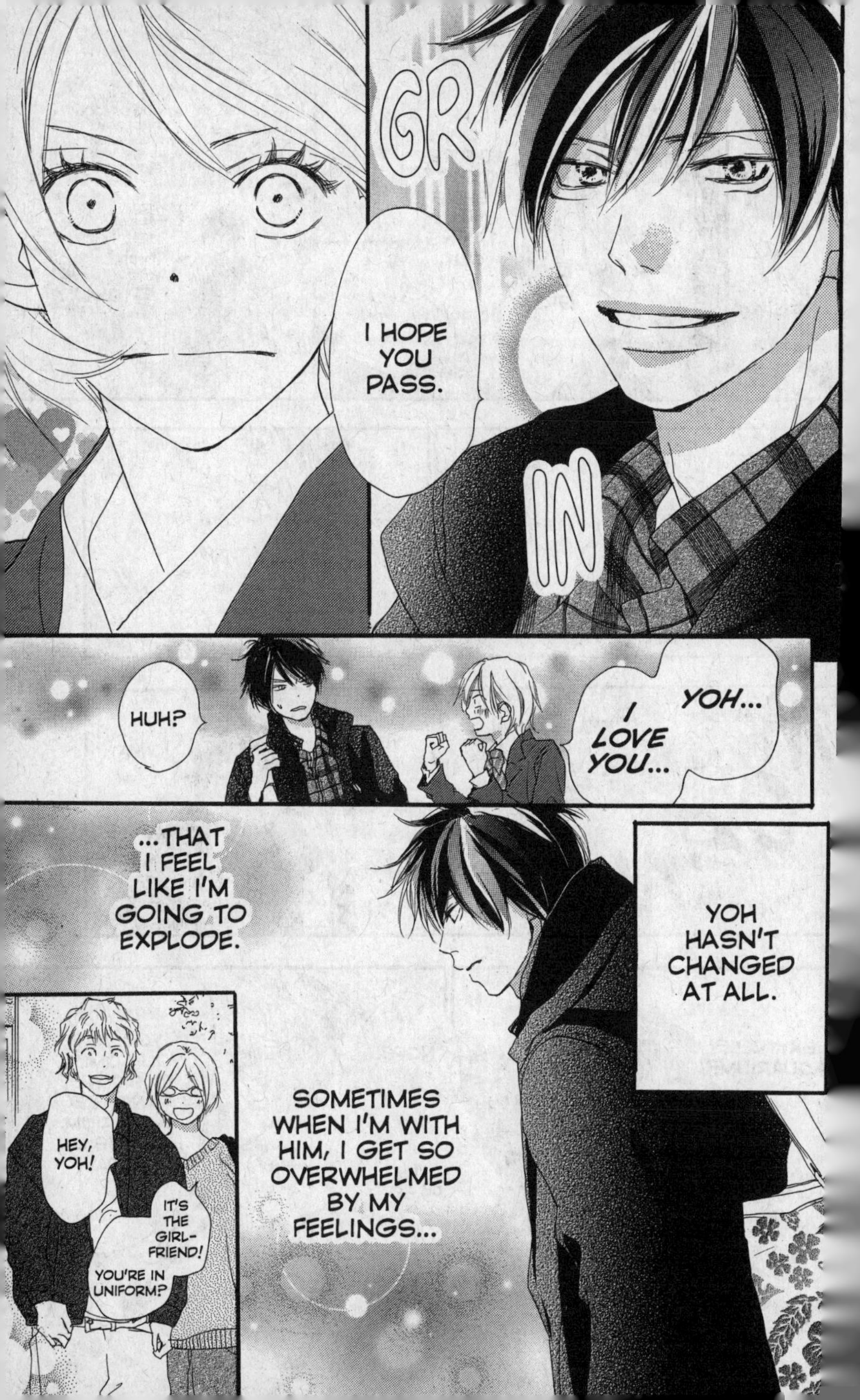
GR
I HOPE YOU PASS.
IN
YOH... I LOVE YOU...
HUH?
YOH HASN'T CHANGED AT ALL.
SOMETIMES WHEN I'M WITH HIM, I GET SO OVERWHELMED BY MY FEELINGS...
...THAT I FEEL LIKE I'M GOING TO EXPLODE.
HEY, YOH!
IT'S THE GIRL-FRIEND!
YOU'RE IN UNIFORM?

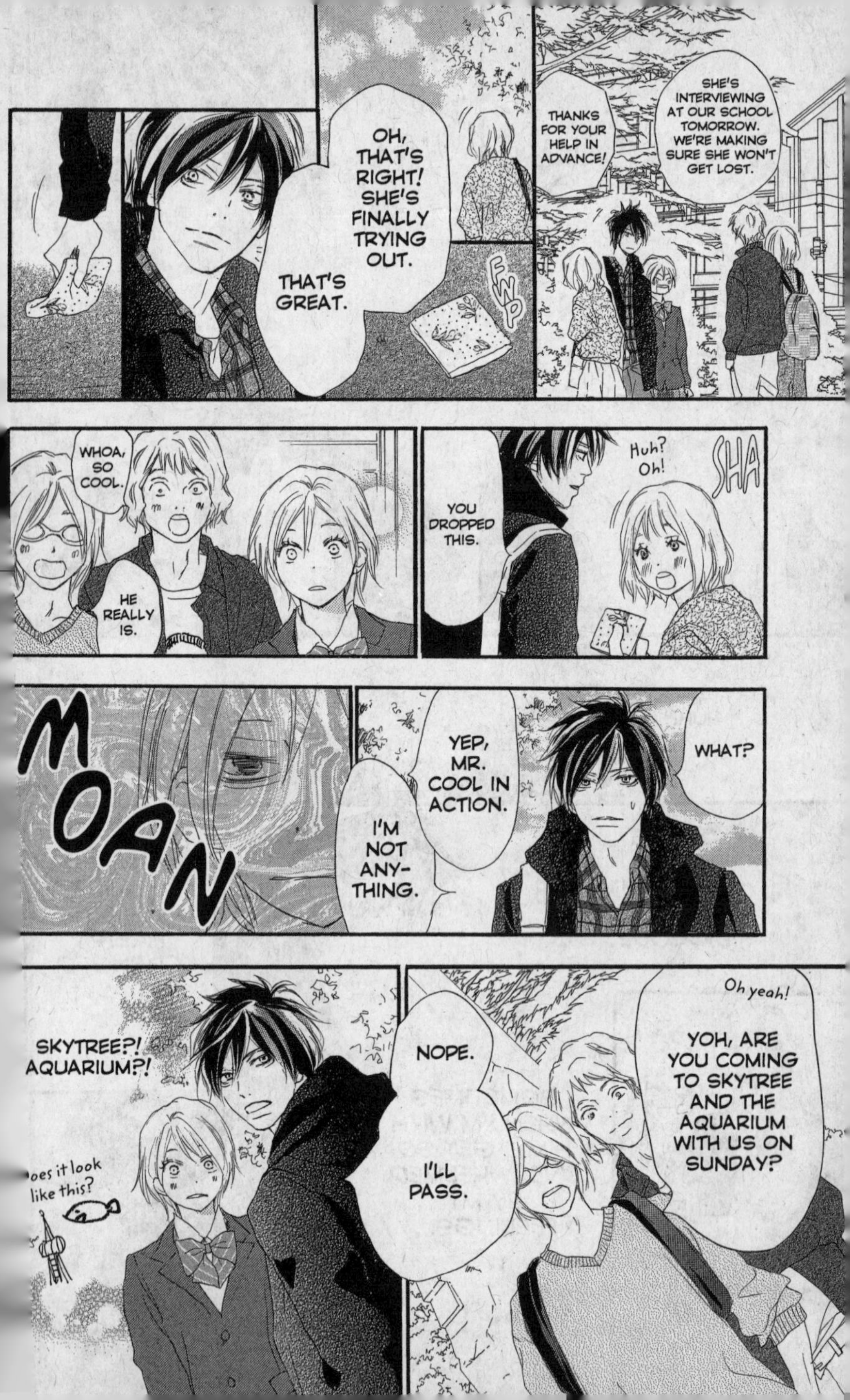
SHE'S INTERVIEWING AT OUR SCHOOL TOMORROW. WE'RE MAKING SURE SHE WON'T GET LOST.
THANKS FOR YOUR HELP IN ADVANCE!
FWP
OH, THAT'S RIGHT! SHE'S FINALLY TRYING OUT.
THAT'S GREAT.
SHA
Huh? Oh!
YOU DROPPED THIS.
WHOA, SO COOL.
HE REALLY IS.
WHAT?
YEP, MR. COOL IN ACTION.
I'M NOT ANY-THING.
MOAN
Oh yeah!
YOH, ARE YOU COMING TO SKYTREE AND THE AQUARIUM WITH US ON SUNDAY?
NOPE.
I'LL PASS.
SKYTREE?! AQUARIUM?!
oes it look like this?

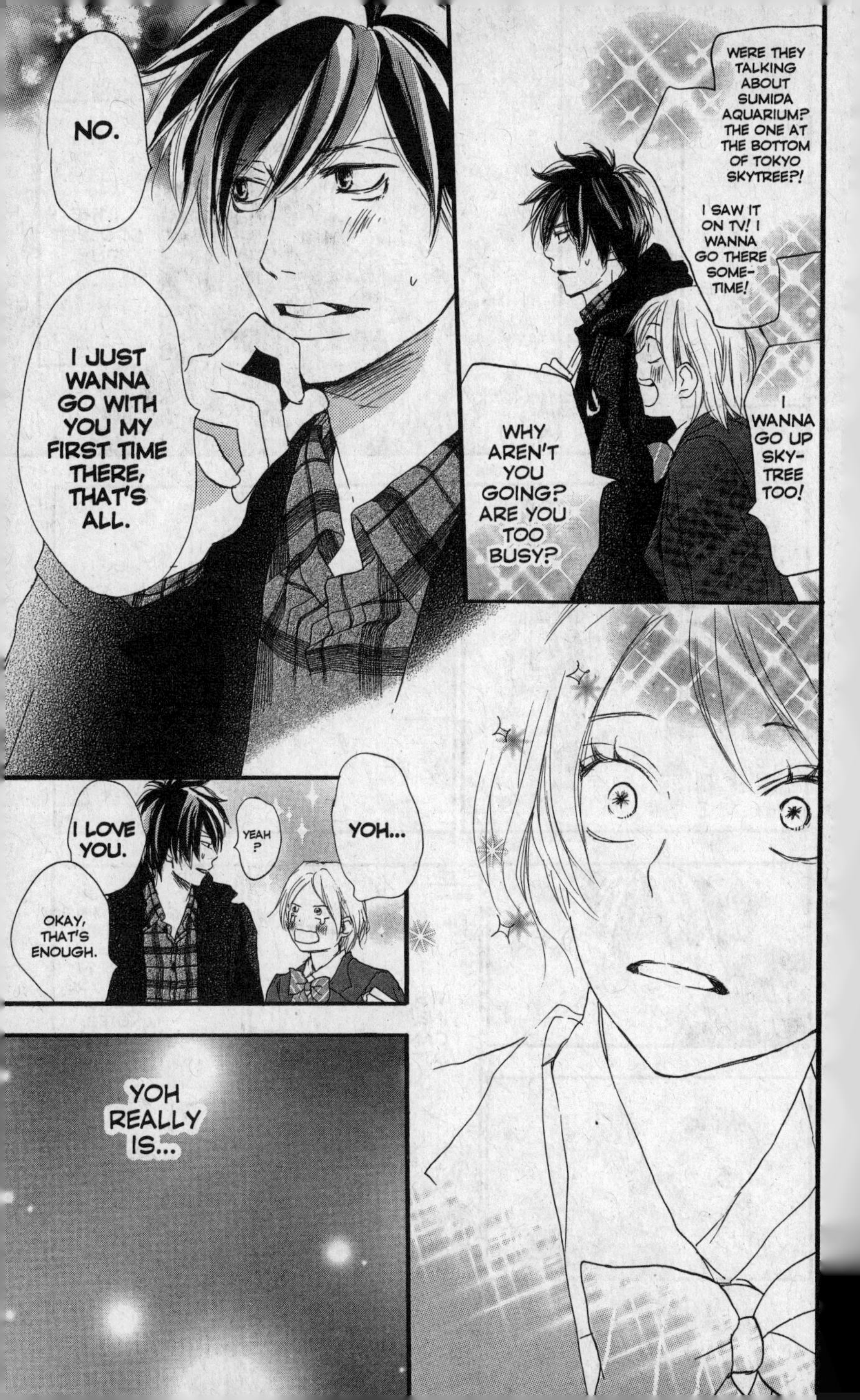
WERE THEY TALKING ABOUT SUMIDA AQUARIUM? THE ONE AT THE BOTTOM OF TOKYO SKYTREE?!
I SAW IT ON TV! I WANNA GO THERE SOME-TIME!
I WANNA GO UP SKY-TREE TOO!
WHY AREN'T YOU GOING? ARE YOU TOO BUSY?
NO.
I JUST WANNA GO WITH YOU MY FIRST TIME THERE, THAT'S ALL.
YOH...
YEAH?
I LOVE YOU.
OKAY, THAT'S ENOUGH.
YOH REALLY IS...

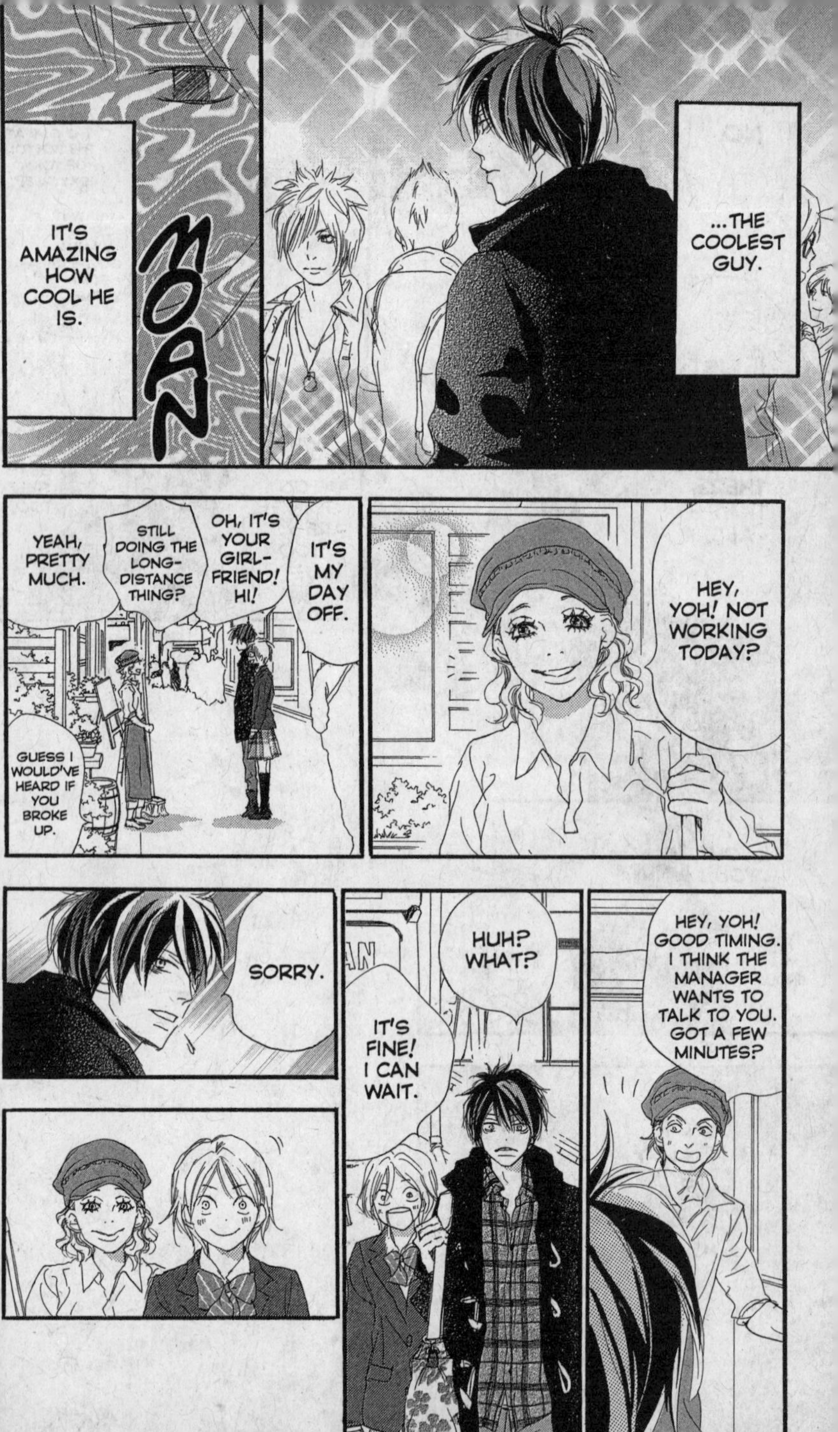
...THE COOLEST GUY.
IT'S AMAZING HOW COOL HE IS.
MOAN
HEY, YOH! NOT WORKING TODAY?
IT'S MY DAY OFF.
OH, IT'S YOUR GIRL-FRIEND! HI!
STILL DOING THE LONG-DISTANCE THING?
YEAH, PRETTY MUCH.
GUESS I WOULD'VE HEARD IF YOU BROKE UP.
HEY, YOH! GOOD TIMING. I THINK THE MANAGER WANTS TO TALK TO YOU. GOT A FEW MINUTES?
HUH? WHAT?
IT'S FINE! I CAN WAIT.
SORRY.

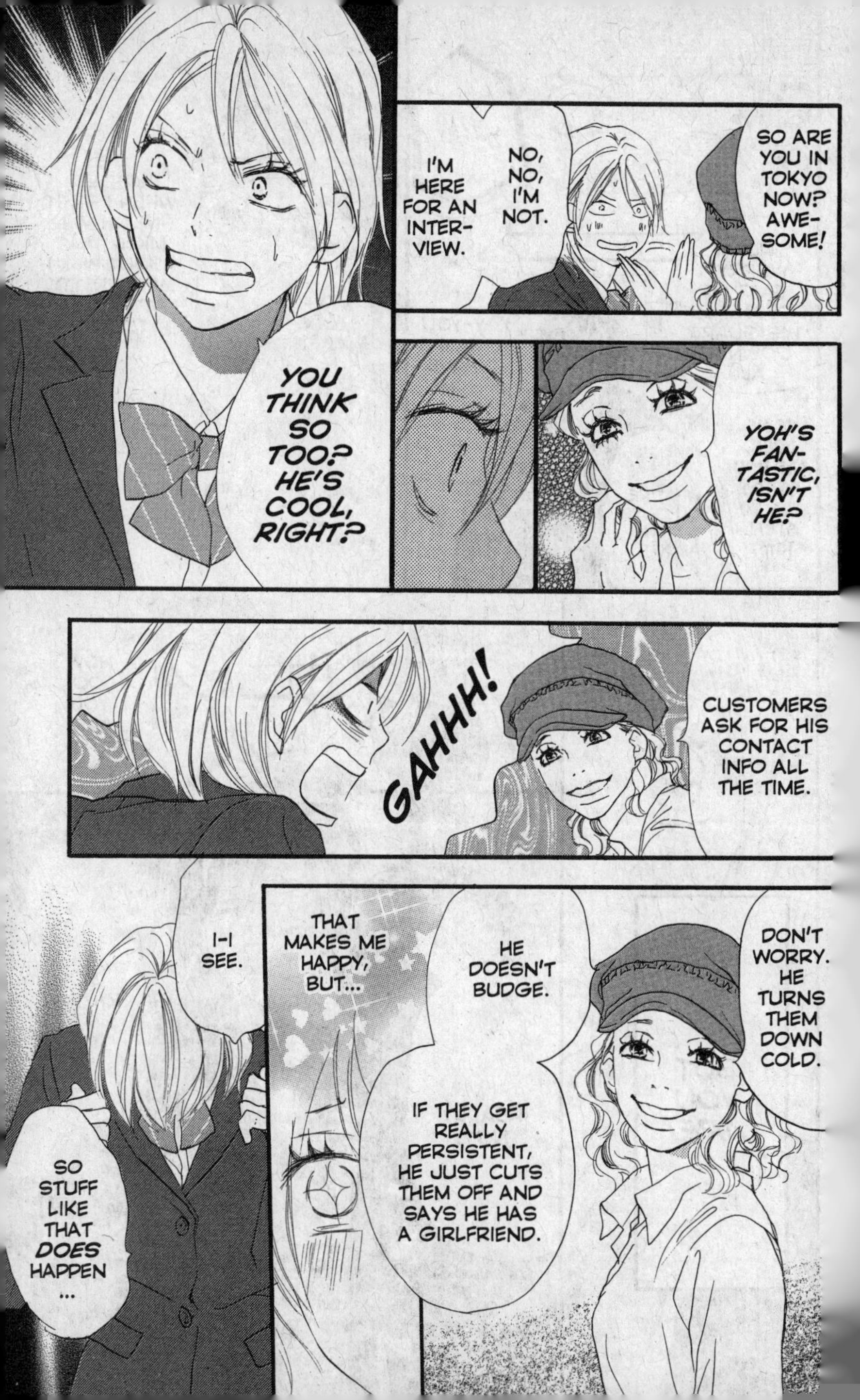
SO ARE YOU IN TOKYO NOW? AWESOME!
NO, NO, I'M NOT.
I'M HERE FOR AN INTERVIEW.
YOH'S FANTASTIC, ISN'T HE?
YOU THINK SO TOO? HE'S COOL, RIGHT?
CUSTOMERS ASK FOR HIS CONTACT INFO ALL THE TIME.
GAHHH!
DON'T WORRY. HE TURNS THEM DOWN COLD.
HE DOESN'T BUDGE.
IF THEY GET REALLY PERSISTENT, HE JUST CUTS THEM OFF AND SAYS HE HAS A GIRLFRIEND.
THAT MAKES ME HAPPY, BUT...
I-I SEE.
SO STUFF LIKE THAT *DOES* HAPPEN...

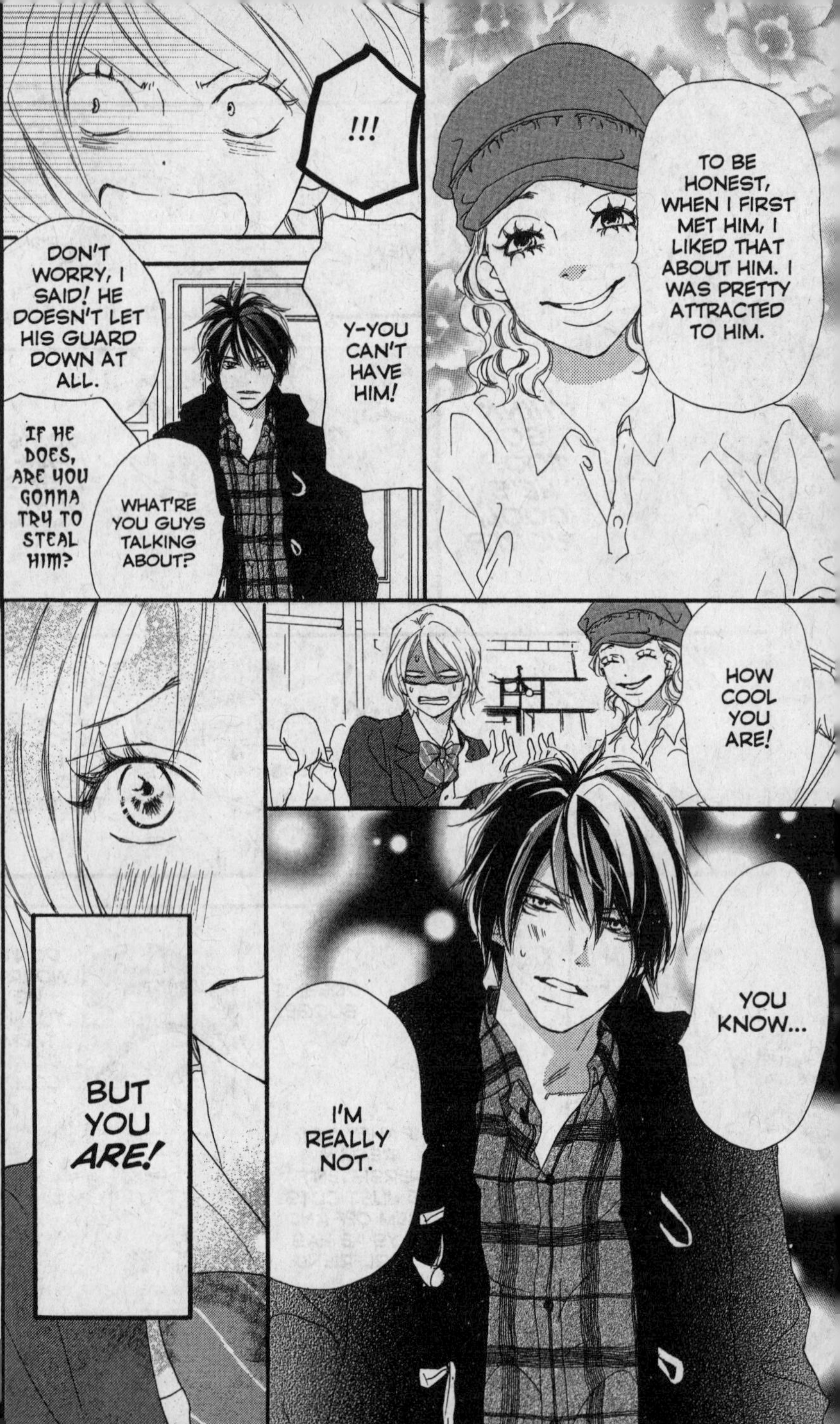
TO BE HONEST, WHEN I FIRST MET HIM, I LIKED THAT ABOUT HIM. I WAS PRETTY ATTRACTED TO HIM.
!!!
Y-YOU CAN'T HAVE HIM!
DON'T WORRY, I SAID! HE DOESN'T LET HIS GUARD DOWN AT ALL.
IF HE DOES, ARE YOU GONNA TRY TO STEAL HIM?
WHAT'RE YOU GUYS TALKING ABOUT?
HOW COOL YOU ARE!
YOU KNOW...
I'M REALLY NOT.
BUT YOU ARE!

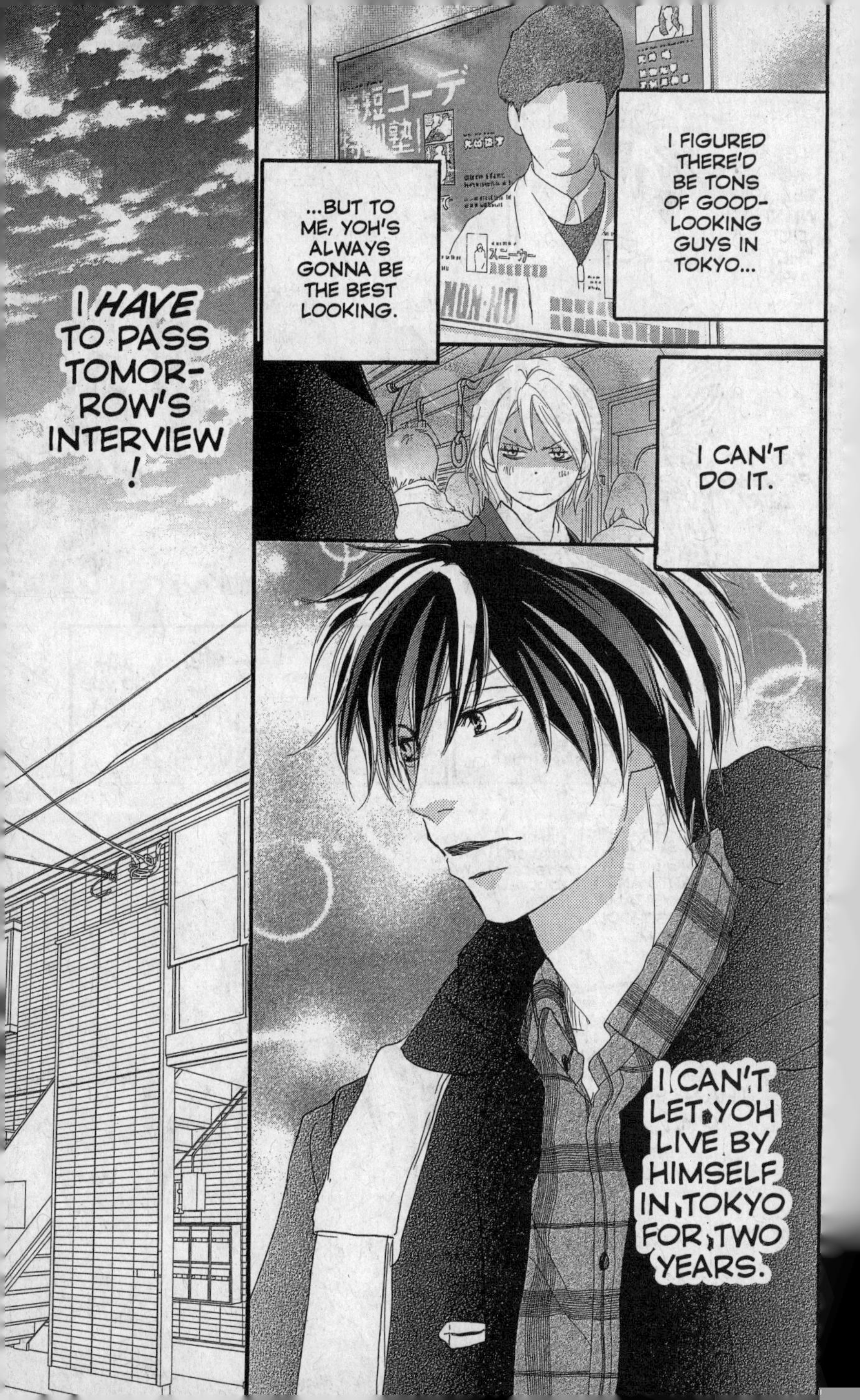
I FIGURED THERE'D BE TONS OF GOOD-LOOKING GUYS IN TOKYO...
...BUT TO ME, YOH'S ALWAYS GONNA BE THE BEST LOOKING.
I CAN'T DO IT.
I CAN'T LET YOH LIVE BY HIMSELF IN TOKYO FOR TWO YEARS.
I *HAVE* TO PASS TOMORROW'S INTERVIEW!

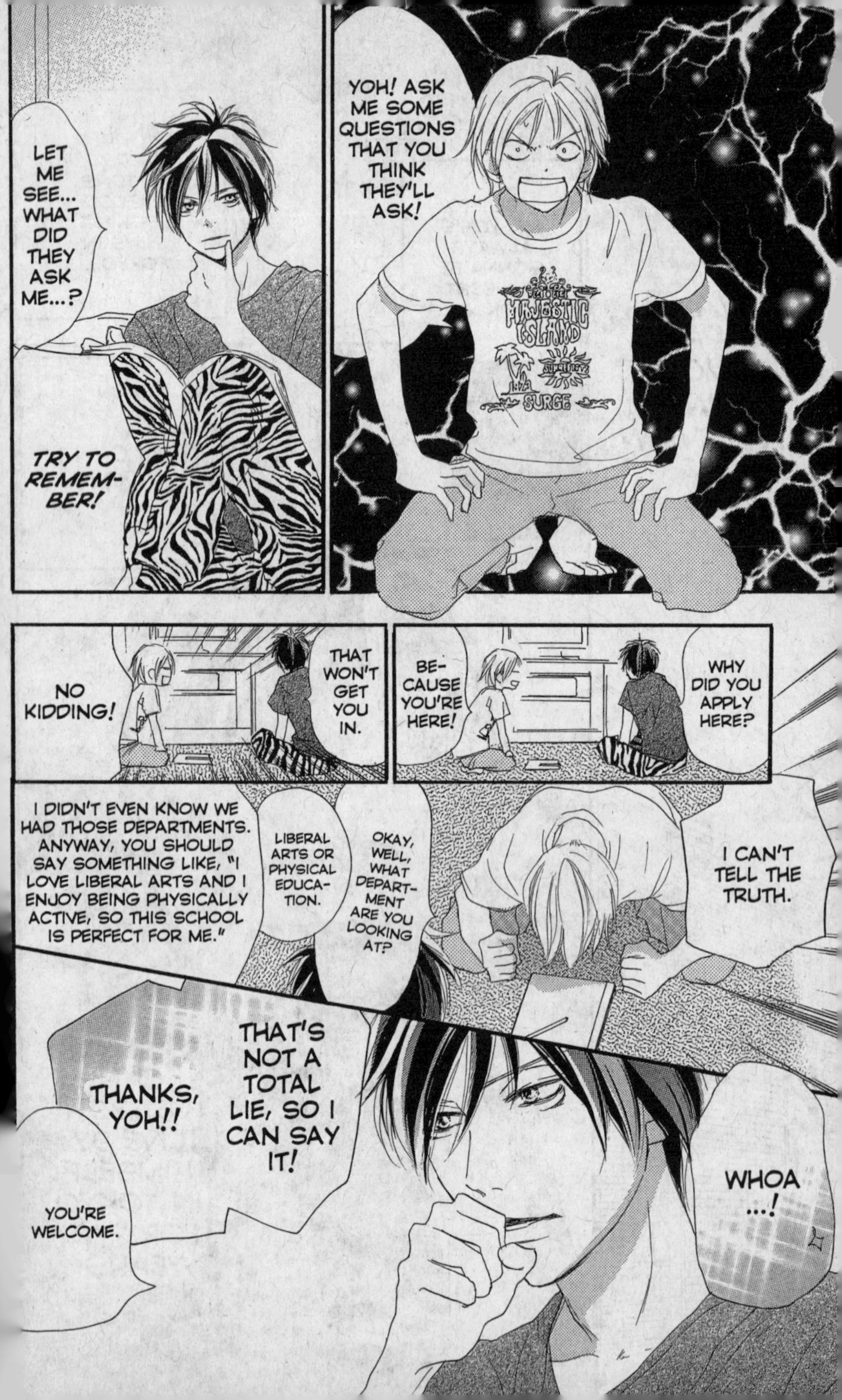

YOH! ASK ME SOME QUESTIONS THAT YOU THINK THEY'LL ASK!
LET ME SEE... WHAT DID THEY ASK ME...?
TRY TO REMEMBER!
WHY DID YOU APPLY HERE?
BECAUSE YOU'RE HERE!
THAT WON'T GET YOU IN.
NO KIDDING!
I CAN'T TELL THE TRUTH.
OKAY, WELL, WHAT DEPARTMENT ARE YOU LOOKING AT?
LIBERAL ARTS OR PHYSICAL EDUCATION.
I DIDN'T EVEN KNOW WE HAD THOSE DEPARTMENTS. ANYWAY, YOU SHOULD SAY SOMETHING LIKE, "I LOVE LIBERAL ARTS AND I ENJOY BEING PHYSICALLY ACTIVE, SO THIS SCHOOL IS PERFECT FOR ME."
WHOA ...!
THAT'S NOT A TOTAL LIE, SO I CAN SAY IT!
THANKS, YOH!!
YOU'RE WELCOME.

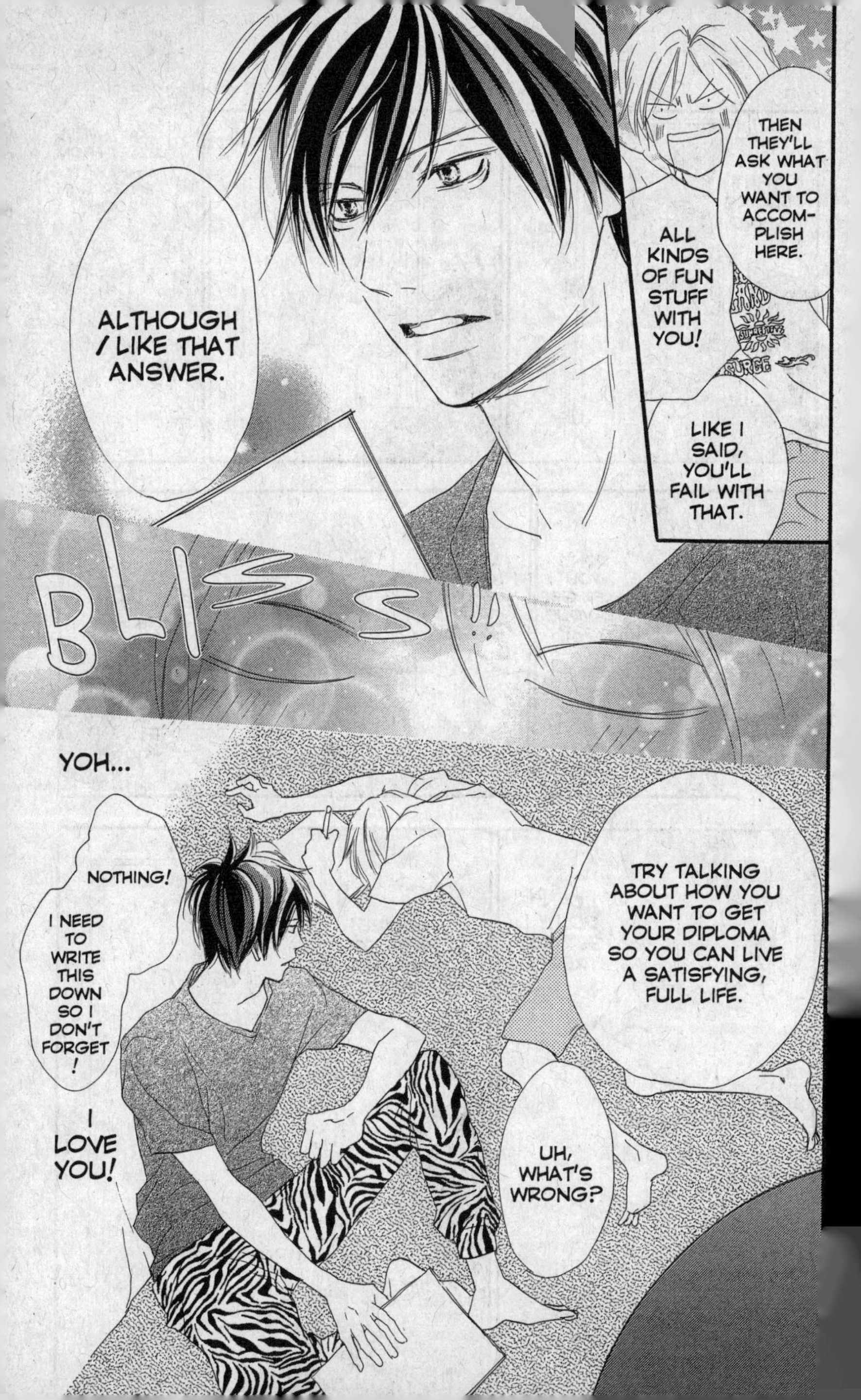
THEN THEY'LL ASK WHAT YOU WANT TO ACCOMPLISH HERE.
ALL KINDS OF FUN STUFF WITH YOU!
LIKE I SAID, YOU'LL FAIL WITH THAT.
ALTHOUGH I LIKE THAT ANSWER.
BLISS
TRY TALKING ABOUT HOW YOU WANT TO GET YOUR DIPLOMA SO YOU CAN LIVE A SATISFYING, FULL LIFE.
UH, WHAT'S WRONG?
YOH...
NOTHING!
I NEED TO WRITE THIS DOWN SO I DON'T FORGET!
I LOVE YOU!

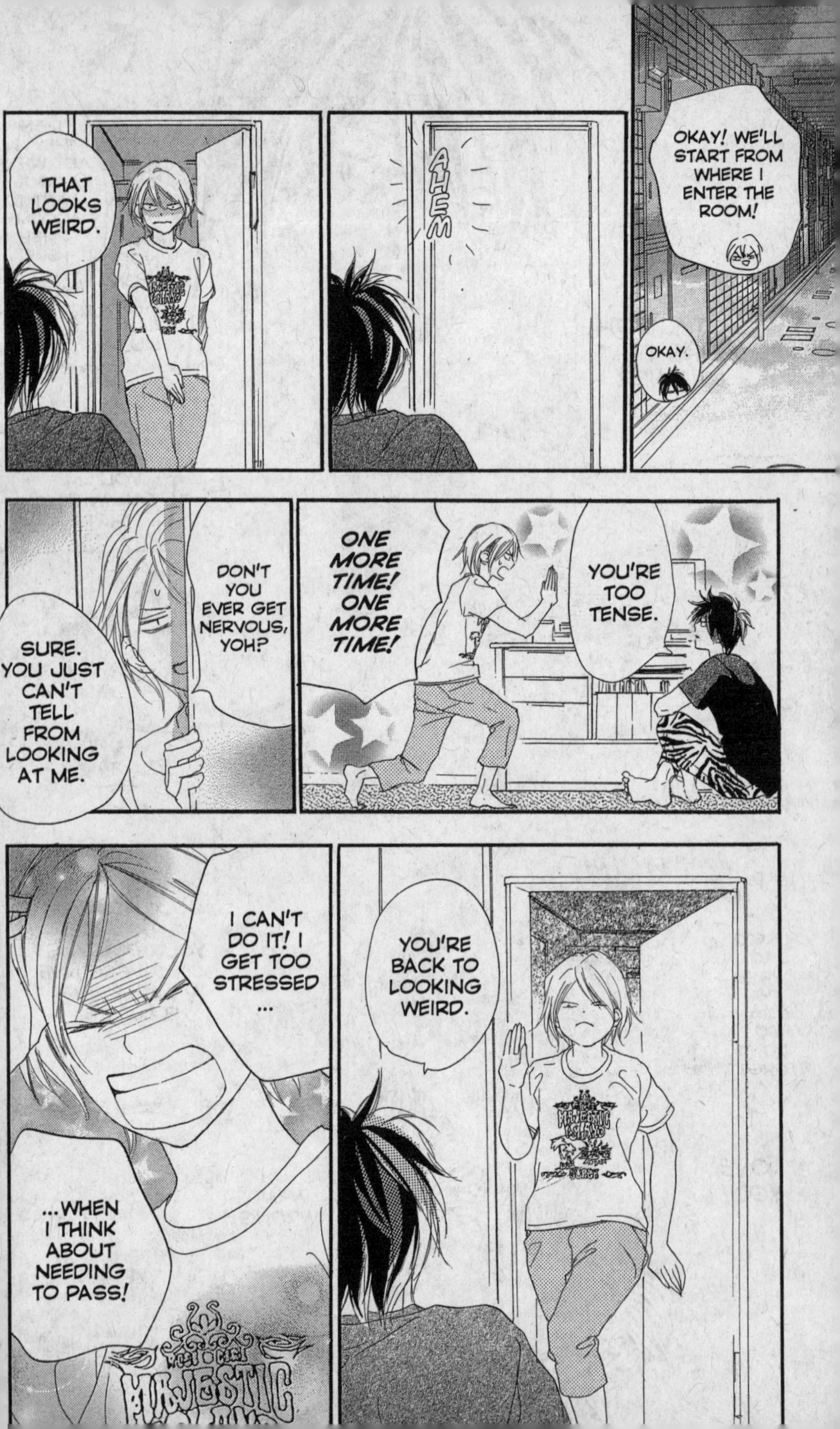
OKAY! WE'LL START FROM WHERE I ENTER THE ROOM!
OKAY.
AHEM
THAT LOOKS WEIRD.
YOU'RE TOO TENSE.
ONE MORE TIME! ONE MORE TIME!
DON'T YOU EVER GET NERVOUS, YOH?
SURE. YOU JUST CAN'T TELL FROM LOOKING AT ME.
YOU'RE BACK TO LOOKING WEIRD.
I CAN'T DO IT! I GET TOO STRESSED ...
...WHEN I THINK ABOUT NEEDING TO PASS!

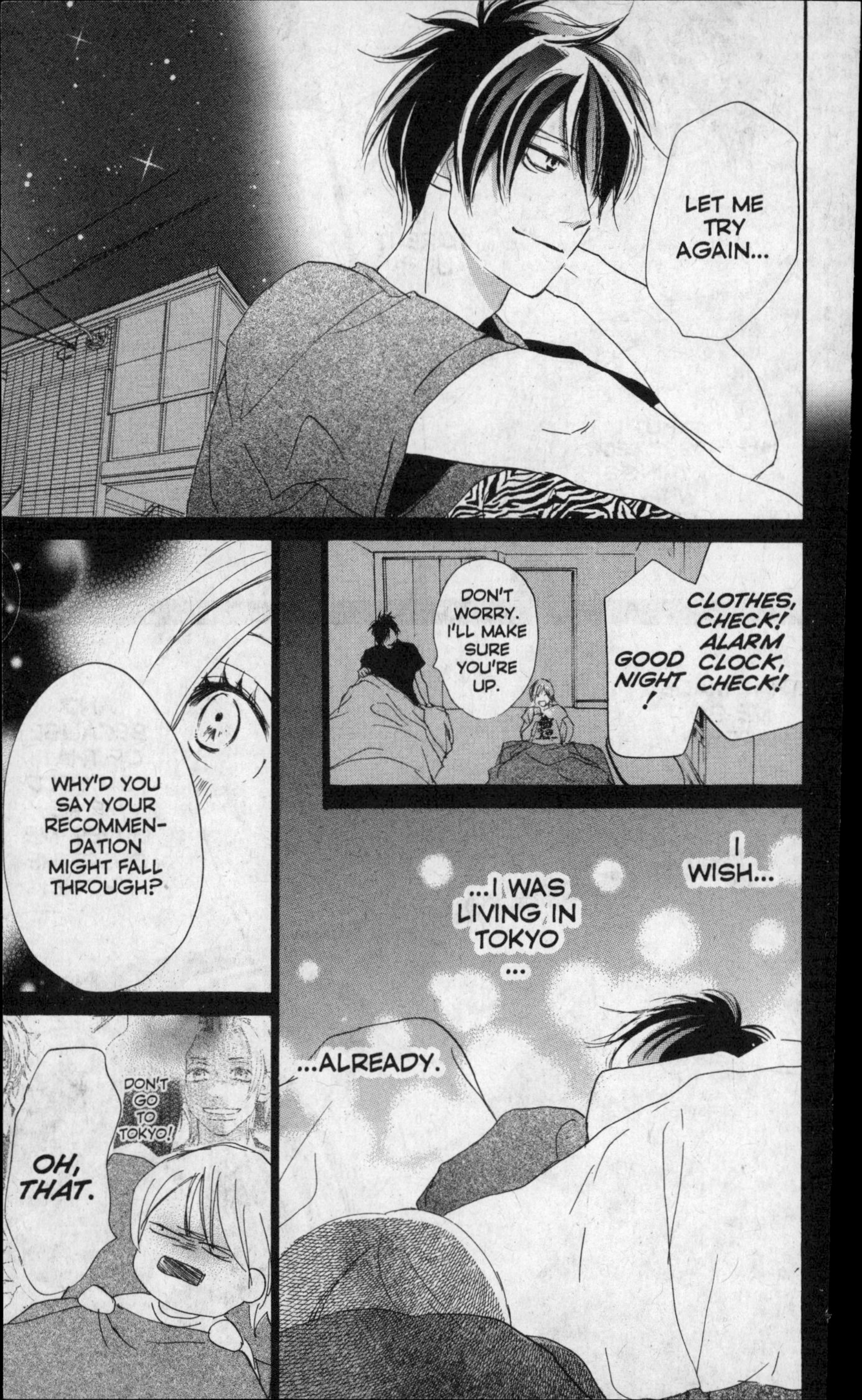
LET ME TRY AGAIN...
CLOTHES, CHECK! ALARM CLOCK, CHECK!
GOOD NIGHT!
DON'T WORRY. I'LL MAKE SURE YOU'RE UP.
WHY'D YOU SAY YOUR RECOMMENDATION MIGHT FALL THROUGH?
I WISH...
...I WAS LIVING IN TOKYO ...
...ALREADY.
DON'T GO TO TOKYO!
OH, THAT.

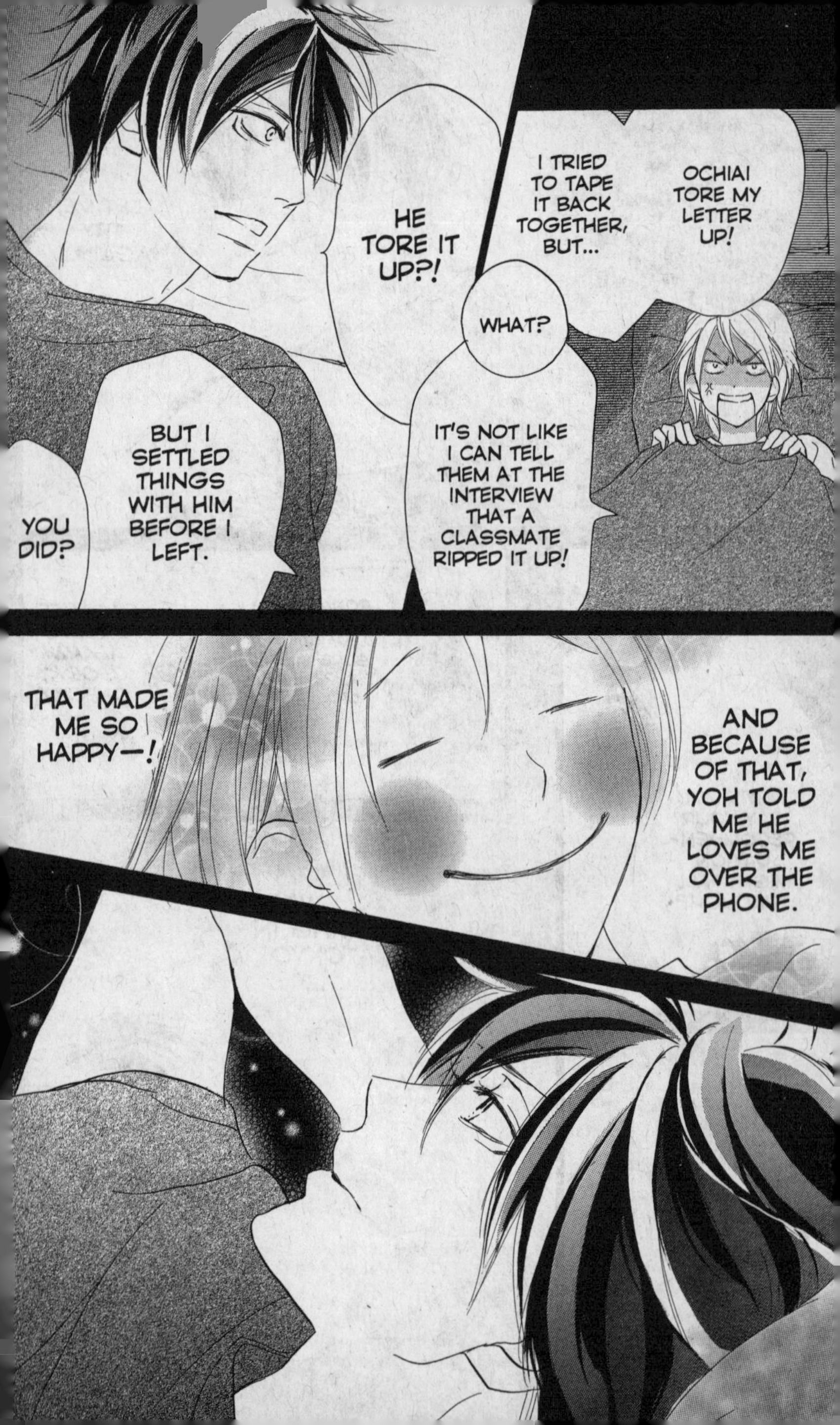
OCHIAI TORE MY LETTER UP!
I TRIED TO TAPE IT BACK TOGETHER, BUT...
WHAT?
HE TORE IT UP?!
IT'S NOT LIKE I CAN TELL THEM AT THE INTERVIEW THAT A CLASSMATE RIPPED IT UP!
BUT I SETTLED THINGS WITH HIM BEFORE I LEFT.
YOU DID?
AND BECAUSE OF THAT, YOH TOLD ME HE LOVES ME OVER THE PHONE.
THAT MADE ME SO HAPPY—!

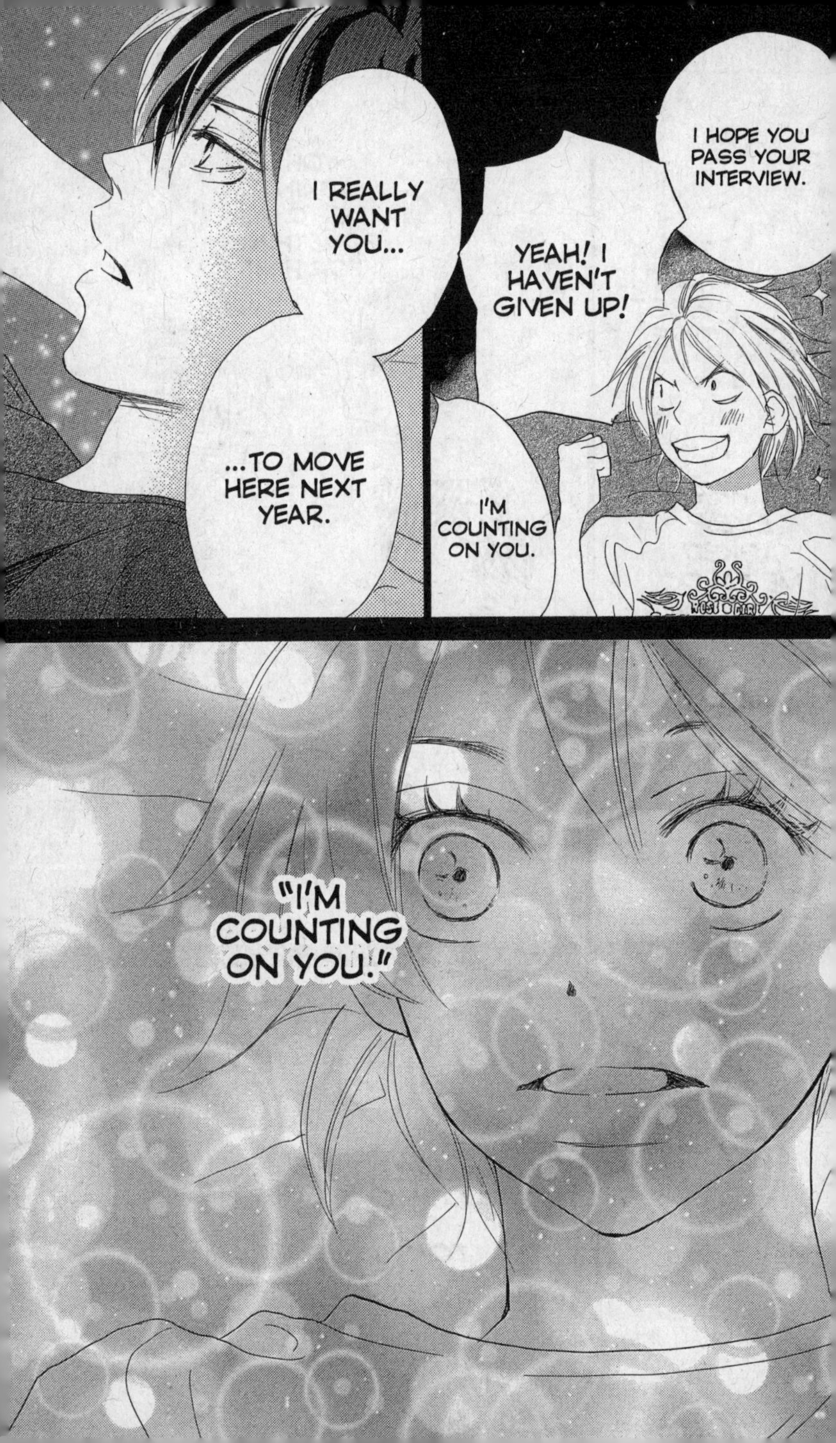
I HOPE YOU PASS YOUR INTERVIEW.
YEAH! I HAVEN'T GIVEN UP!
I'M COUNTING ON YOU.
I REALLY WANT YOU...
...TO MOVE HERE NEXT YEAR.
"I'M COUNTING ON YOU."

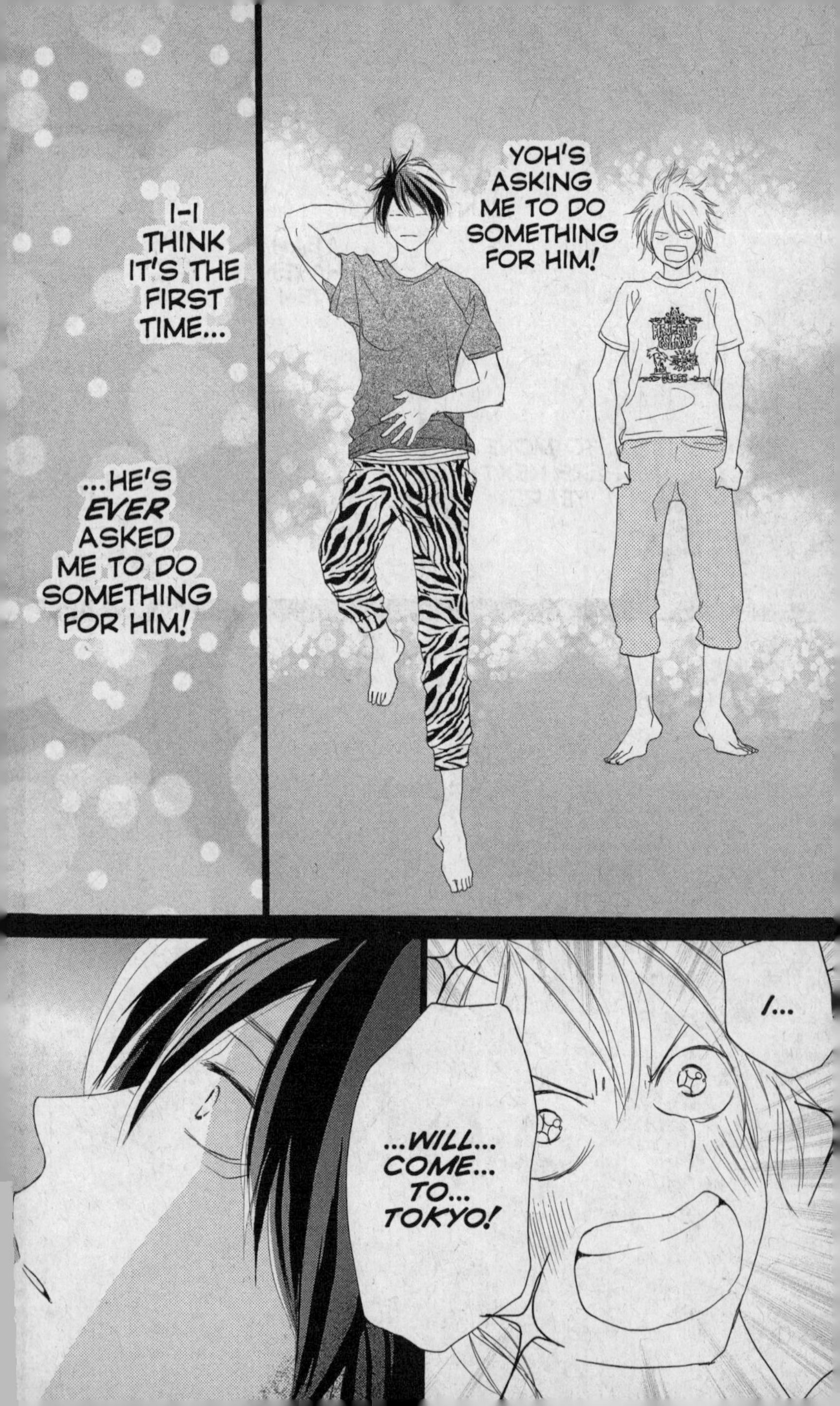
YOH'S ASKING ME TO DO SOMETHING FOR HIM!
I-I THINK IT'S THE FIRST TIME...
...HE'S *EVER* ASKED ME TO DO SOMETHING FOR HIM!
I...
...*WILL... COME... TO... TOKYO!*

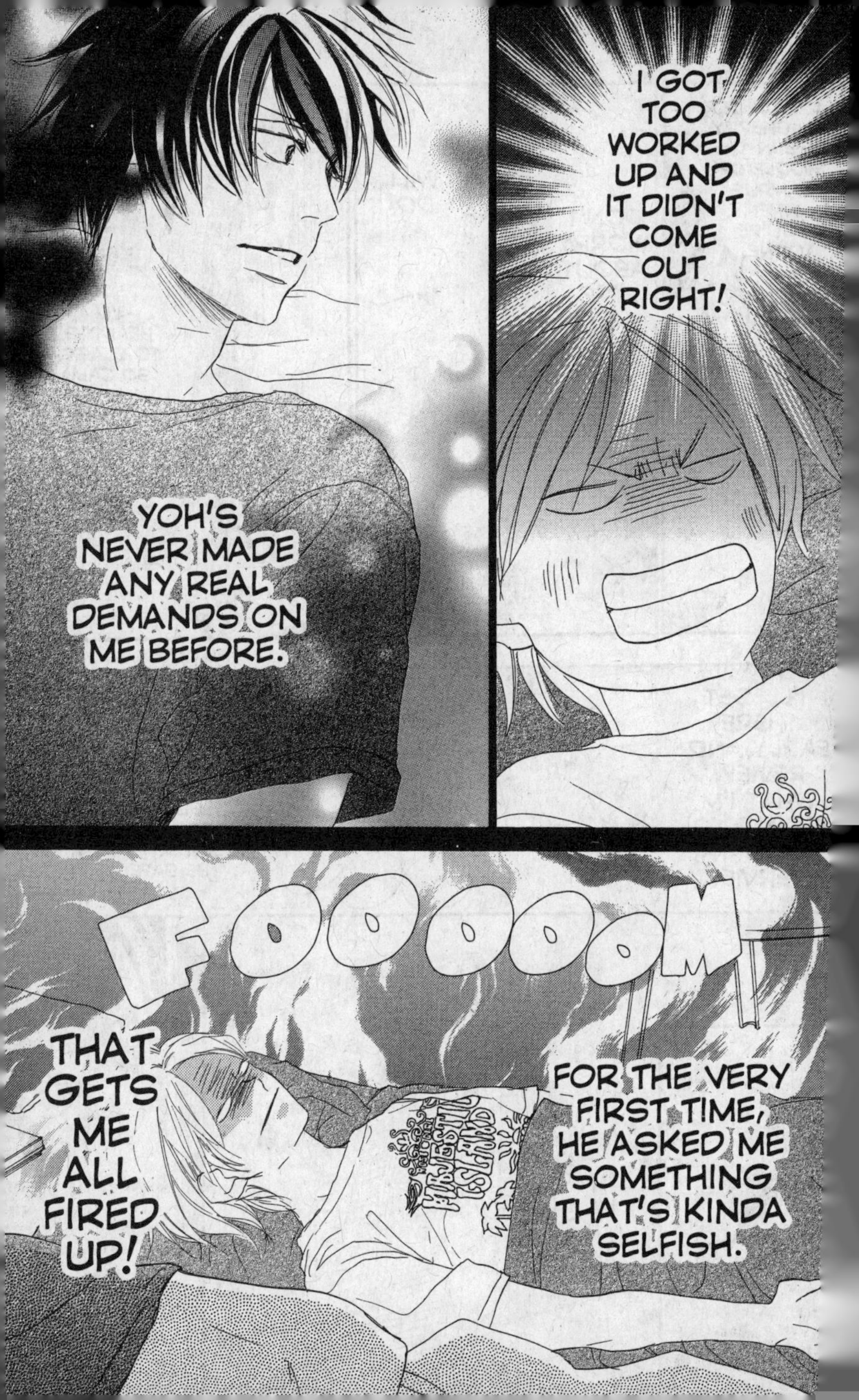
I GOT TOO WORKED UP AND IT DIDN'T COME OUT RIGHT!
YOH'S NEVER MADE ANY REAL DEMANDS ON ME BEFORE.
FOOOOOM
FOR THE VERY FIRST TIME, HE ASKED ME SOMETHING THAT'S KINDA SELFISH.
THAT GETS ME ALL FIRED UP!

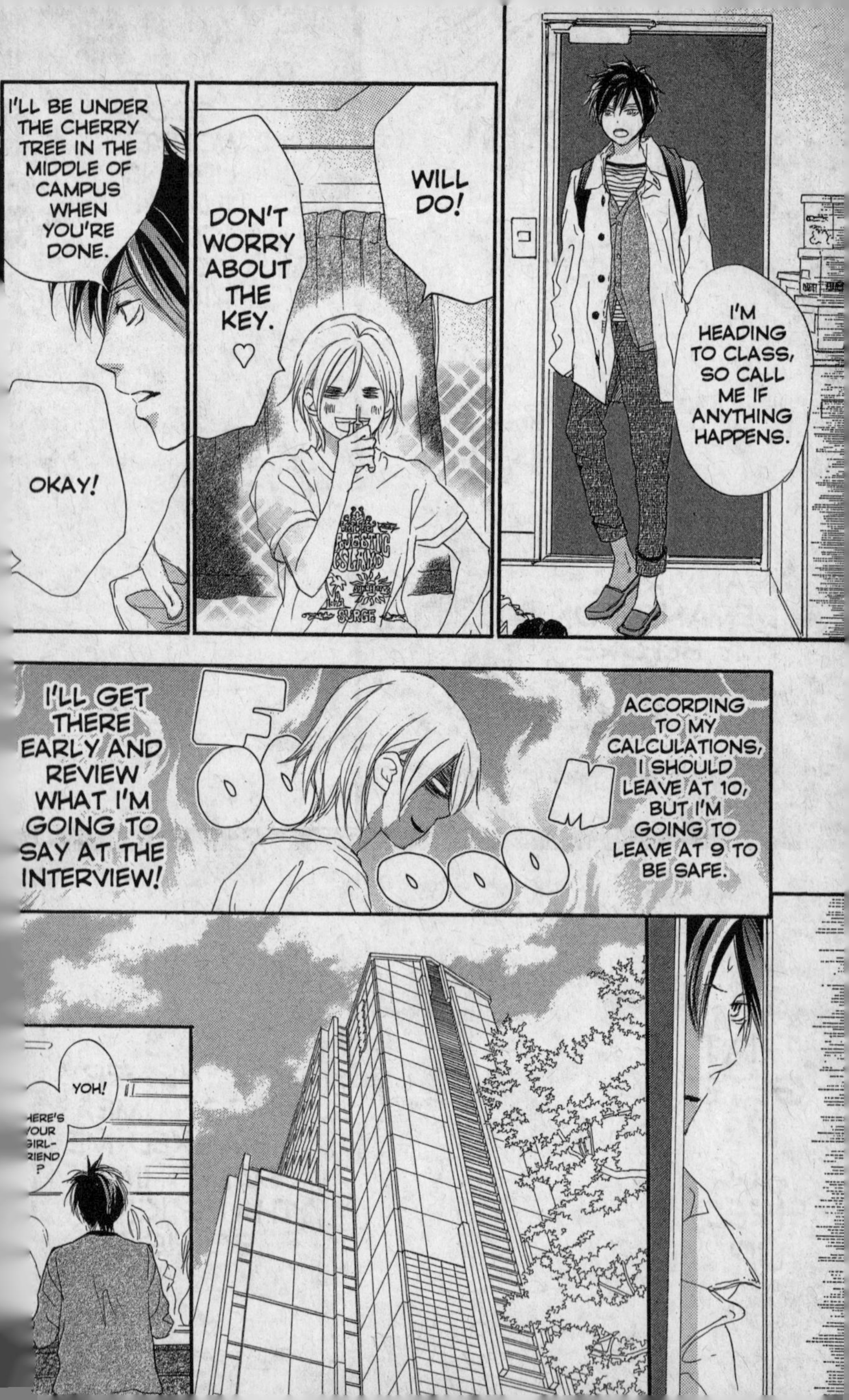
I'M HEADING TO CLASS, SO CALL ME IF ANYTHING HAPPENS.
WILL DO!
DON'T WORRY ABOUT THE KEY. ♡
I'LL BE UNDER THE CHERRY TREE IN THE MIDDLE OF CAMPUS WHEN YOU'RE DONE.
OKAY!
ACCORDING TO MY CALCULATIONS, I SHOULD LEAVE AT 10, BUT I'M GOING TO LEAVE AT 9 TO BE SAFE.
FOOMOOO
I'LL GET THERE EARLY AND REVIEW WHAT I'M GOING TO SAY AT THE INTERVIEW!
YOH!
HERE'S YOUR GIRL-FRIEND ?

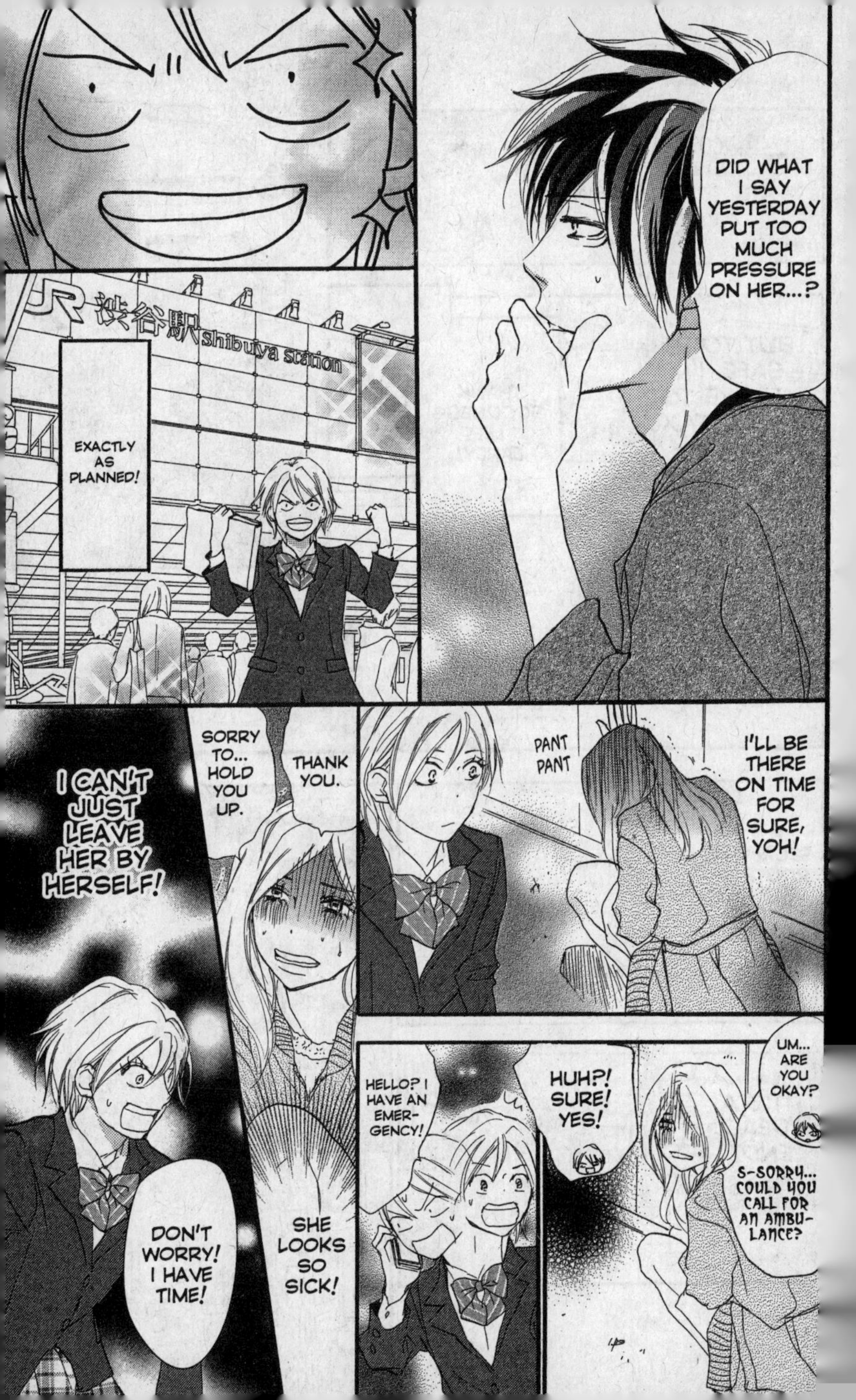
DID WHAT I SAY YESTERDAY PUT TOO MUCH PRESSURE ON HER...?
JR 渋谷駅 shibuya station
EXACTLY AS PLANNED!
I'LL BE THERE ON TIME FOR SURE, YOH!
PANT PANT
UM... ARE YOU OKAY?
S-SORRY... COULD YOU CALL FOR AN AMBULANCE?
HUH?! SURE! YES!
HELLO? I HAVE AN EMERGENCY!
THANK YOU.
SORRY TO... HOLD YOU UP.
SHE LOOKS SO SICK!
I CAN'T JUST LEAVE HER BY HERSELF!
DON'T WORRY! I HAVE TIME!

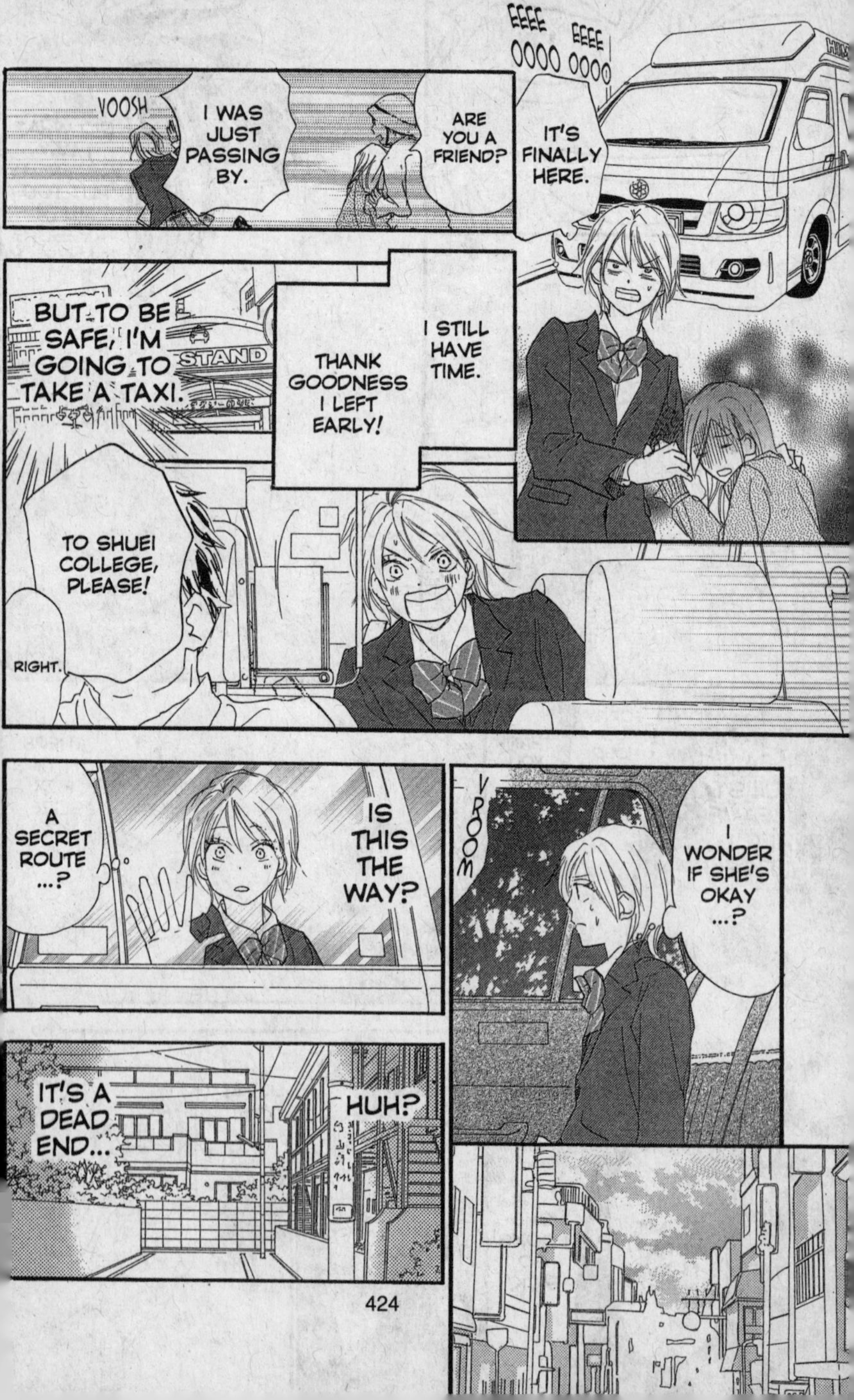
EEEE OOOO EEEE OOOO
IT'S FINALLY HERE.
ARE YOU A FRIEND?
I WAS JUST PASSING BY.
VOOSH
I STILL HAVE TIME.
THANK GOODNESS I LEFT EARLY!
BUT TO BE SAFE, I'M GOING TO TAKE A TAXI.
STAND
TO SHUEI COLLEGE, PLEASE!
RIGHT.
VROOM
I WONDER IF SHE'S OKAY ...?
IS THIS THE WAY?
A SECRET ROUTE ...?
HUH?
IT'S A DEAD END...

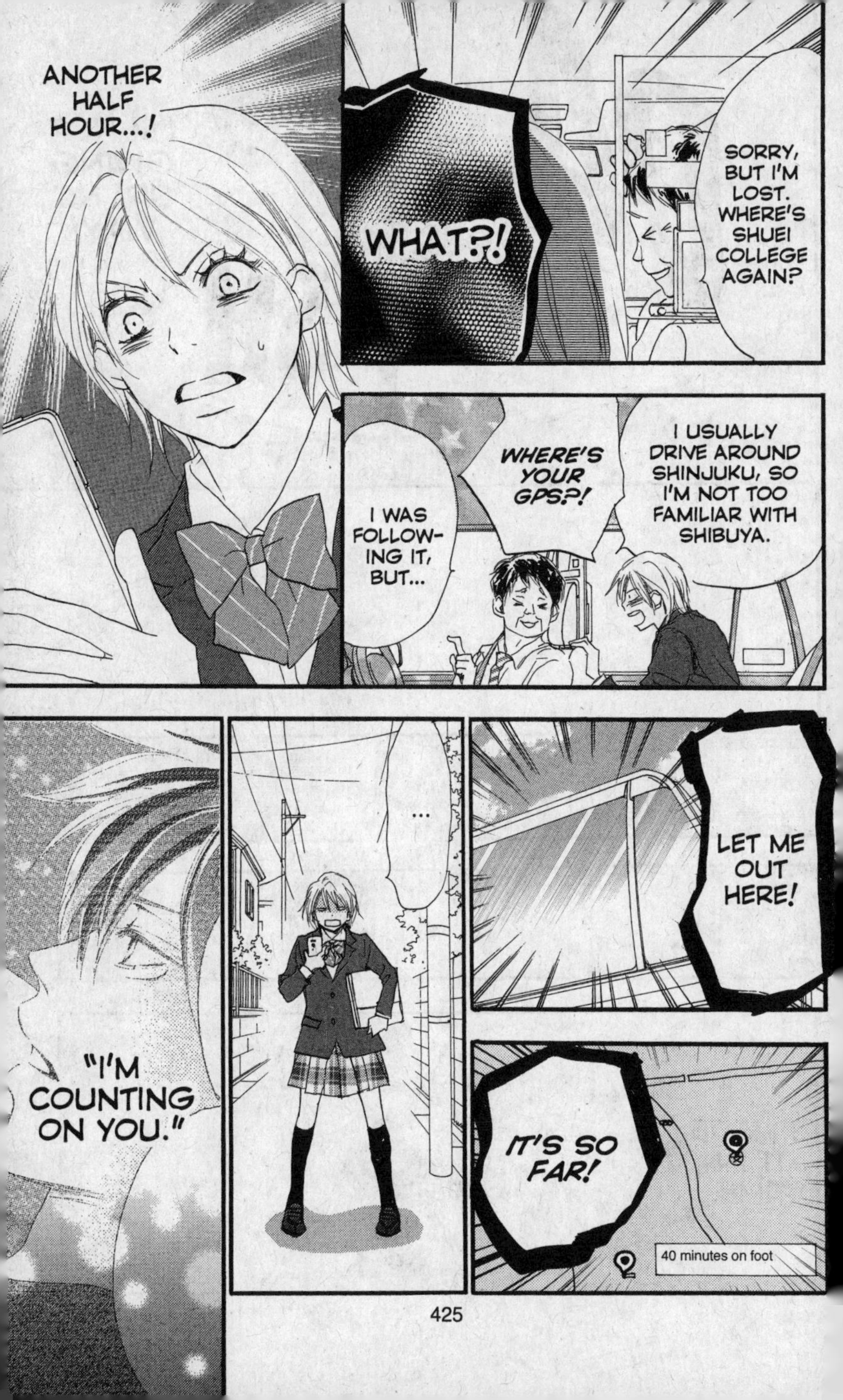
SORRY, BUT I'M LOST. WHERE'S SHUEI COLLEGE AGAIN?
WHAT?!
I USUALLY DRIVE AROUND SHINJUKU, SO I'M NOT TOO FAMILIAR WITH SHIBUYA.
WHERE'S YOUR GPS?!
I WAS FOLLOW-ING IT, BUT...
ANOTHER HALF HOUR...!
LET ME OUT HERE!
IT'S SO FAR!
40 minutes on foot
...
"I'M COUNTING ON YOU."

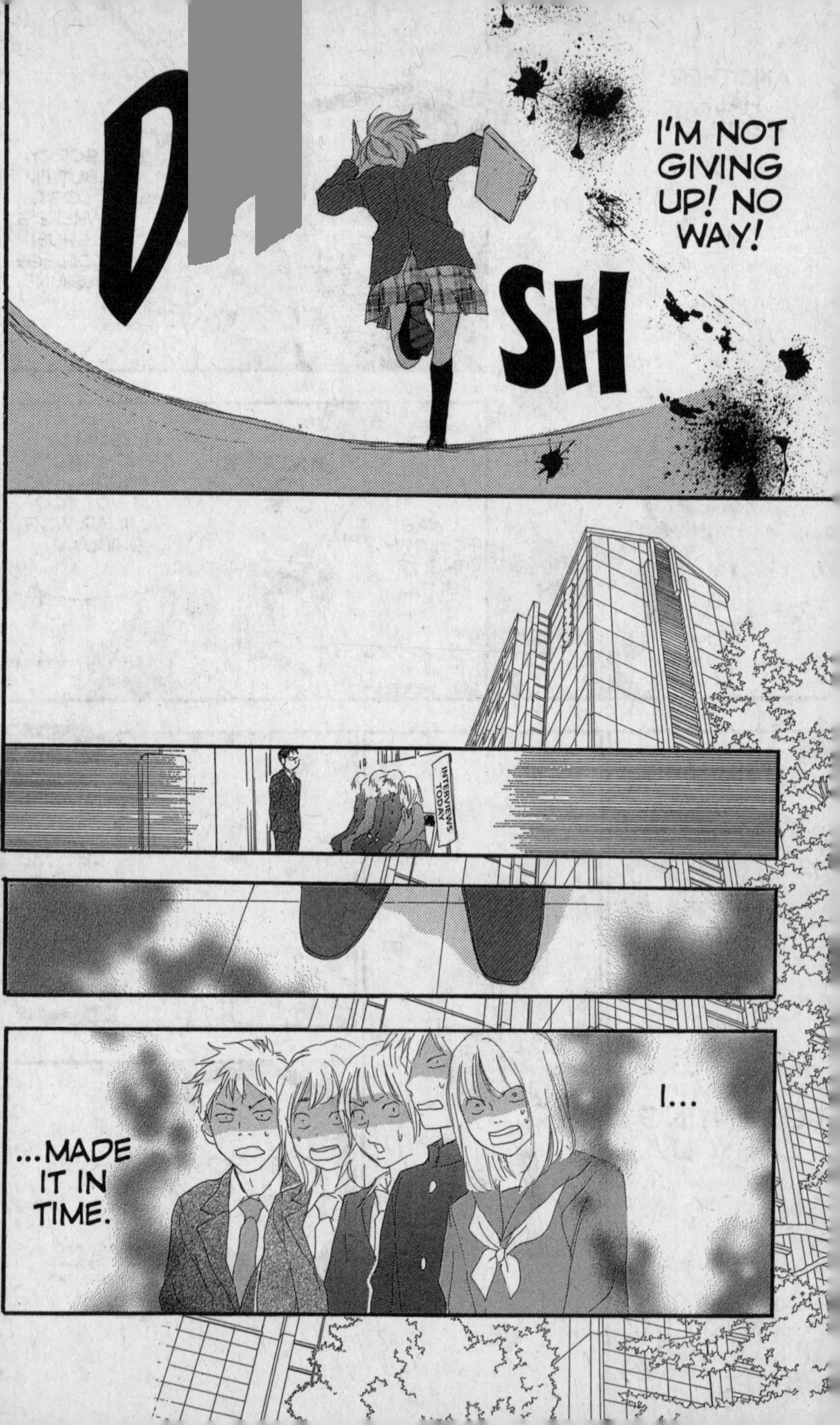
I'M NOT GIVING UP! NO WAY!
D
SH
INTERVIEWS TODAY
I...
...MADE IT IN TIME.

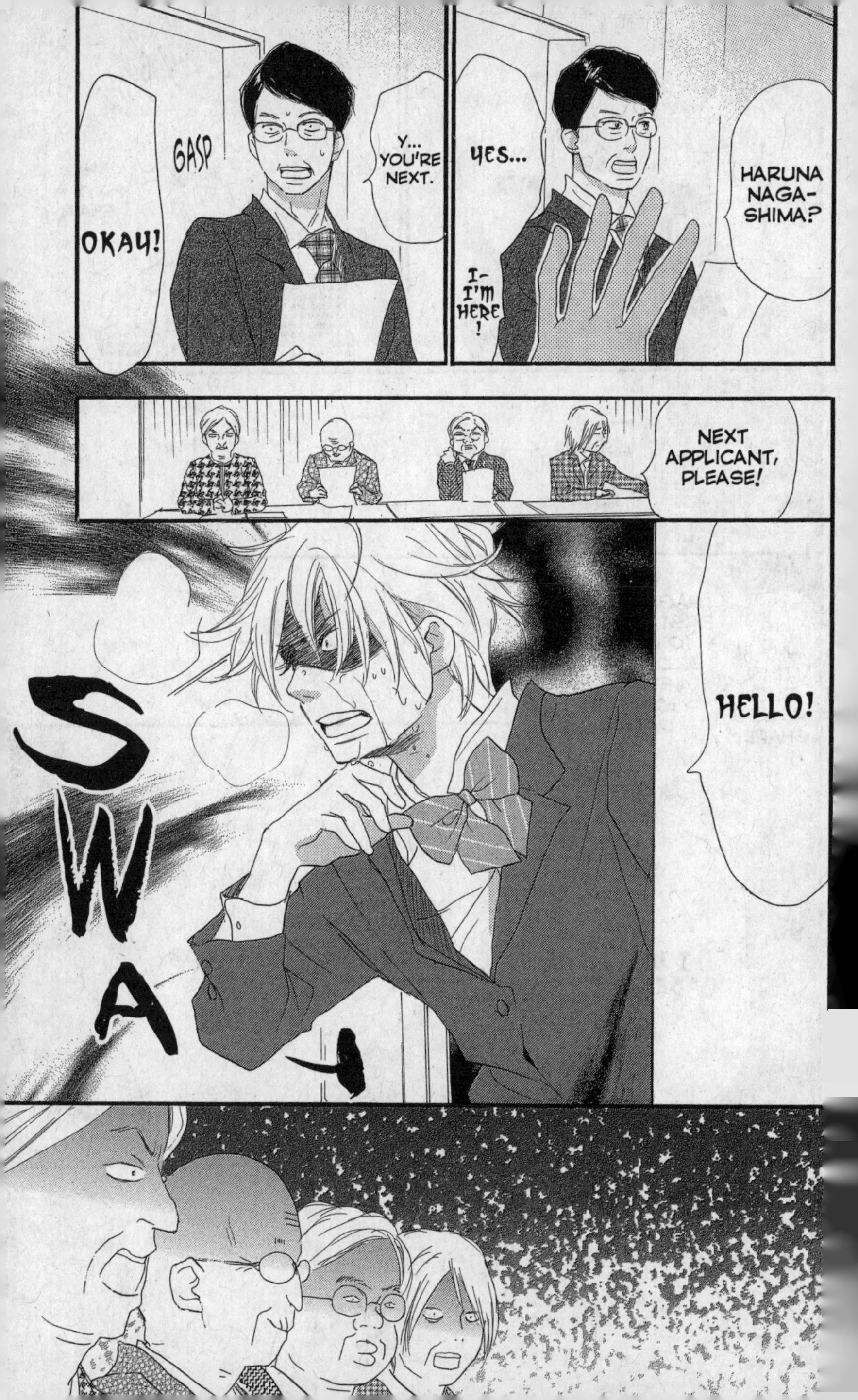
HARUNA NAGA-SHIMA?
YES...
I- I'M HERE!
Y... YOU'RE NEXT.
GASP
OKAY!
NEXT APPLICANT, PLEASE!
HELLO!
SWA

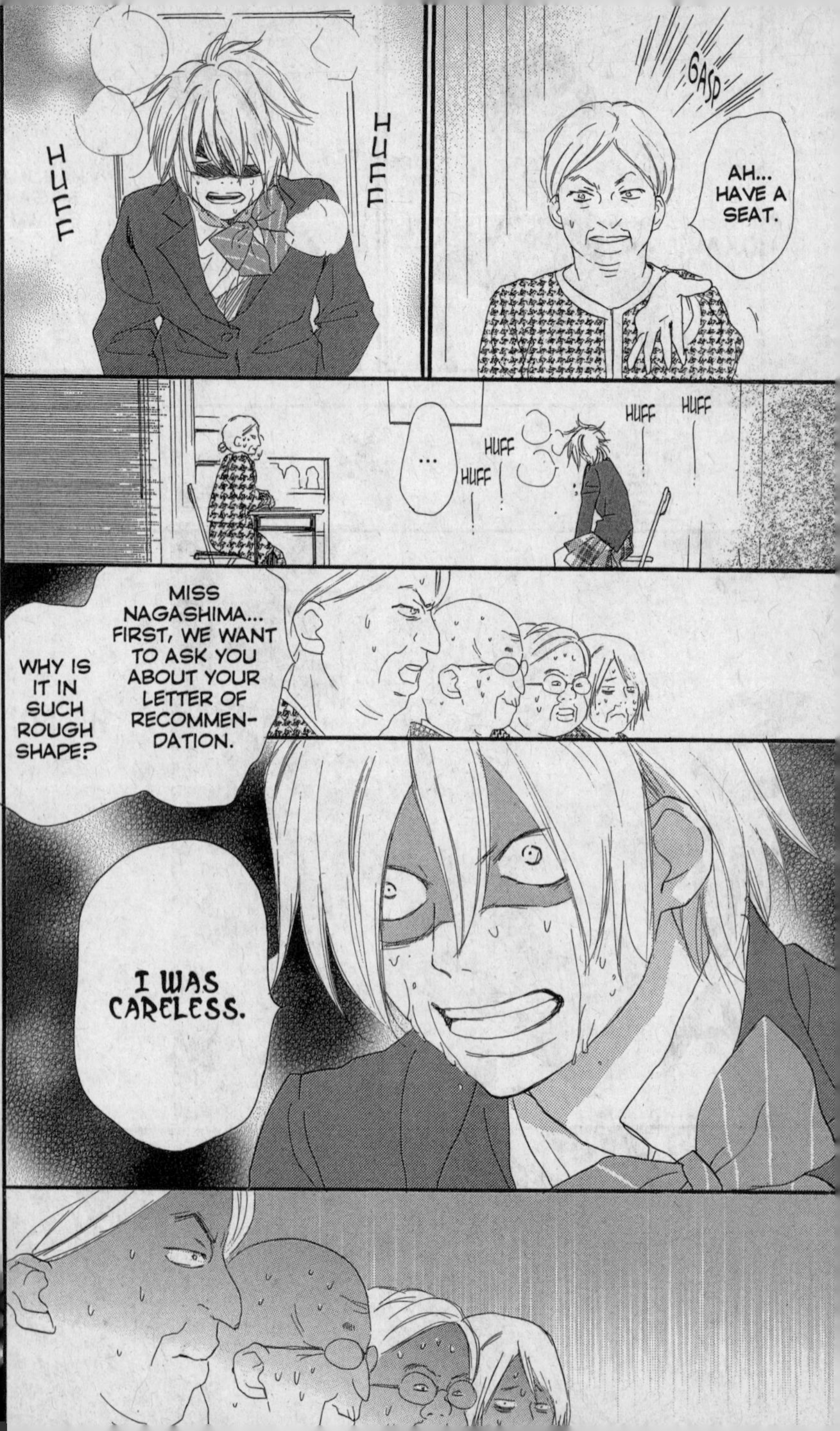
GASP
AH... HAVE A SEAT.
HUFF
HUFF
HUFF
HUFF
HUFF
HUFF
...
MISS NAGASHIMA... FIRST, WE WANT TO ASK YOU ABOUT YOUR LETTER OF RECOMMEN-DATION.
WHY IS IT IN SUCH ROUGH SHAPE?
I WAS CARELESS.

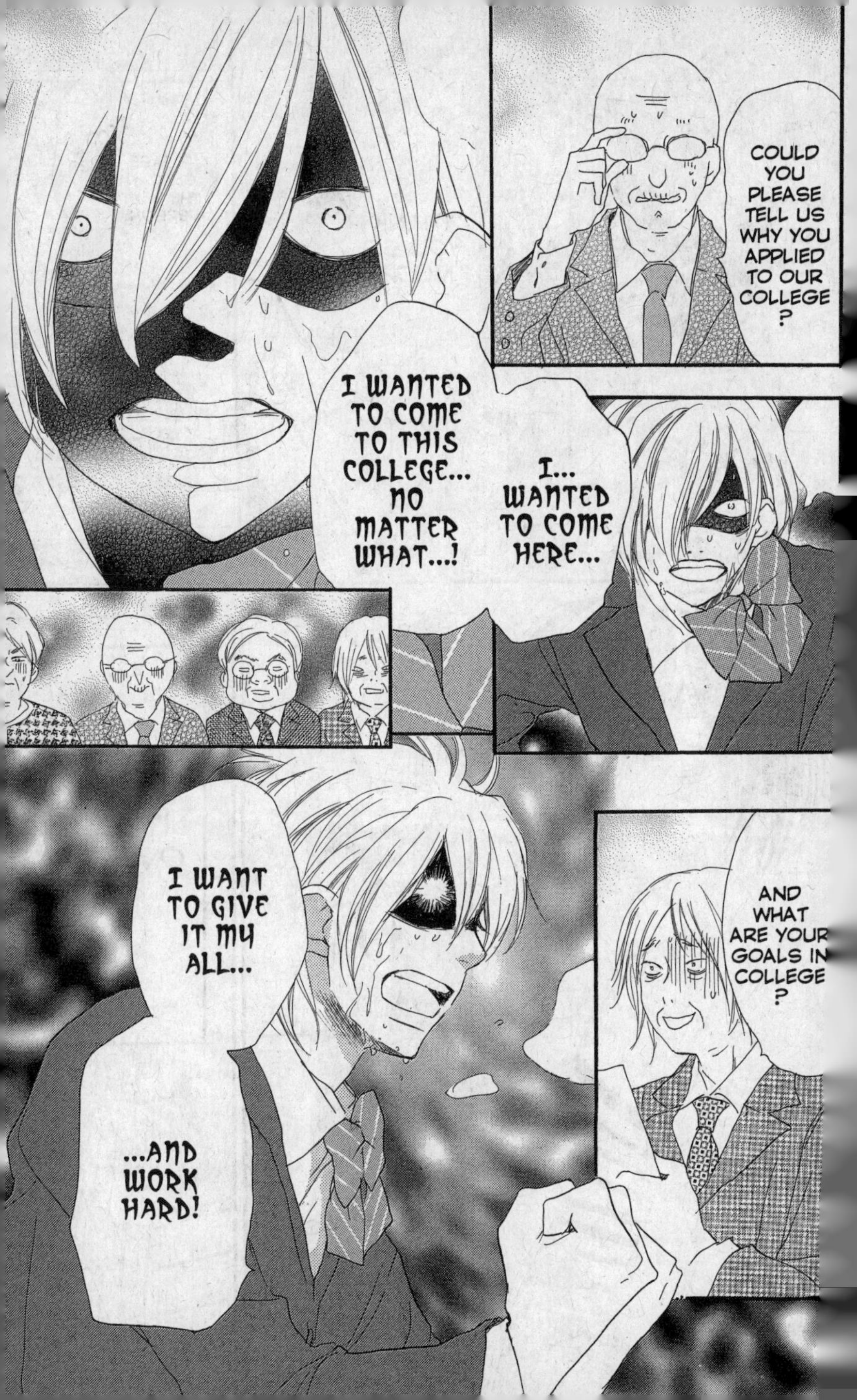
COULD YOU PLEASE TELL US WHY YOU APPLIED TO OUR COLLEGE?
I... WANTED TO COME HERE...
I WANTED TO COME TO THIS COLLEGE... NO MATTER WHAT...!
AND WHAT ARE YOUR GOALS IN COLLEGE?
I WANT TO GIVE IT MY ALL...
...AND WORK HARD!

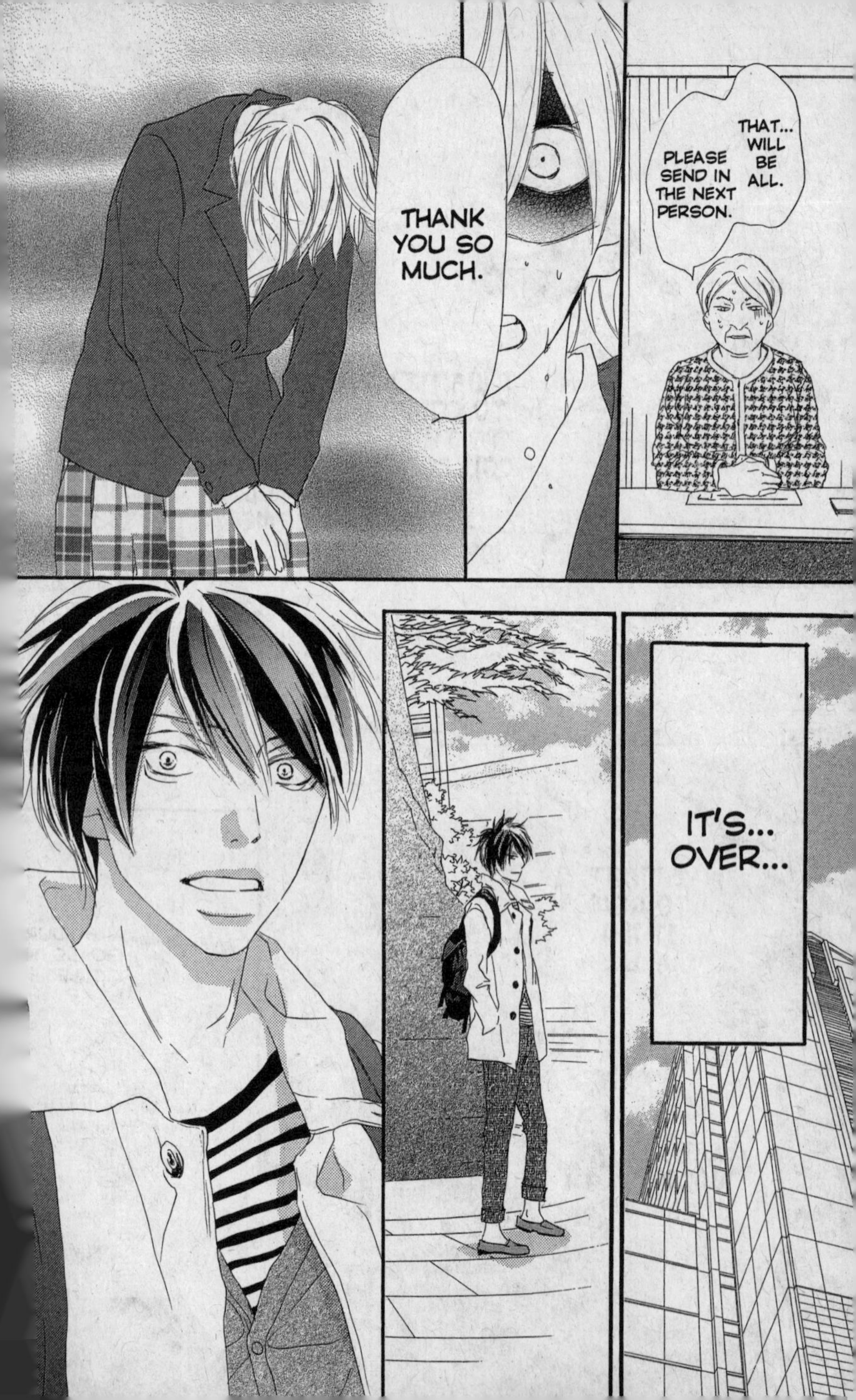
THAT... WILL BE ALL.
PLEASE SEND IN THE NEXT PERSON.
THANK YOU SO MUCH.
IT'S... OVER...

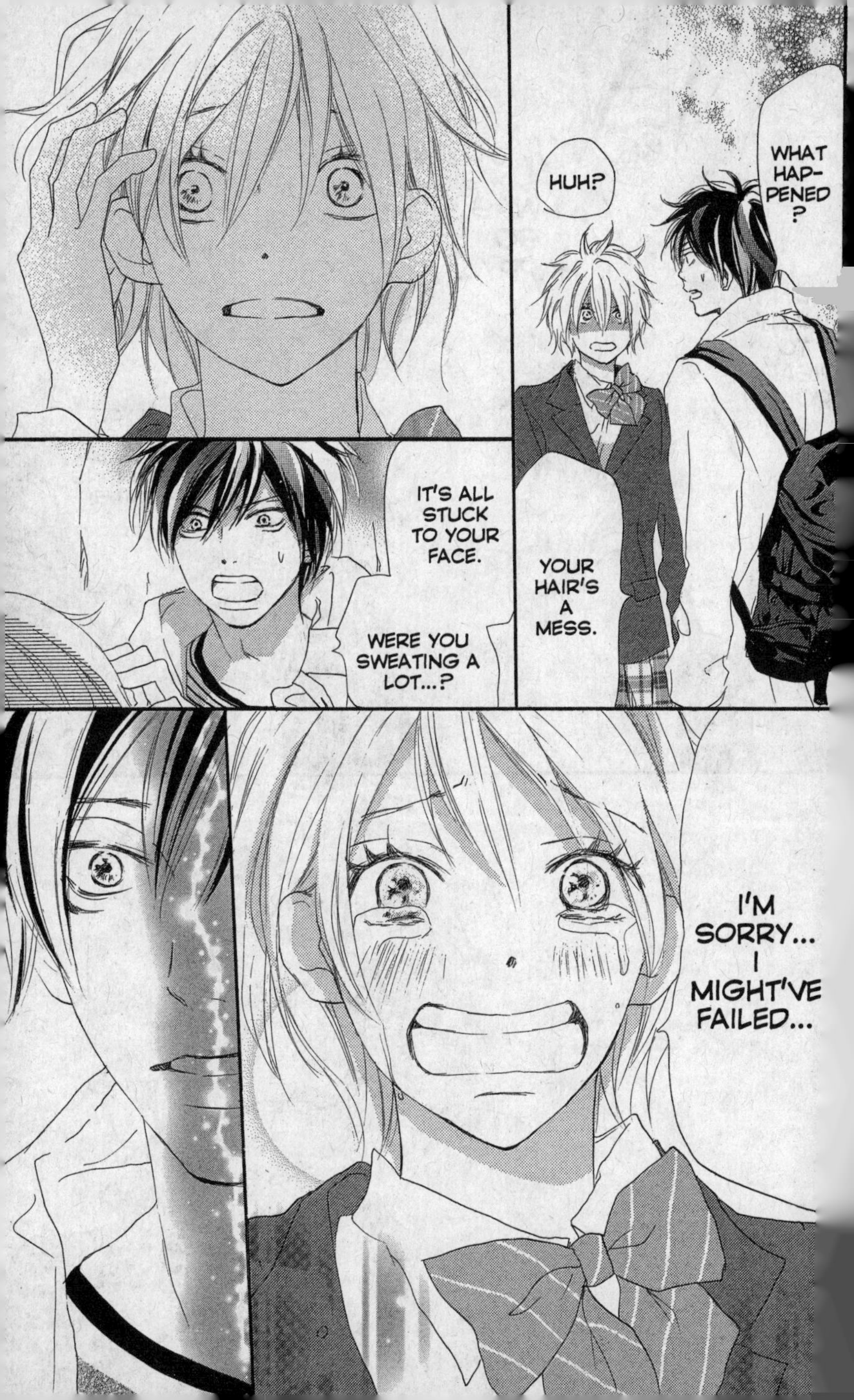
WHAT HAP-PENED?
HUH?
YOUR HAIR'S A MESS.
IT'S ALL STUCK TO YOUR FACE.
WERE YOU SWEATING A LOT...?
I'M SORRY... I MIGHT'VE FAILED...

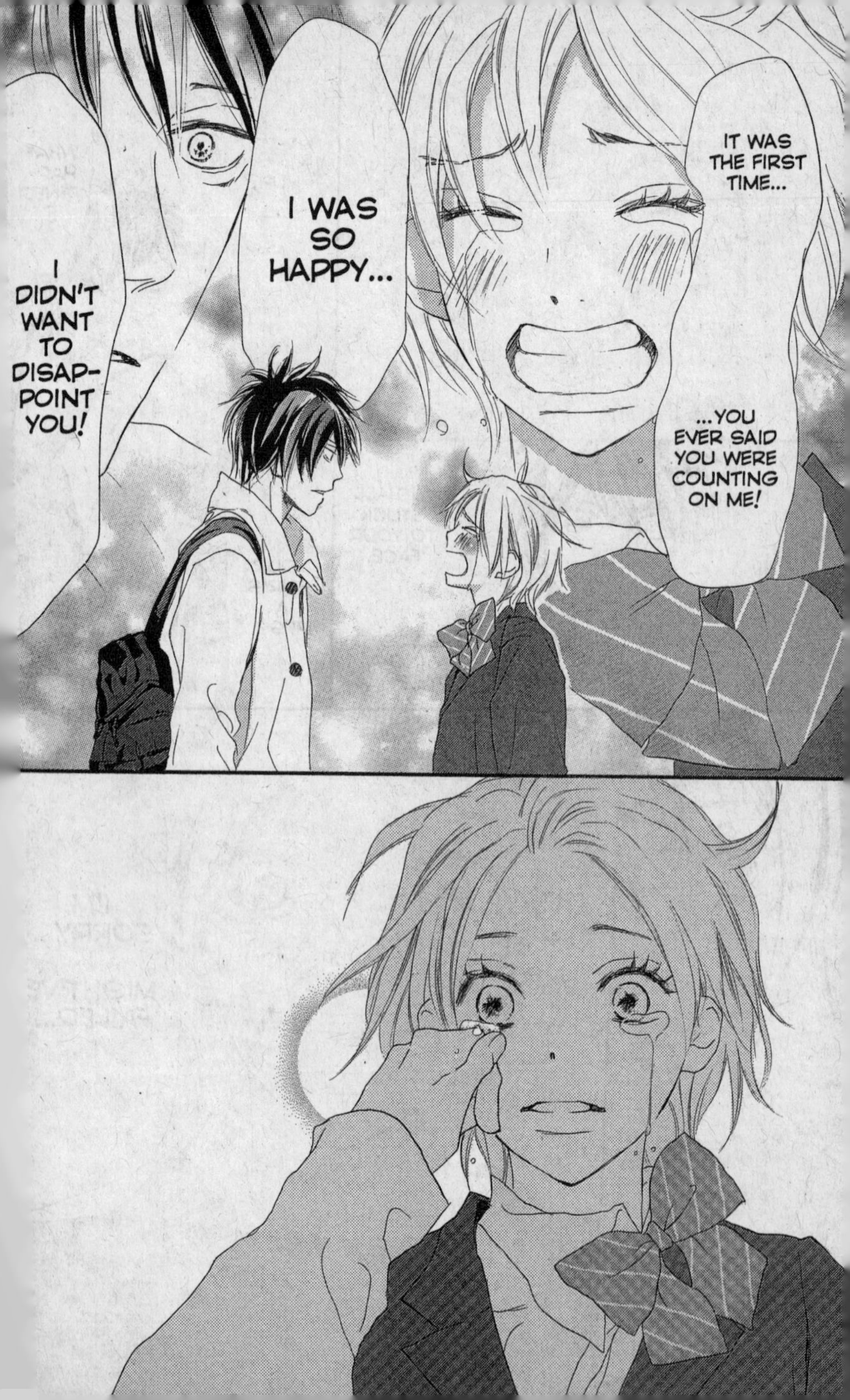
IT WAS THE FIRST TIME...
...YOU EVER SAID YOU WERE COUNTING ON ME!
I WAS SO HAPPY...
I DIDN'T WANT TO DISAP-POINT YOU!

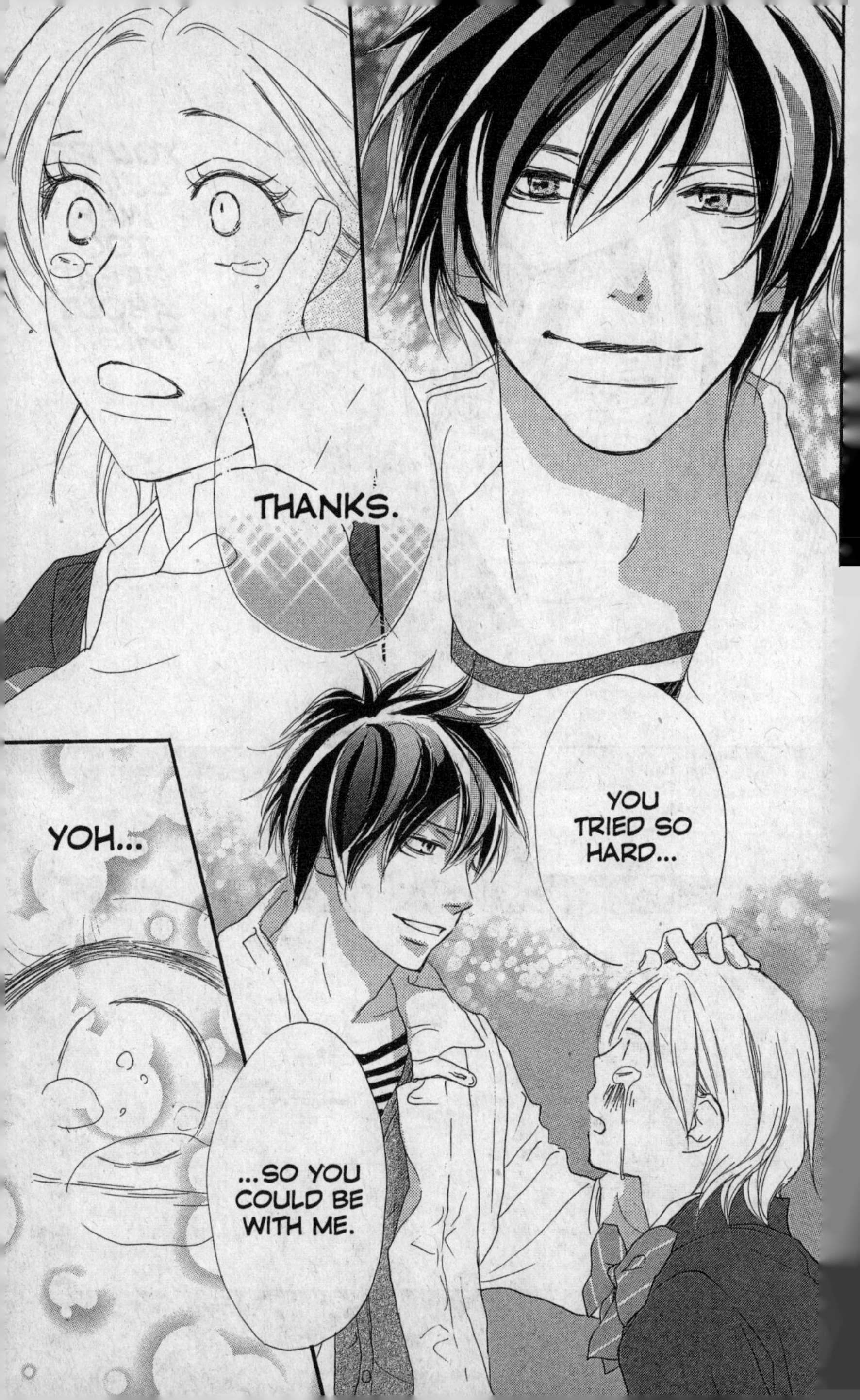
THANKS.
YOU TRIED SO HARD...
...SO YOU COULD BE WITH ME.
YOH...

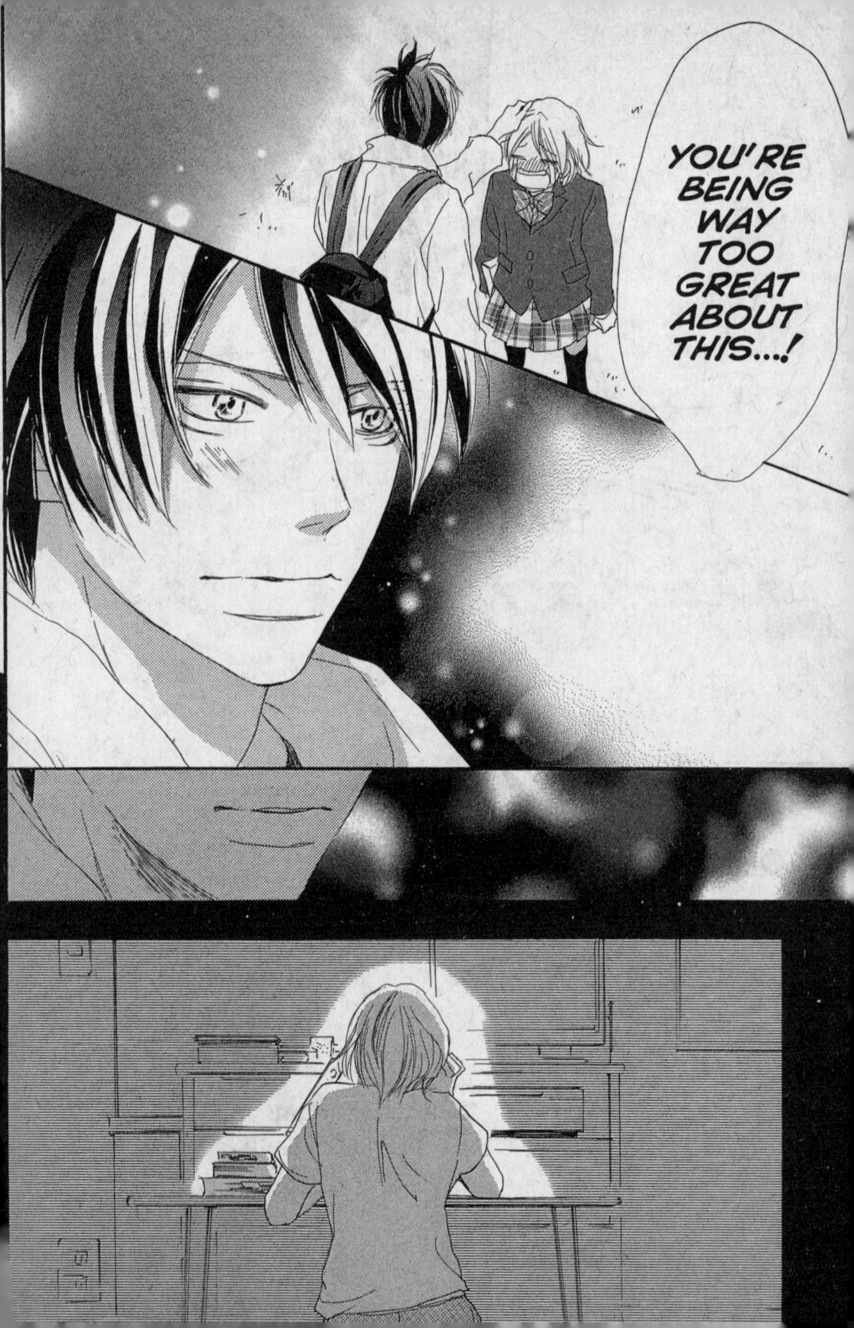
YOU'RE BEING WAY TOO GREAT ABOUT THIS...!

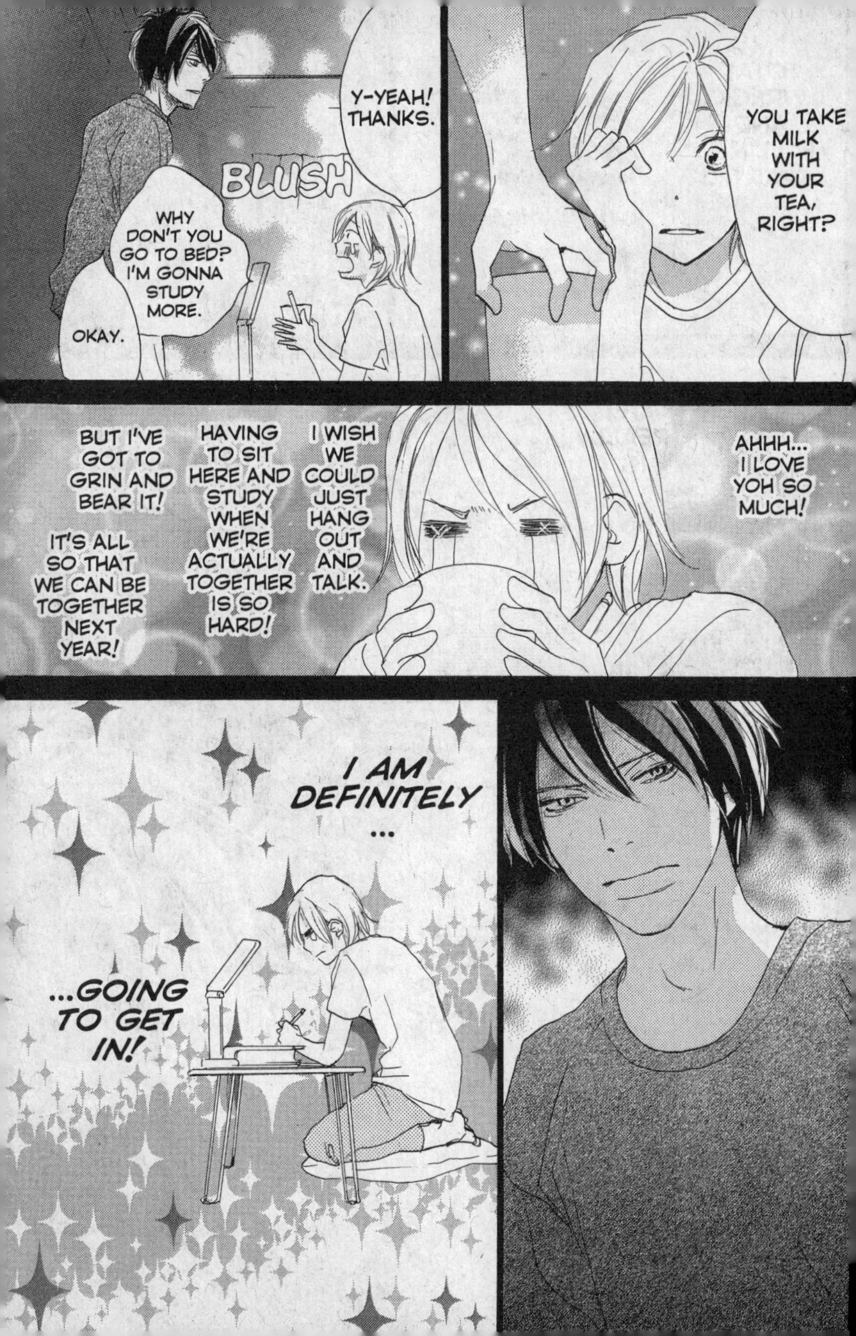
YOU TAKE MILK WITH YOUR TEA, RIGHT?
Y-YEAH! THANKS.
BLUSH
WHY DON'T YOU GO TO BED? I'M GONNA STUDY MORE.
OKAY.
AHHH... I LOVE YOH SO MUCH!
I WISH WE COULD JUST HANG OUT AND TALK.
HAVING TO SIT HERE AND STUDY WHEN WE'RE ACTUALLY TOGETHER IS SO HARD!
BUT I'VE GOT TO GRIN AND BEAR IT!
IT'S ALL SO THAT WE CAN BE TOGETHER NEXT YEAR!
I AM DEFINITELY ...
...GOING TO GET IN!

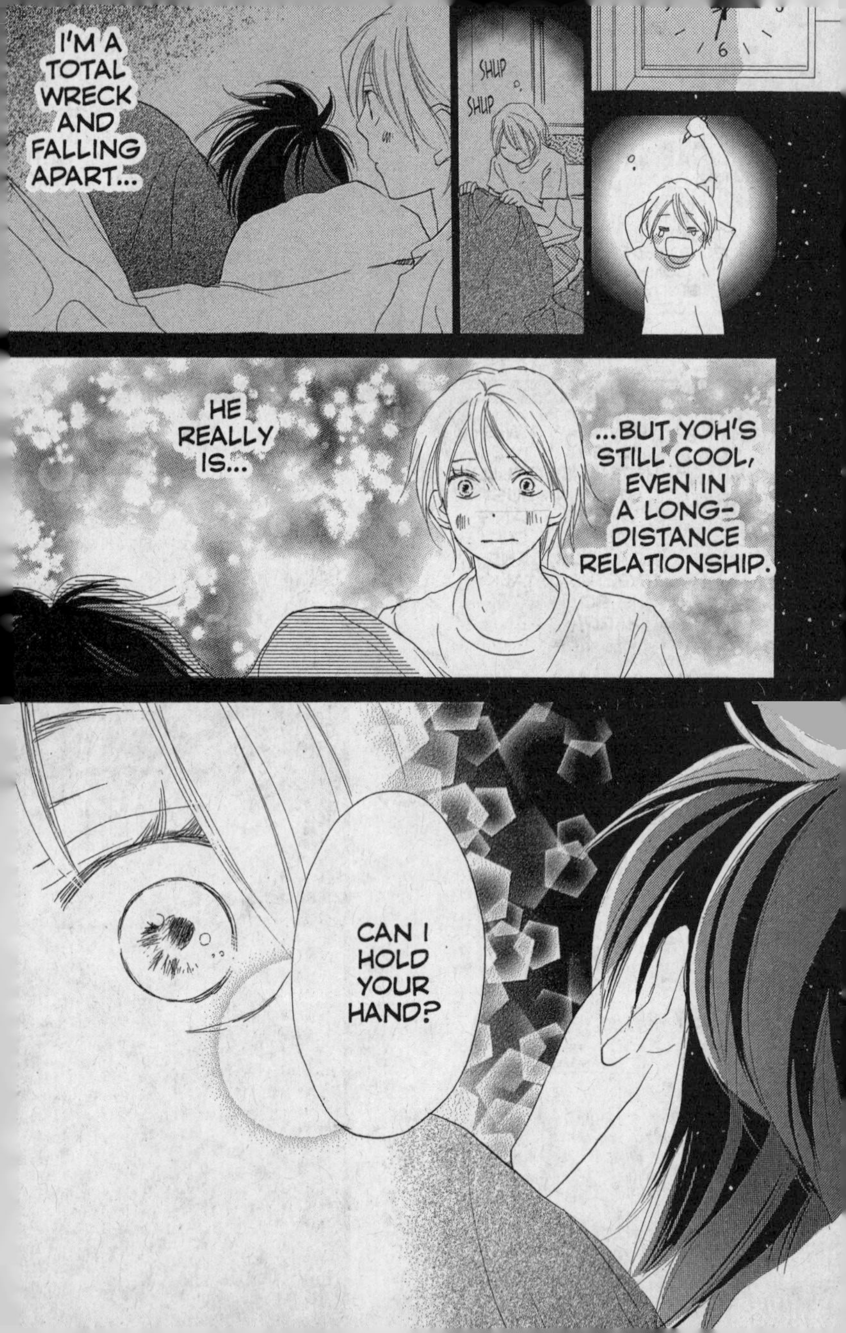
6
SHUP
SHUP
I'M A TOTAL WRECK AND FALLING APART...
...BUT YOH'S STILL COOL, EVEN IN A LONG-DISTANCE RELATIONSHIP.
HE REALLY IS...
CAN I HOLD YOUR HAND?

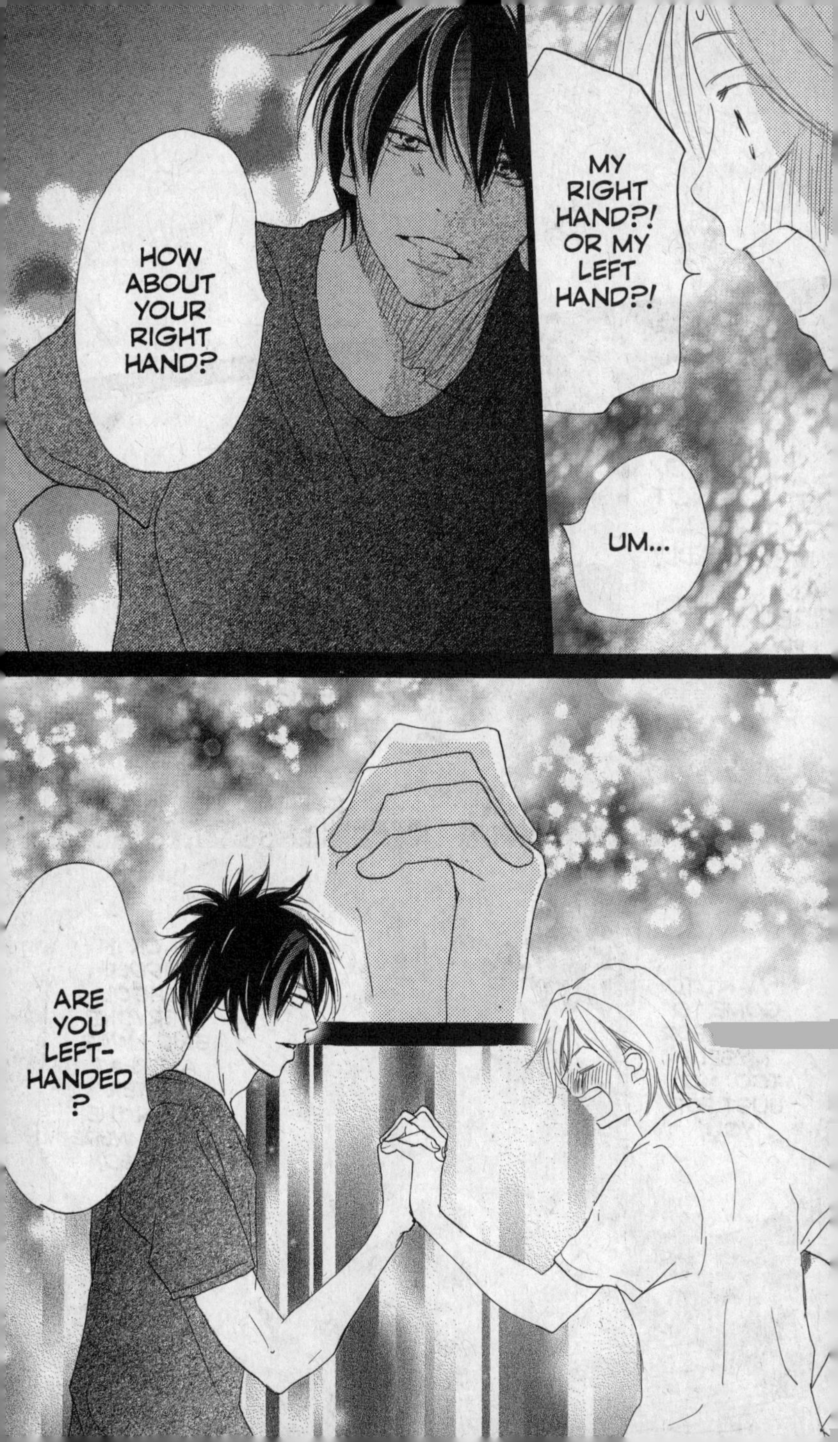
MY RIGHT HAND?! OR MY LEFT HAND?!
UM...
HOW ABOUT YOUR RIGHT HAND?
ARE YOU LEFT-HANDED?

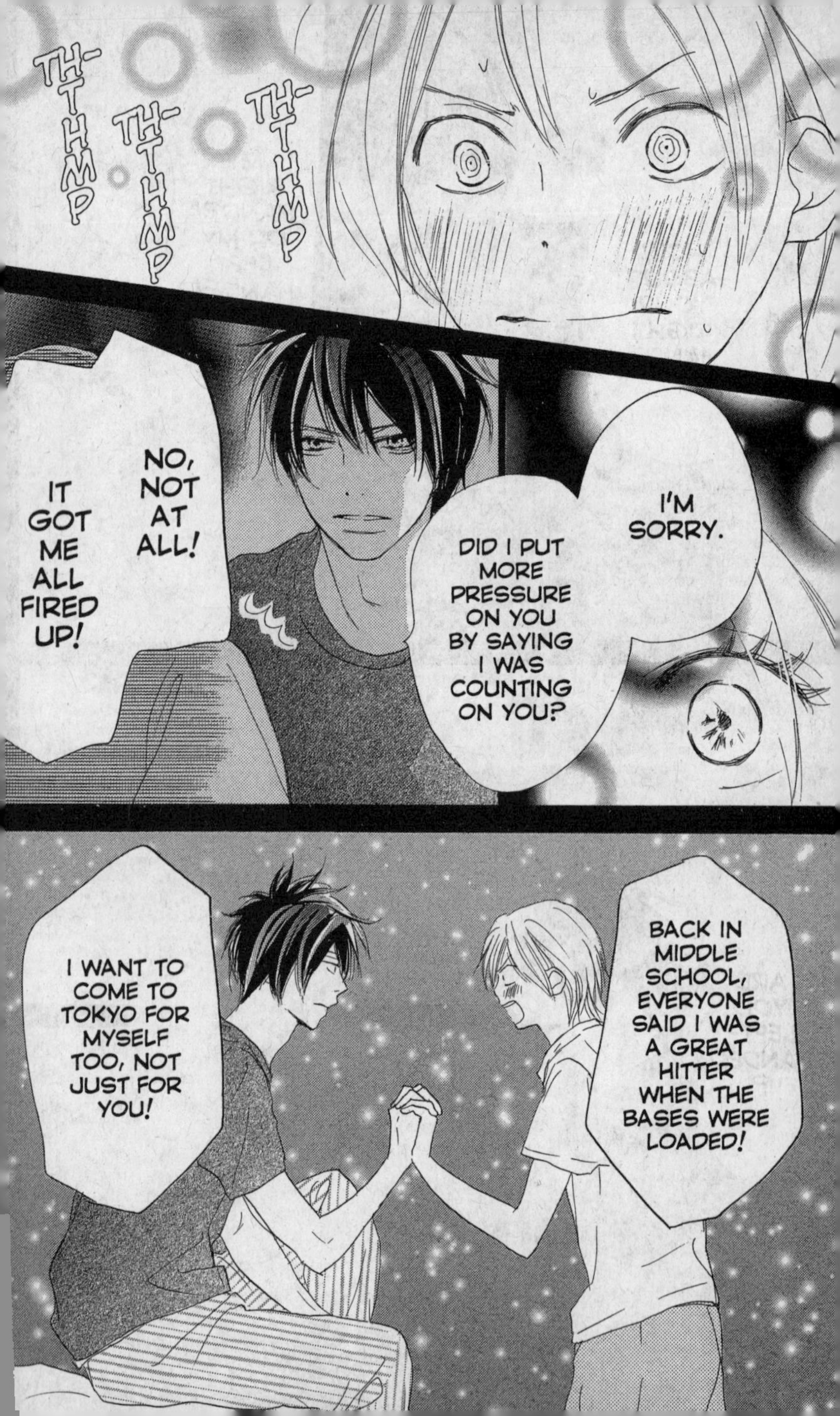
TH-THMP
TH-THMP
TH-THMP
I'M SORRY.
DID I PUT MORE PRESSURE ON YOU BY SAYING I WAS COUNTING ON YOU?
NO, NOT AT ALL!
IT GOT ME ALL FIRED UP!
BACK IN MIDDLE SCHOOL, EVERYONE SAID I WAS A GREAT HITTER WHEN THE BASES WERE LOADED!
I WANT TO COME TO TOKYO FOR MYSELF TOO, NOT JUST FOR YOU!

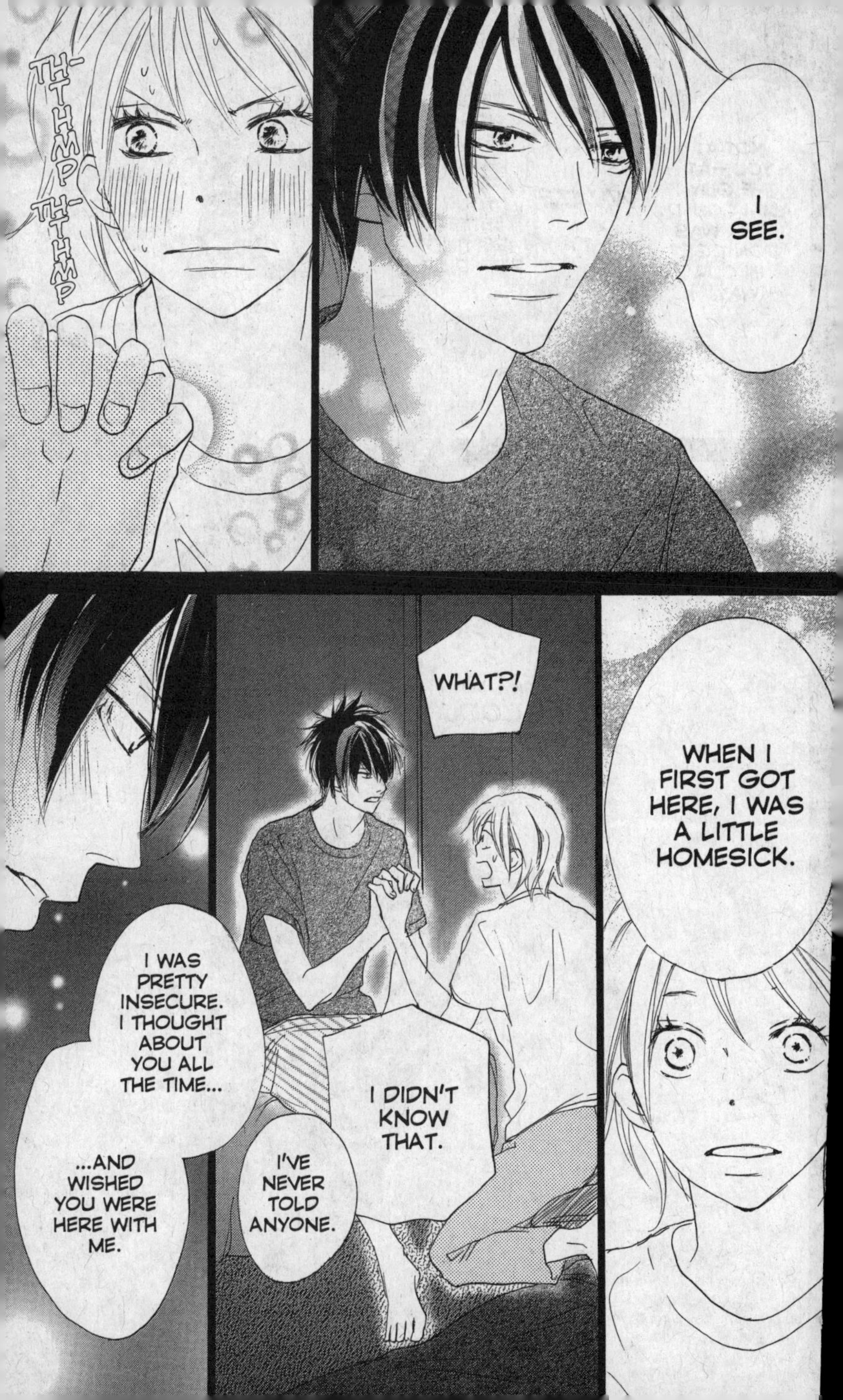
I SEE.
TH-THUMP TH-THUMP
WHEN I FIRST GOT HERE, I WAS A LITTLE HOMESICK.
WHAT?!
I DIDN'T KNOW THAT.
I'VE NEVER TOLD ANYONE.
I WAS PRETTY INSECURE. I THOUGHT ABOUT YOU ALL THE TIME...
...AND WISHED YOU WERE HERE WITH ME.

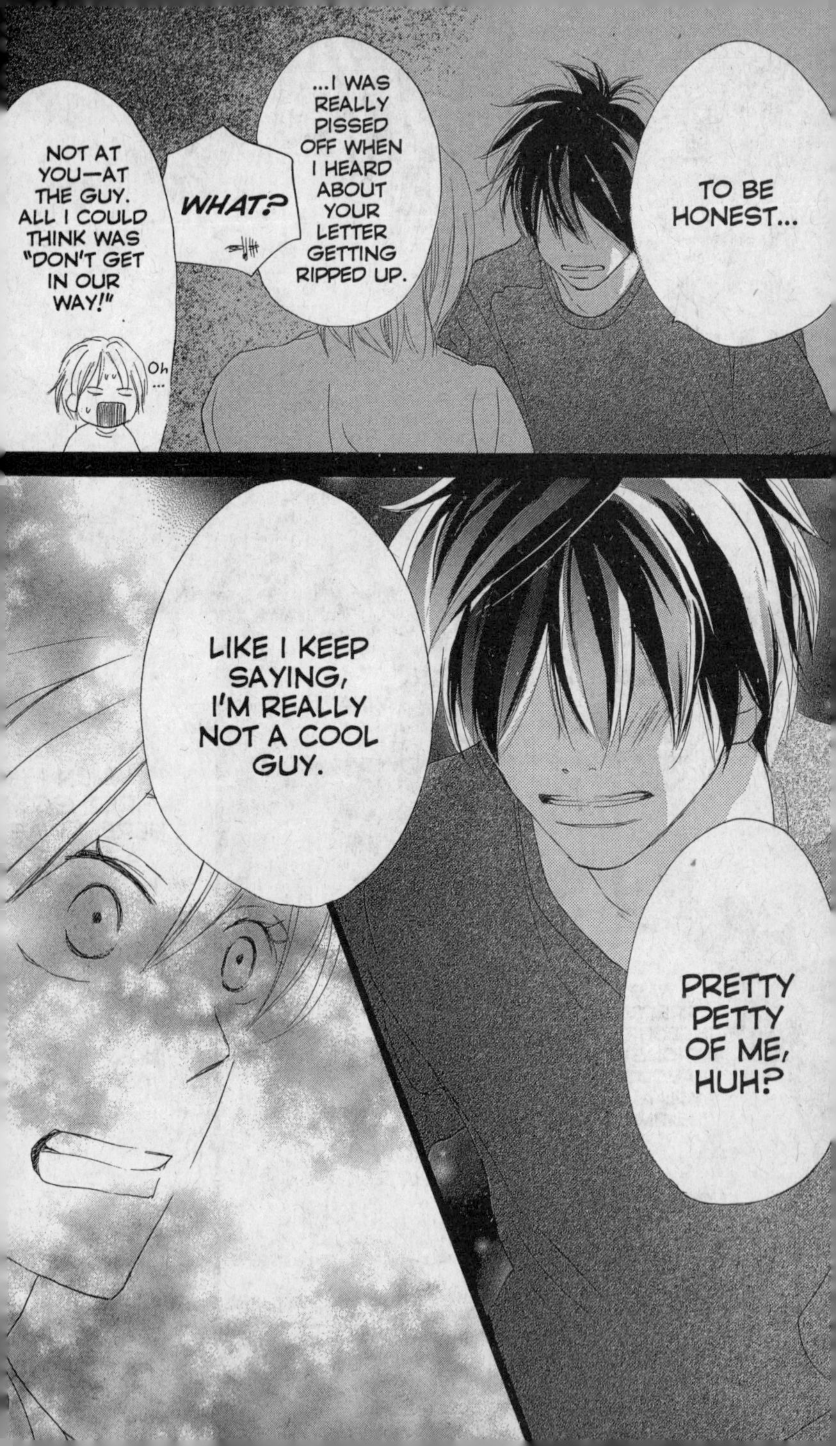
TO BE HONEST...
...I WAS REALLY PISSED OFF WHEN I HEARD ABOUT YOUR LETTER GETTING RIPPED UP.
WHAT?
NOT AT YOU—AT THE GUY. ALL I COULD THINK WAS "DON'T GET IN OUR WAY!"
Oh...
LIKE I KEEP SAYING, I'M REALLY NOT A COOL GUY.
PRETTY PETTY OF ME, HUH?

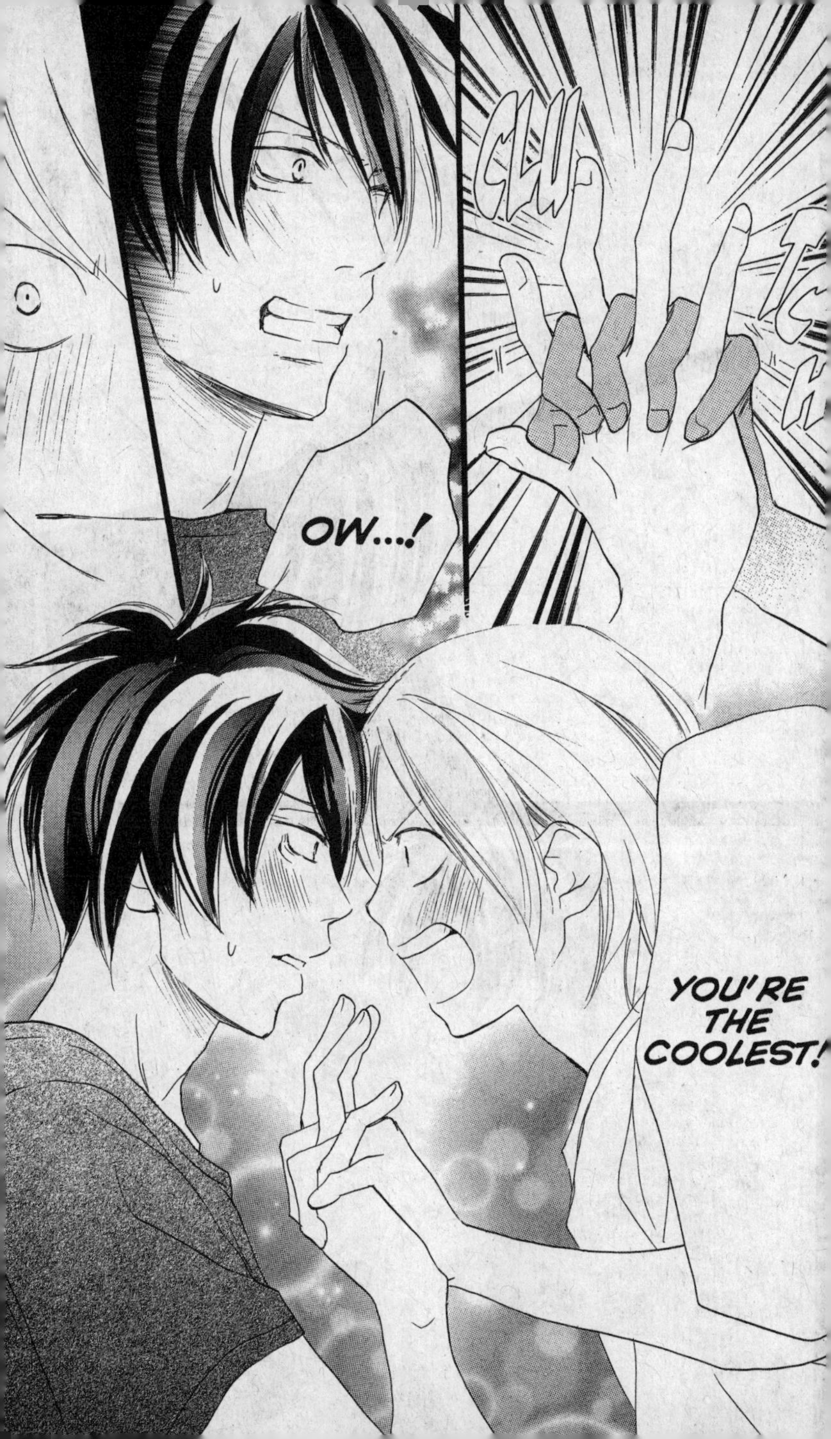
CLU
TCH
OW...!
YOU'RE THE COOLEST!

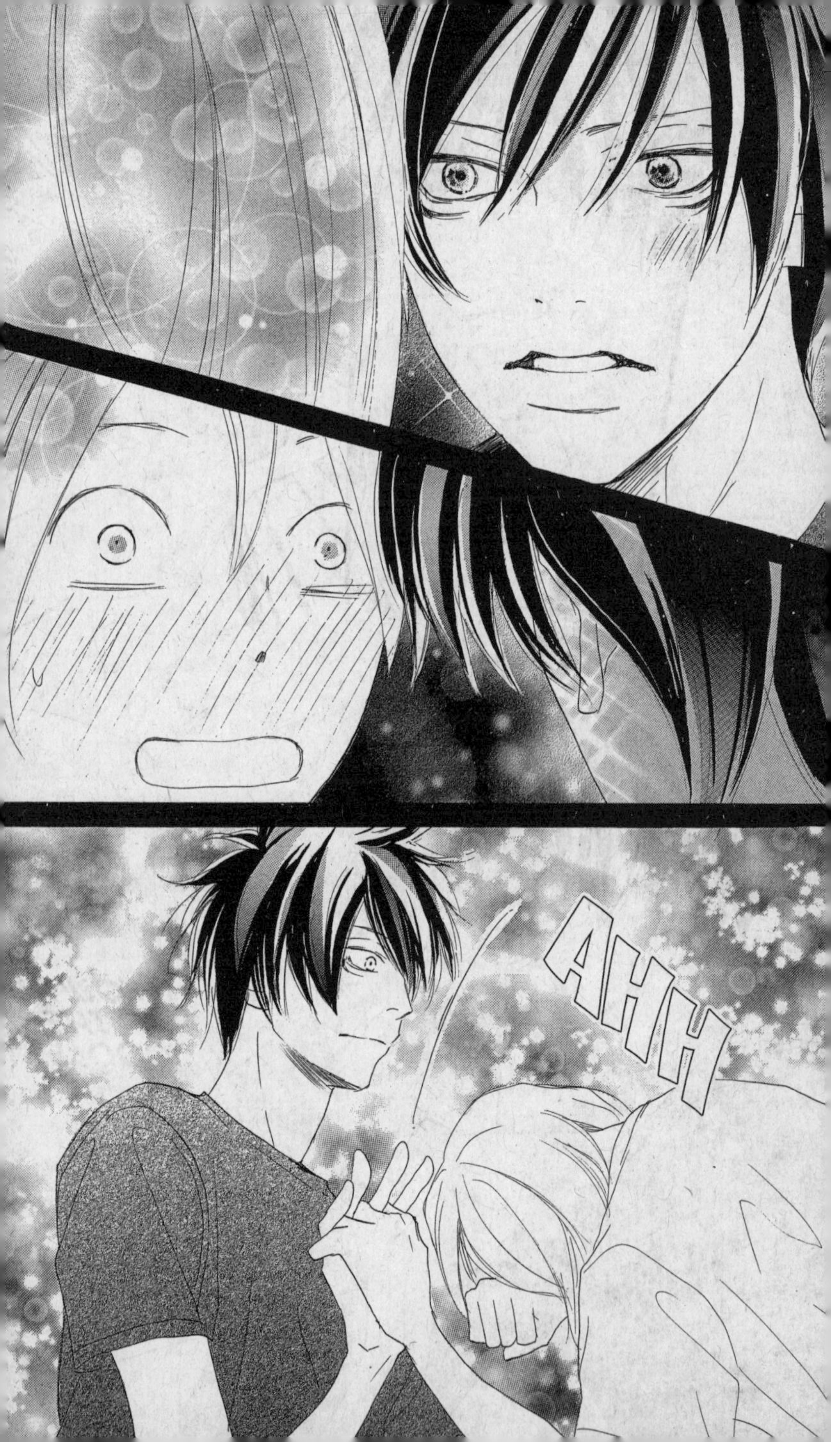
AHH

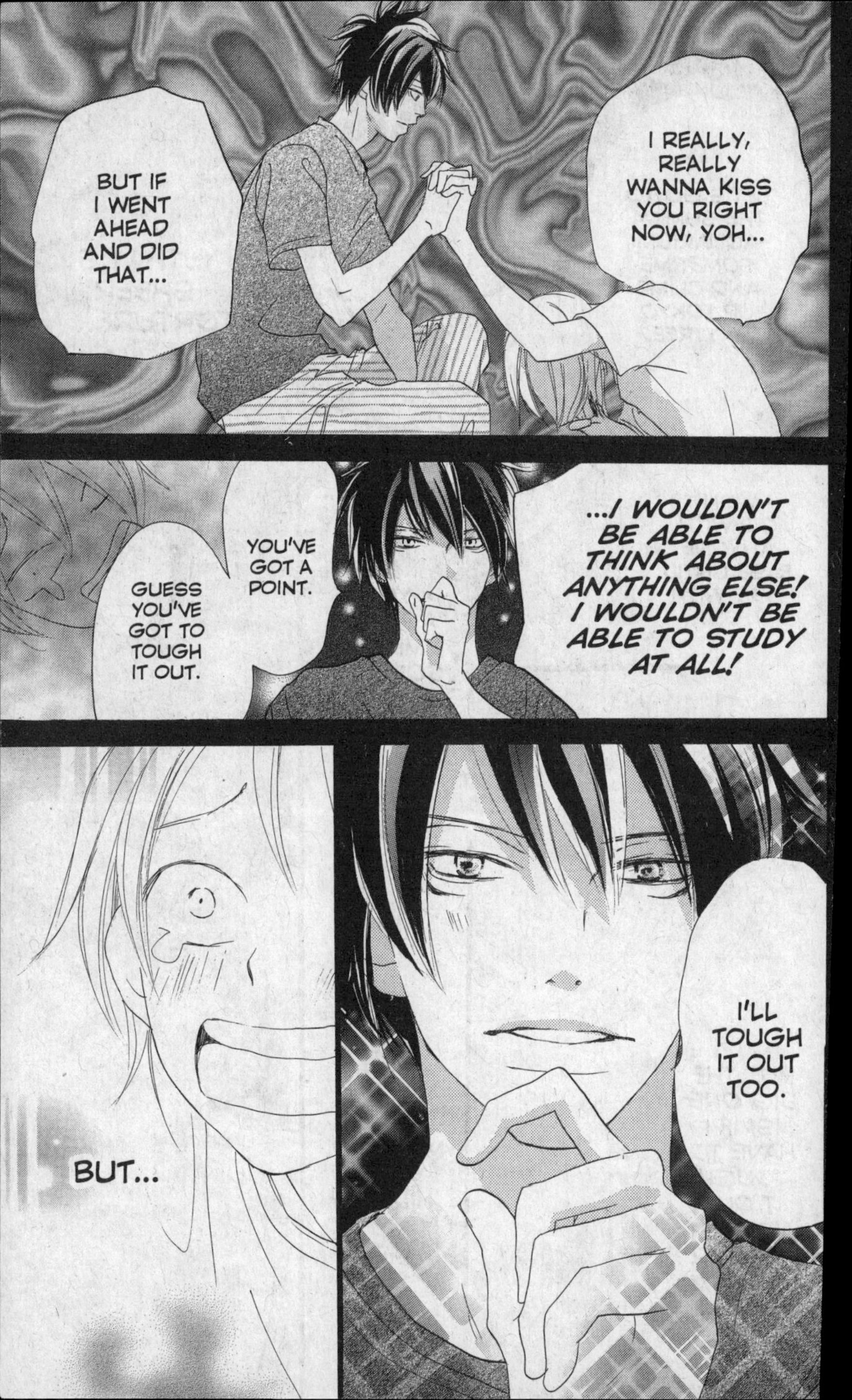
I REALLY, REALLY WANNA KISS YOU RIGHT NOW, YOH...
BUT IF I WENT AHEAD AND DID THAT...
...I WOULDN'T BE ABLE TO THINK ABOUT ANYTHING ELSE! I WOULDN'T BE ABLE TO STUDY AT ALL!
YOU'VE GOT A POINT.
GUESS YOU'VE GOT TO TOUGH IT OUT.
I'LL TOUGH IT OUT TOO.
BUT...

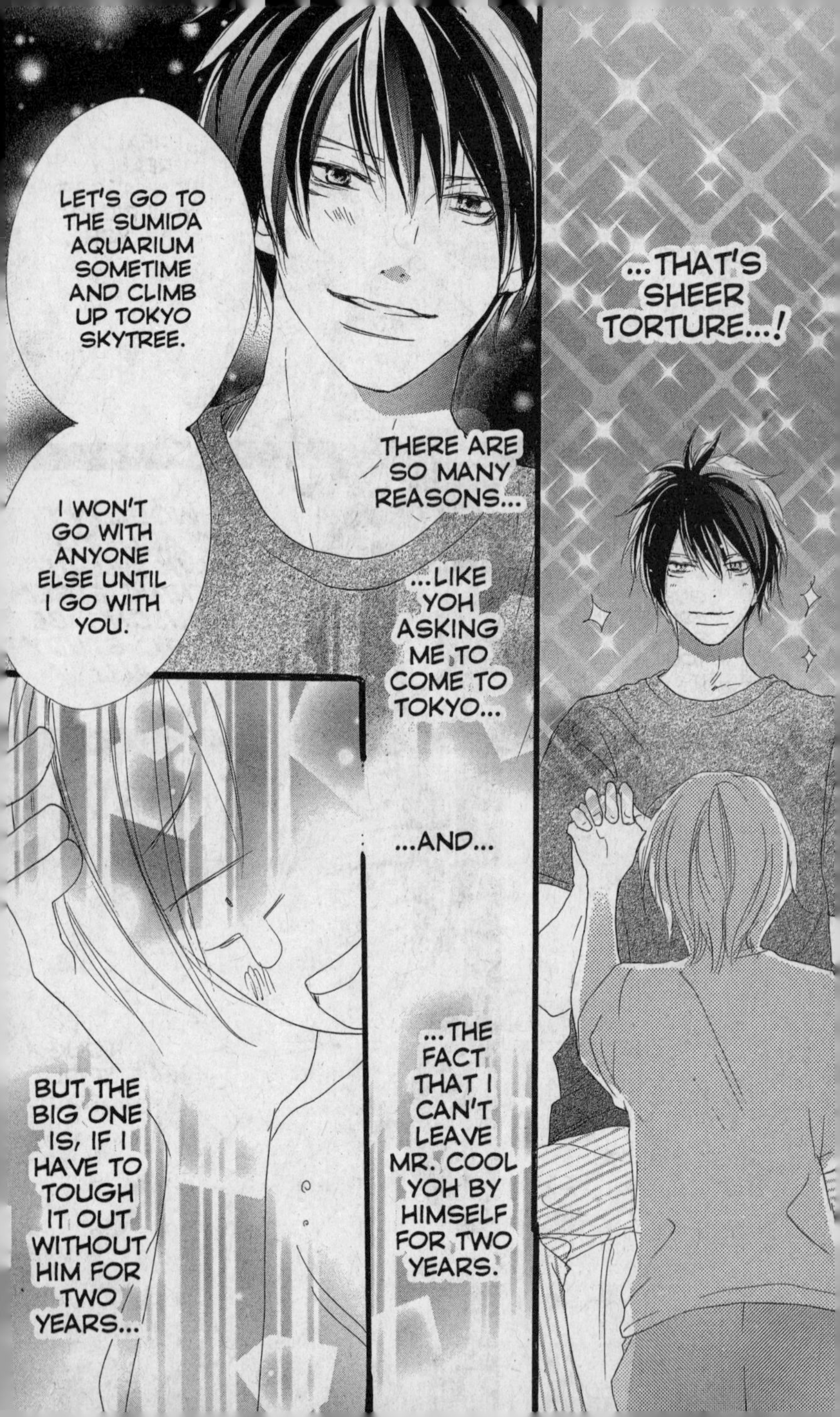
LET'S GO TO THE SUMIDA AQUARIUM SOMETIME AND CLIMB UP TOKYO SKYTREE.
I WON'T GO WITH ANYONE ELSE UNTIL I GO WITH YOU.
THERE ARE SO MANY REASONS...
...LIKE YOH ASKING ME TO COME TO TOKYO...
...AND...
...THE FACT THAT I CAN'T LEAVE MR. COOL YOH BY HIMSELF FOR TWO YEARS.
BUT THE BIG ONE IS, IF I HAVE TO TOUGH IT OUT WITHOUT HIM FOR TWO YEARS...
...THAT'S SHEER TORTURE...!

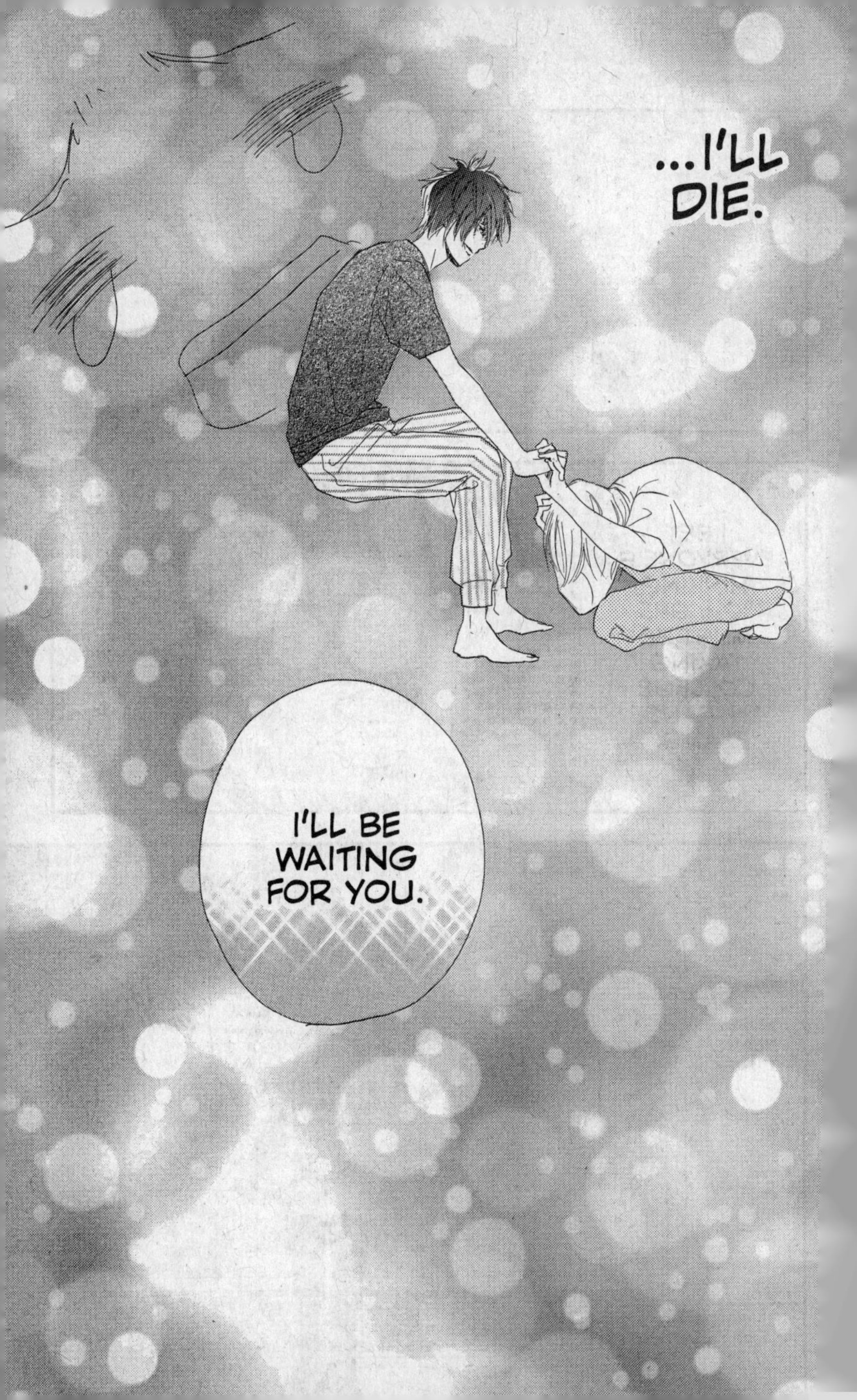
...I'LL DIE.
I'LL BE WAITING FOR YOU.

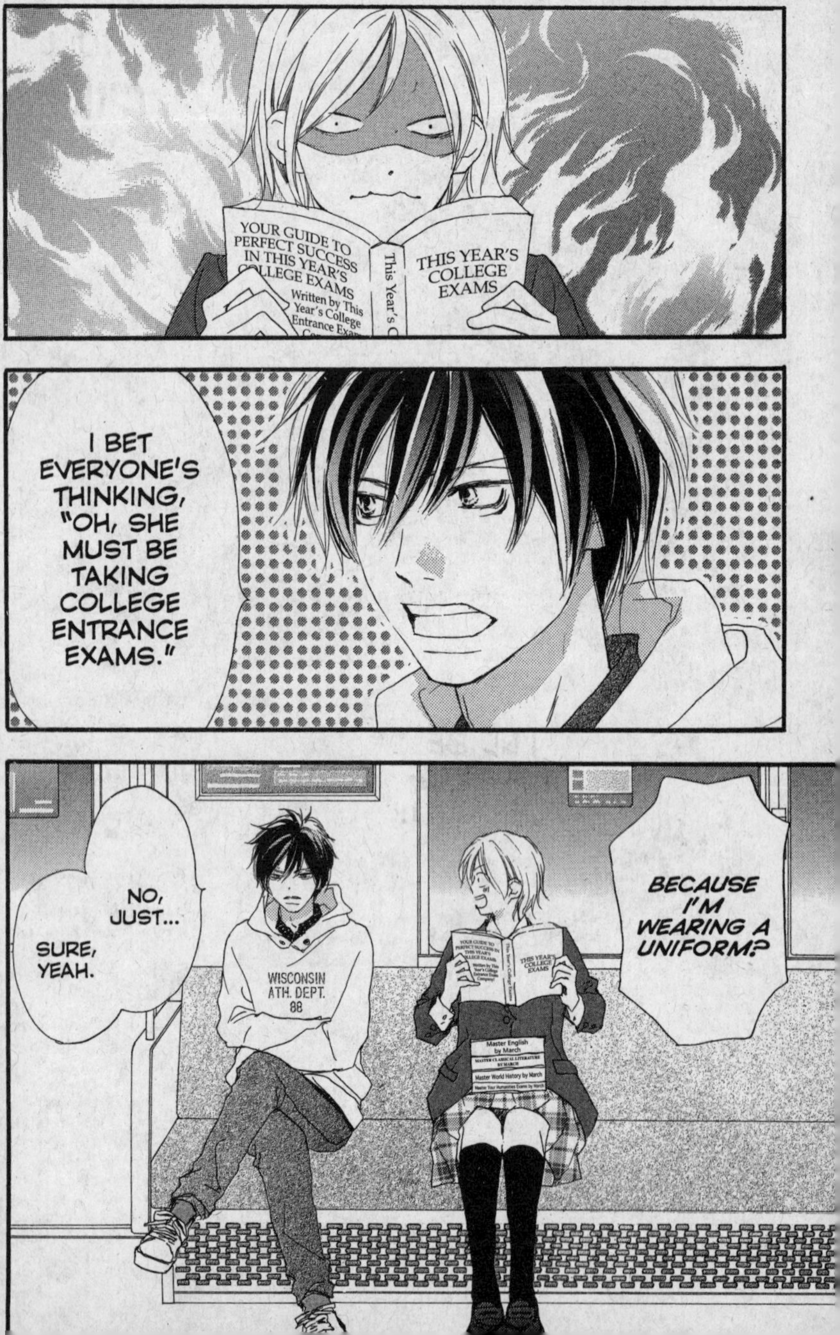
YOUR GUIDE TO PERFECT SUCCESS IN THIS YEAR'S COLLEGE EXAMS
THIS YEAR'S COLLEGE EXAMS
I BET EVERYONE'S THINKING, "OH, SHE MUST BE TAKING COLLEGE ENTRANCE EXAMS."
BECAUSE I'M WEARING A UNIFORM?
NO, JUST...
SURE, YEAH.
WISCONSIN ATH. DEPT. 88
Master English by March
Master World History by March

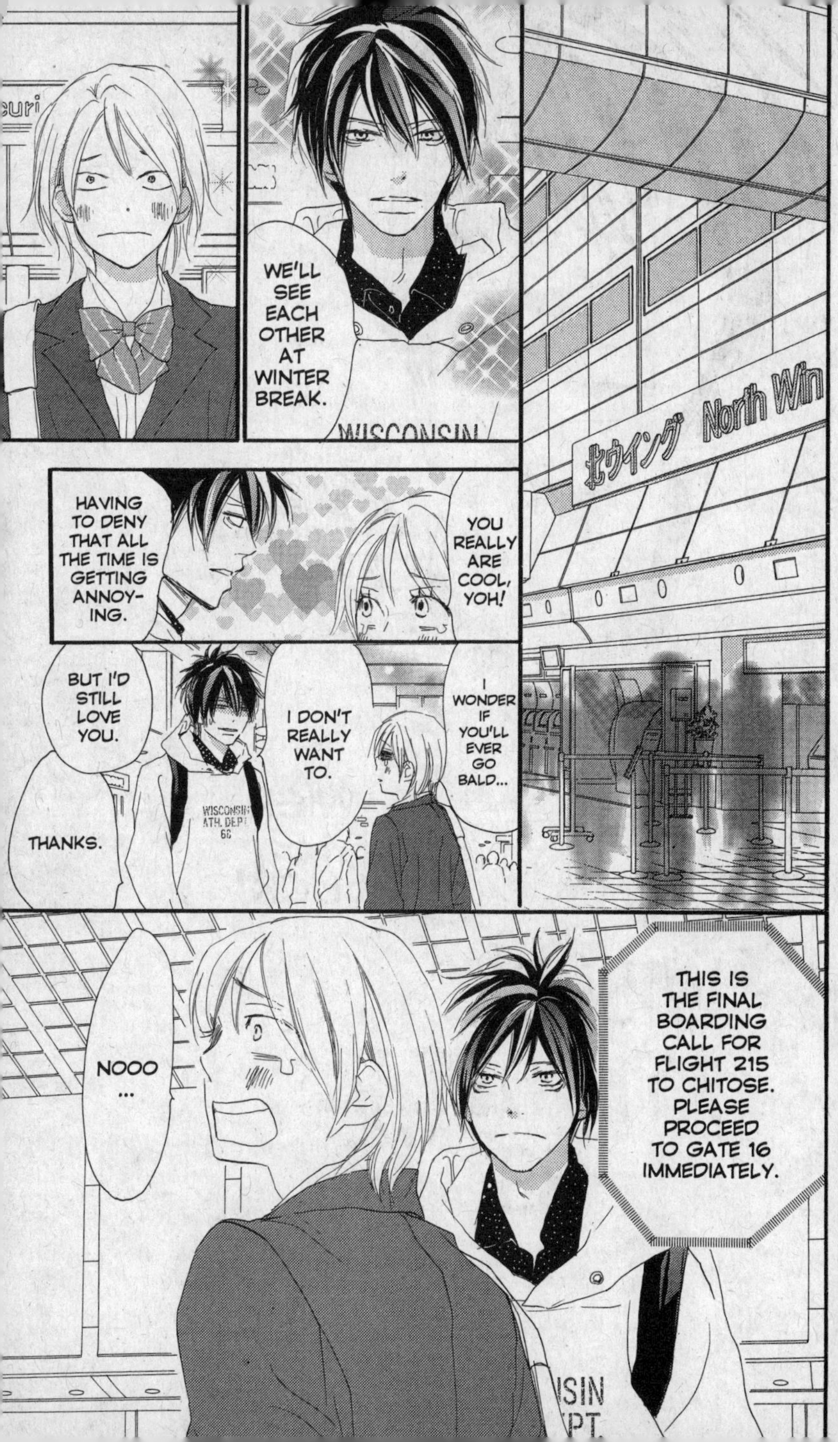
北ウイング North Win
WE'LL SEE EACH OTHER AT WINTER BREAK.
WISCONSIN
YOU REALLY ARE COOL, YOH!
HAVING TO DENY THAT ALL THE TIME IS GETTING ANNOY-ING.
I WONDER IF YOU'LL EVER GO BALD...
I DON'T REALLY WANT TO.
BUT I'D STILL LOVE YOU.
WISCONSIN ATH. DEPT 68
THANKS.
THIS IS THE FINAL BOARDING CALL FOR FLIGHT 215 TO CHITOSE. PLEASE PROCEED TO GATE 16 IMMEDIATELY.
NOOO ...

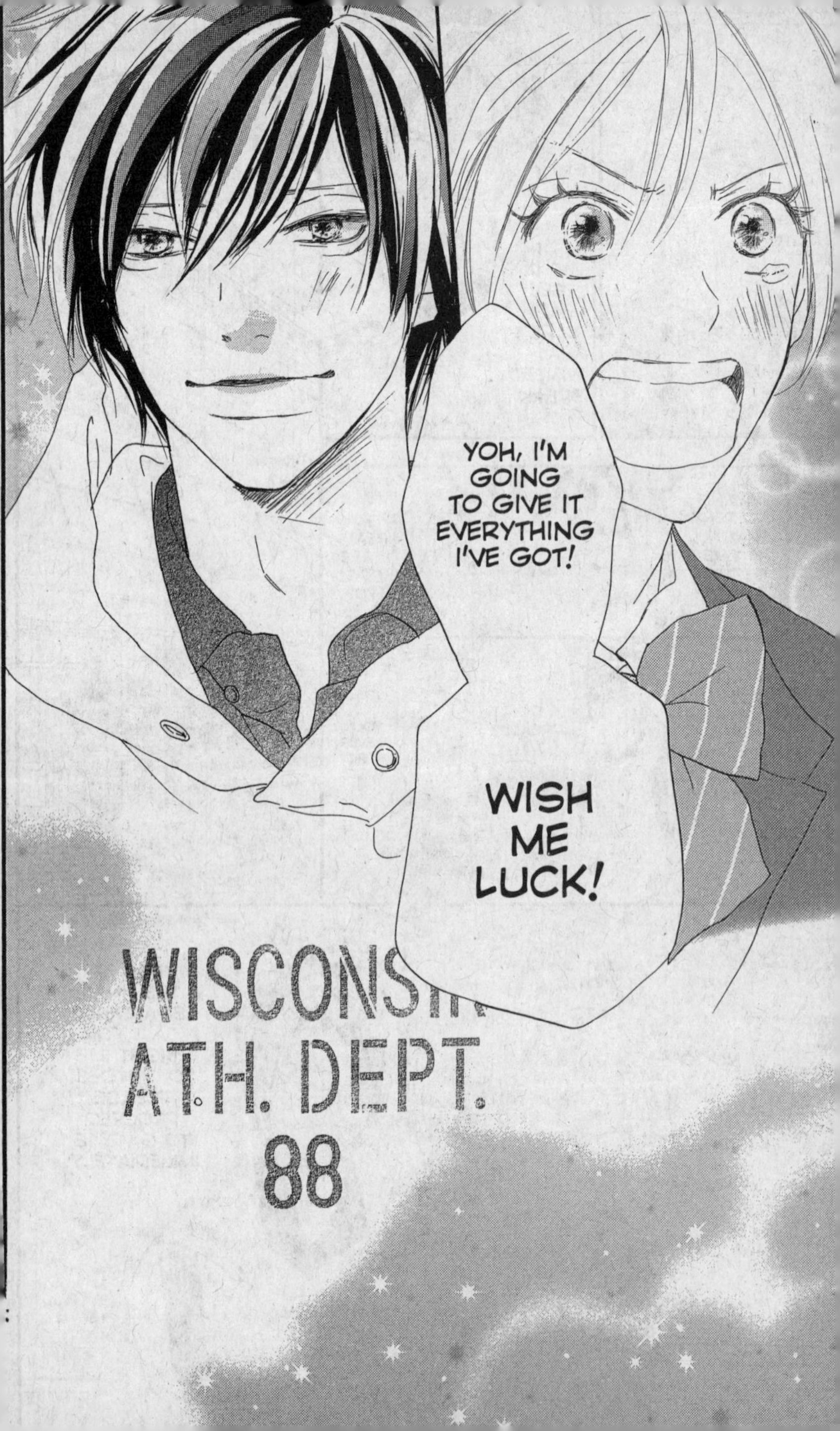
YOH, I'M GOING TO GIVE IT EVERYTHING I'VE GOT!
WISH ME LUCK!
WISCONSIN
A.T.H. DEPT.
88

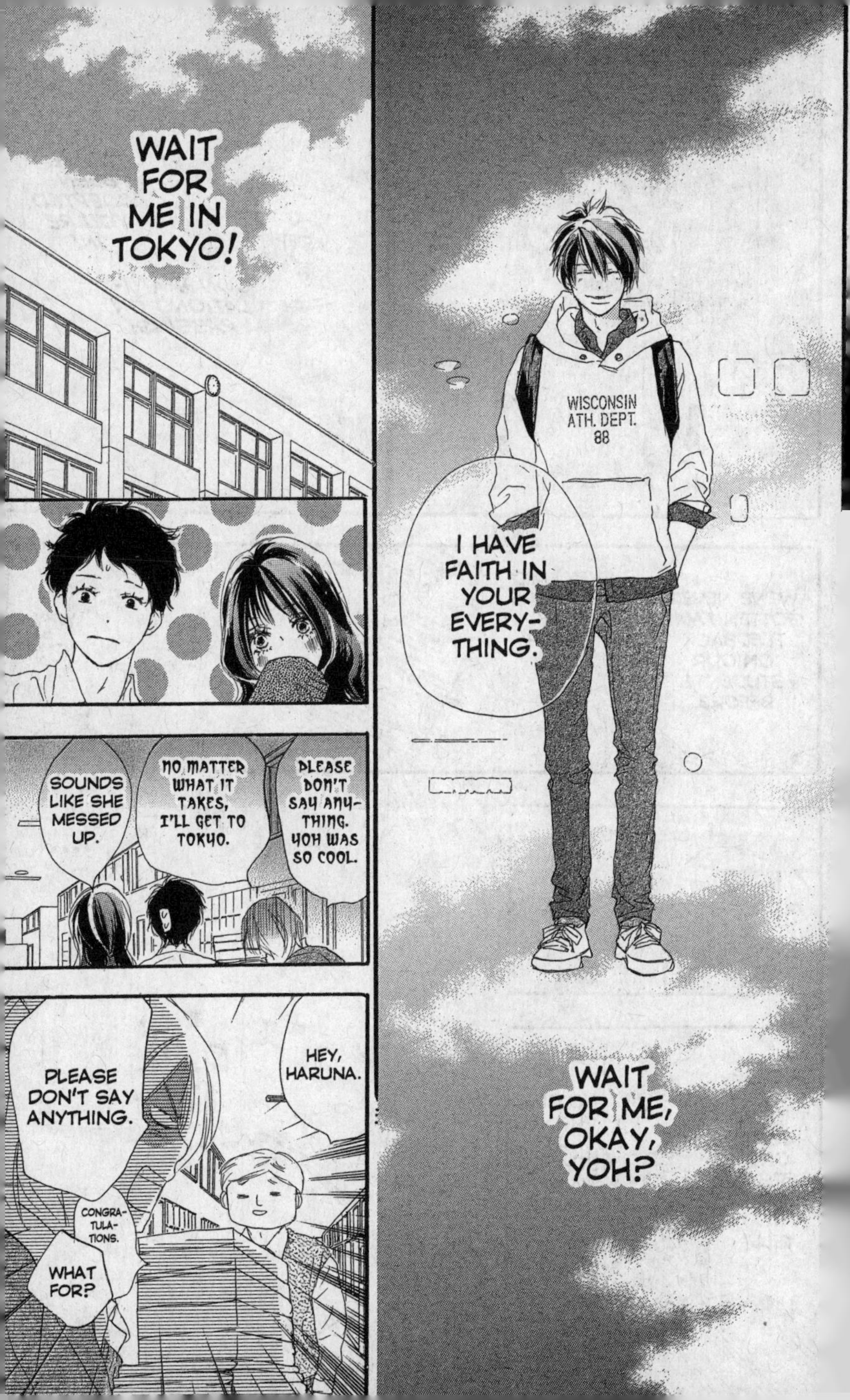
WISCONSIN ATH. DEPT. 88
I HAVE FAITH IN YOUR EVERYTHING.
WAIT FOR ME, OKAY, YOH?
WAIT FOR ME IN TOKYO!
PLEASE DON'T SAY ANYTHING. YOH WAS SO COOL.
NO MATTER WHAT IT TAKES, I'LL GET TO TOKYO.
SOUNDS LIKE SHE MESSED UP.
HEY, HARUNA.
PLEASE DON'T SAY ANYTHING.
CONGRATULATIONS.
WHAT FOR?

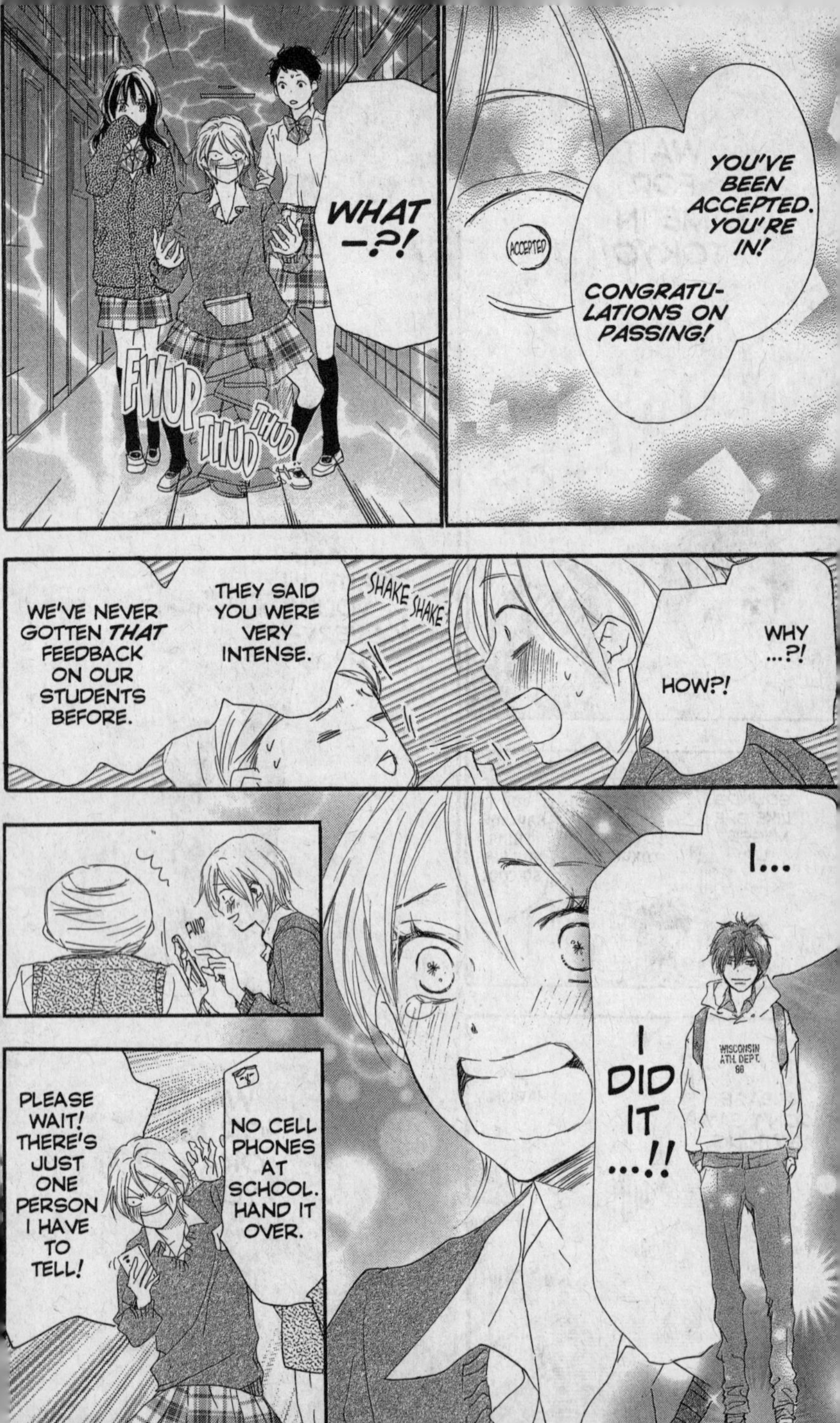
ACCEPTED
YOU'VE BEEN ACCEPTED. YOU'RE IN!
CONGRATULATIONS ON PASSING!
WHAT—?!
FWUP
THUD
THUD
WHY...?!
HOW?!
SHAKE SHAKE
THEY SAID YOU WERE VERY INTENSE.
WE'VE NEVER GOTTEN *THAT* FEEDBACK ON OUR STUDENTS BEFORE.
I...
I DID IT...!!
WISCONSIN ATH. DEPT. 88
FWIP
NO CELL PHONES AT SCHOOL. HAND IT OVER.
PLEASE WAIT! THERE'S JUST ONE PERSON I HAVE TO TELL!

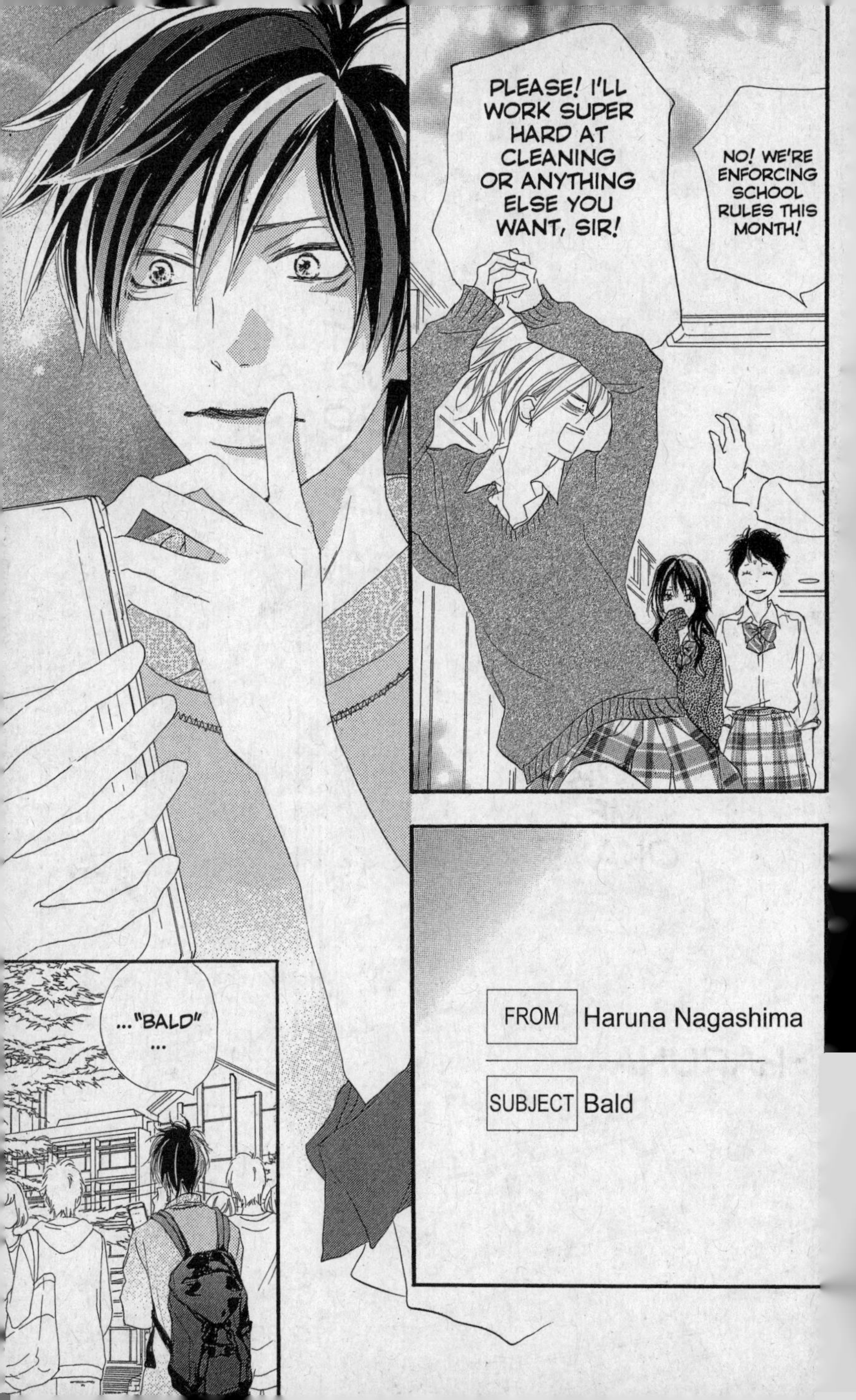
PLEASE! I'LL WORK SUPER HARD AT CLEANING OR ANYTHING ELSE YOU WANT, SIR!
NO! WE'RE ENFORCING SCHOOL RULES THIS MONTH!
FROM Haruna Nagashima
SUBJECT Bald
..."BALD" ...

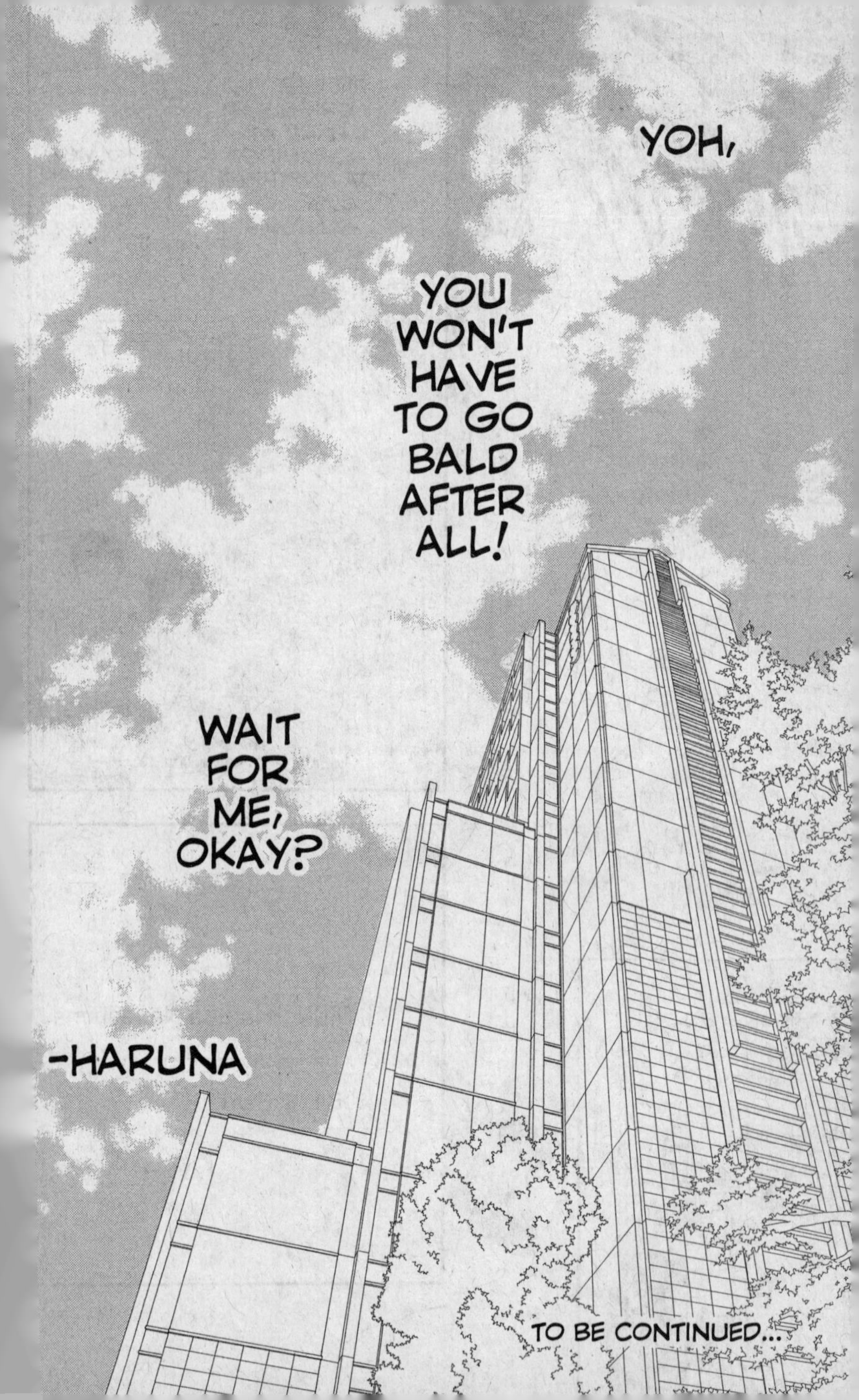
YOH,
YOU WON'T HAVE TO GO BALD AFTER ALL!
WAIT FOR ME, OKAY?
-HARUNA
TO BE CONTINUED...

LONG TIME NO SEE! THANK YOU FOR READING MY BOOK.

AS MANY OF YOU KNOW, HIGH SCHOOL DEBUT WAS MAINLY SERIALIZED IN A MAGAZINE CALLED BESSATSU MARGARET.

SOME PEOPLE HAVE ASKED ME WHY IT'S CALLED "BESSATSU" WHEN IT'S THE MAIN ONE. IT'S TO DISTINGUISH BETWEEN IT AND THE REGULAR MARGARET. I'M AFRAID I WON'T BE ABLE TO PROVIDE AN INTERESTING EXPLANATION, SO LET'S JUST LET THAT BE FOR NOW.

SO BESSATSU MARGARET PUBLISHES AN EXTRA ISSUE CALLED BESSATSU MARGARET SISTER, AND THE FOLLOWING STORIES WERE ALL PUBLISHED IN THESE EXTRA ISSUES AND NOT IN BESSATSU MARGARET. THEY'RE EACH PRETTY SHORT AND WERE WRITTEN LIKE BONUS STORIES, SO IF YOU CAN JUST ENJOY READING EACH OF THEM AS A STAND-ALONE STORY, THAT WOULD BE GREAT.

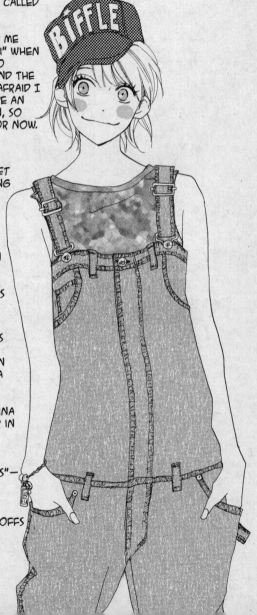

THIS VOLUME ACTUALLY HAS MORE PAGES OF BONUS STORIES THAN OF THE MAIN STORY, SO IT'S MORE LIKE A COLLECTION OF BONUS STORIES. I HOPE YOU LIKE THEM, EVEN THOUGH HARUNA ISN'T THE MAIN CHARACTER IN SOME OF THEM.

I GUESS NOW THEY DON'T CALL THEM "BONUS STORIES"— MORE LIKE SPIN-OFFS. SPIN-OFF... SPIN-OFF...

OKAY, THEN LET THE SPIN-OFFS BEGIN!

IT GETS STARTED ON THE NEXT PAGE!
←

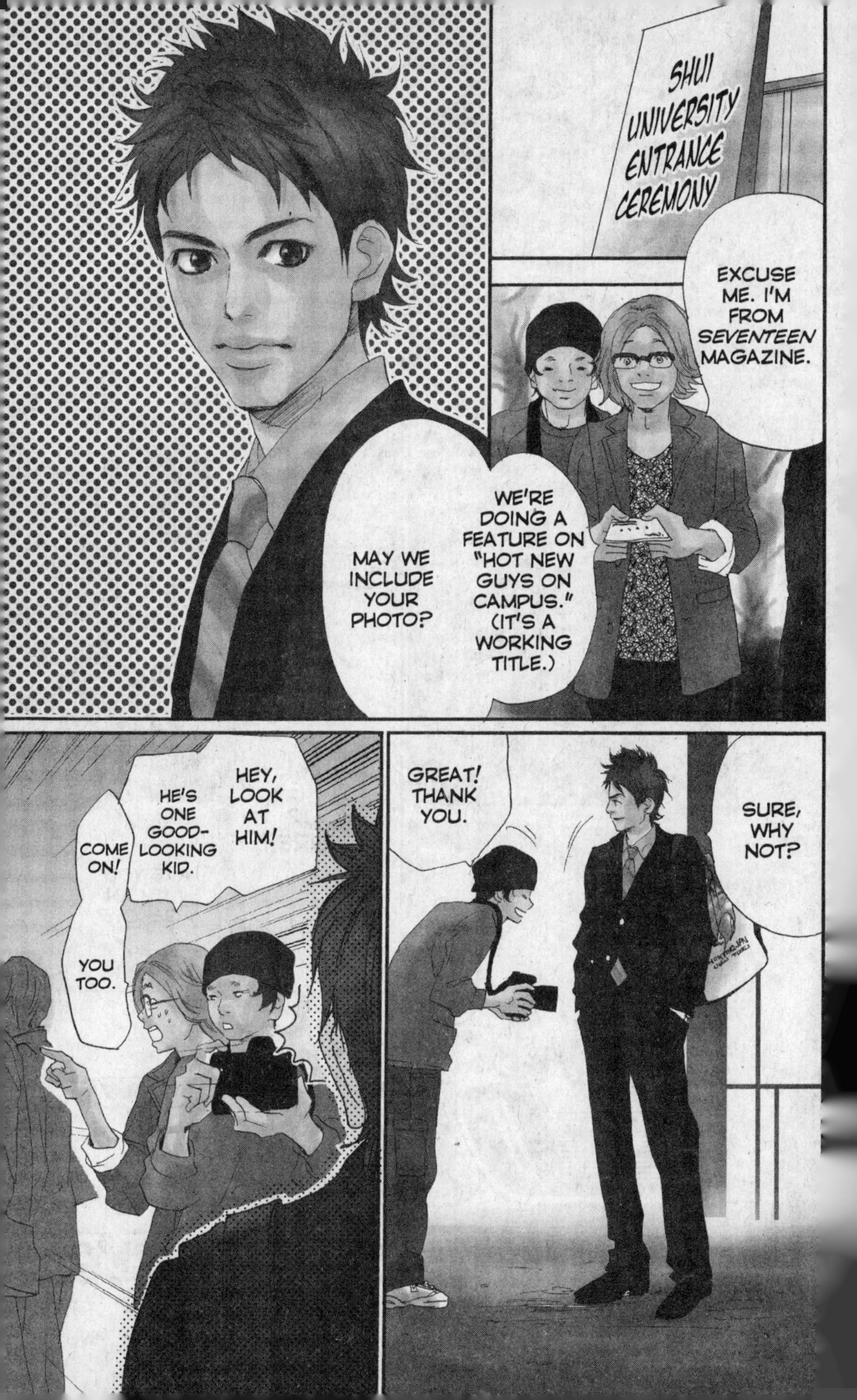
SHUI UNIVERSITY ENTRANCE CEREMONY
EXCUSE ME. I'M FROM SEVENTEEN MAGAZINE.
WE'RE DOING A FEATURE ON "HOT NEW GUYS ON CAMPUS." (IT'S A WORKING TITLE.)
MAY WE INCLUDE YOUR PHOTO?
SURE, WHY NOT?
GREAT! THANK YOU.
HEY, LOOK AT HIM!
HE'S ONE GOOD-LOOKING KID.
COME ON!
YOU TOO.

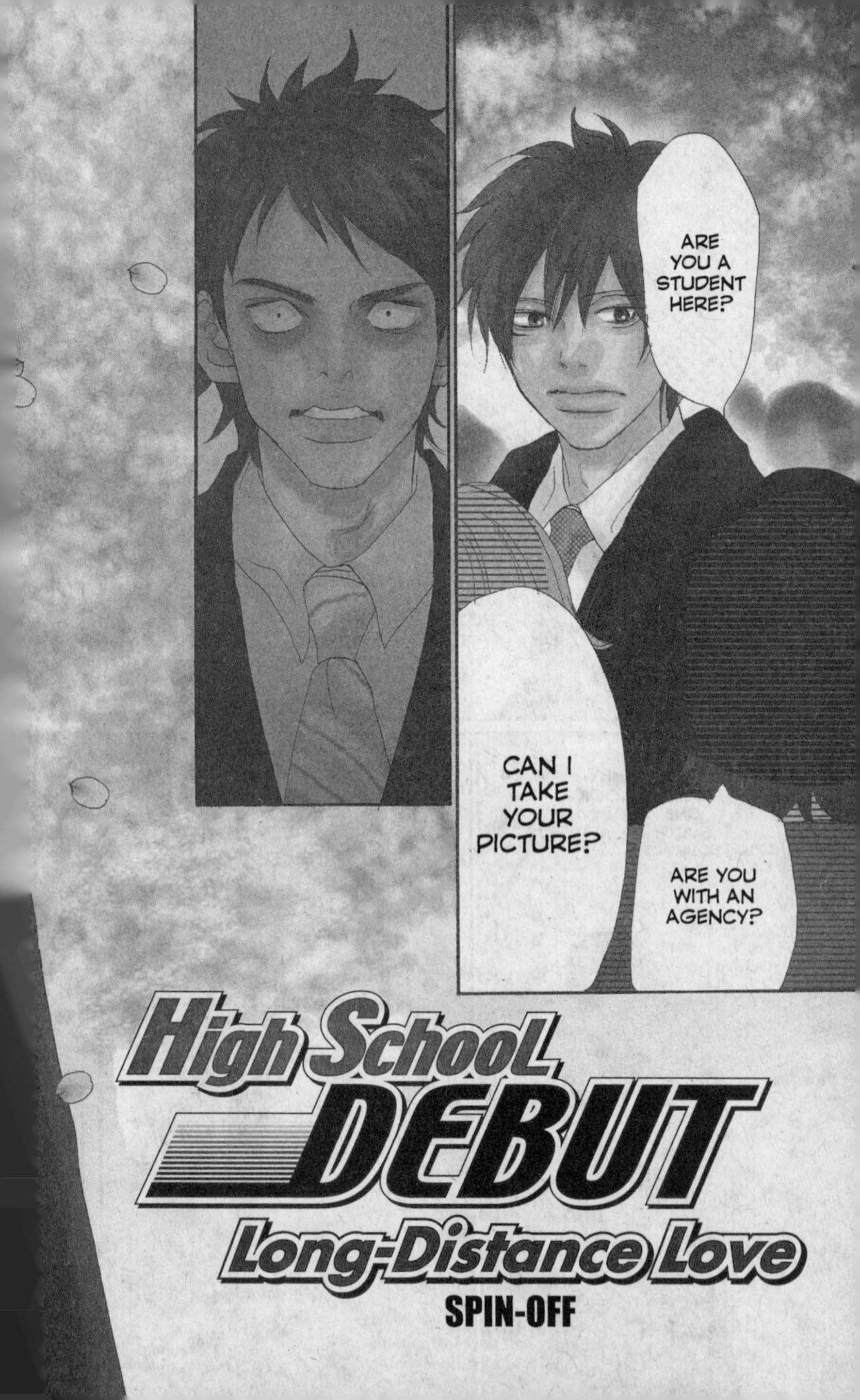
ARE YOU A STUDENT HERE?
ARE YOU WITH AN AGENCY?
CAN I TAKE YOUR PICTURE?
High School DEBUT
Long-Distance Love
SPIN-OFF

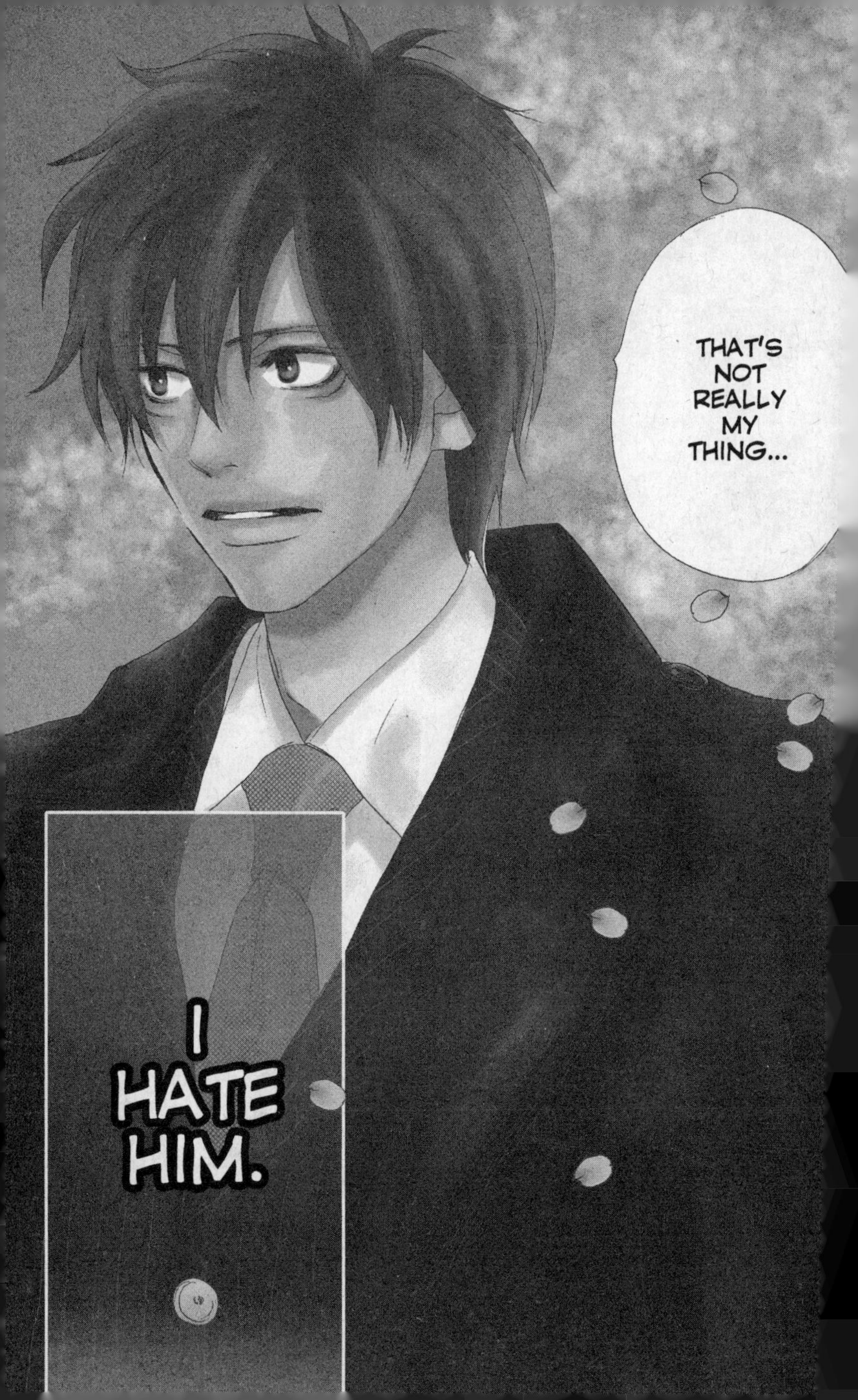
THAT'S NOT REALLY MY THING...
I HATE HIM.

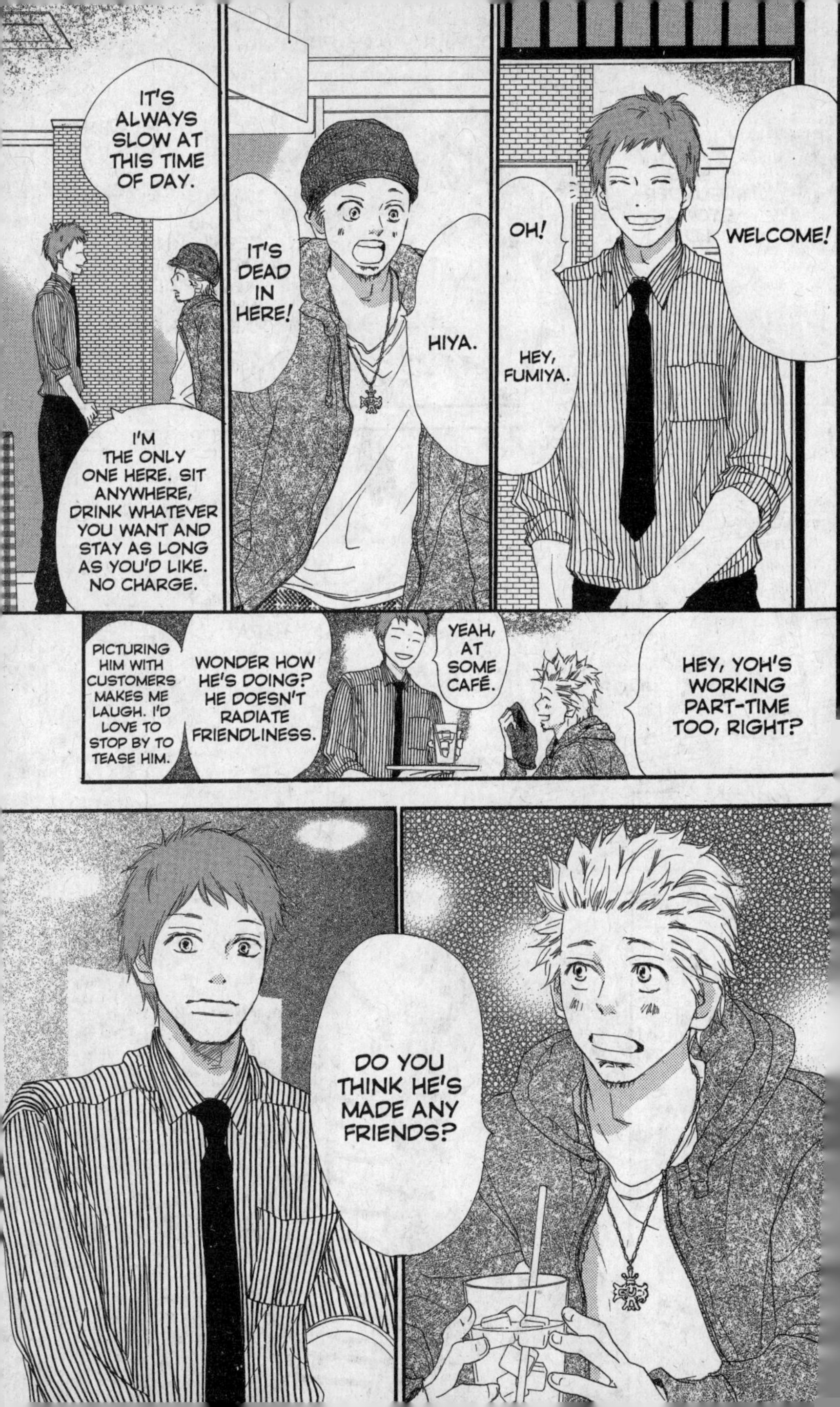
WELCOME!
OH!
HEY, FUMIYA.
HIYA.
IT'S DEAD IN HERE!
IT'S ALWAYS SLOW AT THIS TIME OF DAY.
I'M THE ONLY ONE HERE. SIT ANYWHERE, DRINK WHATEVER YOU WANT AND STAY AS LONG AS YOU'D LIKE. NO CHARGE.
HEY, YOH'S WORKING PART-TIME TOO, RIGHT?
YEAH, AT SOME CAFÉ.
WONDER HOW HE'S DOING? HE DOESN'T RADIATE FRIENDLINESS.
PICTURING HIM WITH CUSTOMERS MAKES ME LAUGH. I'D LOVE TO STOP BY TO TEASE HIM.
DO YOU THINK HE'S MADE ANY FRIENDS?

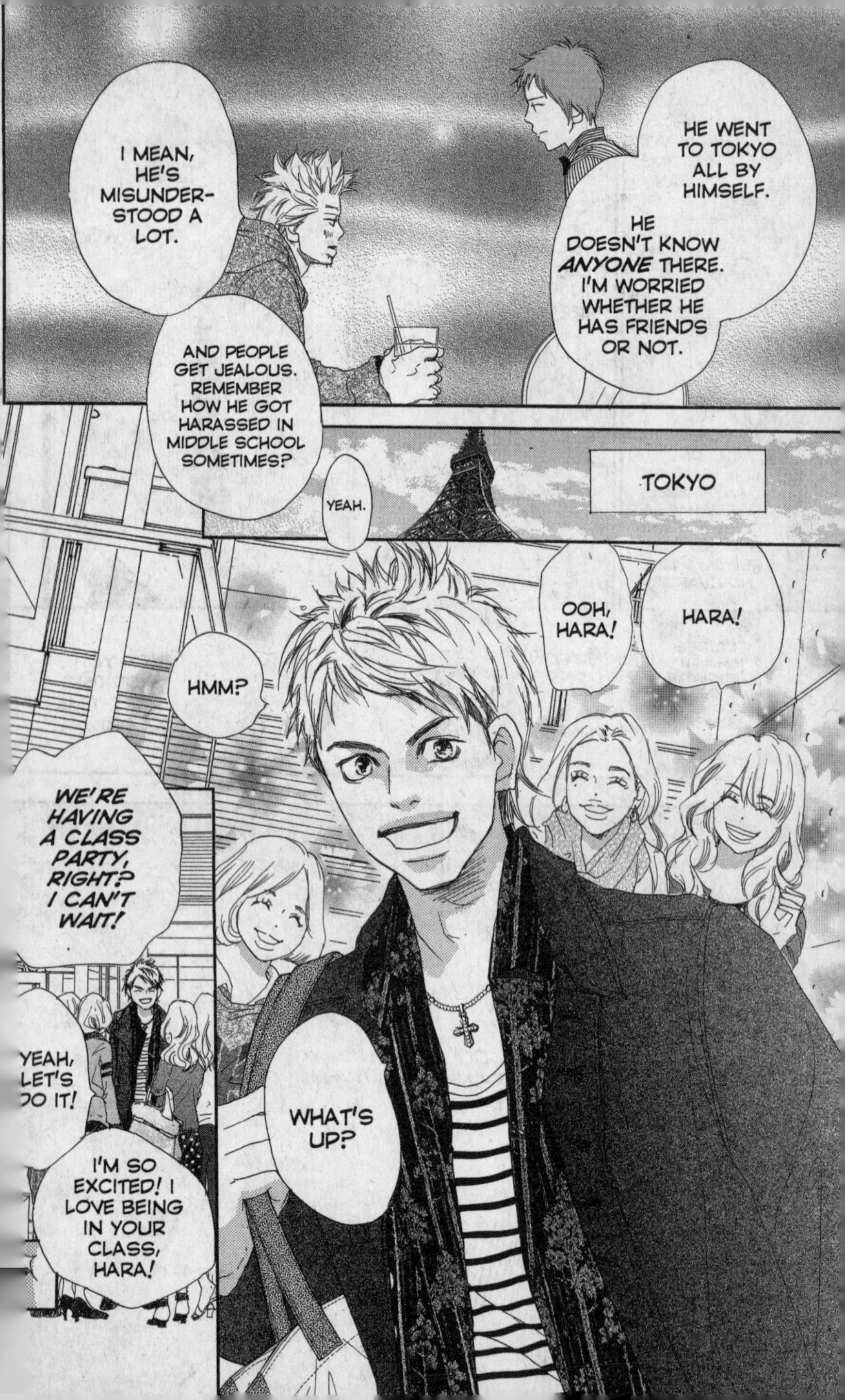

HE WENT TO TOKYO ALL BY HIMSELF.
HE DOESN'T KNOW *ANYONE* THERE. I'M WORRIED WHETHER HE HAS FRIENDS OR NOT.
I MEAN, HE'S MISUNDER-STOOD A LOT.
AND PEOPLE GET JEALOUS. REMEMBER HOW HE GOT HARASSED IN MIDDLE SCHOOL SOMETIMES?
YEAH.
TOKYO
HARA!
OOH, HARA!
HMM?
WHAT'S UP?
WE'RE HAVING A CLASS PARTY, RIGHT? I CAN'T WAIT!
YEAH, LET'S DO IT!
I'M SO EXCITED! I LOVE BEING IN YOUR CLASS, HARA!

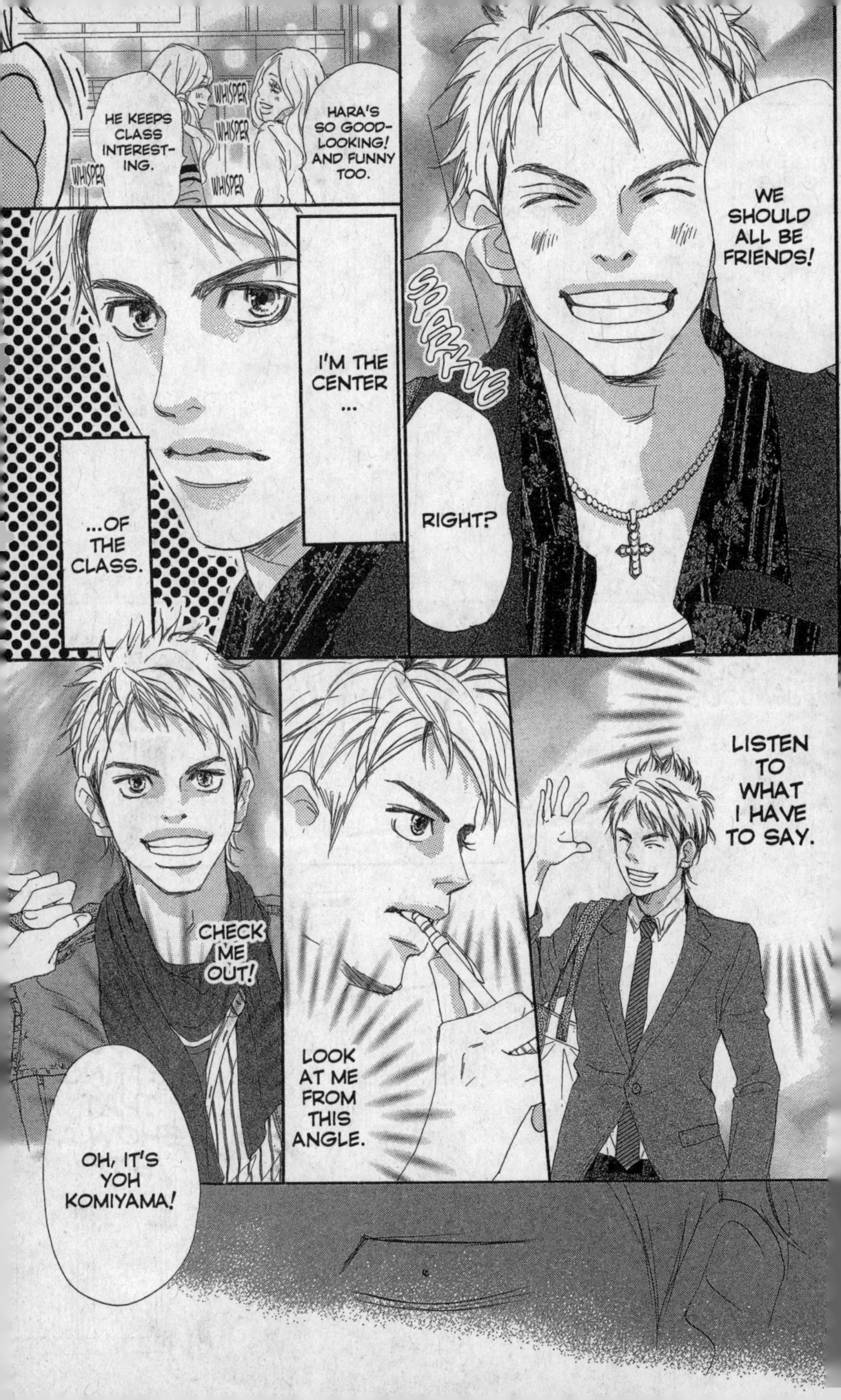
WE SHOULD ALL BE FRIENDS!
SPARKLE
RIGHT?
HARA'S SO GOOD-LOOKING! AND FUNNY TOO.
WHISPER
WHISPER
HE KEEPS CLASS INTEREST-ING.
WHISPER
WHISPER
I'M THE CENTER ...
...OF THE CLASS.
LISTEN TO WHAT I HAVE TO SAY.
LOOK AT ME FROM THIS ANGLE.
CHECK ME OUT!
OH, IT'S YOH KOMIYAMA!

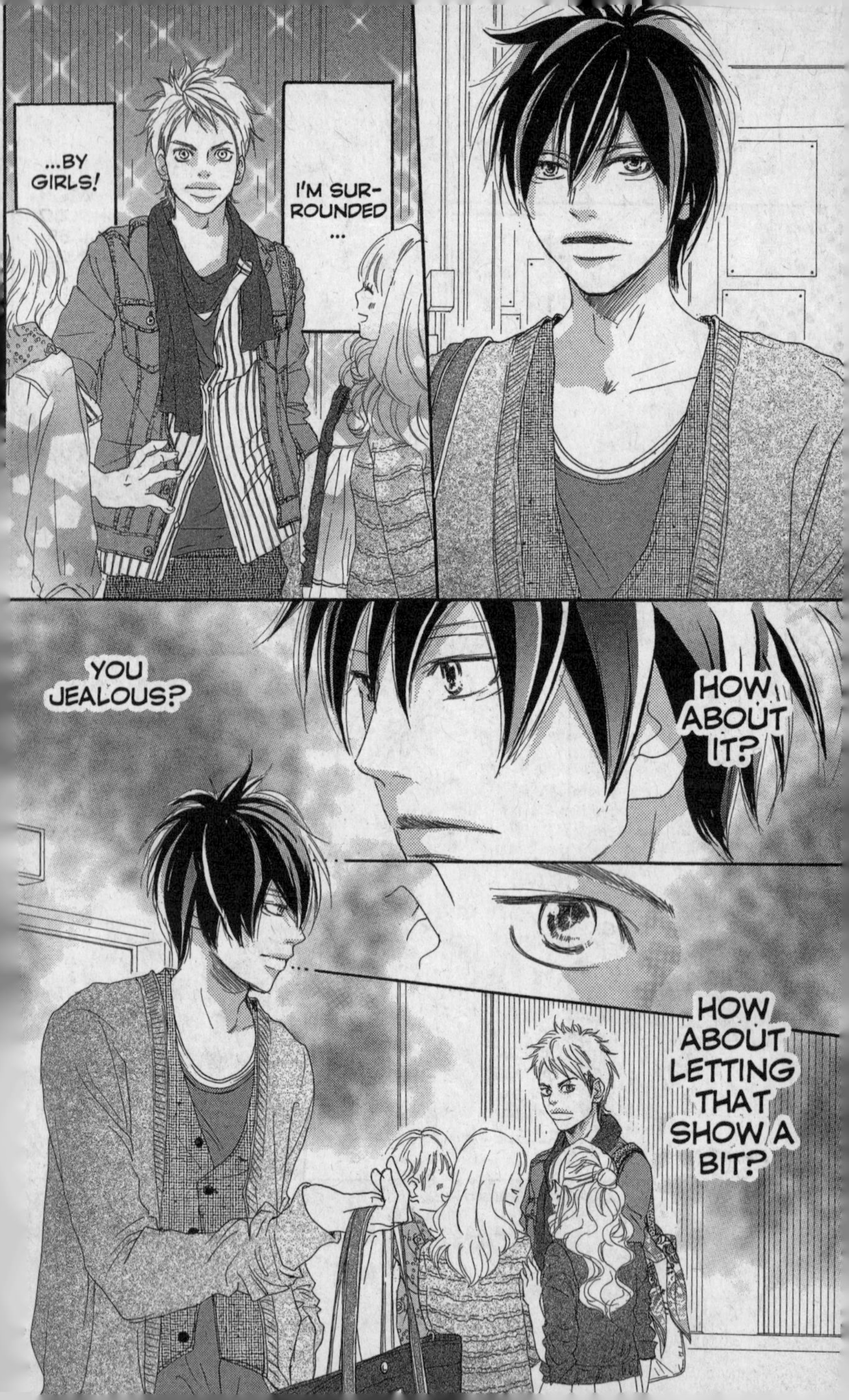
I'M SUR-ROUNDED...
...BY GIRLS!
HOW ABOUT IT?
YOU JEALOUS?
HOW ABOUT LETTING THAT SHOW A BIT?

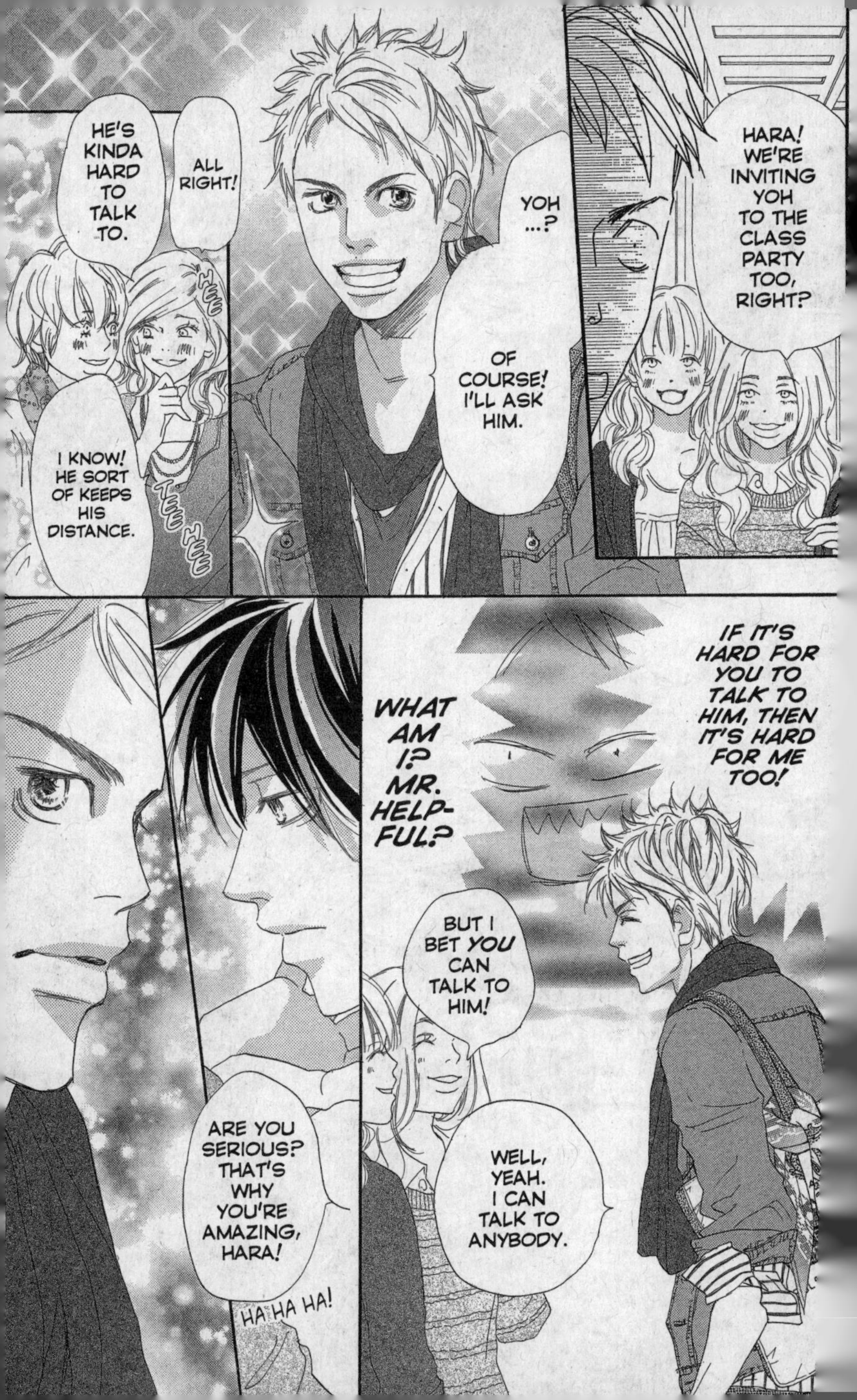
HARA! WE'RE INVITING YOH TO THE CLASS PARTY TOO, RIGHT?
YOH ...?
OF COURSE! I'LL ASK HIM.
ALL RIGHT!
HE'S KINDA HARD TO TALK TO.
HEE HEE
I KNOW! HE SORT OF KEEPS HIS DISTANCE.
TEE HEE
IF IT'S HARD FOR YOU TO TALK TO HIM, THEN IT'S HARD FOR ME TOO!
WHAT AM I? MR. HELPFUL?
BUT I BET YOU CAN TALK TO HIM!
WELL, YEAH. I CAN TALK TO ANYBODY.
ARE YOU SERIOUS? THAT'S WHY YOU'RE AMAZING, HARA!
HA HA HA!

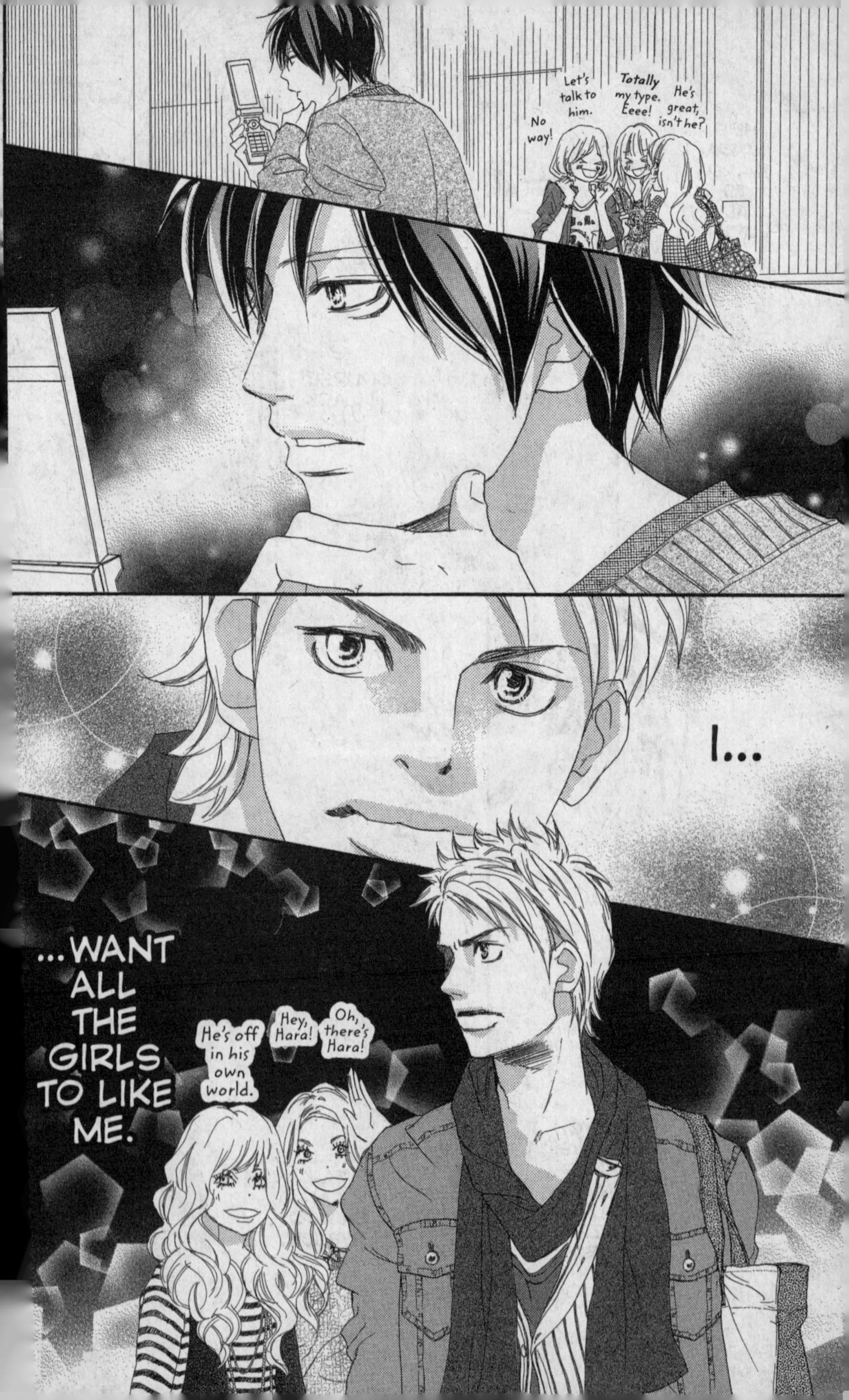
He's great, isn't he?
Totally my type. Eeee!
Let's talk to him.
No way!
I...
Oh, there's Hara!
Hey, Hara!
He's off in his own world.
...WANT ALL THE GIRLS TO LIKE ME.

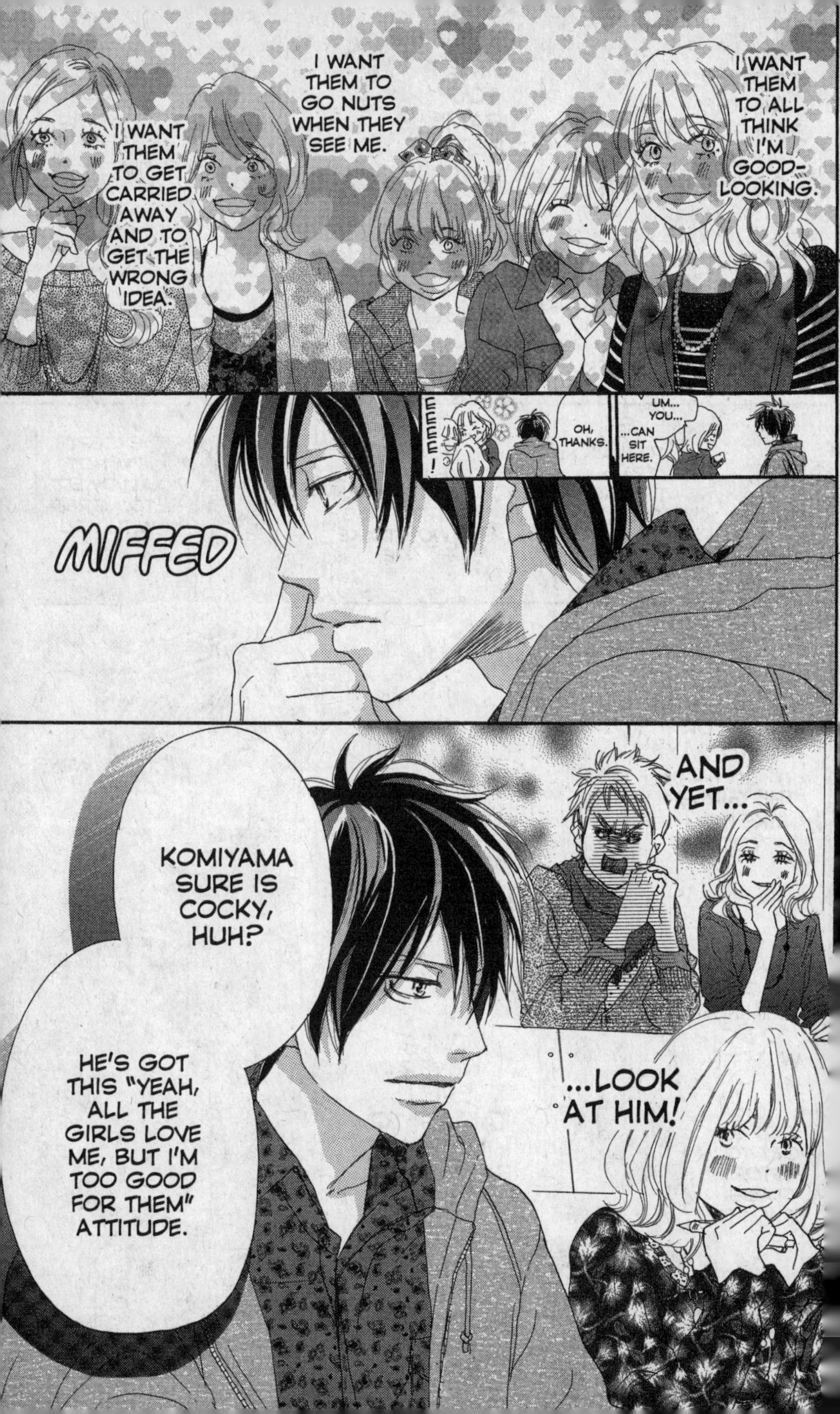
I WANT THEM TO ALL THINK I'M GOOD-LOOKING.
I WANT THEM TO GO NUTS WHEN THEY SEE ME.
I WANT THEM TO GET CARRIED AWAY AND TO GET THE WRONG IDEA.
UM... YOU...
...CAN SIT HERE.
OH, THANKS.
EEEE!
MIFFED
KOMIYAMA SURE IS COCKY, HUH?
HE'S GOT THIS "YEAH, ALL THE GIRLS LOVE ME, BUT I'M TOO GOOD FOR THEM" ATTITUDE.
AND YET...
...LOOK AT HIM!

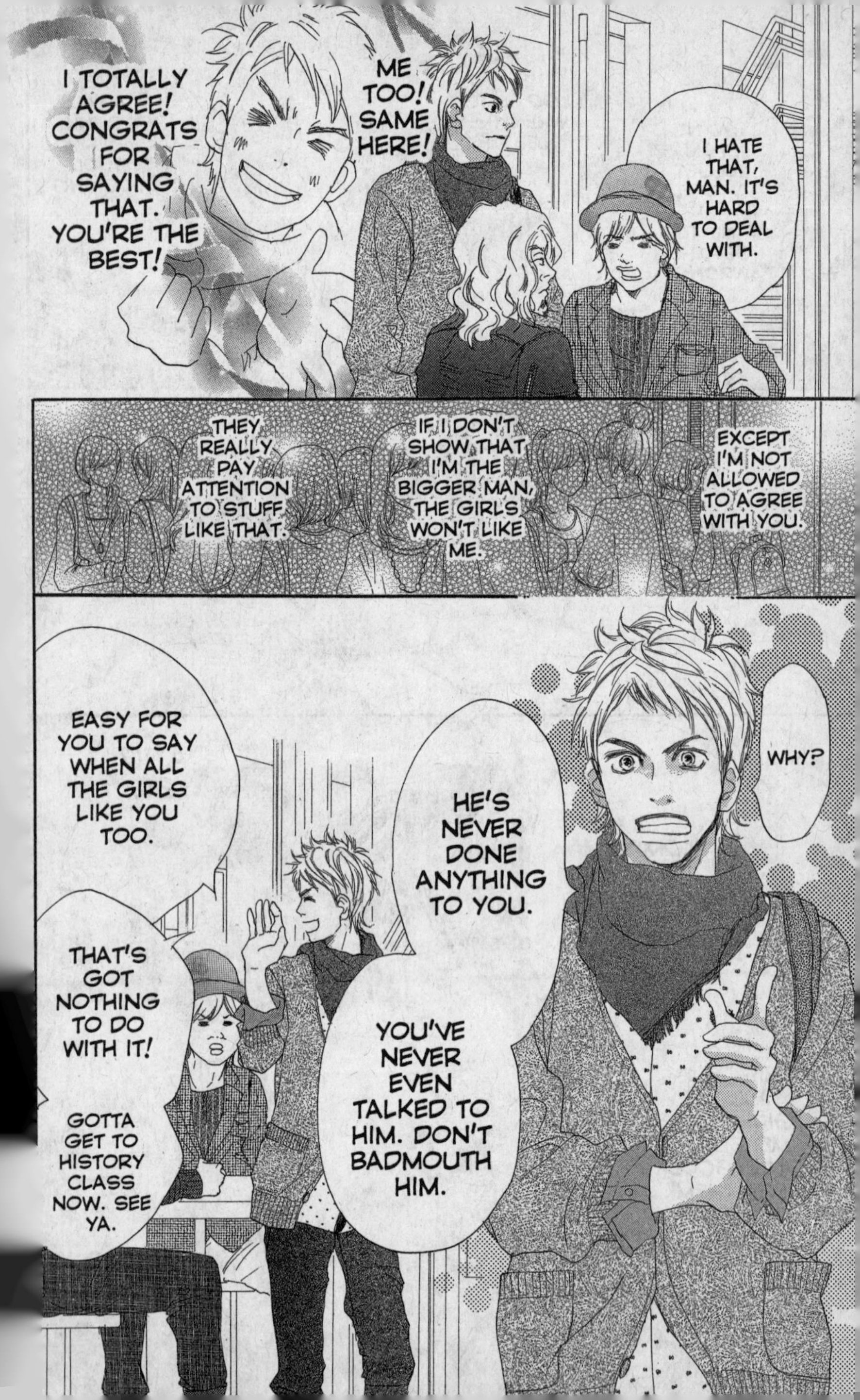
I HATE THAT, MAN. IT'S HARD TO DEAL WITH.
ME TOO! SAME HERE!
I TOTALLY AGREE! CONGRATS FOR SAYING THAT. YOU'RE THE BEST!
EXCEPT I'M NOT ALLOWED TO AGREE WITH YOU.
IF I DON'T SHOW THAT I'M THE BIGGER MAN, THE GIRLS WON'T LIKE ME.
THEY REALLY PAY ATTENTION TO STUFF LIKE THAT.
WHY?
HE'S NEVER DONE ANYTHING TO YOU.
YOU'VE NEVER EVEN TALKED TO HIM. DON'T BADMOUTH HIM.
EASY FOR YOU TO SAY WHEN ALL THE GIRLS LIKE YOU TOO.
THAT'S GOT NOTHING TO DO WITH IT!
GOTTA GET TO HISTORY CLASS NOW. SEE YA.

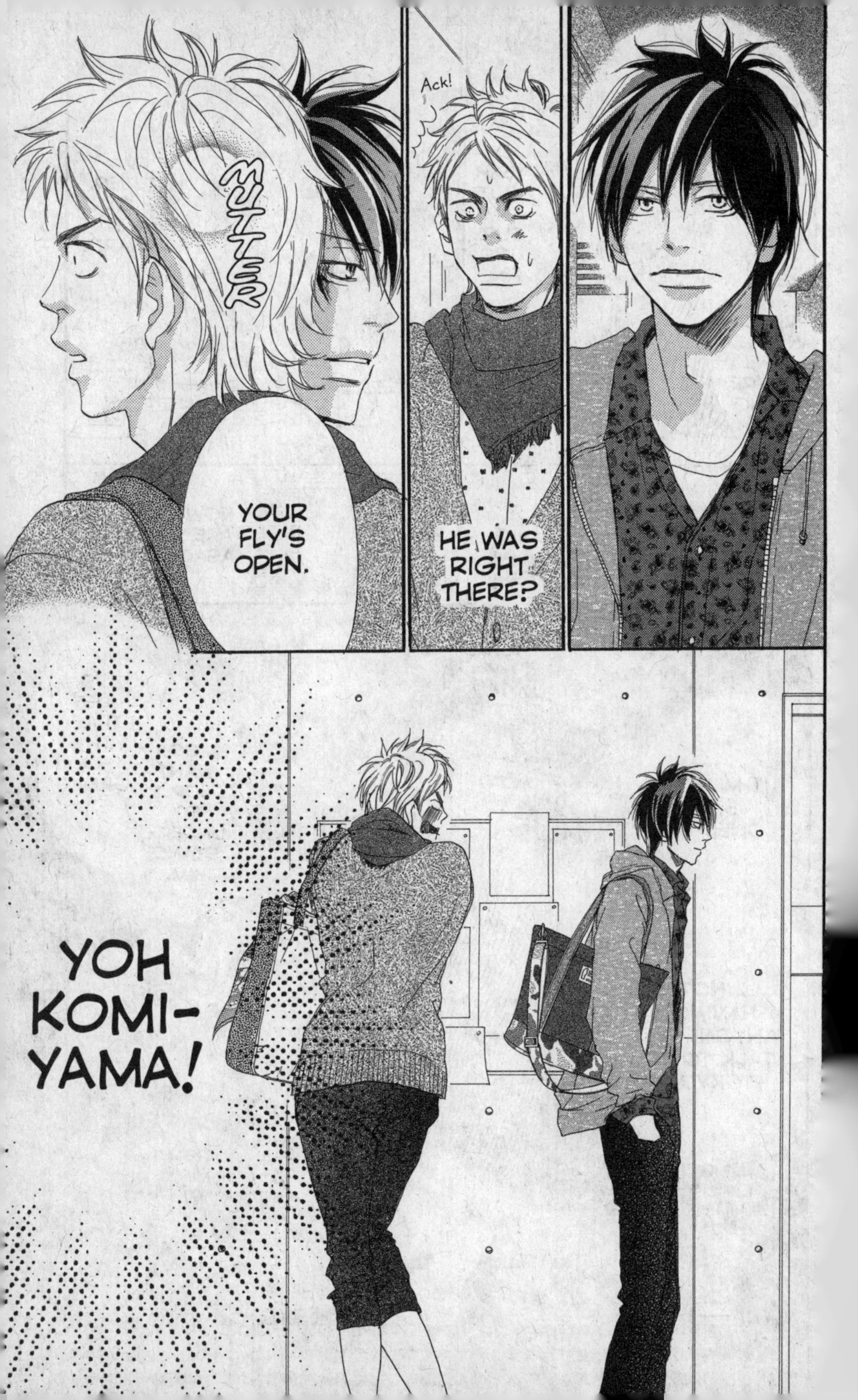
Ack!
HE WAS RIGHT THERE?
MUTTER
YOUR FLY'S OPEN.
YOH KOMI-YAMA!

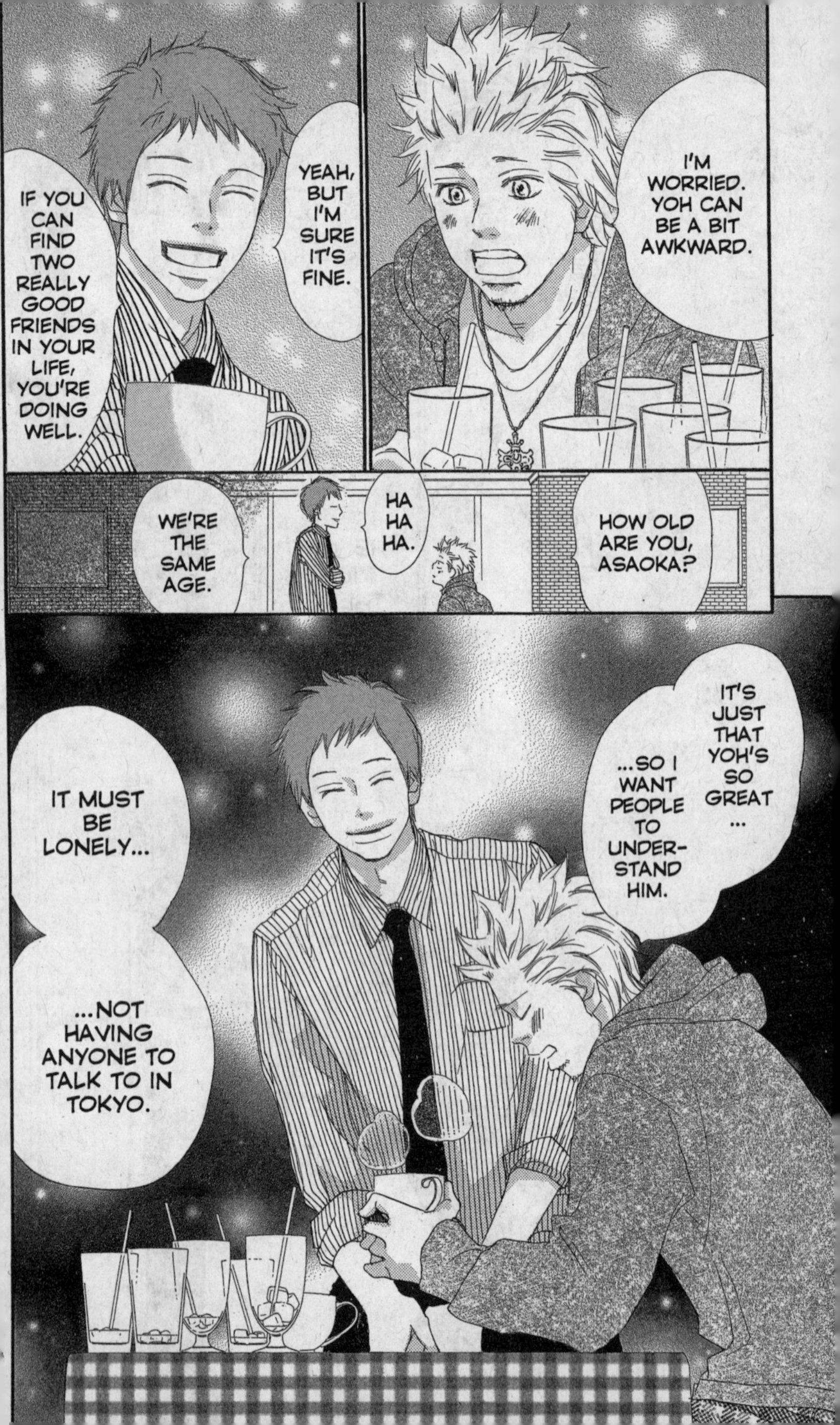
I'M WORRIED. YOH CAN BE A BIT AWKWARD.
YEAH, BUT I'M SURE IT'S FINE.
IF YOU CAN FIND TWO REALLY GOOD FRIENDS IN YOUR LIFE, YOU'RE DOING WELL.
HOW OLD ARE YOU, ASAOKA?
HA HA HA.
WE'RE THE SAME AGE.
IT'S JUST THAT YOH'S SO GREAT...
...SO I WANT PEOPLE TO UNDERSTAND HIM.
IT MUST BE LONELY...
...NOT HAVING ANYONE TO TALK TO IN TOKYO.

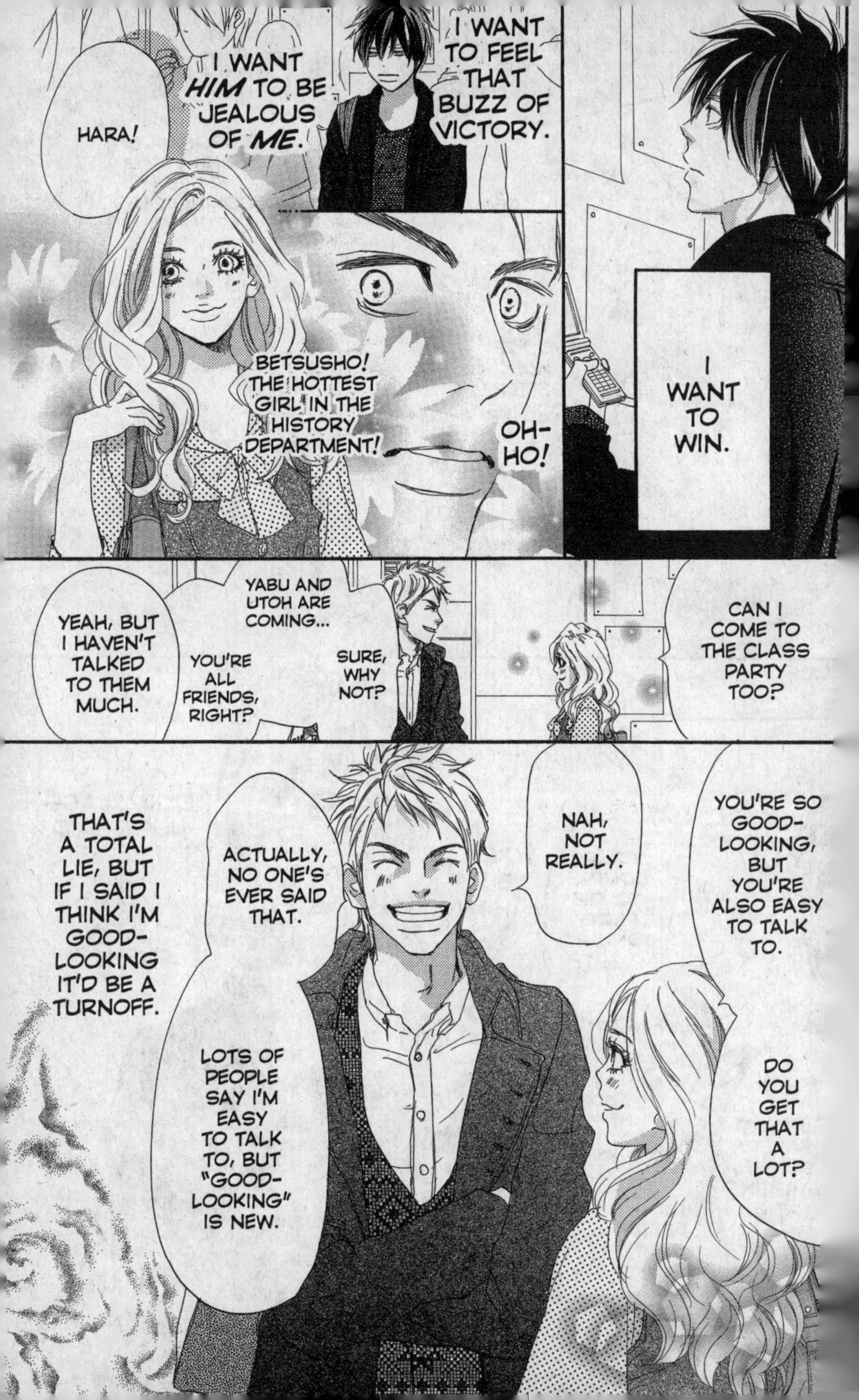
I WANT TO WIN.
I WANT TO FEEL THAT BUZZ OF VICTORY.
I WANT *HIM* TO BE JEALOUS OF *ME*.
HARA!
OH-HO!
BETSUSHO! THE HOTTEST GIRL IN THE HISTORY DEPARTMENT!
CAN I COME TO THE CLASS PARTY TOO?
SURE, WHY NOT?
YABU AND UTOH ARE COMING...
YOU'RE ALL FRIENDS, RIGHT?
YEAH, BUT I HAVEN'T TALKED TO THEM MUCH.
YOU'RE SO GOOD-LOOKING, BUT YOU'RE ALSO EASY TO TALK TO.
DO YOU GET THAT A LOT?
NAH, NOT REALLY.
ACTUALLY, NO ONE'S EVER SAID THAT.
LOTS OF PEOPLE SAY I'M EASY TO TALK TO, BUT "GOOD-LOOKING" IS NEW.
THAT'S A TOTAL LIE, BUT IF I SAID I THINK I'M GOOD-LOOKING IT'D BE A TURNOFF.

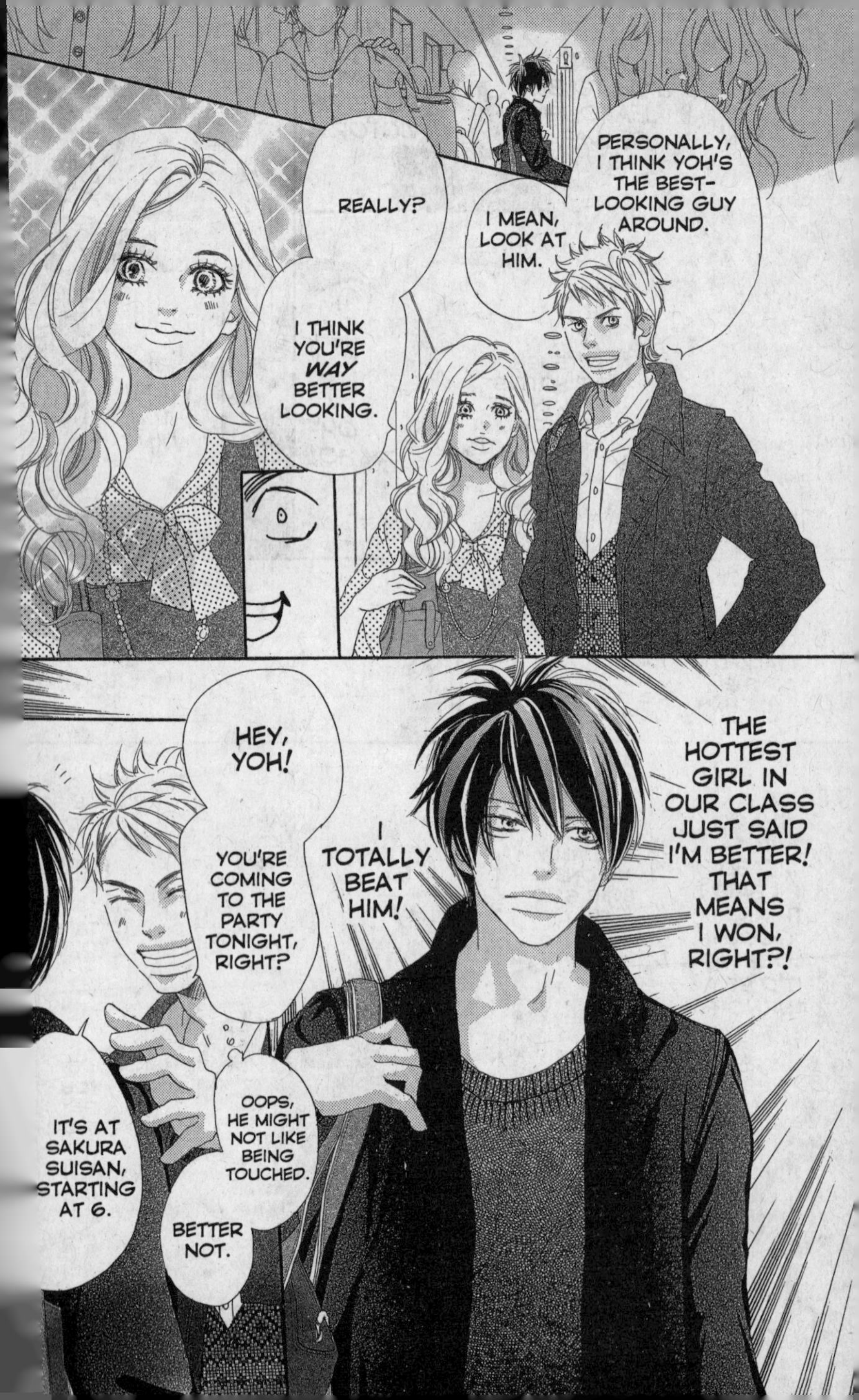
PERSONALLY, I THINK YOH'S THE BEST-LOOKING GUY AROUND.
I MEAN, LOOK AT HIM.
REALLY?
I THINK YOU'RE *WAY* BETTER LOOKING.
THE HOTTEST GIRL IN OUR CLASS JUST SAID I'M BETTER! THAT MEANS I WON, RIGHT?!
I TOTALLY BEAT HIM!
HEY, YOH!
YOU'RE COMING TO THE PARTY TONIGHT, RIGHT?
OOPS, HE MIGHT NOT LIKE BEING TOUCHED.
BETTER NOT.
IT'S AT SAKURA SUISAN, STARTING AT 6.

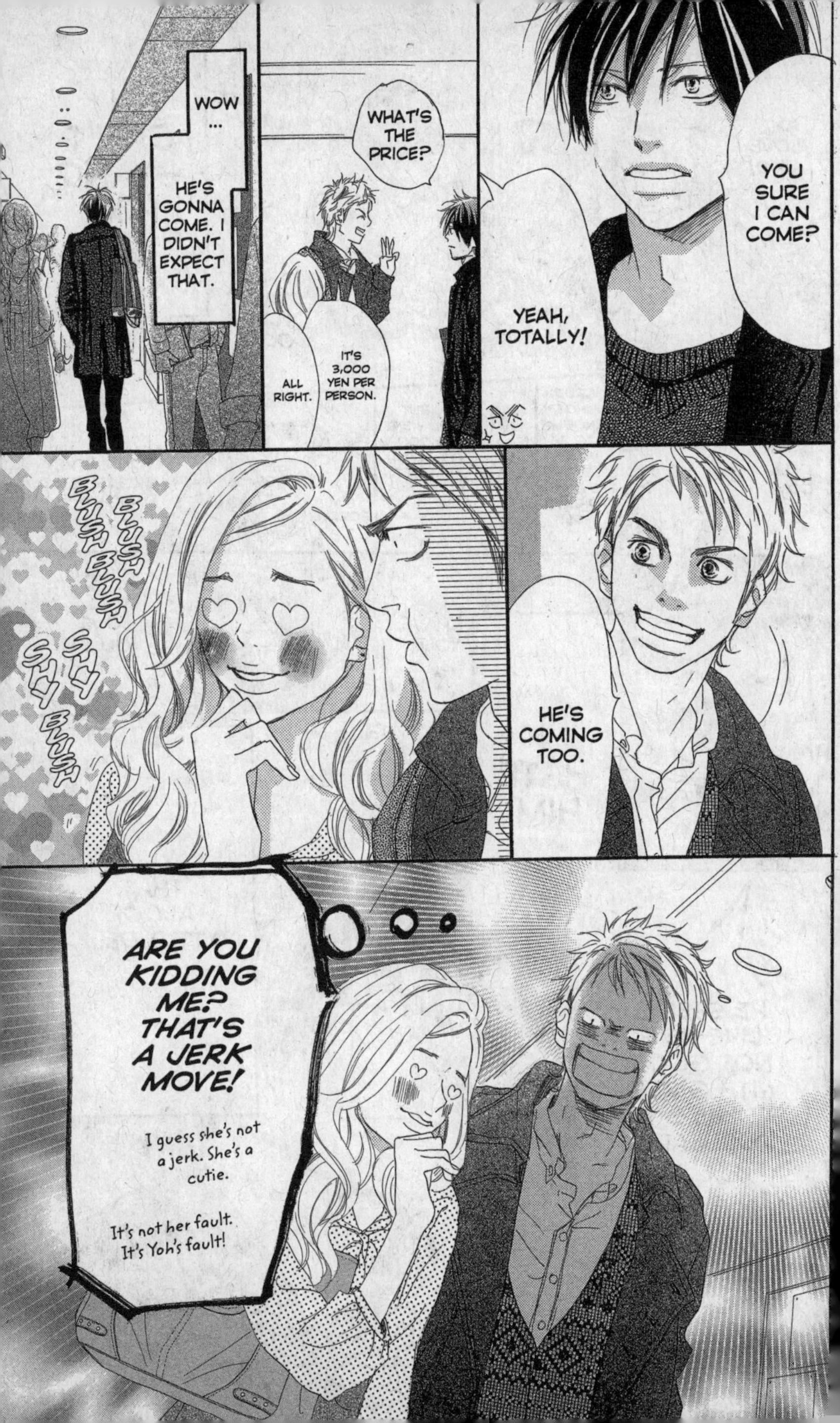
YOU SURE I CAN COME?
YEAH, TOTALLY!
WHAT'S THE PRICE?
IT'S 3,000 YEN PER PERSON.
ALL RIGHT.
WOW ... HE'S GONNA COME. I DIDN'T EXPECT THAT.
HE'S COMING TOO.
BLUSH BLUSH
BLUSH BLUSH
SHY SHY
BLUSH
ARE YOU KIDDING ME? THAT'S A JERK MOVE!
I guess she's not a jerk. She's a cutie.
It's not her fault. It's Yoh's fault!

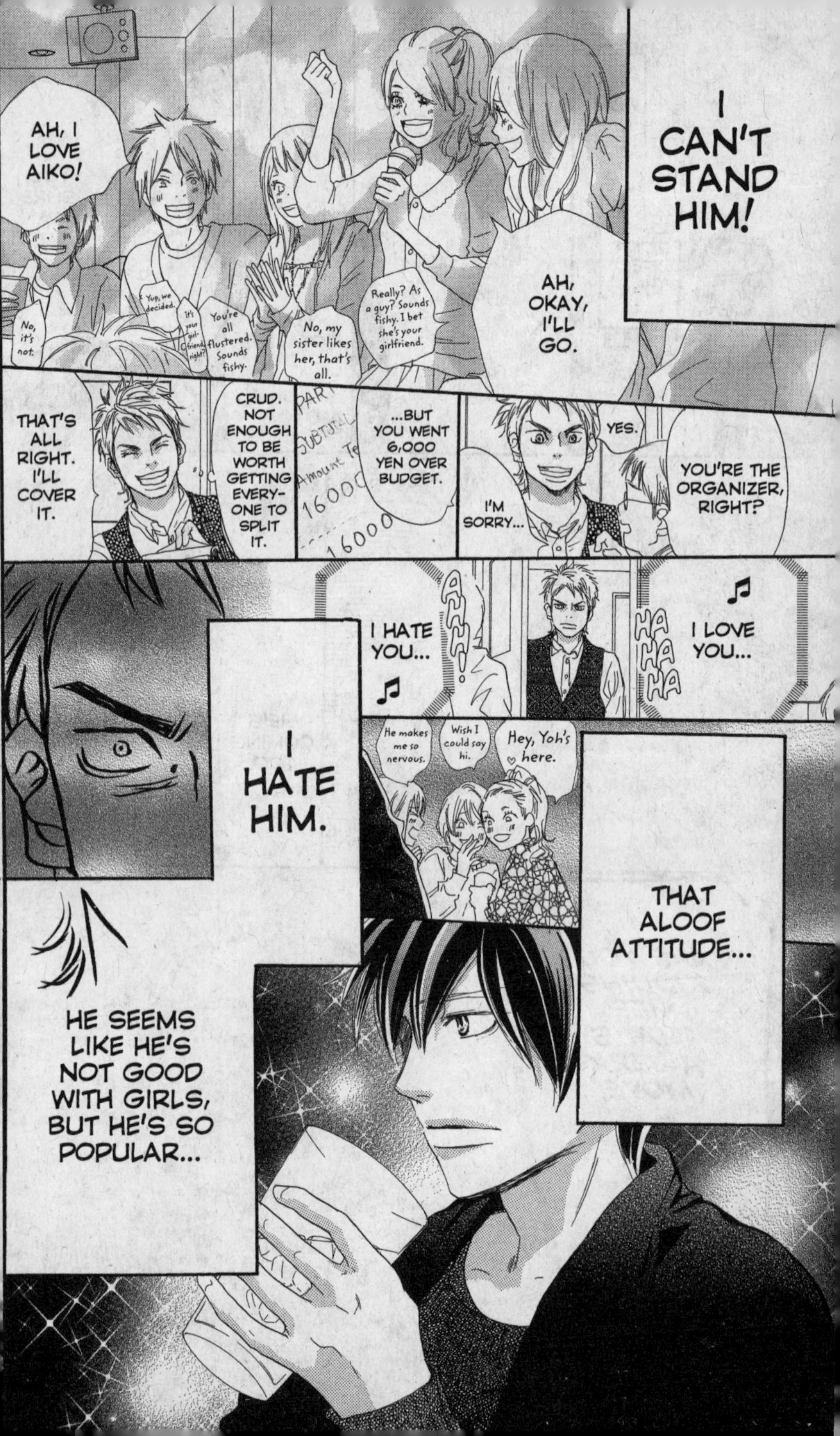
I CAN'T STAND HIM!
AH, OKAY, I'LL GO.
Really? As a guy? Sounds fishy. I bet she's your girlfriend.
No, my sister likes her, that's all.
You're all flustered. Sounds fishy.
It's your girlfriend, right?
Yup, we decided.
AH, I LOVE AIKO!
No, it's not.
YOU'RE THE ORGANIZER, RIGHT?
YES.
I'M SORRY...
...BUT YOU WENT 6,000 YEN OVER BUDGET.
CRUD. NOT ENOUGH TO BE WORTH GETTING EVERY-ONE TO SPLIT IT.
THAT'S ALL RIGHT. I'LL COVER IT.
I LOVE YOU...
HA HA HA HA
AHH!
I HATE YOU...
I HATE HIM.
Hey, Yoh's here.
Wish I could say hi.
He makes me so nervous.
THAT ALOOF ATTITUDE...
HE SEEMS LIKE HE'S NOT GOOD WITH GIRLS, BUT HE'S SO POPULAR...

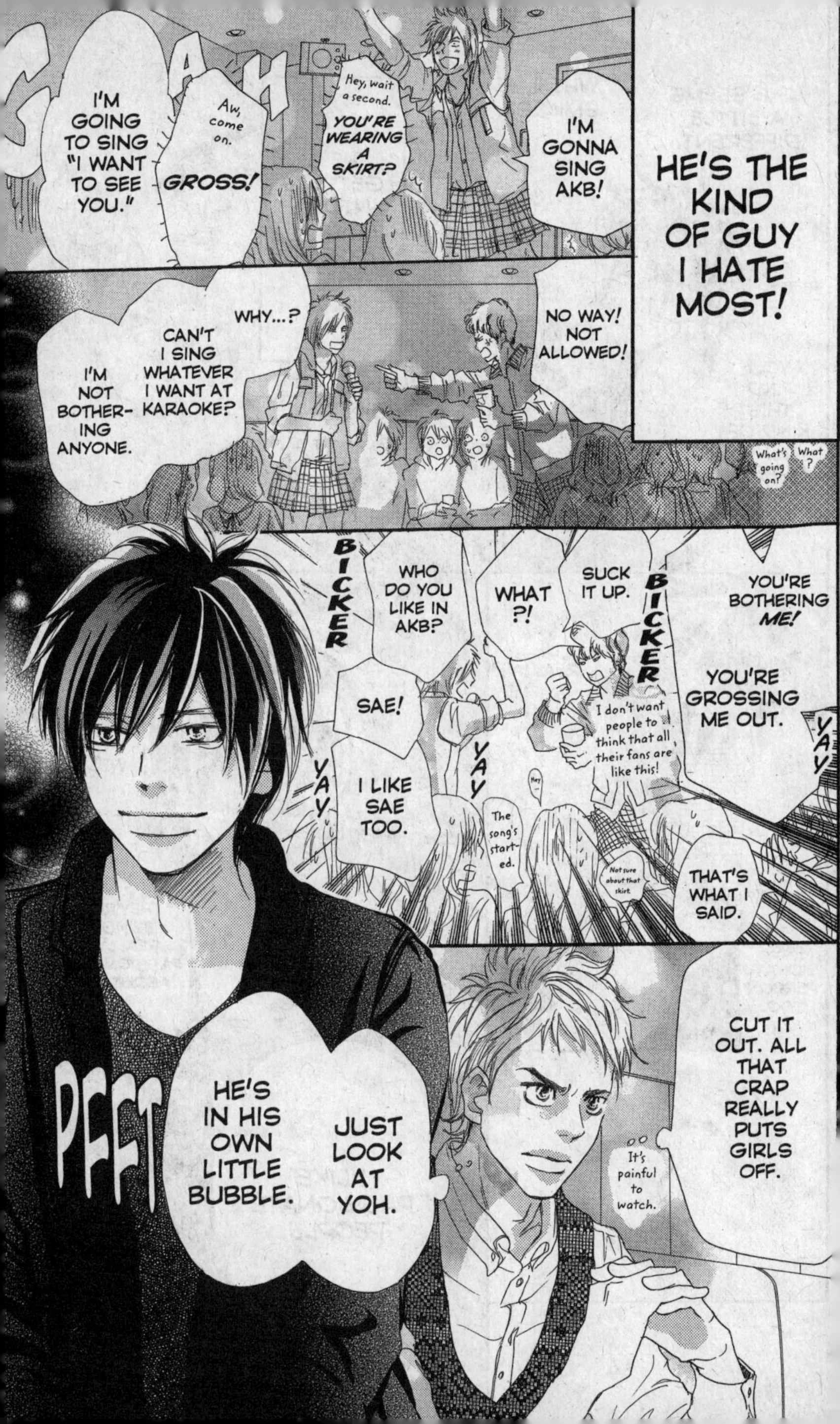
HE'S THE KIND OF GUY I HATE MOST!
I'M GONNA SING AKB!
Hey, wait a second. YOU'RE WEARING A SKIRT?
Aw, come on. GROSS!
I'M GOING TO SING "I WANT TO SEE YOU."
NO WAY! NOT ALLOWED!
WHY...? CAN'T I SING WHATEVER I WANT AT KARAOKE?
I'M NOT BOTHERING ANYONE.
What?
What's going on?
YOU'RE BOTHERING ME!
BICKER
SUCK IT UP.
WHAT?!
WHO DO YOU LIKE IN AKB?
BICKER
YOU'RE GROSSING ME OUT.
I don't want people to think that all their fans are like this!
SAE!
I LIKE SAE TOO.
YAY
YAY
YAY
Hey...
The song's start-ed.
Not sure about that skirt.
THAT'S WHAT I SAID.
CUT IT OUT. ALL THAT CRAP REALLY PUTS GIRLS OFF.
It's painful to watch.
JUST LOOK AT YOH.
HE'S IN HIS OWN LITTLE BUBBLE.
PFFT

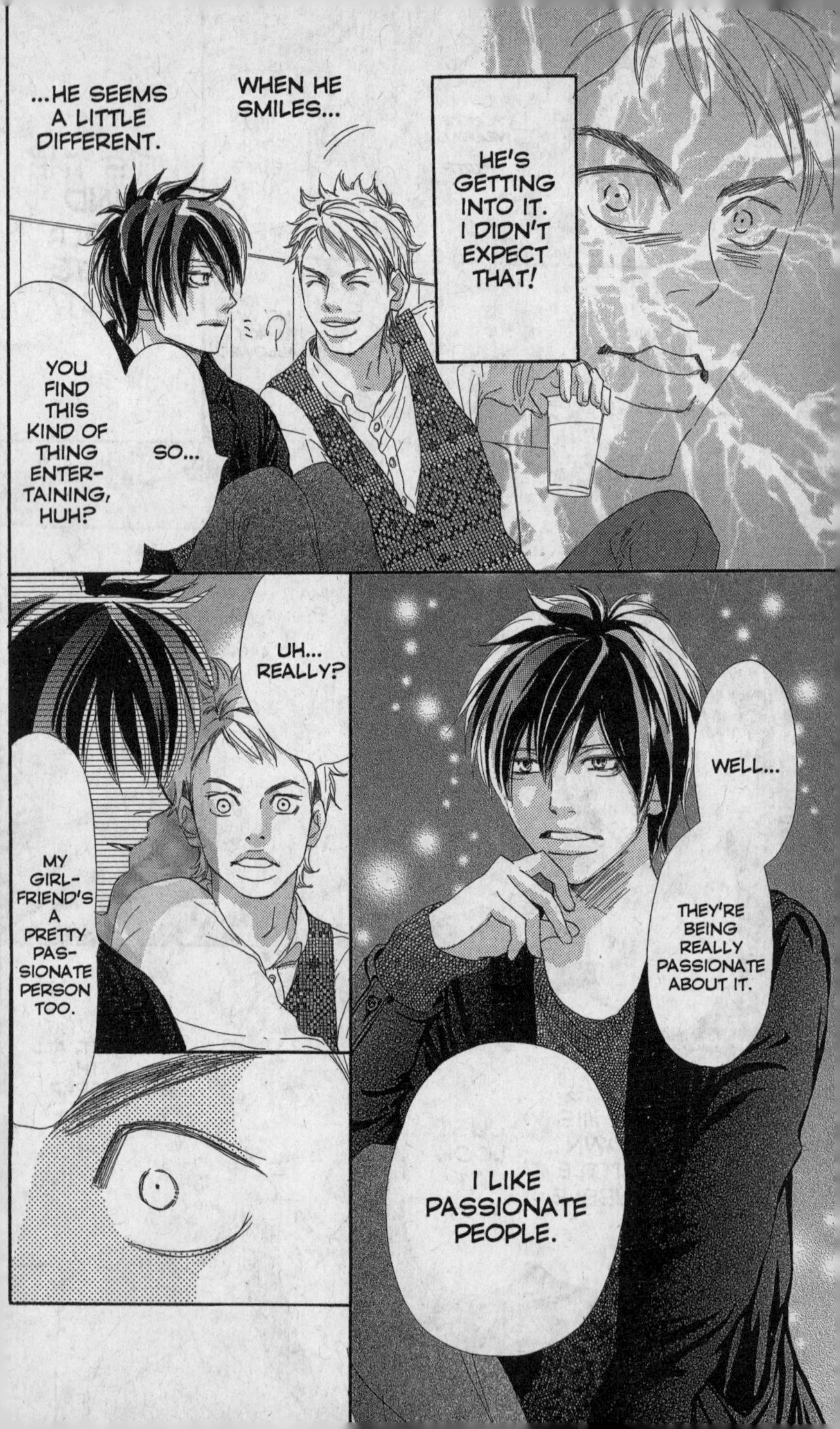
HE'S GETTING INTO IT. I DIDN'T EXPECT THAT!
WHEN HE SMILES...
...HE SEEMS A LITTLE DIFFERENT.
SO...
YOU FIND THIS KIND OF THING ENTER-TAINING, HUH?
WELL...
THEY'RE BEING REALLY PASSIONATE ABOUT IT.
I LIKE PASSIONATE PEOPLE.
UH... REALLY?
MY GIRL-FRIEND'S A PRETTY PAS-SIONATE PERSON TOO.

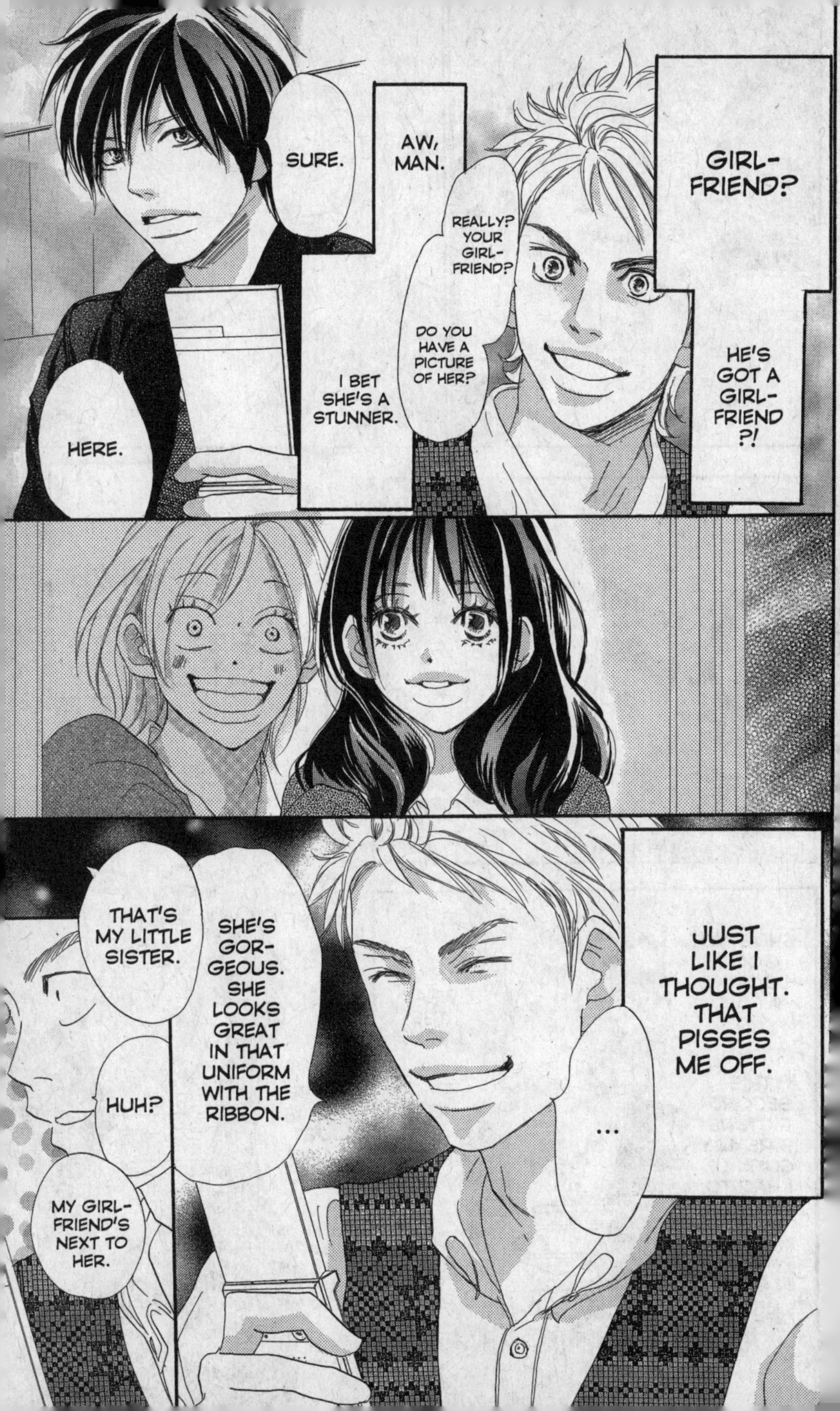
GIRL-FRIEND?
REALLY? YOUR GIRL-FRIEND?
HE'S GOT A GIRL-FRIEND ?!
DO YOU HAVE A PICTURE OF HER?
AW, MAN.
SURE.
I BET SHE'S A STUNNER.
HERE.
JUST LIKE I THOUGHT. THAT PISSES ME OFF.
...
SHE'S GOR-GEOUS. SHE LOOKS GREAT IN THAT UNIFORM WITH THE RIBBON.
THAT'S MY LITTLE SISTER.
HUH?
MY GIRL-FRIEND'S NEXT TO HER.

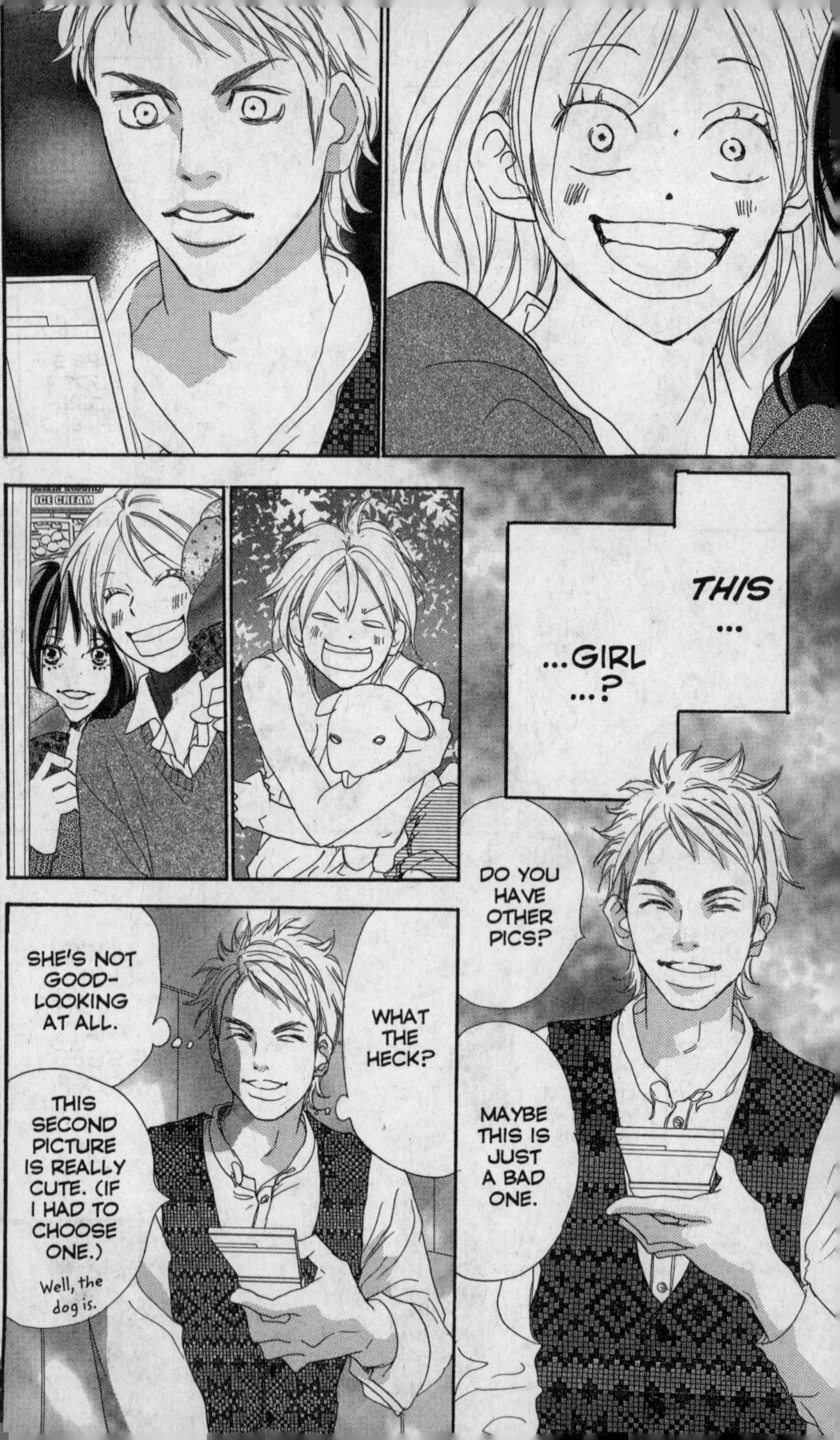
THIS ...
...GIRL ...?
DO YOU HAVE OTHER PICS?
MAYBE THIS IS JUST A BAD ONE.
WHAT THE HECK?
SHE'S NOT GOOD-LOOKING AT ALL.
THIS SECOND PICTURE IS REALLY CUTE. (IF I HAD TO CHOOSE ONE.)
Well, the dog is.
ICE CREAM

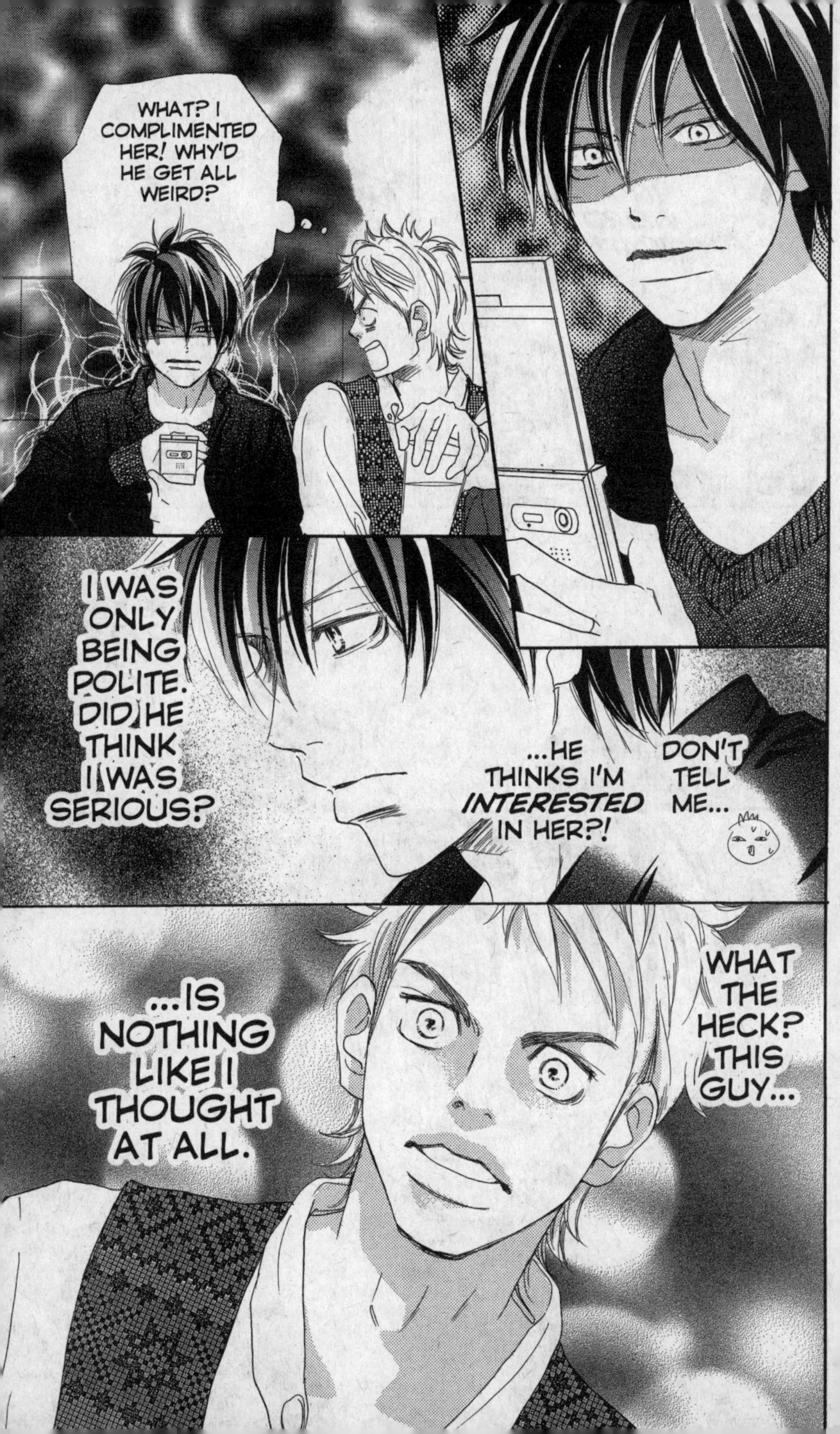
WHAT? I COMPLIMENTED HER! WHY'D HE GET ALL WEIRD?
DON'T TELL ME...
...HE THINKS I'M *INTERESTED* IN HER?!
I WAS ONLY BEING POLITE. DID HE THINK I WAS SERIOUS?
WHAT THE HECK? THIS GUY...
...IS NOTHING LIKE I THOUGHT AT ALL.

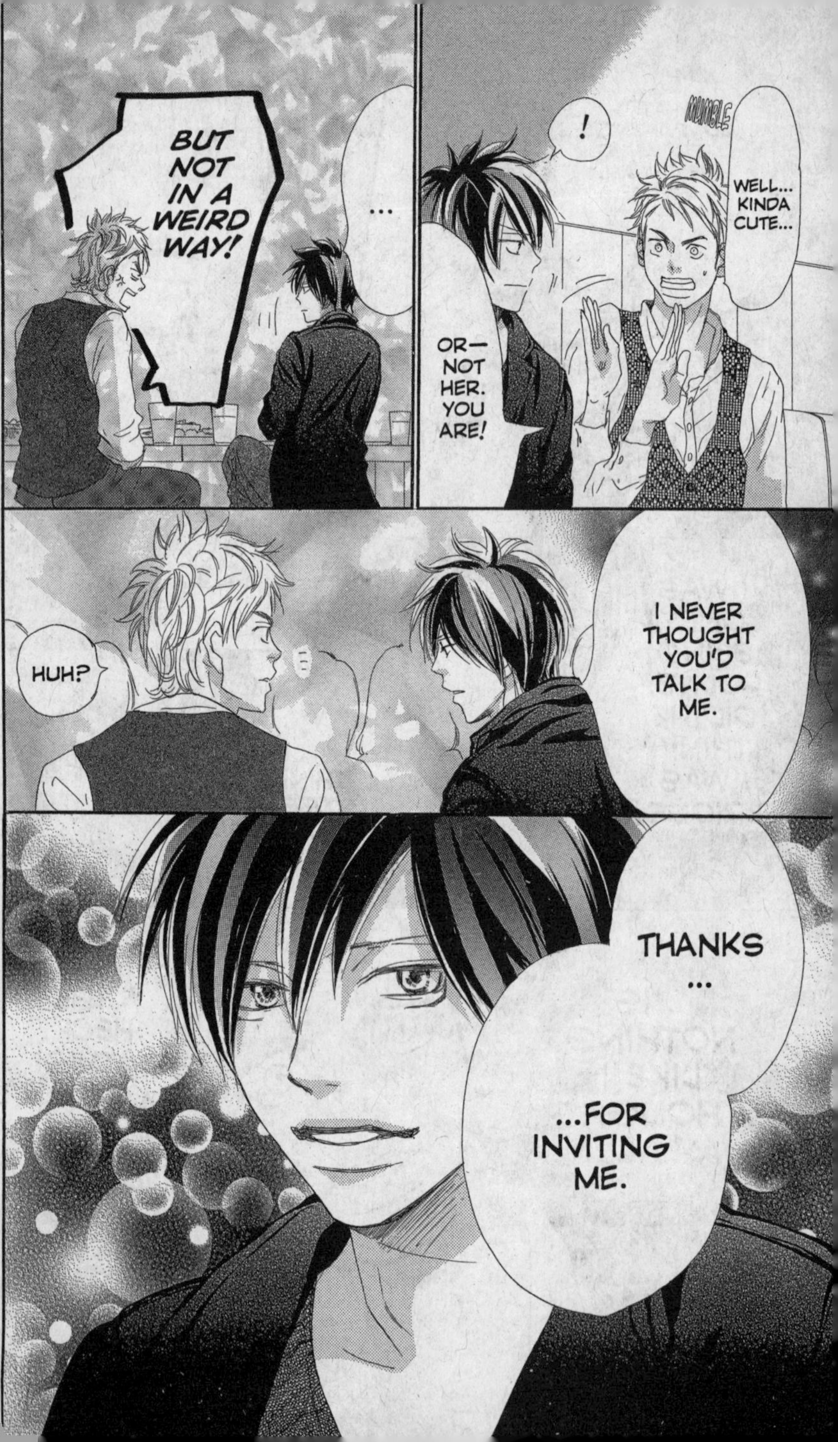
MUMBLE
WELL... KINDA CUTE...
!
OR—NOT HER. YOU ARE!
...
BUT NOT IN A WEIRD WAY!
I NEVER THOUGHT YOU'D TALK TO ME.
HUH?
THANKS...
...FOR INVITING ME.

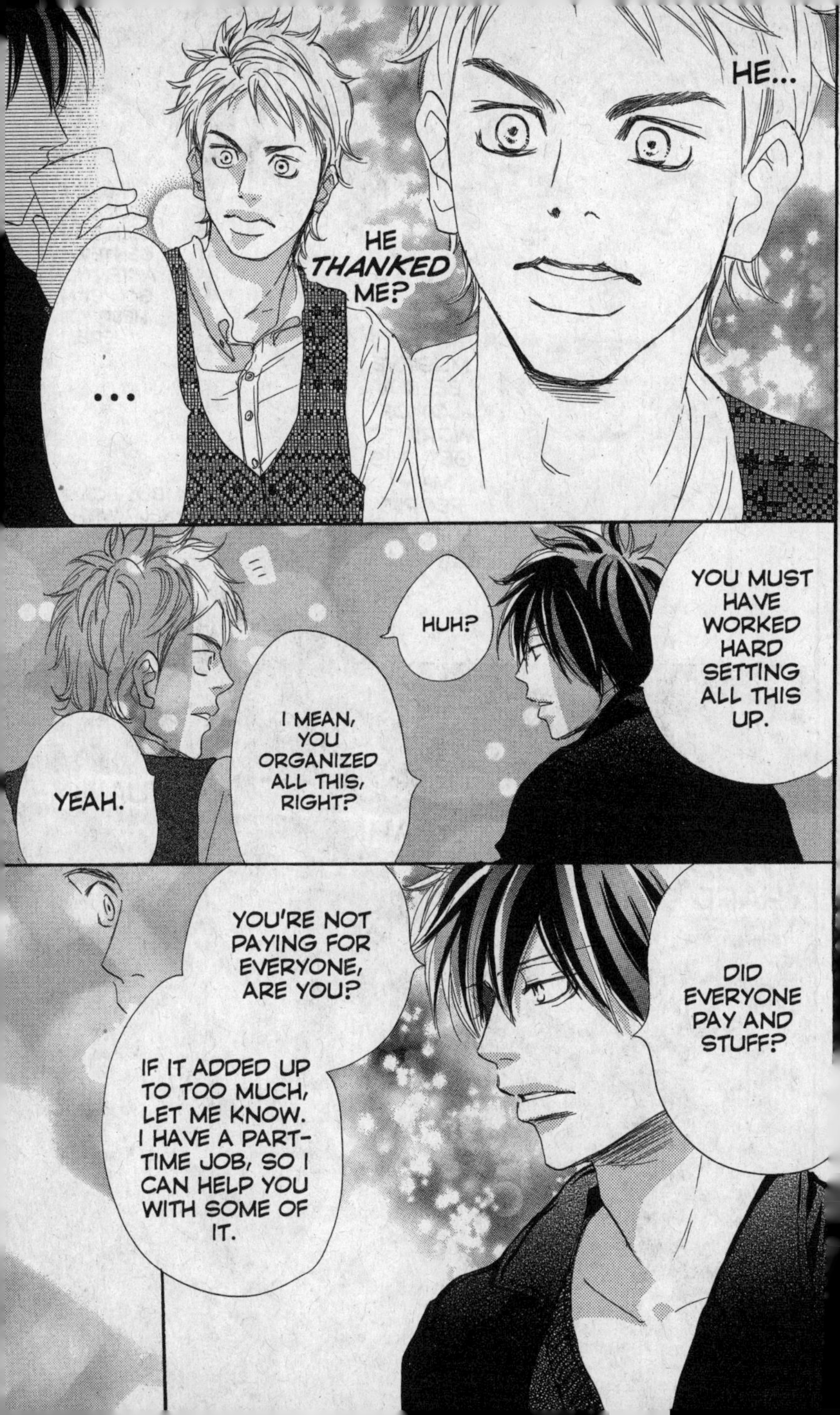
HE...
HE *THANKED* ME?
...
YOU MUST HAVE WORKED HARD SETTING ALL THIS UP.
HUH?
I MEAN, YOU ORGANIZED ALL THIS, RIGHT?
YEAH.
DID EVERYONE PAY AND STUFF?
YOU'RE NOT PAYING FOR EVERYONE, ARE YOU?
IF IT ADDED UP TO TOO MUCH, LET ME KNOW. I HAVE A PART-TIME JOB, SO I CAN HELP YOU WITH SOME OF IT.

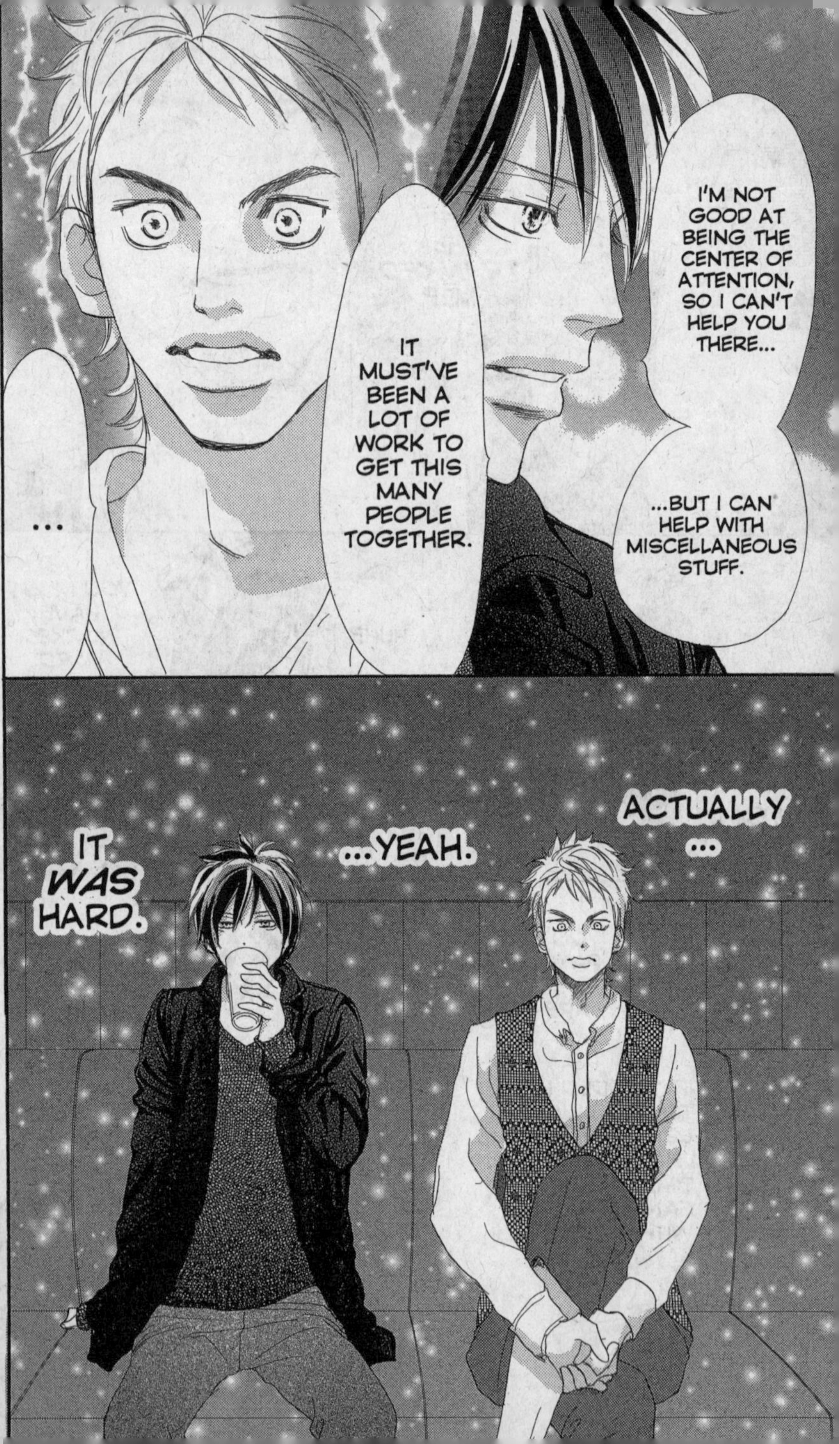
I'M NOT GOOD AT BEING THE CENTER OF ATTENTION, SO I CAN'T HELP YOU THERE...
...BUT I CAN HELP WITH MISCELLANEOUS STUFF.
IT MUST'VE BEEN A LOT OF WORK TO GET THIS MANY PEOPLE TOGETHER.
...
ACTUALLY...
...YEAH.
IT *WAS* HARD.

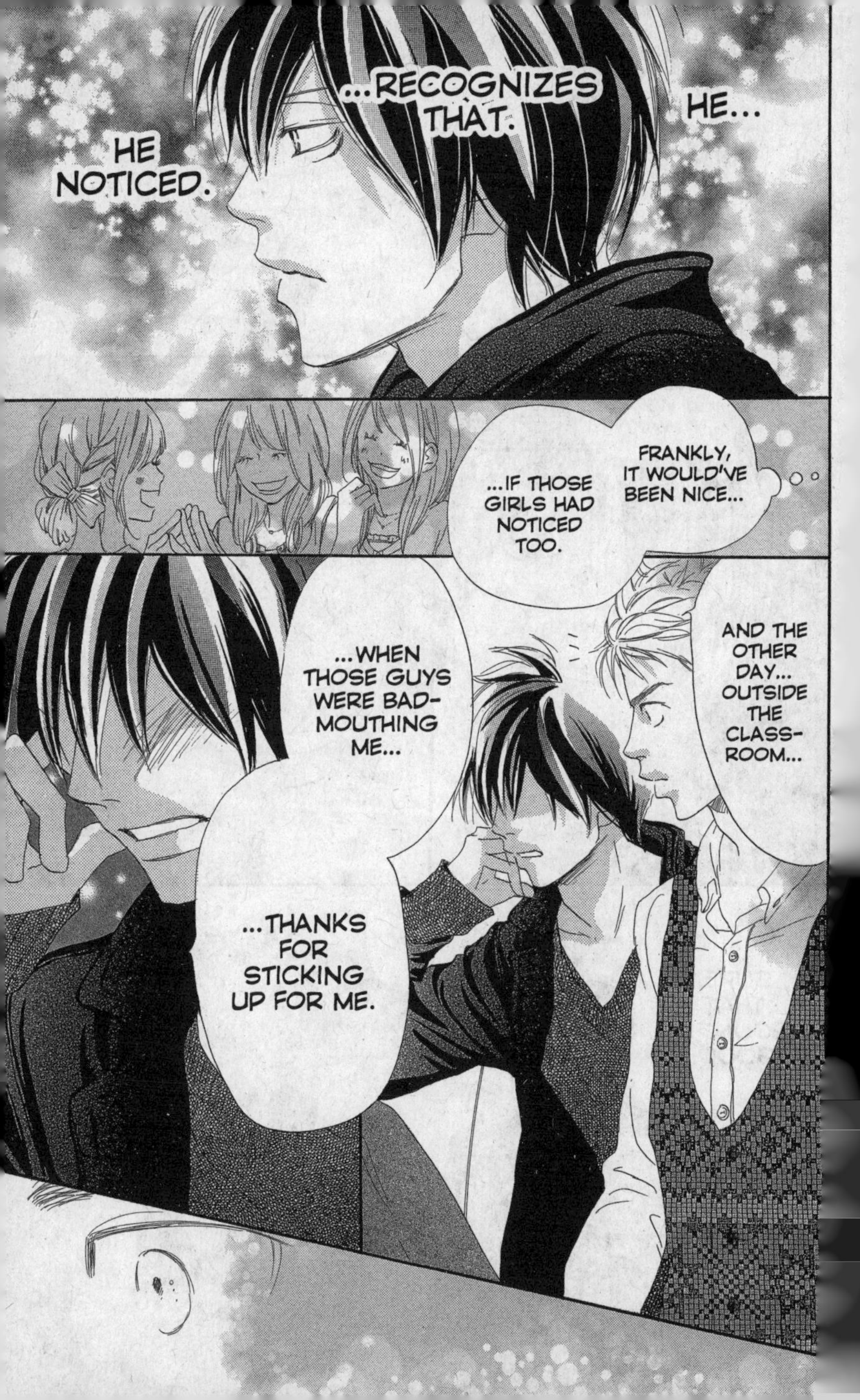
HE...
...RECOGNIZES THAT.
HE NOTICED.
FRANKLY, IT WOULD'VE BEEN NICE...
...IF THOSE GIRLS HAD NOTICED TOO.
AND THE OTHER DAY... OUTSIDE THE CLASS-ROOM...
...WHEN THOSE GUYS WERE BAD-MOUTHING ME...
...THANKS FOR STICKING UP FOR ME.

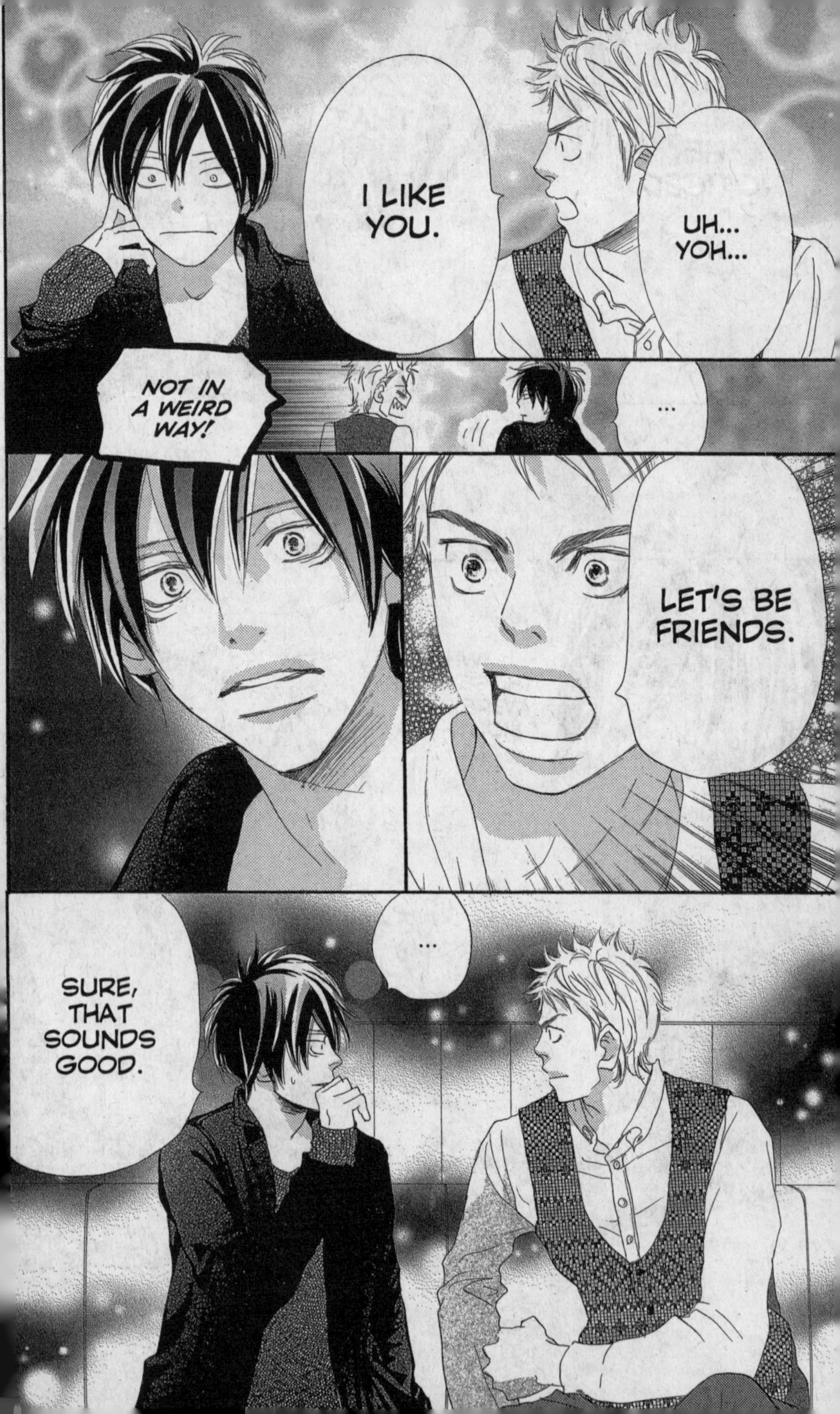
UH... YOH...
I LIKE YOU.
...
NOT IN A WEIRD WAY!
LET'S BE FRIENDS.
...
SURE, THAT SOUNDS GOOD.

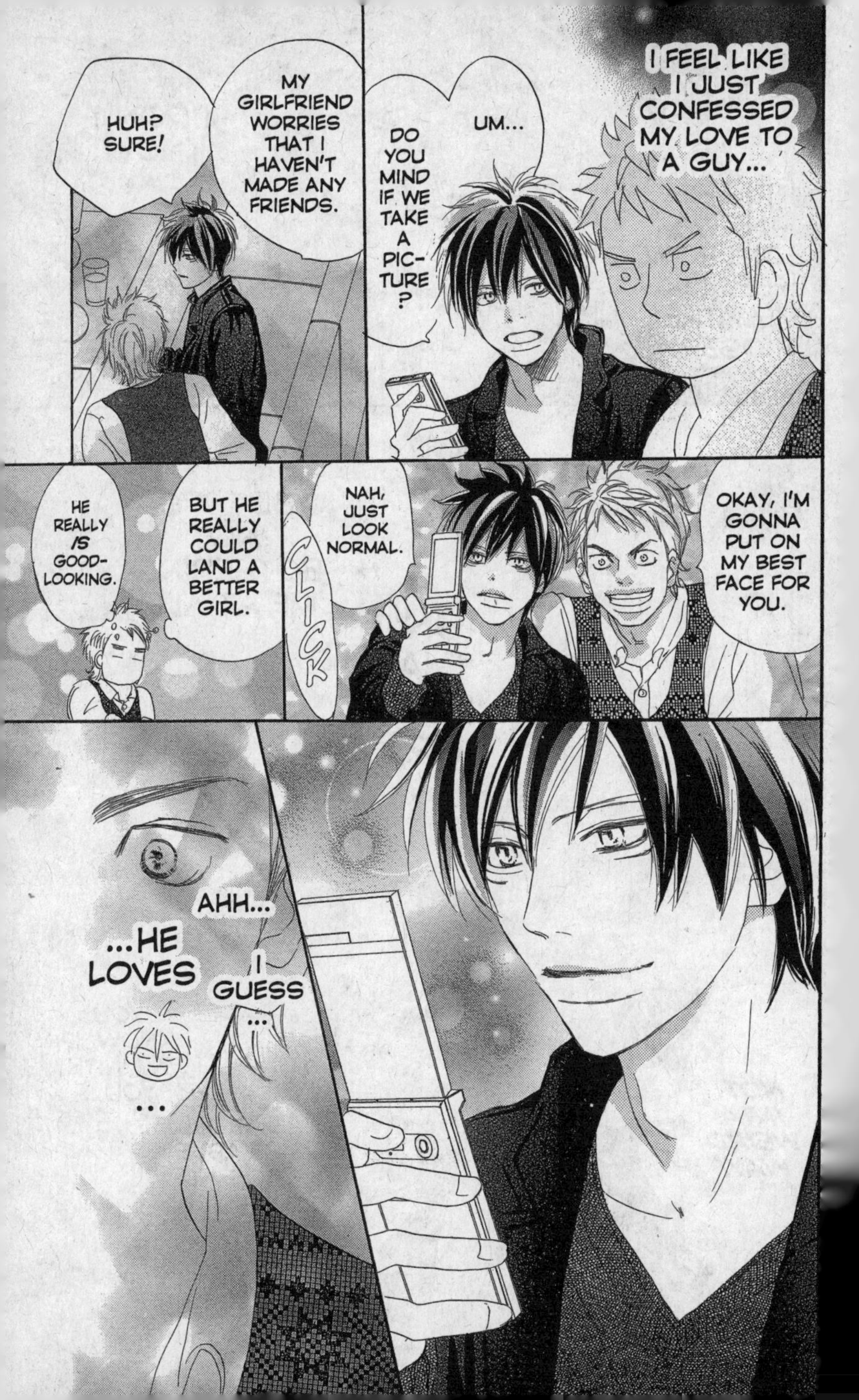
I FEEL LIKE I JUST CONFESSED MY LOVE TO A GUY...
UM...
DO YOU MIND IF WE TAKE A PIC-TURE?
MY GIRLFRIEND WORRIES THAT I HAVEN'T MADE ANY FRIENDS.
HUH? SURE!
OKAY, I'M GONNA PUT ON MY BEST FACE FOR YOU.
NAH, JUST LOOK NORMAL.
CLICK
BUT HE REALLY COULD LAND A BETTER GIRL.
HE REALLY IS GOOD-LOOKING.
AHH...
I GUESS...
...HE LOVES
...

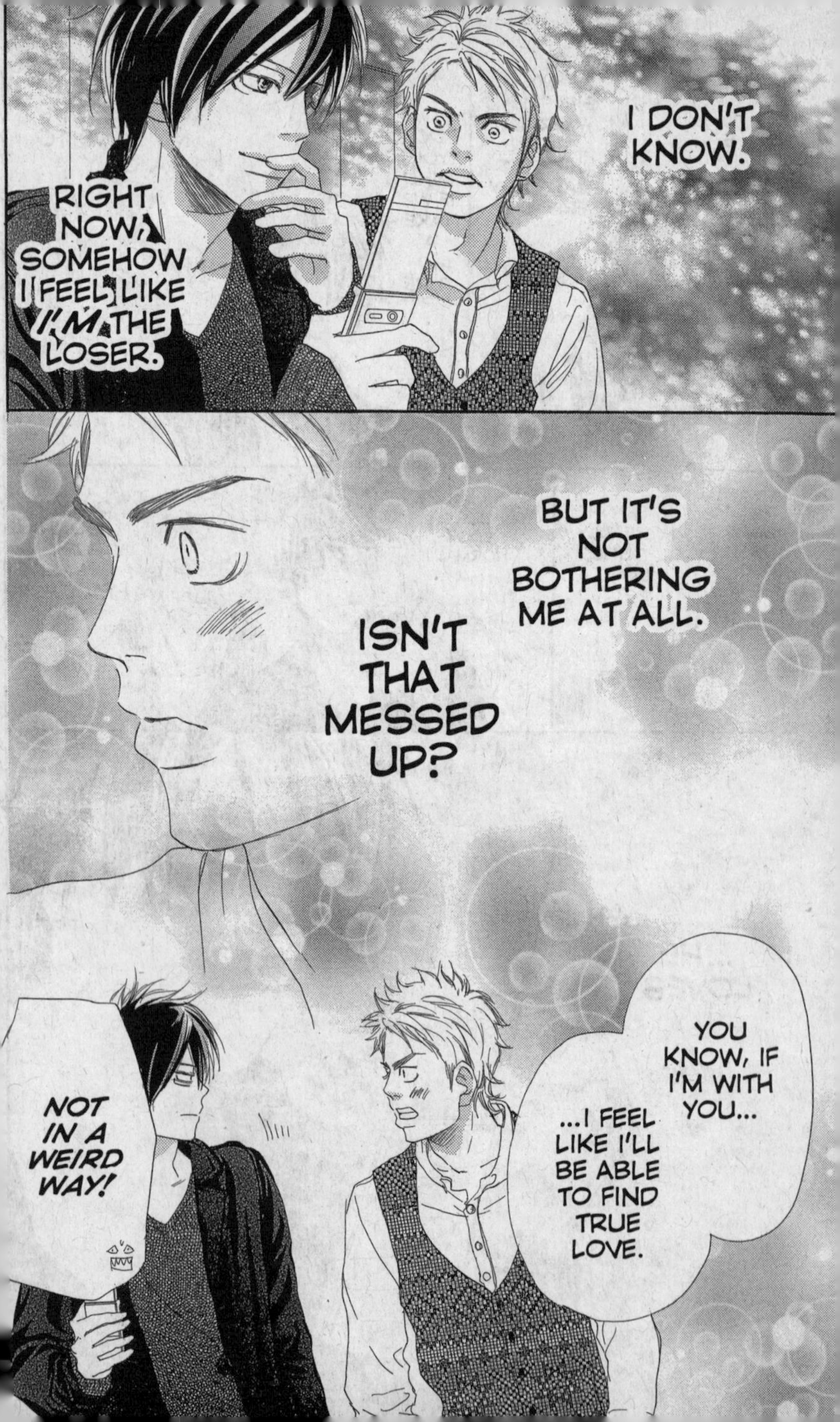

I DON'T KNOW.
RIGHT NOW, SOMEHOW I FEEL LIKE I'M THE LOSER.
BUT IT'S NOT BOTHERING ME AT ALL.
ISN'T THAT MESSED UP?
YOU KNOW, IF I'M WITH YOU...
...I FEEL LIKE I'LL BE ABLE TO FIND TRUE LOVE.
NOT IN A WEIRD WAY!

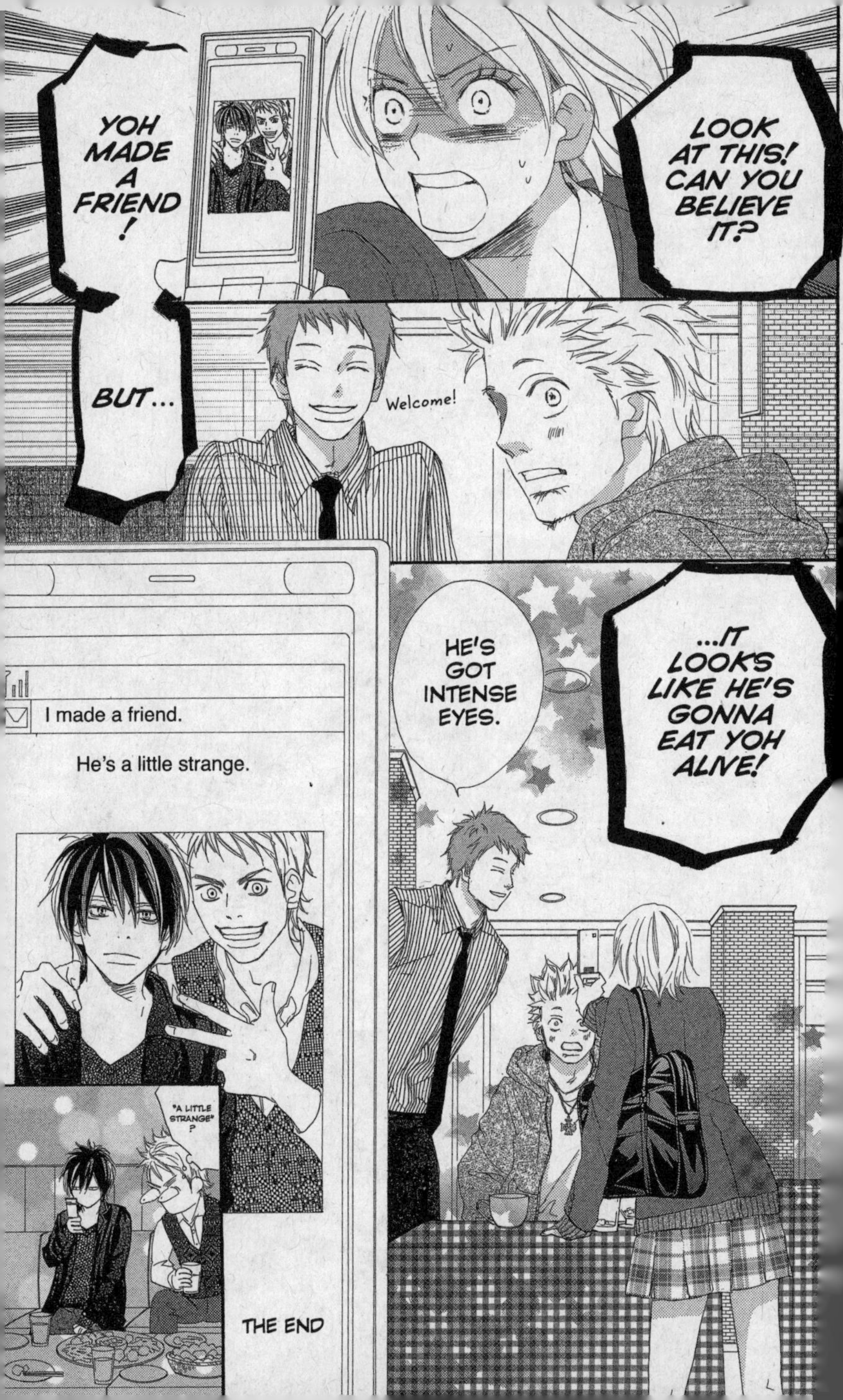
LOOK AT THIS! CAN YOU BELIEVE IT?
YOH MADE A FRIEND!
Welcome!
BUT...
...IT LOOKS LIKE HE'S GONNA EAT YOH ALIVE!
HE'S GOT INTENSE EYES.
I made a friend.
He's a little strange.
"A LITTLE STRANGE"?
THE END

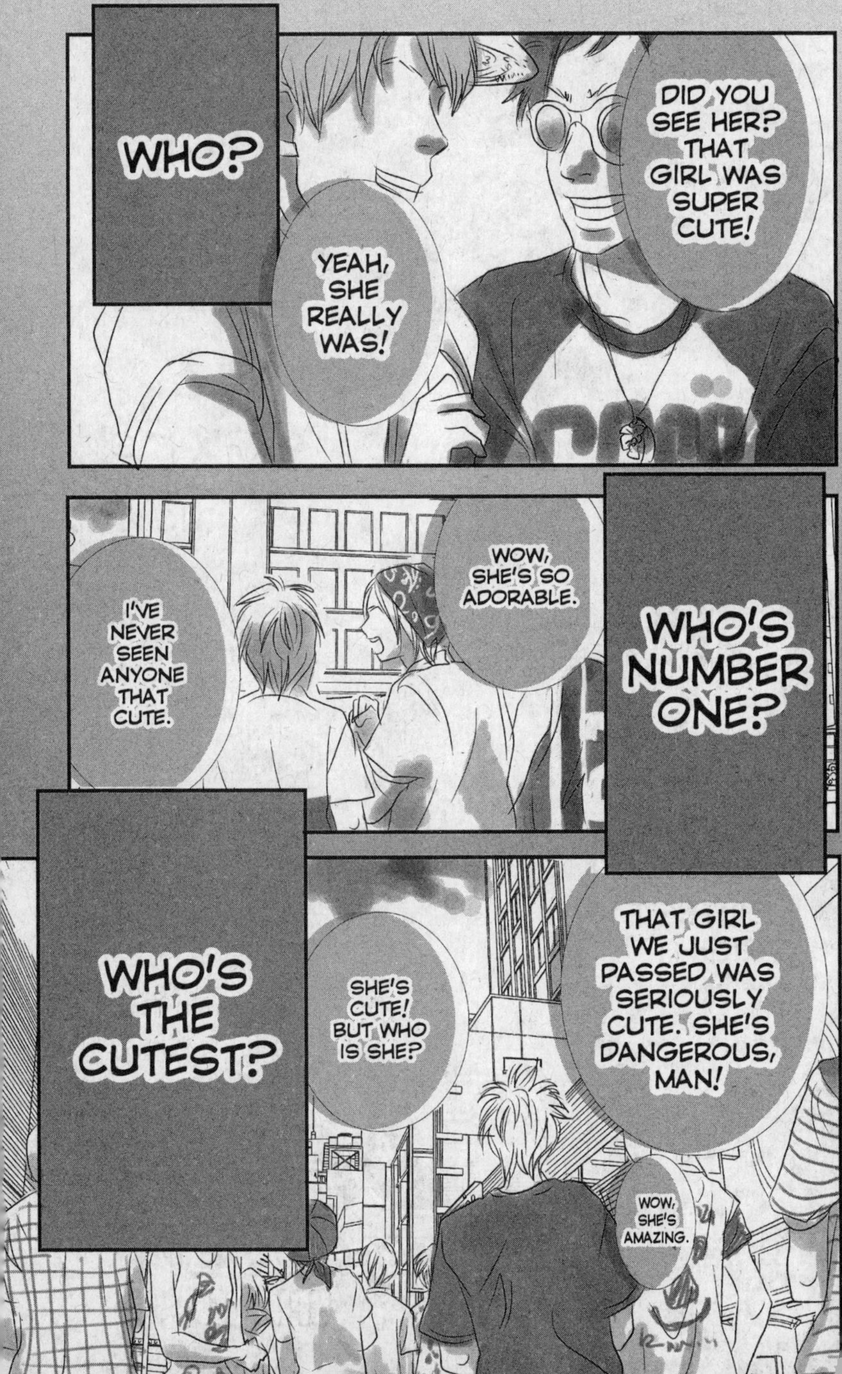
DID YOU SEE HER? THAT GIRL WAS SUPER CUTE!
WHO?
YEAH, SHE REALLY WAS!
WHO'S NUMBER ONE?
WOW, SHE'S SO ADORABLE.
I'VE NEVER SEEN ANYONE THAT CUTE.
THAT GIRL WE JUST PASSED WAS SERIOUSLY CUTE. SHE'S DANGEROUS, MAN!
WOW, SHE'S AMAZING.
SHE'S CUTE! BUT WHO IS SHE?
WHO'S THE CUTEST?

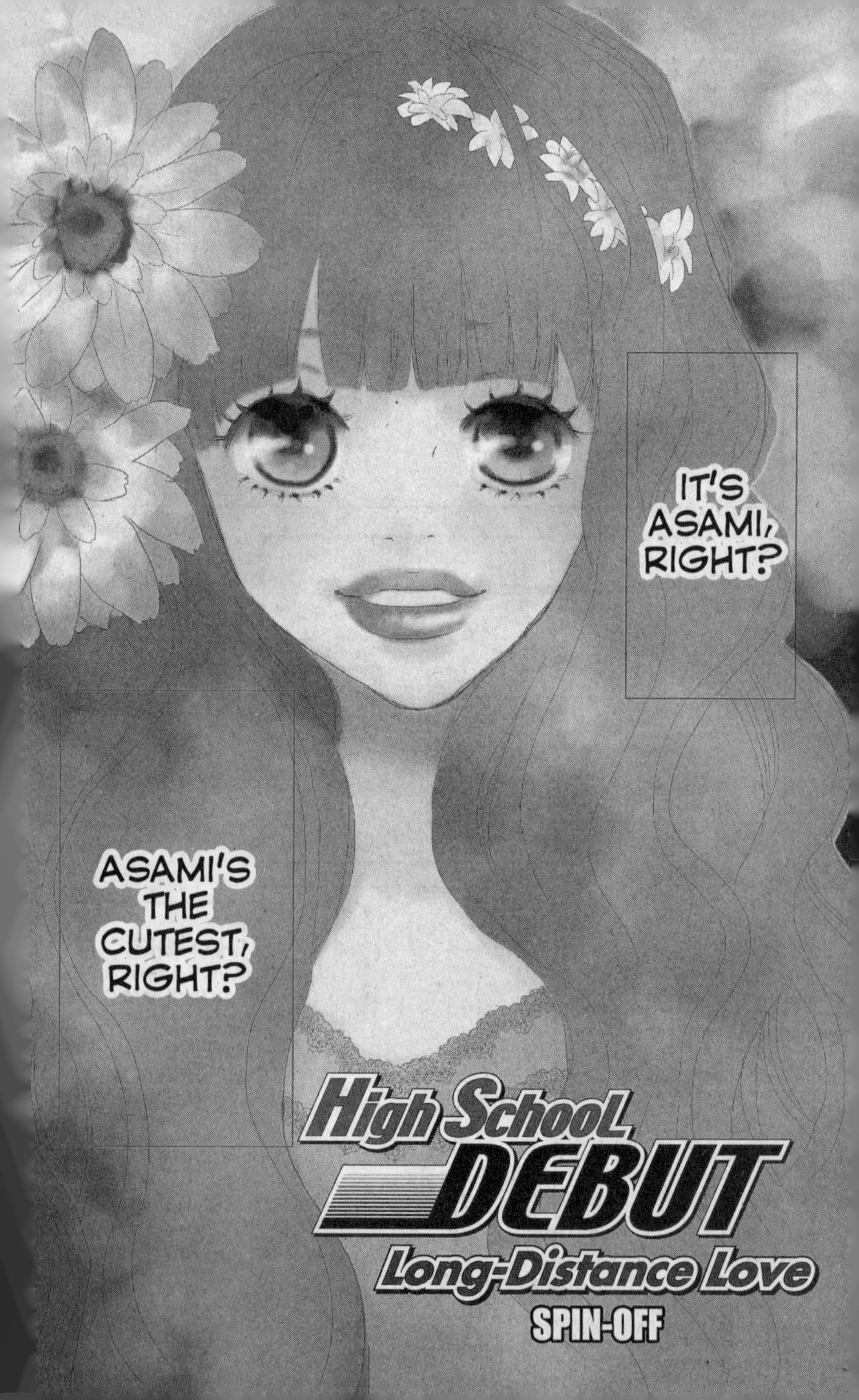

IT'S ASAMI, RIGHT?
ASAMI'S THE CUTEST, RIGHT?
High School DEBUT
Long-Distance Love
SPIN-OFF

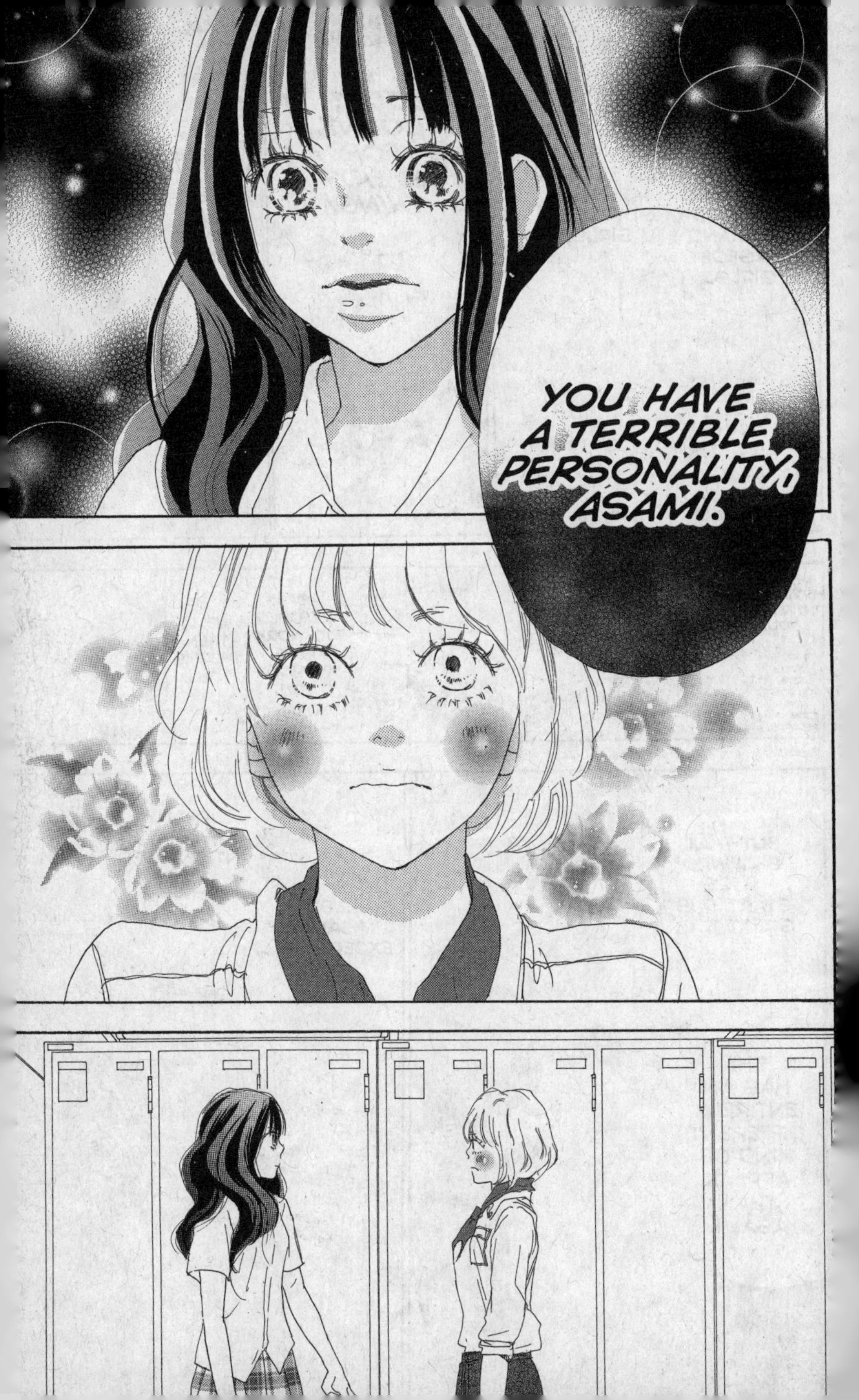
YOU HAVE A TERRIBLE PERSONALITY, ASAMI.

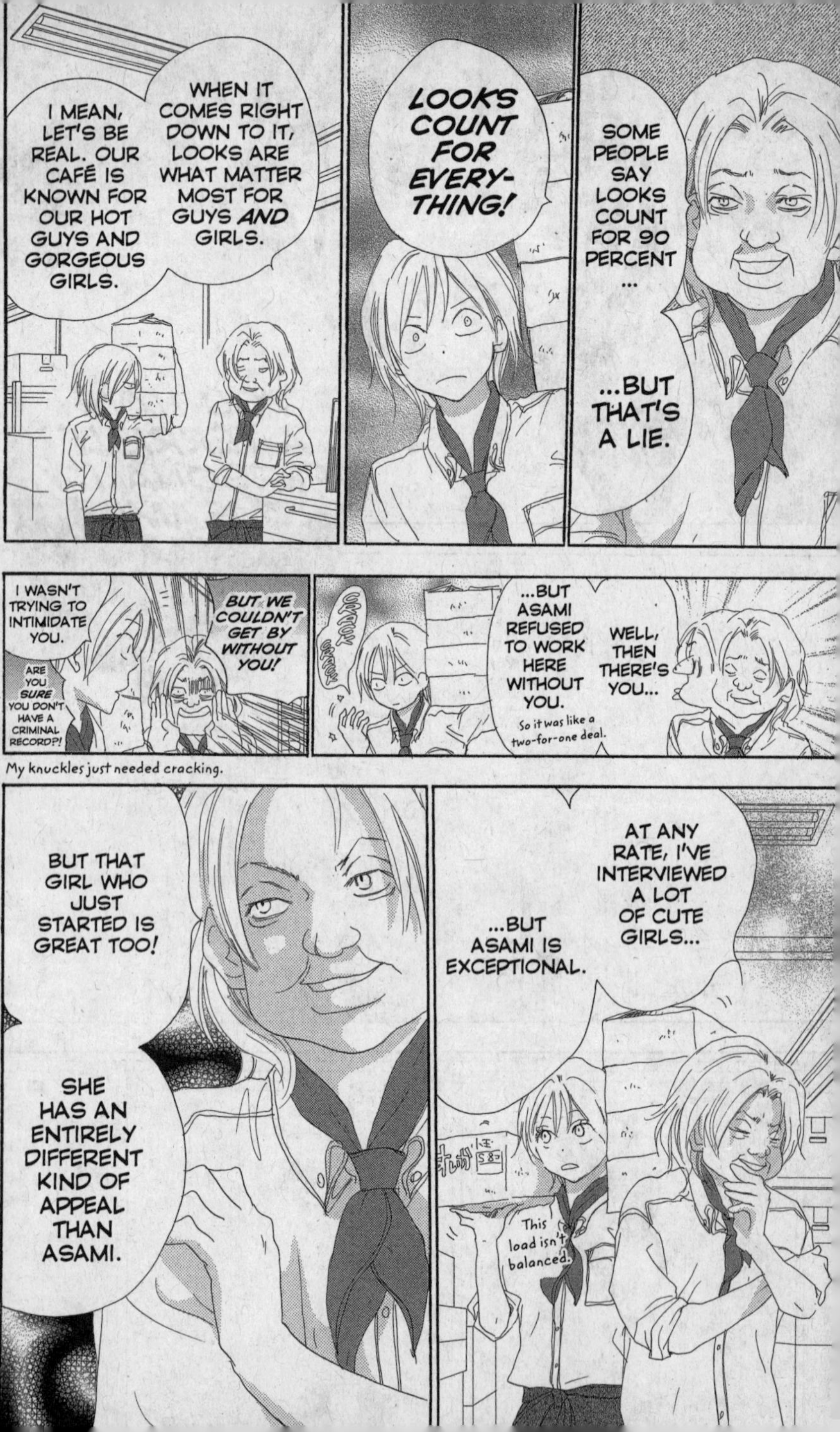
SOME PEOPLE SAY LOOKS COUNT FOR 90 PERCENT...
...BUT THAT'S A LIE.
LOOKS COUNT FOR EVERYTHING!
WHEN IT COMES RIGHT DOWN TO IT, LOOKS ARE WHAT MATTER MOST FOR GUYS AND GIRLS.
I MEAN, LET'S BE REAL. OUR CAFÉ IS KNOWN FOR OUR HOT GUYS AND GORGEOUS GIRLS.
WELL, THEN THERE'S YOU...
...BUT ASAMI REFUSED TO WORK HERE WITHOUT YOU.
So it was like a two-for-one deal.
BUT WE COULDN'T GET BY WITHOUT YOU!
I WASN'T TRYING TO INTIMIDATE YOU.
ARE YOU SURE YOU DON'T HAVE A CRIMINAL RECORD?!
My knuckles just needed cracking.
AT ANY RATE, I'VE INTERVIEWED A LOT OF CUTE GIRLS...
...BUT ASAMI IS EXCEPTIONAL.
This load isn't balanced.
BUT THAT GIRL WHO JUST STARTED IS GREAT TOO!
SHE HAS AN ENTIRELY DIFFERENT KIND OF APPEAL THAN ASAMI.

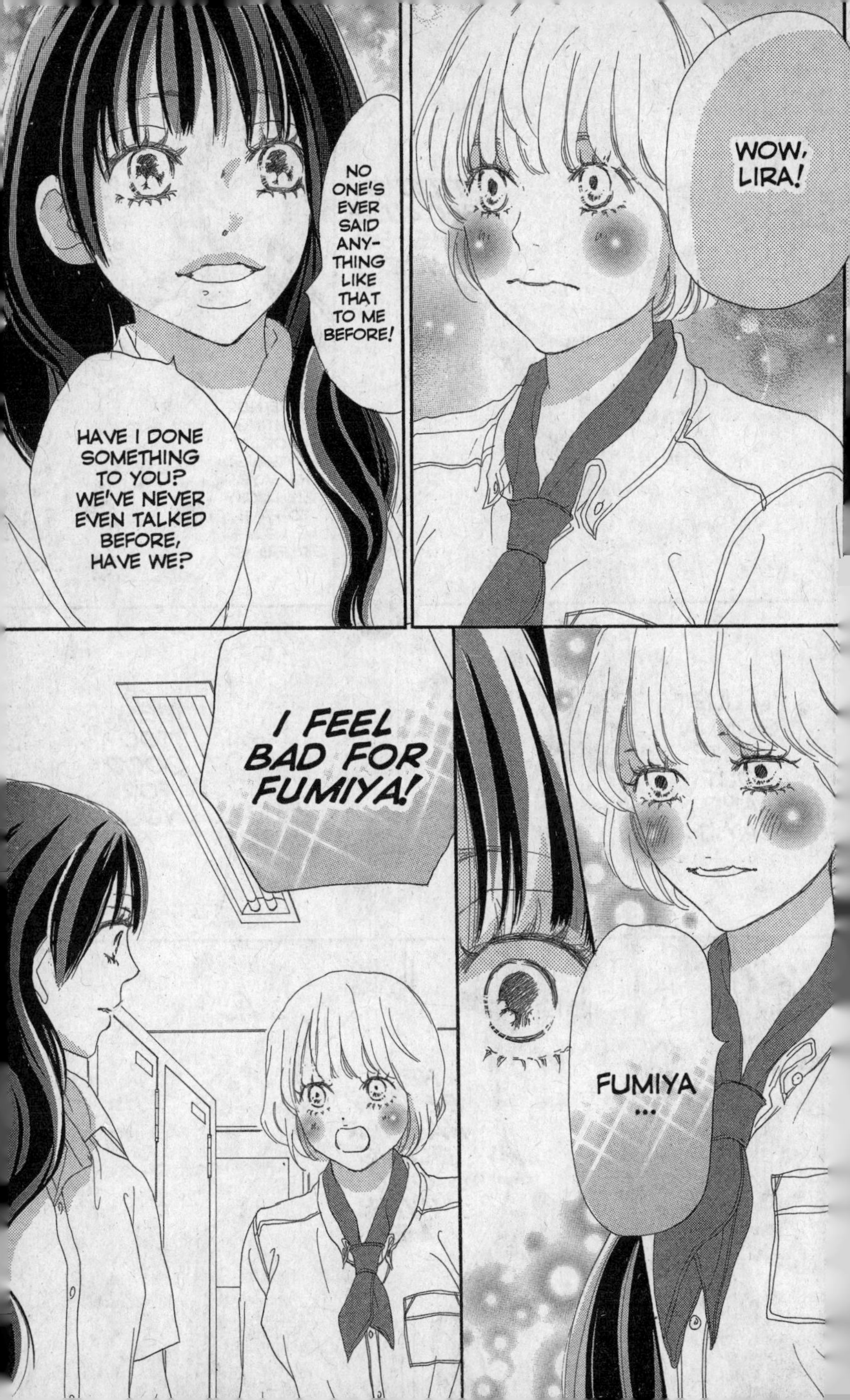
WOW, LIRA!
NO ONE'S EVER SAID ANYTHING LIKE THAT TO ME BEFORE!
HAVE I DONE SOMETHING TO YOU? WE'VE NEVER EVEN TALKED BEFORE, HAVE WE?
FUMIYA...
I FEEL BAD FOR FUMIYA!

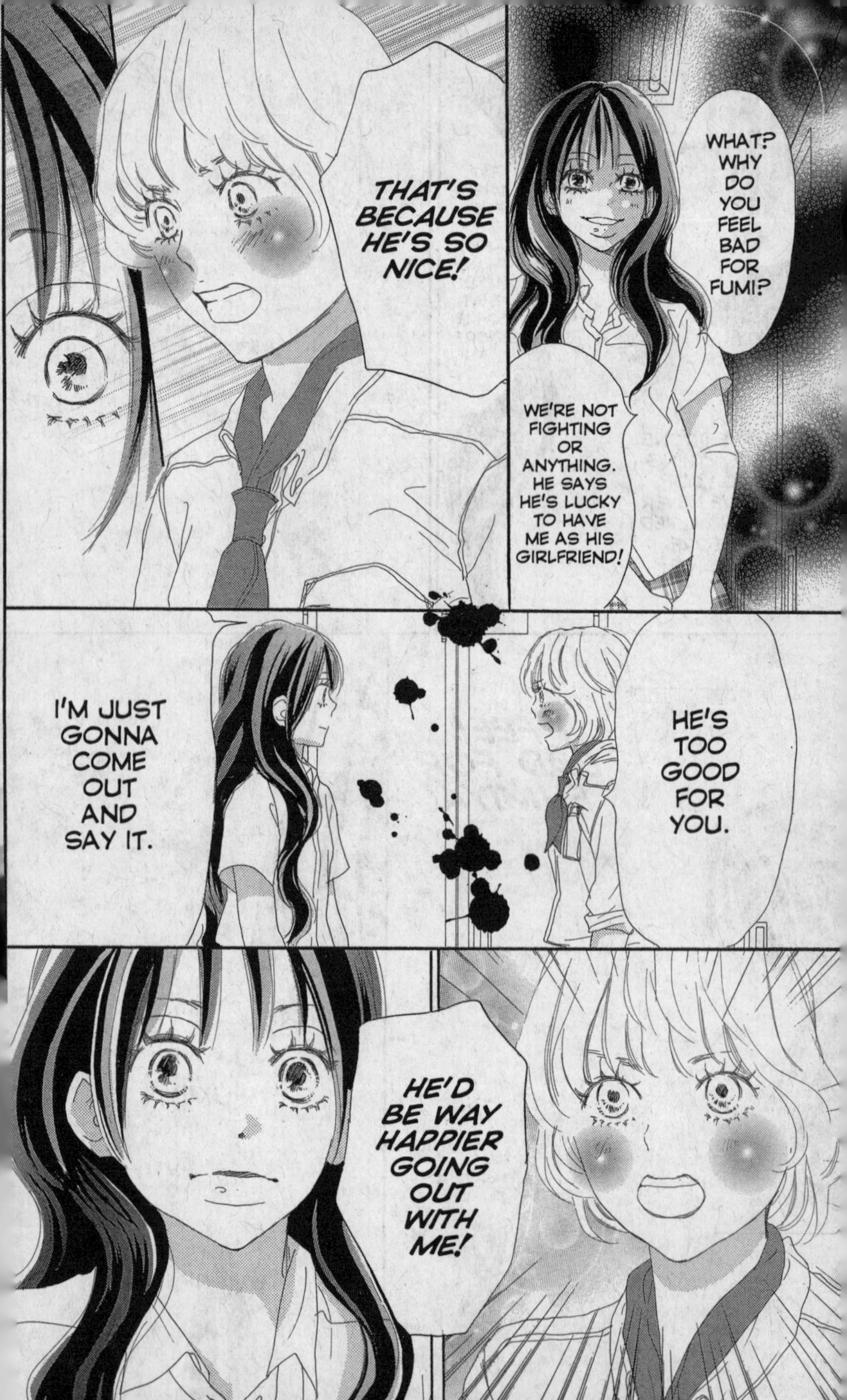
WHAT? WHY DO YOU FEEL BAD FOR FUMI?
WE'RE NOT FIGHTING OR ANYTHING. HE SAYS HE'S LUCKY TO HAVE ME AS HIS GIRLFRIEND!
THAT'S BECAUSE HE'S SO NICE!
HE'S TOO GOOD FOR YOU.
I'M JUST GONNA COME OUT AND SAY IT.
HE'D BE WAY HAPPIER GOING OUT WITH ME!

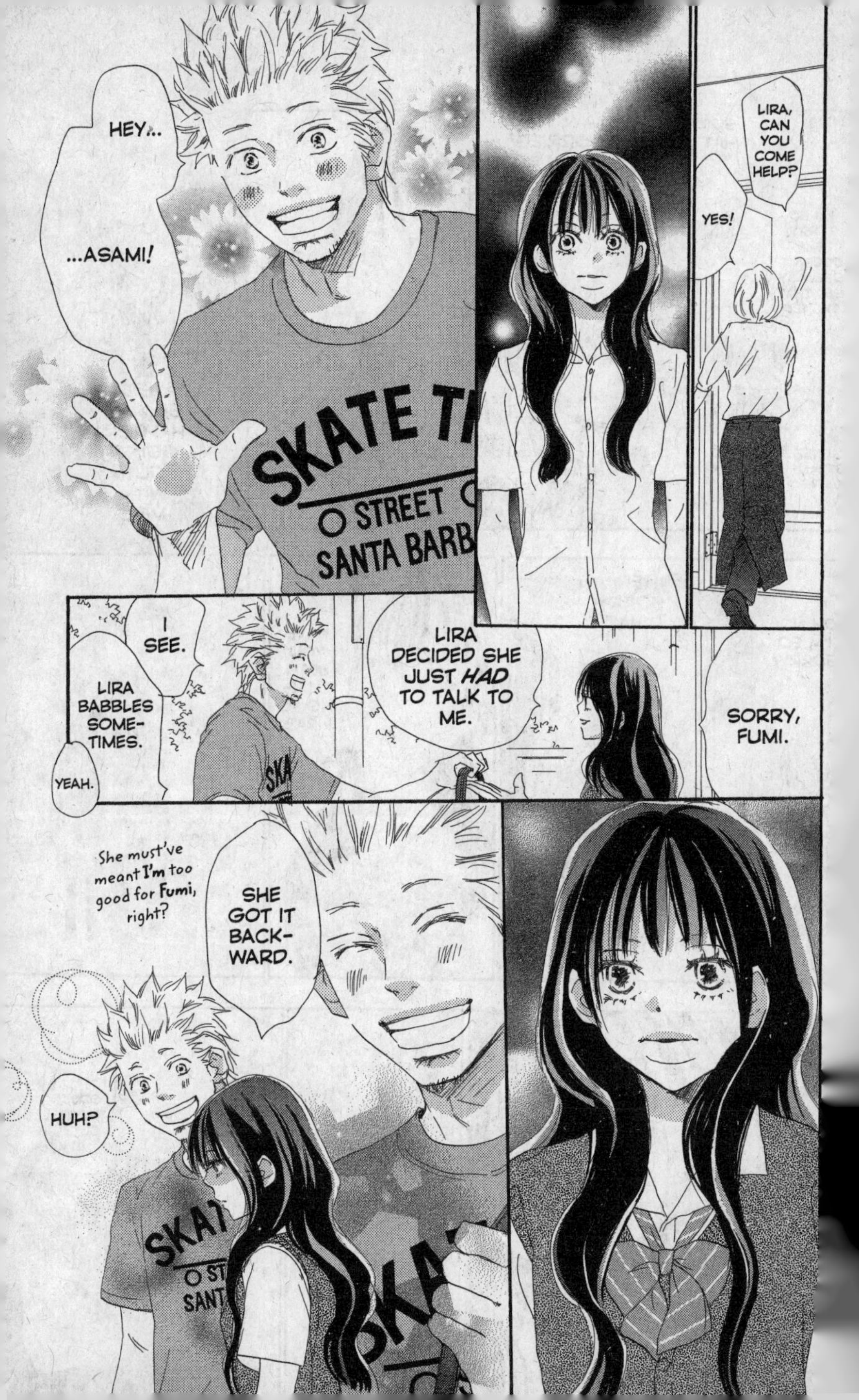
LIRA, CAN YOU COME HELP?
YES!
HEY...
...ASAMI!
SORRY, FUMI.
LIRA DECIDED SHE JUST HAD TO TALK TO ME.
I SEE.
LIRA BABBLES SOMETIMES.
YEAH.
SHE GOT IT BACKWARD.
She must've meant I'm too good for Fumi, right?
HUH?

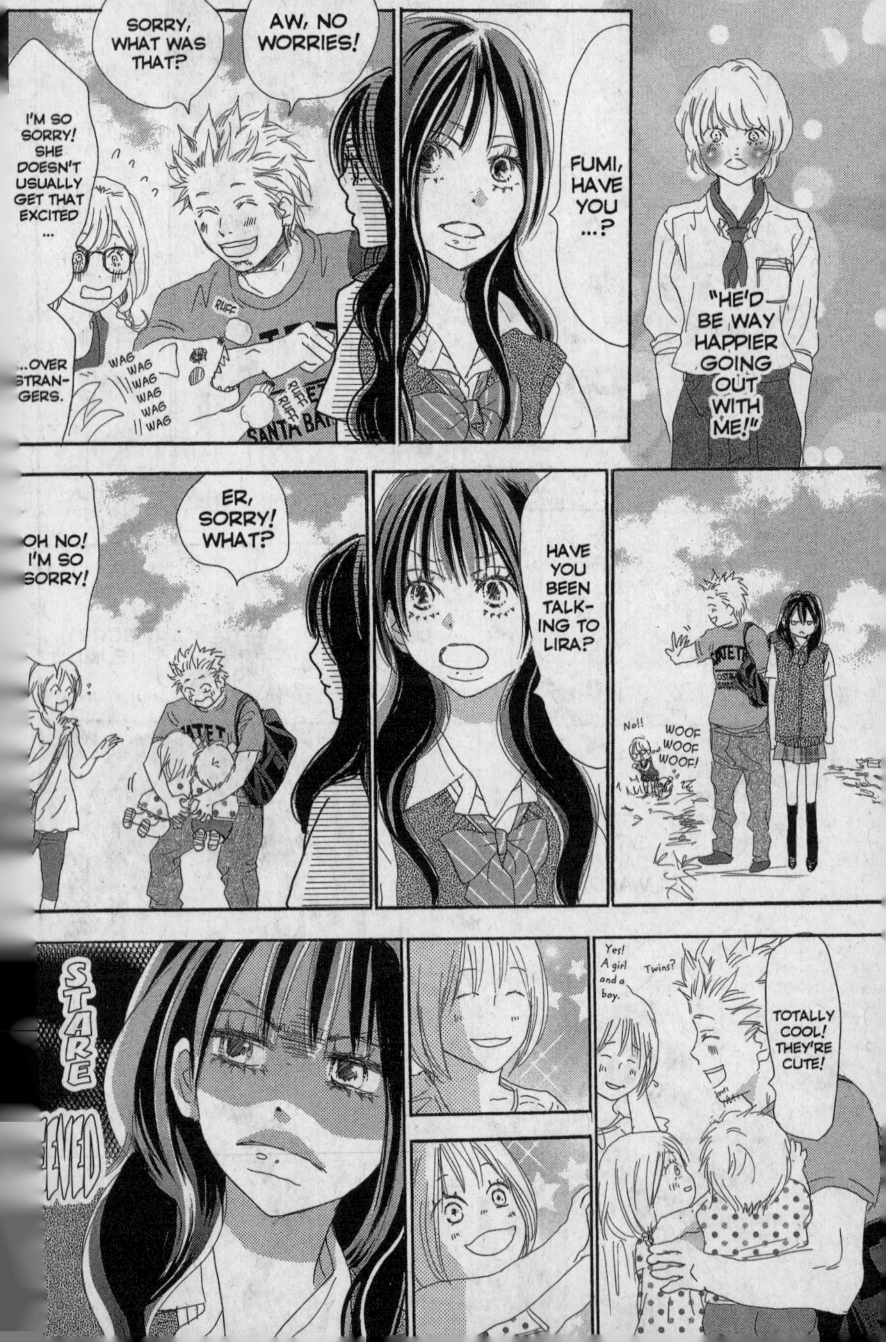
"HE'D BE WAY HAPPIER GOING OUT WITH ME!"
FUMI, HAVE YOU ...?
AW, NO WORRIES!
SORRY, WHAT WAS THAT?
I'M SO SORRY! SHE DOESN'T USUALLY GET THAT EXCITED ...
RUFF
WAG WAG WAG WAG WAG WAG
RUFF RUFF
...OVER STRANGERS.
No!!
WOOF WOOF WOOF!
HAVE YOU BEEN TALKING TO LIRA?
ER, SORRY! WHAT?
OH NO! I'M SO SORRY!
Twins?
Yes! A girl and a boy.
TOTALLY COOL! THEY'RE CUTE!
STARE

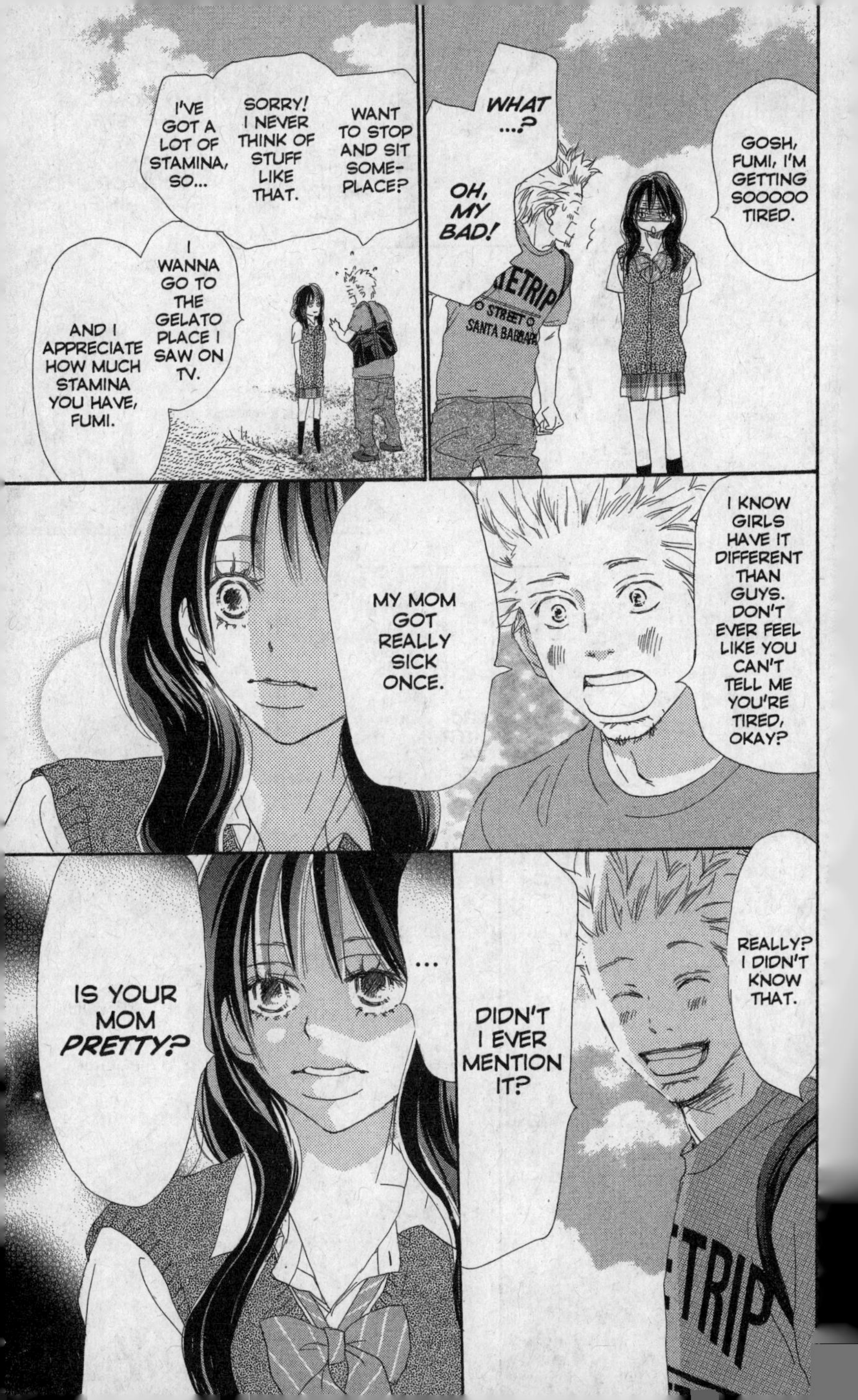
GOSH, FUMI, I'M GETTING SOOOOO TIRED.
WHAT ...?
OH, MY BAD!
WANT TO STOP AND SIT SOME-PLACE?
SORRY! I NEVER THINK OF STUFF LIKE THAT.
I'VE GOT A LOT OF STAMINA, SO...
I WANNA GO TO THE GELATO PLACE I SAW ON TV.
AND I APPRECIATE HOW MUCH STAMINA YOU HAVE, FUMI.
I KNOW GIRLS HAVE IT DIFFERENT THAN GUYS. DON'T EVER FEEL LIKE YOU CAN'T TELL ME YOU'RE TIRED, OKAY?
MY MOM GOT REALLY SICK ONCE.
REALLY? I DIDN'T KNOW THAT.
DIDN'T I EVER MENTION IT?
...
IS YOUR MOM *PRETTY?*

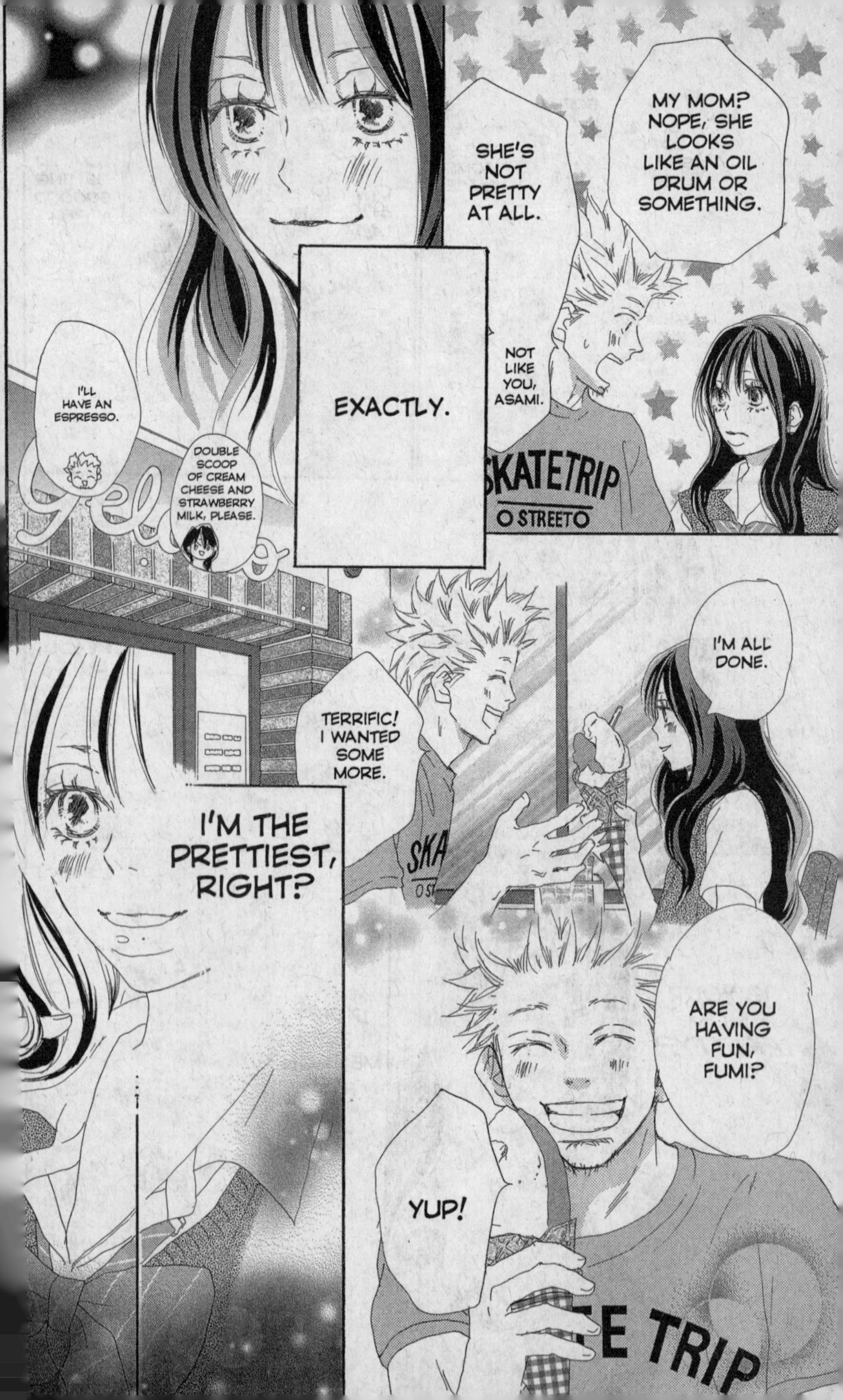
MY MOM? NOPE, SHE LOOKS LIKE AN OIL DRUM OR SOMETHING.
SHE'S NOT PRETTY AT ALL.
NOT LIKE YOU, ASAMI.
SKATETRIP
O STREETO
EXACTLY.
DOUBLE SCOOP OF CREAM CHEESE AND STRAWBERRY MILK, PLEASE.
I'LL HAVE AN ESPRESSO.
I'M ALL DONE.
TERRIFIC! I WANTED SOME MORE.
ARE YOU HAVING FUN, FUMI?
YUP!
I'M THE PRETTIEST, RIGHT?

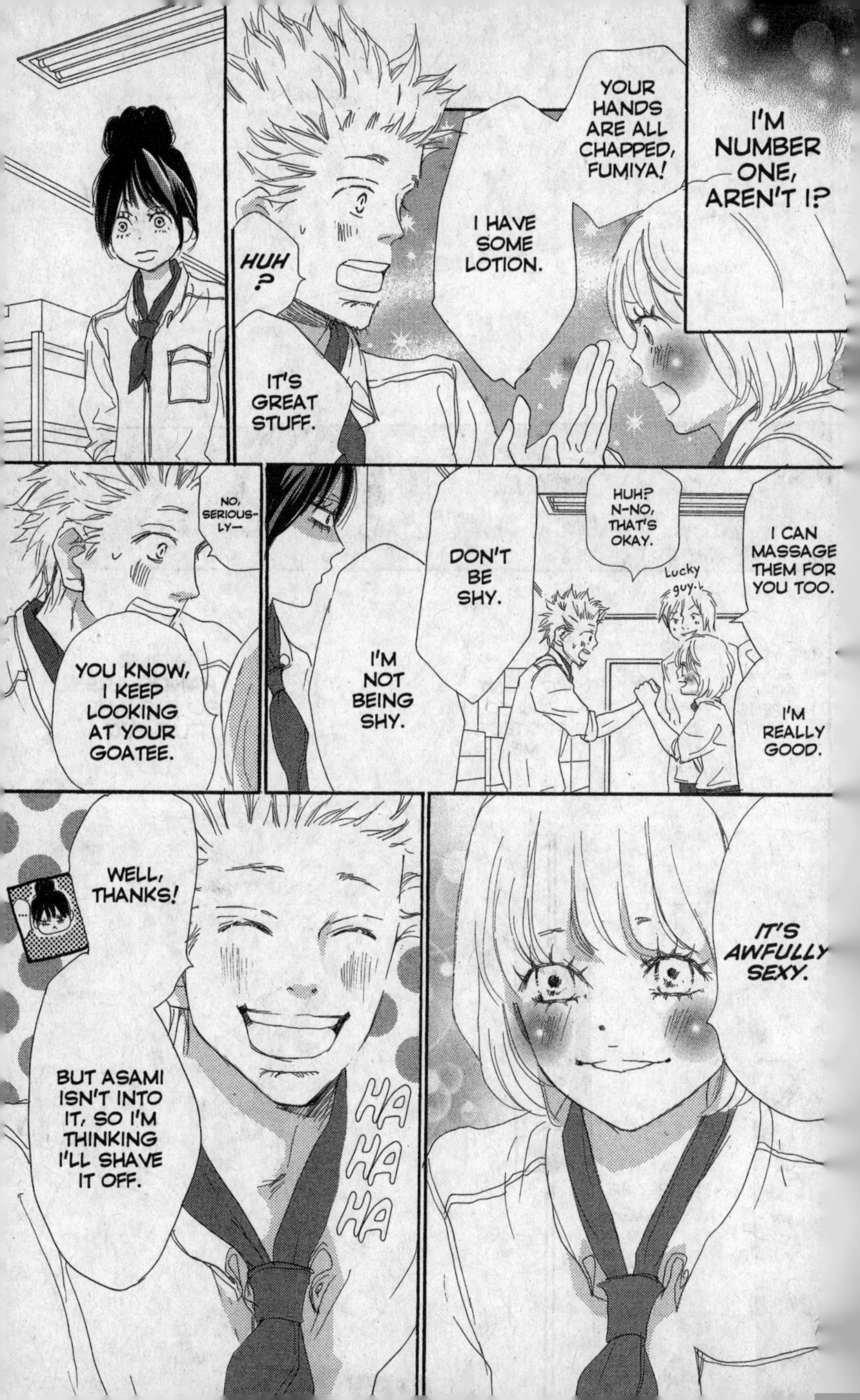
I'M NUMBER ONE, AREN'T I?
YOUR HANDS ARE ALL CHAPPED, FUMIYA!
I HAVE SOME LOTION.
HUH?
IT'S GREAT STUFF.
I CAN MASSAGE THEM FOR YOU TOO.
HUH? N-NO, THAT'S OKAY.
I'M REALLY GOOD.
Lucky guy.
DON'T BE SHY.
I'M NOT BEING SHY.
NO, SERIOUSLY—
YOU KNOW, I KEEP LOOKING AT YOUR GOATEE.
IT'S AWFULLY SEXY.
WELL, THANKS!
BUT ASAMI ISN'T INTO IT, SO I'M THINKING I'LL SHAVE IT OFF.
HA HA HA HA

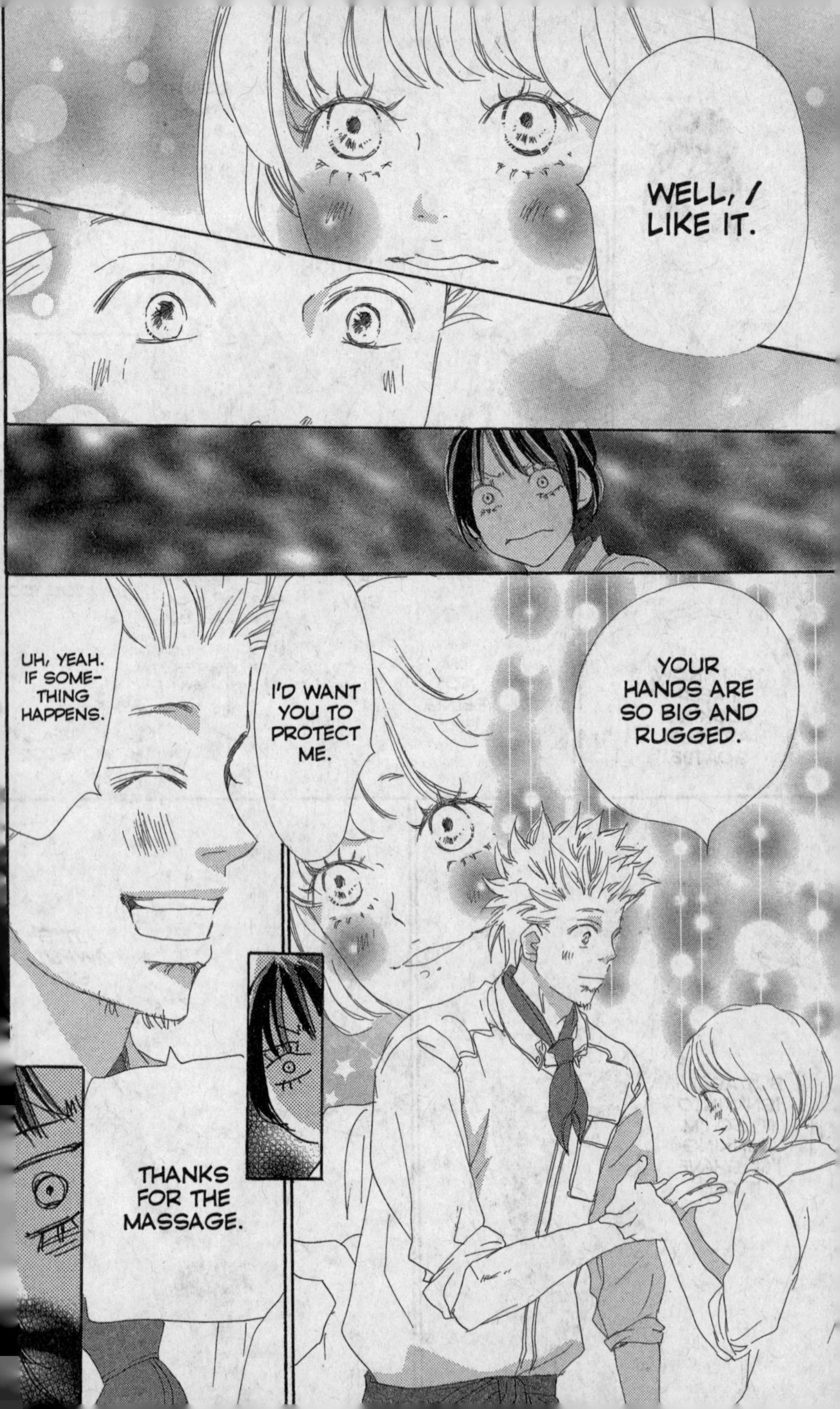
WELL, I LIKE IT.
YOUR HANDS ARE SO BIG AND RUGGED.
I'D WANT YOU TO PROTECT ME.
UH, YEAH. IF SOME-THING HAPPENS.
THANKS FOR THE MASSAGE.

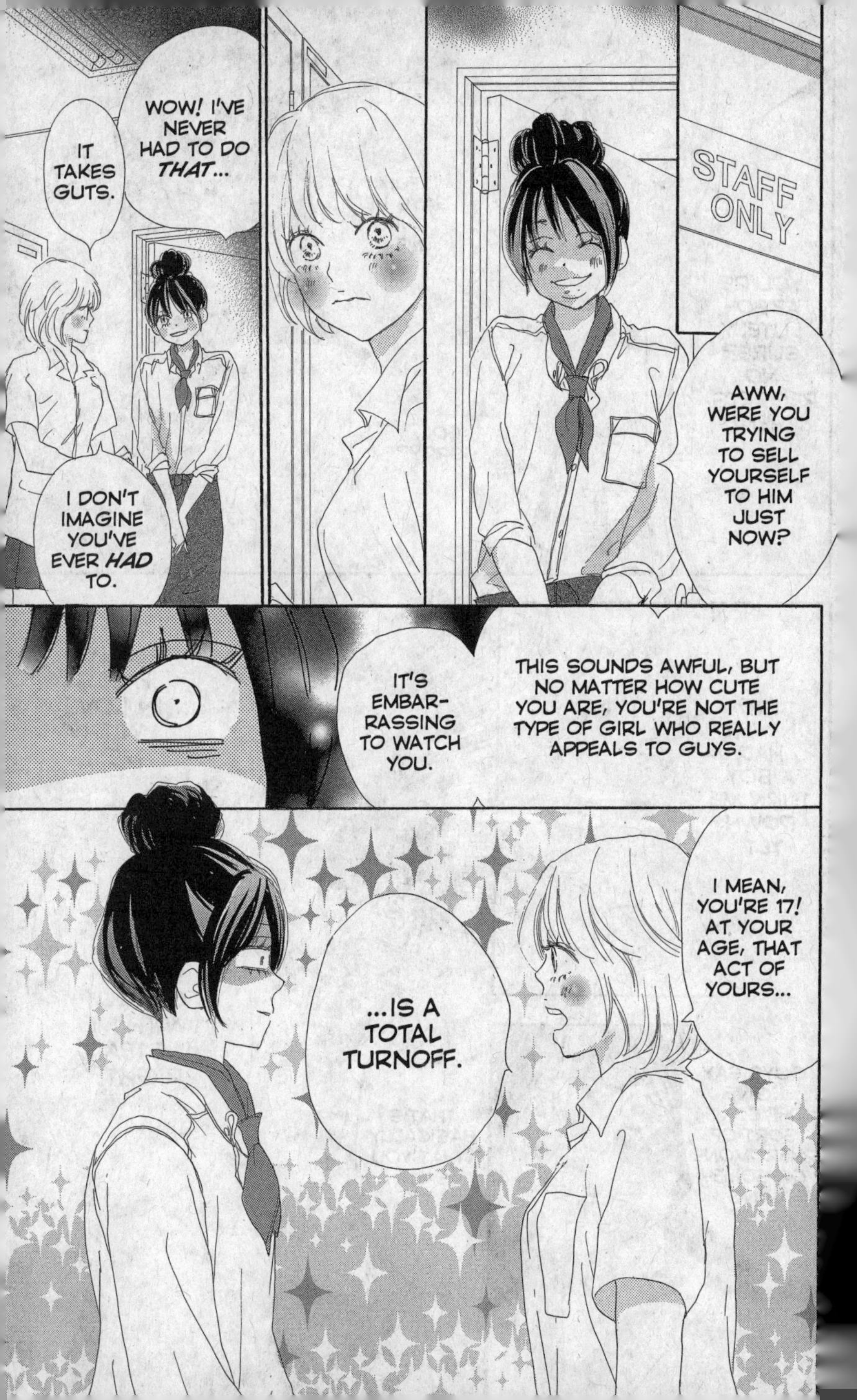
STAFF ONLY
AWW, WERE YOU TRYING TO SELL YOURSELF TO HIM JUST NOW?
WOW! I'VE NEVER HAD TO DO *THAT*...
IT TAKES GUTS.
I DON'T IMAGINE YOU'VE EVER *HAD* TO.
THIS SOUNDS AWFUL, BUT NO MATTER HOW CUTE YOU ARE, YOU'RE NOT THE TYPE OF GIRL WHO REALLY APPEALS TO GUYS.
IT'S EMBAR-RASSING TO WATCH YOU.
I MEAN, YOU'RE 17! AT YOUR AGE, THAT ACT OF YOURS...
...IS A TOTAL TURNOFF.

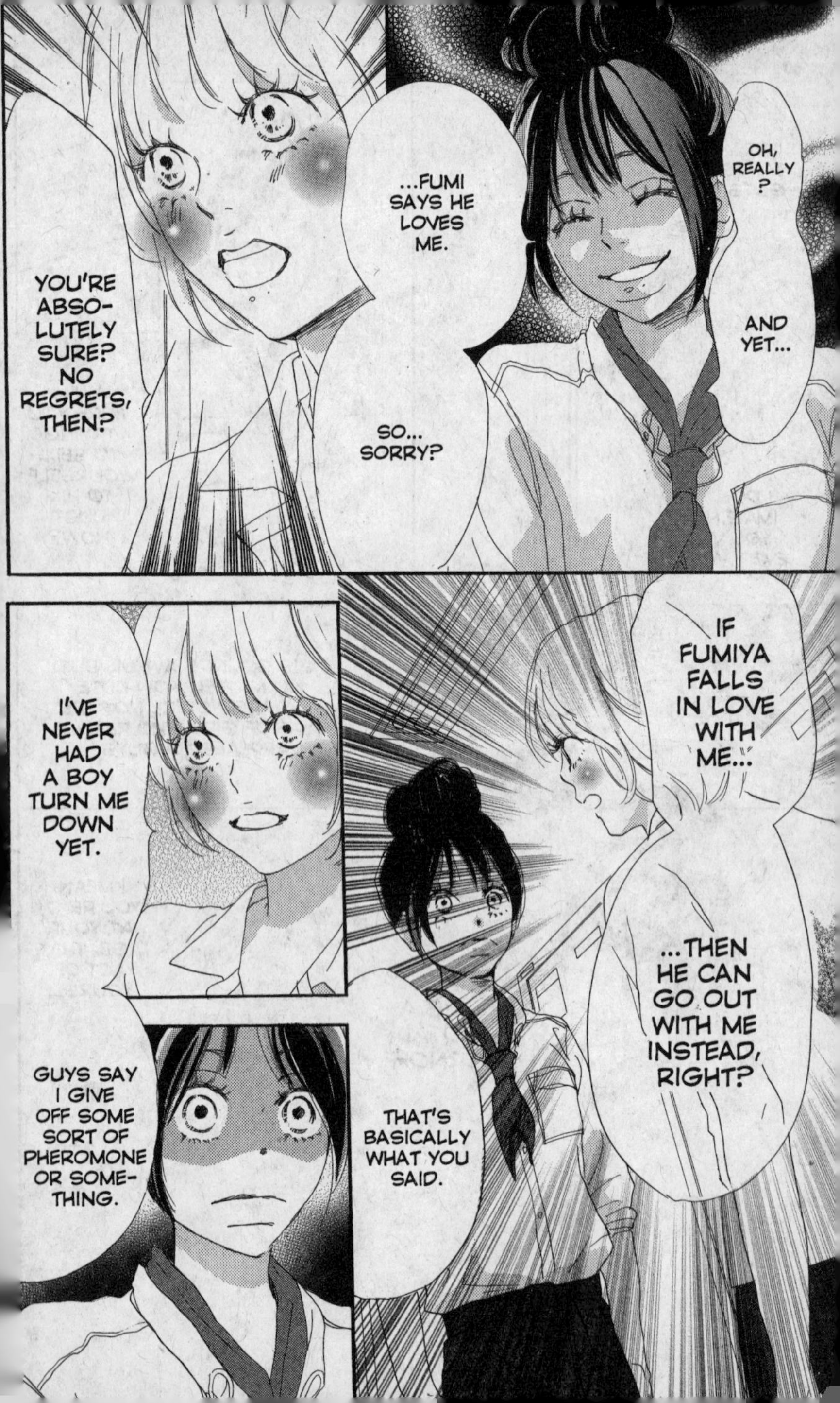
OH, REALLY?
AND YET...
...FUMI SAYS HE LOVES ME.
SO... SORRY?
YOU'RE ABSOLUTELY SURE? NO REGRETS, THEN?
IF FUMIYA FALLS IN LOVE WITH ME...
...THEN HE CAN GO OUT WITH ME INSTEAD, RIGHT?
THAT'S BASICALLY WHAT YOU SAID.
I'VE NEVER HAD A BOY TURN ME DOWN YET.
GUYS SAY I GIVE OFF SOME SORT OF PHEROMONE OR SOMETHING.

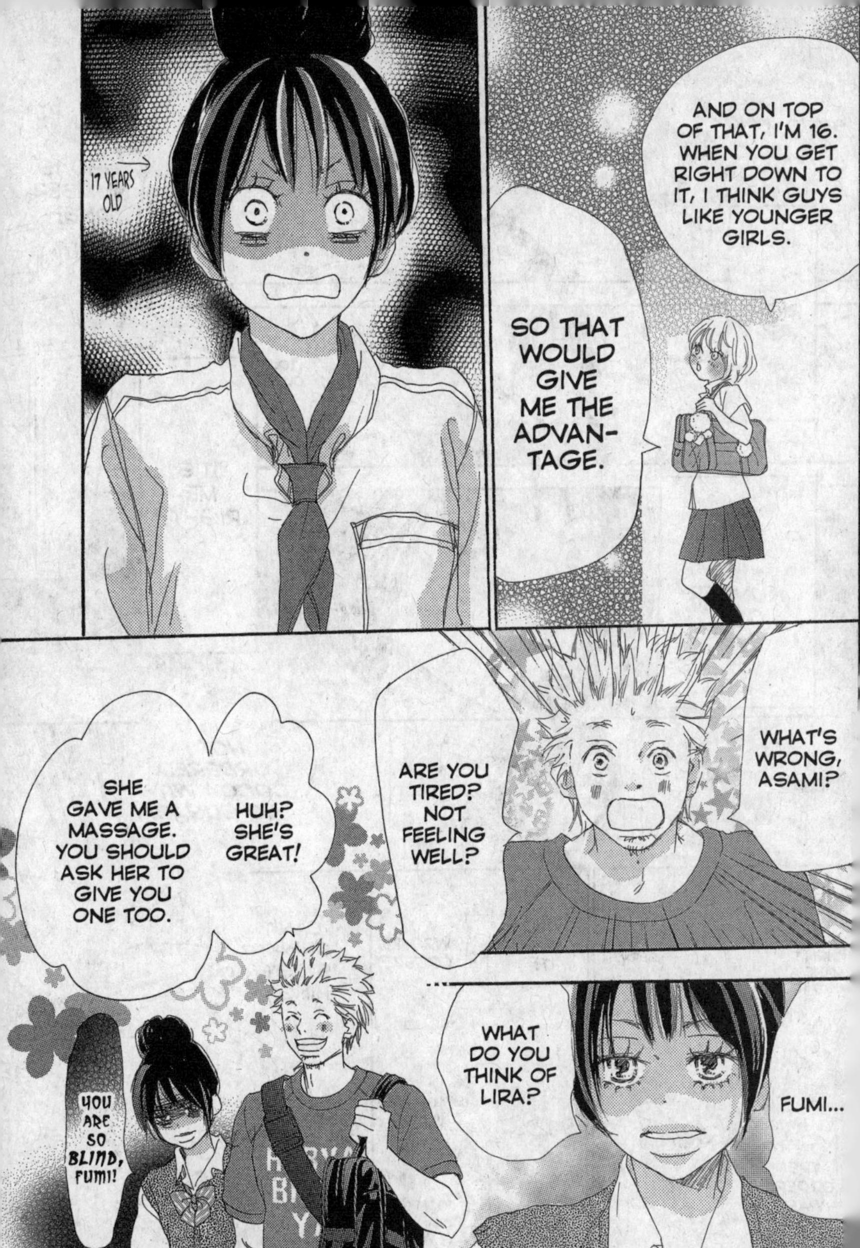
AND ON TOP OF THAT, I'M 16. WHEN YOU GET RIGHT DOWN TO IT, I THINK GUYS LIKE YOUNGER GIRLS.
SO THAT WOULD GIVE ME THE ADVANTAGE.
17 YEARS OLD
WHAT'S WRONG, ASAMI?
ARE YOU TIRED? NOT FEELING WELL?
...
FUMI...
WHAT DO YOU THINK OF LIRA?
HUH? SHE'S GREAT!
SHE GAVE ME A MASSAGE. YOU SHOULD ASK HER TO GIVE YOU ONE TOO.
YOU ARE SO BLIND, FUMI!

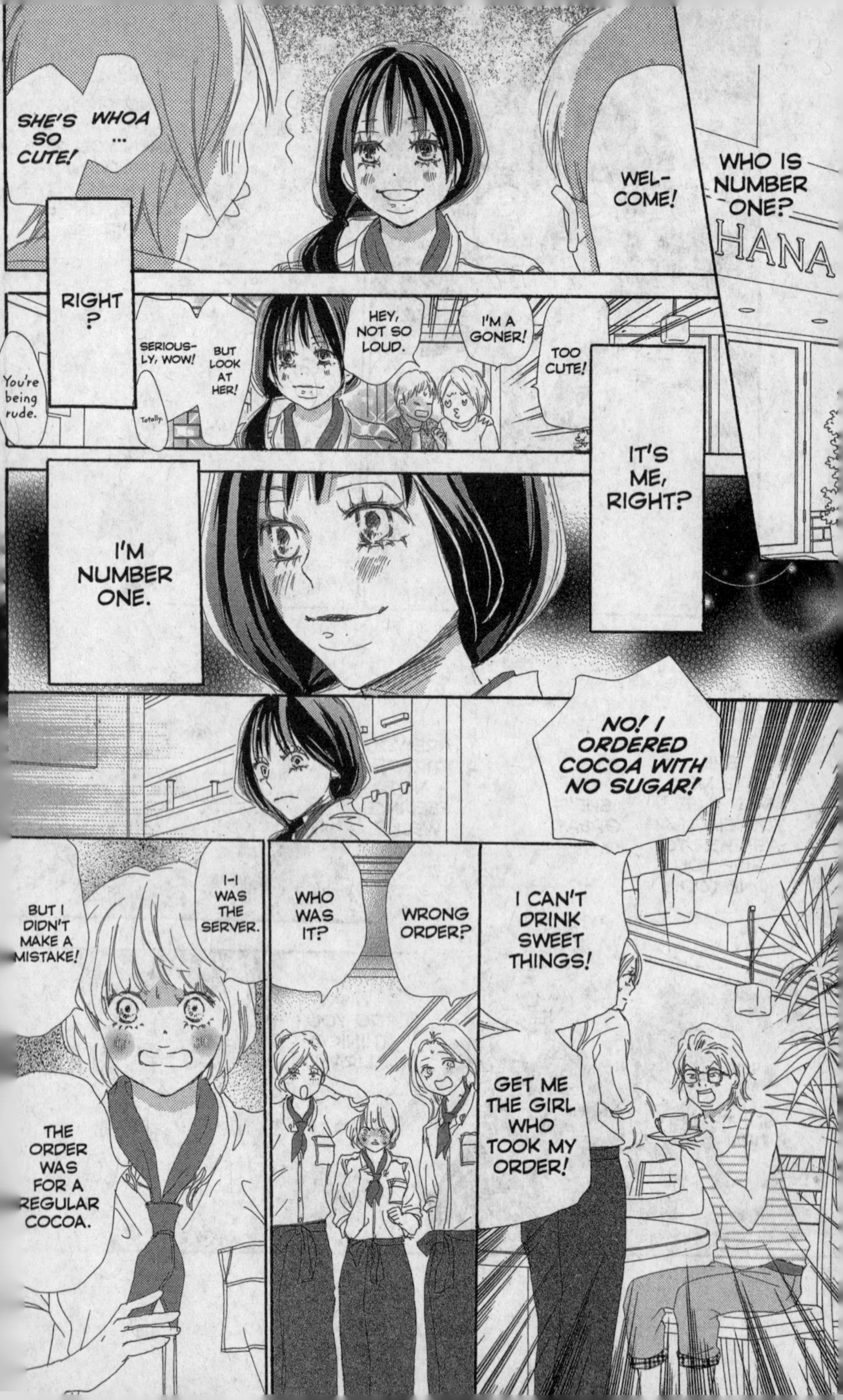

WHO IS NUMBER ONE?
HANA
WEL-COME!
WHOA ...
SHE'S SO CUTE!
RIGHT?
TOO CUTE!
I'M A GONER!
HEY, NOT SO LOUD.
BUT LOOK AT HER!
SERIOUS-LY, WOW!
Totally.
You're being rude.
IT'S ME, RIGHT?
I'M NUMBER ONE.
NO! I ORDERED COCOA WITH NO SUGAR!
I CAN'T DRINK SWEET THINGS!
GET ME THE GIRL WHO TOOK MY ORDER!
WRONG ORDER?
WHO WAS IT?
I-I WAS THE SERVER.
BUT I DIDN'T MAKE A MISTAKE!
THE ORDER WAS FOR A REGULAR COCOA.

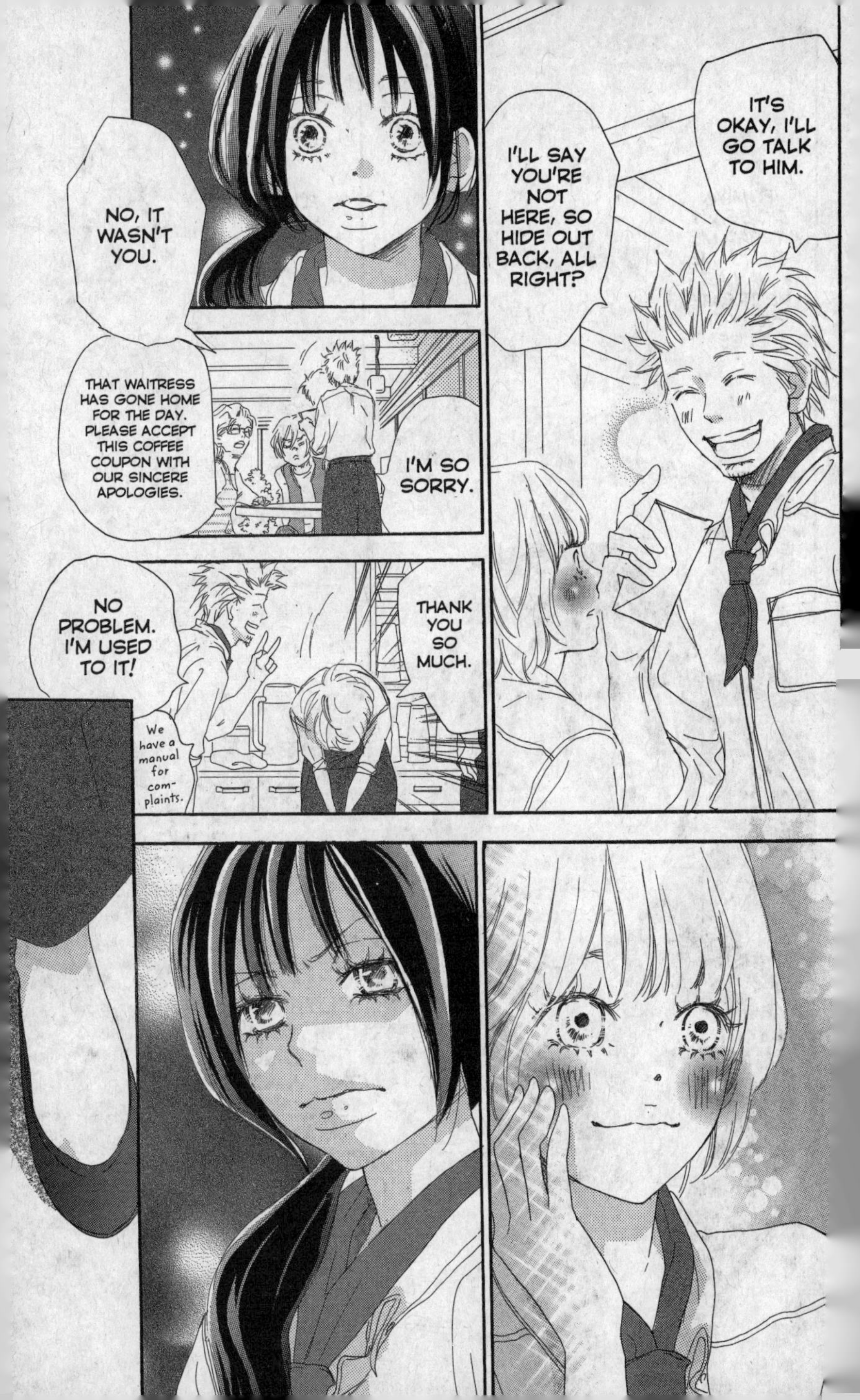
IT'S OKAY, I'LL GO TALK TO HIM.
I'LL SAY YOU'RE NOT HERE, SO HIDE OUT BACK, ALL RIGHT?
NO, IT WASN'T YOU.
I'M SO SORRY.
THAT WAITRESS HAS GONE HOME FOR THE DAY. PLEASE ACCEPT THIS COFFEE COUPON WITH OUR SINCERE APOLOGIES.
THANK YOU SO MUCH.
NO PROBLEM. I'M USED TO IT!
We have a manual for com-plaints.

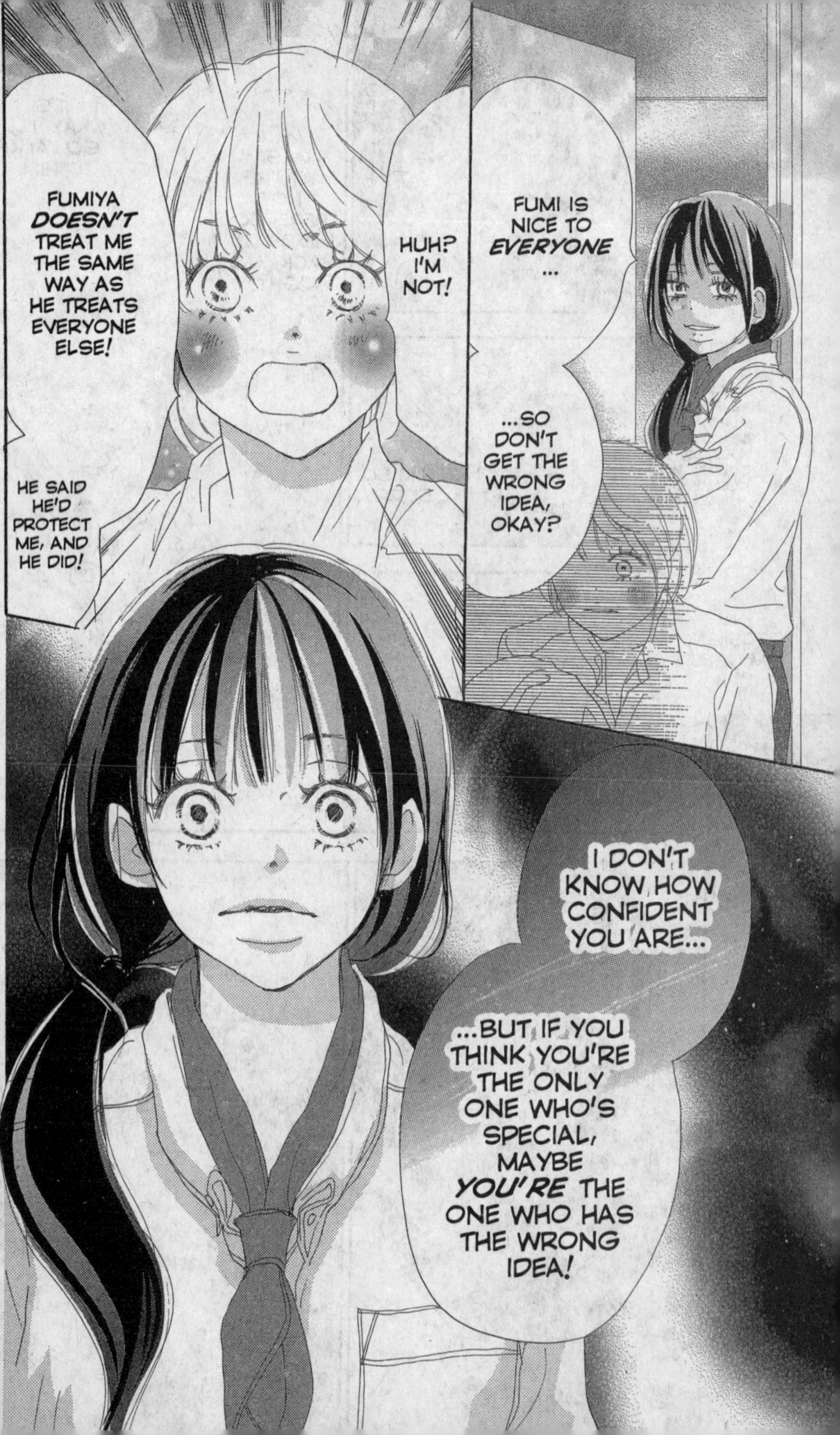
FUMI IS NICE TO *EVERYONE* ...
...SO DON'T GET THE WRONG IDEA, OKAY?
HUH? I'M NOT!
FUMIYA *DOESN'T* TREAT ME THE SAME WAY AS HE TREATS EVERYONE ELSE!
HE SAID HE'D PROTECT ME, AND HE DID!
I DON'T KNOW HOW CONFIDENT YOU ARE...
...BUT IF YOU THINK YOU'RE THE ONLY ONE WHO'S SPECIAL, MAYBE *YOU'RE* THE ONE WHO HAS THE WRONG IDEA!

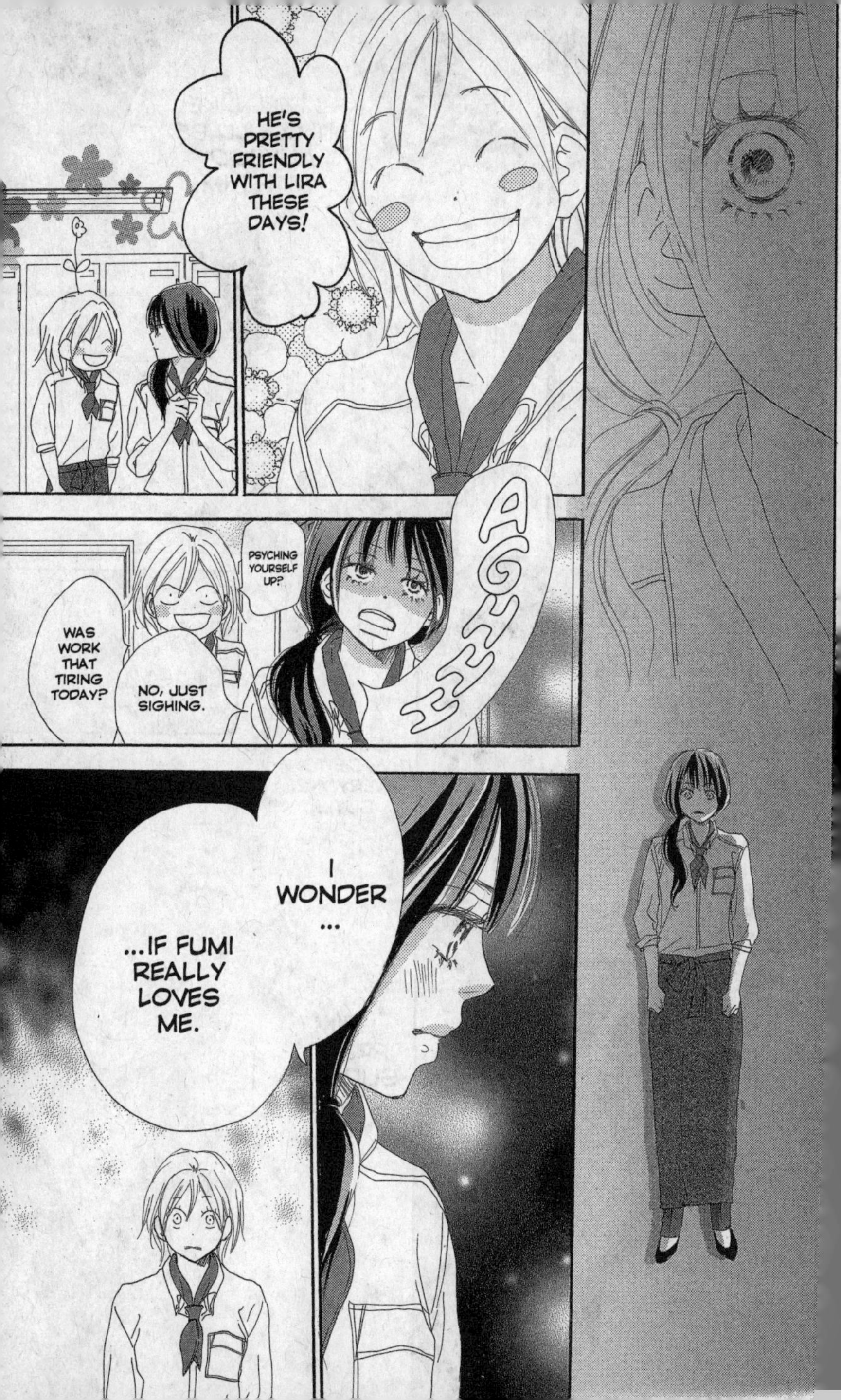
HE'S PRETTY FRIENDLY WITH LIRA THESE DAYS!
AGHHH
PSYCHING YOURSELF UP?
NO, JUST SIGHING.
WAS WORK THAT TIRING TODAY?
I WONDER ...
...IF FUMI REALLY LOVES ME.

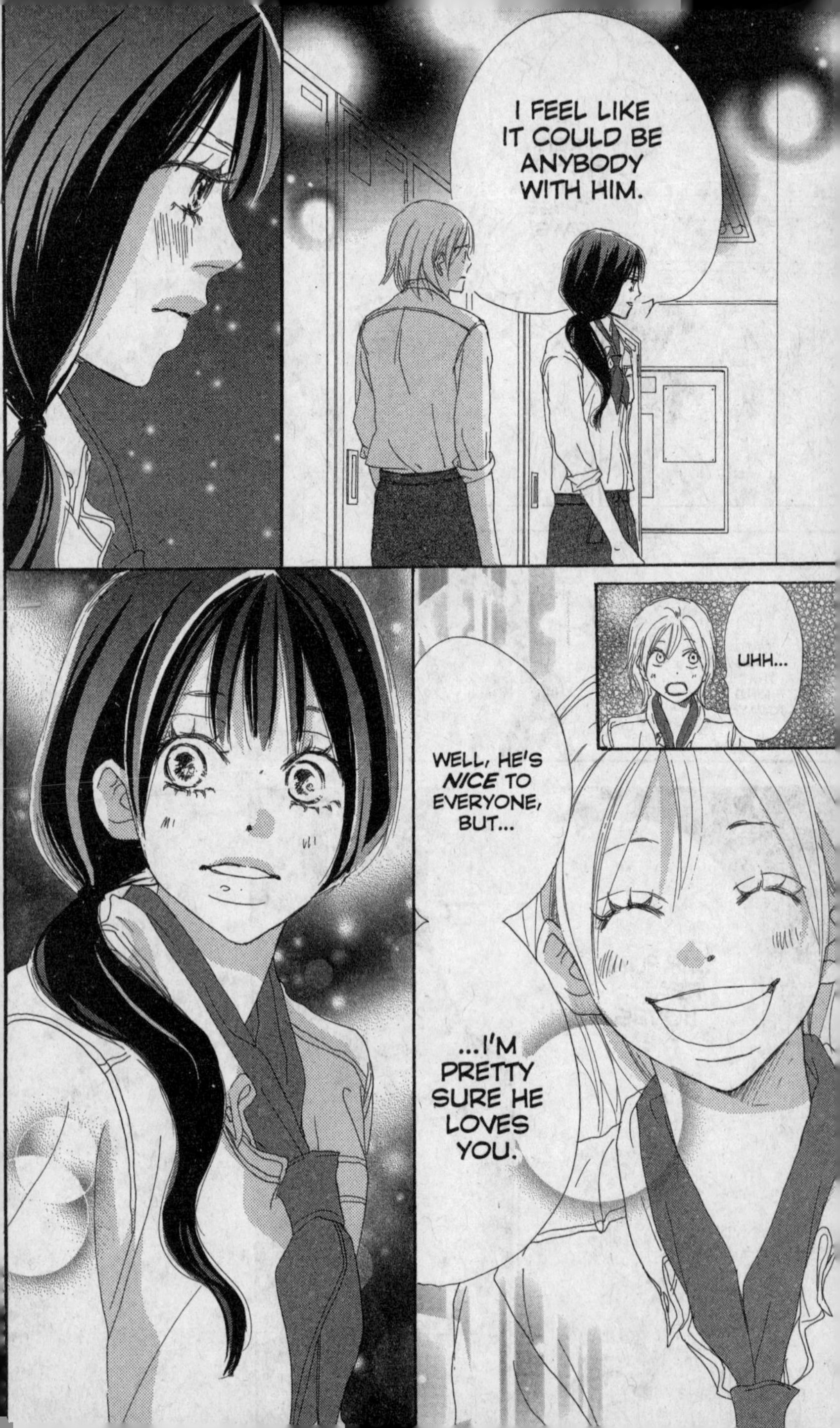
I FEEL LIKE IT COULD BE ANYBODY WITH HIM.
UHH...
WELL, HE'S *NICE* TO EVERYONE, BUT...
...I'M PRETTY SURE HE LOVES YOU.

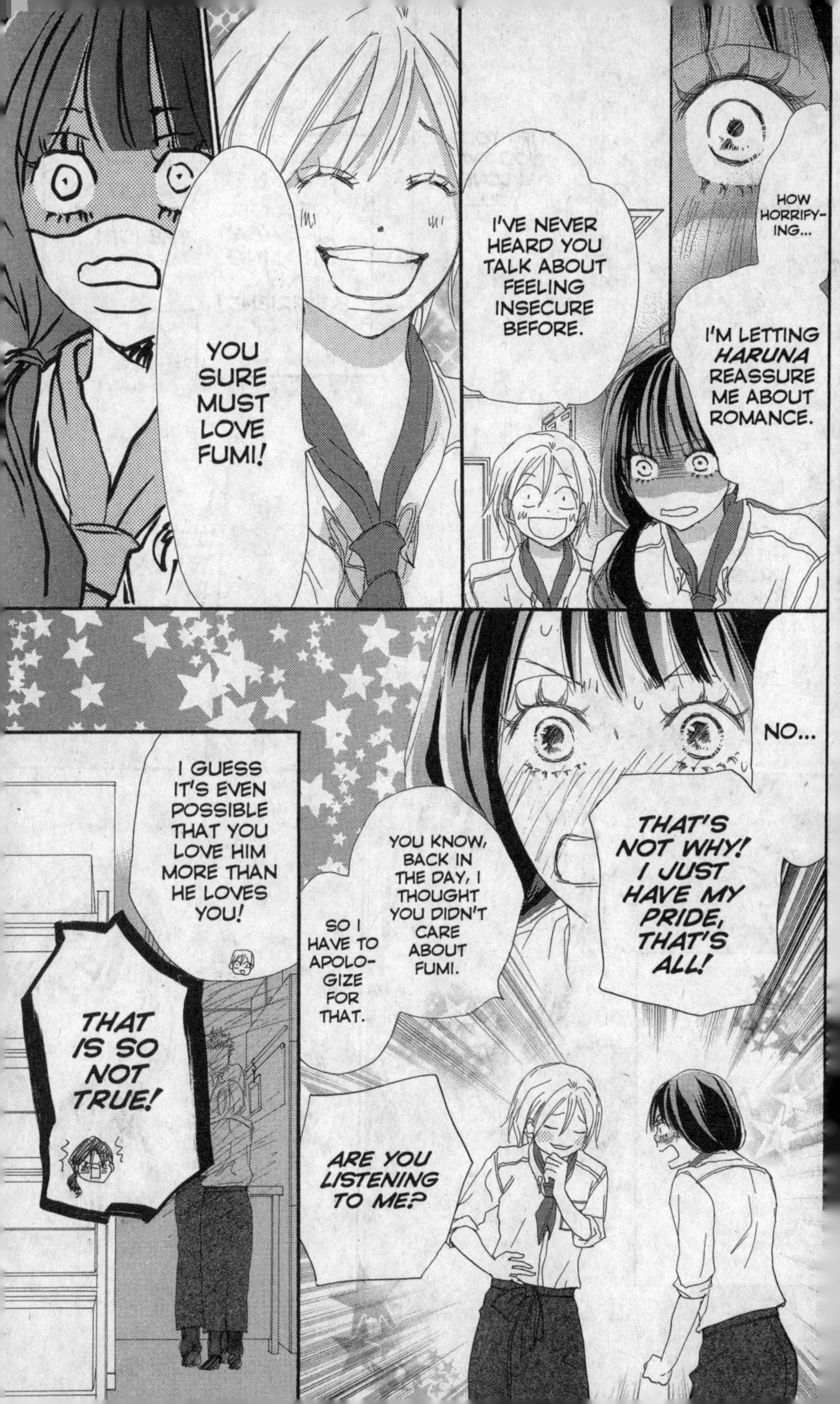
HOW HORRIFYING...
I'VE NEVER HEARD YOU TALK ABOUT FEELING INSECURE BEFORE.
I'M LETTING HARUNA REASSURE ME ABOUT ROMANCE.
YOU SURE MUST LOVE FUMI!
NO...
THAT'S NOT WHY! I JUST HAVE MY PRIDE, THAT'S ALL!
YOU KNOW, BACK IN THE DAY, I THOUGHT YOU DIDN'T CARE ABOUT FUMI.
SO I HAVE TO APOLOGIZE FOR THAT.
ARE YOU LISTENING TO ME?
I GUESS IT'S EVEN POSSIBLE THAT YOU LOVE HIM MORE THAN HE LOVES YOU!
THAT IS SO NOT TRUE!

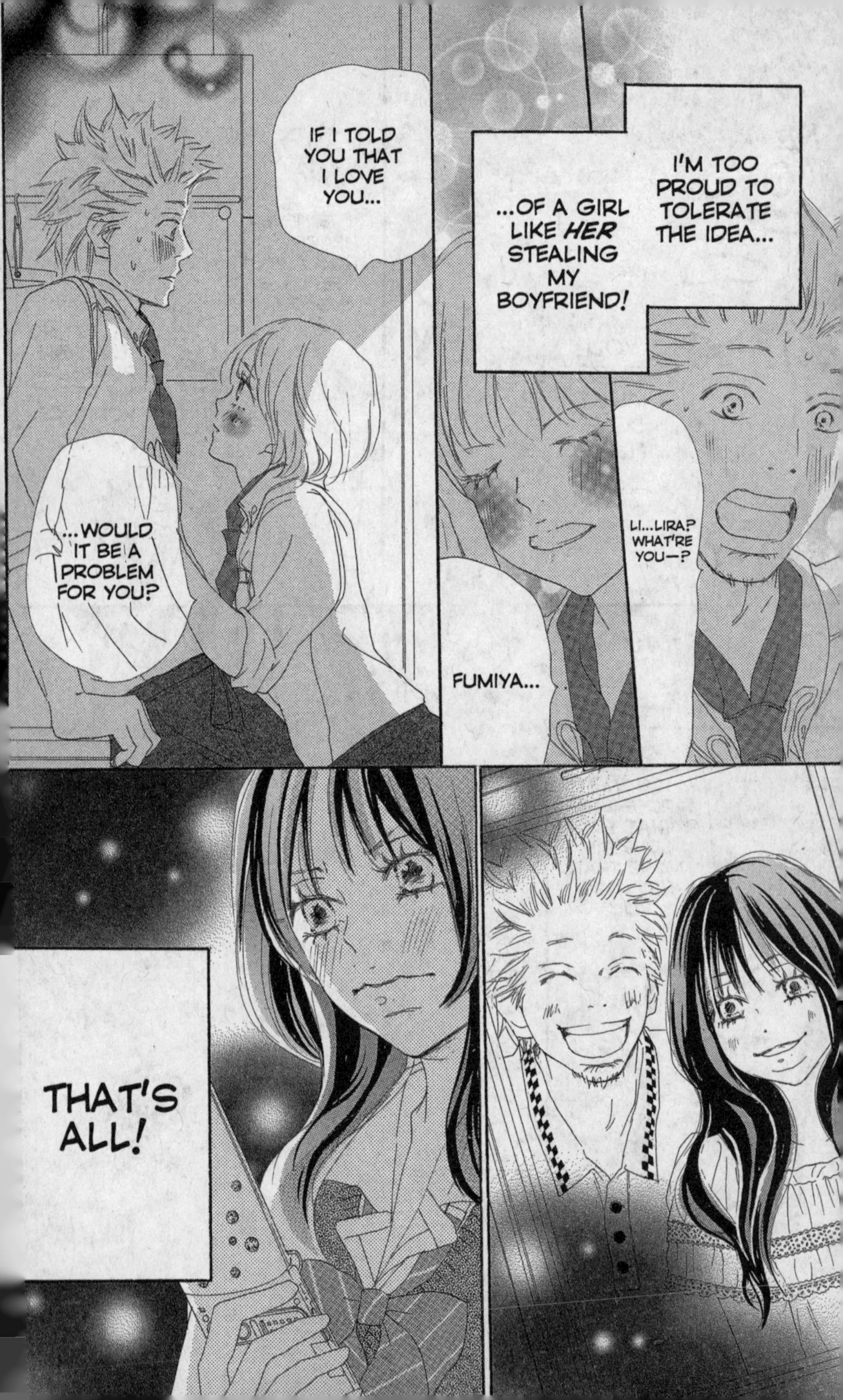
I'M TOO PROUD TO TOLERATE THE IDEA...
...OF A GIRL LIKE *HER* STEALING MY BOYFRIEND!
LI...LIRA? WHAT'RE YOU—?
FUMIYA...
IF I TOLD YOU THAT I LOVE YOU...
...WOULD IT BE A PROBLEM FOR YOU?
THAT'S ALL!

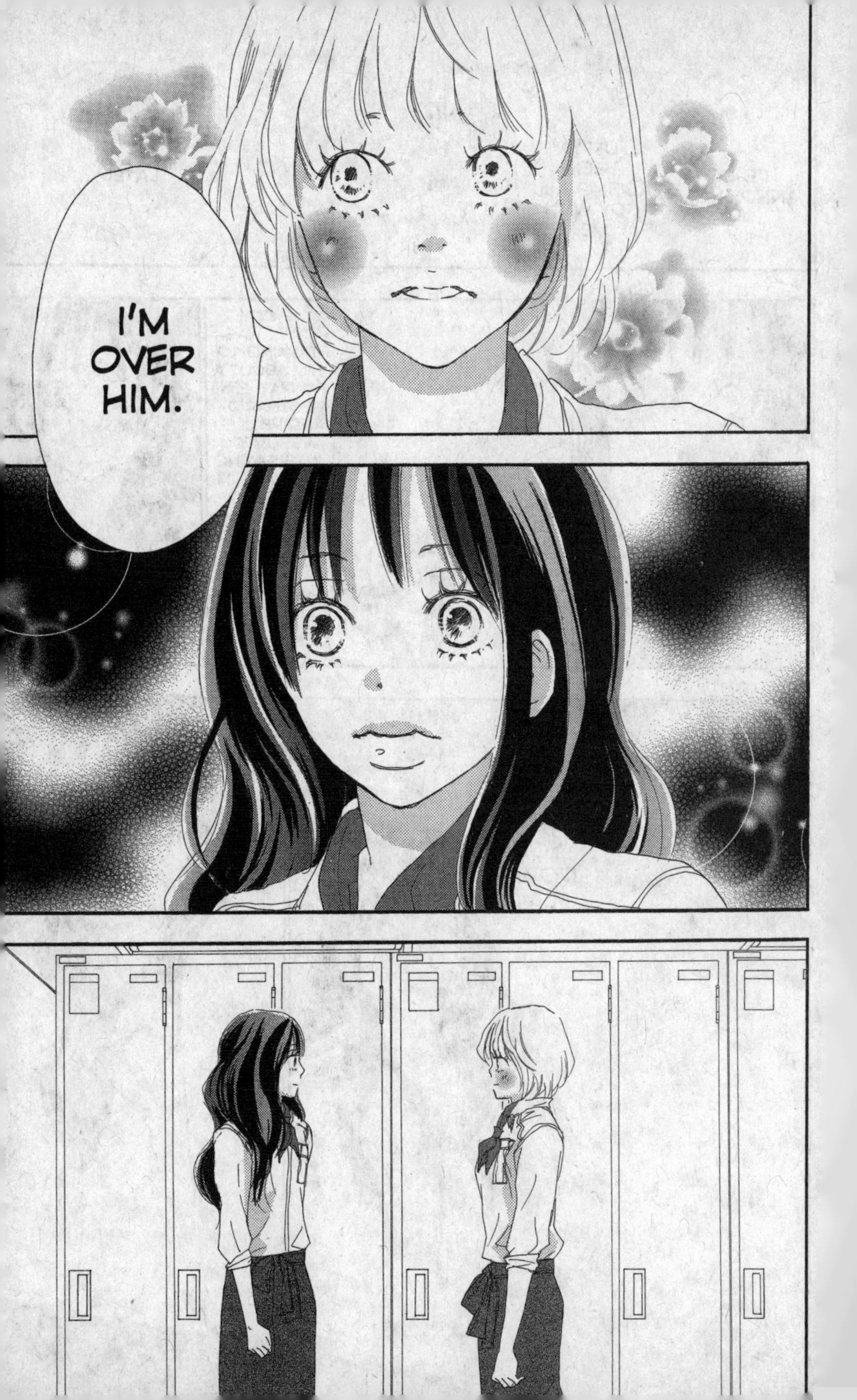
I'M OVER HIM.

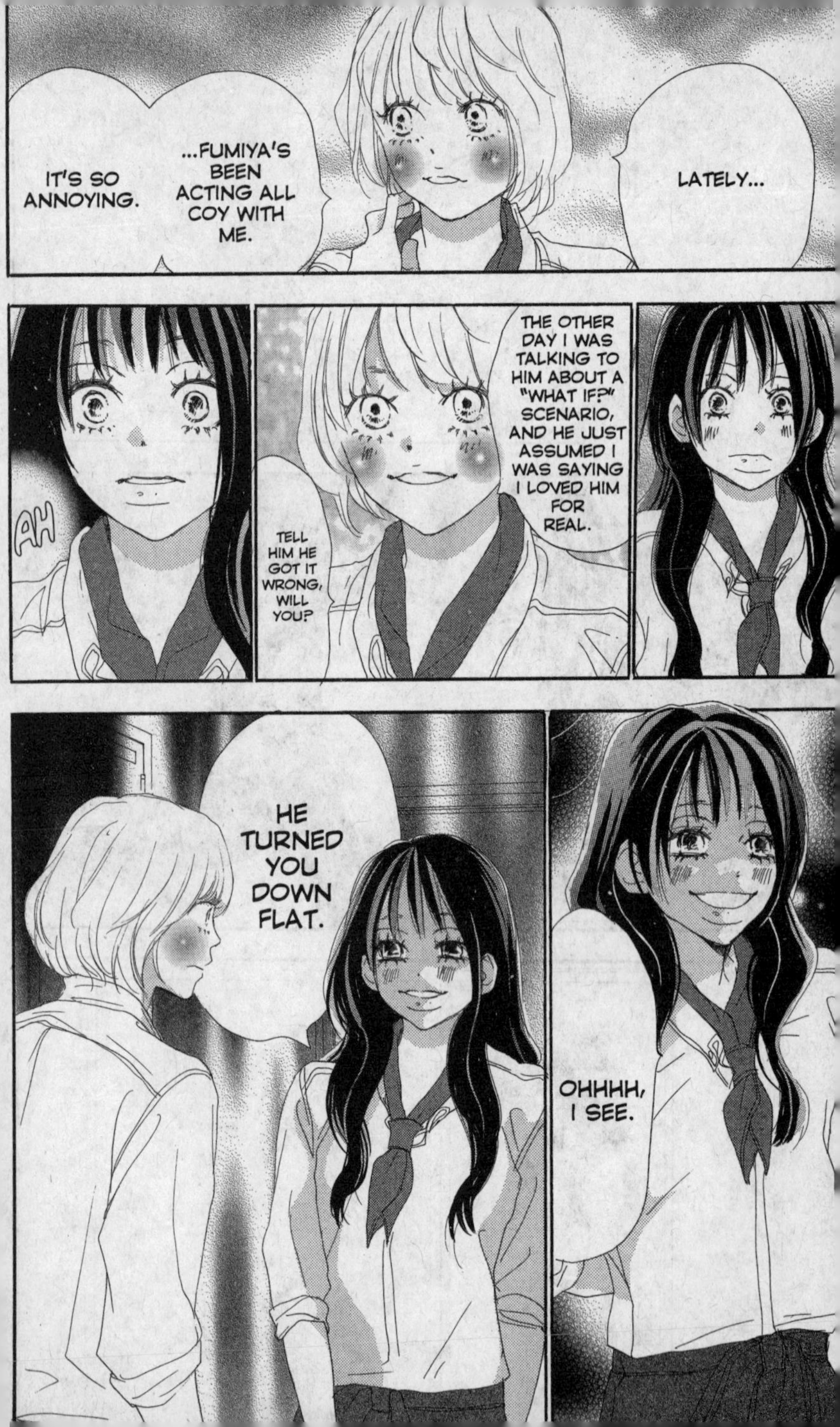
LATELY...
...FUMIYA'S BEEN ACTING ALL COY WITH ME.
IT'S SO ANNOYING.
THE OTHER DAY I WAS TALKING TO HIM ABOUT A "WHAT IF?" SCENARIO, AND HE JUST ASSUMED I WAS SAYING I LOVED HIM FOR REAL.
TELL HIM HE GOT IT WRONG, WILL YOU?
AH
OHHHH, I SEE.
HE TURNED YOU DOWN FLAT.

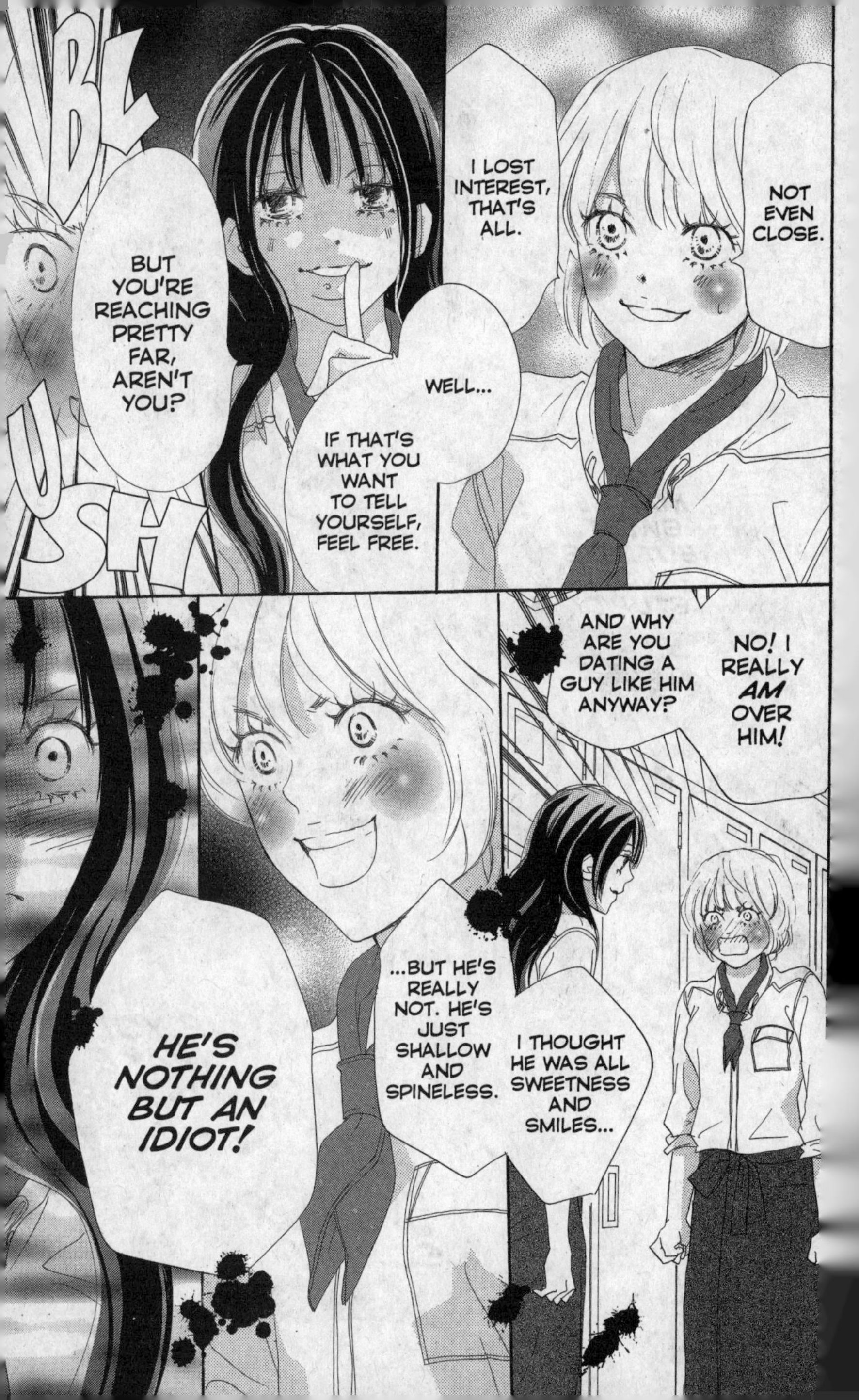
NOT EVEN CLOSE.
I LOST INTEREST, THAT'S ALL.
WELL...
IF THAT'S WHAT YOU WANT TO TELL YOURSELF, FEEL FREE.
BUT YOU'RE REACHING PRETTY FAR, AREN'T YOU?
BLUSH
NO! I REALLY *AM* OVER HIM!
AND WHY ARE YOU DATING A GUY LIKE HIM ANYWAY?
I THOUGHT HE WAS ALL SWEETNESS AND SMILES...
...BUT HE'S REALLY NOT. HE'S JUST SHALLOW AND SPINELESS.
HE'S NOTHING BUT AN IDIOT!

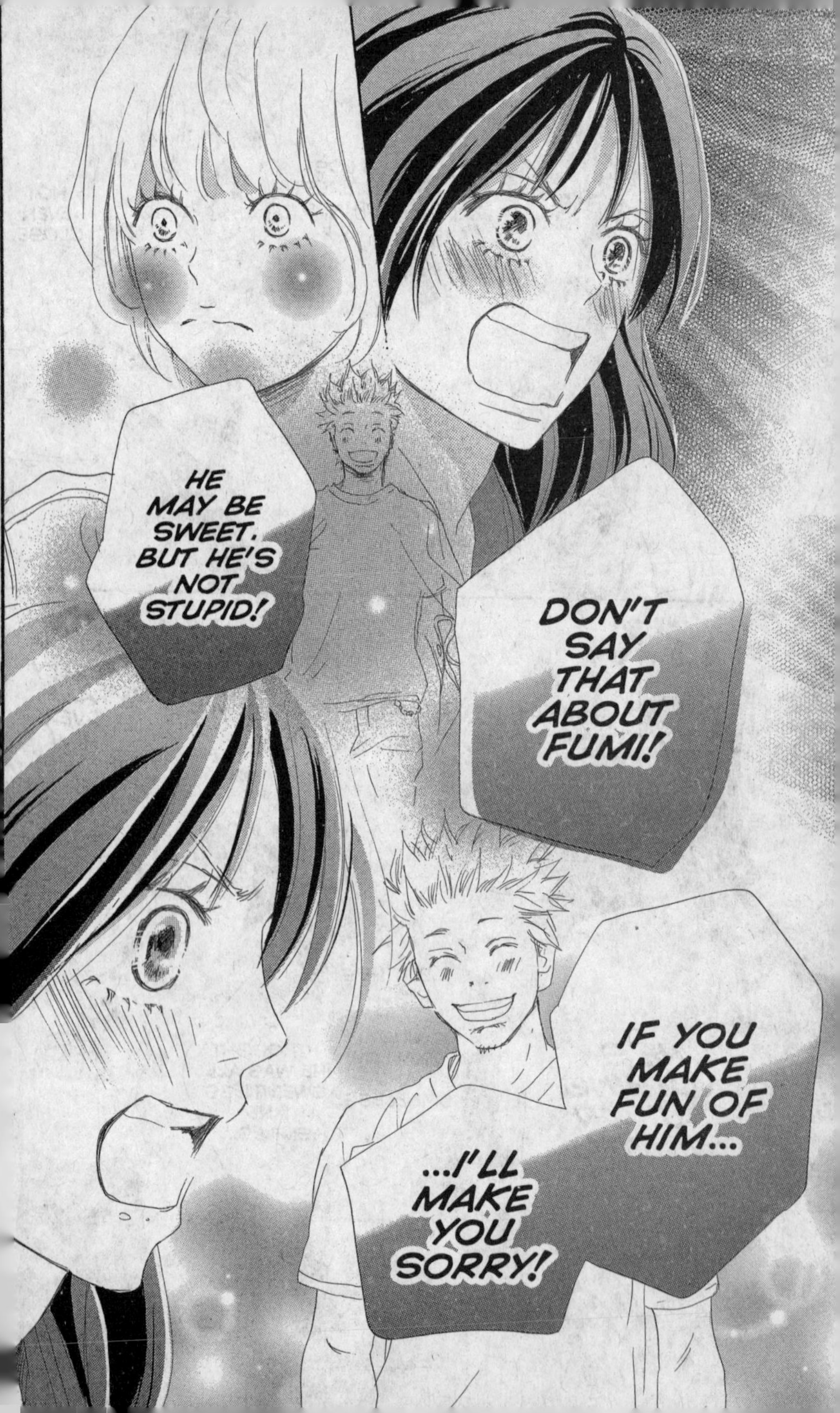
DON'T SAY THAT ABOUT FUMI!
HE MAY BE SWEET. BUT HE'S NOT STUPID!
IF YOU MAKE FUN OF HIM...
...I'LL MAKE YOU SORRY!

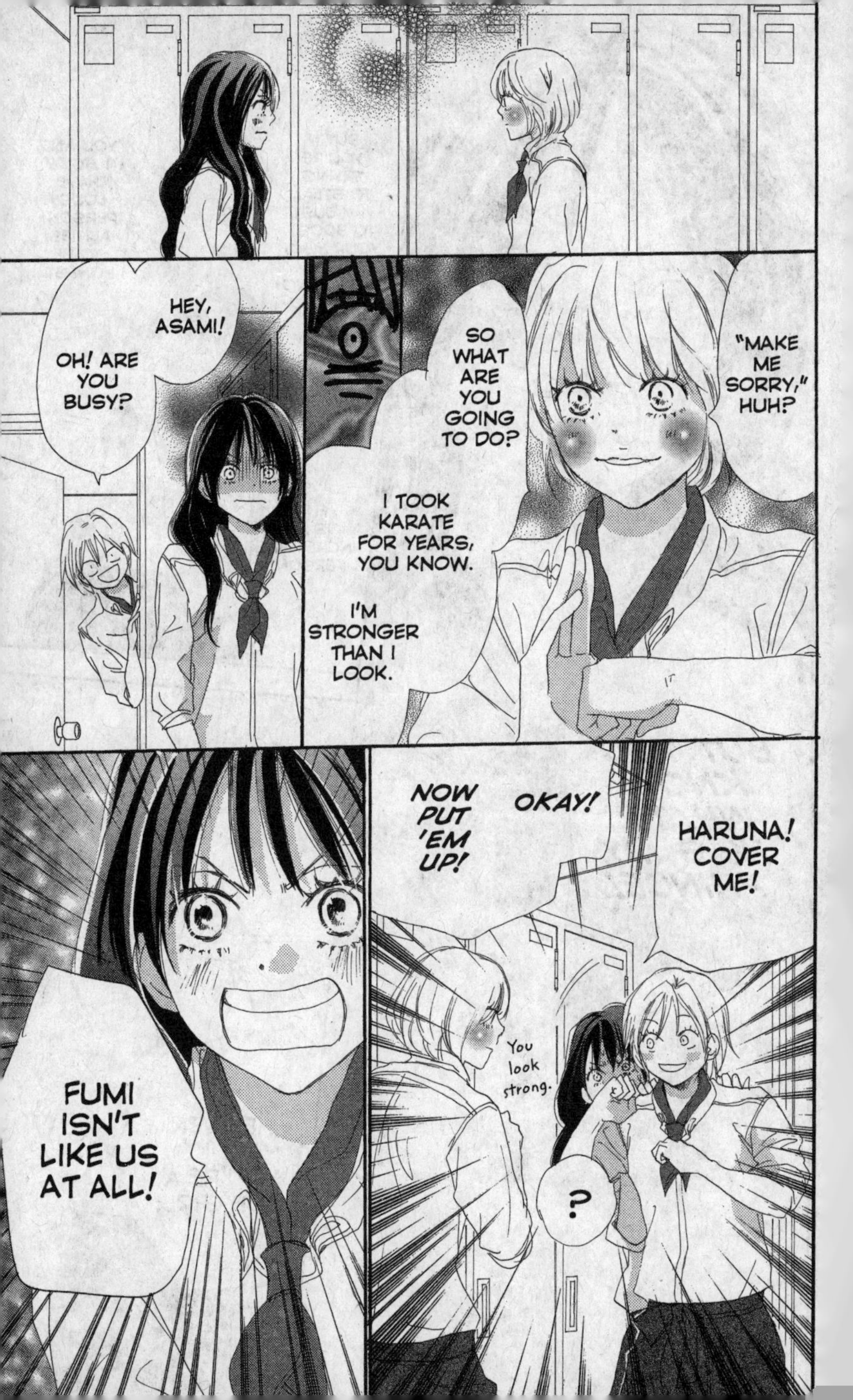
"MAKE ME SORRY," HUH?
SO WHAT ARE YOU GOING TO DO?
I TOOK KARATE FOR YEARS, YOU KNOW.
I'M STRONGER THAN I LOOK.
HEY, ASAMI!
OH! ARE YOU BUSY?
HARUNA! COVER ME!
OKAY!
NOW PUT 'EM UP!
You look strong.
?
FUMI ISN'T LIKE US AT ALL!

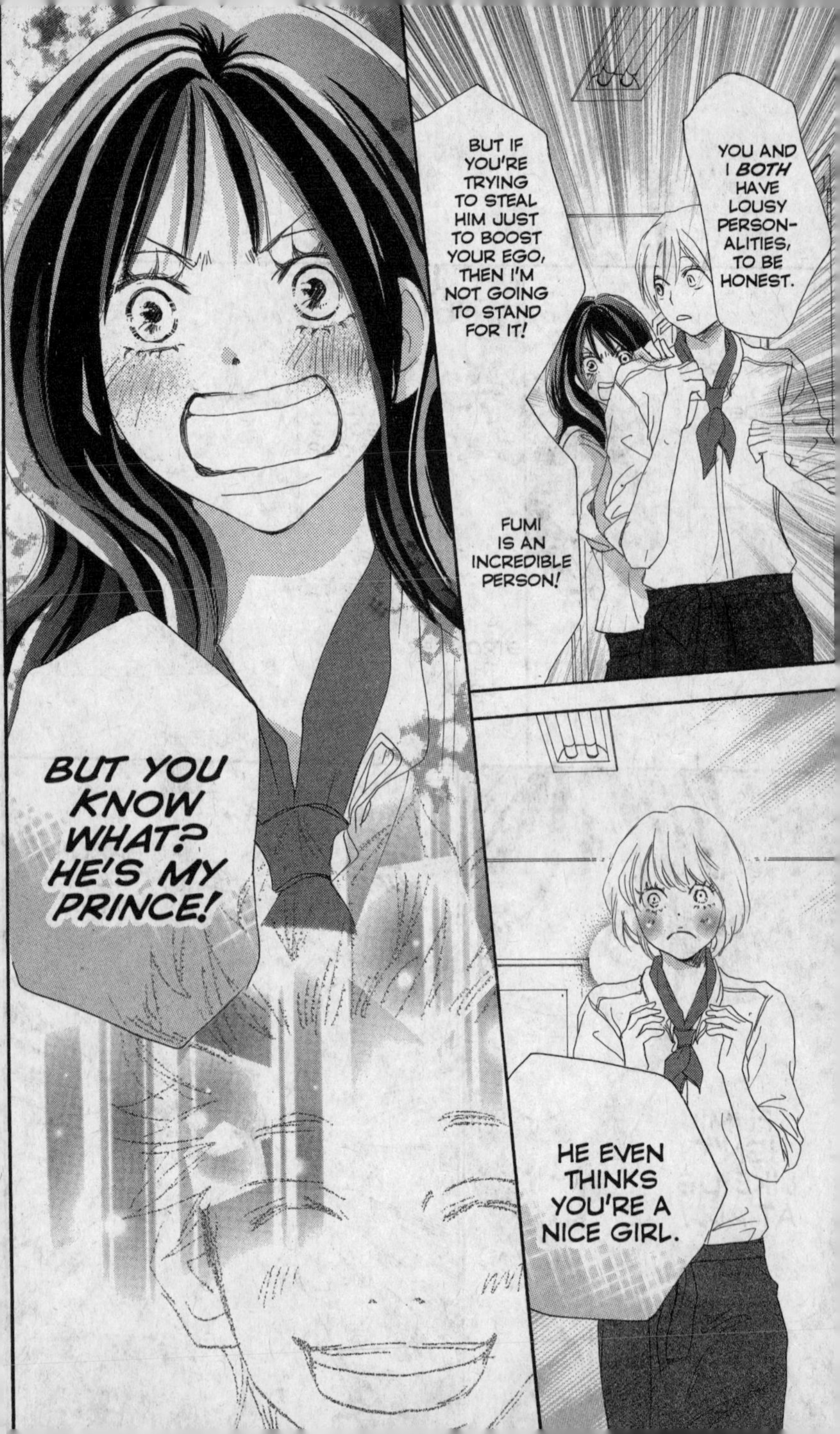
YOU AND I *BOTH* HAVE LOUSY PERSON-ALITIES, TO BE HONEST.
BUT IF YOU'RE TRYING TO STEAL HIM JUST TO BOOST YOUR EGO, THEN I'M NOT GOING TO STAND FOR IT!
FUMI IS AN INCREDIBLE PERSON!
HE EVEN THINKS YOU'RE A NICE GIRL.
BUT YOU KNOW WHAT? HE'S MY PRINCE!

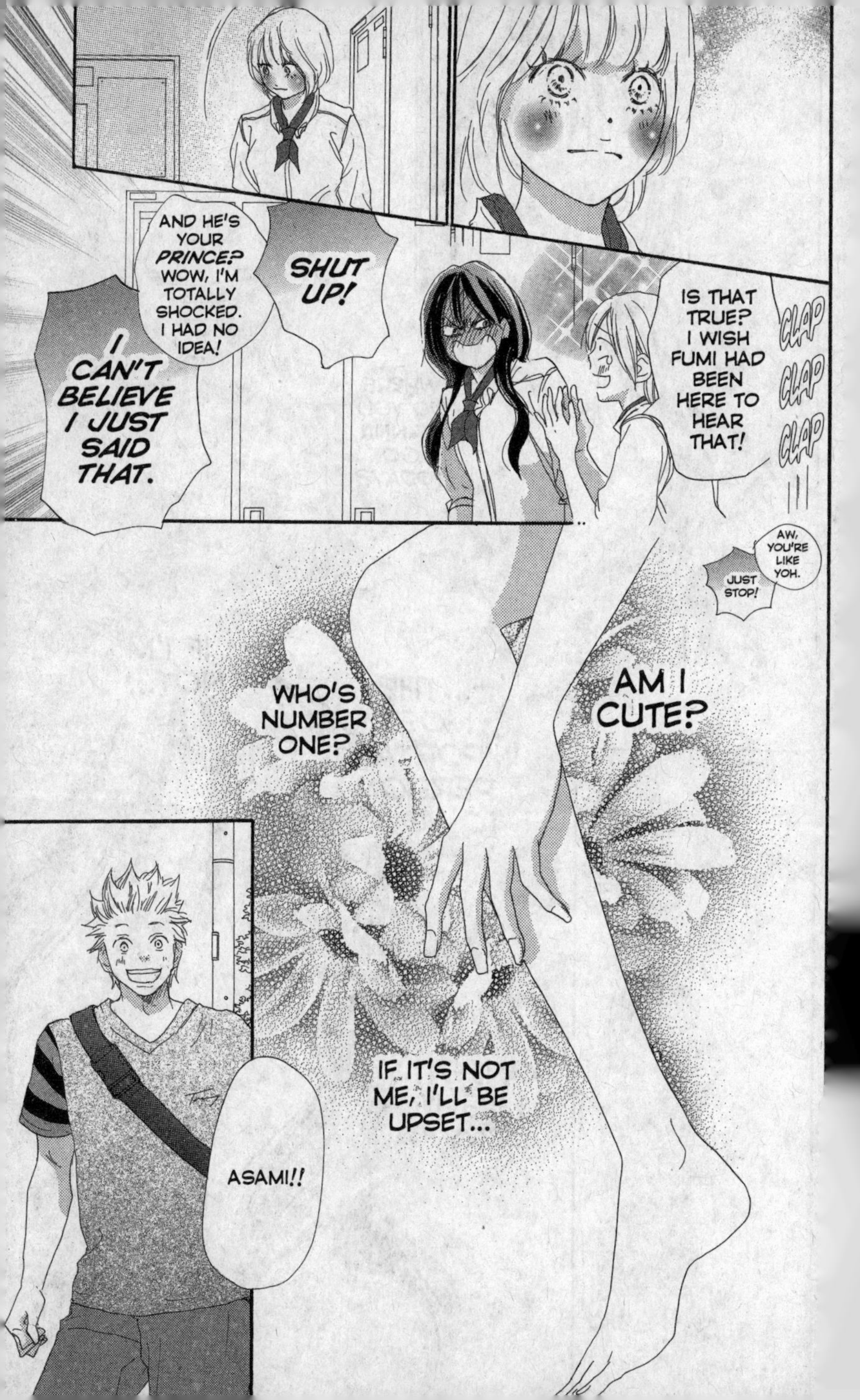
AND HE'S YOUR PRINCE? WOW, I'M TOTALLY SHOCKED. I HAD NO IDEA!
SHUT UP!
IS THAT TRUE? I WISH FUMI HAD BEEN HERE TO HEAR THAT!
CLAP CLAP CLAP
I CAN'T BELIEVE I JUST SAID THAT.
AW, YOU'RE LIKE YOH.
JUST STOP!
AM I CUTE?
WHO'S NUMBER ONE?
IF IT'S NOT ME, I'LL BE UPSET...
ASAMI!!

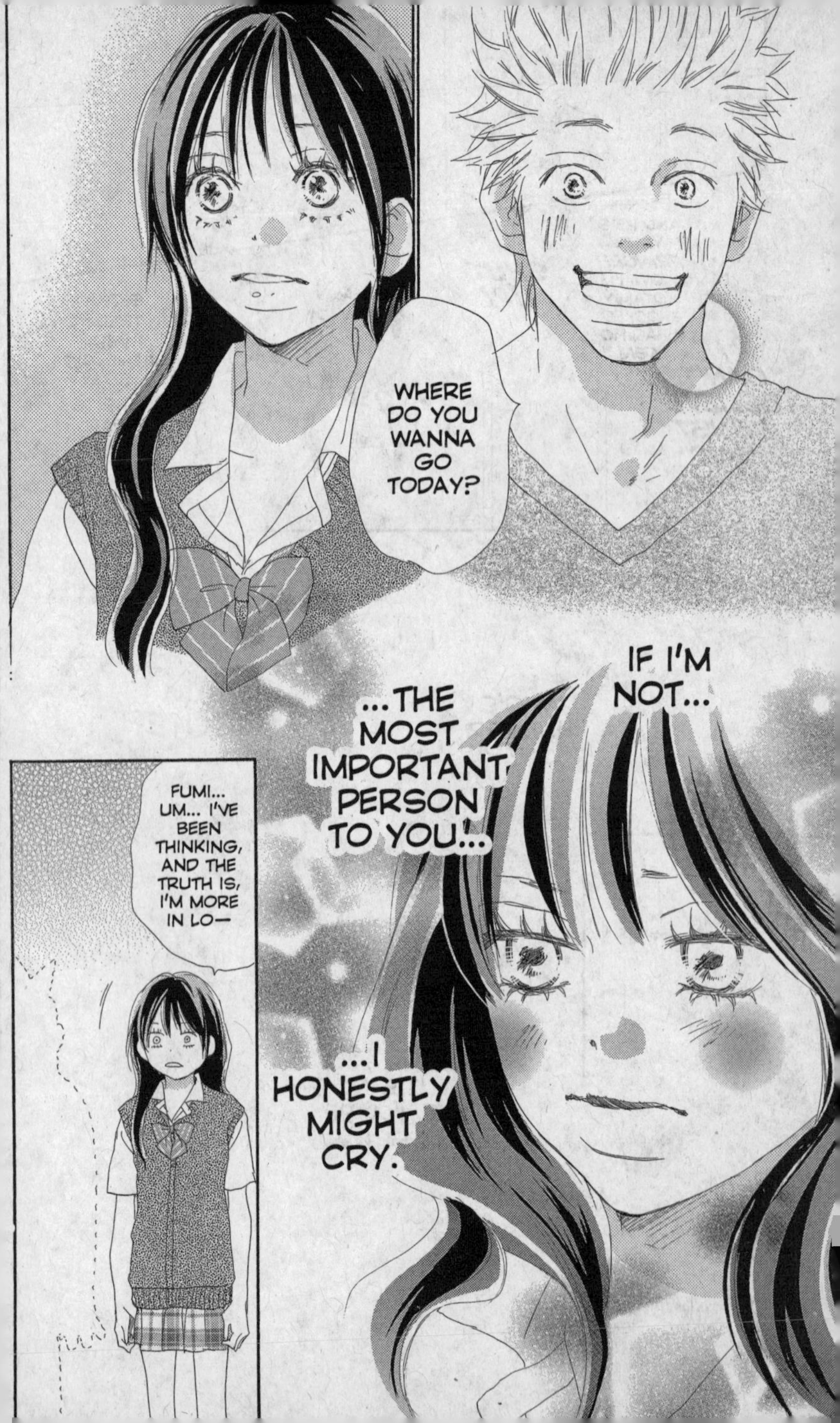
WHERE DO YOU WANNA GO TODAY?
IF I'M NOT...
...THE MOST IMPORTANT PERSON TO YOU...
...I HONESTLY MIGHT CRY.
FUMI... UM... I'VE BEEN THINKING, AND THE TRUTH IS, I'M MORE IN LO—

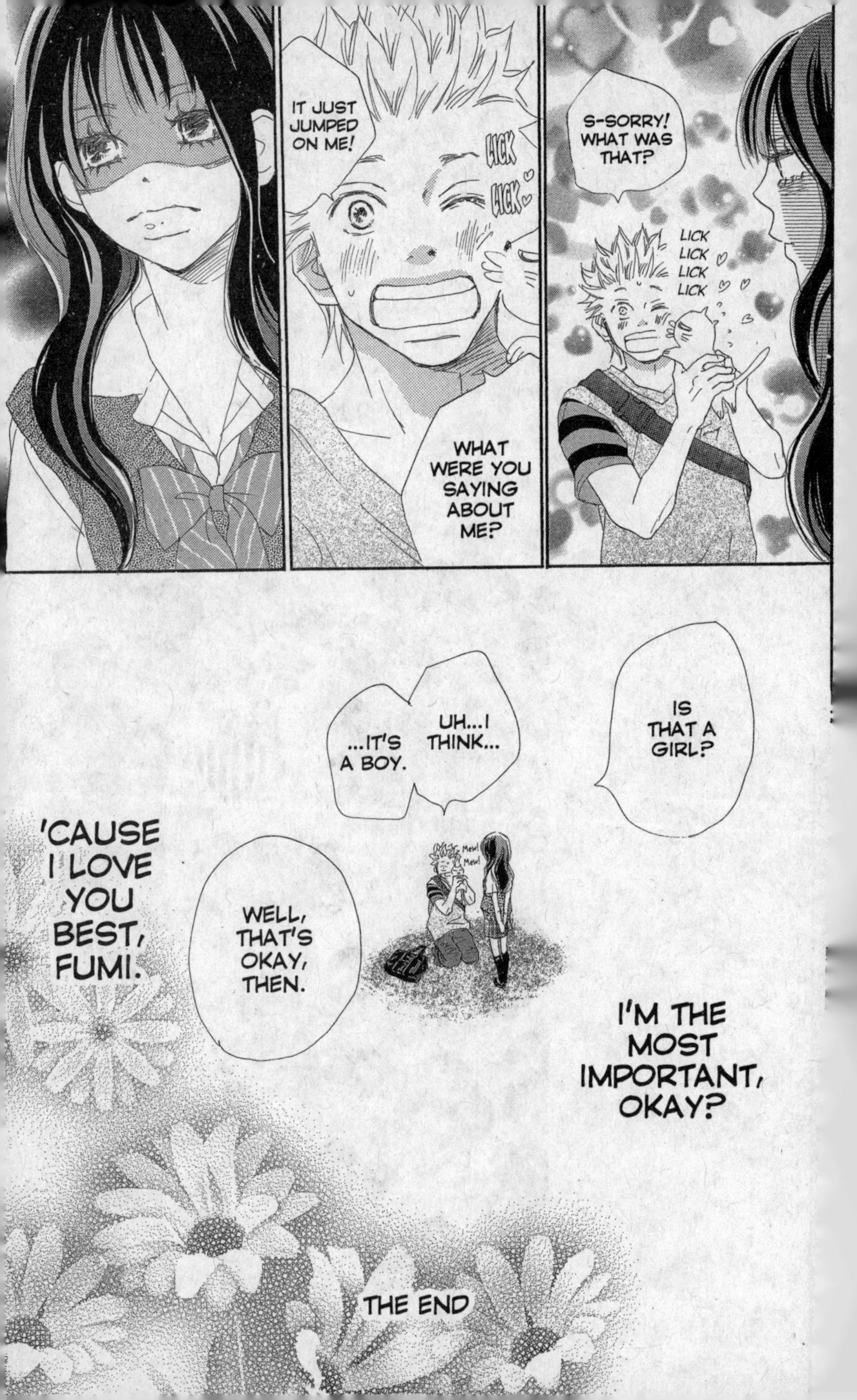
S-SORRY! WHAT WAS THAT?
LICK LICK LICK LICK
IT JUST JUMPED ON ME!
LICK LICK
WHAT WERE YOU SAYING ABOUT ME?
IS THAT A GIRL?
UH...I THINK...
...IT'S A BOY.
Mew! Mew!
WELL, THAT'S OKAY, THEN.
I'M THE MOST IMPORTANT, OKAY?
'CAUSE I LOVE YOU BEST, FUMI.
THE END

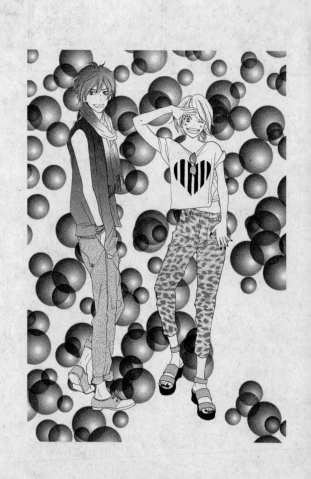

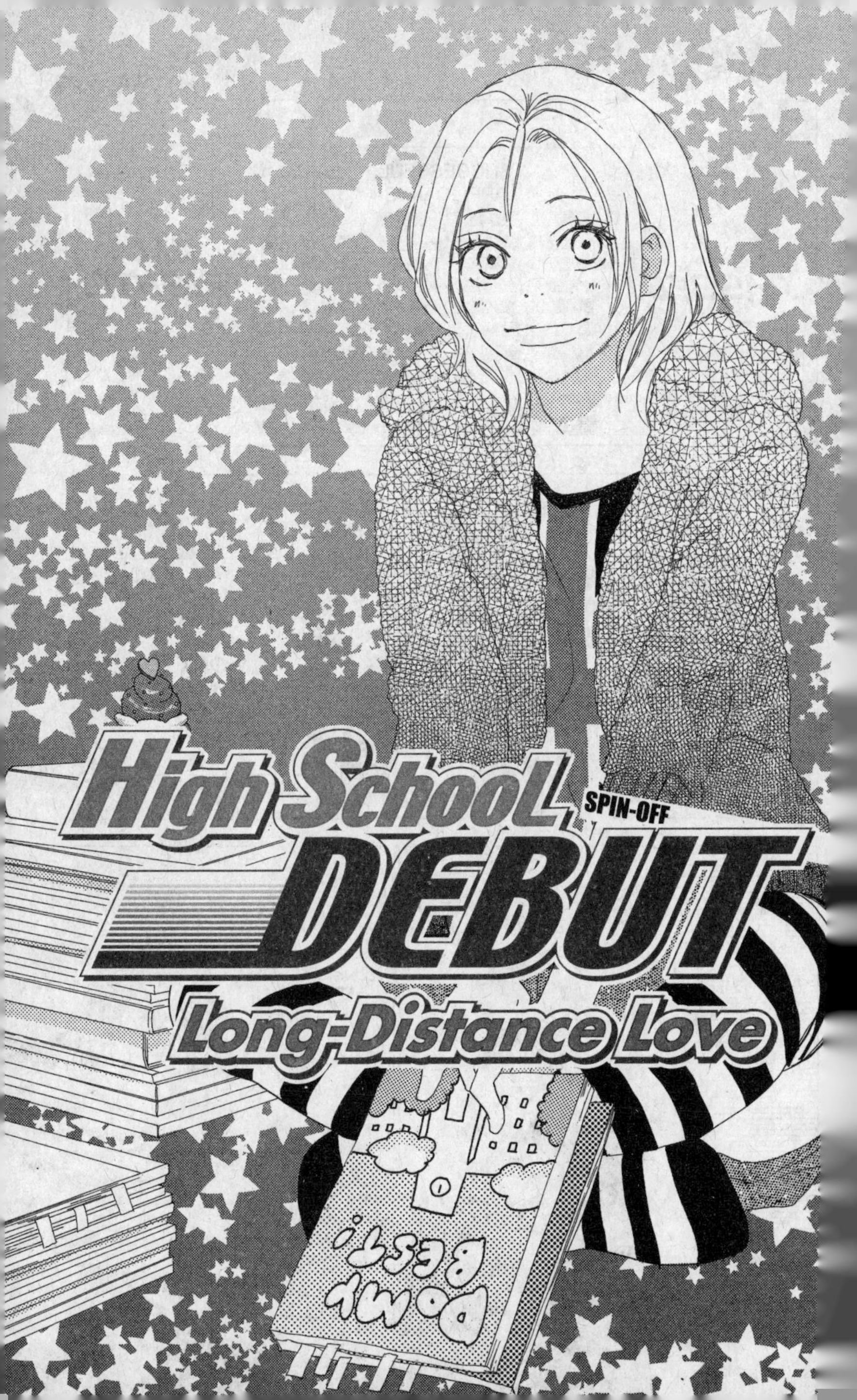
High School DEBUT
SPIN-OFF
Long-Distance Love
MY BEST!

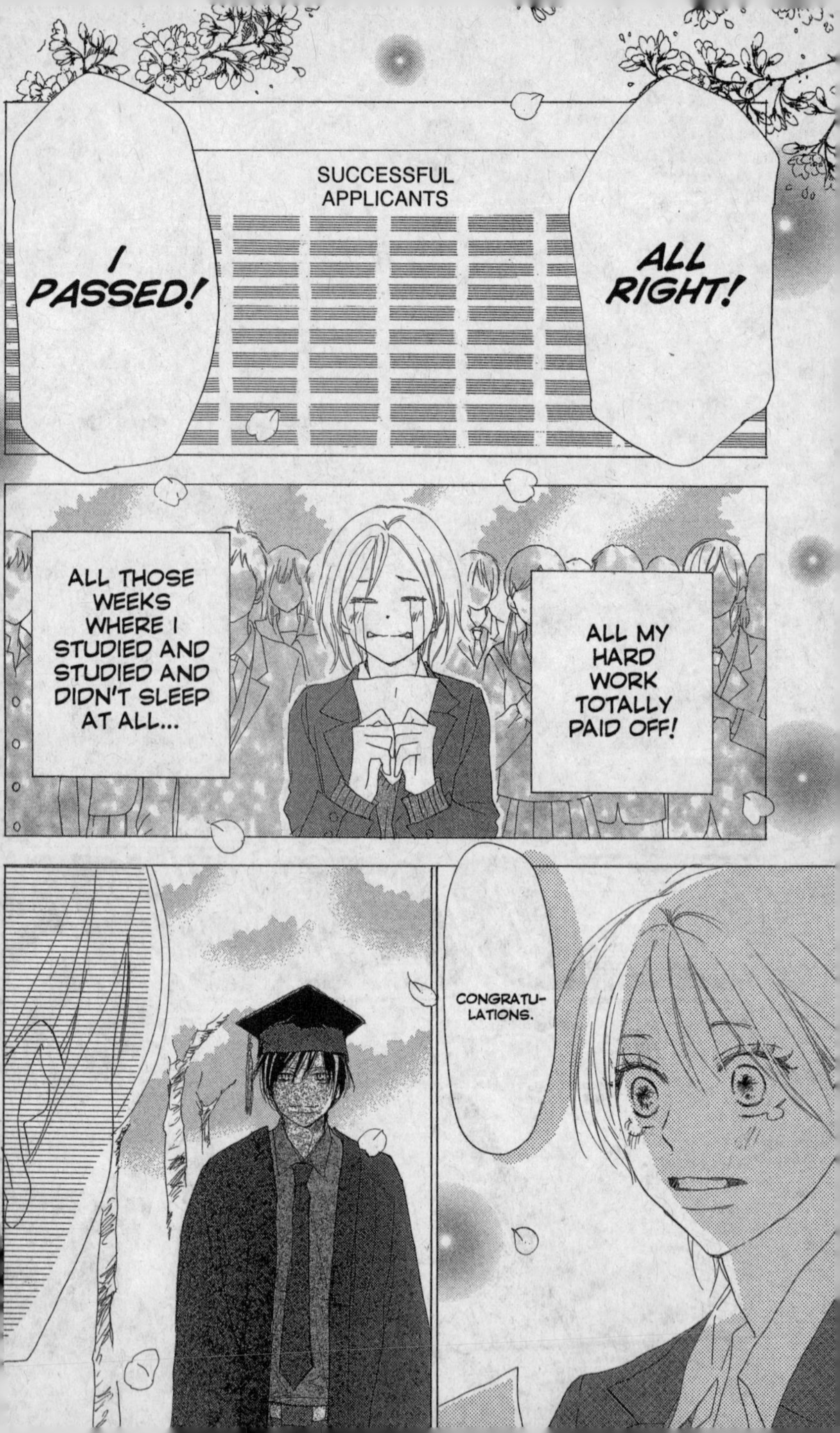
ALL RIGHT!
SUCCESSFUL APPLICANTS
I PASSED!
ALL THOSE WEEKS WHERE I STUDIED AND STUDIED AND DIDN'T SLEEP AT ALL...
ALL MY HARD WORK TOTALLY PAID OFF!
CONGRATU-LATIONS.

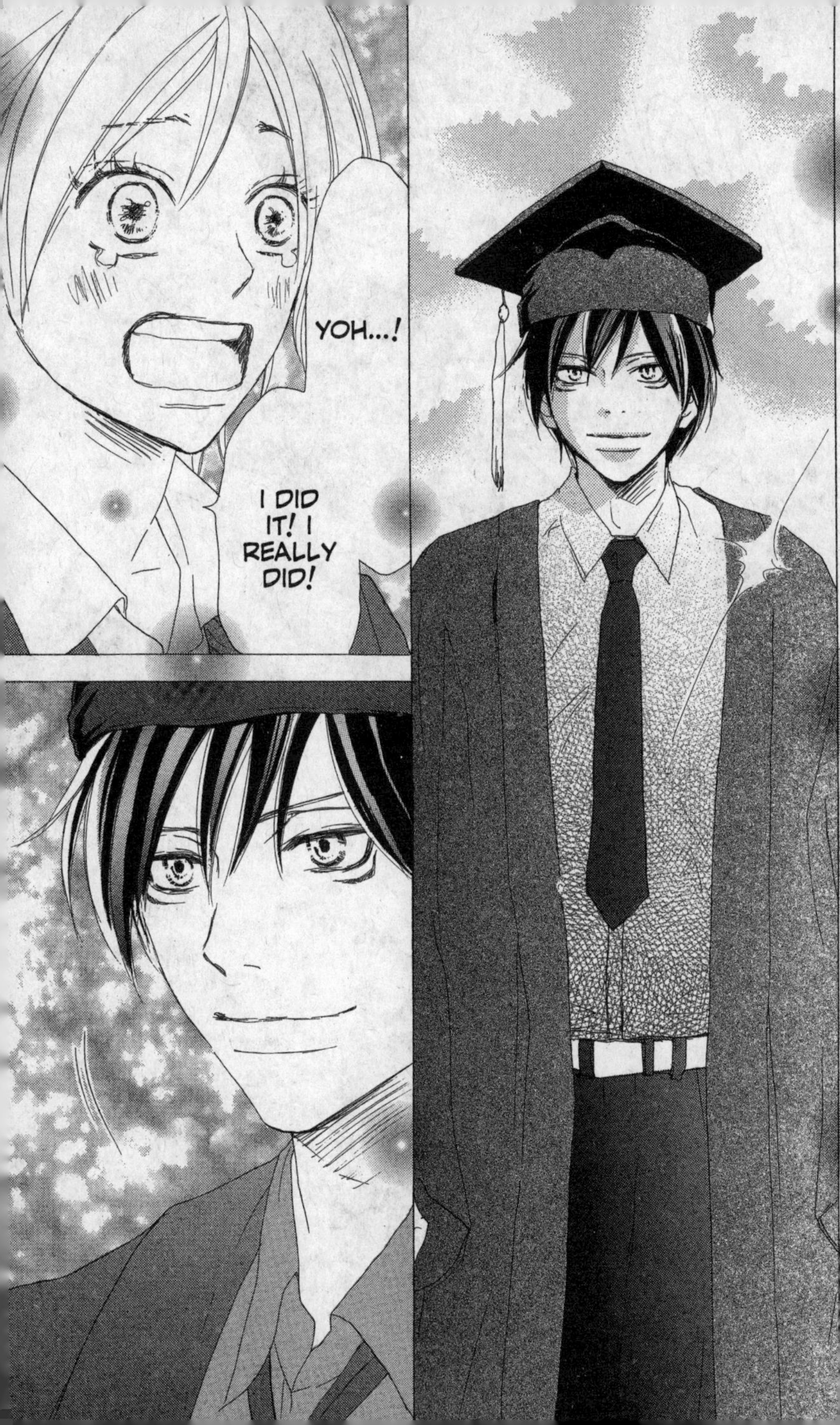
YOH...!
I DID IT! I REALLY DID!

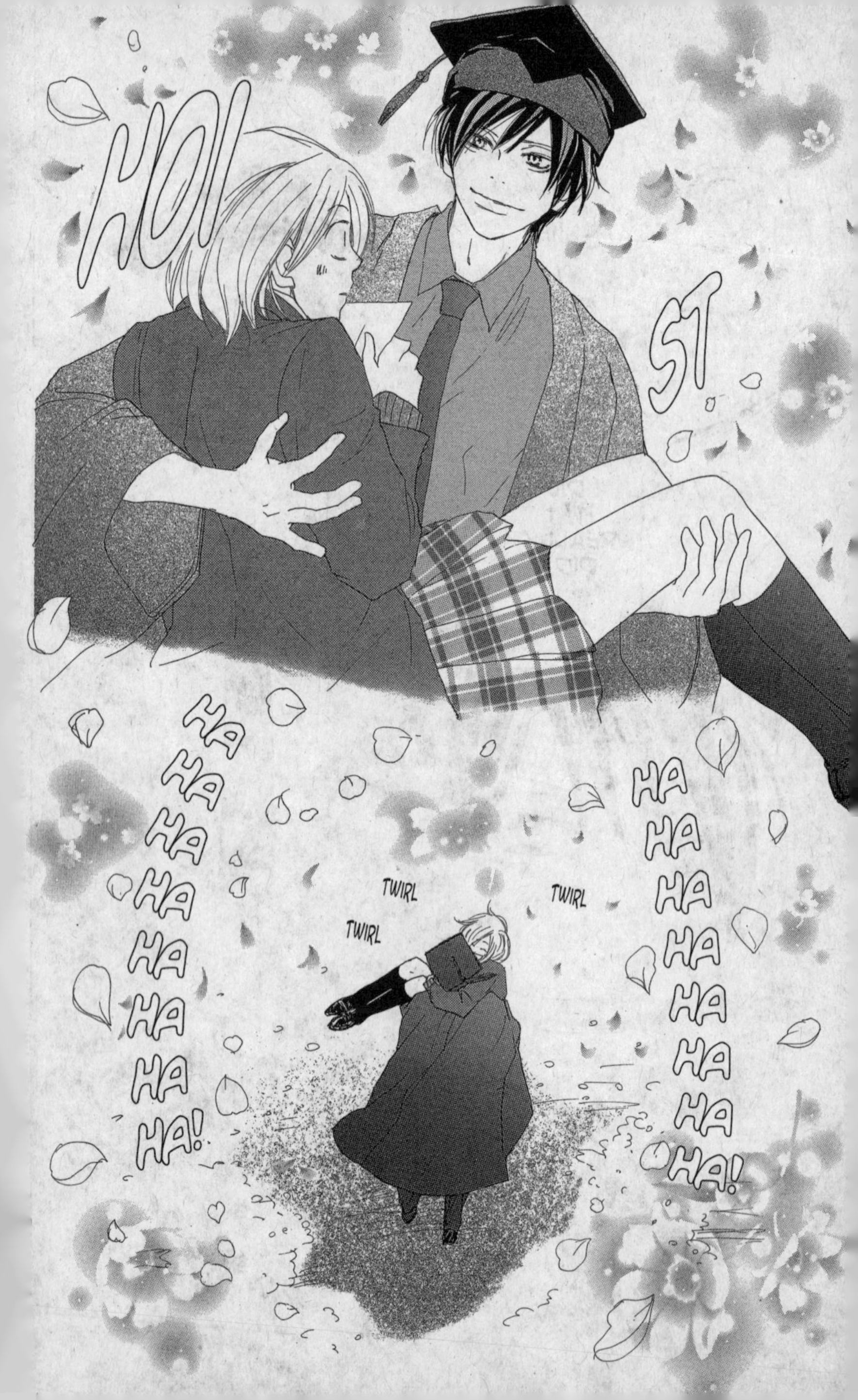
HOI
ST
HA HA HA HA HA HA HA HA!
HA HA HA HA HA HA HA HA!
TWIRL
TWIRL
TWIRL

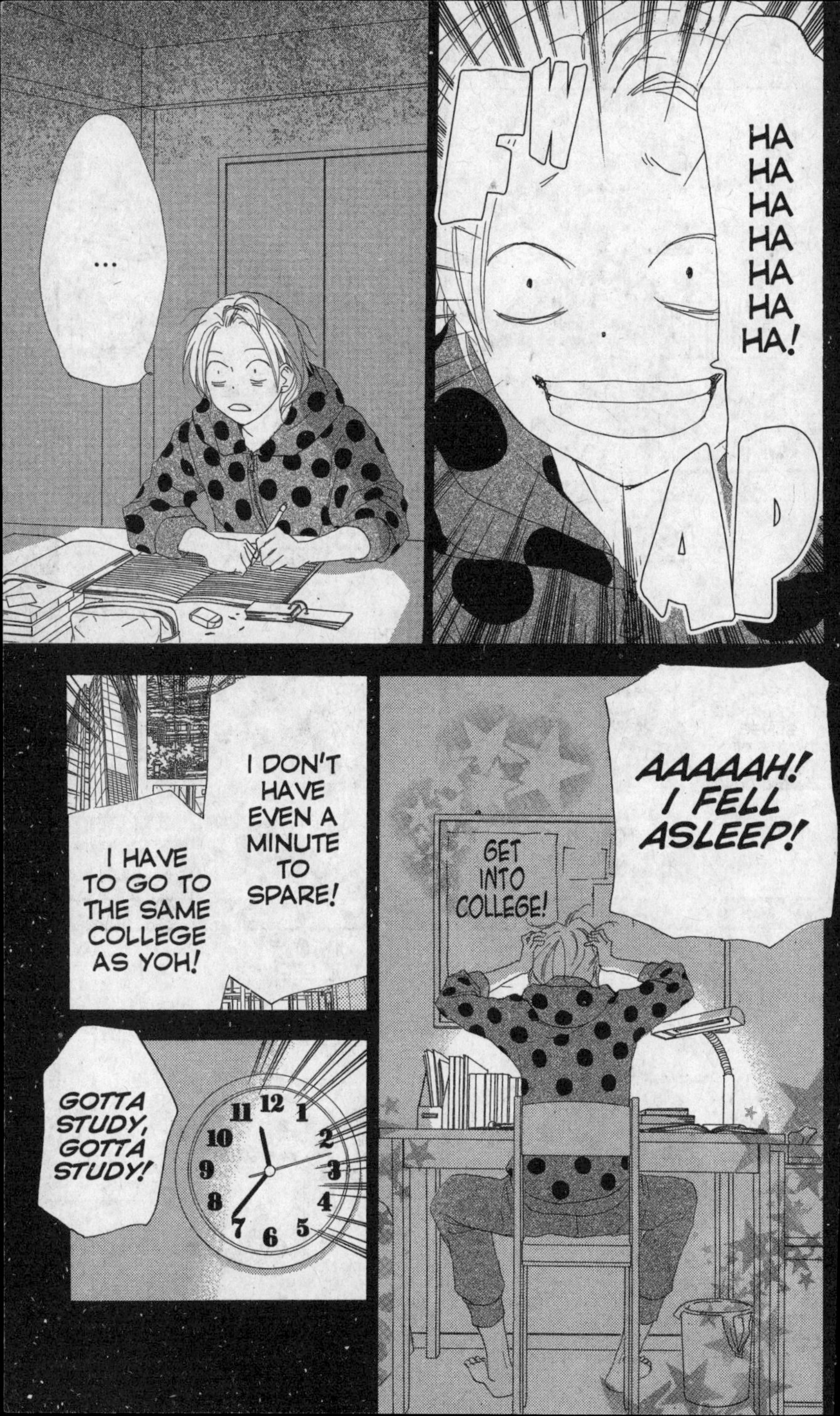
HA HA HA HA HA HA HA!
FWAP
...
AAAAAH! I FELL ASLEEP!
GET INTO COLLEGE!
I DON'T HAVE EVEN A MINUTE TO SPARE!
I HAVE TO GO TO THE SAME COLLEGE AS YOH!
GOTTA STUDY, GOTTA STUDY!

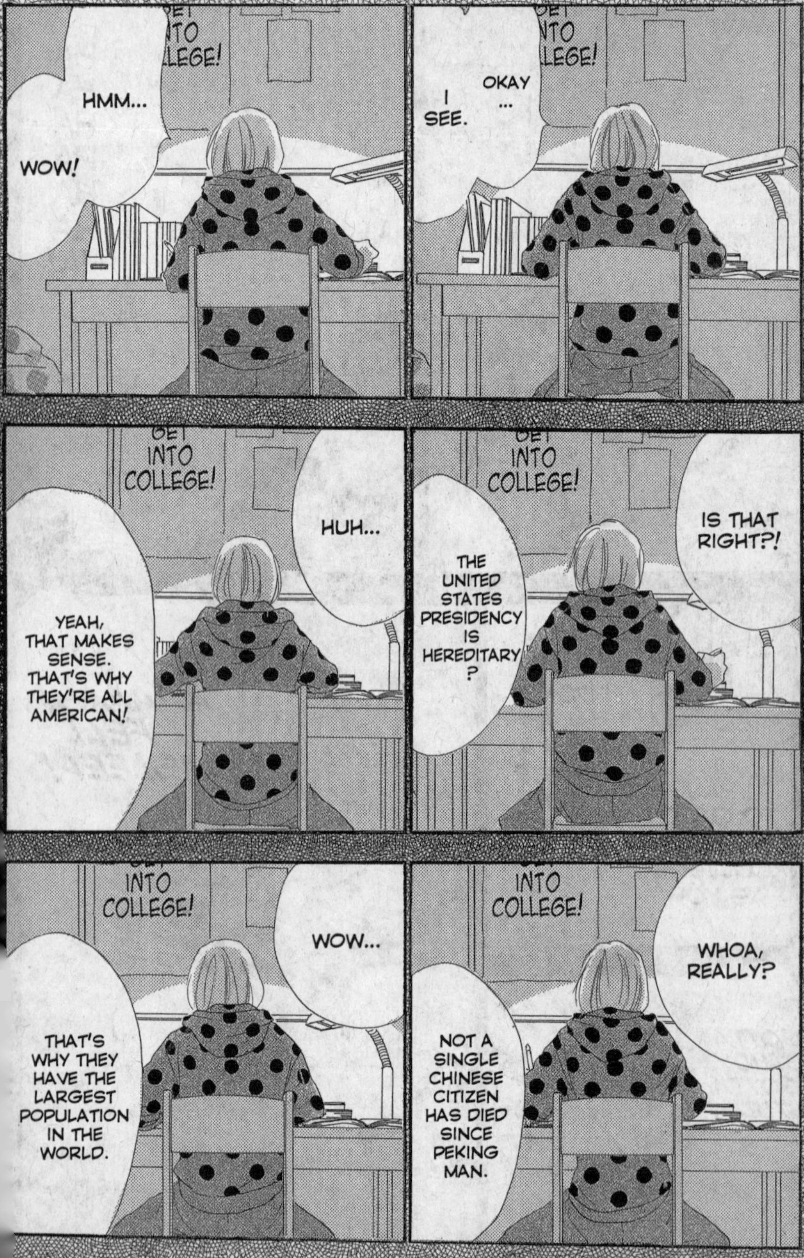

INTO COLLEGE!
OKAY ...
I SEE.
INTO COLLEGE!
HMM...
WOW!
INTO COLLEGE!
IS THAT RIGHT?!
THE UNITED STATES PRESIDENCY IS HEREDITARY?
INTO COLLEGE!
HUH...
YEAH, THAT MAKES SENSE. THAT'S WHY THEY'RE ALL AMERICAN!
INTO COLLEGE!
WHOA, REALLY?
NOT A SINGLE CHINESE CITIZEN HAS DIED SINCE PEKING MAN.
INTO COLLEGE!
WOW...
THAT'S WHY THEY HAVE THE LARGEST POPULATION IN THE WORLD.

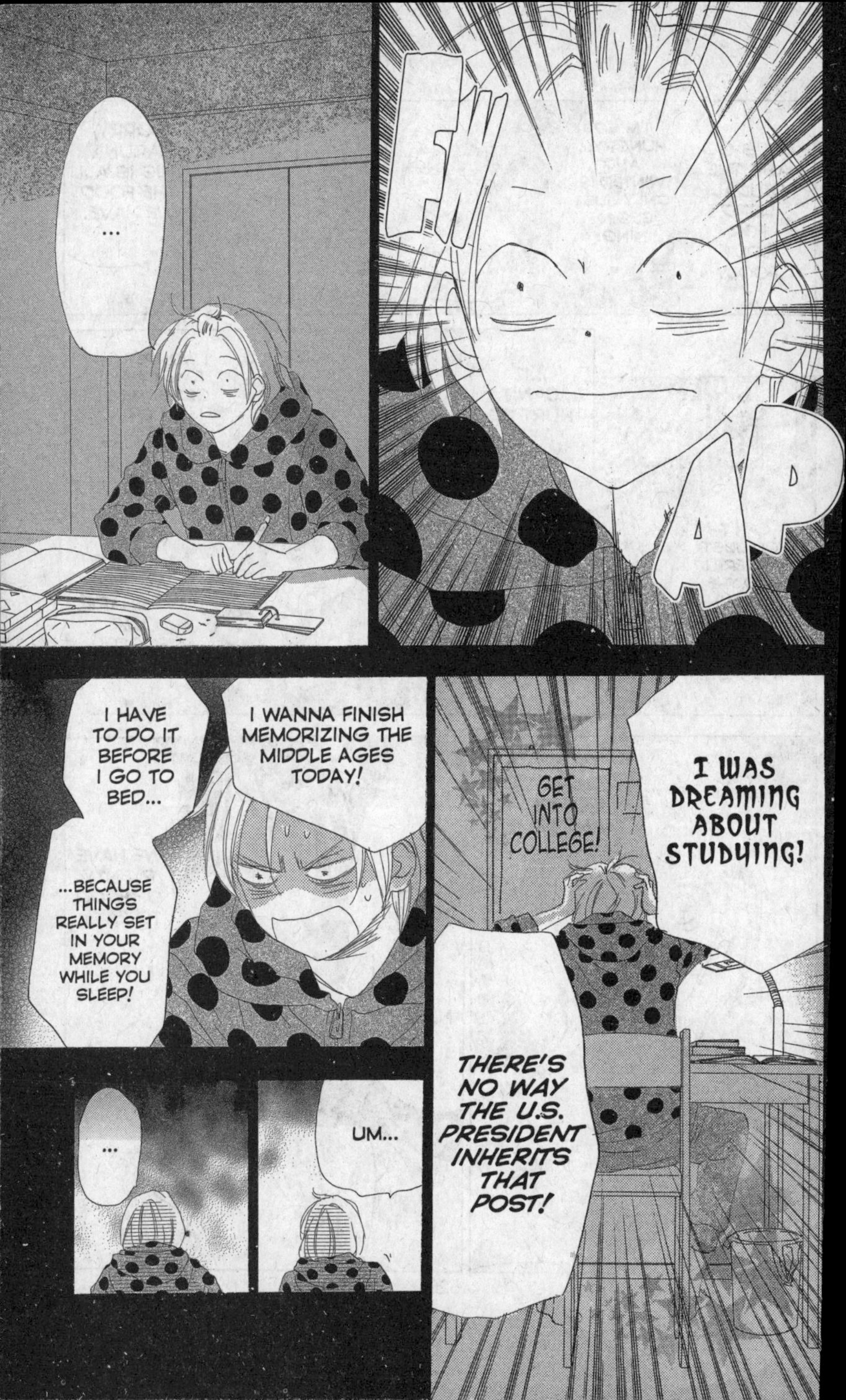
...
I WAS DREAMING ABOUT STUDYING!
GET INTO COLLEGE!
THERE'S NO WAY THE U.S. PRESIDENT INHERITS THAT POST!
I WANNA FINISH MEMORIZING THE MIDDLE AGES TODAY!
I HAVE TO DO IT BEFORE I GO TO BED...
...BECAUSE THINGS REALLY SET IN YOUR MEMORY WHILE YOU SLEEP!
UM...
...

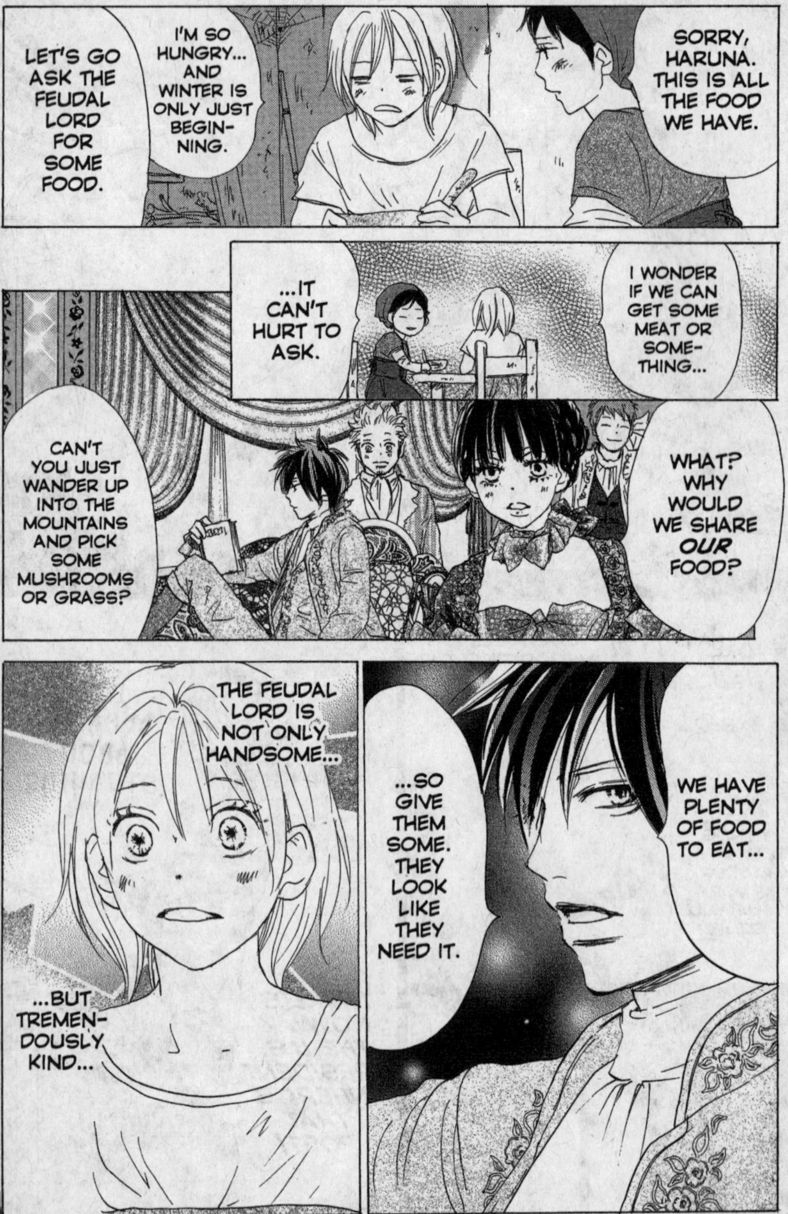
SORRY, HARUNA. THIS IS ALL THE FOOD WE HAVE.
I'M SO HUNGRY... AND WINTER IS ONLY JUST BEGINNING.
LET'S GO ASK THE FEUDAL LORD FOR SOME FOOD.
I WONDER IF WE CAN GET SOME MEAT OR SOMETHING...
...IT CAN'T HURT TO ASK.
WHAT? WHY WOULD WE SHARE ***OUR*** FOOD?
CAN'T YOU JUST WANDER UP INTO THE MOUNTAINS AND PICK SOME MUSHROOMS OR GRASS?
WE HAVE PLENTY OF FOOD TO EAT...
...SO GIVE THEM SOME. THEY LOOK LIKE THEY NEED IT.
THE FEUDAL LORD IS NOT ONLY HANDSOME...
...BUT TREMENDOUSLY KIND...

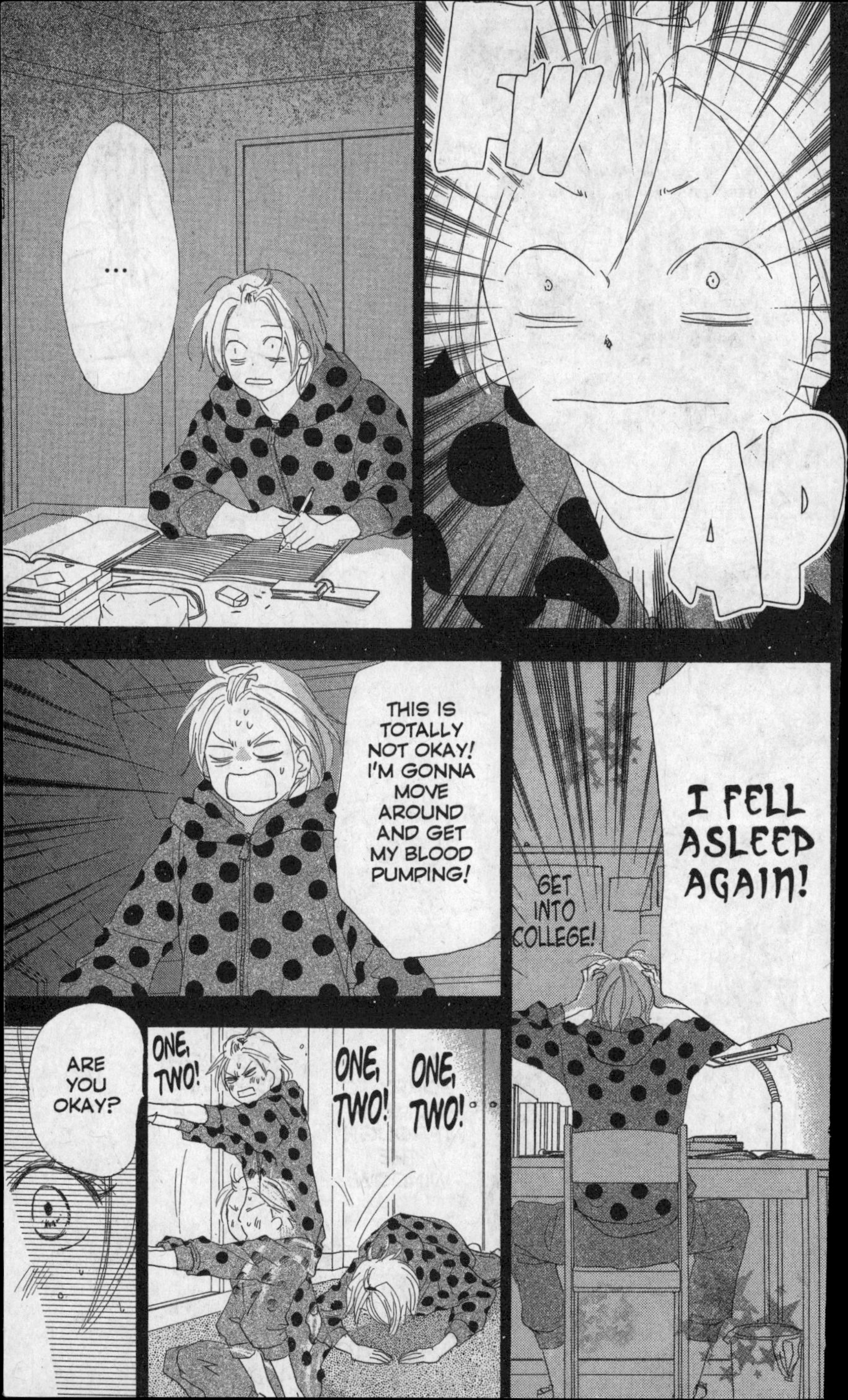
FWAP
...
I FELL ASLEEP AGAIN!
GET INTO COLLEGE!
THIS IS TOTALLY NOT OKAY! I'M GONNA MOVE AROUND AND GET MY BLOOD PUMPING!
ONE, TWO!
ONE, TWO!
ONE, TWO!
ARE YOU OKAY?

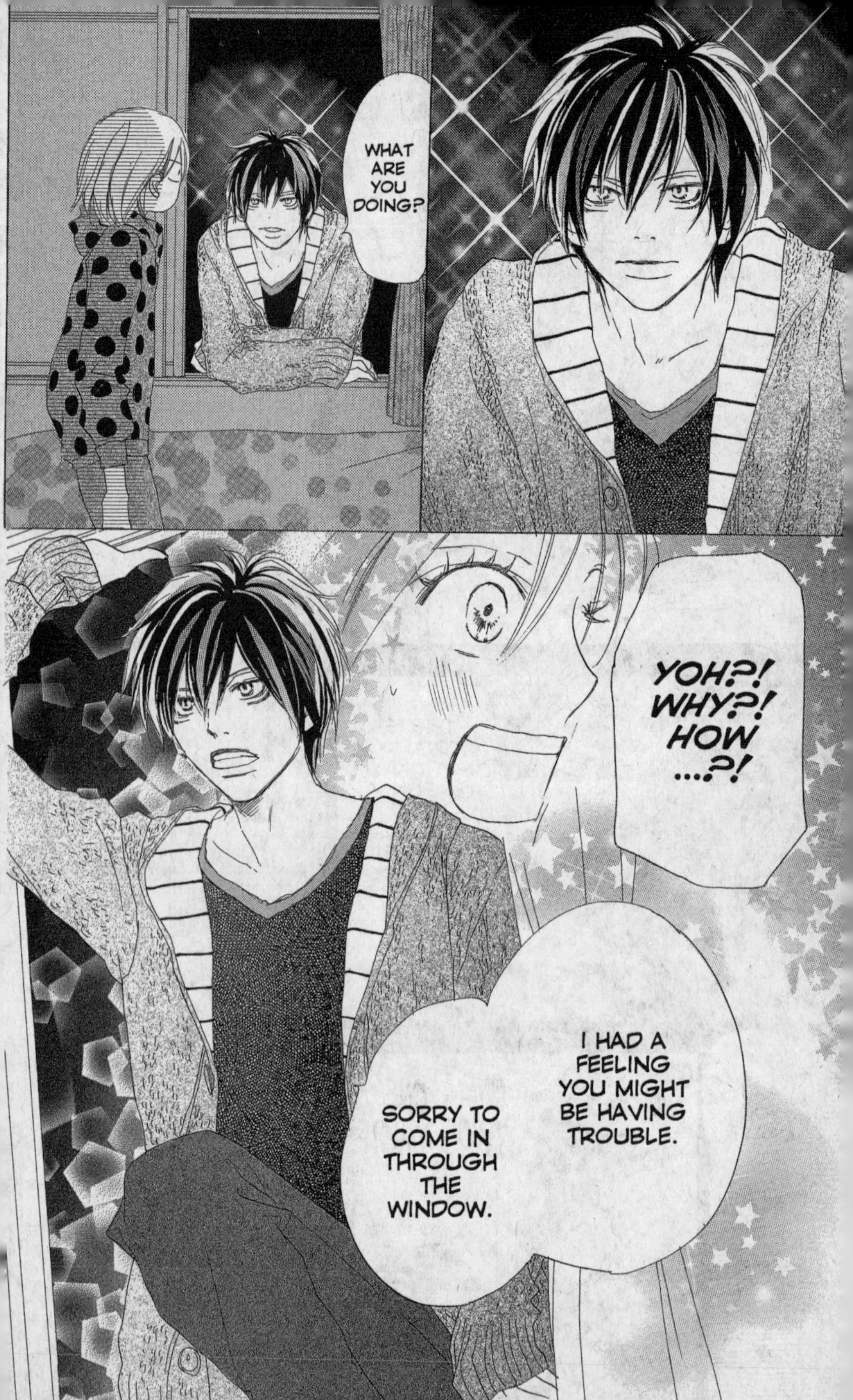
WHAT ARE YOU DOING?
YOH?! WHY?! HOW ...?!
I HAD A FEELING YOU MIGHT BE HAVING TROUBLE.
SORRY TO COME IN THROUGH THE WINDOW.

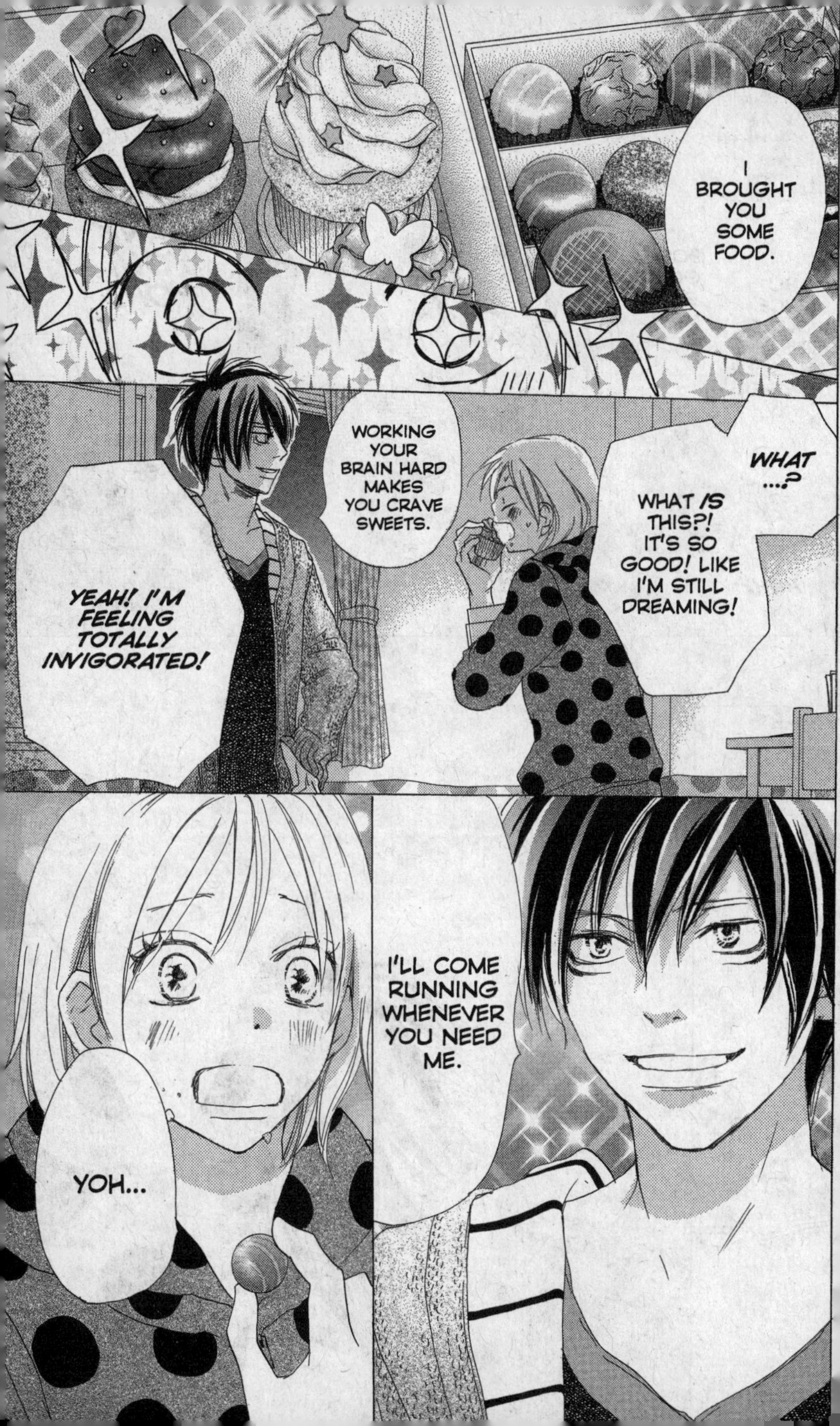
I BROUGHT YOU SOME FOOD.
WHAT ...?
WHAT IS THIS?! IT'S SO GOOD! LIKE I'M STILL DREAMING!
WORKING YOUR BRAIN HARD MAKES YOU CRAVE SWEETS.
YEAH! I'M FEELING TOTALLY INVIGORATED!
I'LL COME RUNNING WHENEVER YOU NEED ME.
YOH...

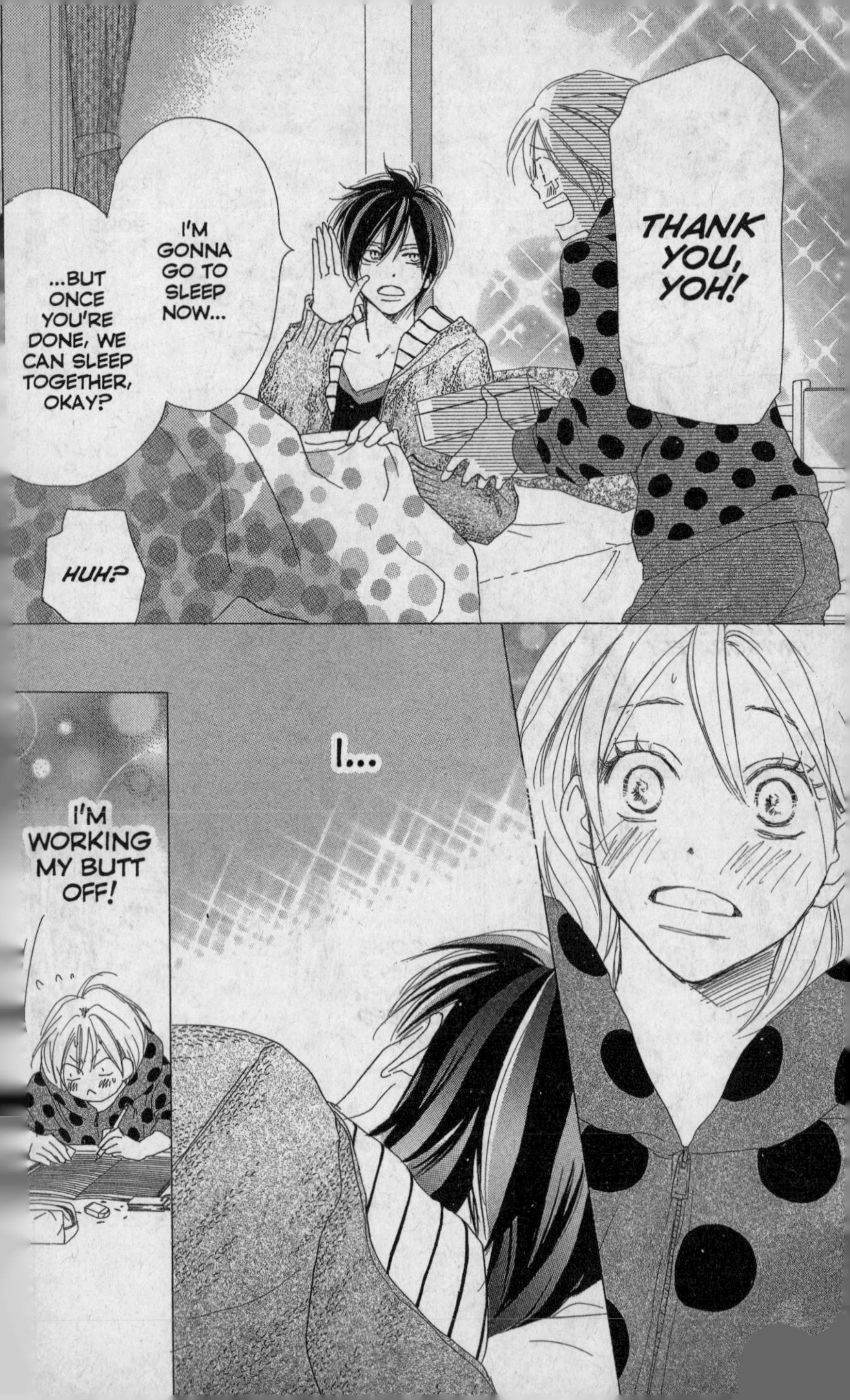
THANK YOU, YOH!
I'M GONNA GO TO SLEEP NOW...
...BUT ONCE YOU'RE DONE, WE CAN SLEEP TOGETHER, OKAY?
HUH?
I...
I'M WORKING MY BUTT OFF!

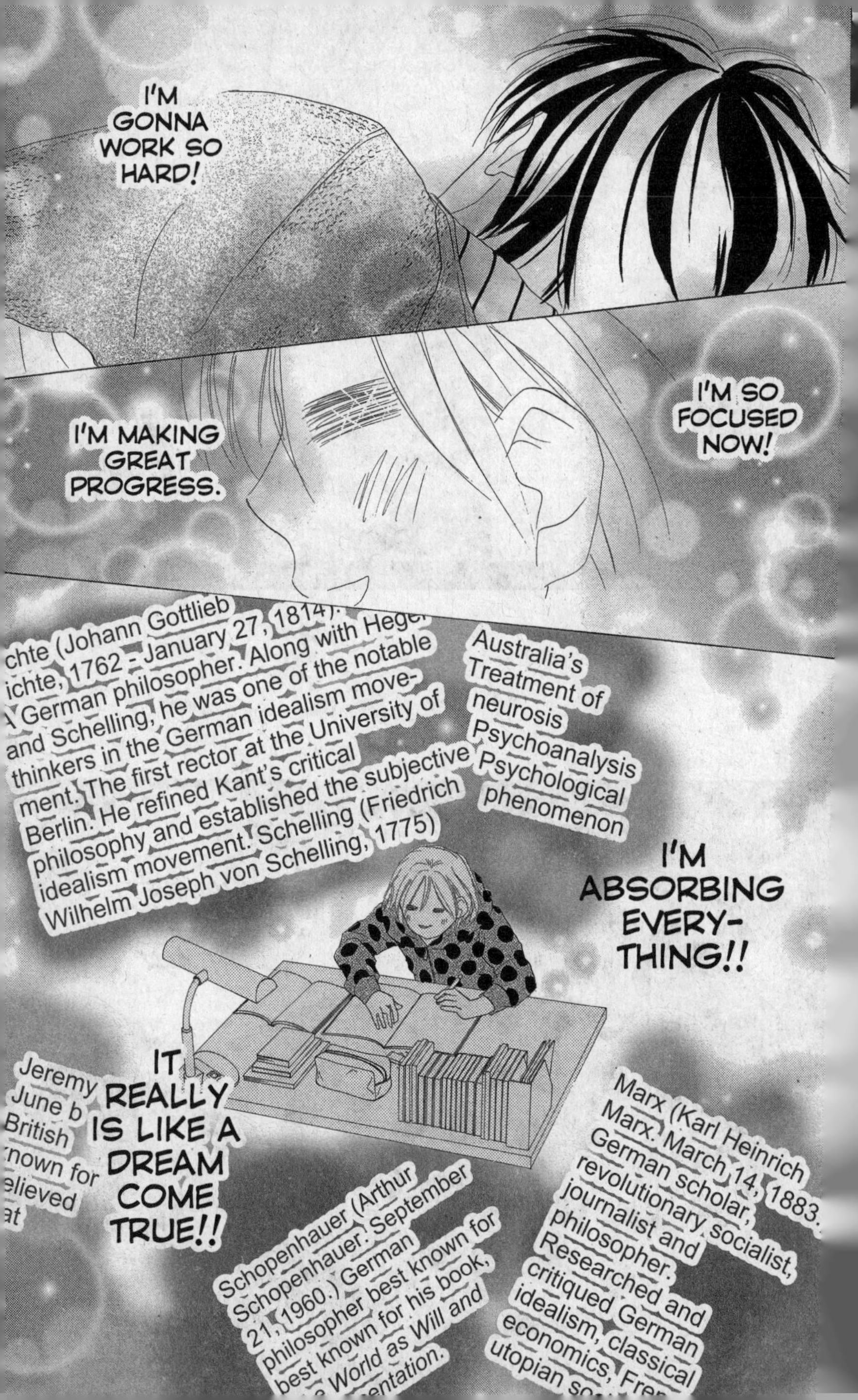
I'M GONNA WORK SO HARD!
I'M SO FOCUSED NOW!
I'M MAKING GREAT PROGRESS.
Australia's Treatment of neurosis Psychoanalysis Psychological phenomenon
ichte (Johann Gottlieb ichte, 1762 - January 27, 1814). A German philosopher. Along with Hegel and Schelling, he was one of the notable thinkers in the German idealism movement. The first rector at the University of Berlin. He refined Kant's critical philosophy and established the subjective idealism movement. Schelling (Friedrich Wilhelm Joseph von Schelling, 1775)
I'M ABSORBING EVERYTHING!!
Marx (Karl Heinrich Marx. March 14, 1883. German scholar, revolutionary socialist, journalist and philosopher. Researched and critiqued German idealism, classical economics, Fren utopian so
IT REALLY IS LIKE A DREAM COME TRUE!!
Jeremy June b British nown for elieved at
Schopenhauer (Arthur Schopenhauer. September 21, 1960.) German philosopher best known for best known for his book, World as Will and entation.

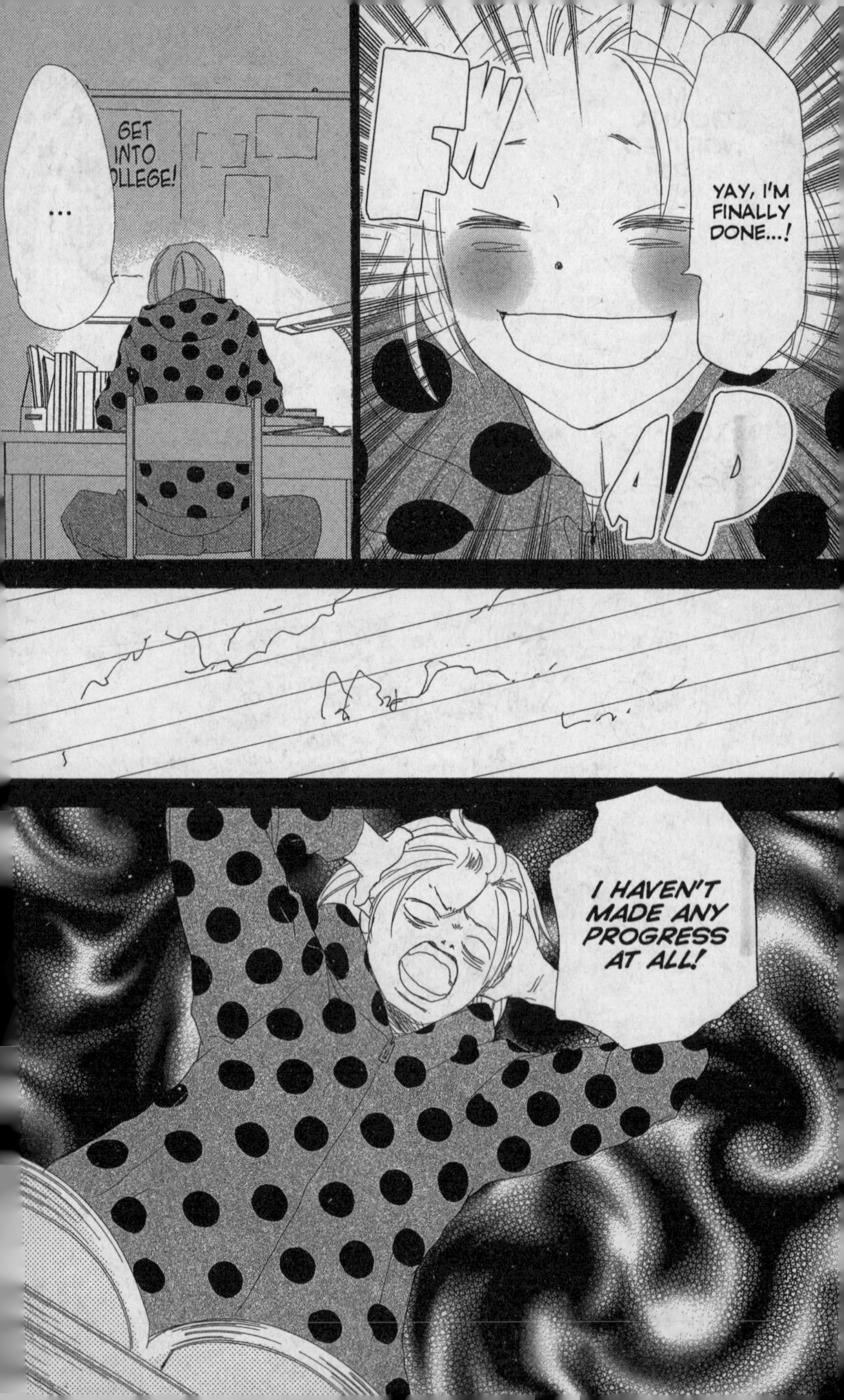
FWAP
YAY, I'M FINALLY DONE...!
...
GET INTO OLLEGE!
I HAVEN'T MADE ANY PROGRESS AT ALL!

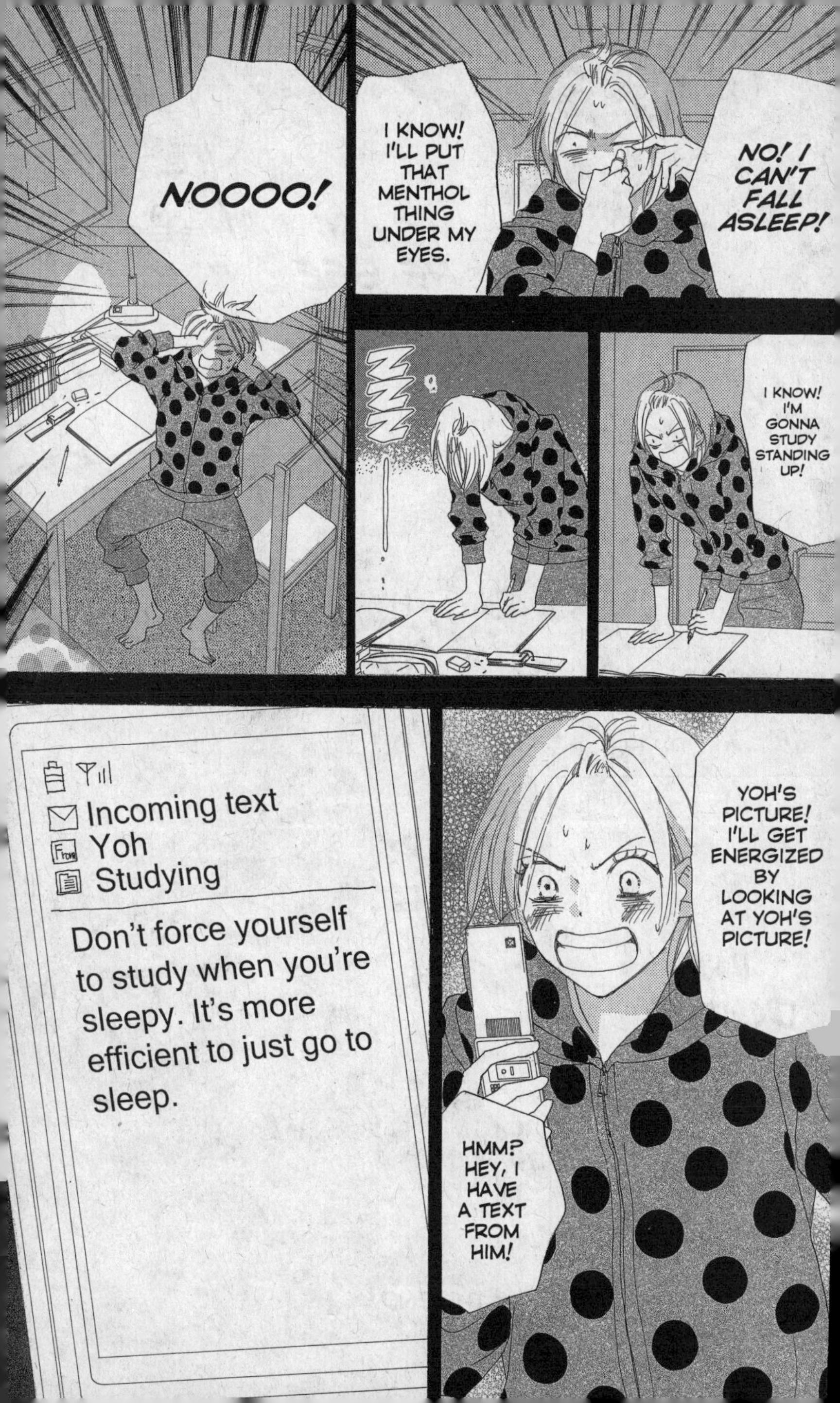
NO! I CAN'T FALL ASLEEP!
I KNOW! I'LL PUT THAT MENTHOL THING UNDER MY EYES.
I KNOW! I'M GONNA STUDY STANDING UP!
ZZZ
NOOOO!
YOH'S PICTURE! I'LL GET ENERGIZED BY LOOKING AT YOH'S PICTURE!
HMM? HEY, I HAVE A TEXT FROM HIM!
Incoming text
Yoh
Studying
Don't force yourself to study when you're sleepy. It's more efficient to just go to sleep.

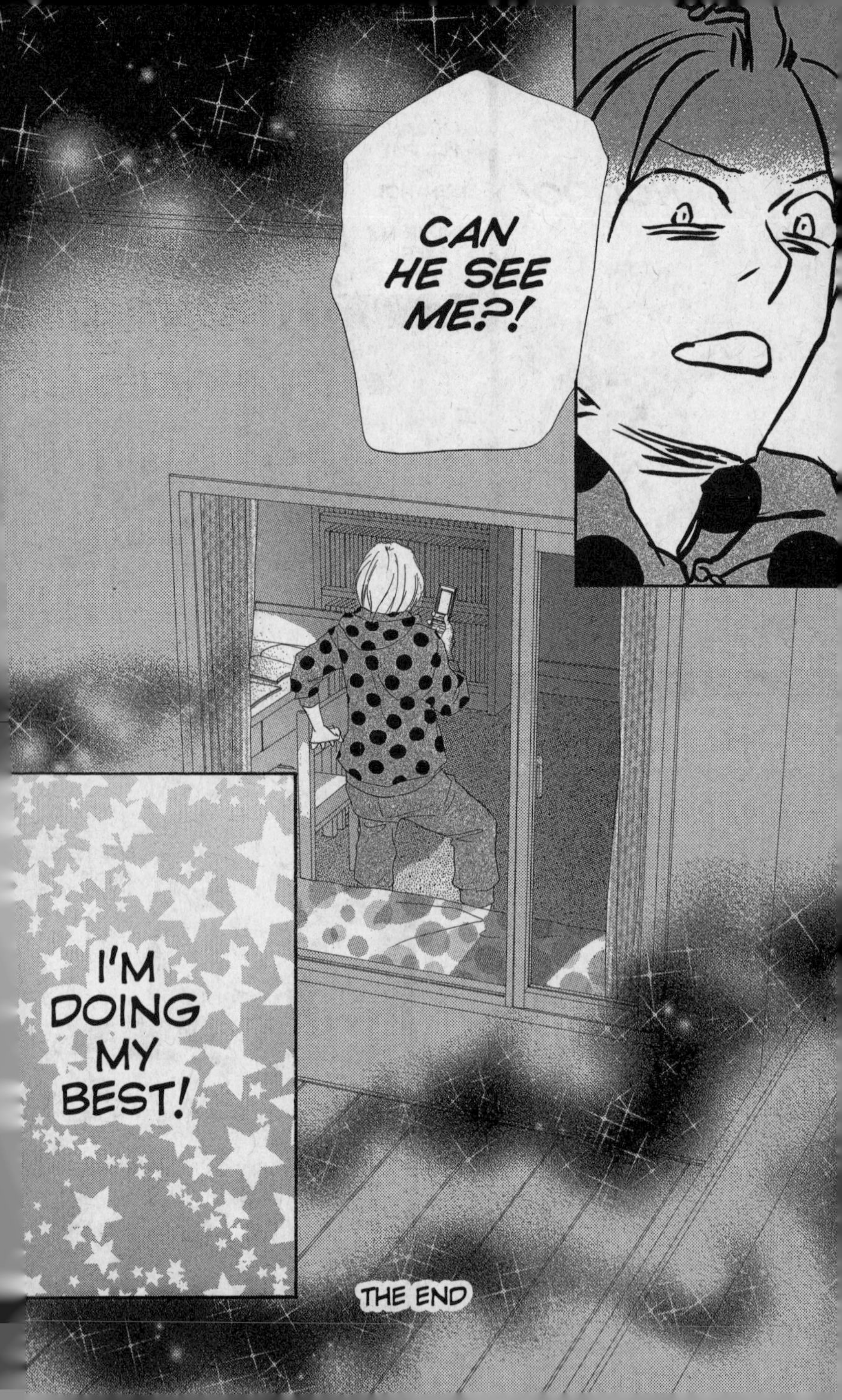
CAN HE SEE ME?!
I'M DOING MY BEST!
THE END

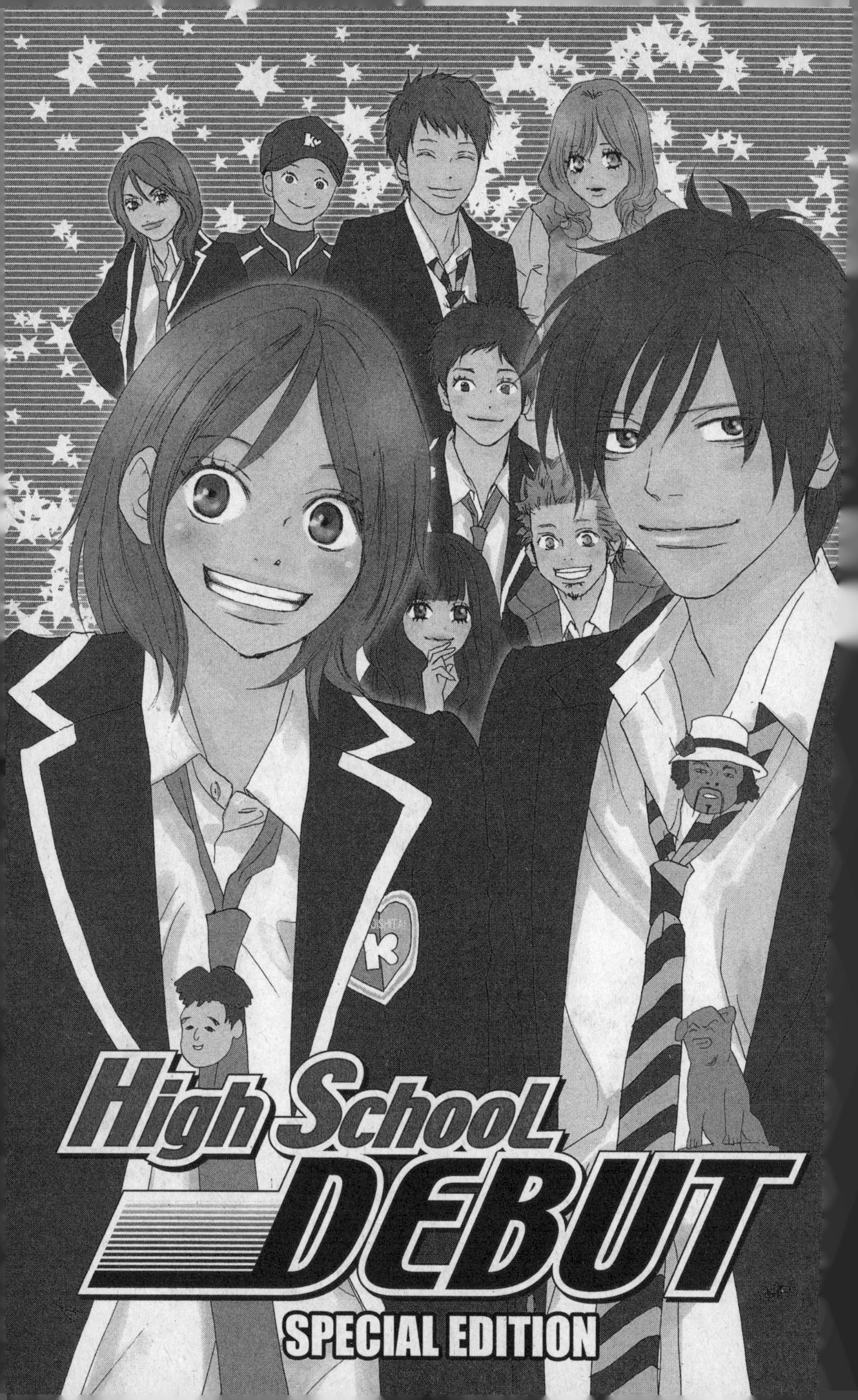
High School
DEBUT
SPECIAL EDITION

TO ALL THE READERS WHO WAIT PATIENTLY FOR MY MANGA TO BE PUBLISHED: THANK YOU VERY MUCH! IT MAKES ME SO HAPPY. THE NEXT VOLUME WILL BE COMING OUT SOON, SO IF YOU HAPPEN TO SEE IT, I'D BE THRILLED IF YOU CHECK IT OUT!

KAZUNE KAWAHARA, 2013

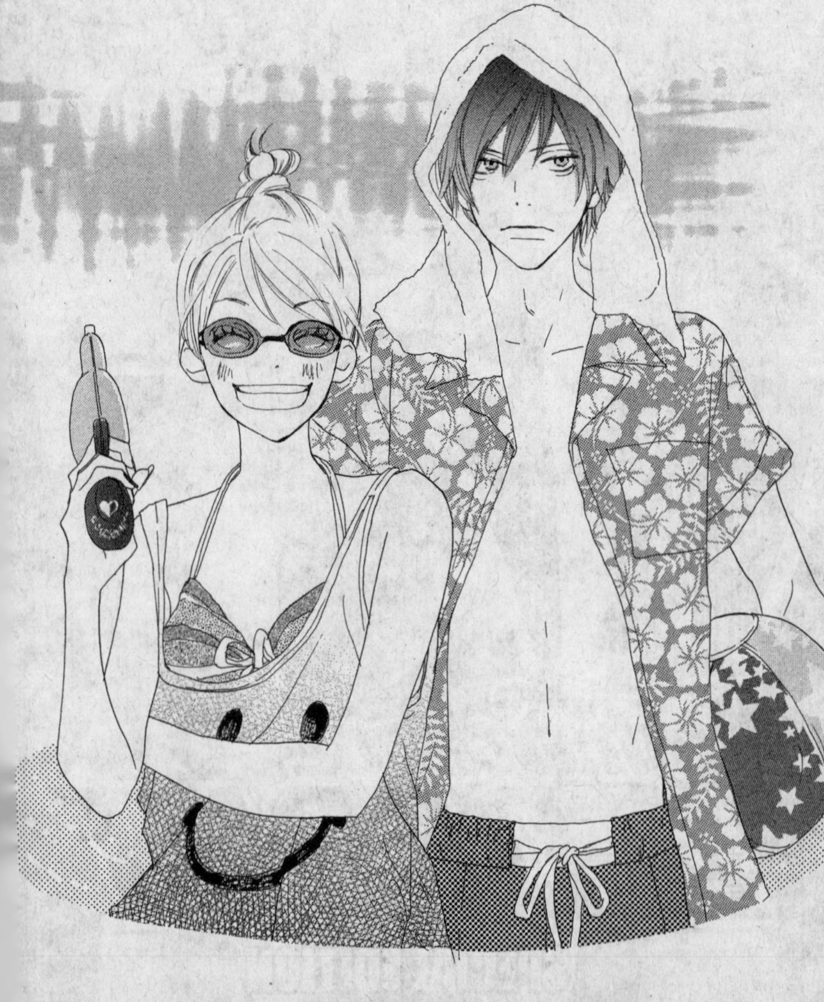

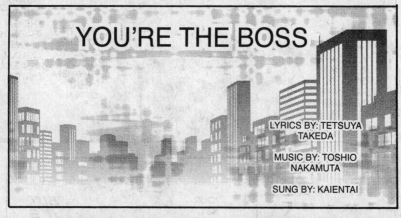

YOU'RE THE BOSS

LYRICS BY: TETSUYA TAKEDA

MUSIC BY: TOSHIO NAKAMUTA

SUNG BY: KAIENTAI

HUH?

YOU'RE STARTING OFF WITH A TETSUYA TAKEDA SONG?

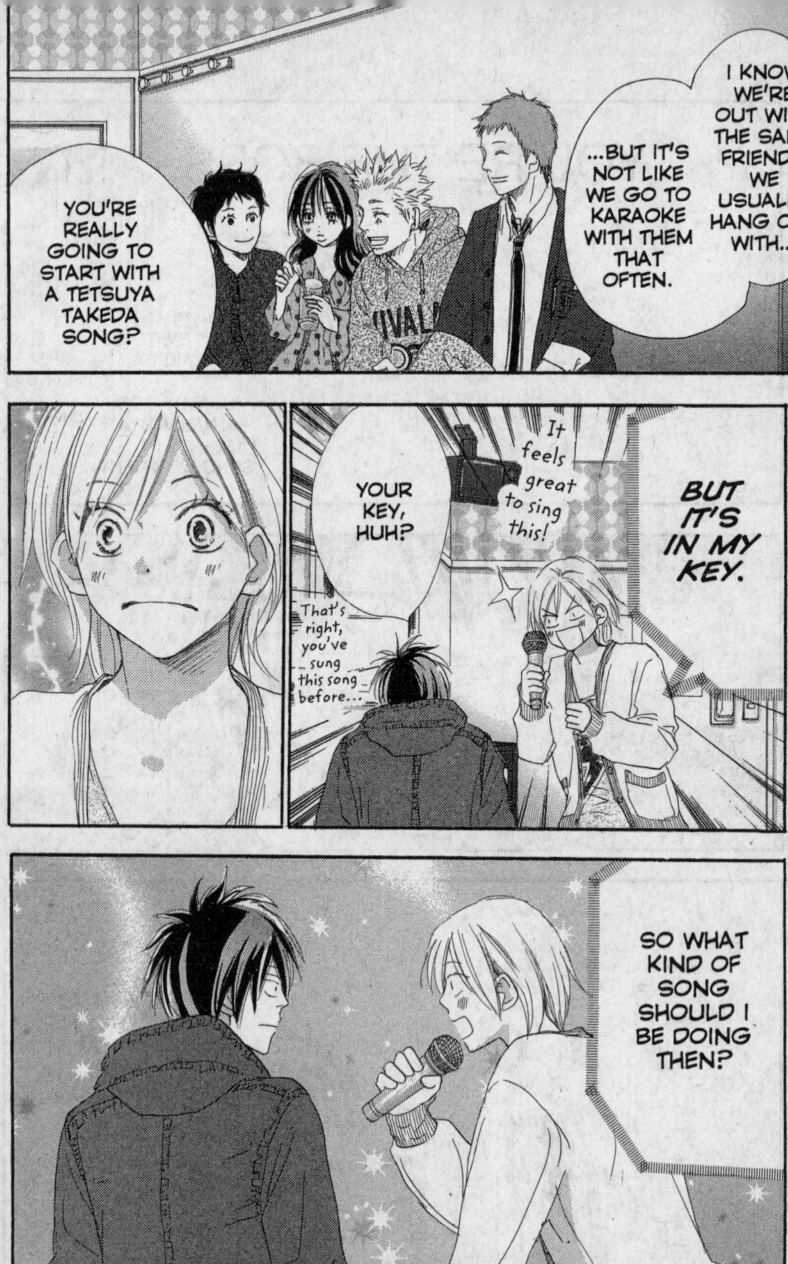
I KNOW WE'RE OUT WITH THE SAME FRIENDS WE USUALLY HANG OUT WITH...
...BUT IT'S NOT LIKE WE GO TO KARAOKE WITH THEM THAT OFTEN.
YOU'RE REALLY GOING TO START WITH A TETSUYA TAKEDA SONG?
BUT IT'S IN MY KEY.
It feels great to sing this!
YOUR KEY, HUH?
That's right, you've sung this song before...
SO WHAT KIND OF SONG SHOULD I BE DOING THEN?

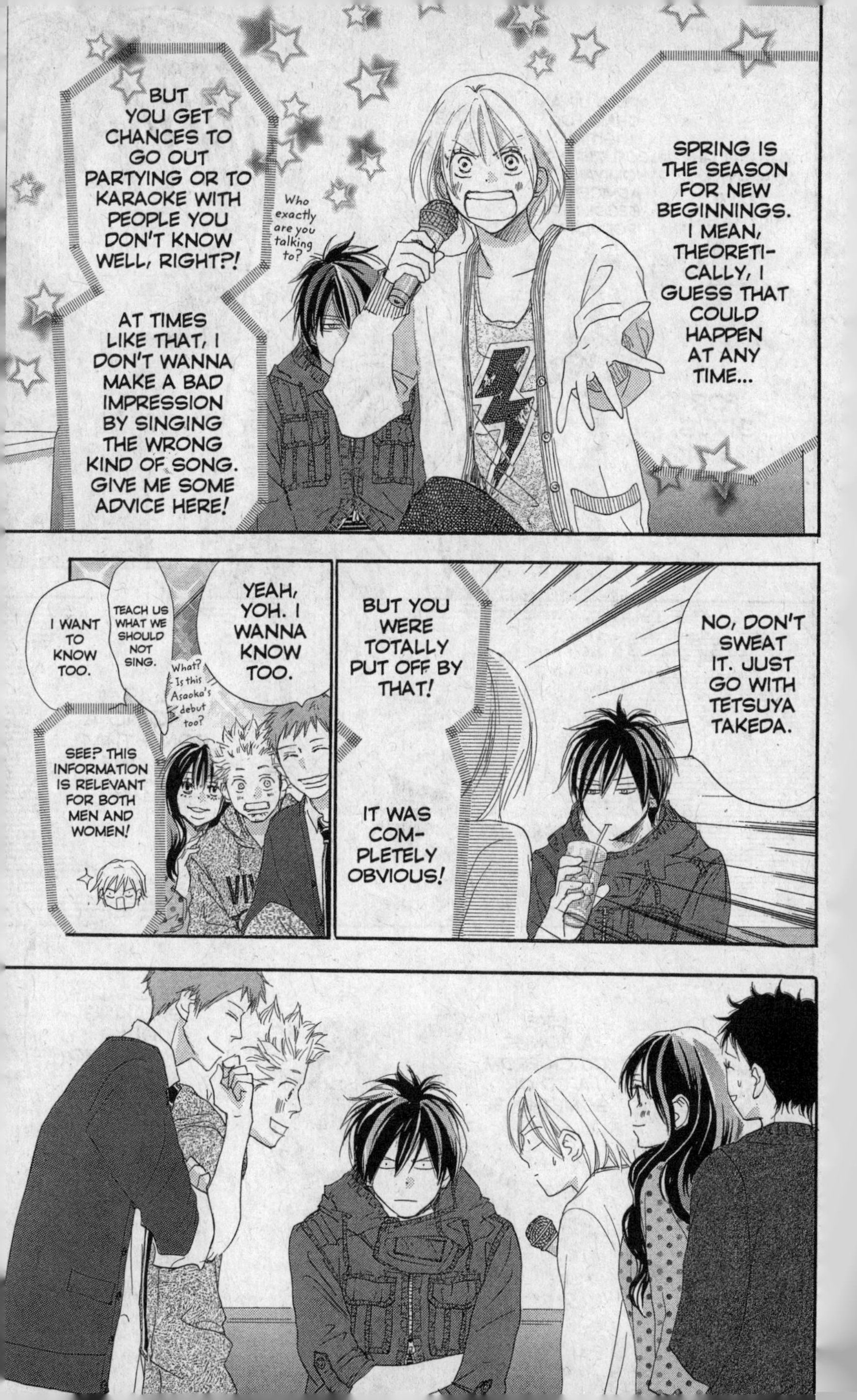
SPRING IS THE SEASON FOR NEW BEGINNINGS. I MEAN, THEORETI-CALLY, I GUESS THAT COULD HAPPEN AT ANY TIME...
BUT YOU GET CHANCES TO GO OUT PARTYING OR TO KARAOKE WITH PEOPLE YOU DON'T KNOW WELL, RIGHT?!
AT TIMES LIKE THAT, I DON'T WANNA MAKE A BAD IMPRESSION BY SINGING THE WRONG KIND OF SONG. GIVE ME SOME ADVICE HERE!
Who exactly are you talking to?
NO, DON'T SWEAT IT. JUST GO WITH TETSUYA TAKEDA.
BUT YOU WERE TOTALLY PUT OFF BY THAT!
IT WAS COM-PLETELY OBVIOUS!
YEAH, YOH. I WANNA KNOW TOO.
TEACH US WHAT WE SHOULD NOT SING.
I WANT TO KNOW TOO.
What? Is this Asaoka's debut too?
SEE? THIS INFORMATION IS RELEVANT FOR BOTH MEN AND WOMEN!

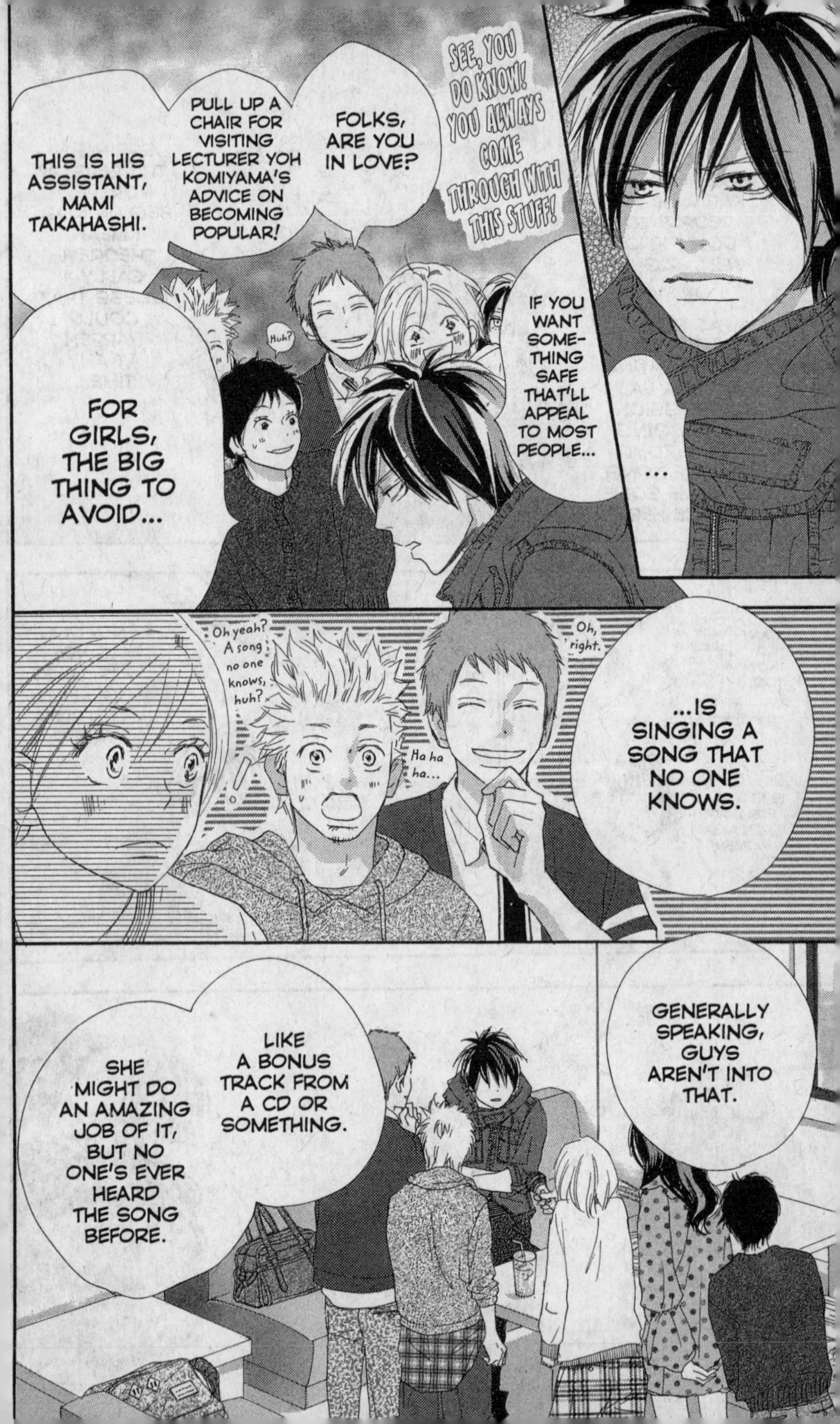
...
SEE, YOU DO KNOW! YOU ALWAYS COME THROUGH WITH THIS STUFF!
IF YOU WANT SOMETHING SAFE THAT'LL APPEAL TO MOST PEOPLE...
FOLKS, ARE YOU IN LOVE?
PULL UP A CHAIR FOR VISITING LECTURER YOH KOMIYAMA'S ADVICE ON BECOMING POPULAR!
THIS IS HIS ASSISTANT, MAMI TAKAHASHI.
Huh?
FOR GIRLS, THE BIG THING TO AVOID...
...IS SINGING A SONG THAT NO ONE KNOWS.
Oh, right.
Ha ha ha...
Oh yeah? A song no one knows, huh?
GENERALLY SPEAKING, GUYS AREN'T INTO THAT.
LIKE A BONUS TRACK FROM A CD OR SOMETHING.
SHE MIGHT DO AN AMAZING JOB OF IT, BUT NO ONE'S EVER HEARD THE SONG BEFORE.

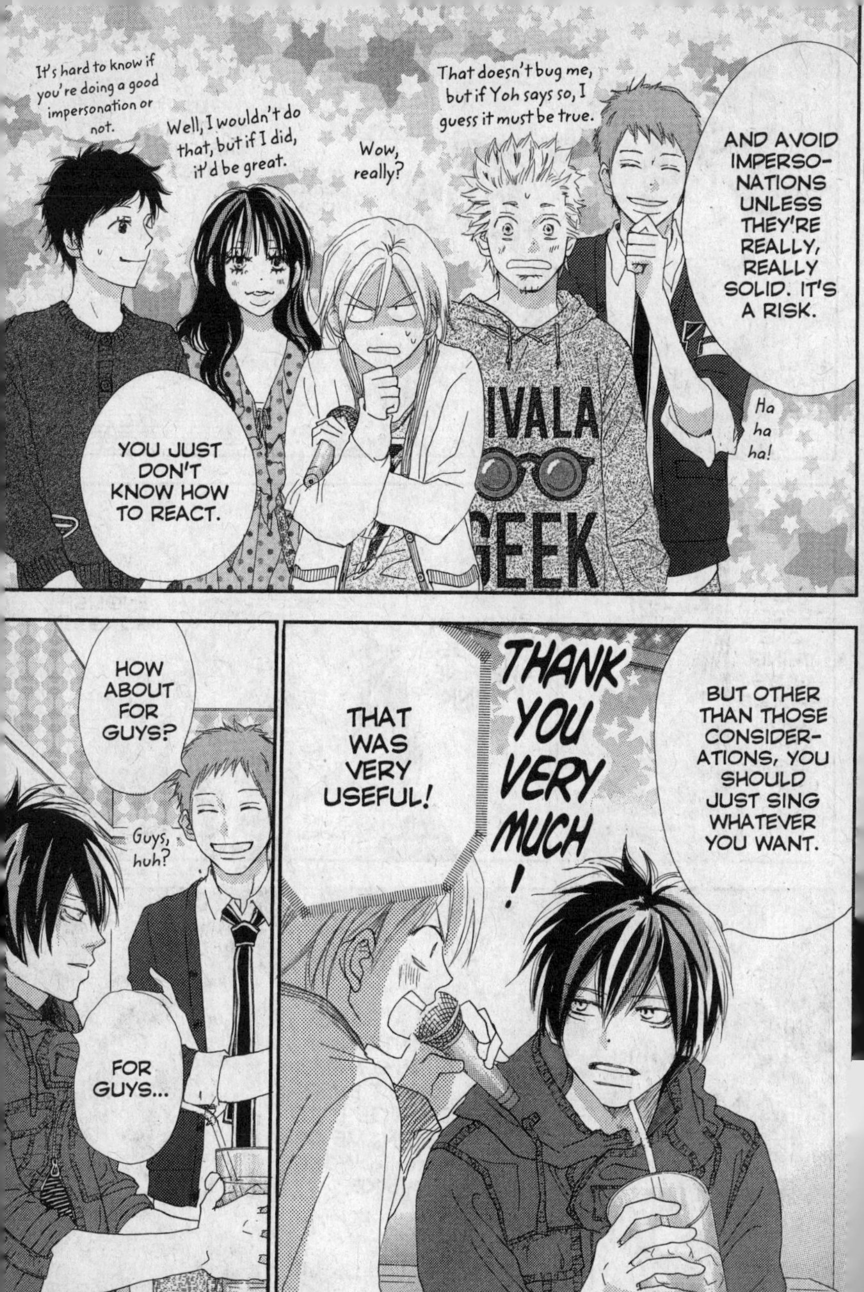
AND AVOID IMPERSONATIONS UNLESS THEY'RE REALLY, REALLY SOLID. IT'S A RISK.
Ha ha ha!
That doesn't bug me, but if Yoh says so, I guess it must be true.
Wow, really?
Well, I wouldn't do that, but if I did, it'd be great.
It's hard to know if you're doing a good impersonation or not.
YOU JUST DON'T KNOW HOW TO REACT.
BUT OTHER THAN THOSE CONSIDERATIONS, YOU SHOULD JUST SING WHATEVER YOU WANT.
THANK YOU VERY MUCH!
THAT WAS VERY USEFUL!
HOW ABOUT FOR GUYS?
Guys, huh?
FOR GUYS...

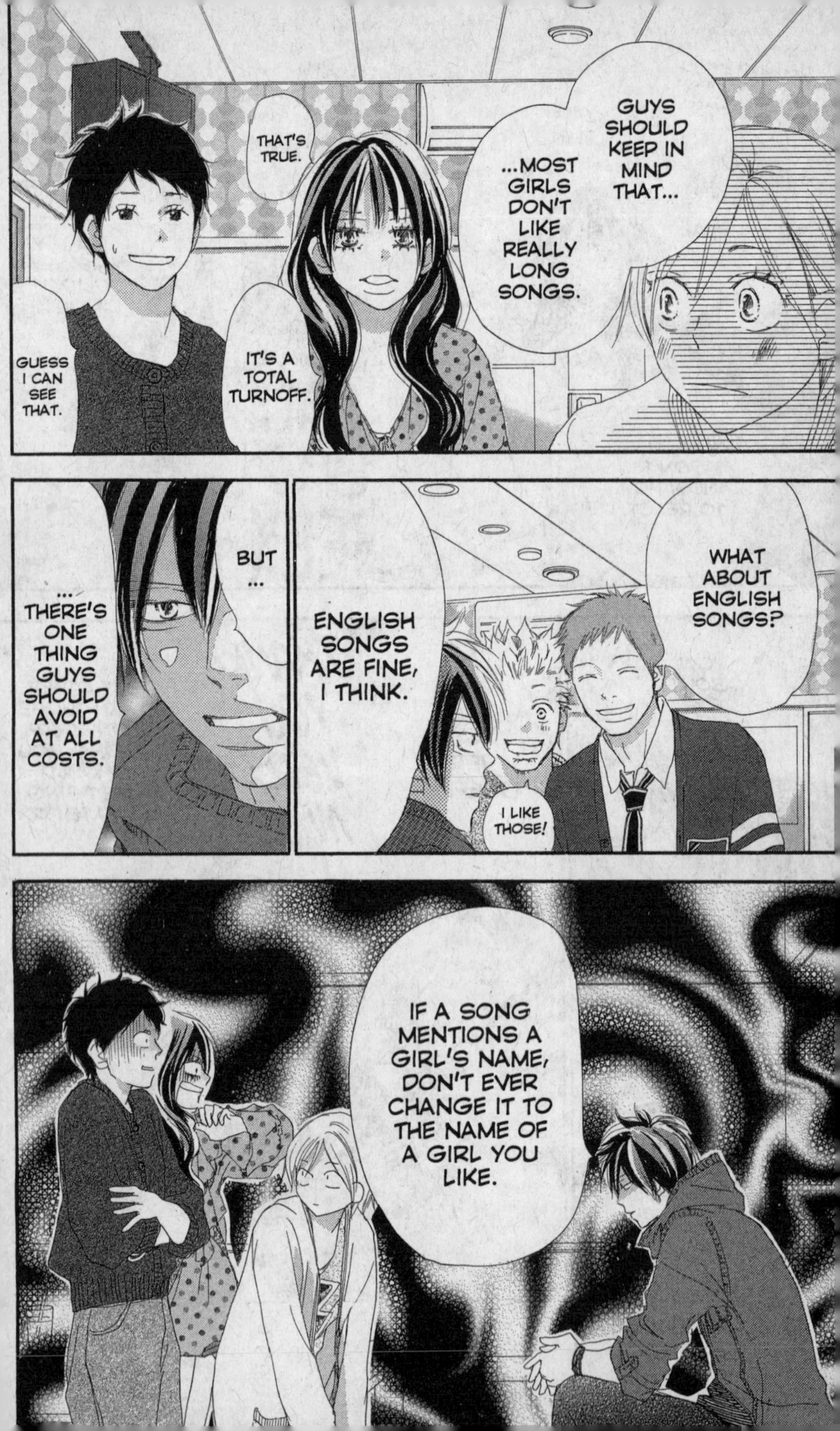
GUYS SHOULD KEEP IN MIND THAT...
...MOST GIRLS DON'T LIKE REALLY LONG SONGS.
THAT'S TRUE.
IT'S A TOTAL TURNOFF.
GUESS I CAN SEE THAT.
WHAT ABOUT ENGLISH SONGS?
ENGLISH SONGS ARE FINE, I THINK.
I LIKE THOSE!
BUT ...
...THERE'S ONE THING GUYS SHOULD AVOID AT ALL COSTS.
IF A SONG MENTIONS A GIRL'S NAME, DON'T EVER CHANGE IT TO THE NAME OF A GIRL YOU LIKE.

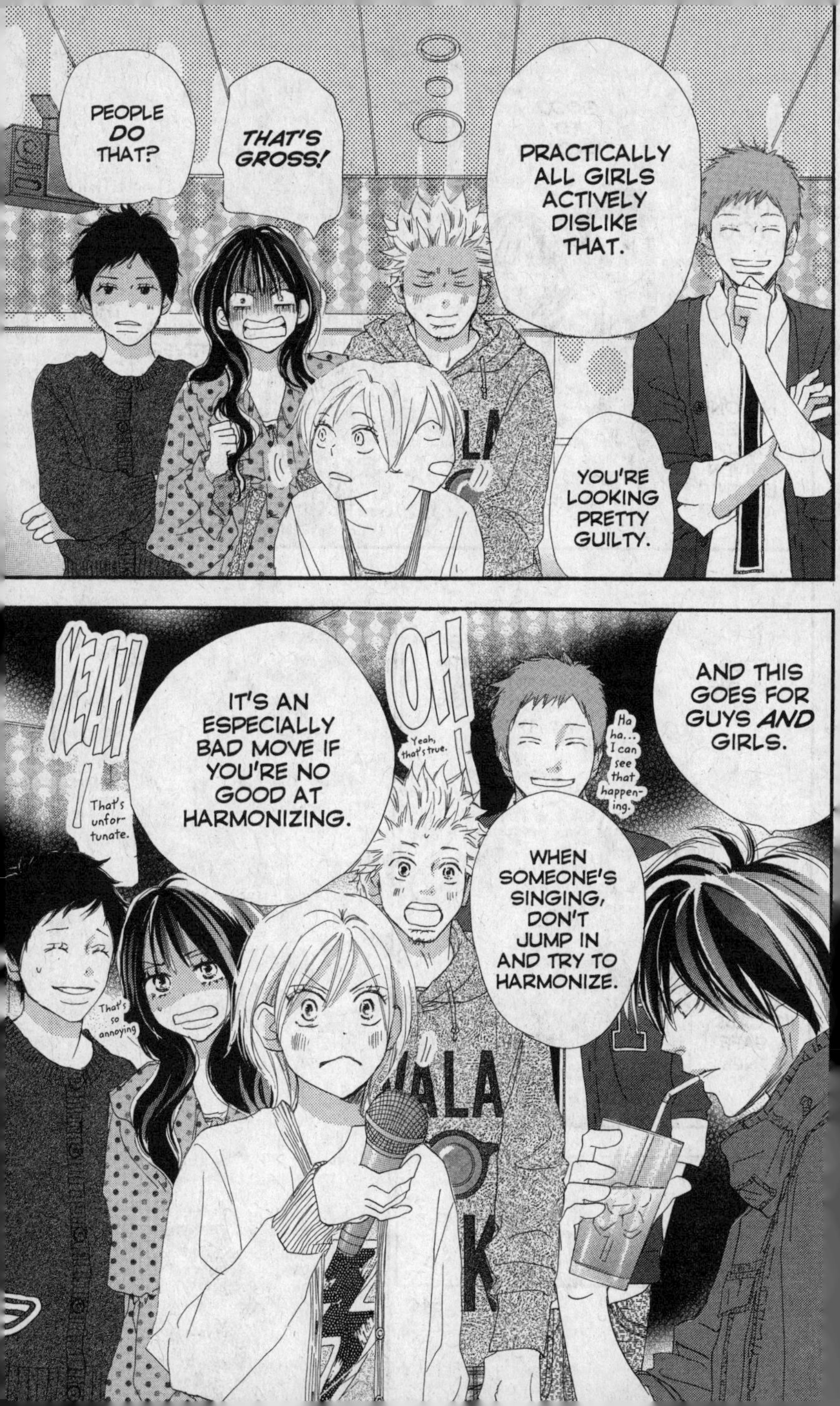
PRACTICALLY ALL GIRLS ACTIVELY DISLIKE THAT.
YOU'RE LOOKING PRETTY GUILTY.
THAT'S GROSS!
PEOPLE *DO* THAT?
AND THIS GOES FOR GUYS *AND* GIRLS.
Ha ha... I can see that happen-ing.
WHEN SOMEONE'S SINGING, DON'T JUMP IN AND TRY TO HARMONIZE.
OH
Yeah, that's true.
IT'S AN ESPECIALLY BAD MOVE IF YOU'RE NO GOOD AT HARMONIZING.
YEAH!
That's unfor-tunate.
That's so annoying

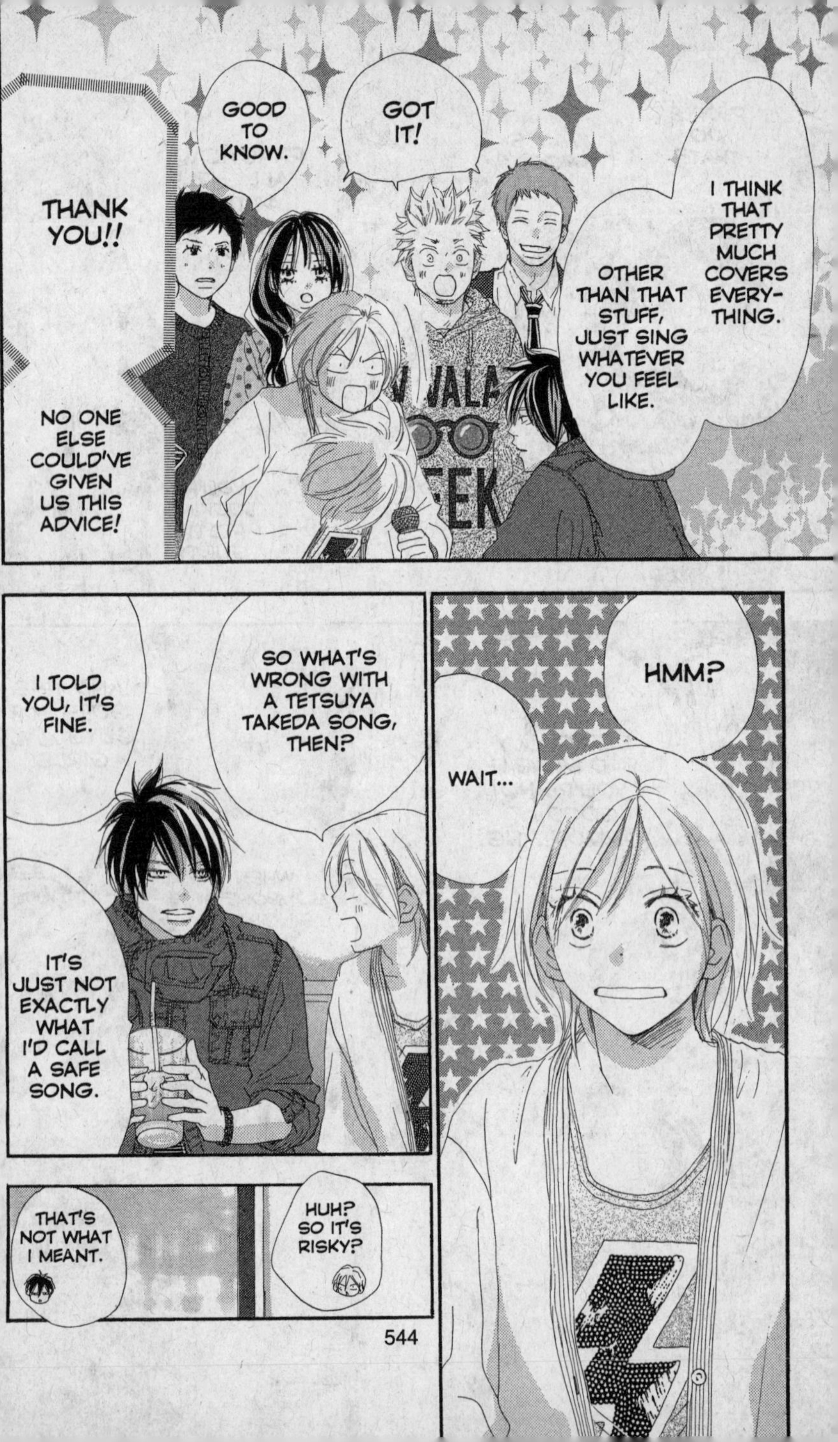
I THINK THAT PRETTY MUCH COVERS EVERY-THING.
OTHER THAN THAT STUFF, JUST SING WHATEVER YOU FEEL LIKE.
GOT IT!
GOOD TO KNOW.
THANK YOU!!
NO ONE ELSE COULD'VE GIVEN US THIS ADVICE!
HMM?
WAIT...
SO WHAT'S WRONG WITH A TETSUYA TAKEDA SONG, THEN?
I TOLD YOU, IT'S FINE.
IT'S JUST NOT EXACTLY WHAT I'D CALL A SAFE SONG.
HUH? SO IT'S RISKY?
THAT'S NOT WHAT I MEANT.

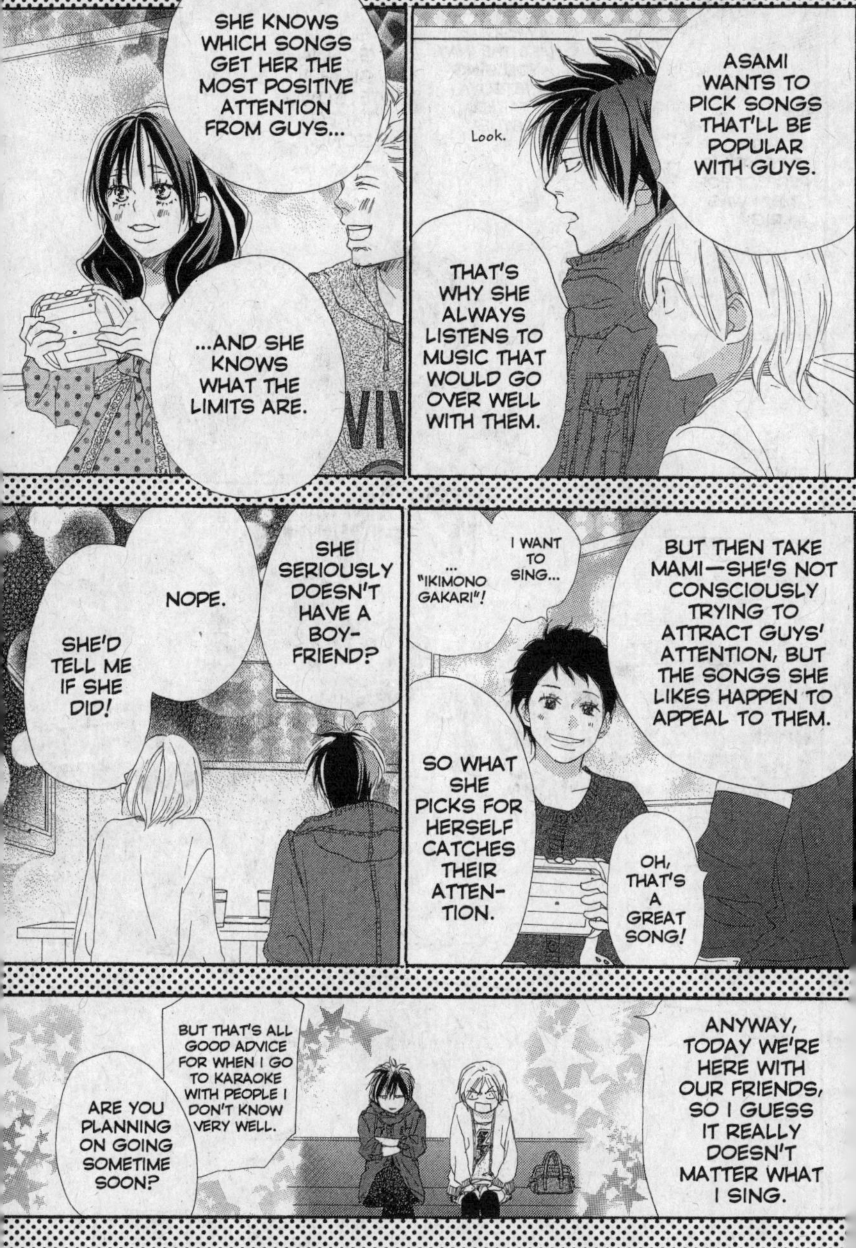
ASAMI WANTS TO PICK SONGS THAT'LL BE POPULAR WITH GUYS.
Look.
THAT'S WHY SHE ALWAYS LISTENS TO MUSIC THAT WOULD GO OVER WELL WITH THEM.
SHE KNOWS WHICH SONGS GET HER THE MOST POSITIVE ATTENTION FROM GUYS...
...AND SHE KNOWS WHAT THE LIMITS ARE.
BUT THEN TAKE MAMI—SHE'S NOT CONSCIOUSLY TRYING TO ATTRACT GUYS' ATTENTION, BUT THE SONGS SHE LIKES HAPPEN TO APPEAL TO THEM.
I WANT TO SING...
... "IKIMONO GAKARI"!
SO WHAT SHE PICKS FOR HERSELF CATCHES THEIR ATTEN-TION.
OH, THAT'S A GREAT SONG!
SHE SERIOUSLY DOESN'T HAVE A BOY-FRIEND?
NOPE.
SHE'D TELL ME IF SHE DID!
ANYWAY, TODAY WE'RE HERE WITH OUR FRIENDS, SO I GUESS IT REALLY DOESN'T MATTER WHAT I SING.
BUT THAT'S ALL GOOD ADVICE FOR WHEN I GO TO KARAOKE WITH PEOPLE I DON'T KNOW VERY WELL.
ARE YOU PLANNING ON GOING SOMETIME SOON?

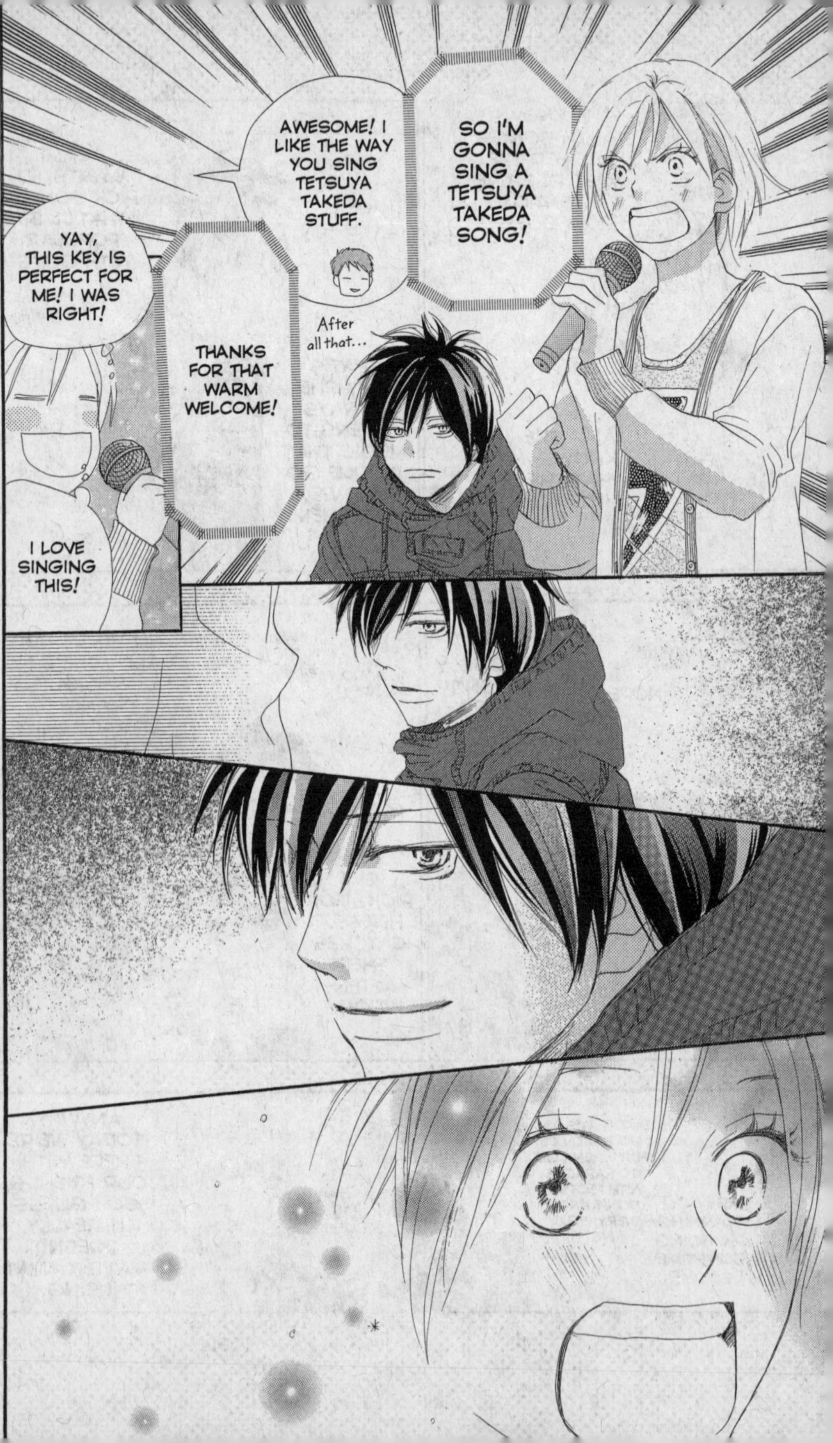
SO I'M GONNA SING A TETSUYA TAKEDA SONG!
AWESOME! I LIKE THE WAY YOU SING TETSUYA TAKEDA STUFF.
After all that...
THANKS FOR THAT WARM WELCOME!
YAY, THIS KEY IS PERFECT FOR ME! I WAS RIGHT!
I LOVE SINGING THIS!

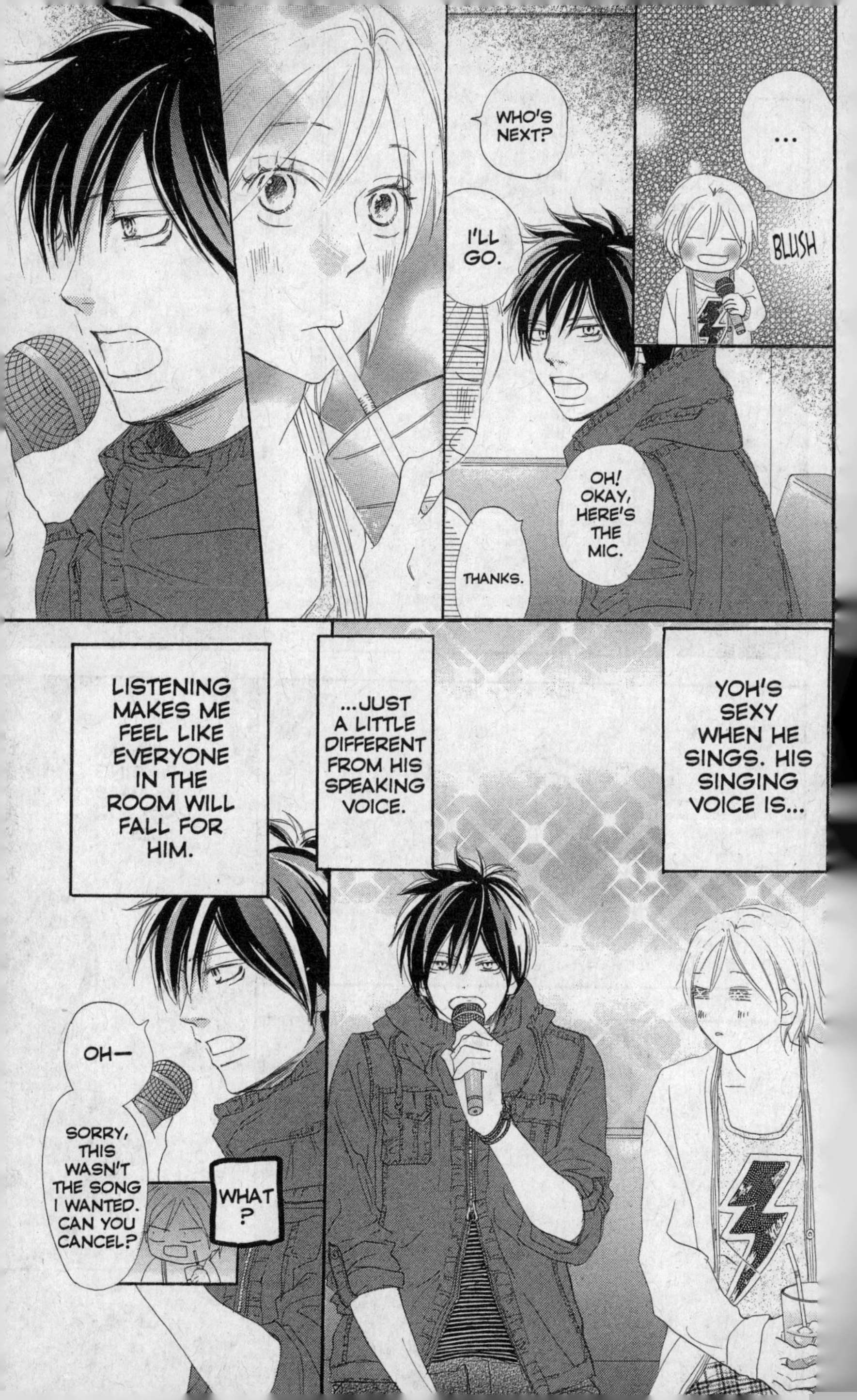

...
BLUSH
WHO'S NEXT?
I'LL GO.
OH! OKAY, HERE'S THE MIC.
THANKS.
YOH'S SEXY WHEN HE SINGS. HIS SINGING VOICE IS...
...JUST A LITTLE DIFFERENT FROM HIS SPEAKING VOICE.
LISTENING MAKES ME FEEL LIKE EVERYONE IN THE ROOM WILL FALL FOR HIM.
OH—
SORRY, THIS WASN'T THE SONG I WANTED. CAN YOU CANCEL?
WHAT?

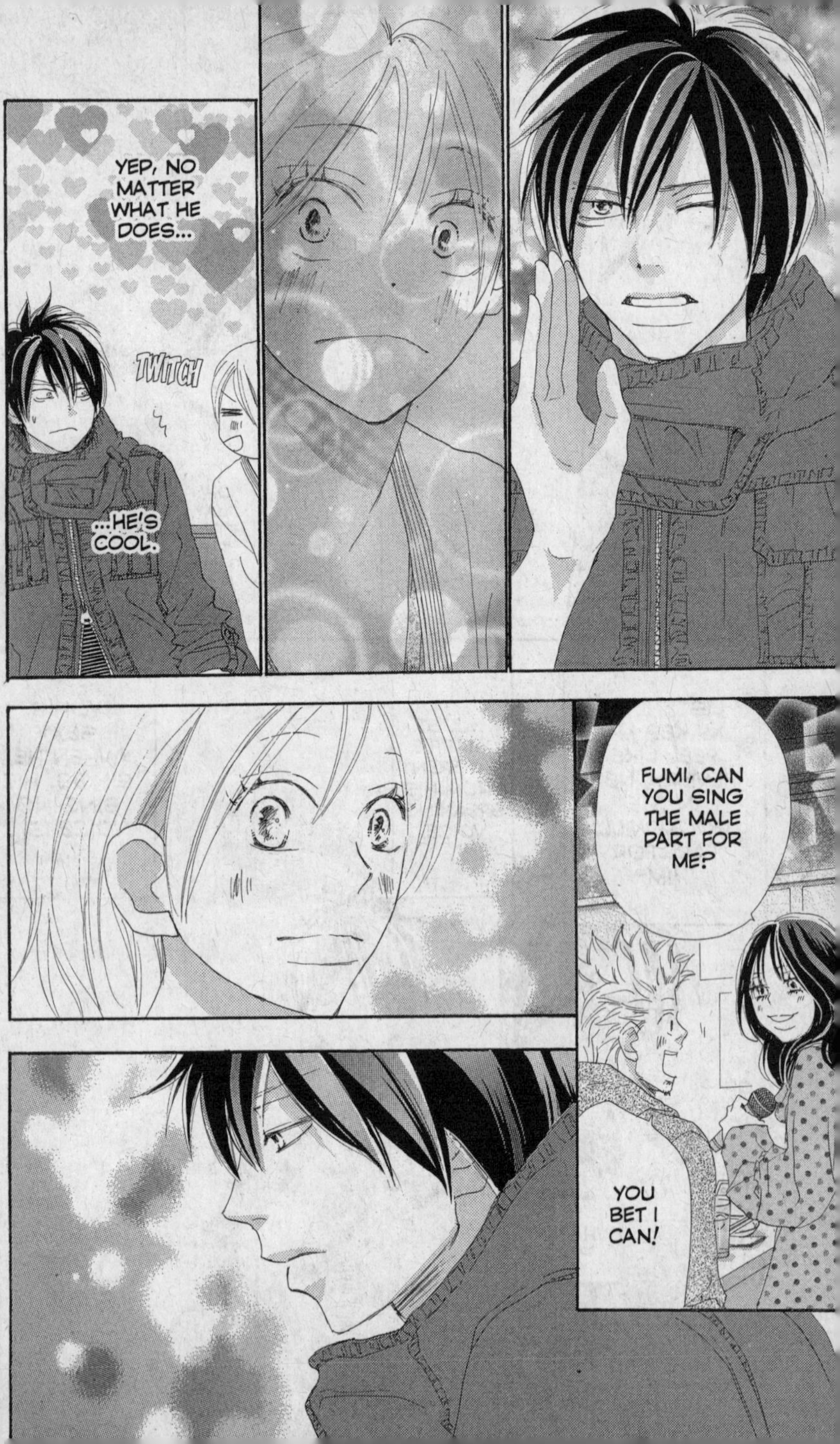
YEP, NO MATTER WHAT HE DOES...
TWITCH
...HE'S COOL.
FUMI, CAN YOU SING THE MALE PART FOR ME?
YOU BET I CAN!

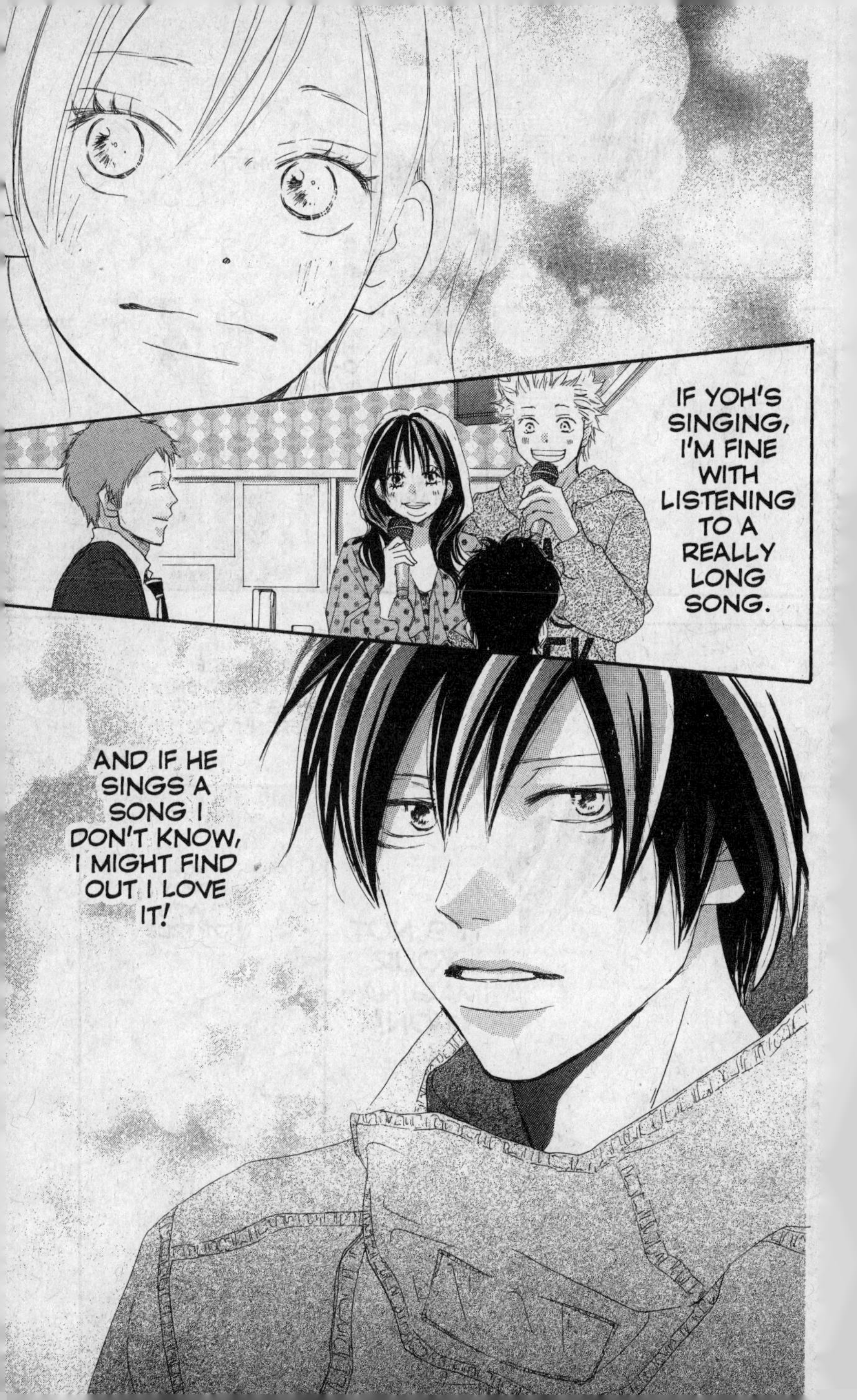
IF YOH'S SINGING, I'M FINE WITH LISTENING TO A REALLY LONG SONG.
AND IF HE SINGS A SONG I DON'T KNOW, I MIGHT FIND OUT I LOVE IT!

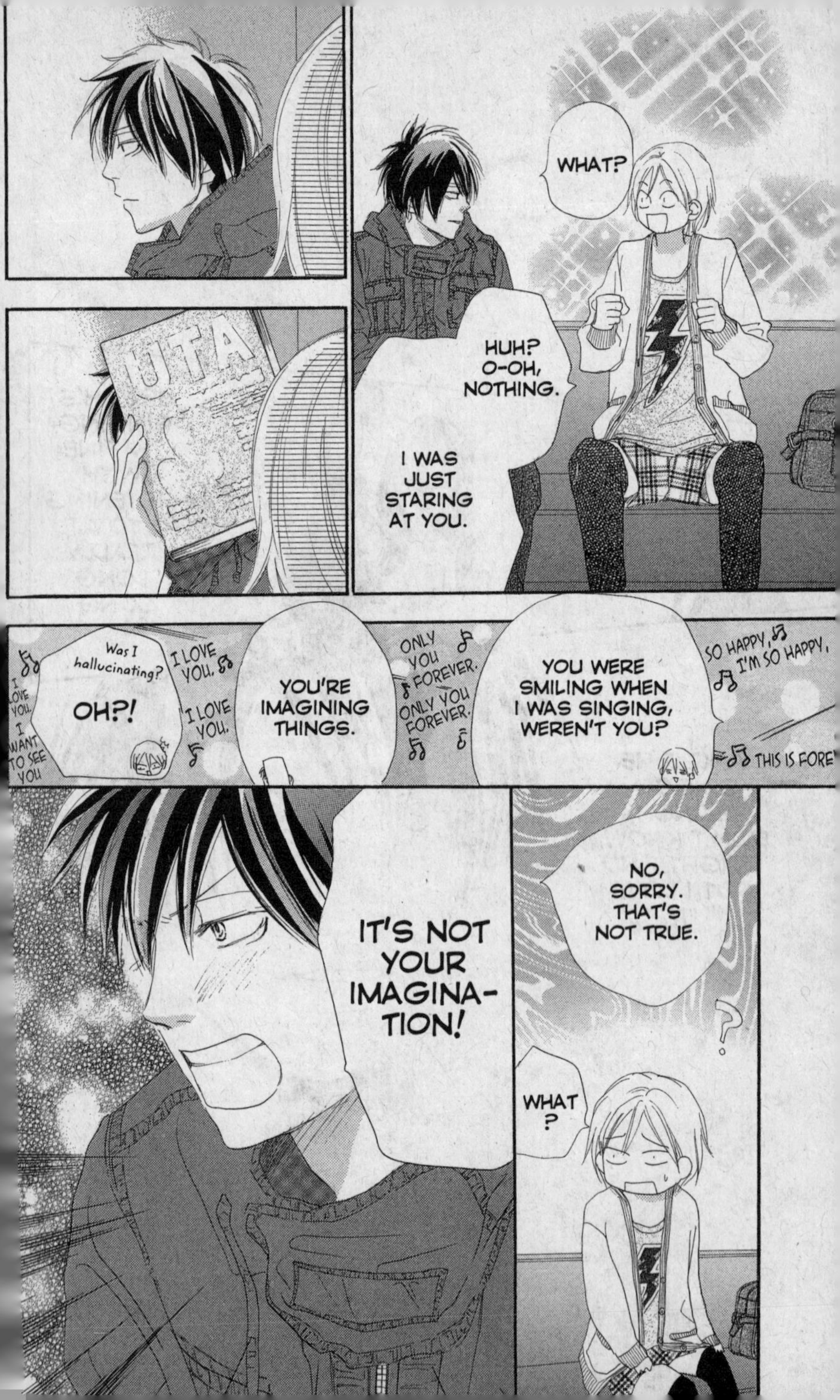
WHAT?
HUH? O-OH, NOTHING.
I WAS JUST STARING AT YOU.
SO HAPPY, I'M SO HAPPY,
THIS IS FORE
YOU WERE SMILING WHEN I WAS SINGING, WEREN'T YOU?
ONLY YOU FOREVER.
ONLY YOU FOREVER.
YOU'RE IMAGINING THINGS.
I LOVE YOU.
I LOVE YOU.
Was I hallucinating?
OH?!
I LOVE YOU. I WANT TO SEE YOU
NO, SORRY. THAT'S NOT TRUE.
WHAT?
IT'S NOT YOUR IMAGINATION!

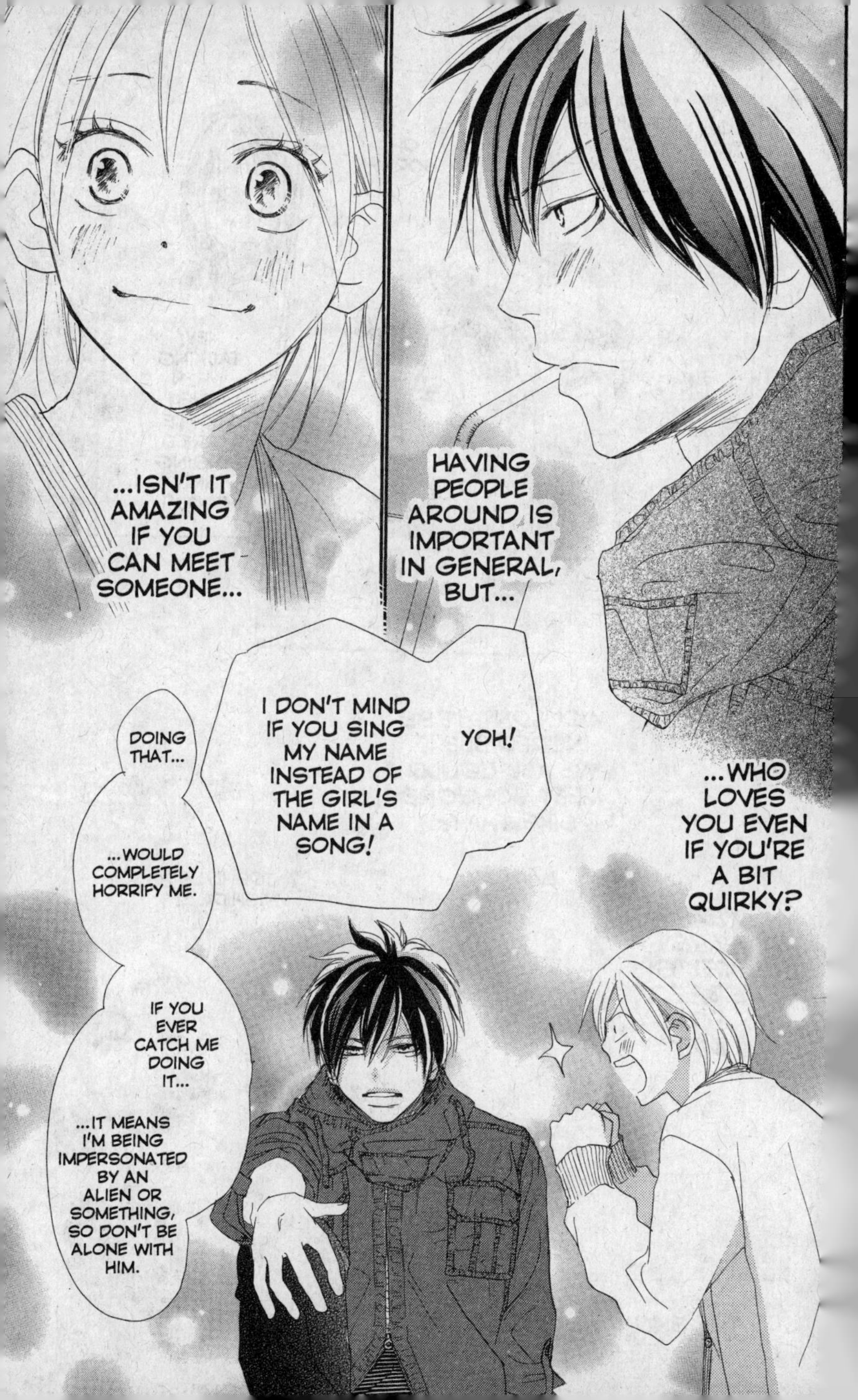
HAVING PEOPLE AROUND IS IMPORTANT IN GENERAL, BUT...
...ISN'T IT AMAZING IF YOU CAN MEET SOMEONE...
...WHO LOVES YOU EVEN IF YOU'RE A BIT QUIRKY?
YOH!
I DON'T MIND IF YOU SING MY NAME INSTEAD OF THE GIRL'S NAME IN A SONG!
DOING THAT...
...WOULD COMPLETELY HORRIFY ME.
IF YOU EVER CATCH ME DOING IT...
...IT MEANS I'M BEING IMPERSONATED BY AN ALIEN OR SOMETHING, SO DON'T BE ALONE WITH HIM.

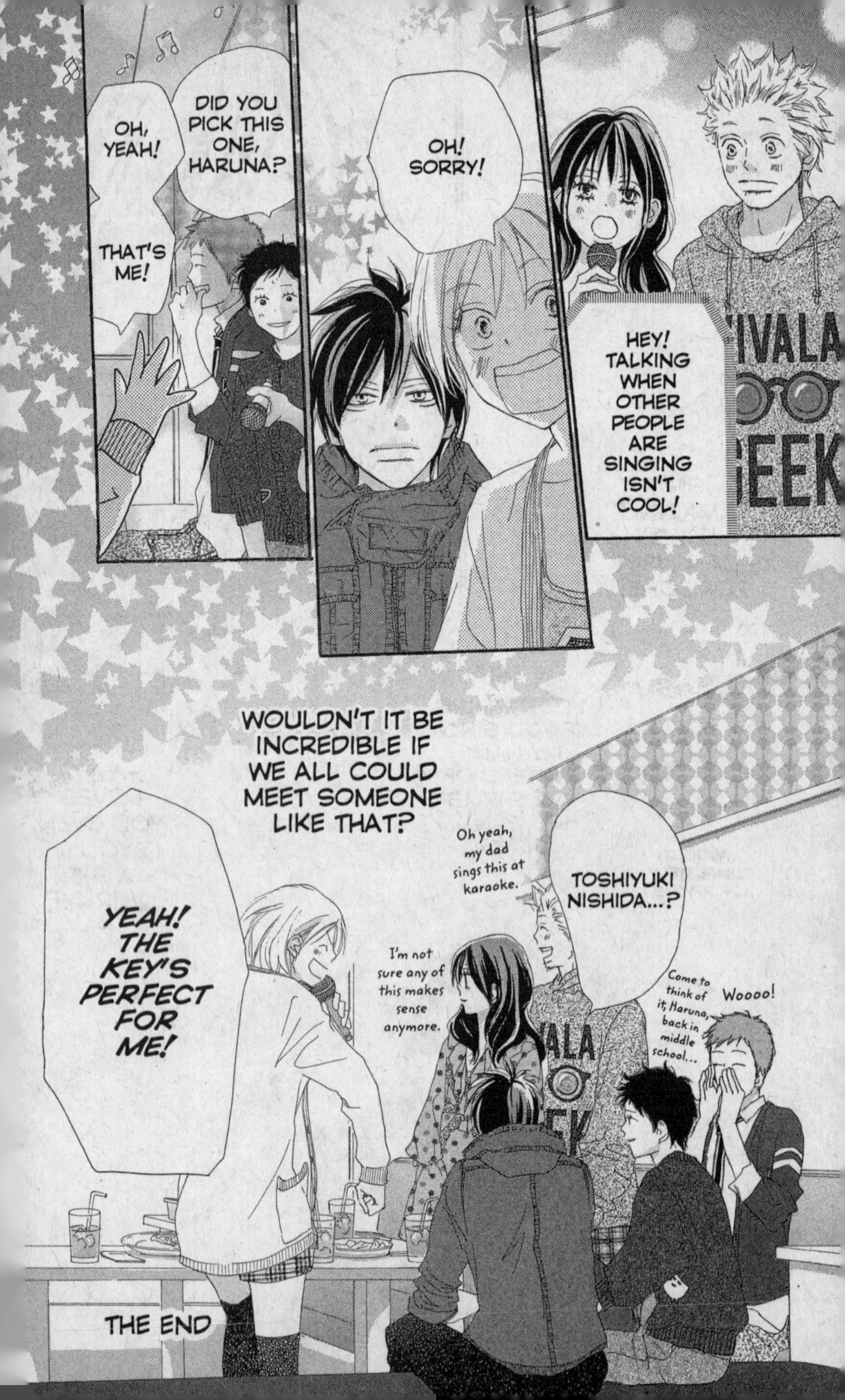
HEY! TALKING WHEN OTHER PEOPLE ARE SINGING ISN'T COOL!
VIVALA GEEK
OH! SORRY!
DID YOU PICK THIS ONE, HARUNA?
OH, YEAH!
THAT'S ME!
WOULDN'T IT BE INCREDIBLE IF WE ALL COULD MEET SOMEONE LIKE THAT?
TOSHIYUKI NISHIDA...?
Oh yeah, my dad sings this at karaoke.
YEAH! THE KEY'S PERFECT FOR ME!
I'm not sure any of this makes sense anymore.
Come to think of it, Haruna, back in middle school...
Woooo!
THE END

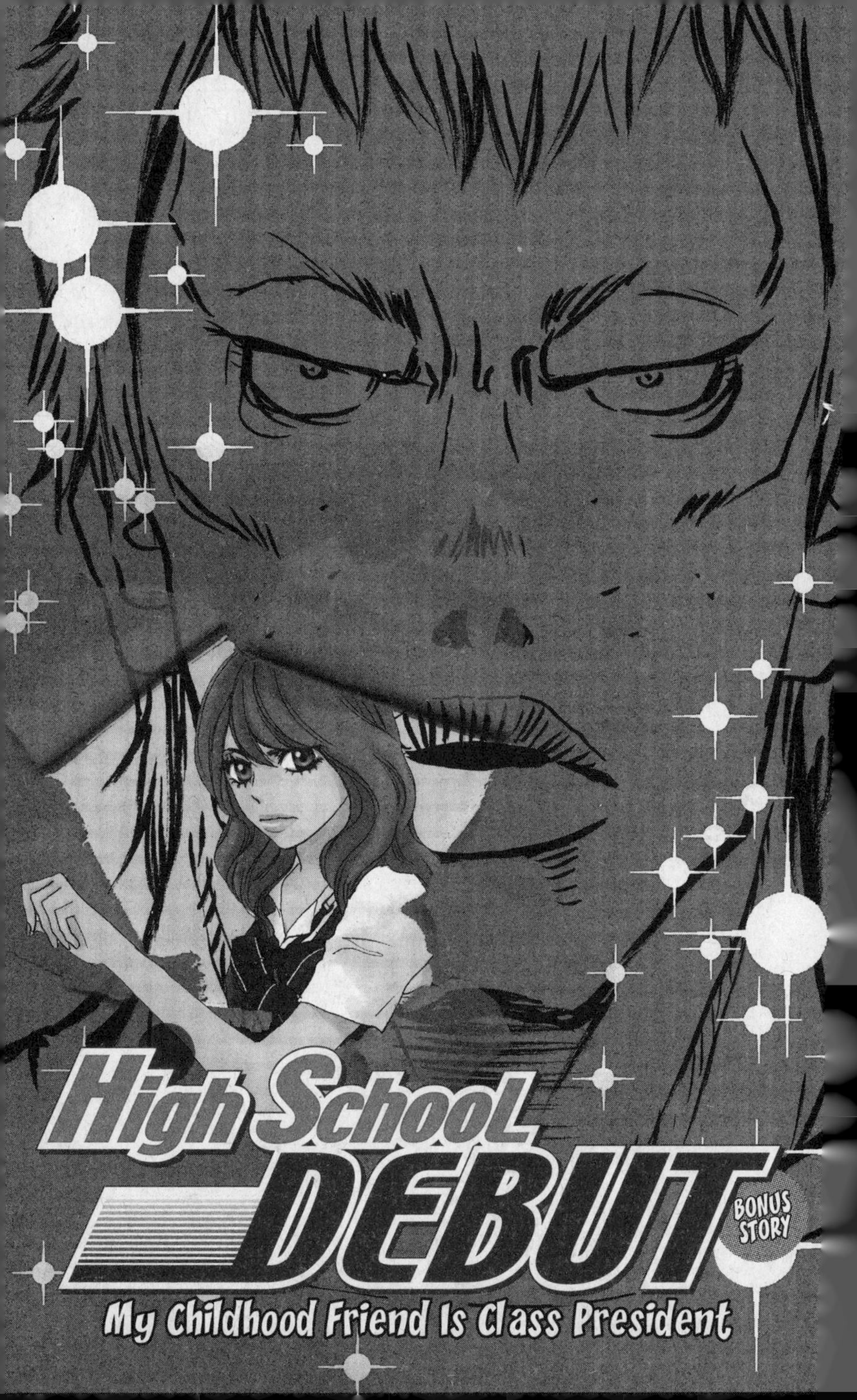
High School
DEBUT
BONUS STORY
My Childhood Friend Is Class President

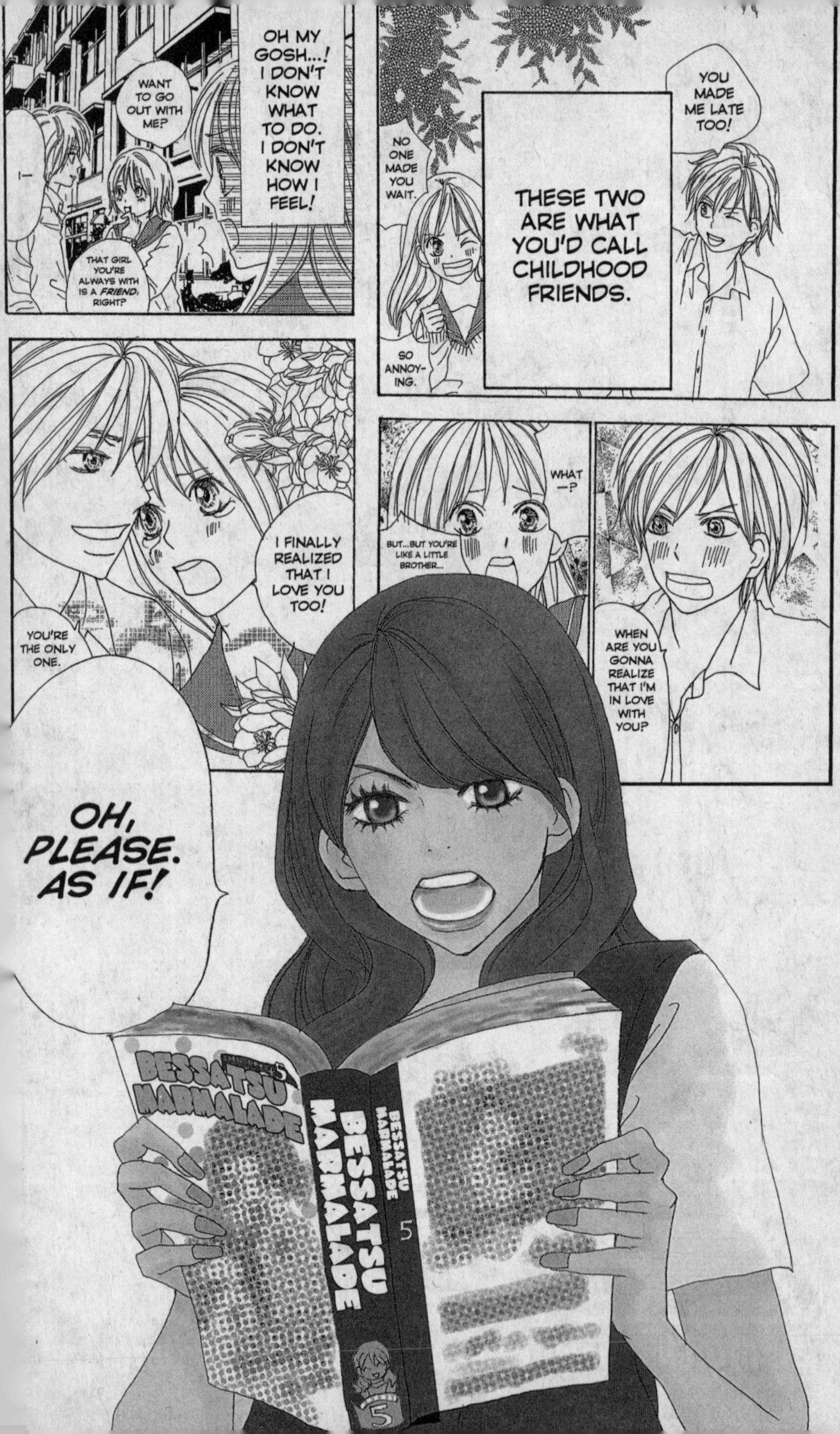
YOU MADE ME LATE TOO!
THESE TWO ARE WHAT YOU'D CALL CHILDHOOD FRIENDS.
NO ONE MADE YOU WAIT.
SO ANNOY-ING.
OH MY GOSH...! I DON'T KNOW WHAT TO DO. I DON'T KNOW HOW I FEEL!
WANT TO GO OUT WITH ME?
I—
THAT GIRL YOU'RE ALWAYS WITH IS A *FRIEND*, RIGHT?
WHEN ARE YOU GONNA REALIZE THAT I'M IN LOVE WITH YOU?
WHAT—?
BUT...BUT YOU'RE LIKE A LITTLE BROTHER...
I FINALLY REALIZED THAT I LOVE YOU TOO!
YOU'RE THE ONLY ONE.
OH, PLEASE. AS IF!
BESSATSU MARMALADE
BESSATSU MARMALADE
BESSATSU MARMALADE 5
5

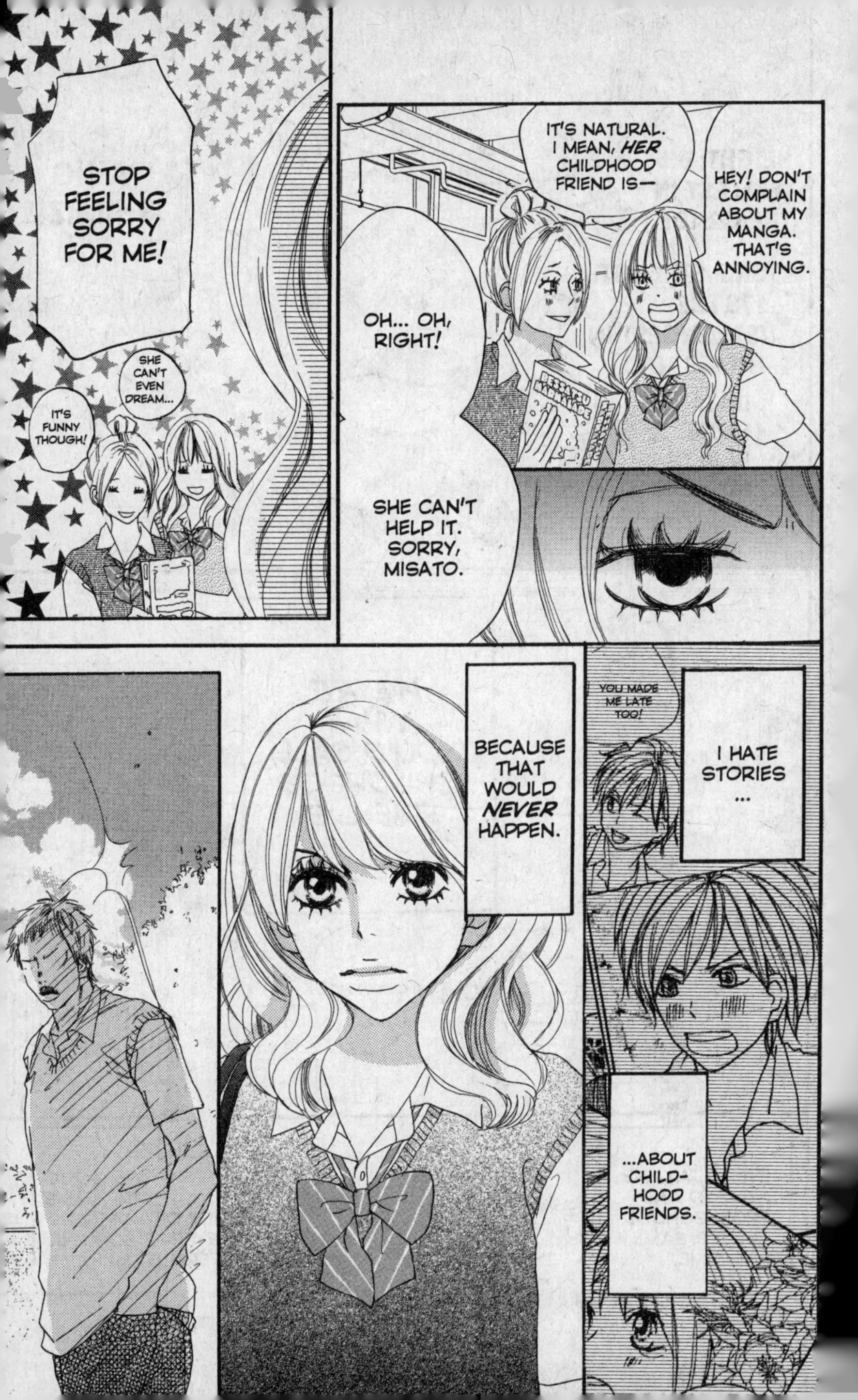
HEY! DON'T COMPLAIN ABOUT MY MANGA. THAT'S ANNOYING.
IT'S NATURAL. I MEAN, *HER* CHILDHOOD FRIEND IS—
BESSATSU MARMALADE
OH... OH, RIGHT!
SHE CAN'T HELP IT. SORRY, MISATO.
STOP FEELING SORRY FOR ME!
SHE CAN'T EVEN DREAM...
IT'S FUNNY THOUGH!
I HATE STORIES ...
YOU MADE ME LATE TOO!
...ABOUT CHILD-HOOD FRIENDS.
BECAUSE THAT WOULD *NEVER* HAPPEN.

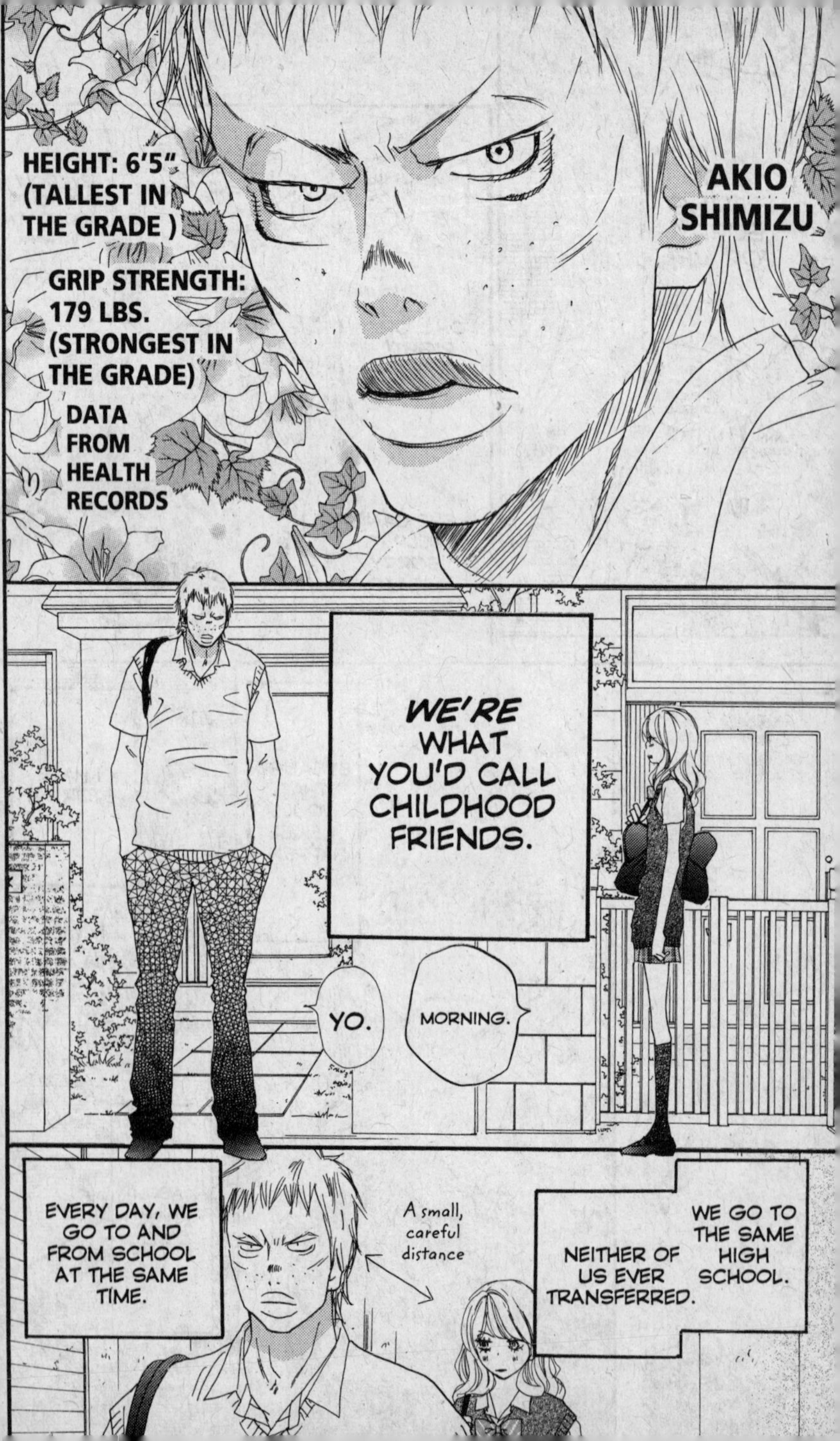
AKIO SHIMIZU
HEIGHT: 6'5" (TALLEST IN THE GRADE)
GRIP STRENGTH: 179 LBS. (STRONGEST IN THE GRADE)
DATA FROM HEALTH RECORDS
WE'RE WHAT YOU'D CALL CHILDHOOD FRIENDS.
MORNING.
YO.
WE GO TO THE SAME HIGH SCHOOL.
NEITHER OF US EVER TRANSFERRED.
A small, careful distance
EVERY DAY, WE GO TO AND FROM SCHOOL AT THE SAME TIME.

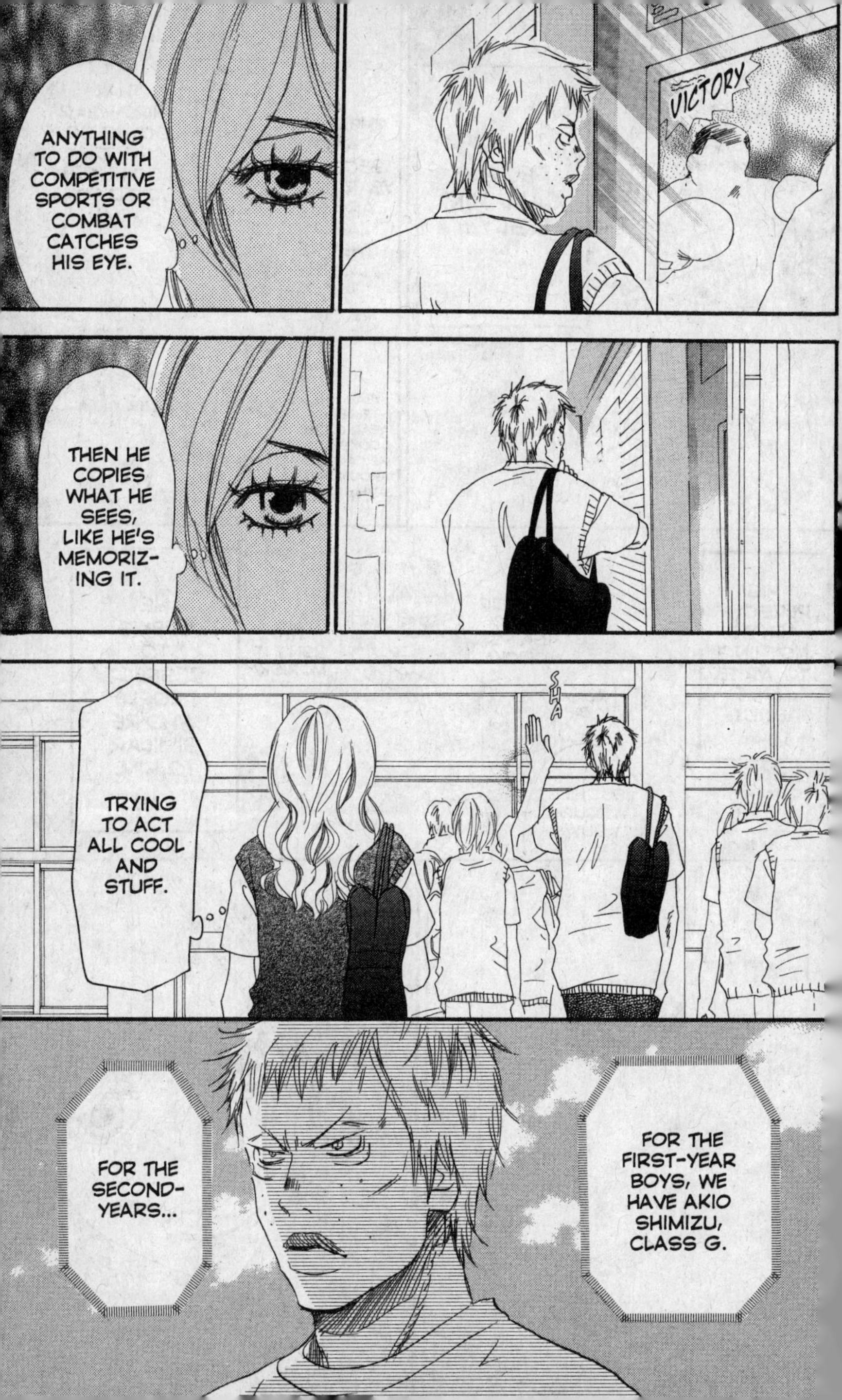
VICTORY
ANYTHING TO DO WITH COMPETITIVE SPORTS OR COMBAT CATCHES HIS EYE.
THEN HE COPIES WHAT HE SEES, LIKE HE'S MEMORIZ-ING IT.
SHA
TRYING TO ACT ALL COOL AND STUFF.
FOR THE FIRST-YEAR BOYS, WE HAVE AKIO SHIMIZU, CLASS G.
FOR THE SECOND-YEARS...

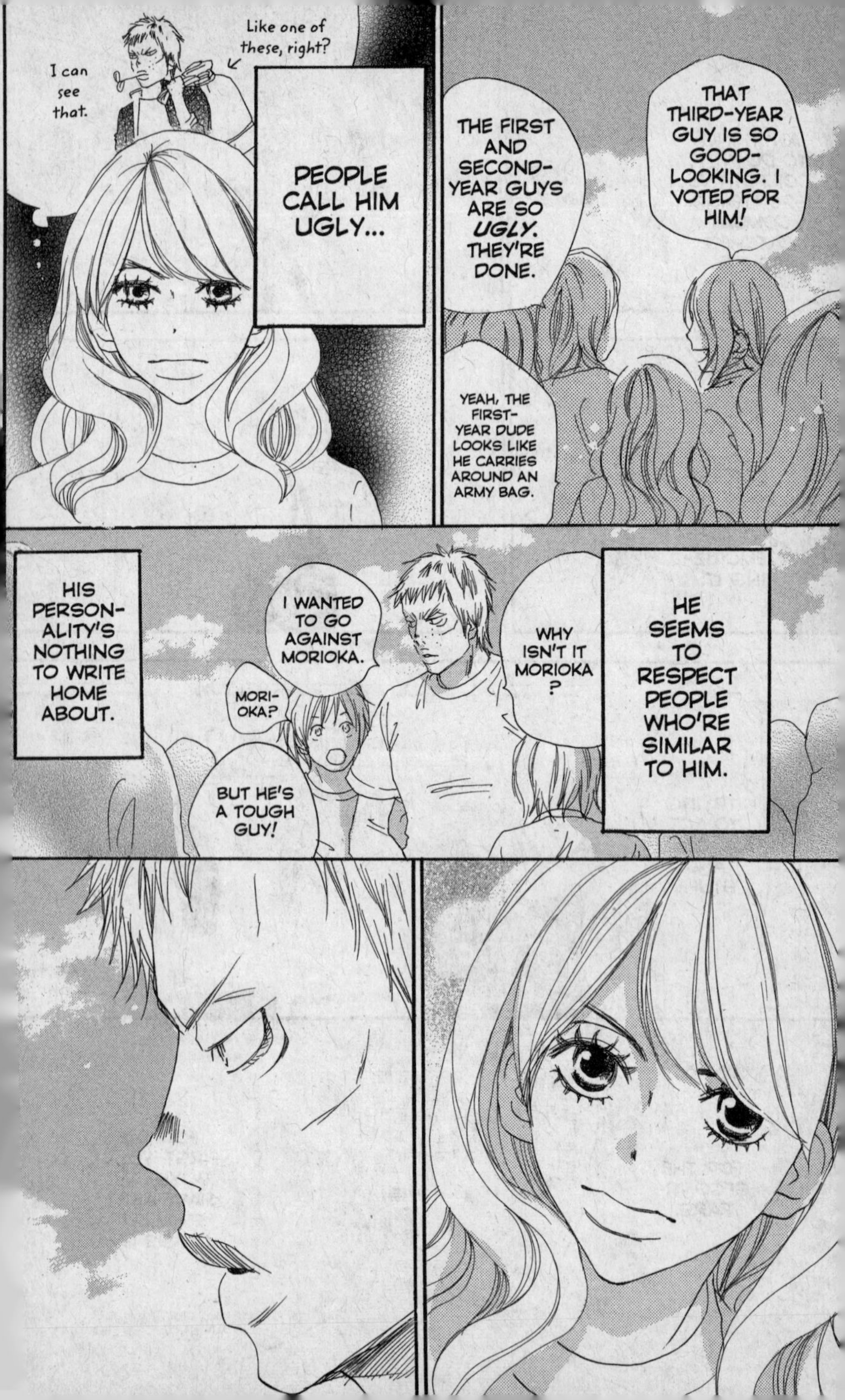
THAT THIRD-YEAR GUY IS SO GOOD-LOOKING. I VOTED FOR HIM!
THE FIRST AND SECOND-YEAR GUYS ARE SO *UGLY*. THEY'RE DONE.
YEAH, THE FIRST-YEAR DUDE LOOKS LIKE HE CARRIES AROUND AN ARMY BAG.
Like one of these, right?
PEOPLE CALL HIM UGLY...
I can see that.
HE SEEMS TO RESPECT PEOPLE WHO'RE SIMILAR TO HIM.
WHY ISN'T IT MORIOKA?
I WANTED TO GO AGAINST MORIOKA.
MORI-OKA?
BUT HE'S A TOUGH GUY!
HIS PERSON-ALITY'S NOTHING TO WRITE HOME ABOUT.

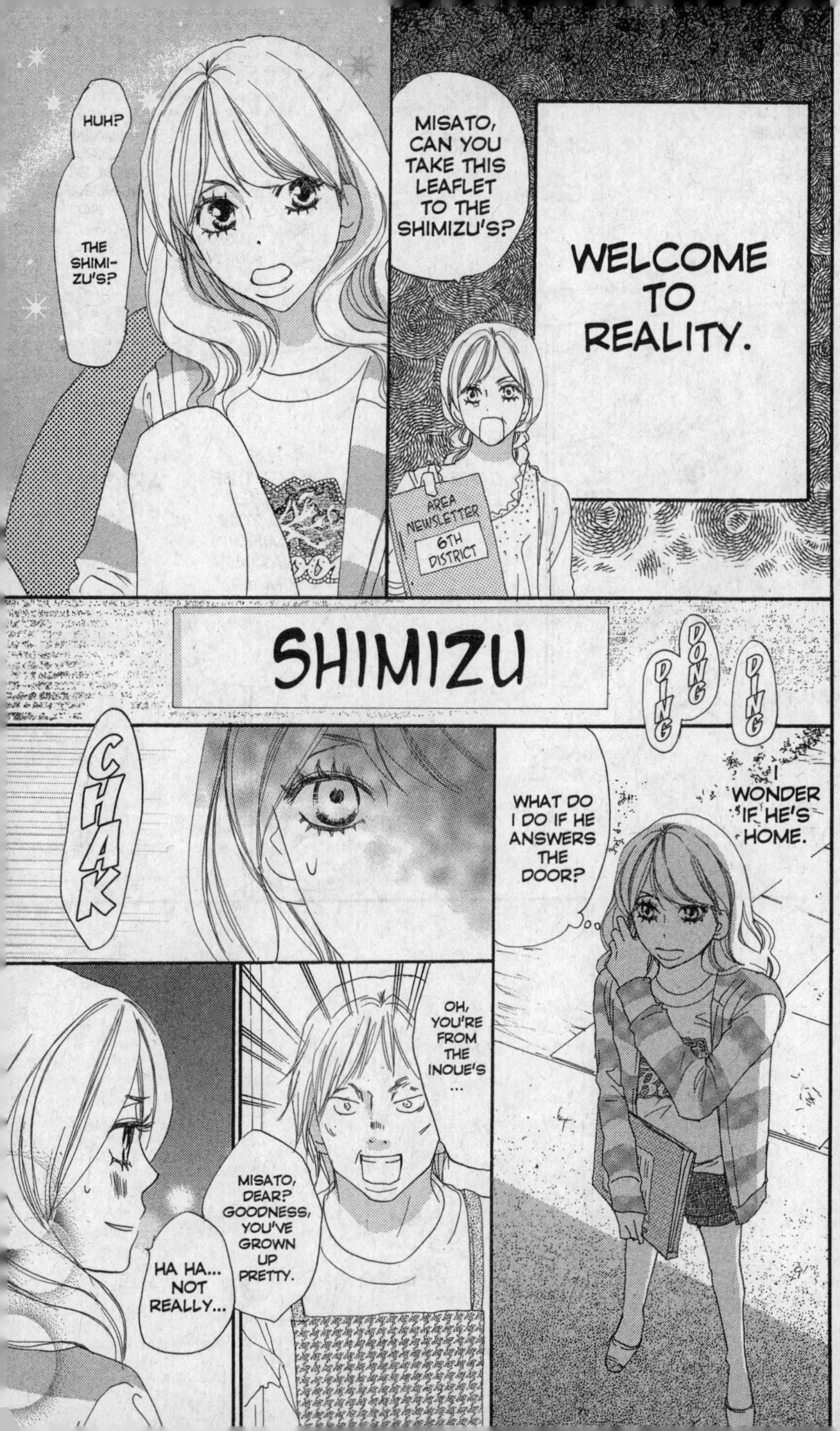
WELCOME TO REALITY.
MISATO, CAN YOU TAKE THIS LEAFLET TO THE SHIMIZU'S?
AREA NEWSLETTER
6TH DISTRICT
HUH?
THE SHIMIZU'S?
SHIMIZU
DING
DONG
DING
I WONDER IF HE'S HOME.
WHAT DO I DO IF HE ANSWERS THE DOOR?
CHAK
OH, YOU'RE FROM THE INOUE'S...
MISATO, DEAR? GOODNESS, YOU'VE GROWN UP PRETTY.
HA HA... NOT REALLY...

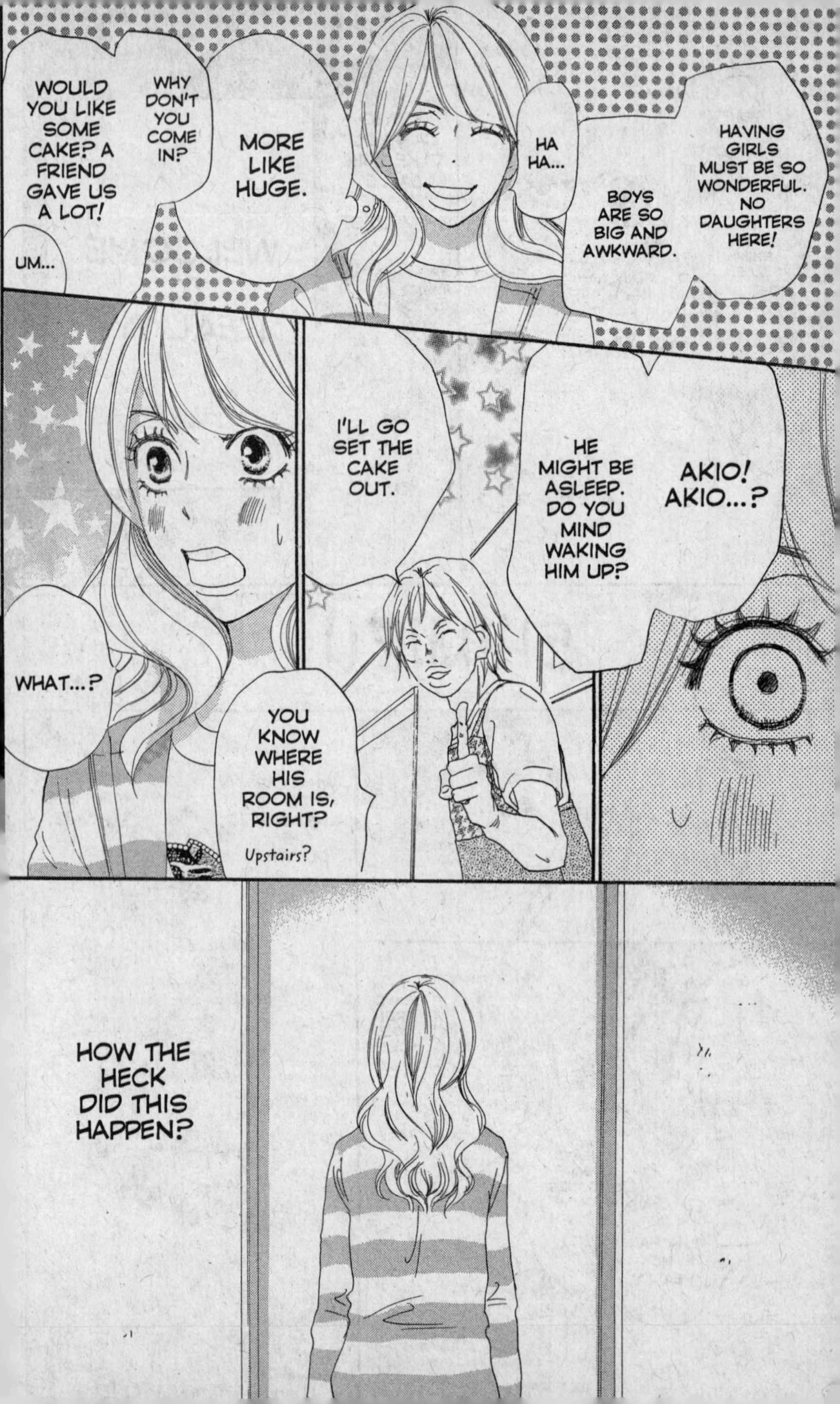
HAVING GIRLS MUST BE SO WONDERFUL. NO DAUGHTERS HERE!
BOYS ARE SO BIG AND AWKWARD.
HA HA...
MORE LIKE HUGE.
WHY DON'T YOU COME IN?
WOULD YOU LIKE SOME CAKE? A FRIEND GAVE US A LOT!
UM...
AKIO! AKIO...?
HE MIGHT BE ASLEEP. DO YOU MIND WAKING HIM UP?
I'LL GO SET THE CAKE OUT.
YOU KNOW WHERE HIS ROOM IS, RIGHT?
Upstairs?
WHAT...?
HOW THE HECK DID THIS HAPPEN?

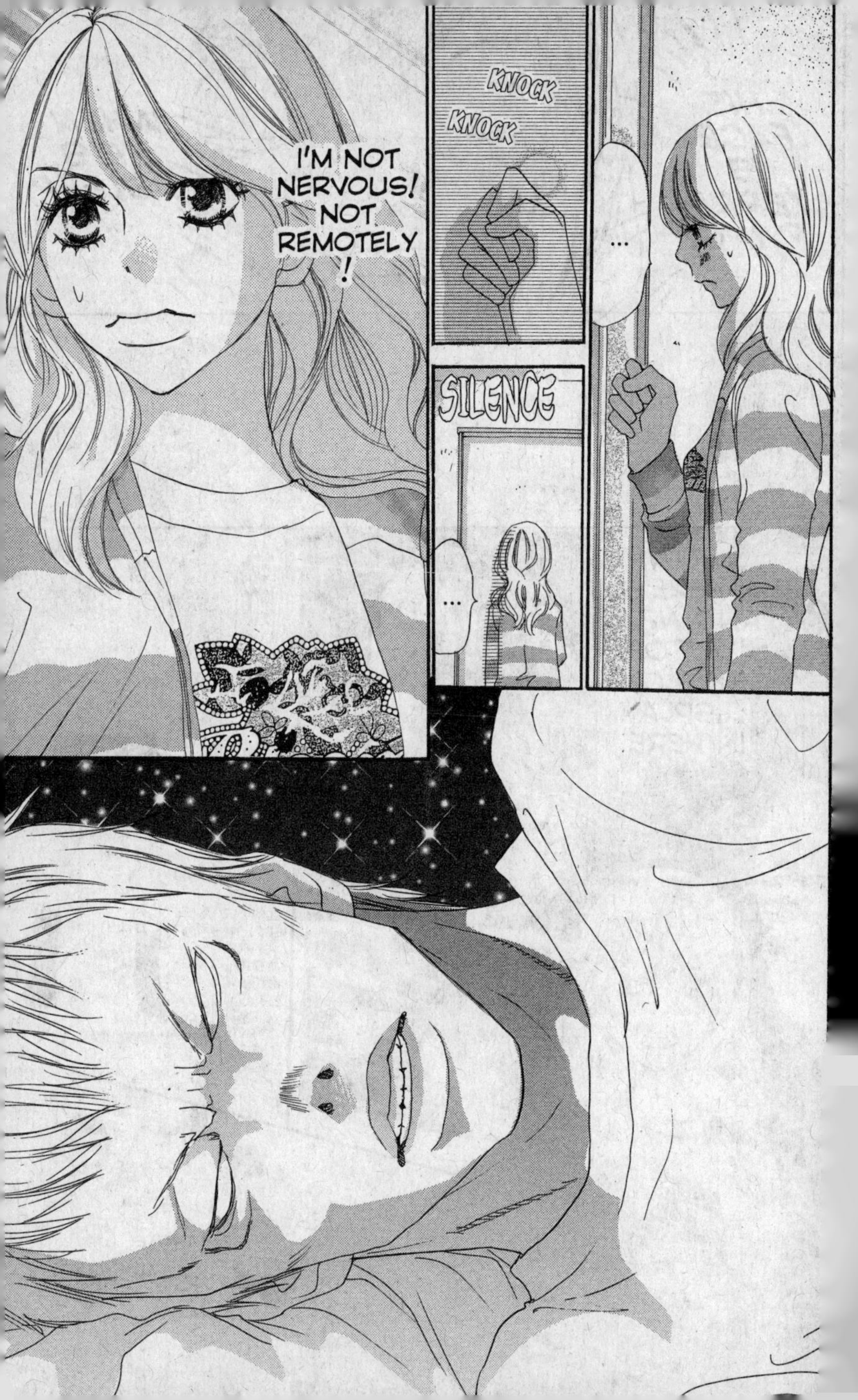
...
KNOCK
KNOCK
SILENCE
...
I'M NOT NERVOUS! NOT REMOTELY!

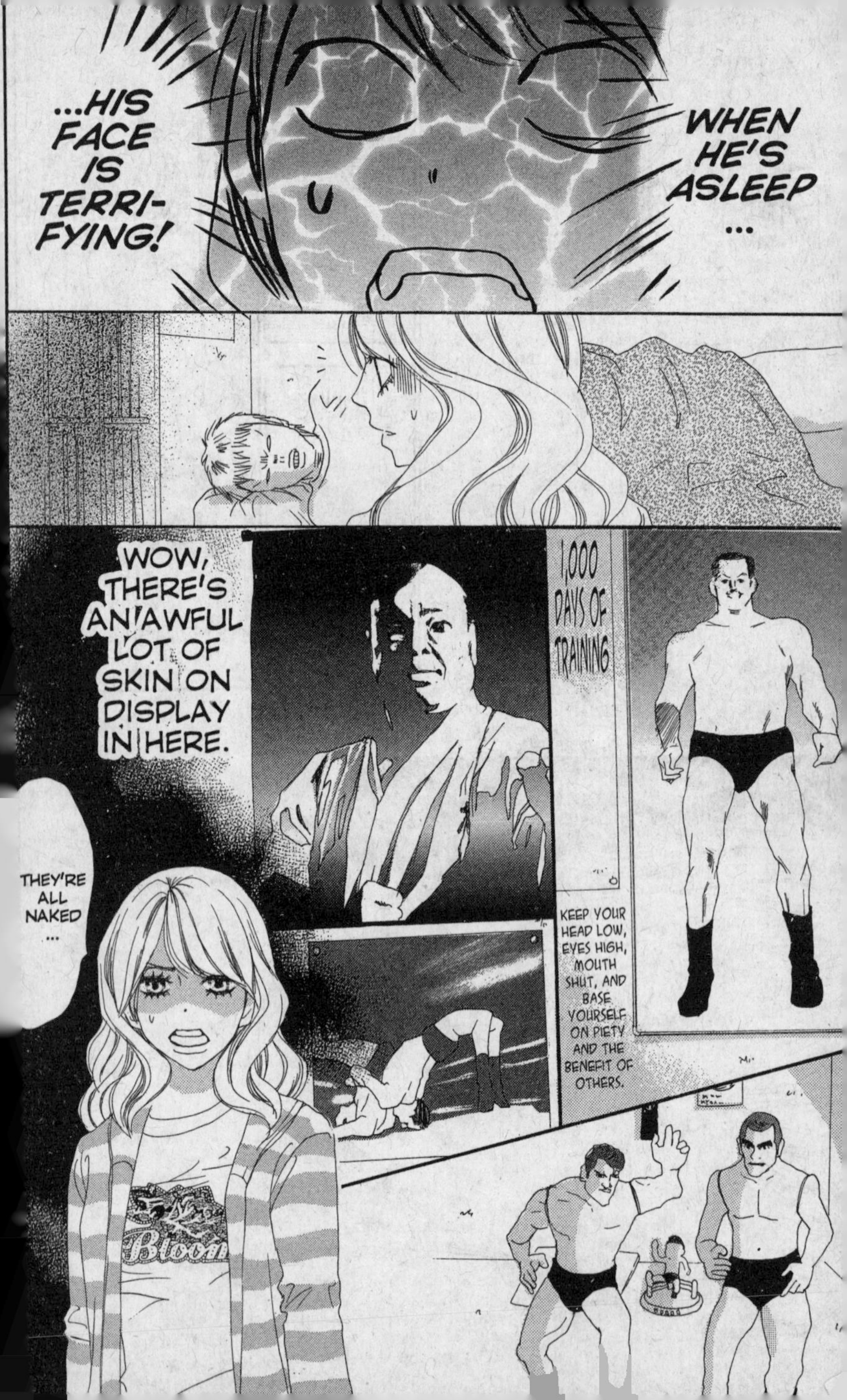
WHEN HE'S ASLEEP ...
...HIS FACE IS TERRI-FYING!
1,000 DAYS OF TRAINING
WOW, THERE'S AN AWFUL LOT OF SKIN ON DISPLAY IN HERE.
KEEP YOUR HEAD LOW, EYES HIGH, MOUTH SHUT, AND BASE YOURSELF ON PIETY AND THE BENEFIT OF OTHERS.
THEY'RE ALL NAKED ...
Bloom

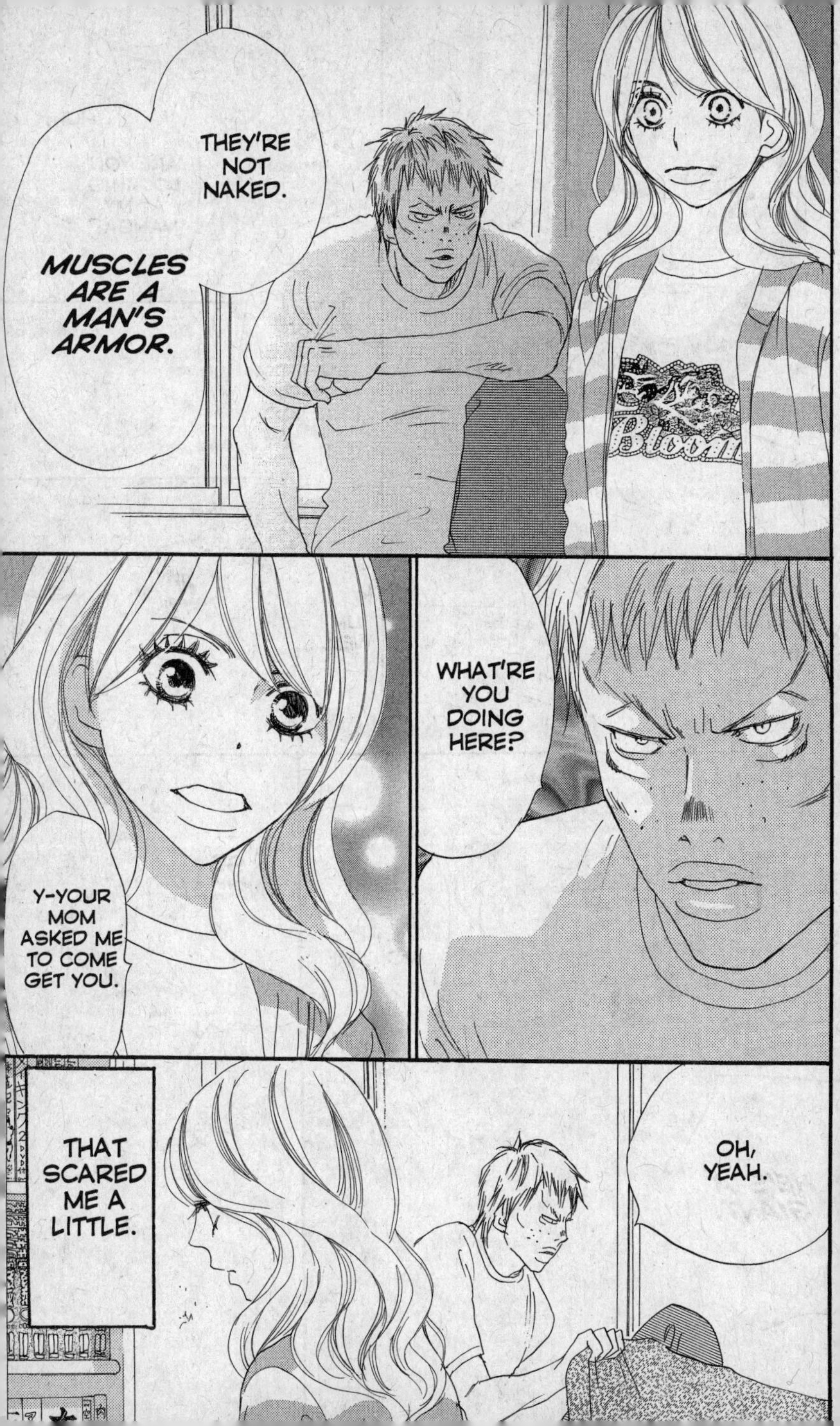
THEY'RE NOT NAKED.
MUSCLES ARE A MAN'S ARMOR.
WHAT'RE YOU DOING HERE?
Y-YOUR MOM ASKED ME TO COME GET YOU.
OH, YEAH.
THAT SCARED ME A LITTLE.

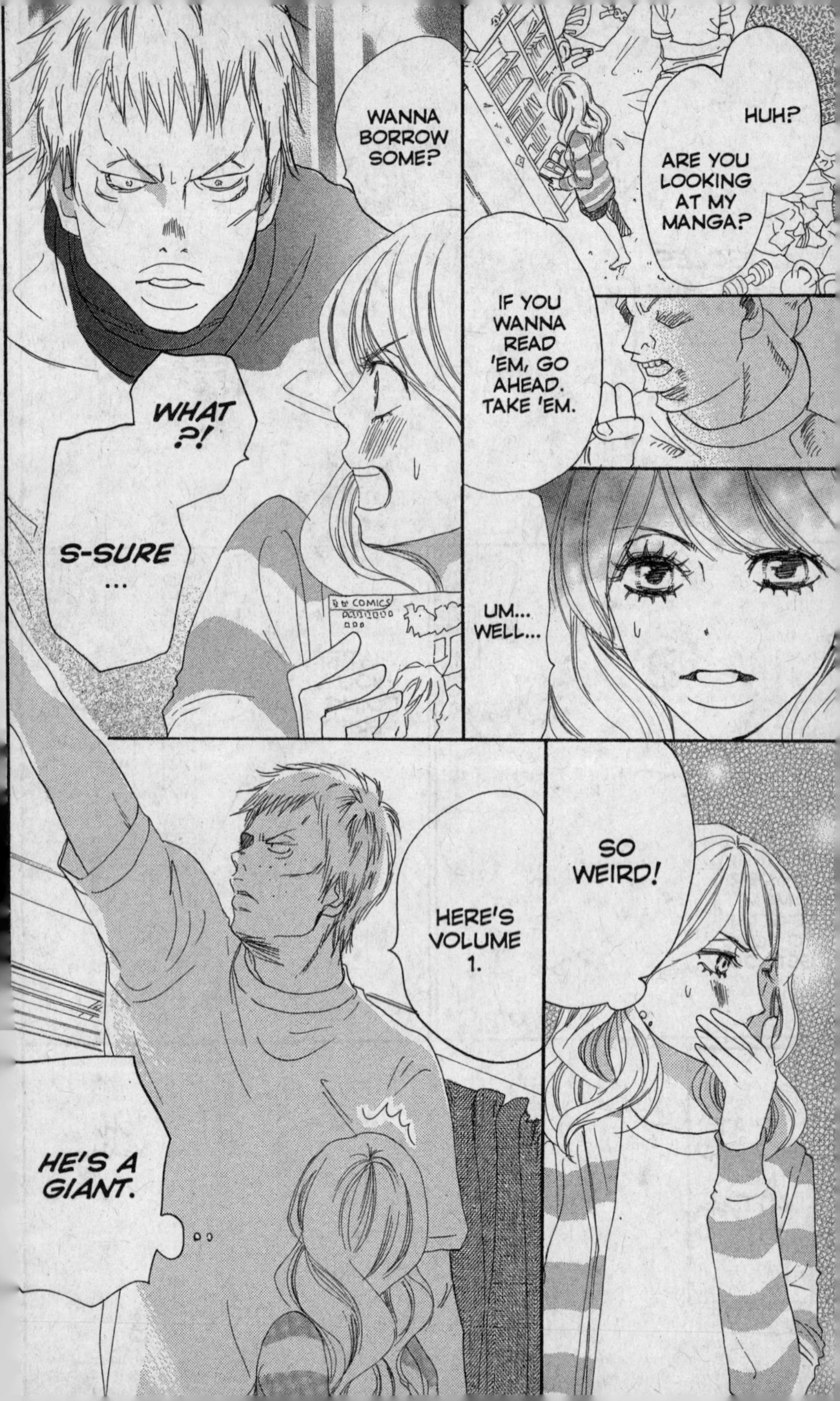
HUH?
ARE YOU LOOKING AT MY MANGA?
IF YOU WANNA READ 'EM, GO AHEAD. TAKE 'EM.
UM... WELL...
WANNA BORROW SOME?
WHAT?!
S-SURE...
SO WEIRD!
HERE'S VOLUME 1.
HE'S A GIANT.

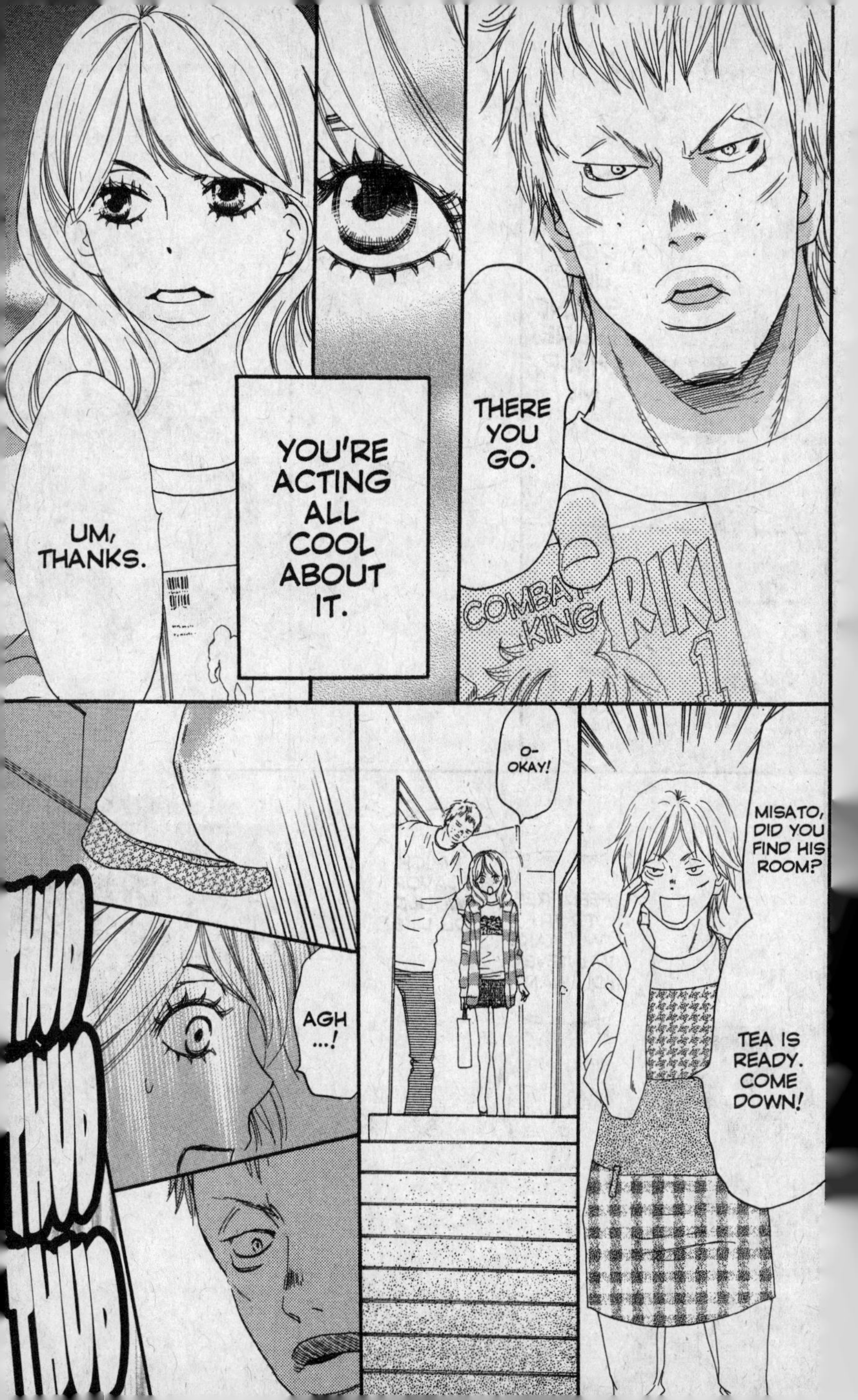
THERE YOU GO.
YOU'RE ACTING ALL COOL ABOUT IT.
UM, THANKS.
MISATO, DID YOU FIND HIS ROOM?
TEA IS READY. COME DOWN!
O-OKAY!
AGH ...!
THUD THUD THUD

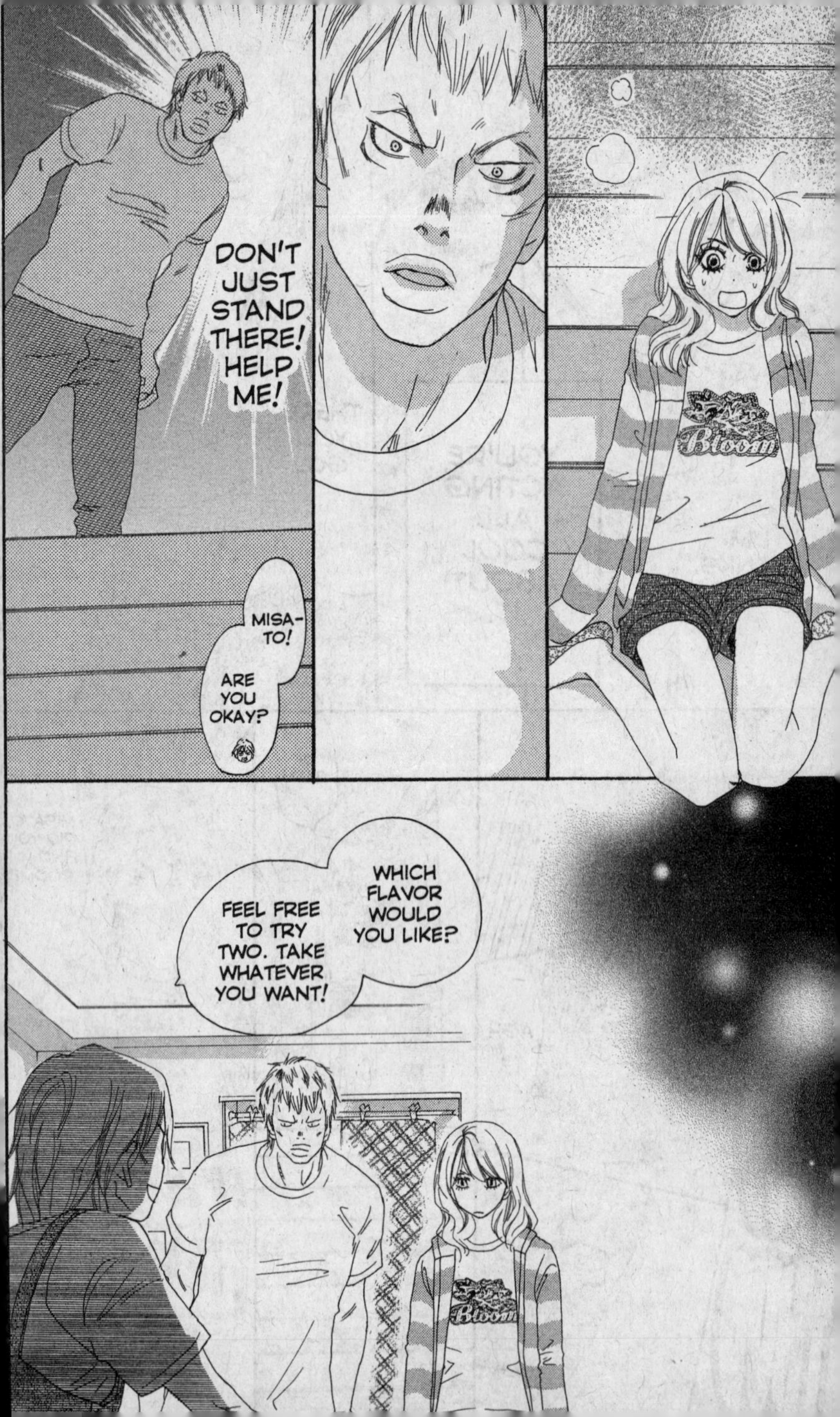
DON'T JUST STAND THERE! HELP ME!
MISA-TO!
ARE YOU OKAY?
WHICH FLAVOR WOULD YOU LIKE?
FEEL FREE TO TRY TWO. TAKE WHATEVER YOU WANT!

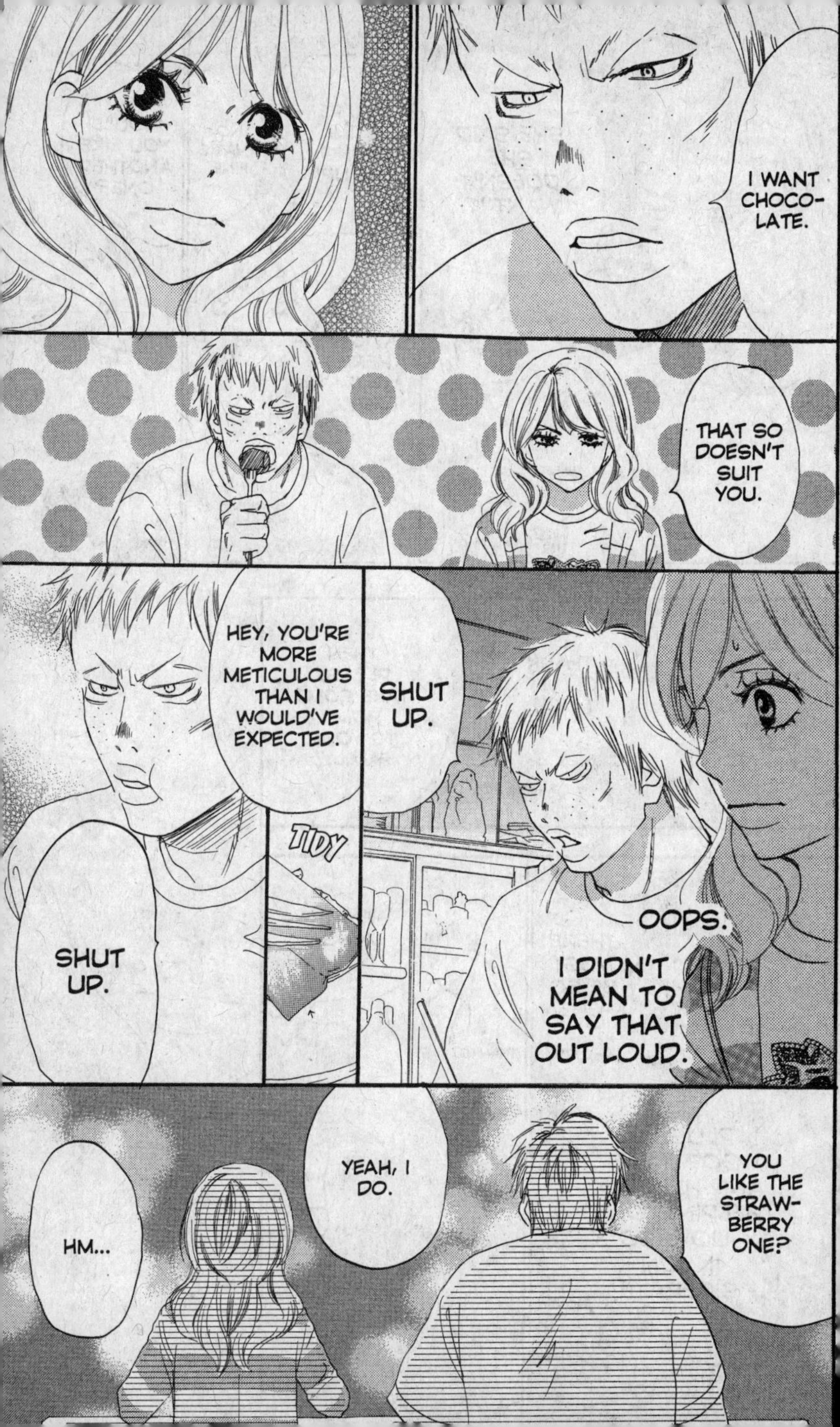
I WANT CHOCO-LATE.
THAT SO DOESN'T SUIT YOU.
SHUT UP.
OOPS.
I DIDN'T MEAN TO SAY THAT OUT LOUD.
HEY, YOU'RE MORE METICULOUS THAN I WOULD'VE EXPECTED.
TIDY
SHUT UP.
YOU LIKE THE STRAW-BERRY ONE?
YEAH, I DO.
HM...

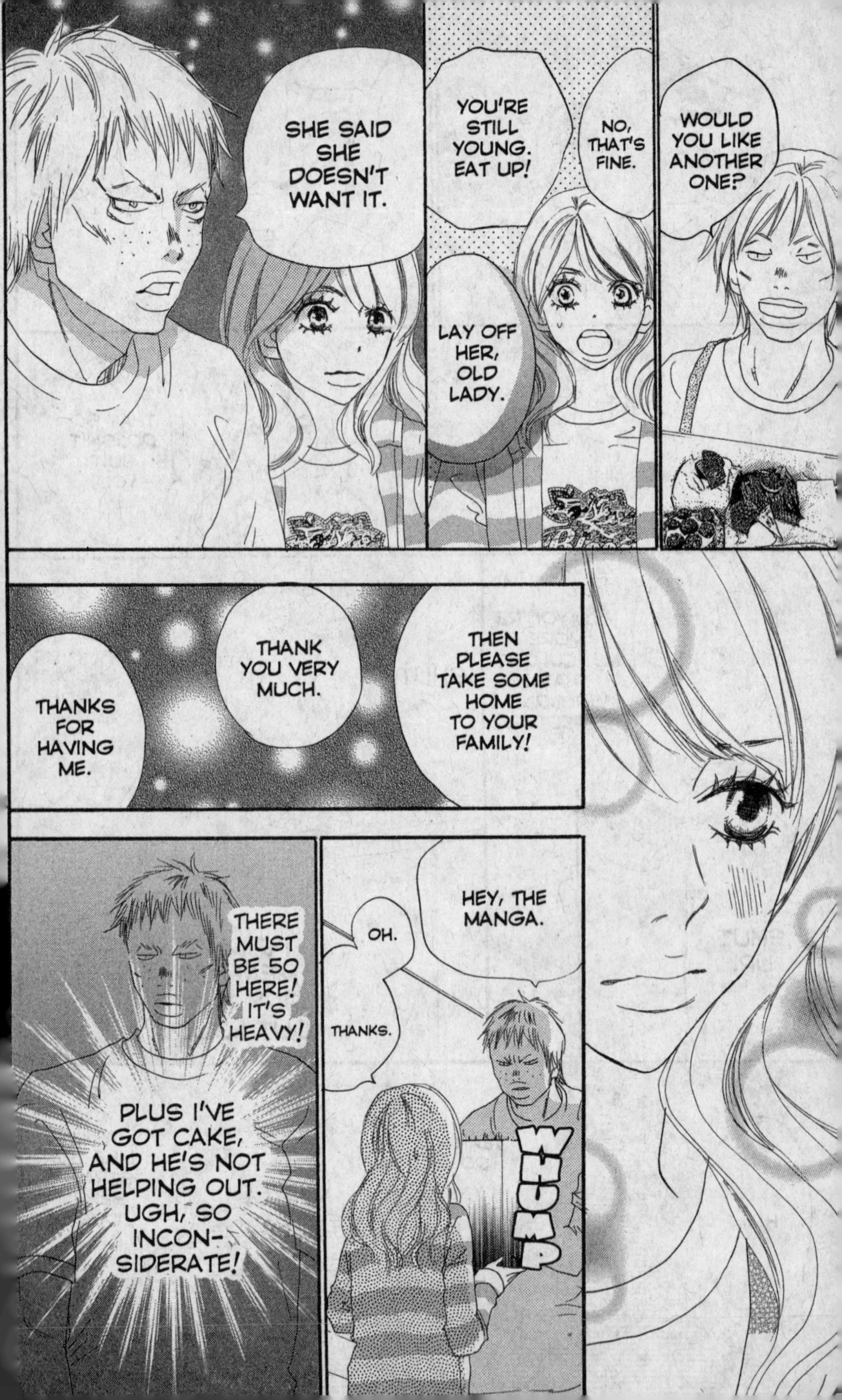
WOULD YOU LIKE ANOTHER ONE?
NO, THAT'S FINE.
YOU'RE STILL YOUNG. EAT UP!
LAY OFF HER, OLD LADY.
SHE SAID SHE DOESN'T WANT IT.
THEN PLEASE TAKE SOME HOME TO YOUR FAMILY!
THANK YOU VERY MUCH.
THANKS FOR HAVING ME.
HEY, THE MANGA.
OH.
THANKS.
WHUMP
THERE MUST BE 50 HERE! IT'S HEAVY!
PLUS I'VE GOT CAKE, AND HE'S NOT HELPING OUT. UGH, SO INCON-SIDERATE!

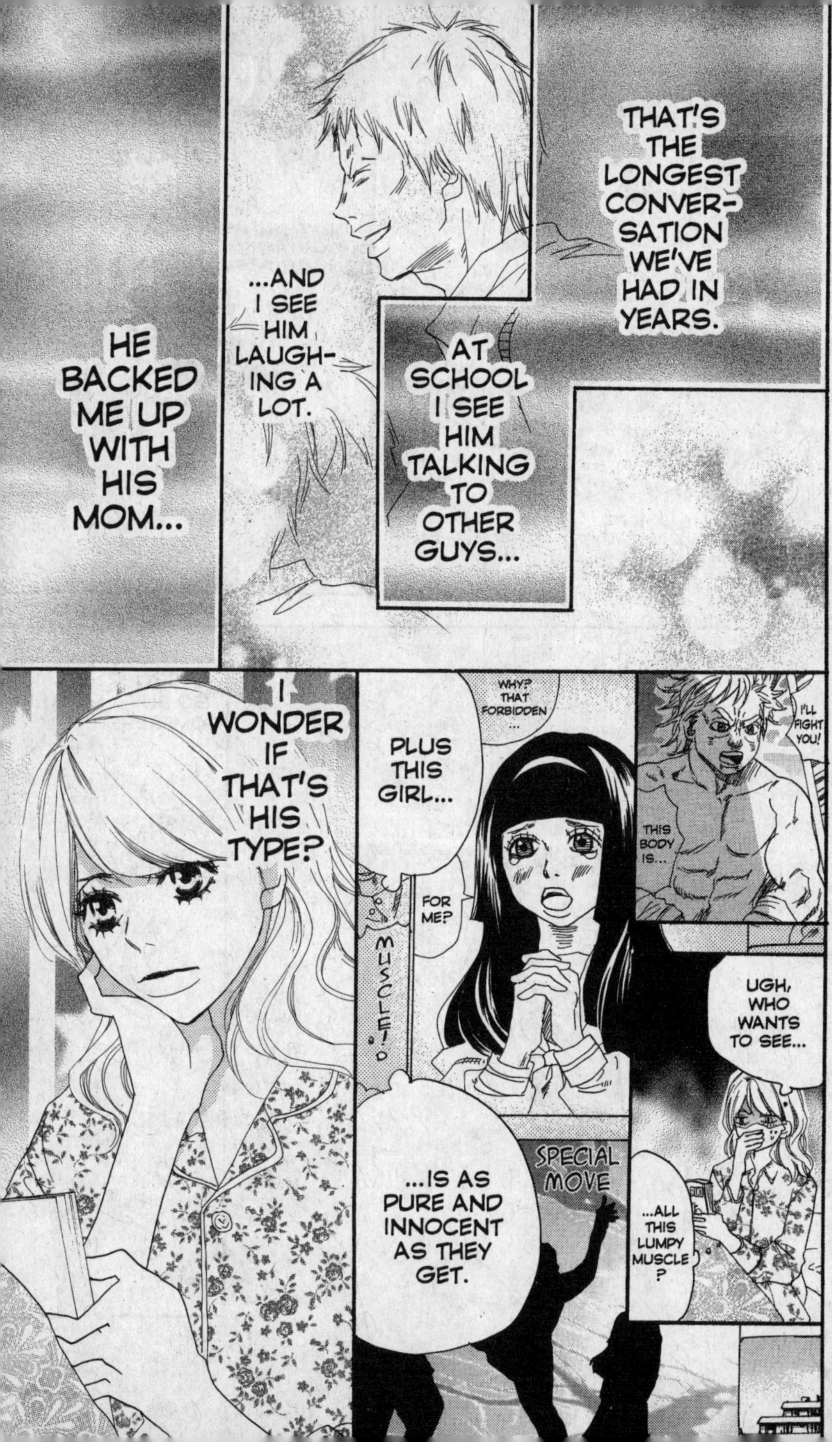
THAT'S THE LONGEST CONVERSATION WE'VE HAD IN YEARS.
AT SCHOOL I SEE HIM TALKING TO OTHER GUYS...
...AND I SEE HIM LAUGHING A LOT.
HE BACKED ME UP WITH HIS MOM...
I'LL FIGHT YOU!
THIS BODY IS...
UGH, WHO WANTS TO SEE...
...ALL THIS LUMPY MUSCLE?
WHY? THAT FORBIDDEN...
PLUS THIS GIRL...
FOR ME?
MUSCLE!
SPECIAL MOVE
...IS AS PURE AND INNOCENT AS THEY GET.
I WONDER IF THAT'S HIS TYPE?

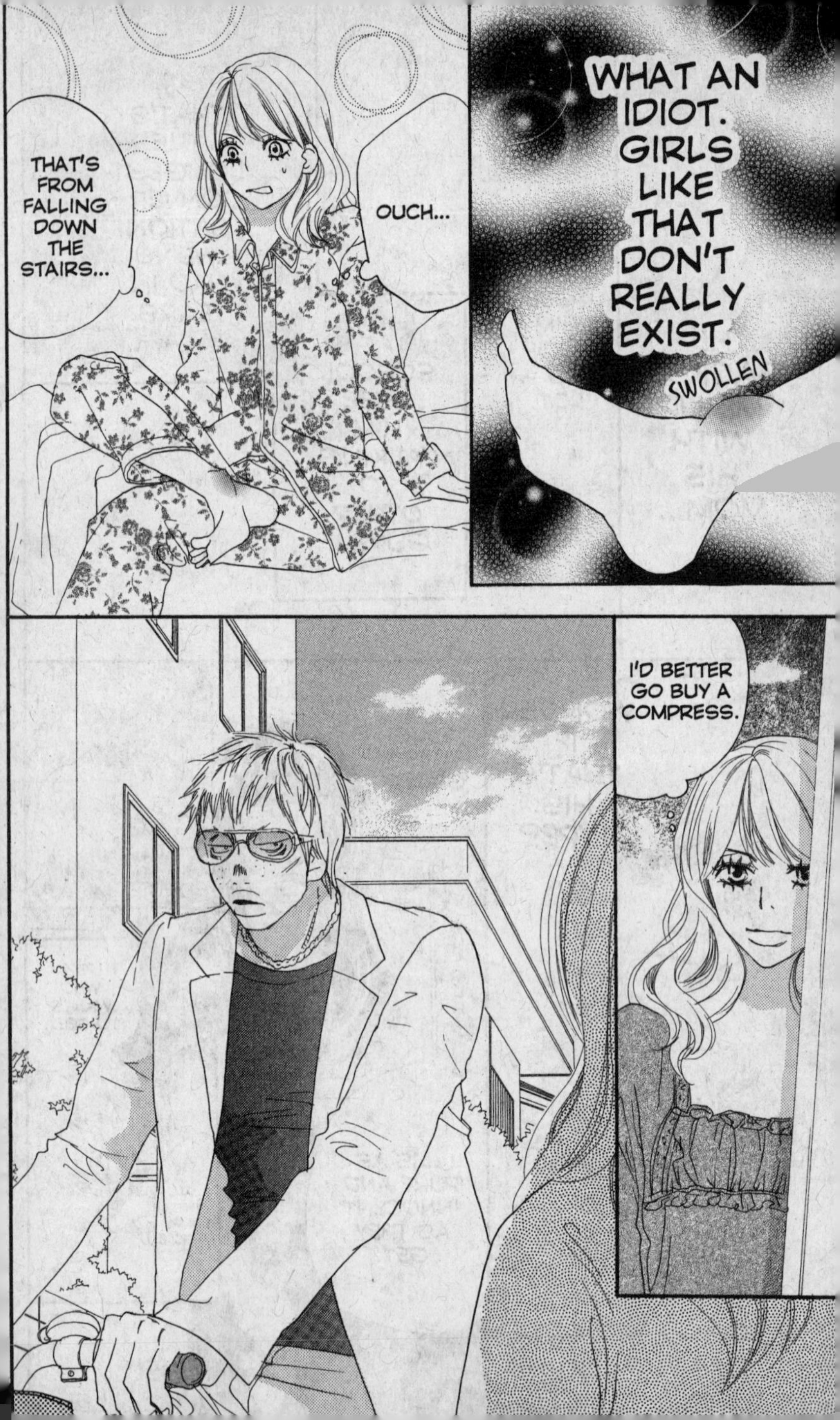
WHAT AN IDIOT. GIRLS LIKE THAT DON'T REALLY EXIST.
SWOLLEN
OUCH...
THAT'S FROM FALLING DOWN THE STAIRS...
I'D BETTER GO BUY A COMPRESS.

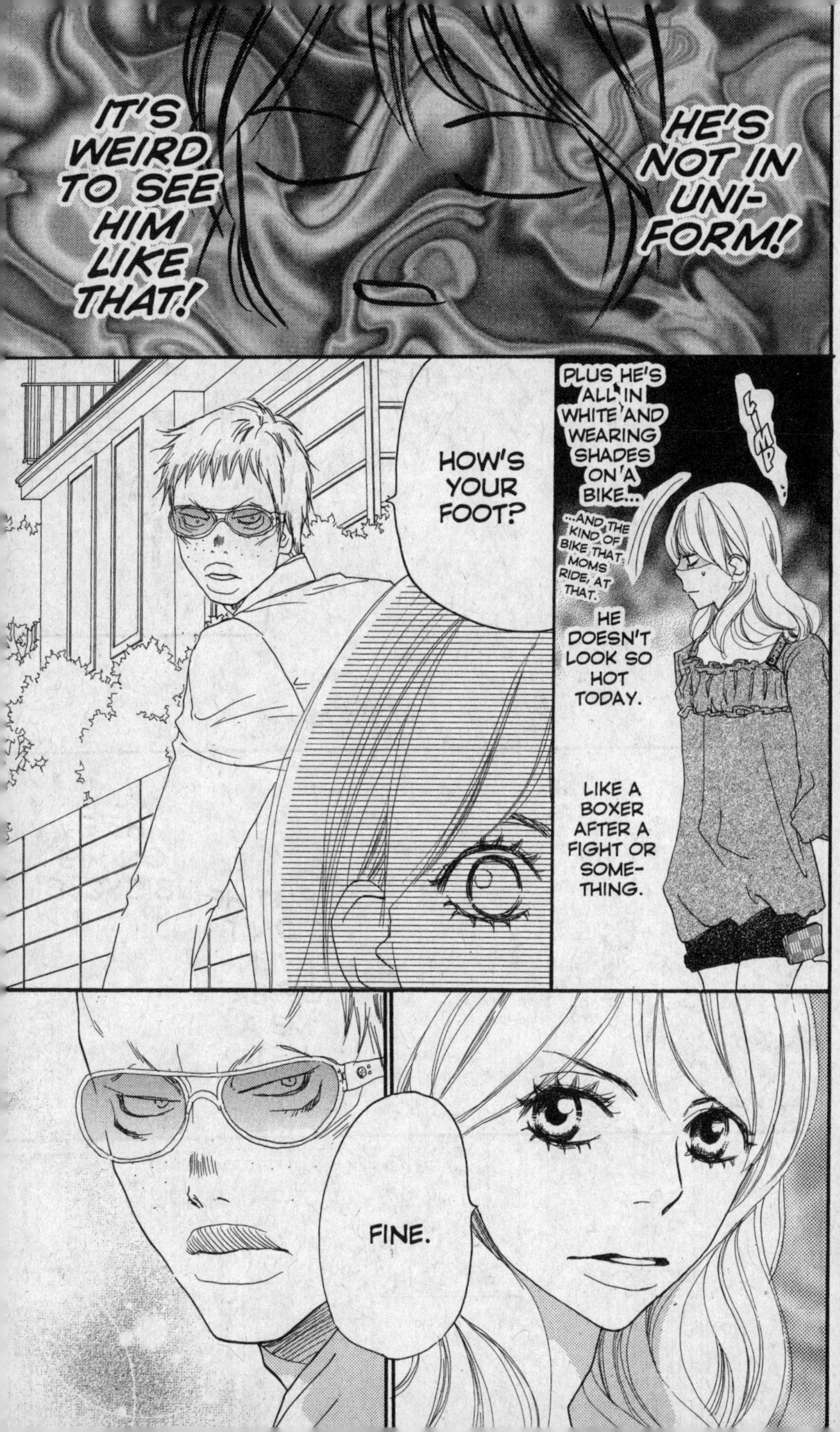
HE'S NOT IN UNI-FORM!
IT'S WEIRD TO SEE HIM LIKE THAT!
PLUS HE'S ALL IN WHITE AND WEARING SHADES ON A BIKE...
...AND THE KIND OF BIKE THAT MOMS RIDE, AT THAT.
LIMP
HE DOESN'T LOOK SO HOT TODAY.
LIKE A BOXER AFTER A FIGHT OR SOME-THING.
HOW'S YOUR FOOT?
FINE.

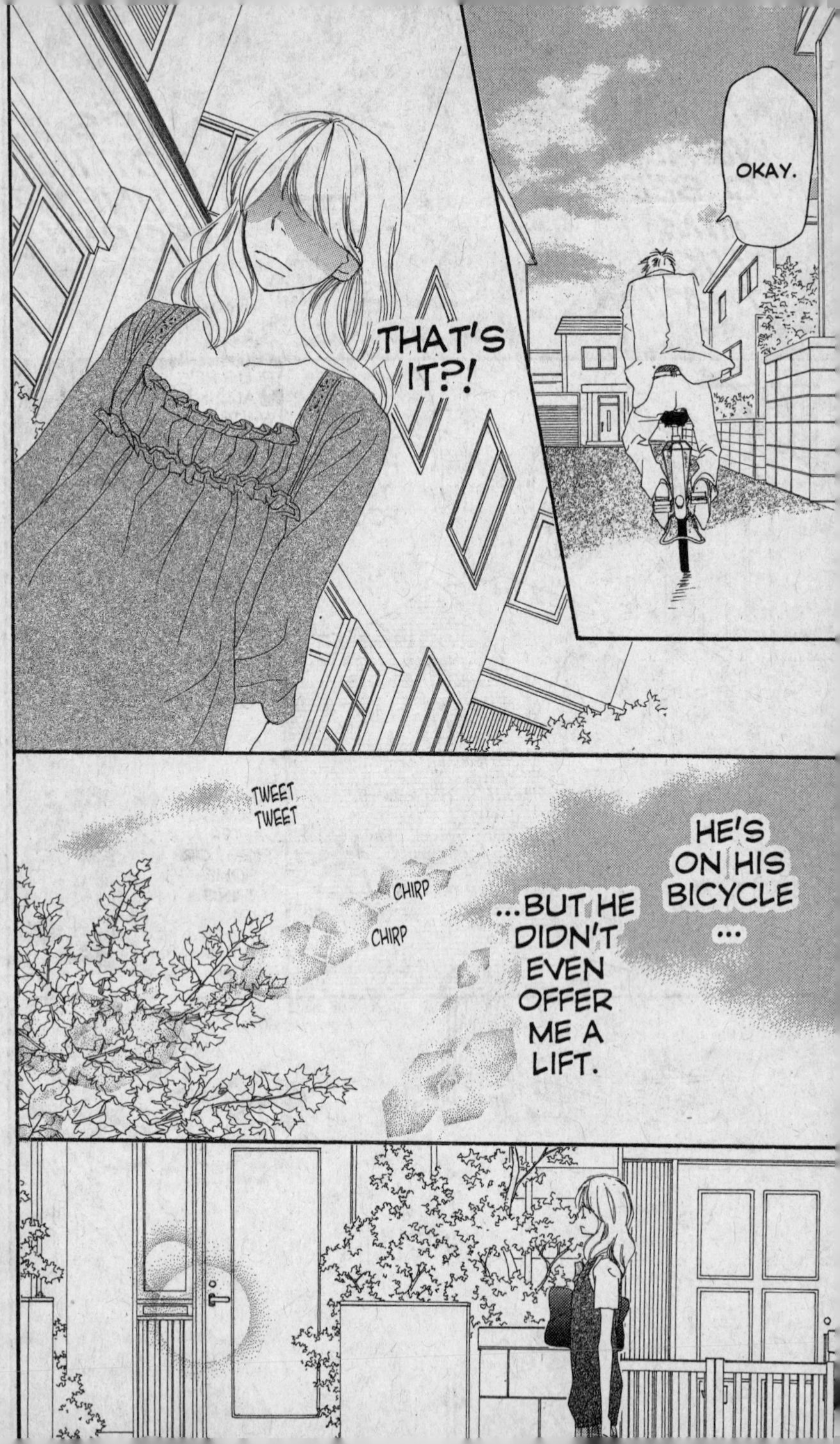
OKAY.
THAT'S IT?!
HE'S ON HIS BICYCLE ...
...BUT HE DIDN'T EVEN OFFER ME A LIFT.
TWEET TWEET
CHIRP
CHIRP

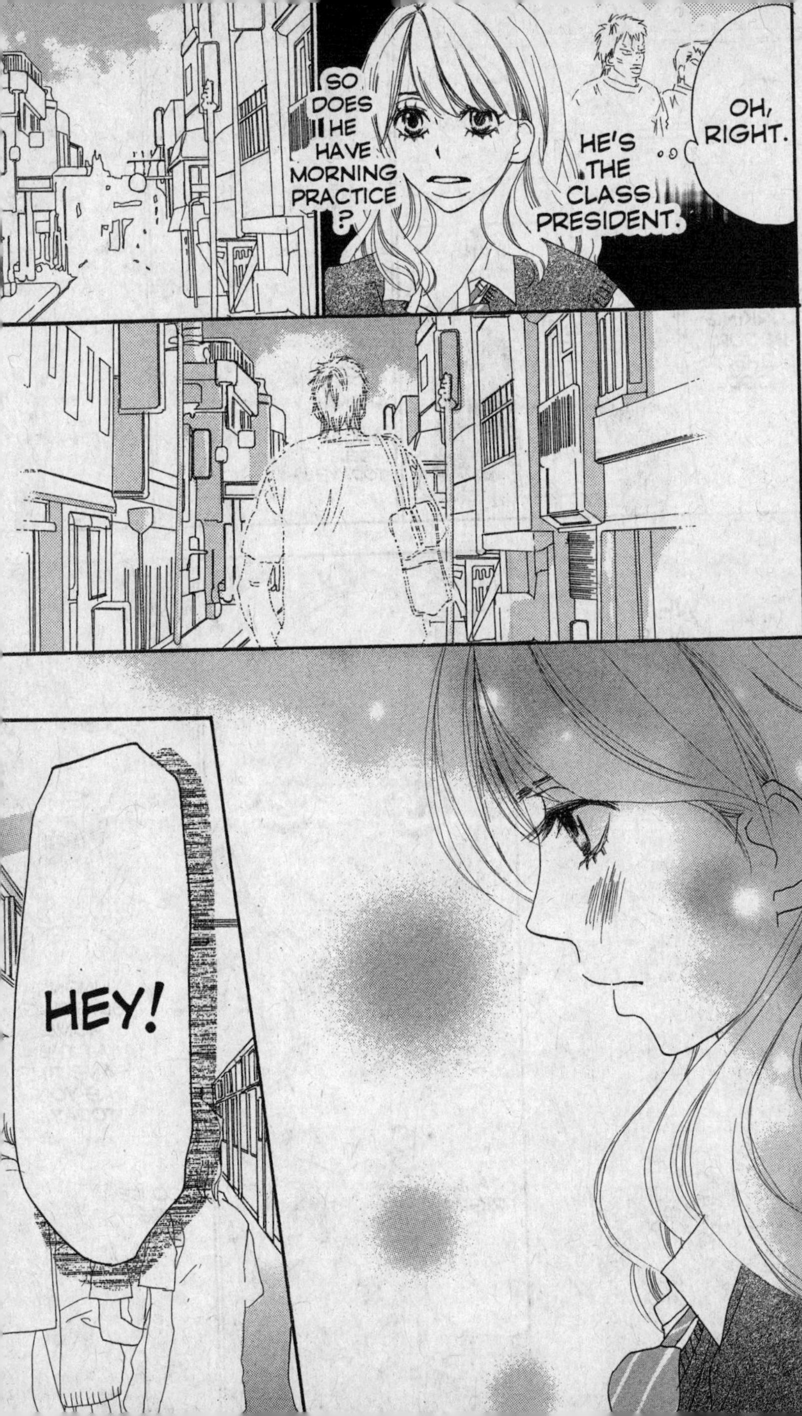
OH, RIGHT.
HE'S THE CLASS PRESIDENT.
SO DOES HE HAVE MORNING PRACTICE?
HEY!

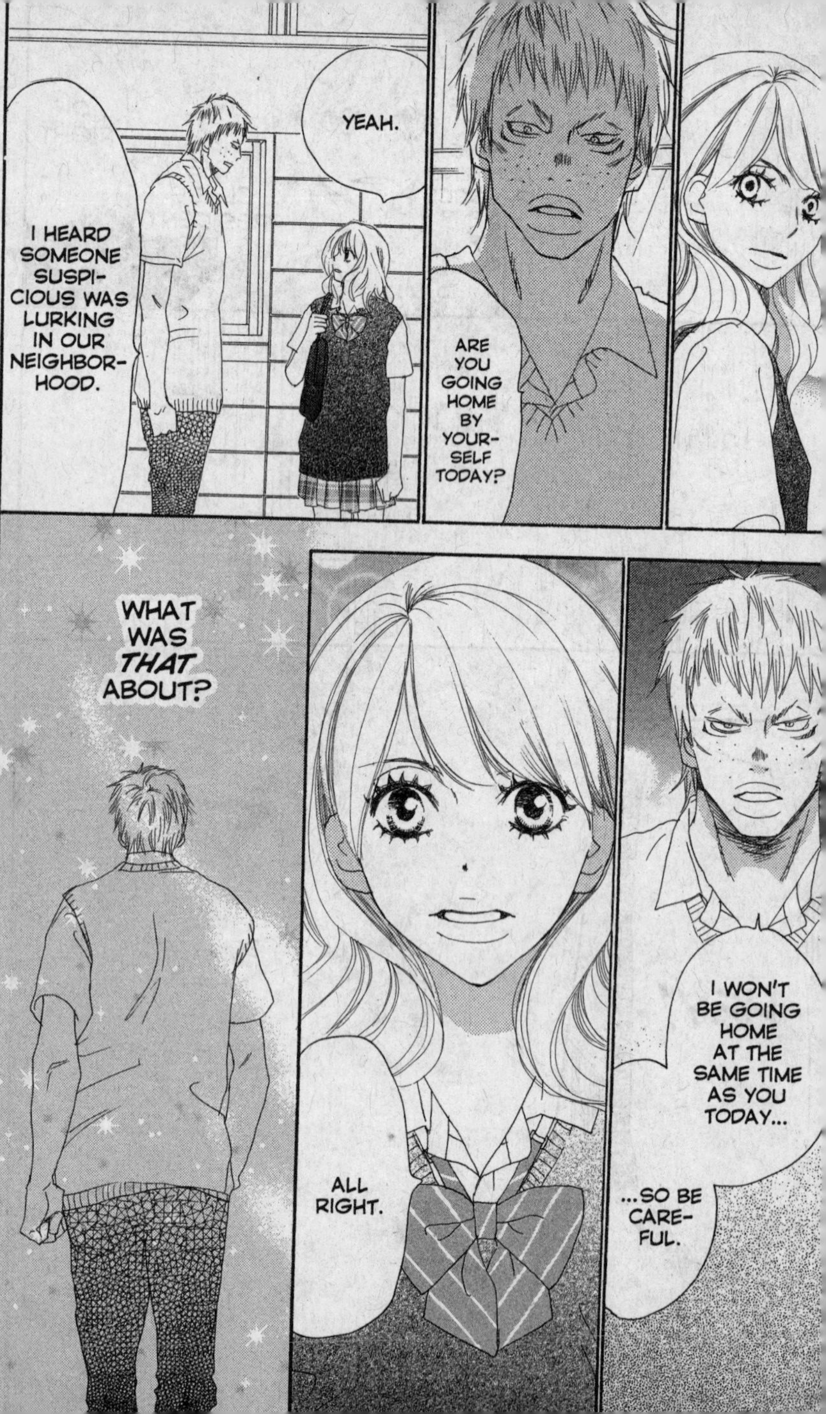
ARE YOU GOING HOME BY YOURSELF TODAY?
YEAH.
I HEARD SOMEONE SUSPICIOUS WAS LURKING IN OUR NEIGHBORHOOD.
I WON'T BE GOING HOME AT THE SAME TIME AS YOU TODAY...
...SO BE CAREFUL.
ALL RIGHT.
WHAT WAS *THAT* ABOUT?

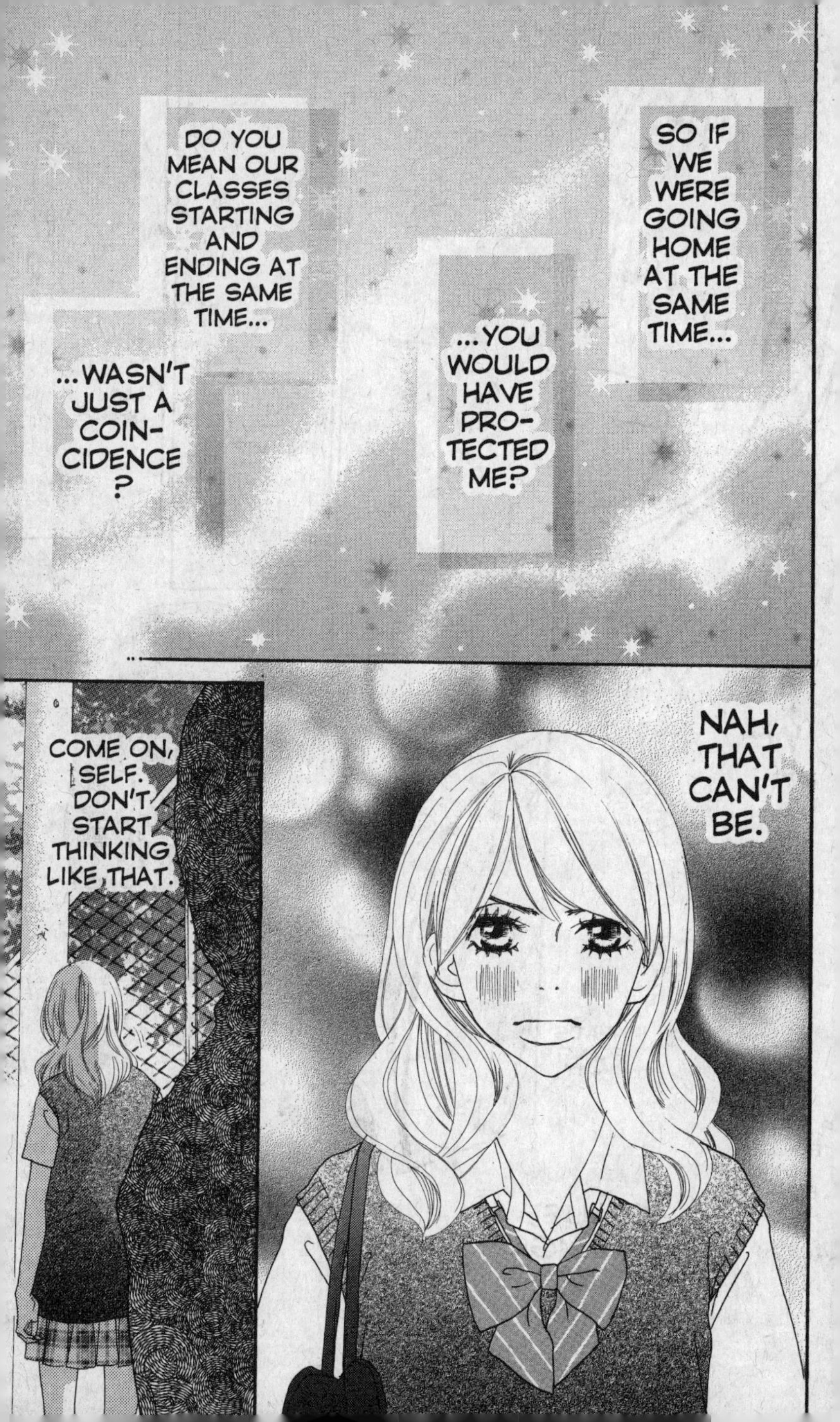
SO IF WE WERE GOING HOME AT THE SAME TIME...
...YOU WOULD HAVE PRO-TECTED ME?
DO YOU MEAN OUR CLASSES STARTING AND ENDING AT THE SAME TIME...
...WASN'T JUST A COIN-CIDENCE ?
NAH, THAT CAN'T BE.
COME ON, SELF. DON'T START THINKING LIKE THAT.

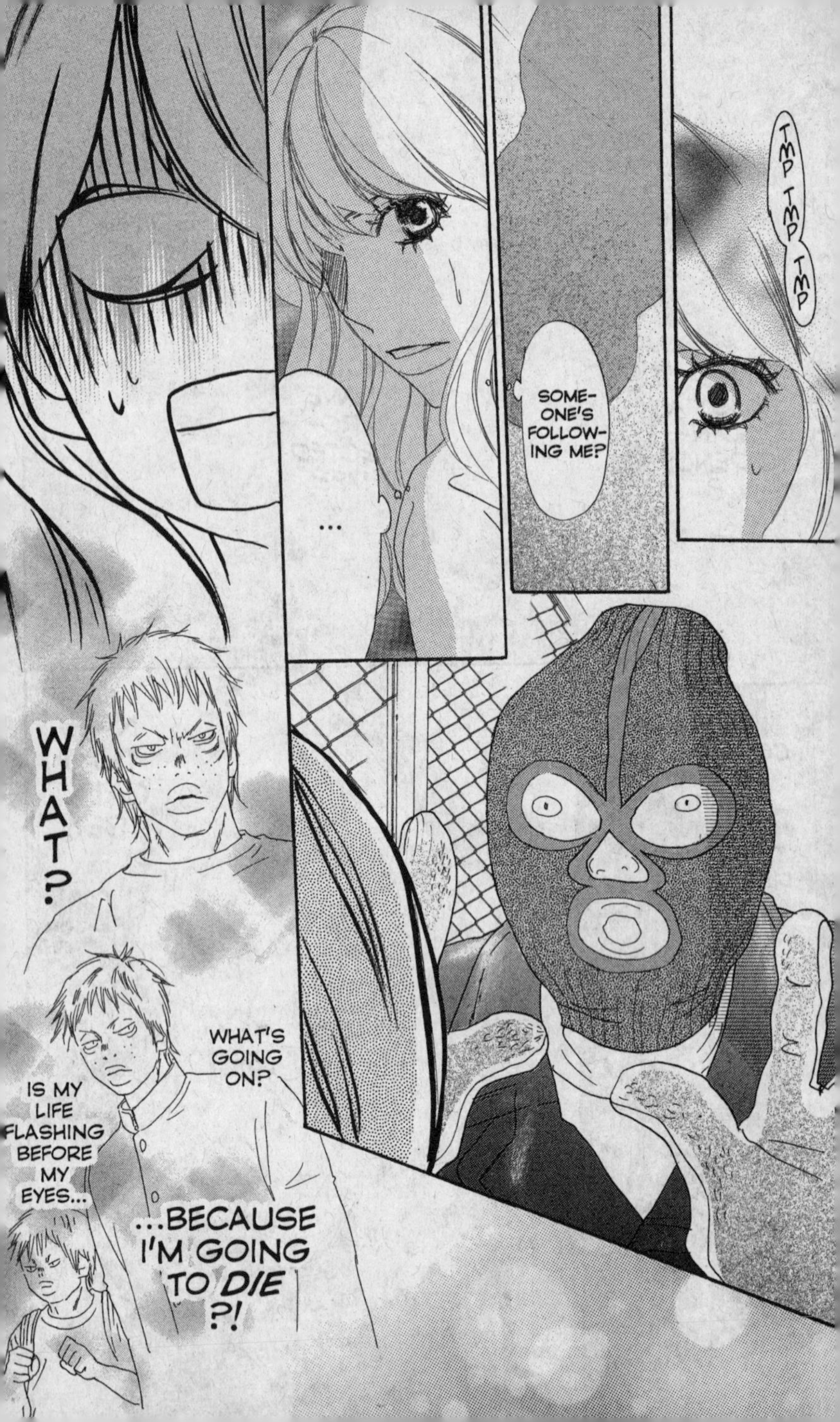
TMP TMP TMP TMP
SOME-ONE'S FOLLOW-ING ME?
...
WHAT?
WHAT'S GOING ON?
IS MY LIFE FLASHING BEFORE MY EYES...
...BECAUSE I'M GOING TO *DIE*?!

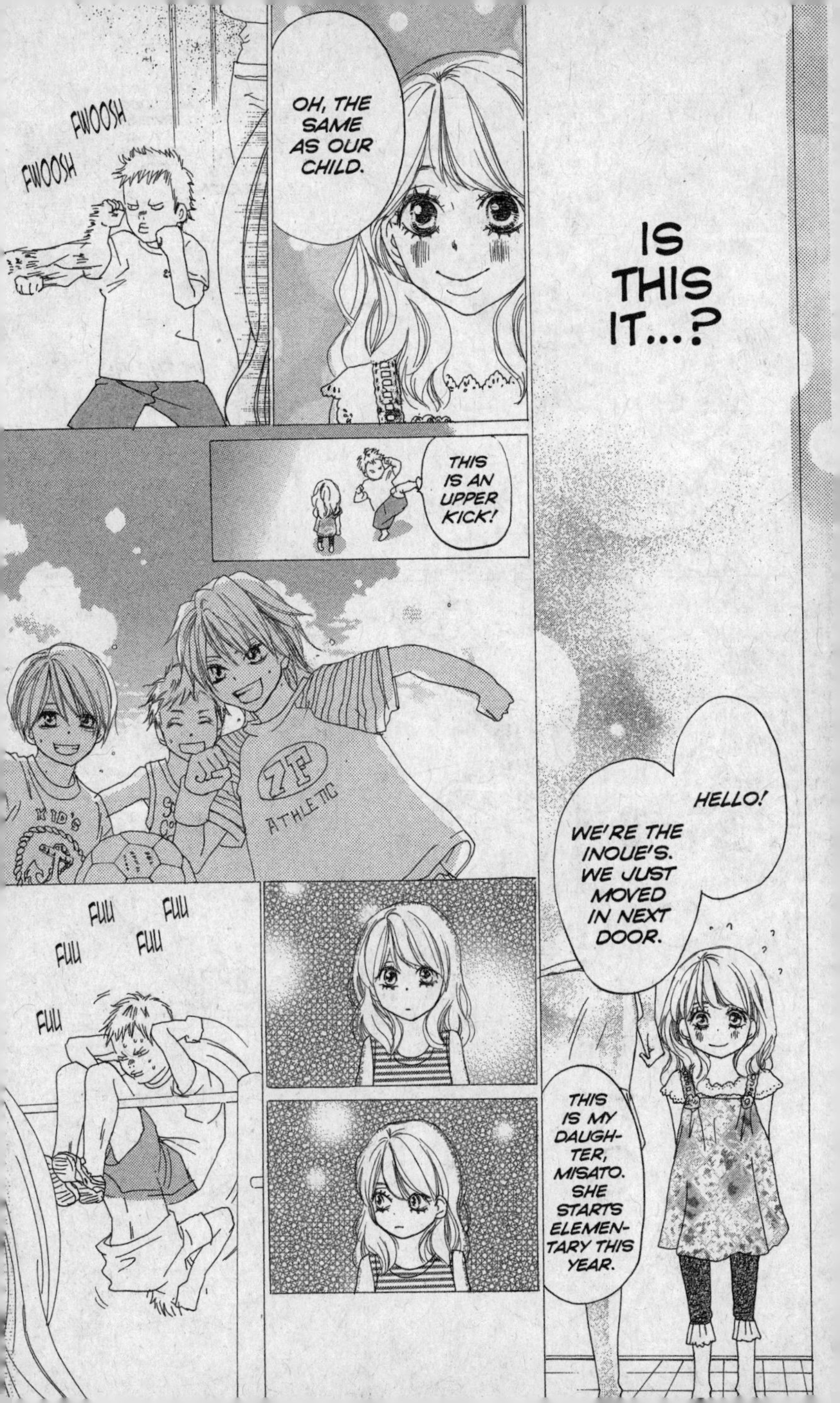

IS THIS IT...?
HELLO!
WE'RE THE INOUE'S. WE JUST MOVED IN NEXT DOOR.
THIS IS MY DAUGHTER, MISATO. SHE STARTS ELEMENTARY THIS YEAR.
OH, THE SAME AS OUR CHILD.
FWOOSH
FWOOSH
THIS IS AN UPPER KICK!
FUU
FUU
FUU
FUU
FUU

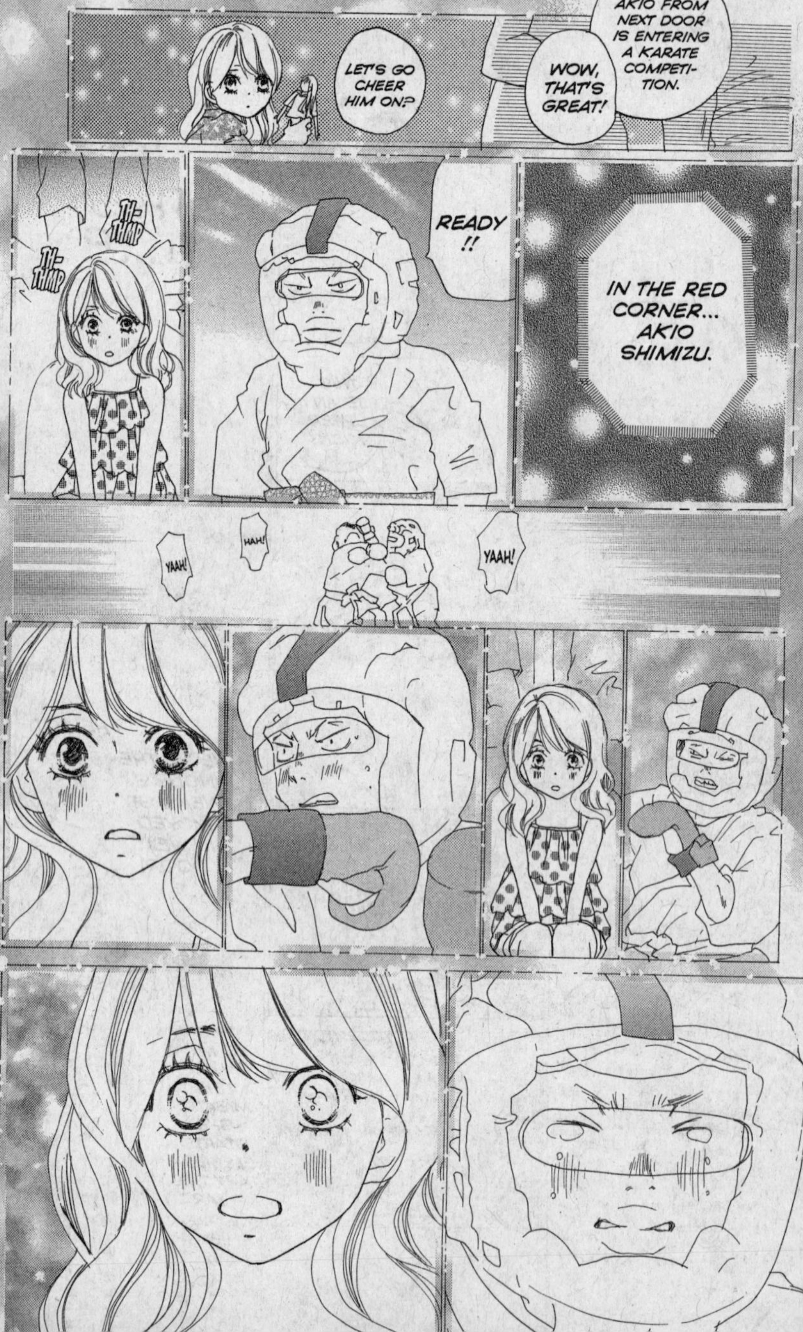
AKIO FROM NEXT DOOR IS ENTERING A KARATE COMPETITION.
WOW, THAT'S GREAT!
LET'S GO CHEER HIM ON?
IN THE RED CORNER... AKIO SHIMIZU.
READY!!
TH-THMP
TH-THMP
YAAH!
HAH!
YAAH!

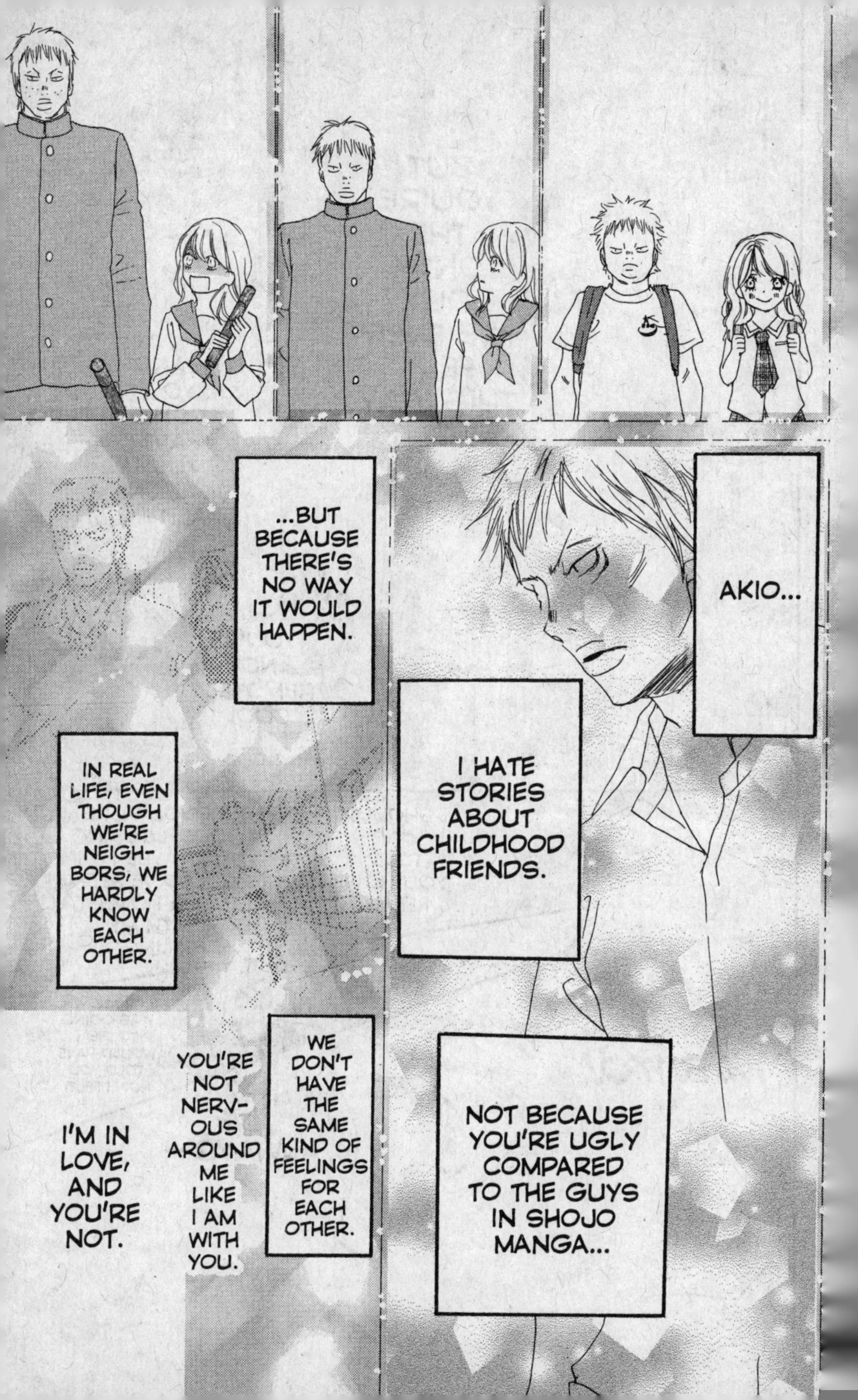
AKIO...
I HATE STORIES ABOUT CHILDHOOD FRIENDS.
NOT BECAUSE YOU'RE UGLY COMPARED TO THE GUYS IN SHOJO MANGA...
...BUT BECAUSE THERE'S NO WAY IT WOULD HAPPEN.
IN REAL LIFE, EVEN THOUGH WE'RE NEIGH-BORS, WE HARDLY KNOW EACH OTHER.
WE DON'T HAVE THE SAME KIND OF FEELINGS FOR EACH OTHER.
YOU'RE NOT NERV-OUS AROUND ME LIKE I AM WITH YOU.
I'M IN LOVE, AND YOU'RE NOT.

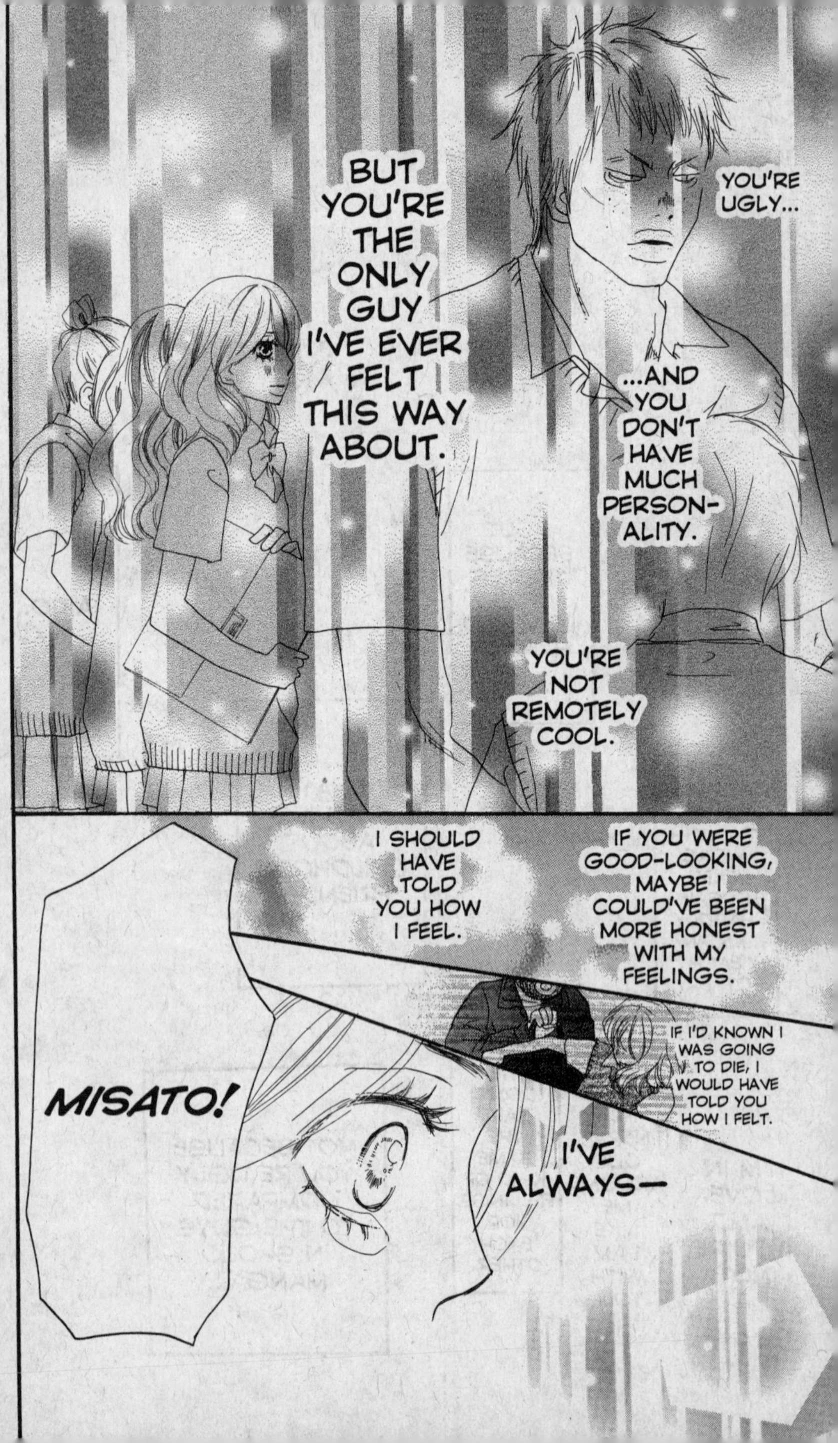
YOU'RE UGLY...
...AND YOU DON'T HAVE MUCH PERSON-ALITY.
YOU'RE NOT REMOTELY COOL.
BUT YOU'RE THE ONLY GUY I'VE EVER FELT THIS WAY ABOUT.
IF YOU WERE GOOD-LOOKING, MAYBE I COULD'VE BEEN MORE HONEST WITH MY FEELINGS.
I SHOULD HAVE TOLD YOU HOW I FEEL.
IF I'D KNOWN I WAS GOING TO DIE, I WOULD HAVE TOLD YOU HOW I FELT.
I'VE ALWAYS—
MISATO!

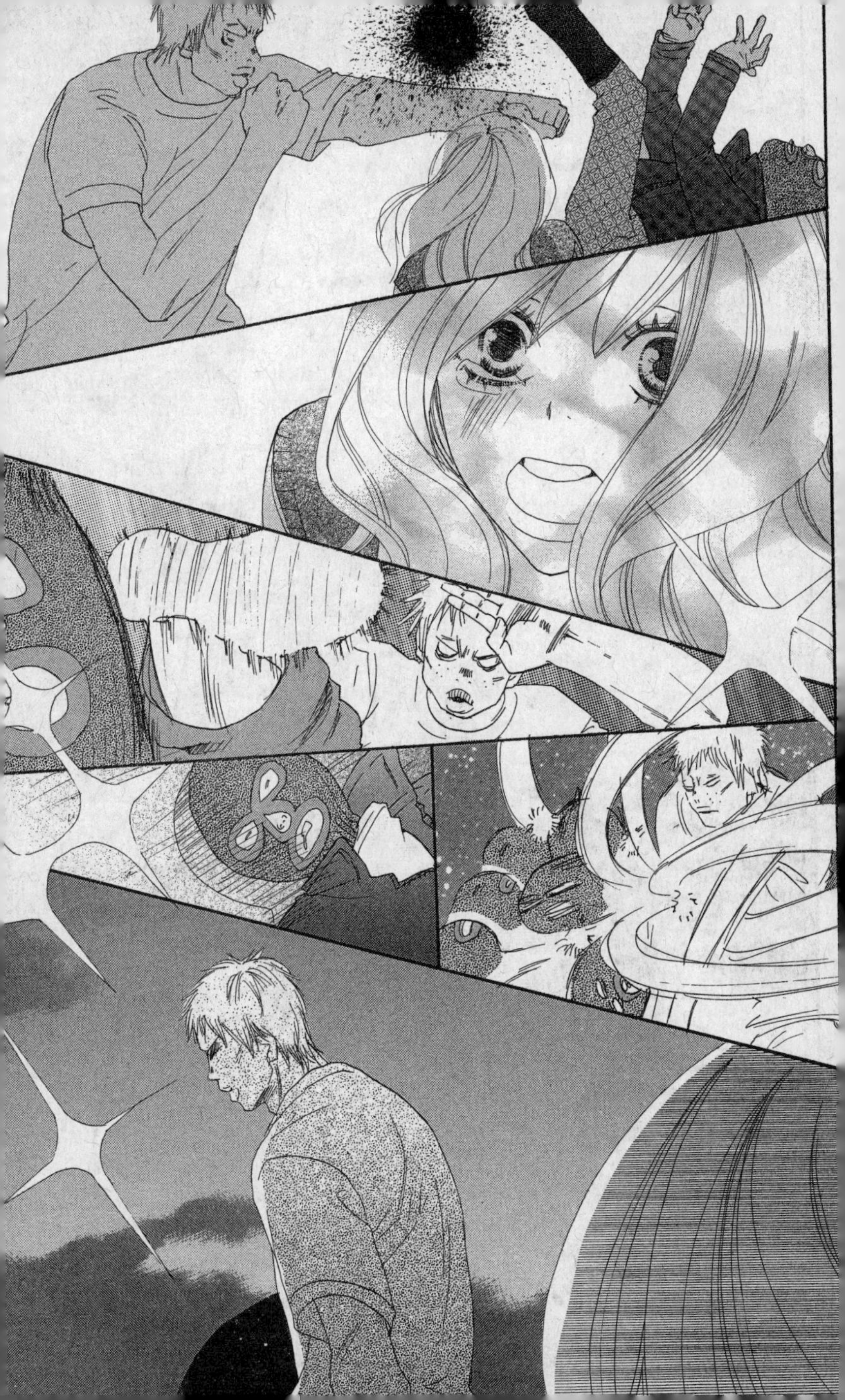

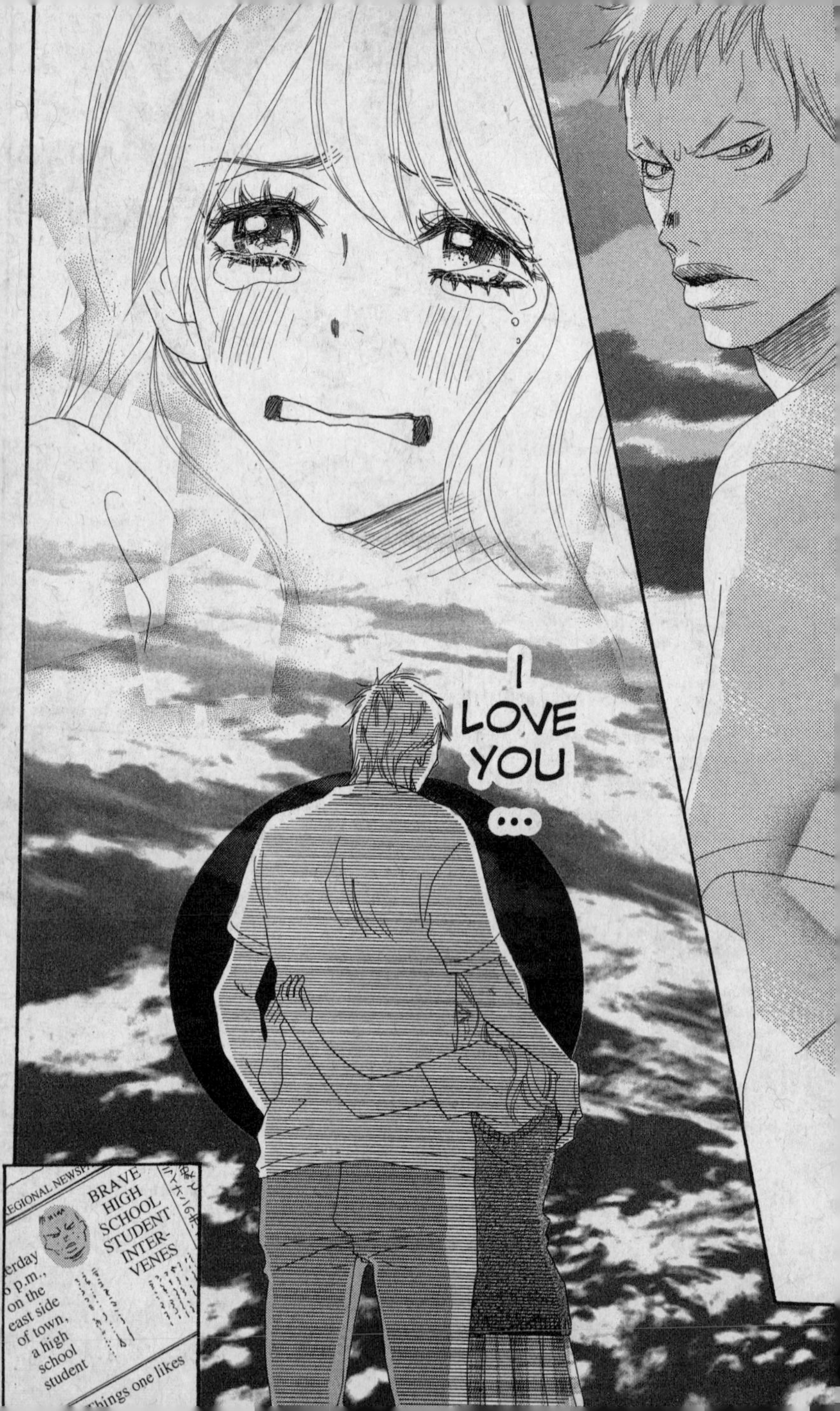
I LOVE YOU ...
BRAVE HIGH SCHOOL STUDENT INTER-VENES
on the east side of town, a high school student
Things one likes

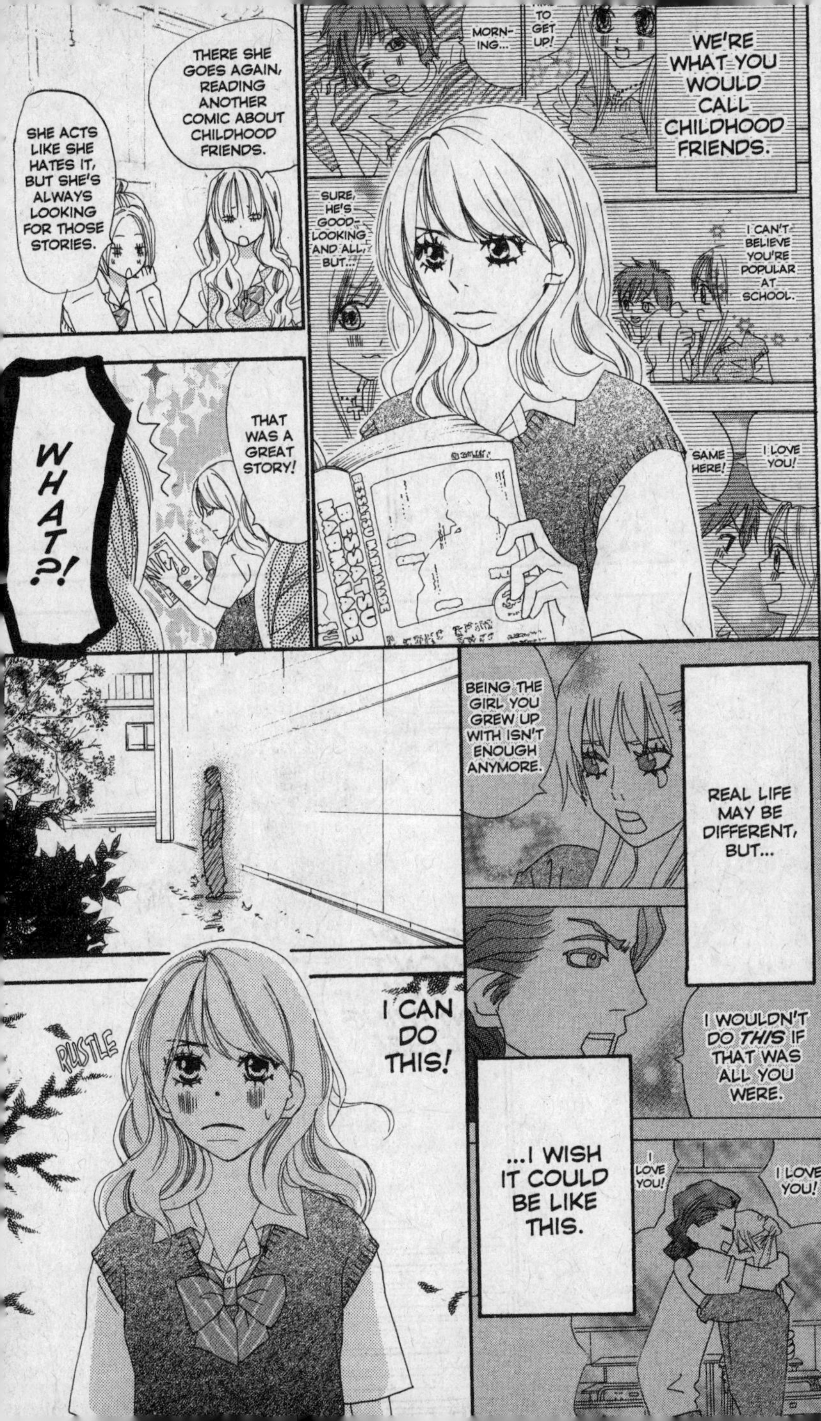
WE'RE WHAT YOU WOULD CALL CHILDHOOD FRIENDS.
TO GET UP!
MORNING...
I CAN'T BELIEVE YOU'RE POPULAR AT SCHOOL.
SURE, HE'S GOOD-LOOKING AND ALL, BUT...
BESSATSU MARMALADE
I LOVE YOU!
SAME HERE!
THERE SHE GOES AGAIN, READING ANOTHER COMIC ABOUT CHILDHOOD FRIENDS.
SHE ACTS LIKE SHE HATES IT, BUT SHE'S ALWAYS LOOKING FOR THOSE STORIES.
THAT WAS A GREAT STORY!
WHAT?!
REAL LIFE MAY BE DIFFERENT, BUT...
BEING THE GIRL YOU GREW UP WITH ISN'T ENOUGH ANYMORE.
I WOULDN'T DO *THIS* IF THAT WAS ALL YOU WERE.
I LOVE YOU!
I LOVE YOU!
...I WISH IT COULD BE LIKE THIS.
I CAN DO THIS!
RUSTLE

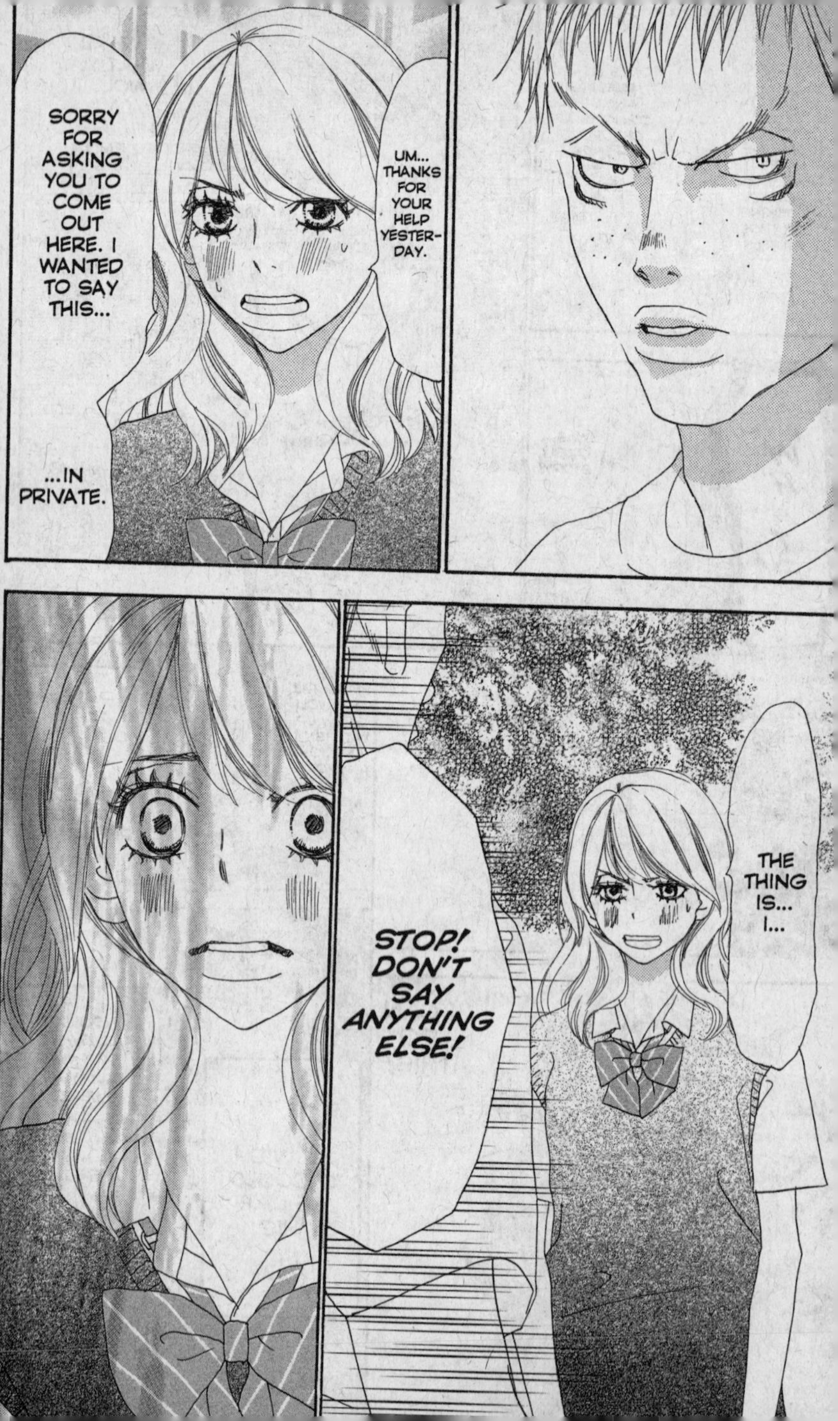
UM... THANKS FOR YOUR HELP YESTER-DAY.
SORRY FOR ASKING YOU TO COME OUT HERE. I WANTED TO SAY THIS...
...IN PRIVATE.
THE THING IS... I...
STOP! DON'T SAY ANYTHING ELSE!

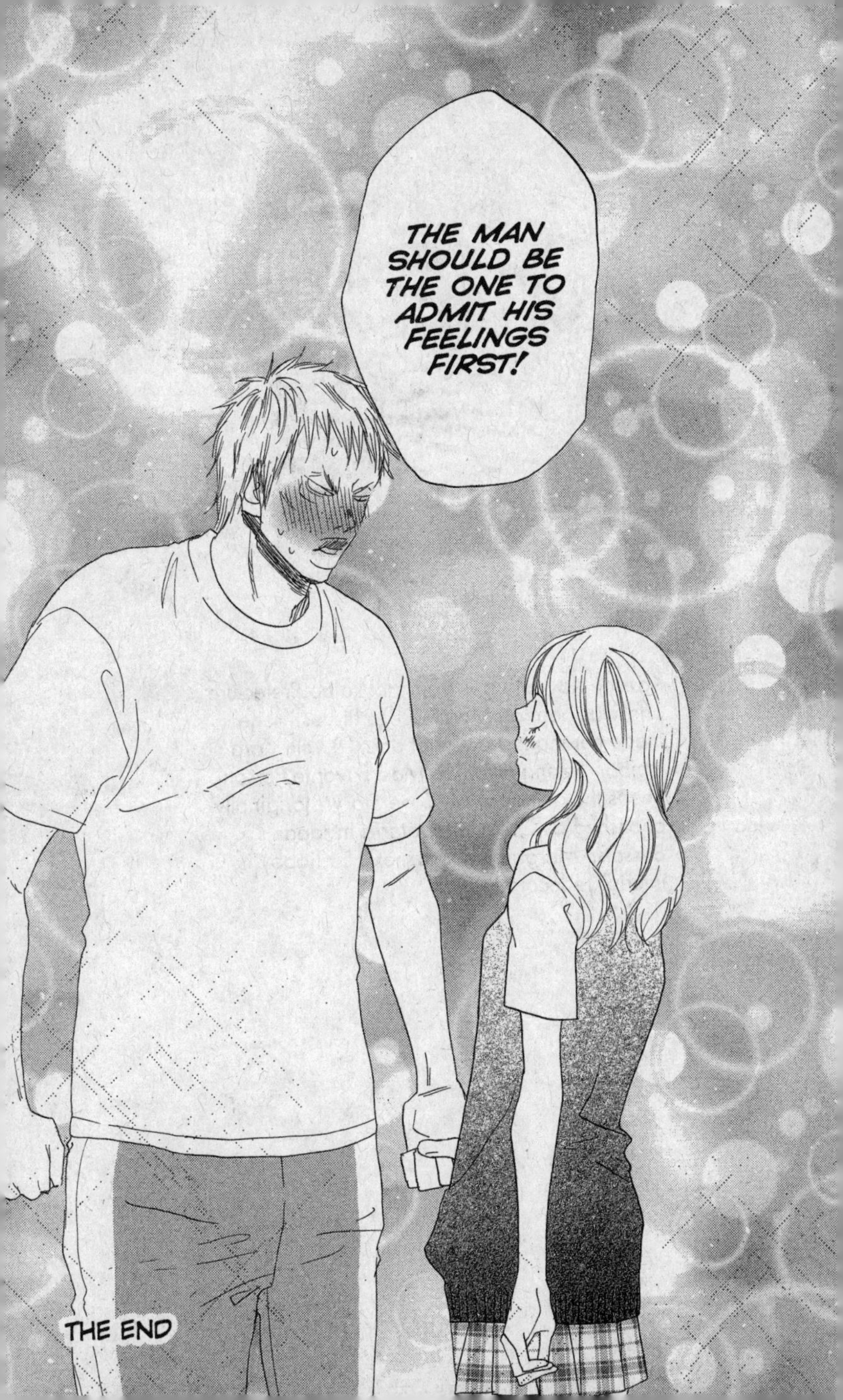
THE MAN SHOULD BE THE ONE TO ADMIT HIS FEELINGS FIRST!
THE END

Kazune Kawahara is from Hokkaido Prefecture and was born on March 11 (a Pisces!). She made her manga debut at age 18 with *Kare no Ichiban Sukina Hito* (His Most Favorite Person). She is the author of *My Love Story!!* (originally published as *Ore Monogatari!!* in Japan's *Bessatsu Margaret* magazine). Her hobby is interior redecorating.

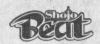

HIGH SCHOOL DEBUT
3-IN-1 EDITION
VOLUME 5
A compilation of graphic novel volumes 13–15

STORY & ART BY
KAZUNE KAWAHARA

Vol.13 English Translation & Adaptation/Gemma Collinge
Vols.14-15 Translation/JN Productions
Vols.14-15 English Adaptation/Ysabet Reinhardt MacFarlane
Touch-up Art & Lettering/Rina Mapa
Design/Courtney Utt, Amy Martin (Graphic Novel Edition)
Design/Yukiko Whitley (3-in-1 Edition)
Editor/Amy Yu

Printed in the U.S.A.

Published by VIZ Media, LLC
P.O. Box 77010
San Francisco, CA 94107

10 9 8 7 6 5 4 3 2 1
First printing, February 2015

www.viz.com

www.shojobeat.com

RATED T FOR TEEN

PARENTAL ADVISORY
HIGH SCHOOL DEBUT is rated T for Teen and is recommended for ages 13 and up. This volume contains suggestive themes.
ratings.viz.com

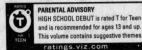

SURPRISE!

You may be reading the wrong way!

It's true: In keeping with the original Japanese comic format, this book reads from right to left—so action, sound effects and word balloons are completely reversed. This preserves the orientation of the original artwork—plus, it's fun! Check out the diagram shown here to get the hang of things, and then turn to the other side of the book to get started!

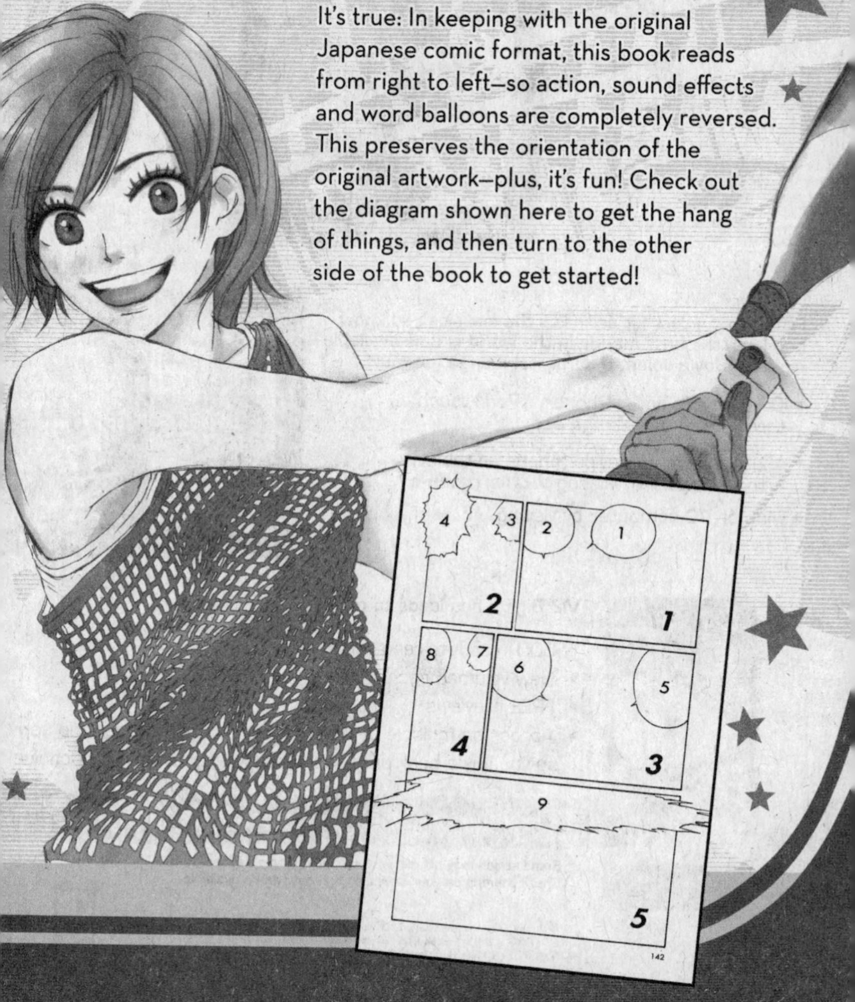

VIZMANGA

Read manga anytime, anywhere!

From our newest hit series to the classics you know and love, the best manga in the world is now available digitally. Buy a volume* of digital manga for your:

- **iOS device (iPad®, iPhone®, iPod® touch)** through the VIZ Manga app
- **Android-powered device (phone or tablet)** with a browser by visiting VIZManga.com
- **Mac or PC computer** by visiting VIZManga.com

VIZ Digital has loads to offer:

- 500+ ready-to-read volumes
- New volumes each week
- FREE previews
- Access on multiple devices! Create a log-in through the app so you buy a book once, and read it on your device of choice!

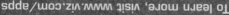

to find love
join force
Risa and Otani
Class clown

By Aya Nakahara

love ★ com